MRCS PART A ESSENTIAL REVISION NOTES

BOOK 1

Edited by
Claire Ritchie Chalmers
BA PhD FRCS
Catherine Parchment Smith
BSc MBChB FRCS

Pas**tes⁺**

© 2016 Pastest Ltd
Egerton Court
Parkgate Estate
Knutsford
Cheshire
WA16 8DX

Telephone: 01565 752000

First published 2012, reprinted 2015, 2016

ISBN: 978 1 905 63582 5
eISBN: 978 1 909 49100 7 MobiPocket
        978 1 908 18570 9 ePUB

A catalogue record for this book is available from the British Library.

The information contained within this book was obtained by the author from reliable
sources. However, while every effort has been made to ensure its accuracy, no
responsibility for loss, damage or injury occasioned to any person acting or refraining
from action as a result of information contained herein can be accepted by the
publishers or author.

Pastest Online Revision, Books and Courses

Pastest provides online revision, books and courses to help medical students and
doctors maximise their personal performance in critical exams and tests. Our in-
depth understanding is based on over 40 years' experience and the feedback of
recent exam candidates.

Resources are available for:
**Medical school applicants and undergraduates, MRCP, MRCS, MRCPCH, DCH,
GPST, MRCGP, FRCA, Dentistry, and USMLE Step 1.**

For further details contact:
Tel: 01565 752000   Fax: 01565 650264
www.pastest.com   enquiries@pastest.com

Text prepared in the UK by Carnegie Book Production, Lancaster
Printed and bound in the UK by Bell & Bain Limited, Glasgow

Contents

Acknowledgements

I would like to thank everyone who has worked so hard to complete this book – Cathy Dickens and the Pastest team. Thanks especially to my fellow editor, Cathy, whose excellent teaching eased my early passage through basic surgical training and whose subsequent advice, friendship and *joie de vivre* is invaluable.

I have been fortunate enough to be surrounded by fantastic friends and colleagues. There are too many to list by name (but you know who you are) and I appreciate all your support.

Thanks also to my family and, last, but c e r t a i n l y not least, thanks to my husband Roy for backing me up and making me laugh – a constant and irreplaceable source of patience and good cheer.

Preface

This book is an attempt to help surgical trainees pass the MRCS exam by putting together the revision notes they need. It was written (in the main) and edited by trainees for trainees and while we do not claim to be authorities on the subjects by any means, we hope to save you some work by expanding our o w n revision notes and putting them in a readable format. Originally written when we were SHOs, as time has passed and we have ourselves climbed the surgical ladder, we have updated the text but have tried to keep the style of the books as accessible and informal as possible. Medical students interested in surgery may also find it a good general introduction to the surgical specialties.

Now in its third incarnation we have refined this edition further to cover the evolving MRCS syllabus in two volumes. These two books have been designed to be used in conjunction with the existing Pastest MRCS Part B OSCEs volume. Although the format of surgical examinations in the UK has changed to include OSCE assessment, the principles of core surgical knowledge remain the same, and often a good exam answer starts with a structured summary followed by expansion of individual points. We have, therefore, arranged each topic in this format, and we have used boxes, bullet points and diagrams to highlight important points. There is additional space around the text for you to annotate and personalise these notes from your own experience.

My dad is fond of saying that the harder you work, the luckier you get, and I have always found this to be true – so GOOD LUCK!

Ritchie Chalmers

Picture Permissions

The following figure in this book has been reproduced with kind permission of Professor Kenneth D Boffard of the University of the Witwatersrand, Johannesburg.

Trauma
Fig 6.4 The metabolic response to trauma

The following figures in this book have been reproduced from Chesser TJS and Leslie IJ (1998) 'Forearm fractures', *Surgery* 16(11): 241–248 by kind permission from the publisher The Medicine Publishing Group (Elsevier).

Trauma
Fig 6.22 Smith's fracture
Fig 6.23 Volar fracture
Fig 6.27 Salter–Harris classification

The following figures in this book have been reproduced from Calder SJ (1998) 'Fractures of the hip' *Surgery* 16(11): 253–258 by kind permission of the publisher The Medicine Publishing Group (Elsevier).

Trauma
Fig 6.24 Blood supply of the femoral head
Fig 6.25 Garden's classification of intracapsular fractures
Fig 6.26 Extracapsular fractures

The following figures in this book have been reproduced from Snell RS (2000) *Clinical Anatomy for Medical Students* (6th edition) by kind permission of the publisher Lippincott Williams and Wilkins (Wolters Kluwer).

Orthopaedic Surgery
Fig 7.7 Femoral triangle and adductor canal in the right lower limb
Fig 7.17 Formation of the neural tube (transverse section) in week 3 of gestation
Fig 7.18 Formation of the neural tube (dorsal view) at days 22 and 23
Fig 7.22 Cervical vertebrae shown from above
Fig 7.25 Some of the intrinsic muscles of the back
Fig 7.30 Some important tendon reflexes

The following figures in this book have been reproduced from Snell RS (1986) *Clinical Anatomy for Medical Students* (3rd edition) by kind permission of the publisher Lippincott Williams and Wilkins (Wolters Kuwer).

Orthopaedic Surgery
Fig 7.2 Muscles attached to the external surface of the right hip
Fig 7.9 Boundaries and contents of the right popliteal fossa
Fig 7.13 Brachial plexus

Fig 7.23 A lateral view of the vertebral column and general features of different kinds of vertebrae
Fig 7.24 Some of the extrinsic muscles of the back
Fig 7.31 Efferent part of autonomic nervous system

The following figure in this book has been reproduced from Dykes MI (2003) *Crash Course: Anatomy* (2nd edition) by kind permission of the publisher Elsevier.

Orthopaedic Surgery
Fig 7.3 Gluteal region

The following figure in this book has been reproduced from Faiz O, Blackburn S, Moffat D (2011) *Anatomy at a Glance* (3rd edition) by kind permission of the publisher Wiley-Blackwell.

Orthopaedic Surgery
Fig 7.4 The greater and lesser sciatic foramina

The following figures in this book have been reproduced from McRae R (1996) *Clinical Orthopaedic Examination* by kind permission from the publisher Churchill Livingstone (Elsevier).

Orthopaedic Surgery
Fig 7.11 Anatomy of the foot
Fig 7.21 Schematic diagram of the vertebra and spinal cord

The following figures in this book have been reproduced from Sadler TW, Langman J (1990) *Langman's Medical Embryology* (6th edition) by kind permission of the publisher Lippincott Williams and Wilkins (Wolters Kluwer).

Paediatric Surgery
Fig 8.1 Sagittal section through the embryo showing formation of the primitive endodermline gut
Fig 8.2 Formation of the GI tract at week 4 of gestation showing foregut, midgut and hindgut
Fig 8.3 The foregut during week 4 of gestation
Fig 8.5 The cloacal region at successive stages in development
Fig 8.8 Transverse section of diaphragm at fourth month of gestation
Fig 8.11 The development of the urinary tract at week 5
Fig 8.12 Development of the urogenital sinus
Fig 8.13 Descent of the testis

Every effort has been made to contact holders of copyright to obtain permission to reproduce copyright material. However, if any have been inadvertently overlooked, the publisher will be pleased to make the necessary arrangements at the first opportunity.

Contributors

Editors

Claire Ritchie Chalmers BA PhD FRCS
Consultant Breast and Oncoplastic Surgeon,
Maidstone and Tunbridge Wells NHS Trust
Infection and Inflammation

Catherine Parchment Smith BSc(Hons) MBChB(Hons) FRCS
Consultant Colorectal Surgeon,
Mid Yorkshire Hospitals NHS Trust

Contributors

David C G Crabbe MD FRCS
Consultant Paediatric Surgeon, Department of
Paediatric Surgery, Leeds General Infirmary,
Leeds
Paediatric Surgey

Brahman Dharmarahah MA MBBS MRCS
Clinical Research Fellow,
Academic Section of Vascular Surgery, Imperial
College and Charing Cross Hospital, London
Postoperative Management and Critical Care

Paul M Brennan BSc (Hons) MB BChir MRCS
ECAT Clinical Lecturer, Honorary Specialist
Registrar Neurosurgery, Edinburgh Cancer
Research Centre, University of Edinburgh
Department of Clinical Neurosciences, NHS
Lothian
*Trauma Part 1: Head, Abdomen and Trunk –
Head injury*

Sylvia Brown MD MRCS MBChB
ST7 in General Surgery,
South General Hospital, Glasgow
Principles of Surgical Oncology

Sebastian Dawson-Bowling MA MSc LLM FRCS(Tr&Orth)
Consultant Orthopaedic Surgeon,
St. George's Hospital, London
Ethics, Clinical Governance and the
Medicolegal *Aspects of Surgery*

Nerys Forester BA BM BCh MRCS FRCR PhD
Consultant Breast Radiologist,
Royal Victoria Infirmary, Newcastle, Tyne & Wear
E*vidence-based Surgical Practice*

Nigel W Gummerson MA FRCS
Consultant Orthopaedic Trauma and Spinal
Surgeon. Department of Orthopaedics and
Trauma, Leeds General Infirmary, Leeds
*Orthopaedic Surgery; Trauma Part
2:Musculoskeletal*

David Mansouri BSc(Med Sci) MBChB MRCS
ST3 General Surgery, Professorial Unit, Western
Infirmary,Glasgow
Surgical Technique and Technology

Tristan McMillan MBChB
Core Surgical Trainee, Department of Plastic
Surgery, Glasgow Royal Infirmary, Glasgow
Perioperative Care

Hayley M Moore MA MBBS MRCS
Clinical Research Fellow, Academic Section of
Vascular Surgery, Imperial College, London
Postoperative Management and Critical Care

Juliette Murray MBChB, MD, FRCS (Gen Surg)
Consultant Surgeon, Wishaw General Hospital,
North Lanarkshire

Stuart J O'Toole MD FRCS(Paeds) FEAPU
Consultant Paediatric Surgeon and Urologist,
Department of Surgical Paediatrics, Royal
Hospital for Sick Children, Glasgow
Paediatric Surgery

Susan Picton BM BS FRCPCH
Consultant Paediatric Oncologist, Leeds
Teaching Hospitals Trust, Leeds
Paediatric Surgery

George Hondag Tse MSc MRCSEd MBChB BSc (Hons)
Clinical Research Fellow, Centre for
Inflammation Research, University of Edinburgh
Trauma Part 1: Head, Abdomen and Trunk

Stuart W Waterston BScMedSci(Hons), MBChB, PGCertMedEd, FRCSEd(Plast)
Fellow in Plastic Surgery/Hand Surgery,
Department of Plastic Surgery, St Andrews
Centre for Plastic Surgery & Burns,
Broomfield Hospital, Chelmsford
*Plastic Surgery; Trauma Part 1: Head, Abdomen
and Trunk – Burns*

Contributors to previous editions

Sam Andrews MA MS FRCS (Gen)
Consultant General and Vascular Surgeon, Department of General and Vascular Surgery, Maidstone Hospital, Maidstone

Amer Aldouri MBChB MRCS
Specialist Registrar in Hepatobiliary and Transplantation Surgery, Hepatobiliary and Transplantation Surgery Unit, St James University Hospital, Leeds

David Crabbe MD FRCS
Consultant Paediatric Surgeon, Clarendon Wing, Leeds General Infirmary, Leeds

Nerys Forester
Specialist Registrar in Clinical Radiology, Yorkshire Deanery

Sheila M Fraser MBChB MRCS
Clinical Research Fellow, Institute of Molecular Medicine, Epidemiology & Cancer Research, St. James's University Hospital, Leeds

Sunjay Jain MD FRCS (Urol)
Clinical Lecturer in Urology, University of Leicester, Leicester

Shireen N. McKenzie MB.ChB MRCS(Ed)
Specialist Registrar in General Surgery, Airdale General Hospital, Keighley, West Yorkshire

Professor Kilian Mellon MD FRCS (Urol)
Professor of Urology, University of Leicester, Leicester

Sally Nicholson BSc MBChB
Senior House Officer in Yorkshire School of Surgery, ENT Department, Leeds General Infirmary, Leeds

Susan Picton BM BS FRCPCH
Consultant Paediatric Oncologist, Leeds Teaching Hospitals Trust, Leeds

Catherine Sargent BM BCh (Oxon) MRCP
Specialist Registrar in Infectious Diseases/ General Medicine, The John Radcliffe Hospital, Oxford

James Brown MRCS
Specialist Registrar in Surgery, South East Thames Surgical Rotation
Neoplasia

Alistair R K Challiner FRCA FIMC.RCSEd DCH
Consultant Anaesthetist and Director Intensive Care Unit, Department of Anaesthetics, Maidstone Hospital, Maidstone, Kent
Intensive Care and Peri-operative Management 1

Nicholas D Maynard BA Hons (OXON) MS FRCS (Gen)
Consultant Upper Gastrointestinal Surgeon, Department of Upper Gastrointestinal Surgery, John Radcliffe Hospital, Headington, Oxford
Peri-operative Management 2

Gillian M Sadler MBBS MRCP FRCR
Consultant Clinical Oncologist, Kent Oncology Centre, Maidstone Hospital, Maidstone, Kent
Neoplasia

Hank Schneider FRCS (Gen. Surg)
Consultant General Surgeon, Department of Surgery, The James Paget Hospital, Great Yarmouth, Norfolk
Trauma

Introduction

A   The Intercollegiate MRCS Examination

Please be aware that from January 2017 there will be changes to the MRCS Part A Examination. Revised Candidate Guidance material is available on the Intercollegiate website: www.intercollegiatemrcsexams.org.uk

The Intercollegiate MRCS examination comprises two parts: Part A (MCQ) and Part B (OSCE)

Part A (written): Multiple Choice Questions (MCQ)

Part A is a 4-hour MCQ examination consisting of two 2-hour papers taken on the same day. The papers cover generic surgical sciences and applied knowledge, including the core knowledge required in all nine specialties. The marks for both papers are combined to give a total mark for Part A although there is also a minimum pass mark for each paper. There are no limits to the number of times that you can attempt this part of the exam.

Paper 1 – Applied Basic Sciences MCQ paper

Paper 2 – Principles of Surgery-in-General MCQ paper

There are 135 questions per paper and two styles of question. The first type of question requires a single best answer. Each question contains five possible answers of which there is only one single best answer. An example of this type of question from the college website is:

A 67-year-old woman is brought to the emergency department having fallen on her left arm.

There is an obvious clinical deformity and X-ray demonstrates a mid-shaft fracture of the humerus. She has lost the ability to extend the left wrist joint. Which nerve has most likely been damaged with the fracture?

A   The axillary nerve
B   The median nerve
C   The musculocutaneous nerve
D   The radial nerve
E   The ulnar nerve

The second type of question is an extended matching question. Each theme contains a variable number of options and clinical situations. Only one option will be the most appropriate response to each clinical situation. You should select the most appropriate option. It is possible for one option to be the answer to more than one of the clinical situations. An example of this type of question from the college website shown overleaf.

Theme: Chest injuries

Options

A   Tension pneumothorax
B   Aortic rupture
C   Haemothorax
D   Aortic dissection
E   Ruptured spleen
F   Cardiac tamponade

For each of the situations below, select the single most likely diagnosis from the options listed above. Each option may be used once, more than once or not at all.

1. A 24-year-old man is brought into the emergency department having been stabbed with a screwdriver. He is conscious. On examination he is tachypnoeic and has a tachycardia of 120 beats/minute. His blood pressure is 90/50 mmHg. He has a small puncture wound below his right costal margin. A central venous line is inserted with ease, and his central venous pressure is 17 cm. A chest Xray shows a small pleural effusion with a small pneumothorax. He has received 2 units of plasma expander, which has failed to improve his blood pressure.
2. A 42-year-old man is admitted following a road traffic accident complaining of pains throughout his chest. He was fit and well prior to the incident. He is tachypnoeic and in considerable pain. His brachial blood pressure is 110/70 mmHg and his pulse rate is 90 beats/minute. Both femoral pulses are present though greatly diminished. A chest Xray shows multiple rib fractures and an appreciably widened upper mediastinum. Lateral views confirm a fractured sternum. An ECG shows ischaemic changes in the V-leads.

Further examples of the two types of question are available as part of the Pastest MRCS Part A online resource, see www.pastest.com/mrcs-part-a/. The questions cover the entire syllabus and are broken down into:

Paper 1

Applied Surgical Anatomy – 45 questions. This includes gross anatomy as well as questions on developmental and imaging anatomy.

Topic	Number of questions
Thorax	6
Abdomen, pelvis, perineum	12
Upper limb, breast	8
Lower limb	6
Head, neck and spine	9
Central, peripheral and autonomic nervous systems	4

Physiology – 45 questions. This includes 12 questions on general physiological principles covering thermoregulation, metabolic pathways, sepsis and septic shock, fluid balance, metabolic acidosis/alkalosis and colloid and crystalloid solutions.

System-specific physiology:

Topic	Number of questions
Respiratory system	6
Cardiovascular system	6
Gastrointestinal system	4
Renal system	6
Endocrine system (including glucose homeostasis)	4
Nervous system	3
Thyroid and parathyroid	4

Pathology – 45 questions. This includes 20–22 questions on general principles of pathology.

Topic	Number of questions
Inflammation	3
Wound healing and cellular healing	1–2
Vascular disorders	3
Disorders of growth	3
Tumours	6
Surgical immunology	3
Surgical haematology	1–2

System-specific pathology (22–26 questions):

Topic	Number of questions
Nervous system	1–2
Musculoskeletal system	3
Respiratory system	1–2
Breast disorders	4
Endocrine systems	1–2
Genitourinary system	3
Gastrointestinal system	5
Lymphoreticular system	1–2
Cardiovascular system	3

Paper 2

Clinical Problem Solving – 135 questions. This includes 45 questions on **Principles of Surgery-in-General** and 90 questions on **Surgical Specialties:**

Principles of Surgery-in-General

Topic	Number of questions
Perioperative care	8
Postoperative care	4
Surgical techniques	6
Management/legal topics	4
Microbiology	6
Emergency medicine	9
Oncology	8

Surgical Specialties Topic	Number of questions
Cardiothoracic	6
Abdominal	9
Upper gastrointestinal	4–5

Hepatobilary and pancreatic	5
Colorectal	6
Breast	4–5
Endocrine	6
Vascular	7
Transplant	3
ENT	6
Oromaxillofacial	2
Paediatrics	6
Neurosurgery	6
Trauma/orthopaedics	7-8
Plastics	6
Urology	7

It is therefore important that you cover the entire syllabus in order to pick up the greatest number of marks.

Part B: Objective Structured Clinical Examination (OSCE)

To be eligible for Part B you must have passed Part A. The OSCE will normally consist of 18 examined stations each of 9 minutes' duration and one or more rest/preparation station. Although the MRCS remains an exam for the Core part of Surgical Training, six of the stations will be examined in a specialty context and the other 12 reflect generic surgical skills. You must specify your choice of specialty context stations at the time of your application to sit the exam.

These stations will examine the following broad content areas:

1. Anatomy and surgical pathology
2. Applied surgical science and critical care
3. Communication skills in giving and receiving information and history taking
4. Clinical and procedural skills

Speciality areas are:
• Head and Neck
• Trunk and Thorax
• Limbs (including spine)
• Neurosciences

Each station is manned by one or two examiners and is marked out of 20 with a separate 'overall global rating' of:
- Pass
- Borderline pass
- Borderline fail
- Fail

There are 4 domains assessed throughout the exam which are areas of knowledge, skill, competencies and professional characteristics that a candidate should demonstrate. These are:
- Clinical knowledge
- Clinical and technical skill
- Communication
- Professionalism

The overall mark is calculated from both the mark out of 20 and the overall global rating. In order to pass the exam you need to achieve the minimum pass mark and also a minimum competence level in each of the four content areas and in each of the four domains.

B   Candidate instructions for Part A (MCQ)

Candidates who are late by no more than 30 minutes for the exam may be allowed entry at the discretion of the senior invigilator but will not be given extra time. You may not leave in the first 60 minutes or the last 15 minutes of the examination and then you must wait until answer sheets and question booklets have been collected from your desk.

Each desk in the examination hall will be numbered and candidates must sit at the desk that corresponds to their examination/candidate number.

Candidates must bring proof of identity to each examination, such as a current passport or driving licence that includes your name, signature and a photograph. Once seated this should be placed on the desk ready for inspection.

Pencils and all stationery will be provided. Mobile phones and electronic devices (including pagers and calculators) must be switched off and are not permitted to be on the desk or on your person during the exam. Failure to comply with this will lead to suspension from the exam.

Dress comfortably. You are allowed to take a small bottle of water or a drink in to the exam hall with you.

There are equal marks for each question. Marks will not be deducted for a wrong answer. However, you will not gain a mark if you mark more than one box for the same item or question. The answer sheets are scanned by machine. If you do not enter your answer to each question correctly and clearly on the answer sheet the machine which scores your paper may reject it. Mark each answer clearly as faint marking may be misread by the machine. If you need to change an answer, you should make sure that you rub it out completely so that the computer can accept your final answer.

Many candidates find it easier to mark their answers on the question booklet first and transfer them to the answer sheet later. If you do this, you should allow time to transfer your answers to the answer sheet before the end of the examination. No extra time will be given for the transfer of answers.

C   Preparing for the MCQ exam

The MRCS exam and syllabus is being constantly updated and the best way to keep up to date with its requirements is via the website 'http://www.intercollegiatemrcsexams.org.uk' which contains information on :

- Examination dates
- Regulations
- Guidance notes
- Domain descriptors
- Application forms
- Syllabus
- Candidate feedback
- Annual reports

Different people prepare for MCQ examinations in different ways. The key to success is to do as many practice questions as possible. You may prefer to revise a topic before undertaking practice questions or use practice questions to highlight areas of lack of knowledge and direct your learning.

Pastest online resources also include over 4,300 practice questions for MRCS Part A. See www.pastest.com/mrcs-part-a/.

D   The Syllabus

The syllabus essentially remains the same although it is structured differently every few years. The most up-to-date version can be found on the intercollegiate website. The syllabus from 2016 has been structured in 10 modules:

Module 1: Basic science knowledge relevant to surgical practice (to include applied surgical anatomy, applied surgical physiology, pharmacology (centred around the safe prescribing of common drugs), applied surgical pathology (principles underlying system-specific pathology), microbiology as applied to surgical practice, imaging (principles, advantages and disadvantages of various diagnostic and interventional imaging methods)

Module 2: Common surgical conditions (under the topics of gastrointestinal disease; breast disease; vascular disease; cardiovascular and pulmonary disease; genitourinary disease; trauma and orthopaedics; diseases of the skin, head and neck; neurology and neurosurgery; and endocrine disease)

Module 3: Basic surgical skills (including the principles and practice of surgery and technique)

Module 4: The assessment and management of the surgical patient (decision making, team working and communication skills)

Module 5: Perioperative care of the surgical patient (preoperative, intraoperative and postoperative care, including the management of complications)

Module 6: Assessment and early treatment of the patient with trauma (including the multiply injured patient)

Module 7: Surgical care of the paediatric patient

Module 8: Management of the dying patient

Module 9: Organ and tissue transplantation

Module 10: Professional behaviour and leadership skills (including communication, teaching and training, keeping up to date, managing people and resources within healthcare, promoting good health and the ethical and legal obligations of a surgeon)

CHAPTER 1
Perioperative Care

Tristan E McMillan

SECTION 1

Assessment of fitness for surgery

Learning point

Before considering surgical intervention it is necessary to prepare the patient as fully as possible.

The extent of pre-op preparation depends on:
- Classification of surgery:
  - Elective
  - Scheduled
  - Urgent
  - Emergency
- Nature of the surgery (minor, major, major-plus)
- Location of the surgery (A&E, endoscopy, minor theatre, main theatre)
- Facilities available

The rationale for pre-op preparation is to:
- Determine a patient's 'fitness for surgery'
- Anticipate difficulties
- Make advanced preparation and organise facilities, equipment and expertise
- Enhance patient safety and minimise chance of errors
- Alleviate any relevant fear/anxiety perceived by the patient
- Reduce morbidity and mortality

Common factors resulting in cancellation of surgery include:
- Inadequate investigation and management of existing medical conditions
- New acute medical conditions

Classification of surgery according to the National Confidential Enquiry into Patient Outcome and Death (NCEPOD):
- **Elective:** mutually convenient timing
- **Scheduled:** (or semi-elective) early surgery under time limits (eg 3 weeks for malignancy)
- **Urgent:** as soon as possible after adequate resuscitation and within 24 hours

Patients may be:
- Emergency: admitted from A&E; admitted from clinic
- Elective: scheduled admission from home, usually following pre assessment

In 2011 NCEPOD published *Knowing the Risk: A review of the perioperative care of surgical patients* in response to concerns that, although overall surgical mortality rates are low, surgical mortality in the high-risk patient in the UK is significantly higher than in similar patient populations in the USA. They assessed over 19 000 surgical cases prospectively and identified four key areas for improvement (see overleaf).

1. **Identification of the high-risk group preoperatively**, eg scoring systems to highlight those at high risk
2. **Improved pre-op assessment, triage and preparation**, proper preassessment systems with full investigations and work-up for elective patients and more rigorous assessment and preoperative management of the emergency surgical patient, especially in terms of fluid management
3. **Improved intraoperative care:** especially fluid management, invasive and cardiac output monitoring
4. **Improved use of postoperative resources:** use of high-dependency beds and critical care facilities

1.1 Preoperative assessment

Learning point

Preoperative preparation of a patient before admission may include:
- History
- Physical examination
- Investigations as indicated:
  - Blood tests
  - Urinalysis
  - ECG
  - Radiological investigations
  - Microbiological investigations
  - Special tests
- Consent and counselling

The preassessment clinic is a useful tool for performing some or all of these tasks before admission.

Preassessment clinics

The preassessment clinic aims to assess surgical patients 2–4 weeks preadmission for elective surgery.

Preassessment is timed so that the gap between assessment and surgery is:
- Long enough so that a suitable response can be made to any problem highlighted
- Short enough so that new problems are unlikely to arise in the interim

The timing of the assessment also means that:
- Surgical team can identify current pre-op problems
- High-risk patients can undergo early anaesthetic review
- Perioperative problems can be anticipated and suitable arrangements made (eg book intensive therapy unit [ITU]/ high-dependency unit [HDU] bed for the high-risk patient)
- Medications can be stopped or adapted (eg anticoagulants, drugs that increase risk of deep vein thrombosis [DVT])
- There is time for assessment by allied specialties (eg dietitian, stoma nurse, occupational therapist, social worker)
- The patient can be admitted to hospital closer to the time of surgery, thereby reducing hospital stay

The patient should be reviewed again on admission for factors likely to influence prognosis and any changes in their pre-existing conditions (eg new chest infection, further weight loss).

Preassessment is run most efficiently by following a set protocol for the preoperative management of each patient group. The protocol-led system has several advantages:
- The proforma is an aide-mémoire in clinic
- Gaps in pre-op work up are easily visible
- Reduces variability between clerking by juniors

However, be wary of preordered situations because they can be dangerous and every instruction must be reviewed on an individual patient basis, eg the patient may be allergic to the antibiotics that are prescribed as part of the preassessment work-up and alternatives should be given.

Preoperative history

A good history is essential to acquire important information before surgery and to establish a good rapport with the patient. Try to ask open rather than leading questions, but direct the resulting conversation. Taking a history also gives you an opportunity to assess patient understanding and the level at which you should pitch your subsequent explanations.

A detailed chapter on taking a surgical history can be found in the new edition of the PasTest book *MRCS Part B OSCES: Essential Revision Notes in Information Gathering under Communication Skills*. In summary, the history should cover the points in the following box.

Taking a surgical history

1. Introductory sentence

Name, age, gender, occupation.

2. Presenting complaint

In one simple phrase, the main complaint that brought the patient into hospital, and the duration of that complaint, eg 'Change in bowel habit for 6 months'.

3. History of presenting complaint

(a) *The story* of the complaint as the patient describes it from when he or she was last well to the present

(b) *Details of the presenting complaint*, eg if it is a pain ask about the site, intensity, radiation, onset, duration, character, alleviating and exacerbating factors, or symptoms associated with previous episodes

(c) *Review of the relevant system(s)* which may include the gastrointestinal, gynaecological and urological review, but does not include the systems not affected by the presenting complaint. This involves direct questioning about every aspect of that system and recording the negatives and the positives

(d) *Relevant medical history*, ie any previous episodes, surgery or investigations directly relevant to this episode. Do not include irrelevant previous operations here. Ask if he or she has had this complaint before, when, how and seen by whom

(e) *Risk factors*. Ask about risk factors relating to the complaint, eg family history, smoking, high cholesterol. Ask about risk factors for having a general anaesthetic, eg previous anaesthetics, family history of problems under anaesthetic, false teeth, caps or crowns, limiting comorbidity, exercise tolerance or anticoagulation medications

4. Past medical and surgical history

In this section should be all the previous medical history, operations, illnesses, admissions to hospital, etc that were not mentioned as relevant to the history of the presenting complaint.

continued overleaf

---

5. Drug history and allergies
List of all drugs, dosages and times that they were taken. List allergies and nature of reactions to alleged allergens. Ask directly about the oral contraceptive pill and antiplatelet medication such as aspirin and clopidogrel which may have to be stopped preoperatively.

6. Social history
Smoking and drinking – how much and for how long. Recreational drug abuse. Who is at home with the patient? Who cares for them? Social Services input? Stairs or bungalow? How much can they manage themselves?

7. Family history

8. Full review of non-relevant systems
This includes all the systems not already covered in the history of the presenting complaint, eg respiratory, cardiovascular, neurological, endocrine and orthopaedic.

Physical examination

Detailed descriptions of methods of physical examination can only really be learnt by observation and practice. Don't rely on the examination of others – surgical signs may change and others may miss important pathologies. See *MRCS Part B OSCEs: Essential Revision Notes* for details of surgical examinations for each surgical system.

Physical examination
General examination: is the patient well or in extremis? Are they in pain? Look for anaemia, cyanosis and jaundice, etc. Do they have characteristic facies or body habitus (eg thyrotoxicosis, cushingoid, marfanoid)? Are they obese or cachectic? Look at the hands for nail clubbing, palmar erythema, etc

Cardiovascular examination: pulse, BP, jugular venous pressure (JVP), heart sounds and murmurs. Vascular bruits (carotids, aortic, renal, femoral) and peripheral pulses

Respiratory examination: respiratory rate (RR), trachea, percussion, auscultation, use of accessory muscles

Abdominal examination: scars from previous surgery, tenderness, organomegaly, mass, peritonism, rectal examination

CNS examination: particularly important in vascular patients pre-carotid surgery and in patients with suspected spinal compression

Musculoskeletal examination: before orthopaedic surgery

1.2 Preoperative laboratory testing and imaging

When to perform a clinical investigation

- To confirm a diagnosis
- To exclude a differential diagnosis
- To assess appropriateness of surgical intervention
- To asses fitness for surgery

When deciding on appropriate investigations for a patient you should consider:

- Simple investigations first
- Safety (non-invasive investigation before invasive investigation if possible)
- Cost vs benefit
- The likelihood of the investigation providing an answer (sensitivity and specificity of the investigation)
- **Ultimately, will the investigation change your management?**

When to perform a preoperative FBC

In practice almost all surgical patients have an FBC measured but it is particularly important in the following groups:

- All emergency pre-op cases – especially abdominal conditions, trauma, sepsis
- All elective pre-op cases aged >60 years
- All elective pre-op cases in adult women
- If surgery is likely to result in significant blood loss
- If there is suspicion of blood loss, anaemia, haematopoietic disease, sepsis, cardiorespiratory disease, coagulation problems

---

Blood tests

Full blood count (FBC)

FBC provides information on the following (normal ranges in brackets):

- Haemoglobin concentration (12–16 g/dl in males; 11–14 g/dl in females)
- White cell count (WCC 5–10 $\times$ 10^9/l)
- Platelet count (150–450 $\times$ 10^9/l)

Also it may reveal details of red cell morphology (eg macrocytosis in alcoholism, microcytosis in iron deficiency anaemia) and white cell differential (eg lymphopenia, neutrophilia).

Urea and electrolytes (U&Es)

U&Es provide information on the following (normal ranges in brackets):

- Sodium (133–144 mmol/l)
- Potassium (3.5–5.5 mmol/l)
- Urea (2.5–6.5 mmol/l)
- Creatinine (55–150 µmol/l)

The incidence of an unexpected abnormality in apparently fit patients aged <40 years is <1% but increases with age and ASA grading (American Society of Anesthesiologists).

When to perform a preoperative U&E

In practice almost all surgical patients get their U&Es tested but it is particularly important in the following groups:

- All pre-op cases aged >65
- Positive result from urinalysis (eg ketonuria)
- All patients with cardiopulmonary disease, or taking diuretics, steroids or drugs active on the cardiovascular system
- All patients with a history of renal/liver disease or an abnormal nutritional state
- All patients with a history of diarrhoea/vomiting or other metabolic/ endocrine disease
- All patients on an intravenous infusion for >24 hours

Amylase

- Normal plasma amylase range varies with different reference laboratories
- Perform in all adult emergency admissions with abdominal pain, before consideration of surgery
- Inflammation surrounding the pancreas will cause mild elevation of the amylase; dramatic elevation of the amylase results from pancreatitis

Random blood glucose (RBG)

- Normal plasma glucose range is 3–7 mmol/l

When to perform an RBG

- Emergency admissions with abdominal pain, especially if suspecting pancreatitis
- Preoperative elective cases with diabetes mellitus, malnutrition or obesity
- All elective pre-op cases aged >60 years
- When glycosuria or ketonuria is present on urinalysis

Clotting tests

Prothrombin time (PT)

- 11–13 seconds
- Measures the functional components of the extrinsic pathway prolonged with warfarin therapy, in liver disease and disseminated intravascular coagulation (DIC)

Activated partial thromboplastin time (APTT)

- <35 seconds
- Measures the functional components of the intrinsic pathway and is prolonged in haemophilia A and B, with heparin therapy and in DIC

International normalised ratio (INR)

- 0.9–1.3 for normal person; range varies for those on warfarin depending on reason for treatment
- INR is a ratio of the patient's PT to a normal, control sample

Sickle cell test

Different hospitals have different protocols, but in general you would be wise to perform a sickle cell test in all black patients in whom surgery is planned, and in anyone who has sickle cell disease in the family. Patients should be counselled before testing to facilitate informed consent.

Liver function tests (LFTs)

- Perform LFTs in all patients with upper abdominal pain, jaundice, known hepatic dysfunction or history of alcohol abuse
- Remember that clotting tests are the most sensitive indicator of liver synthetic disorder and may be deranged before changes in the LFTs. Decreased albumin levels are an indicator of chronic illness and sepsis

Group and save/cross-match

When to perform a group and save:
- Emergency pre-op cases likely to result in significant surgical blood loss, especially trauma, acute abdomen, vascular cases
- If there is suspicion of blood loss, anaemia, haematopoietic disease, coagulation defects
- Procedures on pregnant females

Urinalysis

When to perform pre-op urinalysis:
- All emergency cases with abdominal or pelvic pain
- All elective cases with diabetes mellitus
- All pre-op cases with thoracic, abdominal or pelvic trauma

A **midstream urine** (MSU) specimen should be considered before genitourinary operations and in pre-op patients with abdominal or loin pain.

A **urine pregnancy test** should be performed in all women of childbearing age with abdominal symptoms, or who need a radiograph.

Electrocardiography

A 12-lead electrocardiogram (ECG) is capable of detecting acute or long-standing pathological conditions affecting the heart, particularly changes in rhythm, myocardial perfusion or prior infarction.

Note that the resting ECG is not a sensitive test for coronary heart disease, being normal in up to 50%. An exercise test is preferred.

When to perform a 12-lead ECG:
- Patients with a history of heart disease, diabetes, hypertension or vascular disease, regardless of age
- Patients aged >60 with hypertension or other vascular disease
- Patients undergoing cardiothoracic surgery, taking cardiotoxic drugs or with an irregular pulse
- Any suspicion of hitherto undiagnosed cardiac disease

Radiological investigations

Radiological investigations may include:
- **Plain films:** chest radiograph, plain abdominal film, lateral decubitus film, KUB (kidney, ureter, bladder) film, skeletal views
- **Contrast studies and X-ray screening:** Gastrografin, intravenous (IV) contrast
- **Ultrasonography:** abdominal, thoracic, peripheral vasculature
- **Computed tomography (CT):** intra-abdominal or intrathoracic pathology
- **Magnetic resonance imaging (MRI):** particularly for orthopaedics, spinal cord compression, liver pathology

Chest radiograph

When to perform a pre-op chest radiograph:

- All elective pre-op cases aged >60 years
- All cases of cervical, thoracic or abdominal trauma
- Acute respiratory symptoms or signs
- Previous cardiorespiratory disease and no recent chest radiograph
- Thoracic surgery
- Patients with malignancy
- Suspicion of perforated intra-abdominal viscus
- Recent history of tuberculosis (TB)
- Recent immigrants from areas with a high prevalence of TB
- Thyroid enlargement (retrosternal extension)

Plain abdominal film

Plain abdominal films should be performed when there is:

- Suspicion of obstruction
- Suspicion of perforated intra-abdominal viscus
- Suspicion of peritonitis

The role of radiological investigation in diagnosis and planning is discussed further in Chapter 2, Surgical technique and technology.

Microbiological investigations

The use and collection of microbiological specimens is discussed in *Surgical microbiology*.

Investigating special cases

Coexisting disease

- A chest radiograph for patients with severe rheumatoid arthritis (they are at risk of disease of the odontoid peg, causing subluxation and danger to the cervical spinal cord under anaesthesia)
- Specialised cardiac investigations (eg echocardiography, cardiac stress testing, MUGA scan) used to assess pre-op cardiac reserve and are increasingly used routinely before major surgery
- Specialised respiratory investigations (eg spirometry) to assess pulmonary function and reserve

Investigations relating to the organ in question

- Angiography or duplex scanning in arterial disease before bypass
- Renal perfusion or renal isotope imaging or liver biopsy before transplant
- Colonoscopy, barium enema or CT colonography (CTC) before bowel resection for cancer

1.3 Preoperative consent and counselling

Deciding to operate

It is often said that the best surgeon knows when *not* to operate. The decision to undertake surgery must be based on all available information from a thorough history, examination and investigative tests. All treatment options, including non-surgical management, and the risks and potential outcomes of each course of action must be discussed fully with the patient in order to achieve informed consent. In some specialties, clinical nurse practitioners or other support staff may support the patient (eg a breast-care nurse before mastectomy, a colorectal nurse specialist before an operation resulting in a stoma). This helps to prepare the patient for surgery, gives them an opportunity to ask further questions and provides a support network.

Counselling

Medical staff spend most of their working life in and around hospitals, so it is easy to forget how the public view hospital admission, surgical procedures and the postop stay on the ward. It is important to recognise that all patients are different – in their ages, in their beliefs and in their worries.

Presenting information to patients

- Discuss diagnoses and treatment options at a time when the patient is best able to understand and retain the information
- Use up-to-date written material, visual and other aids to explain complex aspects of surgery
- Use accurate data to explain the prognosis of a condition and probabilities of treatment success or the risks of failure
- Ensure distressing information is given in a considerate way, and offer access to specialist nurses, counselling services and patient support groups
- Allow the patient time to absorb the material, perhaps with repeated consultations or written back-up material

- Ensure voluntary decision-making: you may recommend a course of action but you must not put pressure on the patient to accept it. Ensure that the patient has an opportunity to review the decision nearer the time.

Responding to questions: you must respond honestly to any questions that the patient raises and, as far as possible, answer as fully as the patient wishes.

Withholding information: you should not withhold information necessary for decision-making unless you judge that disclosure of some relevant information would cause the patient serious harm (not including becoming upset or refusing treatment). You may not withhold information from a patient at the request of any other person including a relative.

If a patient insists that he or she does not want to know the details of a condition or a treatment, you should explain the importance of knowing the options and should still provide basic information about the condition or treatment unless you think that this would cause the patient some harm.

Records: you should record in the medical records what you have discussed with the patient and who was present. This helps to establish a timeline and keeps other members of staff informed as to what the patient knows. You must record in the medical records if you have withheld treatment and your reasons for doing so.

General concerns of the surgical patient

Is this the first time the patient has been in hospital?

Never forget that *all* surgical procedures are significant to the patient, no matter how simple we believe the case to be.

Good communication is essential so that the patient knows what to expect beforehand and can make an informed decision:

- Check that you know the patient well enough and understand the problem enough to explain it to him or her
- Choose the setting
- Explain the diagnosis in terms that they will understand
- Explain the possible options
- Explain the difference between between conservative and surgical managements of the condition
- Ask if the patient has any thoughts about the options
- Ask if he or she has any questions
- Give the patient the option to ask you questions later

Think about potential questions from the patient and address them in your explanation:

- **What are the risks of anaesthetic and surgery?**
- Colostomy
- Transplantation
- Amputated limbs
- What if things go wrong?
- How long will I stay in hospital?
- Will I die?

Specific considerations of the individual

Knowledge

- How much does the patient know and understand?
- Is the patient's understanding influenced by what he or she has read (eg on the internet) or by previous experience, either personal or through people whom he or she knows

Employment

- Will surgery affect a return to work?

Social network

- What support does the patient have? Family, friends, carers?
- What responsibilities does the patient have, eg children, dependants
- When can I drive?

Physical issues/deformity

Psychological issues

Recovery and what to expect

- How long will I be in hospital for?

Complications

- What potential complications may result in readmission (eg wound infection, unsuccessful operation)?

Obtaining consent

The General Medical Council gives the following guidelines (GMC 2008).

Ask patients whether they have understood the information and whether they would like more before making a decision. Sometimes asking the patient to explain back to you, in his or her own words, what you have just said clarifies areas that the patient does not really understand and may need more explanation.

The legal right to consent

The ability to give informed consent for different patient ages and groups is discussed fully in Chapter 8, Ethics, Clinical Governance and the Medicolegal Aspects of Surgery.

Obtaining consent

Provide sufficient information:

- Details of diagnosis
- Prognosis if the condition is left untreated and if the condition is treated
- Options for further investigations if diagnosis is uncertain
- Options for treatment or management of the condition
- The option not to treat
- The purpose of the proposed investigation or treatment
- Details of the procedure, including subsidiary treatment such as pain relief
- How the patient should prepare for the procedure
- Common and serious side effects
- Likely benefits and probabilities of success
- Discussion of any serious or frequently occurring risks
- Lifestyle changes that may result from the treatment
- Advice on whether any part of the proposed treatment is experimental
- How and when the patient's condition will be monitored and reassessed
- The name of the doctor who has overall responsibility for the treatment
- Whether doctors in training or students will be involved
- A reminder that patients can change their minds about a decision at any time
- A reminder that patients have a right to seek a second opinion
- Explain how decisions are made about whether to move from one stage of treatment to another (eg chemotherapy)
- Explain that there may be different teams of doctors involved (eg anaesthetists)
- Seek consent to treat any problems that might arise and need to be dealt with while the patient is unconscious or otherwise unable to make a decision
- Ascertain whether there are any procedures to which a patient would object (eg blood transfusions)

1.4 Identification and documentation

Patient identification

Patient identification is essential. All patients should be given an identity wristband on admission to hospital, which should state clearly and legibly the patient's name, date of birth, ward and consultant. He or she should also be given a separate red wristband documenting allergies. Patient identification is checked by the nursing team on admission to theatre.

Documentation

Medical documents (medical notes, drug and fluid charts, consent forms and operation notes) are legal documents. All entries to the notes should be written clearly and legibly. Always write the date and time and your name and position at the beginning of each entry.

Documentation often starts with clerking. Record as much information as possible in the format described above for history and examination. The source of information should also be stated (eg from patient, relative, old notes, clinic letter, GP).

Accurate documentation should continue for each episode of patient contact, including investigations, procedures, ward rounds and conversations with the patient about diagnosis or treatment.

File documents in the notes yourself; otherwise they will get lost. This is important to protect both the patient and yourself. From a medicolegal point of view, if it is not documented then it didn't happen.

1.5 Patient optimisation for elective surgery

Morbidity and mortality increase in patients with comorbidity.

Optimising the patient's condition gives them the best possible chance of a good surgical outcome. Do not forget that this includes nutrition.

In patients with severe comorbidity then NCEPOD recommend the following:
- Discussion between surgeon and anaesthetist before theatre
- Adequate preoperative investigation
- Optimisation of surgery by ensuring:
  - An appropriate grade of surgeon (to minimise operative time and blood loss)
  - Adequate preoperative resuscitation
  - Provision of on-table monitoring
- Critical-care facilities are available

Optimisation of patients for elective surgery

Control underlying comorbidity: specialist advice on the management of underlying comorbidities (cardiovascular, respiratory, renal, endocrinological) should be sought. Individual comorbidities are discussed later in the chapter. Optimisation should be undertaken in a timely fashion as an outpatient for elective surgery, although some may occasionally require inpatient care and intervention before scheduling an elective procedure.

Nutrition: good nutrition is essential for good wound healing. Malnourished patients do badly and a period of preoperative dietary improvement (eg build-up drinks, enteral feeding, total parenteral nutrition or TPN) improves outcome.

1.6 Resuscitation of the emergency patient

It is essential that the acutely ill surgical patient is adequately resuscitated and stabilised before theatre. In extreme and life-threatening conditions this may not be possible (eg ruptured abdominal aortic aneurysm or AAA, trauma) and resuscitation should not delay definitive treatment.

Most emergency patients fall into one of two categories: haemorrhage or sepsis. The management of haemorrhage and sepsis are dealt with in detail in the Chapters 3 and 4 of this book respectively.

General principles of resuscitation are:
- Optimise circulating volume:
  - **Correct dehydration:** many acute surgical patients require IV fluids to correct dehydration and restore electrolyte balance. Establish good IV access. Insertion of a urinary catheter is vital to monitor fluid balance carefully with hourly measurements. Severe renal impairment may require dialysis before theatre. Dehydrated patients may exhibit profound drops in blood pressure on anaesthetic induction and aggressive preoperative fluid management is often required
  - **Correct anaemia:** anaemia compromises cardiac and respiratory function and is not well tolerated in patients with poor cardiac reserve. The anaemia may be acute (acute bleed) or chronic (underlying pathology). If anaemia is acute, transfuse to reasonable Hb and correct clotting. Consider the effects of massive transfusion and order and replace clotting factors simultaneously. Chronic anaemia is better tolerated but may also require correction before theatre

- **Treat pain:** pain results in the release of adrenaline and can cause tachycardia and hypertension. Pain control before anaesthesia reduces cardiac workload
- Give **appropriate antibiotics** early as required in sepsis. These may need to be empirical until antimicrobial treatment can be guided by blood and pus cultures
- **Decompress the stomach:** insert a nasogastric (NG) tube to decompress the stomach because this reduces the risk of aspiration on anaesthetic induction

1.7 The role of prophylaxis

Prophylaxis essentially refers to the reduction or prevention of a known risk. Preoperatively prophylaxis should include:
- **Stopping potentially harmful factors:**
  - Stopping medications (eg the oral contraceptive pill for a month, aspirin or clopidogrel for 2 weeks before surgery)
  - Stopping smoking: improves respiratory function even if the patient can only stop for 24 hours
- **Prescribing drugs known to reduce risks:**
  - Heparin to reduce the risk of DVT
  - Cardiac medications (eg preoperative β blockers, statins or angiotensin-converting enzyme [ACE] inhibitors) to reduce cardiovascular risk

1.8   Preoperative marking

This should be performed after consent and before the patient has received premedication. Marking is essential to help avoid mistakes in theatre. Marking while the patient is conscious is important to minimise error. Preoperative marking is especially important if the patient is having:

- A unilateral procedure (eg on a limb or the groin)
- A lesion excised
- A tender or symptomatic area operated on (eg an epigastric hernia)
- A stoma

Marking for surgery

- Explain to the patient that you are going to mark the site for surgery
- Confirm the procedure and the site (including left or right) with the notes, patient and consent form
- Position the patient appropriately (eg standing for marking varicose veins, supine for abdominal surgery)
- Use a surgical marker that will not come off during skin preparation
- Clearly identify the surgical site using a large arrow

SECTION 2

Preoperative management of coexisting disease

2.1 Preoperative medications

Learning point

If a patient is having surgery:
- Review pre-existing medication:
  - Document preoperative medications
  - Decide which drugs need to be stopped preoperatively
  - Decide on alternative formulations
- Prescribe preoperative medication:
  - Prescribe prophylactic medication
  - Prescribe medication related to the surgery
  - Prescribe premed if needed
- Be aware of problems with specific drugs:
  - Steroids and immunosuppressants
  - Anticoagulants and fibrinolytics

Review pre-existing medication

Perioperative management of pre-existing medication

Document preoperative medications

Decide whether any drugs need to be stopped before surgery
- Stop oral contraceptive (OCP) or tamoxifen 4 weeks before major or limb surgery – risk of thrombosis
- Stop monoamine oxidase inhibitor (MAOI) antidepressants – they interact with anaesthetic drugs, with cardiac risk
- Stop antiplatelet drugs 7–14 days preoperatively – risk of haemorrhage

Decide on alternative formulations for the perioperative period
- For example, IV rather than oral, heparin rather than warfarin

Regular medications should generally be given – even on the day of surgery (with a sip of clear fluid only). If in doubt ask the anaesthetist. This is important, especially for cardiac medication. There are some essential medications (eg anti-rejection therapy in transplant recipients) that may be withheld for 24 hours in the surgical period but this should only be under the direction of a specialist in the field.

Prescribe preoperative medication

> **Medication for the preoperative period**
>
> **Pre-existing medication** (see above for those drugs that should be excluded)
>
> **Prophylactic medication**
> - For example, DVT prophylaxis
> - For example, antibiotic prophylaxis
>
> **Medication related to the surgery**
> - For example, laxatives to clear the bowel before resection
> - For example, methylene blue to aid surgical identification of the parathyroids
>
> **Anaesthetic premedication** (to reduce anxiety, reduce secretions, etc)

Be aware of problems with specific drugs

Steroids and immunosuppression

Indications for perioperative corticosteroid cover
This includes patients:
- With pituitary–adrenal insufficiency on steroids

- Undergoing pituitary or adrenal surgery
- On systemic steroid therapy of >7.5 mg for >1 week before surgery
- Who received a course of steroids for >1 month in the previous 6 months

Complications of steroid therapy in the perioperative period
- Poor wound healing
- Increased risk of infection
- Side effects of steroid therapy (eg impaired glucose tolerance, osteoporosis, muscle wasting, fragile skin and veins, peptic ulceration)
- Mineralocorticoid effects (sodium and water retention, potassium loss and metabolic alkalosis)
- Masking of sepsis/peritonism
- Glucocorticoid deficiency in the perioperative period (may present as increasing cardiac failure which is unresponsive to catecholamines, or addisonian crisis with vomiting and cardiovascular collapse)

Management of patients on pre-op steroid therapy
This depends on the nature of the surgery to be performed and the level of previous steroid use.
- **Minor use:** 50 mg hydrocortisone intramuscularly/intravenously IM/IV preoperatively
- **Intermediate use:** 50 mg hydrocortisone IM/IV with premed and 50 mg hydrocortisone every 6 h for 24 h
- **Major use:** 100 mg hydrocortisone IM/IV with premed and 100 mg hydrocortisone every 6 h for at least 72 h after surgery

Equivalent doses of steroid therapy: hydrocortisone 100 mg, prednisolone 25 mg, dexamethasone 4 mg.

Anticoagulants and fibrinolytics

Consider the risk of thrombosis (augmented by postsurgical state itself) vs risk of haemorrhage.

Warfarin

- Inhibits vitamin K-dependent coagulation factors (II, VII, IX and X) as well as protein C and its cofactor, protein S
- Illness and drug interactions may have unpredictable effects on the level of anticoagulation
- Anticoagulative effects can be reversed by vitamin K (10 mg IV; takes 24 h for adequate synthesis of inhibited factors) and fresh frozen plasma (15 ml/kg; immediate replacement of missing factors)
- Stop 3–5 days before surgery and replace with heparin; depends on indication for anticoagulation (eg metal heart valve is an absolute indication, but atrial fibrillation [AF] is a relative one)
- INR should be <1.2 for open surgery and <1.5 for invasive procedures

Heparin

- Mucopolysaccharide purified from intestine
- Binds to antithrombin III and so inhibits factors IIa, IXa, Xa and XIIa
- May be unfractionated or fractionated (low-molecular-weight heparin [LMWH])

Uses of heparin include:

- General anticoagulant (should be stopped 6 h before surgery)
- Treatment of unstable angina
- Maintenance of extracorporeal circuits (eg dialysis, bypass)
- Flush for IV lines to maintain patency
- In vascular surgery before temporary occlusion of a vessel to prevent distal thrombosis

Unfractionated heparin

- Given by continuous infusion (short half-life)
- Check APTT every 6 h and adjust rate until steady state (ratio of 2:3) achieved

Fractionated heparin (LMWH)

- Inhibits only factor Xa
- Increased half-life and more predictable bioavailability (compared with unfractionated form)
- Can be given once daily (eg tinzaparin) or twice a day (eg enoxaparin)
- Heparin can cause an immune reaction (heparin-induced thrombocytopenia [HIT]); LMWH is less likely to do so
- Effects can be reversed by use of protamine 1 mg per 100 units heparin (may cause hypotension and in high doses, paradoxically, may cause anticoagulation)
- Can be used during pregnancy (non-teratogenic)

Antiplatelet agents

- Increasingly used (eg aspirin, dipyridamole, clopidogrel, abciximab)
- Decrease platelet aggregation and reduce thrombus formation
- May be used in combination
- Should be stopped 7–14 days before major surgery or there is a risk of uncontrollable bleeding

Fibrinolytics

- Examples include streptokinase and alteplase
- Act by activating plasminogen to plasmin, which undertakes clot fibrinolysis
- Used in acute MI, extensive DVT and PE
- Contraindicated if the patient had undergone recent surgery, trauma, recent haemorrhage, pancreatitis, aortic dissection, etc

For discussions of the management of immuno-suppression in the perioperative period see *Transplantation* in Book 2. DVT prophylaxis in the perioperative period is covered in Chapter 3, section 1.2, Surgical haematology.

2.2 Preoperative management of cardiovascular disease

Learning point

Cardiac comorbidity increases surgical mortality (includes ischaemic heart disease, hypertension, valvular disease, arrhythmias and cardiac failure).
Special care must be taken with pacemakers and implantable defibrillators. In general it is necessary to:
- Avoid changes in heart rate (especially tachycardia)
- Avoid changes in BP
- Avoid pain
- Avoid anaemia
- Avoid hypoxia (give supplemental oxygen)
In addition, the details of preoperative assessment before cardiac surgery is covered in Book 2.

The European Society of Cardiology has published guidelines (2009) to cover the preoperative risk assessment and perioperative management of patients with cardiovascular disease. Patient-specific factors are more important in determining risk than the type of surgery but, with regard to cardiac risk, surgical interventions can be divided into low-risk, intermediate-risk and high-risk groups:

- **Low risk** (cardiac event rate 1%): most breast, eye, dental, minor orthopaedics, minor urological and gynaecological procedures
- **Medium risk** (cardiac event rate 1–5%): abdominal surgery, orthopaedic and neurological surgery, transplantation surgery, minor vascular surgery and endovascular repair
- **High risk** (cardiac event rate >5%): major vascular surgery

Laparoscopic surgery has a similar cardiac risk to open procedures because the raised intra-abdominal pressure results in reduced venous return with decreased cardiac output and decreased systemic vascular resistance, and should therefore be risk assessed accordingly.

The Lee Index is a predictor of individual cardiac risk and contains six independent clinical determinants of major perioperative cardiac events:
- A history of ischaemic heart disease (IHD)
- A history of cerebrovascular disease
- Heart failure
- Type 1 diabetes mellitus
- Impaired renal function
- High-risk surgery

The presence of each factor scores 1 point. Patients with an index of 0, 1, 2 and 3 points correspond to an incidence of major cardiac complications of 0.4%, 0.9%, 7% and 11% respectively.

Investigation of patients with cardiac disease

Investigation of patients with previous cardiac disease aims to look at three cardiac risk markers (myocardial ischaemia, left ventricular [LV] dysfunction and valvular abnormality) which are all major determinants of adverse postoperative outcome.

Blood tests

FBC

- Correction of anaemia is essential because it compromises cardiac and respiratory function and is not well tolerated in patients with ischaemic disease
- May require iron supplements or even staged transfusion

Electrolytes

- Potassium and magnesium levels may affect cardiac functioning and should be optimised
- Bear in mind that electrolyte disturbances occur in patients treated with diuretics

Specialist non-invasive tests

Assessing myocardial ischaemia

ECG: remember that ischaemia may be silent. Look for previous infarct, ischaemia at rest, bundle branch block (BBB) or LV hypertrophy (LVH) (evidence of strain) or arrhythmia. Acts as a baseline for comparison in the future, enabling new changes to be distinguished from pre-existing abnormalities.

Exercise testing: physiological exercise gives an estimate of functional capacity, can assess heart rate and BP changes and looks at ischaemia by monitoring dynamic ST segment change.

Dobutamine stress testing or **cardiac perfusion scanning** may also be used for specialist investigation. **CT detection of coronary vessel calcium** and **MR angiography** can also be performed.

Assessing LV function

Echocardiography: provides an estimate of ejection fraction and can assess valvular structure and regions of ventricular wall akinesis suggestive of previous ischaemic damage.

Combined cardiopulmonary testing (CPET): this is a programmed exercise test on a cycle or treadmill with measurement of inspired and expired gases. It assesses peak oxygen consumption and anaerobic threshold and provides an objective measurement of functional capacity.

Always bear in mind that a patient may need his or her cardiac condition optimised by a cardiologist. This may require pharmacological measures such as β–blockers, statins or ACE inhibitors, all of which have been shown to improve surgical outcomes in different groups of patients. It may be necessary to arrange angioplasty, coronary artery bypass graft (CABG) or valvular surgery before other elective procedures are attempted.

Intraoperative considerations for patients with cardiac disease

Cardiac effects of general anaesthesia (GA) include:

- Systemic vascular resistance decreases (induction decreases arterial pressure by 20–30%)
- Tracheal intubation decreases BP by 20–30 mmHg
- Causes myocardial depression (IV agents less than inhaled agents)

- Cardiac irritability increases (increased sensitivity to the catecholamines released in response to surgery predisposes to arrhythmia)

Cardiac effects of regional anaesthesia include:
- Vasodilatation (blocks sympathetic outflow)
- May be combined with GA for pain control

Ischaemic heart disease

Preoperative considerations
Known risk factors must be identified in the history (eg smoking, hypertension, hyperlipidaemia, diabetes, including a positive family history). A careful examination of the heart and lungs must be performed. Remember that **ischaemia may be silent**.

New York Heart Association (NYHA) classification

Grade 1 No limitation on ordinary physical activity

Grade 2 Slight limitation on physical activity; ordinary activity results in palpitations, dyspnoea or angina

Grade 3 Marked limitation of physical activity; less than ordinary activity results in palpitations, dyspnoea or angina

Grade 4 Inability to carry out any physical activity without discomfort; symptoms may be present at rest

---

A recent myocardial infarction (MI) dramatically increases the risk of re-infarction in the perioperative period, ie 80% in the first 3 weeks, 25–40% in the first 3 months and 10–15% in 3–6 months. After 6 months the risk drops to 5% and is normally the minimum time period that is an acceptable risk for an elective procedure.

Obviously the risk must be balanced against any potential benefit of a surgical procedure.

Hypertension

Causes of hypertension
- Essential hypertension
- Pain
- Anxiety (eg white-coat hypertension)
- Fluid overload
- Hypoxia and hypercapnia

If the diastolic blood pressure is >110 mmHg then elective procedures should be discussed with the anaesthetist and possibly postponed until better control can be achieved. After appropriate pain relief take three separate BP readings, separated by a period of at least 1 hour, to help exclude anxiety or discomfort as a cause.

Newly diagnosed hypertension must be assessed for possible reversible aetiological factors (eg renal disease, endocrine diseases such as phaeochromocytoma, pregnancy, the OCP and coarctation of the aorta).

Chronic (long-standing) hypertension puts the patient at increased risk of cardiovascular disease, cerebrovascular events and renal impairment. These patients are also at higher risk of hypertensive crises. These conditions need to be excluded or optimised, if possible, before an elective surgical procedure. LVH (whether clinically, radiologically or electrocardiographically detected) is directly related to myocardial ischaemia. Poorly controlled hypertension in the immediate pre-op period predisposes the patient to perioperative cardiac morbidity and must be avoided.

Valvular disease

Patients with valvular disease are susceptible to endocarditis if they become septic. Prophylactic antibiotics are important. They may also be on long-term anticoagulation.

Aortic stenosis

Associated with a 13% risk of perioperative death (risk increases with increasing stenosis to 50% for patients with critical aortic stenosis). Symptomatic aortic stenosis (AS) produces syncope, dyspnoea and angina. On examination there may be an ejection systolic murmur (radiates to the carotids), a soft or absent second heart sound, and pulsus parvus. The valve needs assessing with echocardiography (valve area <1 cm^2 or gradient of >50 mmHg indicates critical AS).

Mitral stenosis

May predispose to pulmonary hypertension and right cardiac failure. Clinically look for mitral facies, diastolic murmur and atrial fibrillation (AF) (increased pressure chronically enlarges the left atrium). Must be given prophylactic antibiotics for invasive procedures. Minimise fluid overload and changes in cardiac rate.

Arrhythmias

Atrial fibrillation

Common arrhythmia giving an irregularly irregular beat. Due to short-circuiting of the electrical impulses of the atria resulting in disorganised muscle contraction. Causes reduced efficiency of the atria to pump-prime the ventricles.

Common causes of atrial fibrillation

Acute causes
- Fluid overload
- Sepsis (especially chest)
- Ischaemic event
- Alcohol
- Pulmonary embolism (PE)
- Dehydration
- Thyrotoxicosis

Chronic causes
- Ischaemic or valvular disease

Questions to ask yourself about each case of AF

Is it reversible?
- Acute: may be reversible (consider ways to reduce or remove causes listed above)
- Chronic: rarely reversible (eg irreversibly dilated atria, ischaemic disease)

Is the rate compromising cardiac output?
- Indication of the need for and the speed of intervention; consider oral medication (eg digoxin) vs IV medication (eg amiodarone) vs DC cardioversion

Does the patient need anticoagulating?
- AF predisposes to thrombotic events (blood in the auricles of the atria moves sluggishly and forms clots which are then expelled into the systemic circulation – commonly causing a cerebrovascular accident [CVA])

Pacemakers and implanted ventricular defibrillators

Problems during the surgical period include:

- Interactions with diathermy current: electrical interference with device (eg causing resetting, rate increases or inhibition); current travelling down wires and causing myocardial burn
- Effect of anaesthetic agents on pacing and sensing thresholds
- Problems with rate control devices; may not allow physiological responses (eg tachycardia)

Ask yourself the following questions about the device

- Reason for insertion?
- Continuous or demand model?
- If continuous, is it working optimally (ie is the ECG showing captured beats – large electrical spike seen before each ventricular contraction)?

Patients should have the pacemaker evaluated by cardiology before and after surgery because they will be able to assess and advise on any changes required to the settings.

Always use bipolar diathermy if possible and check for deleterious effects. Unipolar diathermy current may pass down pacing wires, causing cardiac burns so advice should be sought from the cardiologist if unipolar diathermy is thought to be necessary.

Cardiac failure

- Due to acute or chronic ischaemic or valvular disease
- Exercise tolerance is a good indictor of cardiac reserve; ask:

- How far can you walk?
- Can you manage a flight of stairs without getting short of breath?
- Morbidity and mortality increase proportionally to severity of congestive cardiac failure (CCF)
- Ask for a cardiology review in order to optimise fully (eg ACE inhibitors, diuretics) before surgery

Care with fluid management in the perioperative period is essential – remember that these patients may require their regular diuretics.

2.3 Preoperative management of respiratory disease

Learning point

- Respiratory disease commonly includes chronic pulmonary obstructive disease (COPD), asthma, cystic fibrosis, bronchiectasis and infections
- Optimise any reversible component of the condition and avoid surgery during infective exacerbations of the disease
- Encourage smoking cessation (even if just for 24 hours preoperatively)

Note that patients with respiratory disease may be on regular long-term steroids.

Chronic obstructive pulmonary disease and asthma

COPD is pathologically distinct, but frequently coexists with bronchospasm. It may be difficult to determine the importance of each condition in an individual. Generalised airflow obstruction is the dominant feature of both diseases.

History and examination of patients with COPD/asthma

Questions should be directed at:
- Patient's exercise tolerance (eg walking distance on the flat)
- Any recent deterioration resulting in hospital admission
- Previous admission to ITU for ventilation
- Need for home oxygen, and present medical therapy (eg need for steroids)
- Current smoking habit, or when smoking was stopped
- Changes on examination (eg are they consistent with chronic lung disease/focal infective exacerbations)

Investigation of COPD and asthma

Assess baseline levels with lung function tests:
- Forced expiratory volume in 1 s/forced vital capacity (FEV_1/FVC) ratio (if <50% the risk of postop respiratory failure is increased)
- Arterial blood gases (ABGs) confirming CO_2 retention in pure chronic bronchitis
- Sputum cultures and sensitivity in the presence of a productive cough
- Chest radiograph

Management of COPD and asthma
- Give preoperative salbutamol (nebulisers)
- Must treat any reversible component (eg infective exacerbations)
- Consider regional anaesthesia for body surface/lower extremity surgery
- Intraoperative nitrous oxide can rupture bullae, leading to a tension pneumothorax, so use opiates in doses that are not associated with pronounced respiratory depression
- Ensure humidification of inspired gases
- Postoperatively, offer advice about smoking; provide chest physiotherapy; administer continuous positive airway pressure (CPAP) in an HDU setting; provide adequate pain relief allowing deep breathing and early mobilisation; nurse in an upright position in bed, monitoring oxygen saturation

Hypoxia in the perioperative setting is most commonly due to inadequate ventilation or respiratory depression with opiates rather than loss of hypoxic drive due to prolonged high-concentration oxygen therapy. However, the latter should always be borne in mind when dealing with patients with chronic respiratory disease.

Tuberculosis

Many patients have evidence of old TB disease or previous anti-TB surgery on chest radiography. This is not usually a problem, but the resulting lung change and reduced respiratory capacity may need consideration.

Active TB should be considered in recent immigrants from areas where TB is endemic, and in immunosuppressed and HIV patients. They may require preoperative chest radiography, sputum culture, Mantoux testing (if they haven't had previous BCG) and treatment if appropriate.

Bronchiectasis and cystic fibrosis

Preoperative sputum culture and ABG are needed to act as baseline information. Input from respiratory physicians is advisable.

Active physiotherapy, bronchodilators and treatment of residual infections are required before elective surgery. Postoperative physiotherapy at least three times per day is essential.

Smoking

Short-term effects of smoking

- Nicotine increases myocardial oxygen demand
- Carbon monoxide reduces oxygen delivery by binding to haemoglobin
- Carboxyhaemoglobin levels fall if stopped before 12 h pre-surgery
- High carboxyhaemoglobin can give false pulse oximetry readings
- Airway irritability and secretions are increased

Long-term effects of smoking

- Reduces immune function, increases mucus secretion
- Reduces clearance and causes chronic airway disease (cessation needs to be longer than 6–8 weeks to bring about an improvement)
- Increased risk of ischaemic heart disease

Intraoperative considerations in patients with respiratory disease

Site and size of incision

Upper abdominal incisions result in an inability to breathe deeply (basal atelectasis) or to cough (retained secretions), and have a higher incidence of respiratory complications compared with lower abdominal incisions (30% vs 3%). In patients with known respiratory disease, think about the optimal incision site (eg transverse rather than midline).

Analgesia

Optimise analgesia using a combination of local and regional techniques to allow deep breaths and coughing as required. Remember local infiltration intraoperatively. Infiltration of local anaesthesia (LA), eg Chirocaine, into the rectus sheath is helpful in upper midline incisions in those with compromised respiratory function.

Anaesthetic agents

Anaesthetic agents have the following effects:
- Reduce muscle tone and thus functional residual capacity
- Increase airway resistance and reduce lung compliance
- Cause atelectasis in dependent zones of the lung, resulting in pulmonary vascular shunting
- Increase ventilatory dead space

2.4 Preoperative management of endocrine disease

Learning point

- Diabetes mellitus
- Thyroid problems
- Parathyroid problems

Preoperative management of diabetes mellitus

Perioperative management of diabetes mellitus

- Avoid hypoglycaemia (especially under anaesthesia – risk of cerebral damage)
- Avoid hyperglycaemia (osmotic diuresis and dehydration)
- Supply enough insulin (prevent ketoacidosis)
- Be aware of increased risks of postoperative complications (infective, arteriopathic, etc)

Reasons for good glycaemic control

- Prevention of ketosis and acidaemia
- Prevention of electrolyte abnormalities and volume depletion secondary to osmotic diuresis
- Impaired wound strength and wound healing when plasma glucose concentration is >11 mmol/l
- Hyperglycaemia interferes with leucocyte chemotaxis, opsonisation and phagocytosis, and so leads to an impaired immune response
- Avoidance of hypoglycaemia in an anaesthetised patient

Preoperative precautions in patients with diabetes

- Full pre-op history and examination (diabetes is associated with increased risk of IHD, hypertension, peripheral vascular disease [PVD], autonomic and peripheral neuropathy, renovascular disease and renal failure, impaired vision, susceptibility to gastric reflux and delayed gastric emptying)
- Check U&Es
- ECG
- Confirm adequate glycaemic control (see below)

Perioperative precautions in patients with diabetes

- Place first on operating list (reduces period of starvation and risk of hypoglycaemia)
- Protect pressure areas (especially with PVD and neuropathy)
- At risk of increased infection and arteriopathic disease (renal, cardiac, neurological, peripheral) postoperatively

- Involve patients themselves in the management of their diabetes during this period; they are usually very knowledgeable and have managed their disease for a long time

---

Assessment of pre-op control of diabetes

- Daily glucose measurements from the patient's diary
- HbA1c measurement (assesses glycaemic control over the last 8 weeks by measuring levels of glycation of haemoglobin)
- Good control <6.5% (<48 mmol/mol)
- Adequate control 6.5–8.0% (48–64 mmol/mol)
- Poor control >8.0% (>64 mmol/mol)

The normal HbA1c reference range for a non-diabetic patient is 4.0–6.0% (20–42 mmol/mol)

Management of diabetes

Management of type 2 diabetes mellitus
Optimise control preoperatively and continue normal oral hypoglycaemic control until the morning of surgery (except chlorpropamide and metformin, which may need to be reduced or stopped 48 hours in advance – can predispose to lactic acidosis). Postoperatively monitor BM regularly and institute a sliding scale of intravenous insulin if the patient is unable to tolerate an oral diet immediately. Restart patients back on their normal oral hypoglycaemic regimen as soon as an enteral diet is recommenced.

Management of type 1 diabetes mellitus

Achieve good pre-op control and admit the patient the night before surgery. Monitor the patient's BM from admission, and commence the patient on a sliding scale of insulin on the morning of surgery. Restart regular insulin once the patient is eating and drinking normally and observe closely for sepsis. Only discharge the patient once his or her control is within recognised limits because the insulin requirements may well increase transiently after a stressful stimulus such as surgery.

Preoperative management of thyroid problems

For more details of thyroid physiology, pathology and management, see the chapter on Endocrine Surgery in Book 2. Problems associated with thyroid disease include:

- **Local effects:** eg large thyroid goitre can cause vocal fold palsy (recurrent laryngeal nerve damage), airway compromise (dyspnoea and stridor), laryngeal deviation and difficult intubation
- **Hormonal effects:** problems arise in patients with poorly controlled hypothyroidism or hyperthyroidism undergoing major emergency procedures (see Endocrine Surgery in Book 2)

Hyperthyroidism

This should be controlled before surgery:

- Propylthiouracil decreases hormone synthesis (but increases vascularity)
- Potassium iodide reduces gland vascularity
- Propanolol reduces systemic side effects of thyroxine

Increased risks associated with lack of pre-op preparation:

- Cardiac: tachycardia, labile BP, arrhythmia

- 'Thyroid crisis' can be precipitated by surgery. This is a syndrome of excessive and uncontrolled thyroxine release which may result in hyperthermia, life-threatening cardiac arrhythmia, metabolic acidosis, nausea, vomiting and diarrhoea, mania and coma

Hypothyroidism

Hypothyroidism reduces physiological responses:

- Low cardiac output and increased incidence of coronary artery disease (hyperlipidaemia)
- Blood loss poorly tolerated
- Respiratory centre less responsive to changes in O_2 and CO_2 partial pressures
- Sensitive to opiate analgesia

Hypothyroidism carries increased risks of:
- Myocardial ischaemia
- Hypotension
- Hypothermia
- Hypoventilation
- Hypoglycaemia
- Hyponatraemia
- Acidosis

Preoperative management of parathyroid problems

For more details of parathyroid physiology, pathology and management, see Chapter 4, Endocrine surgery, Book 2.

Hyperparathyroidism

- **Primary** hyperparathyroidism is due to a secretory parathyroid adenoma
- **Secondary** hyperparathyroidism is parathyroid hyperplasia due to chronic hyperstimulation
- **Tertiary** hyperparathyroidism is autonomous hypersecretion

Problems in hyperparathyroidism

Increased calcium levels; decreased phosphate levels.
Increased risks of:
- Renal impairment (needs careful rehydration and fluid balance, monitoring of catheter and central venous pressure [CVP] line)
- Urinary calcium excretion (which may be enhanced by judicious use of diuretics)
- Hypertension
- Hypercalcaemic crisis (may occur in elderly people or in those with malignant disease)

Hypoparathyroidism

Problems in hypoparathyroidism

Decreased calcium levels; increased phosphate levels.
Increased risks of:
- Stridor
- Convulsions
- Decreased cardiac output

Manage with careful IV calcium replacement.

2.5 Preoperative management of neurological disease

Learning point

- Epilepsy
- Cerebrovascular disease
- Parkinson's disease

Preoperative management of epilepsy

Aim to avoid seizures in the perioperative period by minimising disruption to the maintenance regimen of medication:
- Avoid disturbances of gastrointestinal (GI) function (affects medication absorption and electrolyte balance
- Give usual medications up to the point of surgery
- Replace oral medications with parenteral formulations if required
- Neurology advice may be required for patients whose epilepsy is hard to control

Preoperative management of cerebrovascular disease

- Avoid changes in BP (hypo-/hypertension) and manage fluids carefully because patients with arteriopathy have a relatively rigid vascular system
- Continue anticoagulants in the form of heparin unless contraindicated
- Position neck to avoid syncope
- Examine and carefully document preoperative and early postoperative neurological status
- Delay elective surgery if there has been a recent CVA (risk of subsequent CVA increased 20-fold if surgery is performed in <6 weeks; aim to wait for 6 months)
- Indications for carotid endarterectomy (see Chapter 9, Vascular Surgery in Book 2)

Preoperative management of Parkinson's disease

Parkinson's disease is due to reduced dopaminergic activity in the substantia nigra (may be degenerative, drug-induced, post-traumatic). Typical symptoms include tremor, postural instability, rigidity and dyskinesia.

Perioperative issues include:
- Compromised respiratory function
- Urinary retention
- Confusion, depression, hallucinations
- Difficulties with speech and communication

Preoperative medications and Parkinson's disease

Patients with Parkinson's disease are often on multiple medications and this must be managed carefully. They are at risk of drug interactions. Timing of medications must be optimised to allow the best control of the condition during waking hours ('on' and 'off' periods) because symptoms occur rapidly if doses of regular medications are missed. Consider individual special needs when arranging analgesia (eg may not cope with patient-controlled analgesia). Domperidone is a good antiemetic because it does not have significant antipyramidal effects.

2.6 Preoperative management of liver disease

Learning point

Patients with cirrhosis and liver disease do badly and have a high mortality rate with elective surgery.

Problems to anticipate include:
- Bleeding due to coagulopathy
- Encephalopathy
- Increased risk of infection
- Increased risk of renal failure
- Hypoglycaemia
- Acid–base and electrolyte imbalances
- Underlying cause (eg malignancy, alcohol abuse and withdrawal)

Distinguish between biliary obstruction (cholestatic jaundice) and chronic decompensated liver failure (hepatocellular jaundice), and manage the patient accordingly.

Preoperative management of patients with jaundice

Fluid balance

Hypoalbuminaemia and fluid overload are common in jaundiced patients and lead to pulmonary/peripheral oedema as well as ascites. There may be sodium retention and hypokalaemia due to secondary hyperaldosteronism, which may be further complicated by the use of spironolactone or other diuretics.

Acid–base balance

A combined metabolic and respiratory alkalosis may occur. This will cause the oxygen dissociation curve to shift to the left and decrease oxygen delivery to the tissues.

Clotting

Due to a decrease in vitamin K absorption in cholestatic jaundice, there is reduced synthesis of factors II, VII, IX and X, and there may also be a thrombocytopenia if there is portal hypertension (due to hypersplenism).

Hepatorenal syndrome

Renal failure may be precipitated by hypovolaemia. Hepatorenal syndrome has a very poor prognosis.

Drug metabolism

Many drugs, including anaesthetic agents, undergo metabolism by the liver and may therefore have a prolonged duration of action. Hypoalbuminaemia impairs drug binding and metabolism and may lead to elevated serum levels.

Other complications of jaundice

- Hypoglycaemia may occur due to depleted glycogen stores
- Wound failure and infection are increased in the jaundiced patient
- Risk of infectivity to surgeon and hospital personnel if infective hepatitis (patients require hepatitis screen if considered high-risk)

Preoperative management of cholestatic jaundice

- If possible relieve jaundice before surgery (eg an endoscopically performed sphincterotomy to drain common bile duct stones)

- Keep the patient well hydrated in an attempt to avoid hepatorenal syndrome
- Check the prothrombin time and administer vitamin K 10 mg IV daily (maximum effect after three doses) or fresh frozen plasma within 2 hours of a surgical procedure
- In the presence of biliary obstruction/ anticipated manipulation of the biliary tree administer prophylactic antibiotics to avoid cholangitis

Preoperative management of chronic liver failure

- Fluid and electrolyte management (note that even if there is a low serum sodium these patients have a high total sodium due to secondary aldosteronism, so additional sodium load in fluids should be avoided)
- Management of ascites (consider drainage if gross or refractory ascites, or risk of spontaneous bacterial peritonitis)
- Prevention of encephalopathy (restricted nitrogen, regular lactulose, sedative avoidance, prophylactic antibiotics such as metronidazole)
- Management of coagulopathy (vitamin K and fresh frozen plasma)
- Nutritional support (plus vitamin supplementation)

CHILD'S CLASSIFICATION OF THE SEVERITY OF CHRONIC LIVER DISEASE

	A	B	C
Bilirubin	<35	35–50	>50
Albumin	>35	30–35	<30
Ascites	None		Severe
Encephalopathy	None	Mild	Advanced
Nutrition[a]	Good	Moderate	Poor
Risk of surgery	Good	Average/Fair	Poor
[a]Pugh's modification replaces nutrition with prothrombin time.			

Preoperative management of alcohol withdrawal

- Dangerous
- May cause confusion and aggression
- Symptoms often occur at night

Predicting patients who will suffer from withdrawal allows prescription of a sensible prophylactic regimen (eg reducing dose of chlordiazepoxide from four times per day down to zero over 7–10 days) rather than acute management with large doses of sedatives, which can be dangerous.

2.7 Preoperative management of renal failure

Renal failure may be acute or chronic. Details of the causes, physiology and management of renal failure can be found in the Chapter 3.

Patients in established renal failure pose specific problems in perioperative care. Fluid and electrolyte balance may be deranged and drug/metabolite excretion disturbed. Severe uraemia can directly affect the cardiovascular, pulmonary, haematological, immunological and central nervous systems. Avoid nephrotoxic drugs in those with borderline or impaired renal function.

Classification of renal failure
- **Prerenal**, eg haemorrhage (blood); burns (plasma); vomiting (crystalloid)
- **Renal**, eg diabetes; glomerulonephritis
- **Postrenal**, eg retroperitoneal fibrosis (medially deviated ureters); benign prostatic hyperplasia (with chronic retention); pelvic malignancies

---

Preoperative problems in patients with renal failure

Complications encountered preoperatively in patients with established renal failure may include:
- Fluid overload, oedema
- Hypoalbuminaemia (nephrotic syndrome)
- Electrolyte abnormalities (hyperkalaemia, hyponatraemia)
- Metabolic acidosis
- Higher incidence of arterial disease (ischaemic heart disease and PVD), diabetes and hypertension
- Susceptibility to infection (uraemia suppresses the immune system)

Preoperative management of established renal failure involves:
- Dialysis before surgery with regular monitoring of fluid/electrolyte balance
- Reduce doses of drugs excreted by the kidney (eg morphine)
- Involvement of the renal team

Note that, when establishing IV access in a patient with severe end-stage renal failure, avoid potential arteriovenous fistula sites (eg cephalic vein). Veins on the hands can be used.

2.8 Preoperative management of rheumatoid disease

Rheumatoid disease encompasses a range of disorders from joint arthritis to connective tissue diseases and vasculitis.

Rheumatoid arthritis (RA) is a common relapsing and remitting autoimmune condition resulting in progressive joint swelling and deformity (see Chapter 9, Orthopaedic Surgery). Prevalence is about 3% in females and 1% in males.

Increased risks at time of surgery for RA patients

Cardiac: increased risk of valve disease (valvular inflammation occurs as part of the disease and can damage mitral and tricuspid valves).

Anaemia: of chronic disease.

Respiratory disease: patients often have pleural nodules, pulmonary fibrosis and effusions which may compromise reserve.

Peripheral neuropathy: be careful of pressure areas.

Renal impairment: may be due to nephritis or medication.

Skin: poor wound healing due to underlying disease and steroid use.

C-spine: 15% of RA patients have atlantoaxial instability of the C-spine which may be associated with pathological fracture of the odontoid peg, and which predisposes them to atlantoaxial subluxation (horizontal/vertical); this risk is increased during anaesthesia. Subluxation can result in:

- Medullary compression and sudden death
- Spinal cord compression (acute/chronic); causes difficulty with clumsy hands, stiff legs, gait, balance
- Occipitocervical pain

Patients with neurological symptoms and signs (including tingling of hands or feet) or those with persistent neck pain should have a preoperative C-spine radiograph.

2.9 Preoperative assessment and management of nutritional status

Learning point

Nutritional depletion pre- and post-surgery increases morbidity and mortality. Malnutrition may be due to:
- Decreased intake
- Increasingly catabolic states
- Impaired digestion or absorption of nutrients

Nutritional support improves outcome and follows a hierarchy:
- Oral supplementation
- Enteral tube feeding
- Parenteral nutrition

Body mass index (BMI)

BMI is calculated with the formula below (note that dry weight should be calculated, so exclude extra fluid weight due to ascites, renal failure, etc).

$$BMI = weight\ (kg)/height^2\ (m^2)$$

Body habitus is classified on the basis of BMI as follows:

<16	Severely malnourished
<19	Malnourished
20–27	Normal
27–30	Overweight
30–35	Obese
35–40	Morbidly obese (if also demonstrates comorbidities)
>40–50	Morbidly obese
50–60	Super-obese }
60–70	Super-super-obese }
>70	Ultra-obese }
	{ These are predominantly
	{ American definitions

CHAPTER 1

Information about nutritional status may also be determined by:

- Degree of recent weight loss (>5% mild; 10% moderate; >15% severe)
- Percentage of expected body weight (<85% moderate; <75% severe)
- Physical measurements: mid-arm muscle or triceps skinfold thickness
- Serum albumin levels

Note that albumin is also a negative acute phase protein, the levels of which fall in sepsis and inflammation. Therefore it is not an absolute marker for nutritional status; however, a rising albumin is the most useful as a measure of recovery.

Nutritional requirements

Daily nutritional requirements are shown in the table.

DAILY NUTRITIONAL REQUIREMENTS

	kcal/kg per day	Protein (g/kg per day)
Baseline	25	0.8
Catabolic states	30–35	1.3–2.0
Hypercatabolic states	40–45	1.5–2.5

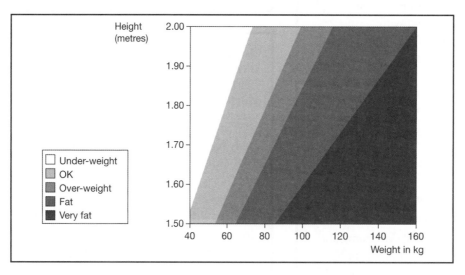

Figure 1.1 Body mass index

Also required are the following micronutrients:
- Electrolytes: sodium, potassium, calcium, chloride, magnesium, phosphate, fluoride
- Vitamins: A, B series, C, D, E, K
- Trace minerals: copper, iodine, iron, manganese, selenium, zinc

Malnutrition

Malnutrition is starvation that induces a low-grade inflammatory state, which causes tissue wasting and impaired organ function. Many patients (especially those with chronic disorders, malignancy and dementia) may be suffering from malnutrition. Surgery may induce anorexia and temporary intestinal failure, exacerbating the problem. The postoperative catabolic state and the stress (inhibition of the normal ketotic response) can cause muscle metabolism and weaken the patient.

Malnutrition in hospital patients is common:
- Up to 40% of surgical patients are nutritionally depleted on admission
- Up to 60% may become nutritionally depleted during admission

Malnutrition has prognostic implications for increased postop complications:
- Poor wound healing and dehiscence
- Immunocompromise leading to infection (chest and wound)
- Organ failure

Causes of malnutrition in the surgical patient

Decreased intake
- Symptoms such as loss of appetite, nausea, vomiting
- Conditions such as alcoholism
- Inability to feed oneself (trauma, stroke, dementia)
- Disease of the mouth, pharynx, or oesophagus
- Primary pathology (eg dysphagia due to tumour)
- Opportunistic infection (eg with Candida spp.)

Increasingly catabolic state
- Due to disease process, eg sepsis, infection and pyrexia (especially if chronic)
- Cachexia due to malignancy (some tumours cause muscle wasting and weight loss out of proportion to their size, eg oesophageal cancers)
- Organ failure (eg renal or hepatic failure)
- Major surgery itself (trauma)

Impaired digestion or absorption
- Primary disease of the GI tract (eg inflammation, obstruction, fistulae)
- Visceral oedema in patients with protein malnutrition
- Ileus
- Post-abdominal surgery
- Intra-abdominal sepsis
- Electrolyte imbalance (eg hypokalaemia, hyponatraemia)

Assessment of malnourished patients

History

- Duration of illness
- Weight loss
- Reduced appetite
- Risk factors (eg alcohol, malignancy)
- Reduced tissue turgor
- Apathy
- Weight loss

Investigation

- Arm circumference/triceps skinfold thickness
- Serum albumin
- FBC
- Transferrin
- Retinol-binding protein

Malnourished patients requiring elective surgery should be considered for preoperative and perioperative feeding.

Obesity

Obese patients are at increased risk of surgical complications for many reasons.

Surgical risks of obesity

Respiratory

- Decreased chest wall compliance, inefficient respiratory muscles and shallow breathing prolong atelectasis, and increase the risk of pulmonary infections
- Oxygen consumption is increased due to metabolic demand from adipose tissue and increased muscular work of breathing
- Increasing obesity causes respiratory impairment and chronic hypoxia, tolerance to hypercapnia and polycythaemia
- Sleep apnoea can result in cardiac failure

Aspiration

- Increased gastric volume and high intra-abdominal pressure predispose to gastric aspiration

Wound healing

- Poor-quality abdominal musculature predisposes to dehiscence
- Increased adipose tissue predisposes to haematoma formation and subsequent wound infection

Technical problems

- Surgery takes longer and is more difficult due to problems of access and obscuring of vital structures by intra-abdominal fat deposits
- Technical problems arise with IV cannulation and subsequent phlebitis

Assessment of obese patients

Obesity increases risks of:
- Hyperglycaemia (insulin resistance)
- Hypertension and ischaemic heart disease
- Gallstones
- Osteoarthritis

For elective surgery in obese patients, the pre-op assessment should include:
- Measurement of the patient's BMI
- Discussion with anaesthetist (may require specialist)
- Referral to a dietitian
- Blood glucose estimation and restoration of glycaemic control
- Measurement of blood gases (hypoxia

and hypercapnia reflect respiratory impairment), and respiratory function tests (FEV_1/FVC) in patients with obstructive pulmonary disease

Consideration of treatment for obesity before major surgery (eg weight-loss regimen, procedure such as gastric bypass in morbidly obese individuals).

Nutritional support

Tailored to the protein, calorific, and micronutrient needs of the patient. It follows a hierarchy, using oral supplementation if possible, enteral tube feeding if oral feeding cannot supply the required nutrients, and parenteral feeding only if enteral feeding is not possible.

Oral supplementation

- Can be used between or instead of meals
- Variety available (milk- or fruit-juice-based)
- High in protein and calories
- Not all contain micronutrients
- Examples include Complan

Enteral tube feeding

Enteral feeding is the best route because it preserves GI mucosal integrity. If the patient cannot take enough nutrients in orally, tube feeding is the next step.

Enteral tube options include:
- NG or nasojejunal (NJ) tube (may be fine-bore)
- Percutaneous endoscopic gastrostomy (PEG) or jejunostomy (PEJ). This may be useful in patients who have had facial, laryngeal or oesophageal surgery, and who cannot have an NG tube
- Feeding gastrostomies or jejunostomies may

be inserted on the ward, under radiological control, endoscopically or at open surgery

Feeds include:
- Polymeric (whole protein, carbohydrate and fat)
- Small-molecule (short peptides, free amino acids and elemental fats)
- Specific feeds (eg low-sodium diets in liver failure)
- Feed is delivered at a pre-set speed by a pump, and gastric residual volume is checked to assess absorption
- A feed-free period allows gastric pH to fall and is important to control bacterial colonisation (see also Bacterial translocation in Chapter 3, Postoperative Management and Critical Care)

> **Complications of enteral feeding tubes**
> - Feeding tube displaced or blocked
> - Metabolic (hyperglycaemia, micronutrient deficiencies)
> - Diarrhoea
> - Aspiration

Parenteral nutrition

This is used only if enteral feeding is not possible or is contraindicated.

Feeding is via venous access, which may be:
- Peripheral vein (long line, peripherally inserted central catheter [PICC] line)
- Central access (jugular or subclavian line)
- Tunnelled, cuffed or with a subcutaneous port

Sterile feeds are made up either to standard or to individual prescription. Feeding may be cyclical or continuous.

Catheter complications
- Risks of insertion
- Thrombosis
- Infection

Metabolic complications
- Hyperglycaemia
- Electrolyte and fluid imbalance
- Hepatic dysfunction
- Immunocompromise
- Metabolic bone disease

Nutritional planning in surgical patients

Preoperative considerations
- Dietitian pre-op assessment of high-risk patients
- Encourage increased oral intake
- Oral supplementation (high-protein and high-calorie drinks, NG/PEG feeding)

Surgical considerations
- Think about placement of tubes for enteral feeding (especially PEJ)

Postoperative considerations

Colorectal surgery
Traditionally the postoperative feeding regimen for bowel surgery was a stepwise progression guided by improving clinical signs (eg passing of flatus) thus: nil by mouth (NBM), sips and small volumes of clear fluids, soft diet, normal diet. This has changed in recent years, with many surgeons allowing free fluids on day 1 and diet as tolerated.
- Early feeding has been shown to improve early outcome measures even in the presence of a bowel anastomosis

- Chart food intake and monitor daily on ward rounds
- Weigh patients regularly
- Patients who have had laparoscopic bowel resections are typically eating and drinking on day 2, and fit for discharge on day 4 or 5

Upper GI surgery
Oesophageal and gastric resections are typically combined with a feeding jejunostomy placed intraoperatively, so that the patient can resume enteral feeding very soon after surgery. Many surgeons will then do a water contrast swallow on day 10 of high-risk anastomoses before allowing oral feeding.

2.10 Risk factors for surgery and scoring systems

There are numerous systems in use in the management of surgical patients that attempt to identify and stratify risk. These commonly include the risk or severity of the underlying condition (eg Ranson's criteria for pancreatitis, the Glasgow Coma Scale (GCS) score, the APACHE score in critical care, etc) or a global indicator of underlying comorbidities such as the ASA grade for anaesthesia.

Increasingly risk assessment has been tailored to combine underlying comorbidity with the type of surgery proposed. This has lead to a number of different models for predicting risk:

- **The POSSUM score** (Physiological and Operative Severity Score for the enumeration of Morbidity and Mortality). The POSSUM score uses 12 physiological and 6 surgical variables for its calculation and can be used pre- and postoperatively to give an initial estimate and calculation of individual risk. There have been some reports of overprediction of mortality risks which has led to specialty-specific modifications:

- V-POSSUM in elective vascular surgery
- O-POSSUM in oesophagogastric surgery
- CR-POSSUM in colorectal surgery

- **ACPGBI** has produced a number of scoring systems including a mortality model for colorectal cancer resection

- **St Mark's lymph node scoring system** for likelihood of lymph node positivity in colorectal cancer
- **Adjuvant! Online** gives an estimate of reduction in the risk of death from breast cancer in patients undergoing chemotherapy

SECTION 3

Principles of anaesthesia

Anaesthesia is the rendering of part (local anaesthesia) or all (general anaesthesia) of the body insensitive to pain or noxious stimuli.

3.1   Local anaesthesia

Learning point

- Local anaesthetic agents work by altering membrane permeability and preventing the passage of nerve impulses
- They can be used in a variety of ways to effect local or regional anaesthesia:
  - Topical
  - Direct infiltration
  - Field block
  - Ring block
  - Individual nerve block
  - Plexus block
  - Intravenous regional anaesthesia
  - Spinal anaesthesia
  - Epidural anaesthesia
- Use of local anaesthetic agents thus has the advantage of avoiding the risks of general anaesthetic

Mode of action of local anaesthetics

- Work by altering membrane permeability to prevent passage of nerve impulses
- Stored as acidic salt solutions (after infiltration the base is released by the relative alkalinity of the tissue – hence LA is ineffective in acidic conditions such as in infected wounds)
- Often used in combination with GA to reduce opiate analgesic and GA requirements
- Ideal LA has low toxicity, high potency, rapid onset and long duration

Local anaesthetic agents

> Dosage of local anaesthetic agents:
> 0.5% = 5 mg/ml
> 1% = 10 mg/ml
> 2% = 20 mg/ml, etc

LAs should be used at their lowest concentration and warmed to body temperature to decrease pain on injection. Adrenaline may be used with LAs to slow systemic absorption and prolong duration of action.

Advantages of local and regional anaesthesia

- No systemic use of drugs (reduced side effects compared with a GA)
- Good depth of analgesia in local area only
- No requirement for mechanical ventilation:
  - Better for patients with chronic respiratory disease
  - No atelectasis and infection risk
  - Less risk of gastric aspiration
- May be used together with reduced level of GA (evidence for reduced morbidity and mortality)
- May be continued for postoperative reasons:
  - Analgesia (eg epidural for laparotomy)
  - Respiratory function (allows deep inspiration and pain-free chest physiotherapy)

DOSAGE AND USES OF LOCAL ANAESTHETIC AGENTS

	Maximum dose	Plus adrenaline/ epinephrine	Uses
Lidocaine	3 mg/kg	7 mg/kg	Infiltration Nerve blocks Epidurals
Bupivacaine (Marcain™)	2 mg/kg	2 mg/kg	Infiltration Nerve blocks Epidurals Spinals – high cardiotoxicity
Prilocaine	6 mg/kg	6 mg/kg	Regional nerve blocks, Bier's block – high cardiotoxicity
Cocaine	–	–	ENT
Ropivacaine	–	–	Like bupivacaine but less cardiotoxic

Note: never use local anaesthetic agents containing adrenaline near end-arteries (eg digits, penis) because this may result in ischaemic necrosis.

- Less cardiac stress during surgery (reduced ST changes seen on ECG)
- Reduced postoperative ileus
- Reduced incidence of DVT

Complications of local anaesthetics

Drug toxicity can be local or systemic.

Local toxicity

- Inflammatory response
- Nerve damage from needle or intraneural injection

Systemic toxicity

- Allergy
- May occur from overdosage, inadvertent IV administration, absorption from highly vascular areas or cuff failure in Bier's block
- Causes perioral tingling and paraesthesia, anxiety, tinnitus, drowsiness, unconsciousness, seizures, coma, apnoea, paralysis and cardiovascular collapse (negatively inotropic and vasodilatation)

Management of toxicity: stop administration of LA, then perform ABC resuscitation – protect airway, intubate and ventilate if necessary. Give IV fluids and consider inotropic support.

Topical local anaesthetic

This is in the form of a cream or a spray and is used for routine procedures where only superficial anaesthesia is required, eg:

- EMLA cream before cannulation in children
- Lidocaine gel before urethral catheterisation
- Xylocaine spray before gastroscopy

Infiltration of local anaesthesia

This is used typically for removal of small skin lesions.

Procedure box: Infiltration of local anaesthetic

- Check that there are no allergies and no contraindication for using a local anaesthetic agent with adrenaline
- Check the maximum safe dose for the patient and draw up only that amount, checking the vial yourself
- Use a fast-acting agent such as lidocaine
- Using an orange or blue needle, first raise a subcutaneous weal along the line of the proposed skin incision (this will be an ellipse around a skin lesion, for example)
- Keeping the needle in the same site as much as possible, inject deeper into the subcutaneous tissue to the level of the estimated dissection, aspirating before you inject in any area where there may be vessels
- If you draw blood, do not inject, because intravenous lidocaine can cause arrhythmias
- Wait a few moments and test the area for sensation with forceps before incision. Remember that even lidocaine takes 10–20 minutes to take full effect
- Use leftover local to infiltrate if the patient reports sensation

3.2 Regional anaesthesia

Field block and ring block

A **field block** is infiltration of a LA agent in such a way as to effect anaesthesia in the entire surgical field. This may involve blocking a nerve that supplies the area, eg when performing an inguinal hernia repair under LA, a surgeon may combine a direct infiltration of local anaesthesia with an injection of LA into the ilioinguinal nerve above the anterosuperior iliac spine.

A **ring block** is a type of field block where the area to be blocked is a digit or the penis. An entire finger or toe can be made completely numb by injecting a millilitre or two of LA just to either side of the proximal phalanx at the level of the web space. The nerve runs here with the digital artery and vein, so adrenaline-containing LA agents should never be used for a ring block, because they might render the digit ischaemic by putting the end-arteries into spasm. A ring block can be used for manipulation of dislocated fingers, ingrowing toenail procedures and postoperative analgesia after circumcision.

Brachial plexus block

The brachial plexus is formed from the nerve roots C5–T1 which unite to form the main trunks (upper, middle and lower) that divide into anterior and posterior nerve divisions at the level of the clavicle. These subdivide into cords as they enter the axilla, and the cords are named according to their position relative to the second part of the axillary artery (medial, lateral and posterior). The cords subdivide as the plexus passes through the axilla.

Brachial plexus blocks may be performed at different levels:
- Interscalene block (trunks)
- Supra-/infraclavicular block (divisions)
- Axillary block (cords)

If injected into the fascial covering of the plexus the anaesthetic will track up and down providing a good block. These blocks are good for postop pain relief because they last for several hours.

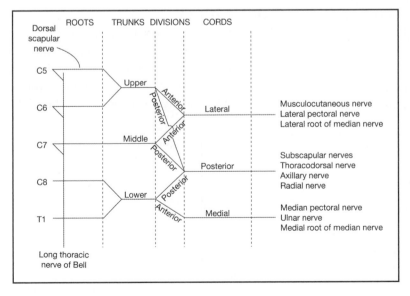

Figure 1.2
The brachial plexus

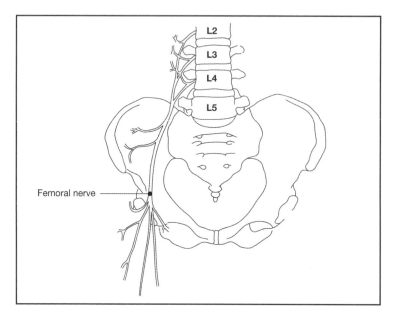

Figure 1.3 The femoral nerve

Femoral block

The femoral nerve arises from L2–4 and passes downwards on the posterior wall in the groove between the psoas and iliacus muscles. It lies on the iliopsoas as it passes under the inguinal ligament to enter the thigh, lateral to the vascular bundle and femoral sheath. The femoral nerve then divides in the femoral triangle and supplies the muscles of the anterior thigh, cutaneous nerves of the anterior thigh and saphenous nerve.

The femoral nerve lies at a point that is 1 cm lateral to the pulsation of the femoral artery as it exits from under the inguinal ligament and 2 cm distal to the ligament. Deep infiltration of LA at this point will produce a femoral block (note: avoid injecting into the femoral vessels). This is suitable for analgesia covering the anterior thigh, knee and femur.

Sciatic block

The sciatic nerve arises from the lumbosacral nerve roots L4–S3 and exits under the biceps femoris muscle. It undergoes early organisation into common peroneal and tibial portions, which run together centrally down the back of the thigh

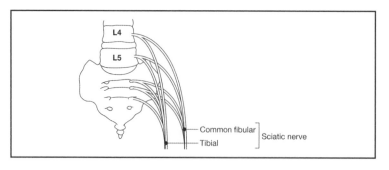

Figure 1.4 The sciatic nerve

under adductor magnus. They usually divide in the distal third of the thigh, although this may occur at a higher level in some individuals.

The sciatic nerve block can be performed by a lateral, anterior or posterior approach, and is suitable for ankle and foot surgery. The sciatic nerve lies 2 cm lateral to the ischial tuberosity at the level of the greater trochanter. Sciatic nerve blocks may be of slow onset (up to 60 minutes) so be patient with your anaesthetist.

Bier's block

This is IV regional anaesthesia, usually into the upper limb.

Technique for Bier's block
- IV access – both arms!
- Exsanguinate limb (eg Eschmark bandage)
- Apply double-cuff tourniquet (with padding)
- Inflate upper cuff to approximately 300 mmHg
- Inject approximately 40 ml 0.5% prilocaine IV into isolated arm
- Inflate lower cuff (over anaesthetised segment)
- Release upper cuff (reduces cuff pain and acts as safeguard)

Intercostal nerve blocks

Useful for invasive procedures (eg chest drain insertion) and analgesia (eg flail chest or fractured ribs, breast surgery). The intercostal nerve runs with the vascular bundle under the overhanging edge of the rib. Feel for the posterior angle of the rib at the posterior axillary line and insert the needle just below the edge of the rib ('walk' the needle off the rib if necessary). Inject local anaesthetic (note: risk of pneumothorax).

Spinal anaesthesia

Useful for lower abdominal, perineal and lower limb surgery. It is contraindicated in patients who are anticoagulated or septic, or who have had previous back surgery or aortic stenosis.
- Introduce via fine-bore needle into spinal (subarachnoid) space at L1–2 level (by the cauda equina)
- Low dose, low volume, rapid (<5 minutes) onset
- Duration 3–4 hours
- Mainly used for perioperative pain relief

Complications of spinal anaesthesia
- Toxicity
- Hypotension (avoid in severe cardiac disease)
- Headache, meningism, neurological disturbance
- Urinary retention

Epidural anaesthesia

This is introduced via a large-bore needle to feed the catheter into the extradural space (as the needle passes through the ligamentum flavum there is a change in resistance signifying placement in the correct location).

- Situated at level of nerve roots supplying surgical site (lumbar for pelvic surgery; thoracic for upper abdominal)
- High dose, high volume, delayed (>5 minutes) onset
- Duration of continuous infusion: up to a few days
- Can be used for peri- and postop pain relief

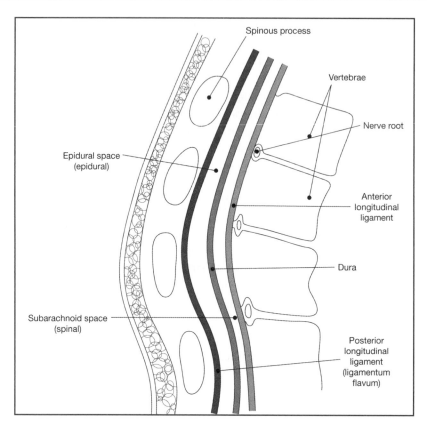

Figure 1.5 Spinal anatomy

Complications of epidural anaesthesia

- Dural tap
- Backache
- Infection
- Haematoma
- Urinary retention

Monitoring the level

Anaesthetic spreads caudally and cranially in both spinals and epidurals.

Level is controlled by:
- Initial level of placement
- Patient positioning (eg head-down tilt)
- Volume and concentration of anaesthetic

Level is described by the dermatome affected:
- Nipples T5
- Umbilicus T10
- Inguinal ligament T12

High block may cause respiratory depression, and impair cough and deep inspiration (respiratory arrest at C4 level).

Spinal haematoma and abscess

- Haematoma may occur on needle insertion and epidural catheter removal
- Catheters should not be removed when the patient is anticoagulated (can be removed 12 hours post low-dose heparin followed by 2 hours delay before any further doses)
- Risk of epidural abscess increases if left in situ for >72 hours

3.3 Sedation

Learning point

Sedation is the administration of drug(s) to alleviate discomfort and distress during diagnostic and therapeutic interventions, with maintenance of patient responsiveness and protective reflexes. Allows for rapid recovery and avoids GA. Sedation can be used:
- As a premedication anxiolytic
- As an amnesiac (eg relocation of dislocated shoulder)
- As an adjunct to regional anaesthesia
- During invasive interventions such as endoscopy
- In critical care (eg to tolerate endotracheal intubation)

Patients must be monitored carefully.
- Supplemental oxygen (mask or nasal cannulae)
- Cardiovascular: ECG leads and monitor
- Respiratory: pulse oximetry
- Central nervous system (CNS): responsive and obeying commands

Avoid sedating high-risk patients (eg elderly patients, obese patients, patients with cardiorespiratory disease). Be prepared for adverse reactions by ensuring the following:
- Presence of an assistant
- Resuscitation equipment ready and nearby
- IV cannula left in for emergencies (**NEVER** use a butterfly needle to administer sedation)
- Drug is titrated slowly against response (especially if combined with opiate because of increased risks of cardiorespiratory depression)
- Monitor until full consciousness is regained and discharge home with a responsible adult

3.4 General anaesthesia

Learning point

General anaesthesia induces
- Narcosis (unconsciousness)
- Analgesia
- Muscle relaxation

It does this in a controlled and reversible manner, so the patient suffers no pain and has no recollection of the experience, and the surgeon has ideal operating conditions.

Stages of general anaesthesia
- Pre-op assessment and preparation
- Induction and muscle relaxation
- Maintenance and monitoring
- Recovery
- Postop monitoring and transfer

Preoperative anaesthetic assessment

The anaesthetist will assess the patient fully preoperatively, ideally to assess and try to minimise risks of general anaesthesia, to counsel the patient and prescribe premedication.

ASA grading (estimation of risk for anaesthesia and surgery)

Class 1 Normal healthy individual

Class 2 Patient with mild systemic disease

Class 3 Patient with severe systemic disease that limits activity but is not incapacitating

Class 4 Patient with incapacitating disease that is a constant threat to life

Class 5 Moribund patient not expected to survive, with or without an operation

Premedication

Objectives and functions of premedication:
- Anxiolytic effect
- Causes sedation and enhancement of hypnotic effect of GA
- Causes amnesia
- Dries secretions
- Antiemetic effect
- Increases vagal tone
- Modification of gastric contents

Benzodiazepines

These are sedative, anxiolytic and amnesic.
- **Midazolam**
  - Induction of anaesthesia
  - Sedation during endoscopy and procedures performed under LA
  - Hypnotic effect
  - Used for premed
  - Used for treatment of chronic pain
  - Is water-soluble, has short duration, gives rapid clear-headed recovery
  - Dose is 0.05–0.1 mg/kg by slow IV injection
  - May cause over-sedation or respiratory depression
  - Can be reversed with flumazenil (which may itself cause seizures)
  - All patients having midazolam sedation should have IV access, pulse oximetry, ECG monitoring and resuscitation facilities available, and should not drive or operate machinery for 24 hours afterwards
- **Temazepam:** 10–20 mg orally 1 hour pre-surgery
- **Diazepam:** oral or IV; longer duration than other benzodiazepines and more difficult to reverse

Droperidol
- A butyrophenone
- Antiemetic, neuroleptic, α blocker
- Prolonged duration action and 'locked in' syndrome may cause problems
- Rarely used

Opioids
- Analgesic and sedative
- Examples are papaveretum (Omnopon) 20 mg IM, morphine 10 mg IM.
- Can be reversed with naloxone (Narcan)

Anticholinergics
- Competitive acetylcholine antagonists at muscarinic receptors
- Dry secretions; prevent reflex bradycardia
- Example: IV atropine 300–600 µg pre-induction

Glycopyrronium
- Less chronotropic effect than atropine
- Doesn't cross the BBB
- 200–400 µg IV/IM pre-induction

Hyoscine (scopolamine)
- As for atropine but more sedative and antiemetic
- May cause bradycardia, confusion, ataxia in elderly people
- 200–600 µg subcutaneously 60 minutes pre-induction

Antacids

These are used to prevent aspiration of gastric contents (causing Mendelson syndrome) in patients at risk (eg pregnancy, trauma patients [not starved], obese, hiatus hernia), eg:
- Cimetidine 400 mg orally 1–2 hours pre-surgery
- Ranitidine 50 mg IV or 150 mg orally 1–2 hours pre-surgery
- Omeprazole 20 mg orally 12 hours pre-surgery

Additional medication

Patients may also be given (according to case):

- Steroids
- Prophylactic antibiotics
- Anticoagulants
- Immunosuppressants (eg if undergoing transplantation)

Induction of general anaesthesia

This is the administration of drug(s) to render the patient unconscious before commencing surgery. It may be intravenous or inhalational. The IV route is quicker, but requires IV access, so inhalation induction may be the method of choice in children, or in people who are needle phobics or difficult to cannulate. IV induction agents are liquid-soluble, and thus hydrophobic. IV induction agents are also used for maintenance of anaesthesia, by slow IV infusion.

- **Thiopental sodium** is a commonly used induction agent. It is a barbiturate that appears as a pale-yellow powder with a bitter taste and a faint smell of garlic. It is given in an alkaline solution (pH 10.8) and so is irritant if injection occurs outside the vein. It causes a smooth and rapid induction but has a narrow therapeutic window and overdose may cause cardiorespiratory depression. It is a negative inotrope and can result in a drop in BP. There is often associated respiratory depression. It sensitises the pharynx and cannot be used with laryngeal airways
- **Propofol** is more expensive than thiopental but has the advantage of a slight antiemetic effect. It is a phenol derivative that appears as a white aqueous emulsion, and may cause pain on injection. It gives a rapid recovery without a 'hangover' and has a lower incidence of laryngospasm, which makes it the agent of choice if using a

laryngeal mask. It causes vasodilatation and is a negative inotrope, resulting in a drop in BP, and therefore it is not recommended for hypovolaemic patients

- **Etomidate** is less myocardial depressive, so is better used in cardiovascularly unstable patients

Inhalational anaesthetics may also be used for induction and are discussed later in this chapter.

Complications of induction agents

Complications include:

- Hypotension
- Respiratory depression
- Laryngeal spasm
- Allergic reactions
- Tissue necrosis from perivenous injection

The effects are especially pronounced in hypovolaemic patients.

Contraindications include previous allergy and porphyria. For a discussion of intubation see Chapter 3.

Muscle relaxants

Depolarising muscle relaxants

Depolarising muscle relaxants work by maintaining muscle in a depolarised (or relaxed) state.

The main example is **suxamethonium**. This has a structure similar to two acetylcholine molecules and acts in the same way as acetylcholine at the neuromuscular junction. The rate of hydrolysis by plasma cholinesterase is, however, much slower, so depolarisation is prolonged, resulting in blockade. Its action cannot therefore be reversed. As it acts on the acetylcholine receptor there is an initial period of muscle fasciculation that may be painful and distressing to the patient.

It is the most rapid-acting of all the muscle relaxants and is therefore useful when rapid tracheal intubation is required (crash induction). It has a duration of 2–6 minutes in normal individuals, but some people have a deficiency of plasma cholinesterase and show a prolonged response (scoline apnoea).

Complications of depolarising muscle relaxants
- Muscle pain
- Hyperkalaemia
- Myoglobinaemia
- Bradycardia
- Hyper- or hypotension
- Malignant hyperpyrexia

Contraindications of depolarising muscle relaxants
- Patients prone to hyperkalaemia, especially burns victims
- History or family history of malignant hyperpyrexia
- History or family history of bronchospasm

Non-depolarising muscle relaxants

All have a slower onset than suxamethonium, but longer duration. Atracurium or benzylisoquinolinium provides intermediate duration.
- **Atracurium** undergoes non-enzymatic metabolism independent of hepatic or renal function and thus has a safety-net advantage for critically ill patients. It does, however, cause significant histamine release in some people, which can cause cardiovascular problems or redness at the site of injection.

Other benzylisoquinoliniums include cisatracurium and gallamine
- **Vecuronium** is an aminosteroid of intermediate duration. Another aminosteroid is pancuronium
- **Reversal agents:** neostigmine is used to reverse non-depolarising neuromuscular blockade, but the resulting muscarinic action may induce a profound bradycardia and it is therefore given with atropine or glycopyrronium

Factors causing prolonged neuromuscular blockade
- Hypothermia
- Acidosis
- Hyperkalaemia
- Increasing age
- Concurrent use of suxamethonium
- Inhalational anaesthetics

People with myasthenia gravis have a lower number of post-synaptic receptors due to auto-antibodies against them; this makes these patients more sensitive to non-depolarising muscle relaxants, but resistant to suxamethonium.

Maintenance of general anaesthesia

Inhalational anaesthetics are usually used for maintenance of anaesthesia, after IV induction, but can be used for induction, eg in children.

- **Halothane**
  - A volatile liquid anaesthetic of the halogenated hydrocarbon class
  - Inhalation is well tolerated and non-irritant, which means that it rarely causes patients to cough or hold their breath

- It is a very potent anaesthetic
- Causes respiratory depression, resulting in the retention of CO_2
- It is a negative inotrope, resulting in a decrease in heart rate and BP
- In addition it is a mild general muscle relaxant
- **Enflurane**
  - A liquid, halogenated methylethyl ether anaesthetic
  - Causes respiratory and myocardial depression, resulting in a decrease in cardiac output and a rise in $PaCO_2$
  - Has been shown to cause EEG changes; it is best avoided in epilepsy
  - Can cause hepatotoxicity and hyperthermia but less commonly than halothane
  - Free fluoride ions are a product of metabolism and may result in the very rare complication of fluoride-induced nephrotoxicity
- **Isoflurane**
  - Also a halogenated ether
  - The inhaled anaesthetic of choice for most surgical procedures
  - It is an isomer of enflurane but only an insignificant amount is metabolised by the patient
  - Hepatotoxicity is rare and malignant hyperthermia is as common as with other agents
  - Respiration is depressed and respiratory tract irritation may occur
  - There is a decrease in systemic vascular resistance due to vasodilatation and BP falls. This may result in an increase in heart rate and rarely in 'coronary steal' syndrome
- **Sevoflurane**
  - A halogenated ether, volatile liquid anaesthetic

- Produces a rapid induction and recovery which means that postop pain relief must be planned well
- **Nitrous oxide**
  - A potent analgesic in concentrations >20%
  - Weak anaesthetic properties
  - Potentiates the effect of other inhalational anaesthetic agents, allowing a reduction in the dose required
  - A mixture of 50% nitrous oxide and oxygen (Entonox) is used for analgesia, especially in obstetrics and emergency departments
  - Nitrous oxide will diffuse into any air-containing space
  - It diffuses more rapidly than nitrogen, and can lead to distension of the bowel
  - It must not be used in those who have recently been diving, exposed to high atmospheric pressures, or who are suspected of having a gas-filled space (eg pneumothorax or pneumocephalus)
  - Avoid prolonged exposure to nitrous oxide as it causes suppression of methionine synthetase, which leads to myelosuppression and a megaloblastic anaemia

Contraindications to inhalational anaesthetics

Pyrexia after administration of halothane or a history of jaundice is an absolute contraindication to its use.

Similar to all inhalational anaesthetics, apart from nitrous oxide, it is also associated with malignant hyperthermia.

INTRAVENOUS VS INHALATIONAL INDUCTION OF ANAESTHESIA

	Intravenous	Inhalational
Advantages	Fast-acting	No IV access required
	Anticonvulsant and antiemetic properties	Slower reflex depression
	Dose titratable	Upper oesophageal tone maintained
	Laryngeal reflex depression	Faster recovery
	Respiration maintained	
Disadvantages	Requires IV access	Slower than IV induction
	Loss of airway control	Irritant
	Risk of hypotension and anaphylaxis	May cause rise in ICP (intracranial pressure)
	Apnoea common	

Patient monitoring during anaesthesia

Patient monitoring during anaesthesia

These are the recommendations for standards of monitoring of the Association of Anaesthetists of Great Britain and Ireland.

- Continuous presence of an adequately trained anaesthetist and clinical observation
- Regular arterial pressure and heart rate measurements (recorded)
- Continuous-display ECG throughout anaesthesia
- Continuous analysis of gas mixture oxygen content (with audible alarm)
- Oxygen supply failure alarm
- Tidal/minute volume measurement
- Ventilator disconnection alarm
- Pulse oximeter
- Capnography with moving trace
- Temperature measurement available

3.5 Complications of general anaesthesia

Problems with intubation

Post-intubation, patients may complain of sore throat due to the endotracheal tube. This usually settles spontaneously but a search for other causes (eg *Candida* spp. in immunocompromised people) should be undertaken if it does not.

Trauma to structures in the mouth, predominantly the soft palate and teeth, may occur. Dislodged teeth may be aspirated. Airway management and intubation may be difficult because of:

- Abnormal anatomy (eg small mouth, large tongue)
- Atlantoaxial instability (eg Down syndrome, rheumatoid arthritis)
- Endocrine disorders causing glycosylation or enlargement of tissues (diabetes, acromegaly)
- Morbid obesity, obstructive sleep apnoea
- Pathology causing tracheal deviation

Options for managing difficult airways include:
- Optimal head position
- Pressure on the larynx
- Bougie
- Fibreoptic intubation (may be performed awake)
- Alternatives such as laryngeal mask

Failed intubation may require the procedure to be abandoned. Failed intubation with inability to ventilate necessitates an alternative airway (eg surgical or needle cricothyroidotomy).

Learning point

- Allergies
- Age
- Anaesthetic agents used (short-acting vs long-acting)
- Accidents
- Problems with intubation
  - Sore throat
  - Damage to structures in the mouth
  - Difficult airways and failed intubation
- Problems with anaesthetic drugs
  - Anaphylaxis
  - Malignant hyperpyrexia
  - Postop nausea and vomiting (PONV)
  - Drowsiness
- Trauma to the unconscious patient
- Cardiovascular complications
  - Myocardial ischaemia
  - Hypo-/hypertension
  - Arrhythmias
- Respiratory complications
  - Airway obstruction
  - Hypoventilation and hypoxia
  - Residual neuromuscular blockade
  - Gastric aspiration

Learning point

Minor complications include:
- Damage to oral cavity and contents (intubation)
- Sore throat (intubation)
- Headache
- PONV
- Urinary retention

Major complications include:
- Death (1 in 160 000)
- Gastric content aspiration
- Hypoxic brain injury
- MI
- Respiratory infection

Problems with anaesthetic drugs

Anaphylaxis

This is a severe allergic reaction to an epitope which is characterised by massive release of histamine and serotonin.

- Commonly occurs as a reaction to muscle relaxants, antibiotics and non-steroidal anti-inflammatory drugs (NSAIDs)
- Clinical features include bronchospasm, angioedema and laryngeal oedema, urticaria and cardiovascular collapse
- Management involves stopping administration of the causative agent, preservation of the airway, IV administration of chlorpheniramine 10–20 mg, hydrocortisone 100–300 mg, and sometimes IM or IV adrenaline is required

Malignant hyperpyrexia

Pathology of malignant hyperpyrexia

This condition may be triggered by all inhalational anaesthetics, except nitrous oxide, and also by suxamethonium. It is a rare life-threatening condition (1 in 150 000) which requires recognition and treatment.

It is a familial disorder thought to be of autosomal dominant inheritance in which there appears to be a rapid influx of Ca^{2+} into muscle cells resulting in actin/myosin activation and muscle rigidity.

Signs include hyperthermia, muscle rigidity, tachycardia, tachypnoea and DIC. There is an increase in oxygen demand and CO_2 production leading to a metabolic acidosis, as well as hyperkalaemia.

Treatment of malignant hyperpyrexia

Dantrolene sodium 1 mg/kg by rapid IV injection, repeated to a maximum dose of 10 mg/kg. Surface cooling and cool IV fluids may be administered. Hyperventilation will help reduce $PaCO_2$. The patient will need to be nursed on ITU and carefully monitored for signs of renal failure. The patient and family must be counselled as to further risks and the possibility of genetic inheritance.

Postoperative nausea and vomiting

Occurs in about 20% patients if no prophylaxis is used.

Aetiology of PONV
- Drugs
  - Anaesthetic agents (eg nitrous oxide, etomidate, ketamine)
  - Opiate analgesics
- Certain procedure groups
  - Gynaecology (especially ovarian)
  - Head and neck, ophthalmic, ENT
  - Bowel and gallbladder surgery
- Early oral intake
- High spinal anaesthesia
- Movement causing disorientation

Management of PONV
- Prophylactic antiemetics
- Follow the analgesic ladder
- Metoclopramide is ineffective – use cyclizine 50 mg three times daily
- Can combine antiemetics (research shows that this is more effective than monotherapy), eg ondansetron and droperidol

Cardiovascular complications
- Myocardial ischaemia
- Cardiac failure
- Hypotension/hypertension
- Arrhythmias

These are covered in more detail in Chapter 3, Postoperative Management and Critical Care.

Respiratory complications

Airway obstruction

May be due to:

- Reduced pharyngeal muscular tone
- Laryngeal oedema
- Laryngeal spasm
- Bronchospasm after extubation

Hypoventilation

- Reduced respiratory drive
  - Sedative drugs and opiate analgesics
  - Anaesthetic agents
- Elevated abdominal pressures due to distension, obesity, abdominal compartment syndrome
- Abdominal pain
- Pre-existing respiratory disease
- Residual neuromuscular blockade occurs due to inadequate reversal at the end of the operation (neostigmine)

Hypoxia

- Hypoventilation
- Pathology causing ventilation–perfusion mismatch
- Increased oxygen requirements

Gastric aspiration

Induction is the riskiest time for gastric aspiration. Even patients undergoing a regional block should be starved preoperatively in case there are complications and the anaesthetic has to be converted to a full GA.

- **Risk factors for aspiration**
  - Raised intra-abdominal pressure (obese, pregnant, intra-abdominal catastrophe)
  - Known GORD or hiatus hernia
  - Trauma
  - Drugs (eg opiates)
  - Children
  - Delayed gastric emptying due to disease
  - Metabolic (diabetes, renal failure)
  - Gastric motility (head injury)
  - Obstruction (at pylorus, due to ileus, mechanical bowel obstruction)
- **Risk reduction**
  - No solids for preceding 6 hours; clear fluids only (no milk)
  - NBM for 4 hours preoperatively
  - Regular medications taken with sips of clear fluids only
  - Decompress the stomach with NG tube if ileus present

SECTION 4

Care of the patient in theatre

4.1 Pre-induction checks

Care of the patient in theatre starts on entering the theatre complex with **pre-induction** – which involves correct identification of patient and name band, operation, site, operation side, information about starving (if for GA), allergies, blood available (if required) and that consent form is signed. Essential preoperative checks should be undertaken under the auspices of the World Health Organisation's Surgical Safety Checklist (see Chapter 2, Surgical Technique and Technology).

4.2 Prevention of injury to the anaesthetised patient

Causes of injury to the anaesthetised patient

General
- Transferring anaesthetised patients on and off the operating table
- Positioning of patients for the duration of surgery

Specific
- Injury to oral cavity during intubation
- Use of diathermy
- Use of laser
- Use of tourniquet
- Pressure area injury
- Joint injury
- Nerve injuries
- Eye injuries
- Skin injuries
- Muscle injuries

Pressure-area injury

- Risk factors: people who are elderly, immobile, on steroids or who have PVD
- Risk areas: sacrum, heels, back of the head
- Prevention: padding, heel protectors

Joint injury

- Risk factors: lithotomy position, 'breaking' the table
- Risk areas: prosthetic hip joints, cervical spine, limbs
- Prevention: coordinated lifting, head support, care with transfers

Eye injury

- Eyes should be closed and taped.
- Pressure injuries on the sphere itself (which can result in blindness) are more likely if the patient is placed prone and measures should be taken to ensure that all pressure is transmitted through the bony prominences of the orbit

Nerve injury

- Risk factor: prolonged pressure at sites where nerves run superficially
- Risk areas: ulnar nerve at the elbow, popliteal nerve at the knee, brachial plexus during abduction
- Prevention of injuries:
  - Brachial plexus: for abduction of <80° pronate hand and turn head
  - Ulnar nerve causing claw hand: excessive flexion, avoid full flexion trauma with poles from stretchers
  - Lateral popliteal causing foot drop: padding nerve of fibula in lithotomy position
  - Femoral nerve causing loss of knee extension: avoid extension of hip

Skin injury

- Burns (may be due to diathermy earth, by patient touching metal on operating table or by use of flammable skin preparation, which may be ignited). Place tape over rings or body piercings to protect site and ensure that there is no patient contact with metal parts of the operating table. Do not use flammable skin preparations
- Allergies (to dressings or skin preparations)
- Explosions (may be caused by flammable skin preparations, or ignition of anaesthetic or colonic gases)

Muscle injury

- Compartment syndromes may occur after prolonged surgery, eg in lithotomy position

4.3 Preserving patient dignity

The operating surgeon and all the staff in contact with the anaesthetised patient have a responsibility to ensure that the patient is cared for in a way that preserves dignity. Try to imagine that the patient is your relative and deal with him or her in a way that you feel is acceptable. Remember that you are the patient's advocate.

In particular:
- Avoid unnecessary exposure of the patient
- Avoid inappropriate comments or personal observations
- Respect clinical confidentiality
- Discourage disrespectful behaviour and report it if it persists

CHAPTER 2
Surgical Technique and Technology

David Mansouri

SECTION 1
Surgical wounds

1.1 Skin anatomy and physiology

All skin has the same basic structure, although it varies in thickness, colour, and the presence of hairs and glands in different regions of the body. The external surface of the skin consists of a keratinised squamous epithelium called the **epidermis**. The epidermis is supported and nourished by a thick underlying layer of dense, fibroelastic connective tissue called the **dermis**, which is highly vascular and contains many sensory receptors. The dermis is attached to underlying tissues by a layer of loose connective tissue called the **hypodermis** or subcutaneous layer. which contains adipose tissue. Hair follicles, sweat glands, sebaceous glands and nails are epithelial structures called **epidermal appendages** which extend down into the dermis and hypodermis. See Figure 2.1.

The four main functions of the skin

- **Protection:** against UV light, and mechanical, chemical and thermal insults; it also prevents excessive dehydration and acts as a physical barrier to microorganisms
- **Sensation:** various receptors for touch, pressure, pain and temperature
- **Thermoregulation:** insulation, sweating and varying blood flow in the dermis
- **Metabolism:** subcutaneous fat is a major store of energy, mainly triglycerides; vitamin D synthesis occurs in the epidermis

Skin has natural tension lines, and incisions placed along these lines tend to heal with a narrower and stronger scar, leading to a more

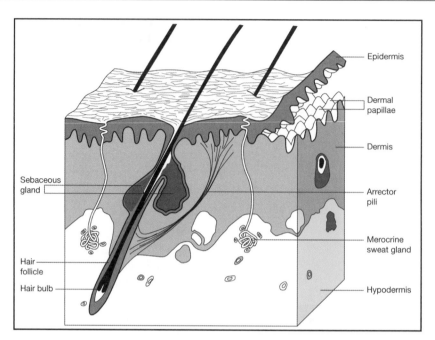

Figure 2.1 Skin anatomy

Epidermis

Dermal papillae

Dermis

Sebaceous gland

Arrector pili

Merocrine sweat gland

Hair follicle

Hair bulb

Hypodermis

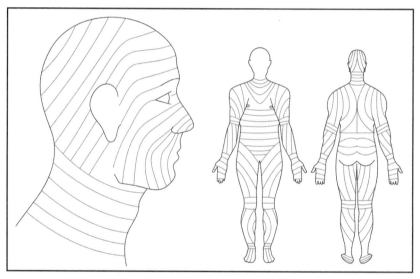

Figure 2.2 Langer's lines: the lines correspond to relaxed skin and indicate optimal orientation of skin incisions to avoid tension across the healing wound

favourable cosmetic result (Figure 2.2). These natural tension lines lie at right angles to the direction of contraction of underlying muscle fibres, and parallel to the dermal collagen bundles. On the head and neck they are readily identifiable as the 'wrinkle' lines, and can easily be exaggerated by smiling, frowning and the display of other emotions. On the limbs and trunk they tend to run circumferentially, and can easily be found by manipulating the skin to find the natural skin creases. Near flexures these lines are parallel to the skin crease.

1.2 Classification of surgical wounds

Learning point

Wounds can be classified in terms of:
- **Depth:** superficial vs deep
- **Mechanism:** incised, lacerated, abrasion, degloved, burn
- **Contamination or cleanliness:** clean, clean contaminated, contaminated, dirty

Depth of wound

Superficial wounds

Superficial wounds involve only the epidermis and dermis and heal without formation of granulation tissue and true scar formation. Epithelial cells (including those from any residual skin appendages such as sweat or sebaceous glands and hair follicles) proliferate and migrate across the remaining dermal collagen.

Examples of superficial wounds:
- Superficial burn
- Graze
- Split-skin graft donor site

Deep wounds

Deep wounds involve layers deep to the dermis and heal with the migration of fibroblasts from perivascular tissue and formation of granulation tissue and subsequent true scar formation. If a deep wound is not closed with good tissue approximation, it heals by a combination of contraction and epithelialisation, which may lead to problematic contractures, especially if over a joint.

Mechanism of wounding

The mechanism of wounding often results in characteristic damage to the skin and deeper tissues. Wounds are categorised as follows:
- **Incised wounds:** surgical or traumatic (knife, glass) where the epithelium is breached by a sharp object
- **Laceration:** an epithelial defect due to blunt trauma or tearing, which results from skin being stretched and leading to failure of the dermis and avulsion of the deeper tissues. It is usually associated with adjacent soft-tissue damage, and vascularity of the wound may be compromised (eg pretibial laceration in elderly women, scalp laceration after a blow to the head)
- **Abrasion:** friction against a surface causes sloughing of superficial skin layers
- **Degloving injury:** a form of laceration when shearing forces parallel tissue planes to move against each other, leading to disruption and separation. Although the skin may be intact, it is often at risk due to disruption of its underlying blood supply. This occurs when, for example, a worker's arm gets caught in an industrial machine
- **Burns**

Contamination of wounds

Wounds may be contaminated by the environment at times of injury. Surgical procedures and accidental injuries may be classified according to the *risk* of wound contamination:
- **Clean** (eg hernia repair)
- **Clean contaminated** (eg cholecystectomy)
- **Contaminated wound** (eg colonic resection)
- **Dirty wound** (eg laparotomy for peritonitis)

1.3 Principles of wound management

> **Learning point**
>
> The principles of wound management are concerned with providing an optimum environment to facilitate wound healing. There are three ways in which wound healing can take place:
> - First (primary) intention
> - Second (secondary) intention
> - Third (tertiary) intention

First (primary) intention

This typically occurs in uncontaminated wounds with minimal tissue loss and when the wound edges can easily be approximated with sutures, staples or adhesive strips, without excessive tension. The wound usually heals by rapid epithelialisation and formation of minimal granulation tissue and subsequent scar tissue.

> **Ideal conditions for wound healing**
> - No foreign material
> - No infection
> - Accurate apposition of tissues in layers (eliminating dead space)
> - No excess tension
> - Good blood supply
> - Good haemostasis, preventing haematoma

Second (secondary) intention

Usually secondary intention occurs in wounds with substantial tissue loss, when the edges cannot be apposed without excessive tension. The wound is left open and allowed to heal from the deep aspects of the wound by a combination of granulation, epithelialisation and contraction. This inevitably takes longer, and is accompanied by a much more intense inflammatory response. Scar quality and cosmetic results are poor. Negative pressure dressings (eg Vac) can facilitate secondary intention healing when large wound defects are present.

Wounds that may be left to heal by secondary intention:
- Extensive loss of epithelium
- Extensive contamination
- Extensive tissue damage
- Extensive oedema leading to inability to close
- Wound reopened (eg infection, failure of knot)

Third (tertiary) intention

The wound is closed several days after its formation. This may well follow a period of healing by secondary intention, eg when infection is under control or tissue oedema is reduced. This can also be called 'delayed primary closure'.

1.4 Pathophysiology of wound healing

> ### Learning point
>
> Wound healing consists of three phases:
> - **Acute inflammatory phase** (see Chapter 4, Infection and Inflammation)
> - **Proliferative phase** (cell proliferation and deposition of extracellular matrix or ECM)
> - **Maturation phase** (remodelling of the ECM)
>
> Different tissues may undergo specialised methods of repair (eg organ parenchyma, bone and nervous tissue).

All surgeons deal with wounds and it is essential to understand fully the exact pathophysiological mechanisms involved in wound healing, how this may be optimised, and how it may be compromised, leading to wound dehiscence, delayed healing and incisional hernia formation.

The aims of wound healing are a rapid restoration of tissue continuity and a rapid return to normal function.

The inflammatory phase

Tissue damage starts a typical acute inflammatory reaction by damage to cells and blood vessels.

> ### The inflammatory phase of wound healing involves:
> - Vasodilatation and increased vascular permeability
> - Influx of inflammatory cells (neutrophils) and fibroblasts
> - Platelet activation and initiation of the coagulation and complement cascades, leading to clot formation and haemostasis

The proliferative phase

The proliferative phase is characterised by migration and proliferation of a number of cell types:
- **Epithelial cells:** within hours of injury epithelial cells at the margins of the wound begin to proliferate and migrate across the defect; epithelial closure is usually complete by 48 hours
- **Fibroblasts:** fibroblasts migrate into the wound, proliferate and synthesise ECM components including collagen and ground substance (4–5 days)
- **Endothelial cells:** the development of new blood vessels (angiogenesis) occurs simultaneously with activation of fibroblasts – proliferation and migration of endothelial cells depend on the proteolytic activity of matrix metalloproteases (for which zinc is an essential cofactor)

Cell types involved in wound healing and time of appearance in wound	
Platelets	Immediate
Neutrophils	0–1 day
Macrophages	1–2 days
Fibroblasts	2–4 days
Myofibroblasts	2–4 days
Endothelial cells	3–5 days

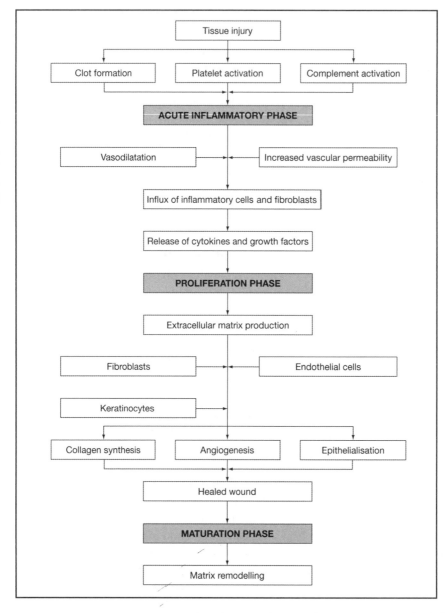

Figure 2.3 Wound healing

Granulation tissue is a temporary structure which forms at this stage. It consists of a rich network of capillary vessels and a heterogeneous population of cells (fibroblasts, macrophages and endothelial cells) within the stroma of the ECM. It has a characteristic pinkish, granular appearance. In addition the wound contracts due to the action of myofibroblasts.

The maturation phase

Matrix remodelling

- This stage lasts for many months after the wound is clinically healed
- The scar becomes less vascular – hence the change in colour

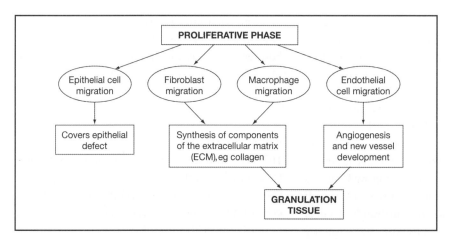

Figure 2.4 The proliferative phase

- The scar tensile strength increases due to modifications made to collagen. The collagen molecule is a triple α helix. Multiple molecules orient to form a fibril. The cross-linkage of collagen fibrils by formation of covalent bonds (aided by the action of vitamin C) increases the tensile strength of the scar

Regaining strength in the wound

During matrix remodelling the scar regains its strength. The tissue types and thickness involved in the scar will determine the length of time needed to regain strength. Bowel and muscle regain near-full strength within 1 month and skin takes up to 6 months. Strength tends to increase very quickly over the first 7–10 days, although full maturation of a scar can take up to 12–18 months. Choice of wound closure materials should reflect this. Abdominal incisions through muscle layers will take many weeks to regain their strength, achieving sufficient strength at 3–4 months to no longer require suture support and about 80% of their former strength after many months. Closure is therefore performed with either loop nylon that will persist in the wound, or a strong, slowly absorbing suture material such as PDS (polydioxanone sulphate) that will support the wound. Superficial skin wounds require minimal support and so can be closed with a quickly absorbable suture material or by interrupted sutures or staples that can be removed within days.

1.5 Healing in specialised tissues

Healing in different tissues

Different tissues heal in a remarkably similar way, albeit at different rates – the scalp and face heal very quickly, at least in part because of increased vascularity. Healing rates are quickest early in life, and decline with advancing years. Surgery performed on the fetus in utero leaves no scarring at all because it occurs by regeneration. Some tissues possess the ability to regenerate their specialised cells after injury, with the result that significant tissue loss can be replaced by regenerated specialised cells, with no – or minimal – loss of function (eg bone, intestine). Conversely, some tissues have little regenerative ability (eg cardiac tissue) and wounds heal by simple scar formation – significant tissue loss will result in significant loss of function. Nervous tissue possesses very limited regenerative capacity – partial function may be regained through slow neuronal growth in peripheral nerve injuries.

Skin

Skin consists of two layers – the keratinised stratified epidermis and the connective tissue of the dermis. After injury to the skin, healing essentially follows the pattern outlined above. Blood lost into the wound clots into a fibrin meshwork (the scab). Inflammatory cells, fibroblasts and capillaries invade the clot to form a contractile granulation tissue that draws the wound margins together. Neutrophils release cytokines and growth factors that activate fibroblasts and keratinocytes, which alter their anchorage to the surrounding cells, ECM and basal lamina. Protease secretion by the keratinocytes allows them to migrate through the fibrin mesh of the clot and the cut epidermal edges to move forward to cover the denuded wound surface. A new stratified epidermis with underlying basal lamina is then re-established. Epidermal appendages (eg sweat glands and hair follicles) do not regenerate. The epithelial layer heals within 48 hours if the edges of the wound are accurately apposed.

Nerve injury and repair

> ### Learning point
>
> **In order of increasing degree of injury:**
> - **Neuropraxia (I):** no axonal disruption
> - **Axonotmesis (II):** axonal disruption/ supportive tissue framework preserved
> - **Neurotmesis (III–V):** supportive tissue framework disrupted
>
> **Principles of surgical repair of nerves:**
> - Accurate apposition of nerve ends
> - Healthy surrounding tissue
> - No tension
> - Minimal dissection

There are many variations of nerve injury. A common classification was described by Seddon, dividing injuries into three groups: neuropraxia, axonotmesis and neurotmesis. Sunderland's classification expands the category of neurotmesis and refers to categories of increasing severity.

Neuropraxia (I)

This is the mildest form of nerve injury, referring to a crush, contusion or stretching injury of the nerve without disruption of its axonal continuity. There is a reduction or block in conduction of the impulse down a segment of the nerve fibre. This may be caused by local biochemical abnormalities. There is a temporary loss of function that is reversible within hours to months of the injury (average 6–8 weeks). Motor function often suffers greater impairment than sensory function, and autonomic function is often retained.

Axonotmesis (II)

This is the loss of the relative continuity of the axon and its covering of myelin with preservation of the connective tissue framework of the nerve (epineurium and perineurium). It is a more serious injury than neuropraxia. Wallerian degeneration occurs and there is a degree of retrograde proximal degeneration of the remaining axon. Recovery occurs through regeneration of the axons (which grow along the existing preserved framework of the nerve). Regeneration requires time and may take weeks or months, depending on the size of the lesion.

Neurotmesis (III, IV and V)

This is the loss of continuity of both axons and nerve structural connective tissue. It ranges in severity, with the most extreme degree of neurotmesis being transection. Most neurotmetic injuries do not produce gross loss of continuity

CHAPTER 2

of the nerve but rather internal disruption of the architecture of the nerve sufficient to involve perineurium and endoneurium as well as the axons and their myelin sheath. There is a complete loss of motor, sensory and autonomic function. If the nerve has been completely divided, axonal regeneration causes a neuroma to form in the proximal stump.

In grade III injuries, axonal continuity is disrupted by loss of endoneurial tubes (the neurolemmal sheaths) but the perineurium is preserved. This causes intraneural scarring and regenerating axons may re-enter the sheaths incorrectly.

In grade IV injuries, nerve fasciculi (axon, endoneurium, perineurium) are damaged, but nerve sheath continuity is preserved.

In grade V injuries the endoneurium, perineurium and epineurium, which make up the entire nerve trunk, are completely transected. This may be associated with perineural haematoma or displacement of the nerve ends.

Bowel

The layers of the bowel involved in the anastomosis heal at different rates. Optimal healing requires good surgical technique and apposition of the layers.

The intestinal mucosa is a sheet of epithelial cells that undergoes rapid turnover and proliferation. It may sustain injury as a result of trauma (from luminal contents or surgery), chemicals (eg bile), ischaemia or infection. Injury to the mucosa resulting in breaches of the epithelial layer is thought to render patients susceptible to bacterial translocation and systemic sepsis syndromes. Minor disruption to the mucosa is thought to be repaired by a process separate from proliferation, called 'restitution', instigated

by cytokines and growth factors and regulated by the interaction of cellular integrins with the ECM. After uncomplicated surgery to the gastro-intestinal (GI) tract, mucosal integrity is thought to have occurred by 24 hours.

The other muscular layers of the bowel undergo the general phases of inflammation, proliferation and maturation as outlined above. Anastomotic healing results in the formation of collagenous scar tissue. Scarring may eventually contract, resulting in stenosis.

Solid organs

Solid organs either heal by regeneration (through a process of cell proliferation) or by hypertrophy of existing cells. Some organs heal by a combination of the two processes. In organs in which the cells are terminally differentiated, healing occurs by scarring or fibrosis.

Liver

The liver has remarkable regenerative capacity. The stimulation for regeneration is reduction in the liver mass to body mass ratio (eg surgical resection) or the loss of liver functional capacity (eg hepatocyte necrosis by toxins or viruses). Regeneration is achieved by proliferation of all the components of the mature organ – hepatocytes, biliary epithelial cells, fenestrated epithelial cells and Kupffer's cells. Hepatocytes, which are normally quiescent and rarely divide, start to proliferate to restore hepatic mass and function. This occurs initially in the areas surrounding the portal triads and then extends to the pericentral areas after 48 hours. After 70% hepatectomy in animal models, the remaining hepatocytes divide once or twice and then return to quiescence. About 24 hours after the hepatocytes start to proliferate, so do all the other cell types and ECM is produced, including the structural protein, laminin. Eventually the cell types restructure into functional lobules over 7–10 days. The stimulus for hepatocyte proliferation is thought to be tumour necrosis factor (TNF) and the interleukin 6 (IL-6) family of cytokines. Subsequently human growth factor (HGF) and transforming growth factor (TGF)-α are responsible for continued cell growth. Regeneration is terminated after about 72 hours by the action of cytokines such as TGF-β_1.

Kidney

The cells of the kidney are highly specialised, reflecting their terminal state of differentiation. Healing in the kidney predominantly occurs by scarring and fibrosis.

Spleen

Splenic regeneration is controversial. Increases in size and weight of the residual splenic tissue have been recognised after partial splenectomy (eg for trauma), and hypertrophy of missed splenunculi after splenectomy for haematological and glycogen storage diseases (eg Gaucher's disease) may also occur. However, there is little evidence that this increase in size of the residual splenic tissue results in functional regeneration and the increase in size may be due to infiltration of the tissue with cells characteristic of the underlying haematological or other disorder.

Heart and lung

Cardiac tissue is commonly damaged by ischaemia and occasionally by trauma. The inflammatory response is particularly important in the healing of cardiac tissue and is instigated by release of cytokines such as TNF- or IL-6 from the damaged myocardium. These cytokines have been implicated in the regulation of myocyte survival or apoptosis, myocyte hypertrophy,

defects in myocyte contractility, proliferation of myofibroblasts and angiogenesis/vasculogenesis and, to a limited extent, progenitor cell proliferation. The cytokine response lasts about a week and the infarcted myocardium is gradually replaced by scar tissue. Within this scar tissue there is a degree of regeneration of myocytes and blood vessels, and current research is focused on facilitating this process for an improvement in myocardial function post-infarct.

Non-regenerative tissues

Non-regenerative tissues, such as the cornea of the eye, heal by collagen deposition and scarring. This is obviously accompanied by complete loss of function.

1.6 Complications of wound healing

> **Learning point**
>
> Wound healing is affected by:
> - **Local factors (factors specific to the wound)**
>   - Wound classification
>   - Surgical skill
> - **General factors (factors specific to the patient)**
>   - Concomitant disease
>   - Nutrition

Factors affecting wound healing

Local risk factors
- Wound infection
- Haematoma

- Excessive mobility
- Foreign body
- Dead tissue
- Dirty wound
- Surgical technique
- Ischaemia
  - Acute: damage to blood supply; sutures too tight
  - Chronic: previous irradiation
  - Diabetes
  - Atherosclerosis
  - Venous disease

General risk factors
- Elderly person
- Cardiac disease
- Respiratory disease
- Anaemia
- Obesity
- Renal (uraemia) or hepatic failure (jaundice)
- Diabetes mellitus
- Smoking
- Malnutrition (vitamins and minerals)
- Malignancy
- Irradiation
- Steroid or cytotoxic drugs
- Other immunosuppressive disease or drugs

Nutritional factors
- Proteins are essential for ECM formation and effective immune response
- Vitamin A is required for epithelial cell proliferation and differentiation
- Vitamin B6 is required for collagen cross-linking
- Vitamin C is necessary for hydroxylation of proline and lysine residues. Without hydroxyproline, newly synthesised collagen is not transported out of fibroblasts; in the absence of hydroxylysine, collagen fibrils are not cross-linked

- Zinc is an essential trace element required for RNA and DNA synthesis and for the function of some 200 metalloenzymes
- Copper plays a role in the cross-linking of collagen and elastin

Optimising wound healing

Wound failure may be minimised by attention to the risk factors listed above. Ensure good delivery of blood and oxygen to the wound (and be aware of the importance of good hydration and respiratory function). Debride devitalised tissues and handle other tissues with care to prevent tissue necrosis. Sutures that are tied very tightly will cause tissue hypoxia. Avoid tension on the wound. Careful aseptic technique should be used. Heavily contaminated wounds or the abdominal cavity should be washed with copious amounts of warmed saline until clean. Patient nutrition is also very important and critically ill patients may require support via either nasogastric (NG) feeding or parenteral nutrition.

On occasions the patient may be in such a poor condition (eg be elderly, have septic shock, be on steroids) and the circumstances of the operation so hostile (emergency, faecal contamination, disseminated malignancy) that the chance of good wound healing is very low. Under these circumstances, there are various surgical options:
- Bring out a stoma rather than perform a primary bowel anastomosis
- Leave the skin and subcutaneous fat open in a heavily contaminated abdomen for delayed primary closure – this wound can then be packed as required (be aware that changing dressings on large wounds may require return visits to theatre)
- Close the wound with additional deep tension sutures

- The abdominal wall itself may be left open (a laparostomy) or partially closed with an artificial mesh to reduce intra-abdominal pressure after surgery for intra-abdominal catastrophe and prevent abdominal compartment syndrome

Wound dehiscence and incisional hernias

Learning point

The same risk factors predispose to:
- Failure of wound healing
- Wound dehiscence
- Incisional herniation

- Wound dehiscence is the partial or total disruption of any or all layers of the surgical wound. Risk factors for wound dehiscence are the same as the factors affecting wound healing
- Evisceration ('burst abdomen') is rupture of all layers of the abdominal wall and extrusion of the abdominal viscera (usually preceded by the appearance of blood-stained fluid – the pink-fluid sign)
- Wound dehiscence without evisceration should be repaired by immediate elective reclosure. Dehiscence of a laparotomy wound with evisceration is a surgical emergency with a mortality rate of >25%. Management involves resuscitation, reassurance, analgesia, protection of the organs with moist sterile towels, and immediate re-operation and closure (usually with deep tension sutures)

Incisional hernias are still common despite modern suture materials. They occur at sites of partial wound failure or dehiscence. Risk factors for incisional hernia are therefore the same as those for dehiscence. Symptoms include visible protrusion of the hernia during episodes of raised intra-abdominal pressure and discomfort. Incisional hernias usually correspond to a wide defect in the abdominal wall and so often do not incarcerate. Treatment depends on symptoms and size of defect (eg conservative measures including a truss/corset and surgical repair). Further details on incisional hernias and methods of repair are covered in the Abdominal Surgery chapter of Book 2.

1.7 Scars and contractures

Learning point

The final appearance of a scar depends on:
- **Wound factors**
  - Site
  - Classification
  - Tissue loss
- **Patient factors**
  - Risk factors for poor wound healing
  - Predisposition to keloid or hypertrophy
- **Surgical factors**
  - Positioning of incisions
  - Correct alignment during closure
  - Correct management of traumatic wounds using the reconstructive ladder

Mechanism of scarring

As a scar forms, the strength increases rapidly within 7–10 days, and it is at this stage that sutures are normally removed. It is usually many months, however, before the scar achieves full strength. As fibrous tissue is laid down, this tissue is continually digested to modify the shape of the scar, and these two competing influences are usually in balance. If too little fibrous tissue is laid down, or excessive breakdown takes place, the wound will fail to heal adequately, and this leads to wound dehiscence (early) or hernia formation (late). Conversely, if excessive scar tissue is laid down, the scar may be hypertrophic or keloid.

Minimisation of scarring

- Use lines of skin tension or hide the scar in naturally occurring lines including:
  - Langer's lines
  - Natural wrinkle lines (nasolabial fold, glabellar wrinkles, forehead wrinkles)
  - Natural junction lines that draw the eye from the scar (eg the junction between nose and face, nostril rim, vermillion border of the lip)
- Hidden sites (eg eyebrow, hairline) where an incision parallel to the hair follicle, rather than perpendicular to the skin, avoids a hairless scar line caused by sectioning the follicles
- Appose tissues correctly (if the wound is irregular, identify landmarks on either side that fit together, allowing the jigsaw to be accurately sutured back together)
- Close in layers to reduce tension (skin may be undermined to improve mobility)
- Clean tissues thoroughly of dirt to prevent infection and tattooing of the skin
- Use the smallest suitable diameter suture (to minimise foreign material in the wound and the inflammatory response, to reduce tissue compression and additional injury)
- Remove sutures as early as possible (tracks will become epithelialised and therefore visible if sutures are left)
- Recommend massage, which prevents adherence to underlying structures and improves the colour of the scar (can be performed after initial healing)
- Advise patient to avoid exposure of new scars to sunshine (causes pigmentation)

Contractures

These occur as the scar shortens. They may lead to distortion of adjacent structures (eg near the eye) or limited flexibility in joints. They may also be caused by extravasation injuries. Contractures can be both prevented and treated by using a Z-plasty to break up the scar. Physiotherapy, massage and even splintage can be used to prevent contractures when scars cross joint surfaces.

Scars

Hypertrophic scars

Most wounds become red and hard for a while but after several months spontaneous maturation leads to a pale soft scar. Occasionally this excessive scar tissue remains, but is limited to the site of the original wound.

- Due to fibroblast overactivity in the proliferative phase; eventually this is corrected (usually by 1 year) and a more normal scar results
- Commonly results from large areas of skin damage (eg abrasion or burns)

Keloid scars

- Excessive scar tissue which **extends beyond** the original wound
- Intense fibroblast activity continues into the maturation phase
- Complications include poor cosmesis, contractures and loss of function
- Prevention: use Langer's lines, ensure meticulous wound closure without undue tension, avoidance of infection and judicious use of pressure garments

Risk factors for hypertrophic and keloid scars

- Young age
- Male sex
- Dark pigmented skin
- Genetic predisposition
- Site (sternum, shoulders, head and neck)
- Tension on wound
- Delayed healing

Treatment of hypertrophic and keloid scars

- Excision (usually leads to recurrence)
- Excision and radiotherapy (not always successful and cannot be repeated)
- Intralesional steroid injection (variable response)
- Pressure garments
- Silastic gel treatment
- CO_2 laser (variable response)

Malignant change in scars

Rarely squamous cell cancers can form in scars (so-called Marjolin's ulcers). Any unusual ulceration or appearance in a scar should be biopsied.

Other scars

Other kinds of scarring may also occur. Scars may be widened and stretched if there is movement in that region that puts tension on the suture line. A scar may become tethered to underlying structures and puckered. Failure to remove dirt or surgical marker pen may result in permanent tattooing of a scar. Failure to properly align tissues and not correctly everting skin edges may result in a scar that appears 'stepped'. Scars can be revised by means of Z-plasty or by direct revision after about 18 months.

SECTION 2

Surgical technique

2.1 Principles of safe surgery and communicable disease

Learning point

Minimise risk to patient
- Asepsis
- Theatre briefing
- Surgical checklist

Minimise risk to staff
- Standard and specialist precautions

Minimising risk to patient

Standard aseptic techniques are used universally to minimise risk of surgical site infections (SSIs).
- Scrubbing
- Skin preparation and draping
- Theatre design

Skin preparation

The choice of surgical scrub is to use either chlorhexidine gluconate-containing or povidone iodine-containing solutions and for these to either be alcohol based or aqueous. Alcohol-based solutions were thought to be quicker acting, more durable and with broader-spectrum antimicrobial activity compared with aqueous solutions; however, they have the potential to be flammable. This flammability can be minimised by allowing the skin time to dry and also avoiding preparation of areas that have excessive body hair, which delays evaporation. Current National Institute for Health and Clinical Excellence (NICE) guidelines show little difference in cover between chlorhexidine and iodine solutions and find alcoholic and aqueous solutions acceptable, provided that appropriate time is allowed for these to dry.

There is no evidence that removing hair before surgery reduces the risk of SSIs; however, if hair removal is preferred by the surgeon then the area should be shaved immediately before theatre and with hair clippers rather than a razor (minimise abrasions to skin that actually increase the risk of SSIs). Using scrub solution, the surgical field should be cleaned from the centre out and 'dirty' areas (eg the groin and perineum) should be cleaned last.

Theatre design

Position

- Theatres ideally should be close to the surgical wards, intensive therapy unit (ITU), sterile supplies unit, A&E and radiology/CT

Layout

- Clean areas and corridors should be separate from dirty areas and sluices
- Anaesthetic rooms should be adjacent to the theatre
- Adequate space is required for such things as storage and staff recreation

Environment

- Ideal temperature of 20–22°C to maintain patient and staff comfort
- Humidity control
- Clean filtered air enters via ceiling, leaves via door flaps (higher pressure in ultra-clean/clean areas; lower in dirty areas)
- Power, piped gas, anaesthetic gas scavenging system, suction
- Adequate lighting

Theatre briefings and checklists

A morning briefing should be performed on the day of surgery and involve all members of the theatre team introducing themselves and then discussing the cases for the day. This provides an opportunity for potential problems to be addressed, including availability of equipment and specific anaesthetic issues, and ensures that all members of the team understand the way that the operating list will run.

All patients should have consent forms and the correct site marked (where appropriate) before being in the theatre complex. A correct site form may also be used.

Preoperative checklists should be performed before the induction of anaesthesia, before starting the operation and before the patient leaves the anaesthetic room. These may vary from hospital to hospital but should incorporate several key elements based on the WHO Surgical Safety Checklist (see Figure 2.5).

The World Health Organisation Surgical Safety Checklist

The WHO Surgical Safety Checklist has been introduced internationally because evidence has shown that the use of a standardised checklist before surgery both reduces surgical errors (such as wrong site surgery) and improves morbidity and mortality (by promoting communication among the surgical team). See Figure 2.5.

Minimising risk to theatre staff

- Wear correct gloves of correct size; if available use indicator undergloves
- Never handle sharps directly, including needles, blades and suture needles
- Scalpels should be passed in a kidney dish or similar
- Scalpel blades should be changed using artery clips or forceps and not handled directly
- Suture needles should have their position in needle holders changed with forceps
- Visors should be worn
- All instrumentation, including diathermy/endoscopes/laparoscopic equipment, should be personally checked by the operating surgeon
- Needles and sharps should be disposed of safely and the operating field left clear of excess instrumentation

Overall risk of contracting a blood-borne virus after a needlestick injury varies in different studies and with different type of injury, but as a general guide there is a 30% risk of hepatitis B, 3% risk of hepatitis C and 0.3% risk of developing HIV. Needlestick injury is discussed further in Microbiology.

2.2 Incisions and wound closures

Figure 2.6 overleaf shows all commonly used incisions and different routes of access to different organs.

The most common reason for a difficult operation is inadequate access. This may be because the organ is difficult to access (gastro-oesophageal junction, gastrosplenic ligament, lower rectum)

or the body shape unfavourable, or because the wrong incision has been used. The surgeon can affect only the last of these, and it is extremely important, having considered the likely course of the operation, to plan the incision before starting. Remember when planning that you may wish to extend your incision if access proves difficult!

If it is considered that different incisions may give identical access, then that incision which leads to better healing and cosmesis should be used. As a general rule, transverse incisions heal better than vertical ones. Plan your closure at the same time as the incision – if the incision is complicated it is valuable to mark lines perpendicular to the incision in ink before you begin. These lines then show how the edges should be brought together accurately for closure.

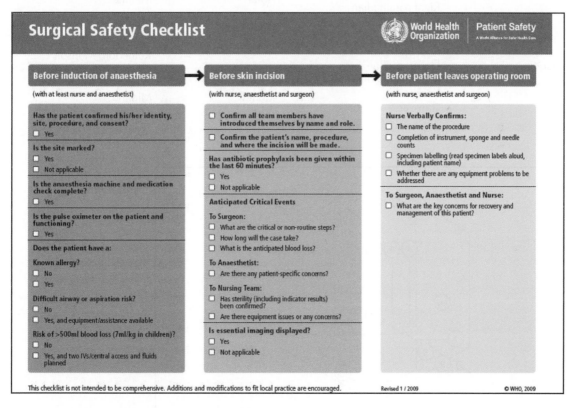

Figure 2.5 WHO's Patient Safety Surgical Checklist

COMMON INCISIONS

Organ	Approach
Oesophagus	Cervical
Upper thoracic	Right 4/5 posterolateral thoracotomy
Mid thoracic	Right 5/6/7 posterolateral thoracotomy
Lower thoracic	Right 5/6/7 posterolateral thoracotomy
	Left 6/7 posterolateral thoracotomy
	Left thoracoabdominal
Abdominal	Left thoracoabdominal
	Rooftop
	Upper midline
Stomach	Left thoracoabdominal
	Rooftop
	Upper midline
Liver	Right thoracoabdominal
Biliary tree	Rooftop
	Upper midline
	Right paramedian
	Kocher
Pancreas	Transverse
	Rooftop
Duodenum	Upper midline
	Right paramedian
	Kocher
	Transverse

Organ	Approach
Small intestine	Midline
	Paramedian
	Transverse
Colon	Right midline
	Right paramedian
	Right transverse
	Rutherford Morison
	Gridiron
Appendix	Gridiron
	Lanz
	Left midline
	Left paramedian
	Left transverse
Rectum	Midline
	Left paramedian
	Left transverse
	Perineal
Uterus, ovaries	Midline
	Pfannenstiel
Aorta	Midline
	Transverse
Iliac vessels	Midline
	Transverse
	Rutherford Morison
Bladder	Lower midline
	Pfannenstiel
Kidney	Midline
Adrenal glands	Kocher
	Twelfth rib incision

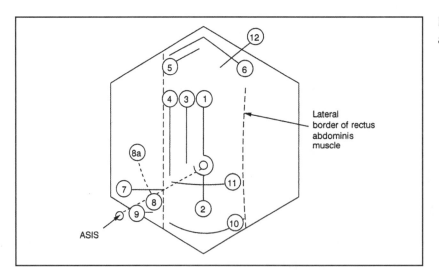

Figure 2.6 Common abdominal incisions

Abdominal incisions

(1) Midline incision through linea alba: provides good access. Can be extended easily. Quick to make and close. Relatively avascular. More painful than transverse incisions. Incision crosses Langer's lines so it has poor cosmetic appearance. Narrow linea alba below umbilicus. Some vessels cross the midline. Can cause bladder damage.

(2) Subumbilical incision: used for repair of paraumbilical hernias and laparoscopic port.

(3) Paramedian incision: 1.5 cm from midline through rectus abdominis sheath. This was the only effective vertical incision in the days when catgut was the only suture material available. Takes longer to make than midline incision. Does not lend itself to closure by 'Jenkins' rule' (length of suture is four times the length of wound). Poor cosmetic result. Can lead to infection in rectus sheath. Other hazards: tendinous intersections must be dissected off; need to divide falciform ligament above umbilicus on the right; if rectus is split >1 cm from medial border, intercostal nerves are disrupted, leading to denervation of medial rectus (avoid by retracting rectus without splitting).

(4) Pararectal 'Battle's' incision: now not used because of damage to nerves entering rectus sheath and poor healing leading to postoperative incisional hernias.

(5) Kocher's incision: 3 cm below and parallel to costal margin from midline to rectus border. Good incision for cholecystectomy on the right and splenectomy on the left – but beware superior epigastric vessels. If wound is extended laterally too many intercostal nerves are severed. Cannot be extended caudally.

(6) Double Kocher's (rooftop) incision: good access to liver and spleen. Useful for intrahepatic surgery. Used for radical pancreatic and gastric surgery and bilateral adrenalectomy.

(7) Transverse muscle-cutting incision: can be across all muscles. Beware of intercostal nerves.

(8) McBurney's/gridiron incision: classic approach to appendix through junction of the outer and middle third of a line from the anterosuperior iliac spine (ASIS) to the umbilicus at right angles to that line. May be modified into a skin-crease horizontal cut. External oblique aponeurosis is cut in the line of the fibres. Internal oblique and transversus abdominis are split transversely in the line of the fibres. Beware: scarring if not horizontal; iliohypogastric and ilioinguinal nerves; deep circumflex artery.

(8a) Rutherford Morison incision: gridiron can be extended cephalad and laterally, obliquely splitting the external oblique to afford good access to caecum, appendix and right colon.

(9) Lanz incision: lower incision than McBurney's and closer to the ASIS. Better cosmetic result (concealed by bikini). Tends to divide iliohypogastric and ilioinguinal nerves, leading to denervation of inguinal canal mechanism (can increase risk of inguinal hernia).

(10) Pfannenstiel incision: most frequently used transverse incision in adults. Excellent access to female genitalia for caesarean section and for bladder and prostate operations. Also can be used for bilateral hernia repair. Skin incised in a downward convex arc into suprapubic skin crease 2 cm above the pubis. Upper flap is raised and rectus sheath incised 1 cm cephalic to the skin incision (not extending lateral to the rectus). Rectus is then divided longitudinally in the midline.

(11) Transverse incision: particularly useful in neonates and children (who do not have the subdiaphragmatic and pelvic recesses of adults). Heals securely and cosmetically. Less pain and fewer respiratory problems than with longitudinal midline incision but division of red muscle involves more blood loss than longitudinal incision. Not extended easily. Takes longer to make and close. Limited access in adults to pelvic or subdiaphragmatic structure.

(12) Thoracoabdominal incision: access to lower thorax and upper abdomen. Used (rarely) for liver and biliary surgery on the right. Used (rarely) for oesophageal, gastric and aortic surgery on the left.

Thoracic incisions

A summary of the important features of these incisions is presented below. For further discussion of thoracic incisions and closures see the Cardiothoracic Surgery chapter of Book 2.

Median sternotomy

This common incision is used in a number of surgical disciplines and is the most frequently used approach to the heart. The patient is placed supine with the neck extended. It is a midline incision extending from 2 cm below the sternal notch to the xiphoid. The sternum is divided using a pneumatic reciprocating saw or a jiggly saw. Gives access to:
- Heart (including aortic and mitral valves)
- Great vessels (especially ascending aorta)
- Structures in the anterior mediastinum (eg thymus, retrosternal thyroid)

Anterolateral thoracotomy

This is the procedure of choice for emergency, resuscitation room procedures for management of cardiac or thoracic injuries, often in the context of major haemorrhage or cardiac arrest.

The incision extends from the lateral edge of the sternum following the rib interspace laterally. It may be performed through the fifth interspace according to indication. Gives access to:
- Heart (control of bleeding)
- Lung hilum (control of bleeding)
- Lung parenchyma (control of bleeding)
- Descending aorta

Posterolateral thoracotomy

Although there are many variants on the thoracotomy, this is the most common incision through which elective thoracic procedures are performed. The incision is curved and passes from the middle of the posterior border of the scapula, below the angle of the scapula, to a point midway between the angle of the scapula and the nipple. This may be performed at either the fifth or the seventh interspace.
- Via fifth interspace:
  - Lung and hilum
  - Mid-oesophagus
- Via seventh interspace:
  - Lower oesophagus
  - Diaphragm
  - Heart and pericardium

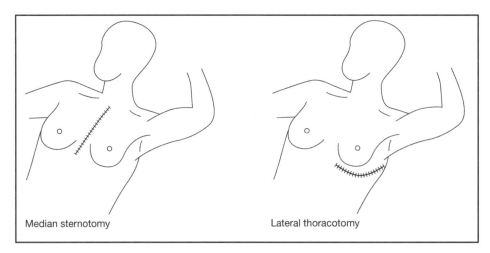

Median sternotomy   Lateral thoracotomy

Figure 2.7 Thoracic incisions

Laparoscopy

Both the abdominal and thoracic cavities can be accessed by means of a laparoscope. The principles of this access are similar, with insertion of a large access port to transmit a camera and a number of smaller instrument ports. Minimal access surgery is discussed later in this chapter.

Closure techniques

Good surgical technique optimises wound healing and cosmesis.

Closure techniques

Principles of wound closure include the following:
- Incise along natural tension lines
- Avoid haematoma and obliterate potential spaces
- Eliminate all dead tissue and infection
- Ensure good apposition of tissues
- Avoid excess wound tension
- Ensure good blood supply
- Handle tissues gently
- Use appropriate suture material
- Choose appropriate closure technique

Abdominal closure

At closure there is an increase in intra-abdominal pressure and some tension on the suture line is inevitable. Abdominal incisions can be closed either in layers or by a mass closure technique. The **mass closure** includes all layers of the abdominal wall except subcutaneous fat and skin, and has been shown to be as strong as a layered closure, with no greater incidence of later wound complications such as dehiscence or incisional hernia formation. This is now the preferred closure method of most surgeons. Other abdominal incisions are closed in layers, apposing the tissues (eg rectus sheath to rectus sheath).

Procedure box: Mass closure of the abdomen

- Carefully reposition abdominal contents into the abdominal cavity and cover with the omentum; abdominal contents may be temporarily protected with a large swab or plastic guard (note that bowel guards must be removed before the closure is complete)
- Use a non-absorbable (eg loop nylon 0/0) or slowly absorbable (eg PDS 0/0) continuous suture on a large curved needle (some surgeons use blunt-ended needles for safety reasons)
- Use a suture that is four times the length of the wound (in practice two or more sutures are used, starting from opposite ends of the wound, meeting in the middle)
- Obey the **Jenkins' 1-cm rule** – each bite of the abdominal wall should be a minimum of 1 cm, and adjacent bites must be a maximum of 1 cm apart. These measurements refer to the rectus sheath only, not the fat or peritoneum or rectus muscle. To develop good technique, before you place each stitch you should identify two things: the site of the last stitch and the cut edge of the anterior rectus sheath. Only then can you apply Jenkins' rule correctly
- Generally in a mass closure you should include in each stitch all layers of the abdominal wall and peritoneum, except subcutaneous fat and skin, but it is important to recognise that it is the fascia of the rectus sheath that gives the wound its strength
- Place each suture under direct vision to avoid accidental damage to the bowel
- Remember that the posterior rectus sheath is deficient in the lower abdomen

CHAPTER 2

Thoracic closure

Thoracic closure is covered in the Cardiothoracic chapter in Book 2. The basic principles include:

- Haemostasis in the chest cavity and of the wound edges
- Closure of the bony layer (with wire for the sternum and heavy nylon ties in a figure-of-eight loop for the ribs in the lateral incisions)
- Closure of the subcutaneous layer
- Closure of the skin

Closure of the subcutaneous layers

Subcutaneous fascial layers (eg Scarpa's fascia) may be apposed accurately with interrupted or continuous absorbable sutures. This aids in the elimination of dead space and helps prevent fluid collections. It also aids subsequent accurate apposition of the skin.

Thick deposits of adipose tissue heal poorly and are susceptible to collection of serous fluid from their large surface area. This predisposes the wound to risks of dehiscence and later hernia formation. Absorbable sutures placed in the deep adipose tissue itself are rarely helpful. If there is a thick layer of adipose tissue (eg in bariatric surgery) a drain may be placed in the subcutaneous layer and large deep tension mattress sutures may be placed across the wound to support the adipose tissue as it heals.

Closure of the skin

There is no evidence that any particular form of skin closure leads to a better cosmetic result in the long term, and the choice is usually down to cost, indication and the surgeon's preference. A good incision made boldly at a perpendicular angle through the skin aids eventual cosmesis. Cross-hatching of scars is not a problem as

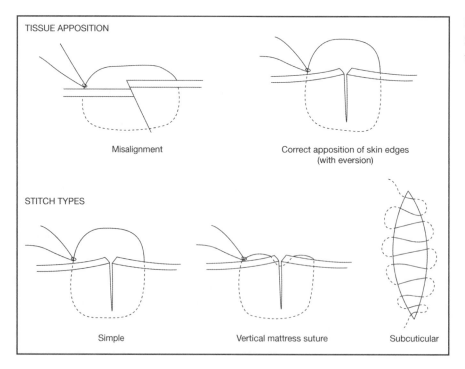

Figure 2.8
Skin closure techniques

TISSUE APPOSITION

Misalignment

Correct apposition of skin edges (with eversion)

STITCH TYPES

Simple

Vertical mattress suture

Subcuticular

long as the sutures or staples are not left in too long. Subcuticular closure is cheaper than using staples but is not suitable for heavily contaminated wounds as wound infection may require drainage of superficial collections of pus.

> **Skin closure options**
> - Staples or skin clips
> - Subcuticular sutures
> - Interrupted or continuous sutures
> - Glue
> - Self-adhesive strips
> - Adequate apposition of tissues under the skin may eliminate the requirement for skin closure

2.3   Diathermy

How diathermy works

Diathermy is used for cutting tissues and for haemostasis. Heat is generated by the passage of high-frequency alternating current through body tissues. Locally concentrated high-density currents generate local temperatures of up to 1000°C. Currents of up to 500 mA are safe at frequencies of 400 kHz to 10 MHz. There is no stimulation of neuromuscular tissue at frequencies above 50 kHz.

Diathermy settings

Cutting

- Continuous output
- High local temperature causes tissue disruption, some vessel coagulation and vaporisation of water

Coagulation

- Pulsed output of high-frequency current at short intervals
- Tissue water vaporisation and vessel coagulation

Blend

- Continuous sine-wave current with superimposed bursts of higher intensity

Monopolar

- High power unit (400 W) generates high-frequency current
- Current passes from active electrode (HIGH current density), which is the tip of the pencil held by the surgeon, through the body, returning via patient plate electrode (LOW current density) to generator

> **Placement of the patient plate electrode**
> - Good contact on dry, shaved skin; kinking must be avoided
> - Contact surface area at least 70 cm² (minimal heating)
> - Away from bony prominences and scar tissue (poor blood supply means poor heat distribution)
> - Normally on patient's thigh or back
> - Avoid metal prostheses (eg hip)
>
> Note that incorrect placement is the most common cause of accidental diathermy burns. Most systems have an alarm system if there is a fault.

Bipolar

- Lower power unit (50 W)
- Current passes between two limbs of diathermy forceps only
- No need for patient plate electrode

- Inherently safer BUT with forceps no use for cutting or touching other instruments to transfer current (buzzing)
- Diathermy scissors are also available where current passes between the scissor blades (eg Prostar)
- Useful for surgery to extremities: scrotum, penis or on digits

Diathermy safety

Safe use of diathermy

- Ensure that the patient is not touching earthed metal (older machines)
- Avoid pooling of inflammable agents (alcohol, inflammable gases)
- Use a pedal
- Use lowest practicable power setting
- Keep active electrode in contact with target tissue and in view
- Do not use too close to important structures (skin, blood vessels, nerves)
- Don't use monopolar on narrow pedicles (penis, digits, dissected tissue block, spermatic cord)
- Place plate away from metallic implants (eg prosthetic hips)

Causes of diathermy burns

- Incorrect plate electrode placement
- Careless technique (eg using alcohol-based skin preparation fluid, not replacing electrode in a quiver after use, failure to observe heated diathermy tip in a laparoscopic field)
- Use of diathermy on appendages (eg penis) where a high current can persist beyond the surgical site
- Use of diathermy on large bowel should be avoided as explosions have been reported

2.4 Laser

Laser is an acronym for **l**ight **a**mplification by the **s**timulated **e**mission of **r**adiation.

Mechanism of action of lasers

Lasers produce light by high-voltage stimulation of a medium, causing it to emit photons that are then reflected around the medium exciting other particles, which release further photons in phase with the initial photons. This process is repeated until a very high density of in-phase photons has been achieved (coherent light), some of which are allowed to escape through a partially reflected mirror (the beam).

At a cellular level the photons vaporise tissue by evaporating water (for cutting or ablation) and coagulate proteins (for haemostasis).

Examples of uses

- Argon-beam laser: eye surgery, endoscopic ablations
- CO_2 laser: ENT ablation surgery, cervical ablation surgery
- Nd:YAG (neodymium:yttrium-aluminium-garnet) laser: endoscopic debulking surgery or GI bleeder coagulation; laparoscopic surgery

Advantages of lasers

Access: can reach difficult areas as the beam can be projected through narrow spaces, or down endoscopes
Selective effects: eg argon lasers selectively absorb red pigments (eg in blood vessels)
Precision: very fine beams can be used for cutting and/or coagulation
Minimal damage to surrounding tissues

Dangers of lasers
- Retinal or corneal damage
- Fire risk
- Damage to structures beyond the target if burns through target
- Burns (patient or operator)
- Beam may be invisible

2.5 Harmonics

Mechanism of action

The harmonic devices work by providing electrical energy to a piezoelectric ceramic plate that expands and contracts rapidly at the frequency of 55 500 Hz. This creates ultrasonic waves which, at a cellular level, lead to the mechanical breakdown of H–H bonds, resulting in protein denaturation and formation of coagulum. The unit consists of a generator and a hand-held and controlled operating device that has a cutting tool attached to the end of it.

There are two power settings:
- Low power: causes slower tissue heating and thus more coagulation effect
- High power: causes rapid tissue heating and thus more cutting effect

Most common usage is in laparoscopic surgery, in particular bowel mobilisation; however, it can be used for open procedures.

Advantages of harmonics
- Low-temperature coagulation with little heat generated
- No risk of electrical energy because no current flow
- Little vapour, smoke or tissue charring
- Minimal damage to surrounding tissues

Disadvantages of harmonics
- Expense
- Only coagulates as it cuts
- Less manoeuvrable than diathermy

2.6 Needles and sutures

Learning point

Choose your suture with regard to:
- **Size of suture** (depends on strength required)
- **Characteristics of materials**
  - Structure (monofilament vs braided – depends on handling vs knotting requirements)
  - Absorbance (non-absorbable vs absorbable – depends on duration of required support)
- Needle (depends on tissue to be sutured)

CHAPTER 2

Sutures and ligatures

Features of ideal suture material
- Monofilament
- Strong
- Easy handling
- Minimal tissue reaction
- Holds knots well
- Predictable absorption

Classification of sutures
- Absorbable vs non-absorbable
- Monofilament vs multifilament
- Synthetic vs natural

Types of sutures

Selection of suture materials

Absorbable sutures for tissues that heal quickly (eg bowel anastomosis)

Non-absorbable sutures for tissues that heal more slowly (eg abdominal wall closure)

Smooth (monofilament) sutures for running stitches (eg vascular surgery) because they slide easily through tissues

Braided sutures for knotting properties (eg ligating pedicles)

Smaller sutures for fine stitching (eg 6/0 or 7/0 Prolene for tibial arteries)

Biological sutures (catgut, silk) cause an inflammatory reaction and fibrosis in the skin and undergo enzymatic absorption, so persistence in the tissues and strength are unpredictable

---

Non-absorbable sutures

Silk
- Biological origin from silk worm
- Braided multifilament
- Dyed or undyed
- May be coated with wax

Linen
- Biological origin from flax plant
- Twisted multifilament
- Dyed or undyed
- Uncoated

Cotton
- Biological origin from cottonseed plant
- Twisted multifilament
- Dyed or undyed
- Uncoated

Polyester
- Synthetic
- Multifilament
- Dyed or undyed
- Coated or uncoated
- Tradenames: Ethibond or TiCron, and Mersilene or Dacron (uncoated)

Polyamide
- Synthetic
- Monofilament or multifilament
- Dyed or undyed
- Tradenames: Ethilon or Dermalon (monofilament), and Nurolon (braided) or Surgilon (braided nylon)

Polypropylene

- Synthetic
- Monofilament
- Dyed or undyed
- Tradename: Prolene

PVDF

- Synthetic
- Monofilament
- Dyed or undyed
- Tradename: Novafil

Steel

- Synthetic
- Monofilament or multifilament

Absorbable sutures

Polyglycolic acid

- Synthetic homopolymer
- Braided multifilament
- Dyed or undyed
- Coated or uncoated
- Tradename: Dexon

Polygalactin 910

- Synthetic copolymer
- Coated with calcium stearate, glycolide and lactide
- Tradename: Vicryl

Polydioxanone sulphate

- Synthetic copolymer
- Monofilament
- Dyed or undyed
- Referred to as 'PDS'

Polyglyconate

- Synthetic copolymer
- Monofilament
- Dyed or undyed
- Tradename: Maxon

Types of needle and their uses

Needles are categorised according to shape, thickness and type.

Shape of needle

- Straight
- Curved
- Circular (proportion of circumference)
- J-shaped

Size of needle

- Needle thickness should be appropriate to the weight of suture selected
- The choice of a larger or smaller curved needle may aid suture placement
- Large for large bites of tissue (eg abdominal closure)
- Small for accurate placement (eg vascular anastomoses)

Point and profile of needle

Blunt needle

- Rounded end helps to prevent splitting tissues
- Advocated by some surgeons for abdominal closure (safety issue)
- Usually also round-bodied

CHAPTER 2

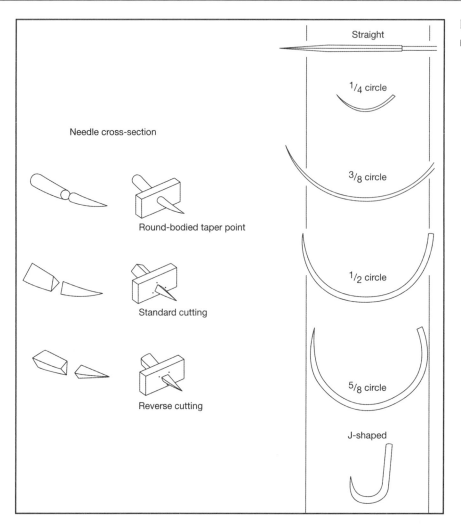

Figure 2.9 Types of needle

Straight

$^1/_4$ circle

Needle cross-section

Round-bodied taper point

Standard cutting

Reverse cutting

$^3/_8$ circle

$^1/_2$ circle

$^5/_8$ circle

J-shaped

Round-bodied needle

- Round profile with a pointed end
- Tend to spread rather than cut tissue (useful for placing sutures in organ parenchyma or viscera)

Cutting needle

- Triangular profile with a cutting edge on either the internal or the external curvature of the needle referred to as 'cutting' or 'reverse cutting' respectively
- Useful for tough fibrous tissue like skin

Staples

Staples now have a variety of uses:

- Skin closure
- Oesophageal, gastric and bowel anastomosis
- Clips for pedicle ligation and haemostasis

They are more expensive than traditional methods but are often much quicker. They are made of titanium and are hypoallergenic.

Staples for skin closure

The teeth of the staples should be used to draw the dermis together and evert the wound edge (misalignment of the closure is a common complication of staple use and impedes wound healing). They are removed with a device that bends the central area of the staple and releases the teeth. Alternate staples may be removed as the wound heals or to allow the escape of pus in infected areas.

Staples for gastrointestinal anastomosis

There are many stapling guns used in GI surgery. Some are linear, some circular and some combined with a cutting device that cuts between two staple lines. Many have been adapted for laparoscopic use.

Staples can be used:

- To divide the bowel without spilling contents and to reduce contamination
- To reduce the risks of anastomotic leakage
- To reduce the incidence of anastomotic stenosis; however, note that the incidence of stenosis is higher in stapled anastomoses if the diameter is small (eg high gastro-oesophageal anastomosis in the chest)
- To improve access if technically difficult (eg circular staples introduced rectally in low anterior resection)
- During laparoscopic surgery
- To add strength (eg stapling of the stomach pouch in bariatric surgery)
- To reduce surgical time

Disadvantages include the potential to damage or split the bowel. Failure of the stapling device often makes it extremely difficult to perform a subsequent hand-sewn anastomosis.

Staples for pedicle ligation and haemostasis

- Clips can be used instead of ties on small vessels (eg laparoscopic cholecystectomy)
- Large pedicles should be tied but some staplers are designed for haemostasis and are useful for division of smaller pedicles

Suture removal

Timing of removal of skin closure materials will vary according to the site of the wound. Good subcutaneous apposition of tissues allows the skin closure material to be removed relatively early, thus minimising scarring. Subcuticular closures with quickly absorbable sutures will not require removal. Areas that have a great deal of mobility may require longer to heal. Infection in wounds may require early removal of the staples or sutures to let pus out.

As a rough guide:

Face	4–5 days
Scalp	6–7 days
Hands and limbs	10 days
Abdominal wounds	10–20 days

2.7 Basic surgical instrumentation

It is out of the scope of this book to explain the eponymous names for all the commonly used surgical instruments. It is, however, important to know the names of some basic instruments so that you are able to communicate effectively with the rest of the scrubbed surgical team. You should be able to identify the key instruments below.

Key instruments

- **Scissors:** as a general rule curved are used for tissue dissection and straight for cutting sutures. Straight Mayo scissors are the

CHAPTER 2

standard for cutting sutures and curved metzebaum are for tissue dissection

- **Dissecting forceps:** a variety of weight of toothed forceps for holding skin edges (eg Adson) and non-toothed for grasping internally. Non-toothed DeBakey atraumatic forceps are favoured by vascular surgeons
- **Needleholders:** again available in a variety of different weights. Note these have criss-crossed teeth in the jaws of the holder in order to grasp the suture well (distinguish from artery/tissue forceps)
- **Retractors:** can either be hand-held or self-retaining. Wide variety of both available from small Langenbeck to larger Deaver or Morris hand-held retractors. Most commonly used abdominal self-retainer is the Balfour with its ability to retract on three sides. A West self-retainer is commonly used for open inguinal hernia repair (also available are Travers and Norfolk and Norwich (larger versions)
- **Tissue forceps:** used to describe artery clips and similar forceps with ratchets to grasp tissue. Artery clips can be straight or curved and of a variety of sizes (eg Dunhill, Mosquito). Other forceps for grasping include Littlewood (have teeth and therefore used for grasping skin edges) and Babcock (atraumatic and therefore useful for grasping bowel (eg when delivering the caecum in an open appendicectomy)
- **Scalpel blades:** attached to a reusable handle (usually Swann–Morton handle). Three different types commonly encountered in general surgery:
  - **10 blade:** most commonly used blade, used for opening the abdomen
  - **11 blade:** pointed, for precision cutting and 'stab' incisions (eg 5-mm laparo-scopic port placement)
  - **15 blade:** general use for smaller incisions than the 10 blade (eg excising a naevus)

2.8 Surgical drains

Learning point

Drains are used for a variety of purposes, and overall the use of drains is reducing. Drains are used:
- **To minimise dead space** in a wound and prevent fluid collecting (eg after axillary nodal clearance, mastectomy, thyroidectomy)
- **When there is a risk of leakage** (eg pancreatic surgery, bowel anastomosis)
- **To drain actual fluid collections** (eg radiologically placed drain for subphrenic abscess)
- **To divert fluid** away from blockage or potential blockage (eg biliary T-tube, suprapubic urinary catheter, ventricular cerebrospinal fluid drain)
- **To decompress** and allow air to escape (chest drain)

Types of surgical drains

- Drains can be **open** (into dressings) or **closed** (into container) systems
- Drains can be **suction** or **non-suction** drains (passive gravity drainage)
- Suction drains provide better drainage but may damage adjacent structures (eg bowel) and precipitate a leak
- Closed systems reduce the risk of introducing infection

Examples of surgical drains:
- Suction drains (closed) – Redivac, Blake, suction chest drain
- Non-suction drains (open) – Penrose drain, corrugated drain
- Non-suction drains (closed) – Robinson drain, T-tube, urinary catheter, chest drain

Complications of surgical drains

- Infection via drain track
- Lets in air (eg chest drain)
- Injury to adjacent structures by drain or during placement (eg bowel)
- Anastomotic leakage
- Retraction of the drain into the wound
- Bleeding by erosion into blood vessel
- Pain (eg chest drain irritating diaphragm)
- Herniation at the drain site

Routine drainage of a bowel anastomosis is controversial. The drains may cause more problems than they solve. They can directly damage the anastomosis and prevent formations of adhesions to adjacent vascular structures, through which the anastomosis would expect to gain an extra blood supply. If the anastomosis is not watertight (eg biliary or urological), a drain is usually used to prevent build-up of a collection that may otherwise hinder healing.

Removal of a drain after an extended period of time results in the formation of a tract of scar tissue circumferentially along the passage of the drain. This mature tract is a fistula and can be created deliberately to allow continued and controlled drainage from a cavity or leaking viscus. The deliberately created fistula will heal spontaneously when the distal obstruction is removed (eg a T-tube in the common bile duct will create a fistula and drain the biliary tree until an obstructing stone can be removed).

2.9 Dressings

Dressings can make a huge contribution to the healing of a wound. The optimum healing environment for a wound is:

- Moist
- Free of infection, with minimal slough
- Free of chemicals and foreign bodies (eg fibres from dressing)
- At the optimum temperature
- Infrequently disrupted (minimal changes of dressings)
- At the correct pH

Learning point

Types of dressings
- Hydrocolloids
- Hydrofibre
- Hydrogels
- Semipermeable film dressings
- Alginates
- Foam dressings
- Antimicrobial dressings
- Artificial and living skin equivalents
- Negative-pressure dressings (eg Vac)

Different dressings are appropriate for different stages of wound healing, and therefore good wound management necessitates a flexible approach to the selection and use of dressings. It is sensible to observe wounds regularly in order to assess changes in requirements.

Requirements of dressings
- Provide protection from infection and trauma
- Allow debridement, both mechanical and chemical
- Are absorbent and remove excess exudates, while keeping wound moist
- Maintain temperature and gaseous exchange
- Are comfortable and cosmetically acceptable
- Stimulate healing
- Are inexpensive and easy to change

Commonly used dressings

Traditional dressings such as gauze and Gamgee have few indications for the modern treatment of wounds. Modern dressings can be classified as follows.

Hydrocolloids

- Available in pastes, granules and wafers
- Consist of a mix of carboxymethylcellulose, pectins, gelatins and elastomers
- Form a gel (on contact with wound secretions) that absorbs secretions
- Example: Granuflex

Hydrofibres

- Consist of carboxymethylcellulose spun into a fibre
- Form a gel (on contact with wound secretions) that absorbs secretions
- Good for heavily exuding wounds
- Example: Aquacel

Hydrogels

- Consist of insoluble polymers, water and propylene glycol
- Absorb large volumes of exudates and are effective at desloughing/debriding
- Available in sheets or gels

Semipermeable film dressings

- Clear polyurethane film coated with adhesive
- Not suitable if excessive exudate

Alginates

- Extracted from seaweed
- Absorb secretions to form gel to optimise moist wound healing
- Available in sheet form or ribbon for packing
- Examples: Kaltostat, Sorbsan

Foam dressings

- Consist of polyurethane or silicone foam
- Very absorbent
- Use for flat wounds and cavity wounds (two forms are available for cavity wounds: liquid foam polymer and hydrocellular cavity dressing)

Antimicrobial dressings

- Usage has declined in recent years
- Little evidence of benefit
- Examples: Inadine, Bactigras

Artificial and living skin equivalents

- Increasing interest in these in recent years
- Can facilitate cell proliferation, production of extracellular matrix (ECM) components and increase concentrations of growth factors in the wound
- Epidermal components (eg Vivoderm)
- Dermal components (eg Dermagraft)
- Composite grafts (epidermal and dermal components) (eg Apligraf)

Negative-pressure dressings

- Used for large defects to allow healing by secondary intention
- Apply negative pressure via a foam or gauze dressing
- Remove wound exudate and reduce fluid pooling in the wound
- Improve blood supply and can stimulate cell proliferation
- Example: Vac dressing

SECTION 3
Surgical procedures

3.1 Biopsy

> ### Learning point
>
> Biopsy is the retrieval of part or all of a tissue or organ for histological evaluation to ascertain future management. Options include:
> - Fine-needle aspiration cytology (FNAC)
> - Brush cytology
> - Core biopsy
> - Endoscopic biopsy
> - Incisional biopsy
> - Excisional biopsy
> - Frozen section

Uses of biopsy

Biopsy is used specifically to:
- Determine tissue diagnosis where clinical diagnosis in doubt (eg Tru-cut liver biopsy for cirrhosis of unknown aetiology)
- Ascertain whether benign or malignant (eg gastric ulcer biopsy)
- Ascertain extent of spread of disease (eg sentinel node biopsy in melanoma)
- Determine different therapeutic pathways (eg lymph node biopsy in lymphoma)
- Excise whole skin lesion for histological analysis and local treatment (eg excision biopsy for rodent ulcer)

Biopsy is merely a form of special investigation and should be interpreted in the light of the clinical picture. Note that biopsy may alter the morphology of a lesion (eg by haemorrhage) and so should be performed AFTER diagnostic imaging wherever possible.

Types of biopsy

Fine-needle aspiration biopsy for cytology

Fine-needle aspiration (FNA) is performed by inserting a fine-bore needle into a lesion, aspirating cells and performing a smear on a slide to allow cytological examination.

It can be performed:
- Directly into a lump (eg thyroid lump FNA)
- Under ultrasound control (eg breast lump FNA)
- Under CT guidance (eg liver lesion FNA)

Advantages of FNA

- Simple and minimally invasive
- Easily repeatable
- Cheap

Disadvantages of FNA

- Gives cytological, but not architectural histology
- Potential for spread of malignant cells
- Sample may be insufficient, or only blood may be aspirated
- May alter morphology of lesion for subsequent imaging
- Depends on expertise of cytologist – can be operator-dependent

---

Procedure box: Fine-needle aspiration for cytology

Use a large syringe (10 ml or 20 ml) and a green needle.

- Fix the mass to be biopsied with your left hand
- Place the needle into the lump and then aspirate, creating suction within the syringe
- Retaining the needle tip in the mass make several passes, maintaining suction on the syringe
- Release the suction before withdrawing the needle
- Pressure on the biopsy site

Brush cytology

This is performed by collecting exfoliated cells, usually using a brush, from intraluminal lesions, and performing a smear on a slide to allow cytological examination.

It can be performed:

- Endoscopically for gastroduodenal lesions
- At endoscopic retrograde cholangiopan-creatography (ERCP) for biliary or pancreatic lesions
- Bronchoscopically for pulmonary or bronchial lesions

Advantages/disadvantages are as for FNAC, except in addition false negatives may occur because the tumour may not be reached or may not shed sufficient cells.

Core biopsy

Uses a circular cutting device to retrieve a core of tissue, either manually or with a trigger device (Tru-cut, Bioptigun). Core biopsy may be direct, or ultrasound- or CT-controlled. Useful for breast, liver and lymph node biopsy.

Advantages of core biopsy

- Simple, easily repeatable
- Provides a core of tissue for architectural and cytological evaluation

Disadvantages of core biopsy

- Insufficient sample for histological examination
- May cause bleeding
- May be painful or distressing to the patient
- Potential for spread of malignant cells
- May alter morphology of lesion for subsequent imaging (always image first)

Procedure box: Core biopsy

- Infiltrate with local anaesthetic (LA)
- Make a small incision through the skin (biopsy needle introduced through the incision)
- Take a core of tissue and place in formalin for formal histology
- Press on the biopsy site if superficial (eg breast)
- Will require patient to remain supine and undergo at least 6 hours of observation with regular haemodynamic measurements to exclude haemorrhage if deep structure biopsied (eg liver)

Endoscopic biopsy

Used for hollow viscus or organ (eg GI tract, airways, sinuses, bladder, uterus).

Advantages of endoscopic biopsy
- Avoids open surgery

Disadvantages of endoscopic biopsy
- Operator-dependent (lesions may not always be seen or reached)
- Bleeding
- Perforation
- Small samples (malignant areas may be missed)

Incisional biopsy

This is where part of a lesion is removed to allow histological diagnosis.

- May be performed laparoscopically or open
- May be useful when other biopsy techniques have failed
- Performed when the lesion is too big or too fixed to allow complete excision

Excisional biopsy

This is performed when the whole lesion is excised to give a histological diagnosis. Usually applies to skin tumours such as basal cell carcinoma and melanoma.

Frozen section

This is where fresh tissue is sent for rapid histological assessment during the course of a surgical procedure, to allow therapeutic decisions to be made at the time of surgery. The tissue is frozen in liquid nitrogen, then rapidly sectioned and examined, and the result phoned back to the theatre.

Advantages and uses
- Assessment of operability (eg to examine lymph nodes in pancreaticoduodenectomy)
- Localise tissues (eg parathyroids)
- Assessment of tumour margins
- Assessment of malignant status where pre-op diagnosis is in doubt and more radical surgery may be required

Disadvantages
- Operator- and histologist-dependent
- Occasional false positives and false negatives
- May delay surgical procedure

3.2 Excision of benign lesions

There are four basic types of lesions likely to be encountered in a standard 'minor operations' list.

- Naevus
- Lipoma:
  - Mobile to overlying skin
  - No punctum
  - 'Rubbery' feel
- Sebaceous cyst:
  - Fixed to overlying skin
  - Overlying punctum
  - Softer consistency
- Warty papillomatous lesions

Procedure box: Excision of a benign skin lesion

Once you have decided which of these lesions you are to remove you can plan your surgery:

- Clean and drape the area
- Use a pen to mark area for incision (Figure 2.10), remember Langer's lines (see Figure 2.2)
- Infiltrate LA
- Skin incision (usually best to chose a 15-mm blade for most small skin lesions)
- **For naevi or sessile skin lesions:**
  - Ensure adequate margin around lesion (at least 1 mm if presumed benign)
  - Cut full thickness through to subcutaneous fat
  - Incision should be at least three times longer than width to ensure closure
  - Raise a corner of your ellipse
  - Work to the other corner, cutting along either side
  - Send ellipse containing lesion in formalin to pathology
  - Some small lesions may also be excised in the round with the circular wound closed, using a single suture because the small dog ears at the edges of these wounds settle over time
- **For lipomas:**
  - Cut full thickness directly over the lesion, extending to the margins, onto the lipoma itself through subcutaneous fat
  - Mild pressure on the side of the lesion can allow it to be 'delivered'
  - If not easily delivered then dissect around lipoma using an Allis or Babcock to grasp it
  - To help with access, incision can be lengthened and retractors used
- **For sebaceous cysts:**
  - Cut ellipse around the overlying punctum the length of the cyst
  - Cut through skin until you reach the cyst wall itself
  - Once down onto cyst wall, use blunt scissors and a combination of blunt and sharp dissection to develop a plane around the cyst
  - Aim to remove cyst intact with overlying skin ellipse
- **For papillomatous lesions** on a narrow stalk – these can usually be held up by a needle and removed at their base with monopolar diathermy
- Ensure adequate haemostasis (pressure and patience before reaching for the bipolar!)
- Adequate skin closure with choice of suture

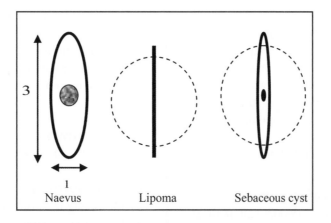

Figure 2.10 Incisions for benign lesions

3.3 Day-case surgery

> **Learning point**
>
> In day-case surgery a patient is admitted for investigation or operation on a planned non-resident basis, but the patient nevertheless requires facilities for recovery. Day-case surgery may be performed under general anaesthetic (GA), regional anaesthetic or LA. Many different procedures are now suitable for day-case surgery. There are advantages and disadvantages when considering a patient for day-case surgery.

Patients should have full verbal and printed instructions, including:

- A brief description of the surgical problem
- An outline of the nature of the surgery to be undertaken
- Preoperative instructions
- Postoperative instructions, as well as details about the nature of possible complications, what to do about them, and when and who to contact for advice
- Advice on when to return to work and other activities
- Instructions about any appropriate appointments for follow-up or suture removal

Advantages of day surgery

- A firm date and time for operation with less risk of cancellation
- Minimum time away from home (especially in paediatric surgery)
- Greater efficiency of operating list scheduling
- Release of inpatient beds
- Cost-effective

Disadvantages of day surgery

- Requirement of adequate aftercare at home
- Restriction of surgery and anaesthesia to experienced staff
- Requirement for inpatient admission or readmission in cases of unexpected complications, inadequate analgesia, etc

patient at home for the first 24–48 hours postoperatively
- At home there is no access to a lift (for an upper floor flat), telephone, or indoor toilet and bathroom

Some common procedures suitable for day-case surgery

General surgery

- Oesophagogastroduodenoscopy (OGD)
- Varicose vein surgery
- Colonoscopy
- Excision of breast lumps
- Hernia repair – inguinal, femoral, umbilical, paraumbilical and epigastric
- Pilonidal sinus

Urological surgery

- Circumcision
- Excision of epididymal cyst
- Cystoscopy ± biopsy
- Reversal of vasectomy
- Hydrocele surgery

Contraindications to day-case surgery

Medical contraindications

- Unfit (American Society of Anesthesiologists [ASA] class >II)
- Obese (body mass index [BMI] >35)
- Specific problems (eg bowel resections)
- Extent of pathology (eg large scrotal hernia)
- Operation >1 hour
- Psychologically unsuitable
- Concept of day surgery unacceptable to patient

ENT surgery

- Myringotomy and insertion of grommets
- Submucous resection
- Submucosal diathermy of turbinates
- Direct laryngoscopy and pharyngoscopy

Social contraindications

- Lives further than a 1-hour drive from the unit
- No competent relative or friend to accompany or drive patient home after surgery and/or to look after the

Orthopaedic surgery

- Carpal tunnel release
- Arthroscopy
- Release of trigger finger
- Amputation of finger or toe
- Dupuytren's contracture surgery
- Ingrowing toenails

Paediatric surgery

- Circumcision
- Repair of umbilical hernia
- Inguinal herniotomy
- Orchidopexy
- Hydrocele surgery

Ophthalmic surgery

- Cataract surgery
- Correction of squint

Plastic surgery

- Correction of 'bat' ears
- Insertion of tissue expanders
- Blepharoplasty
- Nipple and areola reconstruction
- Breast augmentation

Gynaecological surgery

- Dilation and curettage (D&C)
- Laparoscopy
- Termination of pregnancy
- Laparoscopic sterilisation

Other considerations

Day surgery should ideally be performed in dedicated day-case units, controlling their own waiting lists and scheduling. They should ideally be on the ground floor, with their own entrance, wards, theatres and staff. Patient satisfaction, adequacy of postoperative analgesia, complications and admission rates should be regularly audited.

3.4 Principles of anastomosis

> **Learning point**
>
> An anastomosis is a join between two parts of a tubular structure with the result that the lumen becomes continuous. A surgical join occurs commonly between:
> - **Blood vessels** (eg arteries, veins, vascular grafts)
> - **Hollow organs** (eg GI tract, genito-urinary tract)
> - **Ducts** (eg the common bile duct)
>
> Any anastomosis is at risk of infection, leak or rupture.

CHAPTER 2

Vascular anastomosis

Vascular anastomosis may be between arteries, veins, prosthetic materials or combinations of these.

Autologous vein with native vein

- For example, long saphenous vein graft or composite arm vein graft for femoropopliteal bypass
- For example, vessels of a free flap graft for reconstruction (eg tram flap)

Donated organ vessels to native vessels

- For example, anastomosis of the recipient vena cava to the donor liver vena cava in transplantation

Prosthetic graft to connect native vessels

- For example, Gore-Tex graft for AAA (abdominal aortic aneurysm) repair
- For example, PTFE (polytetrafluoroethylene) graft for femorofemoral crossover

Principles of vascular anastomoses

- Non-absorbable monofilament suture with continuous stitches only (eg Prolene)
- Use smallest needles and suture strong enough to hold anastomosis
- Evert edges to prevent intimal disruption (reduces thrombogenicity)
- Adequate graft length to eliminate tension
- Place sutures, drawing the needle from the inside of the vessel to the outside of the vessel
- Prophylactic antibiotics (especially anti-staphylococcal cover and especially if prosthetic material implanted)
- No holes or leaks (good surgical technique)

Early complications of vascular anastomosis

- Haemorrhage or leak
- Thrombosis

Late complications of vascular anastomosis

- Infection
- Stenosis (fibrosis, disease recurrence, neointimal hyperplasia)
- Pseudoaneurysm formation at the suture line
- Rupture

Hollow organs: GI and genitourinary anastomosis

Principles of anastomosis in a hollow organ

- Good blood supply
- Good size approximation (avoid mismatch) and accurate apposition
- No tension
- No holes or leaks (good surgical technique)

Good surgical technique

- Do not perform anastomoses in areas supplied by a vascular 'watershed'
- Ensure adequate mobilisation of the ends
- Invert the edges to discourage leakage and appose mucosa
- Consider pre-op bowel preparation to prevent mechanical damage to the anastomosis by passage of faeces
- Consider the type of suture material (absorbable vs non-absorbable, continuous vs interrupted vs stapled)
- Give prophylactic antibiotics: to cover bowel organisms including anaerobes
- Single layer vs double layer: the risk:benefit ratio must be considered. A single-layer anastomosis may be more prone to leak but a double layer is more prone to ischaemia or luminal narrowing

In the presence of the conditions that increase the risk of anastomotic dehiscence, if the bowel is of dubious viability, if there is great size disparity and in more distal anastomoses, it may be worth considering a defunctioning stoma proximal to the anastomosis (eg loop ileostomy in anterior resection). Some size disparity may be overcome by performing a side-to-side anastomosis or cutting the bowel of smaller diameter at an oblique angle to try to match the circumference.

- **Early anastomotic complications**: leak, bleeding
- **Late anastomotic complications**: stricture due to fibrosis or disease recurrence

Duct anastomosis

Good surgical technique

- Do not perform anastomoses in areas supplied by a vascular 'watershed'
- Ensure adequate mobilisation of the ends
- Invert the edges to discourage leakage and appose mucosa
- All ducts should be sutured using monofilament absorbable sutures (eg PDS) to minimise the risk of residual suture creating a nidus for subsequent stone formation
- Many duct anastomoses may be performed over a stent that is removed at a later date (eg ureteric stent, T-tube in the common bile duct [CBD]) to minimise subsequent stenosis

Early complications of anastomosis in a duct

- Anastomotic leak

Late complications of anastomosis in a duct

- Stenosis (fibrosis, disease recurrence, eg tumour)
- Intraductal stone formation (stitch nidus)

Anastomotic dehiscence

Any anastomosis is at risk of leak, particularly oesophageal and rectal.

Predisposing factors for anastomotic leak

General factors

- Poor tissue perfusion
- Old age
- Malnutrition
- Obesity
- Steroids

Local factors

- Tension on anastomosis
- Local ischaemia
- Poor technique
- Local sepsis

Presentation of bowel anastomotic leakage

- Peritonitis
- Bowel contents in wound or drain
- Abscess
- Ileus
- Systemic signs of sepsis
- Occult (eg arrhythmia, urinary tract infection [UTI])
- Fistula

Diagnosis of bowel anastomotic leak

- Not always obvious
- Should have high index of suspicion in the postop period (especially days 5–10)
- May be made at laparotomy
- Radiological contrast study/enema/swallow are helpful to visualise leak

Treatment of bowel anastomotic leak

- Resuscitate
- Conservative (nil by mouth, intravenous fluids, antibiotics, intravenous nutritional support)
- May require radiological drainage
- Surgical repair (may necessitate temporary bypass eg colostomy)

Anastomosis and infection

Bowel preparation

Preparation of the bowel to remove faecal matter and reduce bacterial load has traditionally been performed before colorectal surgery. This minimises the flow of intestinal contents past the join in the bowel while the anastomosis heals. It is thought that this reduces rates of anastomotic leakage and infective complications. Interestingly there is no clear advantage shown in recent meta-analyses looking at bowel preparation for elective surgery. The evidence for on-table preparation in the acute situation is less clear.

Bowel preparation is achieved by:
- Emergency procedure: diversion of the stream (eg proximal defunctioning colostomy) or on-table lavage of the proximal colon
- Elective: the bowel is emptied preoperatively by the use of laxatives and enemas

In recent years, many colorectal surgeons have moved away from routine bowel preparation; however, indications vary with each procedure, patient and surgeon. It is always wise to familiarise yourself with each consultant's preference, and be aware of the commonly used bowel preparation regimens. These regimens consist of:
- Clear fluids only the day before surgery
- Repeated oral laxatives (eg two or three spaced doses) of one of the following:
  - Klean-Prep – polyethylene glycol
  - Fleet, sodium picosulphate
  - Picolax – magnesium sulphate stimulates release of cholecystokinin (CCK) (promotes intestinal motility and thus diarrhoea)
  - Citramag
- Rectal enema (eg phosphate, Fleet microenema, Microlax)

Arguments against bowel preparation

- Quality of bowel preparation may be variable (eg worse in those with chronic constipation)
- Unpleasant for the patient
- Dehydration due to fluid and electrolyte shifts with some agents (may be minimised by oral or intravenous fluid replacement)
- Contamination in modern procedures with stapled anastomoses is less likely

- The advantage of full bowel preparation in a right hemicolectomy or subtotal colectomy, for example, is not clear, because there will not be any large-bowel contents proximal to the anastomosis
- Solid faeces is easier to control than liquid faeces

3.5   Minimal access surgery

Types of minimal access surgery

Minimal access surgery includes laparoscopy, endoluminal and arthroscopic approaches.

Learning point

Minimal access surgery
- Refers to procedures performed through incisions or via orifices, smaller than or remote from those required for conventional surgery
- Conducted by remote manipulation
- Carried out within the closed confines of body cavities (laparoscopy, thoracoscopy); lumina of hollow organs (endoluminal or endoscopy) or joint cavities (arthroscopy)
- Performed under visual control via telescopes which incorporate the Hopkin's rod–lens system linked to charge-coupled device cameras

---

TYPES OF MINIMAL ACCESS SURGERY WITH EXAMPLES

Laparoscopic

Lower GI
- Rectopexy
- Appendicectomy
- Hernia repair
- Right, left or subtotal colectomy
- Anterior resection of rectum

Gynaecology
- Sterilisation
- Investigative laparoscopy

Urology
- Nephrectomy

Upper GI
- Fundoplication
- Gastric bypass
- Staging

Endoluminal

Vascular
- Angioplasty
- Stenting

Upper GI
- ERCP
- Stenting strictures of oesophagus or
- Banding varices
- Haemostasis of ulcers

Lower GI
- Colonic stenting
- Polypectomy
- Banding of haemorrhoids
- TEMS

Urology
- TURP (transurethral resection of the prostate)
- Cytoscopic procedures
- Stenting

Advantages and disadvantages of minimal access surgery

Advantages of minimal access surgery

- Less trauma to tissues (smaller wounds, no damage from retraction)
- Reduced postop pain, leading to:
  - Increased mobility ($\downarrow$ DVT)
  - Improved respiration ($\downarrow$ chest infections)
  - Reduced need for postop analgesia ($\uparrow$ respiration, $\uparrow$ bowel function)
  - Decrease in postop lethargy/mental debilitation
- Decreased cooling and drying of the bowel which may decrease intestinal function and threaten anastomosis; more marked in elderly people and children
- Decreased retraction and handling (which cause iatrogenic injury and tissue compression, leading to decreased perfusion and bowel function)
- Reduced adhesions
- Fewer wound complications (eg infection, dehiscence, hernia formation)
- Reduced risk of hepatitis B and AIDS transmission
- Improved cosmesis
- Better view on monitors for teaching purposes
- Short hospital stay (laparoscopic cholecystectomies can be done as a day case; laparoscopic bowel resections can be discharged on day 4)
- Quicker return to normal activities/shorter rehabilitation

Disadvantages of minimal access surgery

- Lack of tactile feedback
- Problems controlling bleeding

- Needs more technical expertise and thus longer learning curve
- Longer operation times in some cases
- Significant increase in iatrogenic injuries to other organs (may not be seen), eg common bile duct in lap cholecystectomy
- Difficulty removing bulky organs
- Expensive to buy and maintain cameras, monitors, laparoscopic instruments and disposables
- May be impractical due to previous adhesions or contraindications

Contraindications to laparoscopic surgery

Contraindications to laparoscopy
- Patient refusal
- Unsuitable for GA
- Uncontrollable haemorrhagic shock
- Surgical inexperience
- Gross ascites

Increased risk during laparoscopic surgery[a]:
- Gross obesity
- Pregnancy
- Multiple previous abdominal surgeries with adhesions
- Organomegaly (eg spleen or liver)
- Abdominal aortic aneurysm
- Peritonitis
- Bowel distension
- Bleeding disorders

[a]It used to be thought that the conditions listed here were contraindications to laparoscopy. However, with increasing expertise and use of laparoscopic techniques, many of these patients can be safely operated on by an experienced laparoscopic surgeon.

Equipment for minimal access surgery

All laparoscopic procedures require:

- **Imaging system**
  - Video monitor
  - Light source
  - Camera system
  - At least one video monitor should be positioned for ease of viewing by the surgeon, surgical assistant and the scrub nurse. This may be linked to a method for recording the procedure by means of either photographic images or video. A second or 'slave' monitor is often helpful for the assistant, who may be positioned opposite the surgeon

- **Insufflation device**
  - Insufflates the abdominal cavity from a compressed gas cylinder
  - Maximum rate of insufflation and end intra-abdominal pressure can be set by the surgeon (these settings are maintained by the machine throughout the procedure)
- **Gas**
  - Gas used in most abdominal laparoscopic surgery is carbon dioxide although it can lead to hypercardia and acidosis in those with chronic lung disease
  - Helium is a rarely used alternative
- **Energy source**
- **Specialised instruments**

CHAPTER 2

Principles of minimal access surgery

Establishing a pneumoperitoneum

Procedure box: How to establish a pneumoperitoneum

There are two accepted methods: open (Hassan) or closed (Verress). The open method is preferred by the Royal College of Surgeons (Eng). The Verress method is safe in experienced hands.

Indications

Abdominal laparoscopic surgery

Patient preparation and position

Supine patient; usually GA and muscle relaxation.

Prep and drape anterior abdominal wall for open surgery.

Procedure

Small subumbilical incision with scalpel through the skin, then:

***EITHER*: Open (Hassan) method**

- Dissect to the linea alba and incise it
- Grasp the peritoneum with forceps and incise it to reveal the peritoneal cavity
- Insert a port using a blunt trocar through the hole
- Pass a camera into the port to confirm the peritoneal cavity has been entered
- Insufflate with 2–3 litres CO_2 to a final pressure of 15 mmHg
- Subsequent ports can be inserted with a sharp trocar under camera vision

continued overleaf

OR: Closed (Verress) method

- Introduce Verress needle (spring-loaded needle with blunt probe) through tented abdominal wall (you will feel two characteristic 'pops' as it passes through the fascia and then the peritoneum)
- Confirm position by aspirating on the needle and then flushing the needle with 0.9% saline. Place a drop of saline on the end of the needle and elevate the abdominal wall (when abdominal wall is lifted this creates decreased intra-abdominal pressure, sucking the saline into the intra-abdominal cavity)
- Insufflate with 2–3 litres of CO_2 to a final pressure of 15 mmHg
- Place the first port now by introducing a sharp trocar blindly through a small skin incision assuming that the pneumoperitoneum will have established a safe distance between the internal organs and the abdominal wall
- After inserting the camera, subsequent ports can be inserted with a sharp trocar under camera vision

Risks

Early risks

- Iatrogenic damage to intra-abdominal organs or vessels (rates approximately 0.05% for visceral injury and <0.01% for vascular injury)
- Venous gas embolism (rare)
- Conversion to open procedure

Late risks

- Postop abdominal or shoulder-tip pain (minimised by meticulous irrigation and evacuation of gas from the peritoneal cavity – carbonic acid is formed by combination of the CO_2 and water and acts as an irritant)
- Port-site herniation (midline most common)

Hazards

- Placement of ports
- Avoid known intra-abdominal hazards (eg pregnant uterus, previous scars or adhesions, aortic aneurysm, hepatomegaly)
- Avoid vessels of the anterior abdominal wall. The inferior epigastric artery runs from the midinguinal point upwards and medially to a point 2 cm inferolateral to the umbilicus and should be avoided when placing iliac fossa ports

Physiological consequences of a pneumoperitoneum

Laparoscopic surgery induces multiple physiological responses in the patient due to:

- Mechanical effects of elevated intra-abdominal pressure due to insufflation of gas (eg decreased venous return)
- Positioning of the patient to extreme positions (eg head down)
- Absorption of CO_2 and biochemical changes

Physiological changes include:
- ↑ or ↓ changes in cardiac output
- ↑ systemic and pulmonary vascular resistance
- ↑ mean arterial pressure (MAP)
- ↑ central venous pressure (CVP)
- ↑ or ↓ venous return
- ↑ or ↓ heart rate
- ↑ partial pressure of CO_2 (PCO_2)
- ↑ peak inspiratory pressure (due to increased intra-thoracic pressure)
- ↓ urine output

Prolonged pneumoperitoneum may cause large volumes of CO_2 to be absorbed, and this overwhelms the buffering capacity of the blood – causing acidosis. If severe the pneumoperitoneum must be evacuated to allow the CO_2 to wash out of the system. Arrhythmias are relatively common although there is more likely to be a problem in those with less cardiovascular reserve (eg elderly patients) and in very prolonged procedures. There is a degree of venous stasis in the lower limbs induced by the elevated intra-abdominal pressure and so deep vein thrombosis (DVT) prophylaxis is essential.

Placement of laparoscopic ports

Figure 2.11 shows a few examples of typical placement of laparoscopic ports; however, these vary from surgeon to surgeon – there is no 'correct' position. The basic principles are:
- There should be as few ports as possible to do the procedure safely
- Positioning should allow **triangulation** of the instruments at the operating site. In practice this means that the ports should form a diamond, with the target organ at one apex and the camera at the other and one instrument port either side for optimum triangulation, and for minimum fatigue and contortion; the surgeon's operating hands should be about 10 cm apart with the camera between and behind them, and the table should be low enough to avoid elevating the surgeon's elbows
- Patient positioning should allow a good view of all the areas that need to be inspected (eg tilted head down to view pelvic organs in female appendicectomy, tilted head up and with the right side elevated for cholecystectomy); using gravity in this way reduces the requirement for intra-abdominal retractors, which may otherwise need to be placed out of the camera view (increasing the risk of iatrogenic damage)
- A 5-mm port should be used if possible although some 10-mm ports are necessary – usually for the camera, removal of organs (eg the gallbladder) or certain larger instruments
- Placement should avoid known hazards (see Procedure box above)

Closure of laparoscopic port sites

Many surgeons will require that 10-mm ports are closed in layers, including closure of the rectus sheath/linea alba with slowly absorbable or non-absorbable interrupted sutures. This prevents port-site hernias. Skin hooks can be used to facilitate a good view of the fascial defect through the small incision. Skin can be closed with skin staples, non-absorbable or absorbable sutures, glue or Steri-Strips. The 5-mm port sites usually only require skin closure.

Developments in minimal access surgery

Single-port laparoscopy

A single incision is made at the umbilicus to allow access with a single wide-channelled or

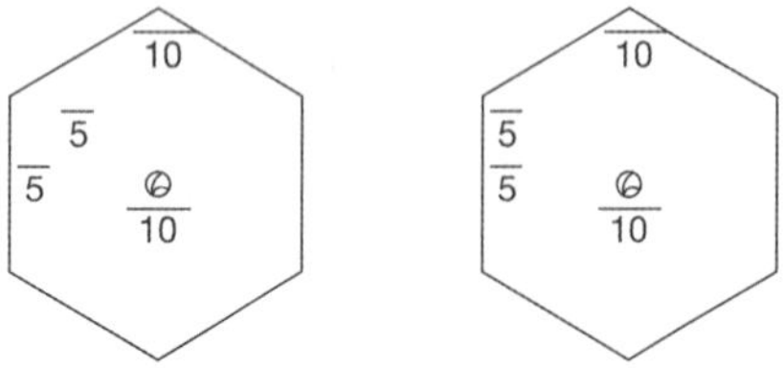

Europe technique

Laparoscopic cholecystectomy: the 10-mm port is inserted in the epigastrium and under the umbilicus for the camera. The placement of 5-mm ports varies with individual preference (common siting shown).

Pelvic appendix   High retrocaecal appendix   Usual placement of ports

Laparoscopic appendicectomy: the 10-mm port is inserted under the umbilicus for the camera. The first 5-mm port is inserted in the left iliac fossa or the suprapubic region and is used to retract the bowel and allow visualisation of the inflamed appendix. The second 5-mm port is inserted in the right upper quadrant (for pelvic appendix) or in the right iliac fossa (for high retrocaecal appendix). Again, placement of ports varies with the surgery.

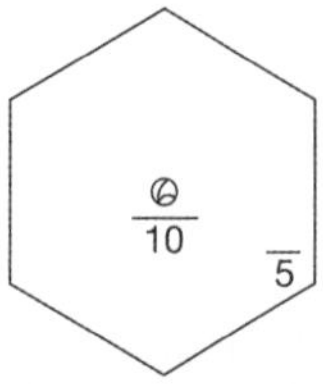

Pelvic diagnostic laparoscopy

Diagnostic laparoscopy: the 10-mm port is inserted under the umbilicus for the camera and a 5-mm port may be sited in the left iliac fossa for the use of instruments to aid organ retraction. A full systematic intra-abdominal inspection must be completed. Further ports can be sited appropriately if pathology is identified.

**Figure 2.11
Port-site insertion
for laparoscopic
surgery**

a single multichannelled port. As mentioned previously, triangulation of instruments is vital in laparoscopic surgery and this is overcome in single-lumen laparoscopy by using articulating instruments.

Advantages
- Smaller incisions
- Better cosmesis
- Improved postoperative pain
- Quicker return to function

Disadvantages
- Increased training
- Equipment costs

NOTES
NOTES is an acronym for Natural Orifice Transluminal Endoscopic Surgery.

It implies surgery performed endoscopically via the transanal, transoral or transvaginal route. A hole is made in the wall of the GI tract/vagina to allow entry into the peritoneal cavity, giving access to perform a variety of operations using multichannel endoscopic equipment (eg appendicectomy, cholecystectomy, fallopian tube ligation). This is currently in the early stages of development with extensive animal model testing and more recently trials of success in human subjects, notably with transvaginal cholecystectomy.

Advantages
- No abdominal wound
- Minimal postoperative pain
- No risk of incisional hernia
- No risk of wound infection
- Quicker return to function

Disadvantages
- Security of access site closure (eg gastric leak)

3.6 Endoscopy
Endoscopy is essentially the examination of a cavity or hollow organ using a fibreoptic flexible tube with an integral camera and lighting system. It is a minimally invasive diagnostic and therapeutic procedure.

Endoscopy includes:
- Bronchoscopy

- OGD
- Enteroscopy
- Colonoscopy
- Choledochoscopy
- ERCP
- Cystoscopy
- Ureteroscopy
- Ductoscopy of the breast

The scope is introduced via a natural orifice where possible, although some forms of endoscopy are performed together with laparoscopic surgery, where a small incision is made in the small bowel or cystic duct to facilitate entry of the scope to inaccessible organs.

The functions of endoscopy are:
- **Diagnostic:** strictures, polyps, varices, malignancy, inflammation, risk lesions
- **Therapeutic:** biopsy, management of haemorrhage, stenting

Endoscopes are either front-viewing or side-viewing (for ERCP). They require cleaning and sterilising between patients. There are three components to the scope:

- **The handpiece:** there are two deflection wheels. A large wheel for up and down movements and a smaller wheel for left to right. There is a valve that allows insufflations of air or water and a valve for suction. There are ports for access to allow introduction of instrumentation for biopsy and injection
- **The flexible shaft:** this transmits the push, pull and torque forces to the tip. The longer the shaft length the more susceptible it is to looping within the lumen
- **The distal tip:** the manoeuvrable tip moves left and right, up and down in response to turning the deflection wheels. It contains:
  - Suction channel

- Light source
- Objective lens
- Water nozzle for washing the lens
- Air nozzle for insufflations
- Water nozzle for washing

Complications of endoscopy:
- Perforation
- Bleeding
- Oversedation
- ERCP-induced pancreatitis

Endoscopy can be combined with ultrasonography (EUS) to visualise the layers of the GI tract and improve diagnostic accuracy of the degree of invasion in malignant disease (eg endoanal ultrasonography) or to look at structures in close proximity (eg EUS evaluation of the biliary tree).

Capsule endoscopy

A small capsule (about the size of a vitamin supplement) contains a tiny camera, battery, light source and transmitter. The camera takes two pictures every second for 8 hours, transmitting images to a data recorder. Capsule endoscopy can be used to investigate such as obscure GI bleeding, malabsorption, chronic abdominal pain and chronic diarrhoea.

3.7   Tourniquets

A tourniquet is an occlusive band applied temporarily to a limb to reduce blood flow.

Uses of tourniquets

- Prevent excessive bleeding in limb surgery, allowing a clear surgical field (eg for vascular anastomosis or orthopaedic surgery)
- Isolation of a limb for perfusion (eg Bier's block)
- Should not be used as a first-aid measure to arrest bleeding

Application of tourniquets

Simple tourniquets:
- Elastic tourniquets for phlebotomy
- Rubber tourniquet for digital surgery (eg ingrowing toenail)

Limb tourniquets:
- Check monitor or cuff before application
- Ensure application to correct limb and adequate-breadth tourniquet (too thin may cause pressure necrosis)
- Apply tourniquet before skin preparation, avoiding vital structures (eg testes)
- Place plenty of padding beneath tourniquet
- Inflate appropriately to 50 mmHg over systolic BP in upper limb, 100 mmHg over systolic BP in lower limb for adults; note the time of application
- The cuff should be deflated to allow reperfusion every 90 minutes (upper limbs) or 120 minutes (lower limb)

Complications of tourniquets

- Damage to skin, soft tissues or joints during application
- Chemical burns due to skin preparation getting under tourniquet
- Pressure necrosis from over-tight tourniquet, insufficient padding on prolonged application
- Distal ischaemia, venous or arterial thrombosis
- Haemorrhage after release

3.8 Managing the surgical list

There are several key considerations when ordering a surgical list:

- **Who should go first?**
  - Patients with diabetes
  - Patients with complicated anaesthetic issues
  - Complex surgical cases
  - Patients with significant allergies (especially latex)
  - Children
- **Who should go last?**
  - Patients with risk of infection (eg HIV)
  - Patients with methicillin-resistant *Staphylococcus aureus* (MRSA)
  - Patients with contaminated wounds

3.9 Operating notes and discharge summaries

Documentation is an essential part of completing an operation. A person reading the formal operation note should be able to replicate the procedure in a stepwise manner. Standard practice in many establishments is to dictate a formal operation note; however, this may not be typed for some time, so a handwritten note should also be entered into the notes. Although this may not be as in-depth as the formal note it should include the salient points from the operation and it may be helpful to include a diagram to help explain (see Figure 2.12).

Key points to include:
- Operating staff involved (eg surgeon, anaesthetist)
- Indications and findings
- Procedural steps
- Estimated blood loss (EBL)
- Any unexpected anaesthetic complications

- Postoperative instructions, eg:
  - Drains
  - Antibiotics
  - Oral intake
  - Dressing changes
  - Postoperative bloods

1/1/12 Theatre note
Surg: Miss A
Asst Surg: Mr B
Anaesth: Dr C
Procedure
Emergency laparotomy, sigmoid colectomy and end-colostomy
Indications: Peritonitic abdomen
Free air on erect chest radiograph
Findings:
- Perforated sigmoid diverticulum
- Faecal peritonitis

Operation:
- GA, supine, ABx on induction
- Midline laparotomy
- Extensive diverticulitis sigmoid colon with perforation
- Sigmoid colon divided with stapler and excised
- Splenic flexure mobilised
- Copious saline lavage
- Suction drain left in pelvis
- Abdomen closed with loop PDS/staples
- End-colostomy fashioned LIF
- EBL: 500 ml

Postop:
- HDU
- NBM tonight
- Continue antibiotics as charted
- Keep suction drain open

CHAPTER 2

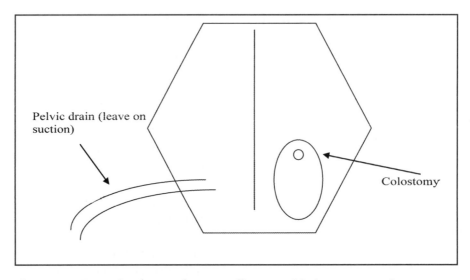

Figure 2.12 Example of an explanatory diagram added to an operation note

Diagnostic and interventional radiology

Imaging has become increasingly important in the diagnosis and management of surgical disease. Although there are some conditions that remain a clinical diagnosis, diagnostic radiology is vital in the assessment of the symptomatic elective or emergency patient.

Interventional radiology is the use of radiological image guidance to precisely target therapy that can then often be performed percutaneously.

The imaging modalities that you should be familiar with include:
- Plain films
- Contrast studies
- Ultrasonography
- Computed tomography (CT)
- Magnetic resonance imaging (MRI)
- Positron-emission tomography (PET)
- Radionuclide scanning
- Angiography

Interventional radiology can be used to:
- Drain collections and abscesses
- Stent or mitigate obstruction (oesophageal, gastric outlet, large bowel, biliary tree, kidney and ureter)
- Ablate tumours (eg radiofrequency ablation of liver metastases)
- Place feeding tubes (gastric and jejunal)
- Stent aneurysms and vascular occlusive disease
- Manage GI haemorrhage by mesenteric angiography and coil embolisation
- Provide targeted thrombolysis (eg vascular embolic events, pulmonary embolism)
- Perform brachytherapy (eg prostate cancer)

4.1 Plain films

Learning point

How do X-rays work?
X-rays are electromagnetic rays that are differentially absorbed by the tissues. Plain films are the result of X-ray exposure onto photographic plates; a negative image is produced. Bone absorbs the most radiation (looks white), soft tissues of different densities and fluids absorb varying amounts (shades of grey) and gas absorbs the least (dark grey and black). A single chest radiograph is the equivalent of 3 days' background radiation and an abdominal film is the equivalent of 150 days'.

Interpretating a chest radiograph

- **Check that the film is technically of good quality, ie:**
  - Not rotated (equal distance between the sinus processes and the end of the clavicle)
  - Adequately exposed (should see vertebrae to mid-cardiac level)
  - Lung fields expanded (should be able to count seven ribs anteriorly and nine ribs posteriorly)
- **Check name, date and orientation** (antero-posterior or posteroanterior?)
- **Follow a systematic approach:** look at the heart, mediastinum, lung fields, diaphragm, other soft tissues and bones
  - **Heart:** cardiothoracic ratio (width of heart: width thorax) should be <50%
  - **Mediastinum:** may be widened in trauma or aortic dissection, trachea should be central
  - **Lung fields:** left hilum should be slightly higher than right; look for hyperex-pansion (chronic obstructive pulmonary disease or COPD); look for masses (eg tumour or old TB), shadowing (eg consolidation or fluid), collapse (eg pneumothorax)
  - **Diaphragm:** right side is usually higher; look for free gas (easier on the right as the stomach bubble is on the left); look for abnormally high diaphragm (eg lobar collapse or traumatic rupture)
  - **Soft tissues:** surgical emphysema (eg from intravenous [IV] line insertion or chest trauma)
  - **Bones:** rib fractures (eg single or flail chest segment)
  - Remember to also take note of the presence of any additional devices (eg pacemaker, endotracheal tube, chest leads, chest drain)

Interpreting an abdominal radiograph

- **Check name and date**
- **Identify bowel regions:** small bowel tends to lie centrally and has valvulae conniventes (lines cross from one wall to the other); large bowel lies peripherally with haustrae (only partially cross the diameter of the bowel).
- **Look at the gas pattern:**
  - Central gas pattern: ascites
  - Dilated bowel: distal obstruction or pseudo-obstruction
  - Extraluminal gas: produces a double-contrast pattern in which the bowel wall is seen clearly because it is highlighted by gas on either side (Rigler's sign)
- **Look for calcification:**
  - Renal or ureteric (best seen on KUB [kidney, ureter, bladder] film), vascular calcification, faecoliths

4.2   Contrast studies

Contrast studies are performed by instilling a radio-opaque compound into a hollow viscus or the bloodstream. Intravenous contrast is commonly used together with CT and MRI and is discussed later. Occasionally patients can have true allergies to intravenous contrast (approximately 1 in a 1000) and intravenous contrast should be used cautiously in patients with renal impairment (see below). Contrast instilled into the lumen of an organ is not nephrotoxic.

- **Upper GI tract contrast studies:** oral contrast agents such as barium and Gastrografin may be used as a 'swallow' to demonstrate tumours, anastomotic leaks, or obstruction in the oesophagus, stomach and small bowel
- **Bowel contrast studies:** barium and Gastrografin may also be used for enema studies to identify tumours, anastomotic leaks, fistulae ('a fistulogram') or obstruction

- **Cholangiography:** contrast is used during ERCP or on-table to demonstrate stones, strictures and tumours of the bile ducts and head of pancreas
- **Renal contrast studies:** intravenous contrast is excreted by the kidneys and thus used to highlight the anatomy of the collecting ducts, ureters and bladder as an intravenous urogram (IVU). This has now largely been superseded by the use of CT. Contrast may also be instilled in a retrograde manner into the bladder to demonstrate urethral rupture after trauma

4.3 Screening studies

X-ray screening involves the production of a continuous image by an image intensifier. Bombardment with X-rays causes fluorescence of phosphor crystals within the machine translated into an image on screen. This allows a procedure to be guided by visualising the needle tip or contrast flow in real time.

Rather than transient exposure to X-rays, screening therefore delivers a higher radiation dose to the patient and surrounding personnel must wear shielding.

4.4 Ultrasonography

> ### Learning point
>
> **How does ultrasonography work?**
> Ultrasonography is the use of pulsed high-frequency sound waves that are differentially reflected by tissues of different densities.
>
> **Uses of ultrasonography**
> Ultrasonography can be combined with Doppler as duplex scanning (to assess blood flow) or with computer technology to form a three-dimensional image. Ultrasonography is commonly used for imaging of the abdomen, pelvis, cardiac anatomy and thorax, and vasculature. It is used for:
> - **Diagnosis**, eg liver metastasis, renal pathology, fluid collections, breast disease
> - **Monitoring**, eg obstetrics, vascular graft patency
> - **Treatment**, eg guiding percutaneous procedures such as drain insertion, radiofrequency ablation

Ultrasonography does not involve exposure to radiation. It works by using pulsed high-frequency sound waves (1–5 MHz) emitted from the ultrasound probe. The sound is generated by vibration of a piezoelectric crystal when a transient electrical field is applied to it. These pulses of sound are differentially reflected by the planes between different tissues (eg tissue and fluid or fluid and air). The higher the density of the object, the more sound is reflected. If all the sound is reflected (eg off a calcified object) then an acoustic shadow appears beyond that object. Reflected waves are identified by the same probe and are analysed by the machine into distance and intensity. This is then displayed as a two-dimensional image on a screen.

The incorporation of the Doppler effect with ultrasonography (called duplex scanning) has allowed assessment of blood flow in peripheral and visceral vessels. The moving blood changes the frequency of the echo reflected to the probe – creating a higher frequency if it is moving towards the probe and a lower frequency if it is moving away from the probe. How much the frequency is changed depends upon how fast the object is moving.

Recent developments in ultrasonography include **three-dimensional imaging**. Several two-dimensional images are acquired by moving the probes across the body surface or by rotating inserted probes. The two-dimensional scans are then combined by computer software to form three-dimensional images.

Contrast-enhanced ultrasonography uses microbubble-based contrast agents to improve the echogenicity of blood flow and allow better visualisation of vascularity.

Advantages of ultrasonography

- No radiation
- Good visualisation of soft tissues, fluids and calculi
- Duplex scanning can be used to assess blood flow

Disadvantages of ultrasonography

- Limited by dense structures that deflect sound waves (eg bone)
- Limited by body habitus (obesity)
- Difficult to accurately visualise the retroperitoneum
- Operator-dependent

4.5 Computed tomography

Learning point

How does CT work?
CT images are created from the integration of X-ray images as the X-ray tube travels in a circle around the patient. The density of different tissues causes differential X-ray attenuation, which is recorded as an image with different levels of grey.

- **Image enhancement:** scanning may be performed with or without IV contrast to demonstrate vessels and enhance vascular lesions
- **Radiation dose:** CT scans represent multiple X-rays, so the cumulative radiation dose is high

CT images are created from the integration of X-ray images. Images are displayed as stacked slices of the whole (similar to slices in a loaf of bread). The X-rays are directed through the slice from multiple orientations as the X-ray tube and detectors travel in a circle around the patient. X-rays are differentially scattered or absorbed due to the density of the different tissues. This X-ray attenuation is recorded by the X-ray detector. A specialised algorithm is then used by the computer to display the X-ray attenuation levels on the screen as different levels of grey. These densities are different for gas, fluid and tissues and can be measured in Hounsfield units. The patient platform then moves an automated distance ready for the next image or slice.

To maximise their effectiveness in differentiating tissues while minimising patient exposure, CT scanners use a limited dose of relatively low-energy X-rays. They acquire data rapidly to minimise artefact created by movement of the patient during scanning (eg breathing, voluntary movement). In order to do this they use high-output X-ray sources and large, sensitive detectors.

The use of contrast in CT scanning

CT may be performed with or without the use of contrast agents. Contrast agents are often iodine-based and so a history of iodine or shellfish allergy must be sought.

Contrast can be given:
- Into hollow organs
  - Orally
  - Rectally (eg CT colonography)
  - Down a percutaneous tube (eg T-tube cholangiogram)
  - Into a fistula
- Intravenously
  - For routine diagnostic work to enhance organ characteristics (may require arterial or venous phase imaging)
  - As a CT angiogram
  - Perfusion studies (eg myocardial perfusion studies)

Intravenous contrast agents: protecting the kidney

Risk factors for contrast-induced nephropathy include pre-existing chronic kidney disease (assessed using estimated glomerular filtration rate [eGFR] not baseline creatinine); diabetes mellitus, renal disease or solitary kidney, sepsis or acute hypotension, dehydration or volume contraction, age >70 years, previous chemotherapy, organ transplantation, vascular disease.
- eGFR ≥60 ml/min: extremely low risk of contrast-induced nephropathy
- eGFR <60 ml/min: low risk of contrast-induced nephropathy
- eGFR <45 ml/min: medium risk of contrast-induced nephropathy
- eGFR <30 ml/min: high risk of contrast-induced nephropathy

Preventive measures

Most radiology departments will have a protocol based on the eGFR but you must consider the following general measures:
- Consider alternative imaging
- Avoid dehydration
- Stop nephrotoxic medications 48 hours before contrast administration
- Stop metformin on the day of contrast administration for at least 48 hours and resume only when eGFR has returned to baseline
- Avoid high osmolar contrast and do not repeat the injection within 72 hours
- Intravenous fluids (0.9% saline) to provide volume loading should be used in all patients with eGFR < 60ml/min if arterial contrast is used and <45 ml/min if venous contrast is used
- Some centres advocate the use of N-acetylcysteine as a renal protective agent, but there is increasing evidence that this may not be very effective

The use of CT has increased exponentially over the last decade. It is important to remember when requesting CT scans that the radiation dose is significant. CT should be used with caution in children and young adults because these groups have a relatively thin anterior abdominal wall and their intra-abdominal organs are relatively exposed to the radiation dose. There is some evidence that this may increase the risk of malignancy in later life.

4.6 Magnetic resonance imaging

> ### Learning point
>
> **How does MRI work?**
> MRI uses a magnetic field to image tissues based on movement of their hydrogen atoms in response to a radiofrequency pulse.
>
> **Pros and cons of MRI**
> Main advantages are the lack of radiation and clarity of soft-tissue imaging.
> However, it is expensive and unsuitable for patients with claustrophobia or metal implants.

MRI uses powerful magnets to detect the movement of hydrogen atomic nuclei. The main magnet creates a stable magnetic field with the patient at the epicentre. This causes the atomic nuclei of hydrogen atoms in the tissues to align in the same direction. A radiofrequency (RF) pulse is then generated by the coil and passed through the tissues, causing the hydrogen atoms to resonate or vibrate. When the RF pulse is turned off, the hydrogen protons slowly return to their natural alignment within the magnetic field and release their excess stored energy. This movement is identified by the coil and sent to the computer system. Different tissues have characteristic readings. In addition, the RF pulse can be altered to produce different responses from normal and abnormal tissues. This 'weights' the images, improving visualisation of different aspects.

- **T1-weighted images:** there is a wide variance of T1 values in normal tissue and so these images show good separation of solid structures and anatomy. Fat has the highest signal intensity (white) and other tissues have varying signal intensities (shades of grey), with fluids giving the lowest intensity (black). These images may be used together with IV contrast such as gadolinium to look at enhancing lesions
- **T2-weighted images:** T2 weighting does not give as much anatomical detail, but it may be better for imaging some pathology. In T2-weighted images fluids give the brightest signal

> **Advantages of MRI**
> - No radiation
> - Can identify vasculature without the use of contrast
> - Can produce images in any plane (eg sagittal and coronal)
> - Less bony artefact than CT

> **Disadvantages of MRI**
> - Expense
> - Claustrophobia
> - Contraindicated in patients with metal implants
> - Not good for bony resolution
> - Longer imaging time than CT

4.7 Positron-emission tomography

> **Learning point**
>
> **How does PET scanning work?**
> A PET scan uses radiation, or nuclear medicine imaging, to produce three-dimensional colour images of the functional processes within the human body. A radiotracer is designed whereby a positron-emitting radionuclide is coupled to a biologically active molecule. This is injected into the body and the machine detects pairs of gamma rays that are emitted indirectly by the radionuclide. The images are reconstructed by computer analysis. Modern machines often use a CT scan which is performed on the patient at the same time in the same machine (PET-CT); this allows accurate anatomical correlation of the images.
> The most common radiotracer is FDG ([^{18}F]fluorodeoxyglucose or FDG), created by tagging a radiolabelled fluoride compound with glucose. Glucose is taken up by metabolically active tissues, highlighting regions of abnormal activity such as primary tumours and metastases

PET-CT is a rapidly changing technology with new evidence for its diagnostic accuracy and cost-effectiveness appearing all the time. Guidelines for its use have been developed because it is currently very expensive. It is predominantly used in cases of known malignancy to look for metastases or an unidentified primary. It is not used as a screening tool; however, it may also be used to look for a source of infection in pyrexia of unknown origin and in specialist centres for the further assessment of vasculitis, cardiac ischaemia and Parkinson's disease.

4.8 Radionuclide scanning (nuclear medicine)

> **Learning point**
>
> A radionuclide (sometimes called a radioisotope or isotope) emits gamma rays. Different radioisotopes have different affinities for certain target organs. Active cells in the target tissue will take up more of the radionuclide and thus emit more gamma rays. Gamma rays are detected by a gamma camera and processed by computer, providing an image of the body with 'hot-spot' identification. The overall radiation dose is low (similar to 2 years' background radiation) but should be avoided if the patient is pregnant or breastfeeding.

Common radionuclide scans include:
- **A bone isotope scan:** the ligand methylene diphosphonate (MDP) can be preferentially taken up by bone. By chemically attaching technetium-99m to MDP, radioactivity can be transported and attached to bone via the hydroxyapatite to identify areas of high osteogenic activity, reflecting metastatic deposits, infection, arthritis or trauma
- **Thyroid scanning** uses iodine-123 (^{123}I) to look for distant metastatic deposits
- **Parathyroid scanning** is undertaken with technetium sestamibi
- **Hepatobiliary excretion studies** can be performed with HIDA (hepatobiliary ^{99m}Tc-labelled iminodiacetic acid) scanning

- **Myocardial perfusion scanning** with thallium-201 (^{201}Tl)
- **Ventilation–perfusion scan** to assess ventilation and perfusion of the lungs in the diagnosis of pulmonary embolism
- **DMSA (^{99m}Tc-labelled dimercaptosuccinic acid) renal scan** identifies renal scarring and can be used to look at differential renal function.

The radioisotope is excreted from the body in a number of ways via:
- Urine
- Faeces
- Saliva
- Sweat
- Lacrimal fluid
- Breast milk

Nuclear medicine can also be used in a therapeutic capacity to target radiation therapy. It is increasingly used for the treatment of non-Hodgkin's lymphoma, palliation of painful bone metastases and radioiodine treatment for thyroid cancer.

4.9 Angiography

Intravenous contrast may be used to image the major vessels. Increasingly, diagnostic angiography is combined with CT or MRI to provide three-dimensional images of the vascular tree.

Percutaneous angiography is an interventional technique whereby access to the arterial tree (usually at the femoral artery) and screening of the angiography process is used to provide a definitive treatment. It can be used to:
- Place stents to treat vessel stenosis or occlusion
- Treat haemorrhage by coil or glue embolisation
- Promote thrombosis of cerebral berry aneurysms
- Target thrombolysis

Digital subtraction angiography (DSA) is a technique providing reverse negative views and requires less contrast to be administered. Many vascular patients have arteriopathy, with poor renal function and so contrast must be used judiciously. **Alternative contrast agents** that are not nephrotoxic include a stream of small CO_2 bubbles which eventually dissolve in the blood and are excreted through the respiratory system.

CHAPTER 3

Postoperative Management and Critical Care

Hayley M Moore and Brahman Dharmarajah

SECTION 1
General physiology

1.1 The physiology of homeostasis

Learning point

Homeostasis is the maintenance of a stable internal environment. This occurs on two levels:
- **Normal cellular physiology** relies on controlled conditions, including temperature, pH, ion concentrations and O_2/CO_2 levels
- **System physiology** within the body requires control of blood pressure and blood composition via the cardio-vascular, respiratory, GI, renal and endocrine systems of the body

These variables oscillate around a set point, with each system drawn back to the normal condition via the homeostatic mechanisms of the body.

Homeostatic feedback works on the principles of:
- Detection via sensors
- Afferent signalling
- Comparison to the 'set point'
- Efferent signalling
- Effector action

The structure of the cell

Learning point

Cells are the building blocks of the body. They consist of elements common to all cells and additional structures that allow a cell to perform specialised functions.

Elements common to all cells include:
- Cell membrane
- Cytoplasm
- Nucleus
- Organelles:
  - Mitochondria
  - Endoplasmic reticulum
  - Golgi apparatus
- Lysosomes

Cell membrane

The cell membrane is a phospholipid bilayer formed by the inner hydrophobic interactions of the lipid tails with the hydrophilic phosphate groups interacting on the outside. Cholesterol molecules are also polarised, with a hydrophilic and hydrophobic portion. This forms a major barrier that is impermeable to water and water-soluble substances, allowing the cell to control its internal environment. The membrane is a fluid structure (similar to oil floating on water) allowing its components to move easily from one area of the cell to another.

There are a number of proteins that are inserted into or span the cell membrane and act as ion channels, transporter molecules or receptors. These transmembrane proteins may be common to all cells (eg ion channels) or reflect the specialised function of the cell (eg hormone receptors).

Cytoplasm

The cytoplasm is composed of:

- **Water:** 70–85% of the cell mass. Ions and chemicals exist in dissolved form or suspended on membranes
- **Electrolytes:** predominantly potassium, magnesium, sulphate and bicarbonate, and small quantities of sodium and chloride
- **Proteins:** the two types are structural proteins and globular proteins (predominantly enzymes)
- **Lipids:** phospholipids and cholesterol are used for cell membranes. Some cells store large quantities of triglycerides (as an energy source)
- **Carbohydrates:** may be combined with proteins in structural roles but are predominantly a source of energy

Under the cell membrane a network of actin filaments provides support to the cytoplasm. There is also a cytoskeleton consisting of tubulin microtubules which enables the cell to maintain its shape and to move by extension of cellular processes called pseudopodia.

Dispersed in the cytoplasm are the intracellular organelles such as the nucleus, mitochondria, Golgi apparatus and endoplasmic reticulum. There are also fat globules, glycogen granules and ribosomes.

The cytoplasm is a complex and busy region of transport between the cell membrane and the intracellular organelles. Binding of molecules to cell-surface receptors activates secondary messenger systems such as cyclic adenosine monophosphate (cAMP) and inositol triphosphate (IP_3) across this network of the cytoplasm.

The nucleus

A double phospholipid membrane surrounds the nucleus and this is penetrated by nuclear pores which allow access to small molecules. The nucleus contains the DNA and is the primary site of gene regulation.

The bases of DNA comprise two purines, adenine (A) and guanine (G), and two pyrimidines, thymidine (T) and cytosine (C); A forms a bond with T, and G forms a bond with C. DNA is a double helix with a backbone of deoxyribose sugars either side of the paired nitrogenous bases, which act as the code.

DNA is stored in the nucleus in a condensed form, wrapped around proteins called histones. When condensed the genes are inactive. The DNA unwinds from the histone protein when the gene becomes activated. The two strands separate to allow transcription factors access to the DNA code. The transcription factor binds to the gene promoter region and allows an enzyme called RNA polymerase to produce complementary copies of the gene in a form known as messenger RNA (mRNA). Messenger RNA is then transported out of the nucleus to the ribosomes for translation into protein.

Mitochondria

These structures generate >95% of the energy required by the cell. Different cells have different numbers. They are bean-shaped, with a double membrane – the internal membrane is folded into shelves where the enzymes for the production of energy are attached. Mitochondria can self-replicate and contain a small amount of DNA.

Endoplasmic reticulum

This is a network of tubular structures, with the lumen of the tube connected to the nuclear membrane. These branching networks provide a huge surface area of membrane and are the site of the major metabolic functions of the cell. They are responsible for most of the synthetic processes, producing lipids and proteins together with the attached ribosomes.

The ribosome is responsible for translating the mRNA into protein. The mRNA travels along the ribosome and may pass through several ribosomes simultaneously, similar to beads on a string. Each amino acid binds to a small molecule of transfer RNA (tRNA), which has a triplet of bases that correspond to the amino acid that it is carrying. These bases are complementary to the bases on the mRNA strand. Energy produced by ATP is required to activate each amino acid. The ribosome then catalyses peptide bonds between activated amino acids.

Golgi apparatus

The Golgi apparatus is structurally similar to the endoplasmic reticulum (ER) and lies as stacked layers of tubes close to the cell membrane. Its function is secretion. Substances to be secreted leave the ER by becoming enclosed in a pinched-off piece of membrane (a vesicle) and travel through the cytoplasm to fuse with the membrane of the Golgi body. They are then processed inside the Golgi to form secretory vesicles (or lysosomes), which bud off the Golgi body and fuse with the cell membrane, disgorging their contents.

Basic cellular functions

Learning point

Basic cellular functions are common to all cells. They include:
- Transport across membranes
- Generation of energy from carbohydrates and lipids
- Protein turnover

Transport across membranes

Molecules may be moved across cell membranes by:
- **Simple diffusion:** this occurs down either a concentration or an ion gradient. It depends on the permeability of the membrane to the molecule. No energy is required for this process
- **Simple facilitated diffusion:** this also occurs down a concentration gradient, but the molecule becomes attached to a protein molecule that facilitates its passage (eg a water-soluble molecule that would be repelled by a cell membrane, attached to a carrier molecule which can pass easily through a cell membrane). There is no energy requirement for this process
- **Primary active transport:** in which energy from ATP is used to move the molecule against a concentration or ion gradient. This is also called a 'pump'
- **Secondary active transport:** in which energy is used to move a molecule against

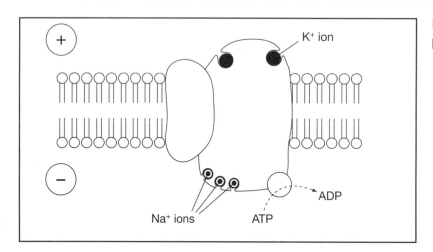

Figure 3.1 The sodium–potassium pump

a concentration or ion gradient. This energy comes from the associated movement of a second molecule down a concentration gradient. If both these molecules are moving in the same direction, this is called 'co-transport'. If they are moving in opposite directions this is called 'counter-transport'

- **Endocytosis and exocytosis:** these processes involve a piece of membrane budding off from the cell membrane to envelop a substance, which is then internalised by the cell (endocytosis). Conversely, secretory vesicles from the Golgi apparatus may fuse with the cell membrane, releasing their contents outside the cell (exocytosis)

The sodium/potassium pump

This pump (also called Na^+/K^+ ATPase) is used by cells to move potassium ions into the cell and sodium ions out of the cell. It is present in all cells of the body and maintains a negative electrical potential inside the cell. It is also the basis of the action potential.

Na^+/K^+ ATPase consists of two globular protein subunits. There are two receptor sites for binding K^+ ions on the outside of the cell and three receptor sites for binding Na^+ on the inside of the cell. When three Na^+ ions bind to the receptors on the inside of the cell, ATP is cleaved to ADP, releasing energy from the phosphate bond. This energy is used to induce a conformational change in the protein, which extrudes the Na^+ ions from the cell and brings the K^+ ions inside the cell. As the cell membrane is relatively impermeable to Na^+ ions this sets up a concentration, and therefore an ion gradient (called the **electrochemical gradient**). Water molecules tend to follow the Na^+ ions, protecting the cell from increases in volume that would lead to cell lysis. In addition, K^+ ions tend to leak back out of the cell more easily than Na^+ ions enter.

Generating energy

Cells generate energy by combining oxygen with carbohydrate, fat or protein under the influence of various enzymes. This is called **oxidation** and results in the production of a molecule of ATP which is used to provide the energy for all cellular processes. The energy is stored in the ATP molecule by two high-energy phosphate bonds and is released when these bonds are broken.

Energy is used for:

- **Synthesis** – synthesis of any chemical compound requires energy. All cells synthesise proteins, phospholipids, cholesterol and the purine/pyrimidine building blocks of DNA. In addition, some cells have specialised secretory roles (eg hormone production)
- **Membrane transport** – active transport of ions and other substances requires energy
- **Mechanical work** – specialised cells (eg muscle cells) require energy for mechanical work. Other cells also require energy for amoeboid and ciliary movement

Energy from carbohydrate

The smallest component of the carbohydrate molecule is its monomer, glucose. Glucose enters the cell via facilitated diffusion using a glucose transporter molecule in the phospholipid membrane. This process is increased by the hormone insulin. Inside the cell, glucose is phosphorylated to form glucose-6-phosphate. Phosphorylated glucose is either stored as a polymer (via glycogenesis to form glycogen) or utilised immediately for energy. Energy is produced from glucose by glycolysis and then oxidation of the end-products of glycolysis (via the tricarboxylate cycle).

In **glycolysis** the glucose molecule is broken down in a stepwise fashion, releasing enough energy to produce one molecule of ATP at each step. This results in two molecules of pyruvic acid, two molecules of ATP and four hydrogen ions. Pyruvic acid is combined with coenzyme A in the mitochondria to form acetyl-coenzyme A (acetyl-coA) and ATP. This combines with water in the tricarboxylate cycle, releasing two molecules of ATP, four molecules of carbon dioxide, 16 hydrogen atoms and coenzyme A which is recycled to be used again. The hydrogen

ions combine with NAD^+ and undergo oxidative phosphorylation to produce most of the ATP.

Energy can also be released in the absence of oxygen by anaerobic glycolysis. When oxygen is not available oxidative phosphorylation cannot take place. Glycolysis to produce pyruvic acid does not require oxygen and so this still occurs, producing a small amount of energy. In the absence of oxygen the pyruvic acid, NAD^+ and hydrogen ions combine to form lactic acid. When oxygen becomes available again the lactic acid breaks down releasing the pyruvic acid, NAD^+ and hydrogen ions, and these can then be used for energy by oxidative phosphorylation.

CHAPTER 3

Energy from lipids

The basic component of a lipid is the fatty acid. Lipids are transported from the intestine to the liver in the blood as small aggregates, called chylomicrons, along the portal vein to the liver. The liver processes lipids to basic fatty acids. It also synthesises triglycerides from carbohydrates and produces cholesterol and phospholipids. Spare fat is stored in adipose tissue (modified fibroblasts; up to 95% of their volume comprises triglycerides).

Lipids can be used as fuel. Triglycerides are hydrolysed to free fatty acids and glycerol in the liver (which enters the carbohydrate pathway described above). Fatty acids are transported into the hepatocyte mitochondria where molecules of acetyl-coA are sequentially released from the fatty acid chains. Each time that a molecule of acetyl-coA is released, four hydrogen ions are also produced and these undergo oxidative phosphorylation, releasing large amounts of ATP. The acetyl-coA condenses to form acetoacetic acid and other ketones, and these are released from the liver into the bloodstream to supply other tissues with energy. Cells take up the

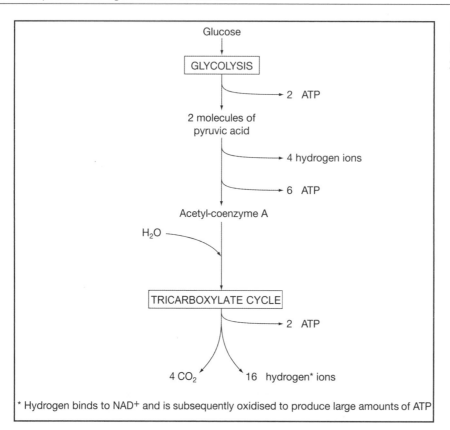

Figure 3.2 Energy production from glucose

Glucose

GLYCOLYSIS

→ 2 ATP

2 molecules of pyruvic acid

→ 4 hydrogen ions

→ 6 ATP

Acetyl-coenzyme A

H_2O

TRICARBOXYLATE CYCLE

→ 2 ATP

$4 CO_2$ 16 hydrogen* ions

* Hydrogen binds to NAD^+ and is subsequently oxidised to produce large amounts of ATP

acetoacetic acid and turn it back into acetyl-coA, which is transported to the mitochondria. Acetyl-coA then enters the tricarboxylate cycle as described above. Usually levels of ketones in the blood are low. If the predominant source of energy comes from fat then these levels rise. This may occur in starvation (when the body is metabolising its own fat stores), diabetes (when a lack of circulating insulin prevents glucose transport into the cells) or in very-high-fat diets.

Protein turnover

Protein synthesis
Proteins are absorbed from the gastrointestinal (GI) tract and transported in the blood as their basic component, amino acids. Amino acids are

taken up by the cells and almost immediately form cellular proteins by creation of peptide linkages directed by the ribosomes.

There are 20 different amino acids – 10 of the amino acids can be synthesised by the body ('non-essential' amino acids) and the other 10 have to be supplied in the diet ('essential' amino acids). The non-essential amino acids are synthesised from ketones. Glutamine acts as an intracellular store which can then be converted into other amino acids by the action of enzymes such as the transaminases.

Protein degradation
Only if cells have achieved maximal protein storage are amino acids 'deaminated' and used

as energy or stored as fat. Ammonia is produced during deamination and converted into urea in the liver. This is then excreted from the bloodstream via the kidney. In severe liver disease this process is insufficient and may lead to the accumulation of ammonia in the blood (resulting in encephalopathy and eventually coma). During starvation, when the body has exhausted its stores of glycogen and fat, amino acids begin to be liberated and oxidised for energy.

Specialised cellular functions

Learning point

Some cells have specialised functions.
They include:
- The action potential
- Synapses
- The neuromuscular junction
- Muscle contraction

The action potential

The transmission of signals along an excitable cell (ie nerve or muscle) is achieved by a self-propagating electrical current known as an action potential.

Generation of an action potential

All cells have an electrochemical gradient maintained by Na^+/K^+ ATPase. This results in a net internal negative charge and a net external positive charge. The difference between the two is called the **resting potential** of the cell membrane and is approximately −70 mV.

The action potential is initiated by a stimulus which alters the resting potential of the membrane. If the stimulus is big enough (usually about 15–35 mV and referred to as the threshold level) it increases the resting potential enough to start a chain of events resulting in a dramatic change in potential (called **depolarisation**), leading to the action potential.

Changes in the resting potential of the membrane alter its permeability to sodium ions. This is thought to be because the resting potential determines whether or not certain ion channels (called voltage-gated sodium channels) are open. When the resting potential increases as a result of a stimulus, the gated sodium channels open and sodium ions flood into the cell down their electrochemical gradient. The membrane potential continues to increase as these positively charged ions enter the negatively charged cell. The gated sodium channels open wider as the membrane potential increases, resulting in a positive feedback loop. At the peak of depolarisation (about 50 mV) the gated sodium channels start to close.

Depolarisation opens voltage-gated potassium channels and potassium moves out of the cell to try and restore the resting potential. This is called **repolarisation**. Depolarisation cannot occur again until the resting potential of the cell membrane has been restored and this is called the **refractory period**.

Differences in the action potential between nerve and muscle

In cardiac and smooth muscle cells there are also calcium channels. In the resting state calcium is pumped out of the cell and so there is a higher concentration in the extracellular fluid than inside the cell. Increases in the membrane potential open voltage-gated calcium channels. These increase the size of the depolarisation but work more slowly than the sodium channels.

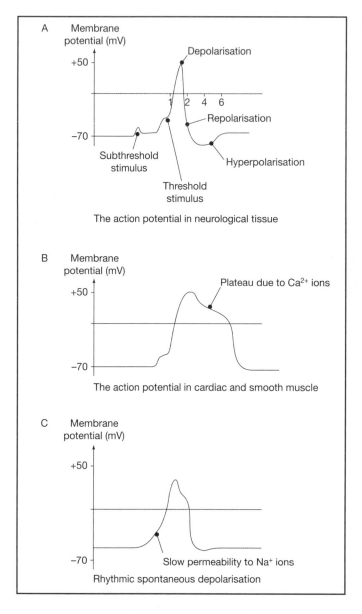

Figure 3.3 The action potential

The action potentials of these cells therefore have a plateau that delays the recovery of the resting potential. This allows for prolonged and complete contraction of the muscle cell compared with the action potential in neurones, which resets itself quickly to transmit repetitive impulses of coded messages. Skeletal muscle has an action potential similar to nerve. Repetitive firing can result in tetany, with multiple sustained contractions and no effective relaxation.

Rhythmical spontaneous depolarisation occurs in some tissues, such as the sinoatrial node of the heart and the smooth muscle cells of the GI tract that are responsible for peristalsis. No stimulus is necessary to cause depolarisation in these cells. This is because the cell membrane is relatively leaky to sodium ions. As sodium ions leak into the cell, the resting potential rises and depolarisation occurs spontaneously. The influx of sodium is seen in the slow up-sweep of the action potential in these cells.

Transmission of the action potential

The action potential can be propagated along the membrane by setting up small local circuits. The stimulus depolarises a small area of the membrane which reverses its polarity. As sodium ions flow into the cell through the depolarised part of the membrane they diffuse locally in either direction. This alters the resting potential of the neighbouring parts of the membrane and acts as a stimulus for depolarisation.

The action potential travels in an 'all or nothing' manner, whereby if a stimulus is sufficient to cause depolarisation then the impulse generated has a fixed amplitude regardless of the strength of the stimulus. The strength of the stimulus is reflected in the frequency of impulses.

Conduction of the action potential

Depolarisation travels smoothly along the membrane in unmyelinated nerve fibres. Myelinated fibres have Schwann cells wrapped around them (similar to Swiss rolls). These cells insulate the membrane and force the depolarisation to jump rapidly from bare area to bare area. These bare areas are called the nodes of Ranvier, and this form of conduction is much faster; it is called saltatory conduction.

Synapses

The synapse is the connection between one neurone and the next. The end terminal of the axon is called the synaptic bulb and this is separated from the postsynaptic membrane by the synaptic cleft. In the end-terminal of the axon are many mitochondria and a Golgi apparatus, which are responsible for the synthesis of chemical neurotransmitters. The neurotransmitter is stored in secretory vesicles in the synaptic bulb.

When an action potential reaches a synapse it stimulates the opening of calcium ion channels. The influx of calcium draws the secretory vesicles to the presynaptic membrane and causes them to exocytose their contents. The neurotransmitter diffuses across the synaptic cleft and stimulates receptors on the postsynaptic membrane. These receptors alter the permeability of the postsynaptic membrane to sodium ions, and this change in the resting potential acts as a stimulus to depolarise the membrane of the target neurone.

Often a single action potential is insufficient to accomplish depolarisation of the postsynaptic neurone, and many action potentials arriving in rapid succession are required. This is called temporal summation. Alternatively, near-simultaneous firing of many synapses onto a single target cell may also be sufficient to result in depolarisation of the target neurone. This is called spatial summation.

A single neurone may have as many as 100 000 synaptic inputs. These may be excitatory or inhibitory. The balance between excitatory inputs (the excitatory postsynaptic potential or EPSP) and inhibitory inputs (the inhibitory postsynaptic potential or IPSP) from other neurones will determine whether the neurone will fire. This integrates information, allowing negative feedback and modifications to be made to the original impulses.

The nerve fibre forms a junction with the muscle fibre at its midpoint. Action potentials

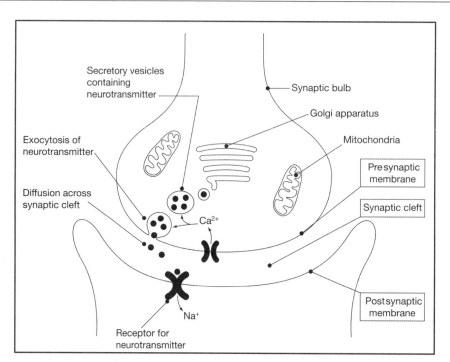

**Figure 3.4
The synapse**

Secretory vesicles
containing
neurotransmitter

Synaptic bulb

Golgi apparatus

Exocytosis of
neurotransmitter

Mitochondria

Presynaptic
membrane

Diffusion across
synaptic cleft

Synaptic cleft

Ca^{2+}

Postsynaptic
membrane

Na^+

Receptor for
neurotransmitter

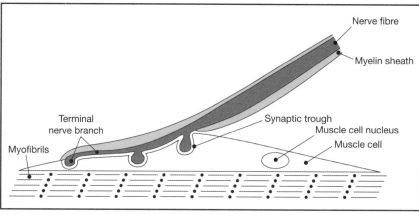

**Figure 3.5
The neuromuscular
junction**

Nerve fibre

Myelin sheath

Terminal
nerve branch

Synaptic trough

Muscle cell nucleus

Myofibrils

Muscle cell

transmitted to the muscle therefore travel in both directions to the either end of the muscle fibre. This is called the motor endplate and it is insulated with Schwann cells. When the action potential reaches the terminal of the nerve it triggers the release of hundreds of secretory vesicles of acetylcholine into the synaptic trough. The muscle membrane of the synaptic

trough has multiple acetylcholine receptors which act as gated ion channels. On binding acetylcholine these channels open, allowing sodium ions to flood into the cell, depolarising the membrane and generating an action potential. The acetylcholine in the synaptic trough is rapidly inactivated by the acetylcholinesterase enzyme in the synaptic trough.

CHAPTER 3

Disease and drugs acting on the neuromuscular junction (NMJ)

Myasthenia gravis: this is an autoimmune condition that involves development of antibodies against the acetylcholine receptor. The endplate potentials are therefore too weak to adequately stimulate the muscle fibres. The hallmark of myasthenia gravis is muscle weakness that increases during periods of activity and improves after periods of rest. Certain muscles, such as those that control eye and eyelid movement, facial expression, chewing, talking and swallowing, are often involved. The muscles that control breathing and neck and limb movements may also be affected.

Acetylcholine mimetic drugs: act in the same manner as acetylcholine but are not sensitive to acetylcholinesterase and so have a longer duration of action. They include methacholine and nicotine.

NMJ blockers: act competitively with acetylcholine for the receptor and are known as the curariform drugs

NMJ activators: inactivate acetylcholinesterase (eg neostigmine, physostigmine) and result in persistence of the acetylcholine in the synaptic trough, with resulting persistence of muscle contraction

Muscle contraction

Skeletal muscle contraction

The structure of skeletal muscle

Skeletal muscles are composed of longitudinal muscle fibres surrounded by a membrane called the sarcolemma. Each muscle fibre is made up of thousands of myofibrils. Myofibrils are composed of actin and myosin filaments, which are polymerised protein molecules that lie in a parallel orientation in the sarcoplasm. They partially interdigitate and so under the microscope the myofibrils appear to have alternating dark and light bands. Between the myofibrils lie large numbers of mitochondria. Wrapped around the myofibrils is a large quantity of modified ER called the sarcoplasmic reticulum.

The ends of the actin filaments are attached to a Z disc. The Z disc passes through neighbouring myofibrils, attaching them together into a muscle fibre. This gives the fibres a striped or 'striated' appearance. The area between the Z discs is called the sarcomere. In the relaxed state the actin molecules overlap very slightly at the ends. In the myofibril, the I band represents areas where the actin molecule does not overlap the myosin, and the A band represents areas where both actin and myosin overlap. Therefore, when the muscle contracts the A band stays the same length but the I bands become much smaller.

The mechanism of contraction of skeletal muscle

The action potential is transmitted through the muscle fibre by invaginations of the membrane deep into the centre of the fibre (called transverse or T-tubules). Depolarisation of the T-tubule membrane stimulates the release of calcium ions from the sarcoplasmic reticulum in the muscle fibre. These calcium ions cause the actin and myosin molecules to slide along one another, resulting in contraction of the myofibrils. This process is called excitation–contraction coupling.

This sliding mechanism works by interaction between the myosin heads and the active site on the actin molecule. The actin fibres are made up

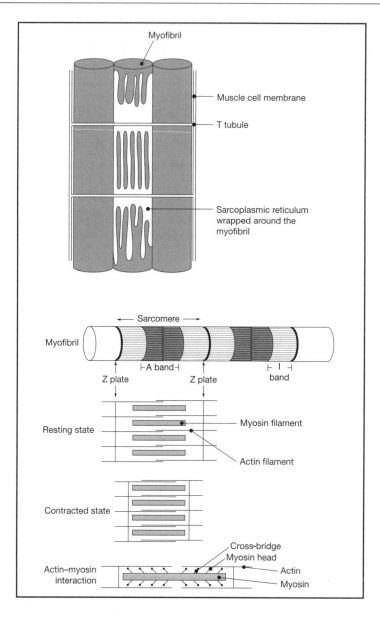

Figure 3.6 The structure of the myofibril

of actin, tropomyosin and troponin molecules. The tropomyosin and troponin form a complex that covers and inhibits the actin active site until it binds with four calcium ions. This induces a conformational change in the molecule which uncovers the actin active site. The myosin molecule has cross-bridges on which there are ATPase heads. These heads bind to the actin active site and ATP is used to enable the myosin molecule to 'walk along' the actin molecules. The calcium ions are then pumped back into the sarcoplasmic reticulum.

Muscles are composed of 'fast-twitch' and 'slow-twitch' fibres and there are other fibres that lie between these two extremes. Depending

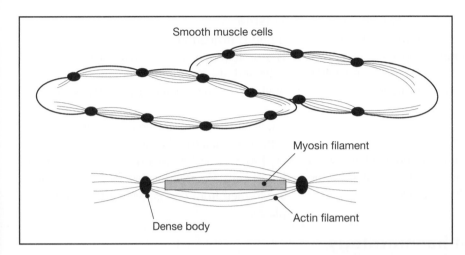

Figure 3.7 The smooth muscle cell

on their function, an entire muscle is made up of a variable mixture of these two types of fibre.

- Slow-twitch fibres (type I) are smaller, with an extensive blood supply, contain myoglobin to act as an oxygen store (and thus appear red) and mitochondria for oxidative phosphorylation. These fibres are used for prolonged or continuous muscle activity
- Fast-twitch fibres (type II) are larger, have extensive sarcoplasmic reticulum for rapid release of calcium ions, and minimal blood supply because they produce energy by glycolysis and not oxidative phosphory-lation. They are used for rapid and powerful muscle contraction. They have no myoglobin and therefore appear white

Smooth muscle contraction

Smooth muscle cells contain muscle fibres that may act as a single or as multiple units. Smooth muscle composed of multiple units is usually richly innervated and under neurological control, compared with single units, which are controlled by non-neurological stimuli. Single-unit smooth muscle is found in the gut, biliary tree, ureters, uterus and blood vessels. These smooth muscle cells are joined by gap junctions, allowing free flow of ions from one cell to the next (known as a syncytium).

Smooth muscle contains bundles of actin filaments attached at either end to a dense body (which serve the same role as the Z disc) and are arranged surrounding a myosin filament. The dense bodies of neighbouring cells may be bonded together to form protein bridges that transmit contractile force from one cell to the next. The actin and myosin in smooth muscle interact as described for skeletal muscle, but there is no troponin molecule – instead they contain the molecule, calmodulin. On binding calcium ions, calmodulin activates myosin kinase, which phosphorylates and activates the myosin cross-bridges. Contraction occurs in a far more prolonged fashion and is halted only when the myosin head is dephosphorylated by another enzyme called myosin phosphatase.

Smooth muscle contraction may be induced by nervous impulses as discussed previously. In addition, smooth muscle may be induced to contract or relax by local tissue factors and hormones, eg local hypoxia, carbon dioxide and increased hydrogen ion concentration all cause smooth muscle relaxation in the blood vessels, which results in vasodilatation. Hormones cause smooth muscle contraction when the smooth muscle contains hormone-specific receptors; these often act as ion gates that open when stimulated by the relevant hormone.

Cardiac muscle contraction

Cardiac muscle is striated and contains actin and myosin filaments which contract in the same manner as skeletal muscle.

1.2 Surgical haematology, coagulation, bleeding and transfusion

Composition of blood

> **Learning point**
>
> The total blood volume in an adult is approximately 5.5 litres.
> Blood is divided into **plasma** and **cells**.
> There are three main types of blood cells:
> - Erythrocytes (red blood cells)
> - Leucocytes (white blood cells), which consist of:
>   - Neutrophils
>   - Eosinophils
>   - Basophils
>   - Lymphocytes
>   - Monocytes
> - Thrombocytes (platelets)
>
> The haematocrit is the percentage of the blood volume formed by erythrocytes.

Plasma

Blood is divided into plasma and cells. Plasma is a protein-rich solution that carries the blood cells and also transports nutrients, metabolites, antibodies and other molecules between organs.

The haematocrit (or packed cell volume – PCV) is the percentage of the blood volume formed by erythrocytes and is usually 45%. Over 99% of blood cells are erythrocytes, so 2.5 litres blood are formed from erythrocytes and 3 litres from plasma.

Stem cells

All blood cells originate from pluripotent stem cells in the bone marrow. At birth the marrow of most bones produces blood cells. In adults the red cell-producing marrow remains only in the axial skeleton, ribs, skull, and proximal humerus and proximal femur. Pluripotent stem cells divide early into lymphoid stem cells, which differentiate into lymphoid and myeloid stem cells – the basis for all other blood cells. Cells of the immune system are discussed later.

Erythrocytes

- Transport oxygen via haemoglobin
- Biconcave disc shape increases surface area to volume ratio and so maximises oxygen exchange
- Contain no nucleus or organelles
- Reticulocytes (immature erythrocytes) contain residual RNA
- Average lifespan is 120 days
- Broken down by macrophages within the spleen, liver and bone marrow
- Synthesis stimulated by erythropoietin production from the kidneys

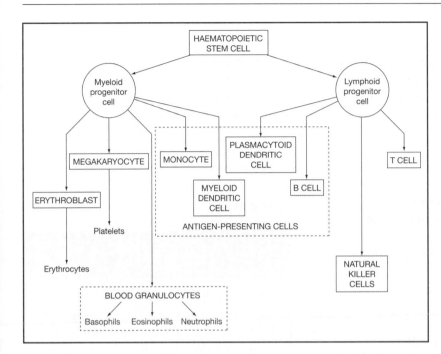

Figure 3.8
Haematopoiesis
(B and T cells are lymphocytes)

CHAPTER 3

Leucocytes

- Part of the immunological defence mechanism of the body
- Transported in the blood; most functions take place when cells have left the blood to enter the tissues
- Five main types:
  - Neutrophils
  - Eosinophils
  - Basophils
  - Lymphocytes
  - Monocytes

Together, neutrophils, eosinophils and basophils are known as polymorphonuclear granulocytes due to the presence of cytoplasmic granules and multilobed nuclei.

Neutrophils

- Most abundant leucocyte (40–70%)
- Spend 14 days in the bone marrow but have a half-life of only 7 hours in the blood
- Major cell in acute inflammation

- Very important role against bacteria
- Migrate from blood to tissues via endothelium

Lymphocytes

- Second most common leucocyte (20–50%)
- Important for specific immune response
- Three types of lymphocyte: B cells, T cells and natural killer (NK) cells
- Activated B cells convert into plasma cells and produce antibodies (the humoral response)
- T cells produce the cell-mediated response. There are three subsets:
  - T-helper cells (activate macrophages and B cells)
  - T-cytotoxic cells (kill target cells)
  - T-suppressor cells (modulate the immune response)
- NK cells are responsible for cell-mediated killing, mainly of viruses and tumour cells

Monocytes

- These account for 15% of leucocytes
- Largest leucocyte, mobile phagocytic cell
- Important in inflammatory reactions
- Located in blood and bone marrow, precursors of macrophages in tissues and lymphoid organs

Eosinophils

- Make up 5% of leucocytes
- Important defence against parasitic infections
- Increase in allergic states (eg hayfever, asthma)

Basophils

- Least common leucocyte (0.5%)
- Probable mast cell precursor – similar structure and function
- Initiate immediate hypersensitivity reactions – anaphylaxis via histamine release

Thrombocytes (platelets)

- Small, discoid, anuclear cells
- Produced from megakaryocytes, the largest cell in the bone marrow, via cytoplasmic fragmentation
- Circulate for 8–10 days
- Essential for normal haemostasis
- Form a platelet plug in response to loss of endothelium lining blood vessels

Surgery and general haematology

There may be changes in haematology as a response to major surgery, including:

- Leucocytosis (usually due to increase in neutrophil count relative to lymphocytes)

- Relative anaemia:
  - Chronic illness
  - Blood loss
  - Impaired erythropoiesis
  - Decreased serum iron
- Relative thrombocytosis
- Increased acute phase reactants including erythrocyte sedimentation rate (ESR) and C-reactive protein (CRP)

Anaemia

Learning point

Anaemia is the reduction in the concentration of circulating haemoglobin below the expected range for age and sex:
- Adult male: <13 g/dl
- Adult female: <11.5 g/dl

It can be acute or chronic.

Causes of anaemia are:

Decreased production
- Impaired erythrocyte formation
- Impaired erythrocyte function

Increased loss
- Blood loss (acute/chronic)
- Decreased erythrocyte lifespan (eg haemolysis)

Physiological anaemia occurs in pregnancy due to a relative increase in plasma volume.

Anaemia may be classified by cause or by the appearance of the cells.

Classification of anaemia

The blood film

Anaemia can be classified according to the morphological appearances of erythrocytes on a blood film.

Look at the mean cell volume (MCV) to determine whether the cells are too small (microcytic), too large (macrocytic) or of the correct size (normocytic).

The intensity of colour of the blood cells as seen on the blood film is also important – cell colour can be decreased, with central pallor (hypochromic), or normal (normochromic).

Causes of anaemia

Microcytic hypochromic red cell appearance

- Thalassaemia
- Iron deficiency
  - Malabsorption
  - Chronic blood loss, usually gastro-intestinal (GI) or genitourinary (GU) tract
  - Decreased dietary intake
  - Increased demand

Normocytic normochromic red cell appearance

- Acute blood loss
- Anaemia of chronic disease
- Endocrine disease
- Malignancy
- Haemolytic anaemia
- Erythrocyte abnormality:
  - Spherocytosis
  - Elliptocytosis
  - Glucose-6-phosphatase dehydro-genase (G6PD) deficiency
- Haemoglobin abnormality
  - Sickle cell anaemia
- Extrinsic factors:
  - Disseminated intravascular coagulation (DIC)
  - Infections
  - Chemical injury
  - Sequestration

Macrocytic red cell appearance

- Megaloblastic (interference with DNA synthesis causing morphological abnormalities)
- Folate deficiency
- Vitamin B12 deficiency
  - Pernicious anaemia
  - Gastrectomy
  - Ileal resection
  - Crohn's disease
- Drugs
  - Azathioprine
  - Hydroxyurea
  - Methotrexate
- Non-megaloblastic anaemia
  - Liver disease
  - Alcohol
  - Pregnancy
  - Hypothyroidism
  - Increased reticulocyte number

Clinical effects of anaemia

Clinically, anaemia becomes apparent when the oxygen demands of the tissues cannot be met without some form of compensatory mechanism. A slowly falling haemoglobin level allows for tissue acclimatisation. Compensatory mechanisms include a tachycardia and increased cardiac output, and chronically a reticulocytosis due to increased erythropoiesis and increased oxygen extraction from the blood.

When the patient is relatively anaemic the blood has a lower haematocrit and decreased viscosity. This improves blood flow through the capillaries and so, in cases of critical illness, patients requiring transfusion may not have their anaemia corrected beyond 9–10 g/dl.

Anaemia is not a diagnosis. If a patient presents with low haemoglobin it is important to look for a cause. When there is no time for further preoperative investigation, correction of anaemia (by transfusion) may be required as part of resuscitation while surgical intervention is ongoing.

Reversible causes of anaemia should be corrected before elective surgery. Mildly anaemic patients who are otherwise well may tolerate general anaesthesia and surgery well. More profound anaemia should be treated by consideration of transfusion, iron supplementation, etc.

Investigating anaemia

History

- Acute or chronic blood loss (eg menorrhagia, per rectal bleeding or change in bowel habit)
- Insufficient dietary intake of iron and folate (eg elderly people, poverty, anorexia, alcohol problems)

- Excessive utilisation of important factors (eg pregnancy, prematurity)
- Malignancy
- Chronic disorders (eg malabsorption states affecting the small bowel)
- Drugs (eg phenytoin antagonises folate)

Further investigation of anaemia

It is important to look at low haemoglobin in relation to the leucocyte and platelet counts, to consider a pancytopenia. A reticulocyte count indicates marrow activity.

Tests for haemolysis include serum bilirubin (unconjugated), urinary urobilinogen, haptoglobin and haemosiderin. A Schilling test is undertaken in suspected vitamin B12 deficiency. A bone marrow biopsy may be considered and other tests where relevant, such as thyroid function tests, urea and electrolytes and γ-glutamyltransferase.

Specific investigations for iron deficiency include blood tests such as ferritin, transferrin and total iron-binding capacity. Vitamin C increases iron absorption by an unknown mechanism. Examine the likely sources of blood loss: GI tract (upper and lower endoscopy), investigation of renal tract (intravenous urogram [IVU], cystoscopy), menorrhagia, etc. Replacement therapies include ferrous sulphate and ferrous fumarate.

Folate deficiency (folate is found in green vegetables and offal) may be due to insufficient intake or excessive utilisation (eg pregnancy – note subsequent deficiency of folate causes fetal neural tube defects). Measurement of red cell folate (<160–640 g/l) is more accurate than serum levels. Exclude vitamin B12 deficiency, because administration of folate will aggravate neuropathy. Replacement therapy should consist of 5 mg folate once daily. If possible, these investigations should be sent off before commencement of iron or a blood transfusion, which will obscure the results.

Polycythaemia

> ### Learning point
>
> Polycythaemia is an increase in erythrocyte concentration, causing a rise in haemoglobin and PCV.
> It may be primary or secondary and the resulting increase in blood viscosity predisposes to thrombotic pathology. Treatment usually requires venesection of a unit of blood at set time intervals.

Causes of polycythaemia

Primary polycythaemia – polycythaemia rubra vera (PRV)
- Excess erythrocyte production despite low erythropoietin levels
- Due to a proliferation of pluripotent stem cells with an associated rise in leucocytes and platelets
- Unknown cause and insidious onset
- Diagnosed with Hb >18 g/dl in males and >16 g/dl in females

Secondary polycythaemia – increase in erythrocytes only

Appropriate increase in erythropoietin production in response to hypoxia
- High altitude
- Cardiac disease
- Pulmonary disease
- Smoking
- Haemoglobinopathy

Inappropriate increase in erythropoietin
- Renal or hepatic carcinoma
- Cerebellar haemangioblastoma
- Renal transplantation
- Large uterine fibroids

Relative (decrease in plasma volume, normal erythrocyte mass)
- Dehydration
- Burns

There is an increase in blood viscosity. Clinically this leads to an increased risk of myocardial infarction (MI), cerebrovascular accident (CVA), peripheral vascular disease (PVD), deep vein thrombosis (DVT) and splenomegaly. Haemorrhagic lesions occur in the GI tract and PRV is associated with peptic ulceration, although the link is unclear.

PRV may result in acute leukaemia (15%), myelofibrosis (30%) or death via a thrombotic complication (30%).

If possible, surgery should be delayed and a haematologist consulted. In an emergency, consider preoperative venesection and store the blood for an autologous transfusion if required.

Neutropenia

> ## Learning point
>
> Neutropenia is a neutrophil count of $<2 \times 10^9/l$.
> Severe neutropenia is a neutrophil count of $< 0.5 \times 10^9/l$.
> It may be primary (rare) or secondary due to drugs or leukaemia. The big risk is that of subsequent infection.
> Note that overwhelming sepsis can lead to failure of the immune system, with a dramatically low white cell count (WCC) and neutropenia. Be very cautious when dealing with a septic patient with a low WCC.

Causes of neutropenia

Primary causes of neutropenia
- Congenital neutropenias are rare. Most are benign; if severe they are usually fatal at a young age
- Beware of ethnic variations; patients of African ancestry often have low neutrophil counts

Secondary causes of neutropenia
- Drugs
  - Immunosuppressives (eg azathioprine)
  - Antivirals (eg zidovudine)
  - Antibiotics (co-trimoxazole and sulfonamides)
  - Chemotherapy
- Disease:
  - Leukaemia
  - Septicaemia
  - Hypersplenism

- Bone marrow failure
- Viral infection
- Rheumatoid arthritis (RA)
- Systemic lupus erythematous (SLE)

Counts of $<0.5 \times 10^9/l$ may result in severe sepsis. Neutropenic infections are usually disseminated, with septicaemia, fungaemia and deep abscess formation.

In hospitals prophylactic measures for a febrile neutropenia are undertaken. These usually consist of reverse barrier isolation, antifungals, antiseptic mouthwash and avoidance of food with a high bacterial load.

Broad-spectrum antibiotics are given in febrile neutropenia. G-CSF (granulocyte colony-stimulating factor) may also be considered, which decreases the number of infective episodes and the duration of neutropenia.

Neutrophilia

> ## Learning point
>
> Neutrophilia is usually caused by infection or inflammation.
> It may also be a result of metabolic disease, haemorrhage, poisoning, malignancy and changes in physiology.

Causes of neutrophilia

Acute infection
- Bacteria (cocci and bacilli)
- Fungi
- Spirochaetes
- Viruses
- Rickettsiae

Infections such as typhoid fever, paratyphoid fever, mumps, measles and tuberculosis are usually not associated with neutrophilia.

Inflammation

- Burns
- Trauma (eg postoperatively)
- MI
- Gout
- Glomerulonephritis
- Collagen vascular disorders
- Hypersensitivity reactions

Postoperatively, neutrophilia may occur for between 12 and 36 hours as a result of tissue injury. Leucocytosis also can occur in intestinal obstruction and strangulated hernia.

Metabolic

- Diabetic ketoacidosis
- Pre-eclampsia
- Uraemia, especially with uraemic pericarditis

Poisoning

- Lead
- Mercury
- Digoxin
- Insect venom

Acute haemorrhage

Acute haemorrhage, especially into body cavities such as the peritoneal cavity, pleural cavity, joint cavity and intracranial cavities (eg extradural, subdural or subarachnoid space) is associated with leucocytosis and neutrophilia. This is probably related to the release of adrenal corticosteroids and/or adrenaline secondary to pain and a degree of local inflammation (blood in body cavities acts as an irritant).

Malignant neoplasms

Neutrophilia can occur in association with rapidly growing neoplasms when the tumour outgrows its blood supply. This is thought to be due to tumour necrosis factor alpha (TNFα). In addition, neutropenia is a common side effect of patients on chemotherapy

Physiological neutrophilia

- Strenuous exercise
- Adrenaline
- Pregnancy and labour
- Neonates

Other causes

- Cushing's disease and corticosteroids
- Haematological disorders – chronic myelocytic leukaemia, polycythaemia vera, myelofibrosis
- Chronic idiopathic neutrophilia
- Hereditary neutrophilia

The differential white cell count

The differential WCC can be very helpful in elucidating the diagnosis (eg differentiating viral from bacterial infection). The following table shows causes of changes in the differential white cell count.

CHAPTER 3

Type of cell	Normal range	↓	↑	↑↑↑
Neutrophil	2.0–7.5 × 10⁹/l	Leukaemia Septicaemia Hypersplenism Bone marrow failure Viral infection SLE and RA	Bacterial infection Inflammation Surgery Trauma Burns Haemorrhage Drugs (eg steroids)	Leukaemia Severe infection Disseminated malignancy
Lymphocyte	1.3–3.5 × 10⁹/l	Stress Malnutrition Infections Immunosuppressants Radiotherapy Primary immunodeficiency Uraemia Bone marrow failure SLE	Viral infection Chronic lymphocytic leukaemia	Epstein–Barr virus (EBV) infection
Eosinophil	0.04–0.44 × 10⁹/l		Asthma Allergy Parasitic infection Skin diseases (eg pemphigus) Malignant disease	
Monocyte	0.2–0.8 × 10⁹/l		Acute or chronic infection Malignant disease Myelodysplasia	
Basophil	0–0.1 × 10⁹/l		Viral infection Urticaria Myxoedema Haemolysis Polycythaemia Ulcerative colitis Malignancy	

Lymphopenia

This is a lymphocyte count of <1 × 10⁹/l. Lymphopenia is associated with opportunistic infections, encapsulated bacterial, fungal and viral infections.

Causes of lymphopenia:
- Stress – trauma, burns, surgery
- Malnutrition
- Infections – TB, HIV, sarcoidosis
- Immunosuppressant drugs, eg steroids
- Radiotherapy
- Primary immunodeficiency syndromes (DiGeorge syndrome, primary antibody deficiencies)
- Uraemia
- Bone marrow failure
- SLE

Lymphocytosis

Lymphocytosis is used to describe lymphocyte counts $>5 \times 10^9/l$. Causes of lymphocytosis:

- Viral infections – especially EBV, cytomegalovirus (CMV), HIV
- Chronic infections – tuberculosis (TB), toxoplasmosis
- Haematological malignancy – chronic lymphocytic leukaemia (CLL), lymphoma
- Acute transient response to stress – 24 hours only

Thrombocytopenia

Learning point

Thrombocytopenia is a platelet number of $<150 \times 10^9/l$. Causes include:
- Production failure
- Decreased thrombocyte survival
- Sequestration

Causes of thrombocytopenia

Platelet production failure
- Aplastic anaemia
- Drugs – cytotoxics
- Alcohol
- Viral infections – EBV, CMV
- Marrow infiltration – leukaemia, myelofibrosis, myeloma, metastatic infiltration
- Hereditary thrombocytopenia

Decreased platelet survival
- Idiopathic thrombocytopenic purpura (ITP)
- Drugs – heparin, penicillamine, gold
- Infections – subacute bacterial endocarditis (SBE), meningococci
- Thrombotic thrombocytopenic purpura (TTP)
- DIC
- Blood transfusions – cause dilutional thrombocytopenia
- Haemolytic uraemic syndrome (HUS)
- Extracorporeal bypass – platelets are activated in the extracorporeal circuit, and are therefore ineffective in haemostasis

Sequestration of platelets
- Caused by hypersplenism (see Abdomen chapter in Book 2)
- Counts of $<70 \times 10^9/l$ are inadequate for surgical haemostasis, and spontaneous bleeding may occur with platelet numbers of $<20 \times 10^9/l$

Clinical conditions in thrombocytopenia

Platelet dysfunction
Excess surgical bleeding may occur with a normal platelet count due to platelet dysfunction. The most common cause in surgical practice is antiplatelet medications such as aspirin and clopidogrel. Patients should be advised to stop these preoperatively if appropriate. Both aspirin and clopidogrel should be stopped 7 days preoperatively to restore normal platelet function.

Disseminated intravascular coagulation
Simultaneous activation of both the coagulation and fibrinolytic systems in the body causes widespread microvascular thrombosis, fibrin deposition, and bleeding due to the consumption of clotting factors and fibrinolysis.

Thrombotic thrombocytopenic purpura

This is a condition of unknown cause, usually affecting young adults. Deposition of widespread hyaline thrombi in small vessels causes microangiopathic haemolysis, renal failure and neurological disturbance.

Haemolytic uraemic syndrome

Usually this occurs after an acute illness, especially URTIs and GI infections. *Escherichia coli* has been implicated. Characteristics include a microangiopathic haemolysis, thrombocytopenia and acute renal failure.

Idiopathic thrombocytopenic purpura

Autoimmune destruction of platelets, due to IgG antibody attack. Two types exist:

- Acute (occurs in children; postviral; usually self-limiting; Henoch–Schönlein purpura)
- Chronic (occurs in adults; female predominance; treated with high-dose steroids; rarely requires splenectomy)

Thrombocytosis

Learning point

Thrombocytosis is a rise in the circulating platelet count. It can be primary or secondary.
Platelets may be numerous but functionally inactive (if functionally active then an antiplatelet agent may be indicated).

Causes of thrombocytosis

Primary thrombocytosis – essential thrombocythaemia

- Related to polycythaemia rubra vera
- Platelet count of $>1000 \times 10^9/l$
- Clinically causes bruising, bleeding and cerebrovascular symptoms
- High platelet count causes splenic atrophy due to recurrent thromboses, after initial hypertrophy

Secondary thrombocytosis

Secondary thrombocytosis is a reaction to:

- Haemorrhage
- Connective tissue disorders
- Surgery
- Splenectomy
- Malignancy
- Myeloproliferative disorders

Patients who have a thrombocytosis and are at risk of a thrombo-occlusive event (such as those who are immobile, have other risk factors for DVT, or have vascular grafts or complex vascular anastomoses) often require treatment with an antiplatelet agent.

Pancytopenia

Learning point

Pancytopenia is a global reduction in the number of erythrocytes, leucocytes and platelets.
Causes include drug reactions, bone marrow infiltration, hypersplenism and aplastic anaemia.
Clinically these patients are **anaemic**, **neutropenic** and **thrombocytopenic**.

Causes of pancytopenia

- Drugs:
  - Causing bone marrow depression
  - Most common cause of pancytopenia while in hospital
  - Includes cytotoxic drugs, immunosuppressants, antiretrovirals
- Bone marrow infiltration:
  - Lymphoma, leukaemia, myeloma, myelofibrosis, metastatic infiltration
- Hypersplenism
- Megaloblastic anaemia
- HIV
- Aplastic anaemia:
  - Reduction in pluripotent stem cells
  - Congenital (Fanconi syndrome, autosomal recessive, 50% 1-year survival rate)
  - Idiopathic
  - Secondary (drugs, infections, radiation, paroxysmal nocturnal haemoglobinuria)

Clinical effects of pancytopenia

Anaemia: may require transfusion to maintain Hb. Repeated transfusion may drop the platelet count further.

Neutropenia: pancytopenic patients may require a neutropenic regimen if their neutrophil count is <0.5 × 10⁹/l. They are at risk of neutropenic sepsis.

Thrombocytopenia: platelet counts of <40 × 10⁹/l put patients at risk of traumatic bleeding. Platelet counts <20 × 10⁹/l put the patient at risk of spontaneous bleeding. Transfusion may be required.

Sickle cell disease

Learning point

Sickle cell disease is due to a genetic mutation (commonly inherited) causing changes in haemoglobin structure and altered oxygen binding.
It may be homozygous or heterozygous (sickle cell trait). The disease has predominance in Africa and is found in India and the Middle East.
Clinical problems include:
- Haemolytic anaemia
- Vaso-occlusive crises

Genetics of sickle cell

- At birth the majority of the haemoglobin in the body is fetal haemoglobin – HbF
- By the age of 6 months 80–90% of this is replaced by adult haemoglobin – HbA

Haemoglobin is made up two α and two β chains. An inherited genetic mutation of the α chain leads to the formation of sickle cell haemoglobin, HbS. This is a single amino acid substitution. Glutamine at position 6 on the β chain is replaced by valine. This changes the oxygen-binding capacity of the molecule.

- Sickle cell haemoglobin can be present as a trait in the heterozygous state – HbAS
- Or as sickle cell disease in the homozygous state – HbSS

The disease usually manifests itself at the age of 6 months, when HbF levels fall.

Clinical aspects of sickle cell disease

Deoxygenated HbS is insoluble and polymerises, causing the red blood cells to form rigid, inflexible shapes. Repeated exposure to low oxygen tensions while travelling through capillaries causes red blood cells to adopt a rigid sickle shape. This is primarily reversible with reoxygenation (and so responds to oxygen therapy).

This results in:

- Haemolytic anaemia and sequelae such as pigment gallstone formation due to the hyperbilirubinaemia
- Vaso-occlusive crises
- Infarction and severe ischaemic pain, commonly seen in: bones, especially fingers (dactylitis), chest, kidney, liver and penis (priapism)

In the long term there is an increased susceptibility to infections, especially *Streptococcus pneumoniae* and salmonella meningitis, chronic renal failure and blindness.

Sickle cell disease and surgery

Diagnosis is via a full blood count (FBC), peripheral blood film and sickle solubility test. This is confirmed by Hb electrophoresis.

It is important in surgery to try to avoid precipitating factors. These include hypothermia, hypoxia, infection, hypotension, dehydration and acidosis – all common problems in surgical patients.

Sickle cell trait is usually asymptomatic. Cells do not sickle unless oxygen saturations are <40%, which is very rare. Anaesthetists should be made aware of patients with the trait preoperatively in order to avoid any degree of hypoxia.

Many hospitals have a protocol whereby patients from at-risk populations (such as Africans or those of Middle Eastern descent) have a routine sickle cell test before surgery.

Thalassaemias

Learning point

Thalassaemias are inherited disorders of defective synthesis of globin chains in haemoglobin.
They cause haemolysis, anaemia and ineffective erythropoiesis.
They are found mainly in Africa, the Mediterranean, Asia and the Middle East.
Types include:

- β-Thalassaemia major (homozygous)
- β-Thalassaemia minor (heterozygous)
- α-Thalassaemia

Beta-thalassaemia

The most common of the thalassaemias, β-thalassaemia minor is the heterozygous state. It produces a symptomless microcytosis, which may be accompanied by a mild anaemia.

Beta-thalassaemia major is the homozygous form, with either none or a much-reduced number of β chains. It presents as a severe anaemia from 3 months onwards, needing regular transfusions. Clinically there is a failure to thrive with recurrent infections. Extramedullary haematopoiesis causes hepatosplenomagaly and bone expansion, leading to frontal bossing and a characteristic appearance.

The aim should be to transfuse to an Hb level of >10 g/dl, while preventing iron overload with desferrioxamine, an iron-chelating agent. Folate supplements are required. Splenectomy for hypersplenism and bone marrow transplantation can be considered.

Alpha-thalassaemia

Four genes are responsible for the α chains and the disease is caused by gene deletions. If all four genes are deleted the condition is fatal. A three-gene deletion causes moderate anaemia and splenomegaly – HbH disease. Patients are not usually transfusion-dependent. Two-gene deletion causes a microcytosis, which may be associated with a mild anaemia. This is the α-thalassaemia trait.

Apart from sickle cell and thalassaemia there are other variants of haemoglobin. The most common are:
- HbC – causes a mild haemolytic anaemia
- HbE – causes a mild microcytic anaemia

Haemostasis and coagulation

Learning point

Haemostasis is the cessation of bleeding. Physiological haemostasis consists of a series of complex interrelated events involving:
- Endothelial cells
- Platelets
- The clotting cascade
- Fibrinolysis

Key events in haemostasis
- Vascular injury with exposure of subendothelial tissue factor and collagen
- Vasoconstriction
- Platelet adherence and aggregation at the injury site (platelet plug)
- Activation of the coagulation cascade
- Platelet plug stabilised with cross-linked fibrin
- Fibrinolysis and vasodilatation
- Regulatory feedback mechanisms achieve a balance between haemostasis and fibrinolysis

Role of endothelial cells in haemostasis

Endothelial cells form a barrier between their enveloping connective tissues and the blood. They also produce thrombotic and antithrombotic factors.

149

Factor	Action
Antithrombotic factors	
Prostacyclin (PGI$_2$)	Inhibitor of platelet aggregation and vasodilator
Thrombomodulin	A glycoprotein bound to the endothelial cell membrane. On complexing with thrombin it activates protein C (co-factor of protein S), which degrades factors Va and VIIIa. It thus reduces fibrin formation
Nitric oxide	Vasodilator and inhibitor of platelet aggregation and adhesion
Tissue plasminogen activator (tPA)	Regulates fibrinolysis
Thrombotic factors	
Von Willebrand's factor (vWF)	Cofactor for platelet adhesion and factor VIII
Platelet-activating factor (PAF)	Platelet aggregation and activation
Plasminogen activator inhibitor	A tPA inhibitor

Role of platelets in haemostasis

Platelets play a crucial role in haemostasis:
- At sites of vascular injury they bind, via vWF, to subendothelial collagen
- On activation they secrete the contents of their α and dense granules; fibrinogen and ADP induce aggregation and thromboxane A$_2$ causes vasoconstriction
- Aggregation of platelets forms a platelet plug
- Their cell membrane becomes procoagulant by providing binding sites for coagulation factors and fibrin

- The platelet plug becomes stabilised with cross-linked fibrin

The clotting cascade
Antithrombin III inactivates thrombin in the presence of heparin. It also inactivates factors VIIa, IXa, Xa and XIa, kallikrein and plasmin.

Fibrinolysis
Fibrinolysis occurs in response to vascular injury. Plasminogen is converted to the serine protease plasmin by a number of activators. Plasmin not only cleaves fibrin but also fibrinogen, factors V and VIII (Figure 3.9).

Disorders of haemostasis and coagulation

Learning point

The relationship between thrombosis and fibrinolysis is finely balanced. Disorders result from disruption of this equilibrium with over-emphasis or deficiency in one system relative to the other.
Disorders of haemostasis result in a predisposition to haemorrhage (see 'Common bleeding disorders' below) or predisposition to thrombosis (thromboembolic disorders).
In addition to a thorough history and physical examination, a number of simple tests can be employed to assess a patient's haemostatic function.

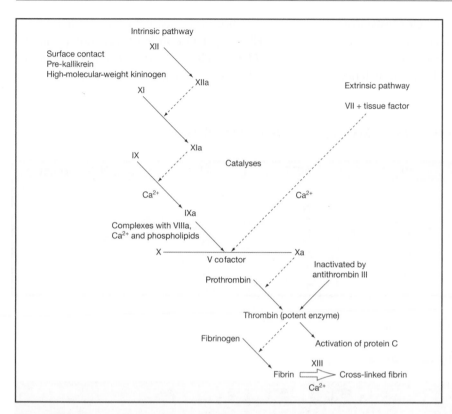

Figure 3.9 The coagulation system

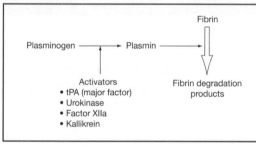

Figure 3.10 Fibrinolysis: tissue plasminogen activator (tPA) is released from endothelial cells. Its action is enhanced by the presence of fibrin, hence plasmin formation is localised to the site of the fibrin clot

Screening tests for clotting disorders

- **FBC and film:** thrombocytopenia is a common cause of abnormal bleeding. If a patient is suspected of having platelet dysfunction then specific assays can be performed. The bleeding time is a crude assessment of platelet function
- **Activated partial thromboplastin time (APTT):** measures the intrinsic as well as the common pathway factors (X to fibrin).

Normal time is approximately 30–40 s
- **Prothrombin time (PT):** assesses the extrinsic system factor (VII) as well as the common pathway factors. It is often expressed as the international normalised ratio (INR)
- **Thrombin time (TT):** this detects deficiencies of fibrinogen or inhibition of thrombin. Normal time is approximately 14–16 s

- **Specific coagulation factor tests:** assess genetic disorders of coagulation predisposing to haemorrhage, such as:
  - Haemophilia (factor VIII deficiency)

- Christmas disease (factor IX deficiency)
- **Fibrinogen and fibrin degradation product (FDP) levels:** useful for detection of ongoing intravascular coagulation (eg DIC)

RESULTS OF BLOOD TESTS IN COMMON BLEEDING DISORDERS

	PT	APTT	TT	Platelet count
Liver disease	↑	↑	N	↓
Warfarin	↑	N	N	N
Heparin	N	↑	↑	N
Factor VII deficiency	↑	N	N	N
Factor VIII deficiency	N	↑	N	N
Factor IX deficiency	N	↑	N	N
DIC	↑	↑	↑	↓

↑ = increased; ↓ = decreased; N = normal.

Common bleeding disorders

Learning point

Bleeding disorders may be congenital or acquired.

Congenital
Haemophilia A and B
Von Willebrand's disease
Platelet function disorders

Acquired
Thrombocytopenia
Platelet function disorders
Vitamin K deficiency
Hepatic failure

Renal failure
Acquired vascular defects

Congenital bleeding disorders

Haemophilia A

Haemophilia A is an X-linked recessive disorder that results from a deficiency or an abnormality of factor VIII. It affects 1 in 10 000 males (females can also rarely be affected) and up to 30% of cases are due to spontaneous mutations. It is characterised by bleeding into soft tissues, muscles and weight-bearing joints, the onset of which may be delayed by several hours after the injury. The functional level of factor VIII determines the severity of the disorder.

Severe disease
- <1% factor VIII
- Frequent bleeding after minor trauma

Moderate disease
- 1–5% factor VIII
- Less frequent bleeding

Mild disease
- 5–25% factor VIII
- Persistent bleeding, usually secondary to trauma

Most affected individuals have factor VIII levels <5%; 10–20% of patients develop antibodies to factor VIII. Treatment depends on the severity of the disorder and the proposed surgery. Factor VIII concentrate may have to be given repeatedly or continuously to maintain factor VIII levels. Desmopressin can be used transiently to raise the factor VIII level in patients with mild haemophilia.

Haemophilia B

Haemophilia B, also known as Christmas disease, is an X-linked disorder. It is clinically indistinguishable from haemophilia A. It occurs in 1 in 100 000 male births and is due to a defect or deficiency in factor IX. Treatment involves either prothrombin complex concentrate, which contains all of the vitamin K-dependent clotting factors, or factor IX concentrate.

Von Willebrand's disease

Von Willebrand's disease is the most common of the congenital bleeding disorders, occurring in as many as 1 in 800–1000 individuals. Von Willebrand factor (vWF) is a plasma glycoprotein that has two main functions: it aids platelet adhesion to the subendothelium at sites of vascular injury, and it serves as the plasma carrier protein for factor VIII. Three main disease subtypes have been described:
- Type I (most common): autosomal dominant (quantitative reduction of vWF)
- Type II: variably inherited (qualitative defects in vWF)
- Type III (very rare): autosomal recessive (almost no vWF)

Patients with the disease develop mucosal bleeding, petechiae, epistaxis and menorrhagia similar to patients with platelet disorders. Treatment depends on the symptoms and the underlying type of disease. Cryoprecipitate, factor VIII concentrate or desmopressin can be used.

Congenital platelet function disorders

These are very rare. They include:
- Bernard–Soulier syndrome (defect in platelet plasma membrane)
- Grey platelet syndrome (defect in storage granules)
- Cyclo-oxygenase and thromboxane synthetase deficiency

Acquired bleeding disorders

Thrombocytopenia

- Normal platelet count is $150–400 \times 10^9/l$
- Spontaneous bleeding uncommon if $40–100 \times 10^9/l$
- Spontaneous bleeding often severe if $<20 \times 10^9/l$

Causes of thrombocytopenia include:
- Decreased production (marrow aplasia, marrow infiltration, uraemia and alcoholism)

- Decreased survival (drugs, ITP)
- Increased consumption (DIC, infection, heparin therapy)

Platelet function disorders

These can be caused by:
- Non-steroidal anti-inflammatory drugs (NSAIDs)
- Heparin
- Alcohol
- Haematological malignancy

Vitamin K deficiency

Vitamin K is a fat-soluble vitamin that is absorbed in the small intestine and stored in the liver. It serves as a cofactor for γ-carboxylase in the production of coagulation factors II, VII, IX and X, and protein C and protein S. The normal liver contains a 30-day store of the vitamin, but the acutely ill patient can become deficient in 7–10 days.

Causes of vitamin K deficiency are:
- Inadequate dietary intake
- Malabsorption
- Lack of bile salts
- Hepatocellular disease
- Cephalosporin antibiotics

Parenteral vitamin K produces a correction in clotting times within 8–10 hours. Fresh frozen plasma (FFP) should be administered to patients with ongoing bleeding.

Hepatic failure

Hepatocellular disease is often accompanied by impaired haemostasis. This is because of:
- Decreased synthesis of coagulation factors (except factor VIII)
- Decreased synthesis of coagulation inhibitors (protein C, protein S and antithrombin III)
- Reduced clearance of activated coagulation factors, which may cause either DIC or systemic fibrinolysis
- Impaired absorption and metabolism of vitamin K
- Splenomegaly and secondary thrombocytopenia

Renal failure

Renal failure causes a decrease in platelet aggregation and adhesion.

Acquired vascular defects

This is a heterogeneous group of conditions characterised by bruising after minor trauma and spontaneous bleeding from small blood vessels. Examples include:
- **Senile purpura:** due to atrophy of perivascular supporting tissues
- **Scurvy:** defective collagen due to vitamin C deficiency
- **Steroid purpura**
- **Henoch–Schönlein purpura**
- **Ehlers–Danlos syndrome:** hereditary collagen abnormality

Thromboembolic disorders

Learning point

Thrombophilia refers to conditions predisposing to thrombosis.
Congenital prothrombotic disorders include:
- Factor V Leiden mutation
- Antithrombin III deficiency
- Protein C and protein S deficiency

Acquired prothrombotic disorders include:
- DIC
- Hyperviscosity of any cause
- Thrombocytosis (see page 146)
- A predisposition to thrombosis increases the risk of DVT, pulmonary embolism (PE) and recurrent miscarriage

Thrombophilia

Investigating thrombophilia

Clinical presentation of thrombophilia is with atypical or recurrent thrombosis. These patients are often young, may have a family history of thrombosis and present with thrombotic conditions such as DVT/PE, recurrent miscarriage and mesenteric thrombosis.

Thrombophilia screen

These tests assess genetic disorders of coagulation predisposing to thrombosis:
- Factor V Leiden mutation
- Antithrombin III
- Protein C
- Protein S

Identifying a genetic predisposition to thrombophilia should prompt screening of family members and giving advice about minimising other risk factors for thrombosis (eg avoiding use of the oral contraceptive pill).

Congenital prothrombotic disorders

Factor V Leiden mutation
- A genetic mutation in the factor V gene causes a change in the factor V protein, making it resistant to inactivation by protein C
- Factor V Leiden is inactivated by activated protein C at a much slower rate, leading to a thrombophilic state (propensity to clot) by having increased activity of factor V in the blood
- Common in northern European populations (4–7% of the general population is heterozygous for factor V Leiden and 0.06–0.25% of the population is homozygous for factor V Leiden)

Antithrombin III deficiency
- Rare autosomal dominant disorder
- Antithrombin III inactivates thrombin, factors VIIa, IXa, Xa and XIa, kallikrein and plasmin
- Antithrombin III level is measured by immunological assay
- <70% of the normal value increases risk of venous thrombosis
- Deficiency is also associated with liver disease, DIC, nephrotic syndrome and heparin therapy
- Prophylaxis and treatment involves antithrombin III concentrate and anticoagulation

Protein C and protein S deficiencies

- Autosomal dominant disorders with variable penetrance
- Protein C is activated by thrombin binding to thrombomodulin, a glycoprotein bound to the endothelial cell membrane; this causes a reduction in fibrin formation by the degradation of factors Va and VIIIa; protein S acts as a cofactor
- Protein C and protein S levels can be assessed by immunoassay techniques
- Treatment involves replacement of protein C or protein S and anticoagulation

Acquired prothrombotic disorders

Disseminated intravascular coagulation

DIC is a systemic thrombohaemorrhagic disorder. It is the pathological response to many underlying conditions.

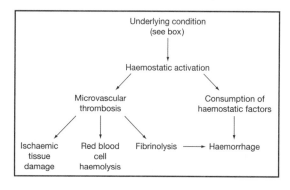

Figure 3.11 Disseminated intravascular coagulation

The clinical presentation is extremely variable. Most patients present with easy bruising and haemorrhage from venepuncture and intramuscular injection sites. This may progress to profuse haemorrhage from mucous membranes and shock. Although haemorrhage is the most common presentation, about 10% present with widespread thrombosis and resultant multiorgan failure.

Conditions associated with DIC
- Malignancy
- Massive tissue injury and trauma
- Obstetric complications (eg placental abruption, septic abortion, intrauterine fetal death, amniotic fluid embolism)
- Infections (especially Gram-negative bacteria)
- Miscellaneous (eg acute pancreatitis, drug reactions, transplant rejection, acute respiratory distress syndrome [ARDS])

Laboratory features of DIC
- Thrombocytopenia
- Prolonged PT, APTT, TT
- Increased fibrin degradation products (also increased after surgery)
- Reduced fibrinogen level
- Fragmented red blood cells

Management of DIC
- Diagnosis and treatment of the underlying disorder
- Shock exacerbates DIC so adequate fluid resuscitation is essential
- Use FFP, cryoprecipitate and platelet concentrates as required; be guided by regular laboratory screening

Use of heparin is controversial; it has been given in an attempt to reduce thrombin formation via antithrombin III activation, but trials have shown little benefit; however, if thrombosis is the predominant feature, heparin should be used at a relatively early stage.

Aetiology of venous thromboembolism

Venous thrombosis occurs in response to factors described by Virchow's triad. The relative importance of these factors to each other is still under debate. Venous thrombosis develops due to activation of coagulation in an area of venous stasis, as an imbalance between thrombogenesis and the circulating inhibitors of coagulation. Thus, prophylactic regimens are based on minimising stasis and providing anticoagulation.

> ### Virchow's triad
> - Endothelial damage (eg smoking, previous DVT)
> - Reduced venous flow or stasis (eg immobility, obstruction to flow)
> - Hypercoaguability (eg hereditary coagulopathy, smoking, malignancy)

Clots usually start in the deep veins around cusps or occasionally in larger vessels after direct venous wall trauma. They either:
- Dissolve spontaneously (with or without treatment), or
- Propagate proximally (20%)

DVT occurs in 50% of patients undergoing major abdominal or pelvic surgery if no prophylactic measures are taken. It is also common in joint replacement surgery and elderly people.

Around 20% of those with DVT are at risk of developing a PE. The risk of embolus from a below-knee DVT is very small; it increases substantially if the clot extends to above the knee; the risk of subsequent embolism is very high if the iliofemoral segment is involved.

Deep venous thrombosis

Venous thrombosis or DVT is common in surgical patients. It can cause pulmonary embolism, which carries a high mortality and therefore should be prevented. It may also cause a post-phlebitic limb with swelling, pain and ulceration many years later.

Factors predisposing to DVT

These can be divided into patient factors and factors involving the disease or surgical procedure.

RELATIVE RISKS OF THROMBOEMBOLISM FOR PATIENT FACTORS

Status	Relative risk of venous thrombosis
Normal	1
OCP use	4
Factor V Leiden, heterozygous	6
Factor V Leiden, homozygous	80
Prothrombin gene mutation, heterozygous	3
Prothrombin gene mutation, homozygous	20
Protein C deficiency, heterozygous	7
Protein C deficiency, homozygous	Severe thrombosis at birth
Protein S deficiency, heterozygous	6
Protein S deficiency, homozygous	Severe thrombosis at birth
Antithrombin III deficiency, heterozygous	5
Antithrombin III deficiency, homozygous	Fatal in utero
Homocysteinaemia	3

CHAPTER 3

Patient factors

- Age
- Previous DVT or PE
- Immobility
- Obesity
- Pregnancy
- Thrombophilia (eg protein C and protein S deficiencies, lupus anticoagulant and factor V Leiden)
- The oral contraceptive pill (OCP)

Factors involving the disease or surgical procedure

- Trauma or surgery, especially of the pelvis and lower limb
- Malignancy, especially pelvic and abdominal
- MI
- Congestive heart failure
- Polycythaemia
- Inflammatory bowel disease (IBD)
- Nephrotic syndrome
- Length of operation

Risks of deep venous thrombosis according to procedure

Low risk

- Any minor surgery (<30 minutes)
- No risk factors other than age with major surgery (>30 minutes)
- Age <40 with no other risk factors other than minor trauma or medical illness

Moderate risk

- Major general, urological, gynaecological, cardiothoracic, vascular or neurological surgery; age >40 or other risk factors
- Major medical illness; heart or lung disease; cancer; IBD
- Major trauma or burns
- Minor surgery, trauma or illness in patients with previous DVT, PE or thrombophilia

High risk

- Fracture or major orthopaedic surgery of pelvis, hip or lower limb
- Major pelvic or abdominal surgery for cancer
- Major surgery, trauma or illness in patients with previous DVT, PE or thrombophilia
- Lower limb paralysis
- Major lower limb amputation

INCIDENCE OF DVT AFTER COMMON SURGICAL PROCEDURES WITHOUT PROPHYLAXIS

Type of operation	Incidence of DVT (%)
Knee surgery	75
Hip fracture surgery	60
Elective hip surgery	50–55
Retropubic prostatectomy	40
General abdominal surgery	30–35
Gynaecological surgery	25–30
Neurosurgery	20–30
Transurethral resection of prostate	10
Inguinal hernia repair	10

Symptoms of deep venous thrombosis

DVT may be asymptomatic and difficult to diagnose. You must have a high level of suspicion in patients at risk. Symptoms may be a combination of those below.

Below-knee symptoms

- Swelling
- Pain and calf tenderness (from inflammation around the thrombus; can be demonstrated by Homan's sign of increased pain on dorsiflexion of the foot but this is very non-specific)
- Calf erythema
- Grumbling mild pyrexia

Above-knee symptoms

- May be asymptomatic and difficult to diagnose. Again you must have a high level of suspicion in patients at risk
- Swelling
- Pain and tenderness
- Grumbling mild pyrexia
- Phlegmasia caerulea dolens is a painful, purple, congested and oedematous lower limb associated with extensive iliofemoral DVT (there is usually underlying pelvic pathology)

Well's criteria

Well's criteria are used to determine the probability of spontaneous DVT (from a meta-analysis published by Anand et al 1998).
Each clinical sign is assigned one point:

- Active cancer (treatment within 6 months or palliative)
- Paralysis, paresis or recent lower limb POP
- Recently bedridden for >3 days or major surgery within last 4 weeks
- Localised calf tenderness
- Entire leg swelling
- Calf swelling >3 cm larger than the other limb
- Pitting oedema (more than other limb)
- Collateral superficial veins (non-varicose)

A high probability of an alternative diagnosis scores minus 2.

Overall score

- High probability of DVT: Scores ≥3
- Moderate probability of DVT: Scores 1–2
- Low probability of DVT: Scores <1

Investigating DVT

- Duplex Doppler US
- Ascending contrast venography (gold standard)
- ^{125}I-labelled fibrinogen scanning (research only)

Differential diagnosis of DVT

- Lymphoedema
- Cellulitis
- Ruptured Baker's cyst

Outcomes of DVT

- Pulmonary embolism
- Post-phlebitic limb
- Resolution without complication

Prevention of DVT

The highest risk of thromboembolism occurs at and immediately after surgery. Measures are therefore required to prevent venous thrombo-embolism in the perioperative period.

CHAPTER 3

General preventive measures against thromboembolism

- Early postoperative mobilisation
- Adequate hydration in the perioperative period
- Avoid calf pressure
- Stop the oral contraceptive pill 6 weeks preoperatively (advise alternative contraception)

Specific preventive measures against thromboembolism

- **Graded elastic compression stockings**: these should be well fitting, applied pre-surgery, and left on until the patient is mobile, except in cases of peripheral vascular ischaemia (eg patients for femorocrural bypass)
- **Intermittent pneumatic calf compression**: various devices available
- **Electrical calf muscle stimulation**
- **Postoperative leg elevation and early ambulation**
- **Heparin prophylaxis:** traditional unfractionated heparin, 5000 units subcutaneously given 2–4 hours before surgery and continued twice daily until patient is mobile. This has been largely superseded by low-molecular-weight (LMW) heparin. Various regimens are available. The advantages of LMW heparin are: less propensity to bleeding; longer half-life; only needs once daily administration; lower incidence of heparin-induced thrombocytopenia and heparin-induced osteoporosis. Heparin prophylaxis should be discontinued 24 hours before administration or withdrawal of epidural anaesthesia, to prevent bleeding into the epidural space
- Other agents affecting blood coagulability: antiplatelet agents (eg aspirin, dipyridamole, dextran) have been tried. Although they do reduce platelet activity, none is widely used for DVT prophylaxis. Oral anticoagulants (eg warfarin) are not used for surgical DVT prophylaxis because of the unacceptably high risk of haemorrhage

In principle, the method used should be simple to use, acceptable to patients, and have minimal adverse effects.

- All hospital inpatients need to be assessed for clinical risk factors and risk of thrombo-embolism; they should be administered graded prophylaxis depending on the degree of risk
- Low-risk patients should be mobilised early
- Moderate- and high-risk patients should be mobilised early AND receive specific prophylaxis

In practice, the methods used vary between clinicians and units but it is important that each centre has specific policies regarding prophylaxis.

Pulmonary embolus

Symptoms and signs of pulmonary embolus

Symptoms and signs of pulmonary embolism (PE) depend on the size and number of emboli. Pulmonary emboli vary from multiple small emboli to a large solitary embolus impacting at a bifurcation as a 'saddle' embolism. Small emboli may be completely asymptomatic. Clinical features of PE include:

- Shortness of breath
- Increased respiratory rate
- Pleuritic chest pain
- Decreased oxygen saturations
- Sinus tachycardia
- Haemoptysis
- Shock and circulatory collapse
- Cardiac arrest with pulseless electrical activity (PEA)

Investigating pulmonary embolism

ECG changes

- Commonly a sinus tachycardia is seen
- May be signs of right-heart strain (eg right bundle branch block or RBBB)
- Classic pattern of S1 Q3 T3 is very rarely seen

Chest radiograph changes

- Acutely there may be no changes seen (but alternative diagnoses can be excluded)
- A wedge of pulmonary infarction may be visible in the days after the PE

Arterial blood gases

- Acute hypoxia and type I respiratory failure in the absence of chest radiograph signs should also raise the suspicion of PE, especially in a preoperative patient

Diagnosis of pulmonary embolism

- Ventilation–perfusion scan (not accurate in those with pre-existing COPD)
- CT pulmonary angiography ('gold standard')
- Pulmonary angiogram
- ECG changes (as above)

Complications of pulmonary embolism

- Pulmonary hypertension (multiple small emboli over a period of time)
- PEA cardiac arrest (eg large saddle embolus) – cause of 10% of hospital deaths

CHAPTER 3

Treatment of DVT and PE
- **Analgesia**
- **Graduated compression stocking**
- **Anticoagulation with heparin** (LMW heparin is commonly used). Long-term anticoagulation is undertaken with warfarin: the length of anticoagulation after surgery depends on the underlying cause of the DVT and the continued presence of any risk factors; a simple DVT due to transient immobility usually requires 3 months' anticoagulation
- **Caval filter:** to reduce the risk of fatal PE when an extensive DVT is present (eg iliofemoral) or when there have been multiple emboli; a filter may be placed into the inferior vena cava (IVC) (this looks like the bare spokes of an umbrella on imaging)
- **Fibrinolytic agents** may be used in cases of very extensive DVT (note: not after major surgery)

Anticoagulation

> ## Learning point
>
> Many surgical patients are pharmacologically anticoagulated because of associated co-morbidity either pre- or postoperatively.
> In addition some patients have pathological defects in clotting, eg due to liver disease.
> Perioperative management of anticoagulation is important because poor management leads to a risk of haemorrhage or thrombosis.
> Pharmacological anticoagulants include:
> - Heparin (eg unfractionated and LMW)
> - Warfarin
> - Antiplatelet agents (eg aspirin, dipyridamole, clopidogrel)

Anticoagulants

Many preoperative elective surgical patients are on some form of anticoagulation. Management depends on the type of anticoagulation and the reason for the anticoagulation.

For elective surgical patients on oral anticoagulation, the challenge is to balance the risk of haemorrhage if the INR is not reduced, against the risk of thrombosis if the INR is reduced for too long or by too great an amount.

Antiplatelet agents

Aspirin

Usually this is given as prophylaxis against cerebrovascular disease, ischaemic heart disease and peripheral vascular disease.

Low-dose aspirin irreversibly acetylates the enzyme cyclo-oxygenase. Affected platelets are therefore unable to synthesise thromboxane A_2 and become inactivated throughout their 7-day lifespan. Other NSAIDs cause a reversible effect that lasts 3–4 days.

It is often safe to leave patients on aspirin through the perioperative period but in certain procedures, where there is a special risk of bleeding (eg thyroidectomy, transurethral resection of the prostate or TURP), it should be stopped. Due to its long half-life it should be stopped 1 week before the proposed date of surgery.

Other antiplatelet agents

Dipyridamole: this may be used as secondary prophylaxis against thrombosis in patients with ischaemic heart disease, transient ischaemic attack (TIA)/CVAs or PVD who are intolerant to, or have had side effects from, aspirin.

Clopidogrel: this drug is also used in the prevention of thrombotic events in patients with known ischaemic heart disease and TIA/CVAs. There may be slight benefit in combining clopidogrel with aspirin but this raises the risk of catastrophic bleeding. This drug must be stopped 1 week or more before surgery.

Heparin

Heparin is a potent anticoagulant that binds to and activates antithrombin III, thus reducing fibrin formation. Heparin is neutralised with IV protamine (1 mg protamine for every 100 U heparin). It can only be given parenterally or subcutaneously. The dose is monitored by measuring the ratio of the patient's APTT to control plasma. LMW heparins are given on the basis of the patient's weight and do not require monitoring.

LMW heparin (LMWH) is usually given subcutaneously throughout the perioperative period for DVT prophylaxis. It may be stopped 24 hours before the proposed date of surgery in procedures with special risks of bleeding, or where the use of epidural anaesthesia is anticipated. IV heparin has a more profound anticoagulant effect, but a shorter half-life, and only needs to be discontinued 6 hours before a procedure.

Warfarin

Warfarin blocks the synthesis of vitamin K-dependent factors. It prolongs the PT and may slightly elevate the APTT. It is highly plasma-protein-bound, so caution must be exercised when giving other drugs because these may potentiate its effects. Treatment of major bleeding consists of the administration of vitamin K and FFP.

The dose is adjusted to maintain the INR (ratio of the patient's PT to that of control plasma) at a level between 1 and 4, according to the degree of anticoagulation required. Warfarin has a more prolonged effect on anticoagulation. It is usually given to patients at special risk of thrombosis, such as those with artificial heart valves, thrombophilia, previous DVT or PE.

Warfarin's effect is monitored by INR measurement:

INR of 0.8–1.2 Normal coagulation
INR of 1.2–2.0 Mild anticoagulation – moderate risk of surgical bleeding
INR of 2.0–3.5 Normal therapeutic range – severe risk of surgical bleeding
INR of >3.5 Severely anticoagulated – surgery should not be contemplated until INR is reduced

Transfusion medicine

Learning point

Blood products are a scarce and expensive resource, and they are not without risks to the recipient.
- Safety of blood products is maintained by donor selection criteria and screening of all samples
- Compatibility of transfusion is based on the ABO and rhesus D typing

Blood components include:
- Red cell concentrates
- Platelet concentrates
- Granulocytes
- Fresh frozen plasma (FFP)
- Albumin solutions
- Coagulation factors

Use of blood products can be minimised by:
- Autologous transfusion (eg cell saver)
- Pharmacological methods

Adverse effects of transfusion include:
- Immunological reaction (incompatible red cells, white cells, platelets, granulocytes, plasma antibodies)
- Infection

Blood collection, grouping and administration

Blood collection

In the UK, the supply of blood and plasma is based entirely on the goodwill of voluntary, healthy blood donors. Donation from individuals at high risk of viral transmission is excluded and measures are taken to ensure that samples of blood are collected in a sterile and accountable manner.

Over 90% of donated blood is separated into its various constituents to allow prescription of individual components and preparation of pooled plasma from which specific blood products are manufactured.

Blood grouping

Red blood cells carry antigens, typically glycoproteins or glycolipids, which are attached to the red cell membrane. Over 400 groups have been identified, the most important of which are the:

- ABO system
- Rhesus system

ABO system

- Consists of A, B and O allelic genes
- A and B control synthesis of enzymes that add carbohydrate residues to the cell surface glycoproteins
- Antibodies occur naturally in the serum, appropriate to the missing antigen as shown in the table below

Blood group	Antigen on cells	Antibody in plasma
A	A	Anti-B
B	B	Anti-A
AB	A and B	None
O	No A or B antigens	Anti-A and anti-B

Transfusion of red cells expressing an antigen against which the recipient possesses an antibody causes a massive immune response, resulting in clumping and destruction of the donor cells. This causes multisystem failure and is usually fatal.

Transfusion of plasma containing an antibody against an antigen expressed on the red cells

of the recipient will also cause an immune response, but of a lesser degree because the antibody concentration is significantly diluted by the recipient's own plasma.

Antibodies to the ABO antigens are naturally occurring, whereas antibodies to other red cell antigens appear only after sensitisation by transfusion or pregnancy. The rhesus system is an example of this.

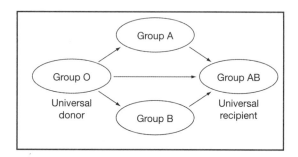

Figure 3.12 The ABO system. Arrows denote compatible transfusion. Group O is termed the 'universal donor' because it is compatible with all three of the other groups. Group AB is termed the 'universal recipient' because these patients can receive blood from any group

Rhesus system

Rhesus-positive (Rh+) patients express the rhesus antigen on their red cells. Rhesus-negative (Rh−) patients do not have antibodies to this antigen unless they have previously been exposed to Rh+ blood (due to previous transfusion or birth of an Rh+ child).

Eighty-five per cent of people are rhesus positive.

All Rh− females of childbearing age should be given Rh− blood because the development of antibodies to the rhesus antigen will cause haemolytic disease of the newborn in any future Rh+ pregnancies.

Blood compatibility testing

Donor and recipient ABO and rhesus type must be compatible. Subsequent testing is to identify additional antibodies in the recipient's serum that may react with the donor's red cells. This can be achieved in one of two ways:

- **Antibody screening:** tests for the presence of antibodies in the recipient's serum to a number of test red cells of the same ABO and rhesus grouping. Agglutination of the test cells indicates the presence of an unusual antibody and this must be characterised further in order to choose compatible red cells for transfusion
- **Cross-matching:** a direct test of compatibility between donor red cells and the recipient's serum

Administration safety

There are a number of safety measures to ensure that ABO-incompatible transfusion does not occur.

Ordering blood products
- Identify the recipient
- Provide adequate information on the request card (name, age, date of birth, hospital number, gender, diagnosis, previous transfusion, pregnancies)
- Ensure adequate labelling of the recipient's blood sample as soon as it is taken to minimise error

When the blood arrives on the ward
- Identify the recipient (name, age, date of birth, hospital number) both verbally, if possible, and by means of the hospital ID bracelet – this must be done by two separate members of staff
- Check that the ABO and rhesus grouping on the front of the unit is compatible with the patient's blood group
- Double-check anything that you aren't comfortable about with the laboratory before commencing transfusion

When transfusing blood, monitor temperature and pulse every 30 minutes
- A sharp spike of temperature (>39°C) at the start of transfusion suggests intravascular haemolysis and the transfusion should be stopped
- Slow elevation of temperature may be due to antibodies against white cells and the infusion should be slowed

If there is any evidence of a severe transfusion reaction
- Stop the infusion
- Recheck patient identity against the unit
- Send the unit back to the blood bank with a fresh sample taken from the patient for comparison
- Supportive management of the patient. Severe reactions may result in cardiovascular collapse

CHAPTER 3

Use of blood products

Learning point

Blood components

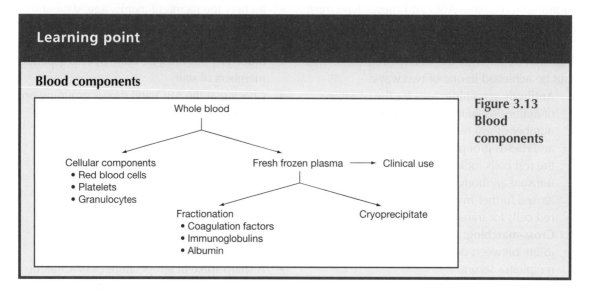

Figure 3.13
Blood
components

Red blood cell concentrates

In whole blood granulocytes and platelets lose function, many coagulation factors lose activity, and aggregates of these dead cells, platelets and other debris are formed unless it is used within a few days.

Red blood cell (RBC) concentrates or packed cells consist of whole blood from which the plasma has been removed. RBCs are suspended in a solution (SAG-M) containing sodium chloride, adenine, glucose and mannitol. The volume of one unit is 350 ml and its shelflife is 35 days at 4°C.

Storage changes include increases in potassium and phosphate concentrations, decreases in pH, haemolysis, microaggregation of dead cells and loss of clotting factor VIII and V activity.

Washed RBCs are used in patients who cannot tolerate granulocyte and platelet debris normally present in RBC concentrates.

Units of **rare blood types** may be stored for up to 3 years at −65°C in glycerol-containing media.

Transfusion of RBC concentrates may occur when Hb <8 g/dl (unless severe ischaemic heart disease when transfusion may occur if Hb <10 g/dl). RBC concentrates should simply be used to increase the oxygen-carrying capacity of the blood. Whole blood should be used for transfusion when there is significant bleeding leading to hypovolaemia, because this replaces volume and clotting factors as well as red cells.

Platelet concentrates

- These are platelets suspended in plasma
- Shelf life is 5 days at room temperature

> **Indications for transfusion of platelets**
> - **Thrombocytopenia** before an invasive procedure
> - **Significant haemorrhage** in the presence of thrombocytopenia
> - **Consumptive coagulopathy** (eg DIC, significant haemorrhage)
> - **Prophylactic transfusion** in patients with thrombocytopenia due to bone marrow failure, chemotherapy or radiotherapy
> - **Prophylactic or therapeutic transfusion** in patients with primary platelet function disorders

Platelet concentrates should be ABO-group-compatible. Anti-D immunoglobulin should be given to premenopausal RhD-negative women to prevent sensitisation.

Granulocytes
- Shelf life is very short – 24 hours at room temperature
- Prepared from a single donor or a pooled collection

Fresh frozen plasma
- Prepared by centrifugation of donor whole blood within 6 hours of collection and frozen at –30°C
- Contains all coagulation factors
- Shelf life is 12 months at –30°C
- Unit volume is about 250 ml (use at a dose rate of 10–15 ml/kg initially)
- Should be used within 1 hour of thawing
- Also high in sodium, glucose and citrate
- Cryoprecipitate is produced by the slow thawing of FFP; this is rich in factors VIII and XIII, fibrinogen and vWF

- Individual clotting factors, immunoglobulins and plasma proteins may be isolated from plasma

> **Indications for FFP transfusion**
> - **Prophylaxis or treatment of haemorrhage** in patients with specific coagulation factor deficiencies for which the specific factor is unavailable
> - **DIC** – together with cryoprecipitate and platelets
> - **Haemorrhage secondary to over-anticoagulation** with warfarin (treatment with vitamin K or prothrombin complex and factor VII may be more effective)
> - **After replacement of large volumes of blood** (eg >4 units) where coagulation abnormalities often occur (guided by APTT)
> - **Thrombotic thrombocytopenic purpura**
> - **Correction of intrinsic clotting disorder** (eg liver coagulopathy) before invasive investigation or surgery

FFP is not indicated in hypovolaemia, plasma exchange, nutritional support or immunodeficiency states.

Group-compatible FFP should be used to prevent Rh immunisation. RhD-compatible FFP should be used in premenopausal women.

Albumin solutions
Albumin should not be used as a general-purpose plasma volume expander; it has no proven benefit over other much cheaper colloid solutions. In addition it should not be used as

parenteral nutrition, or in impaired protein production or chronic protein loss disorders.

The only proven indications for the administration of 20% albumin is diuretic-resistant oedema in hypoproteinaemic patients and in cirrhosis associated with ascites in situations of hepatorenal syndrome, spontaneous bacterial peritonitis and post-paracentesis syndrome.

Coagulation factors

- **Cryoprecipitate:** used in haemorrhagic disorders with a fibrinogen deficiency (eg DIC)

- **Factor VIII concentrate:** for treatment of haemophilia A and von Willebrand's disease
- **Factor IX concentrate:** contains factors IX, X, and XI. It is used in the treatment of haemophilia B and congenital deficiencies of factors X and XI. When combined with factor VII concentrate it is more effective than FFP in the treatment of severe haemorrhage due to excessive warfarinisation and liver disease
- **Other specific coagulation factors:** are available including anticoagulant factors, protein C and antithrombin III

Pharmacological strategies to minimise use of blood products
- **Aprotinin:** haemostatic agent; precise mechanism of action unknown; shown to decrease re-operation secondary to bleeding in cardiac surgery
- **Tranexamic acid/ε-aminocaproic acid:** lysine analogues that inhibit fibrinolysis
- **Desmopressin (DDAVP):** analogue of vasopressin that elevates factor VIII levels and promotes platelet aggregation (Note: can cause vasodilatation and hypotension)
- **Erythropoietin (EPO):** renal hormone that induces red cell progenitor proliferation and differentiation; it can be used to raise haematocrit pre-op but there are concerns about thrombotic side effects

---

Autologous transfusion

Concerns over the potential complications associated with blood transfusions mean that autotransfusion has become more popular. There are three methods of administering an autologous transfusion:
- **Pre-deposit:** blood is taken from the patient in the weeks before admission for elective surgery
- **Haemodilution:** blood is taken immediately before surgery and then reintroduced postoperatively
- **Intraoperative:** blood lost during the operation is processed and

re-infused immediately (eg cell saver). Contraindications are exposure of the blood to a site of infection, or the possibility of contamination with malignant cells

Autologous transfusion (by the first two methods) is contraindicated in patients with active infection, unstable angina, aortic stenosis or severe hypertension. Due to patient restriction and high administration costs, autotransfusion has a limited role in the UK although it is used extensively overseas (especially in areas with high risks of viral transmission).

CHAPTER 3

Adverse effects of blood transfusions

Early complications of blood transfusion – immunological complications

Incompatible red cells

The mortality associated with the transfusion of blood products is around 1 per 100 000 U transfused. ABO incompatibility is the most common cause of death and is predominately due to clerical errors.

Learning point

Adverse effects of blood transfusion may be classified by:
- **Timescale** (early vs late)
- **Volume** (complications of large-volume transfusion)
- **Repetition** of transfusion

Early complications:
- Immunological complications
- Incompatible red cells (acute haemolytic reaction)
- Incompatible white cells (pyrexia)
- Incompatible platelets (purpura)
- Reaction to plasma (anaphylaxis)
- Fluid overload
- Transfusion-related acute lung injury (TRALI)

Late complications:
- Infection
- Delayed hypersensitivity reaction
- Volume complications: the effects of massive transfusion
- Citrate toxicity
- Acidosis
- Hypocalcaemia
- Hyperkalaemia
- Hypothermia
- Clotting abnormalities
- Repetitive transfusion complications
- Iron overload

Immediate haemolytic transfusion reactions
- Most severe haemolytic transfusion reactions are due to ABO incompatibility
- 5–10 ml of blood is sufficient to cause a reaction
- Symptoms: rigors, substernal pain, restlessness
- Signs: fever, hypotension, bleeding, haemoglobinuria, oliguria, jaundice
- Rhesus incompatibility does not cause complement activation and is usually milder

Delayed haemolytic transfusion reactions
- Typically occur 5–10 days after transfusion
- Occur in approximately 1 in 500 transfusions
- Due to a secondary response; occurs in patients who have been immunised to a foreign antigen by a previous transfusion or pregnancy, but in whom tests before the transfusion do not detect the low antibody concentration
- Signs are minimal: unexplained pyrexia, jaundice, unexplained drop in Hb (anaemia), urobilinogenuria
- Management includes:
  - Blood film (shows spherocytosis or reticulocytosis)
  - Direct antiglobulin test
  - Check liver function tests (LFTs), clotting and red cell antibody screens

CHAPTER 3

Incompatible white cells

- Febrile reactions
- Relatively common in patients who have had previous transfusions or have been pregnant
- Symptoms: facial flushing and fever shortly after commencing the transfusion
- Due to the recipient's leucocyte antibodies complexing with donor leucocytes and causing the release of pyrogens from monocytes and granulocytes
- Most reactions respond to slowing the transfusion and giving aspirin or paracetamol

Incompatible platelets

Post-transfusion purpura may occur in patients who have been previously sensitised to a foreign platelet antigen. On subsequent exposure they mount a secondary response, which causes destruction of the patient's own platelets.

Adverse reactions to plasma

- Urticaria results from a patient's IgE antibody complexing with a protein present in the donor's plasma; it usually responds to slowing the transfusion rate and administering an antihistamine
- Anaphylactic reactions rarely occur; they are usually due to anti-IgA antibodies in the patient's plasma binding to normal IgA in the donor's plasma; the incidence of anti-IgA individuals is about 1 in 1000

Transfusion-related acute lung injury (TRALI)

This is the result of incompatibility between donor antibodies and recipient granulocytes.
- Clinical picture similar to ARDS
- Can occur 30 minutes to several days after transfusion

- Fever, dyspnoea, cough
- Chest radiograph: shadowing in perihilar and lower lung fields
- Treat as for ARDS

Late complications of blood transfusion

Infectious complications

- Hepatitis viruses (HBV and HCV)
- HIV
- Syphilis
- Variant Creutzfeldt–Jakob disease (vCJD)
- CMV
- Parvovirus:
  - Can cause aplastic crisis in a patient with sickle cell anaemia
- Bacteria:
  - Very uncommon
  - Incidence less than 1 in 1×10^6 units
  - *Yersinia enterocolitica* and *Pseudomonas* spp. are the most common
  - Usually caused by delayed administration of donated blood (when stored at room temperature, blood is an excellent culture medium)
- Parasites
  - Recent travel to regions where malaria is endemic is a contraindication to blood donation
  - *Plasmodium malariae* has a long incubation period so a few cases of transfusion-related malaria still occur

Screening of donations

- **Anti-HCV and anti-HBsAg** (anti-hepatitis B surface antigen): incidence of hepatitis B transmission is about 1 in 200 000 units transfused; the risk of hepatitis C transmission is between 1 in 150 000 and 1 in 200 000

- **Anti-HIV-1 and anti-HIV-2**: since the 1980s all blood has been screened for HIV. Some patients (eg those with haemophilia) who received regular transfusion before this time have been infected. Risk of transmission is now less than 1 in 2×10^6 units
- Syphilis
- Variant CJD is a prion disease and the transmissible element (the prion) has been found in leucocytes. All blood for transfusion from 2000 onwards is now leucocyte-depleted

Complications associated with massive transfusion

This is defined as transfusion of the total blood volume in <24 hours. It can result in:

- Cardiac abnormalities (ventricular arrhythmias) due to low temperature, high potassium concentration and excess citrate with low calcium concentration
- ARDS/acute lung injury
- DIC

Citrate toxicity

- Neonates and hypothermic patients find it difficult to excrete citrate
- Citrate binds ionised calcium and also potentially lowers serum calcium levels
- Need cardiac monitoring

Acidosis

- Lactic acid produced by red cell glycolysis
- Can exacerbate acidosis of the acutely shocked patient
- Transfusion usually improves acidosis due to reversal of hypoxia and improved tissue perfusion

Hypocalcaemia

- Citrate normally rapidly metabolised so effects not normally seen
- Corrected by 10% calcium gluconate if the patient has an abnormal ECG

Hyperkalaemia

- Plasma potassium content of blood increases with its storage
- More problematic during massive transfusion

Hypothermia

- From rapid transfusion of stored blood
- Use blood warmers

Clotting abnormalities

- Lack of platelets and clotting factors in stored blood
  - Give FFP during massive transfusions
  - Consider platelets if level $<50 \times 10^9/l$
- DIC

Complications associated with repetitive transfusions

When patients undergo repetitive transfusions they may develop antibodies to lesser-known blood groups. It is therefore important if the patient has undergone multiple transfusions (either in the past or at present admission) to indicate this on the request card so that direct compatibility between donor and recipient blood can be made. This minimises the risks of transfusion reactions. Multiple antibodies can make the patient very difficult to cross-match.

CHAPTER 3

Miscellaneous complications of blood transfusion

- Fluid overload
- Air embolus
- Iron overload
- Immunosuppression: there is some evidence that blood transfusion results in a poorer prognosis in patients with colorectal cancer
- Graft-versus-host disease (GVHD) – immunodeficient patients at risk

Lymphoreticular malignancy

Leukaemia

Learning point

Leukaemias are a group of neoplastic disorders of white blood cells. The cells replace the bone marrow and may spill over into the blood or infiltrate other organs. The leukaemias can be divided into:
- Myeloid or lymphoid
- Acute (blastic) or chronic

	Myeloid	Lymphoid
Acute	**Acute myelogenous leukaemia (AML)** Group of neoplastic disorders of the haematopoietic precursor cells of the bone marrow	**Acute lymphocytic leukaemia (ALL)** Malignant proliferation of lymphoblasts
Chronic	**Chronic myelogenous leukaemia (CML)** Group characterised by an uncontrolled proliferation of granulocytes	**Chronic lymphocytic leukaemia (CLL)** Monoclonal expansion of lymphocytes

Clinical features of leukaemia

Presentation depends on whether the condition is acute or chronic (chronic is often asymptomatic but may have an acute 'blastic' phase or crisis, eg CML).

Constitutional symptoms
- Malaise
- Weakness
- Fever
- Polyarthritis

Bone marrow failure causing pancytopenia
- Anaemia
- Infection (neutropenia)
- Oral ulceration and gingival overgrowth
- Bleeding (thrombocytopenia)

Leukaemic infiltration
- Bone pain
- Central nervous system (CNS) symptoms (eg cranial nerves, cord compression)
- Splenomegaly
- Hepatomegaly
- Lymphadenopathy

Pathology of leukaemia

A clone of malignant cells may arise at any stage of maturation in either the lymphoid, myeloid or pluripotential stages. Aetiology is thought to be:
- Genetic: correlations seen in twin studies and Down syndrome; the Philadelphia chromosome is seen characteristically in CML
- Environmental: viruses, radiation exposure, chemicals, drugs (eg alkylating chemotherapeutic agents)

Diagnosis of leukaemia

There are characteristic cells in blood and bone marrow (BM):

- ALL: characterised by a homogeneous infiltrate of at least 30% lymphoblasts; usually small with scant cytoplasm, no granules and indistinct nucleolus
- AML: BM aspirate shows blast cells of myeloid origin. Multiple large nucleoli, delicate chromatin, grey–blue cytoplasm and Auer rods (presence of Auer rods is virtually diagnostic of AML)
- CLL: BM infiltration exceeds 30% lymphocytes, which are mature with <55% atypical or blast forms. The nuclei are round, cytoplasm is scant, chromatin is compact, nucleoli are inconspicuous and mitotic figures are rare
- CML: BM is hypercellular, with expansion of the myeloid cell line (ie neutrophils, eosinophils, basophils) and its progenitor cells

Specific forms of leukaemia

Acute lymphocytic leukaemia

- Predominantly a disease of childhood (occurrence in adults has worse prognosis)
- May be pre-B-cell, T-cell or null-cell type
- Tends to present with bone pain or pancytopenia due to BM infiltration with malignant cells
- Often there is neutropenia and fever
- Treated with chemotherapy. Remission occurs in 65–85%. BM transplantation is considered for relapsing disease (eg allogeneic sibling donor or unrelated)

Acute myelogenous leukaemia

- Increasing incidence with age (median 65 years)
- More common in men
- Long-term complication of previous chemotherapy (eg for lymphoma)
- Tends to present with pancytopenia and hepatosplenomegaly
- Treatment with chemotherapy ± BM transplantation

Chronic lymphocytic leukaemia

- Usually >40 years
- 25% leukaemias
- Twice as common in men
- Presents with lymphadenopathy
- 99% are B-cell malignancies (1% T cell)
- Staging relates to presence of BM failure and correlates well with survival

Chronic myelogenous leukaemia

- Commonly occurs age 40–50
- Slight male preponderance
- 15% leukaemias
- Presents with leucocytosis and splenomegaly
- Constitutional symptoms common
- Has three phases: chronic (responsive to treatment), accelerating or transitional (unresponsive to treatment) and blastic (pre-terminal)

Lymphoma

Learning point

- Lymphoma is a cancer of the reticulo-endothelial system
- Lymphoma may be subclassified into Hodgkin's lymphoma and non-Hodgkin's lymphoma
- Hodgkin's lymphoma predominantly affects young people and generally has a good prognosis
- Non-Hodgkin's lymphoma generally affects middle-aged and elderly people

Rye classification of Hodgkin's lymphoma

1	Lymphocyte-predominant	15%
2	Nodular sclerosing	40%
3	Mixed cellularity	30%
4	Lymphocyte-depleted	15%

The prognosis worsens from 1 to 4

Hodgkin's lymphoma

Demographics of Hodgkin's lymphoma

Common in:
- Males
- Young adults

Clinical features of Hodgkin's lymphoma
- Painless progressive lymph node enlargement (cervical/supraclavicular)
- Malaise, fever, weight loss, pruritus
- Superior vena cava (SVC) obstruction
- Bone pain (extranodal disease)
- Splenomegaly, hepatomegaly

Pathology of Hodgkin's lymphoma
- Must have Reed–Sternberg (RS) cells
- Rubbery nodes
- Can involve bone, lungs and liver

Staging of Hodgkin's lymphoma

Based on the Ann Arbor classification:

A Absence of systemic symptoms (ie weight loss, fever, night sweats)
B Presence of above symptoms
I   Confined to one lymph node site
II In more than one lymph node site but confined to one side of the diaphragm
III Nodes above and below the diaphragm
IV Spread beyond lymphatic system (eg liver and bone)

Diagnosis of Hodgkin's lymphoma
- Node excision biopsy
- Chest radiograph: mediastinal nodes
- IVU: retroperitoneal nodes compressing renal calyces
- CT scan

Staging laparotomy is now rarely done due to improved imaging techniques.

Treatment of Hodgkin's lymphoma
- Stage I: radiotherapy
- Stages II–IV: combination chemotherapy

Has an 80% cure rate in good prognostic groups (ie lymphocyte-predominant stage I).

Non-Hodgkin's lymphoma

Non-Hodgkin's lymphomas (NHLs) are tumours originating from lymphoid tissues, mainly of lymph nodes. They are a progressive clonal expansion of B cells (85%) or T cells, NK cells or macrophages. This is a very diverse group of conditions, each with distinct and different clinical features.

- Usually present in patients aged >50 but some aggressive NHLs can be seen in children
- Classification is based on morphology and grade (low, medium, high)
- Staging is based on the Ann Arbor stages discussed above

Treatment consists of chemotherapy ± radiotherapy of the involved field. BM transplant may be considered for relapse.

Poor prognostic factors include:
- Age >60 years
- More than one region affected
- Stage >II
- Longer time for response to chemotherapy (eg more than three cycles)

Multiple myeloma

Learning point

Multiple myeloma is a neoplastic proliferation of plasma cells resulting in gradual replacement of the bone marrow with cancer cells.
It causes pancytopenia, bone symptoms, hypercalcaemia and renal impairment.

Multiple myeloma is a malignant proliferation of monoclonal plasma cells with production of an individual paraprotein. Common in the 65–70 age group with a male:female ratio of 3:2.

Clinical features of multiple myeloma

- BM replacement with proliferating plasma cells causes pancytopenia (anaemia, bleeding secondary to thrombocytopenia)
- Lytic bone lesions (bone pain, risk of pathological fractures, hypercalcaemia, spinal cord compression)
- Soft-tissue masses
- Over-production of antibodies causes:
  - Renal impairment
  - Hyperviscosity
  - Amyloidosis
- Impaired humoral immunity (susceptible to infection with encapsulated organisms)
- Asymptomatic patients may be identified through screening (consider this diagnosis if total protein level is more than albumin + globulin)

Pathology of multiple myeloma

Aetiology is thought to be a combination of:
- Genetic factors
- Environmental exposure to chemicals in agriculture
- Radiation exposure

Investigating multiple myeloma

- FBC – normal, or evidence of pancytopenia
- ESR – virtually always very high
- Urea and electrolytes (U&Es) (evidence of renal failure)
- Calcium (often raised)
- Uric acid (may be normal or raised)
- 24-hour urine collection for Bence Jones protein (λ light chains)

CHAPTER 3

- Plasma electrophoresis for paraprotein band
- β_2-microglobulin and CRP are prognostic indicators
- Skeletal radiographs or targeted MRI (osteoporosis, crush fractures, osteolytic lesions)
- Pepper-pot skull is characteristic

Classification of multiple myeloma
This is based on the monoclonal product:
- 55% IgG
- 25% IgA
- 20% light-chain disease

Staging of multiple myeloma
- Stage I involves all of the following:
  - Haemoglobin >10 g/dl
  - Calcium <12 mg/dl
  - Radiograph showing normal bones or solitary plasmacytoma
  - Low M protein values (IgG <5 g/dl, IgA <3 g/dl, urine <4 g/24 h)
- Stage III involves any one of the following:
  - Haemoglobin <8.5 g/dl
  - Calcium level >12 mg/dl
  - Radiograph showing advanced lytic bone disease
  - High M protein value (IgG >7 g/dl, IgA >5 g/dl, urine >12 g/24 h)
- Stage II is anything in-between

These three stages are subclassified according to renal function (A = normal creatinine; B = elevated creatinine).

Mean survival
- 60 months for stage I
- 42 months for stage II
- 23 months for stage III

Diagnosis of multiple myeloma
- Monoclonal band on plasma electrophoresis
- Bence Jones protein in urine
- Plasma cells on BM biopsy
- Osteolytic bone lesions

Cannot diagnose on the basis of paraproteinaemia alone.

Treatment of multiple myeloma
- Myeloablative therapy (high-dose radiotherapy and chemotherapy) with autotransplantation of BM stem cells
- Plasmapheresis for renal failure
- Hydration and bisphosphonates for hypercalcaemia
- Radiotherapy for bone pain (myeloma is highly radiosensitive)
- Vaccinate against encapsulated organisms

1.3 Fluid balance and fluid replacement therapy

Learning point

Body fluids are predominantly composed of:
- Water
- Ions
- Proteins

The movement of fluids within the body and across capillary membranes depends on the relative concentration of these three components in each compartment. Different concentrations of these components exert forces across cell membranes. The net movement of fluid depends on the balance of these forces. These forces include:
- Osmotic pressure
- Hydrostatic pressure

Body fluid composition

Water distribution within the body

Water makes up about 60% of a man and 50% of a woman (due to higher body fat) and 75% of a child. The majority of water in the body is from oral intake. In addition, a small volume (150–250 ml/day) is produced as the result of oxidation of hydrogen during the oxidative phosphorylation phase of metabolism.

- **Total body water** (TBW) is the total volume of water in the body
- **Extracellular fluid** (ECF) is the fluid outside the cells
- **Intracellular fluid** (ICF) is the fluid inside the cells (TBW – ECF)
- **Plasma** is blood without cells, containing proteins, water and electrolytes

Transcellular fluid is defined as being separated by a layer of epithelium; it includes cerebrospinal fluid (CSF), intraocular, pleural, synovial and digestive secretions, and gut luminal fluid. Volume is relatively small. If the transcellular compartment is very large, it may be called the 'third space' because fluid in this compartment is not readily exchangeable with the rest of the ECF.

- Intravascular volume is the fluid within the vascular compartment
- Interstitial fluid is the fluid within tissues (ECF – intravascular volume)

Distribution of water in a 70-kg man
Total body water is 45 l (57%).
One-third is extracellular fluid (15 l):
- Plasma (3.5 l)
- Interstitial/tissue fluid (8.5 l)
- Lymph (1.5 l)
- Transcellular fluid (1.5 l)

Two-thirds is intracellular fluid (30 l) found in the cell cytoplasm

---

Distribution of ions in the body

ION COMPOSITION OF BODY FLUIDS		
Ions	Extracellular fluid (mmol/l)	Intracellular fluid (mmol/l)
Cations		
Na^+	135–145	4–10
K^+	3.5–5.0	150
Ca^{2+} ionised	1.0–1.25	0.001
Ca^{2+} total	2.12–2.65	–
Mg^{2+}	1.0	40
Anions		
Bicarbonate	25	10
Chloride	95–105	15
Phosphate	1.1	100
Organic anions	3.0	0
Protein	1.1	8

In ICF:
- K^+ and Mg^{2+} are the main cations
- Phosphate, proteins and organic ions are the main anions

In ECF:
- Na^+ is the main cation
- Chloride (Cl^-) and bicarbonate (HCO_3^-) are the major anions

Regulation of potassium (K^+)

Potassium is the main intracellular cation and its levels inside the cell are maintained by the Na^+/K^+ ATPase pump which was discussed earlier in this chapter. Plasma levels of potassium are tightly regulated because hypokalaemia and hyperkalaemia may manifest in abnormalities of cardiac function.

Control of potassium levels in the plasma

Potassium levels in the plasma are controlled by:
- **Dietary intake:** foods that are high in potassium include bananas, chocolate,

avocado, baked beans, lentils, tomatoes and milk

- **Renal excretion:** filtration of potassium in the renal tubule depends on the plasma concentration. However, the resorption of sodium in the collecting ducts depends on exchange for potassium. This is controlled by aldosterone, which is produced in response to low plasma sodium and low blood pressure. Aldosterone may also be produced in response to high plasma potassium levels
- **Plasma pH:** hydrogen ions move in and out of cells in exchange for potassium ions. When hydrogen levels in the plasma rise, hydrogen enters the cell in exchange for potassium, thus raising the plasma potassium levels. When hydrogen levels in the plasma fall, hydrogen leaves the cell in exchange for potassium, thus lowering the plasma potassium levels. In addition, in an attempt to retain hydrogen ions in alkalotic states the kidney preferentially secretes potassium
- **Hormones:** insulin, adrenaline and aldosterone stimulate cellular uptake of potassium. Hyperaldosteronism (in renal artery stenosis, cirrhosis, nephrotic syndrome and severe heart failure) is associated with hypokalaemia

---

Drugs that affect potassium levels in the body

Drugs that increase potassium levels
- Angiotensin-converting enzyme (ACE) inhibitors
- Angiotensin II receptor antagonists
- Ciclosporin
- Potassium salts

Drugs that decrease potassium levels
- Loop and thiazide diuretics
- Corticosteroids
- β_2 Agonists
- Amphotericin
- Theophylline

Control of sodium levels in the plasma

Sodium is the most common extracellular cation and it is important in regulating the amount and distribution of water in the body. Excess sodium results in water retention and too little sodium may result in neuromuscular dysfunction. Total body sodium levels depend on amounts ingested and the amount of renal excretion. The concentration of sodium in the body depends on the amount of total body water. Non-renal excretion (eg sweat, faeces) is usually small but may be significant if there is prolonged diarrhoea or large surface area burns.

- **Sodium intake:** high sodium levels stimulate the hypothalamus and generate thirst. The addition of salt to food and consumption of high-sodium food depends on dietary habits
- **Sodium excretion:** sodium is filtered freely through the glomerular membrane of the kidney and so the sodium concentration in the filtrate depends on the plasma sodium; 65% of the sodium filtered is passively reabsorbed in the proximal convoluted tubule and the remainder is actively reabsorbed by the Na^+/K^+ pump in the ascending limb of the loop of Henle. Atrial natriuretic peptide (ANP) is produced in response to fluid overload and promotes sodium excretion by decreasing resorption. Antidiuretic hormone (ADH) is produced in response to increased plasma osmolality and acts to increase water resorption in the distal nephron, so restoring sodium concentration.

Fluid movement across the capillary membrane

Plasma proteins

The capillary barrier is readily permeable to ions but impermeable to proteins, so plasma proteins determine the osmotic pressure within the capillary. Albumin accounts for 75% of this osmotic pressure within the capillary lumen.

The capillary

The capillary is the site of fluid and solute exchange between the interstitium of the tissues and the bloodstream. Arterioles become meta-arterioles and then capillary beds. The flow through each capillary is regulated by a precapillary sphincter which controls flow through the capillary bed. A capillary wall is a single layer of endothelial cells surrounded by a basement membrane. There are potential spaces between adjacent cells and their size regulates permeability to solutes.

Osmotic pressure

Osmosis is a form of diffusion of water molecules across a semipermeable membrane when there is a different concentration (osmolality) of solutes on either side. This is because the number or concentration of particles in solution on either side of the membrane generates osmotic pressure. Water is drawn by osmotic pressure, moving from regions of low osmotic pressure to regions of higher osmotic pressure. Osmotic pressure can be generated by ions (eg Na^+ or Cl^-) or by proteins.

- **Capillary osmotic pressure** refers to the pressure generated by the plasma proteins inside the capillary. It is sometimes called colloid osmotic pressure, or even oncotic pressure
- **Tissue osmotic pressure** refers to the pressure generated by the interstitial fluid. The oncotic pressure of the interstitial fluid depends on the interstitial protein concentration and the permeability of the capillary wall to proteins. The more permeable the capillary barrier is to proteins, the higher the tissue osmotic pressure

Hydrostatic pressure

Hydrostatic pressure is the difference between the capillary pressure (ie perfusion pressure generated by the blood pressure) and the pressure of interstitial fluid within the tissues.

- **Capillary hydrostatic pressure** is determined by the blood pressure and the differential between arterial and venous pressures
- **Tissue hydrostatic pressure** is determined by the interstitial fluid volume and the

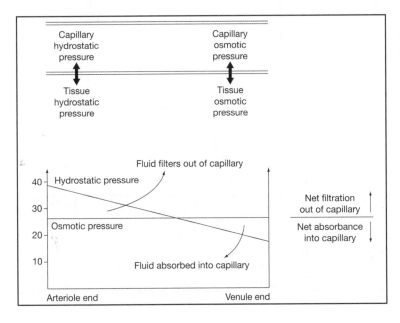

Figure 3.14 The movement of fluids across the capillary membrane

compliance of the tissue, which is related to the ability of the tissue volume to increase and accommodate more fluid

Movement of fluid across capillary membranes: the Starling hypothesis

The distribution of ECF between plasma and the interstitial space is regulated at the membrane of the capillaries and lymphatics.

The movement of fluid at the capillary membrane is shown in Figure 3.14. In normal tissue there are few proteins in the interstitial fluid and the capillary is impermeable to plasma proteins and so the osmotic pressure across the membrane is considered to be constant (about 25 mmHg).

In addition the tissue hydrostatic pressure is relatively constant. The capillary hydrostatic pressure is high at the arterial end of the capillary, favouring net filtration of fluid into the interstitium. As fluid moves along the capillary towards the venous end, the hydrostatic pressure falls.

There tends to be a net flow of water out of the capillary into the interstitium at the arteriolar end of the capillary, and a net flow back into the capillary at the venular end of the capillary.

Starling's equation

Movement of fluid across capillary:

K = outward pressure − inward pressure

where:

K = filtration constant for the capillary membrane

Outward pressure = capillary hydrostatic pressure + tissue osmotic pressure

Inward pressure = tissue hydrostatic pressure + capillary osmotic pressure

---

Oedema

This describes the clinical observation of excess tissue fluid (ie interstitial fluid).

The causes of oedema include:
- Increased capillary hydrostatic pressure (eg venous obstruction, fluid overload)
- Decreased capillary oncotic pressure (eg causes of hypoproteinaemia such as nephrotic syndrome or cirrhosis)
- Increased tissue oncotic pressure (eg resulting from increased capillary permeability due to burns or inflammation)
- Decreased tissue hydrostatic pressure

Fluid management

DAILY FLUID AND ELECTROLYTE MAINTENANCE REQUIREMENTS

Electrolyte/ water	Total average 70-kg male adult (mmol)	Per kg body weight (mmol)
Na$^+$	70–140	1–2
K$^+$	70	1.0
Cl$^-$	70	1.0
PO$_4^{3-}$	14	0.2
Ca^{2+}	7.0	0.1
Mg^{2+}	7.0	0.1
Water	2500 ml	35 ml

AVERAGE DAILY WATER BALANCE FOR SEDENTARY ADULT IN TEMPERATE CONDITIONS

	Input (ml)		Output (ml)
Drink	1500	Urine	1500
Food	750	Faeces	100
Metabolic	350	Lungs	400
Total	2600	Total	2600

Fever increases maintenance fluid requirement by 20% of the daily insensible loss for each 1°C rise. Most clinicians give an extra 1 litre per 24 hours for each 1°C rise.

In general, fluid maintenance needs can be gauged by maintaining an adequate urine output (>0.5 ml/kg per hour). The patient's daily weight is also essential for adequate assessment.

(Note that mechanical ventilation also increases insensible fluid loss).

DAILY GI SECRETIONS AND ELECTROLYTE COMPOSITION

	Volume (ml/24 h) (range)	Na$^+$ (mmol/l)	K$^+$ (mmol/l)	Cl$^-$ (mmol/l)	HCO$^-$ (mmol/l)
Saliva	1500 (1000–15 000)	10	26	10	30
Stomach	1500 (1000–2500)	60	10	130	–
Duodenum	Variable (100–2000)	140	5	80	–
Ileum	3000 (100–9000)	140	5	104	–
Colon	Minimal	60	30	40	–
Pancreas	500 (100–800)	140	5	75	115
Bile	800 (50–800)	145	5	100	35

Summary of fluid balance considerations

- Patient size and age
- Abnormal ongoing losses, pre-existing deficits or excesses, fluid shifts
- Renal and cardiovascular function
- Look at fluid balance charts over preceding 24 hours
- Check serum electrolytes

Fluid loss and surgical trauma

Surgical trauma
↓
ADH release and aldosterone from adrenal glands
↓
Water conservation, Na$^+$ retention, K$^+$ excretion

Therefore perioperative fluid balance must be carefully monitored in relation to electrolytes and volume.

Sources of excess fluid loss in surgical patients

- Blood loss (eg trauma, surgery)
- Plasma loss (eg burns)
- GI fluid loss (eg vomiting, diarrhoea, ileostomy, bowel obstruction)
- Intra-abdominal inflammatory fluid loss (eg pancreatitis)
- Sepsis
- Abnormal insensible loss (eg fever, mechanical ventilation with no humidification)

It is essential for an accurate fluid chart to be kept. This records all fluid intake (oral and IV) and all output (urine, drain fluid, GI contents, etc), and provides a balance for each 24 hours, once insensible loss has been estimated.

Assessing fluid depletion

Patient evaluation

History
- Thirst, obvious fluid loss
- Fluid intake, fluid output
- Check charts for fluid balance

Examination
- Dry mucous membranes
- Reduced capillary refill time
- Sunken eyes
- Low skin elasticity
- Low urine output
- Increase in heart rate
- Low BP/pulse pressure
- Confusion

Routes of fluid replacement

Enteral fluids

Oral fluid replacement is suitable if the GI tract is functioning and the deficiency is not excessive (ie post-obstructive diuresis). However, this is not always possible (eg paralytic ileus after surgery).

Parenteral fluids

IV fluid replacement is needed if the GI tract is not functioning properly or if rapid fluid replacement is required. Parenteral fluids can broadly be divided into crystalloid, colloid and blood.

Fluid administration

Types of fluid replacement

Water

This is given as a 5% dextrose solution. Dextrose is a carbohydrate monomer and is metabolised, leaving net pure water.

Crystalloid solutions

All are isotonic with body fluid.
- **Physiological saline** (0.9%) contains 154 mmol/l Na^+, 154 mmol/l Cl^-
- **5% dextrose** contains 278 mmol/l dextrose (calorific content is negligible)
- **Dextrose saline** (0.18% saline; 4% dextrose) contains 30 mmol/l Na^+, 30 mmol/l Cl^-, 222 mmol/l dextrose
- **Hartmann's solution** contains 131 mmol/l Na^+, 5 mmol/l K^+, 29 mmol/l HCO_3^-, 111 mmol/l Cl^-, 2 mmol/l Ca^{2+}
- **Ringer's solution** contains 147 mmol/l Na^+, 4 mmol/l K^+, 156 mmol/l Cl^- and 2.2 mmol/l Ca^{2+}

Colloid solutions

- Albumin (4.5%)
  - Natural blood product
  - M_r 45 000–70 000 (natural, therefore broad-range M_r)
  - No clotting factors
  - Small risk of anaphylaxis
  - Limited availability/expensive
- Gelatins (Haemaccel/gelofusine/Volplex)
  - Modified gelatins (from hydrolysis of bovine collagen)
  - Half-life 8–10 hours
  - Low incidence allergic reaction

Note that Haemaccel contains K^+ and Ca^{2+} so, if mixed with citrated blood in a giving set, leads to coagulation of the residual blood.

Dextrans

- Glucose polymers
  - Dextran 40: average M_r is 40 000
  - Dextran 70: average M_r is 70 000
- Half-life 16 hours
- Dextran 40 is filtered by the kidney but Dextran 70 is not, so Dextran 70 stays in circulation for longer

- Dextran interferes with cross-matching blood and coagulation (forms red blood cell rouleaux) – it is also nephrotoxic and can cause allergic reactions

- Low incidence anaphylaxis and no interference with cross-matching
- Expensive

Hetastarch

- 6% hetastarch in saline
- Half-life 16–24 hours
- M_r 120 000
- Must limit dose to 1500 ml/kg (excess leads to coagulation problems)

Use of common fluids

When prescribing fluid regimens for patients, we need to consider three aspects of fluid replacement:

- Basal requirements
- Continuing abnormal losses over and above basal requirements
- Pre-existing dehydration and electrolyte loss

Basal fluid requirements

Common daily maintenance regimens for a 70-kg adult in a temperate environment

Regimen A

- 1 litre physiological saline (0.9%) + 20 mmol KCl over 8 hours
- 1 litre 5% dextrose + 20 mmol KCl over 8 hours
- 1 litre 5% dextrose + 20 mmol KCl over 8 hours

This provides: 3 litres water, 60 mmol K⁺, 150 mmol Na⁺

Regimen B

- 1 litre dextrose saline + 20 mmol KCl over 8 hours
- 1 litre dextrose saline + 20 mmol KCl over 8 hours
- 1 litre dextrose saline + 20 mmol KCl over 8 hours

This provides: 3 litres water, 60 mmol K⁺, 90 mmol Na⁺

Note that metabolism of dextrose may lead to effectively administering hypotonic saline. Therefore, regimen B is suitable only in the short term.

Correction of pre-existing dehydration

Patients who are dehydrated will need to be resuscitated with fluid over and above their basal requirements. The important issues are:

- To identify from which compartment or compartments the fluid has been lost
- To assess the extent of the dehydration

The fluid used to resuscitate the patient should be similar to that which has been lost. It is usually easy to decide where the losses are coming from. Bowel losses come from the ECF, pure water losses come from the total body water and protein-containing fluid is lost from the plasma. There is frequently a combination of these.

Fluid regimens and potassium (K⁺)

In the first 24 hours after non-cardiac surgery, potassium is often omitted from the IV fluid regimen. There is a tendency for potassium to rise during and after surgery because of:

- Cell injury (high intracellular potassium concentration released into plasma)
- Blood transfusions
- Decreased renal potassium clearance due to transient renal impairment in the immediate postop period
- Opposed action of insulin by 'stress hormones' tends to cause potassium release from the cells

However, potassium should be replaced in patients who are on intravenous fluids for prolonged periods of time.

Therefore perioperative fluid balance must be carefully monitored in relation to electrolytes and volume.

It is essential for an accurate fluid chart to be kept. This records all fluid intake (oral and IV) and all output (urine, drain fluid, GI contents, etc), and provides a balance for each 24 hours, once insensible loss has been estimated.

1.4 Surgical biochemistry and acid–base balance

Acid–base balance

Acids, bases and buffers

Normal physiological function depends on a narrow range of pH (7.35–7.45). The major products of metabolism are acids (CO_2 and organic acids). The body prevents the pH level straying too far from the ideal with the use of buffering systems and by excretion of the excess acid via the lungs and the renal system.

A buffering system usually consists of a weak acid and its conjugate base.

Learning point

The products of metabolism are predominantly acids (CO_2 and organic acids). Maintenance of a stable pH is initially achieved by buffer systems. The excess acid is then excreted via the lungs and kidneys.

- An acid is a proton or hydrogen ion donor
- An alkali is a base or hydrogen ion acceptor
- **Acidaemia** is an arterial blood pH of <7.35
- **Alkalaemia** is an arterial blood pH of >7.45
- **Acidosis** is an abnormal condition demonstrated by a decrease in arterial pH
- **Alkalosis** is an abnormal condition demonstrated by an increase in arterial pH
- **pH** is the logarithm (to the base 10) of the reciprocal of the hydrogen ion concentration, thus: $pH = \log_{10} 1/[H^+] = -\log_{10} [H^+]$
- **pK$_a$** is the pH of a buffer at which half the acid molecules are undissociated and half are associatedw

$$HB \Leftrightarrow H^+ + B^-$$

Where HB is a weak acid, H^+ is the hydrogen ion and B^- is the conjugate base.

This resists changes in pH because the addition of any acid reacts with the free base ions (and the reaction moves to the left to provide replacement B^- ions for those in solution that have just been used to neutralise the acid). Conversely, the addition of alkali reacts with the free H^+ ions (and the reaction moves to the right to provide replacement H^+ ions for those in solution that have just been used to neutralise the base).

Intracellularly, proteins and phosphates act as buffers. Extracellularly, the bicarbonate buffer system is of major importance. This is illustrated by the Henderson–Hasselbach equation.

The Henderson–Hasselbach equation

The Henderson–Hasselbach equation is based on the relationship between CO_2 and bicarbonate (HCO_3^-) in the blood. In the bicarbonate buffer system, the weak acid and base are carbonic acid and bicarbonate:

$$H_2CO_3 \Leftrightarrow H^+ + HCO_3^-$$

The carbonic acid (H_2CO_3) dissociates in the blood to form $CO_2 + H_2O$:

$$CO_2 + H_2O \Leftrightarrow H_2CO_3$$

Therefore:

$$CO_2 + H_2O \Leftrightarrow H_2CO_3 \Leftrightarrow H^+ + HCO_3^-$$

The addition of acid will shift this equation to the left to provide replacement HCO_3^- ions for those in solution that have just been used to neutralise the acid. The addition of alkali will shift the equation to the right to provide replacement H^+ ions for those in solution that have just been used to neutralise the alkali.

The Henderson–Hasselbach equation

The equation is given by:
$$pH = pK_a + \log [base]/[acid]$$
That is:
$$pH = pK_a + \log\{[HCO_3^-]/[H_2CO_3]\{$$
This equation describes the relationship of arterial pH to bicarbonate and $PaCO_2$. It is derived from the reaction of CO_2 with water, thus:
$$CO_2 + H_2O \Leftrightarrow H_2CO_3 \Leftrightarrow H^+ + HCO_3^-$$

The carbonic acid can be expressed as CO_2, thus:
$$pH = pK_a + \log\{[HCO_3^-]/pK_a CO_2\}$$

where pK_a is a constant.
This buffer system aims to minimise pH change, so if $PaCO_2$ goes up then HCO_3^- goes down, and if $PaCO_2$ goes down then HCO_3^- goes up.

Excretion of excess acid and alkali

The bicarbonate buffering system will not restore large changes in pH. Excess H^+ and HCO_3^- ions are excreted via the lungs and the kidneys.

Excretion via the lungs

The respiratory mechanism is a rapid-response system that allows CO_2 to be transferred from pulmonary venous blood to alveolar gas and excreted in expired gas. Brainstem respiratory centres respond directly to the levels of CO_2 by detecting H^+ in the blood.

High levels cause an increase in the rate of respiration, blowing off CO_2, thus decreasing acidity. Dysfunction of the mechanics or control of ventilation can lead to retention of CO_2 and a rise in H^+ (respiratory acidosis) or over-excretion of CO_2 and a fall in H^+ (respiratory alkalosis).

Excretion via the kidneys

Excretion of excess acid and alkali occurs more slowly by renal compensation. The body produces more acid than base each day and so the urine is usually slightly acidic (pH 6.0). It relies on the excretion of hydrogen ions in the urine by secretion of H^+ ions in the distal nephron. In addition, HCO_3^- ions are generated in the renal tubules. Renal dysfunction prevents H^+ excretion, resulting in a metabolic acidosis.

The excretion of excess acid requires buffer systems in the urine. These are phosphate and ammonia:

$$H^+ + H_2PO_4^- \Leftrightarrow H_3PO_4$$

$$H^+ + NH_3 \Leftrightarrow NH_4^+$$

Respiratory acidosis

Respiratory acidosis results in a primary disturbance of increased PCO_2 leading to a decrease in pH and a compensatory increase in HCO_3^-.

Causes of respiratory acidosis

Depression of the respiratory centre
- CVA
- Cerebral tumour
- Drugs (opiates/sedatives)
- Encephalitis

Decreased chest wall movement
- Neuromuscular disorder (eg myasthenia gravis)
- Trauma/surgery
- Ankylosing spondylitis

Pulmonary disease (causing type II respiratory failure)
- COPD
- Pneumonia

Respiratory alkalosis

Respiratory alkalosis results from the primary disturbance of a decreased $PaCO_2$, leading to an increase in pH and a compensatory decrease in HCO_3^-.

Causes of respiratory alkalosis

Stimulation of the respiratory centre
- CNS disease (eg CVA, encephalitis)
- Hypermetabolic state (eg fever, hyperthyroidism, sepsis)
- Exercise
- Hypoxia (eg pneumonia, pulmonary oedema, pulmonary collapse)

Excess ventilation
- Anxiety
- Certain drugs (eg aspirin)

Metabolic acidosis

Metabolic acidosis results from the primary disturbance of a decreased HCO_3^- or increased H^+ leading to a decrease in pH and a compensatory decrease in $PaCO_2$.

Causes of metabolic acidosis

Increased anion gap (ie another source of acid production)

- Renal glomerular failure
- Overdose (eg salicylate – also causes respiratory alkalosis; see above)
- Lactic acidosis – inadequate tissue perfusion (hypovolaemia, ischaemic gut)
- Ketoacidosis – diabetic or alcoholic
- Renal tubular acidosis
- Acetazolamide therapy
- Ureterosigmoidostomy

Normal anion gap

- Excess acid intake (eg parenteral nutrition)

Metabolic alkalosis

This occurs in diarrhoea, fistulae and proximal renal tubular acidosis. It results from the primary disturbance of an increase in HCO_3^- or a decrease in H^+, leading to an increase in pH and a compensatory increase in $PaCO_2$ (although clinically this effect is small).

Causes of metabolic alkalosis

Excess alkali intake

- Alkali abuse
- Over-treatment of acidosis

Excess loss of acid

- Vomiting

Increased urinary acidification

- Diuretics
- Excess aldosterone
- Hypokalaemia

Compensation in acid–base balance

During a disturbance in the acid–base status there is an attempt by the body to try to correct the disturbance. There are two main mechanisms:

- Manipulation of $PaCO_2$ by the respiratory system: this is rapid but not as effective as renal compensation
- Manipulation of HCO_3^- by the kidneys: this is slow but more effective than respiratory compensation

Note that compensatory changes do not bring the pH to normal; they simply change the pH towards the normal range.

Interpretation of acid–base balance

From the Henderson–Hasselbach equation it can be seen that, if a patient has a change in acid–base status, three parameters also change:

- pH
- HCO_3^- concentration
- $PaCO_2$

Blood gas machines measure PO_2, pH and PCO_2 directly. Bicarbonate is calculated from the Henderson–Hasselbach equation.

Other important variables given by the blood gas machine include:

- **Actual bicarbonate:** the concentration of bicarbonate measured in the blood sample at the $PaCO_2$ of the patient
- **Standard bicarbonate:** the concentration of bicarbonate in the blood sample when the $PaCO_2$ is normal (ie if there was no respiratory disturbance). Therefore this gives information about metabolic changes

Normal standard bicarbonate is 22–26 mmol.

- >26 mmol **metabolic alkalosis**
- <22 mmol **metabolic acidosis**

Standard base excess is the amount of acid/base needed to be added to the sample to return the pH to the normal range.

CHAPTER 3

Normal ranges of arterial blood gases	
pH	7.35–7.45
H^+	36–44 mmol/l
PO_2	10–14 kPa (75–100 mmHg)
PCO_2	4–6 kPa (35–42 mmHg)
HCO_3^-	22–26 mmol/l

Interpretation of the ABG

When interpreting the arterial blood gas it helps to follow a logical scheme such as the one below:

1. Is the patient hypoxic?

- PO_2 <10 kPa (type I respiratory failure <8 kPa)

How much inspired O_2 is the patient on?

2. Is the patient acidotic or alkalotic?

Look at the pH:

- Normal arterial blood pH = 7.35–7.45
- Acidotic pH <7.35
- Alkalotic pH >7.45

3. Is the primary disturbance respiratory or metabolic?

Look at the PCO_2 and the serum HCO_3^-.

- A respiratory disturbance primarily alters the arterial PCO_2
- A metabolic disturbance primarily alters the serum HCO_3^-

Compensation occurs within the two systems when the pH becomes disturbed. This occurs rapidly in the case of the respiratory system by changing the rate of respiration to 'blow off' or conserve CO_2. The kidney is responsible for metabolic compensation and this responds more slowly (approximately 4 hours with maximal compensation at 4 days) with the net gain or loss of HCO_3^- ions.

The anion gap

The anion gap is the calculated difference between negatively charged (anion) and positively charged (cation) electrolytes. It provides diagnostic information in cases of metabolic acidosis. Normally this is 10–16 mmol/l.

In the body, to maintain electrical chemical neutrality, the number of cations equals the number of anions. The main cations in the body are sodium and potassium. The main anions in the body are chloride, bicarbonate, proteins, phosphates, sulphates and organic acids. Usually the ions that are measured are sodium, potassium, bicarbonate and chloride.

CALCULATING THE ANION GAP

Cations	Concentration	Anions	Concentration
Na^+	140 mmol/l	Cl^-	105 mmol/l
K^+	5 mmol/l	HCO_3^-	30 mmol/l
Total	145 mmol/l	Total	135 mmol/l

In the example shown in the table the difference is 10 mmol/l and therefore the anion gap is 10 mmol/l.

This anion gap is made up of anions that are not usually measured (eg proteins, phosphate).

Why is this important?
- An increased anion gap = metabolic acidosis
- The cause of this metabolic acidosis will be due to retention of acid other than HCl (eg lactic acid) and is particularly useful in diagnosing ketoacidosis in diabetics.

1.5 Metabolic abnormalities

The metabolic response to surgery

Learning point

Trauma can be defined as any stress to the body (including surgery itself). This provokes a metabolic and physiological response. This response occurs:
- Locally (inflammation and wound repair)
- Generally, with systemic involvement (ebb and flow pattern)

It involves an initial **catabolic** phase followed by a rebuilding **anabolic** phase. Metabolism = anabolism + catabolism Catabolism is a destructive mechanism in which large organic molecules are broken down into their constituent parts, providing material for synthesis and ATP release.

Anabolism is a constructive mechanism in which small precursor molecules are assembled into larger organic molecules with utilisation of an energy source, ATP.

Stress provokes a metabolic response. Stress may include:
- Injury
- Surgery
- Sepsis
- Dehydration
- Starvation
- Hypothermia
- Anaesthesia
- Severe psychological stress

CHAPTER 3

The nature, severity and duration of the metabolic response are variable and depend on:

- Nature and degree of trauma
- Presence of sepsis
- Coexisting systemic disease
- Drugs
- Age (reduced in children and elderly people)
- Gender (reduced in young women)
- Nutritional state (malnutrition reduces metabolic response)

The response to injury can be considered to occur as both local and general phenomena:

- Local response: management of wounds (inflammation and subsequent wound healing)
- General response: acts to conserve fluid and provide energy for repair processes

It is described as an ebb and flow pattern by Cuthbertson (1932).

The ebb and flow phases of the metabolic response to trauma

The ebb phase

- Occurs in the first few hours (<24 hours)
- Acts as a protective mechanism, conserving circulating volume and minimising demands on the body
- Effects include:
  - ↓ oxygen consumption
  - ↓ enzymatic activity
  - ↓ cardiac output
  - ↓ basal metabolic rate
  - ↓ body temperature
  - ↑ production of acute phase proteins
- Modulated by catecholamines, cortisol and aldosterone

The flow phase

- Occurs later (>24 hours)
- Describes a hypermetabolic state
- Effects include:
  - ↑ oxygen consumption
  - ↑ glucose production
  - ↑ cardiac output
  - ↑ basal metabolic rate
  - ↑ body temperature
  - ↓ weight loss
- Initially this phase is **catabolic** (3–10 days), which allows mobilisation of the building blocks of repair; it is controlled by glucagons, insulin, cortisol and catecholamines
- Subsequently the process becomes **anabolic** (10–60 days) with repair of tissue, repletion of stores of fat and protein, and weight gain; it is controlled by growth hormones, androgens and ketosteroids (growth hormone and insulin-like growth factor are dependent on calorie intake)

Energy sources in catabolism

- **Glucose:** glucose is released from the liver by glycolysis from glycogen stores and seriously ill patients may develop a state of glucose intolerance. Serum glucose is high and the turnover rapid. The liver produces glucose from the catabolism of proteins and fats to maintain the high serum levels
- **Fat:** this is initially released from adipose tissue under control of interleukins and TNF. Lipases release glycerol and fatty acids from triglycerides. Glycerol is used for gluconeogenesis and fatty acids are oxidised for energy
- **Protein:** skeletal muscle breakdown occurs at an increased rate due to a proteolysis-inducing factor (PIF) secreted after trauma. Muscle loss results in a supply of alanine and glutamine. Amino acids are used for

gluconeogenesis and synthesis of acute phase proteins. This results in a negative nitrogen balance because up to 20 g/day of nitrogen is excreted in the urine and it peaks after several days

Severe loss of muscle mass causes a reduction and eventually failure in immunocompetence, predisposing to overwhelming infection. Gut mucosal integrity also relies on a supply of amino acids and a reduction in this supply (especially of glutamine) predisposes to bacterial translocation.

Glucose is incredibly important in the response to trauma and the metabolic response is geared to providing as much as possible. Nutritional support for patients in shock is therefore composed of 65–70% glucose, with the rest of the calories supplied by means of emulsified fat.

Management of the metabolic response

- Minimise the initial insult if possible (eg minimal access surgery)
- Aggressive fluid and electrolyte management to prevent a decrease in tissue perfusion and fluid shifts
- Provide sufficient oxygen (by respiratory support and ventilation if necessary)
- Control glucose levels
- Control pain (pain and anxiety cause hormonal release and potentiate an increase in the metabolic response)
- Manage body temperature (warming/ cooling, medication)
- Prevent and control associated sepsis
- Optimise nutrition to provide energy for repair
- Support failing organ systems (renal replacement therapy, respiratory support, cardiac support)

Production and utilisation of energy in the body

Energy produced from catabolism of food is utilised as:
- Energy for necessary synthesis and anabolism
- Energy for heat
- Energy storage
- Energy for external work

Energy is measured in joules or calories. These are essentially measures of heat (1 kilocalorie or kcal is the amount of heat needed to produce a rise of 1°C in 1 kg of water.

Energy supplied by different food types:
- 1 g carbohydrate = 4.1 kcal
- 1 g protein = 5.3 kcal
- 1 g fat = 9.3 kcal

Energy production by the body can be measured by direct or indirect calorimetry:
- Direct calorimetry relies on measurement of the heat released by the body; this is difficult to do and so remains experimental (eg Atwater–Benedict chamber)
- Indirect calorimetry measures bodily processes associated with the consumption and production of energy (eg oxygen consumption and CO_2 production with Benedict apparatus)

The respiratory quotient (*RQ*) is the ratio of O_2 consumption to volume of CO_2 produced per unit of time. It reflects the fuel used to produce the energy (a diet of pure carbohydrate produces a *RQ* of 1.0, of pure protein 0.8 and of pure fat 0.7).

CHAPTER 3

Metabolic rate

Learning point

The **basal metabolic rate (BMR)** is the minimal calorific requirement to sustain life. It can be measured in kcal/m² per hour.
It is affected by a number of different factors (eg age, sex, temperature and catabolic states such as burns).

Measurement of BMR

BMR is measured in kcal/m² per hour (about 35–40 kcal/m² per hour for an adult male). Calorific requirement can also be estimated by the equation:

$$BMR = \text{body mass (kg)} \times 20 \text{ kcal}$$

Around 20 kcal are required to maintain 1 kg of body mass. Thus, for example, a 70-kg man will have a baseline daily requirement of 1400 kcal if he sleeps all day. The energy required for external work is not taken into account and so additional calories are required for movement.

BMR increases in injury states when the body is catabolic (eg burns, where the BMR doubles to about 45 kcal/kg of body mass).

Factors affecting BMR
- Age (higher in the young due to higher lean body mass)
- Height (taller people have higher BMRs)
- Surface area (higher with greater surface area)
- Sex (lower by 10% in women)
- Race (higher in white than in Asian people)
- Growth states (higher in children and pregnancy/lactation)
- Body composition (higher BMR with more lean tissue)
- Pyrexia (↑ BMR)
- Environmental temperature (both heat and cold ↑ BMR)
- Malnutrition and starvation (↓ BMR)
- Food (protein ↑ BMR)
- Hormones (catecholamines and thyroxine ↑ BMR)
- Stress and mental status (stress ↑ BMR; depression ↓ BMR)
- Physical exercise (can ↑ BMR 10–20-fold)
- Sleep (↓ BMR)

CHAPTER 3

1.6 Thermoregulation

Control of body temperature

Learning point

Body temperature control is essential for optimal functioning of intracellular enzymes. Aberrations in body temperature compromise organ function.

Body temperature is controlled by balancing heat production against heat loss. The body has mechanisms for reducing temperature when it is too hot, and increasing temperature when it is too cold.

'Normal' temperature is actually a range from 36°C to 37.5°C. It oscillates minutely around a 'set point' determined by the hypothalamus.

- **Pyrexia** is temperature >37.5°C
- **Hypothermia** is temperature <36°C

Physiological control of normal body temperature

The deep tissues of the body or the 'core' remain at a constant temperature (unless there is a febrile illness). The temperature of skin and subcutaneous tissues or 'peripheral' tissue rises and falls with the surroundings:

- Climate (hot vs cold; humid vs dry)
- Exercise (mild vs strenuous)

Heat production in the body

Heat is an essential by-product of metabolism, and so the rate of its production is determined by the metabolic rate. Factors affecting the metabolic rate will therefore affect the rate of heat production.

Most of this heat is produced in the deep tissues of the body, such as the liver, heart, brain and skeletal muscle (eg fulminant liver failure is often associated with hypothermia).

The production of heat requires oxygen consumption and this is important in critically ill individuals, particularly in neonates, who have difficulty with body heat regulation. The 'thermo-neutral zone' is a temperature at which the oxygen requirement for temperature regulation is at a minimal level. Nursing neonates at this temperature allows the infant to optimise their use of the available oxygen.

Elevation of temperature when the body is cold

This is achieved by:

- Cutaneous vasoconstriction
- Piloerection (elevation of body hairs to increase insulating layer of air next to the skin)
- Increased heat production by:
  - Shivering
  - Sympathetic excitation
  - Thyroxine secretion
  - Brown fat heating
  - Behavioural modification (eg clothing)

Heat loss from the body

Core heat is conducted to the periphery and lost through the skin into the surrounding environment. Two factors predominantly control the rate of this loss:

- **Insulation:** fat conducts heat only a third as well as other tissues and so it acts as an insulator. It allows the temperature of the skin to approach that of the surroundings, with no loss of core temperature
- **Cutaneous blood flow:** blood vessels penetrate the fat to lie directly beneath the skin in a continuous venous plexus.

This plexus is also supplied directly by small arteries through arteriovenous anastomoses. The rate of blood flow (and thus heat exchange) from the core to the periphery can therefore be controlled by sympathetic vasoconstriction or dilation of the vessels (blood flow can vary from zero to 30% of the cardiac output). In a thermo-neutral environment the blood vessels of the skin are sufficiently vasodilated so that each litre of blood loses 1°C in heat as it passes through the skin capillaries. Vasoconstriction of the blood supply to the skin results in net heat conservation and vasodilatation results in net heat loss. Heat loss can be promoted by a factor of 10 during the vasodilatation of vigorous exercise.

Heat loss from the skin is via:
- **Radiation:** this occurs if the ambient temperature is lower than the skin; 60% of total heat loss via infrared heat rays
- **Conduction:** conduction of heat as motion to the surrounding air molecules causes these heated molecules to move away from the skin as a convection current, replacing the layer of air in contact with the skin with cold air. This occurs if the ambient temperature is lower than that of the skin. Hairs on the skin help to hold a layer of air in place which is heated by the body to form an insulator zone. This is displaced if the air is moving (eg wind chill). The insulator layer cannot form water molecules and so more heat is lost by conduction in cases of submersion
- **Evaporation:** when the vasculature is fully dilated and the body needs to lose further heat then it does so by sweating. Sweating occurs when the ambient temperature rises >30–31°C, and/or when internal body temperature rises >37°C, allowing

the body to lose heat by evaporation. The amount that you sweat rises linearly with the temperature; 0.58 kcal is used to allow evaporation of 1 g water from the surface of the skin. This may be insensible loss from the skin and lungs or due to sweat. Sweating is controlled by the autonomic nervous system (stimulation of the anterior hypothalamus by excess heat causes cholinergic sympathetic stimulation of sweat glands). Sweating occurs even if the ambient temperature is the same or higher than that of the skin

Reduction of temperature when the body is hot
This is achieved by:
- Sweating
- Cutaneous vasodilation
- Inhibition of heat-producing mechanisms (eg shivering, chemical thermogenesis)
- Behavioural modification (eg clothing, seeking shade)

The physiology of abnormal body temperature

Pyrexia
Elevation of the body temperature may be caused by:
- **Toxins** that result from:
  - Infection – eg release of bacterial endotoxins
  - Trauma – eg release of cytokines involved in inflammation and repair
- **Damage to thermoregulatory structures in the brain**, eg tumours or surgery in the region of the hypothalamus

Toxins or pyrogens can cause the set point in the hypothalamus to rise. This initially brings heat-conserving mechanisms into play and the body temperature rises to the new set point. This is especially true of interleukins IL-1 and IL-6 released by lymphocytes in response to bacterial toxin.

The activation of these heat-conserving mechanisms causes rigors – vasoconstriction, piloerection, shivering and chattering teeth occur despite the presence of a high core temperature.

Removal of the causative agent results in re-setting of the hypothalamus and stimulation of heat-loss mechanisms into play. There is vasodilatation of the skin and excess sweating to reduce the body temperature back down to the new set point.

Heat stroke occurs if the environmental conditions prevent sufficient heat loss by convection and sweating (ie low air currents and high humidity). The symptoms (dizziness, abdominal pain, loss of consciousness) are exacerbated by a degree of circulatory shock due to fluid loss. Hyperpyrexia for short periods causes damage and local haemorrhage in all organs but particularly the brain.

Hypothermia

When core temperature falls <30°C the ability of the hypothalamus to regulate temperature is lost. The chemical and enzymatic activity within the cells is decreased several-fold, reducing heat production still further. Reduced conscious level and coma depress the activity of the CNS and prevent activation of heat-preserving mechanisms such as shivering.

After surgery or trauma patients often have evidence of a pyrexia and their blood picture demonstrates an acute phase response in the first 24 hours. This is due to:
- Tissue damage necrosis and acute inflammatory response
- Basal atelectasis due to general anaesthesia and posture (bed-bound)

Loss of control of thermoregulation due to drugs

Thermoregulatory control can also be disrupted by drugs and this is especially relevant during anaesthesia. Volatile anaesthetics and propofol cause vasodilatation. Fentanyl and opiates cause depression of the thermoregulatory control centre in the hypothalamus. Neuromuscular blockade compromises shivering. Conversely malignant hyperthermia is triggered by an autosomal dominant gene causing skeletal muscular spasm, and thus heat generation in response to halogenated anaesthetics and depolarising neuromuscular blocking agents.

CHAPTER 3

SECTION 2

Critical care

2.1 The structure of critical care

When considering postoperative monitoring, it is necessary to consider what level of care a patient will require. In order to decide this, a basic knowledge of the structure of critical care is essential.

Learning point

Critical care provision is classified into four levels:

Level 0 Normal ward

Level 1 Enhanced care. Nurse:patient ratio of approximately 3:1. Monitored

Level 2 High dependency. Nurse:patient ratio of 2:1. Single organ failure (not ventilated)

Level 3 Intensive care. Recovery units. Nurse:patient ratio of 1:1. Multiorgan failure. Ventilation

---

Recovery units

After a general anaesthetic, patients are routinely transferred to a recovery unit that provides level 3 critical care before transfer to the ward. The recovery unit provides continued invasive monitoring for:

- Detection of continuing effects of anaesthetics
- Detection of early complications of surgery (eg haemorrhage, severe pain)

Criteria for discharge to ward:

- Spontaneous airway maintenance
- Awake and non-drowsy
- Comfortable and pain-free
- Haemodynamically stable and well perfused
- No evidence of haemorrhage

The high-dependency unit

The HDU provides level 2 critical care. It is appropriate for patients who require more input than a general ward can give or who have single organ failure but do not require ITU care or ventilation. These patients benefit from a higher ratio of nurses to each patient, allowing for increased levels of monitoring and therapy.

Outreach services may provide early access to skilled advice and allow earlier initiation of critical care.

The intensive therapy unit

The ITU provides level 3 critical care. ITU beds in the UK account for 1% of the total beds. An ITU should have a minimum of four beds to be efficient and they often have 8–12 beds. Bed occupancy should be around 70% but is often much higher due to insufficient capacity.

The ITU should ideally be near and on the same floor as:

- A&E (accident and emergency)
- Theatres
- Radiology
- Blood bank

Admission to ITU

- For elective, emergency or prophylactic treatment
- For potentially reversible conditions
- For specialised or high level of monitoring
- For mechanical support of organs (eg ventilation, dialysis)
- For failure of more than one organ system

Discharge from ITU

- Discharge to HDU can occur sooner than to a general ward
- Decided by senior ITU staff
- Care is handed over to specialty team

Staffing in critical care

Medical staff

- **ITU director:** should have speciality training in intensive care medicine (CCST in intensive care medicine will be required in the future), and base specialty from anaesthetics, medicine, surgery or A&E. More than 80% of consultants are from anaesthetics
- **ITU consultants:** covering all daytime sessions and on-call rota
- **Junior medical staff:** 24-hour dedicated cover by SHOs (senior house officers), SpRs (specialist registrars) or Fellows from the above specialities. It is recommended that trainees in acute specialities should have at least 3 months' training in ITU
- **Nursing staff:** there should be about seven whole-time equivalents per ITU bed. Nurses have an increasing degree of autonomy with roles in fluid therapy, weaning and ventilation, and inotrope titration

Costs of critical care

- Approximately £1000–1800 per bed per day

Rationale for critical care

Reasons for poor outcome in the critically ill

- Inadequate ward care
- Late referral to ITU
- Cardiac arrest (it is estimated that in up to 80% cases cardiac arrest could have been predicted)

Improvement in survival

This is possible because of:

- Earlier critical care intervention
- Better training of medical and nursing staff in critical care principles
- Early warning systems and protocols to identify physiological deterioration early
- ITU staff are expanding their roles into the wards and emergency departments

CHAPTER 3

2.2 Scoring systems in critical care

Early warning and scoring systems

These are needed to recognise ill patients on the ward early and institute critical care. They can be based on a physiological core including parameters such as:

- Airway compromise
- Respiratory rate
- Oxygen saturation
- Heart rate
- BP
- Urine output
- Temperature
- GCS

Examples of early warning systems

Many hospitals use a medical early warning system (MEWS) in order to identify the critically ill patient and highlight deterioration of a previously stable patient. The MEWS system converts vital signs into a numerical score. Nursing staff have a set threshold at which a doctor must be called to assess the patient.

The MEWS score takes into consideration:

- Haemodynamic parameters (pulse and BP)
- Temperature
- Urine output
- Respiratory rate
- Level of consciousness

Scoring systems

Scoring systems enable comparison between units and evaluation of new/existing treatments by case-mix adjustment for differences in the severity of illness of patients. Average mortality rate in ITUs is 25–30%.

- **Standardised mortality ratio (SMR):** calculated on the unit for diagnostic groups and can be compared with national standards (eg ICNARC)
- **Acute physiology, age and chronic health evaluation** (APACHE I, II and III). This has three point-scoring components:
  - Acute physiology based on GCS, blood results, haemodynamic and urine output variables
  - Age
  - Chronic health
- **Simplified acute physiology score (SAPS):** reduces the APACHE scoring system to 14 variables

Other scoring systems:

- **Injury severity score (ISS)** correlates severity of injury in three anatomical areas, scoring up to 5 and squaring the result. Maximum score is 75. Used for audit
- **Revised trauma score (RTS)** where TRISS = ratio of RTS and ISS
- **Mortality prediction model** or mortality probability model (MPM)
- **Standardised mortality ratio (SMR)** is the ratio of estimated deaths (MPM) and actual deaths
- **Therapeutic intervention scoring system (TISS)** is used to measure nursing workload; points are attributed to different therapeutic interventions received by patients
- Quality-of-life data, eg quality-adjusted life-years (QALYs)

Transportation of critically ill patients

The standard of care provided during interhospital transfer for critically ill patients must be the same as that provided on the ITU.

Patients should be transported:
• When adequately resuscitated
• When as stable as possible
• With a secure airway (ie endotracheal intubation) if mechanical ventilation is required
• With adequate IV access (at least two large-bore cannulas)
• With full monitoring capability (pulse, BP, oxygen sats, end-tidal CO_2)
• With appropriately qualified staff in attendance (doctor and ITU nurse or operating department practitioner [ODP]). Some specialties, especially paediatrics, have specialist patient retrieval teams
• With all the equipment and drugs that may be needed for resuscitation

Communication between sending and receiving centres must be exemplary. All the involved medical and surgical teams should have a written and verbal doctor-to-doctor handover, and all relevant radiology, lab results and notes should be sent with the patient.

Documentation of the transfer period must also be completed.

2.3 Cardiovascular monitoring and support

Cardiovascular physiology

> **Learning point**
>
> • The **blood pressure** (BP) is regulated by the systemic vascular resistance (SVR) and the cardiac output (CO)
> • **Peripheral vascular resistance** depends on compliance of the blood vessels, predominantly the arterioles
> • **Cardiac output** is measured by multiplying the stroke volume (SV) and the heart rate (HR)
> • **Stroke volume** depends on venous return (Starling's law)

Systemic vascular resistance

Systemic vascular resistance depends on vascular compliance and the haemodynamics of blood flow.

Factors such as heart rate (HR) and stroke volume (SV) affect arterial pressure by altering the cardiac output (CO):

$$CO = HR \times SV$$

The less compliant the system is (with stiff arteries) the more work the heart must do to pump a given stroke volume. Compliance decreases with age, when elastic fibres are partially replaced with collagen and there is a decrease in the number of smooth muscle cells in the arterial walls.

CHAPTER 3

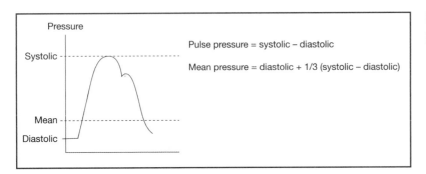

Figure 3.15 The arterial pressure wave

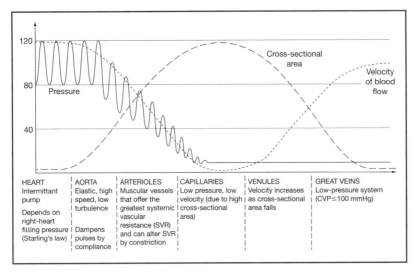

Figure 3.16 Basic vascular physiology

Blood pressure

The pressure in arteries depends on both the rate of blood entering and the rate of blood leaving the system, and the compliance of the vessels. Flow of blood through the vascular system requires a pressure gradient to be generated across the area where flow is to be established.

Stroke volume

Starling's law

Cardiac muscle cells (similar to skeletal muscle cells) are made up of sarcomeres. Sarcomeres contain thick filaments (myosin) and thin filaments (actin) as discussed in the section on muscle contraction in this chapter.

The filaments slide over each other (expending energy) and so shorten the sarcomere (therefore shortening of several sarcomeres is the mechanism by which the muscle cell contracts). The force that the muscle sarcomere can exert depends partly on the length of the sarcomere (which, in turn, is a reflection of the degree of overlap of the thick and thin filaments).

- When the sarcomere is very short, the high degree of overlap interferes with contraction and the force is therefore reduced
- When the sarcomere is very long, the relative lack of overlap means that less force can be exerted between these two extremes
- A length of sarcomere exists where the overlap is high enough to produce

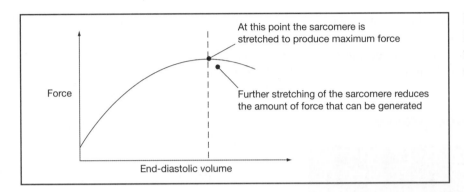

At this point the sarcomere is stretched to produce maximum force

Force

Further stretching of the sarcomere reduces the amount of force that can be generated

End-diastolic volume

Figure 3.17 End-diastolic volume (Starling's curve)

maximum force, but not high enough to interfere with force production from sarcomere shortening

This has implications for the force that the heart can exert to pump blood (known as the 'Frank–Starling mechanism' or 'Starling's law of the heart').

End-diastolic volume (EDV) refers to the amount of blood that the ventricle of the heart holds at its maximum (ie just before it contracts).

Regulation of stroke volume
Stroke volume can be regulated by:
- **Pre-load**, which is dependent on:
  - Venous filling time
  - Diastolic filling time
  - Atrial systole (ie in fibrillation)
  - Myocardial/pericardial distensibility (compliance)
- **Contractility**, which is increased by:
  - Pre-load
  - Nerves (sympathetic stimulation increases contractility as well as heart rate)
  - Hormones (the following all increase contractility: adrenaline, thyroxine, glucagon)
  - Drugs (inotropic)

- And decreased by:
  - Hypoxia
  - Ischaemia and cardiac disease
  - Acidosis and alkalosis
  - Parasympathetic stimulation (mainly by suppressing the sinoatrial node)
  - Electrolyte imbalance (K^+, Ca^{2+})
  - Reduced filling (Starling's law)
  - Drugs (anaesthetics)
- **After-load**, which is increased by:
  - Aortic stenosis
  - Raised systemic vascular resistance (SVR) as in shock
  - Increased ventricular volume (greater tension to contract, Laplace's law)
  - (Increased after-load increases cardiac work and oxygen consumption)
- And decreased by:
  - Vasodilator drugs
  - Vasodilator mediators (eg septic shock)

Heart rate

Regulation of heart rate
The heart rate is controlled by the autonomic nervous system:
- Sympathetic nerve fibres (from C8 to T5) cause noradrenaline release at nerve endings, which acts on cardiac β receptors, increasing heart rate (chronotropic) and contractility force (inotropic)

- Parasympathetic nerve fibres (in the vagus nerve) cause acetylcholine release at nerve endings, acting on muscarinic receptors, causing a slowing of heart rate

Control of blood pressure

Learning point

- In the short term blood pressure is controlled by neurological mechanisms with reflexes that can detect abnormalities and respond rapidly
- Long-term control and regulation of the blood pressure occurs by the regulation of blood volume by the kidney

Short-term regulation of BP

Short-term changes in blood pressure (a time frame of seconds to minutes) are mediated by the autonomic nervous system.

Arterial BP sensors

Mean arterial pressure is monitored by baroreceptors, primarily in the aortic arch and carotid sinus. They mediate rapid responses to changes in blood pressure (eg getting up from a chair) and their failure is a cause of postural hypotension.

These are the sensors for two temporally different (but integrated) reflex pathways, which act as feedback loops. Information from the baroreceptor is transmitted to the medulla oblongata where the vasomotor centre and the cardioinhibitory control centre lie and the efferent response originates.

The vasomotor centre predominantly activates sympathetic nerves to increase the BP:

- Increases heart rate and contractility to increase cardiac output (CO)
- Releases noradrenaline to cause vasoconstriction and venoconstriction, which increases SVR and decreases hydrostatic pressure in the capillaries (favouring fluid resorption from the interstitium and thus volume expansion)

The cardioinhibitory centre activates vagal parasympathetic nerves to:

- Slow the heart rate
- Reduce the cardiac output
- Reduce the blood pressure

Increases in arterial pressure result in decreased sympathetic outflow to the vasculature (decreasing systemic resistance) and increased parasympathetic stimulation to the heart (decreasing the heart rate).

Decreased arterial BP increases sympathetic outflow to the vasculature (increasing systemic resistance) and decreases parasympathetic stimulation to the heart (increasing the heart rate).

The range in which these two types of baroreceptor are active is slightly different: carotid sinus baroreceptors have a lower range of 60–180 mmHg and aortic arch baroreceptors detect higher pressures of 90–200 mmHg. Persistent elevation of the blood pressure results in re-setting of the baroreceptor range and blunting of the response.

Venous BP sensors

Baroreceptors located in the great veins, atria and pulmonary trunk are stretch receptors sensitive to changes in blood volume rather then

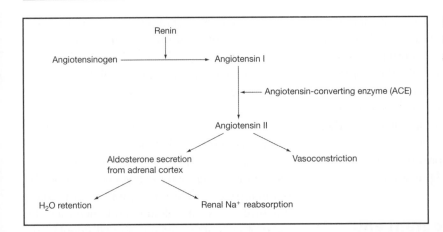

Figure 3.18 The renin–angiotensin–aldosterone axis

CHAPTER 3

pressure. Increased stretch of these receptors reduces sympathetic outflow and promotes vasodilatation. In addition, the Bainbridge reflex results in a decrease in heart rate when the stretch receptors in the right atrium detect higher blood volumes.

Chemoreceptors

Chemoreceptors found in the aortic and carotid bodies are predominantly sensitive to tissue oxygen and carbon dioxide levels. Low arterial pressure results in poor tissue perfusion and activation of these receptors, which promote vasoconstriction in order to increase SVR.

Hormonal control of the BP

Catecholamines: sympathetic stimulation to the adrenal medulla results in the secretion of catecholamines (adrenaline and noradrenaline) which cause increased heart rate, contractility and peripheral vasoconstriction.

Antidiuretic hormone (ADH) is released from the posterior pituitary causing vasoconstriction and renal water reabsorption to increase the blood volume.

Long-term regulation of the BP

Long-term changes in blood pressure (hours to days) are primarily mediated by hormonal factors that control blood volume by regulating sodium and water retention. The reflex pathways are described below.

The renin–angiotensin–aldosterone axis

Reduced arterial BP is sensed as decreased renal blood flow by the juxtaglomerular apparatus (JGA) of the nephron. The JGA secretes renin, a proteolytic enzyme, which acts on angiotensinogen as shown in Figure 3.18. High sympathetic outflow also causes an increase in renin secretion.

Natriuretic peptides

Blood volume changes also promote the release of atrial natriuretic peptide (ANP) from the right atrium. A second natriuretic peptide (brain natriuretic peptide or BNP) is synthesised within the ventricles (as well as in the brain, where it was first identified). BNP is apparently released by the same mechanisms that release ANP, and it has similar physiological actions. This peptide is used as a clinical diagnostic marker for heart failure. Natriuretic peptides are involved in the long-term regulation of sodium and water balance, blood volume and arterial pressure. This hormone decreases aldosterone release by the adrenal cortex, increases the glomerular filtration rate (GFR), produces natriuresis and diuresis (potassium sparing), and decreases renin release, thereby decreasing angiotensin II. These actions contribute to reductions in volume and therefore central venous pressure (CVP), cardiac output, and arterial blood pressure.

The electrocardiogram and cardiac conduction

Cardiac conduction

The heart has three different types of excitatory tissue: atrial muscle, ventricular muscle and the specialised conducting system. The heart also has a large number of mitochondria. This means that energy for heart muscle function can be continuously generated via aerobic metabolism.

Rhythmical spontaneous depolarisation occurs in cardiac tissue. The sinoatrial (SA) and atrioventricular (AV) nodes of the heart have the highest rates of spontaneous activity but the cardiac muscle itself has intrinsic activity. No stimulus is necessary to cause depolarisation in these cells. This is because the cell membrane is relatively leaky to Na^+ ions. As Na^+ ions leak into the cell, the resting potential rises and depolarisation occurs spontaneously.

In addition to the release of Ca^{2+} ions into the sarcoplasm, large quantities of extra Ca^{2+} ions also diffuse into the tubules (tubules of cardiac muscle have a diameter 5 times greater than skeletal muscle, with a volume 25 times greater). Free intracellular calcium ions are the most important factor in regulating the contractility of the myocardium.

- Increased intracellular calcium will increase the force of myocardial contraction
- Decreased intracellular calcium will decrease the force of myocardial contraction

Many drugs that increase cardiac muscle contractile force involve increasing intracellular calcium. For example, cardiac glycosides inhibit the sodium pump and the myocyte responds by pumping out Na^+ in exchange for Ca^{2+}. This loads the myocyte with calcium and increases the force of contraction when the cell depolarises. Catecholamines also increase the calcium influx to the myocyte, whereas acidosis reduces it.

The electrocardiogram (ECG)

- Records the sum of the electrical impulses generated by the heart during depolarisation and contraction
- Provides information on the rate and rhythm of heart contraction, as well as information on pathological processes (eg infarction, inflammation)
- A standard ECG consists of 12 'leads', best thought of as extensions of the direction of electrical flow from the heart, which can be measured. A positive deflection on the ECG (upwards) shows that electrical current is conducted towards that electrode and vice versa

Parts of the ECG waveform and their normal dimensions

P wave
- Depolarisation of the atria
- <2.5 mm height
- >0.1 s duration
- Repolarisation is hidden within the QRS

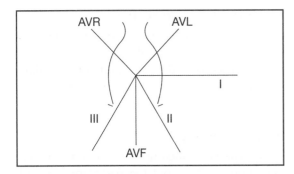

Figure 3.19 12-lead ECG. The six V leads look at the heart in a horizontal plane from the front and left side

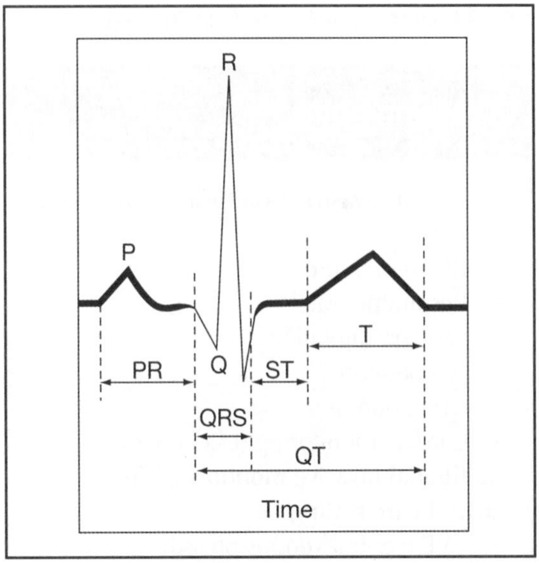

Figure 3.20 The important deflections and intervals of a typical ECG

QRS complex
- Depolarisation of the ventricles
- If first deflection is downwards it is called a Q wave
- First upward deflection (whether preceded by a Q wave or not) is called the R wave, and usually has increasing amplitude from V1 to V6
- First downward deflection after the R wave is called the S wave
- The QRS should be <0.10 s (three small squares) in duration
- An S wave in lead I suggests right axis deviation; an S wave in lead II suggests left axis deviation. Normal axis is −30 to +90
- A wide QRS (>0.12) occurs when depolarisation does not pass down the Purkinje fibres as in bundle branch block and complexes of ventricular origin (ectopics and third-degree block)

PR interval
- Represents the (normal) conduction delay between the atria and the ventricles

- Should be 0.12–0.20 s (three to five small squares)
- >0.2 s represents first-degree heart block
- A variable PR occurs in second-degree heart blocks and complete dissociation of P wave and QRS complex represents third-degree heart block

T wave
- Represents repolarisation of the ventricles

ST segment
- The period between the S wave and the T wave
- Usually isoelectric (ie level with the baseline of the ECG)
- May be elevated acutely when MI is present
- May be depressed when myocardial ischaemia is present
- Note that the ST segment may be normal despite the presence of either infarction or ischaemia

Postoperative monitoring

Learning point

Basic non-invasive monitoring comprises:
- Pulse
- Blood pressure
- Respiratory rate
- Oxygen saturations
- Temperature
- Urine output
- Cardiac monitoring (ECG trace)

Additional invasive monitoring (in a critical care setting):
- CVP (central venous pressure)
- Invasive peripheral arterial monitoring for BP and ABGs (arterial blood gases)
- Cardiac output measurement
- Minimally invasive: oesophageal Doppler (transoesophageal echocardiogram or TOE)
- Invasive: Swan–Ganz catheter and pulmonary artery or wedge pressures

Pulse and BP monitoring

This is mandatory throughout induction of anaesthesia, maintenance and recovery. Heart rate can be obtained from ECG monitoring, pulse oximetry or intra-arterial BP monitoring.

BP can be estimated by manual sphygmomanometry, automatic sphygmomanometry measurement or directly by intra-arterial pressure monitoring via a catheter placed into a peripheral artery, usually the radial.

Cardiac/ECG monitoring

Postoperatively, patients may be monitored by cardiac monitor, especially in a critical care setting. This provides a continuous cardiac rhythm trace and measurement of the pulse rate.

Pulse oximetry

Pulse oximeters measure the arterial oxygen saturation (SaO_2) – not the partial pressure of oxygen (PaO_2). Probes are attached to either the fingers or earlobes and contain two light-emitting diodes (one red, one infrared) and one detector.

The instrument pulses infrared light of wavelengths 660–940 nm through the tissues. A constant 'background' amount is absorbed by skin, venous blood and fat, but a changing amount is absorbed by the pulsatile arterial blood. The constant amount is subtracted from the total absorbed to give the amount absorbed by arterial blood. As oxygenated Hb and deoxygenated Hb absorb differing amounts at the two wavelengths, the instrument is able to calculate a percentage of saturated Hb from the ratio of the two. Skin pigmentation does not affect the readings.

However, observation of the haemoglobin dissociation curve may show that a significant fall in the PaO_2 occurs before the SaO_2 decreases (15- to 20-second delay).

Problems with pulse oximetry

- **Delay:** calculations are made from a number of pulses so there is a delay of about 20 seconds between the actual and displayed values
- **Abnormal pulses:** atrial fibrillation, hypotension/vasoconstriction, tricuspid incompetence (pulsatile venous component)
- **Abnormal Hb or pigments:** carbon monoxide poisoning (eg smoke inhalation); methaemoglobinaemia; bilirubin that also saturates Hb and therefore produce a falsely elevated SaO_2 measurement
- **Interference:** movement/shivering, electrical equipment (eg diathermy), bright ambient light (eg in theatre)
- **Poor tissue perfusion**
- **Nail varnish** (coloured or not)

Note that pulse oximetry only measures Hb saturation, ie oxygenation, not ventilation. CO_2 content of blood is a reflection of ventilation (measured using a capnograph or ABGs).

Urine output

Renal perfusion is closely linked to cerebral perfusion. Urine output is a good indicator of renal perfusion and thus of overall fluid balance and adequate resuscitation in a sick patient.

Catheterisation and hourly urine measurement is mandatory in:
- Massive fluid or blood loss
- Shocked patients – all causes
- Major cardiac, vascular or general surgery
- Surgery in jaundiced patients (hepatorenal syndrome)

- Pathology associated with major fluid sequestration – 'third space loss' (eg bowel obstruction, pancreatitis)

Invasive monitoring

Intra-arterial BP monitoring

Indications for intra-arterial monitoring
- Critically ill or shocked patients
- Major surgery (general, vascular, cardio-thoracic, orthopaedic or neurosurgery)
- Surgery for phaeochromocytomas
- Induced hypotension
- Those requiring frequent blood gas analysis (ie severe pre-existing lung disease)
- Monitoring use of inotropes

Complications of intra-arterial monitoring
- Embolisation
- Haemorrhage
- Arterial damage and thrombosis
- AV fistula formation
- Distal limb ischaemia
- Sepsis
- Tissue necrosis
- Radial nerve damage

Central venous pressure monitoring

CVP is a guide to circulating volume status and myocardial contractility. CVP lines are normally placed with the tip in the SVC from either an internal jugular or a subclavian venous approach using an ultrasound-guided Seldinger method.

The normal CVP range for adults is 8–12 cmH$_2$O.

CHAPTER 3

The CVP can be read intermittently with a manometer, or continuously using a transducer connected to an oscilloscope. It is essential when the measurement is taken for the transducer to be at the level of the right atrium, and for the reading to be taken during respiratory end-expiration.

CVP lines can also be used for administering total parenteral nutrition (TPN) or toxic drugs (eg chemotherapy) or for haemofiltration.

They are indicated in critically ill patients and in major surgery if there is likely to be a complicated postoperative course, or in patients with a poor cardiac reserve where fluid balance may prove difficult to assess correctly.

Fluid challenge using CVP monitoring

The CVP is more useful as a trend in response to the rapid administration of a set volume of colloid (250–500 ml) rather than as an absolute number. The fluid challenge assesses the compliance of the vascular system. The end-point is return of normal BP and tissue perfusion, eg urine output representing a normovolaemic vascular system. Poor response in BP or tissue perfusion despite adequate filling may require inotropic or vasopressor support.

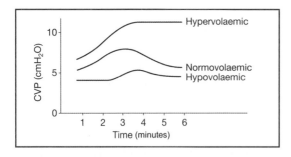

Figure 3.21 Changes in CVP in response to an IV fluid bolus

Complications of central venous lines

> **Complications of CVP lines**
> **Common complications:**
> - Sepsis
> - Pneumothorax
> - Incorrect placement (position should be confirmed with a CXR)
>
> **Less common complications:**
> - Brachial plexus injury
> - Phrenic nerve injury
> - Carotid or subclavian artery puncture
> - Thoracic duct injury
>
> **Uncommon but potentially fatal complications:**
> - Tension pneumothorax
> - Air embolism (head-down position in ventilated patient employed during insertion, aspirate blood before flushing lines)
> - Haemothorax
> - Lost guidewire

Transoesophageal Doppler measurement

Ultrasound records the change in the frequency of the signal that is reflected off the red blood cells travelling in the ascending aorta and thus measuring velocity. This is multiplied by the cross-sectional area of the aorta to give stroke volume. The stroke volume is multiplied by the heart rate to give cardiac output.

Pulmonary artery wedge pressure

Pulmonary artery pressure (Swan–Ganz) catheters may be required when the CVP does not correlate with pressure in the left atrium as

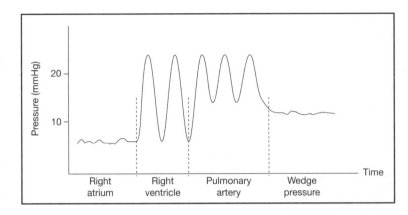

Figure 3.22 Pressure waves as catheter is passed through the heart

in the following conditions:
• Left ventricular failure
• Interstitial pulmonary oedema
• Valvular heart disease
• Chronic severe lung disease
• Pulmonary hypertension
• Pulmonary embolus

They are also of value for the calculation of cardiac output and SVR. Most catheters have at least four lumens:
• Distal lumen (at the tip), which should lie in a peripheral pulmonary artery
• Proximal lumen approximately 25 cm from the tip, which should lie in the right atrium
• Balloon lumen
• Thermistor lumen, which is used to measure temperatures

The catheter is inserted into a central vein, connected to an oscilloscope and advanced into the right atrium (shown by the venous waveform). The balloon is inflated with air and floated into the right ventricle and then into the pulmonary artery. Further advancement will occlude a branch of the pulmonary artery and show a typical 'wedging' waveform. When occluded there is a column of fluid from the end of the catheter to the left atrium and the left arterial pressure can be measured. The

balloon is then deflated to prevent pulmonary infarction.

It can be used to measure cardiac output by the thermodilution method (Fick's principle) and once this is known it can be used with other cardiovascular measurements (CVP, PAWP, MAP, PAP) to calculate the SVR, PVR (pulmonary vascular resistance) and ventricular stroke work. A bolus (10 ml) of cold dextrose is injected and a thermistor at the catheter tip measures a temperature drop proportional to cardiac output. Knowledge of the cardiac output and SVR is useful in helping to determine if a critically ill patient who is in shock has a myocardial, hypovolaemic or septic (vasodilatory) cause, and for guiding inotropic therapy. Other measurements include oxygen delivery and consumption.

Measurement of cardiac output
Pulmonary artery catheters were the first reliable monitors for CO in the ITU. Once CO is measured the SVR can be calculated from data from an arterial line and CVP lines.
• **Continuous CO from PA catheter:** rather than using a cold bolus of fluid as indicator, a coil around the catheter warms the blood as it flows past and the drop in temperature is analysed continuously

- **PiC CO:** thermodilution from cold fluid injected via a CVP line and analysed via a modified arterial line containing a thermistor. By a double-indicator method it shows continuous CO_2, intrathoracic blood volume and pulmonary extravascular lung water. From the latter two values the requirement for fluids or inotropes can be judged
- **Lithium dilution and pulse contour analysis:** similar to Fick's principle technique using small doses of lithium as the indicator with a lithium electrode attached to an arterial line. This calibrates the software, which calculates continuous CO by pulse wave analysis
- **Echo Doppler:** measures blood flow in the aorta via an oesophageal probe; hence it gives an indication of contractility and CO. Patients need to have a patent oesophagus and be sedated to use this technique. From the Doppler waveform, CO and contractility can be deduced
- **Echocardiography:** by visualisation of the ventricle a trained operator can assess filling, myocardial wall motion and ejection fraction (EF is normally 50–70%). May be used transthoracically or oesophageally

2.4 Ventilatory support

Anatomy of the thorax

The thoracic cage

Sternum

This consists of three parts:

- **Manubrium:** jugular notch (upper concave margin); articulates with the clavicles, first costal cartilages and upper halves of second costal cartilages; first costal cartilage joint is

a primary cartilaginous joint (not synovial)
- **Body:** upper border is the manubriosternal symphysis, which is bridged by the second costal cartilage; each lateral border has 5½ facets for articulation with costal cartilages 2–7
- **Xiphoid process:** posterior attachment of diaphragm; anterior attachment of rectus abdominis

Ribs

- **Head:** two facets for articulation with the two adjacent thoracic vertebrae (thoracic vertebra of the same number plus the one above) (note that the first rib's head has just one facet for articulation with T1 only)
- **Neck:** the tubercle has one facet for articulation with the transverse process of the vertebra; the body continues anteriorly as the costal cartilage

Costal cartilages

- 1–7 articulate directly with the sternum
- 8, 9 and 10 run into one another and then into 7 to articulate with the sternum
- 11 and 12 float free

The intercostal spaces

Intercostal muscles

There are three muscle layers (as with the abdomen):

- **Outer:** external intercostal muscles (+ serratus posterior muscles and levator costae)
- **Middle:** internal intercostal muscles
- **Inner:** innermost intercostal muscles (+ transversus thoracis and subcostal muscles)

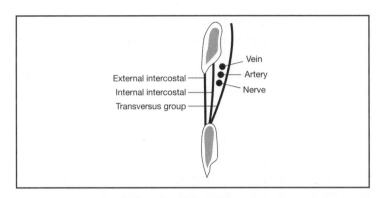

Figure 3.23 Vertical section through an intercostal space

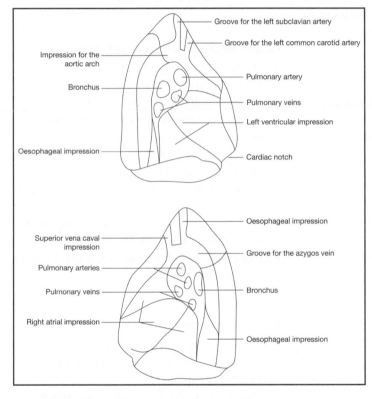

Figure 3.24 Mediastinal surface of the right and left lungs

External intercostals
- Run obliquely downwards and forwards
- Replaced by the anterior intercostal membrane anteriorly

Internal intercostals
- Run downwards and backwards

- Complete anteriorly but replaced posteriorly by the posterior intercostal membrane

Innermost intercostals
- Cross more than one intercostal space
- Innermost layer includes transversus thoracis and subcostal muscles

Neurovascular bundle

- Between internal intercostals and innermost intercostals
- Under protection from the lower border of the ribs, so drains or needles should always be sited above a rib

The pleura

There are two layers, separated by a small amount of fluid in a closed space. They couple the lungs and chest wall and allow the lungs to slide in the thorax during respiration.

Parietal pleura

- Outer layer covers the inside of the thoracic cavity
- Reflects around the root of the lung to be continuous with the visceral pleura

Visceral pleura

- The inner layer is firmly adherent to the surface of the lungs themselves
- The pulmonary ligament is a loose fold of pleura that hangs from the lung root, allowing movement of the lung root during respiration

Nerve supply of the pleura

- Parietal pleura:
  - Intercostal nerves
  - Phrenic nerves
- Visceral pleura:
  - Autonomic innervation only

The lungs

- **Left lung:** two lobes separated by oblique fissure
- **Right lung:** three lobes separated by oblique and horizontal fissures

Lung roots

- Pulmonary artery lies superiorly
- Bronchus lies posteriorly
- Pulmonary veins lie inferiorly

Lobar and segmental bronchi

- The right (shorter and more vertical) and left main bronchi branch and become lobar bronchi, which continue to branch to become segmental bronchi and then bronchioles
- Each lung has 10 bronchopulmonary segments: 5 per lobe on the left and 3 (upper), 2 (middle) and 5 (lower) in the right lung
- Each branch of a bronchus is accompanied by a branch of the pulmonary artery
- Blood supply to the bronchial tree is from its own small bronchial arteries

Surface anatomy of the thorax

- Diaphragm (in full expiration): extends from the fourth intercostal space on the right to the fifth rib on left
- Pleura and lungs: lung roots correspond to the level of the costal cartilages 3 and 4 (or T5–T7) at sternal edges

Remember 2, 4, 6, 8, 10 and 12 – they correspond to the relevant surface points that demarcate the lungs, as shown in the diagram.

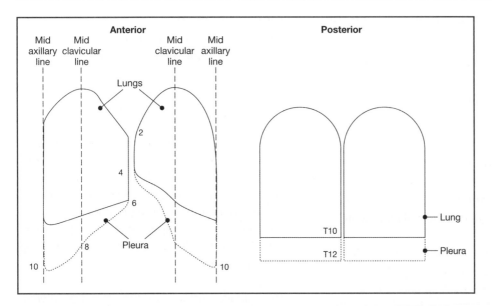

Figure 3.25 Surface anatomy of the lungs

Respiratory physiology

The physiology of ventilation

The mechanics of breathing

The function of the airways

Air passes through the larynx, trachea, bronchi and bronchioles to the alveoli. The functions of the airways are:

- **Conduits for gas passage:** the flow of gas depends on the pressure gradient between the alveoli and the atmosphere and the compliance and resistance of the airways. Normal resistance is low but constriction and dilation of the airways occurs under autonomic control to alter airway resistance
- **Protection of the lungs:** air is filtered by nasal hair and the mucociliary escalator of the upper airway. In addition the vocal folds of the larynx and the cough reflex protect against aspiration. The upper airways also warm and humidify the air

The action of inspiration and expiration

Muscles used in inspiration

- Diaphragm (main respiratory muscle)
- External intercostals
- Accessory inspiratory muscles:
  - Scalenes
  - Sternomastoid
  - Pectoralis
  - Latissimus dorsi

Action of inspiration

- The diaphragm contracts, flattening its domes
- The ribs swing up in a bucket-handle fashion, around their vertebral joints, pushing the sternum up and out, so increasing the cross-sectional area of the thorax
- Both of the above increase the thoracic volume, leading to a reduced intrathoracic pressure. This is subatmospheric and so air flows passively into the lungs. Forced inspiration uses accessory muscles to further increase the intrathoracic volume and generate a lower intrathoracic pressure

Muscles used in expiration

- Expiration is passive in quiet respiration as elastic recoil produces a positive intra-alveolar pressure
- Muscles of forced expiration: abdominal wall muscles; internal intercostals generate higher intra-alveolar pressures and drive air out

Action of expiration

- The diaphragm relaxes
- The lungs and chest wall recoil
- The thoracic volume reduces, leading to a raised intrathoracic pressure causing airflow out of the lungs

Airway compliance

This is the 'elasticity' or 'stretchiness' of the lungs and it refers to the lungs and/or the chest walls.

$$\text{Compliance} = \text{change in lung volume}/\text{change in pressure}$$

A high or good compliance means that the lungs are easily inflated. Poor or low compliance means that the lungs are stiff, difficult to inflate and do not reach normal volumes. Poor compliance is caused by lung disease (eg pulmonary fibrosis, sarcoidosis, acute respiratory distress syndrome [ARDS]) or by disease of the chest wall (eg thoracic scoliosis).

The surface tension in the spherical alveoli tends to cause them to collapse. To counteract this and minimise the additional work required to re-inflate collapsed alveoli, the pneumocytes produce surfactant, which decreases the surface tension to that of a simple ionic solution.

The work of breathing

The work of breathing is usually performed only during inspiration because expiration is a passive phenomenon. It comprises:
- Work to expand the lung against elastic and surface tension forces
- Work to overcome airway resistance (may be high in disease)
- Movement of the chest wall

Respiratory capacity

Respiratory capacity is dependent on the volume of gas moved and the respiratory rate at which this occurs.

Respiratory volumes

The amount of gas moved during respiration depends on age, sex, build and level of fitness. Spirometry measures functionally important changes in lung volumes.

Definitions used in spirometry

- **TV** is tidal volume (0.5 l) – the volume of air moved in quiet respiration
- **IRV** is inspiratory reserve volume (3 l) – the maximum volume inspirable
- **ERV** is expiratory reserve volume (2.1 l) – the maximum volume expirable after TV expiration
- **RV** is residual volume (1.9 l) – the volume remaining in the lungs after maximum expiration
- **FRC** is functional residual capacity (1.9 l) – the is sum of ERV + RV (ie the volume in which gas exchange takes place)
- **VC** is vital capacity (5.6 l) – the volume that can be expired after a maximal inspiratory effort
- **FVC** is forced vital capacity
- **FEV_1** is forced expiratory volume – the volume expired in the 1st second of a forced expiration FVC measurement
- **TLC** is total lung capacity (6 l) – the sum of VC + RV
- **PEFR** is peak expiratory flow rate – a cheap and easy measure of airway resistance

All of the above except RV (and hence TLC) can be measured by spirometry.
To measure RV (or TLC) requires helium dilution methods or whole-body plethysmography.
Note that the above volumes are only meant as guides and relate to fit young adults.

Respiratory rate

The amount of air brought into the lungs per minute is the respiratory minute volume.

Minute volume = tidal volume × respiratory rate

Not all inspired air participates in gas exchange. Some occupies 'dead space':

- **Anatomical dead space:** mouth, nose, pharynx, larynx, trachea, bronchi
- **Alveolar dead space:** volumes of diseased parts of lung unable to perform gaseous exchange
- **Physiological dead space:** anatomical dead space plus alveolar dead space

As atmospheric PCO_2 is practically zero, all the CO_2 expired in a breath can be assumed to come from the communicating alveoli and none from the dead space. By measuring the PCO_2 in the communicating alveoli (which is the same as that in the arterial blood) and the PCO_2 in the expired air, one can use the Bohr equation to compute the 'diluting', non-PCO_2-containing volume, the physiological dead space. Normal value is 0.3 litres.

Dead space usually accounts for 150 ml but may be higher in disease states. Gas exchange depends on alveolar ventilation.

Alveolar ventilation rate = (tidal volume – dead space) × respiratory rate

Therefore any increase in dead space requires an increase in respiratory minute volume to achieve the same alveolar ventilation rate. This is very important in disease states with high physiological dead space and in patients on ventilators with high anatomical dead space (due to lengths of tubing).

CHAPTER 3

215

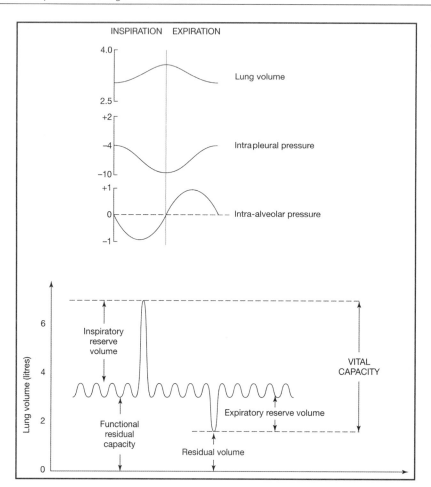

Figure 3.26 Respiratory volumes and alveolar pressures

The FEV₁:FVC ratio

The **FVC** gives an idea of the vital capacity. It is reduced in restrictive lung disease (eg fibrosis or collapse).

FEV₁ is the volume of gas expelled in the first second of forced expiration. It is reduced in obstructive airway disease because the gas cannot be forced out quickly.

- Normal value 0.7 (or 70%)
- Obstructive picture <70%
- Restrictive picture >70% or ratio stays the same with a reduced overall FVC compared with expected values

Peak expiratory flow rate (PEFR) measurement indicates airflow resistance but depends on patient effort and technique.

Control of respiration

Learning point

Respiratory control is regulated by neurological control and feedback mechanisms involving:
- Chemoreceptors
- Stretch receptors

Neurological control of respiration

Neurones controlling respiration are located in the medulla. Respiratory centres located nearby in the pons modify their activity. Inspiratory neurones have spontaneous rhythmical activity. Expiratory neurones are usually inactive unless forced expiration is required.

Chemoreceptors

Chemoreceptors detect chemical changes in the blood due to either changes in the partial pressure of oxygen or the local concentration of H^+ ions (which may be generated by dissolved CO_2 or metabolic products).

Central (medulla)	Peripheral
Detect changes in pH CO_2 crosses blood–brain barrier and dissolves in CSF Receptors detect the increase in CSF H^+ concentration	Carotid bodies via cranial nerve IX (and less important aortic bodies via X) Primarily detect changes in PaO_2 Less important detectors of changes in $PaCO_2$

Stretch receptors

In the Hering–Breuer reflex, negative feedback from lung stretch receptors as the lung inflates causes termination of inspiration. These send inhibitory impulses through the vagus nerve to prevent over-inflation.

The physiology of gas exchange

Gaseous exchange

- Occurs by simple diffusion across the alveolar–capillary interface
- Driven by the partial pressure of the gases involved

- Also depends on the solubility of the gas (CO_2 is more soluble than O_2)
- Usually not a rate-limiting step
- Measured using CO_2 uptake techniques

The transfer coefficient (KCO_2) depends on the diffusing capacity of lungs for CO_2 ($DLCO_2$) and the accessible alveolar volume (VA) and can be calculated thus:

$$KCO_2 = DLCO_2/VA$$

The ventilation–perfusion ratio ($\dot{V}/\dot{Q}$ ratio)

Normal gas exchange requires adequate ventilation and perfusion. Usually most alveoli will be both ventilated and perfused. There is some functional redundancy in the system and in the healthy state blood flow is diverted to the regions of the lung that are well perfused. This is a ventilation–perfusion match.

$$\dot{V}/\dot{Q} \text{ ratio = alveolar ventilation rate/pulmonary blood flow}$$

If significant regions of the lung are perfused but not ventilated (ventilation–perfusion mismatch) then there is a decrease in the ratio, with a tendency for a decrease in O_2 and CO_2 exchange and a gradual decrease in O_2 and increase in CO_2 in the arterial blood.

If significant regions of the lung are ventilated but not perfused there is an increase in the ratio and these regions add to the physiological dead space.

The oxyhaemoglobin dissociation curve

Oxygen is not very soluble in plasma and most of the oxygen is therefore carried bound to Hb molecules. Most O_2 is carried by Hb. A small amount of O_2 is dissolved in plasma and this is described by the PaO_2 value.

Haemoglobin readily binds oxygen at the capillary–alveolar interface and releases oxygen at the capillary tissue interface. It is capable of changing its affinity for oxygen under these two different conditions because of the shape of the oxyhaemoglobin dissociation curve.

The haemoglobin molecule
- Molecular weight 66 500 kDa.
- Normal blood serumconcentration is 15 g/dl
- Porphyrin ring attached to an Fe^{2+} ion
- Binds four molecules of O_2 per molecule of Hb
- 1 g Hb binds 1.34 ml of O_2 when fully saturated
- O_2 saturation refers to the number of O_2-bound haem molecules expressed as a percentage of the total number available; it can be measured by pulse oximetry

---

The relationship between O_2 saturation and PaO_2 is described by the O_2 dissociation curve. The sigmoid shape is formed because as each haem binds an oxygen molecule, it increases its binding capacity at the other three sites in a phenomenon called 'cooperativity'. When all the sites are full the Hb is saturated and the curve plateaus. When the Hb reaches the tissues, the dissociation of one molecule of oxygen makes it easier for the remaining molecules to dissociate.

The Bohr effect

The Bohr effect describes the factors that alter the position of the oxyhaemoglobin dissociation curve. In the lungs CO_2 diffuses from the blood into the alveoli and the H^+ concentration falls. This pushes the curve to the left where the quantity of O_2 that can bind with the Hb is increased, resulting in a higher saturation of the blood with O_2.

When the blood reaches the tissues it absorbs the products of metabolism in the form of CO_2 and this increases the H^+ ion concentration. The concentration of 2,3-diphosphoglycerate (2,3-DPG) increases with hypoxia and these factors shift the curve to the right, which favours release of the O_2 molecules and delivers O_2 to the tissues at a higher O_2 partial pressure than would otherwise occur.

Factors that shift the curve

To the left, ie increased affinity for O_2	To the right, ie reduced affinity for O_2
Decreased $PaCO_2$	Increased $PaCO_2$
Decreased H^+ ion concentration	Increased H^+ ion concentration
Decreased 2,3-DPG levels	Increased 2,3-DPG levels
Decreased temperature	Increased temperature
Increased fetal Hb (HbF)	
Increased carboxyhaemoglobin	

Transport of CO_2

CO_2 is transported in three ways:
- Dissolved as free CO_2 in plasma (10%)

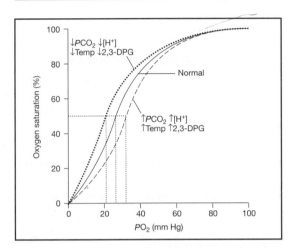

Figure 3.27 The O$_2$ dissociation curve

- Reacts with amine side groups of deoxy-Hb to form carbamino-Hb (30%)
- Reacts with H$_2$O of plasma to form H$^+$ and HCO$_3^-$, catalysed within the red blood cells by carbonic anhydrase. Inside the RBC the H$^+$ ions bind to the Hb protein which acts as a buffer. In order to maintain electrical neutrality, the bicarbonate diffuses out of the red cells in exchange for chloride ions (chloride shift)

The **Haldane effect** reflects the observation that, as the partial pressure of O$_2$ increases, the amount of CO$_2$ that is carried by the blood falls. This is because deoxy-Hb (venous) is a weaker acid than oxy-Hb and can hence carry more CO$_2$ in the carbamino-Hb form.

Oxygen delivery and consumption

Oxygen delivery

Oxygen delivery = Cardiac output × Arterial oxygen content

Oxygen delivery (DO_2) is the total amount of oxygen delivered to the tissues per unit time. It can be calculated using the formula:

$$\text{Oxygen delivery } (DO_2) = CO \times \{(Hb \times SaO_2 \times 1.34) + (PaO_2 \times 0.003)\}$$

Hb = haemoglobin (usually 15 g/dl or 1.5 g/ml in males)
SaO_2 = saturation of Hb with oxygen in arterial blood (usually 99% or 0.99)
PaO_2 = partial pressure of oxygen in arterial blood.

The amount of dissolved oxygen (ie the PaO_2 is usually negligible compared with the amount carried by the haemoglobin. It is approximately 13 kPa and 0.003 is the amount in millilitres of oxygen carried per kilopascal. However, PaO_2 also affects SaO_2

So, arterial oxygen content (ml/min):

= (1.5 g/ml × 0.99 × (1.34) + (13 kPa × 0.003)
≅ 2 ml O$_2$/ml of blood/min
≅ 0.2 L O$_2$/l of blood/min
Cardiac output is approximately 5 litres/min. So oxygen delivery:

≅ 5 l/min × 0.2 l/min
≅ 1 l/min

Oxygen consumption

Oxygen consumption is the oxygen content of arterial blood (CaO_2) minus the oxygen content of venous blood (CvO_2) multiplied by the cardiac output:

$$\textbf{O}_2 \textbf{ consumption} = (\textbf{CaO}_2 - \textbf{CvO}_2) \times \textbf{Cardiac output}$$

CvO_2 is measured by substituting mixed venous saturations (SvO_2 which is usually 75%) and PvO_2 (which is usually 4–5 kPa) into the equation for content. The values are measured directly via a blood-gas analyser with blood obtained from the tip of a pulmonary artery (PA) catheter. This provides true mixed venous blood. Some PA catheters have an oximeter at the tip to give continuous values.

CvO_2 is approximately 150 ml/l and hence O_2 consumption is normally 250 ml/min. It can be seen that there is more oxygen delivered than is consumed. There is an excess of supply over demand in healthy states. However, in low-delivery states and in critical illness, oxygen consumption is initially supply-dependent.

Respiratory investigations

Imaging

On ITUs radiographs are almost always anteroposterior (AP) views, so the heart size is unreliable. They are also frequently supine films, hence pneumothorax and effusions may not appear in the classic positions. CT of the thorax can provide detailed information and ultrasonography can help with isolation of effusions (including marking sites for drainage).

Remember:
- Label (check patient details)
- Adequacy of image (exposure; thoracic vertebrae just visible)
- Attached equipment (ECG leads, CVP/PA line, nasogastric [NG] tube)
- Heart size
- Mediastinum
- Endotracheal (ET) tube
- Hilar regions
- Diaphragm

- Lungs:
  - Look for silhouette sign
  - Consolidation: air bronchogram, no volume change
  - Atelectasis: shift of fissures, decreased volume, compensatory hyperinflation
- Bones
- Soft tissues
- Special areas (apices, behind heart, look for pneumothorax)
- Effusions (may appear at apex if supine)

Lung function tests
These tests measure for lung volumes, airway resistance and gas transfer. These have been discussed previously in this chapter.

Respiratory failure
The definition of respiratory failure is when pulmonary gas exchange is sufficiently impaired to cause hypoxia, with or without hypercapnia, ie PaO_2 <8 kPa or $PaCO_2$ >7 kPa.
- **Type I respiratory failure:** this is low PaO_2 <8 kPa with normal or low $PaCO_2$. It is caused by diseases that damage lung tissue, eg pulmonary embolus
- **Type II respiratory failure:** this is low PaO_2 <8 kPa with high $PaCO_2$ >7 kPa . It is caused by ventilation being insufficient to excrete sufficient CO_2, eg COPD, exhaustion, restrictive airway disease, failure to compensate for increased CO_2 production

Management of respiratory failure
- Exclude any airway problem and resuscitate as appropriate
- Give oxygen: in type I failure continuous positive airway pressure (CPAP) can improve PaO_2 if high-flow oxygen is inadequate; in type II failure ventilation can be improved

with bi-level positive airway pressure (BiPAP)
- Involve senior and ITU staff early for mechanical ventilatory support
- Take history (if possible) and examine thoroughly
- Regularly monitor arterial blood gases (ABGs) and consider arterial line insertion
- Adjust inspired O_2 according to ABGs
- Give bronchodilators (nebulised or IV), steroids, and antibiotics as appropriate
- Ensure high-level supervision – HDU or ITU[a]
- Make repeated assessments

[a]Patients with a requirement of >40% oxygen to keep oxygen saturation of >94% should be considered for observation on HDU/ITU (a Hudson oxygen mask, without a reservoir attached, can deliver at most about 40% oxygen).

Note that, as students, we all remember being told that high concentrations of inspired oxygen can ultimately stop a patient breathing due to loss of hypoxic drive (low PaO_2 rather than raised $PaCO_2$ drives respiration in some patients with COPD). However, in reality this is unusual and the junior doctor should not be afraid to give a hypoxic patient high-flow oxygen when O_2 saturations are <90%. Respiratory depression in this situation does not occur immediately and delivery of oxygen is more important at this stage. These patients should be carefully monitored during O_2 therapy.

ITU-specific pathologies that may result in respiratory failure

Learning point

Causes of respiratory failure in the ITU
- Respiratory infection
- ARDS

Specific respiratory infections in the ITU

Aspiration
- Current management depends on what is aspirated into the lungs. Look out for:
  - Particulate small-airway obstruction
  - Acid damage to alveolar membrane
  - Possible infected material
- Management of aspiration:
  - Observe, oxygen, physiotherapy; ventilation if necessary
  - No antibiotics unless definitely infected material (as promotes resistant organisms)
  - Do not use steroids

Lung abscess
- Often caused by aspiration and hence anaerobic organisms
- Can be caused by: bronchial obstruction; pneumonia; infected pulmonary infarcts; haematogenous spread
- Treatment: antibiotics, postural drainage and physiotherapy; <10% need surgical drainage

CHAPTER 3

Opportunistic pneumonia
- Relatively common on ITUs
- May require bronchial lavage ± transbronchial biopsy to identify organism
- Most common infections are Gram-positive organisms but include Gram negatives
- After use of antibiotics *Candida* spp. may colonise and cause infection

Empyema
- Accumulation of pus in pleural cavity
- 50% caused by pneumonia, 25% by post-surgical infections
- Gram-negative bacteria including *Pseudomonas* spp. often found, as well as staphylococci
- Acutely, low-viscosity fluid accumulates, then becomes more turbid, with increased WCC; at this point a fibrous peel develops on the lung surface, limiting expansion – after 6 weeks this peel becomes organised with fibroblasts
- Diagnosis: thoracocentesis: pH <7, low glucose, lactate dehydrogenase (LDH) >1000 IU/l and Gram stain, chest radiograph and CT scan
- Treat with antibiotics and chest drain in the acute phase but if there is failure to respond then open formal surgical drainage may be required

Acute lung injury and ARDS

Clinical features of acute lung injury
There is a spectrum of acute lung injury (ALF) from mild to severe. Severe ALI is called ARDS. ARDS is a term used to describe the respiratory component of systemic inflammatory response syndrome (SIRS) or multiorgan dysfunction syndrome (MODS) (see section 3.6 of this chapter).

Lung injury causes an inflammatory response, leading to damage to the alveolar capillary membrane and microcirculatory changes. This results in an increased pulmonary vascular permeability, leading to thickened alveolar membranes and leakage of fluid into the interstitium and alveoli. This process may be the pulmonary manifestation of whole-body capillary leak syndrome in MODS. This gives poorer lung volumes, compliance and gaseous exchange capabilities of lungs. There are three areas of the lung in this condition:
- Collapsed solid lung with consistency similar to the liver
- Ventilated and perfused lung (termed 'baby lung' because much smaller than normal)
- Potentially recruitable alveoli – this is where ventilatory techniques may be beneficial

It may resolve with or without pulmonary fibrosis.

Diagnostic features of acute lung injury
- Pulmonary infiltrates on CXR
- Pulmonary artery wedge pressure (PAWP) is <18 (so infiltrates are not due to cardiac pulmonary oedema)
- Hypoxaemia with ratio PaO_2/FiO_2 <40. ARDS criterion is severe hypoxaemia, ie PaO_2/FiO_2 <27
- A known cause (eg pancreatitis, aspiration, massive transfusion)

Other features include respiratory distress and decreased compliance.

Causes of ALI and ARDS	
Direct	**Indirect**
Chest trauma	Hypovolaemia
Aspiration	Sepsis
Inhaled irritants (eg smoke)	Burns
	Pancreatitis
	Fat embolism
	Radiation
	DIC

Management of acute lung injury

General management

- Almost entirely supportive
- Treat underlying cause if possible
- Reposition patient (eg prone)
- Careful fluid restriction/diuresis
- Corticosteroids in fibrosis stage
- Trial of blind antibiotics (controversial)

Ventilatory management

Optimisation of oxygenation is achieved by:
- Increasing mean airway pressure
- Increasing FiO_2
- Increasing airway pressure:
  - Increased peak inspired pressure limited to about 34 cmH_2O
  - Increased positive end-expiratory pressure (PEEP)
  - Increased inspiratory time, even so far as reversing the inhalation to exhalation ratio to 2:1
- Increasing FiO_2: levels >0.5 (50%) increase risk of oxygen toxicity, hence the above measures are used to minimise the inspired oxygen and targets of PaO_2 of 8 kPa and saturations of 90% are acceptable

The usual method is pressure-control ventilation, with PEEP and sometimes reverse ratio. To limit the peak pressures a low tidal volume can be allowed, hence the $PaCO_2$ can be allowed to increase (permissive hypercapnia). The tidal volume should also be restricted to around 6 ml/kg because excessive volumes cause shear stress damage to the alveoli.

In severely hypoxaemic patients, nitric oxide (NO) may be used to reduce the FiO_2 and improve oxygenation. The mainstay of therapy is, however, pressure support and PEEP to recruit collapsed alveoli and maintain them.

Ventilation in the prone position for periods of 4–8 hours may improve regional pulmonary $\dot{V}/\dot{Q}$ matching and improve oxygenation. This is due to non-homogeneous distribution of damage, which tends to be in the dependent lung. Despite this benefit, in some patients there are risks of dislodging the ET tube, catheters, and other monitoring lines and drains.

Fluid balance: this is difficult because over-hydration is deleterious to injured lung but adequate cardiovascular performance is required. Judicious use of ventilation, fluids and inotropes is needed.

Nitric Oxide (NO) therapy

NO is a vasodilator that is formed naturally in almost all tissues (constitutive). It is also produced in excess in sepsis, causing vascular dilatation.

Side effects include pulmonary toxicity due to nitric acid formation when oxidised. It causes vasodilatation in ventilated lung only, improving ventilation–perfusion match and thus preventing systemic vasodilatation and reversal of pulmonary hypoxic vasoconstriction. NO has a very high affinity for haemoglobin, and combined this becomes methaemoglobin, which deactivates NO and prevents systemic effects.

Outcome of ARDS
- 50–60% mortality rate
- Those who recover may be left with diffuse interstitial fibrosis

Respiratory monitoring and support

> **Learning point**
>
> Management of a compromised airway should be carried out according to Advance Life Support (ALS) guidelines (or Advance Trauma Life Support [ATLS] guidelines)
> Definitive airway management in critical care patients who are unable to maintain their own airway or who require mechanical ventilation is intubation:
> - **Nasal intubation** is preferred for paediatric ITU – there is an increased risk of haemorrhage in adults and risk of sepsis from sinus infection
> - **Endotracheal** or **pretracheal intubation** is the mainstay of management

Nasotracheal intubation

This technique is contraindicated in the apnoeic patient and in patients in whom midface or basal skull fractures are suspected.

Guiding the tip of the tube into the trachea is achieved blindly by auscultation for the point of maximum breath sounds, which is not as reliable as visualisation of the vocal folds using the orotracheal route. An alternative method is fibreoptic-guided insertion of the nasotracheal tube, but these endoscopes are costly and not widely available. This technique would seldom be advised in the acute trauma situation where speed and reliability are paramount.

Orotracheal intubation

Characteristics of the ET tube
- Internal diameter: 8–9 mm for males; 7–8 mm for females
- Length: 23 cm to teeth in males; 21 cm in females

The cuffed end:
- Creates a seal
- Helps prevent aspiration
- Can cause stenosis and tracheomalacia if high pressure (pressures should be monitored)

Procedure box: Endotracheal intubation

Indications
- Unconscious patient who cannot maintain own airway (GCS <8)
- Where there is a risk of upper airway obstruction
- Impaired gag reflex
- To prevent rise in ICP (iatrogenic hyperventilation)
- Requirement for mechanical ventilation (severe hypoxia or metabolic acidosis)
- Anaesthesia for surgery
- To enable suction of secretions

Contraindications
- Severe lower facial trauma may be better managed with a surgical airway

Patient positioning
- Supine with head in the 'sniffing the morning air' position
- Unconscious or under GA

Procedure
- Familiarise yourself with the technique and check all equipment before starting – laryngoscope, suction, ET tube (size 7–8 for females; 8–9 for males), Ambu-Bag, oxygen supply, assistant, muscle relaxant, sedation, IV access
- Pre-oxygenate the patient with 100% oxygen for 3–4 minutes
- Allow a maximum of 30 seconds for each attempt at insertion (hold your own breath!)
- Slide the laryngoscope into the right side of the mouth, sweeping the tongue to the left
- Place the tip of the blade in the groove between the epiglottis and the base of the tongue and draw the laryngoscope gently upwards (don't lever it on the teeth). Directly visualise the vocal folds and slide the ET tube into the trachea
- Check position of tube by auscultation of both lungs and the epigastrium
- End-tidal CO_2 monitors help verify correct position
- Secure tube by tying in place (average length is 21–23 cm to teeth for females, 23–25 cm for males)

Hazards
- Oesophageal intubation (a fatal complication if it goes unnoticed. If in any doubt about the position of the tube, remove it, pre-oxygenate the patient and start again)
- Tube advanced too far down, entering the right main bronchus
- Airway damage or rupture

Post-procedure instructions
- Always ensure that the tube is correctly positioned, allowing adequate ventilation of both lungs. If in any doubt or if the tube becomes displaced, it may have to be removed and the procedure repeated

Complications
- Early (see 'Hazards' above): damage to mouth and teeth; equipment failure; inability to intubate
- Late: erosion; stenosis of the trachea and larynx

Anaesthetic induction for intubation

This requires:

- **Skilled operator** trained in anaesthesia
- **Preparation of equipment**
- **Prevention of pressor response** on laryngoscopy with IV fentanyl or lidocaine, especially if risk of raised intracranial pressure (ICP)
- **Cricoid pressure:** application of pressure to the cricoid, the only complete ring of cartilage in the airway, causes it to impinge onto the body of C6; this will prevent passive regurgitation once induced
- **Induction agent:** if haemodynamically unstable there may be a precipitous drop in BP; etomidate is reasonably cardio-stable, as is ketamine (which has the added value of bronchodilation)
- **Muscle relaxant:** suxamethonium has rapid onset (<1 minute) characterised by fasciculations and is short acting; side effects include anaphylaxis and hyperkalaemia, especially after burns or in patients with paralysis, when cardiac arrest can occur

Alternative airways

- Emergency surgical airway: cricothyroidotomy
- Elective surgical airway: surgical tracheostomy
  - Percutaneous tracheostomy
  - Open surgical tracheostomy

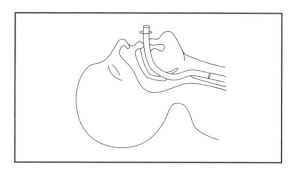

Figure 3.28 Orotracheal intubation

Tracheostomy

An open surgical tracheostomy is slow, technically more complex, with potential for bleeding, and requires formal operating facilities. It is not appropriate in the acute trauma situation, but is better suited to the long-term management of a ventilated patient. It is performed when a percutaneous tracheostomy would be difficult (eg abnormal or distorted anatomy).

Percutaneous tracheostomy is also time-consuming and requires hyperextension of the neck. In addition the use of a guidewire and multiple dilators make it an unsuitable technique in the acute trauma situation.

CHAPTER 3

Procedure box: Percutaneous tracheostomy

Indications
- Prolonged ventilation (reduces risk of tracheal stenosis from long-term orotracheal intubation). Aids weaning from the ventilator
- Patients who are unable to maintain their own airway due to long-term disease (eg bulbar palsy)

Contraindications
- Coagulopathy, abnormal anatomy, unstable patient

Patient positioning
- Supine with the neck extended
- Most are already intubated and ventilated under sedation or GA
- The surgical area is infiltrated with 10 ml 1% lidocaine with adrenaline to reduce bleeding

Procedure
- A bronchoscope is inserted into the trachea and the ET tube is withdrawn to the level of the vocal folds by an anaesthetist
- The tracheal stoma should be located between the second and fourth tracheal rings and a superficial 2-cm horizontal incision is made at this level
- A large-bore needle is inserted into the trachea through the incision and its location verified by aspiration of air through a syringe
- A guidewire is passed into the trachea under direct vision by the bronchoscope. Lubricated sequential dilators are passed over the guidewire to enlarge the stoma to an appropriate size
- A cuffed tracheostomy tube is passed over the guidewire and into the trachea. Once secure, the ET tube is removed completely

Hazards
- Haemorrhage from subcutaneous blood vessels
- Failure to cannulate the trachea

Complications
Early
- Asphyxia
- Aspiration
- Creation of a false track, leading to subcutaneous/mediastinal emphysema and/or haemorrhage/haematoma
- Laceration of the oesophagus or trachea

Late
- Vocal fold paralysis/hoarseness
- Cellulitis
- Laryngeal stenosis
- Tracheomalacia

Mini-tracheostomy

A small tracheostomy tube may be inserted through the cricothyroid membrane – to aid suctioning of secretions and physiotherapy. This is not suitable as a definitive airway because the tube is not cuffed.

Mechanically assisted ventilation

Indications and aims of mechanical ventilation

- Elimination and control of CO_2
- Improve oxygenation – reduces 'work' of respiration and therefore O_2 consumed
- Enables high levels of inspired O_2 to be administered
- Can open collapsed alveoli by raising pressure during inspiration and maintaining pressure during expiration

Complications of mechanical ventilation

- Airway complications (see above)
- Barotrauma (pneumothorax, pneumo-mediastinum, pneumoperitoneum, surgical emphysema)
- Cardiovascular – reduced venous return (high intrathoracic pressure)
- Increased pulmonary vascular resistance
- Gastric dilatation/ileus (gastric tube must be inserted)
- Accidental disconnection or wrong setting of ventilator
- Na^+ and H_2O retention – increased ADH and ANP
- Atrophy of respiratory muscles if no spontaneous effort
- Infection/pneumonia

Positive end-expiratory pressure

- Achieved by adding a valve to an assisted breathing circuit
- Expiratory pressure is not allowed to fall below a certain level (2.5–20 cmH$_2$O)
- Pressure prevents alveolar collapse at the end of expiration and recruits collapsed alveoli

Advantages: increases lung volumes and improves oxygenation. Can be used with the patient breathing spontaneously (see CPAP and BiPAP) or with mechanical ventilation.

Disadvantages: reduces physiological shunting, but further reduces venous return and increases barotrauma.

Continuous positive airway pressure

- Used in spontaneously ventilating patients (may or may not require airway management)
- If the patient is conscious and making respiratory effort this requires a tightly fitting mask to maintain positive pressure
- If the patient is not conscious or is tiring, intubation with a cuffed ET tube is required
- Same advantages and disadvantages as PEEP but also reduces respiratory effort
- Reduces cardiac work by reducing transmural tension

Bi-level positive airway pressure

- Allows separate adjustment of the pressures delivered during inspiration and expiration
- Allows lower overall airway pressures to be used (reduces barotrauma compared with CPAP)
- Tolerated better because the high pressure corresponds to inspiration, and a lower

CHAPTER 3

pressure during expiration makes this phase easier for the patient
- May also have a spontaneous timed setting; if the patient fails to initiate a breath then the machine will initiate that breath for them

Intermittent positive-pressure ventilation

Ventilators on ITU have a choice of mode and mandatory or spontaneous features; all have pressure limitation cut-off and sophisticated alarms.

Controlled mechanical ventilation (CMV)
- Sets rate for breaths and breath volume by either volume or pressure control
- Allows no spontaneous respirations (eg as in anaesthetic ventilators)

Intermittent mandatory ventilation (IMV)
- Delivers 'mandatory' minute volume but allows the patient to take spontaneous breaths between mechanical breaths
- Can be synchronised with spontaneous breaths (SIMV) thus preventing stacking of breaths. This occurs when a mechanical breath is imposed after a spontaneous one. Sensors in the ventilator detect the patient's own breaths. This is the main mode used in ITU

Mandatory-type ventilator features
This determines how breaths are delivered, as either a set volume or a set pressure.

Volume control
- Tidal volume to be delivered is set on the ventilator. Normal settings are 10 ml/kg. This is the usual mandatory type; however, if compliance is poor the inspired pressure will be very high, with risk of barotrauma. Therefore it is not suitable in ARDS and asthma

Pressure control
- An inspiratory pressure is set on the ventilator and tidal volume is dependent on compliance
- This type is used in ARDS; the inspiratory pressure is set to a value to achieve a satisfactory measured tidal volume but peak pressures are usually limited to 34 cmH$_2$O to avoid barotrauma

Spontaneous-type ventilator features

Pressure support
- This adjunct supports spontaneous breaths with a set pressure to increase their tidal volumes
- Allows very small breaths produced by the patient to be boosted to adequate volumes as an aid to weaning
- Sensitivity of breath detection can be altered via the trigger sensitivity and type
- Trigger for supported breaths is usually a drop in pressure, but flow triggering is more sensitive if required

Assist-control (trigger) ventilation
- Uses patient's own respiratory rhythm to trigger delivery of a set tidal volume

CHAPTER 3

Weaning from assisted ventilation

- Patient must have recovered from original problem requiring ventilation
- Conscious level, metabolic state, cardio-vascular function and state of mind are to be considered
- SIMV mode aids weaning with pressure support (PS). As the patient starts taking spontaneous breaths the SIMV rate is reduced until all breaths are spontaneous and supported by PS. PS is then reduced until the patient self-ventilates without support
- The longer the time spent on a ventilator, the longer (more difficult) the weaning

Before extubation the patient may be placed on a T-piece, which allows oxygenation without support. CPAP is sometimes helpful.

The most successful method of weaning is with spontaneous breaths from the patient supported by pressure support.

Extubation

The patient must:

- Be able to breathe spontaneously indefinitely
- Have an effective cough reflex and be able to protect their airway
- Be conscious enough to cooperate

Other factors include adequate tidal volume (TV) without tachypnoea (ie respiratory rate/TV <100).

Physiotherapy

It is essential that secretions are cleared in ventilated patients who cannot cough, especially those with pneumonia. Chest physio with suctioning should be carried out frequently.

2.5 Pain control

Pain and its management

Learning point

Pain is an unpleasant sensory and emotional experience associated with actual or potential tissue damage. It is a protective mechanism.

The physiological experience of pain is called **nociception**. It comprises four processes:

- Transduction (anti-inflammatories act here)
- Transmission (local anaesthetics act here)
- Modulation (transcutaneous electrical nerve stimulation [TENS] machine exploits pain gating)
- Perception (opiates act here)

The physiological aspects of pain may be modified by pharmacological means.

Transduction of pain stimuli

This is the translation of a noxious stimulus into electrical activity at the sensory endings of nerves. A noxious stimulus can be mechanical, chemical or thermal. The pain receptors in the skin and other tissues are all free nerve endings. The noxious stimulus results in tissue damage and inflammation. Non-steroidal analgesics reduce pain by inhibiting prostaglandins, which sensitise pain receptors to noxious stimuli.

Nociceptive neurones can change in their responsiveness to stimuli, especially in the presence of inflammation.

- In areas of damaged tissue the nociceptive threshold is decreased; normally noxious

stimuli result in an exaggerated response (**primary hyperalgesia**) as in the extreme sensitivity of sunburned skin
- In damaged tissue there can be a lower pain threshold in areas beyond the site of injury (**secondary hyperalgesia**)
- In damaged tissue normally innocuous stimuli (eg light touch) can cause pain (allodynia), eg a light touch in peritonitis can cause severe pain
- In damaged tissue pain is prolonged beyond the application of the stimuli (**hyperpathia**)

Transmission of pain impulses

Impulses travel in A fibres (fast) and C fibres (slow): A fibres transmit acute sharp pain; C fibres transmit slow chronic pain. This 'dual system' of pain transmission means that a painful stimulus results in a 'double' pain sensation, a fast sharp pain, followed by slow burning pain. 'Fast' pain involves a localised reflex flexion response, removing that part of the body from the injurious stimulus, therefore limiting tissue damage. Although C-fibre pain is not well localised, it results in immobility, which enforces rest and therefore promotes healing of the injured area.
- A fibres terminate at two places in the dorsal horn: lamina 1and lamina 5
- C fibres terminate in lamina 2 and lamina 3 of the dorsal horn (an area called the **substantia gelatinosa**)
- These primary afferent fibres synapse onto second-order neurones in the dorsal horn (the neurotransmitter here is **substance P**)
- Most of these second-order neurones cross over in the **anterior white commissure** about one segment rostrally and ascend as the **lateral spinothalamic tract**; in the brainstem this is called the **spinal lemniscus**
- The second-order neurones eventually synapse in the thalamus (**ventral postero-lateral nucleus**)

- From here the third-order neurones pass through the **internal capsule** to the somaesthetic area in the **postcentral gyrus** of the cerebral cortex, for conscious perception and localisation of the pain. This projection is **somatotropic**
- Although A fibres project to the cortex, the C fibres nearly all terminate in the reticular formation, which is responsible for the general arousal of the CNS

Modulation of pain

Central mechanisms

Sometimes these central mechanisms are called the descending anti-nociceptive tract. The tract originates in the periaqueductal grey and periventricular area of the midbrain, and descends to the dorsal horn of the spinal cord; here enkephalins are released which cause presynaptic inhibition of incoming pain fibres.

Throughout the descending anti-nociceptive tract there are receptors that respond to morphine; the brain has its own natural opiates known as endorphins and enkephalins which act along this pathway (opiate analgesics act via these opioid receptors).

Spinal mechanisms

Opioids act directly at the spinal laminae inhibiting the release of substance P (the neurotransmitter involved between the primary and secondary afferent fibres). This is the mechanism exploited by epidural injection.

Mechanical inhibition of pain

Stimulation of mechanoreceptors in the area of the body where the pain originates can inhibit pain by stimulation of large A fibres. (This is why

CHAPTER 3

analgesia is induced by rubbing the affected part or by applying TENS.) TENS involves applying a small electrical current over the nerve distribution of the pain, which activates the large sensory fibres and inhibits pain transmission through the dorsal horn. This is known as 'pain gating'.

Perception of pain

This occurs in the thalamus and sensory cortex.

Referred pain

This is when pain is perceived to occur in a part of the body topographically distinct from the source of the pain. Branches of visceral pain fibres synapse in the spinal cord with some of the same second-order neurones that receive pain fibres from the skin. Therefore when the visceral pain fibres are stimulated, pain signals from the viscera can be conducted through second-order neurones which normally conduct pain signals from the skin. The person then perceives the pain as originating in the skin itself.

Visceral pain

Viscera have sensory receptors for no other modality of sensation except pain. Localised damage to viscera rarely causes severe pain. Stimuli that cause diffuse stimulation of nerve endings in a viscus can cause pain that is very severe (eg ischaemia, smooth muscle spasm, distension of a hollow viscus, chemical damage to visceral surfaces).

- Visceral pain from the thoracic and abdominal cavities is transmitted through sensory nerve fibres which run in the sympathetic nerves – these fibres are C fibres (transmit burning/aching pain)
- Some visceral pain fibres enter the spinal cord through the sacral parasympathetic

nerves, including those from distal colon, rectum and bladder
- Note that visceral pain fibres may enter the cord via the cranial nerves (eg the glossopharyngeal and vagus nerves) which transmit pain from the pharynx, trachea and upper oesophagus

If a disease affecting a viscus spreads to the parietal wall surrounding the viscera, the pain perceived will be sharp and intense. The parietal wall is innervated from spinal nerves, including the fast A fibres.

Localisation of pain

Visceral pain is referred to various dermatomes on the body surface. The position on the surface of the body to which pain is referred depends on the segment of the body from which the organ developed embryologically, eg the heart originated in the neck and upper thorax, so the visceral pain fibres from the surface of the heart enter the cord from C3 to T5. These are the dermatome segments in which cardiac pain may be perceived. Pain from organs derived from the foregut is felt in the upper abdomen. Pain from organs derived from the midgut is felt in the mid-abdomen, and pain from organs derived from the hindgut is felt in the lower abdomen.

Parietal pain (eg from parietal peritoneum) is transmitted via spinal nerves which supply the external body surface. A good example is acute appendicitis:

- A colicky umbilical pain appears to 'move' to the right iliac fossa (RIF) and becomes constant
- Visceral pain is transmitted via the sympathetic chain at the level of T10; this pain is referred to the dermatome corresponding to this area, ie around the

umbilicus; this is colicky pain associated with obstruction of a hollow viscus (the appendix)

When the inflamed appendix touches the parietal peritoneum, these impulses pass via spinal nerves to level L1–2. This constant pain will be localised in the RIF (at McBurney's point, a third of the distance from anterosuperior iliac spine to the umbilicus).

Acute pain

Methods of assessing acute pain

Subjective measures of acute pain
- Verbal scale:
  - None
  - Mild
  - Moderate
  - Severe
- Visual analogue score:
  - Ranging from worst pain ever (10) to no pain at all (0)
  - Smiley faces, sad faces (for children)

Objective measures of acute pain
- Most are indirect (eg blood pressure variations, vital capacity)

Inadequate analgesia
Inadequate post-op pain relief may be due to:
- Expectation (of the patient, nursing staff or medical team)
- Prescription method: prescribe prophylactically and regularly rather than on demand
- Inability to use or intolerance of the pain relief method (eg if the patient is immobile, arthritic or confused and so unable to use patient-controlled analgesia [PCA])

Harmful effects of undertreated acute pain

Cardiovascular effects
- Tachycardia
- Hypertension
- Increased myocardial oxygen consumption

Respiratory effects
- Splinting of the chest wall and therefore decreased lung volumes
- Basal atelectasis

Gastrointestinal effects
- Reduced gastric emptying and bowel movement

Genitourinary effects
- Urinary retention

Musculoskeletal effects
- Muscle spasm
- Immobility (therefore increased risk of DVT)

Psychological effects
- Anxiety
- Fear
- Sleeplessness

Neuroendocrine effects
- Secretion of catecholamines and catabolic hormones, leading to increased metabolism and oxygen consumption, which promotes sodium and water retention and hyperglycaemia

Management of postoperative pain

The realistic aim of pain relief is not to abolish pain completely, but to ensure that the patients are comfortable and have return of function with a more rapid recovery and rehabilitation. Two fundamental concepts prevail:

- Preventing the development of pain is more effective than treating established pain – give pre-emptive analgesia, before surgical trauma, with parenteral opioids, regional blocks or NSAIDs
- It is difficult to produce safe, effective analgesia for major surgery with a single group of drugs (monomodal therapy). Better analgesia is achieved with combinations of drugs that affect different parts of the pain pathway (multimodal therapy) – usually a combination of local anaesthetics, opioids and NSAIDs

Note that, if possible, the choice should be of the least painful incisions (eg lower abdominal or transverse incisions).

Postoperative analgesia

- Multimodal therapy
- Use regular non-opioid analgesic initially (eg paracetamol or NSAID, if not contraindicated) for minor surgery
- Use regional or local analgesia techniques (eg epidural or peripheral nerve blocks); they are especially effective in the immediate post-anaesthetic period
- In major surgery, opioids will be needed as an addition to the above to enhance analgesia; they are especially useful in the immediate postop period and are still the mainstay for routine postop pain relief. IV opioids are preferred as dose delivery of IM injections is erratic and has greater complications
- IV opioids are best administered in the form of PCA

The acute pain service (APS)

Each hospital should have an acute pain service team who should be responsible for the day-to-day management of patients with postop pain. This is a multidisciplinary team using medical, nursing and pharmacological expertise. Anaesthetists have a major role to play, since they not only initiate postoperative analgesic regimens such as PCA and epidural infusions, but also are very familiar with the drugs and equipment. Protocols for the strict management of PCA and epidural regimens are essential.

Chronic pain

Chronic pain is pain that persists after a time period when it would be expected that healing were complete.

The aetiology involves physical neural system rewiring and behavioural and psychosocial factors. It is very difficult to manage and requires specialist knowledge (often an anaesthetic subspeciality).

Management strategies include:

- Assessment of chronic pain states
- Multimodal therapy
- Pain clinics

Aetiology of chronic pain

Neural system rewiring

In chronic pain states, there are microscopic neural changes in the dorsal horn, spinal cord and brain. Neural connections are altered, resulting in central plasticity. These changes result in a reduced pain threshold, in which there is exaggerated local response to mildly painful stimulus termed 'hyperalgesia' or connection of mechanoreceptive neurones to pain pathways in which non-painful stimuli are perceived as painful, resulting in allodynia. Examples of plasticity of the neural system are phantom limb pain and the pain of peripheral neuropathy.

Behavioural and psychosocial issues
Depression or anxiety occurs in 58% of chronic pain patients and there is a higher than normal incidence of personality disorder. Psychological issues may represent aetiological factors or occur as the sequelae to an unpleasant condition.

Types of chronic pain
- May be skeletal, spinal, joint, muscle or neuropathic (eg burning)
- Commonly back pain and headaches

Assessment of chronic pain
- History of injury, medication use and comorbid illness (physical and psychological)
- Pain history (amount, duration, constant vs intermittent, description, eg shooting vs burning)
- Identify effects of condition on physical, psychological, social and financial aspects of the patient's life to establish functional status
- Exclude a treatable underlying medical condition
- Identify behaviour patterns that may respond to behaviour modification techniques
- Identify realistic treatment goals and time course

Multimodal therapy for chronic pain
- Functional rehabilitation (multidisciplinary team [MDT] approach – nurses, psychologists, physiotherapists and occupational therapists) coordinated in the pain clinic

- Medication:
  - NSAIDs and moderate opioids, eg tramadol or codeine for flare-ups
  - Long-acting opioids (eg morphine sulphate tablet [MST], transdermal fentanyl) for analgesia maintenance
  - Antiepileptics (gabapentin, lamotrigine) and antidepressants (tricyclic antidepressants [TCAs] or serotonin selective reuptake inhibitors [SSRIs]) for neuropathic pain

Pain in malignancy
Pain from malignancy is a combination of:
- Neuropathic pain (due to invasion of nerves)
- Nociception (due to tissue damage)

Management of malignant pain:
- Follow the WHO analgesic ladder (may require opioid analgesia)
- Aim for regular, oral medication
- Regional blocks (eg coeliac plexus block)
- Radiotherapy can provide pain relief
- CT-guided stereotactic percutaneous destructive procedures

Pharmacology of pain

The WHO analgesic ladder
Step 1   Simple analgesics (paracetamol, NSAIDs)
Step 2   Compound analgesics (eg co-codamol, co-dydramol)
Step 3   Opiates (oral morphine remains drug of choice)

Routes for administration of analgesics	
Oral	Sublingual
Intramuscular	Rectal
Intravenous	Inhalational
Subcutaneous	Epidural
Transdermal	Spinal

Paracetamol
- Mildly analgesic and antipyretic orally
- Given intravenously, 1 g paracetamol has been shown to be as effective as 10 mg morphine

Side effects of paracetamol:
- Overdose can cause liver damage and/or failure

Non-steroidal anti-inflammatory drugs
- Examples: diclofenac, ibuprofen
- Anti-inflammatory, analgesic and antipyretic actions
- Mainly act peripherally but have some central action
- Mechanism of action is by inhibition of the enzyme cyclo-oxygenase (this therefore inhibits synthesis of prostaglandins which sensitise pain receptors to noxious stimuli)

Side effects of NSAIDs:
- Prostaglandins are important in gastric mucus and bicarbonate production, so gastric irritation and peptic ulceration may result if their production is inhibited (especially in elderly patients)
- Nephrotoxicity: chronic use can cause interstitial nephritis, papillary necrosis and urothelial tumours
- Increased bleeding results from decreased platelet adhesiveness because of inhibition of thromboxane production
- Bronchospasm in patients with asthma (use should be avoided)
- May cause gout (especially indomethacin)
- May displace warfarin or other drugs from plasma proteins
- Aspirin overdosage causes metabolic acidosis and respiratory alkalosis

Opioid analgesics
- Examples: morphine, diamorphine, fentanyl
- Cause analgesia, euphoria and anxiolysis
- Act centrally and peripherally at opiate receptors
- Three main types of receptor: mu (μ), kappa (κ) and delta (δ)

Side effects of opiates:
- **Central** side effects of opiates:
  - Respiratory depression (by acting on respiratory centre)
  - Nausea and vomiting (by acting on chemoreceptor trigger zone)
  - Hypotension, especially if hypovolaemic or if taking vasodilating drugs (common cause of postoperative hypotension)
  - Miosis
  - Tolerance and addiction
- **Peripheral** side effects of opiates:
  - Constipation
  - Delayed gastric emptying
  - Urinary retention
  - Spasm of the sphincter of Oddi
  - Pruritis

Routes of administration of opiates
- Oral opioids:
  - Codeine phosphate, tramadol, oral morphine sulphate solution
  - Not useful immediately after major surgery because of nausea and vomiting and delayed gastric emptying
  - Very useful after day-case surgery and 3–4 days after major surgery
- Intramuscular opioids:
  - Most common form of postop analgesia, even though they are ineffective in providing effective analgesia in up to 40% of patients
  - There is a fivefold difference in peak plasma concentrations among different patients after administration of a

standard dose of morphine, with the time taken to reach these levels varying by as much as sevenfold
- The minimum effective analgesic concentration (MEAC) may vary by up to fourfold between patients
- The 'standard' dose is likely to be optimal for a minority of patients
- Intravenous opioids:
  - Continuous infusion leads to effective analgesia, but with significant risk of respiratory depression
  - PCA is the safest form
- Epidural opioid analgesia (see below)
- Slow-release oral opioids:
  - MSTs have modified release over 12 hours (therefore given twice daily)
  - To calculate dose: titrate oral dose required to provide relief, then divide total daily oral dose into two daily MST doses
  - Always provide additional oral morphine sulphate solution when required for breakthrough pain

Management of analgesia
Remember to work up the ladder toward opiates. There are often substitutions that can be made:
- Paracetamol should be given regularly as a starting point
- Non-opioids (eg aspirin, NSAIDs, paracetamol) can control bone pain
- Co-codamol two tablets four times daily is equivalent to morphine 6–8 mg 4-hourly
- The starting dose of morphine should be titrated to pain (eg 10 mg 4-hourly) unless the patient is elderly or has hepatorenal impairment.
- Transdermal fentanyl or alternative oral drugs (eg OxyNorm) are useful if tolerance is poor

With opiates, always prescribe:
- Antiemetic for first 2 or 3 days
- A laxative to prevent constipation

Patient-controlled analgesia
- Now widely used for postoperative analgesia
- Administered via a special microprocessor-controlled pump, connected to the patient via an intravenous line, which is triggered by pressing a button in patient's hand
- A pre-set bolus of drug is delivered, and a timer prevents administration of another bolus for a specified period (lock-out interval)

Advantages of PCA
- Dose matches patient requirements
- Decreased nurse workload
- Painless (no IM injections)
- Additional placebo effect from patient autonomy

Disadvantages of PCA
- Technical error can be fatal (be very wary of background infusions)
- Expense of equipment

Cautions in the use of PCA
- A dedicated IV cannula should be used to ensure that the drug from the PCA does not accumulate retrogradely
- Monitor respiratory rate and level of sedation
- Patient must be orientated and fully understand how to use the system for it to be effective; use may be difficult for some patients (eg rheumatoid arthritis or learning difficulties)

CHAPTER 3

Sedation

Sedation can also be used in critical care as an adjunct to analgesia

Aims of sedation

- Relieve anxiety
- Help synchronisation with the ventilator
- Encourage natural sleep
- Permit unpleasant procedures

Routes for sedation

- Bolus dosing: prevents over-sedation but is inconvenient
- Infusion: risk of over-sedation. Can be discontinued each day until rousable then restarted as necessary

Drugs for sedation

- Benzodiazepines (eg midazolam): reduce anxiety and are amnesic. Can accumulate with infusions and are inexpensive
- Propofol: rapid elimination. Does not accumulate but is expensive (however, avoiding increased length of stay due to over-sedation may offset cost). May cause hypotension

2.6 Intravenous drug delivery

> **Learning point**
>
> Venous access may be achieved:
> - Peripherally: by insertion of cannulas into peripheral veins of the extremities (includes venous cut-down)
> - Centrally: by insertion of a cannula through the peripheral system into a central large-bore vessel or direct cannulation of central vessels

Peripheral venous access

In most patients requiring venous access for IV medication or fluids, a peripheral vein is the appropriate route. Peripheral venous cannulation may be a life-saving procedure in hypovolaemic shock.

Cannula sizes range from 12 G (the largest, for rapid infusion in hypovolaemia) to 24 G (the smallest, for children).

Note that flow is proportional to r^4 (where r is the radius of the lumen of the cannula). High flow requires a large bore.

Indications and contraindications for peripheral access

Indications for peripheral venous access

- Fluid/blood infusion
- Blood sampling
- Drug administration
- Central venous line via peripheral route, eg percutaneous indwelling central catheter (PICC) line
- Peripheral venous feeding

Contraindications for peripheral venous access

- Local sepsis
- Puncture of potential arteriovenous fistula sites in haemodialysis patients

Complications of peripheral venous access

- Infection (local or systemic introduction of pathogens)
- Thrombophlebitis (usually chemical, eg erythromycin, cytotoxic agents)
- Subcutaneous haematoma

- Extravasation (may just cause oedema, but cytotoxic agents can cause considerable tissue damage)
- Accidental arterial cannulation

Common sites used for peripheral venous access

- Dorsum of hand
- Median basilic, median cephalic, basilic veins at antecubital fossa (avoid in haemodialysis patients)
- External jugular vein
- Long saphenous vein at the ankle (avoid in patients with coronary artery disease)
- Dorsum of foot
- Scalp veins in infants or neonates

Venous cut-down

Patients in hypovolaemic shock often have collapsed peripheral veins, resulting in difficult cannulation. In such circumstances rapid access can be gained by open cut-down onto a vein and cannulation. The most common veins used for this are the antecubital veins and the long saphenous vein. Of the antecubital veins, the median basilic vein is most commonly used. It is found 2 cm medial to the brachial artery.

Procedure box: Venous cut-down

Indications
- IV access in cases of circulatory collapse when attempts to establish peripheral venous access have failed
- Useful in trauma and burns

Patient positioning
- Supine, with medial side of the ankle exposed

Procedure
- Prepare the ankle on the medial side with antiseptic and drapes
- Infiltrate LA into the skin over the long saphenous vein (unless immediate access is required)
- Make a transverse incision 1–2 cm anterior to the medial malleolus
- Using blunt dissection, isolate the vein and free it from surrounding tissue
- Ligate the distal end of the mobilised vein
- Pass a tie around the proximal aspect of the vein
- Make a small transverse venotomy
- Dilate this with closed haemostatic forceps
- Insert a large-bore cannula and secure it with the proximal tie
- Close the wound with interrupted sutures and apply a sterile dressing

Post-procedure
- Standard wound care
- Observe for infection

Complication
- Haemorrhage due to lack of vascular control

CHAPTER 3

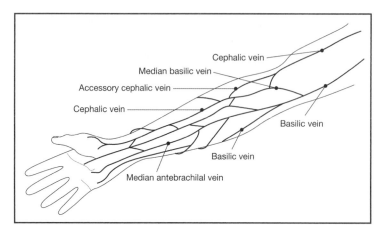

Figure 3.29 Peripheral venous access – veins of the forearm

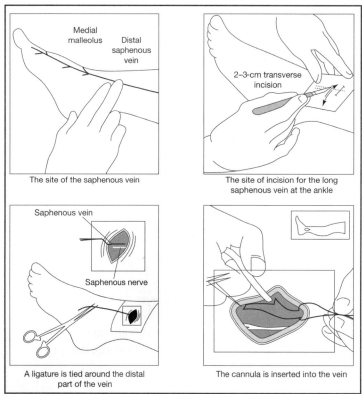

Figure 3.30 Venous cut-down into long saphenous vein

Central venous access

Central venous cannulation is a potentially dangerous procedure, particularly in a hypovolaemic patient, and should be performed only by (or supervised by) an experienced practitioner.

Central venous catheters may reach the SVC or right atrium via the basilic, cephalic, subclavian, external and internal jugular veins. The most common sites are the subclavian and internal jugular veins. Insertion of catheters into the IVC via the long saphenous or femoral veins is associated with a high incidence of DVT and PE and should be considered only as a last resort.

Catheters may be introduced with the 'through cannula' technique, whereby a short plastic cannula is first introduced into the vein:

- Needle introduced into vein
- Cannula advanced over needle and needle withdrawn
- Catheter inserted through cannula and cannula withdrawn

The Seldinger technique uses a flexible metal guidewire as an intermediate step to prevent the catheter coiling up on itself inside the vein:

- Needle introduced into vein
- Guidewire advanced through needle and needle withdrawn
- Catheter advanced over guidewire and guidewire withdrawn

Catheters may be Teflon or Silastic – Silastic catheters are more expensive, but induce less reaction, are more flexible, and are most suitable for long-term central venous access. Wide-bore Silastic catheters (single-, double- or triple-lumen) (eg Hickman) are suitable for long-term parenteral nutrition or chemotherapy and are introduced percutaneously or surgically and the skin tunnelled (to reduce catheter-related sepsis) to an exit site on the chest wall.

Central venous anatomy

Catheters are usually inserted percutaneously, but may be placed under direct vision after surgical exposure of the vein.

The subclavian vein

The axillary vein continues as the subclavian vein as it crosses the outer border of the first rib behind the clavicle, and it ends behind the sternoclavicular joint where it joins the internal jugular vein (IJV) to form the brachiocephalic vein. It is closely related to the subclavian artery above and behind it and to the dome of the pleura below and behind it. The thoracic duct enters the brachiocephalic vein at its origin on the left and cannulation of the right side is therefore safer.

The internal jugular vein (IJV)

As the IJV runs down in the neck, it comes to lie lateral to the internal and common carotid arteries deep to sternomastoid muscle and joins the subclavian vein to form the brachio-cephalic vein behind the sternoclavicular joint. The vein may be punctured from three sites: the posterior border of sternomastoid muscle, the anterior border of sternomastoid muscle and near its lower end between the two heads of the sternomastoid muscle; the first route is the most commonly used.

CHAPTER 3

241

Insertion of central venous access

Procedure box: Central venous access

Indications
- Fluid infusion
- Drug infusion
- Cytotoxic drugs which would damage peripheral veins
- Inotropic drugs
- TPN (hypertonic solution would damage peripheral veins)
- Pacemaker electrode insertion
- Monitoring of central pressures (eg CVP, pulmonary artery pressure)

Contraindications
- Local sepsis
- Severe coagulation disorders

Patient positioning
- The patient should be supine, with arms by the side, head turned to the opposite side
- Prepare all your equipment and only then place the patient head down, just before you start the procedure

Procedure (Seldinger technique)
You will need:
- Skin preparation
- 10 ml plain LA in a 10-ml syringe with a blue needle (22 G) attached
- 10 ml 0.9% saline in a 10-ml syringe with a green needle attached (you must be able to differentiate between the syringe containing anaesthetic and the one containing saline)
- 10 ml 0.9% saline to flush the line at completion
- A CVP line kit complete with large-bore needle, guidewire, dilator and CVP line
- Small scalpel blade
- Silk suture and fixative dressings
- Sterile surgical drape
- Sterile gown and gloves
- Ultrasonography for identification of target vessel
- Prepare the CVP line itself by opening all the taps on the three lumens and flushing the line through with 0.9% saline to remove the air
- Close all the taps except the lumen that the guidewire will emerge through (commonly marked with a brown bung)
- Position the patient. Patients should be supine with a head-down tilt of 20–30° to prevent air embolism and distension of the vein. Make sure that you have prepared all equipment before tilting the patient, because critically ill patients may not tolerate this position for long periods. The procedure should be performed under aseptic technique so glove and gown and drape the patient with sterile drapes
- After infiltration of LA, and using the syringe filled with saline, introduce the green needle through the skin

continued opposite

Subclavian approach

- Immediately below the junction of the lateral third and medial two-thirds of the clavicle; advance the tip towards the suprasternal notch, 'walking' the needle tip along the under-surface of the clavicle

Internal jugular approach

- Palpate the sternomastoid muscle and place the fingertips of your left hand on the pulsatile right carotid artery. You can gently displace the artery medially as you introduce the needle at the midpoint of the anterior border of sternomastoid. Direct the needle tip away from your fingers (protecting the artery) and towards the ipsilateral right nipple of the patient. The needle should be angled at 30° to the skin surface

Technique for line insertion for both approaches

- Aspirate gently as the needle advances, until there is free aspiration of blood, indicating that the vein has been entered. You now know the depth and location of the vein
- Attach the syringe to the large-bore needle and follow the track of the green needle with the large-bore needle until blood is aspirated easily
- Leaving the large-bore needle in the vein, detach the syringe and advance the guidewire through the needle (some kits allow the guidewire to be advanced through the syringe without its removal from the needle), checking that it advances freely, with no obstruction; then remove the needle over the guidewire, ensuring that control of the guidewire is maintained at all times
- Make a small nick in the skin with a scalpel blade at the site of entry and dilate up the tract by passing the dilator over the guidewire
- Railroad the catheter over the guidewire (you must always hold on to the distal part of the guidewire by the patient's neck until the proximal end emerges from the lumen of the catheter)
- Check that the catheter advances freely with no obstruction, to its required length (approximately 20 cm)
- Remove the guidewire, suture the catheter to the adjacent skin and check that blood can be aspirated freely from all lumens. Flush the line with 0.9% saline

Post-procedure

- Take a chest radiograph in expiration to exclude a pneumothorax and to check the catheter tip is in the optimal position (SVC or right atrium)

Complications of central venous catheterisation

Complications of insertion

- Pneumothorax
- Haemothorax (due to laceration of intrathoracic vein wall)
- Puncture of adjacent artery causing subcutaneous haematoma, arteriovenous fistula or aneurysm
- Thoracic duct injury
- Brachial plexus damage
- Cardiac complications (arrhythmias, perforation of right atrium)
- Malposition of the catheter (eg into neck veins, axillary vein or contralateral veins)

Complications of use

- Catheter-related sepsis
- Catheter occlusion
- Catheter embolisation (due to migration of detached catheter)
- Central vein thrombosis

Subcutaneously implanted vascular access systems

These consist of a stainless steel (Port-a-Cath) or plastic (Infuse-a-Port) reservoir with a silicone septum buried in a subcutaneous pocket and connected to a Silastic central venous catheter. Access to the reservoir is with a percutaneous needle, which pierces the self-sealing septum without coring. Used for long-term antibiotics or chemotherapy.

Intraosseous puncture

This is an emergency technique for fluid resuscitation.

Procedure box: Intraosseous puncture

Indication
- Used in emergency situations in children aged 6 years or younger in whom venous access by other means has failed on two attempts.

Contraindications
- Local sepsis
- Ipsilateral fractured extremity

Complications
- Misplacement of the needle (this usually involves incomplete penetration of the anterior cortex or over-penetration, with the needle passing through the posterior cortex)
- Epiphyseal plate damage
- Local sepsis
- Osteomyelitis

Technique of intraosseous puncture
- Identify the puncture site – approximately 1.5 cm below the tibial tuberosity on the anteromedial surface of the tibia
- Clean and drape the area
- If the patient is awake infiltrate the area with LA
- Direct the intraosseous needle at 90° to the anteromedial surface of the tibia
- Aspirate bone marrow to confirm the position
- Inject with saline to expel any clot and again confirm the position; if the saline flushes easily with no swelling the needle is correctly placed
- Connect the needle to a giving set and apply a sterile dressing

Post-procedure
- Discontinue as soon as reliable venous access has been established

CHAPTER 3

Infuse and pump

Learning point

The principles of cardiovascular support in circulatory failure follow the VIP rule:
- **V**entilate
- **I**nfuse
- **P**ump

The ventilatory support has been covered earlier, intravenous access has been achieved, so now the 'infuse and pump' principle aims to maximise blood flow and perfusion to vital organs by means of:
- Appropriate fluid management
- Drugs

Infuse
- Fluid challenge using invasive monitoring
- Use of colloids as tighter dose response relationship
- Always ensure adequate filling before vasoactive support (Starling's)

Fluids: the crystalloid–colloid controversy

Crystalloids
- Consist of salt ions in water
- Of the volume infused, about a third stays intravascular and two-thirds pass to ECF, hence risk of tissue oedema
- Examples: 0.9% sodium chloride, Hartmann's solution
- Advantage: ECF fluid deficit in shock is replaced

Colloids
- Consist of osmotically active particles in solution
- Expand plasma volume by volume infused
- May leak into interstitium in capillary leak syndrome
- Examples: gelofusine, Haemaccel (gelatine-based, half-life about 4 hours)
- Dextrans (degraded dextrose; interfere with cross-matching)
- Starches (long half-life in some cases; 10% solutions hyperoncotic hence increase plasma volume more than volume infused; some may have benefit in reducing capillary leak syndrome)
- Albumin (pasteurised; suppresses albumin synthesis; normally some albumin leaks through the capillary membrane)
- Blood (plasma-reduced has haematocrit of about 70%)

A combination of crystalloids and colloids is probably the best approach.

Dextrose-containing fluids are not useful for intravascular volume replacement because they only replace water, which, as the sugar is metabolised, redistributes to intracellular and extracellular compartments. The dextrose allows water to be isotonic for IV infusion.

Potassium is replaced at a maximum rate of 20 mmol/hour in a monitored ITU environment. In hypokalaemic patients this reflects a large total intracellular deficit.

Magnesium replacement should be considered, aiming for a serum level of 1 mmol/l.

Volume-expanding fluids should be considered separately from maintenance fluids. See section 1.3 of this chapter for further detail on maintenance of fluid balance.

Pump

The first priority in shock of any cause is to restore perfusion pressure; the second is to optimise cardiac output.

Blood pressure

- Aim for MAP >60 mmHg or systolic BP >90 mmHg (elderly people often require higher pressure to perfuse vital organs due to pre-existing hypertension)
- An adequate perfusion pressure should maintain urine flow
- If systemic vascular resistance (SVR) is low then a vasopressor such as noradrenaline is indicated to improve perfusion pressure once normovolaemia has been reached
- Vasoconstriction may mask hypovolaemia,

so closely monitor filling pressures and cardiac output, especially during inotropic infusion

Cardiac output

- Drugs may be used to increase cardiac output by positive inotropic effect or increase perfusion to a specific organ system (eg renal and mesenteric blood flow is increased by dopexamine infusion at a rate of 0.5–1 µg/kg per minute; no evidence for prevention of renal failure)
- Monitor effect via DO_2, lactate, pH, urine output, cardiac output
- **Adrenaline:** inotrope, vasopressor, chronotrope. Activates β receptors, increasing intracellular cAMP. At low dose it has β effects mostly, and as doses increase has greater effect on α receptors; $β_2$ effects cause vasodilatation in skeletal muscle beds, lowering SVR
- **Dobutamine:** inotrope, vasodilator, synthetic. Predominant $β_1$ effect increases heart rate and force of contraction, and hence cardiac output. Mild $β_2$ and α effects overall, causing vasodilatation
- **Dopamine:** up to 5 µg/kg per minute has dopamine receptor activity causing renal dilatation; 5–10 µg has mostly a β-inotropic effect. Above 15 µg has mostly an α-vasoconstrictive effect. Unpredictable ranges in different patients. Problems with dopamine include: gut ischaemia, growth hormone suppression, immunosuppression
- **Dopexamine:** mesenteric and renal vasodilatation via dopamine receptors, and also has $β_2$ effects. Synthetic. Anti-inflammatory effect. May protect the gut against ischaemia in the presence of vasoconstrictors. Used at a dose of 0.5–0.9 mg/kg per minute for mesenteric protection

- **Noradrenaline:** vasopressor effect predominates. Mild inotropic β_1. Increases SVR to improve perfusion pressure but may suppress end-organ and skin perfusion due to capillary vasoconstriction. Used to increase perfusion pressure in septic shock
- **Isoprenaline:** chronotrope used to increase heart rate in heart block while awaiting pacing; β_1 and β_2 effects
- **Phosphodiesterase inhibitors:** milrinone, enoximone. Increase intracellular cAMP by decreasing its breakdown. Increase inotropic and vasodilatation (inodilator and lusiotropic). Increased cardiac output, lowered pulmonary artery occlusion pressure and SVR, but no significant rise in heart rate or myocardial oxygen consumption
- **Hydralazine:** mostly arterial vasodilatation; to control BP
- **Nitroprusside:** arterial vasodilator with short half-life given as infusion
- **Nitrates:** venodilators, reducing pre-load

Cardiac drugs
- **Inotropes:** increase force of ventricular contraction (usually a β effect)
- **Lusiotropes:** enhance myocardial relaxation
- **Vasopressors:** vasoconstrict blood vessels (α effect)
- **Vasodilators:** vasodilate blood vessels (arterial, venous or both)
- **Chronotropes:** increase heart rate (β effect)

Usually infused in micrograms per kilogram per minute. Dose ranges and individual effects are unpredictable in the critically ill patient.

CHAPTER 3

SECTION 3

Postoperative complications

3.1 General surgical complications

Learning point

Postoperative complications may be classified by **time of occurrence:**
- Immediate
- Early
- Late

They may also be classified according to their **underlying cause:**
- **General complications of surgery**
  - Haemorrhage
  - Pyrexia
  - Venous thromboembolism
  - Wound complications and surgical site infection
- **Complications specific to the operation:**
  - Anastomotic leak after bowel resection
  - Infection of prosthetic material after joint replacement
  - Hypocalcaemia after parathyroid surgery
- **Complications related to patient comorbidity**
  - Can affect any system: cardiac, respiratory, GU, GI, neurological

---

Risk factors for postoperative complications

- Extremes of age
- Obesity
- Cardiovascular disease
- Respiratory disease
- Diabetes mellitus
- Liver disease
- Renal disorders
- Steroids and immunosuppressant drugs

Complications may be immediate, early or late and may also be specific to the operation or general to any operation.

- **Immediate complications** occur within 24 hours of surgery
- **Early complications** occur within the 30-day period after the operation or during the period of hospital stay
- **Late complications** occur after the patient has been discharged from hospital or more than 30 days after the operation

---

Remember:
- Prophylaxis
- Early recognition
- Early management

General complications of surgery

Haemorrhage

- **Primary haemorrhage** occurs during the operation; it should be controlled before the end of the operation
- **Reactionary haemorrhage** occurs usually in the first few hours after surgery, eg clot disturbance with raised BP
- **Secondary haemorrhage** occurs a number of days after the operation; the cause is usually infection-related, but can also be related to sloughing of a clot or erosion of a ligature

Predisposing factors for haemorrhage

- Obesity
- Steroid therapy
- Jaundice
- Recent transfusion of stored blood
- Disorders of coagulation
- Platelet deficiencies
- Anticoagulation therapy
- Old age
- Severe sepsis with DIC

Prevention of haemorrhage

- Recognise patients at risk
- Reverse risk factors if possible
- Liaise with haematologist about managing coagulative disorders
- Control of infection
- Meticulous surgical technique

Management of haemorrhage

- Resuscitate
- Correct coagulopathy
- Consider blood transfusion
- Surgical or interventional radiology haemostasis if necessary
- Packing may be necessary

Postoperative pyrexia

Pyrexia is a common complication. Consider:
- Is it a correct measurement?
- How was the temperature measured?

What is the trend?

- New onset?
- Persistent elevation?
- 'Swinging'?

Is it due to an infection?

- DVT and PE can present with low-grade pyrexia
- Compartment syndrome may cause pyrexia
- Early pyrexia may be a response to surgical trauma or blood transfusion

Is there evidence of systemic involvement?

- Rigors
- Shivering
- Sweating

Is it related to drugs or infusions?

- Allergy
- Blood transfusion reaction
- Gelofusine can cause reactions

Recent culture results?

- Tailor the correct antibiotic specific to the bacteria grown

Different causes tend to manifest at different time points in the postoperative period. However, these are not absolute and you should consider all causes.

Postoperative pyrexia

Day 1–3
- Atelectasis
- Metabolic response to trauma
- Drug reactions (including to IV fluids)
- SIRS
- Line infection
- Instrumentation of a viscus or tract causing transient bacteraemia

Day 4–6
- Chest infection
- Superficial wound infection
- Urinary infection
- Line infection

Day 7 onwards
- Chest infection
- Suppurative wound infection
- Anastomotic leak
- Deep abscess
- DVT

Note: in the 24 hours after surgery, CRP will almost always be raised due to trauma and so should not be measured routinely; an upward trend in CRP measurements is a sensitive marker of infection (CRP increases within 24 hours of an insult).

Wound complications

Risk factors for wound complications
- Type of operation
- Potentially contaminated operations (eg elective operations on GI tract)
- Contaminated operations (eg perforated duodenal ulcer)
- Dirty operations (eg faecal peritonitis)
- Obesity
- Haematoma
- Diabetes
- Steroids
- Immunosuppression
- Malnutrition
- Obstructive jaundice
- Foreign material
- Vascular grafts
- Joint replacements
- Heart valves
- Hernia mesh

Note that the effects of infection in cases with implanted prosthetic material can be devastating.

Investigation of a postop pyrexia
- Bloods, including WCC, neutrophil count and CRP
- Septic screen
- Blood for culture (take from peripheral site and a separate sample through any potentially infected line; if removing lines send line tips for culture)
- Urinalysis
- Wound swab
- Sputum culture
- Stool culture (eg antibiotic-associated colitis)
- Tailor special investigations to examination findings (eg chest radiograph for respiratory symptoms or signs; abdominal CT to look for deep abscess)

Prophylaxis for wound infections
- Identify patients at risk
- Reduce/control risk factors
- Meticulous surgical technique
- Antibiotic prophylaxis
- Bowel preparation

Treatment of wound complications

Wound infections
- Ensure adequate drainage
- Send fluid/pus for culture and sensitivity
- Debride if necessary
- Appropriate dressings
- Antibiotics only if acute infection (cellulitis, septic)
- Dehiscence requires urgent surgical repair

Abscesses
- Drain – radiological, surgical
- Treat underlying cause (eg anastomotic leak)

Septicaemia/septic shock
- Early recognition
- Treat and/or remove source of sepsis
- Organ support as required on HDU/ITU

Complications of specific surgery

Complications of GI surgery
- Anastomotic haemorrhage or leak (± peritonitis or abscess)
- Visceral injury (due to adhesions)
- Ileus
- Oesophageal surgery: reflux, fungal infections, strictures
- Gastric surgery: 'dumping syndrome', nausea, pancreatitis
- Biliary surgery: leaks, bile duct injuries, strictures
- Small-bowel surgery: short-gut syndrome, malabsorption
- Colorectal surgery: stoma formation, anastomotic leaks, wound infection

Complications of vascular surgery

Carotid surgery
- TIA/CVA
- Hyperperfusion syndrome
- Patch dehiscence and secondary haemorrhage
- Cranial nerve injuries

AAA repair
- Damage to adjacent structures (eg left renal vein)
- Prosthetic infection
- Acute ischaemic colitis
- Retroperitoneal haematoma
- Impotence
- Spinal ischaemia (in thoracic aneurysmal procedures)
- Endoleaks and stent migration (for endovascular aneurysm repair procedures)

Arterial by-pass grafting
- Anastomotic leaks or rupture
- Graft thrombosis and failure (± amputation)
- False aneurysm formation
- Compartment syndrome
- Disease progression
- Graft infection

Venous surgery
- Damage to nerves (saphenous and sural)
- DVT
- Major venous injury (to femoral vein)
- Recurrence

Complications of cardiothoracic surgery

Cardiac surgery

- Arrhythmia
- Anastomotic bleeding/blow-out
- Low cardiac output
- MI

Pulmonary surgery

- Persistent air leak
- Atelectasis
- Bronchopleural fistula
- Empyema

Complications of orthopaedic surgery

- Prosthetic infection
- Joint dislocation
- Periprosthetic fracture
- Malunion
- Non-union
- DVT

Complications of urological surgery

Renal surgery

- Haemorrhage
- Arteriovenous fistula
- Urinary leaks

Ureteric surgery

- Stenosis
- Obstruction
- Hydronephrosis

Bladder surgery

- Ileus
- Rectal injury

Complications of plastic surgery

- Unsightly scarring
- Flap failure and necrosis

Complications of breast surgery

- Damage to axillary structures
- Seroma, haematoma and wound infection
- Lymphoedema and limited movement of arm
- Nerve damage
- Breast deformity

Rehabilitation

For surgeons the ultimate goal is success of surgery. However, this does not just mean getting patients off the operating table; it includes postoperative care and rehabilitation during that time, and eventually getting the patient successfully back into the community with any adjustments and help that are necessary.

- What is the physical injury or operation?
- What is the likely outcome and effect on physical status?
- What is the existing home/work situation?

Things to consider include:

- Multidisiplinary team (MDT) input
- Communication with:
  - Patient
  - Relatives
  - Nurses
  - Physiotherapists
  - Occupational therapists
  - Social services
- Transfer possibilities:
  - Home (± increased level of care)
  - Increased level of care (residential home or nursing home)
  - Hospice
  - Rehabilitation unit

Specific rehabilitation needs

Some injuries or procedures have specific rehabilitation needs, eg:

- Multiple trauma
- Head injuries
- Stoma patients

- Amputation
- Mastectomy
- Transplant recipients

Consider the following:
- Age and pre-hospital function
- Understanding and acceptance of injuries
- Long-term analgesia requirements
- Goal setting (ideal vs realistic)
- Early physiotherapy
- Occupational therapy (time frame)
- Employment and income issues
  - If self-employed:
    - More likely to want to restart work early, whether their rehab is complete or not
    - Family need money
  - If company-employed:
    - Sick pay
    - Stigma of 'being on the sick'
- Psychological issues
  - Psychiatric review
  - Social worker
  - Support groups

3.2 Respiratory failure

Postoperative respiratory complications

Risk factors for respiratory problems

Patient factors
- Age
- Pre-existing respiratory disease
- Smoking
- Obesity
- Pre-existing cardiac disease
- Immobility
- Postoperative pain

Anaesthetic factors
- Reduced residual capacity resulting from supine position and raising of diaphragm
- Ventilation–perfusion mismatching: **increased shunt** – perfused but not ventilated; **increased dead space** – ventilated but not perfused
- One-lung ventilation
- Excessive sedation
- Residual anaesthetic agents (muscle relaxants)
- Impaired host defences: impaired protective reflexes (eg gag and cough); dry anaesthetic gases hinder ciliary function

Perioperative factors
- Upper abdominal/thoracic wounds
- Analgesia/sedatives (eg opiates)
- Pain restricting respiratory effort and adequate cough
- Lying supine

Trauma factors
- Cord lesions
- Analgesia
- Pain
- Rib fractures/resection
- Pneumothorax
- Lung contusion

CHAPTER 3

Common respiratory postoperative pathology

- Basal atelectasis (most common)
- Bronchopneumonia
- PE
- Pleural effusion
- Pneumothorax
- Respiratory failure
- ARDS/acute lung injury

Investigating postop respiratory problems

- Chest radiograph
- ABGs (see earlier for interpretation of ABGs)
- ECG to exclude cardiac cause

Management of postop respiratory problems

- Risk factors corrected before surgery
- Adequate postoperative analgesia (epidural is ideal for major abdominal surgery)
- Minimal sedation
- Early and regular physiotherapy
- Early mobilisation
- Antibiotics if evidence of infection
- Drainage of effusion/pneumothorax
- Ventilatory support if necessary

3.3 Acute renal failure

Renal physiology

Learning point

The kidney has multiple functions.
Homeostasis of the extracellular fluid: control of water and electrolyte balance by plasma filtration followed by excretion and resorption of ions and water.
Excretion: elimination of waste products of metabolism (eg ammonium-containing compounds) and foreign substances (eg drugs).
Metabolism: vitamin D hydroxylation and activation.
Endocrine: production of erythropoietin and control of the renin–angiotensin–aldosterone system.

Renal blood flow

The kidneys receive 20–25% of the cardiac output, ie approximately 1200 ml/min, yet only represent 0.5% of the body mass. This is called the renal fraction. The kidneys contribute to local control of renal blood flow by production of several hormones (eg renin, prostaglandins, nitric oxide and the kallikrein cascade).

Factors influencing renal blood flow include:
- **Increased flow:**
  - Hormones (ANP)
  - Drugs (dopamine, dobutamine, captopril, furosemide)
- **Decreased flow:**
  - Hormones (ADH, renin)
  - Anatomy (renal artery stenosis)
  - Drugs (β blockers, indomethacin)

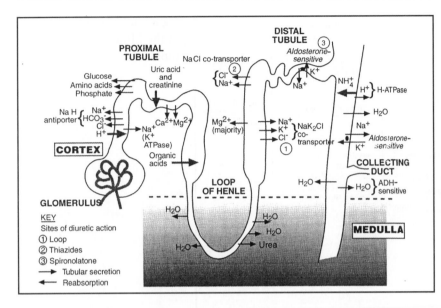

Figure 3.31 The structure of the nephron

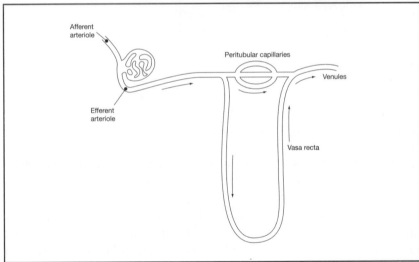

Figure 3.32 The vasculature surrounding the nephron

The nephron

Each kidney has about 1 million functional units or nephrons arranged in parallel (Figure 3.31). The nephron has two main regions – the glomerulus and the tubule. The glomerulus handles blood flow to the kidney and initial plasma filtration. The tubule further filters and processes the filtrate, reabsorbing water and solutes, and excreting others.

Structure and function of the glomerulus

The glomerulus is a coiled capillary bed nestling inside Bowman's capsule. It is supplied with blood via an afferent arteriole and initial filtration of the plasma occurs through the fenestrated capillary endothelium and the basement membrane of the capillary. The major barrier to flow is the basement membrane. The total area available for filtration in the kidney

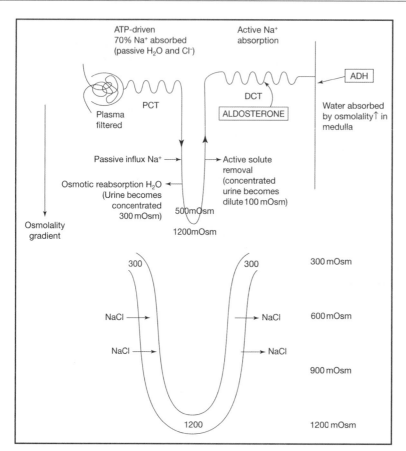

Figure 3.33 Modifications of the filtrate in the renal tubule

is 1 m². The blood then passes to the efferent arteriole, which forms a second capillary bed around the tubules (peritubular capillaries) to allow for reabsorption from the filtrate. The peritubular bed lies in the renal cortex and has long looping capillaries (vasa recta) which project down into the medulla along with the juxtamedullary nephrons. Of the blood flow to the kidneys 1–2% passes through the vasa recta and flow here is relatively sluggish. Blood then drains back into the renal venules.

Structure and function of the renal tubule

This extends from Bowman's capsule around the glomerulus to the collecting ducts (eventually draining into the ureter). Initially ultrafiltrate from Bowman's space drains through the podocyte 'foot' processes of the capsule into the proximal convoluted tubule (PCT). The PCT leads to the loop of Henle, which has both thin descending and ascending limbs followed by a thick ascending limb. Subsequently, the distal convoluted tubule (DCT) joins the cortical collecting duct, which runs into the medulla, forming the medullary collecting duct. At each stage the filtrate is progressively modified by secretion and resorption of water and electrolytes (Figure 3.33).

There are two types of nephrons with different functions:

- **Superficial cortical nephrons** (80%): these

have glomeruli lying close to the kidney surface and short loops of Henle reaching only the outer medulla

- **Deeper juxtamedullary nephrons** (20%): these have long loops of Henle which plunge deep into the medulla. They are accompanied by the vasa recta, which are capillary loops derived from the efferent glomerular arterioles. The vasa recta are involved in a countercurrent system that maintains a high solute concentration in the renal medulla. They are used to concentrate urine and thus preserve water

The ultrafiltrate is modified in the tubules by a combination of passive and active processes:

- Three sodium ions are **actively transported** out of the lumen by exchange for two K^+ ions via an ATP-driven ion pump in the tubule wall
- This creates an electrical sodium gradient, encouraging simple diffusion of sodium out of the filtrate. Other compounds such as glucose, chloride and some urea are also reabsorbed in this way
- Sodium carrier proteins pull additional molecules (eg amino acids or glucose) into the cell with the Na^+ ions. This is called 'co-transport'
- Water is drawn out of the tubules by means of passive osmosis

SUMMARY OF FILTRATE MODIFYING ACTIONS WITHIN THE TUBULE

Nephron region		Resorbs	Secretes
Proximal convoluted tubule	Absorbs about 65% of filtrate Lined with a brush border of villi Extensive membrane area Many transporter molecules (both absorb and secrete)	Na^+, Cl^-, H_2O, HCO_3^-, glucose, K^+, PO_4^{3-}	Organic acids and bases H^+ Some NH_4^+
Loop of Henle (descending)	No villi (site of simple diffusion)	H_2O	
Loop of Henle (ascending)	Thick portion has a brush border Site of active resorption	Na^+, Cl^-	
Distal convoluted tubule	Brush border with specialised 'brown cells'	Cl^-	H^+ NH_4^+ K^+
Collecting ducts	Specialised brown cells secrete H^+	Na^+, Cl^- (aldosterone) H_2O (ADH)	H^+ NH_4^+

Concentration and dilution of urine

The degree of urinary concentration is controlled by ADH (see 'Renal hormones and their actions' page 259). In the absence of ADH, the ascending loop of Henle, the DCT and the collecting ducts are relatively impermeable to water, so a higher proportion of the water in the filtrate is excreted. Concentration of urine is performed by the countercurrent mechanism and occurs in the long loops of Henle of the juxtamedullary nephrons and the vasa recta. The renal medulla has a very hyperosmolar interstitial fluid, maintained by active transport of NaCl. As the filtrate passes down the loop of Henle, water is drawn out by the high medullary osmotic pressure. In the ascending limb, additional sodium and chloride are actively transported out of the filtrate. Under the influence of ADH, the distal convoluted tubule and collecting ducts become highly permeable to water. This portion of the nephron passes through the hyperosmolar medulla, so allowing resorption of additional water and concentration of the urine.

Glomerular filtration rate

This is the net flow of filtrate across the basement membrane per unit time. It is the most sensitive indicator of renal function. There is great functional reserve within the human kidney, and plasma levels of urea and creatinine may be preserved despite massive loss of functioning nephrons. A representative value for GFR in adults is about 125 ml/minute or 180 litres/day. This value varies according to age, sex and body surface area.

GFR depends on:

- The difference in **hydrostatic pressure** between the glomerular capillary and Bowman's space (fluid hydrostatic pressure is higher in the capillary, promoting filtration of the plasma). Hydronephrosis causes an increase in the hydrostatic pressure of Bowman's capsule, reducing the difference between them and effectively reducing GFR
- The difference in **colloid osmotic pressure** between the glomerular capillary and Bowman's space (the colloid osmotic pressure is that pressure exerted by the protein content of the fluid; here this is effectively the colloid pressure of the plasma because very few proteins are filtered into Bowman's capsule – this opposes filtration)
- The **ultrafiltration coefficient** is a constant related to the area and conductivity of the basement membrane; it may be altered in conditions such as glomerulonephritis

As the glomerular capillary bed has an arteriole at either end (a unique situation) the hydrostatic pressure in the capillaries is determined by both afferent and efferent arteriolar resistance. This allows very precise regulation of capillary pressure and therefore glomerular filtration.

- **Afferent arteriolar vasoconstriction** decreases both GFR and glomerular plasma flow
- **Efferent arteriolar vasoconstriction** reduces glomerular plasma flow, and also increases glomerular pressure, so increasing GFR

Autoregulation holds the glomerular filtration pressure relatively constant despite variation in mean arterial blood pressure over the range 80–180 mmHg. The mechanism for autoregulation is not completely understood. However, it still occurs in denervated and isolated perfused kidney preparations, suggesting that it is intrinsic to the kidney.

If renal perfusion pressure increases, afferent arteriolar resistance also increases, so that glomerular blood flow and GFR remain constant. Conversely, when blood pressure falls the afferent arteriole decreases in resistance, but the efferent arteriolar resistance increases to maintain GFR.

Juxtaglomerular apparatus

Tubuloglomerular feedback is another mechanism by which GFR is regulated. This is a negative feedback system whereby the GFR is inversely related to fluid delivery to the distal nephron. It is controlled by specialist cells in the juxtaglomerular apparatus (JGA). The JGA is located in the initial portion of the DCT where the DCT bends upwards, and is situated between the afferent and efferent arterioles of the glomerulus.

The JGA contains three cell types:
- Macula densa cells (cells of the tubule involved in feedback)
- Juxtaglomerular cells (smooth muscle cells of the arterioles which secrete renin)
- Extraglomerular mesangial cells

Measurement of GFR

There are a number of ways of measuring GFR. Each requires the use of a solute that is:
- Detectable in plasma and urine
- Freely filtered by the kidney
- Not absorbed or secreted
- Not toxic
- Does not alter renal blood flow

This solute may be administered exogenously (eg inulin, which requires continuous infusion for a steady plasma state) or may be produced endogenously (eg creatinine, which fulfils most of these requirements apart from a degree of tubular secretion).

Creatinine clearance therefore gives an approximation of GFR. To calculate GFR:

$$GFR = [U \times V]/P$$

where V is the volume of urine produced, P is the concentration of the solute in the plasma and U is the concentration of the solute in the urine.

The filtration fraction is the proportion of plasma filtered by the glomerulus. It is expressed as the relationship between GFR and renal blood flow and is normally about a fifth of the value of GFR.

Renal blood flow (RBF) can be calculated if it is considered that renal plasma flow (RPF) is equal to the GFR, thus:

$$RBF = RPF/(1 - haematocrit)$$

Diuretics

Diuretics work by increasing urine volume. This can be achieved either by increasing renal tubular excretion of sodium and chloride, which draws water with it, or by giving an osmotically active substance such as mannitol.

Thiazides (eg bendroflumethiazide)

These act by inhibiting NaCl resorption in the DCT (thus exchanging urinary sodium loss for potassium loss) by acting on tubular ATPase ion pumps. Side effects include hypokalaemia, hyperuricaemia (alteration in the excretion of uric acid), glucose intolerance and hyperlipidaemia.

Loop diuretics (eg furosemide, bumetanide)

These act by inhibiting the co-transport of sodium, chloride and potassium in the thick ascending loop of Henle. Potassium is lost in preference to sodium and so the hypokalaemic effect can be pronounced.

Potassium-sparing diuretics (eg spironolactone, amiloride)

These act as aldosterone antagonists and therefore prevent resorption of sodium in the DCT. These drugs do not cause the body to exchange sodium loss for potassium loss and therefore do not cause hypokalaemia. Care must be taken in the elderly not to cause hyperkalaemia.

Renal hormones and their actions

ADH/arginine vasopressin (AVP)

This hormone is produced by the cells of the supraoptic nucleus of the hypothalamus and is stored in the posterior pituitary gland.

CHAPTER 3

It is released by a number of stimuli:
- Increased plasma osmolality (sensed by osmoreceptors in the brain)
- Decreased blood pressure (sensed by baroreceptors in the great vessels)
- Decreased circulating volume (stretch receptors and increased ANP)

Alcohol, opiates, prostaglandins, oestrogens and stress all decrease ADH secretion. ADH (AVP) acts to increase salt and thus water reabsorption in the DCT, and to increase the permeability of the collecting system and thus increase the amount of water reabsorbed as the filtrate passes through the medulla. This concentrates the urine and reduces its volume.

Renin–angiotensin–aldosterone system

Renin is produced and stored in the smooth muscle cells of the JGA. It is released when arterial pressure falls. It has several intrarenal functions and acts enzymatically on a plasma protein, angiotensin I.

Angiotensin I is fast converted to angiotensin II by angiotensin-converting enzyme (ACE) in lung endothelium. Angiotensin II has three major actions:
- It is a powerful vasoconstrictor, increasing arterial pressure
- It acts directly on the kidney to conserve sodium and water and to decrease renal blood flow, which reduces urine volume, gradually increasing arterial pressure
- It stimulates the production of aldosterone by the adrenal glands

Aldosterone causes increased sodium retention by the kidney tubules, which expands the ECF compartment by causing retention of water.

Atrial natriuretic peptide

Over-stretching of the atrial wall by high volumes is sensed by stretch receptors and results in the release of ANP into the bloodstream. This acts on the kidneys to increase sodium and water excretion and thus reduce blood volume by increasing urine output.

Renal failure

Learning point

Renal failure is defined as failure of the kidneys to maintain the correct composition and volume of the body's internal environment. Patients undergoing major surgery are at risk of developing renal failure, particularly in the postoperative period, where inadequate fluid rehydration is not uncommon.

Anuria is the absence of urine output. In most surgical patients, sudden anuria is more likely to be due to a blocked or misplaced urinary catheter rather than to acute renal failure.

Oliguria is defined as a urine output of <0.5 ml/kg per hour. This is a much more likely presentation of impending renal failure in surgical patients than anuria. It is not uncommonly seen after inadequate fluid replacement.

Non-oliguric renal failure can also occur. It has a much lower morbidity.

Acute renal failure (ARF) is a rapid reduction in renal function (best measured by decrease in GFR or increase in serum creatinine) that may or may not be accompanied by oliguria. The abrupt decline in renal function occurs over hours or days.

The most useful classification system divides renal failure into:
- Prerenal
- Renal
- Postrenal

Prerenal causes of renal failure

- Volume depletion (eg haemorrhage, GI losses, dehydration, burns)
- Abnormal fluid distribution (eg distributive shock, cirrhosis, congestive cardiac failure (CCF)
- Local renal ischaemia, eg renal artery stenosis or prostaglandin inhibitors such as NSAIDs
- Low-output cardiac failure
- Raised intra-abdominal pressure (abdominal compartment syndrome)

Inadequate perfusion of the kidneys is the most common cause of renal failure in hospital.

Hypovolaemia is classified according to aetiology:
- Loss of whole blood (haemorrhage)
- Loss of plasma (burns)
- Loss of crystalloid (dehydration, diarrhoea, vomiting)

Note that as far as possible one should replace like with like, ie blood after haemorrhage or water (given as 5% dextrose) in dehydration. However, in many hypovolaemic patients, the priority is initially to rapidly replace lost circulating volume. This is with blood, colloid or isotonic crystalloid, such as 0.9% saline. The remaining fluid deficit can be made up more slowly with whatever fluid most closely resembles the fluid losses.

The typical mechanism is that hypoxaemia and hypoperfusion reduce sodium absorption in the ascending loop of Henle, which is a high-energy-consuming process. Hence the JGA detects increased filtrate sodium concentration, and so reduces renal blood flow to conserve blood volume, resulting in reduced urine output. Appropriate treatment should reverse this process before ischaemic damage and acute tubular necrosis (ATN) occurs.

Renal causes of renal failure

Intrinsic renal pathology:
- ATN due to prolonged ischaemia or tubular toxins, including drugs (eg gentamicin)
- Glomerulonephritis or vasculitis (eg SLE, polyarteritis nodosa, Wegener's granulomatosis)
- Goodpasture syndrome (anti-glomerular basement membrane antibodies)
- Interstitial nephritis
- Vascular lesions: hypertension, emboli, renal vein thrombosis
- Infections such as pyelonephritis
- Contrast-induced nephropathy

Postrenal causes of renal failure

Obstruction to the flow of urine along the urinary tract:
- Pelvicalyceal: usually at pelviureteric junction (PUJ) (eg bilateral PUJ obstruction)
- Ureteric: luminal/intramural extrinsic obstruction; retroperitoneal fibrosis, stone
- Bladder/urethral outflow obstruction: urinary retention, prostatic enlargement, high pressure or atonic bladder, urethral stricture, blocked catheter, cervical prostatic neoplasm

CHAPTER 3

> **The most important causes of renal failure that must not be missed** (because they are so easily treatable) are prerenal, especially hypovolaemia/dehydration, and postrenal (particularly prostate or catheter problems). Also, inadequate rehydration of a postobstructive diuresis commonly results in prerenal failure.

Prevention of renal failure

- Prevention of hypotension or hypovolaemia
- Prevention of dehydration (especially in patients who continue to receive their 'normal' diuretic medication)
- Early treatment of sepsis
- Caution with potentially nephrotoxic drugs (eg NSAIDs, gentamicin): in all cases monitor renal function closely, substitute these drugs with non-nephrotoxic equivalents if there is any indication of deterioration in renal function
- Prophylactic intravenous fluid hydration 24 hours pre- and post-contrast administration in those with pre-existing renal disease and consider use of an antioxidant, eg *N*-acetylcysteine

Assessment of acute renal failure

Differentiating causes: renal and prerenal failure

This is initially on the basis of a history and examination (postrenal failure is usually clinically evident and the main differentiation exists between establishing renal from prerenal failure).

- **History**
- **Examination**

- **Serum urea and creatinine**
- **Blood gases:** a metabolic acidosis may occur
- **Paired urinary and serum** measures of osmolality and sodium
- **Response to fluid challenge:** this may distinguish between prerenal and renal causes. If no diuresis occurs with adequate fluid replacement, consider a renal cause
- **Bladder scanning for residual volume and catheterisation:** this diagnoses retention
- **Renal tract ultrasonography and Doppler:** these show renal blood flow, and evidence and level of hydronephrosis

---

Urine analysis and serum biochemistry

Where there is still a query as to the cause of renal failure, an analysis of the urine and serum biochemistry is performed. This is one of the simplest and most effective ways of differentiating prerenal from intrinsic renal failure.

Measurement	Prerenal	Renal
Urinary sodium	Low: <20 mmol/l	High: >40 mmol/l
Urine Serum osmolarity ratio	>1.2	<1.2
Serum creatinine ratio	High: > 40	Low: <20
Urine osmolality	>500	<350

Normally functioning kidneys, in the presence of hypotension or hypovolaemia, will concentrate urine and conserve sodium (meaning that there will be less in the urine). If there is intrinsic renal pathology, the kidney will be unable to concentrate the urine or conserve sodium.

Management of renal failure

The important steps in the management of oliguria are:

- **Exclude obstruction:** insert catheter or flush existing catheter
- **Correct hypovolaemia and hypotension:** may need CVP ± PA catheter and assessment of response of CVP to fluid boluses. When optimally filled, inotropes or vasopressor may be required to provide adequate perfusion pressure (perfusion pressure may need to be increased in people with hypertension)
- **Fluid maintenance after resuscitation:** includes infusing volume equivalent to urine output each hour plus insensible losses (about 1000 ml/24 hours). Insensible losses will be increased in pyrexia
- **Treat the cause or any contributing factors:** eg stop NSAIDs and ACE inhibitors. Prostaglandin inhibition by NSAIDs causes renal vasoconstriction

In addition, various treatments are often used to try to reverse/prevent renal failure. Examples of such treatments are:

- **Dopamine or dopexamine:** cause stimulation of dopamine receptors
- **Sodium loading with NaHCO₃** to reduce oxygen-dependent sodium retention by the nephron
- **Mannitol:** increases urine output by osmotic diuresis. Does not prevent renal failure; some evidence of nephrotoxicity. Used successfully to reduce renal damage in jaundice and rhabdomyolysis. Be aware that induced diuresis can cause hypovolaemia and reduce renal perfusion

However, none of these treatments has been proved to prevent renal failure and the other measures described above are much more important.

Review of drug therapy for patients with renal failure

All drug therapy given to patients in renal failure needs to be regularly and thoroughly reviewed.

- Drugs that may exacerbate renal failure or its complications (eg NSAIDs, ACE inhibitors, gentamicin and potassium-sparing diuretics) should be avoided
- Many drugs need dose adjustment to prevent overdosage because they, or their active metabolites, are excreted by the kidneys (this includes most antibiotics)
- If possible, serum drug levels should be checked and drug doses adjusted accordingly

Optimisation of serum biochemistry in renal failure

The following biochemical abnormalities commonly occur:

- Progressive rise in urea and creatinine
- Hyperkalaemia
- Hyponatraemia (due to relative water overload)
- Acidosis
- Hypocalcaemia
- Hyperphosphataemia
- Hyperuricaemia

The abnormalities requiring most urgent correction are hyperkalaemia and acidosis.

Treatment of hyperkalaemia

- 10 ml IV 10% calcium chloride (does not reduce potassium levels but reduces risk of cardiac arrhythmia)
- 10 units IV insulin + 50 ml 50% dextrose
- Sodium bicarbonate infusion
- Salbutamol or other β agonist
- Calcium resonium: orally or per rectum (reduces total body potassium, but poorly

tolerated orally and works slowly)

- Stop potassium-containing infusions (which may include TPN or enteral feed)
- Stop drugs such as potassium-sparing diuretics

Insulin, β agonists and sodium bicarbonate do not reduce total body potassium. They increase intracellular potassium and so reduce the serum potassium. This reduces the risk of a fatal arrhythmia, but is only a short-term measure; haemofiltration/haemodialysis will be required medium/long-term to prevent hyperkalaemia unless renal function improves.

Treatment of acidosis

- If artificially ventilated, increase the minute ventilation
- Sodium bicarbonate infusion (but this is controversial; may paradoxically increase intracellular acidosis and is only a short-term measure)
- Artificial renal support

Nutritional requirements in patients with renal failure

High-calorie diet needed, with adequate high-quality protein. Maximum of 35 kcal/kg per day (about 2500 kcal) plus 14 g nitrogen/day.

Treatment of infection in patients with renal failure

Infection and generalised sepsis may already be apparent as the cause or contributing factor in the development of renal failure. If the cause of renal failure (or other organ system failure) is sepsis it is unlikely to improve until the source of the sepsis is eradicated (eg intra-abdominal collection).

Renal replacement therapy

In established renal failure, artificial support may be required. This is commonly achieved by haemodialysis.

Indications for renal replacement therapy

- Hyperkalaemia (persistently >6.0 mmol/l)
- Metabolic acidosis (pH <7.2) with negative base excess
- Pulmonary oedema/fluid overload without substantial diuresis
- High urea (30–40 mmol/l)
- Complications of chronic uraemia (eg pericarditis/cardiac tamponade)
- Creatinine rising >100 μmol/l per day
- The need to 'make room' for ongoing drug infusions and nutrition, and to aid clearance of drugs already given (eg sedatives)

Methods of renal replacement therapy

CAVH	Continuous arteriovenous haemofiltration
CVVH	Continuous venovenous haemofiltration
CVVHD	Continuous venovenous haemodiafiltration
HD	Haemodialysis

In the ITU, both haemofiltration and haemodiafiltration are commonly performed via a large-bore dual-lumen central venous cannula (CVVH). As the flow of blood is both from and to the venous side of the circulation, a pump is required. The blood flow is in the region of 250 ml/minute and alarms are incorporated to prevent air embolism. Anticoagulation is needed and heparin is usually used as an infusion or

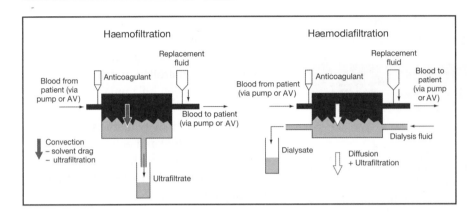

Figure 3.34
Haemofiltration and haemodialysis

prostacyclin if thrombocytopenia develops. Previously, arteriovenous systems were used, but a large-bore catheter needs to be placed in an artery and filtration depends on arterial pressure. These techniques provide slow fluid shifts and maintain haemodynamic stability.

In haemofiltration the blood is driven under pressure through a filter (a semipermeable membrane). The 'ultrafiltrate' derived from the blood (which is biochemically abnormal) is disposed of and replaced with a replacement fluid. Small molecules such as sodium, urea, creatinine and bicarbonate pass through the filter with water but large molecules such as proteins and cells do not. The usual volume of filtrate produced is 1–2 l/hour and this volume is replaced with an electrolyte solution containing ions and buffer. The replacement fluid is buffered with lactate, acetate or freshly added bicarbonate. The system provides a clearance equivalent to 10 ml/minute and if solute clearance is inadequate then augmentation with dialysis can be used (CVVHD).

In haemodiafiltration (CVVHD) the dialysate augments clearance by diffusion by running an electrolyte solution on the outside of the filter. The clearance increases to about 20 ml/minute. Fluid balance over 24 hours can be manipulated using these filters. If the patient is oedematous then removal of 2 litres may be appropriate and

can be achieved by replacing 84 ml less per hour than is filtered.

In HD blood is pumped through the machine on one side of a semipermeable membrane, in a manner similar to haemofiltration. However, in HD dialysis fluid is also pumped through the machine, on the other side of the semipermeable membrane, to the blood. The biochemistry of the blood equilibrates with that of the dialysis fluid by diffusion, although some ultrafiltration also occurs.

HD tends to be more effective in terms of correcting acidosis and abnormal biochemistry in a short period of time. However, it is associated with more circulatory instability; continuous haemofiltration is often better tolerated in patients with circulatory instability.

Continuous ambulatory peritoneal dialysis (CAPD) is becoming more common. Fluid is instilled into the peritoneum by a special catheter (eg Tenckhoff catheter). The peritoneum acts as the dialysis membrane. Increasingly this method is chosen by patients because they can perform it at home, but it is unsuitable for inpatients or those on ITU.

3.4 Systemic inflammatory response syndrome

Learning point

Systemic inflammatory response syndrome (SIRS) is a disseminated inflammatory response that may arise as a result of a number of insults.

It is described as a syndrome because the symptoms and signs can be produced by processes other than just infection.

SIRS is a harmful, excessive reaction of acute phase response. It is defined by two or more of the following:

- Tachycardia >90 beats/minute
- Respiratory rate >20 breaths/minute or $PaCO_2$ >4.3 kPa
- Temperature >38°C or <36°C
- WCC >12 or <4 × 10^3/mm^3

Pathophysiology of SIRS

SIRS is a disseminated inflammatory response that may arise as a result of a number of insults:

- Infection and sepsis
- Ischaemia–reperfusion syndrome
- Fulminant liver failure
- Pancreatitis
- Dead tissue

Any localised injury stimulates an inflammatory response. This response involves recruitment of inflammatory cells (such as macrophages and neutrophils) to the area, release of inflammatory mediators (eg cytokines, IL-1, IL-6, IL-8, TNF-α), and changes in vascular permeability.

- These localised inflammatory responses are responsible for minimising further damage (eg from infection) and optimising conditions for healing

- Under certain conditions (eg major trauma) the extent of the inflammatory activity throughout the body is activated in an apparently uncontrolled manner, with an imbalance between inflammatory and anti-inflammatory responses
- The widespread activity of this systemic inflammation (SIRS) and activation of a mediator network is such that it damages organs throughout the body, potentially initiating MODS

Important components of the inflammatory response

Oxygen free radicals

- Occur after initial hypoxic injury and subsequent reperfusion (ie reperfusion injury)
- Mechanism involves the formation of xanthine oxidase during ischaemia from xanthine dehydrogenase which converts adenosine to hypoxanthine
- When oxygen becomes available the hypoxanthine is metabolised to uric acid via the enzyme xanthine oxidase and oxygen free radicals are formed in the process
- Cause direct endothelial damage and increased permeability

Cytokines

- Peptides released by various cell types which are involved in the immune response
- Produced by macrophages
- TNF: central mediator in sepsis, produces deleterious effects similar to effects of infection; pivotal role in host response
- IL-1: synergistic with TNF; initiator of host response; stimulates T-helper cells
- IL-6/IL-8: reparative processes; production of acute phase proteins

Macrophages

- Phagocytosis of debris and bacteria
- Act as antigen-presenting cells to T lymphocytes
- Release inflammatory mediators, endothelial cells and fibroblasts

Neutrophils

- Migrate to inflamed tissue from the blood
- Release mediators
- Release proteolytic and hydrolytic enzymes, which cause vasodilatation, increased permeability, myocardial depression and activation of clotting mechanisms

Inducible intercellular adhesion molecules (ICAMs)

- Mediation of adhesion and migration of neutrophils through endothelium
- Induced by lipopolysaccharides (LPSs) and cytokines

Platelet-activating factor (PAF)

- Released by neutrophils and monocytes
- Cause hypotension, increased permeability and platelet aggregation

Arachidonic acid metabolites

- Essential fatty acid
- Metabolised by cyclo-oxygenase to form prostaglandins and thromboxane, and by lipoxygenase to form leukotrienes (LTs)

Vascular endothelium

- Increased permeability, allowing both inflammatory cells and acute phase proteins from the blood to reach the injured (inflamed) area

- Complex organ in its own right, involved in vascular tone, permeability, coagulation, phagocytosis and metabolism of vascular mediators
- Nitric oxide: induced form stimulated by TNF and endotoxin via nitric oxide synthase; causes sustained vasodilatation
- Endothelin-1: powerful vasoconstrictor, increased in trauma and cardiogenic shock

Complement cascade

- Occurs in early septic shock via the alternative pathway
- Attracts and activates neutrophils

Vasodilatation

- Allowing increased recruitment of inflammatory cells from the blood

> In the systemic inflammatory response syndrome, it is these changes in the vascular endothelium which, when widespread, cause circulatory failure and hypotension, contributing to MODS.

The 'two-hit' hypothesis and the role of the gut

The gut is thought to have an important role in the development of SIRS and a 'two-hit' theory has been postulated. The initial cellular insult (cellular trauma or shock states) sets up a controlled inflammatory response. A second insult is then sustained by the patient (eg repeated surgery, superimposed infection, bacteraemia or persistent cellular damage). This creates a destructive inflammatory response and results in loss of intestinal mucosal integrity, allowing translocation of bacteria and endotoxin into the

CHAPTER 3

portal circulation which further feeds back into the immuno-inflammatory cascade.

3.5   Sepsis and septic shock

Definitions in sepsis

- **Infection:** microbiologically proven clinical condition with host response
- **Sepsis:** the body's response to infection in the presence of SIRS
- **Severe sepsis:** sepsis with evidence of organ dysfunction or hypoperfusion
- **Septic shock:** severe sepsis with hypotension (<90 mmHg) despite fluid resuscitation
- **Septicaemia:** clinical signs and symptoms associated with multiplying bacteria in the bloodstream
- **Bacteraemia:** bacteria in bloodstream but not necessarily symptomatic or requiring treatment
- **Endotoxin:** toxin that remains within the cell wall of bacteria. Heat stable. Lipid A conserved among different organisms acts to trigger various mediators responsible for sepsis
- **Exotoxin:** toxin actively secreted by a bacterium, with specific effects according to organism
- **Carriage:** two consecutive surveillance samples of throat and rectum that are positive for microorganisms
- **Colonisation:** presence of microorganisms in a normally sterile organ without host response (eg throat, gut)

> ### Factors predisposing to sepsis in critical care
> **Impaired barriers**
> - Loss of gag reflex – reduced level of consciousness, drugs
> - Loss of cough reflex – drugs, pain
> - Ciliary function – high inspired O_2, dry O_2, intubation
> - Gut mucosal barrier – ischaemia, change in gut flora (antibiotics)
> - Urinary catheters predispose to urinary tract infection
> - IV/arterial lines breach skin barrier
>
> **Impaired defences**
> - Cell-mediated immunity
> - Humoral immunity
> - Reticuloendothelial system
> - Caused by trauma, shock, postop, sepsis, age, malnutrition, malignancy, splenectomy (humoral), immunosuppressive drugs

Gram-positive bacteria are the most common cause of infection (eg staphylococci), having taken over from Gram negatives such as *Pseudomonas* spp., *Escherichia coli* and *Proteus* spp. Organisms such as *Acinetobacter* spp. are a particular problem on ITUs after use of broad-spectrum antibiotics or in immunosuppression, as are fungal infections (eg *Candida* and *Aspergillus* spp.).

Local antibiotic policy on ITUs should be formulated by collaboration with the microbiologist so that appropriate antibiotics for local organisms are used, as well as being based on culture and sensitivity.

Typical policies follow patterns such as:

cephalosporin + metronidazole ± gentamicin
(renal toxicity)

↓

If unsuccessful

↓

Broad-spectrum anti-pseudomonals such as:

piperacillin + tazobactam

ciprofloxacin

ceftazidime

or

imipenem/meropenem

Antibiotic policy should be guided by culture
and sensitivity of sputum, blood, wound and
urine samples, but quite often these are not
available, so broad-spectrum agents are used
in the first instance. Take advice from your
microbiologist.
- For MRSA: teicoplanin, or vancomycin
  (beware toxicity)
- For fungal infections: fluconazole followed
  by amphotericin if resistant or *Aspergillus*
  spp.

Infection on ITUs
- Community acquired: tend to be sensitive
  organisms
- Nosocomial: tend to be resistant species
- Gram-positive organisms are more
  common, but *Pseudomonas* spp. and other
  Gram negatives still occur
- EPIC (European Prevalence of Infection
  in Intensive Care) study showed 21% of
  infections are acquired within ITUs

Septic shock
Classically this is a combination of high cardiac
output, low systemic resistance, maldistri-
bution of blood flow and increased vascular
permeability. There is suppression of cardiac
contractility but tachycardia increases the
cardiac output. Vasodilatation results from nitric
oxide production. The physiological effects seen
in septic shock result from the cytokines of the
inflammatory response and therefore may also
be due to an inflammatory rather than infective
stimulus (eg pancreatitis).

Clinical features of septic shock
- Pyrexia
- Tachycardia
- Peripherally warm, flushed
- Hypotensive, low CVP
- Acidotic (lactic acidosis)

Note that NSAIDs and corticosteroids can
mask pyrexia. Corticosteroids may also mask
peritonitis.

Management of septic shock
Management of sepsis-induced shock, defined
as tissue hypoperfusion (hypotension persisting
after initial fluid challenge or blood lactate
concentration ≥4 mmol/l) essentially comprises:
- Identify and treat the cause
- Support organ function

CHAPTER 3

The Surviving Sepsis Campaign and management of septic shock

The Surviving Sepsis Campaign has published international guidelines (2008) on the recognition and management of severe sepsis in an attempt to decrease the high mortality rates. Its recommendations are:

Initial resuscitation (first 6 hours)

Begin fluid resuscitation and high-flow oxygen immediately in patients with hypotension or elevated serum lactate ≥4 mmol/l; aim to achieve haemodynamic goals of:

- Central venous pressure 8–12 mmHg
- Mean arterial pressure (MAP) ≥65 mmHg
- Urine output ≥0.5 ml/kg per hour
- Central venous (SVA) or mixed venous oxygen saturation ≥70% or ≥65%, respectively

If venous oxygen saturation target is not achieved:

- Consider further fluid
- Transfuse packed red blood cells if required to hematocrit of ≥30%, and/or
- Start dobutamine infusion, maximum 20 μg/kg per minute

Diagnosis

- Obtain appropriate cultures before starting antibiotics provided that this does not significantly delay antimicrobial administration
- Obtain two or more blood cultures
- One or more blood cultures should be percutaneous
- One blood culture from each vascular access device inserted ≥48 hours ago
- Culture other sites as clinically indicated (urine, the tip from any line that you change, pus after drainage of collections, etc)
- Perform imaging studies promptly to confirm and sample any source of infection, if safe to do so

Antibiotic therapy

- Begin IV antibiotics as early as possible and always within the first hour
- Broad-spectrum: one or more agents active against likely bacterial/fungal pathogens and with good penetration into presumed source
- Reassess antimicrobial regimen daily with culture results to optimise efficacy, prevent resistance, avoid toxicity and minimise costs
- Duration of therapy typically limited to 7–10 days, longer if response is slow or there are undrainable foci of infection or immunological deficiencies
- Stop antimicrobial therapy if cause is found to be non-infectious

Source identification and control

- A specific anatomical site of infection should be established as rapidly as possible. Look for a focus of infection amenable to active treatment such as surgical resection, percutaneous or open abscess drainage, tissue debridement, etc (noted exception: infected pancreatic necrosis, where surgical intervention is best delayed)
- Remove intravascular access devices if potentially infected and send the tip for culture

Additional critical care management

- **Transfusion:** give packed red cells if Hb <7 g/dl
- **Hyperglycaemia:** should be managed with sliding-scale IV insulin
- **Prophylaxis:** use LMWH for DVT prophylaxis and H_2-receptor blocker for stress ulcer prophylaxis
- **Steroids:** consider IV hydrocortisone (dose should be ≤300 mg/day) for septic shock if hypotension responds poorly to fluid and vasopressors but do not use steroids to treat sepsis in the absence of shock. Steroids can be stopped once vasopressors are no longer needed
- **Recombinant human activated protein C (rhAPC):** consider rhAPC in adult patients with sepsis-induced organ dysfunction with clinical assessment of high risk of death (typically APACHE II ≥25 or multiorgan failure)
- **Nutrition:** use enteral nutrition unless not absorbing; consider TPN

Complications of sepsis and septic shock

- Metabolic acidosis
- DIC
- MODS/MOF (multiorgan failure)
- Hypercatabolic state and hyperglycaemia
- Stress ulcers
- Pulmonary hypertension

Septic shock has approximately a 50% mortality rate.

3.6 Multiorgan dysfunction syndrome

Definitions of individual organ system failure

Cardiovascular failure (one or more of the following)

- Heart rate <54 beats/minute or symptomatic bradycardia
- MAP <49 mmHg or (>70 mmHg requiring inotropic support)
- Occurrence of ventricular fibrillation or tachycardia (VT or VF)
- Serum pH <7.24 with normal PCO_2

Respiratory failure

- Respiratory rate <5 or >49 breaths/minute
- $PaCO_2$ >6.65 kPa
- Alveolar–arterial gradient >46.55
- Ventilator-dependent on day 4 in ITU

Renal failure

- Urine output <479 ml in 24 hours, or <159 ml in 8 hours
- Urea >36 mmol/l
- Creatinine >310 µmol/l
- Dependent on haemofiltration

Haematological failure

- White cell count <1/mm³
- Platelets <20 × 10⁹/l
- Haematocrit <0.2%
- DIC

Neurological failure

- GCS <6 in the absence of sedation

Gastrointestinal failure

- Ileus >3 days
- Diarrhoea >4 days
- GI bleeding
- Inability to tolerate enteral feed in absence of primary gut pathology

Skin failure

- Decubitus ulcers

Endocrine failure

- Hypoadrenalism or abnormal thyroid function tests

Multiple system failures

MODS may also be referred to as MOF and is an important cause of death in intensive care. It refers to the process whereby more than one organ system has deranged function and requires support. Patients do not often die from single organ failure but from the development of MOF following the initial insult.

The degree of dysfunction can be difficult to quantify (eg dysfunction of the GI tract) or easily quantifiable (eg renal dysfunction, quantified by the degree of oliguria, serum biochemistry and acid–base status).

When assessing the degree of dysfunction, account must be taken of the support being provided for the organ system (eg for respiratory failure the concentration of inspired oxygen and ventilatory support must be considered when assessing PaO_2).

MOF is a process that develops over a period of time, and can be in response to an initial severe stimulus (eg major burn, sepsis, multiple trauma, major surgery) or after several seemingly minor insults.

The development of MOF depends more on the pre-existing physiological reserve of the organs and the body's response to a given stimulus than the stimulus itself. This may explain why different patients, with seemingly similar pathology or injuries, differ in their tendency to develop MOF.

Outcome of MOF

The prognosis of established multiorgan failure is extremely poor:

- In two-organ failure, the mortality rate is in the region of 50% and increases to 66% on day 4
- In three-organ failure, the mortality rate is around 80% on the first day, increasing to 96% if it does not resolve
- In four-organ failure, survival is unlikely

Pre-existing medical condition and age must be considered in the outcome of MOF.

Treatment and prevention of MOF

The emphasis must be on identifying at-risk patients early, and intervening quickly to prevent MOF.

In order to optimise the chances of recovery, the initial insult (eg intra-abdominal sepsis) must be treated if possible. Supportive treatment for specific organ systems is the mainstay of treatment. Early nutritional support, particularly via the gut (enteral feeding), is increasingly being recognised as important in improving outcome.

Various anti-inflammatory treatments have been attempted, affecting different parts of the inflammatory response (eg anti-endotoxin antibodies, IL-1 antibodies), but in clinical trials none seems to have any effect on the outcome. This is due to the complex and multiple pathways involved.

CHAPTER 4

Infection and Inflammation

Claire Ritchie Chalmers

SECTION 1

Inflammatory processes

1.1   Acute inflammation

Causes of acute inflammation

Inflammation is the essential response of living tissue to trauma. It destroys and limits the injury and is intimately related to the process of repair. It is therefore an integral component of the body's defence mechanisms, and without it there would be no defence against foreign organisms and no wound healing.

Acute inflammation is usually beneficial, although it can occasionally be harmful (eg anaphylaxis, acute lung injury, systemic inflammatory response syndrome).

Causes of acute inflammation include:
- Trauma (mechanical, thermal, radiation, chemical – includes stomach acid, bile and blood when free in the peritoneal cavity)
- Infection (bacteria, virus, parasite, fungus)
- Ischaemic injury
- Immunological attack (autoimmunity, graft vs host disease)
- Foreign body response (eg mesh in hernia repair)

Mechanism of acute inflammation

Vasodilatation and vascular permeability

After the initial injury there is a rapid and transient arteriolar vasoconstriction (reduces blood loss in case of vascular injury). Damage to the vasculature results in a collection of blood and activation of the clotting cascade. The resulting clot fills the wound and consists of a mesh-like fibrin plug in which are trapped a number of activated platelets. Activation of the platelets results in the release of a number of inflammatory mediators. Platelet activation may also activate the complement cascade.

The plasma contains four interlinked enzyme cascades – the **clotting cascade**, **fibrinolysis cascade**, **complement cascade** and **kinin system**. These cascades are interrelated and can be activated by each other's products. They are discussed in detail in Chapter 3.

Important inflammatory mediators released by platelets
- Prostaglandins
- Leukotrienes
- Histamine
- Serotonin

The release of prostaglandins (PGs) and nitric oxide results in persistent arteriolar smooth muscle relaxation and therefore increased local blood flow ('rubor' and 'calor'); 5HT, histamine, leukotrienes and complement proteins (C3a and C5a) cause activation of the endothelium, resulting in increased vascular permeability and exudation of fluid and plasma proteins. Increased oncotic pressure in the interstitial fluid draws water out from the vessels and causes tissue oedema – 'tumour'.

Vessel permeability

Due to three different responses
- The **immediate-transient response** begins at once, peaks at 5–10 minutes, and is over by 30 minutes. It is due to chemical mediators (prostaglandins, histamine, 5HT). It involves only the venules and is due to contraction and separation of endothelial cells

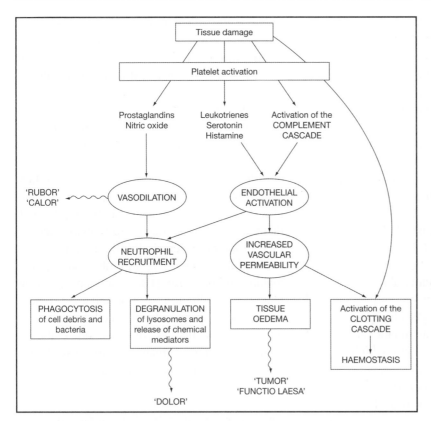

Figure 4.1 Acute inflammation

- The **immediate-prolonged reaction** is seen only when the injury is severe enough to cause direct endothelial cell damage (eg trauma to the blood vessel). It persists until the clotting cascade ends it

- The **delayed-prolonged leakage phenomenon** is seen only after hours or days. Venules and capillaries exude protein because their junctions separate due to apoptosis of the endothelial cells

In addition, endothelial cells are damaged as the leucocytes squeeze through the capillary walls and there is a degree of endothelial cell apoptosis. As the tissues heal, new blood vessels are formed which are, in themselves, leaky. This leakage of fluid from the vessels causes sludging or stasis in the capillary blood flow because there is a relative increase in the viscosity (thus the application of plasma viscosity measurement in inflammatory states).

Cellular events in acute inflammation

Initially neutrophils, and later macrophages, rapidly migrate to the injured area. Their subsequent activities involve the steps as shown in the box overleaf.

Recruitment of inflammatory cells

Margination: as blood flow decreases, leucocytes move from the centre of the vessel to lie against the endothelium.

Pavementing: adhesion molecules on leucocytes (eg integrins) bind to corresponding molecules on the endothelium (eg intercellular adhesion molecule 1 [ICAM-1] – see below); expression of these adhesion molecules is upregulated by specific inflammatory mediators (C5a, interleukin 1 [IL-1], tumour necrosis factor [TNF]) in the locality of the inflammation.

Diapedesis or emigration: adherent leucocytes pass through interendothelial junctions into the extravascular space; neutrophils are the predominant cell type in the first 24 hours, after which monocytes predominate.

Chemotaxis: leukocytes move to the injury site along a chemical gradient assisted by chemotactic factors (bacterial components, complement factors, leukotriene [LT]–B4).

Phagocytosis and intracellular degradation: opsonised bacteria (opsonins IgG and C3b) attach via Fc and C3b receptors to the surface of neutrophils and macrophages; the bacteria/foreign particle is then engulfed to create a phagosome, which then fuses with lysosomal granules to form a phagolysosome, and the contents of the lysosome degrade the ingested particle.

ICAM-1, ICAM-2 and integrins

ICAM-1 and ICAM-2 are cell adhesion molecules belonging to the Ig gene superfamily. They are expressed on endothelial cells (upregulated by inflammatory mediators) and act as receptors for β_2-integrin (expressed on neutrophils, eosinophils and T cells). The integrin 'hooks on' to the ICAM molecule and this interaction allows the leucocyte to adhere to the endothelium and emigrate into the tissue from the bloodstream. Integrins thus allow cell–cell interactions and cell–extracellular matrix (ECM) interactions.

The ICAM family is upregulated in certain disease states such as allergy (eg atopic asthma, allergic alveolitis), autoimmunity (eg type 1 diabetes mellitus, systemic lupus erythematosus [SLE], multiple sclerosis [MS]), certain cancers (eg bladder, melanoma), and infection (eg HIV, malaria, tuberculosis [TB]), allowing increased leucocyte infiltration of non-inflamed tissue. Reduction in the numbers of cellular adhesion molecules occurs in disease (eg diabetes, alcoholism, steroid treatment) and results in a reduced immune response to bacterial infection.

Cellular components of the inflammatory infiltrate

The neutrophils are the predominant cell type in the inflammatory phase in the first 24 hours. They degranulate, releasing their lysosomal contents, and also initiate phagocytosis of bacteria and cell debris. Phagocytosis requires that the particle be recognised and attach to the neutrophil. Most particles must be coated (opsonised) by IgG or complement protein C3b. There are receptors for both on the neutrophil surface. The particle will then be engulfed and a lysosome membrane fused with the phagosome membrane, causing digestion within the phagolysosome. Macrophages become the predominant cell type after 48 hours. They continue the process of phagocytosis and secrete growth factors (cytokines) which are instrumental in ECM production. Macrophages are also responsible for fibrosis, and heavy or prolonged inflammatory infiltrates are associated with severe scarring.

Inflammatory mediators in acute inflammation

The inflammatory response to trauma is mediated by chemical factors present in the plasma and produced by the inflammatory cells, as shown in the following table.

Mediators of the inflammatory response

Plasma	Cells
Complement system	Vasoactive amines (eg histamine, serotonin)
Kinin system	Lysosomal enzymes
Coagulation pathway	Arachidonic acid derivatives
Fibrinolytic system	Cytokines (eg TNF-α, interleukins)
	Free radicals

Important cytokines responsible for chemotaxis

- Transforming growth factor β (TGF-β)
- Basic fibroblast growth factor (bFGF)
- Platelet factor 4 (PF-4)
- β-Thromboglobulin (β-TG)
- Vascular endothelial growth factor (VEGF)
- Platelet-derived growth factor (PDGF)
- Monocyte chemotactic protein 1 (MCP-1)
- Keratinocyte growth factor (KGF)
- Epidermal growth factor (EGF)
- Fibroblast growth factor (FGF)

Complement system

The complement system consists of over 20 component proteins.

- The **classical pathway** is initiated by antigen–antibody complexes
- The **alternative pathway** is activated by endotoxins, complex polysaccharides and aggregated immunoglobulins

Both pathways convert C3 to C3a and C3b.

- C3b initiates the lytic pathway that produces the membrane attack complex (MAC), which forms destructive pores in the membranes of target cells
- C3a and C5a increase vascular permeability by causing release of histamine from granulocytes, mast cells and platelets. C5a is also chemotactic

The biological functions of complement are as follows:

- It yields particles that coat microorganisms and function as adhesion molecules for neutrophils and macrophages (opsonins)
- It leads to lysis of bacterial cell membranes via the MAC
- It yields biologically active fragments that influence capillary permeability and chemotaxis

Kinin system

Activation of coagulation factor XII produces factor XIIa. This converts prekallikrein into the active enzyme kallikrein, which produces bradykinin from high-molecular-weight kininogen. Bradykinin is a potent vasodilator and increases vascular permeability.

CHAPTER 4

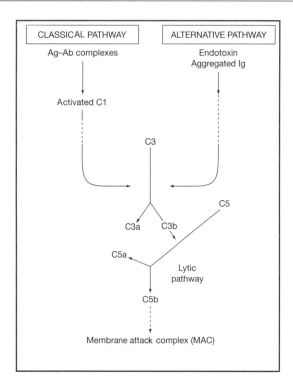

Figure 4.2 Activation of the complement pathways – classical and alternative

Coagulation and fibrinolysis

The clotting cascade and fibrinolysis are discussed in detail in Chapter 3.

Vasoactive amines

Histamine and serotonin

- Mast cells, basophils and platelets contain the amines histamine and 5HT
- Release from mast cell granules is stimulated by C3a and C5a, IgE immunological reactions and IL-1
- Release from platelets is caused by contact with collagen, thrombin, ADP and by PAF
- Both amines cause vasodilatation and increased vascular permeability

Nitric oxide (NO)

- Found to be of increasing importance in health and disease
- Synthesised by nitric oxide synthase (NOS) during oxidation of arginine to citrulline
- Produced by three NOS genes in neurones, endothelial cells and the immune system
- Acts to reduce intracellular calcium (smooth muscle dilatation, decreased cardiac contractility, reduced platelet and inflammatory cell activation)
- Appears to have protective beneficial effects when produced in neurones and endothelial cells, but pathological activity in inflammatory states:
- Has multiple actions in inflammation:
  - Local vasodilator
  - Bactericidal activity
  - Downregulatory effects on neutrophil function
  - Prolongs neutrophil lifespan
  - Causes apoptosis in macrophages

Lysosomal enzymes

Leucocytes degranulate at the site of infection, setting up a cycle of bacterial phagocytosis, tissue destruction and recruitment of increasing numbers of immune cells.

- Cationic proteins: increase vascular permeability and act as chemotactants
- Acid proteases: most active at about pH 3
- Neutral proteases: degrade extracellular matrix

Arachidonic acid metabolism

Arachidonic acid is a 20-carbon polyunsaturated fatty acid present in cell membranes. After activation, arachidonic acid is released from the membrane by phospholipases. It is then metabolised via two main pathways: the cyclooxygenase (COX) pathway and the lipoxygenase pathway.

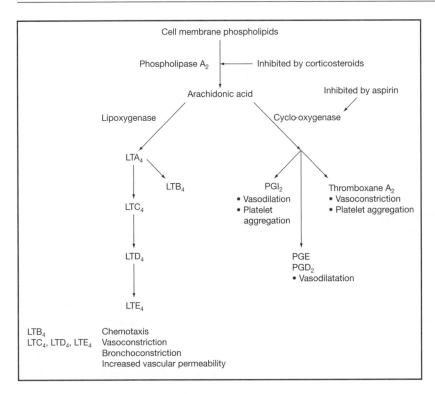

Figure 4.3 Arachidonic acid metabolism

COX pathway → prostaglandins PGE$_2$ and PGI$_2$

- Cause vasodilatation and increased vascular permeability
- The E-series prostaglandins are hyperalgesic

Lipoxygenase pathway→ leukotrienes

- Produced by all of the inflammatory cells except lymphocytes
- LTC$_4$ (plus products LTD$_4$ and -E$_4$) increase vascular permeability and constrict smooth muscle
- LTB$_4$ makes neutrophils adhere to endothelium and is a potent chemotactic agent

See section 1.4 for a discussion of anti-inflammatory pharmacology.

Interleukins, cytokines and monokines

- **Polypeptides:** produced by activated monocytes (monokines), lymphocytes (lymphokines) and other inflammatory cells
- **Interferons:** viral infection induces the synthesis and secretion of interferons; they confer an antiviral state on uninfected cells
- **Interleukins:**
  - IL-8 is a chemokine produced by monocytes, T lymphocytes, endothelial cells and platelets, which mediates the rapid accumulation of neutrophils in inflamed tissues
  - IL-1 is secreted by numerous cell types (monocytes, macrophages, neutrophils, endothelial cells); it promotes T- and B-cell proliferation, tissue catabolism and the acute phase response, and also acts as a pyrogen (see Section 2, The immune system)

- **TNF-α**
  - Produced by monocytes and macrophages, particularly if stimulated by bacterial endotoxins
  - Plays an important part in host defence against Gram-negative sepsis
  - When endotoxin present at a low dose TNF-α enhances macrophage killing, activation of B white blood cells and cytokine production
  - When endotoxin is present at a high dose TNF-α is an extremely potent mediator in the pathogenesis of endotoxin-related shock
- **PAF:**
  - A wide variety of cells produces PAF, including mast cells, neutrophils, platelets and macrophages
  - It has a multitude of effects and increases vascular permeability, leucocyte aggregation and exudation, smooth muscle constriction and cellular degranulation
  - Research into anti-PAF agents is ongoing

Free radicals

- Neutrophils release collagenase, alkaline phosphatase, elastase, myeloperoxidase, acid hydrolases, α_1-antitrypsin and lysozyme
- Monocytes produce acid hydrolases, collagenase and elastase

Outcomes of acute inflammation

> **Outcomes of acute inflammation**
> - Resolution
> - Abscess and pus formation
> - Scarring and fibrosis
> - Chronic inflammation

Resolution

Resolution occurs when no structural tissue component has been lost, with restoration of normal cellular and tissue function.

Abscesses and pus formation

- Pus is a body fluid containing neutrophils and necrotic debris
- Chemicals and enzymes released by inflammatory cells damage surrounding tissue and may even cause liquefaction necrosis – the mediators released by neutrophils are the worst offenders (predominantly these are proteases and free radicals)
- Collections of pus tend to find their own way out through tissue planes as the pressure inside the abscess builds; there is an increase in osmotic pressure due to the increasing number of molecular products being generated by the continuous action of proteases (eg formation of sinuses in osteomyelitis)

Scarring and fibrosis

Scarring means laying down of dense (type I) collagen in chronic inflammation ± wound healing. Degree of scarring is determined by repair vs regeneration.

- **Repair** occurs by laying down of fibrous tissue (fibroblasts produce ground substance, fibronectin and initially type III collagen, which is replaced with type I collagen as the scar matures)
- **Regeneration** can occur only in certain cell types:
  - Labile cells are continuous replicators (eg intestinal mucosa, hair follicles)
  - Stable cells are discontinuous replicators and can divide when required to do so (eg fibroblasts and endothelial cells)
  - Permanent cells are non-replicators and cannot divide (eg neurones)

1.2   Chronic inflammation

Chronic inflammation is characterised by
three features:
- **Infiltration of tissue with
  mononuclear inflammatory cells**
  (monocytes, lymphocytes ± plasma
  cells)
- **Ongoing tissue destruction**
- **Evidence of healing** (scarring,
  fibroblast proliferation, angioblast
  proliferation, angiogenesis)

It can be non-specific, autoimmune or
granulomatous. Granulomatous disease
includes TB, syphilis, leprosy and
schistosomiasis.

Chronic inflammation results from:
- Persistence of the acute inflammatory
  stimulus (eg cholangitis leading to chronic
  liver abscess)
- Deranged inflammatory response (eg
  autoimmune conditions such as rheumatoid
  arthritis or SLE)
- Recurrent episodes of acute inflammation
  (eg recurrent cholecystitis or pancreatitis
  resulting in pseudocyst formation)

Non-specific chronic inflammation

This is when acute inflammation fails to end in
resolution or repair, as a result of:
- Persistence of injurious agent (eg chronic
  osteomyelitis, peptic ulcer due to
  Helicobacter pylori)
- Failure of removal of pus and foreign
  material (eg undrained abscess)

- Inadequate blood supply or drainage (eg
  ischaemic or venous ulceration)
- Inadequate drainage of an exocrine gland
  (eg chronic sialoadenitis)

Pathology of non-specific chronic inflammation
- Tissue macrophages are almost all recruited
  directly from bloodstream monocytes
- T-helper cells activate B lymphocytes to
  produce plasma cells (via IL-4)
- Plasma cells produce antibodies against
  the persistent antigen or the altered
  tissue components; they divide under the
  influence of IL-1 from macrophages
- Some degree of scarring always occurs in
  chronic inflammation; IL-1 also activates
  fibroblasts, resulting in scarring
- Fibrosis is stimulated by TGF-β

Cellular response to chronic inflammation

The predominant cell in the inflammatory
infiltrate varies according to the cause of
inflammation:
- **Neutrophils** predominate in inflammation
  caused by common bacteria
- **Lymphocytes** predominate in viral infections
  and autoimmune diseases
- **Plasma cells** predominate in spirochaetal
  diseases (syphilis and Lyme disease)
- **Macrophages** predominate in typhoid
  fever, TB and fungal infections (except
  candidiasis)
- **Eosinophils** predominate in inflammation
  secondary to allergic reactions, parasites (ie
  worms) and in most inflammations of the
  gut

CHAPTER 4

Autoimmune chronic inflammation

Autoimmune diseases are characterised by the production of antibodies against 'self'. These antibodies cause chronic tissue damage and necrosis, and may be deposited as antibody complexes. This feeds a state of chronic inflammation. In autoimmune diseases the primary immune cell in the inflammatory infiltrate is the lymphocyte.

Autoimmunity is discussed in detail in section 2.3 of this chapter.

Granulomatous chronic inflammation

This is characterised by small collections (granulomas) of modified macrophages called 'epithelioid cells'. T-helper cells are stimulated by the persistent antigen to produce activating cytokines, which recruit and activate macrophages (eg by interferon [IFN]-α, TNF-α, etc). Persistence of the causative organism or substance causes the macrophages to surround the offending particle, effectively walling it off. These are then termed 'epithelioid cells'. Epithelioid cells may fuse over several days to form giant multinucleated cells (Langerhans' or foreign-body giant cells).

Granulomatous inflammation may be associated with suppuration (pus-filled cavity), caseation or a central foreign body. It is usually a low-grade smouldering response, occurring in the settings listed in the box.

Causes of granulomatous inflammation

Persistent infection
- Mycobacteria (TB, syphilis, leprosy)
- Atypical fungi

Prolonged exposure to non-degradable substances
- Pulmonary asbestosis
- Silicosis
- Talc

Immune reactions
- Autoimmune disorders (eg rheumatoid arthritis)
- Wegener's granulomatosis
- Sarcoidosis
- Reactions to tumours (eg lymphomas and seminomas)

Tuberculosis

Organism

Mycobacterium tuberculosis hominis or *Mycobacterium bovis*.
- Identified as acid-fast bacilli (AFBs) in sputum or pus smears by Ziehl–Neelsen stain
  - Needs special growth conditions (grow very slowly) so must be specifically requested
  - Three consecutive samples required (bacteria often sparse)
  - Early-morning samples best (sputum or urine)
- Waxy, hard to kill and resistant to drying (they remain infectious)

Transmitted commonly by droplet inhalation or dust containing dried sputum; can also be ingested.

Demographics of TB

Incidence increasing worldwide (increased drug resistance, HIV, non-compliance with treatment). WHO data show that TB is common in Southeast Asia (33% of cases) and is increasing in sub-Saharan Africa (secondary to HIV causes highest mortality per capita). There is an increased risk in populations who are malnourished, overcrowded and economically deprived, in those who have HIV and are immunosuppressed (eg due to steroids), and in alcoholism.

- **Bacille Calmette–Guérin (BCG)** vaccination (live attenuated virus) is used in some countries and is most effective in protecting children from TB meningitis
- **Tuberculin (or Mantoux/Heaf) tests** for infection or previous effective immunisation. Intracutaneous injection or topical application of purified tuberculin protein causes a type IV hypersensitivity reaction if there has been previous exposure. (Note that very immunosuppressed patients cannot mount this response and so the test may be negative despite florid TB.) The interpretation of the result of these tests also depends on whether the patient has been immunised with BCG

Symptoms and signs of TB

TB is a multisystem disease, with the following signs and symptoms:

- **General:** weight loss, night sweats, fever, malaise, 'consumption'
- **Pulmonary:** caseating cavities, empyema, progressive lung destruction, miliary form; cough, haemoptysis (chest radiograph: granulomas and thickening of pleura in upper lobes; diffuse shadowing in miliary form)
- **Gastrointestinal:** commonly ileocaecal; features similar to Crohn's disease ± RLQ (right lower quadrant) mass

- **Adrenal:** usually bilateral. Tissue destruction can lead to Addison's disease
- **Peritoneal:** primary peritonitis
- **Urinary:** sterile pyuria, renal involvement, predisposes to transitional cell carcinoma (TCC) in bladder
- **Hepatic:** miliary involvement
- **Skin:** may look like carcinoma
- **Bone:** Pott's disease is vertebral TB (± neurological compromise); joints (commonly knee and hip)
- **CNS:** meningeal pattern involving base of brain (cranial nerve signs)
- **Lymph nodes:** lymphadenitis of the cervical nodes (scrofula)
- **Cardiovascular:** usually pericarditis

Primary TB

- Often occurs in childhood
- Caseating granuloma surrounds primary infective focus (often subpleural); associated hilar lymphadenopathy and the initial granuloma together are referred to as the Ghon complex
- Disease may resolve, calcify or remain dormant and reactivate later in life (often due to subsequent immunocompromise)
- Rarely florid

Secondary TB

- Seen commonly in adults (re-infection/reactivation when bacilli escape the walled-off Ghon focus)
- Commonly at apex of lung
- Active florid infection with spread throughout the pulmonary tree and sequelae such as haemoptysis, erosion into bronchioles and 'open infection'

CHAPTER 4

'Cold abscess'

- Develops slowly so very little associated inflammation (ie 'cold')
- Becomes painful when pressure develops on surrounding areas
- Often affects musculoskeletal tissues
- Pus may track down tissue planes and present as a swelling some distance away
- Can be drained by percutaneous catheter or surgically

Treatment of TB

- Multiple drug therapy (rifampicin, isoniazid, pyrazinamide, ethambutanol) given as triple or quadruple therapy initially
- Requires directly observed therapy to ensure compliance
- Should also give pyridoxine to avoid isoniazid-induced neuropathy

Syphilis

Organism

- *Treponema pallidum*
- Transmitted: sexually (bacterium is fragile and moves from open genital sore to skin/mucous membrane of recipient); vertically (transplacental); via blood transfusion
- Risks: increases risk of transmitting HIV three- to fivefold; teratogenicity

Symptoms of syphilis

These are divided into primary, secondary and tertiary stages.

- **Primary syphilis**
  - Ulceration at site (chancre) within 2–6 weeks
  - May occur on genitalia, lips, tongue or cervix
  - Chancre disappears after a few weeks regardless of treatment
  - 30% progress to chronicity
- **Secondary syphilis**
  - Skin rash (large brown sores) on palms and soles of feet
  - Fever, headache, sore throat, lymphadenopathy
  - Lasts for a few weeks and may recur over next 1–2 years
- **Tertiary syphilis**
  - Damage to heart, eyes, brain, nervous system, bones and joints
  - Development of gummas (granulomas with coagulative necrosis; often in liver, testes, bridge of the nose)

Diagnosis of syphilis

- In early stages the disease mimics many others (called 'the great imitator')
- Diagnosed by two separate blood tests on different occasions (VDRL test)

Treatment of syphilis

- Intravenous (IV) penicillin

Leprosy (Hansen's disease)

Organism

- *Mycobacterium leprae*
- Multiplies very slowly (difficult to culture)

Demographics of leprosy

- WHO data show 90% of cases are in Brazil, Madagascar, Ethiopia, Mozambique, Tanzania and Nepal
- Transmission probably involves respiratory droplet infection

Symptoms of leprosy

- Disfiguring skin lesions, peripheral nerve damage (sensory loss and muscle weakness), loss of sweating and progressive debilitation (loss of sensation results in repeated injury and damage to hands and feet)
- Predisposes to amyloidosis A

Diagnosis of leprosy

- Classic appearance
- Skin scraping for AFBs

Classification of leprosy

- **Paucibacillary leprosy:** mild with hypopigmented skin papules
- **Multibacillary leprosy:** symmetrical skin lesions, nodules, plaques and thickened dermis, nerve damage and disability
- **Tuberculoid leprosy:** infection is controlled by the patient's T cells forming granulomas similar to TB (especially in nerve sheaths, leading to damage)
- **Lepromatous leprosy:** the patient's T cells are unable to control the infection and lesions become diffuse with large disfiguring lesions and bacterial invasion of supporting cells of the nervous system

Treatment of leprosy

- Multidrug therapy (eg rifampicin, dapsone, ethionamide)
- Early treatment reduces infectivity and minimises debilitation

Granulomas and exposure to non-degradable substances

Persistence of any non-degradable substance may lead to granuloma formation as the body 'walls it off'. Granulomas may form around the deposition of endogenous substances (such as ingrown hairs or ruptured epidermoid cysts) or around foreign bodies (such as asbestos fibres and schistosome eggs). Any foreign body may result in granuloma formation.

Asbestosis

- Asbestosis results from prolonged heavy exposure to asbestos fibres or dust (usually occupational)
- The asbestos fibre is long and pierces through the lung tissue, coming to lie near the pleura
- Pathology: there is marked peribronchiolar and alveolar interstitial fibrosis.
- Granulomas form early in involved areas, and undergo fibrosis as the disease progresses
- Asbestos exposure is also associated with bronchial carcinoma and mesothelioma

Schistosomiasis

- Granuloma formation in gastrointestinal (GI) and urinary tracts due to reaction instigated by deposition of schistosomal ova (fluke)
- Sequelae include bleeding, fibrosis and stricture
- Commonly causes liver involvement and portal hypertension

Immune reactions and granulomas

Granulomas form as a result of immune reactions, typically:

- Type IV hypersensitivity reactions
- Unusual immune reactions: Wegener's granulomatosis, sarcoidosis, Crohn's disease, primary biliary cirrhosis
- Immune reactions to tumours: usually those affecting lymph nodes, such as lymphoma or seminoma

CHAPTER 4

Wegener's granulomatosis

Wegener's is a granulomatous vasculitis. Any organ may be involved and granuloma is commonly seen in the respiratory tract. Also commonly causes glomerulonephritis and generalised arteritis. See discussion of vasculitides in Chapter 9, Vascular Surgery in Book 2.

Sarcoidosis

Sarcoidosis is characterised by non-caseating granulomas of unknown cause. It primarily affects young adults of African or Caribbean descent, with a female preponderance. It is commonly found in the chest, causing bilateral hilar lymphadenopathy. Extrathoracic disease is more serious. It may affect a number of organ systems:

- **Respiratory:** bilateral hilar lymphade-nopathy ± cough, fever, malaise, arthralgia and erythema nodosum. May eventually lead to pulmonary fibrosis
- **Central nervous system (CNS):** uveitis (may cause blindness), cranial nerve palsies, diffuse CNS disease or space-occupying lesions, granulomatous meningitis
- **Renal:** nephropathy and renal calculi (due to hypercalcaemia)
- **Cardiovascular:** sudden death, tachyar-rhythmias, cardiomyopathy, pericardial effusion

It is diagnosed by biopsy and its characteristic granulomatous histology. Steroids are used to prevent pulmonary fibrosis, blindness and nephropathy.

1.3 Clinical indicators of inflammation

Examination findings

The cardinal signs of acute inflammation are 'rubor' (redness), 'calor' (heat), 'dolor' (pain), 'tumour' (swelling) and 'functio laesa' (reduction in function). Increased blood flow due to vasodilatation causes redness and heat. Increased vascular permeability results in tissue oedema and swelling with loss of functional capacity. The presence of inflammatory mediators from the complement cascade and neutrophil lysosomal contents, and those released from injured tissue, cause pain.

Pyrexia may also be a feature and is a CNS response to circulating inflammatory mediators.

Generalised inflammation or the systemic inflammatory response syndrome (SIRS) is discussed in Chapter 3.

Investigations for inflammation

Leucocytosis

Leucocytosis in inflammation is predominantly a neutrophilia (ie increase in neutrophils). Initially circulating neutrophils are attracted to the site of inflammation. Subsequently cytokines cause increased release of immature neutrophils from the bone marrow and there are increases in the overall circulating level of neutrophils (called a 'left shift' after the position of columns on the old haematologists' counting pad).

Erythrocyte sedimentation rate

The erythrocyte sedimentation rate (ESR) increases as a result of increased plasma viscosity in inflammatory conditions. It is less useful in sepsis because values rise slowly (more useful in chronic inflammatory states). ESR is a fairly non-specific test but can be used to monitor inflammatory states over a period of days to years.

- Value is higher in women than in men, in elderly people, during pregnancy, and in anaemia and obesity
- Values also high in widespread malignancy

Acute phase proteins

These are about 40 different plasma proteins that are synthesised in the liver in response to the inflammatory state – referred to as the acute phase response.

- Include clotting proteins, complement factors, transport proteins and anti-proteases
- Many can be measured as serial markers in acute and chronic disease

C-reactive protein

C-reactive protein (CRP) is produced by the liver. It binds to molecules exposed during cell death or on surface of pathogens, and it:

- Acts as an opsonin (aiding phagocytosis)
- Activates classical complement pathway
- Upregulates adhesion molecules
- Increases release of proinflammatory cytokines

CRP plasma levels:

- Normal range 0–10 mg/ml
- Levels >300 mg/ml are an independently poor prognostic sign
- Levels are sensitive and respond rapidly (can be used <24 hours so good for acute inflammatory states such as sepsis)

- Mildly elevated levels are associated with increased risk of atherosclerosis and colon cancer
- Elevated levels are a common response to surgical trauma (so interpret with care in the first 24 hours postoperatively)

Fibrinogen

Component of the clotting cascade. Leaks out of vessels during inflammation and acts as a framework for:

- Trapping blood cells to form clot
- Confining inflammatory cells to the site of inflammation
- Trapping bacteria, so impeding dissemination around body
- Subsequent scar formation

Plasma levels increase with inflammatory stimuli (normal 200–400 mg/dl).

1.4 Anti-inflammatory pharmacology

Steroids

Glucocorticoids inhibit expression of many of the genes involved in inflammatory and immune responses (including those encoding cytokines, chemokines, cell-surface receptors, adhesion molecules, tissue factor, degradative proteases, COX-2 and inducible NO synthase [NOS]). They bind to a glucocorticoid receptor (GR) in the cell and this interacts directly with DNA at glucocorticoid response elements (GREs) to activate or inhibit transcription of the factors outlined above.

CHAPTER 4

Side effects of steroids

> **Side effects of steroids**
> **Mineralocorticoid effects**
> - Hypertension
> - Fluid retention
>
> **Glucocorticoid effects**
> - Diabetes
> - Osteoporosis
> - Mental disturbance and psychosis
> - Muscle wasting (proximal myopathy)
> - Peptic ulceration
> - Adiposity (altered distribution)
> - Thin skin

Adrenal suppression

Withdrawal after long periods causes acute adrenal insufficiency (see Endocrine Surgery in Book 2). Steroids must be weaned gradually or replaced with equivalent IV supply if they have been taken long term (approximate equivalent doses to 5 mg prednisolone are 750 μg dexamethasone, 20 mg hydrocortisone, 4 mg methylprednisolone). Patients on long-term steroids will require IV replacement if they become acutely unwell or require surgery.

Cushing syndrome

Signs include moon face, striae, abnormal fat distribution (buffalo hump, supraclavicular fossae), acne and hypertension. Remember that Cushing 'syndrome' refers to excessive glucocorticoids and may be iatrogenic. Cushing's 'disease' is due to ACTH secretion by pituitary tumour (see Endocrine Surgery in Book 2).

Non-steroidal anti-inflammatory drugs

Types of NSAIDs

The differences in anti-inflammatory activity of the different non-steroidal anti-inflammatory drugs (NSAIDs) are small but individual patients show considerable variation in their tolerance and response to different NSAIDs.

- Aspirin (salicylate hydrolysed in the body to salicylic acid)
- Indometacin
- Diclofenac sodium
- Naproxen
- Ibuprofen
- Ketorolac (for postop pain)
- Celecoxib, rofecoxib, valdecoxib and etoricoxib (arthritides)

The side effects of the NSAIDs vary, and the newer NSAIDs (eg COX-2 inhibitors) have been developed with improvement in the GI safety profile in mind. However, there have been recent concerns about the cardiovascular safety of the COX-2 inhibitors.

Pharmacology of the NSAIDs

All NSAIDs have similar pharmacology:
- Absorbed passively in the stomach and small intestine
- Detectable in plasma at 30–45 minutes. Peak levels occur in inflamed tissue slowly but the compounds persist in inflammatory exudates long after they have been removed from the plasma (ie delayed onset but prolonged action)
- Activity occurs mainly in the peripheral nervous system, although they do have some CNS effects
- Ceiling to their analgesic effect
- Can be used to reduce or eliminate requirement for steroid use

- Variability between individuals in response (thought to have a genetic basis)

There are two components to their mechanism of action:

1. The drug molecule inserts into the cell lipid bilayer (more lipophilic at low pH as seen in inflamed tissue). This disrupts cellular signals so, for example, in neutrophils this reduces aggregation and enzyme release
2. The drug acts on the COX pathway, targeting the isoenzymes COX-1 and COX-2. This suppresses production of PGE_2 and prostacyclin (PGI_2) so these drugs act as antipyretic, analgesic and anti-inflammatory agents. This effect does not prevent inflammation itself but acts to suppress the positive feedback of continued prostaglandin production
- **COX-1** is constitutively expressed and produces prostaglandins important for mucosal integrity in the GI tract and for renal perfusion in the kidney
- **COX-2** is the inducible form. Production is dramatically upregulated by cytokines, mitogens and inflammation. The currently available NSAIDs vary in their potency as inhibitors of COX-2, but virtually all

are far more potent inhibitors of COX-1 than COX-2. COX-2-selective drugs have been developed (eg rofecoxib, celecoxib, valdecoxib, parecoxib) which have an improved GI safety profile – although recent evidence suggests that there may be an increase in thromboembolic complications in patients taking long-term COX-2 inhibitors. It is unclear how much the prostaglandins produced by COX-1 may contribute to pain and inflammation; it is also possible that COX-2 produces some beneficial prostaglandins

---

Side effects of NSAIDs

Side effects of the NSAIDs are:
- GI toxicity (duodenal or gastric ulceration, nausea, dyspepsia)
- Renal toxicity
- Fluid retention and hypertension
- Hypersensitivity reactions (especially bronchospasm in patients with asthma)
- Tinnitus

CHAPTER 4

SECTION 2

The immune system

> **Learning point**
>
> The primary function of the immune system is to eliminate infectious agents and to minimise the damage they cause.
>
> The immune system consists of non-specific defences and specific (acquired) immunity.
>
> | **Non-specific defences** | **Specific (acquired) immunity** |
> |---|---|
> | Skin and mucous membranes | Lymphocytes: special |
> | Commensal organisms | features include specificity, |
> | Bactericidal body fluids (gastric acid) | adaptation, memory |
> | Complement system | |
> | Phagocytes: neutrophils, PMNs and natural killer (NK) cells | |
> | Inflammatory cells: eosinophils, basophils and mast cells | |
> | **Characteristics** | **Characteristics** |
> | Antigen-independent | Antigen dependent |
> | Immediate maximal response | Lag time between exposure and response |
> | No immunological memory | Immunological memory |

2.1 Non-specific mechanisms of immunity

Skin and mucous membranes

Physical barrier to penetration by bacteria. Often contain an outpost of the immune system for early antigen recognition (mucosa-associated lymphoid tissue or MALT), eg Peyer's patches, intraepithelial T cells. May employ movement to flush out bacteria (eg intestinal peristalsis, bronchopulmonary mucociliary escalator, urinary voiding).

Commensal organisms

Normal commensals may be overwhelmed by a pathogen due to the use of antibiotics or changes in their growth environment (eg pH). A common example is the loss of normal gut flora with broad-spectrum antibiotics and an increase in colonisation with *Clostridium difficile*.

Bactericidal body fluids

Bactericidal activity is due to:
- pH – often due to this (eg stomach acid, vaginal secretions)
- Enzymatic action, eg lysosyme in lacrimal secretions
- Thiocyanate in saliva
- Low-molecular-weight fatty acids in the bowel
- Bile acids

Complement system

Components of the complement system are the pharmacological mediators of inflammation. The system is concerned with the initial elimination of foreign microorganisms, involving opsonisation and chemotaxis.

Phagocytes

All phagocytes have receptors for a variety of molecules: IgG Fc, complement, IFN, TNF and some ubiquitous bacterial proteins. Target cells and organisms become coated in these molecules and the phagocyte is stimulated to engulf the target. Bacteria produce *N*-formylmethionine which acts as a phagocyte chemoattractant.

Neutrophils

- Neutrophils are polymorphonuclear cells (PMNs)
- Seen as large abundant lymphocytes with a lobed nucleus and multiple cytoplasmic granules (lysosomes)
- Immature neutrophils contain primary azurophilic granules with proteases
- Mature neutrophils contain secondary granules

Mononuclear phagocytes

- Have smooth nuclei and also contain granules in the cytoplasm
- Cells include:
  - Monocytes in circulation
  - Tissue histiocytes
  - Microglial cells (brain)
  - Kupffer cells (liver)
  - Macrophages (serous cavities and lymphoid organs)

Natural killer cells

- Class of cytotoxic lymphocytes that carry marker CD16 but no unique receptors for antigenic targets
- Lyse virus-infected cells and tumour-derived cells by recognising Fc fragments
- Release perforins which punch holes in infected cells (causing cell lysis or a channel for the injection of protease enzymes)
- Use a dual receptor system to lyse cells that do not express major histocompatibility complex (MHC) class I molecules (downregulated in cancer and viral infections) or that express stress-related proteins (infection and tumours produce the human MHC class I chain-related genes *MICA* and *MICB*)
- Have no immunological memory
- Actions are enhanced by IFNs and IL-2

Bone-marrow-derived inflammatory cells

- Eosinophils, basophils and mast cells release inflammatory mediators in response to infection (prostaglandins, vasoactive amines, leukotrienes and signalling proteins such as cytokines)

2.2 Specific mechanisms of immunity

The immune system is adaptive. When a new antigen is encountered cells undergo genetic rearrangements to generate a subgroup of cells capable of attacking the source. These undergo clonal expansion. After resolution, the system retains some of these cells as memory cells. The memory cells provide a background production of specific immunoglobulins and a population of T cells that can be reactivated quickly. This leads to a reduction in subsequent susceptibility to that disease in the future.

This acquisition of increased resistance to a specific infectious agent is known as acquired specific immunity, and forms the basis for many immunisation programmes.

Acquired specific immunity provides the ability to:

- Recognise the difference between self and non-self
- Mount a response that is specific to foreign material
- Remember previous responses so that a subsequent response to previously encountered foreign material will be faster and larger

---

Cell-mediated immunity (CMI) has distinct roles.

Role of CMI in bacterial infection

- Specific recognition of antigen by T cells
- Non-specific lymphokine production, which upregulates macrophages and activates cytotoxic T and B cells

Role of CMI in viral infection

- Upregulation of macrophages and killer cells for cell killing
- Production of interferons

All class I antigens and most of the class II antigens evoke the formation of antibodies in genetically non-identical individuals.

Antigen presentation

An antigen is a substance capable of inducing a specific immune response. When a host encounters an antigen two things may occur:

- Proliferation of T lymphocytes
- Antibody formation by plasma cells

Dendritic cells and macrophages process antigens and present peptide fragments in association with MHC molecules on the cell surface. These can then be recognised by receptors on T cells. Antigen-presenting cells (APCs) are located in the lymphoid system and in all organs. They present antigens to the rest of the immune system in a manner dependent on the source of the antigen:

- **Endogenous proteins** (or viral proteins) are processed and presented bound to MHC class I molecules (and this combination is then recognised by CD8+ T cells)
- **Exogenous proteins** (taken up by phagocytosis or pinocytosis) are processed and presented bound to MHC class II molecules (and this combination is recognised by CD4+ T-helper cells)

Major histocompatibility complex

This important set of genes is on the short arm of chromosome 6. The genes code for the human leucocyte antigens (HLAs) which are present on cell membranes and are specific to each individual.

They consist of α and β chains which combine to provide a peptide-binding cleft in which the antigen fragment is displayed. The HLA system is the most polymorphic genetic system in humans (>1000 alleles) and contributes to a huge array of different possible peptide-binding clefts.

The recognition by the recipient's immune system of HLAs on the surface of donor cells forms the basis of rejection following organ transplantation.

MHC gene products
Based on their structure, distribution and function, the MHC gene products are classified into three groups.

Class I antigens
- Found on all nucleated cells and platelets as cell-surface molecules
- Coded by three loci, designated HLA-A, HLA-B and HLA-C

Class II antigens
- Found on dendritic cells, macrophages, B lymphocytes and activated T cells
- Coded for in a region known as HLA-D
- Antigens are HLA-DR, HLA-DQ and HLA-DP
- These are proteins involved in antigen processing

Class III proteins
- Components of the complement system coded for within the MHC (includes C4 and heat shock protein, HSP)

Role of T lymphocytes
T lymphocytes recognise the combination of antigen and MHC molecule via their specialised receptor, the TCR (T-cell receptor). The TCR is also composed of α and β chains. During T-cell development the gene segments encoding these chains are rearranged, generating a huge diversity in their capacity to recognise peptide fragments.

The CD4 or CD8 molecule is associated with the TCR and its distal portion recognises either MHC class I or MHC class II, respectively. This ensures that the correct type of T cell is brought into contact with the source of the antigen (see below).

Cytotoxic T lymphocytes
CD8+ cells are cytotoxic T lymphocytes:
- Recognise antigen + MHC class I
- Kill cells infected with viruses or intracellular bacteria
- Memory cytotoxic T cells persist after recovery

Helper T lymphocytes
These CD4+ cells recognise antigen + MHC class II. They produce these soluble mediators:
- IFN-γ activates macrophages
- IL-2 stimulates proliferation of B and T cells
- IL-4 promotes differentiation of CD4+ T and B cells
- IL-5 stimulates activation of eosinophils
- IL-6 promotes differentiation of B and T cells
- IL-10 suppresses proinflammatory cytokine production by macrophages
- IL-12 promotes cytotoxic action of T and NK cells

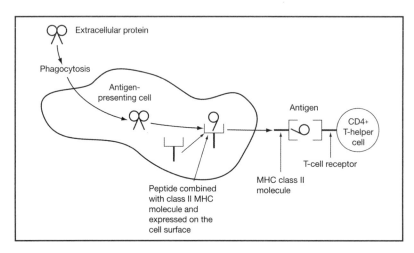

Figure 4.4 Activation of CD4⁺ T lymphocytes

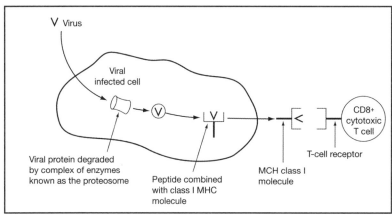

Figure 4.5 Activation of CD8⁺ T lymphocytes

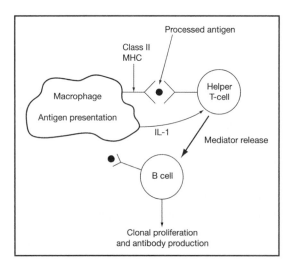

Figure 4.6 T and B cell interaction

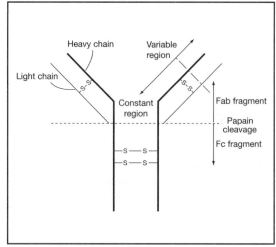

Figure 4.7 Antibody structure

Role of B lymphocytes

The B-cell receptor for antigen is the antibody molecule. Activated B cells differentiate into plasma cells, which secrete immunoglobulins. B cells have a unique ability to produce an almost endless array of antibodies to an enormous number of antigens.

- T-helper cells promote immunoglobulin production
- All have similar monomeric structure except IgM (pentameric structure)

An immunoglobulin molecule is a four-polypeptide chain structure with two heavy and two light chains linked covalently by disulphide bonds (S–S). Digestion with papain produces antigen-binding fragments (Fab) and one Fc fragment, which is involved with complement and macrophage binding.

Light chains are either kappa (κ) or lambda (λ).

There are five main classes of immunoglobulin, based on the Fc fragment of the heavy chain. These are IgG (γ), IgM (μ), IgA (α), IgD (δ), IgE (ε).

Antibodies binding to antigen leads to:

- Agglutination and lysis of bacteria (IgM)
- Opsonisation of such organisms
- Initiation of the classical complement pathway
- Blocking the entry or passage of microorganisms from the respiratory tract, gut, eyes and urinary tract into deeper tissues
- Killing the infected cell by antibody-dependent cell-mediated cytotoxicity
- Neutralising bacterial toxins and products

Functions of macrophages

Macrophages are generated from blood monocytes and are present in most tissues. Functions include:

- **Antigen presentation:** macrophages present antigen to T lymphocytes as processed peptides associated with MHC class II molecules
- **Phagocytosis:** macrophages ingest bacteria opsonised by immunoglobulin ± complement; this leads to the release of toxic molecules into the phagosome and death of the microorganism
- **Secretion:** activated macrophages secrete numerous factors, including neutral proteases, lysosyme, cytokines, chemotactic factors, arachidonic acid metabolites and complement components

Immune tolerance

As immune cells develop in the bone marrow and thymus they are exposed to self-antigens. Cells expressing receptor molecules that have the potential to recognise self-antigens are deleted to prevent the development of autoimmunity. Some antigens, those in immuno-logically privileged sites (such as the testis and eye), are not represented during this process and damage to these areas later in life will expose these antigens to the mature immune system for the first time.

CHAPTER 4

2.3 Disorders of immunity

> **Learning point**
>
> **Hypersensitivity:** tissue damage results from an inappropriate immune response to an exogenous antigen
>
> **Autoimmunity:** immune response against the host's own antigens
>
> **Immune deficiency:** inadequate immune response (may be due to a congenital or acquired defect)
>
> **Neoplastic proliferations:** uncontrolled production of various elements of the immune system is a haematopoietic neoplasm
>
> **Transplant-specific problems:** implantation of transplanted material may result in rejection or graft-versus-host disease

Hypersensitivity reactions: Gell and Coombs' classification

Type I (anaphylactic or immediate)

Exposure to allergen leads to formation of IgE. IgE binds to mast cells and basophils, and then re-exposure to allergen leads to release of mediators from these cells.

- **Mediators** include:
  - Histamine (causes bronchial constriction, increased vascular permeability and increased mucous gland secretion)
  - Leukotrienes (LTC_4, LTD_4, LTE_4 are 1000 times more potent than histamine)
  - Eosinophil and neutrophil chemotactic factors
  - Neutral proteases
  - PAF

- **Examples:** asthma and peanut allergy, anaphylactic shock

If you have a patient with a suspected anaphylactic reaction it is useful to send a blood sample to immunology 30 minutes after the reaction begins for tryptase enzyme levels. This can confirm anaphylaxis. Sodium cromoglicate and steroids are thought to inhibit mediator release by stabilising lysosomal membranes.

Type II (cytotoxic)

Mediated by antibodies against intrinsic or extrinsic antigens absorbed on the cell surface or on other components. Tissue damage results from complement-dependent reactions and antibody-dependent cell-mediated cytotoxicity.

Complement-dependent reactions

- Antibody complexes with antigen present on the cell surface activate the complement system. The cell then becomes susceptible to phagocytosis by the antibody or C3b present on the cell surface. In addition, cellular damage may be secondary to the formation of the membrane attack complex (MAC)
- **Examples:** transfusion reaction, autoimmune thrombocytopenia, drug reactions

Antibody-dependent cell-mediated cytotoxicity

- Cells complexed with antibody are lysed by non-sensitised cells (NK cells, neutrophils, and monocytes)
- **Examples:** parasitic infections, graft rejection

Type III (immune complex-mediated)

- Mediated by immune complexes (antigen–antibody) formed either in the circulation or at extravascular sites. Immune complex leads to complement activation and thence to neutrophil activation, with release of lysosomal enzymes, resulting in tissue damage
- **Examples:** SLE, acute glomerulonephritis, serum sickness

Type IV (cell-mediated/delayed)

- Mediated by sensitised T lymphocytes. Sensitised T cells lead to cytotoxic T-cell activation plus release of lymphokines from T-helper cells, and thence to recruitment and activation of macrophages and monocytes, resulting in cell damage
- **Examples:** TB Mantoux test, transplant rejection

Type V (stimulatory)

- Anti-receptor antibodies lead to stimulation of cell function
- **Examples:** Graves' disease, myasthenia gravis

Autoimmunity

Autoimmune disorders result from a defect in self-tolerance. Autoimmunity may be tissue-specific or systemic. They are usually relapsing and remitting conditions.

Mechanisms of development of autoimmunity are unclear but it can result from:

- Defects in suppressor cell numbers or function
- Microorganisms eliciting antibodies that cross-react with self-antigens (molecular mimicry)
- Alteration of self-antigens by drugs or microorganisms, exposing new antigenic sites
- T-cell-independent emergence of B cells that are capable of mounting an autoimmune response

CHAPTER 4

Major autoimmune diseases	
Disease	**Autoantibodies present against**
Organ-specific diseases	
Hashimoto's thyroiditis	Thyroglobulin, thyroid microsomes
Graves' disease	Thyroid-stimulating hormone receptor (thyroid-stimulating Igs)
Atrophic gastritis	Parietal cells
Pernicious anaemia	Intrinsic factor
Goodpasture syndrome	Basement membrane (lungs and kidneys)
Myasthenia gravis	Acetylcholine receptor
Non-organ-specific disease	
SLE	Antinuclear antigen (ANA), DNA, smooth muscle
Rheumatoid arthritis	Rheumatoid factor
Scleroderma	Centromere

Individual diseases are typically linked to a specific class I or II HLA antigen (but not both). Diseases linked to class I locations are more common in men, eg ankylosing spondylitis and Reiter syndrome (HLA-B27) and psoriasis (HLA-Cw6), and those linked to class II are more common in women, eg pernicious anaemia, Hashimoto's thyroiditis (HLA-DR5) and rheumatoid arthritis (HLA-DR4).

Monozygotic twins of patients are at increased risk of developing an autoimmune disease (around 25%) and siblings have a slightly increased risk (because they have a slightly different arrangement of HLA alleles).

Autoantibodies

These should be requested only after discussion with an immunologist, when a certain diagnosis is in mind.
* ANA should be requested only if SLE or Sjögren syndrome is suspected. ANA is sensitive and SLE is unlikely in the absence of a positive ANA
* Anti-Ro and anti-La (associated with Sjögren syndrome)
* Anti-centromere (associated with CREST syndrome)
* Anti-Scl70 (associated with scleroderma)

In general, older patients, even when healthy, will have higher autoantibody levels.

Important autoimmune diseases

See other sections for discussions of:
* Hashimoto's thyroiditis and Graves' disease (Endocrine Surgery in Book 2)
* Atrophic gastritis and pernicious anaemia (Abdomen in Book 2)
* Rheumatoid arthritis (Chapter 9, Orthopaedic Surgery)

Systemic lupus erythematosus

Often affects young women. More common in Africa, the Caribbean and Southeast Asia.

The aetiology of SLE is unclear. There are many theories but it appears to be due to autoantibodies against a variety of normal cell nuclear constituents. These also form complexes that are deposited in other organs, causing chronic inflammation. 'Lupus anticoagulant' is an autoantibody generated against membrane phospholipids. It is prothrombotic (it affects the intrinsic clotting cascade) and results in cerebrovascular accidents (CVAs), multiple miscarriages, deep venous thromboses (DVTs) and pulmonary emboli (PEs). Lupus anticoagulant is positive in a third of lupus patients.

SLE is a multisystem disease. It commonly presents with a number of symptoms (eg a 23-year-old woman from Thailand presenting with urticarial rash, mucosal ulceration, arthralgia, alopecia, pleuritic chest pain, fever and weight loss) of the following systems:
* **Dermatological:** may manifest with many types of rash, classically butterfly or lupoid skin rash/discoid rash and/or photosensitivity
* **Mucous membranes:** ulceration, serositis
* **Cardiovascular:** acute necrotising vasculitis, endocarditis, pericarditis
* **Respiratory:** pleurisy
* **Renal:** immune complexes deposited in the glomeruli (chronic renal failure), acute renal failure (ARF)
* **Joint:** arthritis/arthralgia
* **Haematological:** anaemia, thrombocytopenia, neutropenia
* **CNS:** mental changes, psychosis, convulsions, CVA

Management should be by specialist only. It is steroid-based (causing immunosuppression).

Sjögren syndrome

Mild illness due to autoimmune damage to joints and glandular structures (predominantly salivary and lacrimal but occasionally vulval glands and renal tubules).

Scleroderma

Slowly progressive disorder characterised by a vasculitis and excessive fibrosis. It affects multiple organ systems (skin changes and Raynaud's phenomenon, GI tract and replacement of the smooth muscle with collagen, synovitis, renal damage).

CREST syndrome is a variant: **c**alcinosis, **R**aynaud's phenomenon, **o**esophageal dysfunction, **s**clerodactyly and **t**elangiectasia.

Immune deficiency

May affect specific immunity (eg a T- or B-cell problem) or non-specific immunity (eg NK cells or complement). Classification is into primary and secondary disorders.

- **Primary immune deficiencies:** hereditary disorders that typically manifest between 6 months and 2 years of age as maternal antibody protection is lost (eg an 18-month-old boy presenting with recurrent pneumonia, several episodes of otitis media and sinusitis over the last year, failure to thrive; chest radiograph reveals bronchiectasis and serum Igs reveal hypogammaglobulinaemia)
- **Secondary immune deficiencies:** altered immune response secondary to malnutrition, ageing, infection, irradiation, splenectomy, medication (chemotherapy, steroids) or immunosuppression – recurrent, persistent or atypical infections suggest an immune deficiency disorder

CHAPTER 4

Examples of immune deficiency include

IgA deficiency
- Common disorder (1 in 600 people affected)
- Congenital or acquired after viral infection
- Usually asymptomatic
- Recurrent pulmonary and GI infections
- 40% have antibodies to IgA

Common variable immune deficiency
- Congenital
- Hypogammaglobulinaemia (especially IgG)
- May include disorder of T-cell regulation in addition to B-cell function
- Typically presents after the first decade of life with recurrent pyogenic infections
- Prone to autoimmune diseases and lymphoid malignancies

X-linked agammaglobulinaemia of Bruton
- X-linked primary immunodeficiency disorder
- Lack of mature B cells and nearly no immunoglobulin
- T-cell function and numbers are normal
- Recurrent bacterial infections
- Most viral and fungal infections are handled appropriately

continued overleaf

CHAPTER 4

DiGeorge syndrome
- Congenital disorder due to fetal damage to the third and fourth pharyngeal pouches
- Syndrome involves thymic hypoplasia/aplasia, parathyroid hypoplasia, congenital heart disease and dysmorphic facies
- T-cell deficiency (prone to viral and parasitic infections)
- B cells and Ig levels are normal

Severe combined immunodeficiency disease (SCID)
- Group of autosomal or X-linked recessive disorders
- Characterised by lymphopenia and defects in T- and B-cell function
- Death usually occurs within 1 year from opportunistic infection (unless treated by bone marrow transplantation)

Complement factor deficiencies
- C3 deficiency predisposes to bacterial infections
- C2 deficiency increases risk of autoimmune connective tissue disorders
- C5–8 defects lead to recurrent *Neisseria* infections (eg recurrent meningitis)

Acquired immune deficiency syndrome (AIDS)
- See section 3.2

2.4 Management of the immunocompromised patient

Learning point

- A patient may be immunocompromised due to a congenital or an acquired cause
- The trauma of surgery itself may cause the patient to be immunocompromised
- Immunocompromised patients may exhibit attenuated signs of infection
- Patterns of susceptibility to infection depend on the immunological defect (may be truly pathogenic organisms or opportunists)

The immunocompromised patient may exhibit attenuated signs of infection, whereby the patient:
- May not be pyrexial
- May not generate a haematological response (raised lymphocyte count)
- May not generate localised inflammation (and consequently may have poor wound healing)
- May have masking of clinical signs (eg corticosteroid treatment often masks acute abdominal pain)

The pattern of infection depends on the defect in the immune system.

Generalised immune dysfunction
- Drugs (eg ciclosporin, corticosteroids)
- Trauma, burns, surgical stress
- Blood transfusion

Cell-mediated immunity dysfunction

- Specific B- and T-cell defects
- Widespread malignancy impairs T- and B-cell functions
- Haematological malignancy impairs cell-mediated immunity
- Malnutrition is associated with decreased lymphocyte function

Non-specific immunity dysfunction

- Diabetes impairs neutrophil activity
- Vitamin deficiency affects NK cells
- Ig and complement deficiencies affect phagocytosis (eg splenectomy predisposes to encapsulated bacteria)

Immunocompromised patients are susceptible to two forms of infection:

- The same bugs that cause infection in everyone
- Opportunistic infections (less virulent organisms, viruses and fungal infection)

All infections in immunocompromised patients can cause:

- Chest infection
- Urine infection
- Line infection
- Wound infection – macrophage dysfunction predisposes to wound infection (impaired phagocytosis of debris, etc)

Management of immunocompromised patients

- Prophylactic preop antibiotics
- Aggressive treatment of any preop infection
- Consider diagnoses that may be masked by immune compromise
- Some immunosuppressive medication may be required throughout the operative period (eg transplant recipients, long-term steroid use)
- Good surgical technique
- Early identification of postop problems (sepsis screen if pyrexial, requires careful wound management)

CHAPTER 4

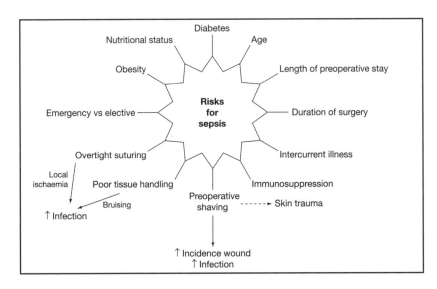

**Figure 4.8
Risks for sepsis**

Splenectomy

Splenectomy results in immunocompromise. Patients are particularly vulnerable to encapsulated organisms. Splenectomy is discussed in the Abdomen chapter of Book 2.

Overwhelming post-splenectomy infection

Caused by infection by one of the encapsulated organisms normally destroyed by the spleen. These are *Streptococcus pneumoniae*, *Neisseria meningitidis* and *Haemophilus influenzae*. Infection with these pathogens can lead to overwhelming sepsis with a mortality rate of 50–90%. Incidence is about 2% in children and 0.5% in adults, the highest incidence being in those undergoing splenectomy for lymphoreticular malignancy. All patients should have prophylaxis after splenectomy. Interestingly there are some reports that the risk of infection is lower if splenectomy is performed for trauma due to seeding of cells from the damaged spleen around the peritoneal cavity.

Current guidelines for post-splenectomy prophylaxis

The following should be carried out:

- Explanation of risk to patient, with card to carry
- Immunisation with Pneumovax, Hib and meningococcal vaccines (at least 2 weeks before elective splenectomy or a few weeks after emergency surgery; remember boosters at 5–10 years)
- Antibiotic prophylaxis with phenoxymethylpenicillin (or erythromycin) until age 15 only – lifelong prophylaxis should be offered but is particularly important for the first 2 years
- Patients should commence amoxicillin at the first sign of febrile illness

CHAPTER 4

SECTION 3

Disease-causing organisms

Learning point

Infection may be due to:
- Pathogenic organisms
- Infection with normal body commensals
- Infection with saprophytic organisms from soil, plants, etc

The pathogenicity of surgical infections depends on the:
- Virulence of the pathogen
- Level of host defence
- Nature of the infection

- **Conventional infections** affect previously healthy individuals
- **Opportunistic infections** affect immunosuppressed hosts
- **Colonisation** refers to a bacterial carrier state without clinical symptoms or signs of infection
- **Infection** refers to a bacterial carriage with clinical symptoms and signs of infection
- **Bacteraemia** is the presence of bacteria in the bloodstream
- **Septicaemia** is the presence of bacterial products in the bloodstream (eg toxins)

causing a clinical syndrome of septic shock. This term has been superseded by the more accurate terms 'sepsis', 'septic syndrome' and 'septic shock'

3.1   Bacteria

Mechanisms of bacterial virulence

Exotoxins
- Usually Gram-positive bacteria (eg *Clostridium* spp.)
- Highly toxic, highly antigenic polypeptides
- Specific target sites
- Excreted by living bacteria
- Neutralised by antitoxins
- Include enterotoxins (eg *Staphylococcus aureus, Escherichia coli*)

Endotoxins
- Lipopolysaccharide molecules in outer layer of Gram-negative cell walls
- Stimulate non-specific release of mediators from inflammatory cells
- Severe endotoxaemia is life-threatening

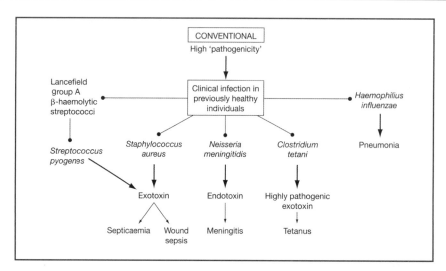

Figure 4.9 Disease-causing organisms – conventional pathogens

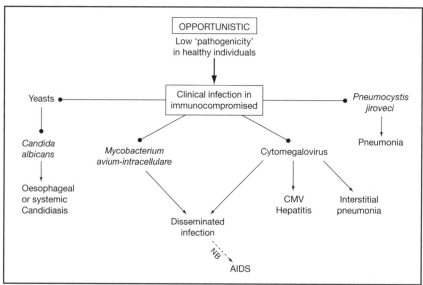

Figure 4.10 Disease-causing organisms – opportunistic pathogens

Capsules

- Capsule enhances invasiveness
- Increased resistance to phagocytosis
- Reduced effectiveness of bacterial killing within macrophages and polymorphs

Damage to tissues

- Fast-growing bacteria deprive host tissues of nutrients and lower tissue pH

- Secretion of exotoxins
- Destruction of cell walls produce endotoxins (cause systemic response, fever, increased capillary permeability, shock and even disseminated intravascular coagulation or DIC)
- Some bacteria express 'superantigens' which activate all of the B or T cells (some, for example, *S. aureus* as in toxic shock syndrome; some streptococci)

- Activation of phagocytosis causes systemic release of mediators from cells

Gram-positive bacteria

Stain blue/purple/black.

Gram-positive cocci

Aerobic cocci

- Staphylococci (clusters): presence of coagulase enzyme = virulence factor:
  - Coagulase-positive *S. aureus*
  - Coagulase-negative skin flora (eg *S. epidermidis*)
- Streptococci (chains/pairs): virulence (ability to lyse red blood cells [RBCs])
  - α-Haemolytic streptococci: partial lysis of RBCs; altered haemoglobin causes green colour around each colony on blood agar (eg *Streptococcus pneumoniae* = diplococcus; *S. viridans* group)
  - β-Haemolytic streptococci: complete lysis of RBCs around each colony
- Lancefield grouping
- Used mainly for β-haemolytic streptococci:
  - Based on specific polysaccharide antigen extracted from streptococcal cell walls
  - Lancefield group A (eg *S. pyogenes*)
  - Lancefield group B (eg *S. faecalis*)
  - Other Lancefield groups (C and G)
  - γ-Haemolytic streptococci: no lysis of RBCs (eg *S. faecalis* (most common) and *S. bovis*)

Anaerobic cocci

- Anaerobic streptococci:
  - Gut flora
  - *Enterococcus faecalis*

Gram-positive bacilli

Aerobic bacilli

- Diphtheroides:
  - *Corynebacterium diphtheriae*
  - *Listeria monocytogenes*
  - *Bacillus* spp.

Anaerobic bacilli

- *Clostridium* spp. (spore-forming)
  - *C. botulinum* (botulism)
  - *C. perfringens* (gas gangrene)
  - *C. tetani* (tetanus)
  - *C. difficile* (pseudomembranous colitis)
- Actinomycetes (non-spore forming; 'sulphur granules'):
  - *Actinomyces israelii* (actinomycosis: cervicofacial, pulmonary, pelvic)

Gram-negative bacteria

Stain pink/red.

Gram-negative cocci

Aerobic cocci

- *Neisseria* spp. (pairs):
  - *N. meningitidis*: meningococcus (meningitis and septicaemia)
  - *N. gonorrhoeae*: gonococcus (gonorrhoea)
- *Moraxella* spp.: *M. catarrhalis* (atypical pneumonia)

Gram-negative bacilli

This is a large group.

Aerobic bacilli

- *Pseudomonas (P. aeruginosa)*: immunocompromised host, hospital-acquired infection, associated with respirators, drainage tubes, catheters

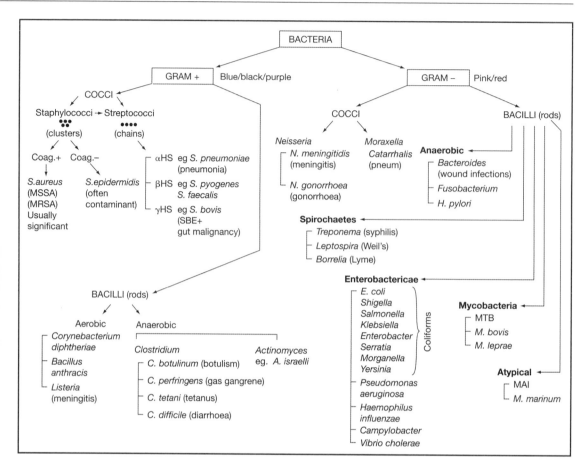

Figure 4.11 Classification of bacteria

- *Vibrio* spp. (*V. cholerae*)
- *Campylobacter* spp. (*C. jejuni*): human infection of small bowel
- Parvobacteria:
  - *Haemophilus influenzae*
  - *Yersinia enterocolitica* (gastroenteritis) and *Y. pseudotuberculosis* (mesenteric adenitis)
  - *Bordetella pertussis*
  - *Brucella* spp.
- *Legionella* spp.:
  - *L. pneumophila*
  - Enterobacteria (coliforms; gut flora)

- Lactose fermenters 'facultative anaerobes' (can grow without oxygen):
  - *E. coli*
  - *Klebsiella* spp.
  - *Enterobacter* spp.
  - *Shigella* spp. (late lactose fermenter)
  - *Citrobacter* spp.
- Non-lactose fermenters:
  - *Proteus* spp.
  - *Salmonella* spp.

Anaerobic bacilli

- *Bacteroides* spp. (eg *B. fragilis*)

3.2   Viruses

Learning point

- Viruses are genetic material with protein coats that are able to integrate themselves into eukaryotic cells in order to replicate
- They are dependent on cells for their life cycle
- They may carry DNA or RNA as their genetic material

Pathological viral cycle

The pathological viral cycle involves the following:
- Virion particle attaches to the cell
- Virion enters cell
- Loses protein capsule
- Integrates with cell RNA or DNA
- Virus replicates genetic material
- Virions are produced using host cell's own materials
- Virions are released into the surrounding tissues and blood cells

Some viruses integrate into the cell genome (becoming a 'pro-virus'). These are often DNA viruses. Others remain in the cytoplasm (most RNA viruses, except those with reverse transcriptase). The virus replicates with the cell or hijacks cellular machinery to produce multiple copies of its own genetic material. Viral inclusions (aggregates of viral proteins) become visible in the nucleus or cytoplasm of infected cells. Virions are released from the cell (often by cellular lysis) so shedding multiple copies into surrounding tissues and the bloodstream.

Pathological effects of viruses

Pathological effects occur by:
- Death of the host cell by lysis to release virions
- Rendering infected cells less or non-functional
- Stimulating cell-mediated immunity, which kills infected cells
- Stimulating cell proliferation (which may result in carcinogenesis and neoplasia, eg Epstein–Barr virus (EBV)

Viral infections usually resolve without treatment unless the patient is immunocompromised. Topical applications exist for localised infection (eg aciclovir cream for herpesvirus eruptions). Intravenous treatments are reserved for systemic infections in immunocompromised individuals.

Intravenous treatments commonly include:
- Nucleoside analogues
- Reverse transcriptase inhibitors (against HIV, eg lamivudine and AZT [azidothymidine])
- Protease inhibitors
- Interferons

Classification of viruses

Classification of DNA and RNA viruses

Double-stranded DNA viruses	RNA viruses
Adenovirus family	**Rotavirus** (gastroenteritis)
Hepatitis B	**Coronavirus**
Herpesviruses	Influenza
CMV	**Picornavirus**
EBV	**Enteroviruses**
Herpes simplex	Coxsackie
Herpes zoster	Polio
Pox viruses	**Echoviruses**
Molluscum contagiosum	Rhinovirus (common cold)
Smallpox	Hepatitis A

RNA viruses

Paramyxoviruses

Measles

Mumps

RSV

Retroviruses

HIV-1

HIV-2

HTLV

Togaviruses

Rubella

Hepatitis C

Hepatitis G

Immune responses to viruses

Three parts of the immune response to viruses
- Humoral response (neutralising antibodies, produced during immunisation or initial exposure)
- Interferon production
- Cellular response (T-cell response for destruction of infected cells)

Specific important viruses

Influenza viruses
- A, B and C strains
- Symptoms 1–2 days after exposure (fever, myalgia, headache)
- New strains are appearing and periodically cause severe outbreaks (eg avian flu) with large numbers of fatalities (often secondary to pneumonitis)
- Vaccine is available and is useful in young people, but less so in elderly people

Coxsackie viruses
- Coxsackie A causes sore throat with blistering, hand, foot and mouth disease
- Coxsackie B causes pleurisy, myocarditis

Morbillivirus (measles)
- Incubation period 14 days after droplet infection
- Starts as a cold followed by conjunctivitis, Koplik's spots, lymphoid hyperplasia and rash
- Complications can be severe: pneumonitis, autoimmune encephalitis (may cause brain damage)

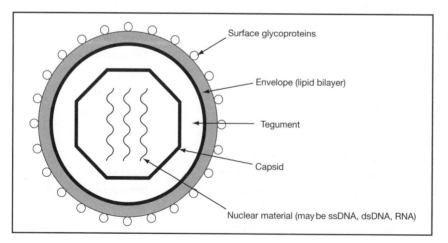

Figure 4.12 The virion

- Vaccine included in the MMR (measles, mumps, rubella) triple vaccine given in the first year of life in many countries. There has been an increased incidence of measles and mumps in recent years as a result of reduced uptake in the MMR vaccine among parents (after publication of a single spurious paper finding a link to autism). The result was devastating because many children and immunocompromised individuals have been infected with these preventable illnesses. In some cases the results are fatal

Mumps virus

- Mumps usually occurs in childhood: usually with inflammation of salivary glands ± mild meningitis
- Adults may also get orchitis and infertility, oophoritis and pancreatitis
- Vaccine included in the MMR

Rubella (German measles)

- Mild illness transmitted by droplet infection
- Causes rash, arthritis and is teratogenic (can cause congenital blindness, deafness, heart defects, hepatospenomegaly and thrombocytopenia in Gregg syndrome)
- Vaccine included in the MMR

Herpesviruses

Herpesviruses types 1–8 are DNA viruses that integrate into the human genome and periodically reactivate throughout life.

- **Herpes simplex virus 1 (HSV-1):** persists in nervous tissue causing cold sores (reactivated by sunlight, intercurrent illness and stress). In the immunocompromised host it can also cause fulminant pneumonitis and encephalitis

- **Herpes simplex virus 2 (HSV-2):** causes genital herpes. It is sexually transmitted. The infection is fulminant if passed to a newborn during birth or to an immunocompromised person
- **Varicella-zoster virus (VZV) or herpes (chickenpox virus):** spread by droplet infection and often contracted in childhood. It causes a vesicular rash and can cause pneumonitis and encephalitis in immunocompromised people. It resides in a nerve root and can reactivate as shingles later in life with a vesicular rash on the corresponding skin dermatome, paraesthesia, or hyperaesthesia and pain. May also involve the cornea (a serious complication). A vaccine is available but not commonly used in Europe (there is increasing use in the USA). Contraction of the disease in the first trimester can cause fetal abnormalities and pregnant women who have not previously had chickenpox must consider treatment with VZV antibodies if exposed to the disease
- **Epstein–Barr virus (herpesvirus 4):** EBV infects the B cells and integrates into the genome. Infected cells are eventually eliminated by the T cells of the immune system. EBV causes infectious mononucleosis (also called glandular fever or 'the kissing disease' because it passes via saliva from teenager to teenager). It is also common in gay men. The incubation period is around 6 weeks and the disease features fever, malaise and generalised lymphadenopathy. There may be a mild hepatitis and thrombocytopenia. EBV is also linked to lymphoma (especially Burkitt's lymphoma and lymphomas of the brain), squamous cell carcinoma (SCC) of the throat and salivary gland cancers. There may also be a link to multiple sclerosis

- **Cytomegalovirus (CMV) (herpesvirus 5):** a very common infection, often acquired *in utero* or in infancy. It can also be acquired from sexual activity, blood transfusion or transplantation; 80% of adults have positive serology
  - May cause a mononucleosis-type infection initially
  - Remains latent until immunosuppression occurs
  - May cause pneumonia, GI tract perforation, chorioretinitis (in AIDS) or encephalitis, and is the most common precipitating factor for Guillaine–Barré syndrome (commonly in immunocompromised individuals such as those with AIDS)
  - May cause fetal abnormalities
  - CMV status of donor and recipient is important in organ transplantation. CMV-positive organs are generally not given to CMV-negative recipients. Post-transplantation immunosuppression may reactivate the virus, resulting in the conditions listed above
- **Herpesvirus 8:** Kaposi's sarcoma virus is caused by this virus

Hepatitis viruses

The first hepatitis virus was isolated in 1969 and six major viruses are now known (hepatitis viruses A–G). Other common viruses also affect the liver (eg CMV, mumps, rubella).

- **Hepatitis A virus:** an RNA virus transmitted by the faecal–oral route. It is often picked up through travel. After 6 weeks it causes jaundice, weakness, fever and flu-like symptoms with tender lymphadenopathy. The disease usually resolves spontaneously, and is occasionally fulminant. It may relapse. Immunisation with IgG is effective

- **Hepatitis B virus:** a DNA virus with many subtypes. It is transmitted parenterally, vertically or sexually. Acute illness resolves within a few weeks. Fulminant hepatitis may occur in <1% cases. The disease progresses to chronicity in 5% of cases. Chronic hepatitis B may cause an active hepatitis with eventual cirrhosis. Treatments for chronic hepatitis B include IFN and lamivudine but these have limited efficacy. Three-stage immunisation is mandatory for healthcare workers and for anyone likely to be exposed to the virus (eg gay men). Hepatitis B immunoglobulins (HBIgs) can be given in cases of emergency exposure (eg newborn from infected mother; needlestick or sharps injury)
- **Hepatitis C virus:** a single-stranded RNA virus. Risk factors for transmission include exposure to blood (transfusion, needlestick injury), IV drug use, tattoos and body piercings, and multiple sexual partners. Often there are no risk factors identified. The acute phase occurs 6 weeks after infection with flu-like illness ± jaundice. Chronicity occurs in 50–60%; the disease may progress to chronicity with no symptoms until end-stage liver disease. IFN and ribavirin combination therapy may be given under the care of an experienced hepatology team; transplantation may be required for end-stage disease
- **Hepatitis D virus:** a co-infection that occurs with hepatitis B virus infection and is usually associated with parenteral transmission
- **Hepatitis E:** similar to hepatitis A virus and causes acute but not chronic illness
- **Hepatitis G:** very similar to hepatitis C virus but does not seem to be pathogenic in humans

Human immunodeficiency viruses (HIV) and AIDS

Pathophysiology of AIDS

AIDS is caused by the human immunodeficiency virus (HIV) – a retrovirus. There are two classes:

- HIV-1 is responsible for the global pandemic
- HIV-2 is less virulent

There are various subtypes of HIV-1 (types A–O) with different geographical distributions. The HIV membrane contains the glycoprotein gp120, which has a high affinity for the CD4 antigen on T-helper cells, monocytes and macrophages. There is also a molecule called gp41 that stimulates fusion of the HIV virion to the target cell membrane. HIV complexes with the target cell, the virus invades a cell, its single-stranded RNA genome is copied as double-stranded DNA by the viral reverse transcriptase system, and viral DNA integrates into the host genome.

Key genes in HIV

- *Env* codes for the production and processing of envelope proteins (gp120 and gp41)
- *Gag* forms matrix protein and proteins of the core capsid and nucleocapsid
- *Pol* directs synthesis of the enzymes (integrase, protease, reverse transcriptase)
- *Nef* is a virulence factor

Viral propagation occurs (via the viral protease system) with subsequent T-cell activation. There is an extremely high degree of viral turnover (20% per day) throughout the course of infection, including the latent period. The virus often changes its capsid through mutation, producing different strains (even in the same

patient) and so development of a vaccine is difficult. Most anti-HIV drugs inhibit either reverse transcriptase or protease synthesis.

CD4+ T-cell depletion increases susceptibility to opportunistic infections and malignancies.

Transmission of HIV

Sexual transmission occurs when the presence of other sexually transmitted infections aids transmission of the virus (due to ulceration and inflammation of mucosa).

Vertical transmission occurs from mother to child transplacentally (risk is about 25% without prophylaxis) or via breast milk (risk is 5–15%). This risk is reduced with antiretroviral treatments.

Parenteral transmission is through exposure to infected blood products (transfusion, contaminated needles, etc).

Demographics of HIV infection

Up-to-date information on the incidence and prevalence of HIV in different countries can be accessed via the World Health Organisation website (www.who.int/hiv).

There is new evidence that adult HIV infection rates have decreased in certain countries and that changes in behaviour to prevent infection (such as increased use of condoms, delay of first sexual experience and fewer sexual partners) have played a key part in these declines. This predominantly relates to the situation in Africa – 40% HIV infection prevalence in South Africa (higher in sub-Saharan Africa); incidence rates in Kenya have fallen from 10% in 2003 to 7% in 2005, and a similar pattern has been seen in Zimbabwe and in some Caribbean countries.

CHAPTER 4

Overall, trends in HIV transmission are still increasing, and far greater HIV prevention efforts are needed to slow the epidemic. Increasing incidence of infection has been documented in Southeast Asia and Eastern Europe. In addition, the incidence of HIV infection in young heterosexual women in the UK has doubled in the past 5 years. The incidence of HIV in the USA is also increasing – 50% of heroin users in New York, USA are HIV-positive and 1.5% women of childbearing age in the USA are HIV-positive.

Around 1% of cases have occurred in people with haemophilia who received infected blood (most cases occurred before the advent of routine screening of blood products in the 1980s and most of these patients have now died).

HIV testing

The routine HIV test is ELISA (enzyme-linked immunosorbent assay), which detects antibody directed towards HIV. In the early stages (before seroconversion, in the first 12 weeks or so) the test may be negative but the patient is highly infectious. All patients should give informed consent and be counselled before and after HIV testing.

Clinical symptoms of HIV infection

HIV infection is initially asymptomatic. **AIDS** is a syndrome characterised by:

- **Vulnerability to infections** by opportunistic microorganisms (ie those that do not produce severe disease in humans with a normal immune system)
- **Systemic features:** generalised lymphadenopathy (cervical, occipital, epitrochlear and submental), fever, weight loss (accelerates in the terminal phases)
- **Tumours** (Kaposi's sarcoma and non-Hodgkin's B-cell lymphoma)

- Variable degree of **nervous system damage** (attacks the brain, spinal cord, and peripheral nerves) causing PML (progressive multifocal leukoencephalopathy)

Opportunistic infections in HIV infection

Respiratory tract infection

- *Pneumocystis jiroveci*: causes pneumonia; rarely disseminates outside the lung. Symptoms include fever, non-productive cough and dyspnoea. Chest radiograph shows perihilar infiltrates and diffuse shadowing. Diagnosed on bronchoalveolar lavage (BAL)
- *Mycoplasma tuberculosis*: TB is common in HIV patients. Causes pulmonary infection (commonly miliary form but may present atypically). May also cause extrapulmonary TB (joints, bone and GI tract). Multidrug resistance is a problem. *Mycobacterium avium* complex infection is pathognomonic for HIV
- CMV: Once a common opportunistic infection seen in AIDS. Often disseminated. Causes pneumonitis, GI and CNS disease (including retinitis and blindness). Fortunately with HAART these are rarely seen in developed countries now

CNS infection

- *Toxoplasmosis gondii*: most common CNS problem in AIDS; causes multiple brain abscesses visible as ring-enhancing lesions on CT/MRI
- *Cryptococcus neoformans*: causes insidious meningitis in advanced disease; treat with fluconazole (may need lifelong secondary preventive treatment)
- *Herpes simplex*: causes encephalitis and blistering of mucosal areas

GI tract infection

- *Candida albicans*: causes irritation and ulceration in the mouth and oesophagus in advanced disease. Treated with nystatin or amphotericin orally (or fluconazole systemically)
- *Cryptosporidium*: causes diarrhoea (advise patients to boil water)
- *HIV enteropathy*: small-bowel enteropathy caused by the virus itself; causes villus atrophy with malabsorption

Autoimmune phenomena

The HIV virus causes an increase in autoimmune phenomena, possibly due to effects on B cells (eg pancreatic damage leading to diabetes).

Surgical conditions in HIV

Essentially these are infections and tumours, as shown in the box below.

Surgical conditions in HIV/AIDS
Infections
- Abscesses
- Empyema
- Peritonitis
- Perianal disease
- Osteomyelitis

Tumours
- **Non-Hodgkin's lymphoma:** usually high-grade B cell lymphoma; 2% get cerebral lymphoma. Often have EBV as an additional aetiological agent
- **Kaposi's sarcoma:** there are nodules of abnormal vessels and spindle-shaped cells in the dermis. This sarcoma is aggressive and infiltrates other organs (lungs, body cavities and GI system). Caused by herpesvirus 8

Natural history of HIV disease

Up-to-date information about the natural history of HIV can be found on the WHO website (www.who.int).

Clinical staging is for use where HIV infection has been confirmed (ie there is serological and/or virological evidence of HIV infection). The clinical stage is useful for assessment at baseline (first diagnosis of HIV infection) or entry into HIV care. It is also useful in the follow-up of patients in care and treatment programmes.

Clinical staging of HIV infection
Primary HIV infection
- Asymptomatic
- Acute retroviral syndrome

Clinical stage 1 (asymptomatic established HIV)
- Asymptomatic
- Persistent generalised lymphadenopathy

Clinical stage 2 (mild symptoms)
- Moderate unexplained weight loss (<10% of presumed or measured body weight)
- Recurrent respiratory tract infections (sinusitis, tonsillitis, bronchitis, otitis media, pharyngitis)
- Herpes zoster
- Angular cheilitis
- Recurrent oral ulceration
- Papular pruritic eruptions
- Seborrhoeic dermatitis
- Fungal nail infections

Clinical stage 3 (advanced symptoms)
- Unexplained severe weight loss (>10% of presumed or measured body weight)
- Unexplained chronic diarrhoea for >1 month

continued overleaf

- Unexplained persistent fever (intermittent or constant for longer than 1 month)
- Persistent oral *Candida* infection
- Oral hairy leukoplakia
- Pulmonary tuberculosis
- Severe presumed bacterial infections (eg pneumonia, empyema, pyomyositis, bone or joint infection, meningitis, bacteraemia, excluding pneumonia)
- Acute necrotising ulcerative stomatitis, gingivitis or periodontitis
- Unexplained anaemia (<8 g/dl), neutropenia (<500/mm³) and or chronic thrombocytopenia (<50 000/mm³)

Clinical stage 4 (severe/very advanced symptoms)

- HIV-wasting syndrome
- *Pneumocystis* pneumonia (PCP)
- Recurrent severe (presumed bacterial pneumonia)
- Chronic herpes simplex infection (orolabial, genital or anorectal, of more than 1 month's duration or visceral at any site)
- Oesophageal candidiasis (or Candida infection of trachea, bronchi or lungs)
- Extrapulmonary tuberculosis
- Kaposi's sarcoma
- CMV infection (retinitis or infection of other organs)
- CNS toxoplasmosis
- HIV encephalopathy
- Extrapulmonary cryptococcosis including meningitis
- Disseminated non-tuberculous *Mycobacteria* infection
- Progressive multifocal leukoencephalopathy

- Chronic cryptosporidiosis
- Chronic isosporiasis
- Disseminated mycosis (extrapulmonary histoplasmosis, coccidioidomycosis, penicilliosis)
- Recurrent septicaemia (including non-typhoidal *Salmonella*)
- Lymphoma (cerebral or B-cell non-Hodgkin's)
- Invasive cervical carcinoma
- Atypical disseminated leishmaniasis

CD4 counts

The pathogenesis of HIV virus infection is largely attributable to the decrease in the number of T cells (a specific type of lymphocyte) that bear the CD4 receptor. The immunological status of the HIV-infected infant, child, adolescent or adult can be assessed by measurement of absolute number or percentage of T cells expressing CD4, and this is regarded as the standard way to define the severity of HIV-related immunodeficiency. Progressive depletion of CD4+ T cells is associated with progression of HIV, and an increased likelihood of opportunistic infections and other clinical events associated with HIV.

- At a **CD4 count of 200–350 × 10⁶/l** infections with common organisms begin to occur (particularly *S. pneumoniae*, *H. influenzae*, *M. tuberculosis* and *Candida* spp.); patients may present with weight loss, diarrhoea, fever, fatigue and myalgia
- At a **CD4 count of <200 × 10⁶/l** there is increased risk of opportunist infections and tumours (commonly *P. jiroveci* pneumonia; (incidence decreasing with use of prophylaxis); cerebral toxoplasmosis; Kaposi's sarcoma; and candidiasis)
- At a **CD4 count of <50 × 10⁶/l** multiple, concurrent infections with organisms of low

virulence are common (commonly atypical mycobacterial infections, systematic fungal infections, CMV infection, AIDS–dementia complex and lymphoma)

Prognosis in HIV infection

The course of infection depends on viral and host factors, and more recently on treatment options. The mean time from infection with HIV to diagnosis of a major opportunistic infection or tumour is 11.2 years; the mean time to death is around 18–24 months after this (without treatment). With HAART patients can expect to have a much longer life expectancy (50–60 years or maybe longer).

Antiviral treatments for HIV/AIDS

In affluent countries, the progression of HIV disease has been markedly slowed by the use of HAART. This refers to combined therapy with three or more drugs, usually two that target the reverse transcriptase and one that targets the viral protease.

Reverse transcriptase inhibitors

- **Nucleoside analogues:** by mimicking a nucleoside these drugs become incorporated into the growing DNA strand by the viral reverse transcriptase. This then halts further DNA synthesis. Examples include zidovudine (AZT; Retrovir), lamivudine (Epivir) and didanosine (Videx)

Other anti-HIV drugs

- **Protease inhibitors:** these block the viral protease so that the proteins needed for assembly of new viruses cannot be cleaved from the large protein precursor. Examples include indinavir (Crixivan), saquinavir (Invirase) and ritonavir (Norvir)
- **Fusion inhibitors:** the viral protein gp41 penetrates the host plasma membrane by a process involving non-covalent binding between two segments of its chain (HR1 and HR2). Fusion inhibitors (eg enfuvirtide, Fuzeon) act as a competitive inhibitor, binding to HR1 and thus preventing binding of HR2
- **Integrase inhibitors:** drugs that inhibit the HIV-1 integrase; have been shown to slow disease progression in experimental animals (monkeys)

Problems with drug treatment

Drug treatment has been shown to slow the progression of the disease, transiently reverse the symptoms of the late stages of the disease and reduce vertical transmission, preventing the infection of babies born to infected mothers. However, the problems with drug therapy include:

- Expense (£5000–10 000/year per patient)
- Side effects (eg nausea, diarrhoea, hepatic damage)
- Complicated dosing regimen
- Resistance: drug treatment selects for the emergence of drug-resistant virions in the patient. This is particularly serious because of the speed at which mutations occur in HIV

3.3 Fungi

> ### Learning point
>
> **Fungal infections**
> Fungi can be categorised as:
> - Yeasts (eg *Candida* spp., cryptococci)
> - Moulds (eg *Aspergillus* spp.)
> - Dimorphic fungi (eg histoplasmosis)
>
> They cause different types of disease:
> - Local superficial (eg ringworm, tinea versicolor, tinea pedis)
> - Subcutaneous (eg sporotrichosis)
> - Systemic infections (mycoses; occur in immunocompromised people)

Fungal species

Most fungi are opportunists. They are capable of causing systemic disease in immunocompromised hosts/people.

Candida spp.

- Most common human fungal disease
- *Candida albicans* is a normal commensal
- Overgrowth occurs when the host has:
  - Normal flora eradicated by antibiotics
  - Hyperglycaemia (in diabetes; vaginally during pregnancy)
  - Wet skin (eg groin creases in the obese)
  - Immune dysfunction
- It occurs as white patch ± ulceration on mucosal surfaces
- Oesophageal candidiasis is a sign of serious underlying immune compromise

Cryptococci

- Yeasts with a polysaccharide coating

- Responsible for meningitis, pneumonia and GI infections
- Any organ can be involved

Aspergillus spp. (aspergillosis)

- Invasive fungus (*Aspergillus fumigatus* or *A. niger*)
- Filamentous with septate branching hyphae
- Produces aflatoxin (carcinogen)
- Forms balls of fungus in the lungs (aspergilloma)
- Capable of invading blood vessels
- Causes allergic aspergillosis (asthmatic reaction to airborne spores)
- Causes invasive aspergillosis (systemic; often fatal in immunosuppressed individuals)

Histoplasma spp. (histoplasmosis)

- Tiny non-encapsulated yeast
- Spores are inhaled from soil, bird or bat droppings
- Spores lodge in the lungs, causing mild fever and symptoms of a cold ('primary histoplasmosis')
- Chronic reactivated histoplasmosis causes pulmonary cavities and granulomas – very similar to TB pattern
- Systemic histoplasmosis is often fatal in immunocompromised people

Sporothrix spp. (sporotrichosis)

- Occurs while gardening or from rose-thorn injury
- May be superficial or deep and spreading

Pneumocystis jiroveci

- Described as a fungus
- Usually harmless in immunocompetent adults

- Increasingly seen in immunocompromise (especially AIDS)
- Organisms damage pneumocytes and alveolar spaces fill with organisms and dead cells producing pneumonia (PCP)
- Treatment with co-trimoxazole

Treatment of fungal infection

Options for treatment of fungal infection include:

- **Polyene antifungals:** not absorbed orally and used to treat infections such as *Candida albicans* topically (eg nystatin). Amphotericin is used for systemic infections and is given parenterally
- **Imidazole antifungals:** used for vaginal candidiasis and local oral infections (eg ketoconazole, miconazole)
- **Triazole antifungals:** well absorbed and achieve good penetrance into the tissues including the CNS (eg fluconazole)

3.4 Parasites

Learning point

Parasitic infections
Protozoa may be:
- Luminal (amoebiasis, cryptosporidosis, giardiasis, trichomoniasis)
- Blood-borne (malaria, trypanosomiasis)
- Intracellular (Chagas' disease, leishmaniasis, toxoplasmosis)

Helminths (worms) may be:
- Platyhelminths (flatworms)
- Cestodes (tapeworms), eg *Echinococcus* spp. (hydatid disease)
- Trematodes (flukes), eg *Schistosoma* spp., the liver flukes
- Nematodes (roundworms), eg *Ascaris* spp.

Protozoa

Amoeba (eg *Entamoeba histolytica*)

- *E. histolytica* causes colonic inflammation and diarrhoea
- May be commensal
- Acquired by ingestion of cysts
- Affects right side of the colon (amoeba penetrate the mucosa through the crypts and spread out underneath it causing ulceration and eventually sloughing; occasionally the bowel perforates)
- May cause extra-intestinal disease, predominantly in the liver with formation of abscesses (see Abdomen chapter in Book 2) and may also spread to the heart, lungs and brain
- Treatment is with metronidazole

Giardia lamblia

- Usually acquired by ingestion
- Accumulates in the duodenum; cysts excreted in the stool
- May be asymptomatic or cause diarrhoea and malabsorption
- Treatment is with metronidazole

Cryptosporidium spp.

- Lodges in the brush border of the villi
- Common cause of diarrhoea in children
- Increasingly common in AIDS patients

Trichomonas spp. (trichomoniasis)

- Flagellate organism transmitted sexually
- May be asymptomatic or cause discharge from vaginitis, urethritis and prostatitis

Plasmodium spp. (malaria)

- Four *Plasmodium* spp.: *P. malariae*, *P. ovale*, *P. vivax*, *P. falciparum*

CHAPTER 4

- Intracellular parasites carried by female mosquitoes (humans are intermediate hosts)
- Parasites travel from subcutaneous region to the liver where they multiply and enter RBCs; further parasite multiplication occurs here and then the cells undergo lysis to release the organism (life cycle of 24 hours)
- Symptoms depend on plasmodium type; symptoms of *P. falciparum* include:
  - Pyrexia and rigors
  - Massive haemolysis
  - Hepatosplenomegaly
  - Raised intracranial pressure (ICP) in cerebral malaria
- 'Blackwater fever' (*P. falciparum*) is due to haemoglobinuria, which precipitates renal failure and diffuse thrombotic events

Trypanosoma spp. (trypanosomiasis)

- Flagellate parasites
- Responsible for African sleeping sickness and Chagas' disease
- Carried by tsetse flies
- Results in damage to the brain and organ dilatation (megacolon, cardiac dilatation, mega-oesophagus) possibly by an autoimmune process

Leishmania spp. (leishmaniasis)

- Variety of syndromes caused by tiny protozoa
- Found in Africa and South America
- Causes cutaneous (spontaneous healing sores) or mucocutaneous leishmaniasis (non-healing ulceration)

Toxoplasma spp. (toxoplasmosis)

- Intracellular parasite associated with cat faeces
- 50% people have positive serology

- Dangerous for fetuses and immunocompromised people

Helminths

Nematodes (roundworms)

- Eggs are ingested and larvae hatch in the stomach; they pass through the lungs and are coughed up and re-swallowed to settle in the gut
- Can grow to great lengths (up to 30 cm)
- Balls of worms can cause intestinal obstruction or perforation

Cestodes (tapeworms)

- Found in uncooked food
- Worm attaches to the bowel wall
- Uses up vitamin B12 and may cause vitamin deficiency and weight loss

Trematodes (flukes)

- *Schistosoma* spp. (schistosomiasis): lives in the bloodstream, but pathology is from tissue reaction where eggs are laid (500 per day!). Acquired from infected water. Symptoms depend on affected tissue:
  - Hepatic fibrosis and cirrhosis
  - Urothelium, causing SCC and renal failure
- Treatment with praziquantel 40–60 mg/kg; three doses over 1 day are effective
- *Filaria* spp. (filariasis; elephantiasis): larvae carried by mosquitoes and mature worms plug the lymphatics, causing obstruction and eventual fibrosis

Treatment of helminth infections is typically with mebendazole (100–200 mg three times daily, for 3–5 days) or with albendazole.

SECTION 4

Surgical infections

Learning point

You will come across infections that are:
- **Primary conditions** (eg any surgical condition ending in -itis)
- **Community-acquired** (eg UTI, gastroenteritis)
- **Hospital-acquired** (nosocomial)

Always attempt to identify the organism in order to tailor antibiotic treatment, ie send specimens before starting empirical treatment.

Do not delay treatment if clinically septic (ie treat with a 'best guess' antibiotic after sending specimens).

Take advice from microbiologists. This is essential in immunocompromised individuals and patients previously treated with multiple antibiotics.

4.1   Recognition of a septic patient

Definitions of 'sepsis'
- **Sepsis:** clinical evidence of infection
- **Sepsis syndrome:** clinical evidence of infection plus evidence of altered organ perfusion
- **Septic shock:** septic syndrome plus evidence of decreased blood pressure unresponsive to fluid therapy

Clinical indicators of infection

Consider sepsis as a diagnosis in cases of:
- Changes in core temperature
  - Fever: >37.8°C
  - Hypothermia: <36°C (especially in elderly people)
- Unexplained hypotension
- Oliguria
- Confusion

Patients should be thoroughly examined and a septic screen performed.

Examination for sepsis

> ### Possible foci of infection
> **Abdominal examination**
> - Bowel: eg inflammatory bowel disease, perforation, anastomotic leak, abscess
> - Hepatobiliary: eg cholecystitis, cholangitis, hepatitis
> - Genitourinary: eg urinary tract infection (UTI), pyelonephritis
>
> **Respiratory examination** (eg pneumonia)
> **Cardiovascular examination** (eg endocarditis)
> **Skin:** surgical wound inspection, percutaneous lines including Venflon, abscesses
> **Joints:** septic arthritis, prosthetic infection
> **CNS:** meningitis, encephalitis
> **Haematological:** recent travel (eg malaria)

> ### Septic screen
> **Blood tests**
> - Full blood count (for leucocytosis)
> - Acute phase proteins: C-reactive protein, fibrinogen
> - Urea, creatinine and electrolytes
> - Liver function tests (LFTs)/amylase
> - Clotting
> - Arterial blood gases (ABGs) for acidosis
>
> **Radiology**
> - Chest radiograph
> - Abdominal radiograph
> - CT
> - Cardiac echo
>
> **Microbiology**
> - Blood cultures
> - Sputum
>
> **Urine**

Septic screen

The nature of the septic screen should be directed by findings at patient examination. In particular, radiological investigation of sepsis should be targeted to the most likely focus.

Blood tests for sepsis

Leucocytosis

The white cell count (WCC) may be elevated, referred to as 'leucocytosis'. Differential diagnosis of leucocytosis is discussed in Chapter 3. Features of leucocytosis pertinent to sepsis will be outlined here. Very high WCCs may be indicative of abscess formation (>20). The WCC may be low if there is overwhelming sepsis (NB, the elderly may exhibit signs of sepsis without a rise in the WCC).

- **Neutrophils:** increases in the neutrophil count are commonly due to bacterial infection. Neutropenia may occur due to underlying conditions (eg immune deficiency, chemotherapy) or to overwhelming sepsis. Chemical mediators produced by leucocytes cause increased numbers of neutrophils to form in the bone marrow; these are released early into the bloodstream, producing a neutro-philia indicative of an acute inflammatory response
- **Lymphocytes:** a low lymphocyte count is indicative of sepsis; a high lymphocyte count may indicate viral illness

Acute phase proteins

CRP is commonly used as a marker for sepsis as levels respond within 24 hours to inflammatory change (compared with the ESR, which takes days). The range for CRP is commonly <8 to >285 in most labs. Elevated CRP of >100 is strongly indicative of bacterial infection. CRP is commonly elevated postoperatively (as an acute response to trauma) so should be interpreted with care. Fibrinogen levels are also elevated postoperatively.

U&Es and LFTs

Urea, creatinine and electrolytes are important to assess renal function (severe sepsis can result in ARF). Renal function is also important in the administration of certain antibiotics (eg gentamicin). Albumin levels fall in acute sepsis and LFTs may become elevated in cholangitis or sepsis syndrome. Elevation in amylase may occur as a result of pancreatitis or inflammation near the pancreas.

Arterial blood gases

ABGs are important to demonstrate acidosis. Metabolic acidosis may occur in sepsis as a result of low BP and poor tissue perfusion.

Clotting screen

There may also be a non-specific thrombocytosis (increased platelet count). It is not clear whether this translates into increased risk of thrombosis. Sepsis may also result in DIC, with deranged clotting parameters such as increasing prothrombin time (PT) and falling platelet count.

Radiology

Chest radiograph may show consolidation or demonstrate free intra-abdominal gas (indicative of perforation of a viscus). Remember that changes in the chest radiograph may lag behind clinical signs. Abdominal collections are best demonstrated by CT but can sometimes be seen on ultrasonography.

Microbiology

See section 4.6, Specimen collection page 329.

4.2 Fever in a postoperative patient

Postoperative pyrexia

A low-grade pyrexia postoperatively often doesn't require further investigation. However, if pyrexia persists you should investigate potential foci of infection.

Common postop infections
- Surgical site infection
- Respiratory infection
- Urinary tract infection
- Line-associated infection

While a patient remains systemically well with stable haemodynamic and respiratory parameters, there is time to perform adequate septic screen investigations and seek microbiological advice in order to define appropriate antibiotic therapy. Patients who are unstable or demonstrating septic syndrome or shock should have microbiological specimens taken and then be treated with a 'best guess' antibiotic (see Section 6).

For a discussion of sepsis, systemic inflammatory response syndrome (SIRS) and multiorgan dysfunction syndrome (MODS) see Chapter 3.

CHAPTER 4

Surgical site infection

> ## Surgical site infection includes:
> Superficial wound infection
> Deep abscess formation:
> - Intra-abdominal abscess after abdominal surgery
> - Intrathoracic abscess after cardio-thoracic surgery
> - Intracranial abscess after neurosurgery
> - Periprosthetic infection/abscess formation (eg around orthopaedic prosthesis or vascular graft)

Implantation of prosthetic materials carries a higher risk of infection, and such infection is often very difficult to eradicate. For detailed discussions of infection in vascular surgery see Chapter 9, Vascular Surgery in Book 2, and for infection in orthopaedic surgery see Chapter 9, Orthopaedic Surgery.

Common organisms in surgical site infection

Organism related to wound type
- Clean wounds – skin commensals (eg *Staphylococcus epidermidis*, *S. aureus*, enterobacteria)
- Contaminated wounds – site-specific organisms (eg from soil, saliva after bites, perforated viscus)
- Dirty wounds – site-specific organisms
- Necrotising fasciitis – mixed flora or group A streptococci
- Infected prostheses – may be skin flora or nosocomial
- Burns – *Pseudomonas* spp.
- Nosocomial infection, eg meticillin-resistant *S. aureus* (MRSA)

Management includes:
- Wound swab ± blood cultures if indicated
- Empirical treatment with a broad-spectrum agent likely to cover organisms involved (see Section 6)
- Pus won't resolve with antibiotics – it needs formal radiological or surgical drainage

Note that surgical site infections may be due to an organism resistant to the antibiotic administered prophylactically.

Respiratory infection

Postoperative respiratory tract infection may be due to nosocomial infection or aspiration (in the critically unwell). Patients are more prone to respiratory infection after surgery due to:
- General anaesthetic and basal atelectasis
- Supine positioning (prevents full expansion of lung bases)
- Immunosuppression (comorbid conditions)

Common organisms in respiratory infection
- **Community-acquired:** *Streptococcus pneumoniae*, *Haemophilus influenzae*, *Mycoplasma pneumoniae*
- **Nosocomial:** often aerobic Gram-negative bacteria – includes *Klebsiella* spp., *Escherichia coli*, *Enterobacter* spp., *S. aureus*
  - Common in ventilated patients (50% prevalence)
  - May be opportunistic infection in the immunosuppressed (eg *Pneumocystis jiroveci*)
- **Empyema (pus in thoracic cavity):** commonly due to *S. pneumoniae* but occasionally *S. aureus* secondary to:
  - Primary lung infection
  - Haematogenous or lymphatic spread
  - Direct extension from diaphragmatic, mediastinal or cervical foci

- Inoculation by penetrating trauma
- **Lung abscesses:** result from aspiration (anaerobic organisms) or granulomatous disease (eg TB)

Urinary infection

See also Urology and Transplantation chapters in Book 2.

Common organisms in urinary tract infection

- Community-acquired: commonly *E. coli*; may also be due to *Proteus* and *Klebsiella* spp.
- Abnormalities of the renal tract: *Pseudomonas* spp.
- Catheterisation/instrumentation of the renal tract: *Staphylococcus epidermidis*, *Enterococcus faecalis*

Line-associated infection

Common organisms in line-associated infection

- *S. aureus*, coagulase-negative staphylococci, streptococci, enterococci and Gram-negative species
- Incidence increases with length of time since line insertion (keep sites clean, record date of insertion, observe site regularly, change lines before they become infected, re-site if infection documented)

Management includes:
- Change lines if evidence of infection: may require at least 24-hour antibiotic treatment before re-insertion of tunnelled lines. NEVER pass a guidewire through an infected line and insert a new line along the same guidewire

- Take blood cultures from two separate sites (one through the infected line before it is removed and one from a distant peripheral site; label them accordingly)
- Discuss antibiotic choice with on-call microbiologist

Possible causes of PUO

Infection (23%)
- Abscesses (lung, liver, subphrenic, perinephric, pelvic)
- Empyema
- Endocarditis
- Unusual bacterial infection (*Salmonella*, *Brucella*, *Borrelia* spp. or leptospirosis)
- TB and other granulomatous diseases (actinomycosis, toxoplasmosis)
- Parasites (amoebic liver abscess, malaria, schistosomiasis)
- Fungi
- HIV

Neoplasia (20%)
- Lymphoma
- Solid tumour (GI, renal cell)

Connective tissue diseases (22%)
- Rheumatoid arthritis
- SLE
- Still's disease
- PAN (polyarteritis nodosa)
- Kawasaki's disease

Drugs (3%)

Other causes (14%)
- Pulmonary emboli
- Inflammatory bowel disease (Crohn's/ulcerative colitis)
- Sarcoid
- Amyloid

It is impossible to reach a diagnosis in up to 25% cases.

Pyrexia of unknown origin

Pyrexia of unknown origin (PUO) is defined as a prolonged fever (of >3 weeks) that remains undiagnosed after sufficient hospital investigation (about a week). Management should involve an infectious diseases physician.

4.3   Abscess management

Learning point

An abscess is a localised collection of pus in a cavity. The cavity may be naturally occurring or caused by tissue destruction or displacement.
If there is pus about, let it out!

Diagnosis of abscesses

Abscess may be difficult to distinguish from cellulitis. The former require surgical drainage, the latter may respond to antibiotics. Abscess may be inferred if the area is pointing or the centre is fluctuant. If in doubt, needle aspiration or ultrasonography may help. Left alone, many abscesses will drain spontaneously. Pus may track through tissue planes, causing the base of the abscess to be much deeper than initially thought.

Common sites for superficial abscesses

- Infection of a pre-existing sebaceous cyst
- Axillary:
  - Exclude hidradenitis suppurativa
  - Exclude breast disease
- Anorectal (eg perianal, ischiorectal):
  - Exclude inflammatory bowel disease by rigid sigmoidoscopy ± biopsy
  - Exclude fistula in ano by proctoscopy
- Groin (beware the femoral pseudoaneurysm masquerading as groin abscess in IV drug users – get an ultrasound scan before incising it!)

Treatment of abscesses

Superficial skin abscesses may be lanced. Local anaesthetics do not work satisfactorily in inflamed tissue (because the injection is more painful, there is a risk that the needle track will spread the infection, and inflamed tissue has a low pH, reducing the dissociation and binding of the anaesthetic compound). Deeper abscesses under the skin require a surgical procedure under general anaesthetic (GA). Abscesses deep in body cavities may be drained percutaneously under radiological guidance or at open surgery.

Procedure box: Superficial abscess drainage

Indications
- Area of fluctuance
- Pointing of an abscess
- Identification of a superficial collection of pus by imaging
- Region (axilla, anorectal, groin)

Patient position
- Anaesthetic: the skin may be frozen with ethyl chloride spray or the patient placed under GA
- Anorectal abscesses should only be drained under GA because they require thorough colorectal investigation for underlying cause
- Positioning should be appropriate to the site of the abscess, thus:
  - Perianal and ischiorectal abscesses require the patient to be placed in the lithotomy position
  - Axillary abscesses require elevation of the arm

Procedure
- Make a cruciate incision over the point of greatest fluctuance (this should be extended into a circular incision once the cavity is defined to deroof the abscess and allow easier packing)
- Release pus (and send for microbiological analysis; targeted antibiotics can then be started if cellulitis persists)
- The cavity may be irrigated or curetted down to the base (removes dead tissue)
- Gently pack the cavity (eg with gauze ribbon soaked in Betadine)
- Note that packs are changed frequently until the cavity closes and this is performed initially on the ward and then by the district nurse – it is essential that the incision allows for this to be done with ease. The cavity will granulate from the base regardless of its size but the abscess will recur if its 'roof' (ie the skin) closes before the cavity has healed. Antibiotics are not usually indicated

Risks
- Inadequate drainage (especially loculated abscesses)
- Recurrence
- Persistent cellulitis (may require antibiotics)

Hazards
- Consider the relationship to nearby important structures, eg:
  - Anal sphincters in anorectal abscesses
  - Cervical and mandibular branches of facial nerve around the jaw
  - Femoral vessels in the groin

For a detailed discussion of anorectal abscess, incision and drainage see the abdominal surgery chapter in Book 2.

CHAPTER 4

Special cases

- **Neck abscesses** may be due to simple abscess, furuncle, infected epidermal cysts or branchial cysts, abscess in lymph node, dental abscesses, actinomycosis or TB (cold abscess). They should be operated on by a suitably experienced surgeon
- **Perianal abscesses** are usually infection in the anal glands (other causes include fistulae, Crohn's disease, tumours and HIV). See Abdomen chapter in Book 2. An on-table rigid sigmoidoscopy should always be performed
- **Breast or axillary abscesses** are occasionally related to underlying malignancy. A biopsy should always be sent and follow-up should always be arranged in a breast clinic
- **Groin abscesses** may be due to suppurating lymph nodes, TB or psoas abscess (tracking down from the kidney or lumbar spine). An ultrasound scan should be done on anyone at risk of an infected femoral artery aneurysm (such as drug addicts) before incision

4.4 Necrotising fasciitis

This is an infection that spreads along fascial planes, secondarily affecting muscle, subcutaneous tissue and skin.

Aetiology of necrotising fasciitis

- Typically polymicrobial (streptococci; haemolytic staphylococci; *Bacteroides* spp.; coliforms)
- Postop
- Trauma
- Untreated perineal wound
- Contaminated needle

Pathology of necrotising fasciitis

- Appears benign in initial stages
- If untreated: results in massive subcutaneous oedema and dermal gangrene
- Fournier's gangrene is dermal gangrene of scrotum and penis

Management of necrotising fasciitis

- Rapid aggressive resuscitation
- Broad-spectrum antibiotics
- Skin incisions down to fascia
- Aggressive debridement of soft tissue with excision of necrotic tissue
- Colostomy if perineal area is involved
- Nutritional support
- Mortality rate is 30%

4.5 Gangrene

Gangrene is essentially irreversible tissue death due to loss of its blood supply.

Causes of gangrene

- Progressive tissue ischaemia (eg vascular disease)
- Trauma (eg crush injury, burns, frostbite)
- Infection resulting in tissue necrosis

Differentiating between dry and wet gangrene

Gangrene may be dry, resulting in mummification of the tissues, or wet, in which the tissues become infected and purulent. Odour is associated with infection. Gas gangrene occurs when infection occurs by a gas-forming organism such as *Clostridium perfringens* and gas may be palpable or visible between the tissue planes on plain film.

Investigations for gangrene

- Proximal blood supply (eg arteriogram)
- Cultures for infective organism
- Plain film for gas tracking between tissue planes

Management of gangrene

- Gangrene is painful due to tissue ischaemia so pain relief is essential
- Dry gangrene can be managed expectantly because digits usually autoamputate
- Wet gangrene will need debriding back to healthy tissue

4.6 Specimen collection

The microbiological data available from specimens are often related to the manner of collection and should be interpreted in the light of the patient's clinical condition. Most specimens are processed during working hours but specimens that will be processed out of hours in most labs include:

- Cerebrospinal fluid (CSF)
- Aspirates of sterile sites (eg intra-abdominal abscess, thoracic cavity, joints)
- Intraoperative specimens from deep surgical infections (eg debridement of osteomyelitis)
- HIV/hepatitis B and C in transplant donors (recipient status usually known)

Skin swabs

- **Wound infections:** overt infections (with pus) can be swabbed for causative organism to tailor therapy. Often the organism is related to the site of surgery (eg bowel flora in abdominal wounds) but swabs may exclude organisms such as MRSA
- **Ulcers:** little value in swabbing ulceration because this gives only an indication of colonising organisms and will not help in tailoring therapy
- **Abscess cavities:** may be of use if taken from deep in the abscess cavity. Remember that abscesses do not respond to antibiotics but require surgical drainage of pus. Surrounding cellulitits may benefit from therapy tailored to the causative organism

Urine samples

- **Midstream urine (MSU):** this is optimal because it is a clean-catch sample and results may determine antibiotic choice
- **Catheter-stream urine (CSU):** urine from catheters may demonstrate colonisation rather than overt infection (particularly if the catheter is long term). Treat only if the patient is symptomatic

Stool samples

- **Stool culture:** useful in the returning traveller with diarrhoea. Document region of travel and duration of request card
- *Clostridium difficile* **toxin (CDT):** useful in patients who develop diarrhoea on antibiotics. It is a highly sensitive assay. Document antibiotic treatment and specifically request a CDT test. The test remains positive after treatment so there is little point in repeating it

Blood cultures

Blood cultures should be taken if the patient is presumed to be septic before the start of empirical treatment. Cultures do not have to be taken during a temperature 'spike' because patients will remain bacteraemic for many hours. Cultures can be sent even if the patient is afebrile but has other features of sepsis and may provide the elusive diagnosis in elderly people.

> ## Taking a blood culture
> Use aseptic technique with gloves and swab the skin several times with alcohol before puncture to prevent skin contamination.
>
> Try to take two sets from different peripheral venepuncture sites (eg antecubital fossa) – groin and line cultures are likely to be contaminated (however, cultures can also be taken from intravenous lines, eg arterial lines, central venous pressure [CVP] lines, and may help in the diagnosis of line infection).
>
> If considering endocarditis, three sets of cultures should be taken from three sites at three separate times.
>
> Inoculate aerobic and anaerobic bottles with 10 ml blood each (do not touch the bottle lids). Label each bottle with the patient details, site of venepuncture, time of sample, any current antibiotic therapy and current diagnosis. Indicate if the sample is high risk (eg hepatitis, HIV).

Processing of blood cultures

Once in the lab

- Specimens are placed in an oscillating incubator
- Bacteria present produce CO_2 which reacts with a disc at the bottom of the bottle, producing a colour change that is detected by the machine, flagging the sample up as being positive
- Blood is aspirated from positive bottles for Gram staining (positive or negative) and microscopy (rods or cocci)
- Blood is inoculated on to Agar plates with discs impregnated with common antibiotics
- After 24 hours bacterial growth has occurred apart from in the region of antibiotics to which the organism is sensitive
- Additional tests may be employed to identify the organism
- The microbiologists phone positive results and antibiotic sensitivities to the ward (so it is important to correctly identify this on the request form)

Common results from blood cultures

Growth in both bottles

- Staphylococci: in the face of sepsis these are likely to be a significant finding. In a hospital setting this may represent MRSA bacteraemia, so microbiological advice may include a dose of vancomycin
- Coliforms: almost always significant. Consider GI and urosepsis. Will require tailored antibiotic therapy

Growth in one bottle

- May represent contamination and should be interpreted in the light of the clinical context
- May therefore require repeat sample

Joint aspirates

Joint aspiration technique is discussed in the Orthopaedics chapter. It should be performed using aseptic technique to produce a sterile specimen.

Sputum

These are poor-quality specimens and usually represent oral flora. For this reason many labs do not process these. Specimens obtained by BLA are, however, of much higher quality and can be used to tailor antibiotic therapy (eg in a critical care setting).

Advice from your microbiologist

To get the best advice and answers to questions such as *Which antibiotic?* or *How long should we continue antibiotics for?* the microbiologist will want to know:

- Patient age, gender and occupation
- Date of admission
- Premorbid conditions (eg diabetes, malignancy, steroid or other immuno-suppressant, elderly, pregnant)
- Date and details of surgery or injury
- Current and previous antibiotic therapy
- Results or outstanding microbiological samples
- MRSA status
- Details of current clinical condition: examination findings (temperature, haemodynamic status, chest/abdo/cardiovascular exam)
- Results of septic screen (blood results with WCC differential)
- Allergies (confirmed or suspected)

SECTION 5

Prevention and control of infection

5.1 Infection control

Identify patients at risk

All patients need careful thought and planning to prevent infection. Some are at increased risk if they have or undergo:
- Trauma (including major surgery itself)
- Burns
- Shock
- Pre-existing sepsis syndrome
- Coexisting metabolic disease (diabetes mellitus, renal failure, liver failure)
- Haematological problems
- Nutritional problems (malnutrition, obesity)
- Malignancy
- Chemotherapy and/or radiotherapy
- Immunosuppression (steroids, previous splenectomy, transplantation, congenital or acquired immune deficiency)

Infection control teams and hospital policy

Infection control teams are multidisciplinary and should include:
- A consultant microbiologist
- Infection control nurses
- Representatives from medical and surgical specialities
- Occupational health personnel
- Management personnel

The infection control team should:
- Meet regularly
- Perform audit evaluations of current hospital status, by:
  - Surveillance of nosocomial infection rates
  - Comparison with published countrywide rates
  - Implementation of alterations to policy
- Advise and implement hospital policy

Patient isolation and ward discipline

Patient isolation
Patients may be isolated because they are:
- Infectious (and require barrier nursing to protect others from the spread of transmissible infection)

- At increased risk of infection (and require 'reverse' barrier nursing to protect them from the spread of transmissible infection; barrier nursing and reverse-barrier nursing are essentially the same – they use barrier methods to prevent the spread of infection, eg gloves, plastic aprons, filtered air and masks to prevent droplet infections)

Ward discipline

- After examining every patient always wash your hands or use an alcohol rub
- Always wear gloves to handle or change dressings, take blood, etc
- Observe isolation procedures
- For MRSA-positive patients always wear gloves and an apron and spray stethoscope with alcohol after examining
- Contact infection control team if there are any doubts

5.2   Skin preparation

Learning point

Preparation of the patient
- Skin (shaving, skin disinfection, adhesive wound drapes)
- Bowel (laxatives/enemas)

Preparation of the theatre
- Cleanliness, airflow issues, personnel movements

Preparation of the surgical team
- Scrubbing up, caps, gowns, gloves, masks, shoes

Preop skin preparation

Antiseptics

- Include Betadine (iodine-based) and chlorhexidine (colourless)
- Should be applied to the skin in circular or sweeping motion (friction on the skin removes some bacterial colonisation)
- Apply several times to high-risk areas:
  - Perineum
  - Groin
  - Axilla
- There is no evidence that Betadine placed in the wound during closure reduces the rate of wound infection
- Alcoholic antiseptics are much more effective than aqueous preparations but pooled areas on the skin may can ignite if using diathermy

Preop shaving

- Causes skin abrasion
- Disrupts deeper flora layers; increased bacterial count on skin surface
- Increased tendency to postop wound sepsis
- Therefore shave immediately preoperatively with surgical clippers or use depilatory cream before theatre

Adhesive wound drapes

- Do not prevent infection
- Reported to reduce wound contamination by 50% BUT no decrease in wound infection
- Trapped bacteria may multiply

CHAPTER 4

Preparation of theatre

Theatre design
Theatre design is discussed in Chapter 1, Perioperative care.

Control of air quality
- Aim: to decrease number of airborne particles carrying bacteria from skin flora
- Positive pressure-filtered ventilation (PPFV) prevents bacteria gaining entry to the air
- Laminar flow plus ultraclean air systems give twofold reduction in postop wound infections

Greater numbers of people in theatre and movement through doors have been correlated with infection rates.

Preparation of the surgical team

Scrub up
- Aim: to decrease bacterial skin count
- Chlorhexidine gluconate or povidone-iodine solutions: stiff brushes damage the epidermis; use on fingernails only
- One nail scrub at beginning of operating list is sufficient

Clothing
- Cotton gowns reduce the bacterial count in the air by only 30%
- Bacteria-impermeable fabrics may reduce bacterial air counts by 40–70%. There is no evidence of reduced wound infection

Caps
- Useful because *S. aureus* can be carried on the scalp
- Prevents hair from falling in the wound

Masks
- Deflect forceful expirations such as coughs and sneezes that carry bacteria (normal speech does not expel bacteria)
- May rub off bacteria-carrying skin squames from the face
- No effect on infection rates
- Prudent use in implant surgery

Gloves
- Effective hand disinfection before gloving up
- Glove punctures or tears do not affect incidence of wound infection
- Double-glove if implanting prosthesis (eg orthopaedic) or if high-risk patient

Shoes
- Plastic overshoes have not been proved to reduce wound infection

5.3 Asepsis and sterilisation

Learning point

- **Asepsis** is prevention of introduction of bacteria to the surgical field
- **Antisepsis** is destruction of pre-existing bacteria in the surgical field
- **Sterilisation:** complete destruction of all viable microorganisms, including spores and viruses by means of heat, chemicals or irradiation. Inanimate objects only (eg not skin because it damages tissue)
- **Disinfection:** treatment of tissue or hard surface in an attempt to decrease the bacterial count
- **Antiseptics:** disinfectants used in living tissue
- **Cleaning:** physically removes contamination – does NOT necessarily destroy microorganisms

Asepsis

Development of asepsis

In the1860s Joseph Lister introduced carbolic acid as a disinfectant for hands and surgical instruments and to be sprayed into the air. A few years later he published in *The Lancet* a reduction in mortality rates during major amputations of from 45% to 15%.

Principles of asepsis

Invasive procedures should always be performed in line with aseptic techniques (may be incomplete in times of life-threatening emergency).

Principles of asepsis

- Skin preparation with disinfectant
- Bowel preparation preoperatively
- Draping to surround the sterile field
- 'Scrubbing up' with disinfectant
- Use of sterile gloves and gowns
- Use of sterile instrumentation and no-touch technique
- Good surgical technique

Sterilisation

Sterilisation methods

Autoclave sterilisation
- Saturated steam at high pressure
- Kills ALL organisms, including TB, viruses, heat-resistant spores
- Holding times depend on temperature and pressure (eg 134°C at 30 lb/in^2 has a 3-minute holding time; 121°C at 15 lb/in^2 has a 15-minute holding time)
- Wrapped instruments: use a porous load autoclave – steam penetration monitored with Bowie–Dick test
- Unwrapped instruments: use a Little Sister II portable autoclave
- Fluids: use a bottle autoclave

Dry heat sterilisation
- Hot-air ovens
- For moisture-sensitive instruments (no corrosion), non-stainless metals, surgical instruments with fine cutting edges

- Able to process airtight containers and non-aqueous liquids
- Effective BUT inefficient (160°C for at least 2 hours kills ALL microorganisms)
- Monitor with Browne's tubes type III

Ethylene oxide sterilisation
- Highly penetrative gas
- Kills vegetative bacteria, spores and viruses
- Effective at ambient temperatures and pressures
- Effective as a liquid or a gas
- Efficient for heat-sensitive equipment (eg rubber, plastics, electrical equipment, lenses)
- Used for sutures and single-use items
- Flammable if vapour >3% volume in air
- Toxic, irritant, mutagenic, carcinogenic
- Limited availability and expensive (predominantly industrial process)

Low-temperature steam and formaldehyde sterilisation
- Physicochemical method
- Kills vegetative bacteria, spores and viruses
- 73°C for heat-sensitive items
- NOT suitable for sealed, oily or greasy items

Irradiation sterilisation
- Use of gamma rays limited to industry
- Use for large batches of single-use items (catheters, syringes)

Disinfection
Disinfection aims to bring about a reduction in the number of viable organisms. Some viruses and bacterial spores may remain active.

Disinfection of inanimate objects can be carried out with:
- Low-temperature steam
- Boiling water
- Formaldehyde gas

Alcohols
- Broadest spectrum at 70% concentration
- Rapidly effective against Gram-positive and Gram-negative bacteria; some antiviral activity
- No residual activity
- Relatively inactive against spores and fungi
- Denature proteins
- Use of alcohols: skin preparation (note: ensure dryness before using diathermy – explosions – and pooling may irritate sensitive areas such as the groin)

Diguanides

Chlorhexidine
- Good activity against *S. aureus*
- Moderate activity against Gram-negative bacteria
- Some activity against *Pseudomonas aeruginosa*, although may multiply in deteriorating solutions
- Non-toxic to skin and mucous membranes
- Poor activity against spores, fungi and viruses
- Inactivated by pus, soap and some plastics
- Causes bacterial cell-wall disruption
- Uses of chlorhexidine:
  - In local antisepsis
  - 4% chlorhexidine in detergent (Hibiscrub)
  - Chlorhexidine-cetrimide mixture for some dirty wounds
  - 0.5% chlorhexidine in 70% alcohol

Iodophors and iodine

- Broad spectrum of activity against bacteria, spores, fungi and viruses (including hepatitis B and HIV)
- Easily inactivated by blood, faeces and pus
- Need optimum freshness, concentration and pH <4
- Stains skin and fabrics
- Irritant; may cause local hypersensitivity
- Use of iodophors and iodine:
  - Preoperative skin disinfection
  - Wound antisepsis

Hydrogen peroxide

- Only weak bactericidal activity

Aldehydes (glutaraldehyde and formaldehyde)

- Rapidly active against vegetative bacteria and viruses (including hepatitis B and HIV)
- Slowly effective against spores
- Only fair activity against tubercle bacilli
- Exposure of at least 3 hours to kill ALL microbes (most bacteria killed in <10 minutes)
- Toxic, with sensitivity reactions in skin, eyes and lungs (glutaraldehyde is safer)
- Endoscopes are heat-sensitive – disinfect by immersion in 2% glutaraldehyde between each case

5.4   Surgical measures to reduce infection

If you become aware of changes in the rate of postop infections you should contact the infection control team. They will analyse the cases and identify any linking factors. This is often reassuring because cases often only represent a statistical cluster rather than a true increase.

Learning point

Surgical infection may be caused by:
- Endogenous organisms
- Exogenous organisms

Surgical infection can be reduced or prevented by:
- Environmental factors
- Patient factors
- Surgeon factors
- Surgical technique
- Prophylactic antibiotics

Endogenous infection

This is clinical infection with organisms normally found in the patient as commensals. All surgical procedures result in a transient bacteraemia. Good preparation, surgical technique and prophylactic antibiotics minimise the chance of these becoming a significant problem.

- **Lower GI tract:**
  - 'Coliforms' (eg Gram-negative bacilli such as *E. coli*, *Klebsiella* and *Proteus* spp.)
  - Enterococci
  - Anaerobes (eg *Bacteroides fragilis*)
  - *Pseudomonas* spp.
  - *Enterobacter* spp.
- **Urogenital tract:**
  - Vagina: anaerobes, lactobacilli
  - Urethra: skin flora (eg staphylococci, diphtheroids)
- **Upper respiratory tract:**
  - Streptococci, *Haemophilus* spp., *S. aureus*, diphtheroids

Conditional pathogens colonise when use of antimicrobials destroys normal flora – this is known as **superinfection**.

CHAPTER 4

> **Prevention of endogenous infection**
> Patient preparation
> - Skin disinfection
> - Bowel preparation
> - Appropriate antibiotic prophylaxis
>
> Avoid disrupting normal flora (give antibiotics only for specific infection). Treat sepsis with full course of antibiotics, not prophylaxis (inadequately treated infections encourage bacterial resistance).

> **Prevention of wound sepsis**
> **In exogenous infection**
> - Control of surgical conditions
> - Sterilisation (air and instruments)
> - Aseptic technique
> - Good surgical technique
> - Preparation of patient and surgeon
>
> **In clean wounds**
> - No-touch technique
> - Careful and gentle dissection
> - Careful haemostasis
> - Minimisation of operation duration
> - Skin preparation
> - Prophylactic antibiotics (only if insertion of prosthetic material)
>
> **In clean–contaminated wounds**
> Measures as for clean wounds plus:
> - Single-shot antibiotic prophylaxis
> - Minimisation of spillage (swabs, suction)
>
> **In contaminated wounds**
> - Full course of antibiotics
> - Debridement of devitalised tissues (samples to microbiology for causative organism and sensitivity)
> - Removal of foreign material
> - Cleaning of tissues
> - Lavage
>
> **In dirty wounds**
> - Full course of antibiotics
> - Thorough removal of pus
> - Wound debridement
> - Thorough lavage
> - Simplest shortest operation (life-saving)
> - Avoidance of anastomosis (eg Hartmann's procedure)
> - Consideration of delayed primary closure

Exogenous infection

This is clinical infection acquired from an external source. Incidence is low (2%), affecting:
- Hospital staff
- Hospital environment
- Other patients

Wound sepsis

Asepsis means no organisms are present during surgery. A truly aseptic environment is needed in immunocompromised patients. **Antisepsis** involves prevention of sepsis. Total abolition of organisms is not achieved.

Clean wounds
- Incise through non-inflamed tissue
- Ensure no entry into genitourinary, GI or respiratory tracts
- Contamination rate <2% (exogenous sepsis)

Clean–contaminated wounds
- Entry into a hollow viscus other than the colon, with minimal, controlled contamination
- Contamination rate 8–10%

Contaminated wounds

- Breaching of hollow viscus with more spillage: opening the colon, open fractures, penetrating animal or human bites
- Contamination rate 12–20%

Dirty wounds

- Gross pus, perforated viscus (eg faecal peritonitis) or traumatic wounds >4 hours
- Contamination rate >25%

5.5   Vaccination

Learning point

Vaccines act by inducing active or passive immunity. Vaccination is used in groups who are susceptible to certain diseases:
- Children (diseases of childhood)
- Travellers to endemic areas of disease
- Healthcare professionals exposed to high-risk patients

Principles of immunisation

Active vs passive immunisation

Active immunisation stimulates the immune system to produce a response, resulting in the formation of immunological memory and thus protection against subsequent exposure. Antigens used for immunisation:

- Live-attenuated organism (bacterium or virus such as TB (BCG), MMR)
- Dead organism (eg tetanus, pneumococci, influenza virus)
- Characteristic protein from organism (eg purified viral protein coat)

Passive immunisation involves the transfer of preformed antibodies to provide immediate protection against disease exposure, eg:

- Maternal transfer of immunoglobulin in breast milk
- Immunoglobulins, eg against hepatitis, tetanus, varicella zoster, hepatitis A, rabies

Reasons for immunisation

- For eradication of dangerous childhood disease
- For those who are immunocompromised or who have increased susceptibility (eg splenectomy, extremes of age)
- For healthcare professionals with exposure to infection
- For travel to areas of endemic disease

Immunisation of surgical patients

Consider immunisation in the following surgical patients.

Patients with dirty or soil-contaminated wounds

- Tetanus toxoid (intramuscularly)
- Human tetanus immunoglobulin

Splenectomy patients

- Give *Haemophilus influenzae* type b (Hib), meningococcal and pneumococcal vaccines
- Re-immunise every 5–10 years
- Give annual influenza vaccine
- For elective cases give immunisations at least 2 weeks preoperatively
- For traumatic cases immunise after a few weeks to maximise immune response

CHAPTER 4

Immunisation of healthcare professionals

The most serious health risks are posed by blood-borne viruses:

- Hepatitis B
- Hepatitis C
- HIV

Infections may be passed in either direction:

- From patients to healthcare staff (many infections may be undiagnosed – adopt universal protective precautions at all times)
- From healthcare staff to patients during exposure-prone procedures when there is a risk of exposure to blood (eg cuts) or accidental injury to hands (eg bony spurs, sharp instruments)

Common mode of transmission is exposure to any bodily fluid

- Blood (needlestick or sharps injury; bleeding, eg haematemesis, melaena, epistaxis; invasive procedures; spray from arteries during surgery; bone fragments, eg trauma and orthopaedic surgery)
- Saliva
- Urine and stools
- CSF
- Semen

Healthcare professionals should be immunised against the following diseases capable of nosocomial transmission:

- Hepatitis B
- Varicella zoster
- ± Rubella
- ± Measles
- ± Mumps

Additional immunisation may be required for workers dealing with outbreaks of disease (eg influenza pandemics, meningococcal C disease) or workers commonly encountering other diseases in endemic countries or among certain patient groups (eg hepatitis A).

The Hospital Infection Control Practices Advisory Committee (HIPAC) guidelines suggest that the following personnel should be immunised, or be capable of demonstrating immunity to the diseases listed above (as all may come into contact with needles or bodily fluids):

- Doctors
- Nurses
- Emergency service personnel
- Dental professionals
- Students (medical and nursing)
- Laboratory personnel
- Hospital volunteers
- Housekeeping personnel

5.6   Sharps injury

Causes of sharps injury

Needlestick or sharps injury may occur in situations involving:

- Syringes and hypodermic needles
- Taking of blood/venous access
- Invasive procedures
- Suturing
- Sharp instruments

It commonly occurs with practices such as:

- Re-sheathing needles
- Transferring body fluids between containers
- Poor disposal of needles (use sharps bins)

Post-injury procedure

In the event of sharps injury follow hospital protocol, which involves:

- Encouraging bleeding by squeezing the wound
- Washing with water/soap/disinfectant (do not suck the wound)
- Reporting the incident (to on-call microbiologist if out of hours)
- Attending the appropriate department immediately (occupational health, A&E)
- Counselling and testing of recipient and donor (for hepatitis B, hepatitis C and HIV status) if required
- Postexposure prophylactic treatment (eg triple therapy started immediately in the event of high-risk exposure to HIV) – this should be discussed with a microbiologist or infectious disease physician

High-risk patients

Note that many infectious patients do not exhibit symptoms and signs of the disease so precautions should be taken with all patients (eg wear gloves for taking blood and for cannulation, catheterisation and intubation).

Precautions in hepatitis and HIV patients

Surgeons, anaesthetists, theatre nurses, operating department practitioners and other theatre personnel also need protection from potentially infectious agents, in the following situations:

- Contact (with blood, saliva, urine, tears, CSF, stools)
- Air (eg after use of power tools)
- Inoculation (via sharps, scalpel or bone fragment injuries)

Universal precautions

These precautions serve to protect theatre staff from infection in all cases (eg surgical gloves, gowns, masks, no-touch surgical technique).

Special precautions

These are used for high-risk surgical patients (eg hepatitis and HIV patients). In an ideal world all procedures would be performed using special precautions, but in practice the level of precaution is limited by expense, time, etc. Precautions include:

- Disposable drapes and gowns
- Double-gloving and 'indicator' glove systems
- Face visors
- Blunt suture needles
- Passing of instruments in a kidney dish
- No-touch technique
- Minimal theatre staff
- Only vital equipment in theatre

Some of the special precautions should be undertaken with all patients (eg high-risk patients or in high-risk areas). Special precautions are also used for infective cases to prevent spread of infection to other patients (eg MRSA).

CHAPTER 4

SECTION 6

Antibiotic control of infection

6.1 Types of antibiotic

Learning point

Antibiotic action is either:
- **Bactericidal** (results in death of current bacterial population) or
- **Bacteriostatic** (prevents bacterial replication)

These actions may be achieved by inhibition of protein synthesis, nucleic acid synthesis or membrane functions. Different classes of antibiotics have different spectrums of activity against different organisms.

Mode of action of antibiotics

Bactericidal antibiotics
- Include β-lactams, vancomycin, aminoglycosides and chloramphenicol
- Indications for bactericidal antibiotics include:
  - Life-threatening sepsis
  - Infective endocarditis
  - Opportunistic infections in immunocompromised patients

Bacteriostatic antibiotics
- Include tetracycline, erythromycin, clindamycin and chloramphenicol
- Bacteria can multiply again
- Final elimination of pathogens depends on host defence mechanisms with effective phagocytosis

Mechanisms of action

Inhibition of cell-wall synthesis
- Leads to osmotic lysis of bacteria with defective peptidoglycan molecules in the cell wall. Antibiotics with bactericidal action:
  - β-Lactams (penicillin, ampicillin, cephalosporin)
  - Vancomycin

Inhibition of protein synthesis
Occurs at the following stages of the bacteria life cycle:
- Transfer RNA – amino acid attachment (eg by tetracyclines, bacteriostatic agents)
- Translocation (eg by chloramphenicol and erythromycin, which are bacteriostatic at low concentration; clindamycin and fusidic acid, which are bactericidal at high concentrations)

SPECTRUM OF ACTIVITY OF ANTIMICROBIALS

| Drug | Gram-negative | | Gram-positive | | |
	Cocci	Bacilli	Cocci	Bacilli	Others
Beta-lactams	*Neisseria meningitides*	Produce β-lactamases	Streptococci:	*C. perfringens*	*T. pallidum*
Benzylpenicillin			*S. pyogenes*	*S. pyogenes*	
Penicillin V	*N. gonorrhoeae*		*S. viridans*	*S. viridans*	
1st generation cephalosporins			Anaerobic cocci	Anaerobic cocci	
Anti-staphylococcal penicillins			*S. aureus* (produces beta-lactamase)		
Methicillin					
Cloxacillin					
Flucloxacillin					
Aminoglycosides		*Escherichia coli*	*S. aureus*		
Gentamicin		*Klebsiella*	(especially gentamicin)		
Tobramycin		*Proteus*			
		Coliforms			
		P. aeruginosa			
Macrolides		*Campylobacter* spp.	Streptococci including *S. pneumoniae* (may produce β-lactamase)	*C. diphtheriae*	*M. pneumoniae*
Erythromycin					
Vancomycin			*S. aureus*	*C. difficile*	
Metronidazole (active only against anaerobic protozoa and bacteria)		*Bacteroides* spp.	Anaerobic cocci	*Clostridium* spp.	

BROAD-SPECTRUM ANTIBIOTICS

| Drug | Gram-negative | | Gram-positive | | |
	Cocci	Bacilli	Cocci	Bacilli	Others
Aminopenicillins	*N. meningitides*	*E. coli* and other coliforms (not *Klebsiella*)	Streptococci including *S. pneumoniae*	*Clostridium* spp.	*T. pallidum*
Amoxycillin	*N. gonorrhoeae*				
Ampicillin					
Clavulanic acid		*H. influenzae*	(beta-lactamase producing)		
Broad-spectrum antibiotics		*P. aeruginosa* Coliforms			
Piperacillin					
Cephalosporins (2nd generation; β-lactamase stable)	*N. gonorrhoeae*	*E. coli* and other coliforms (including *Klebsiella*)	Streptococci Staphylococci	*Clostridium* spp.	
Cefuroxime					
Ceftazidime					
Tetracyclines	*N. gonorrhoeae*	*H. influenzae*	Streptococci Staphylococci	*Clostridium* spp.	*M. pneumoniae* Chlamydia
Ciprafloxacin	*N. gonorrhoeae*	*Haemophilus P. aeruginosa* Coliforms	*S. aureus* and some streptococci		

CHAPTER 4

- Attachment of mRNA to ribosome (eg by aminoglycosides, bactericidals)

Inhibition of nucleic acid synthesis
Bactericidal mechanisms include:
- Decreased RNA replication, eg by:
  - Sulfonamides
  - Trimethoprim
  - Quinolones (ciprofloxacin, nalidixic acid)
  - Metronidazole
- Decreased mRNA, eg by:
  - Rifampicin

Alteration of cell membrane function
- Antibiotics called ionophores alter the permeability of bacterial cell membranes causing lysis. Polymyxin has bactericidal actions against Gram-negative bacilli

Antibiotic classes

β-Lactams
- **Penicillins:**
  - Examples: benzylpenicillin, flucloxacillin, ampicillin
  - Bactericidal
  - Good penetrance of tissues and body fluids
  - Renal excretion
  - Hypersensitivity (rash alone) occurs in up to 10% of patients (anaphylaxis in 0.05%) and may occur with other β-lactams (similar molecular structures). There is a 1 in 10 risk of hypersensitivity to cephalosporins in patients with penicillin hypersensitivity
  - May cause antibiotic-associated colitis
- **Cephalosporins:**
  - Broad-spectrum antibiotics (for septicaemia, pneumonia, meningitis, biliary tract and urinary tract infections)
  - Pharmacology similar to penicillins
  - 10% penicillin-allergic patients will be hypersensitive to cephalosporins
  - First-generation cephalosporins include cephradine
  - Second-generation cephalosporins include cefuroxime
  - Third-generation cephalosporins include cefotaxime, ceftazidime, ceftriaxone
- **Other β-lactam agents:**
  - Carbapenems, eg imipenem, meropenem
  - Broad spectrum activity against anaerobes and aerobic Gram-positive and Gram-negative bacteria

Tetracyclines
- Examples: tetracycline, doxycycline, minocycline
- Work by attacking bacterial ribosomes (note increasing bacterial resistance)
- Used against *Chlamydia* spp., *Haemophilus influenzae*, *Rickettsia* and *Brucella* spp. and spirochaetes
- Generally safe but should not be used in pregnancy

Aminoglycosides
- Examples: gentamicin, neomycin, streptomycin
- Active against Gram-negative and some Gram-positive organisms
- Not absorbed from the gut (given intravenously)
- Excreted via the kidney
- Side effects are dose-related (ototoxicity, nephrotoxicity) – as a general guide you can give a single dose of 5–7 mg/kg if renal function is normal; reduce to 3 mg/kg if there is any compromise in renal function

Macrolides

- Examples: erythromycin, clarithromycin
- Antibacterial spectrum similar to penicillins (used for respiratory infections, *Campylobacter* spp., Legionnaires' disease, *Chlamydia* spp.)
- Clarithromycin has higher tissue concentrations than erythromycin
- Side effects include nausea, vomiting and diarrhoea

Glycopeptides

- Examples: first line vancomycin, second line teicoplanin
- Anaerobes and aerobes; Gram-positive bacteria – used against MRSA
- Side effects are dose-related (ototoxicity, nephrotoxicity) – dose should be reduced in renal failure

Sulfonamides

- Examples: co-trimoxazole, trimethoprim
- Used for PCP, urinary and respiratory tract infections, and *Salmonella* infection
- Side effects include nausea, vomiting and diarrhoea

Metronidazole

- Effective against anaerobic and protozoal infections

Quinolones

- Examples: ciprofloxacin, norfloxacin
- Ciprofloxacin is particularly active against Gram-negative bacteria
- Used for respiratory tract and biliary infections

- Same bioavailability orally as intravenously (and much cheaper)
- Side effects include GI disturbance, rash, headache, tendinitis
- Avoid in elderly people and people with epilepsy (lowers seizure threshold)

6.2 Empirical treatment

Sometimes it is not possible to wait for microbiological results to guide your choice of antibiotics. The following should act as a guide. If in doubt, discuss with your local microbiologist.

Which antibiotic? Narrow-spectrum or broad-spectrum?

Narrow-spectrum antibiotics

These are selected for specific infections. They cause less disturbance of normal flora and are associated with:

- Reduced risk of superinfection
- Fewer resistant strains

Broad-spectrum antibiotics

Use of these is associated with acquiring *Clostridium difficile* (pseudomembranous colitis).

Wound infection and cellulitis

Wound infection

- Clean wounds: flucloxacillin (to cover skin flora)
- Traumatic or abdominal surgical wounds: intravenous cefuroxime 1.5 g three times daily and metronidazole 400 mg three times daily
- Animal bites: co-amoxiclav

CHAPTER 4

If considering necrotising fasciitis (sepsis, delirium, rapidly progressive pain, systemic upset out of keeping with erythema) seek microbiological advice because this is commonly group A streptococci – give cefuroxime (or clindamycin) and gentamicin.

Cellulitis

Most likely organisms are staphylococci and streptococci.

- If not systemically unwell consider oral clindamycin 300 mg four times daily (oral flucloxacillin is not very effective)
- If systemically unwell consider intravenous flucloxacillin 2 g four times daily

Management of ulceration should include imaging to exclude bony involvement. If systemically unwell can consider intravenous cefuroxime 1.5 g three times daily and metronidazole 400 mg three times daily.

Intra-abdominal sepsis

Most intra-abdominal organisms will be covered by intravenous cefuroxime 1.5 g three times daily and metronidazole 400 mg three times daily. If there is a history of rigors, hypotension or suspected cholangitis then you should also consider a one-off single dose of gentamicin (5 mg/kg – but check renal function is normal).

Pneumonia

Community-acquired pneumonia

Treatment should be guided by severity. The CURB criteria are a useful guide:

    Confusion
    Urea
    Respiratory rate
    Blood pressure

For mild pneumonia give oral amoxicillin 500 mg three times daily. For moderate pneumonia (one or two criteria) give oral amoxicillin 500 mg three times daily and oral erythromycin 500 mg four times daily. For severe pneumonia (more than two criteria) give intravenous cefuroxime 1.5 g three times daily and oral erythromycin 1 g four times daily.

Hospital-acquired pneumonia

Usually treated with intravenous cefuroxime 1.5 g three times daily. If there is worsening of respiratory function or fever on cefuroxime, then consult microbiology (commonly change to intravenous meropenem 500 mg four times daily or Tazocin 4.5 g three times daily).

Urinary tract infection

Simple UTI

If there is no systemic upset then consider 3 days of oral treatment. The choice depends on local policy (which reflects resistance patterns):

- Nitrofurantoin 50 mg four times daily
- Trimethoprim 200 mg twice daily
- Ciprofloxacin 100 mg twice daily

Complicated UTI

UTI involving urosepsis or pyelonephritis generally presents with rigors and loin pain. Generally best treated with intravenous cefuroxime 1.5 g three times daily plus a single dose of gentamicin (5 mg/kg – but check renal function is normal).

Catheter-related sepsis

Treatment is not required for asymptomatic bacterial colonisation. Indications for treatment include urinary symptoms, fever, signs of sepsis or high WCC. When changing long-term indwelling catheters it is advisable to give 1.5 mg gentamicin as a single dose (check renal function is normal) or oral ciprofloxacin 500 mg 1 hour before the procedure.

Diarrhoea

Diarrhoea after antibiotic therapy

Send stool for CDT. Treat with metronidazole 400 mg three times daily (commonly for 2 weeks). Failure to respond to metronidazole – can give oral vancomycin 125 mg four times daily.

Diarrhoea after food poisoning

May not require treatment. Traveller's diarrhoea (with associated pyrexia) or after food poisoning may respond to oral ciprofloxacin 500 mg twice daily.

Septic arthritis

Obtain an aspirate to guide treatment. It is likely to require joint wash-out. Give empirical treatment with intravenous cefuroxime 1.5 g three times daily.

Meningitis

Uncommon unless in neurosurgical setting. Should give intravenous ceftriaxone 2 g twice daily (dose before lumbar puncture). Guidelines now also give consideration to dexamethasone administration. If the patient is elderly, immuno-compromised or pregnant then consider intravenous ceftriaxone 2 g twice daily with amoxicillin 2 g four times daily (to cover *Listeria* spp.) ± steroids.

6.3 Antibiotic prophylaxis

> **Learning point**
>
> **Prophylactic antibiotics**
> - Reduce surgical site infection
> - Should be given early (before or just after anaesthetic)
> - Can be given as a single dose at therapeutic concentration
> - Must be broad spectrum and appropriate to probable organisms

The most important aspect of good antibiotic prophylaxis is to obtain high levels of systemic antibiotics at the time of the procedure and to maintain this for the duration of surgery. Prophylactic antibiotics should not be continued beyond this. This measure aims to reduce the incidence of surgical site infection, particularly during implantation of prosthetic material. The aim of antibiotic prophylaxis is to prevent bacteria from multiplying without altering normal flora.

Prophylaxis should be started preoperatively, ideally within 30 minutes of anaesthesia, and antibiotics should be given intravenously. Early administration of the antibiotic allows time for levels to accumulate in the tissues before they are disrupted by surgery (eg application of tourniquets, opening hollow organs).

A single dose of the correct antibiotic at its therapeutic concentration is sufficient for most purposes. Prophylaxis may be continued for a set duration (eg 24 hours) as a matter of policy in certain circumstances but it should not be inappropriately prolonged.

CHAPTER 4

Choice of antibiotic may be set by hospital policy or surgeon preference, but the prophylaxis chosen must be broad spectrum and cover the organisms likely to be encountered. Policies for surgical prophylaxis that recommend β-lactam antibiotics as first-line agents should also recommend an alternative for patients with allergy to penicillins or cephalosporins.

> **Issues for consideration**
> - Is it needed?
> - For what pathogen and where?
> - Which route of administration?
> - Is the patient immunocompromised?

Indications for antibiotic prophylaxis

- Where procedure commonly leads to infection (eg colectomy)
- In reducing postop infections from endogenous sources (proven value)
- Where results of sepsis would be devastating, despite low risk of occurrence (eg vascular or other prostheses)

It has no value in clean procedures where the risk of sepsis from an exogenous source is <2%.

Administration of antibiotic prophylaxis

- Choice of antibiotic: bacteriostatic or bactericidal (if immunocompromised)
- Give short courses <24 hours
- Dosage:
  - Single dose (used if 3–6% postop infection rate) or
  - Multiple dose (used if 6% postop infection rate)

- Timing of administration:
  - Within 1 hour preoperatively or at induction (15–20 minutes before skin incision or tourniquet inflation)
  - Second dose if operation >4 hours to maintain adequate tissue levels

Note: beware of the following when giving antibiotic prophylaxis:
- Toxicity
- Side effects
- Routes of excretion
- Allergies

Examples of antibiotic prophylaxis

- Upper GI surgery: cefuroxime and metronidazole; ciprofloxacin
- Lower GI surgery: cefuroxime and metronidazole
- Orthopaedic surgery:
  - Open fractures: first-generation cephalosporin plus benzylpenicillin (plus gentamicin if grade III or very heavily contaminated)
  - Joint replacement: cefuroxime
- Vascular surgery: cefuroxime, gentamicin and metronidazole
- Cardiothoracic surgery: flucloxacillin and gentamicin

CHAPTER 4

6.4   Microbial resistance

Learning point

- Hospital-acquired (nosocomial) infection is increasing in incidence (sicker patients, rapid patient turnover, etc)
- Antibiotic resistance is increasing, acquired by spontaneous mutation, transformation and plasmid transfer
- There are clinical measures to help reduce the acquisition of both nosocomial infection and antibiotic resistance

Bacterial antibiotic resistance and multiresistant organisms

Bacterial resistance is increasing. Data from the USA show that in intensive therapy unit (ITU) patients up to 30% of hospital-acquired infections are resistant to the preferred antibiotic for treatment. Increasing MRSA incidence has been documented (and use of vancomycin results in emerging *S. aureus* resistance to vancomycin). Resistance results from selective survival pressure on bacteria.

Mechanisms of resistance

Resistance may occur by:
- Alteration of bacterial cell-wall proteins to prevent antibiotic binding (eg penicillin resistance)
- Alteration of ribosome structure to prevent antibiotic binding (eg erythromycin, tetracycline, gentamicin)
- Production of antibiotic-destroying proteins

Resistance is passed on to all subsequent bacterial progeny. Resistance may be conferred against multiple antibiotics.

Bacteria acquire resistance genes by three mechanisms

- **Spontaneous mutation:** rapid replication times cause spontaneous mutations to arise in bacterial DNA; some of these mutations may confer resistance
- **Transformation:** one bacterium takes up DNA from another and splices it into its genome using enzymes called integrases, allowing passage of resistance genes against antibiotics, disinfectants and pollutants
- **Plasmids:** these are small circles of DNA (similar to small chromosomes) which can be transmitted from bacterium to bacterium and cross bacterial phylogeny

Potential causes of resistance
- Inappropriate prescription
- Failure to finish the course of antibiotics: microbes that are relatively drug-resistant will not be killed in the first few days and will become preferentially selected
- Addition of antibiotics to agricultural feed (entry into the food chain)
- Extensive use of antibiotics in sick patients with multiple organisms may promote resistance and transmission between individuals
- Natural evolution of bacteria

CHAPTER 4

Meticillin-resistant *S. aureus*

During the last 20 years the prevalence of MRSA in hospitals has fluctuated – it is now nearly 50% in UK hospitals. Beta-lactam antibiotics inhibit bacterial cell-wall synthesis by inactivating penicillin-binding proteins (PBPs); MRSA strains produce an alternative PBP (*mecA* gene) that allows continued cell-wall synthesis.

Prevention of MRSA transmission

- Use of preventive measures (handwashing, alcohol gels, etc)
- Patient screening (especially important if having elective surgery with prosthetic implants)
- Isolation of carrier or infected patients (barrier nursing)
- Removal of any colonised catheters
- Eradication of carriage (nasal: mupirocin; chlorhexidine hair and body wash; hexachlorophene powder)

Systemic MRSA infections

May require appropriate antibiotics if isolated from sterile site (eg MRSA detected in abdominal cavity or in blood cultures). An antibiotic regimen that includes intravenous vancomycin 1 g twice daily should be considered. If the patient is systemically unwell a single dose of gentamicin 5 mg/kg should act as a holding measure until further cultures are back.

Vancomycin-resistant enterococcus

There are two types of vancomycin resistance in enterococci:

- Low-level intrinsic resistance (eg *Enterococcus gallinarum*)
- Acquired resistance by transfer of genes (*vanA*, *vanB*, etc) commonly seen in *E. faecalis*

Vancomycin-resistant enterococci (VREs) can be carried in the gut without disease (colonisation) and can be picked up by screening.

CHAPTER 5

Principles of Surgical Oncology

Sylvia Brown

SECTION 1

Epidemiology of common cancers

1.1   Epidemiology studies

> **Learning point**
>
> **Epidemiology** is the study of disease
> frequency in populations. In cancer
> epidemiology, useful concepts include:
> **Measures of frequency**
> - **Prevalence:** proportion of population
>   with a condition at a given time
> - **Incidence:** proportion of population
>   developing a condition in a given time
>
> **Measures of risk**
> - **Risk factor:** an agent or characteristic
>   predisposing to the development of a
>   condition
> - **Relative risk:** strength of association
>   between risk factor and condition
>
> **Measures of outcome**
> - **Disease-free survival:** an outcome
>   measure in oncology for the time
>   period from completion of treatment
>   to detection of recurrence
> - **Life table:** a calculation predicting the
>   cumulative probability of surviving
>   a given number of years (eg 5-year
>   survival rate)
> - **Survival curve:** plot of probability of
>   survival against time (eg Kaplan–Meier
>   curve)

1.2   Cancer registries

> **Learning point**
>
> **Cancer registries**
> - Monitor levels and changes in different
>   cancers in the population
> - Collate information from death
>   certificates about deaths from each
>   cancer type

These registries are set up to monitor the
incidence and mortality of various cancers in
the population, and to determine any changes
in these parameters.

Information from death certificates is collated
by the National Cancer Registry in England
and Wales and is followed up by case-note
analysis and postmortem diagnoses, etc.
Statistical information from cancer registries
should be viewed with caution due to potential
errors arising from differences in accuracy of
data collection, geographical variations, and
differences in diagnosis and postmortem rates,
for example.

1.3   Common cancers

Learning point

Cancer is a common disease affecting a third of the population in their lifetime.
- There are 250 000 new cases diagnosed per year
- 65% of cancer affects the >65 age group
- Common cancers are different for different age groups (adults, teenagers and children)
- Smoking and diet are the main environmental aetiological factors (thought to be responsible for a third of cancer cases each)

Specific clinical information about most common cancers is covered in Book 2.

Cancer incidence by age and gender

Common cancers in adults

Fifty per cent of adult cancer involves the **big four** – breast, prostate, lung, large bowel.

Remember that the incidence of a cancer is not the same as the death rate from that cancer. Incidence data can be expressed as the number of new cases per 1000 per year or as a percentage.

There is a different incidence of certain cancers in men and women.

COMMON CANCERS ACCORDING TO GENDER (incidence expressed as a percentage of all newly diagnosed cases of cancer per year)					
Men			**Women**		
	Incidence (%)	Lifetime risk		Incidence (%)	Lifetime risk
Prostate	25	1 in 9	Breast	30	1 in 8
Lung	14	1 in 14	Large bowel/rectum	12	1 in 9
large bowel/rectum	14	1 in 15	Lung	5	1 in 9
Bladder	4.7	1 in 40	Ovary	4.4	1 in 54
Stomach	3	1 in 61	Uterus	4	1 in 46
Melanoma	3.5	1 in 61	Non-Hodgkin's lymphoma	3.6	1 in 62
Non-Hodgkin's lymphoma	4.1	1 in 52	Melanoma	2.7	1 in 60
Oesophagus	3.3	1 in 58	Pancreas	2.7	1 in 79
Kidney	3.5	1 in 61	Stomach	2.3	1 in 120
Leukaemia	3	1 in 71	Leukaemia	2.2	1 in 108
Others (individually <1%)	20		Others (individually < 1%)	22	

Common cancers in teenagers

- Testicular cancer
- Brain tumour
- Melanoma
- Leukaemia

Common cancers in children

The risk of cancer in childhood (<15 years) is 1 in 500 in the UK. For a detailed discussion of oncology in childhood see the Paediatrics chapter.

Commonly these cancers are:

- **Haematological:** 25% of childhood cancers are acute lymphocytic leukaemia (ALL). Incidence of Hodgkin's lymphoma peaks in teenagers
- **Brain and spinal cord:** eg astrocytoma and primitive neuroectodermal tumour
- **Embryonal tumours:** occur in different parts of the body and are referred to as ' blastomas', eg medulloblastoma (brain), nephroblastoma (Wilms' tumour), retinoblastoma
- **Bone tumours:** osteosarcoma and Ewing's sarcoma. Bone tumour incidence peaks at 14–15 years

Cancer incidence by geographical region

Different cancers have different incidences in different countries and in different ethnic groups.

- **Breast cancer:** much less common in the developing than in developed countries. Its incidence is highest in the West and second-generation immigrants from areas of low incidence (they acquire the elevated risk of their new country)

- **Hepatocellular carcinoma:** most common where hepatitis B infection is common (Far East, sub-Saharan Africa) regardless of race. Iron overload and aflatoxin also contribute in these regions
- **Stomach cancer:** common in Japan and Chile. First-generation immigrants to the West retain this high rate but second-generation immigrants adopt the lower rate of their new country, which suggests that dietary factors may be important (eg salt/nitrates)
- **Colon cancer:** westernised countries with low-fibre diets have increased risks of colon cancer
- **Prostate cancer:** highest in African-Caribbean people and lowest in Japan
- **Oesophageal cancer:** common in China, former USSR and poor nations. The reasons may be dietary
- Epstein–Barr virus: is ubiquitous around the world, but **Burkitt's lymphoma** is an African disease, and its distribution corresponds to regions where malaria is endemic. Immigrants to Africa are susceptible, as are the indigenous black people
- **Skin cancers:** (notably melanomas) are most common in light-skinned people who have heavy sun exposure at low latitudes and/or high altitudes
- **Cervical cancer:** incidence follows that of sexually transmitted infections (STIs) (aetiological agent is human papillomavirus or HPV). It may be less common in areas where men are circumcised
- **Squamous cell carcinoma of the bladder:** caused by schistosomiasis and so is common in endemic areas (eg Egypt)

CHAPTER 5

Changes in cancer incidence in Europe

Factors impacting on incidence of cancer

Behavioural factors
- Women starting to smoke in the 1940s (increase in lung cancer)
- Sunbathing and tanning became fashionable (increase in melanoma)
- Changing fertility patterns (increase in breast cancer)

Environmental exposure
- Asbestos: the EU ban on use of asbestos products in 2005 may reduce mesothelioma rates only in around 35 years' time due to the long latency period after exposure

Diagnostic tests
- Introduction of prostate-specific antigen (PSA) as a test for occult and asymptomatic prostate cancer

Screening
- Initial increase in incidence often seen (by detection of asymptomatic tumours)
- May decrease incidence (by detection of precursor lesions that can be treated before the tumour develops, eg colorectal polyps, carcinoma in situ of the cervix)

There is a variable lag period before the effects of changes in behaviour or environmental exposure are seen. Implementation of new diagnostic tests or screening programmes may have a much more rapid impact on the incidence figures.

Increasing incidence of cancer in Europe
Data from Europe over the last decade show increasing incidence in the following cancers:
- Melanoma (54% and 37% increases in incidence in men and women respectively)
- Prostate (60% increase; note: remember introduction of PSA testing)
- Uterus (23% increase in incidence)
- Kidney
- Non-Hodgkin's lymphoma
- Breast
- Leukaemia
- Ovary

Decreasing incidence of cancer in Europe
Incidence is decreasing in the following cancers:
- Large bowel (6–8% decrease)
- Pancreas
- Bladder
- Stomach (28% decrease)
- Lung
- Cervix (24% decrease)

For discussion of survival and mortality rates please refer to the clinical sections on individual cancers in Book 2.

CHAPTER 5

SECTION 2

Molecular basis of cancer

Learning point

The word 'tumour' means 'swelling.'
The swelling is either physiological or
pathological.

Physiological swelling
- The pregnant uterus, for example

Pathological swelling
- Neoplastic
- Non-neoplastic (eg pus, inflammatory,
  bony callus)

Neoplasia is an abnormal mass of tissue,
the growth of which is uncoordinated,
exceeds that of the normal tissues
and persists in the same manner after
cessation of the stimuli that evoked the
change.

Tumours are **similar** to the organ in which they
arose:
- They consist of both parenchymal and
  stromal elements but come from a single
  'cell of origin' in the parent tissue (ie they
  are clonal)
- They may continue to perform some of the
  functions of the parent organ (eg mucin
  production in colorectal tumours; hormone
  production in endocrine tumours; IgG
  production in myeloma)
- Individual cells look similar to the parent
  cells; the degree of similarity depends on
  the degree of differentiation of the tumour

However, they also **differ** in some ways:
- Deranged histological architecture
- No controlled functional contribution to the
  body
- Can proliferate rapidly (unlike other differ-
  entiated cell groups)
- Can develop metastatic potential

2.1   Normal cell growth

Learning point

Cells fall into several different categories according to their propensity to divide and their degree of differentiation:

- **Labile cells:** constantly renewed (eg stratified squamous epithelium of the skin)
- **Stable cells:** usually quiescent but can be stimulated to divide (eg hepatocytes)
- **Permanent cells:** do not undergo mitosis in postnatal life (eg neurones, skeletal muscle tissues, glomeruli)

Cells divide as they progress through the cell cycle. There are many regulatory points inherent in the cycle, and disruption of regulatory genes results in uncontrolled replication.

The cell cycle

DNA structure

Deoxyribonucleic acid (DNA) is a strand-like molecule consisting of four building blocks – adenine (A), thymine (T), cytosine (C) and guanine (G). These are paired (A with T, and C with G) and their affiliation for each other zips the two strands of DNA into the double helix.

DNA is stored in the cellular nucleus as a folded form called **chromatin**. This is wrapped around proteins called **histones** to form complexes called **nucleosomes** (which look like a bead on a string). Active genes unwrap from the histones, opening out the DNA for access by transcriptional proteins. When the cell divides, the nucleosomes become very tightly folded, condensing into **chromosomes**.

The nucleus of most human cells contains two sets of chromosomes, one set given by each parent. Each set has 23 single chromosomes – 22 autosomes and a sex chromosome (X or Y). There are therefore 46 chromosomes in each cell.

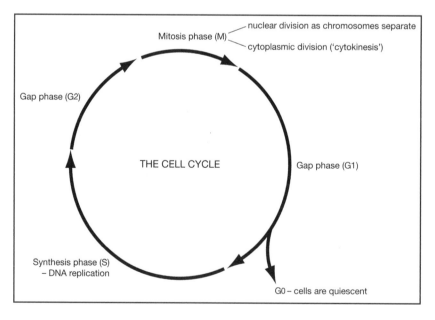

**Figure 5.1
The cell cycle**

Phases of the cell cycle

The cell cycle is divided into phases:

G1	Pre-synthetic
S	DNA synthesis (chromosome replication)
G2	Premitotic
M	Mitotic (cell division)
G0	Quiescent (resting phase)

Mitosis is divided into several phases:

- **Interphase:** this comprises phases G1, S and G2 of the cell cycle when the cell is in preparation for division. The chromosomes have replicated and there are two copies of each in the cell (ie 92 chromosomes)
- **Prophase:** the chromatin begins to condense and is seen as chromosomes. Centrioles move to opposing ends of the cell and fibres stretch between them, forming the mitotic spindle
- **Prometaphase:** the nuclear membrane dissolves and the chromosomes start to move towards the centre of the cell under the control of microtubules
- **Metaphase:** the spindle fibres align with the chromosomes along the metaphase plate (this allows accurate separation of the paired replicated chromosomes to the two cells)
- **Anaphase:** the paired chromosomes separate and are dragged to the opposite sides of the cell by the microtubules
- **Telophase:** the chromatids arrive at the opposite poles of the cell and disperse after new nuclear membranes are formed
- **Cytokinesis:** an actin fibre forms around the centre of the cell and contracts, pinching it into two daughter cells, each with 23 pairs of chromosomes

Control of the cell cycle

There are regulatory points between the different phases of the cell cycle.

Most adult cells are in G0 (ie outside the cell cycle) and quiescent. The length of the G1 phase is variable. The length of the S, G2 and M phases are fairly constant because these processes have a limit as to how quickly they can be performed.

Entry of G0 cells into the cycle and transition from G1 to S phase are the two crucial regulatory points of the cell cycle. They are controlled by:

- **Intracellular enzymes:** cyclin-dependent kinases (CDKs) cause cells to move from G1 to S and also from G2 to M. They are:
  - Upregulated by platelet-derived growth factor (PDGF), epidermal growth factor (EGF) and insulin-like growth factor 1 (IGF-1) in the serum
  - Downregulated by transforming growth factor β (TGF-β)
- **Protein p53:** this protein blocks the cell cycle in G1 phase if DNA is damaged. This allows for DNA repair or, if the damage is severe, cellular apoptosis. High levels of p53 are seen in damaged cells and loss of p53 activity by gene mutation or deletion is associated with tumour development

Cellular differentiation

This is a complex and incompletely understood process occurring during development of the fetus and occurs continuously in certain systems of the body (eg haematopoiesis).

Definitions relating to differentiation

- **Differentiation:** cell specialisation that occurs at the end of the developmental pathway. Selective genes are activated to produce the differentiated phenotype

CHAPTER 5

- **Stem cell:** a cell from an embryo, fetus or adult that can reproduce itself for long periods of time and can give rise to specialised cells and tissues
- **Totipotent cell:** a cell capable of expressing any of the genes of the genome (can give rise to any part of the later embryo or adult). In humans, the fertilised egg is totipotent until the eight-cell stage
- **Pluripotent cell:** a cell with the potential to generate cell types and tissues from all three primary germ layers of the body
- **Plasticity:** the ability of a stem cell of one tissue type to generate cells from another tissue type
- **Progenitor or precursor cell:** occurs when a stem cell divides into two partially differentiated cells, neither of which can replicate itself but which may continue along the path of differentiation

Process of differentiation
Irreversible transition from stem cell to a predetermined differentiated cell type can take one of two pathways:
- A totipotent or pluripotent stem cell may **proliferate and its daughters progress to terminal differentiation**. As this process progresses these cells lose their ability to divide again. Once committed to this pathway cells cannot change their lineage, resulting in mature differentiated cells that have specific functions and do not divide (eg cells of the blood)
- After trauma some tissues may **selectively replicate to replenish tissues**. This can occur because the stimulus causes some of the cells to de-differentiate, re-enter the cell cycle and replicate rapidly

Regulation of differentiation
There is usually an inverse relationship between cell replication and cell differentiation. Differentiation is complex and is regulated by a number of factors.

Soluble factors
- Hormones (eg glucagon, hydrocortisone)
- Interferon
- Vitamin D
- Calcium ions

Cell–cell interactions
- Effects of high cell density and proximity
- Through gap junctions

Cell–matrix interactions
- Matrix attachments may regulate gene expression

These regulators affect gene expression in the differentiating cell. Gene expression is controlled by a combination of:
- **DNA methylation:** this causes the gene to be silenced
- **Chromatin structure:** regulation of the acetylation of histones causes changes in chromatin configuration that allow genes to be increasingly or decreasingly accessible to transcription

2.2 Disorders of cell growth

Developmental disorders of cell growth

- **Hypoplasia:** the organ doesn't reach its full size
- **Agenesis:** vestigial structure only or no development at all
- **Atresia:** failure of canalisation in a hollow lumen causing congenital obstruction (eg gastrointestinal [GI] tract)
- **Ectopia:** location of normal differentiated tissue in an abnormal location (eg thyroid tissue may develop anywhere along the thyroglossal tract)

- **Heteroplasia:** anomalous differentiation of tissues within an organ (eg the presence of sebaceous glands within the mouth) is referred to as heteroplasia
- **Hamartoma:** overgrowth of mature cells that are usually found within the tissue but with disordered architecture (eg haemangioma)

Acquired disorders of cell growth

Hyperplasia

Increase in the number of cells.

The cells mature to normal size and shape. This can occur in response to inflammation, increased workload, excess endocrine drive or increased metabolic demand, eg:
- Benign prostatic hyperplasia
- Renal hyperplasia (in response to contra-lateral dysfunction)

Hypertrophy

Increase in cell size but not in number.

This occurs in response to a demand for increased function, eg:
- Increased skeletal muscle volume in athletes
- Increased cardiac muscle volume in hypertension
- Pregnant uterus

Note that hyperplasia and hypertrophy can occur simultaneously.

Teratoma

Growth of cells originating from more than one germline cell.

CHAPTER 5

Teratomas contain a variety of tissues in a variable state of differentiation. They arise in the gonads or the midline of the body (eg mediastinum, retroperitoneum, base of skull). They can behave in a benign or malignant manner.

Atrophy

Loss of cell substance causing a reduction in cell size. These are the different types:

- **Physiological atrophy:** shrinkage of a well-differentiated structure when it is no longer required (eg ductus arteriosus after birth)
- **Pathological atrophy:** occurs with age (eg musculature, brain tissue)
- **Local atrophy:** often due to reduced blood flow or neurological input (eg nerve damage) to that region
- **Disuse atrophy:** often musculature, due to trauma, immobility or age

Metaplasia

Reversible replacement of one differentiated cell type with another.

This is an adaptive response and the replacement cells are of the same tissue type. It can be due to chronic irritation or altered cell function. There is greater susceptibility to neoplastic transformation (via dysplasia) but it is not inevitable (eg squamous epithelium changing to gastric type in the distal oesophagus – Barrett's oesophagus).

Dysplasia

Disordered cellular development characterised by increased mitosis and pleomorphism. This is frequently preneoplastic and it may follow metaplasia. May also be called carcinoma in situ, intraepithelial neoplasia, incipient neoplasia or pre-cancer.

Neoplasia

'Transformed' is a word that is used to describe the process by which a normal cell becomes neoplastic. The processes involved are called carcinogenesis. Transformed cells adopt the abnormal growth patterns consistent with neoplasia (discussed in section 2.4).

2.3 Carcinogenesis

Learning point

A tumour (neoplasm) is an overgrowth of tissue formed by a clone of cells bearing cumulative genetic injuries. Each of these genetic injuries confers an additional growth advantage to the clone that possesses it (Cole and Nowell, 1976). These mutations can be:

- **Congenital:** already present in the genome (heritable cancers)
- **Acquired:** additional mutations brought about by exposure to a carcinogen
- (sporadic cancers)

The multistage process of carcinogenesis

Carcinogenesis is a generic term for the acquisition of a series of genetic mutations that lead up to the expression of full malignant potential. As cells undergo carcinogenesis and become neoplastic they become **transformed.**

Cole and Nowell described the multistep process of tumorigenesis in their article in *Science* in 1976. Essentially:

- Neoplasms are monoclonal (they arise from a single cell)

- Neoplasms arise due to cumulative genetic injury
- Neoplasms may develop more aggressive sub-clones as genetic injuries accumulate
- Genetic injuries confer growth advantages:
  - Increased proliferation (failure of control of division)
  - Immortalisation (failure of cell senescence)
  - Loss of apoptotic control
- Genetic injuries may include:
  - Point mutations
  - Amplifications
  - Deletions
  - Changes in control regions (eg gene promoters, enhancer sequences)
  - Translocations of chromosomal material

Carcinogens

> **Learning point**
>
> **Carcinogens** can be divided into three types:
> - Chemical
> - Physical
> - Infectious (oncogenic viruses, bacteria, protozoa)

Chemical carcinogens

Chemical carcinogens may act directly to damage DNA (eg alkylating agents) whereas the majority require metabolic conversion from a pro-carcinogen state to become activated (eg polycyclic hydrocarbons [smoke], aromatic amines, amides and azo dyes, natural plant products and nitrosamines). The carcinogen is often activated by metabolism via the hepatic cytochrome P450 mixed function oxidase system of the liver.

Chemical carcinogens can be either **mutagens** (irreversibly directly damage DNA) or **non-mutagens** (reversibly promote cell division). Some heavy metals depolymerise DNA.

The process of **initiation** is exposure to a carcinogen that causes irreversible DNA damage but does not directly lead to a change in phenotype, which is followed by the process of **promotion**; this allows initiated cells to grow into tumours by promoting cell division (eg hormonal influences on tumour growth).

Chemicals are tested for mutagenicity by a variety of in-vitro and in-vivo procedures:
- Production of mutations in bacteria colonies (eg the Ames test), yeast colonies and in cultured mammalian cells
- Charting unexpected DNA synthesis in cultured mammalian cells
- Use of higher plants to look at chromosome damage

Physical carcinogens
These consist of a wide range of agents:
- Electromagnetic radiation (ultraviolet [UV] light, ionising radiation)
- Extremes of temperature
- Mechanical trauma
- Foreign bodies and implants

The mechanism of carcinogenesis is thought to be centred around long-term inflammation causing proliferation. There may also be direct DNA damage by radiation. Selection of clones with growth advantages then leads to neoplasia. There are a few reported cases of sarcomatous change around foreign bodies and surgical implants (this is very rare).

CHAPTER 5

Infectious carcinogens

Infection causing persistent inflammation may result in neoplastic transformation (eg bladder schistosomiasis resulting in transitional cell carcinoma [TCC] of the bladder in endemic areas such as Egypt; malaria and Burkitt's lymphoma).

Viral infection may also result in neoplastic transformation. This may be caused by insertion of viral genomic material into the cell (eg Epstein–Barr virus [EBV] incorporation into the genome) or cell lysis due to viral infection stimulating cell turnover and proliferation (eg hepatitis and cirrhosis leading to hepatocellular carcinoma [HCC]).

EXAMPLES OF CARCINOGENS (HISTORICAL AND CONTEMPORARY) AND THEIR EFFECTS

Carcinogen	Associated carcinoma	Examples of groups affected
Chemical agents		
β-Naphthylamine	Bladder carcinoma	Dye workers
Benzopyrene	Lung carcinoma	Painters, printers
Aflatoxin	Hepatocellular carcinoma	Peanut farmers
Asbestos	Mesothelioma	Builders, shipbuilders
Chromium, arsenic, nickel	Lung carcinoma	Miners, smelters
Vinyl chloride monomers	Angiosarcoma of liver	
Diethylstilbestrol	Adenocarcinoma of the vagina	
Benzol/benzene	Blood and lymphatic cancers	
Nitrates	Gastric cancer	
Physical agents		
UV light	Melanoma (especially UVB) Basal cell carcinoma Squamous cell carcinoma	
Ionising radiation	Leukaemia (blood) Bone Breast Thyroid Skin, tongue, tonsil	Radium workers
Viruses, bacteria and protozoa		
HIV	Leukaemias, lymphomas, Kaposi sarcoma	
Hepatitis B, C	Hepatocellular carcinoma	
EBV	Nasopharyngeal carcinoma	
	B-cell lymphoma, Burkitt's lymphoma, Hodgkin's lymphoma, post-transplant lymphoma	
HPV-16, HPV-18	Cervical cancer	
Helicobacter pylori	Gastric cancer	
Schistosoma spp.	Squamous cell carcinoma of the bladder	

Genes involved in carcinogenesis

Four classes of genes can be affected to produce a neoplasm:

- Oncogenes
- Tumour suppressor genes
- Anti-apoptotic genes
- DNA mismatch-repair genes

Oncogenes

Normal genes involved in cell division are called **proto-oncogenes**. These genes may become permanently activated by point mutation, translocation or an increase in the copy number (amplification). This results in permanent upregulation. Activation of these genes causes cell division and promotes growth in a dominant manner (ie the damaged gene over-rides signals from its undamaged normal counterpart). These genes code for growth factors and their receptors, signal transducing proteins, transcription factors and cell cycle regulators.

Examples of commonly mutated oncogenes include:

- *Ras* oncogene (over-expression of growth factor p21)
- *ERB1* and *ERB2* (over-expression of growth factors)
- Telomerase (important for cellular immortality)

Tumour suppressor genes (anti-oncogenes)

These are normal genes that tell cells when not to divide. They are downregulated by mutations. They tend to act in a recessive manner (ie usually the malignant phenotype is expressed only when both copies are damaged or missing).

Examples of commonly mutated tumour suppressor genes include:

- *APC* (results in familial adenomatous polyposis or FAP)
- E-cadherin
- *TP53* (mutated in up to 50% of tumours)

Anti-apoptotic genes

Normal tissues are subject to genes regulating programmed cell death (apoptosis). Neoplasia is associated with changes in cell senescence and immortalisation of the cell line. Loss of these normal controls results in a reduction in cell death. This occurs when the genes controlling apoptosis are downregulated by mutation.

Commonly affected apoptosis genes include *Bcl-2* (inhibits apoptosis).

DNA mismatch-repair genes

After normal cellular replication, there are genes responsible for recognising and excising mutated gene segments. If these genes themselves undergo mutation they become downregulated, allowing accumulation of mutations within the cell.

Commonly affected DNA repair genes include *MSH-2*.

There is also a level of interaction between all these gene products, exemplified by the role of p53. This protein is upregulated by cellular and DNA damage, and high levels can be identified in damaged cells. The p53 protein upregulates a CDK inhibitor molecule, causing inhibition of the CDK family. This halts the cell cycle in G1. In addition p53 upregulates transcription of GADD-45, which is a DNA-repair enzyme, and the BAX protein, which binds to *Bcl-2* allowing apoptosis to occur if the DNA is not repaired.

CHAPTER 5

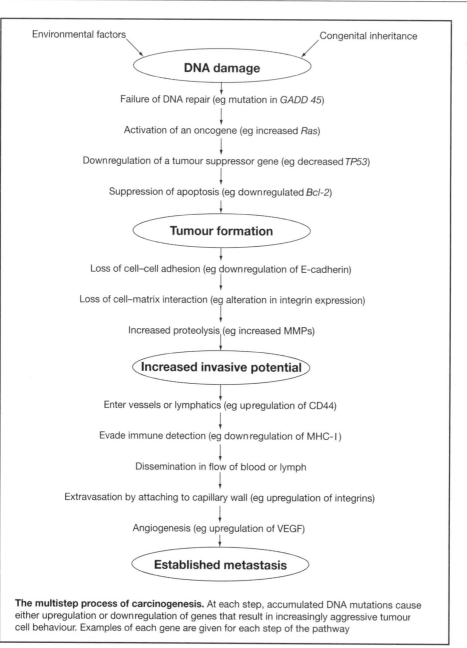

**Figure 5.2
Overview of
carcinogenesis**

The multistep process of carcinogenesis. At each step, accumulated DNA mutations cause either upregulation or downregulation of genes that result in increasingly aggressive tumour cell behaviour. Examples of each gene are given for each step of the pathway

The Knudson two-hit hypothesis

This hypothesis describes the role of recessive genes in tumorigenesis. Both normal alleles of the *Rb* gene on chromosome 13q14 have to be lost before retinoblastoma develops. One may be inherited as a mutated copy, but the tumour will develop only if the second copy undergoes mutation.

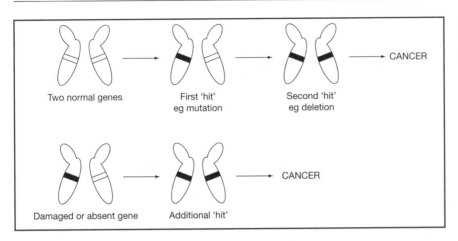

**Figure 5.3
The Knudson
two-hit hypothesis**

The Knudson two-hit hypothesis also helps to explain the development of familial cancer.

Familial and sporadic cancers

Familial cancers – congenital mutations

Defective or mutated genes may be inherited via the cell germline. People carrying this defective gene copy are at high risk of developing a tumour. These genes may be dominant or recessive.

It is estimated that 5–10% of common solid adult tumours may be attributable to an inherited defective gene. The rest (and therefore the majority) are sporadic.

Clinical aspects of familial tumours

Familial cancers include:

- Breast cancer (+ ovarian or ± sarcoma)
- Colorectal cancer
- Ovarian cancer
- Uterine cancer
- Multiple endocrine neoplasia (MEN) syndromes

Suspect a familial cancer if:

- Multiple family members are affected
- Age of onset is early
- Multiple primaries are identified within the same individual
- Cancer is bilateral
- Cancer is rare form

It is helpful to draw a detailed family tree and mark affected members because this can help identification of transmission patterns.

Management of familial cancers

Referral to a genetics service should be appropriate to the guidelines for your region. For the purposes of genetics, **close relatives** are considered to be:

- Parent (mother/father)
- Sibling (brother/sister)
- Child (son/daughter)
- Grandparent (grandmother/grandfather)
- Aunt/uncle (note not by marriage; only consider siblings of the parents)

CHAPTER 5

GENES RELATED TO FAMILIAL CANCER SYNDROMES
(all are available for genetic testing)

Syndrome	Clinical presentation	Gene
Oncogenes		
Familial malignant melanoma	Melanoma	CDK-4
Hereditary GIST syndrome	Stromal tumours of GI tract from oesophagus to rectum	KIT
Hereditary papillary renal carcinoma	Bilateral papillary renal carcinoma	MET
Multiple endocrine neoplasia type 2	Medullary thyroid carcinoma, phaeochromocytoma, parathyroid adenoma	RET
Tumour-suppressor genes		
Familial adenomatous polyposis	Multiple colonic adenomas	APC
Familial breast and ovarian cancer	Breast cancer Ovarian cancer Prostate cancer Colon cancer	BRCA-1, BRCA-2
Retinoblastoma	Retinoblastoma Osteosarcoma Pinealoma	Rb1
Multiple endocrine neoplasia type 1	Parathyroid adenomas Pancreatic adenomas or malignant gastromas Pituitary adenomas	MEN 1
Neurofibromatosis	Neurofibromas Schwannomas of cranial nerves	NF-1 NF-2
Von Hippel–Lindau	Haemangioblastoma Renal cell carcinoma Phaeochromocytoma	VHL
Li–Fraumeni	Breast cancer Soft-tissue sarcoma Leukaemia Osteosarcoma Melanoma Colon cancer Pancreas	TP53
DNA-repair genes		
Hereditary non-polyposis colorectal cancer (HNPCC)	Colorectal cancer Endometrial cancer Ovarian cancer Gastric cancer	MLH-1 MSH-2 MSH-3 PMS-1 PMS-2

Guidelines for referral to genetics services

- **Breast cancer**
  - One relative (aged <40 years at diagnosis)
  - One relative with bilateral disease
  - One male relative
  - Two relatives (aged <60 years at diagnosis)
- **Ovarian cancer**
  - Two relatives (any age at diagnosis)
- **Colorectal cancer**
  - One relative aged <45 years at diagnosis
  - Two relatives aged <70 years at diagnosis
  - Three relatives with GI, uterine or ovarian cancers
  - Suspected familial adenomatous polyposis (FAP)
- **Multiple primary tumours** in an individual
- **Three close relatives** have had cancers of the GI tract, breast, ovary, prostate, pancreas, thyroid or melanoma

---

Patients who test positive for a defective gene may require:

- Increased surveillance
- Watchful waiting
- Screening (eg mammography, colonoscopy, PSA)
- Prophylactic measures:
  - Lifestyle changes (eg exercise, fat intake)
  - Medical prophylaxis (eg drugs)
  - Surgical prophylaxis (eg mastectomy for *BRCA-1* and *BRCA-2*; total colectomy for FAP)

Sporadic cancers – acquired mutations

Mutations may accumulate with advancing age and with exposure to an environmental mutagen (a carcinogen). Carcinogens act by causing additional genetic mutations within the cell that eventually accumulate sufficiently for the development of neoplasia.

2.4 Abnormalities in neoplastic cell behaviour

Learning point

Neoplastic cells exhibit different behaviour from normal cells in terms of:
- Proliferation
- Differentiation
- Immortality
- Apoptosis
- Karyotype and progression
- Stimulation of angiogenesis

For discussion of normal cell behaviour please read section 2.1 first.

CHAPTER 5

Tumour cell proliferation

The rate of cell proliferation within any population of cells depends on three things:

- **The rate of tumour cell division:** tumour cells can be pushed into the cell cycle more easily because there is loss of the regulation that controls movement from one phase of the cycle to the next
- **The fraction of cells within the population undergoing cell division (growth fraction):** this is the proportion of cells within the tumour cell population that are in the replicative pool. Not all cells within a tumour are actively replicating and many are quiescent. The growth fraction is only 20% even in rapidly growing tumours
- **The rate of cell loss from the replicating pool due to differentiation or apoptosis:** overall growth depends on balance between production and loss by apoptosis. In general tumour cells grow faster than they die off

Entry of G0 cells into the cycle and transition from G1 to S phase are the two crucial regulators of the cell cycle. They largely regulate the growth fraction of a cell population. As discussed previously, these points are regulated by CDK, which is regulated:

- Positively by platelet-derived growth factor (PDGF), epidermal growth factor (EGF) and insulin growth factor (IGF)-1
- Negatively by transforming growth factor (TGF)-β

Neoplastic cells may:

- Upregulate their receptors
- Mutate intracellular pathways (eg retinoblastoma gene and *TP53*) to evade the requirement for these signals

Neoplasms initially grow exponentially and then slow down as they increase in size. This is called **gompertzian growth** (Figure 5.4). Several mechanisms have been invoked to explain this change in growth rate with larger tumours:

- Decrease in the growth fraction
- Increase in cell loss (eg exfoliation, necrosis)
- Nutritional depletion of tumour cells resulting from outgrowth of available blood supply (under adverse conditions tumours may enter G0 until conditions improve)

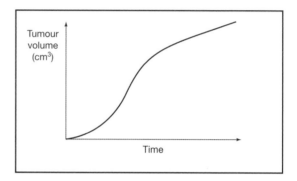

Figure 5.4 Gompertzian growth curve. Initially growth of a small tumour is exponential but as the tumour enlarges this pattern of growth is unsustainable. Tumour-cell doubling time therefore reduces and overall growth slows

Latent period: accumulation of cells is slow, so it can take several years for a single cell to proliferate into a clinically detectable mass.

Chemotherapy: chemotherapy drugs are most effective on cycling cells; tumours with a high growth fraction are more susceptible to antinuclear agents. Debulking tumours or treating with radiation pushes more cells into the cell cycle and therefore increases the number of susceptible cells.

Tumour cell differentiation

Tumour cells may:

- Arise at any stage during the process of differentiation and their progeny can replicate while still retaining the characteristics of that stage of differentiation
- Lose the inverse relationship between proliferation and differentiation
- De-differentiate
- Change lineage
- Hypomethylate or hypermethylate genes that would control their replication (eg *TP53* is often silenced in this way)

Tumour cell apoptosis

The role of apoptosis

Apoptosis is the process of programmed cell death. It is a controlled sequence of steps that is activated by a number of signals and results in 'suicide' of the cell. Most importantly it acts to balance mitotic processes within the body. Apoptosis may be physiological or pathological.

Physiological apoptosis

- Development: to create organs of normal size and function (eg creation of web spaces between digits)
- Homeostasis: eg loss of the uterine lining during menstruation or of the tips of the intestinal villi
- Immune function: to recognise antigens that are foreign and not 'self'

Pathological apoptosis

- Cell damage (eg peeling skin caused by sunburn)
- Cell infection

The process of apoptosis

Apoptosis occurs as a result of activation of one of two pathways.

Intrinsic pathway

- Activated from within the cell as a result of DNA damage or other stress
- Regulated by the **bcl-2** family of proteins (pro-apoptotic and anti-apoptotic members) that stabilise the mitochondrial membrane
- Mitochondria release cytochromes which bind to apoptotic factors and activate cell death via the caspases

Extrinsic pathway

- Activated by apoptotic messages via receptors
- Via **tumour necrosis factor (TNF)** superfamily of proteins and CD95

Common final apoptotic pathway

Activation of a cascade of proteolytic **caspase enzymes** is the final common pathway to cellular destruction. This manifests as:

- Chromatin condensation
- DNA fragmentation
- Protein cleavage
- Reduction in cellular size and membrane blebbing
- Fragmentation of the cell into membrane-enclosed apoptotic bodies (without release of the cell contents into the surrounding environment)
- Phagocytes engulf and destroy the apoptotic bodies without causing an inflammatory reaction

Loss of the apoptotic pathway is responsible for increased levels of genetic instability and accumulation of genetic mutations. This leads to tumour progression by the expansion of clones with more aggressive phenotypes. It also confers

CHAPTER 5

resistance to chemotherapy, radiation, and immune-mediated cell destruction.

The **Bcl-2 gene** is particularly important in tumours. The products of this gene represent a superfamily that associate with each other by homo- and heterodimerisation. Some dimers are pro-apoptotic and others anti-apoptotic. The ratio of anti-apoptotic:pro-apoptotic dimers is important for determining resistance of a cell to apoptosis. Mutations causing upregulation of anti-apoptotic dimers (or loss of pro-apoptotic dimers) result in an overall resistance to apoptosis. Tumours may evade apoptosis by disruption of the control mechanisms for apoptosis, such as mutation of genes such as *Bcl-2* and *BAX*.

Tumour cell karyotype

The term 'karyotype' refers to the chromosomal arrangement of the genetic material in the cell. Virtually all solid tumours, including non-Hodgkin's lymphomas, have an abnormal karyotype or chromosomal abnormality. Some of these abnormalities are limited to a given tumour type, almost like a 'genetic fingerprint'. A good example of this is the Philadelphia chromosome, which is characteristic of chronic myelocytic leukaemia (CML).

Types of chromosome abnormality

- Gain/loss of whole chromosome (aneuploidy)
- Partial deletion
- Translocation from one chromosome to another
- Inversion of a segment of chromosome

Rearranging genetic material in this fashion has implications for the control of expression of the genes in the abnormal segment. It may place oncogenes in a highly transcriptionally active region of the genome or lead to deletion of tumour suppressor genes.

Tumour angiogenesis

Nutrients can diffuse to tumour cells only over a limited distance, so an adequate blood supply is critical for a tumour to grow >1–2 mm in diameter. The process by which a tumour recruits and sustains its own blood supply is called angiogenesis.

The majority of endothelial cells in the body are quiescent. Physiological angiogenesis in the adult occurs only as a response to trauma and tissue repair or at certain times (eg the menstrual cycle). Pathological angiogenesis occurs when there is persistent proliferation of endothelial cells in response to a stimulus (eg from a tumour).

The angiogenic switch

Tumours recruit endothelial cells from surrounding vessels and progenitor cells in the circulation. These cells are stimulated to grow into the tumour from the outside. When this occurs this stage is called 'the angiogenic switch'. The genetic determinant of the angiogenic switch remains unknown. The angiogenic phenotype of a tumour depends on the net balance between pro-angiogenic and anti-angiogenic growth factors in the region of the tumour. These growth factors may be produced by the tumour itself or by stromal or immune cells in the tumour vicinity.

Promoters of angiogenesis

Angiogenic factors are secreted by tumour cells and tumour-associated macrophages. The most important naturally occurring angiogenesis promoters include:
- Fibroblast growth factors (FGFs)
- Vascular endothelial growth factor (VEGF)
- Angiopoietins (Ang-1 and Ang-2; the ratio between them is likely to be important)

Inhibitors of angiogenesis

Naturally occurring proteins:

- Angiostatin
- Endostatin
- Thrombostatin

For discussion of angiogenesis as a target for cancer therapy see Section 5.5.

2.5 Neoplastic progression – invasion and metastasis

Learning point

Neoplastic progression is a term that refers to the generation of subclones within the tumour. These subclones occur by accumulation of further genetic mutations and have an increasingly aggressive phenotype, allowing invasion and metastasis to distant sites.

Neoplastic invasion

Learning point

The ability to invade and spread determines the difference between a benign and a malignant phenotype. **Invasion** is due to:

- Changes in adhesion molecules
  - Cell-to-cell interactions
  - Cell-to-matrix interactions
- Proteolysis
- Migration and chemotaxis

Changes in adhesion

Loss of cell-to-cell adhesion

E-cadherin is the major cell adhesion molecule in epithelia; these cell adhesion molecules are downregulated in several carcinomas.

Loss of cell-to-matrix interactions

Integrins and cadherins bind epithelial cells to the basement membrane; loss of integrins is associated with increased invasive potential. In particular the integrin v3 mediates adhesion to laminin, fibronectin and fibrinogen. It is over-expressed on the basement membrane of new blood vessels and its activation results in increased cell motility and proteolysis.

Cell adhesion to basement membrane

In normal epithelial cells laminin receptors are expressed on one side of the cell and bind to laminin on the basement membrane; tumour cells have increased numbers of laminin receptors on all sides.

Proteolysis

Degradation of collagen by proteolytic enzymes is a vital step. Upregulation of proteolytic enzymes groups; the matrix metalloproteases (MMPs) and tissue plasminogen activators (tPAs) correlate with increased invasiveness.

Tumour cell migration

Tumour cells coordinate proteolysis with migration. Migration consists of intermittent and limited attachment and detachment. The direction of migration is stimulated by chemotaxis driven by:

- Host growth factors, eg IGF, human growth factor (hGF), fibroblast growth factor (FGF) and TGF-β

CHAPTER 5

- Tumour-secreted factors (called autocrine motility factors)
- Gradient of degraded extracellular matrix components

Neoplastic metastasis

Learning point

Natural history of a typical malignant tumour
- Neoplastic transformation of a cell
- Clonal expansion
- Local invasion
- Distant spread

Tumour spread may be:
- Direct extension (eg direct invasion of bladder from adenocarcinoma of the sigmoid colon)
- Transcoelomic (eg ovary)
- Lymphatic (eg axillary nodes from carcinoma of the breast)
- Haematogenous (eg bone metastases from follicular carcinoma of the thyroid)
- Spillage of tumour cells during surgery

Haematogenous metastasis comprises:
- Entry to the circulation
- Dissemination
- Extravasation
- Establishment of a distant site
- Angiogenesis

Lymphatic metastasis

Basement membranes of the lymphatics do not contain collagen or laminin and so are easier for the tumour cell to invade. This is a common method of metastasis for carcinomas. Cells may become trapped in the filtering lymph nodes draining the site of the primary tumour, where

they are either destroyed or form deposits and start to grow.

Many primary tumours have well-defined regional lymph nodes that are examined for signs of metastasis during resection of the primary. See Section 5.1 for discussion of management of these nodes.

Haematogenous metastasis

Entry to the circulation
Tumour cells squeeze through gaps between endothelial cells to enter the circulation in a manner similar to that employed by cells of the immune system in inflammation (remind yourself from Chapter 4). Many of the same molecules have been implicated in this process (eg CD44).

Dissemination in the circulation
Malignant cells avoid detection by decreased expression of MHC I. They also shed intercellular adhesion molecule (ICAM)-1 which interacts with cytotoxic T-cell receptors, stopping their destruction.

Extravasation
Cells attach to the vessel wall and migrate through it (eg increased expression of integrin VLA-4 in melanoma); reduced expression of the *nm23* gene is associated with increased metastases of breast cancer, but its mechanism of action is unknown.

Establishment of metastasis
This is poorly understood. Traditionally it has been described in terms of the 'seed and soil hypothesis'. This may also go some way to explain common sites for development of metastasis

CHAPTER 5

from specific tumour types. Other common sites for metastasis reflect the vascular drainage of the primary tumour (eg cells shed from a colonic tumour travel via the portal circulation to the liver, where they have an impact in the capillaries). Millions of cells may be shed into the circulation daily, but only a small fraction is successful at initiating colonies. Development of a distant metastasis also requires initiation of an angiogenic process at the chosen site.

Metastasis may be established as an early or late event in the development of the tumour (eg distant spread with no identifiable primary). This may reflect different molecular processes going on in subclones within the tumour.

Common patterns of metastasis

Site of metastasis	Possible primary source
Liver	GI
	Pancreas
	Lung
	Breast
	Genitourinary
	Malignant melanoma
Skeletal	Lung
	Breast
	Prostate (osteosclerotic)
	Kidney
	Thyroid
Brain	Lung
	Malignant melanoma
	Breast
Adrenal	Lung
	Breast
Transcoelomic	Stomach
	Colon
	Ovary
Lung	Kidney
	Breast
	Colorectal
	Ovary

2.6 The immune system and neoplasia

Learning point

The immune system and neoplasia
- Malignant transformation is associated with the expression of tumour antigens
- These antigens may be recognised as foreign by the immune system, resulting in destruction of the tumour cell (theory of immune surveillance)
- Tumour cells may practise immune evasion

The theory of immune surveillance

The process of malignant transformation may be associated with the expression of molecules on the cell membrane that can be distinguished as foreign by the immune system. These are called **tumour antigens** and they include:
- Products of point mutations in normal genes
- Over-expression of self-antigens (previously expressed at a low enough level not to induce tolerance)
- Viral antigens
- Products of silent genes not usually expressed as protein (eg *MAGE, BAGE* and *GAGE*)
- Products of fetal proteins (oncofetal antigens)

Tumour antigens may thus be recognised by either arm of the immune system; the cellular and humoral components and the abnormal cells are destroyed before tumours develop. The success of this strategy depends on the immunogenicity of the tumour cells.

CHAPTER 5

This is the **immune surveillance theory**. In particular, tumours are targeted by the complement system, IgG and components of the cellular system: cytotoxic T lymphocytes, natural killer (NK) cells and macrophages. Cytotoxic T cells recognise antigens displayed in complexes with MHC class I molecules. Macrophages and dendritic cells engulf tumour cells, presenting their antigens to T cells in complex with MHC molecules. The T-helper cells respond by secreting cytokines and recruiting other immunological cells. Tumours producing interferon (IFN) specifically stimulate NK cells which lyse their targets. IFN-α concentration also affects the way that antigens are processed within the cell and this alters their immunogenicity.

Evading the immune system

Tumours may evade the immune system by means of:

- Secretion of anti-inflammatory and immunosuppressive factors such as interleukins IL-4, IL-6 and IL-10, prostaglandin PGE_2, $TGF-\beta_1$ and macrophage colony-stimulating factor (M-CSF)
- Induction of apoptosis in immunological effector cells: tumour cells display Fas ligand which induces apoptosis in the T cell when it binds to its own surface Fas molecule (this exploits the body's system of inducing tolerance)
- Utilisation of immunological ignorance mechanisms:
  - Displaying peptides that are not immunogenic
  - Downregulating MHC class I molecules
  - Shedding large volumes of antigen into the circulation to swamp the T-cell receptors

SECTION 3

Screening programmes

3.1 Cancer screening

> **Learning point**
>
> There are criteria for screening programmes and for the screening test used. Current NHS screening programmes are nationally coordinated and include:
> - Breast screening
> - Cervical screening
> - Colorectal cancer screening
>
> Go to www.cancerscreening.nhs.uk for further information.

Screening programmes

Criteria for screening programmes

A screening programme needs to fulfil certain criteria (defined by the WHO in 1966). These criteria are:
- The condition is an important health problem
- Its natural history is well understood
- It is recognisable at an early stage
- Treatment is better at an early stage
- A suitable test exists
- An acceptable test exists
- Adequate facilities exist to cope with the abnormalities detected
- Screening is done at repeated intervals when the onset is insidious
- The chance of harm is less than the chance of benefit
- The cost is balanced against benefit

Criteria for screening tests

The screening test must detect the condition at an earlier stage than it would clinically present. This means that there should be a detectable latent or preclinical phase during which interventional treatment is possible.

The screening test should:
- Be simple and cheap/cost-effective
- Be continuous
- Be highly sensitive (few false negatives)
- Be highly specific (few false positives)
- Have a high positive predictive value
- Be safe
- Be non-invasive
- Be acceptable to patients
- Be offered to a group agreed to be at high risk
- Be easy to perform and analyse

There should also be adequate resources to deal with the workload for both screening and treatment of specific programmes.

3.2 UK screening programmes

Breast screening

The WHO's International Agency for Research on Cancer (IARC) concluded that mammography screening for breast cancer reduces mortality. The IARC working group determined that there is a 35% reduction in mortality from breast cancer among screened women aged 50–69 (ie the number needed to screen to save one life is 500). See www.cancerscreening.nhs.uk for more information.

Women aged 50–70 are routinely invited for breast screening every 3 years. After the upper age limit women are invited to make their own appointments. A randomised controlled trial of age extension to women aged 47–49 and 70–73 is under way.

There are over 90 breast screening units across the UK, each responsible for an average population of around 45 000 women. These can be mobile, hospital based or permanently based in another convenient location (eg a shopping centre).

The total budget in England is £96 million (£45.50 per woman screened).

Cervical screening

This is essentially a smear test, sent for cytology looking for early precursor abnormalities that may be treated to prevent the development of cervical cancer.

All women between the ages of 25 and 64 are invited for a cervical smear test every 3–5 years. Women aged 25–49 are screened every 3 years and women aged 50–64 are screened every 5 years.

The total budget (including the cost of treating cervical abnormalities) is around £150 million a year (£37.50 per woman screened).

Colorectal cancer (CRC) screening

The English CRC screening pilot was recently completed. It assessed the feasibility of CRC screening using the faecal occult blood (FOB) test for patients aged 50–69. This was positive in about 2% and these people were offered colonoscopy. Based on the success of this programme, an FOB screening programme has been rolled out in England, aimed at men and women aged 60–69 (screened ages are 50–74 in Scotland and 60–74 in Wales).

Prostate cancer screening

There is no UK screening programme for prostate cancer; prostate-specific antigen (PSA) screening does not fulfil the WHO screening criteria and European studies have suggested that it results in high levels of over-treatment of the disease.

CHAPTER 5

SECTION 4

Clinical and pathological grading and staging of cancers

4.1 Tumour grade

This is an assessment of the degree of **differentiation** of a tumour and corresponds to the **aggressive behaviour** of the tumour. Tumours are graded as:

- Well differentiated
- Moderately differentiated
- Poorly/undifferentiated/anaplastic

Many different grading systems exist for different tumours that take into consideration growth patterns as well as differentiation status, eg Gleason grade for prostate cancer.

Differentiation refers to the degree to which neoplastic cells resemble their tissue of origin. Features of poor differentiation are:

- Increased nuclear pleomorphism
- Atypical mitoses
- Hyperchromatic nuclei
- Increased nuclear:cytoplasmic size ratio
- Possible presence of giant cells

Tumour grading is important for prediction of tumour behaviour and prognosis. In general, the less differentiated the tumour, the more aggressive its biological behaviour.

4.2 Tumour staging

This refers to the size and spread of the neoplasm as assessed by clinician, pathologist or radiologist. It is used to determine prognosis and is pivotally important for deciding on appropriate management, including the need for adjuvant therapy after surgery.

Examples:

- Dukes' classification for colorectal carcinoma
- Clarke's classification for malignant melanoma
- TNM (tumour, node, metastasis) system

Staging often requires extensive investigations of the sites most likely to be involved in disease and is aimed at assessing degree of tumour spread to regional nodes and distant sites:

- Blood tests (eg liver function tests [LFTs], tumour markers)
- Cytology or biopsy for histology
- Chest radiograph or computed tomography (CT)
- Abdominal ultrasonography or CT
- Magnetic resonance imaging (MRI)
- Isotope bone scanning

- Positron emission tomography (PET)
- Diagnostic or staging laparoscopy
- Full staging may not be possible until after surgery to resect the tumour, when regional lymph nodes can be inspected histologically for tumour deposits.
- Failure to identify distant metastasis at the time of staging does not necessarily mean that the patient is free from all tumour cells after resection of the primary. Tumour cells continue to be present in the circulation until the primary is removed and there may be tiny, as yet undetectable, metastatic deposits in other organs or lymph nodes.

TMN staging system

The TNM classification was first developed by the American Joint Committee on Cancer Staging and End Result Reporting and has now been modified for systems for most solid tumours, eg breast, colon, thyroid.

The TNM staging system

T = primary tumour
- T0 = no primary tumour
- Tis = in situ primary tumour
- Tx = unknown primary
- T1–4 sizes of primary tumour

N = nodal metastasis
- N0 = no nodes
- N1 = few node(s)
- N2–3 relates to number, fixity or distant lymph node group involvement

M = distant metastasis
- M0 = no metastasis
- M1 = distant metastasis present
- Mx = unknown if metastasis present

Solid organ tumours have their own individual numbering for T and N stage, which can be determined non-surgically, eg by CT or MRI,

or by a pathologist on a resected specimen. For example, a pathologist studying a colonic resection specimen may report the primary lesion as a T2 N2 tumour – the tumour has invaded the muscularis propria (T2) and cancer is found in four or more lymph nodes (N2). Other prefixes used in the TNM classification are a 'p' before the T stage (as in 'pT4 tumour'), which indicates that the T stage had been determined pathologically rather than by any other modality, and 'y' before the staging, which indicates that neoadjuvant therapy had been given before the surgery.

Dukes' staging (A–D) is still in common usage as an adjunct to TNM staging in determining the management of colorectal cancer. The Roman numeral cancer staging system has not been completely superseded by the TNM classification, and is still in common usage; this stratifies tumour stage from 0 (carcinoma in situ) to IV (distant metastasis present). In breast cancer the Nottingham Prognostic Index is calculated for each tumour, taking into account various tumour characteristics, and is pivotally important in guiding treatment.

4.3 Tumour markers

Learning point

Tumour markers are substances in the blood that may be useful in monitoring of specific cancers. Markers include:
- **Epithelial proteins**, eg prostate-specific antigen (PSA)
- **Hormones**, eg β-human chorionic gonadotrophin (β-hCG)
- **Oncofetal antigens**, eg carcinoembryonic antigen (CEA)

Tumour markers are useful in diagnosis, staging, treatment, detection of recurrence.

PSA

- A prostatic epithelial protein
- Elevated if >4 ng/dl (in general)
- Used together with digital rectal examination, transrectal sonography and needle biopsy for 'screening', diagnosis and monitoring of treatment for prostatic cancer
- It is also elevated in benign prostatic hyperplasia, prostatitis, prostatic infarction, urinary retention, instrumentation and even ejaculation
- Thought *not* to rise significantly after rectal examination
- PSA velocity measures rate of change of PSA with time (>0.75 ng/dl per year suggests malignancy)
- PSA density compares PSA value with volume of prostate (>0.15 suggests malignancy)
- Age-related PSA (older patients have a higher 'normal' cut-off)
- Free total PSA ratio (<25% suggests malignancy)

CEA

- An oncofetal antigen, normally expressed in embryonic gut, liver, pancreas
- Elevated in colorectal carcinoma in 60–90% of cases
- May also be elevated in ovarian and breast carcinoma
- Also occasionally elevated in cirrhosis, alcoholic hepatitis, inflammatory bowel disease, pancreatitis
- Not specific or sensitive enough to be used as a screening tool
- Used to monitor efficacy of therapy and detection of recurrence

Alpha-fetoprotein (α-FP)

- An embryonic antigen
- Elevated in carcinoma of liver (also in cirrhosis, chronic hepatitis, normal pregnancy, fetal neural tube defects)
- Also elevated in non-seminomatous germ-cell tumour of the testes (NSGCT)

Beta-human chorionic gonadotrophin (β-hCG)

- A hormone that is elevated in pregnancy
- Elevated in choriocarcinoma, non-small-cell germ-cell tumour (NSGCT) and in 7% of seminomas where syncytiotrophoblastic elements are present

CA antigens

- CA-125: for non-mucinous ovarian cancers. A high concentration is more likely to be associated with malignancy. Can be used to monitor therapy. Can be raised in other conditions (eg pancreatitis, endometriosis, breast and pancreatic carcinomas)
- CA-15-3: a glycoprotein, occasionally elevated in breast carcinoma
- CA-19-9: a glycoprotein sometimes elevated in pancreatic and advanced colorectal carcinoma

Thyroglobulin

- Elevated in some thyroid carcinomas

Calcitonin

- Elevated in medullary thyroid carcinoma

Adrenocorticotropic hormone/antidiuretic hormone

- Elevated in some small-cell lung carcinomas

SECTION 5

Principles of cancer treatment

Learning point

The management of cancer patients is usually decided in the context of a **multidisciplinary team**. Many therapies are combined on the basis of tumour type, grade and stage.
Therapies include:
- Surgery
- Radiotherapy
- Chemotherapy
- Hormonal therapy
- Additional and experimental therapies
- Immunomodulation
- Monoclonal antibodies
- Cryotherapy and radioablation
- Gene therapy
- Anti-angiogenic treatment

Learning point

- Surgery is used in diagnosis, staging, treatment and palliation of cancer
- Surgical design is driven by local invasion and tumour spread (resection en bloc)

Surgical design is influenced by the degree of invasion and spread of the tumour. The two most important principles of curative oncological surgery are **resection en bloc** (ie without surgical disruption of the plane between the tumour and potentially locally infiltrated tissue and without disruption of the lymphatics draining the region of the tumour) and **resection margins that are free from tumour cells**.

Details of surgical resection of individual tumours are discussed in the relevant chapters in Book 2.

5.1 The role of surgery in neoplasia

Surgery has a diagnostic, staging and therapeutic role in neoplasia. It may be curative or palliative. It forms a primary treatment for many solid tumours.

Curative surgery

Curative surgery involves removal of the entire tumour with an intact perimeter of normal tissue, leaving resection margins free of tumour cells.

It may demand an aggressive approach that has higher risks of postoperative complications. Actual or likely directions of tumour spread must be known in order to clear the surgical field (eg mesorectal excision for rectal cancer). If the regional lymph nodes are involved or suspected and lymph node clearance is planned, then this should be performed en bloc (ie without disrupting lymphatic connections between tumour and nodes or between tumour and locally infiltrated tissue).

Curative surgery may be preceded by **neoadjuvant therapies** such as radiotherapy or chemotherapy to 'downstage' disease before surgery, increasing the chance that surgery will be curative; similarly it is increasingly followed by **adjuvant therapies** aimed at reducing recurrence rates.

Surgical management of draining lymph nodes

Learning point

Management of the regional lymph nodes may take many forms:
- Surgical lymph node sampling to predict involvement (eg sentinel node biopsy)
- Surgical lymph node clearance

The role of the regional lymph nodes in cancer is still up for discussion. Many believe that these nodes may not act as filters for malignant cells and that fairly large tumour emboli may skip the regional nodes altogether. These nodes may have an important role in the early immune response to tumours, allowing appropriate antigen recognition and prevention of widespread tumour cell dissemination.

For many tumours, elective lymph node resection has not shown any survival benefit. However, the presence of lymph node metastases is an important prognostic sign and requires treatment, hence there has been much research directed at ways of ascertaining lymph node stage without the need for full regional lymphadenectomy.

There has been much recent interest in directed methods of lymph node sampling, in order to gain information about tumour staging in as sensitive and specific a manner as possible. Sentinel node biopsy is one such method.

Sentinel node biopsy

Essentially there is a single node through which lymphatic drainage from the primary tumour passes to reach the chain of regional lymph nodes. The node that predominantly drains the site of the primary tumour (the sentinel node) is identified by the injection of a tracer substance into the area of the primary tumour. This may be a visible blue dye or radioactive substance (eg human albumin nanocolloid).

Sentinel nodes can then be identified either visually and/or by a hand-held gamma probe at open surgery. There is more than one sentinel node in up to 50% of patients. These nodes are excised and sent for histopathology to look for metastatic deposits. The residual nodes are also scanned for evidence of radioactivity (should have a ratio of at least 3:1 radioactivity for sentinel node vs other nodes in vivo, and 10:1 ex vivo).

CHAPTER 5

Following the success of the Almanac trial (Goyal et al. 2004), the principle of sentinel node detection for breast cancer has been adopted as a mainstay of staging. This is associated with a significant reduction in postoperative morbidity and loss of function when compared with radical axillary dissection. It is also applied selectively to patients with malignant melanoma.

For further discussion about sentinel node biopsy see Chapter 2, Breast Surgery in Book 2.

Lymph node clearance

Regional lymph node clearance may be indicated for:

- Visible involvement by tumour
- Symptomatic involvement by tumour
- Occult involvement by tumour (eg identified by lymphoscintigraphy above)
- For staging (eg Dukes' stage of colorectal cancer)
- Prophylactically when shown to improve prognosis

It is associated with a higher morbidity, eg lymphoedema in axillary dissection.

It is associated with improved prognosis in certain tumour types (eg malignant melanoma).

Reconstructive surgery

May be performed at the same time as primary surgery or later. Includes:

- Reconstruction or remodelling (eg breast reconstruction)
- Restitution or restoration (eg continuity of the bowel)
- Replacement or substitution (eg free flaps)

Sugery in advanced disease

In general metastatic disease is indicative of systemic tumour spread and surgery has little role. However, some metastatic disease is amenable to surgical resection. Resection of liver and lung metastases from colorectal cancer is potentially curative, with 5- and 10-year survival rates post-resection of 25% and 10% respectively. Metastatic disease to the liver may also be treated by radiofrequency ablation. Some solitary brain metastases (eg from breast cancer) may be managed with surgical resection.

In advanced disease surgery may be used to palliate symptoms, eg colonic bypass or stoma creation, or to debulk disease, either to prolong survival or to allow use of another treatment modality. Stenting is often carried out as a combined surgical and radiological procedure to palliate symptoms of oesophageal, colonic or pancreaticobiliary cancers.

5.2 Radiotherapy

Types of radiation

Particulate: does not penetrate the tissue deeply and is used predominantly to treat cutaneous and subcutaneous conditions:

- Electrons
- Protons
- Neutrons
- α Particles
- Pi mesons

Electromagnetic: penetrates tissue deeply and is therefore used to treat deep tumour tissue:

- X-rays
- Gamma rays

Learning point

This is the therapeutic use of ionising radiation for the treatment of malignant conditions.

Radiotherapy
- Radiation may be particulate or electromagnetic
- Radiotherapy kills tumour cells by generating high-energy molecular movement
- Tumour susceptibility is related to tumour oxygenation and radiosensitivity of the individual cells
- Radiotherapy may be used as a primary, neoadjuvant, adjuvant or palliative therapy
- It causes damage to normal as well as tumour cells, resulting in local and systemic complications

Mechanism of action

Radiation kills cells by causing high-energy interactions between molecules:
- DNA damage is via release of kinetic energy from free radicals (an oxygen-dependent process)
- Causes deletions and strand breaks within the DNA
- May trigger apoptosis in some cells due to severe DNA damage
- Cells are most sensitive during S phase

Killing cells leads to stimulation of other cells to divide, ie to enter the S phase:
- **Repair:** normal cells take 4 hours to recover (6+ hours for central nervous system [CNS]); malignant cells take longer
- **Repopulation:** more cells are stimulated to divide due to death of others, after about 3–4 weeks of standard fractionated treatment
- **Redistribution:** pushes cells into the S phase – more radiosensitive
- **Re-oxygenation:** oxygen is a radiation sensitiser; cell death facilitates re-oxygenation – increases cytotoxicity

The degree of tumour destruction by radiotherapy is related to:
- **Radiosensitivity of tumour**
  - Sensitive: seminoma, Hodgkin's lymphoma,
  - Resistant: tendency to repair DNA damage (eg melanoma)
  - Similar tumour types tend to have similar radiosensitivity (eg all carcinomas)
  - Slow-growing tumours may not respond or only respond slowly to radiotherapy
- **Tolerance of normal tissue:** surrounding tissue may be very sensitive to treatment (eg nervous tissue, small bowel), which limits the amount of radiotherapy that can be delivered
- **Tumour size:** larger tumours have areas of low oxygen tension and necrosis, and are more resistant. They require more cycles and larger treatment volumes, which exposes normal tissue to higher doses of radiation

Administration of radiotherapy

- **Locally,** ie the source can be implanted into tissue to be treated (eg brachytherapy for prostate cancer) or into a cavity, eg uterus
- **Systematically** (eg iodine-131 for thyroid cancer)
- **External beam** radiation via linear accelerator

CHAPTER 5

Fractionation describes the number of individual treatments and their time course. The **therapeutic ratio** is the relationship between the amount of radiation tolerated by the normal tissues and that delivered to the tumour.

For radical treatments, aim for maximum possible dose in the smallest volume which will encompass all the tumour and probable occult spread. This is called the **treatment volume** and it comprises:

- Macroscopic tumour
- Biological margin (0.5–1 cm)
- Technical margin (allows for minute variations in positioning and set-up)

The site is accurately localised by imaging and permanent skin markings applied to ensure reproducibility at subsequent sessions.

Complex multi-field arrangements divide the tumour into cubes. The radiation is targeted to divide the dose between surrounding normal tissues, because different tissues can tolerate different amounts of radiation (eg liver is more resilient than kidney). It is usually delivered intermittently, allowing normal tissues to recover. This takes at least 4 hours, whereas malignant tissues take longer.

Improved imaging techniques now allow precise targeting of a tumour shape, which is important if it is located near sensitive structures. Techniques are being refined so that there is an increase in the number of sessions that can be given within a short period of treatment time; this is known as **accelerated radiotherapy** (eg multiple sessions per day for 2 weeks).

Stereotactic radiotherapy is commonly used for brain tumours. The patient's head is placed in a frame and an accurate three-dimensional image of the tumour is obtained using high-resolution MRI. The beam of radiation is focused on the tumour but rotation of delivery means that the surrounding normal tissues receive minimal doses.

Uses of radiotherapy

Primary treatment

- Sensitive tumours
- Better cosmetic/functional result
- Inoperable or high mortality/morbidity with surgery
- Patient not fit for surgery

Adjuvant radiotherapy

- Postoperative
- Can be given at site of disease in order to reduce risk of local recurrence, eg in high-risk tumours or those with compromised resection margins. The disease sites addressed may include the primary tumour and any involved lymph nodes. Intraoperative clips placed around the tumour bed can help direct therapy

Neoadjuvant radiotherapy

- Preoperatively, can downstage tumours to allow surgery to be technically feasible and increase the chance of a clear margin (eg circumferential margin in rectal tumours)
- Can reduce risk of seeding at operation
- Does not cause additional surgical morbidity if performed within 4 weeks of surgery

Palliation

- Palliative radiotherapy aims for symptom relief, from either primary or metastatic disease (eg relief of bone pain, bleeding, dyspnoea, cord compression, superior vena caval obstruction)
- It is given as short courses of treatment, with simple set-ups, to minimise toxicity
- Single fractions are often used to control bone pain

Complications of radiotherapy

Local complications

- Itching and dry skin
- Ulceration
- Bleeding
- Radiation enteritis
- Fibrosis and stricture formation
- Delayed wound healing
- Lymphoedema
- Alopecia
- Osteoradionecrosis

Systemic complications

- Lethargy
- Loss of appetite
- Premature menopause
- Oligospermia
- Acute leukaemia
- Myelosuppression
- Hypothyroidism/renal failure – after many years' treatment

5.3 Chemotherapy

Learning point

Chemotherapeutics are drugs that are used to treat cancer by affecting cell proliferation. They may be used as primary, neoadjuvant or adjuvant therapies.
Chemotherapeutic drugs include:
- Alkylating agents
- Antimetabolites
- Antibiotics
- Vinca alkaloids
- Taxanes
- Topoisomerase inhibitors

Side effects may be acute (related to dose) or chronic (related to duration of treatment). Tumours may eventually become resistant to individual chemotherapeutics.

Chemotherapeutics are drugs that are used to treat cancer that inhibit the mechanisms of cell proliferation. They are therefore toxic to normally proliferating cells (ie bone marrow, GI epithelium, hair follicles). They can be:

- **Cycle-specific:** effective throughout the cell cycle
- **Phase-specific:** effective during part of the cell cycle

Tumour susceptibility depends on the concentration of drug delivered, cell sensitivity and cell cycling of tumour. Drugs are less effective in large solid tumours because of:

- Fall in the growth fraction
- Poor drug penetrance into the centre
- Intrinsic drug resistance of subclones

CHAPTER 5

Indications for chemotherapy

> **Indications for chemotherapy**
> - **Primary treatment** (eg lymphoma)
> - **Neoadjunctive treatment** to decrease tumour bulk before surgery
> - **Adjunctive treatment** for prevention of recurrence
> - Advanced disease and **palliation**
> - **Maintenance** treatment (eg leukaemia)

Important treatment in:
- Haematological malignancy
- Germ cell tumours
- Ovarian cancer
- Small-cell lung cancer
- Breast cancer (locally advanced)

Important neoadjuvant in:
- Colorectal liver metastasis
- Low rectal cancers

Important adjuvant in:
- Colorectal cancer primaries (Dukes' C)
- Breast cancer

Methods of delivering chemotherapy

> **Methods of delivery for chemotherapeutic agents**
> - Intravenous
> - Oral
> - Intra-arterial (eg for HCC)
> - Intramuscular
> - Intrathecal
> - Intracavitary (eg intravesicular for TCC of the bladder)
> - Intralesional

Doses are based on body surface area; affected by hepatic metabolism and renal excretion.

Efficacy of treatment for different tumours may be improved by:
- Pulsed treatment
- Combinations of drugs with different modes of action (synergy, reduces drug resistance)
- Alternating cycles
- High-dose treatment with subsequent replacement of normal tissues (eg bone marrow transplantation)
- Scheduling with continuous low dose

Chemotherapeutic agents

Alkylating agents

Classic alkylating agents
Act by forming covalent bonds with nucleic acids, proteins, nucleotides and amino acids, and so inactivate the enzymes involved in DNA production and protein synthesis.

Non-classic alkylating agents
Act by causing cross-linkage of DNA strands.

Side effects of classic alkylating agents

Indications	Side effects
Mustargen	
Hodgkin's lymphoma	Very toxic so rarely used
Non-Hodgkin's lymphoma	Vomiting
Chronic myelocytic leukaemia (CML)	Bone-marrow depression
Chronic lymphatic leukaemia (CLL)	
Cyclophosphamide	
Many cancers including:	
Lymphoma	Bone marrow depression
Breast	Nausea and vomiting (mild unless high dose)
Lung	Haemorrhagic cystitis (high doses)
Ovary	Pulmonary interstitial fibrosis
Chlorambucil	
CLL	Bone marrow suppression
Non-Hodgkin's lymphoma (low-grade)	Nausea, vomiting, diarrhoea
Ovary	Jaundice, pulmonary fibrosis
Melphalan	
Multiple myeloma	Bone marrow depression
	Nausea and vomiting
	Diarrhoea
	Rash
	Pulmonary fibrosis

Side effects of non-classic alkylating agents

Indications	Side effects
Cisplatin (C-DDP) (toxic to cycling and resting cells)	
Testis cancer	Renal failure
Ovary cancer	Electrolyte disturbance (hypomagnesaemia)
Head and neck cancer	Peripheral neuropathy
Bladder cancer	Ototoxicity
Lung cancer	Bone marrow depression
Oesophageal cancer	
Stomach cancer	
Carboplatin	
Ovary cancer	Less toxic analogue, but more bone marrow suppression
Lung cancer	
Seminoma	

CHAPTER 5

Side effects of antimetabolites

Indications	Side effects
Methotrexate (S-phase specific)	
Acute lymphocytic leukaemia (ALL)	Bone marrow depression
Breast cancer	GI symptoms
Lung	Stomatitis
Renal failure	Hepatic failure
5-Fluorouracil (5-FU) (toxic to resting and cycling cells)	
Colon	Bone marrow depression
Breast	GI symptoms
Stomach	Alopecia
Oesophagus	Rash
Pancreas	Palmar–plantar syndrome and cardiotoxicity with high-dose infusional treatments
Gemcitabine	
Pancreas	Nausea
Lung	Flu-like symptoms
	Oedema

Antimetabolites

Act by interfering with purine or pyrimidine synthesis and hence interfere with DNA synthesis.

Antibiotics

Act by intercalating between base pairs and prevent RNA production. There are several groups with differing actions.

Anthracycline antibiotics

Complex actions (not fully understood):
- Intercalate into DNA strands
- Bind membranes
- Produce free radicals

- Chelate metals – producing cytotoxic compounds
- Alkylation

Non-anthracycline antibiotics

Act by intercalation, free radical production and/or alkylation.

Vinca alkaloids

Act by inhibiting mitosis, by preventing spindle formation. M-phase-specific.

Note that intrathecal administration of vinca alkaloids is fatal!

Side effects of anthracycline antibiotics

Indications	Side effects
Doxorubicin	
Acute leukaemia	Bone marrow depression
Lymphoma	Nausea and vomiting
Breast cancer	Alopecia
Small-cell lung cancer	Cardiac-dose-dependent congestive cardiac failure
Sarcoma	
Bladder cancer	
Ovary cancer	
Wilms' tumour	
Neuroblastoma	
Epirubicin	
Breast	Doxorubicin analogue with less cardiac toxicity

Side effects of non-anthracycline antibiotics

Indications	Side effects
Mitozantrone	
Breast cancer	Bone marrow depression
	Congestive cardiac failure
	Alopecia
	Nausea and vomiting
Bleomycin	
Lymphoma	Bone marrow sparing
Testicular cancer	Pneumonitis and pulmonary fibrosis
Head and neck cancer	Rash
	Fever
Mitomycin C	
Breast cancer	Bone marrow depression
Bladder cancer (intravesical)	Renal failure (haemolytic–uraemic syndrome with tamoxifen)
Pancreatic cancer	Stomatitis, rash, alopecia
Gastric cancer	Nausea and vomiting

CHAPTER 5

Side effects of vinca alkaloids

Indications	Side effects
Vincristine	
Acute leukaemia	Highly vesicant
Lymphoma	Neuropathy
Neuroblastoma	Bronchospasm
Wilms' tumour	
Rhabdomyosarcoma	
Vinblastine	
Testis	Highly vesicant
Hodgkin's lymphoma	Bone marrow depression
Non-Hodgkin's lymphoma	Bronchospasm
Choriocarcinoma	Abdominal pain and ileus (mimics acute abdomen)
Peripheral neuropathy	
Vinorelbine	
Breast	Highly vesicant
Lung	Bone marrow depression
	Abdominal pain and constipation
	Local phlebitis

Taxanes

Act by inhibiting mitosis through stabilisation of microtubules.

Topoisomerase inhibitors

Inhibit topoisomerase I, an enzyme involved in DNA replication.

Side effects of topoisomerase inhibitors

Indications	Side effects
Irinotecan	
Colorectal cancer	Cholinergic syndrome
	Profuse diarrhoea (may be life-threatening)

Side effects of taxanes

Indications	Side effects
Docetaxel	
Breast cancer	Allergic reaction
Ovarian cancer	Severe neutropenia
	Alopecia
	Peripheral oedema
	Myalgia
	Peripheral neuropathy
Paclitaxel	
Ovary cancer	Anaphylaxis
Breast cancer	Severe neutropenia
Lung cancer	Sudden total alopecia
	Myalgia
	Peripheral neuropathy

Side effects of chemotherapy

Acute complications

- Nausea and vomiting
- Diarrhoea or constipation
- Mucositis
- Alopecia
- Bone marrow suppression
- Cystitis
- Phlebitis
- Renal and cardiac toxicity

Chronic complications

- Carcinogenesis (especially alkylating agents that cause leukaemias; risk proportional to dose)
- Pulmonary fibrosis
- Infertility

Drug resistance in tumours

- Reduced drug uptake
- Increased concentrations of target enzymes to minimise the effects of enzyme inhibition
- DNA-repair mechanisms (eg melanoma)
- Mutations coding for cell pumps which extrude the drug
- Salvage pathways
- Drug inactivation

5.4 Hormonal therapy

Up to 15% of tumours may have hormone-responsive elements.

Prostate tumours

- Subcapsular orchidectomy (bilateral)
- Anti-androgens
- Luteinising hormone-releasing hormone (LHRH) analogues
- Stilbestrol (oestrogen)

Breast tumours

- **Tamoxifen:** pre- and postmenopausal women if oestrogen receptor (ER) and/or progesterone receptor (PR) positive
- **Aromatase inhibitors:** prevent oestrogen production from peripheral fat – no effect on ovarian oestrogens, so postmenopausal only. Recent evidence of superior disease-free survival even in early disease compared with tamoxifen for third-generation aromatase inhibitors (eg anastrazole)
- **Progestogens:** now tend to be used third line, because aromatase inhibitors are superior
- **LHRH analogues:** monthly goserelin in premenopausal women (3-monthly preparation does not reliably suppress menstruation in all)

Thyroid tumours

- Thyroxine to suppress thyroid-secreting hormone secretion
- Liothyronine used

5.5 Additional therapies

Learning point

Additional potential therapies include:
- Immunomodulation: used in renal cell carcinoma, bladder carcinoma
- Monoclonal antibodies
- Cryotherapy and radiofrequency ablation

Experimental therapies include:
- Gene therapy
- Anti-angiogenic therapy

Immunomodulation

Renal cancer

- Radioresistant
- Chemoresistant
- Some success with IL-2 and IFN-α

Bladder cancer

- BCG vaccine used intravesically
- Used in treatment of carcinoma in situ and high-grade (non-invasive) tumours
- May be used long term as 'maintenance therapy'

Monoclonal antibodies

The first two monoclonal antibodies in clinical use are rituximab and trastuzumab:

- **Rituximab** (MabThera) is a monoclonal antibody that causes lysis of B lymphocytes and is licensed for treatment of relapsed or advanced low-grade lymphoma, and as 'maintenance' therapy in the disease
- **Trastuzumab** (Herceptin) is now licensed for use as an adjuvant therapy for breast cancer in high-risk tumours that over-express human epidermal growth factor receptor -2 (HER-2). Around 16–18% are likely to be strongly HER-2-positive.

Infusion-related side effects are common with both (chills, fever, hypersensitivity reactions) and both can exacerbate chemotherapy-related cardiotoxicity.

Bevacizumab (Avastin) binds to VEGF and works as an anti-angiogenic agent. It is used in advanced CRCs.

Cryotherapy and radiofrequency ablation

Probe inserted into tumour either percutaneously under radiological control or intraoperatively.

- Freezing temperature causes 'ice ball'
- Mainly used in palliation
- Increasing use in primary treatment for liver tumours

Experimental therapies

Gene therapy

There are ongoing trials of gene therapy with glioblastoma.

Anti-angiogenic agents

Most of the endothelial cells in an adult are quiescent during health. Therapies targeting the process of angiogenesis are therefore directed specifically at tumour growth.

Current options include:

1. Targeting endogenous pro-angiogenic factors, such as:
    - Anti-VEGF antibodies (trials of adjuvant use of anti-VEGF agents in colorectal cancer are ongoing in the USA)
    - Anti-angiogenic pharmacology (eg cyclo-oxygenase [COX]-2 inhibitors)
2. Administering endogenous anti-angiogenic compounds or molecules, eg angiostatin, endostatin

SECTION 6
Palliative care and care of the dying

Learning point

Palliation is the care of patients who are not responsive to curative treatment and have a terminal condition.

Palliative care (from the Latin *palliare*, to cloak) aims to address physical, mental and spiritual needs, and achieve the highest quality of life possible (with the emphasis on quality rather than quantity), in a manner that promotes dignity and provides support to both the patient and those close to them.

Patients may be nursed at home, in a hospice or as a hospital inpatient.

6.1 The palliative care team

Although providing support for patients with terminal disease is an important skill for all health professionals, access to a multidisciplinary palliative care team with specialist skills, eg in control of symptoms, is recognised as improving the quality of end-of-life care. The team usually includes palliative care consultants and specialist palliative care nurses, and may include pharmacists, physiotherapists and occupational therapists with a special interest. On an inpatient basis, the team is contacted by the medical or surgical team in charge of a patient with palliative care needs. These may vary from control of symptoms, to psychological support or financial advice. The National Institute for Health and Clinical Excellence (NICE) guidelines advise that 24-hour access to palliative care advice should be available, eg out-of-hours telephone advice may be given by local hospice staff. On an outpatient basis the patient's family may become a key part of the palliative care 'team'; district nurses, community palliative nurses and social workers are also involved in providing palliative care in the community.

6.2 Symptomatic control in palliative care

> ### Common symptoms in palliative care
> - Pain
> - Shortness of breath
> - Fatigue
> - Dry mouth
> - Appetite loss, nausea, vomiting, diarrhoea and cachexia
> - Anxiety, depression and confusion
>
> The Edmonton Symptom Assessment System (ESAS) is one of the scoring systems that can be used to assess these ongoing symptoms. It comprises nine variables, each scored from 1 to 10, and can be completed by the patient or a caregiver and plotted on a graph.

Managing pain

Assessing and managing pain
- Determine the cause by history and examination
- Grade the degree of pain
- Is there a psychological component?
- Use the analgesic ladder
- Specific medications may be useful in particular kinds of pain (see below)
- Teach the family how to give painkillers and oral morphine
- Consider adjuncts to pharmacological pain relief:
  - Emotional support
  - Touch: stroking, rocking, vibration, massage
  - Cognitive methods: distraction, music etc

Analgesics in palliative care
- **By mouth** (where possible)

- **By the clock** (prescribe regularly, as prn, meaning *pro re nata*, Latin for 'as needed', but to help = **p**ain **r**elief **n**egligible!). The next dose of analgesia should be given before the last dose has worn off and there should be an optional extra for breakthrough pain
- **By the analgesic:**
  - Start with simple analgesia (regular paracetamol, ibuprofen)
  - Add in codeine (with a laxative unless the patient has diarrhoea)
  - Substitute an opioid (such as morphine) for codeine and titrate the dose. There is no maximum limit

Parenteral analgesia
- For patients who cannot take things by mouth
- Subcutaneous (SC) administration has been shown to be as effective as intramuscular in terminal care and is less painful
- Diamorphine is the drug of choice:
  - May need antiemetic in pump if not previously on opiate
  - Diamorphine SC dose is equivalent to a quarter to a third of the oral dose of morphine
  - SC infusion preferable to intravenous (IV) infusion
- Less potentiation
- Easier management
- Can discharge to home/hospice with SC pump

Potential problems with pumps
- Miscalculations of rate and delivery when setting pump
- Mechanical failure of pump
- Reaction at injection site (IV/SC)

CHAPTER 5

Managing other symptoms

Managing symptoms in palliative care

Pain

Colic	Loperamide 2–4 mg four times daily
Gastric distension	Domperidone
Muscle spasm	Relaxant (eg diazepam, baclofen)
Nerve pain–compression	Dexamethasone
Nerve irritation	Amitriptyline, carbamazepine, TENS, nerve blocks
Liver pain (capsular stretching)	Dexamethasone

Respiratory

Dyspnoea	Morphine, diazepam, dexamethasone
Excess respiratory secretions	Hyoscine
Cough	Morphine (short-acting better than MST)

GI

Hiccoughs	Antacid, metoclopramide, chlorpromazine
Anorexia	Prednisolone, dexamethasone, Megace
Constipation	Lactulose, co-danthrusate
Nausea and vomiting	Haloperidol (due to morphine)

Skin/mucous membranes

Pruritus	Antihistamine
Dry mouth	Artificial saliva, oral candidiasis treatments

Neurological

Headache	Dexamethasone if raised intracranial pressure
Hypoxia	Oxygen
Confusion/sedation	Consider drugs/hypercalcaemia/brain metastases
Confusion/agitation	Phenytoin, carbamazepine, rectal diazepam
Convulsions	Haloperidol, chlorpromazine

CHAPTER 5

Preventive palliative care

All patients should have:
- Regular oral care
- Bathing as required
- Prevention of bedsores by changes in position
- Prevention of stiffness in joints by regular active or passive mobilisation

Other needs

Both patient and their families may have financial, psychological, social and spiritual concerns.

Many people don't want to die in hospital and every effort should be made for them to be discharged either to a hospice or to their own home.

There are a variety of charities and organisations that can help in the provision either of additional or respite care for patients who are at home or financially.

- **Sue Ryder:** offers specialist palliative and long-term care for people living with cancer, multiple sclerosis, Huntington's disease, Parkinson's disease, motor neurone disease, stroke, brain injury and other life-changing illnesses: www.sueryder.org/pages/care.html
- **Macmillan Cancer Support:** works in a huge number of ways to improve the lives of people affected by cancer. The charity offers a comprehensive range of services including practical and emotional support at home and in cancer care centres: www.macmillan.org.uk/Home.aspx

The Liverpool Care Pathway

The Liverpool Care pathway (LCP) is an integrated care pathway that was designed to use the best of hospice care techniques to improve the quality of care delivered to the dying patient in other settings such as hospitals and care homes.

The advantages of an integrated pathway are:
- Explicit statement of the key elements of care based on evidence and best practice
- Facilitates communication between members of the medical team and with the patient and family
- Coordinates and clarifies care and activities of the members of the medical team
- Standardises documentation into a single generic type for use by all team members
- Enables identification of resources

The recognition and diagnosis of dying are always complex and uncertainty is part of dying. There are always times when a patient who is thought to be dying lives longer than expected or vice versa. Regular assessment, involvement of senior clinical decision-makers and the experience of the palliative care team are essential. The diagnosis of dying should be made by the multidisciplinary team and not an individual. Good communication between team members and the patient and their family is also essential. The LCP is designed neither to hasten nor postpone death, and its use should be discussed with the patient and family if possible.

Key features of using the LCP
- Non-essential medications should be stopped
- Non-essential investigations (eg blood tests) should be stopped
- Oral nutrition is supplied as tolerated
- Fluids and antibiotics may be used but should be prescribed on an individual basis in the patient's best interests
- The LCP document provides guidance on the types and regimens of suitable medications for symptom control
- Records daily status, symptoms and treatments provided
- Records and prompts daily care measures such as mouth care, prevention of bedsores, hygiene

---

The 'Do not resuscitate' order

These decisions should be made by the most senior member of the team and should be discussed with the patient and family. These can be difficult discussions and require excellent communication skills. Survival to discharge rates after inpatient cardiac arrest remain low and a 'Do not resuscitate' (DNR) order reflects the likelihood of the patient surviving such an attempt. DNR orders should be recorded on

CHAPTER 5

a standardised form, and all members of the nursing and medical team should be aware of the patient's resuscitation status.

It is vital that everyone caring for the patient understands that **DNR does not mean 'Do not treat'**.

6.3 Oncological emergencies

> **Learning point**
>
> Oncological emergencies include:
> - Neutropenia and sepsis
> - Hypercalcaemia
> - Superior vena cava (SVC) obstruction
> - Spinal cord compression

Neutropenia and sepsis

Neutropenia may result from:
- Pancytopenia due to bone marrow replacement with malignant cells
- Treatment resulting in bone marrow suppression

These patients may be complicated and require aggressive antibiotic management. Discuss with microbiology for advice before initiating therapy.

Hypercalcaemia

Often seen in tumours of the breast, bronchus, prostate, myeloma, kidney and thyroid. May be due to bone metastases or ectopic parathyroid hormone (PTH) secretion.

Presentation of hypercalcaemia in neoplasia

Clinically – 'bones, moans, stones and groans':
- Malaise
- Nausea and vomiting
- Constipation
- Abdominal pain
- Polyuria/polydipsia
- Bone pain
- Renal stones
- Psychosis

Management of hypercalcaemia in neoplasia

- May resolve with treatment of the primary malignancy
- Optimise fluid balance
- Stop thiazide diuretics
- May use oral phosphates, calcitonin or non-steroidal anti-inflammatory drugs (NSAIDs)

SVC obstruction

Typically occurs with lung carcinoma or lymphoma.

Presentation of SVC obstruction in neoplasia

- Plethoric congested facies
- Obstructed dilated neck veins (if the patient elevates the arms then the veins on the affected side do not empty)
- Dizziness on bending forwards
- Dyspnoea and pulmonary oedema
- Headache
- Risk of venous thrombosis (stagnation of blood)

CHAPTER 5

Management of SVC obstruction in neoplasia

- Diagnosis of underlying cause
- Local radiotherapy
- Dexamethasome 4 mg every 6 hours may help

Spinal cord compression

Distribution of malignant spinal cord compression is 70% thoracic, 20% lumbosacral and 10% cervical. For further discussion see Chapter 9, Orthopaedic Surgery.

Presentation of spinal cord compression in neoplasia

- Back pain (worse on straining or coughing)
- Leg weakness
- Upper motor neurone and sensory signs
- Urinary retention

Management of spinal cord compression in neoplasia

- Emergency MRI for diagnosis
- Discuss with neuro-orthopaedics
- Radiotherapy to vertebrae may be helpful
- May require surgery if histological diagnosis unclear or the spine is mechanically unstable
- High-dose steroids may be helpful

6.4 The psychological effects of surgery

Postoperative confusion

Acute confusional states are common after surgery, although reports of incidence vary.

Learning point

The psychological effects of surgery should be considered in all patients. All require a degree of counselling and rehabilitation. Psychological problems after surgery include:
- Confusion
- Depression
- The effects of chronic pain
- Long postoperative recovery

Risk factors for postop confusion

- Male > female
- Elderly > young
- Alcohol abuse
- Preoperative dementia or cognitive impairment
- Electrolyte imbalance

Exacerbating factors for postop confusion

- Hypotension and poor cerebral perfusion
- Sepsis
- Hypoxia
- Electrolyte imbalances
- Drug effects, interactions and withdrawal
- Pain and anxiety
- Cerebral events (eg cerebrovascular accident [CVA] or transient ischaemic attack [TIA])

Management of postop confusion

- Assess and correct underlying causes if possible
- Be careful with prescription of sedatives in elderly people; small doses of medication can be given pre-emptively rather than large doses in the middle of the night
- See section on management of delirium tremens

Postoperative depression

This affects 4.5% of surgical patients. Preoperative psychiatric illness, people with complications of surgery and long-stay patients are at high risk of developing depression. Certain procedures are more strongly associated with its development:

- Cancer surgery
- Cardiothoracic surgery
- Transplantation
- Breast surgery

Clinical features include low mood, tearfulness, insomnia, apathy and anorexia. Management should be together with psychiatric referral and includes supportive measures and medication.

Chronic pain may contribute to depression.

Long-stay patients also have high levels of depression. Factors affecting the long-stay patient also include:

- Immobility (eg complications, bed sores, deep venous thrombosis [DVT])
- Colonisation (eg meticillin-resistant *Staphylococcus aureus* [MRSA])
- Institutionalisation

Response to surgery and disease

Factors influencing the response to surgery and disease are:

- Preoperative emotional state
- Accuracy of expectations

- Ability to choose and feelings of control over the outcome
- Personality traits (eg type A personality is associated with catecholamine release; optimists have better outcomes than pessimists)
- Coping and relaxation strategies
- Social support

Additional sources of psychological support

- Nurses
- Social services (eg ward-based social workers)
- Physiotherapists (encouragement and aims)
- Counsellors and psychotherapists
- Chronic pain team
- Drugs (eg antidepressants)

The effects of critical care

There are physical and psychological effects of a period spent in critical care.

Physical complications of critical care

- Reduced function due to disease process or pathology
- Muscle wasting and weakness
- Joint stiffness
- Nerve injuries or peripheral neuropathy
- Pressure sores
- Sleep disturbance and loss of diurnal rhythm
- Tracheal stenosis

Psychological impact of critical care

Do not underestimate the psychological impact of critical care. After recovery patients feel that they have lost a portion of their memory or their memory may be hazy and disjointed. They may

CHAPTER 5

401

recall pieces of conversation held around their bedside and have memories during periods of drifting in and out of consciousness. They often feel a loss of control. They may experience anxiety, depression and nightmares.

Some ITUs run a post-discharge clinic where patients can attend to talk about their experiences. Patient feedback may help the ITU to minimise the impact by altering practice.

6.5 Communication skills in surgery

Communication skills in surgery are covered in depth in the MRCS Part B OSCEs book of the *Essential Revision Notes* series and are not discussed further here.

6.6 Breaking bad news

This is discussed in more detail in MRCS Part B OSCEs book of the *Essential Revision Notes* series.

Compassion and honesty are required.

Breaking bad news should **not** be done on the ward round in front of large groups of people, and remember that the curtains around the bed are **not** soundproof.

If possible take the patient to an office or private space or return at the end of the round in order to speak to the patient personally. Many patients already expect the worst and you should sound out their expectations. They may not wish to have full knowledge of their diagnosis and prognosis, and you should identify how much they want to be told by giving information in small amounts and assessing their reaction. Patients may need information to be repeated several times in different ways at a later date.

The six steps to breaking bad news

Getting started
- **Get the physical context right.** In person, not by phone or letter
- **Where?** In a private room. Curtains drawn around the bed. Both sitting down
- **Who should be there?** A relative, friend or nurse, as the patient wishes
- **Starting off.** Normal courtesies apply: say hello, use the patient's name, introduce yourself. Start with a general question to get a two-way conversation going, assess the patient's mental state and make the patient feel that you care: How are you today? Are you up to having a chat for a few minutes?

Find out how much the patient knows
- How much has the patient been told? How much has he or she understood?
- What is the style of the patient's statements? This will guide you to the level at which you have to pitch your information. Does he or she talk in simple terms? Or is he or she very well educated with good medical knowledge and a wide vocabulary?
- What is the emotional content of the patient's statements? Distressed, anxious, brave, off-hand and defensive, hostile or in denial?

Find out how much the patient wants to know
You could ask the patient:
- Would you like me to give you the full details of the diagnosis?
- Are you the type of person who wants to know all the details of what's wrong, or would you prefer if I just tell you what's going to happen next?

CHAPTER 5

- If your condition is serious, how much would you like to know about it?
- That's fine. If you change your mind or want any questions answered at future visits, just ask me at any time. I won't push information at you if you don't want it

Share information

- **Decide on your agenda** (diagnosis, treatment plan, prognosis, support)
- **Start from the patient's starting point** (aligning)
  - Repeat to patients what they have said to you and reinforce those things that they have said that are correct. This shows them that you take their point of view seriously and respect them
  - Give them the information that you need to, clearly, to educate them
  - Give information in small chunks with warning shots: Well, the situation does appear to be more serious than that
  - Do not use jargon: say tumour AND THEN cancer, not space-occupying lesion or malignancy
  - Check how they receive this and clarify: Am I making sense? Do you follow what I'm saying?
  - Make sure that you both mean the same thing: Do you understand what I mean when I say it's incurable?
  - Repeat the important points
  - Use diagrams and written messages
  - Use any printed or recorded information available
  - Check your level: Is it too complicated or too patronising?
  - Listen for the patient's agenda: Is there anything that you particularly want to talk through or are worried about?
  - Try to blend your agenda with the patient's agenda

- Be prepared for a 'last minute' query, a hidden question or the patient trying to 'lead' the interview

Respond to the patient's feelings

- Identify and acknowledge the patient's reaction
- Allow silence if needed
- Denial is perfectly natural and should be challenged only if causing serious problems for the patient
- Anger and blame need to be acknowledged; exploring the causes can follow later
- Despair and depression must be acknowledged. Allow the patient to express his or her feelings and offer support
- Awkward questions such as 'How long have I got?' may have no honest answer and you may have to reply with an open question, an empathic response or silence in some situations
- Collusion, where relatives ask the doctor not to tell the patient, is a common request. It must be made clear that the duty of the doctor lies first to the patient, but the reasons for collusion need to be explored

Planning and follow-up

Planning for the future is a good way to alleviate the bewildered, dispirited, disorganised thoughts of a patient who has just received bad news.

- Demonstrate an understanding of the patient's problem list
- Identify problems that are 'fixable' and those that are not
- Make a plan: put 'fixable' problems in order of priority and explain what you are going to do about each one
- Prepare the patient for the worst and give them some hope for the best
- Identify coping strategies for the patient and reinforce them
- Identify other sources of support for the

CHAPTER 5

patient and incorporate them
- Make a contract and follow it through
- Summarise the plan that you have formulated
- Check that there are no outstanding issues
- Outline what will happen next and what the patient is expected to do
- Make sure that you leave an avenue open for further communication (eg follow-up appointment with doctor or associated medical professional, such as a breast-care nurse)

Grief

Be aware of the normal stages of grief as shown in the box.

Response to bad news or grief
- Denial
- Anger
- Bargaining
- Depression
- Acceptance

These responses to bad news may not occur in a predefined order and there is no predictive timeline for how long these feelings will last. The intensity of the reaction may depend on the intensity of the feeling of loss on hearing the bad news.

6.7 Dealing with death

Withdrawal of treatment

Over the duration of admission to the ITU and after a period of stabilisation and treatment it may become apparent that the patient will not recover.

Decisions may be taken that active treatment may be withdrawn, reduced or not increased. Withdrawal of supportive treatment such as

inotropes, ventilatory support or renal replacement therapy may be considered. Most units also have an upper threshold for certain types of treatment (eg inotrope doses) that represents what they consider to be maximal support.

In cases where there is a consensus from the medical and nursing staff that continued treatment would be futile, there is no medicolegal requirement to continue with treatment. This should be discussed in depth between the relevant family members and members of the medical and nursing teams caring for the patient.

Deaths that should be reported to the coroner

Report to the coroner all deaths occurring:
- Within 24 hours of admission
- Related to surgery or anaesthesia
- In theatre
- Due to accidents and trauma (report all cases of fractured neck of femur)
- Due to self- or external neglect
- Due to poisoning or drugs
- Due to industrial or notifiable diseases

If in doubt, discuss the case informally with the coroner's office. They are an invaluable source of help and advice. You will need to tell them all the patient's details, the dates of admission and death, and give an outline summary of the case with suggested causes for completion of the death certificate.

It is very important that death certificates are filled in correctly because a great deal of epidemiological information is garnered from them and this has effects as far-reaching as funding for service provision.

CHAPTER 6

Trauma
Part 1: Head, Abdomen and Trunk

George Hondag Tse

Head injury: Paul Brennan
Burns: Stuart W Waterston

SECTION 1

Overview of trauma

1.1 Historical perspective

Trauma care and surgery have been inextricably entwined since the beginnings of society. Battlefield surgeons such as Ambrose Paré (1510–1590) used empirical observation, common sense and 'hands-on' personal experience to improve the treatment of battle wounds during the Napoleonic Wars. The plastic surgeon Archibald Hector McIndoe (1900–1960) improved the treatment of burns in RAF pilots during World War II. He noted that those who ditched in the sea had less scarring and infection of their burn sites, leading to the use of saline soaks instead of tannins. Both men found that conventional practice was inadequate and sought to improve care and techniques for the sake of their patients and for the common good.

In 1976 an orthopaedic surgeon crashed his light aircraft in Nebraska, resulting in the death of his wife and injuring his children. The emergency care that he and his family received was inadequate and this became the impetus for the development of the Advanced Trauma Life Support (ATLS) training course.

The Royal College of Surgeons of England was one of the first bodies outside the USA to implement ATLS training (in November 1988).

This system has provided a framework and approach to acute trauma care so that trauma team personnel can communicate and prioritise in a similar way, allowing parallel or simultaneous treatment in the multiple injury patient, by a coordinated team approach. This has increased the speed with which injuries are identified and treated, making the most use of the 'golden hour', in order to improve survival and patient outcome.

1.2 The trimodal distribution of death

> **Learning point**
>
> Mortality from trauma can be considered in three phases – immediate, early and late (Figure 6.1). Of deaths caused by trauma 50% occur in the first 10 min after the accident.

- **Immediate-phase death:** these deaths are almost always unpreventable. They include massive brain injuries, or great vessel injuries (eg aortic avulsion associated with

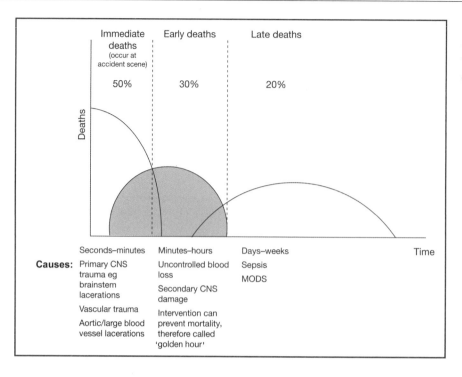

Figure 6.1 Mortality from trauma – trimodal distribution

a fall from a height), airway occlusion, cord transection and exsanguination

- **Early-phase death:** occurs within the first few minutes to hours when the opportunity for prompt and appropriate diagnosis and intervention can prevent loss of life or limb (the so-called 'golden hour'). The ATLS system mainly addresses this phase of care, and emphasises the need for rapid assessment and resuscitation
- **Late-phase death:** occurs days to weeks after the injury, during which time deaths can occur due to sepsis and multiple organ system failure, or complications arising as a consequence of the initial injury or surgery. The quality of care in phases 1 and 2 will obviously have an impact on mortality in phase 3, and on overall outcome

1.3 Pre-hospital care

Learning point

The primary role of pre-hospital care is to:
- Temporarily stabilise the patient
- Expedite transport of the severely injured patient to the site of definitive treatment

Pre-hospital treatment is driven by rapid assessment and the principles of ATLS.

Pre-hospital care in the UK is delivered in a variety of ways depending on illness or injury severity. These include:
- **NHS Direct:** this scheme provides information via the telephone or internet from senior nurses on minor illness or

injury, with the emphasis on self-care. Patients may be diverted to primary care or the ambulance service if necessary

- **Minor injury units:** care is delivered by emergency nurse practitioners and these centres have links with local accident and emergency departments (A&E) and radiology services
- **Primary care:** general practitioners may manage minor injury
- **Road ambulance service:** the emergency ambulance service is usually mobilised by telephone (999) from either the patient or a witness at the scene. Vehicle tracking is used to mobilise the nearest resource, and clinical information is relayed to the ambulance team. Calls are prioritised according to clinical need (A for life-threatening, B for serious but not life-threatening and C for neither serious nor life-threatening) by computer software used in the ambulance control room. Road ambulances are usually staffed by a paramedic and a technician, and an ambulance officer or manager may also be sent to manage the scene of complex incidents. Clinical care at the scene is delivered in accordance with national clinical protocols. Clinical information is relayed by ambulance staff at the scene to the proposed A&E to allow advance preparation of facilities and staff to receive the patient (eg preparation of the resus room and trauma call). Patients are usually delivered to the nearest A&E but some may subsequently require secondary transfer to a tertiary referral centre for definitive care
- **Air ambulance:** air ambulances are primarily staffed by suitably trained paramedics and technicians, but in some regions these teams also include trained senior doctors and nurses (eg the Helicopter Emergency Medical Service [HEMS] in London)

- **Mobile medical teams (MMTs):** these teams consist of trained medical personnel, often from the A&E of the nearest hospital, or doctors trained by organisations such as the British Association for Immediate Care (BASICS). They may be mobilised to entrapments or major incidents. Extrication requires close coordination between medical and fire services

The techniques of pre-hospital care vary from country to country. In the USA, pre-hospital care personnel are taught to 'scoop and run', with the aim of delivering the patient to the place of definitive care as quickly as possible. This may involve bypass of the local facilities and targeting of tertiary facilities (eg delivery of cardiothoracic injuries direct to a cardiothoracic unit). In France, pre-hospital care involves the mobilisation of intensive therapy units (ITUs) to the scene with more emphasis on stabilising the patient before transfer.

The value of information obtained from the emergency agencies in the field cannot be underestimated. Detailed and early information allows mobilisation of the trauma team, including laboratory services, porters and the radiology department. Advance knowledge of the number of casualties and the type and extent of injuries allows for preparation of the appropriate equipment (such as chest drains, thoracotomy sets and O-negative blood), so that they are available as soon as the patient arrives. Ideally, continual updates should be provided by the emergency services so that the receiving team is appropriately prepared.

Principles of immediate care

The principles of immediate care have been outlined by the American College of Surgeons' Committee on Trauma (ACS-COT) in a format similar to ATLS.

CHAPTER 6

- **Assess potential safety issues** at the scene and take steps to make it as safe as possible
- **Quickly assess the patient:** observe vital signs and level of consciousness, determine the nature of accident and probable mechanism of injuries

---

Indications of potential significant trauma

- **Penetrating injury** to thorax, abdomen or head
- **Major bony injury:** two or more proximal long-bone fractures, pelvic fracture, traumatic amputation proximal to wrist or ankle
- **Burns** involving more than 15% of the body surface area or to face and potentially to airway
- **Evidence of high-energy impact:**
  - Fall from a height (>6 metres)
  - Pedestrian in a road traffic accident (RTA) (hit at more than 20 mph or thrown by impact)
  - Car occupant in an RTA (unrestrained; speed >20 mph, intrusion into passenger compartment of >30 cm, ejection of passenger from vehicle, roll-over of vehicle, death of another car occupant, extrication time >20 minutes)

Pre-hospital resuscitation follows ATLS principles:

- **C-spine immobilisation:** in-line immobilisation with a hard collar, sandbags and tape
- **Airway management:** can be difficult. Can often be maintained with basic measures. Intubation without anaesthesia and rapid-sequence induction is ill-advised because it can induce vomiting and raise intracranial pressure
- **Breathing:** give oxygen
- **Circulation:** haemorrhage should be controlled with direct pressure; ensure good venous access before releasing from vehicle. Fluid resuscitation should be given to a systolic blood pressure of 90 mmHg
- **Disability:** fractured limbs should be splinted and the patient prepared for transport
- **Analgesia:** can be achieved with ketamine or Entonox (contraindicated if possibility of pneumothorax or basal skull fracture)

Initial hospital care

Most Emergency Departments in the UK that deal with trauma cases have a designated area for receiving trauma cases. This is obviously essential for rapid access to specialist equipment and services.

ESSENTIAL RESOURCES FOR TRAUMA MANAGEMENT

Airway management	Circulatory support	Infrastructure
Laryngoscope	Large-bore cannulas	Rapid communication links
Endotracheal (ET) tubes	Warmed crystalloid solutions	Laboratory support
Fully stocked anaesthetic trolley	O-negative blood	Radiology – immediate access
Suction	Giving sets	Designated trauma team of medical personnel
Oxygen	Blood sampling equipment	

1.4 Triage and major incidents

Triage

> **Learning point**
>
> **'Triage is the sorting of patients based on the need for treatment and the available resources to provide that treatment'** (definition from the ATLS manual).
>
> Triage is a system for dealing with a large number of casualties. The aim is to offer the most medical treatment to the largest number of patients, resulting in the best possible outcome.
>
> To be of use triage needs to be **quick**, **efficient** and **reproducible**. It should involve continual reassessment of patients by appropriate medical staff, with regular readjustment of patient priorities.

There are usually two types of triage.

When there is sufficient treatment capacity to deal with multiple casualties, patients with life-threatening and multisystem injuries are treated first. Essentially this sort of triage occurs in the Emergency Department all the time – as patients present to the department they are rapidly assessed and prioritised by a member of the nursing team. The categories are based on order of priority (eg accidents prioritised 1 to 5; medical emergencies prioritised 1 to 5). All patients in category 1 are seen first, followed by those in category 2, and so on.

When there is insufficient treatment capacity to deal with multiple casualties, patients with the greatest chance of survival are treated first. This form of triage was originally invented by the military to deal with multiple battlefield casualties. Triage in this situation is usually performed by personnel who assess casualties without giving treatment, often by categorising them into life-threatening or limb-threatening, urgent, serious and minor groups.

Major incidents

All hospitals have a major incident plan (MAJAX) that details management within each department should a major incident occur, such as management in A&E and creating bed space in the ITU. In general, all available personnel are asked to congregate in the A&E where they will be assigned tasks by the coordinator.

1.5 Trauma severity scoring

> **Learning point**
>
> **Trauma scoring systems may be used for:**
> - Communication about the status of individual patients
> - Monitoring improvement or deterioration in an individual
> - Prognostic information about an individual
> - Triage of multiple casualties
>
> **They include the:**
> - Injury severity score (ISS)
> - Revised trauma score (RTS)
> - Trauma score–injury severity score (TRISS)

CHAPTER 6

Injury severity score (ISS)

- Anatomical description
- Score of 0–6 is given to each body region depending on severity of injury; the three highest scores are squared and added together to produce the ISS score
- Disadvantage: the score is static (needs absolute diagnosis before score can be calculated)
- Subjective

Revised trauma score (RTS)

- Physiological description
- Score calculated using the Glasgow Coma Scale (GCS), respiratory rate and systolic BP
- Flexible (varies with patient's progress)
- Objective (little interobserver variability)

Trauma score–injury severity score (TRISS)

- Combined ISS and RTS scoring
- Also includes age of patient and mechanism of injury (ie penetrating or blunt)
- Indicator of patient prognosis

SECTION 2
Injury and shock

2.1 The biomechanics of injury

In all cases injury results from a transfer of energy to the tissues. This energy travels as a shock wave which travels at different speeds through air, fluid and tissues of different densities. Maximal disruption occurs at a site of interface between these media due to differential compression and re-expansion. Objects travelling at speed (eg bullets) cause cavitation of tissues as the tissue particles absorb energy and move away from the site of impact.

Blunt trauma

RTAs are the most common cause of blunt trauma and are usually associated with simultaneous head and neck (50%), chest (20%), or abdominal and pelvic trauma (25%).

A careful history of the mechanism of injury, combined impact speed, whether a seat belt was worn or an airbag inflated, whether pedestrian or motorcyclist, will enable the trauma surgeon to develop an idea of which areas of the body and underlying organs are at risk. Investigations are useful but should not delay an essential laparotomy, which is necessary in about 10% of blunt trauma patients.

The physical examination should include:
- **Inspection:** bruising, seat-belt marks and distension may all denote underlying injury
- **Palpation:** signs of peritonism due to blood, urine or faeces in the peritoneal cavity
- **Percussion:** a crude indicator of the presence of free fluid
- **Auscultation:** essential in evaluating the chest

CHAPTER 6

Penetrating injury

Can be due to blades, glass or metal fragments, shrapnel, bullets, and so may be associated with other mechanisms of trauma.

- May be solitary or multiple injuries
- Cause damage only in the direct area (eg stabbing) or in a cone related to explosive force and speed of travel (eg high-velocity vs low-velocity bullets)
- The process of cavitation associated with high-velocity missiles sucks dirt, clothing and skin into the wound, increasing the risk of secondary infection

Blast injury

A blast injury is due to an explosion (eg gas, chemical, bomb) and so has multiple mechanisms of injury:

- **Pressure wave:** travels faster than the speed of sound and can cause rupture of air-filled structures, eg tympanic membrane, lungs ('blast-lung syndrome'), bowel
- **Penetrating injury** from shrapnel
- **Falls** (the body may be thrown by the blast wind)
- **Crush injuries** from disruption of the environment, eg falling masonry
- **Burns**, eg thermal, chemical

Deceleration injury

Occurs on impact in vehicular accidents and falls from a height. Relatively mobile structures avulse from the site at which they are anchored:

- Cervical spine
- Brain
- Main bronchus
- Thoracic aorta
- Renal vessels
- Transverse mesocolon

Crush injury

Initial injury plus sustained compression of the tissues causes ischaemia and muscle necrosis.

Crush syndrome may be a feature of any severe injury, which results in ischaemia of large amounts of soft tissue. Results in fluid loss, disseminated intravascular coagulation (DIC), and release of myoglobin from muscle (rhabdomyolysis) and toxins from damaged tissue. Can clog the renal tubules causing acute tubular necrosis (ATN) and renal failure requiring dialysis. Treat with large volumes of fluid, watch urine output and plasma K^+.

Burn injury

Burn injury requires specialist management and is therefore discussed separately in Section 5.

Hypothermia

Hypothermia may be accidental (usually due to environmental exposure) or intentional (eg cardiac bypass).

It is associated with the use of alcohol, illicit drugs, overdoses, psychiatric conditions and major trauma. Symptoms:

- **Mild hypothermia (32–35°C):** lethargy, confusion, amnesia, shivering, loss of coordination and fine motor skills, dysarthria
- **Moderate hypothermia (28–32°C):** delirium, stupor, slowed reflexes, bradycardia
- **Severe hypothermia (<28°C):** coma, dilated pupils, dyspnoea, arrhythmia or cardiac arrest

The management of hypothermia occurs in two stages: initial pre-hospital care and definitive hospital management by rewarming.

On scene: reduce further heat loss from evaporation, radiation, conduction or convection. Remove wet clothing and replace it with dry blankets or sleeping bags. Move the patient to a sheltered environment. Rewarm with heat packs or skin-to-skin contact.

Definitive management: this is by rewarming. It may be undertaken slowly or rapidly. There is some evidence that, in severe hypothermia, rapid rewarming provides the best prognosis. Options for rewarming include:

- Warmed blankets and heat lamps
- Heated intravenous (IV fluids) such as saline (fluid temperatures up to 65°C have been used)
- Heated humidified oxygen
- Warmed gastric, thoracic or peritoneal lavage
- Cardiopulmonary bypass (CPB)
- Warm water immersion (Hubbard technique)

Management of arrhythmia or cardiac arrest: defibrillation is ineffective at hypothermic core temperatures. Use IV bretylium (if available) followed by extended cardiopulmonary resuscitation (CPR) until active rewarming begins and successful defibrillation is more likely. Death cannot be declared until the patient is warm.

Hyperthermia

Hyperthermia occurs when the body loses its ability to respond to heat. Inability to respond to heat manifests as a spectrum of illnesses from heat rash, to heat exhaustion and heat stroke. The normal body response to heat is discussed in Chapter 3.

Heat exhaustion is an acute heat injury with hyperthermia caused by dehydration. It occurs when the body can no longer dissipate heat adequately because of extreme environmental conditions or increased endogenous heat production. It may progress to heat stroke when the body's thermoregulatory mechanisms become overwhelmed and fail.

Heat stroke is extreme hyperthermia with thermoregulatory failure. The condition is characterised by serious end-organ damage with universal involvement of the central nervous system (CNS). Heat stroke is defined as pyrexia (>41°C) associated with anhidrosis and neurological dysfunction. However, these criteria are not absolute. Heat stroke occurs in two forms:

- **Exertional heat stroke:** usually in young fit individuals undertaking strenuous activity in a hot environment for a prolonged period of time. Anhidrosis is not always a factor. Associated with abdominal and muscular cramping, nausea, vomiting, diarrhoea, headache, dizziness, dyspnoea and weakness. Risk factors include preceding viral infection, dehydration, fatigue, obesity, lack of sleep, poor physical fitness and exercise at altitude
- **Non-exertional heat stroke:** an impaired response to temperature seen in elderly, chronically ill and very young individuals. Associated with confusion, delirium, hallucinations, seizures and coma

Barotrauma

Barotrauma refers to injuries caused by pressure changes. These may be due to explosions or diving injuries and have been reported after deployment of airbags during RTAs. Barotrauma affects regions of the body that contain air, such as the middle ear and the lungs, perhaps leading to rupture of the eardrum or a pneumothorax. Barotrauma sustained from an explosion may be complicated by other mechanisms of trauma, eg penetrating or crush injuries, burns and smoke inhalation.

CHAPTER 6

2.2 The physiology of shock

Hypovolaemic shock

Pathophysiology of hypovolaemic shock

In hypovolaemic shock the reduction in blood flow leads to decreased tissue perfusion, causing hypoxia and lactic acidosis, both of which lead to further circulatory collapse, and the result may be the multiorgan dysfunction syndrome (MODS). Haemorrhage is the acute loss of circulating blood volume and is the cause of hypovolaemic shock in trauma patients.

This model of hypovolaemic shock hinges on the fact that acidosis leads to actual cellular destruction, which is caused by dysfunction of the cell membrane's Na^+/K^+ pump in the acidotic environment. Normally, intracellular Na^+ is exchanged for extracellular K^+. When this system fails Na^+ accumulates intracellularly, taking water with it, and causing the cell to swell. The intercellular spaces enlarge as the cells pull away from each other, allowing fluid to escape into the interstitium and disrupting the integrity of the individual organs.

In situations where there is inadequate cardiac output despite fluid replacement, inotropes (such as dopamine, dobutamine or adrenaline) may be considered.

Learning point

Shock occurs when tissue perfusion is insufficient to meet metabolic requirements and leads to disordered physiology. Shock is characterised by hypotension.

Types of shock

- Hypovolaemic
- Neurogenic
- Cardiogenic
- Septic
- Anaphylactic

In trauma cases, hypotension is always assumed to be hypovolaemia due to haemorrhage until proved otherwise. This leads to a typical picture of a patient who is cold, pale, clammy, anxious or confused, and peripherally 'shut down'.

Monitored variables in types of shock

	(HR)	CVP/ PAOP	CO	SV	SVR
Hypovolaemic	↑	↓	↓	↓	↑
Cardiogenic	↑	↑	↓	↓	↑
Septic	↑	↓	↑	↓	↓
Tamponade	↑	↑↑	↓	↓	↑
Neurogenic	↓	–	↓	–	↓

CO, cardiac output; CVP, central venous pressure; HR, heart rate; PAOP, pulmonary artery occlusion pressure; SV, stroke volume; SVR, systemic vascular resistance.

Remember

- CO = SV × HR (normal value is 6 l/min)
- SBP = DBP + PP

CO is cardiac output, SV stroke volume, HR heart rate, SBP systolic blood pressure, DBP diastolic blood pressure, PP pulse pressure and PVR peripheral vascular resistance.

This demonstrates that PP, a major determinant of SBP, is governed in part by the PVR, which will be raised due to peripheral vasoconstriction after hypovolaemic insult. Therefore the SBP will appear normal in a situation where the CO may be much reduced. This is especially true in the young fit patient who is compensating for the blood loss.

PHYSIOLOGICAL RESPONSES TO HYPOVOLAEMIA

	Class I	Class II	Class III	Class IV
Volume loss (ml)	0–750	750–1500	1500–2000	>2000
Loss (%)	0–15	15–30	30–40	>40
Pulse (beats/min)	<100	>100	>120	>140
Blood pressure	Unchanged	Unchanged	Decreased	Decreased
Pulse pressure	Unchanged	Decreased	Decreased	Decreased
Urine output (ml/h)	>30	20–30	5–15	Anuric
Respiratory rate (breaths/min)	14–20	20–30	30–40	>40
Mental state	Restless	Anxious	Anxious/confused	Confused/lethargic
Fluid replacement	Crystalloid	Colloid and crystalloid	Colloid and blood	Colloid and blood

These values refer to the 'average' 70-kg man with a blood volume of 5 litres. Values are irrespective of body fat proportions. Calculate fluid replacement in an obese patient to be the same as the predicted weight, to avoid overfilling.

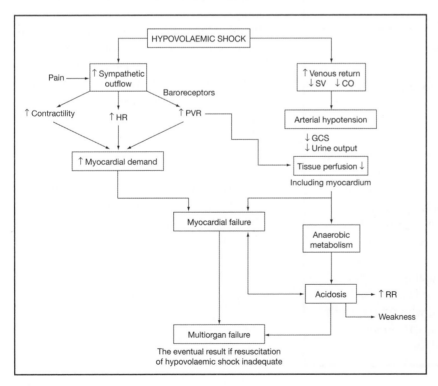

Figure 6.2 Pathophysiology of hypovolaemic shock

The principles of immediate management of hypovolaemic shock are to stop the bleeding and to replace the volume lost.

1. Control any obvious haemorrhage
- Direct pressure
- Elevation of injured limb
- Head-down tilt

2. Establish IV access
Two 16-gauge cannulas, or if this is not possible:
- Forearm antecubital veins
- Cut-down to great saphenous vein
- Intraosseous access in children (<6 years) if initial IV access fails

Central access only after the patient is more stable; this is useful as a guide to fluid replacement after the initial resuscitation but is not an effective route for resuscitation.

3. Follow ATLS guidelines for fluid replacement and identification of cause of hypovolaemia (see Sections 3 and 4 of this chapter)

Remember

CVP may be falsely raised in tension pneumothorax, pericardial effusion, air embolus, pericardial effusion or myocardial infarction (MI).

Physiological responses may be distorted by β blockers, coronary heart disease, pacemakers, age, opiates, anatomical location of injury, pre-hospital fluid replacement, pneumatic anti-shock garment, spinal injury or head injury.

Transient responders are patients who initially respond favourably to a bolus of fluid with a trend toward normalisation of their physiology but who subsequently deteriorate again. This is an important sign of ongoing blood loss.

Fluid replacement in hypovolaemic shock

Crystalloid vs colloid

There is a great deal of debate about the use of crystalloid or colloid in the initial resuscitation of the patient with hypovolaemic shock. Traditionally in the UK colloid has been used, whereas in the USA crystalloid is preferred. The following advice is taken from the ATLS guidelines. Use an initial bolus of 1–2 litres of Ringer's lactate (equivalent to Hartmann's solution). Titrate fluid resuscitation thereafter to response following the initial bolus.

- **Physiological (0.9%) saline:** 25% remains in the intravascular compartment. Excess may lead to hyperchloraemic acidosis and sodium overload
- **Haemaccel, Gelofusine and Volplex** exert greater oncotic pressure than isotonic crystalloid solutions, so fluid tends to remain in the intravascular compartment for longer
- **Blood:** if the patient has obviously lost large volumes of blood then blood replacement is indicated, even if the Hb measurement is normal. There is a delay in the fall of serum Hb in acute haemorrhage because it takes time for fluid shifts to occur. Cross-matched blood is rarely available immediately

The patient's response to fluid resuscitation is indicated by improvement of the following signs and evidence of organ perfusion:
- Pulse (Figure 6.3)
- Blood pressure
- Skin colour
- CNS state

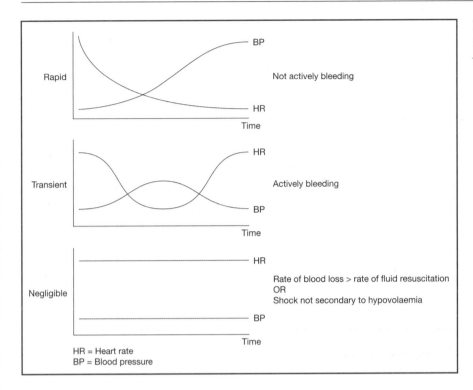

Figure 6.3
Response to initial fluid resuscitation

BP

Rapid

Not actively bleeding

HR

Time

HR

Transient

Actively bleeding

BP

Time

HR

Negligible

Rate of blood loss > rate of fluid resuscitation
OR
Shock not secondary to hypovolaemia

BP

Time

HR = Heart rate
BP = Blood pressure

Urine output in hypovolaemic shock

This is a sensitive and quantitative indication of progress of resuscitation and reflects end-organ perfusion. A normal urine output reflects that resuscitation has been sufficient to reach the renal autoregulatory threshold, and achieve normal renal blood flow. A urinary catheter can be placed quickly and safely in the trauma patient, in the absence of a urethral injury.

Expect the following values for urine output:
Adult   0.5 ml/kg per hour
Child   1.0 ml/kg per hour
Infant   2.0 ml/kg per hour

Acid–base balance in hypovolaemic shock

Initial respiratory alkalosis occurs due to increased respiratory rate. Later, metabolic acidosis ensues if there is uncompensated tissue hypoperfusion or insufficient fluid replacement leading to anaerobic metabolism. This will be reflected by a lowered pH, a progressive base deficit and low bicarbonate. Adequate fluid resuscitation, oxygen administration and transfusion to maintain adequate oxygen delivery can correct this process.

Occult haemorrhage

'In the chest, in the belly, or on the road' – possible locations of significant 'hidden haemorrhage' are in the thorax, the abdomen (including the retroperitoneal space) and pelvic fractures. If there are multiple long-bone fractures there may be enough soft-tissue haemorrhage to cause hypotensive shock. In compound fractures expect double the blood loss. This illustrates the importance of adequate pre-hospital information and the clinical history.

CHAPTER 6

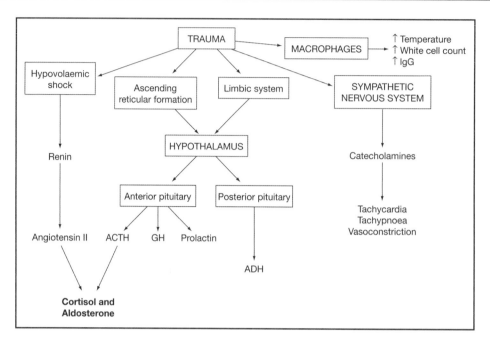

Figure 6.4 The metabolic response to trauma

Pneumatic anti-shock garment (PASG)

For discussion of pelvic fractures see Chapter 9, Orthopaedic Surgery.

Indications

- Splinting pelvic fractures with concomitant haemorrhage and hypotension
- Interim support for a shocked patient with abdominal trauma en route to theatre
- Support for lower-limb fractures

Contraindications

- Pulmonary oedema
- Suspected diaphragmatic rupture
- Haemorrhage above the PASG

Complications

- Compartment syndrome and skin problems associated with prolonged use
- Deflation accompanied by sudden hypotension (therefore deflate gradually and resuscitate accordingly)

Neurogenic shock

Injury to the descending sympathetic pathways can lead to loss of vasomotor tone with pooling in capacitance vessels and failure to generate a tachycardic response. This results in profound hypotension, which in the trauma setting may mistakenly be attributed to hypovolaemia. Appropriate treatment requires the selective use of inotropic agents, rather than aggressive and inappropriate volume replacement, which may result in pulmonary oedema. Atropine may be necessary to counteract an associated bradycardia.

CHAPTER 6

Other shock syndromes

Shock syndromes all tend to result in hypotension. Hypotension is due to:

- Loss of volume in hypovolaemic shock
- Loss of vasomotor tone in neurogenic shock
- Impaired cardiac function in cardiogenic shock
- Loss of peripheral vascular tone due to vasodilatation in septic and anaphylactic shock

Cardiogenic shock is discussed in Chapter 3 and sepsis and anaphylaxis are discussed in Chapter 4.

The metabolic response to trauma

Trauma results in activation of the sympathetic nervous system, immune system and CNS. These systems work in concert to minimise the effects of volume loss and maintain the blood pressure (by raising the heart rate) to conserve fluid volume (by activation of the renin–angiotensin axis and secretion of antidiuretic hormone [ADH]) and to tackle infection.

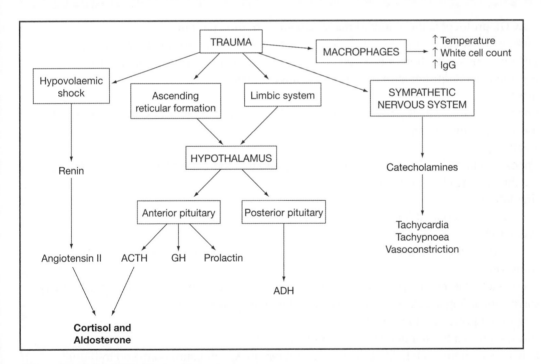

Figure 6.5 The metabolic response to trauma

SECTION 3

Resuscitation: the primary survey

Learning point

The ABCDE protocol is the standard management of trauma patients.
The aim of this system is to save 'life before limb', ie to preserve heart, brain and lung oxygenation and circulation. It is based on the ATLS format and involves continuous reassessment and adjustment in response to changing needs.

A (airway)
- Check that the airway is patent and protect it. Ensure that the cervical spine is protected, especially in the unconscious patient

B (breathing)
- Check that there is adequate bilateral air entry and that there are no clinical signs of life-threatening chest conditions

C (circulation)
- Detect shock and treat if present. Appropriate access is essential

D (disability)
- Briefly assess the neurological status using the 'AVPU' mnemonic (see Section 3.4)

E (exposure)
- Completely undress the patient. Inspect the entire body along guidelines for the secondary survey, including the spine, with a 'log roll'. Keep the patient warm

The important principles to remember are:
- Always assess a trauma patient in this order (ABCDE)
- If there is an immediately life-threatening problem in A, you cannot proceed to B until the airway is secured. If there is an immediately life-threatening problem in B, you cannot proceed to C unless it is dealt with. In a severely injured patient you may never get to E

3.1   Airway and C-spine

Learning point

Assessment of the airway in the primary survey
Is the airway compromised?
- No ventilatory effort
- Cyanosis, stridor, use of accessory muscles
- Patient unable to speak although conscious

If so, it must be made safe immediately by one of the following:
- Clear mouth of foreign bodies or secretions
- Chin lift, jaw thrust
- Establish oral or nasopharyngeal airway with bag-and-mask ventilation
- Definitive airway (intubation) and ventilation
- Surgical airway and ventilation

Is the airway at risk but currently not compromised?
- Decreased GCS score
- Facial trauma
- Burn to face

If so, call for anaesthetic/ENT support and be prepared to provide a definitive airway if needed. Constantly reassess the situation.

Is the airway safe?
- Patient speaking
- Good air movement without stridor

If so, give oxygen and move on to assess breathing.

Control of the C-spine in the primary survey
- In-line survey manual immobilisation (assistant holds patient's head with both hands)

or
- Hard cervical spine collar with sandbag and tape

The C-spine should be controlled by one of the above methods throughout the primary survey until it is safe to fully assess it clinically and, if necessary, radiologically.

Hypoxia is the quickest killer of trauma patients, so maintenance of a patent airway and adequate oxygen delivery are essential. Remember that all trauma patients must be assumed to have a cervical spine injury until proved otherwise.

Recognition of a compromised airway
- Risk factors (eg head injury, drugs, alcohol)
- Clinical signs (eg stridor, cyanosis, accessory muscle use)
- If a patient can speak, his airway is patent

CHAPTER 6

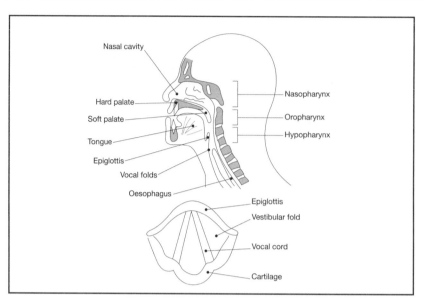

Figure 6.5 Anatomy of the upper airway

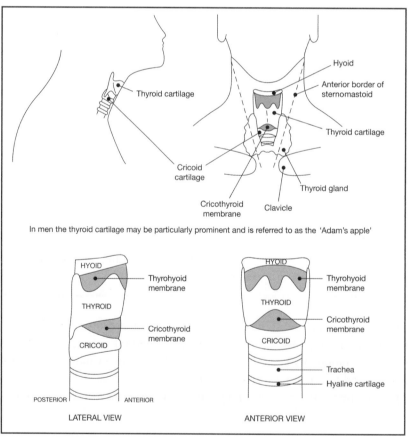

Figure 6.6 Surface markings of the larynx and trachea

Management of a compromised airway

- Chin lift and jaw thrust
- Guedel airway
- Nasopharyngeal airway
- Definitive airway:
  - Nasotracheal
  - Orotracheal
  - Cricothyroidotomy
  - Tracheostomy

Remember, if the airway is obstructed you cannot move on to assess breathing until the airway is secured.

Anatomy of the airway

The anatomy of the airways is illustrated in Figures 6.5 and 6.6.

Recognition of a compromised airway

Airway obstruction can be gradual or sudden and the clinical signs (tachypnoea, cyanosis and agitation) may be subtle. An altered level of consciousness due to head injury, drugs, alcohol or these factors combined makes airway compromise particularly likely, especially from the risk of aspiration of stomach contents.

Vomiting or the presence of stomach contents in the oropharynx requires immediate suction and turning the patient into the lateral 'recovery' position.

Associated chest injuries may reduce ventilation/ oxygenation and injuries of the neck may cause airway compromise by pressure from oedema or an expanding haematoma or tracheal perforation.

LOOK   Facial or airway trauma, agitation, cyanosis, use of accessory muscles

LISTEN   Stridor, gurgling, snoring or hoarseness

FEEL   Chest wall movement

Administer supplemental oxygen at 15 litres/ minute with reservoir bag.

Management of an obstructed airway

The following must be achieved with simultaneous immobilisation of the cervical spine. In the unconscious patient, the airway may be obstructed by vomit, dentures, broken teeth or the tongue falling backwards. The mouth should be gently opened and inspected. A gloved finger may be used to remove debris and a Yankauer sucker used for secretions.

The 'chin lift' and 'jaw thrust'

Both these manoeuvres are aimed at maintaining the patency of the upper airway (eg when the tongue has fallen backwards). To perform a jaw thrust, place your hands on either side of the patient's head. Your thumbs should lie on the patient's chin. Find the angle of the mandible with the tips of your index fingers. Maintaining the neutral position of the C-spine, grip the mandible and lift it forwards and upwards. This lifts the base of the tongue away from the airway. This position is sometimes called 'sniffing the morning air'.

- **Advantages:** no additional equipment needed. Holding both sides of the head may be combined with temporary in-line stabilisation of the C-spine. Can be used in a conscious patient
- **Disadvantages:** requires practice to maintain airway. Difficult to maintain for long periods of time

CHAPTER 6

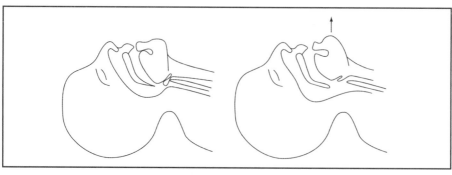

Figure 6.7 'Chin lift' and 'jaw thrust'

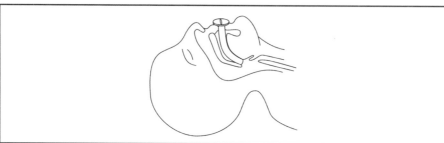

Figure 6.8 Guedel airway

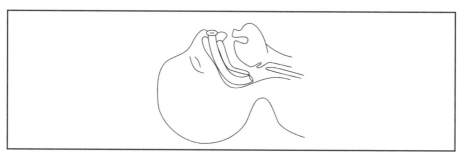

Figure 6.9 Nasopharyngeal airway

The Guedel airway

Used for temporary bag-and-mask ventilation of the unconscious patient before intubation.

- **Advantages:** easy to insert, widely available, various sizes
- **Disadvantages:** sited above vocal folds so does not prevent airway obstruction at this site. Can provoke gag reflex. Does not prevent aspiration of stomach contents

The nasopharyngeal airway

Used to prevent upper airway obstruction (eg in a drowsy/still-conscious patient).

- **Advantages:** fairly easy to insert; unlikely to stimulate gag reflex in comparison with oropharyngeal (Guedel) airway
- **Disadvantages:** less widely available, uncomfortable for the patient, sited above the vocal folds. Insertion dangerous if facial trauma present. Does not prevent aspiration of stomach contents

The definitive airway

If the above measures are insufficient then a definitive airway is indicated. This will ensure free passage of oxygen to the trachea, distal to the vocal folds.

Orotracheal intubation

A definitive airway may be secured by orotracheal intubation using an endotracheal (ET) tube. In cases of oral trauma, nasotracheal intubation may be preferred.

For discussion of nasotracheal and orotracheal intubation see Chapter 3.

Surgical cricothyroidotomy

This technique is quick and can be performed without hyperextension of the potentially injured cervical spine. It provides a large-calibre airway that can be secured, and it is therefore the technique of choice for a surgical airway in the early management of trauma patients.

Indications for a definitive airway

- Apnoea
- Hypoxia refractory to oxygen therapy
- Protection from aspiration pneumonitis
- Protection of the airway from impending obstruction due to burns/oedema/facial trauma/seizures
- Inability to maintain an airway by the above simpler measures
- Head injury with a risk of raised intracranial pressure (ICP)
- Vocal fold paralysis

Types of definitive airway

- Orotracheal intubation
- Nasotracheal intubation
- Surgical airway (eg tracheostomy or cricothyroidotomy)

Procedure box: Surgical cricothyroidotomy

Indications

May be needle cricothyroidotomy or open surgical cricothyroidotomy. Indication is failed orotracheal intubation due to:

- Severe oedema of the glottis
- Fracture of the larynx
- Severe oropharyngeal haemorrhage obstructing passage of a tube past the vocal folds

Contraindications

(Relative) surgical cricothyroidotomy is not recommended in children aged <12 in whom the cricoid cartilage provides the only circumferential support for the upper trachea.

Patient positioning

- Supine with neck extended

Procedure

Needle cricothyroidotomy

- Skin preparation with Betadine or chlorhexidine
- Identify the relevant landmarks: the cricoid cartilage and thyroid cartilage with the cricothyroid membrane between

continued overleaf

CHAPTER 6

- Puncture the skin in the line with a 12- or 14-G needle attached to the syringe, directly over the cricothyroid membrane. A small incision with a no. 11 blade may facilitate passage of the needle through the skin
- Direct the needle at a 45° angle inferiorly, while applying negative pressure to the syringe, and carefully insert the needle through the lower half of the cricothyroid membrane
- Aspiration of air signifies entry into the tracheal lumen
- Remove the syringe and withdraw the needle while advancing the catheter downward into position, being careful not to perforate the posterior wall of the trachea
- Attach the oxygen tubing over the catheter needle hub

Intermittent **jet ventilation** can be achieved by occluding an open hole cut into the oxygen tubing with your thumb for 1 second and releasing it for 4 seconds. After releasing your thumb from the hole in the tubing, passive exhalation occurs. This can be used for temporary ventilation (30–40 minutes) until a definitive airway can be established. CO_2 gradually accumulates due to inadequate exhalation and this technique cannot be used with chest trauma. It is not recommended for children.

Open surgical cricothyroidotomy
- Skin preparation with Betadine or chlorhexidine
- Identify the relevant landmarks: the cricoid cartilage and thyroid cartilage with the cricothyroid membrane between
- If the patient is conscious the surgical field is infiltrated with 10 ml of local anaesthetic (LA) with adrenaline to reduce haemorrhage
- Stabilise the thyroid with the left hand
- Make a transverse skin incision over the cricothyroid membrane. Carefully incise through the membrane
- Insert the scalpel handle into the incision and rotate it 90° to open the airway or use a pair of artery forceps to dilate the tract
- Insert an appropriately sized, cuffed ET tube or tracheotomy tube into the cricothyroid membrane incision, directing the tube distally into the trachea
- Inflate the cuff and ventilate the patient
- Observe lung inflation and auscultate the chest for adequate ventilation

Hazards
- Haemorrhage
- Damage to cricoid and thyroid cartilages

Post-procedure instructions
Observe for haemorrhage because clots may obstruct airway.

Complications
This is a temporary airway. A formal tracheostomy is more suited to long-term management.

CHAPTER 6

Tracheostomy

An open surgical tracheostomy is slow, technically more complex, with potential for bleeding, and requires formal operating facilities. It is not appropriate in the acute trauma situation, but is better suited to the long-term management of a ventilated patient. It is performed when a percutaneous tracheostomy would be difficult (eg abnormal or distorted anatomy).

Percutaneous tracheostomy is also time-consuming and requires hyperextension of the neck. In addition the use of a guidewire and multiple dilators make it an unsuitable technique in the acute trauma situation.

For discussion of tracheostomy see Book 2, Head and Neck.

Cervical spine control

In the first part of the primary survey of a trauma victim cervical spine control is vital. The patient's head should be held with in-line traction immediately if the neck is not immobilised on a spinal board. A hard cervical collar alone is not sufficient to control the cervical spine: sandbags and tape should be used.

3.2 Breathing

Learning point

Assessment of breathing in the primary survey: if the airway is safe or has been secured, you can move on to assessing breathing:
- Full examination
- Check saturation and/or arterial blood gases
- Provide supplemental oxygen
- Identify any of the six immediately life-threatening chest injuries and treat them immediately, before moving on with the primary survey (the recognition and management of these conditions is covered in section 4.3):
- Airway obstruction (see section 3.1)
  - Tension pneumothorax
  - Sucking chest wound and/or open pneumothorax
  - Massive haemothorax
  - Flail chest
  - Cardiac tamponade
- Ensure ventilation is adequate before moving on to assess circulation

Supplemental oxygen must be delivered to all trauma patients.

CHAPTER 6

Spontaneous breathing may resume when the airway is protected. If an ET tube has been inserted then intermittent positive-pressure ventilation (IPPV) must be commenced because the diameter of the tube dramatically increases the work of breathing.

Ventilatory support may be required:
- Bag-and-mask assistance
- IPPV

Examine the chest:
- Expose and observe
- Palpate
- Percuss
- Auscultate

Injuries that may compromise ventilation are:
- Thoracic injuries:
  - Pneumothorax (simple, open or tension)
  - Haemothorax
  - Pulmonary contusion
  - Rib fractures and flail chest
- Abdominal injuries: pain causes splinting of the abdominal wall and diaphragm
- Head injuries

Injuries compromising breathing must be dealt with early. This often requires insertion of a chest drain, which is discussed in Section 4.3 of this chapter.

3.3 Circulation

Learning point

Assessment of the circulation in the primary survey

If the airway is safe and ventilation is adequate, you can move on to assessing circulation.
- Assess haemodynamic status
- Identify sites of haemorrhage
- Establish IV access
- Send off blood for cross-matching and other investigations
- Give a bolus of intravenous fluid if the patient is shocked

If the patient is haemodynamically unstable and losing blood, action must be taken before moving on with the primary survey. This may mean transferring the patient to the operating theatre at this stage of the primary survey if there is uncontrolled internal bleeding.

Assess the patient's haemodynamic status:
- Pulse and BP
- Conscious level (cerebral perfusion)
- Skin colour (peripheral perfusion)

Remember to assess the patient's likely premorbid condition, bearing in mind AMPLE history (see Section 3.6), age group (elderly person, child), medication (eg β blocker), lifestyle (athletic).

Hypotension should be presumed to be secondary to haemorrhage until proved otherwise.

Identify sites of haemorrhage

- External
- Internal (thoracic cavity, abdominal cavity, extremities due to fractures)
- Occult

Establish IV access

Establish IV access with a cannula of sufficient diameter to allow large-volume fluid resuscitation:

- Two large-gauge (brown or grey) cannulas, one in each antecubital fossa
- Venous cut-down
- Intraosseous line
- Femoral venous catheterisation

Central lines tend to be of narrow diameter and are not ideal for administering large volumes of fluid quickly.

You can send venous blood for baseline tests as soon as access is established:

- Full blood count (FBC)
- Cross-match
- Urea and electrolytes (U&Es)

Management of the individual traumatic pathologies that can cause haemorrhage are dealt with in Sections 4.2–4.6.

Signs and symptoms of class I–IV shock are discussed in Section 2.2.

3.4 Disability

> **Learning point**
>
> **Assessment of disability in the primary survey**
> If the airway is safe, ventilation is adequate and there is no uncontrolled haemorrhage, you can move on to assessing disability:
> - Neurological status (AVPU)
> - Pupils
>
> Remember, shock can cause decreased consciousness.

Neurological status

Briefly assess neurological status using the acronym **AVPU**:

Alert
Verbal stimuli (responds to)
Pain (responds to)
Unresponsive

Pupils

Check pupils for:

- Size
- Symmetry
- Response to light

The anatomy, physiology, pathology and management of head injuries are discussed in Section 4.2.

CHAPTER 6

3.5 Exposure and environment

> ### Learning point
>
> **Exposure in the primary survey**
> If the airway is safe, ventilation is adequate, and there is no uncontrolled haemorrhage or evidence of severe or progressing head injury, you can move on to exposing the patient and attending to his or her environment:
> - Undress fully
> - Keep warm
> - Prepare for full inspection, log-roll and examination in the secondary survey

The patient should be fully exposed in order to look for hidden injuries in the secondary survey. Remember that the patient may already be hypothermic and maintenance of their body temperature is essential:
- Warmed fluids
- Warm resus room
- External warming devices (blankets, bear-hugger, etc)

3.6 Monitoring and important investigations

> ### Learning point
>
> **Completing the primary survey: monitoring and investigations**
> If the airway is safe, ventilation is adequate, there is no uncontrolled haemorrhage or evidence of severe or progressing head injury, and the patient is exposed with attention to his or her environment, the time has come to complete the primary survey and move on to the secondary survey. Before this is done you must:
> - Take an AMPLE history
> - Give analgesia
> - Set up:
>   - Pulse oximetry
>   - ECG leads
> - Monitor:
>   - Urine output
>   - Conscious level
> - Send blood investigations if not already done
> - Do the three trauma radiographs:
>   - Anteroposterior (AP) chest
>   - Pelvis
>   - C-spine
> - Fully reassess the ABCDEs
> You are now ready to progress to the secondary survey.

CHAPTER 6

History

It is important to take a medical history from the patient in the primary survey. Use the mnemonic AMPLE to remind you of each section.

AMPLE mnemonic
- **A**llergies
- **M**edication
- **P**ast medical history
- **L**ast meal
- **E**vents of the injury

Don't forget to consider analgesia for the patient at this point – it does not affect diagnosis of the injury, and it is not ethically acceptable to leave the patient in pain.

Monitoring in the resuscitation room
- Pulse oximetry and arterial blood gases (ABGs)
- ECG leads
- Conscious level
- Urinary output

Initial urgent investigations
- Blood tests (FBC, cross-match, U&Es)
- ABGs
- Imaging: radiographs (AP chest, pelvis, C-spine) are usually performed rapidly and may help in the assessment of injuries

CHAPTER 6

SECTION 4

Assessment: the secondary survey

Learning point

The secondary survey starts after the initial resuscitation as the patient begins to stabilise. It is carried out while continually reassessing ABC. Immediately life-threatening conditions should already have been detected and treated.

- Obtain a complete medical history
- Perform a sequential and thorough examination of the body, starting at the head and working down the body, looking for hidden injuries
- Obtain all necessary investigations: bloods, radiographs (of cervical spine, chest and pelvis)
- Perform any special procedures
- Monitor patient's response to treatment

Follow up with 'Fingers and tubes in every orifice'

- Per rectum
- Per vaginam
- Check ENT
- Nasogastric (NG) tube insertion (if no skull fracture)
- Urinary catheter insertion if no evidence of genitourinary trauma

4.1 Patient overview

Learning point

The role of the secondary survey is to obtain an overview of the patient's injuries and proceed to treat each one. This ensures that minor but potentially problematic injuries are not overlooked in the severely injured patient. The secondary survey should only be attempted on completion of the primary survey when life-threatening injuries have been managed and the patient is stable. Start at the top and systematically work down.

- Head
- Neck
- Thorax
- Abdomen
- Pelvis
- Extremities
- Spine
- Tetanus

Documentation is vital at this stage.

The patient should be fully exposed in order to look for any hidden injuries in the secondary survey. Remember that the patient may already be hypothermic and so maintenance of their body temperature is vital:

- Warmed fluids
- Warm resuscitation room
- External warming devices (blankets, bear-hugger etc)

Secondary survey of the head

- Neurological state
  - Full GCS assessment
  - Pupils
- Eyes
- Examination of the face
  - Check facial bones for stability
  - Loose or absent teeth
- Examination of the scalp
  - Presence of soft-tissue injuries/haematoma
- Signs of skull fracture
  - Periorbital haematoma
  - Scleral haematoma with no posterior margin
  - Battle's sign
  - Cerebrospinal fluid (CSF)/blood from ears or nose

Secondary survey of the neck

- Risk factors for cervical spine injury
  - Any injury above the clavicle
  - High-speed RTA
  - Fall from height
- Neck examination
  - Thorough palpation of bony prominences
  - Check for soft-tissue swellings
  - Check for muscle spasm
- Radiograph of C-spine
- Exclude:
  - Penetrating injuries of the neck
  - Subcutaneous emphysema
  - Elevated jugular venous pressure (JVP)

Secondary survey of the thorax

- Exclude pathology (pneumothorax, haemothorax, rib fractures, mediastinal injury, cardiac contusion)
- Examine the full respiratory system, especially reassessing air entry
- Inspect chest wall (bony or soft tissue injury, subcutaneous emphysema)
- Chest radiograph
- ECG
- ABG should be obtained to monitor whether ventilation is adequate

Secondary survey of the abdomen

- Examine thoroughly (abdominal wall injury suggests internal viscus injury)
- Insertion of a NG tube to decompress the stomach is suggested as long as there are no facial fractures or basal skull fractures
- Involve surgeons early if suspect internal injury
- After general resuscitation the main decision to be made in this area is whether a laparotomy is necessary

Secondary survey of the pelvis

- Check for bony instability which indicates significant blood loss
- Identify any genitourinary system injuries suggested by: high-riding prostate felt per rectum; blood found on rectal examination; blood found on vaginal examination; blood at external urethral meatus; gross haematuria
- Urethral catheterisation is performed only if there is no evidence of genitourinary injury

Secondary survey of the extremities

- Examine the full extent of each limb (remember hands and feet, including individual fingers and toes)

- Exclude soft-tissue injury, bony injury, vascular injury, neurological injury
- Control haemorrhage; elevate limb; apply direct pressure (tourniquets are not favoured)
- Correct any obvious bony deformity because this will decrease: fat emboli; haemorrhage; soft-tissue injury; requirement for analgesia; skin tension in dislocations
- Caution: check and document neurovascular supply to limb before and after any manipulation

Secondary survey of the spine

- Examine the spinal column for alignment, stepping and tenderness
- Examine the peripheral and central nervous systems
- Exclude sensory or motor deficits

Tetanus status and prophylaxis

- Check tetanus status, as shown in the table

Documentation

Document ABCDE status, observations, history of injury, AMPLE history, and site and nature of all injuries seen. All A&Es will have trauma proforma sheets available to assist with this.

TETANUS STATUS

Tetanus status	Minor injuries	Major injuries
Unknown or fewer than three doses	Tetanus toxoid only	Tetanus toxoid and tetanus IgG
Full course received with last booster <10 years ago	No treatment needed	No treatment necessary
Full course received with last booster >10 years ago	Tetanus IgG	Tetanus IgG

4.2   Head injury

Head injuries account for approximately 10% of A&E attendance in the UK. Around 50% of trauma deaths are associated with head injury.

The anatomy of the brain and skull is discussed in Elective Neurosurgery in Book 2.

Learning point

Head injuries may involve skull fracture, focal injury or diffuse brain injury. They may be classified according to severity, mechanism of injury or (most usefully) pathology.

The five aims of emergency management:

1. Assessment
2. Resuscitation
3. Establishing the diagnosis
4. Ensuring that metabolic needs of the brain are met
5. Preventing secondary brain damage

CHAPTER 6

Classification system for head injuries

Patients with head injuries are a very diverse group and their injuries may be classified in a number of ways.

Severity of injury

- Minor: GCS 8–15
- Major: GCS <8

Mechanism of injury

- Blunt injuries
- Penetrating injuries

Pathology of injury

- Focal/diffuse
- Primary/secondary
- Skull/intracranial lesions
- **Primary brain injury** is neurological damage produced by a causative event
- **Secondary brain injury** is neurological damage produced by subsequent insults (eg haemorrhage, hypoxia, hypovolaemia, ischaemia, increased ICP, metabolic imbalance, infection)

The main aim of treatment is to:

- Diagnose a primary brain injury and provide optimum conditions for recovery
- Minimise/prevent secondary brain injury by maintaining brain tissue oxygenation

Intracranial haemorrhage causes destruction of tissue immediately adjacent to the injury and compression of surrounding structures (see below).

Mechanisms of brain damage

Hypoxia/ischaemia

Permanent damage occurs within 3–4 min.

Contusion

The brain has a soft consistency and is poorly anchored within the cranial cavity. It moves during acceleration/deceleration and keeps going when the skull stops. Contact with the skull can cause bruising (contusions). The frontal and temporal lobes are particularly vulnerable. Contre-coup injury refers to injury on the opposite side of the brain to the impact (eg damage to frontal lobes after impact on the back of the head). This is due to the mobility of the brain within the skull vault.

Diffuse axonal injury

Axonal tracts may be torn by shearing forces, resulting in a spectrum of damage that can be reversible or irreversible. Transient LOC (concussion) is due to a mild form of stretch injury, through disruption of neuronal physiology and possibly also actual cell damage. Severe tract injury, depending on its site, can cause persistent vegetative states.

CHAPTER 6

Mild	Coma lasting 6–12 hours	Concussion
Moderate	Coma lasting >24 hours	No brainstem dysfunction (mortality rate 20%)
Severe	Coma lasting >24 hours	With brainstem dysfunction (mortality rate 57%)

Intracranial haemorrhage

> **Focal injuries**
> - Extradural haematoma
> - Subdural haematoma
> - Intracerebral haematoma

Extradural haematoma

This results from trauma (of varying severity), with injury to the temporal or parietal bone causing rupture of the underlying middle meningeal artery). Children and young adults are more susceptible because the dura becomes more adherent to the skull with advancing age. Initial concussion is typically followed by a 'lucid interval' as the expanding haematoma is accommodated. Rapid decompensation may then follow when the ICP rises as the inner edge of the temporal lobe descends into the tentorial opening. Herniation of the uncus of the temporal lobe across the tentorial edge compresses the third cranial nerve, resulting in pupillary dilatation. Extension of the haematoma is limited by dural attachments at the suture lines, giving the clot a characteristic biconvex appearance on imaging.

Acute subdural haematoma

A severe head injury may leave a layer of clot over the surface of the brain in the subdural space, by rupture of a bridging vein due to either shearing forces or laceration of brain substance. In either case there is usually severe underlying primary brain damage and deterioration is more rapid than with an extradural haematoma. Prognosis is also poorer.

Intracerebral haematoma

These injuries are the least remediable of the compressing intracranial haematomas. They are usually associated with cerebral laceration, contusion, oedema and necrosis, all of which contribute to their compressive effects. Removal of such clots has unpredictable and often disappointing results. (Its value is under investigation in the STICH II trial.)

Raised intracranial pressure

Intracranial pressure

Normal ICP = 10 mmHg
Abnormal ICP >20 mmHg

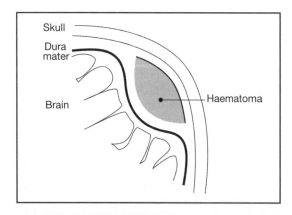

Figure 6.10 Extradural haematoma

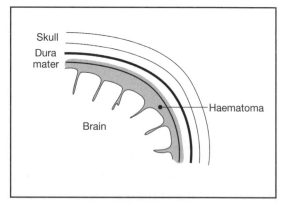

Figure 6.11 Acute subdural haematoma

CHAPTER 6

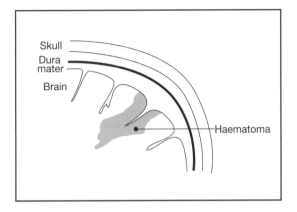

Figure 6.12 Intracerebral haematoma

The Monro–Kellie doctrine explains intracranial compensation for an expanding intracranial mass.

The addition of a mass (eg haematoma) within the constant volume of the skull results initially in extrusion of an equal volume of CSF and venous blood in order to maintain a normal ICP. However, when this compensatory mechanism reaches its limit, the ICP will increase exponentially with the increasing volume of the haematoma. Normal ICP does not therefore exclude a mass lesion.

Causes of raised ICP

- Haematoma
- Focal oedema secondary to contusion/haematoma
- Diffuse cerebral oedema secondary to ischaemia
- Obstruction of CSF flow (rarely an acute problem in trauma)
- Obstruction to venous outflow, eg from tight cervical collar

---

Effects of raised intracranial pressure

- Temporal uncal herniation across the tentorium results in third nerve compression and pupillary dilatation
- Motor weakness as a result of corticospinal tract compression
- Compression of vital cardiorespiratory centres against the bone occurs as the brainstem is squeezed through the foramen magnum

---

Rising ICP causes Cushing's response

- Respiratory rate decreases
- Heart rate decreases
- Systolic BP increases
- Pulse pressure increases

Death results from respiratory arrest secondary to brainstem infarction/haemorrhage. Direct measurement of ICP has proved more reliable than waiting for clinical signs to develop. ICP can be monitored extradurally, subdurally and intraventricularly.

Cerebral blood flow

- CPP = MAP – ICP

CPP is cerebral perfusion pressure, MAP mean arterial pressure and ICP intracranial pressure. Cerebral perfusion pressure is maintained by a phenomenon called autoregulation. Blood flow to the brain (Figure 6.14) is increased by:

- Rising CO_2 levels
- Rising extracellular K^+ levels
- Decreased PO_2

Autoregulation is severely disturbed in head injury, and CPP <70 mmHg is associated with poor outcome. Therefore the priority with a head

CHAPTER 6

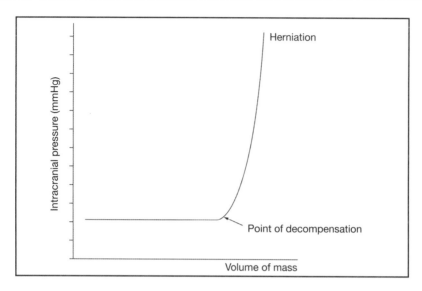

Figure 6.13 Volume–pressure curve

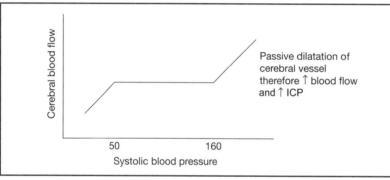

Figure 6.14 Control of cerebral blood flow

injury is to maintain cerebral perfusion, because these patients are susceptible to secondary brain injury due to hypotension.

Management of raised ICP

- CT scan for diagnosis of underlying cause
- Definitive management of underlying cause if possible

Non-surgical management

- Sedate and intubate
- Nurse the patient with tilted head up (aids venous drainage)

- Maintain normal PCO_2 (approximately 3.5–4.0 kPa)
- Establish monitoring with an ICP bolt and transducer
- Aim to maintain CPP at 60–70 mmHg by:
  - Optimal fluid management
  - Judicious use of inotropes
- Aim to maintain ICP at 10 mmHg by:
  - Mannitol (0.5 g/kg) (usually 100–200 ml 20% mannitol given rapidly may result in a transient mild reduction in ICP
  - Hyperventilation to PCO_2 4.5kPa
  - Thiopental infusion (15 mg/kg)
  - Hypothermia (controversial as to whether 'cool' to only normoxia or lower)
- Emergency burr holes or craniotomy

Burr holes

A burr hole is a small hole through the skull. If placed over the site of an intracranial haematoma, then partial evacuation of a clot can be made and ICP reduced. Only a small volume of haematoma (often gelatinous and clotted) can be evacuated but this can dramatically reduce ICP and be life-saving while awaiting definitive treatment. Placement of burr holes should not delay definitive neurosurgical intervention. It should be performed only if training has been received from a neurosurgeon.

Procedure box: Burr holes

Indications
Patients with signs of severe elevated ICP and impending herniation (eg pupil dilatation) due to epidural or subdural haematoma.

Contraindications
Presence of facilities for definitive neurosurgical intervention.

Patient positioning
- Supine, under general anaesthetic (GA)

Procedure
- Identify the location of the haematoma (usually frontal or temporal)
- In the absence of a CT scan, place a burr hole on the side of the dilated pupil, two finger-widths anterior to tragus of ear and three fingerwidths above
- Perform a straight scalp incision with haemostasis and insert a self-retainer
- Elevate the periosteum with a periosteal elevator
- Drill a hole through the skull to the dura with an automatic perforator or a manual Hudson brace
- Hook the dura up through the hole and open the dura with a cruciate incision
- Slowly decompress the haematoma with gentle suction and irrigation using Jake's catheter until the returning fluid is clear (this catheter can be left in situ for drainage)
- Close the scalp with clips to skin
- More than one burr hole may be placed to evacuate large haematomas

Post-procedure instructions
- Transfer to neurosurgical care
- Nurse flat for 48 hours (to reduce pneumocephalus) and observe drain output
- Rescan if the patient's GCS score deteriorates

Hazards
- Damage to underlying tissues (brain, blood vessels)

Complications
- Bleeding (scalp, bone edges)
- Damage to brain
- Failure to evacuate sufficient haematoma

CHAPTER 6

Monitoring after head injury and surgical interventions

Assessment of conscious level

Consciousness is controlled by the reticular activating system located in the upper portion of the brainstem.

Causes of altered conscious level
- Trauma
- Poisons
- Shock
- Epilepsy
- Opiates
- Infection
- Psychiatric disorders
- Alcohol
- Raised ICP
- Metabolic disorders (eg uraemia)

The Glasgow Coma Scale

The GCS offers a reproducible, quantitative measure of the patient's level of consciousness.

GLASGOW COMA SCALE

Best motor response	6	Obeys commands
	5	Localises to pain
	4	Withdraws from pain
	3	Abnormal flexion
	2	Extension
	1	None
Best verbal response	5	Orientated
	4	Confused
	3	Inappropriate
	2	Incomprehensible sounds
	1	None
Best eye-opening response	4	Open spontaneously
	3	Open to speech
	2	Open to pain
	1	None

Pupil size

Assessment of pupil size and symmetry on admission and subsequently at least hourly is important. Sudden unilateral pupil dilatation ('blowing a pupil') may be indicative of raised ICP.

ICP monitoring

Monitoring ICP may be performed as an **invasive** procedure.
- **Parenchymal:** a transducer is inserted through a bolt placed in a small hole drilled in the skull and then into the brain parenchyma. This can be combined with tissue oxygen and temperature monitoring
- **Ventricular cannula:** placement of a cannula into the ventricular system gives a measure of ICP using a manometer. Useful because therapeutic CSF drainage can be performed, particularly if hydrocephalus present.
- Various methods are being developed to monitor ICP **non-invasively**, although none has yet impacted significantly on clinical practice, eg two-depth transcranial Doppler for measurements of ICP through the ophthalmic artery
- **Transcranial Doppler ultrasonography of major intracranial vessels**

ICP monitoring is useful in clinical management. Perfusion essentially ceases when the ICP exceeds the diastolic BP.

Problems associated with ICP monitoring include:
- Cost
- Infection – although this is rare
- Haemorrhage – which can exacerbate ICP problems.
- ICP can be monitored a lot more easily than it can be controlled
- Control of ICP does not guarantee good patient outcomes

CHAPTER 6

Management of head injuries

Treatment priorities and management decisions depend on whether the head injury is minor or major.

Minor head injuries

The management aim is to detect those at risk of developing a clinically significant intracranial haematoma, or other case of raised ICP. Even those with so-called mild head injuries can have neuropsychological deficits that impact on their recovery.

RISK OF HAEMATOMA FOLLOWING MINOR HEAD INJURY

	Skull fracture	No skull fracture
Fully conscious	1 in 45	1 in 7900
Confused	1 in 5	1 in 180
Coma	1 in 4	1 in 27

Criteria for CT after recent head injury (eg SIGN guidelines)

Immediate CT scanning (adults)

- Eye opening only to pain or not conversing (GCS 12/15 or less)
- Confusion or drowsiness (GCS 13/15 or 14/15) followed by failure to improve within 2 hours of injury
- Base of skull or depressed skull fracture and/or suspected penetrating injuries
- A deteriorating level of consciousness or new focal neurological signs
- Full consciousness (GCS 15/15) with no fracture but other features, eg severe and persistent headache and two distinct episodes of vomiting
- History of coagulopathy and neurological deficit

Adults with impaired consciousness and an indication for CT head imaging should also have cervical spine CT from the craniocervical junction to T4.

Any patient who is admitted for assessment and fails to improve or develops new deficits/reduced consciousness or seizures should be re-imaged and discussed with the regional neurosurgical unit.

Children can be more difficult to reliably assess and CT can be particularly useful. Criteria for scanning are similar to those in adults.

Criteria for admission of the patient with a head injury

- Impaired consciousness
- Neurological symptoms/signs, worsening headache, nausea or vomiting
- For management of other injuries, eg long bone fractures.
- If the patient has a significant medical problem such as anticoagulant use
- Difficulty in assessment (eg in alcohol intoxication)
- No responsible adult at home
- Similar criteria apply to children who have sustained a head injury, but admission is also necessary if there is any suspicion of non-accidental injury
- Patients who are sent home should be discharged in the care of a responsible

adult, and given written instructions about possible complications and appropriate actions should their condition deteriorate

Major head injuries

The aim of management is prevention of secondary cerebral damage. Major head injuries often have concomitant cervical spine injury so ensure that imaging is done and precautions taken.

Management of major head injury

Maintain ventilation with PaO_2 >13 kPa and $PaCO_2$ 4–5 kPa

- Intubation is appropriate when gag reflex is absent, or PaO_2 <9, $PaCO_2$ >5.3
- Use rapid-sequence intubation
- Exclude any pneumothoraces before ventilation
- Remember that a talking patient indicates a reduced risk of complications because this indicates a patent airway

Maintain adequate MAP

- Note: CPP = MAP – ICP

Mannitol

- 0.5–1 g/kg over 10–30 minutes to help reduce ICP

Metabolic

- Correct any potential metabolic contributors to impaired consciousness such as hypoglycaemia

Antibiotics

- Skull fractures do not routinely require antibiotics, but they may be indicated for compound injuries

---

Criteria for consultation with a neurosurgical unit

- Fractured skull in combination with any abnormal neurology
- Confusion or other neurological disturbance that persists for >12 hours
- Coma that continues after resuscitation
- Suspected open injury of the vault or the base of the skull
- Depressed fracture of the skull
- Deterioration of the patient's GCS score
- Significant radiological abnormality on imaging

Note: never assume that impaired consciousness in a patient who has taken alcohol or drugs is due to intoxication if they have a head injury. Assume that it's the head injury!

4.3 Facial injuries

Learning point

An appreciation of the anatomy of the face is needed.
Initial management of facial injury
- History of injury
- Mechanism of injury
- Loss of consciousness
- Visual disturbance (flashes of light, photophobia, diplopia, blurry vision, pain or change in vision present with eye movement)
- Hearing (tinnitus or vertigo)
- Difficulty moving the jaw
- Areas of facial numbness

Examination
- ABCDE

Inspect for:
- Asymmetry
- Abrasions and cuts
- Bruising
- Missing tissue
- Teeth and bite for fracture and malocclusion

Palpate for bony injury (tenderness, crepitus and step-off) especially orbital rims, zygomatic arch, medial orbital area, nasal bones, mandibular length and teeth
- Place one hand on the anterior maxillary teeth and the other on the nasal bridge: movement of only the teeth indicates a Le Fort I fracture; movement at the nasal bridge indicates a Le Fort II or III fracture

Ear canal examination: look for discharge, Battle's sign, integrity of the tympanic membrane and lacerations.

Eye examination (see below).

Cranial nerve exam.

axillofacial surgery is a speciality not covered in this text. A basic knowledge of the bones, soft tissues, blood supply and nerve supply of the face should be appreciated. The muscles and nerve supply of the face are discussed in Chapter 5, Head and Neck Surgery, Book 2. The bones and blood supply of the face are described below.

Bones of the face

The bones of the face include:
- Facial skeleton
- Naso-orbital complex
- Bones of the orbit (see Chapter 5, Book 2)
- Temporal bone
- Temporomandibular joint
- Zygomatic arch

CHAPTER 6

- Pterion
- Mandible
- Hard palate

Facial skeleton

The bones of the face are shown in Figure 6.15. The face can be divided into three zones:

- **Upper zone:** the frontal bone
- **Mid-zone:** between the frontal bone and mandible, including the orbit, nasal cavity, maxillary and ethmoid
- **Lower zone:** mandible

Naso-orbital complex

This consists of:
- Nasal bones (right and left)
- Lacrimal bones (right and left)
- Maxillary bones (right and left)
- Ethmoid bone

These bones are important because fracturing them may damage the nasal septum, ethmoidal sinuses or the cribriform plate.

Temporal bone

The temporal bone contributes structurally to the cranial vault. It is one of the most complex bones of the body. It consists of five parts: the squamous, mastoid, tympanic, zygomatic and petrous segments. It is intimately related to the dura of the middle and posterior fossae. Anteriorly, it communicates with the middle ear. Many important structures are found within or passing through the bone:
- Part of the carotid artery
- Jugular venous drainage system
- Middle ear
- Vestibulocochlear end-organs
- Facial nerve

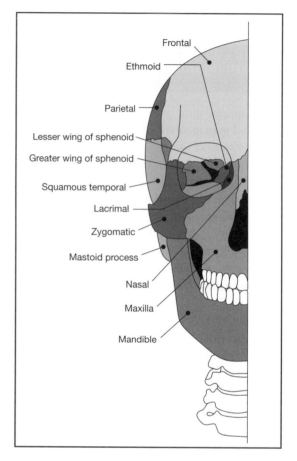

Figure 6.15 Bones of the face

Temporomandibular joint

The temporomandibular joint (TMJ) is a sliding joint, formed by the condyle of the mandible and the squamous part of the temporal bone. The articular surface of the temporal bone consists of a convex articular eminence anteriorly and a concave articular fossa posteriorly. The articular surface of the mandible consists of the top of the condyle. The articular surfaces of the mandible and temporal bone are separated by an articular disc, which divides the joint cavity into two small spaces.

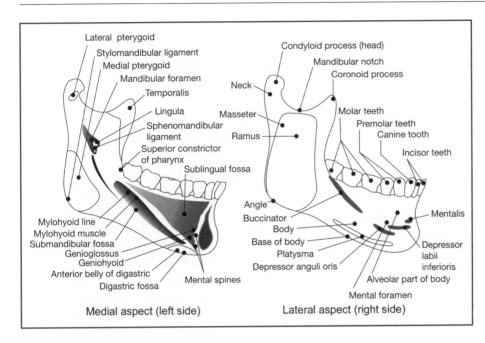

**Figure 6.16
Anatomy of the
mandible and
the teeth**

Medial aspect (left side)   Lateral aspect (right side)

Zygomatic arch

This is made up of the zygomatic processes of the following:

- Temporal bone
- Malar (zygoma)
- Maxilla

The zygomatic branch of the facial nerve runs along the midportion of the arch where it is susceptible to damage by fractures (causing inability to close the eyelid by denervation of the orbicularis oculi).

Pterion

This is the name of an area where three bones meet:

- Greater wing of the sphenoid
- Squamous temporal bone
- Parietal bone

Mandible

This has several parts, namely:

- **Symphysis:** the bone of the chin, extending back bilaterally to an imaginary line drawn vertically at the base of the canine teeth
- **Body:** the bone between the angle and symphysis
- **Ramus:** the bone between the coronoid, condyle and mandibular angle
- **Mandibular angle** (Figure 6.16)
- **Alveolar ridge:** the horseshoe of bone directly beneath the teeth
- **Coronoid process**
- **Condyle of TMJ**

The inferior alveolar nerve provides sensation to the lower gums, lower lip and skin of the chin.

CHAPTER 6

447

Blood supply of the face

The facial artery is a branch of the external carotid artery. It passes the side wall of the pharynx, upper surface of the submandibular gland and inferior border of the masseter, towards the medial angle of the eye, giving off superior and inferior arteries among other branches. Other arteries that supply the face include:

- **The superficial temporal artery** (from the external carotid)
- **The supraorbital and supratrochlear** branches of the ophthalmic artery (from the internal carotid)

The venous drainage of the face is into the internal and external jugular veins. There is a communication with the cavernous sinus via the ophthalmic veins.

Bony facial injury

Frontal bone fractures

The frontal bone is very thick and fractures result from a great deal of force with direct impact to the forehead (so are often associated with other injuries). The patency of the nasofrontal duct is of great importance (because blockage can cause abscess formation). Anterior sinus wall fractures require fixation if they are displaced. Posterior sinus wall fractures are examined for dural tears and CSF leakage.

Nasal bone fractures

> **Trauma to the nose**
> **May result in:**
> - Epistaxisis
> - Fractured nasal bones
> - Septal fracture or dislocation
> - Septal haematoma
>
> **Fractured nasal bones**
> A broken nose should only be treated if there is deformity. Initial simple manipulation may be sufficient to straighten the nose. Otherwise refer the patient for plastic surgery 7–10 days after the injury (time for the swelling to reduce) with a recent pre-injury photo. The nasal bones can be reduced under GA, or a formal rhinoplasty may be required.
>
> **Septal injury**
> Deviation of the septum may cause:
> - Airway obstruction
> - Septal haematoma (must be drained urgently as can lead to septal abscess and saddlenose deformity)

Naso-ethmoidal fractures

These extend from the nose to the ethmoid bone and can result in damage to the medial canthus, lacrimal apparatus or nasofrontal duct. They also can result in a dural tear at the cribriform plate. Fractures with associated dural tears require neurosurgical review, and patients should be admitted for observation and IV antibiotics.

Temporal bone fractures

- Tend to be managed several weeks after presentation
- Fractures can be longitudinal (80%) or transverse (20%)

CHAPTER 6

Signs of longitudinal fractures
- Swollen external auditory canal
- Tear of the tympanic membrane
- Bleeding from the ear
- CSF otorrhoea
- Facial nerve palsy (less commonly)

Signs of transverse fractures
- Haemotympanum
- 50% have facial nerve palsy
- Sensorineural hearing loss
- Vertigo
- Nystagmus
- Cranial nerve IX, X, XII palsies

Management of temporal bone fracture
- Hearing test
- Electromyography (EMG) (if facial nerve palsy)
- Surgical decompression and grafting of facial nerve (may be indicated)

TMJ dislocation

Most cases of dislocation occur spontaneously when the jaw is opened wide (eg while yawning, yelling, eating, singing or during prolonged dental work) or during a seizure. Some patients are susceptible because of a shallow joint.

Traumatic dislocations occur when downward force is applied to a partially opened mandible. Most dislocations are anterior.

Exclude a fracture before manipulating. It is uncomfortable for the patient but can often be reduced fairly easily by a combination of downward and forward traction on the mandible (place your thumbs inside the mouth and support the bone with your fingers as you pull).

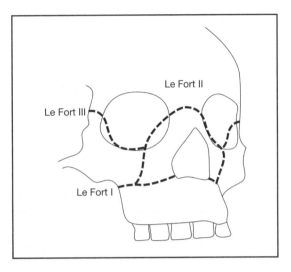

Figure 6.17 Le Fort injury

Zygomatic arch fractures

Isolated fractures may be undisplaced and treated conservatively. If the fracture is displaced it may impinge on the coronoid process of the mandible and require reduction and fixation.

Maxillary fractures

Le Fort classification of maxillary fracture (Figure 6.17) is as follows:
- **Le Fort I:** severs the tooth-bearing portion of the maxilla from the upper maxilla. Signs include crepitus on manipulation. It causes epistaxis but rarely threatens the airway
- **Le Fort II:** the middle third of the facial skeleton is driven back and downwards. If the bite is open, the airway is at risk
- **Le Fort III:** the fracture extends into the anterior fossa via the superior orbital margins. There may be CSF rhinorrhoea

If displaced, then open reduction and intermaxillary fixation may be performed to establish correct occlusion, followed by rigid fixation.

CHAPTER 6

Mandibular fractures

These can occur in multiple locations secondary to the U-shape of the jaw and the weak condylar neck. Fractures often occur bilaterally at sites apart from the site of direct trauma. The most common sites of fracture are at the body, condyles and angle: body 40–21%; condyle 20–15%; angle 31–20%; symphysis and parasymphysis 15–10%; ramus 9–3%; alveolar ridge 5–3%; and coronoid process 2–1%. Temporary stabilisation is performed by applying a Barton bandage (wrap the bandage around the crown of the head and jaw). A fracture of the symphysis or body of the mandible can be wired (controls haemorrhage and pain).

Soft-tissue facial injury

- **Facial lacerations:** should be cleaned meticulously. Alignment of the tissues must be exact to produce a good cosmetic result. Refer complex lacerations to plastic surgery
- **Dog bites:** clean well and give appropriate antibiotic cover. Do not use primary closure
- **Rugby player's ear:** aspirate haematoma (repeat every few days) and then strap orthopaedic felt pressure pads against the head
- **Ruptured ear drum:** refer to ENT; advise against letting water into the external auditory meatus
- **Avulsed teeth:** may be replaced. If inhaled, arrange expiratory chest radiograph
- **Bleeding socket:** bite on an adrenaline-soaked dressing or use sutures

Complications of facial injuries

- Aspiration
- Airway compromise
- Scars and permanent facial deformity
- Nerve damage resulting in loss of sensation, facial movement, smell, taste or vision

- Chronic sinusitis
- Infection
- Malnutrition
- Weight loss
- Non-union or malunion of fractures
- Malocclusion
- Haemorrhage

4.4 Chest Trauma

Learning point

Life-threatening thoracic trauma
- Causes 25% trauma deaths in the UK
- Fewer than 15% will require surgery
- May be blunt, penetrating or crush injury

Essential techniques for thoracic trauma
- Chest drain insertion
- Pericardiocentesis
- Emergency thoracotomy

Likely pathologies for thoracic trauma
- Flail chest
- Pulmonary contusion
- Pneumothorax:
  - Tension pneumothorax
  - Open pneumothorax
- Massive haemothorax
- Mediastinal injury
- Myocardial contusion
- Cardiac tamponade
- Aortic disruption
- Diaphragmatic rupture
- Oesophageal trauma

Types of trauma

- **Blunt** chest trauma as a result of RTAs predominates in the UK

CHAPTER 6

- **Penetrating** trauma of the chest has a greater incidence in countries such as South Africa and the USA
- **Crush** trauma of the chest may be associated with cerebral oedema, congestion and

petechiae due to superior vena cava (SVC) compression

Many of the conditions discussed in the following pages should be identified in the primary survey.

Procedure box: Insertion of a chest drain

Indications
Compromise in ventilation due to the presence of one of the following in the thoracic cavity:
- Air
- Blood
- Pus
- Lymph
- Fluid (transudate/exudate)

Patient positioning
The site of the drain insertion depends upon the site of the fluid collection to be drained. Ultrasonography may be used to locate fluid collections, and a mark placed on the skin to show an ideal site for drainage. Do not change the patient's position after marking. Alternatively a pigtail catheter inserted using a Seldinger technique may be placed for small fluid collections or small pneumothoraces but this is contraversial.

In general the drain may be inserted with the patient supine and the arm elevated. If there is grave respiratory distress and the patient is conscious, the patient may be positioned sitting up and leaning forwards during the procedure.

Procedure
- Perform under aseptic technique (skin preparation, gown, gloves, sterile drapes)
- Identify insertion site (for large fluid collections this is usually the fifth intercostal space just anterior to the axillary line – remember the long thoracic nerve runs down the axillary line and should be avoided)
- Infiltrate area with LA, taking care to site the area just above the rib – remember the intercostal neurovascular bundle runs in a groove in the underside of the lower rib border
- Make a 2- to 3-cm transverse incision through the skin and bluntly dissect through the tissues to the parietal pleura
- Puncture the parietal pleura and insert a finger into the thoracic cavity to sweep away adhesions, lung tissue and clots
- Clamp the chest tube at the distal end and advance it through the incision, angled downwards towards the diaphragm for fluid collections and upwards towards the neck for collections of air

continued overleaf

CHAPTER 6

- **Never use the trocar because there is a high risk of damage to the lung and mediastinum**
- Connect the chest drain to an underwater sealed receptacle and confirm that the level swings with respiration
- Suture the drain in place (you may use a purse-string to ensure that the tissues are closed tightly around the drain entry site)

Post-procedure instructions
- Chest radiograph to ensure position of drain

Hazards
- Never use the trocar
- Never clamp a chest drain (high risk of tension pneumothorax)
- Rapid drainage of fluid can result in pulmonary oedema

Complications
- Damage to intrathoracic organs (lung, blood vessels, mediastinal structures)
- Damage to structures of the chest wall (intercostal neurovascular bundle, long thoracic nerve)
- Introduction of infection
- Introduction of air to the thoracic cavity (leak around entry site; leak at site of apparatus)
- Incorrect tube position

Chest wall injuries result in an inability to generate a negative intrathoracic pressure due to the mechanics of a flail segment, pneumothorax or haemothorax. Pain inhibits the ability to move the chest wall to breathe and secondary complications of hypoxia, collapse of alveoli and infection.

Damage to the trachea, bronchi or bronchioles results in the impedance of air flow even in the presence of negative intrathoracic pressure and may be due to the presence of blood or direct trauma. Leak from airspaces may result in pneumothorax, pneumomediastinum or subcutaneous emphysema.

Injury to the lung parenchyma is a result of contusion and haemorrhage into the alveoli and interstitial spaces. This results in ventilation – perfusion mismatch.

Blunt cardiac injury can result in contusion, rupture of valves or chambers and the risk of dysrythmia is greatest in the first 24 hours post injury. Traumatic aortic disruption is a common cause of sudden death after blunt trauma, if partially contained then surgery may be life-saving.

Flail chest

This is when a segment of the chest wall loses bony continuity with the rest of the thoracic cage due to multiple rib or sternal fractures. There will always be a degree of underlying lung contusion.
- Paradoxical chest wall movement means that the tidal volume decreases
- Dramatic hypoxia commonly seen due to severe underlying pulmonary contusion

Signs of flail chest
- Respiratory distress
- Paradoxical chest wall movement
- Crepitus of ribs
- Hypoxia
- Hypovolaemia if associated with significant blood loss

Treatment of flail chest
- Main aim of treatment is respiratory support
- IPPV is indicated if there is failure to maintain adequate oxygenation

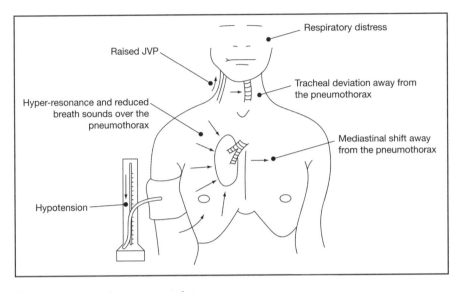

Figure 6.18 Tension pneumothorax

- Drainage of any haemopneumothorax
- Adequate analgesia (epidural often helpful; intercostal block may be adequate)
- Careful fluid management essential because patients are prone to pulmonary oedema
- Surgical intervention for stabilisation rarely indicated

Pulmonary contusion

Signs of pulmonary contusion
- Bruising of lung tissue
- Usually blunt trauma
- Insidious onset of symptoms and signs
- Respiratory distress
- Increased airway resistance
- Decreased lung compliance
- Increased shunting leading to hypoxia
- Atelectasis

Treatment of pulmonary contusion

- Support the respiratory system including intubation and IPPV if necessary

Tension pneumothorax

Signs of tension pneumothorax
- Respiratory distress
- Tracheal deviation AWAY from the side of injury
- Unilaterally decreased breath sounds
- Raised JVP
- Electromechanical dissociation (EMD) cardiac arrest

Treatment of tension pneumothorax

- Immediate decompression: if tension pneumothorax is suspected it should be decompressed immediately, BEFORE chest radiograph is performed
- Aspiration with a 14-G Venflon in the second intercostal space, clavicular line
- IV access
- Formal chest drain insertion

CHAPTER 6

453

Open pneumothorax

This is a chest wound that is associated with air in the pleural space.

Signs of open pneumothorax
- Respiratory distress
- Sucking chest wound: decreased air entry; increased percussion note over affected side

---

Treatment of open pneumothorax

- Occlude wound with sterile dressing; fix three sides only (flutter valve)
- Using different site, insert chest drain
- Surgical closure usually indicated

Massive haemothorax

This is 1500 ml or more blood drained from chest cavity on insertion of chest drain.

Signs of massive haemothorax
- Hypovolaemic shock (decreased BP, tachycardia; peripheral vasoconstriction)
- Absent breath sounds
- Dull percussion note
- Signs of penetrating wound
- Increased JVP if concomitant tension pneumothorax
- Decreased JVP if hypovolaemic shock prevails

Cause of massive haemothorax

- Usually penetrating injury

Treatment of massive haemothorax

- Simultaneous drainage of haemothorax and fluid resuscitation
- Chest drain must be wide bore (>32 Fr) AAL (anterior axillary line) fifth intercostal space
- Thoracotomy indicated if immediate loss >2000 ml or continuing loss >200 ml/hour

---

If there are any signs of penetrating injury medial to the nipples/scapula posteriorly, assume damage to the great vessels or hilar structures.

Mediastinal injury

This is injury of any or all of the mediastinal structures:
- Heart
- Great vessels
- Tracheobronchial tree
- Oesophagus

Chest radiograph signs of mediastinal injury
- Subcutaneous emphysema
- Unilateral or bilateral haemothoraces
- Pleural cap
- Widened mediastinum
- Free air in the mediastinum

Cardiac trauma

Learning point

- Blunt trauma
- Iatrogenic trauma
- Penetrating trauma

CHAPTER 6

Blunt trauma

Myocardial contusion

The leading cause of blunt trauma to the heart is RTAs (blunt trauma/deceleration injury). Various injuries can occur, such as:

- **Myocardial contusion** (in which the myocardium is bruised and may be akinetic)
- **Coronary artery dissection** (which causes myocardial ischaemia, infarction and arrhythmias)
- **Cardiac rupture** (usually from the atrium, which may lead to tamponade)

Cardiac blunt trauma may also be associated with other intrathoracic injuries (eg lung contusion, avulsion of vessels, aortic transection, pneumothorax).

- Myocardial contusion is the most common undiagnosed fatal injury
- Right ventricle is more often injured than the left
- Damaged heart tissue behaves similarly to infarcted myocardium

Cardiogenic shock is possible, in which case:

- Treat it early
- Treat aberrant conduction with a pacemaker if needed
- ECG changes include: premature ventricular ectopics or complexes (PVCs); sinus tachycardia; atrial fibrillation, ST changes; T-wave abnormalities; right bundle branch block (RBBB)

All cardiac blunt trauma may also be associated with other intrathoracic injuries, including **lung contusion**, **avulsion of vessels**, **aortic transection** and **pneumothorax**.

Management of blunt trauma

- Commence resuscitation. Place an endotracheal tube. Initiate volume replacement. If a cardiac injury is suspected, investigate by echocardiography if there is time
- Emergent left anterolateral thoracotomy is justified if there is pericardial tamponade or uncontrolled bleeding

Iatrogenic trauma

The rise in percutaneous coronary interventions has led in turn to more interventional complications. These include:

- Coronary dissection
- Coronary perforation causing tamponade

Penetrating trauma and cardiac tamponade

In the UK the most common penetrating cardiac traumas result from stabbing with a knife. Cardiac chamber injury is often associated with injury to other intrathoracic regions (eg pulmonary parenchyma, hilum). The chambers most often injured are the left ventricle and the right ventricle, and injury to multiple chambers is common.

Cardiac chamber injuries proceed rapidly to pericardial tamponade. Associated chest or abdominal injuries cause hypovolaemia and pneumothorax. Failure to respond to thoracostomy tube drainage should lead to the diagnosis of pericardial tamponade being considered.

CHAPTER 6

Cardinal signs of cardiac tamponade

- Raised JVP, low BP, muffled heart sounds (Beck's triad)
- Kussmaul's sign (JVP raised on inspiration)
- EMD cardiac arrest

Treatment of cardiac tamponade

Pericardiocentesis is both a diagnostic and a therapeutic manoeuvre, and can decompress the pericardial space until formal cardiac surgery can be performed. A plastic cannula can be left in situ for repeated aspirations until thoracotomy is feasible. There is, however, a high false-negative diagnostic rate (50%) and a high rate of perforation of previously uninjured cardiac chambers. In one in four cases clotted blood is encountered that cannot be aspirated, although the removal of just 15–20 ml blood can provide temporary relief.

Procedure box: Pericardiocentesis

Indications
- Cardiac tamponade
- Large pericardial effusions
- Diagnostic pericardial fluid

Contraindications
- Small, loculated or posterior effusions

Patient positioning
- Supine, tilted head-up by 20°

Procedure
- Performed under strict aseptic technique (gloves, gown, sterile drapes) and with full resuscitative measures in place
- Infiltrate the field with 10 ml, LA
- Aspirating continuously, advance an 18-G needle (plastic sheathed, Seldinger catheter or spinal needle) from the left subxiphoid approach, aiming towards the left shoulder tip
- Keep an eye on the ECG as you advance the needle. An ECG lead can also be attached to the needle, which will demonstrate increased T-wave voltage when the needle touches the epicardium
- Blood is aspirated from the pericardial space and then a guidewire can be passed through the needle
- A plastic sheath or catheter can be passed over the guidewire and left in situ (sutured in place) until urgent thoracotomy can be performed

Complications
- Pneumothorax
- Cardiac arrhythmia (VT)
- Cardiac damage (myocardial puncture, damage to the coronary arteries)

CHAPTER 6

Surgical management of penetrating trauma

> ### Initial management of tamponade
> Give lots of volume (it raises venous pressure and improves cardiac filling).
> Open the pericardium wide.
> Put a finger in the hole.
> Call for senior help.
> Definitive management.

The level of urgency is judged on the patient's clinical state. With some injuries there is enough time to perform a chest radiograph or CT, and to get the patient to a properly prepared operating theatre with trained cardiothoracic surgeons to perform a median sternotomy. In more urgent cases a left anterolateral thoracotomy may be performed in the resuscitation room. If the patient presents after prolonged cardiac arrest, the chances of saving life at this stage may be very slim. As this procedure carries risk to the surgeon (in terms of needlestick/sharps injury and cuts from broken ribs) thoracotomy may not always be justified. Initial surgical management involves:

- Relief of tamponade (see box)
- Over-sewing the defect, usually with pledgetted polypropylene
- Open cardiac massage if output is inadequate

For complex injuries (eg ventricular septal defect [VSD] or coronary artery injury) it may be necessary to cannulate for CPB and perform an extended procedure.

Aortic disruption

In aortic disruption:
- 90% are immediately fatal

- Deceleration injury mechanism is most common
- Site of rupture is usually ligamentum arteriosum
- Early diagnosis is essential for survival

> ### Signs of aortic disruption
> - Hypovolaemia
> - Chest radiograph (widened mediastinum the only consistent finding)

Treatment of aortic disruption

- Involves fluid resuscitation while maintaining BP >100 mmHg systolic
- Definitive treatment is surgical or stenting

Diaphragmatic rupture

Blunt trauma causes large defects in the diaphragm (radial tears that allow herniation of abdominal viscera). Penetrating injuries are small and rarely life-threatening.

> ### Signs of diaphragmatic rupture
> - Left side affected more than the right (right protected by liver; left more easily diagnosed)
> - Bilateral rupture is rare
> - Differential diagnoses include acute gastric dilatation, raised hemidia-phragm, loculated pneumothorax
> - If chest radiograph ambiguous consider contrast radiography or CT

Treatment of diaphragmatic rupture is by surgical repair.

CHAPTER 6

Oesophageal trauma

This is usually penetrating. Can follow blunt trauma to the upper abdomen (the oesophagus distends with gastric contents, producing a linear tear).

Clinical signs of oesophageal trauma
- Mediastinitis
- Empyema

Confirmation of oesophageal trauma is by contrast studies, endoscopy and CT.

Treatment of oesophageal trauma
- Surgical repair
- Drainage of the empyema
- Drainage of the pleural space

Emergency thoracotomy

This is commonly an **anterolateral thoracotomy**, the procedure of choice for emergency, resuscitation room procedures, for management of cardiac or thoracic injuries, often in the context of major haemorrhage or cardiac arrest. This is discussed further in the Cardiothoracic chapter of Book 2.

Following penetrating injury the indications for emergency thoracotomy are:
- >1500 mls of blood drained on chest drain insertion
- >200 mls / hour of blood drained for 4 hours

Resuscitative thoracotomy allows the surgeon to:
- Evacuate pericardial blood causing tamponade
- Control intrathoracic haemorrhage
- Perform open cardiac massage
- Cross clamp the aorta to slow bleeding below the diaphragm and preserve cardiac and cerebral perfusion.

4.5   Abdominal trauma

Blunt abdominal trauma

Blunt abdominal trauma is usually due to an RTA, a fall from a height or a sports injury (eg rugby). The impact causes a crushing force to be applied to the organs which may result in rupture of distended hollow organs. Patients who have been involved in an RTA are also likely to have deceleration injuries.

Learning point

Abdominal trauma is often missed and frequently underestimated; therefore management should be aggressive. CT may be helpful but may also miss the early signs of a ruptured hollow viscus such as the small bowel.

Laparotomy is necessary in about 10% of blunt trauma patients, 40% of stab wound victims and 95% of patients with gunshot wounds.

Trauma may be **blunt** or **penetrating**.
Damage may be to the:
- Abdominal viscera
- Spleen
- Liver
- Pancreas
- Intestine and mesentery
- Renal and genitourinary systems

Investigating blunt abdominal trauma

- **Baseline blood tests (including amylase):** FBC may be normal in the acute phase even with significant haemorrhage when dilution and equilibration has not yet occurred. ABG estimation may provide evidence of shock in terms of acidosis or a significant base deficit

- **Erect chest radiograph and abdominal radiograph:** these may reveal a haemothorax or pneumothorax, diaphragmatic rupture, rib fractures associated with splenic or hepatic trauma, gas under the diaphragm associated with visceral perforation, and pelvic fractures associated with massive blood loss
- **Ultrasonography:** a portable scanner may provide a rapid, inexpensive way of detecting free fluid in the abdomen, with a sensitivity of 86–97%. This is often called a FAST scan
- **CT scan:** this is suitable for patients who are haemodynamically stable, but it is slow to complete. It involves moving the patient into the scanner, and relies on specialist interpretation. It provides good imaging of the retroperitoneum and is 92–98% accurate in guiding the decision to operate. It should be used only if the patient is haemodynamically stable and may miss occult injuries such as the early signs of ruptured hollow organs, eg the small bowel

Diagnostic peritoneal lavage

Diagnostic peritoneal lavage (DPL) provides a rapid way of determining whether an unstable patient with abdominal trauma requires a laparotomy. It does not reveal retroperitoneal blood loss, however, and carries a 1% complication rate, even in experienced hands. It is made more difficult by obesity, but can be up to 98% sensitive. It is used less often with the advent of FAST ultrasonography in the resus room.

FAST scan (focused assessment with sonography for trauma)

The FAST scan is a rapid, bedside ultrasound examination performed by suitably trained personnel to identify intraperitoneal haemorrhage or pericardial tamponade. It is used to assess patients who have suffered blunt abdominal and thoracic trauma.

Ultrasonography is poor at identifying and grading solid organ injury, bowel injury and retroperitoneal trauma. The FAST examination is directed purely at detecting free intraperitoneal fluid or the presence of cardiac tamponade.

FAST examines four areas for free fluid:
- Perihepatic and hepatorenal space
- Perisplenic
- Pelvis
- Pericardium

Indications for DPL
- Multiply injured patient with equivocal abdominal examination
- Suspicion of injury with difficult examination
- Refractory hypotension with no other obvious sites of haemorrhage

Contraindications to DPL
- Absolute – decision already made for laparotomy
- Relative – previous abdominal surgery, obesity, advanced cirrhosis, coagulopathy, pregnancy

CHAPTER 6

Procedure box: Technique of diagnostic peritoneal lavage

This is illustrated in Figure 6.19. Empty the stomach and bladder with an NG tube and a Foley catheter, respectively. Prep and drape the lower abdomen. Infiltrate LA with adrenaline at the site of incision, in the line, a third of the distance from umbilicus to pubic symphysis. Make a 2- to 3-cm vertical incision (long enough to expose the linea alba and peritoneum under direct vision) and dissect down in the line. Elevate the peritoneum between haemostats and carefully incise. Thread DPL catheter gently into the pelvis and aspirate gently. If blood is found, proceed to laparotomy. Otherwise, instil 1 litre warm saline, and then allow this to drain back into the bag under gravity.

- If macroscopic blood or contamination is seen, proceed to laparotomy
- If macroscopically clear, send sample to the lab for analysis

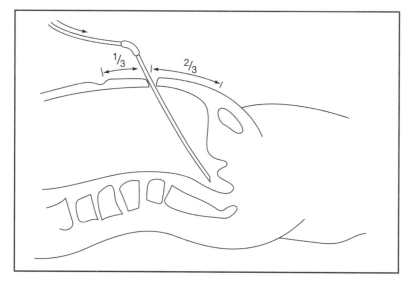

Figure 6.19 Diagnostic peritoneal lavage

Positive results of diagnostic peritoneal lavage

- Red blood cells (RBCs) >100 000/mm³
- Gram stain showing organisms
- Peritoneal lavage fluid found in urinary catheter or chest drain
- White cell count (WCC) >500/mm³
- Gastrointestinal (GI) tract contents aspirated on DPL

Penetrating abdominal trauma

- Low velocity, eg knives – 3% cause visceral injury
- High velocity, eg bullets – 80% cause visceral injury

These injuries commonly involve:

- Liver 40%
- Small bowel 30%
- Diaphragm 20%
- Colon 15%

Gunshot injuries are also likely to involve intra-abdominal vascular structures in 25% of cases.

Trauma to abdominal viscera

The management of trauma to individual intra-abdominal viscera is discussed in the Abdomen chapter of Book 2. A general outline only will be given here.

Trauma to the spleen

The spleen is one of the most commonly injured abdominal organs. Injury usually results from blunt trauma to the abdomen/lower ribs. Injury may arise from more minor trauma in children (due to the proportionally larger spleen and less robust rib cage) or in adults with splenomegaly. The injury is tolerated better in children.

- Main signs are those of haemorrhage
- Investigation depends on whether or not the patient is haemodynamically stable
- Management depends on the degree of injury (conservative vs surgical)
- Post-splenectomy prophylaxis against infection is vital

If the patient is haemodynamically stable the possibility of splenic injury can be assessed with USS or CT (both have diagnostic accuracy of >90%) although most trauma protocols recommend CT to exclude intra-abdominal injuries.

If the patient is unstable with obvious abdominal injuries, laparotomy is indicated after initial attempts at resuscitation. DPL is indicated only if there is doubt as to the cause of hypovolaemia (eg in unconscious, multiply injured patients); some argue that it has **no role**, because less invasive investigations can be carried out if the patient is stable and immediate laparotomy is indicated if the patient is unstable.

Management is conservative unless there are signs of continuing haemorrhage, where laparotomy with splenectomy is indicated. Currently, there is a trend towards conservative management to avoid subsequent complications of overwhelming sepsis.

Long-term prophylaxis against encapsulated organisms is essential in order to prevent post-splenectomy sepsis syndrome. Immunisation with Pneumovax, Hib vaccine and Meningovax should be administered in the postop period. Long-term penicillin prophylaxis may also be advisable for susceptible people.

Trauma to the liver

The liver is the most frequently injured intra-abdominal organ. Mechanisms of injury include:
- **Penetrating injuries:** knife and gunshot wounds
- **Blunt injuries:** deceleration in falls from a height or RTAs

There is a hepatic injury scale that grades the liver damage from grade I (small laceration or subcapsular haematoma) to grade VI (avulsion, incompatible with survival).

Management includes simultaneous assessment and resuscitation along ATLS guidelines. If surgery is indicated, it should be performed promptly and by an appropriately experienced surgeon. Transfer to a liver unit may be necessary before or after surgery. The initial management should be along ATLS guidelines (see Section 1.1).

Trauma to the pancreas

Blunt trauma to the pancreas is increasingly common and it is usually due to a compressive injury against the vertebral column from a direct

CHAPTER 6

461

blow (eg RTA, handlebar injury). It is a difficult diagnosis to make because the retroperitoneal location may mask symptoms.

- **Major injury:** proximal gland damage involving the head with duct disruption
- **Intermediate injury:** distal gland damage with duct disruption
- **Minor injury:** contusion or laceration that does not include damage to the main ducts

Amylase level may or may not be elevated; abdominal radiograph may show associated duodenal injury and free gas; CT scan may be required.

Surgical intervention is reserved for major injuries. Lesser injuries can be treated with haemostasis alone. Distal injuries may require resection of the tail. Proximal injuries may require pancreaticoduodenectomy.

Trauma to the intestine and mesentery

Blunt injury leads to shearing, compression or laceration injuries. Injuries can be direct, or secondary to devitalisation when the mesenteric blood supply is compromised. Damage occurs in three ways:

- Bursting due to sudden rises in intra-abdominal pressure
- Crush injury against the vertebral column
- Deceleration injury at points where viscera are tethered (ie become intraperitoneal from retroperitoneal, or vice versa)

Penetrating injuries may cause perforation of the bowel (eg those caused by a blade) or large areas of damage (eg those from a gunshot).

Management of trauma to the intestine and mesentery

Conservative management of intestine and mesentery trauma

- With repeated observation and early intervention if required (peritonism may be slow to develop)

Surgical management of intestine and mesentery trauma

- Primary repair of small perforation (safer in right-sided injuries than in left-sided)
- Resection with end-to-end anastomosis (if early intervention and minimal peritoneal soiling)
- Defunctioning colostomy (usually due to gross contamination in a hostile abdomen)

Renal trauma

Learning point

Injuries to the genitourinary tract account for 10% of all renal trauma.

Most often renal trauma is due to blunt trauma, especially RTAs, and is associated with other abdominal injuries (eg liver or spleen). Penetrating trauma accounts for <10% but has a higher association with requirement for intervention.

Injury is more common in children who have relatively larger kidneys and less surrounding fat and muscle bulk than adults and in those with previously abnormal kidneys (eg hydronephrosis or cysts).

Assessment of renal trauma

Clearly these may be multiply injured patients and the ATLS principles of acute trauma should be applied.

- The mechanism of injury is important (eg deceleration in high-speed RTA)
- **Gross haematuria means mandatory imaging**. Microhaematuria should be sought either by dipstick or microscopy

Investigating renal trauma

Experience in the USA has shown that not all patients with microscopic haematuria have significant renal injury and therefore imaging is not indicated in all patients. Be suspicious if there is associated systemic shock and loin pain as severe renal pedicle injury may present with only microscopic haematuria. A perinephric haematoma may be palpable. Plain abdominal radiograph may show loss of psoas shadowing, an enlarged kidney, fractures of overlying ribs or transverse processes of lumbar vertebrae, or scoliosis to the affected side due to muscle spasm.

Criteria for renal imaging

- Any penetrating trauma to the flank or abdomen associated with haematuria
- Blunt trauma with gross haematuria
- Blunt trauma with microscopic haematuria and a systolic BP <90 mmHg at any stage
- Deceleration injury (classically associated with renal devascularisation and therefore may not present with haematuria)
- Associated major intra-abdominal injury and microscopic haematuria
- Any child with any degree of haematuria

Standard imaging is a CT scan with intravenous contrast (in a *stable* patient). An intravenous urogram (IVU) may be used, but CT has advantages in that it more accurately stages renal injuries and it also identifies other intra-abdominal injuries. It also aids in the decision to manage the patient conservatively.

Classification of renal trauma based on the American Association for the Surgery of Trauma Staging System

Grade 1 Contusion, subcapsular haematoma but intact renal capsule

Grade 2 Minor laceration of the cortex not involving the medulla or collecting system

Grade 3 Major laceration extending through the cortex and the medulla but not involving the collecting system

Grade 4 A major laceration extending into the collecting system

Grade 5 A completely shattered kidney or renal pedicle avulsion leading to renal devascularisaton

---

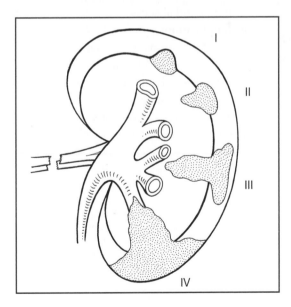

Figure 6.20 The four stages of renal trauma

Management of renal trauma

Of blunt renal injuries 98% are managed non-surgically (hospital admission and bedrest until gross haematuria clears). Serial ultrasonography may be used to monitor haematoma.

Absolute indications for renal exploration include:

- Persistent hypotension despite resuscitation
- Expanding haematoma
- Disruption of the renal pelvis with leakage of urine

Recent experience suggests that not all penetrating trauma requires exploration; 40% of stab wounds and 75% of gunshot wounds were managed non-surgically in one large American series.

Complications of renal trauma

Early complications

- Haemorrhage
- Urinary extravasation (leading to urinoma and abscess)

Late complications

- Penetrating trauma may leave residual arteriovenous (AV) fistula
- Hypertension due to renal ischaemia or renal artery stenosis
- Fibrotic change causing obstruction at the renal pelvis and hydronephrosis

---

Ureteric trauma

Learning point

Most ureteric injury is iatrogenic; 50% of iatrogenic injuries to the ureter occur during gynaecological surgery due to the nearby uterine artery.

Management options include stenting or repair, depending on whether the injury is diagnosed immediately or diagnosis is delayed.

Damage to the ureter after external violence is rare but may be due to penetrating injury.

Most ueretic injuries are due to damage at surgery and include ligation, crush injury due to clamps, complete or partial transection, or devascularisation:

- 50% of iatrogenic ureteric injuries occur during gynaecological surgery, especially during hysterectomy (the ureter lies very close to the uterine artery)
- The remaining 50% occur in colorectal, vascular or urological surgery
- Damage during ureteroscopy occurs in approximately 5% of patients

Presentation of ureteric trauma

- **Early recognition:** often a transected ureter may be obvious at the time of surgery. If ureteric injury is suspected during surgery then the ureter can be directly inspected or a retrograde ureterogram obtained
- **Late recognition:** postoperative ureteric injury may present with loin pain and unexplained pyrexia due to abdominal collection of urine or drainage of urine (from a wound drain or per vaginam)

Investigating ureteric trauma

IVU is the first-line investigation. It may show hydronephrosis or delayed excretion of contrast. Urinary extravasation may also be seen.

Management of ureteric trauma

This depends on whether the ureteric injury is recognised at the time of damage, or the diagnosis is delayed.

Immediate recognition of surgical ureteric injury

- **Ligation of the ureter:** treat by removing the ligature and observation. A ureteric stent should be placed across the area of damage to reduce risk of stricture formation
- **Transection recognised immediately:** this may be managed by direct end-to-end repair.

The ureter should be spatulated, bearing in mind that the blood supply may be tenuous. If there is likely to be any degree of tension the bladder should be mobilised to allow it to be brought up towards the ureteric injury, with subsequent ureteric re-implantation (methods include the **Boari flap** and the **psoas hitch**). A TVV may also be considered. Once again, the ureter is stented to allow for healing without stricturing.

Delayed recognition of surgical ureteric injury

The options are stenting and surgical repair. Occasionally a stent can be passed retrogradely via the bladder. If this is unsuccessful, percutaneous drainage of the kidney (nephrostomy) should be performed, both to relieve obstruction and to prevent urine leak. Subsequent surgical repair should be carried out (about 6 weeks after injury).

Options for repair include:
- **Re-implantation:** if this is feasible
- **Transureteroureterostomy:** anastomosis of the damaged ureter to the normal one on the other side
- **Ureteric substitution** using ileum
- **Autotransplantation** of the kidney to the iliac fossa
- **Nephrectomy:** sometimes this is the simplest solution if there is thought to be associated renal damage and the contra-lateral kidney has normal function

Ureteroscopic injury

This can usually be treated by insertion of a ureteric stent.

Bladder trauma

Learning point

Blunt trauma can cause injury to the bladder.
- 80% of bladder injuries have an associated pelvic fracture
- 10% of pelvic fractures have an associated bladder injury
- Penetrating injury is rare in the UK

The bladder is also at risk when distended and full from blunt trauma to the abdomen. The tear often occurs at the dome. Iatrogenic injuries may occur during surgery, eg open pelvic surgery such as caesarean section, or endoscopic surgery such as transurethral resection of bladder tumour (TURBT).

CHAPTER 6

Presentation of bladder trauma

Macroscopic haematuria is present in 95–100% of patients with blunt bladder injury. There may be lower abdominal pain and oliguria or anuria. There may be urinary peritonitis if the diagnosis is made late. Extravasation of urine may also cause a rise in blood urea level due to reabsorption.

Investigating bladder trauma

Retrograde cystography is the most accurate method of diagnosing bladder injury. There are two main steps:

- Fill the bladder with contrast via urethral catheter (at least 400 ml)
- Obtain post-drainage views (otherwise small leaks may be missed)

Intraperitoneal and extraperitoneal rupture can be distinguished according to distribution of contrast. Most bladder injuries cause extraperitoneal rupture.

Management of bladder trauma

Extraperitoneal perforations require catheter drainage for 14 days. Healing should be confirmed with a repeat cystogram. Intraperitoneal bladder perforations all require open surgical repair.

Note that bladder injuries may coexist with urethral injuries so care should be taken with catheterisation if there is blood at the urethral meatus. If there is any doubt then a retrograde urethrogram should be performed. If a catheter cannot be inserted due to urethral injury a CT cystogram should be performed. If there is an extraperitoneal leak a suprapubic catheter should be inserted under radiological guidance or an open cystotomy performed.

Trauma to the urethra and male genitals

Learning point

Urethral injuries can be anterior (associated with fall-astride injuries or instrumentation) or posterior (associated with pelvic fractures). They may present with the classic triad of symptoms or with characteristic bruising.

A safe method of investigation is by urethrogram followed by careful urethral catheterisation by an experienced urologist, or suprapubic catheterisation at open cystotomy with inspection of the bladder.

Post-traumatic strictures may need reconstruction.

Classification of urethral trauma

Urethral trauma can be divided into anterior and posterior urethral injuries:

- **Anterior injuries:** these usually affect the penile and bulbar urethra and are often associated with instrumentation of the urinary tract or 'fall astride' injuries
- **Posterior injuries:** these usually affect the membranous urethra and are common sequelae of pelvic fracture (occurring in 4–14%). Some 10–17% of posterior urethral injuries have associated bladder rupture

Presentation of urethral trauma

Urethral trauma may present with the classic triad of:

- Blood at the urethral meatus
- An inability to void
- A palpably full bladder

CHAPTER 6

This triad occurs in a minority of patients, and indeed 50% of patients with significant urethral injury will not have blood at the urethral meatus. Anterior urethral injuries may produce classic **butterfly bruising** of the perineum. Bruising is confined by Colles' fascia, which fuses posteriorly with the perineal body and extends a little way down each thigh.

Investigating urethral trauma

If there is blood at the urethral meatus there are two schools of thought.

Option 1: try to gently pass a urethral catheter. This should be performed by a urologist and attempts should be abandoned at the slightest resistance. The risk here is the conversion of a partial injury to a complete injury.

Option 2: perform an **immediate urethrogram**. This is done by inserting a 12-Fr catheter just inside the urethral meatus and slightly inflating the balloon with 1–2 ml water. Water-soluble contrast is then injected.

Management of urethral trauma

If a catheter cannot be passed, urethral injuries should be treated by **suprapubic catheterisation**. Ideally this should be carried out via an open formal cystotomy, at which time the bladder is inspected. Subsequent management will depend on the extent of urethral stricture that develops after conservative management. Injuries may heal with only a small amount of residual stricturing. Severe strictures may be treated with urethral reconstruction at a later stage (reduced incidence of long-term stricturing compared with primary repair).

Penile and scrotal trauma

Scrotal haematoma and testicular rupture may occur after a direct blow. Mild haematoma is treated conservatively but a ruptured testis requires surgical reconstruction of the overlying coverings. Penile fracture (ie rupture of the corpus cavernosum) requires surgical intervention to prevent fibrosis and erectile dysfunction.

4.6　Trauma to the soft tissues and skin

Learning point

The key issues in the management of traumatic wounds are:
- Assessment of devitalised tissue
- Contamination:
  - Micro (bacteria)
  - Macro (foreign bodies)
- Debridement
- Antibiotics and tetanus prophylaxis

Never treat a contaminated wound with primary closure.

Recognition of viable tissue

Skin viability

Look for:
- Colour and capillary return
- Bleeding from the dermal edge

Muscle viability

Accurate initial assessment of muscle viability is difficult. Debridement of dead muscle tissue

CHAPTER 6

is important to prevent infection. Traditionally assessment is by the **4Cs:**

Colour
Capillary bleeding
Consistency
Contractility

Colour is the least reliable sign – discoloration may occur due to dirt, contusion, haemorrhage or local vasoconstriction. Transient capillary vasospasm may prevent bleeding in otherwise healthy tissue. Muscle consistency is the best predictor of viability: healthy muscle springs back into shape when compressed with forceps; non-viable muscle loses this ability and becomes gelatinous. Viable muscle fibres should twitch when squeezed with forceps.

Bone viability

Look for:
- Degree of soft-tissue and periosteal stripping
- Pinpoint bleeding from debrided edges

See Chapter 11 on Plastic Surgery for discussion of:
- Wound contamination
- Wound debridement
- Antibiotics and tetanus prophylaxis
- Skin loss and reconstruction

4.7 Trauma to the peripheral nerves

Acute injury to peripheral nerves is usually the result of direct mechanical trauma:
- Blunt (pressure)
- Penetrative (laceration)
- Traction (RTA and fracture)

Nerve damage is often missed, so assume injury present until proved otherwise. Chronic nerve injuries are more common. Leprosy is the most common cause of chronic loss of sensation worldwide, but diabetes is more common in developed countries.

Commonest causes of sensation loss

In the UK	Worldwide
Diabetes mellitus (DM)	Leprosy
Peripheral vascular disease (PVD)	
Radiotherapy	

Structure of peripheral nerves

- **Endoneurium:** connective tissue around individual axons, containing collagen, capillaries and lymphatics. Protects from stretching forces
- **Perineurium:** dense connective tissue surrounding fascicle. Strong mechanical barrier. Diffusion barrier protects nerve fibres from large ionic fluxes
- **Epineurium:** outermost layer of connective tissue. Binds fascicles together and forms thick protective coat. Forms 25–75% cross-sectional area of nerve. Thicker over joints

Nerve disruption and healing

The classification of nerve lesions and process of healing is discussed in Chapter 3, Surgical technique and technology.

Diagnosis and investigation of nerve injuries

Arterial bleeds suggest the possibility of nerve injury. Check the individual peripheral nerves, as detailed in the table.

CHAPTER 6

PERIPHERAL NERVE CHECKS

	Sensory nerves	Motor nerves
Upper limb nerves		
Axillary	Regimental badge area (lateral upper arm)	Abduction of shoulder
Musculocutaneous	Lateral area of forearm	Flexion of elbow
Median	Palmar aspect of index finger	Abductor pollicis brevis
Radial	Dorsal web space between thumb and index finger	Wrist extension
Ulnar	Little finger	Index finger abduction
Lower limb nerves		
Femoral	Anterior aspect of knee	Knee extension
Obturator	Medial aspect of thigh	Hip adduction
Superficial peroneal	Lateral aspect of foot dorsum	Ankle eversion
Deep peroneal	Dorsal aspect of first web space	Ankle and toe dorsiflexion
NB: Sensation can be maintained for 72 hours so look for sensation distortion.		

Comparison of peripheral nerve function

- Hypersensitivity
- Reduced two-point discrimination
- Test with light touch
- Vasomotor function (reduced sweat production; disturbance of sympathetic function is an important early sign of nerve damage)

Treatment of nerve injuries

Aim to maximise the chance of recovery. Primary repair is always favourable as the outcome is better.

Nerve recovery

- Stump oedema occurs after 1 hour
- Axons start to sprout filopodia from the proximal to the last node of Ranvier and rely on the myelin sheath to guide them to the end-organ (day 3)
- Chromatolysis (regenerative response of cell body whereby cell body enlarges) occurs in response to the increased metabolism (days 14–20)

- Distal axon undergoes wallerian degradation (complete in 6 weeks)
- Muscle innervated by the injured nerve wastes over time

During examination of the progress of a peripheral nerve injury, **Tinel's sign** represents painful paraesthesia on percussion over the area of regeneration.

Open injuries

- Always surgically explore and debride the wound thoroughly
- Clean cuts should be repaired or marked with 6/0 nylon
- Crushed/torn nerves are lightly opposed and reoperated on at 2–3 weeks

Note that vascular and orthopaedic injuries take priority over nerve injuries.

CHAPTER 6

469

Closed injuries

- Mostly axonotmesis or neuropraxia
- Late surgery scar tissue should be excised; clean-cut ends should be anastomosed
- Use nerve grafts
- Use limb splints to decrease tension

Techniques for repairing nerves

- Epineural
- Fascicular
- Grouped fascicular
- Mixed repair

All wounds should be free of foreign bodies and nerves aligned with no tension.

4.8 Spinal cord injuries

Learning point

The major trauma patient must be safely immobilised until the spine is cleared. At the end of the secondary survey you should have lateral C-spine X-rays and a clinical assessment of the spinal cord, which will lead you to one of the following conclusions:

1. The history, mechanism of injury and lack of clinical signs in a conscious patient who has no pain on palpation and no restriction of movement excludes a significant spinal injury
   Action: C-spine may be cleared clinically with or without adequate X-rays
2. There is a significant mechanism of injury but the patient is conscious and has no clinical signs
   Action: C-spine may be cleared clinically but adequate imaging is advised
3. There is a significant mechanism of injury and the patient is not fully conscious or has significant distracting pain
   Action: It is difficult to clear the C-spine clinically and full imaging (which may include a CT) may be necessary
4. There are clinical signs of spinal injury, such as pain on palpation or restriction of movement or focal neurology, but no radiological signs on lateral C-spine X-rays
   Action: Full imaging is needed before clearing the C-spine (usually CT)
5. There is radiological evidence of spinal injury on C-spine X-rays
   Action: Urgent discussion with neurosurgeons, keep patient immobilised, and image the rest of the spine

The overriding concern with spinal injuries is the risk of the trauma team either *causing* or *completing* an injury to the spinal cord, which can result in devastating and permanent neurological injury. This causes tragedy at a personal level, and has a long-term economic impact on medical resources. Utmost caution and vigilance should therefore be exercised when dealing with trauma victims at risk of having a spinal injury.

CHAPTER 6

Trauma cases at risk of a spinal injury

- Unconscious/head injury (10% risk of associated C-spine injury)
- High-speed RTA
- Injury above the clavicle
- Sensory or motor deficit
- Brachial plexus injury
- Fall from heights more than 3 times patient's height

National Institute for Health and Clinical Excellence Head Injury guidelines 2007.

Indications for immediate three-view radiograph:

- Patient cannot actively rotate neck to 45 degrees to left and right (if safe to assess the range of movement in the neck)
- Not safe to assess range of movement in the neck
- Neck pain or midline tenderness plus: age ≥ 65 years, or dangerous mechanism of injury
- Definitive diagnosis of cervical spine injury required urgently (for example, prior to surgery)

Indications for immediateCT imaging:

- GCS < 13 on initial assessment
- Has been intubated
- Plain film series technically inadequate (for example, desired view unavailable), suspicious or definitely abnormal
- Continued clinical suspicion of injury despite normal X-ray
- Patient is being scanned for multi-region trauma

Learning point

Assess the motor and sensory function below the level of the injury.
Complete injury: there is no motor or sensory function below the level of the injury.
Incomplete injury: there is partial motor and sensory function below the level of the injury (may also demonstrate sacral sparing with perianal sensation).

Neurological assessment

Motor function

The assessment of motor function should reflect active movement by the patient related to each spinal level.

Movement related to spinal level

C3, C4 and C5 supply the diaphragm
C5 flexes the elbow C6 extends the wrist
C7 extends the elbow C8 flexes the fingers

T1 spreads the fingers
T1–T12 supply the chest wall and abdominal muscles

L2 flexes the hip
L3 extends the knee
L4 dorsiflexes the foot
L5 wiggles the toes

S1 plantar-flexes the foot
S3, S4, S5 supply the bladder, bowel, anal sphincter and other pelvic muscles

CHAPTER 6

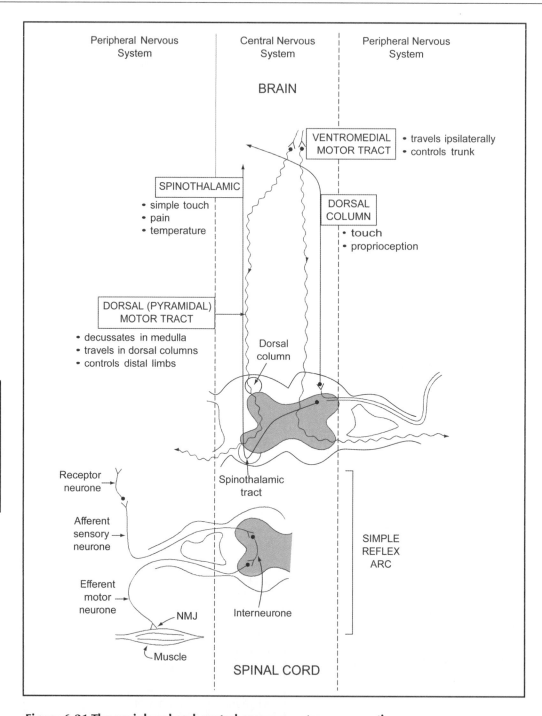

Figure 6.21 The peripheral and central nervous systems – somatic

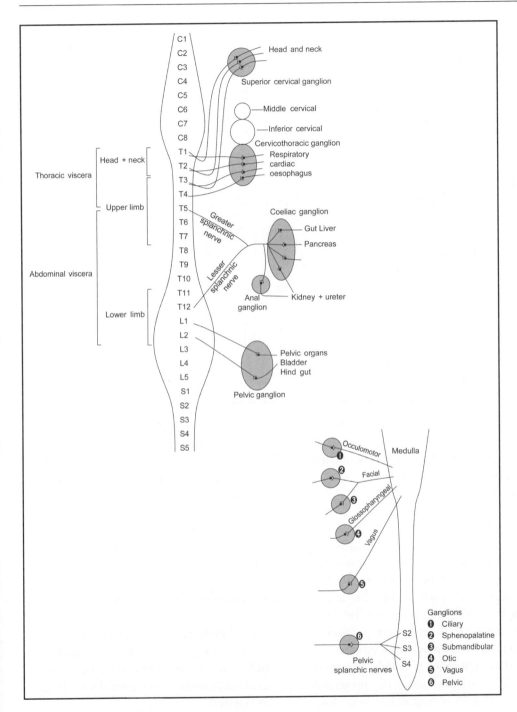

Figure 6.22 The peripheral nervous system – autonomic

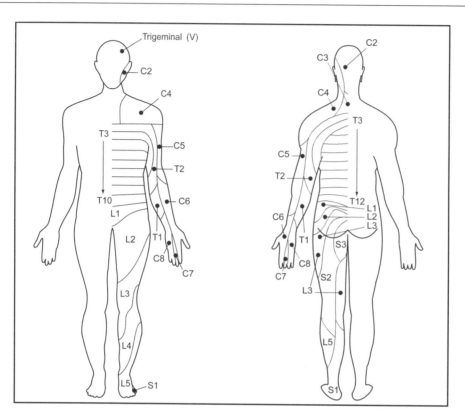

**Figure 6.23
Sensory levels**

Motor function is conveyed by the ventromedial and dorsal motor tracts (see Fig. 6.21). It is important to remember where the fibres of each tract decussates in the spinal cord.

Sensory function

Pain and temperature perception are conveyed by the spinothalamic tract which supplies the contralateral side of the body (see Fig. 6.21). Deep and superficial pain should be tested for separately (the pinch test and pricking with a broken tongue depressor, respectively). Superficial pain and light touch must be carefully distinguished as light touch is widely conveyed in the spinal cord and may be preserved when superficial pain sensation has been lost, enabling the diagnosis of a partial (as opposed to complete) spinal cord injury. Partial injuries have some potential for recovery, whereas complete

injuries carry a dismal prognosis. In extreme cases the perianal and scrotal areas may be the only regions preserved (sacral sparing) and these should be carefully tested for sensation and anal contraction.

NB: loss of sensation below the level of spinal injury may obscure the diagnosis of other life-threatening injury.

The sensory levels are shown in Fig.6.23

- **Motor function:** this is transmitted via the corticospinal tracts which run on the ipsilateral side. Voluntary movement and involuntary response to painful stimuli can be assessed
- **Proprioception:** this is subserved by the posterior columns on the ipsilateral side and can be tested by joint position sense, and

CHAPTER 6

vibration sense using a tuning fork

- **Reflexes:** these should be assessed in the standard fashion, using a reflex hammer, and carefully documented for serial evaluation
- **Autonomic function:** evidence of damage to the autonomic nervous system can manifest as priapism and/or incontinence

Injury to the cervical spine

> ### Learning point
>
> Clinical findings that suggest C-spine injury in an unconscious patient include:
> - Flaccid areflexia
> - Abdominal breathing (use of accessory muscles of respiration)
> - Elbow flexion without extension
> - Grimaces to pain above the clavicle (but not to pain below the clavicle)
> - Hypotension with bradycardia (and euvolaemia)
> - Priapism
>
> NB: Accurate repeated documentation of clinical findings is essential in order to establish a baseline with which to compare trends of improvement or deterioration.

Assessment of the cervical spine

If a cervical spine injury is suspected then strict immobilisation must be maintained until accurate assessment can be performed by an adequately qualified individual. Assessment should include an accurate history, with careful consideration of the mechanism of injury and energy of impact.

Clinical symptoms in a conscious patient may include pain and neurological deficit. Clinical signs may include deformity (a palpable 'step off'), bruising, crepitus, and muscle spasm. A full radiological assessment (AP and lateral C-spine, visualisation of C7 with an effective pull-down, or a swimmer's view, and additional CT scanning if necessary).

Only when there is an absence of clinical and radiological evidence of a C-spine injury should spinal precautions be dispensed with. The cervical spine, if injured, is at particular risk during endotracheal intubation, 'log rolling', and transfer onto the operating table. During these manoeuvres, extreme caution must be exercised. For example: fibreoptic intu- bation avoids extending the neck from the neutral position; log rolling should be the minimum necessary to complete the secondary survey and only performed with an adequate number of trained assistants (four) in order to maintain in-line stabilisation of the C-spine

In the first hour

Lateral C-spine radiographs are obtained as part of the standard trauma series (C-spine, chest, pelvis). Adequate views from the base of the skull to T1 must be obtained and the region of C7/T1 requires either a 'pull-down' technique, or a swimmer's view for proper assessment. The area of the atlas and axis can be rapidly assessed during CT scanning for a head injury.

It must be noted that portable films taken in the emergency setting miss up to 15% of fractures, therefore if a spinal injury is suspected on clinical grounds, then such an injury should be assumed to be present until proven otherwise. If a C-spine injury is present, then the rest of the spine needs to undergo radiological assessment.

CHAPTER 6

Secondary evaluation

After the acute phase of the patient's assessment and resuscitation, if a C-spine injury is suspected or proven, then specialist evaluation by the orthopaedic or neurosurgical team will follow. This will include AP and oblique views of the C-spine, odontoid views, and CXR. Bony fragments within the spinal canal can be revealed by CT or MRI scanning. Flexion/extension views of the C-spine may also be deemed necessary and should only be performed under the strict supervision of an experienced specialist.

Specific types of cervical spine fracture

- **C1 atlas fracture:** axial loading can cause a blow-out of the ring of C1 (Jefferson fracture) best seen on the open-mouth view. A third of these are associated with a fracture of C2, but cord injuries are uncommon. These fractures are unstable and require specialist referral and management
- **C1 rotary subluxation:** usually presents in a child as torticollis. Odontoid views show the peg to be asymmetric with respect to the lateral masses of C1. No attempt should be made to overcome the rotated position of the head, and specialist referral and management is required
- **C2 odontoid dislocation:** bony injury may be absent and dislocation may be due solely to disruption of the transverse ligament on C1. Suspect this when the space between the anterior arch of C1 and the odontoid is more than 3 mm (Steel's rule of three: adjacent to the atlas, one third of the spinal canal is occupied by the odontoid, one third intervening space, one third spinal cord). This condition is unstable with a high risk of cord injury. Strict immobilisation and specialist management are mandatory

- **C2 odontoid fractures:** all require strict immobilisation and specialist referral:

  Type 1   Above the base

  Type 2   Across the base (NB: childhood epiphysis may resemble this on X-ray)

  Type 3   Fracture extends onto the vertebral body

- **'Hangman's' fracture:** this results from an extension–distraction injury plus axial compression, and involves the posterior elements of C2 (in judicial hanging the slip knot was placed under the chin). This is a highly unstable injury and traction is strictly contraindicated. Strict immobilisation and specialist referral are essential
- **C3 to C7 injuries:** these can arise through a variety of mechanisms and, apart from obvious bony injury and clinical signs, they may be revealed by a haematoma reducing the space between the anterior border of C3 and the pharynx (normally < 5 mm). In children this distance is normally two thirds the width of C2 and increases on Valsalva. These require strict immobilisation, followed by specialist referral and management
- **Facet dislocations:** these may be unilateral (suspect them if the displacement between adjacent vertebral bodies is 25%) or bilateral (displacement of 50%). You may also see displacement of the spinous processes on AP views with unilateral dislocation
- **Cervical cord injuries:** at risk are injuries associated with a bone fragment from the anterior/inferior vertebral body which give the classic 'tear drop' appearance on X-ray. The posterior vertebral fragment may displace into the canal and cause cord damage

Thoracic spine injuries

These usually result in wedge fractures from hyperflexion injuries. Cord injury is uncommon but, because the canal is narrow in this region, cord injury is frequently complete when present. Thoracic spine injury more commonly occurs with a rotational injury. Wedge fractures of the thoracic vertebrae are splinted by the rib cage and only require internal fixation if the kyphosis exceeds 30° or if a neurological deficit is present.

Thoracolumbar injuries

Usually these result from hyperflexion and rotation, and they are commonly unstable. The cauda equina is at risk and will produce bladder and bowel signs, and deficits in the lower limbs. These patients are at high risk during log rolling so this may need to be minimised or deferred until X-ray studies are obtained.

Paralysis

Injury to any part of the motor pathway from the cerebrum, brain stem, spinal cord and motor unit may cause paralysis. Spinal cord injuries may be classified as 'complete' where sensory and motor loss may both occur or 'incomplete' where some functions are spared below the the level of injury.
- Paralysis is a loss of motor function.
- Paraplegia comes from greek meaning 'half-striking' and implies motor function loss in the lower extremities. Quadraplegia is paralysis of the upper limbs in conjunction. Hemiplegia is paralysis of one half of the side of the body.

Cerebral, midbrain, pontine or medullary injuries may result in contralateral hemiplegia or monoplegia. Remember it is important to elicit upper mototr neuron signs in detecting the level of cord damage as lower motor signs may result from segmental damage or root damage at a higher level.

Brown-Sequard syndrome

This syndrome results from hemisection of the spinal cord or disease processes affecting only one half of the cord. It results in ipsilateral motor dysfunction and contralateral sensory dysfunction below the level of the lesion. This occurs because motor fibres travel ipsilaterally in the spinal column and decussate in the brainstem. However, sensory fibres decussate in the spinal cord before ascending to the brain.

In the immediate post-injury phase, the injured spinal cord may appear completely functionless with resulting flaccidity and loss of reflexes. Several days or weeks later characteristic spasticity, hyperactive reflexes, and up-going plantar response supersede the flaccid state.

CHAPTER 6

4.9 Vascular Trauma

Learning point

Vascular trauma is most commonly iatrogenic

Trauma may be **blunt** or **penetrating**.

Arterial injury results in:

Acute limb ischaemia

Pseudo-aneurysm

Haematoma

Hypovolaemic shock

Venous injury results in:

Deep vein thrombosis

Chronic venous insufficieny

Haematoma

Hypovolaemic shock

Effects of blunt and penetrating injuries to arteries and veins

Arterial injury

The sequelae following arterial injury will be dependent on which layers of the arterial wall are injuried. Remember the artery is composed of

- Tunica Intima - comprises of the endothelium, a single cell layer in contact with blood, supported by the internal elastic lamina.
- Tunica Media – made up of smooth muscle cells and elastic fibres
- Tunica Externa or Adventitia – composed of collagen and the external elastic lamina. The collagen acts to anchor the vessel into surrounding tissue.

In the upper limb the areas of greatest concern are the axilla, medial and anterior upper arm, and antecubital fossa because of the superficial location of the axillary and brachial arteries in these regions. Injuries distal to the bifurcation of the brachial artery are less likely to result in serious limb ischemia due to the radial and ulnar anastomosis. Injuries to a single distal artery can often be managed by ligation alone if the palmar arches are complete.

In the lower extremity below the inguinal region, medial thigh, and popliteal fossa particularly are considered high-risk locations. Below the knee, the popliteal artery trifurcates to form the anterior and posterior tibial arteries and the peroneal artery. Arterial wounds affecting a single vessel distal to the trifurcation are unlikely to produce serious limb ischemia. If distal collateralization is adequate, injuries to a single branch may therefore be managed by ligation.

The result of blunt injury is dependent on the calibre of vessel affected.

- Rupture smaller arteries but are less likely to rupture larger vessels as larger vessels contain an increasing amount of elastic tissue. Rupture of smaller vessels will lead to localised bleeding and haemtoma formation.
- Larger vessels trauma may result in rupture of atherosclerotic plaques (found between the intima and media), instigating thrombosis within the vessel and emboli beyond this.
- Dissection of a larger vessel may occur with blood flow between the intima and media.
- External compression from a foreign body or following limb fracture may cause distal limb ischaemia and compartments syndrome.

Penetrating arterial injuries are likely to traverse all three layers of the vessel, this may result in:

- Life threatening haemorrhae and hypovolaemic shock
- Distal ischaemia of a limb or organ
- Haematoma
- Pseudo-aneurysm occurs when a breach of all three layers causes a persistent defective in continuity with a haematoma. The result is a pulsatile swelling with a wall consisting of connective tissue and compacted thrombus.
- Arterio-venous fistula

Arterial repair should be carried out were possible. Primary repair by suture may be possible in clean penetrating injuries with straight edges. However where segmental loss has occurred repair with vein or prosthesis should be considered. Ligation of an artery should only be considered in life threatening haemorrhage and may be followed by repair if the limb has not been rendered ischaemic for too long a period. Embolectomy of distal thrombo-embolus may also be required at time of operation.

Where there is a significant risk of limb loss, stroke, gut ischaemia or other serious consequence of ligation, intraluminal shunts may be employed to temporarily restore flow.

Venous injury

Veins are thinner walled and more fragile then arteries so may rupture more readily. Following blunt injury, however the pressure within them is lower and compression gains control of haemorrhage much more readily. Damage to the venous endothelium and media may instigate venous thrombosis as described in Virchows triad (thrombosis dependent on wall component, blood constituents and flow).

Concomitant arterial and venous injury is the most common finding following penetrating trauma. The most commonly injured vessels in order of frequency are superficial femoral vein, inferior vena cava, internal jugular vein, brachial vein then popliteal vein.

Most surgeons agree that the best management of major axial vein injuries is to repair them if possible. Even complex repairs are possible in patients who have minimal injuries and can tolerate additional operative time. For patients in extremis, where decisions of life over limb need to be made, repair of even major extremity veins becomes less important and ligation of the vein can be performed.

There is currently no evidence that repair of venous injuries leads to a higher incidence of venous thromboembolic complications. However limb swelling and oedema should expected and chronic venous insufficiency, defined by venous hypertension with resultant skin damage, may occur in the long term.

Assessment of vascular injury

Assessment of vascular injuries will be performed during the circulatory assessment in the ATLS protocol. Ischaemia is a limb-threatening or life-threatening condition.

Palpate peripheral pulses bilaterally for quality and symmetry in character, volume and rate.
- Dorsalis pedis
- Posterior tibial
- Femoral
- Radial
- Brachial
- Carotid

Document findings then re-evaluate peripheral pulses frequently for asymmetry and developing pathology.

CHAPTER 6

Arterial compromised limbs should be assessed for six key features (6 P's).

- Pulseless, pallor and 'perishingly' cold due to interrupted arterial tree.
- Paraesthesia and paralalysis due to ischaemia of the nerves.
- Pain due to ischaemia and lactic acidosis from interrupted arterial tree and nerve iscahemia.

Remember to assess concomitant neurological injury especially in juries to the axilla where the brachial plexus may be injured.

Extremity venous injuries are often difficult to identify unless significant hemorrhage is present, venous injuries are often difficult to diagnosis by physical examination alone. Slow, persistent hemorrhage from open soft tissue wounds may be noted. Venous injuries may require 12 to 24 hours to become symptomatic, usually with the development of swelling, oedema, or cyanosis. In cases of proximal venous injury, swelling may be massive and in extreme situations may be limb threatening and present as *phlegmasia cerulean dolens*.

For arterial injuries vascular supply to ischemic territories should be restored, this can be accomplished by thromboembolectomy, patch angioplasty, primary anastomosis, or bypass grafting. When the injury exceeds 30% of the circumference of the vessel, surgical repair should be performed with means other than simple closure, such as vein patching or grafting.

Treatment of ateriovenous fistulas involves dissection of both vessels and closure of the communication.

Interventional radiology is now fundamental in the management of vascular injuries in both adults and children. Excellent long-term results are achieved with endovascular treatment in several types of vascular injuries and anomalies with the techniques of embolization, coiling and endovascular stenting.

Iatrogenic injuries

Iatrogenic injuries are the most common reason for arteries or veins to be disrupted, the reasons include

- Arterial or venous cannulation for invasive monitoring or drug administration
- Repeated venipuncture, or arterial blood sampling
- Transfemoral or transradial arteriography, have been associated with thromboembolism in the lower extremities.
- During other surgery

Pseudo aneurysm is the most common complication due to the expanding on inerventional radiology and cardiological angiography. However pseudoaneurysms can be treated with percutaneous embolization if they have a small neck, surgical repair involves directly repairing the defect.

In infants and small children these pathologies are distinctly different from that in adults. The small size of their vessels, severe arterial vasospasm, and the consequences of diminished blood flow on limb growth must be considered.

Repair of an iatrogenic injury is dependent on the type of defect in the vascular wall that has been created, if this has occurred at operation simple over-sewing and closure of the defect may suffice, larger defects may need a vein or prosthetic patch to close the defect.

5.1 Burns

Burns

A burn injury is a form of multisystem trauma that may result in airway and breathing problems, circulatory compromise, shock and the consequences of shock, major wounds and wound healing requirements, and lifelong physical and psychological injury. In adults, burn injuries are often associated with other significant forms of trauma, and/or occur in patients with physical and medical comorbidities, particularly alcohol and drug abuse.

Epidemiology and aetiology of burn injury

In the UK about 250 000 burn injuries are sustained each year. The majority are managed as outpatients, but some 13 000 admissions will be required, of which around 10% will be significant enough to warrant fluid resuscitation. Half of this group will be children. Around 300 deaths occur secondary to burns.

Most burns occur in the home, but the aetiology differs between children and adults. Most adult burns are thermal injuries secondary to fire (approximately 50%), followed by scalds (33%). In children, more than two-thirds of injuries are scalds. The possibility of non-accidental injury should always be considered in children and adults with incapacity.

Mechanism of Injury

Burns may be caused by exposure to thermal, chemical, electrical or radiation sources.

- **Thermal injuries** are usually the result of exposure to flames, hot liquids or a heat source, eg radiator. The likelihood of a burn is related to the temperature of the source, duration and location of contact, age of the patient and any first aid received. Flame burns are usually deep injuries. Scalds may cause a mixed type of burn wound, with superficial and deeper areas. Contact burns usually require prolonged exposure to a hot source, and, in adults, may result when the patient has been incapacitated while in contact with the source, eg secondary to alcohol, or a collapse due to a medical event; the cause should be sought. Contact burns may occur in children with a much lesser duration of exposure

481

- **Chemical injuries** may be caused by any number of household and industrial agents. Acids cause a coagulative necrosis of tissue, and alkaline substances cause a liquefactive necrosis that may result in a more severe injury because the alkali continues to penetrate tissue layers. In general, both are managed by removal of contaminated clothing and dilution of the agent by extensive irrigation with water. Some chemicals require specific management and advice can be sought from manufacturers and toxicology services. Hydrofluoric acid burns are an important example because a relatively small burn (approximately 2%) may be fatal, depending on the concentration of the agent. The fluoride component causes extensive liquefactive necrosis, and also systemic effects, eg cardiac, neurological secondary to chelation of calcium ions. Calcium gluconate gel applied topically/injected into burn should be used as part of the management regimen
- **Electrical injuries** may be low voltage (<1000 V), eg domestic electricity, or high voltage (>1000 V). High-voltage injuries tend to be associated with significant coexistent trauma, muscle necrosis, compartment syndrome and renal failure. Low-voltage injuries may cause more localised injuries. Electrical injuries may cause cardiac dysrhythmias, which may be fatal or cause ongoing disturbances. Cardiac monitoring of patients with electrical injury is required if the ECG is abnormal on presentation to hospital, or if there is a history of loss of consciousness
- **Radiation injuries** are most commonly the result of exposure to UV radiation, ie sunburn. Burns may also be sustained secondary to exposure to ionising radiation as the result

of medical or nuclear accidents or nuclear explosions. Victims of nuclear explosions may also sustain extensive thermal injuries

Pathophysiology of burns

Burn injuries result in local and systemic effects. The local response to a burn can be illustrated using the model described by Jackson (1970), in which the burn wound has three zones:

- **Zone of coagulative necrosis** – area closest to heat source. Immediate coagulation of cellular proteins resulting in cell death
- **Zone of stasis** – area with damage to microcirculation caused by local inflammatory mediators, resulting in tissue hypoperfusion. May progress to necrosis, but potentially salvageable with adequate resuscitation/early surgery. May be seen clinically as an area of burn that initially appears viable, but is subsequently necrotic
- **Zone of hyperaemia** – production of inflammatory mediators secondary to burn injury results in widespread vasodilatation and capillary leak, contributing to hypovolaemia and oedema. May involve entire body surface in burns >20% area. Should return to normal

Release of inflammatory mediators results in vasodilatation and increased capillary permeability, and subsequently the development of oedema, which impairs tissue oxygen delivery. Oedema develops secondary to increased capillary permeability, increased capillary hydrostatic pressure, decreased interstitial hydrostatic pressure (a result of the effect of the burn on ground substance constituents) and increased tissue osmotic pressure (mainly due to loss of albumin into interstitium).

Important mediators in the development of the burn injury include histamine (promotes early-phase increase in capillary permeability), prostaglandin E_2 (increased capillary permeability and vasodilatation), bradykinins, leukotrienes and serotonin. Oxygen free radicals also have an important role, both in the response to injury and as a result of reperfusion injury.

A burn injury results in multisystem responses. When the injury is >20% of body surface area, systemic effects may be seen clinically. These include:

- **Hypovolaemia**, secondary to loss of fluid and protein into the interstitial space
- **Reduced cardiac output** – secondary to decreased venous return (vasodilatation, increased capillary permeability), inadequate pre-load (hypovolaemia), decreased myocardial contractility, increased after-load (increased systemic vascular resistance)
- **Respiratory** – risk of development of acute respiratory distress syndrome (ARDS) secondary to inflammatory response, even in the absence of inhalational injury
- **Hypermetabolic state**, secondary to release of stress hormones (catecholamines, cortisol, glucagon) and reduced sensitivity to anabolic hormones (insulin, growth hormone). Impairment of temperature regulation and increased muscle protein breakdown. Seen clinically as tachycardia, hyperthermia and muscle wasting. If burn >40% body surface, hypermetabolic response may continue up to 2 years post-injury. Modification of the hypermetabolic response is possible via environmental, nutritional, pharmacological and surgical interventions:
  - Environmental – control of ambient temperature to 33°C
  - Nutritional – calorie-controlled diet (early feeding also prevents gut dysfunction)

- Pharmacological – clear role for insulin therapy. Use of anabolic steroids and β blockers. Growth hormone in severely burned children
- **Immunosuppression**, resulting in increased susceptibility to infection
- **Gut dysfunction**, resulting in impaired barrier function and bacterial translocation through gut wall, causing systemic infection

Initial assessment and management

Despite the often shocking appearance of the burn victim, initial assessment should be performed as for any other trauma patient, using ATLS principles. Severely burned patients have a high incidence of concomitant trauma, often suggested by the history, eg explosion.

Primary survey

Airway + C-spine

Ensure airway clear and C-spine supported. Possible airway or inhalational injury suggested by history, facial burns, soot around mouth/nose, singeing of nasal hairs or oropharyngeal burns. If suspected, urgent senior anaesthetic review is required. If there is any doubt, patients should be intubated. Facial and oropharyngeal swelling may lead to subsequent respiratory compromise; swelling peaks at 12–36 hours post-injury.

Breathing + ventilation

All trauma patients should receive initial high-flow oxygen via a bag-and-mask system. Breathing may be compromised by mechanical restriction to chest expansion secondary to full-thickness burns (escharotomy required), effects of blast injury/pneumothorax, smoke

CHAPTER 6

inhalation and chemical injury – in particular, carbon monoxide poisoning.

Carbon monoxide (CO) poisoning results in tissue hypoxia. CO has approximately 210 times greater affinity for oxygen than Hb, resulting in a left shift of the $Hb:O_2$ dissociation curve. CO also affects cellular uptake of O_2 by impairment of the mitochondrial cytochrome systems.

Symptoms and signs of CO poisoning vary depending on blood levels of carboxyhaemoglobin, and are relatively non-specific and similar to alcohol intoxication:

Carboxyhaemoglobin (%)	Symptoms/Signs
0–10	None
10–20	Headache, nausea
20–30	Disorientation, irritability, drowsiness
30–40	Confusion, agitation
40–50	Hallucinations, convulsions, coma, respiratory depression
>50	Death

CO poisoning must be excluded in the obtunded burns patient, and should be considered present until proved otherwise. Classic signs, such as 'cherry red' discoloration of the skin, are not often seen. Carboxyhaemoglobin levels can be measured by most A&E blood gas analysers.

Management of CO poisoning is by administration of O_2. CO has a half-life of 250 minutes in room air, but 40 minutes on 100% O_2. O_2 should be continued for at least 24 hours as a secondary washout of cytochrome-bound CO occurs at approximately 24 hours and may lead to further obtundation.

Circulation

Establish IV access via at least two large-bore cannulas, ideally through non-burned tissue. Take blood for FBC, U&Es, coagulation studies and blood grouping. Assess perfusion by tissue capillary refill – beware of circumferential deep burns to limbs, as a tourniquet effect may develop and require release by escharotomy. Burns presenting acutely would not be expected to cause hypovolaemia. If the patient shows signs of hypovolaemia, seek another cause.

Disability

Establish level of consciousness using AVPU or GCS score. A depressed consciousness level may be secondary to neurological injury, hypoxia or hypovolaemia.

Exposure with environmental control

Clothing should be removed and the patient fully examined front and back to assess the full extent of the injury. An estimate of the extent of the burn can be made to guide fluid resuscitation. The patient should be kept warm while this process is completed.

The extent of a burn, as a percentage of the total body surface area (TBSA), may be estimated by a number of methods. Areas of erythema only should not be included in the calculation. For small areas or injuries that are patchy, such as scalds, a useful guide is that the *patient's* hand, with digits extended, represents approximately 1% of TBSA.

The 'rule of nines' divides the body into areas that are multiples of 9 (excluding perineum = 1%). This is not so useful in children and, although there is a paediatric modification of the rule of nines, other more accurate methods should be used.

CHAPTER 6

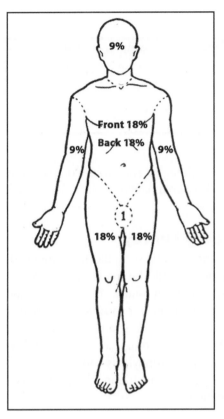

Adult rule of nines

A more accurate estimation of TBSA burned can be obtained using Lund and Browder charts – these are available in both adult and paediatric versions. The paediatric charts allow adjustment for the age of the child.

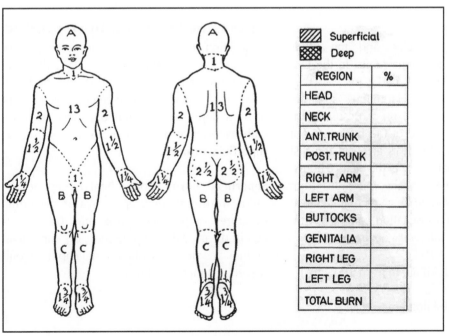

REGION	%
HEAD	
NECK	
ANT. TRUNK	
POST. TRUNK	
RIGHT ARM	
LEFT ARM	
BUTTOCKS	
GENITALIA	
RIGHT LEG	
LEFT LEG	
TOTAL BURN	

LUND AND BROWDER CHART

Area	0 years	1 year	5 years	10 years	15 years	Adult
A = ½ of head	9½	8½	6½	5½	4½	3½
B = ½ of one thigh	2¾	3¼	4	4¼	4½	4¾
C = ½ of one leg	2½	2½	2¾	3	3¼	3½

Fluid resuscitation

Fluid resuscitation for burns is given when the TBSA affected is at least 10% in children and 15% in adults.

The volumes of fluid required for burn resuscitation may be estimated by the use of a number of formulae. The adequacy of resuscitation should be measured by clinical parameters, in particular urine output and capillary refill time, and the volumes of fluid adjusted as required. Urine output of 0.5–1 ml/kg per hour in adults and 1–1.5 ml/kg per hour in children is the target. Other endpoints may be useful in monitoring adequacy of resuscitation, eg serum lactate and arterial base deficit.

Fluid resuscitation formulae and the fluids given vary between individual units. In the UK, the Parkland formula (3–4 ml/kg per % TBSA burn), using crystalloids (Hartmann's solution) initially, is most commonly used. Resuscitation should start from the time of the burn. Half of the calculated fluid volume is given in the first 8 hours, and the remainder over the next 16 hours. Colloid may be given as ongoing fluids from 24 hours. Children should be given maintenance fluids in addition to resuscitation volumes, with, for example, 0.45% saline/5% dextrose.
- 100 ml/kg for first 10 kg
- 50 ml/kg for each kilogram from 10 kg to 20 kg
- 20 ml/kg for each kilogram >20 kg

Trauma series imaging should be completed as for any other trauma patient.

Secondary survey

A full secondary survey should be completed. Particular note should be made of the circumstances of the burn injury, in particular the mechanism, duration of exposure and any first aid given. For major burns, an NG tube should be inserted and feeding commenced when possible. Tetanus prophylaxis should be given. Antibiotics are not given routinely as prophylaxis in burns patients.

Assessment of the burn wound

In addition to estimation of the percentage of the burn, assessment of the depth will guide the requirement for resuscitation and the likely need for surgical management. Assessment of burn depth can be difficult, even for those with experience. Burns may be categorised as **superficial** or **deep**.

Superficial burns should heal by epithelialisation from remaining epidermis or epidermal structures. Superficial burns may be subcategorised as either epidermal or superficial dermal. The presence of a normal capillary refill is seen in superficial burns.

CHAPTER 6

Epidermal burns damage epidermis only, producing a painful erythema. The most common example is sunburn. Blistering is not seen. Erythema should resolve over several days and no scarring should result.

Superficial dermal burns result in blistering. They are usually very painful because nerve endings are exposed. They should heal by re-epithelialisation within 10–14 days. A colour mismatch may result that is more marked in non-white patients.

Deep burns usually require surgical management other than in exceptional circumstances. They may be subcategorised as either **deep dermal** or **full thickness**. Capillary refill is lost, and these burns may be less painful due to more significant nerve damage.

Deep dermal burns tend to be redder in colour, indicating exposure of deeper layers of the dermis. Blistering is less frequent. Full-thickness burns have a white, leathery appearance and texture, no blistering is seen and they are usually painless. Coagulated blood vessels may be seen within the wound.

The use of laser Doppler imaging technology in the assessment of burn wound depth is a useful tool, and has recently been approved by the National Institute for Health and Clinical Excellence (NICE). This assesses blood flow in tissues and gives a pictographic representation of the depth of areas of the burn that may be used to aid decision-making about management.

Initial management of the burn wound

Stopping the burning process and cooling the burn wound may seem like obvious measures, but are not always effectively performed. Clothing and jewellery should be removed. The patient must be kept warm. If presenting within 3 hours of injury, the burn wound should be cooled with cool running water, ideally between 8° and 25°C for 20 minutes. Very cold/iced water may have a detrimental effect because it results in vasoconstriction and potential hypothermia. The burn may be cleaned with saline or 0.1% chlorhexidine, and a simple, non-adherent dressing applied. Clingfilm may be used as a temporary dressing, but care should be taken not to tightly wrap this around a limb. Limbs should be elevated, and patients with head and neck burns should be nursed in an upright position to limit swelling.

Deep burns of the chest may limit chest wall compliance and cause ventilation difficulties. Deep, circumferential burns of the limbs may have a tourniquet effect and result in circulatory compromise distally. In such situations, escharotomy may be required. This is surgical division of burned tissue to subcutaneous tissue, and extending into non-burned skin. In the chest, incisions along anterior axillary lines are connected by transverse incisions below the clavicles and across the upper abdomen. In the limbs, incisions follow midaxial lines, avoiding flexure creases, and taking care not to damage underlying structures, eg ulnar nerve. Escharotomies may result in significant bleeding, and should therefore be performed under controlled circumstances, ideally using surgical diathermy.

CHAPTER 6

Ongoing care and transfer

The British Burn Association has established a standard for referral of injuries to a burn unit:

- Burns >10% TBSA in adults
- Burns >5% TBSA in children
- Burns at the extremes of age – children and elderly people
- Full-thickness burns >5% TBSA
- Burns of special areas – face, hands, feet, genitalia, perineum and major joints
- Circumferential burns of limbs or chest
- Electrical and chemical injuries
- Burns with associated inhalational injury
- Burns in patients with medical comorbidities that may affect management/ recovery/survival
- Burns in patients with associated trauma

Patients should be prepared for transfer as for any other major trauma patient.

Surgical management of the burn wound

Early excision (<72 hours) of the burn wound is indicated in major burns and in smaller burns that are obviously deep/full thickness. Early excision is associated with more rapid healing, decreased blood loss, shorter hospital stays, less hypertrophic scarring and improvement in overall survival. Early removal of burned tissue modulates the inflammatory response. Excision is by tangential excision of burned tissue until healthy tissue is encountered. Alternatively, for large burns, tissue may be excised at a fascial level. This results in a more significant defect but limits blood loss.

Closure of the burn wound is ideally with split-skin autograft; however, this may not be initially achievable in major burns due to a lack of donor sites. In such circumstances, alternatives include use of cadaveric allograft skin, skin substitutes, eg Integra, or autograft/cell suspensions cultured from biopsy of the patient's own skin – this technique has a time lag of at least 1 week.

Management of special areas

Face

Significant facial burns are often accompanied by massive swelling, making airway compromise likely and endotracheal intubation difficult. Such patients should be intubated early to preserve the airway. Tracheostomy may be required. Eyes should be evaluated for injury as soon as is practical. Surgical management of facial burns is controversial. The face has an excellent capacity for healing and it is reasonable to wait for a short period of time before making decisions about excision of facial burns.

Neck

Deep neck burns should be managed aggressively to prevent airway problems, and prevent the development of contractures. Resurfacing of the neck with skin graft or flaps is followed by splinting and physiotherapy to prevent further contracture.

Hands

Burns to the palm of the hand are less likely to require surgical management than burns to the dorsum of the hand. Palmar burns should be managed conservatively initially if possible. Intensive physiotherapy is required.

Perineum

Perineal burns are often managed conservatively, and spontaneous healing is often the outcome. Penoscrotal burns in particular should

CHAPTER 6

be managed conservatively if possible. Patients may require urethral catheterisation if unable to void urine.

Burn reconstruction

Wound contracture is one of the major problems post-burn. Early and aggressive management of the burn wound in association with intensive physiotherapy and splinting regimens may help to prevent contractures, but ongoing management is often still required. In the acute phase of burn management, it may be necessary to manage eyelid, perioral and neck contractures surgically to protect structures and facilitate rehabilitation. Burn reconstruction can be achieved using the techniques of the reconstructive ladder – a detailed description for individual areas is outside the scope of this chapter.

Cold injuries

Cold injuries are the result of exposure to low temperatures resulting in tissue damage. As with thermal injuries caused by heat, a number of factors influence the development of a cold injury. Duration of exposure and rapidity of tissue cooling are important factors. The temperature at which a cold injury occurs is also variable and dependent on other factors such as wind chill and whether the skin is moist or dry.

Cold injury is the result of extra- and intracellular ice crystal formation, resulting in cellular dysfunction, combined with microvascular damage. If blood flow is re-established, a reperfusion injury results in further tissue damage.

Cold injury commonly occurs to the extremities, ears, nose, cheeks and penis. The degree of injury may be classified as first, second or third:

- **First degree** – 'frostnip', superficial freezing of epidermis. Hyperaemia and mild oedema. No formation of blisters/vesicles. Reversible with no true tissue damage
- **Second degree** – 'frostbite', partial-thickness skin injury. Presents with hyperaemia and oedema, pain and paraesthesiae, formation of blisters. No long-term sequelae
- **Third degree** – necrosis of entire skin thickness and variable depth of subcutaneous tissue. Often less pain. Dark/ haemorrhagic blisters that evolve into eschar
- **Fourth degree** – necrosis extends to deeper tissues, eg bone

Management of cold injuries is by **rapid** rewarming in water at around 40°C. This should not be started if there is a risk of refreezing. Patients will require significant analgesia as rewarming can be very painful. Surgical management can be conservative to allow demarcation of parts to occur before amputation.

5.2 Paediatric trauma

Learning point

Accidents are the most common cause of death in children aged >1 year. They account for 150 000 paediatric admissions and 600 deaths per year in the UK. The most common forms of accident resulting in death are RTAs, drowning and house fires.

The assessment and resuscitation of the injured child is the same as for the adult (ABCDE) but take note of the anatomical and physiological differences.

CHAPTER 6

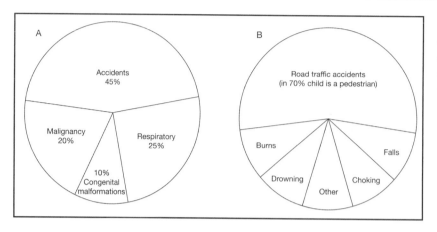

Figure 6.24 Causes of death (A) and accidents (B) in children aged 1–14 years

Causes of trauma in children

The main causes of childhood deaths and accidents are shown in Figure 6.24.

Differences between children and adults with respect to trauma

For more on paediatric physiology see the Paediatric Surgery chapter.

Anatomical differences in children

Children frequently have multisystem trauma because of their small size and shape.

Anatomical differences include:
- Increased force per body area
- Decreased fat layer
- Organs lie in closer proximity
- Rapid thermal losses
- Elastic skeleton often conceals underlying organ damage without fractures
- Effects of injury on growth and development

Physiological differences in children

Children tend to compensate well and therefore serious pathology goes unnoticed until decompensation occurs. Remember that pulse, respiratory rate and urine outputs vary according to the age of the child.

Psychological differences in children

Long-term effects of trauma can be social or affective, resulting in learning disabilities. Communication difficulties can give rise to increased fear. Parents should always be allowed maximal contact.

Airway management

The relatively large occiput causes relatively increased flexion of the cervical spine. Soft tissues such as the tongue and tonsils are relatively large compared with the oral cavity and therefore obstruct the airway easily. A short trachea often results in right bronchus intubation. Nasal passages are narrow. Children aged <6 months are obligate nose breathers.

CHAPTER 6

Intubation

- Use a straight-bladed laryngoscope
- Use uncuffed ET tube to avoid subglottic oedema
- Choose a tube with a size equivalent to the girth of the child's little finger (or use the formula: [age + 4]/4)
- Use of a nasopharyngeal tube is debatable but is often safer during transport of the child

Emergency surgical airway

- In small children (<11 years) needle cricothyroidotomy with jet insufflation is the preferred method (surgical cricothyroidotomy is not performed because the cricoid cartilage provides the sole support for the airway in children aged <11 years)

Breathing

Note these differences when intubating a child compared with an adult:

- Small airways are more easily obstructed (note resistance is proportional to radius of tube)
- Muscles are more likely to fatigue
- The tracheobronchial tree is immature and therefore more sensitive to pressure changes – be careful when using a bag and mask to minimise iatrogenic injury

Circulation

Recognition of shock may be difficult due to the great physiological reserve of children. Often the only signs are reduced peripheral perfusion and tachycardia. Greater degrees of shock may manifest as decreased consciousness and reduced responses to pain.

> **Remember**
> - CO = SV × HR
> CO is cardiac output, SV stroke volume, HR heart rate.
> In infants the SV is small and relatively fixed, so CO varies with HR. Thus the primary response to hypovolaemia is tachycardia and the response to fluid resuscitation is blunted.
> **Caution:** increased HR is compounded by pain and fear.

Other useful features in assessing paediatric circulation are:

- Pulse volume
- End-organ perfusion (skin perfusion, respiratory rate, urine output, mental status)
- Temperature (toe–core gap)

CHAPTER 6

NORMAL VALUES OF BP, HEART AND RESPIRATORY RATES, AND URINE OUTPUT IN CHILDREN

Age (years)	Heart rate (beats/min)	BP (mmHg)	Respiratory rate (breaths/min)	Urine output (ml/kg per hour)
<1	110–160	70–90	30–40	2
2–5	95–140	80–100	25–30	1.5
5–12	80–120	90–110	20–25	1
Children aged >12 years have values very similar to those of adults.				

PHYSIOLOGICAL RESPONSES OF CHILDREN TO HAEMORRHAGE

Organ/system	Blood volume loss		
	<25%	24–45%	>45%
Cardiovascular	Tachycardia	Tachycardia or bradycardia	Hypotension
	Weak and thready		Pulse decreased
CNS	Lethargic	Loss of consciousness	Coma
	Irritable	Dulled response	
	Confused		
Skin	Cool	Poor capillary refill	Pale and cold
	Cold extremities	Clammy	
		Cyanotic	
Kidneys	Low urine output	Minimal urine output	No urine output

Intravenous access in paediatric trauma

After two attempts at percutaneous access, consider:

- In children aged <6 years: intraosseous needle (anterior surface of tibia 2 cm below tuberosity)
- In children aged >6 years: venous cut-down

Fluid resuscitation in paediatric trauma

Give initial bolus of 20 ml/kg crystalloid (warmed whenever possible). Reassess, looking continually for a response to the bolus:

- Decreased HR
- Increased BP
- Increased pulse pressure
- Increased urine output
- Warm extremities
- Improved mental status

If there is no improvement with the bolus, give 20 ml/kg colloid (usually Haemaccel). Children who do not respond to fluids may require blood (10 ml/kg).

Disability after paediatric head trauma

A child's brain is different from that of an adult. The brain grows rapidly over the first 2 years and has an increased water content. The subarachnoid space is relatively smaller and so the brain is surrounded by less CSF to cushion it in the event of impact.

The outcome of head trauma is worse in children aged <3 and these children are particularly vulnerable to secondary brain injury. Children with an open fontanelle are more tolerant to an expanding mass because the ICP does not rise as easily (a bulging fontanelle may be palpated).

The GCS is still useful in children aged >4. In children aged <4 the verbal response score must be modified (eg 5 = appropriate for age, 4 = crying consolably, 3 = crying inconsolably, 2 = agitated, 1 = noiseless).

Exposure

Remember that the relatively large surface area to weight ratio of children means that they lose heat quickly. Overhead heaters and blankets are essential.

Note: remember that all drug dosages should be worked out per kilogram of body weight. The weight estimate in kilograms for those <10 is calculated by: (age + 4) × 2.

Thoracic trauma in children

This occurs in 10% of children (and two-thirds of these will have concurrent injury to the head or abdomen).

- The chest wall is more compliant, so children can have pulmonary contusions without rib fracture; therefore you should actively look for injury (rib fracture requires proportionally more force in a child than in an adult)
- Mobility of the mediastinal structures makes the child more sensitive to tension pneumo-thorax and flail segments
- Chest drain insertion is performed in the same way as for an adult but a smaller diameter tube is used

Abdominal trauma in children

- Decompress the stomach with an NG or orogastric tube (crying causes swallowing of air)
- Children are often managed non-surgically with repeated observation and examination (unless haemodynamically unstable)

Certain injuries are more prevalent in the child:

- Duodenal and pancreatic injuries due to handlebar trauma
- Mesenteric small-bowel avulsion injuries
- Bladder rupture (shallower pelvis)
- Fall-astride injuries to the perineum

Non-accidental injury

Always be aware of the possibility that trauma has been caused by non-accidental injury (NAI). It is estimated that up to 2% of children may suffer NAI during childhood. A number of features should raise your suspicion.

In the history:

- Late presentation
- Inconsistent story
- Injury not compatible with history (eg long bone fracture in children under walking age)
- Repeated injuries

In the examination:

- Abnormal interaction between child and parents
- Bizarre injuries (eg bites, burns and shape of injury such as fingertip bruising)
- Perioral injuries
- Perianal/genital injuries
- Evidence of previous injuries (old scars, healing fractures)

You must refer on to the appropriate authorities, even if in doubt (via your immediate senior and the paediatrics service – these children should be seen by a senior paediatrician). Ensure that your notes are clear and accurate. Describe what you see, not what you infer, eg say 'four circular bruises approximately 1 cm in diameter around the upper arm' rather than 'bruising from fingertips'.

The following investigations should be performed in any case of suspected physical abuse:

- Full skeletal survey – radiology of the whole skeleton to look for old or undiagnosed fractures
- Tests of clotting function, including FBC for platelets
- Biochemistry, including bone biochemistry
- Appropriate investigations of the head if indicated
- Medical photography of any affected area

CHAPTER 6

5.3   Trauma in pregnancy

Learning point

Treatment priorities are the same as for the non-pregnant patient – treat the mother first as the fetus is reliant on her condition. Resuscitation and stabilisation need modification to account for the anatomical and physiological changes that occur in pregnancy.

The fetus may be in distress before the mother shows outward signs of shock.

Anatomical changes in pregnancy

- **First trimester:** uterus is relatively protected by bony pelvis and thick-walled uterus
- **Second trimester:** uterus becomes intra-abdominal and more vulnerable to injury; amniotic fluid cushions fetus
- **Third trimester:** relative decrease in amniotic fluid and thickness of uterus, so fetus is more vulnerable to blunt and penetrative trauma

The placenta contains no elastic tissue and is vulnerable to shearing forces, resulting in incidences of placental abruption and damage to dilated pelvic veins.

Physiological changes in pregnancy

Oestrogen and progesterone have the following effects:

- **↓ smooth muscle tone:** decreased gastric emptying with lower oesophageal sphincter reflux, so risk of aspiration
- **↓ *PaCO$_2$*:** to 4 kPa (30 mmHg). This is the 'physiological hyperventilation of pregnancy' secondary to the respiratory stimulant effect of progesterone. Forced expiratory volume in 1 s/forced vital capacity (FEV$_1$/FVC) remains the same, but tidal volume increases by 40%

- **↑ pulse rate**
- **↑ BP:** by 10–15 mmHg in the second trimester (normalises near term)
- **↑ plasma volume:** by 50%
- **↑ cardiac output:** by 1.0–1.5 l/min (CVP is usually normal despite the increased total volume)

This means that pregnant women have to lose more of their total circulating volume before signs of hypovolaemia develop. Blood is shunted away from the uterofetal circulation to maintain the mother's vital signs. Therefore the fetus may be shocked before maternal tachycardia, tachypnoea or hypotension develop. For these reasons, vigorous fluid replacement is required.

Aortocaval compression

The enlarged uterus can compress the inferior vena cava (IVC) and impair venous return, reducing cardiac output by up to 40%. This can cause a drop in BP unless the pressure is minimised by placing patients in the left lateral position.

Secondary survey in pregnancy

Urgent radiographs (eg of C-spine) are still taken because the priority is to detect life-threatening injuries. The uterus can be protected with lead for all imaging except the pelvic film.

Special considerations in pregnancy

Search for conditions unique to the pregnant patient:

- Blunt/penetrating uterine trauma

- Placental abruption
- Amniotic fluid embolism
- DIC
- Eclampsia
- Uterine rupture
- Premature rupture of membranes in labour
- Isoimmunisation: prophylactic anti-D should be given to rhesus-negative mothers within 72 hours
- The Kleihauer–Betke test (maternal blood smear looking for fetal red blood cells) is specific but not very sensitive, and is therefore of little use

5.4 Post-traumatic stress disorder

Learning point

This occurs when a person has experienced a traumatic event involving actual or threatened death or injury to themselves or others. The individual will have felt fear, helplessness or horror. There are three classic symptoms that usually cluster:

- **Intrusions:** re-experiencing the event via flashbacks or nightmares
- **Avoidance:** the person attempts to reduce exposure to people, places or things that exacerbate the intrusions
- **Hyperarousal:** physiological signs of increased arousal, including hypervigilance and increased startle response

These symptoms must persist for more than 1 month after the event to qualify as PTSD, causing significant distress or impairment of social or occupational situations.

Other symptoms include:
- Insomnia
- Anorexia
- Depression with low energy
- Difficulty in focusing
- Social withdrawal

Lifetime prevalence in the USA is 5–10% (Kessler et al, 1995). This value increases to more than 20% in inner city populations.

Management of PTSD

If symptoms are mild and present for less than 4 weeks, then a period of watchful waiting is recommended.

Psychological therapy: trauma-focused cognitive behavioural therapy should be offered to those with either severe post-traumatic symptoms or severe PTSD in the first month after the traumatic event. These treatments should be offered to everyone with PTSD over the subsequent months and should normally be provided on an individual outpatient basis.

Drug therapy: this should be administered only by a specialist and usually involves antidepressants such as paroxetine.

5.5 Brainstem death

The diagnosis of brainstem death

Definition of brainstem death
- Irreversible cessation of brainstem function
- In the UK, diagnosed by specific tests

Preconditions for diagnosis of brainstem death

- Apnoeic coma requiring ventilation
- Known cause of irreversible brain damage (eg head injury, cerebral haemorrhage)

Exclusions from diagnosis of brainstem death

- Hypothermia (temperature <35°C)
- Depressant drugs (eg sedatives, opiates, muscle relaxants)
- Metabolic derangements (eg sodium, glucose, hepatic encephalopathy)

Tests of brainstem death

These look for activity in the cranial nerves (CNs).

- **Pupil responses:** CN II. No direct or indirect reaction to light
- **Corneal reflex:** CN V and CN VII. Direct stimulation with cotton wool
- **Pain reflex:** in facial distribution; motor; CN V and CN VII. Reflexes below the neck are ignored as they may be spinal reflexes
- **Caloric test:** instillation of cold water into the auditory canal, looking for nystagmus towards the stimulation; CN VIII, CN III and CN VI. Check that canal is not blocked with wax first
- **Gag reflex:** CN IX and CN X
- **Apnoea test:** pre-oxygenate with 100% O_2 then disconnect from the ventilator. Insufflate oxygen into the trachea via catheter at 4 litres/min. Observe for any sign of respiration for 10 minutes until $PaCO_2$ is >6.65 kPa. May need to stop test if sats drop or becomes bradycardic and unstable

If the patient shows no response to the above tests then brain death can be diagnosed after two sets have been performed. Legal time of death is after the first set.

The tests are performed by two doctors, both 5 years post-registration, one of whom must be a consultant, and neither doctor should be a member of a transplant team. There is no set time between the two sets but at least 6 hours should have elapsed between the onset of coma and the first set.

Organ donation after brainstem death

The possibility of donation must be discussed with the relatives, usually after the first set of tests. If they agree to donation then the local transplant coordinator is contacted, who arranges viral and histocompatibility testing. They will come to the hospital and talk in detail with the relatives and liaise with the transplant surgeons. See Chapter 7, Transplantation in Book 2.

5.6 Complications of intravascular drug abuse

Types of drugs which are injected for recreational drug use are: morphine, heroin, cocaine, amphetamine and methamphetamin. Injecting preparations not intended for this purpose is particularly dangerous because of the presence of excipients (fillers), which can cause blood clots. Injecting codeine into the bloodstream directly is dangerous because it causes a rapid histamine release, which can lead to potentially fatal anaphylaxis and pulmonary oedema. Dihydrocodeine, hydrocodone, nicocodeine, and other codeine-based products carry similar risks. To minimize the amount of undissolved material in fluids prepared for injection, a filter of cotton or synthetic fiber is typically used, such as a cotton-swab tip or a small piece of cigarette filter.

Following prolonged drug administration peripheral venous access becomes increasingly difficult due to phlebitis associated with repeated non-sterile injection. The addict eventually attempts to administer drugs into a major deep vein, commonly the groin, with a substantial probability of vascular injury occurring. Direct intra-arterial injection can lead to limb ischaemia, either primarily as a consequence of direct local arterial injury and occlusion or as a result of distal small vessel damage. Infective vascular complications may also result with peri-vascular abscess or formation of an arterial or venous pseudoaneurysm.

Intra-arterial Injection

The effects of intra-arterial injection arise as a combination of particulate emboli, vasospasm in distal vessels, and endothelial injury leading to small vessel vasculitis and venous thrombosis. These changes produce a diffuse tissue ischaemia, which may be exacerbated if the patchy muscle necrosis that results leads to the development of a compartment syndrome with major muscle necrosis. It is predominantly small vessel and venous damage that gives rise to the clinical picture of limb mottling and swelling with muscle tenderness, in the presence of a full complement of pulses.

Supportive medical therapy with systemic heparin is,the best treatment in patients with a full complenient of limb pulses following intra-arterial injection. In the few patients who present with an absent major limb pulse at the site of injection it is probable that thrombosis

has been initiated following direct mechanical and chemical injury of the vessel. Unless major proximal limb pulses are absent investigation with a view to reconstructive vascular surgery are not indicated.

Infective Complications

Superficial thrombophlebitis and deep vein thrombosis are prevalent in injecting drug addicts

Venous pseudoaneurysm is usually present with groin pain, fever, leucocytosis and, sometimes, a fluctuant groin. Preoperative investigation rarely enables the diagnosis to be made before surgery, which consists of excision of the infected pseudoaneurysm with excision and ligation of the infected vein, in most cases this is the common femoral vein.

Arterial infected pseudoaneurysm or 'aneurysmal abscess' is the commonest vascular complications found in drug addicts. The majority of infected pseudoaneurysms develop in the femoral artery although they have been reported to occur in brachial and radial arteries Pseudoaneurysm commonly presents as a painful swelling, with fever and leucocytosis, it may present with intermittent bleeding and, occasionally, massive haemorrhage. The features of an indurated, erythematous swelling may be mistaken for a simple abscess on initial presentation the majority of pseudoaneurysms are pulsatile on examination, with an audible bruit over the swelling. Infected pseudoaneurysms of the upper limb vessels seem to require neither revascularization nor amputation after excision and ligation. Revascularization following ligation and resection of an infected femoral aneurysm often requires the use of a synthetic graft because of the lack of good quality vein

CHAPTER 6

in drug abusers, this has been associated with a significant incidence of graft infection and occlusion.

Duplex ultra-sonography should be performed on any swelling in the vicinity of a major vessel to determine whether or not the lesion contains flowing blood, confirming the diagnosis of pseudoaneurysm.

Bacterial endocarditis should always be considered when assessing intravenous drug users.

5.7   Human and animal bites

Human Bites

Any form of bite should be considered a contaminated wound and management is as for all traumatic wounds. Thorough lavage, removal of foreign bodies and debridement should be performed.

Infection is the major complication of bite wounds and infections of poorly vascularized structures, such as ear cartilage, may be difficult to treat.   Other serious infectious complications such as osteomyelitis of the skull vault, necrotizing fasciitis, infectious tenosynovitis, and septic arthritis have been associated with human bites.

Bacteria that often contaminate human bites include streptococci, Staphylococcus aureus, Haemophilus spp, Eikenella corrodens and Bacteroides spp and other anaerobes. Transmission of viruses (e.g. hepatitis B, hepatitis C, HIV, HTLV-1) following human bites is much less common.

Animal Bites

Dog attacks kill approximately 10-20 people annually in US, most of these fatalities are young children. Local infection and cellulitis are the leading causes of morbidity, sepsis is a potential complication of bite wounds, particularly C canimorsus (DF-2) sepsis in immunocompromised individuals. Dog bites typically cause a crushing-type wound because of their rounded teeth and strong jaws.

The sharp pointed teeth of cats usually cause puncture wounds and lacerations that may inoculate bacteria into deep tissues. Infections caused by cat bites generally develop faster than those of dogs. Pasteurella multocida infection is the most common pathogen contracted from cat bites and may be complicated by sepsis.

Other complications include meningitis, osteomyelitis, tenosynovitis, abscesses, pneumonia, endocarditis, and septic arthritis. When rabies occurs, it is almost uniformly fatal.

CHAPTER 6

Trauma
Part 2: Musculoskeletal

Nigel W Gummerson

CHAPTER 6

Pathophysiology of fracture healing

Bone is unique in its ability to repair itself without scarring, using the processes that occur during normal bone formation and bone turnover. Bone healing may be primary or secondary.

1.1   Primary bone healing

Primary bone healing occurs when the fracture gap is small and there is minimal motion between the fracture fragments. This situation is achieved after anatomical reduction and rigid fixation with absolute stability (eg open reduction and internal fixation [ORIF] of forearm fracture with interfragmentary compression).

New vessels will cross the fracture gap and bone remodelling occurs across the fracture gap with little or no callus formation. Primary bone healing requires a blood supply, and extensive soft-tissue stripping at the time of injury or at the time of surgery will impede the process.

1.2   Secondary bone healing

Secondary bone healing occurs in three phases (others may further subdivide these phases). There is considerable overlap between these phases:

- Inflammatory phase

- Reparative phase
- Remodelling phase

Inflammatory phase

At the time of injury there will be bleeding from both the vessels in the medullary cavity and the vessels in the periosteum. Blood clot will form and the bleeding will stop. Cytokines (platelet-derived growth factor [PDGF], interleukins IL-1 and IL-6, transforming growth factor β [TFG-β], fibroblast growth factor [FGF], insulin-like growth factor [IGF] and bone morphogenetic proteins [BMPs]) are released from the clot, marrow, periosteum and bone, recruiting inflammatory cells (macrophages and neutrophils), fibroblasts and osteoprogenitor cells. This process begins immediately and is well established by day 7, which represents the peak of cellular proliferation at the fracture site. Cell proliferation declines to day 14.

Reparative phase

Fibroblasts, recruited to the fracture site, will lay down a disordered matrix of type II collagen. Chondrocytes will mature and begin chondrogenesis around day 9–14. This produces **callus**, initially a soft material, which bridges the fracture ends. This soft callus will become mineralised (from day 14), increasing in stiffness and strength, to become hard callus. This process is similar to the embryonic process of endochondral ossification. The osteoblasts, which mediate this process, are derived from periosteum, marrow and fracture site. Ossification is enhanced by early motion and (protected) weight bearing. During this time neovascularisation occurs, with new vessels growing into the fracture site.

As ossification continues the callus becomes **woven bone**. Unlike the bone before injury, the woven bone has a random orientation of collagen and haversian systems.

Remodelling phase

Remodelling takes many (1–4) years. it is a normal physiological process for the entire skeleton, allowing it to respond to changes in loading patterns. After injury, remodelling converts woven bone to **lamellar bone** which has an internal architecture ordered in response to the loads across it. This change in bone internal structure in response to load is Wolff's law.

As a very general rule fractures of the upper limb (in adults) take 6–8 weeks to unite. In the lower limb it takes 12–14 weeks.

1.3 Delayed bone healing

There are many factors that can delay bone healing. After internal fixation this may manifest as failure of the instrumentation. For conservatively treated fractures delayed union may manifest as persisting pain and motion or with radiological signs such as hypertrophic callus formation and a persistent fracture gap (suggesting insufficient immobilisation of the fracture) or atrophic/hypotrophic callus (suggesting a biological reason for delayed union).

Factors that delay bone healing

Systemic patient factors
- Diabetes
- Vascular insufficiency
- Malnutrition
- Disorders of vitamin D, calcium or phosphate metabolism
- Drugs, non-steroidal anti-inflammatory drugs (NSAIDs) and steroids

Local factors
- Infection
- Inadequate immobilisation
- Loss of local blood supply

1.4 Systemic effects of trauma

There is a well-recognised inflammatory response after trauma or surgery. The cytokines that stimulate the inflammatory response at the fracture site can also be measured in the circulation where it is thought that they contribute to the systemic response to trauma (particularly IL-6 and TGF-β).

Injured patients will have a rise in cytokine levels immediately after the incident. The cytokine levels will rise again after any surgical procedure. The most frequently studied situation is femoral nailing for femoral fractures. It is thought that this 'second hit' can precipitate acute respiratory distress syndrome (ARDS) or multiorgan failure (MOF). Measurement of cytokines may help determine the optimal timing of reconstructive surgery to minimise the pro-inflammatory systemic effects of the trauma and subsequent surgery.

SECTION 2

Classification of fractures

Many different classification systems have been developed for use in trauma. They each try to describe one or more of the following areas:
- Mechanism of injury
- Location of injury
- Injury morphology
- Functional or physiological consequences of injury
- Damage to surrounding structures in zone of injury

Fracture classifications tend to focus on the location and morphology of injury. Some fracture classifications attempt to provide a comprehensive framework that allows classification of any fracture in any anatomical area (eg the AO classification of long-bone fractures); others are specific to one anatomical location (eg the Garden classification of intracapsular proximal femoral fractures).

There are pros and cons to all these systems. In general any classification system should be reliable, reproducible and relevant – and have some bearing on treatment and prognosis.

Remember, it is more useful for a trainee to be able to describe a fracture accurately than to learn one of the many classification systems.

The age of the patient can help determine which injuries are more or less likely (see box overleaf).

CHAPTER 6

Fracture pattern related to age

The same mechanism of injury may result in a different pattern of pathology depending on the age of the patient. This is because different structures are vulnerable at different stages of development and the weakest structure tends to be injured, eg:

- At age 10–14 years growth plate is vulnerable
- At age 16–35 years ligaments rather than bone are vulnerable
- At age 40–70 years bone is weakest

A fall on the outstretched hand therefore results in typical injuries.

Typical injury from a fall on an outstretched hand at different ages

Age (years)	Typical injury
Child <10	Greenstick fracture (distal radius or radius and ulna)
10–14	Physeal injury (typically Salter–Harris II fracture)
16–35	Fractured scaphoid Scaphoid ligament injury Intra-articular radial head fracture
40–70+	Colles' fracture of the distal radius

2.1 Describing fractures

Nine things to talk about

1. **General features:** age of patient, mechanism of injury, general condition of patient, medical history, etc
2. **Anatomical site:** which bone? Which part of the bone?
3. **Type:** traumatic, pathological or stress fracture?

- **Traumatic** fracture identified by mechanism of injury and absence of pathological features
- **Stress** fractures develop slowly in bones subjected to repetitive loads (eg sports training, military marching)
- **Pathological** fractures are low-energy injuries (not sufficient to fracture a normal bone) resulting in fracture of a bone altered by a disease process that can be:
  - Systemic (osteoporosis, metabolic bone disease, Paget's disease)
  - Localised (primary bone tumour, haematopoietic disorder, metastatic disease)

4. **Intra-articular or extra-articular**
5. **Joints:** congruent, subluxed or dislocated
6. **Physeal injury** (if growth plate still open)
7. **Fracture pattern:**
- Simple (spiral, oblique or transverse)
- Wedge fracture
- Multifragmentary
8. **Deformity and displacement:**
- Rotational deformity
- Shortening or distraction
- Translation (occurs in two planes: for a distal radius this is volar/dorsal and radial/ulnar)
- Angular deformity (occurs in two planes)
- Articular steps
9. **Associated soft-tissue injury:**
- Condition of skin, muscle and tendon
- Open or closed (fracture site communicates with open wound)
- Neurovascular status
- Ligamentous injuries

2.2 Imaging of fractures

Plain radiographs

- Standard investigation to confirm/exclude fracture or dislocation

CHAPTER 6

- Always two views of whole bone with its proximal and distal joints
- If one bone of a pair is broken, look very carefully at the other one
- If there is no fracture look for dislocation
- Look for soft-tissue injuries on radiographs

CT

- Image intra-articular fractures (good resolution of articular fragments)
- Useful for spinal and pelvic injuries
- Can be used to create three-dimensional reconstructions that help preoperative planning

MRI

- The investigation of choice for suspected hip fracture when the plain films are equivocal (NICE guideline)

- Can be used to image articular surface
- Gives information on soft tissues (eg ligamentous and meniscal injuries with tibial plateau fracture)

2.3 Describing plain trauma radiographs

It is possible that you'll be shown a radiograph of a trauma case or complication of a fracture. There are too many possibilities to be covered in this book, but nothing can replace experience in a busy A&E or orthopaedics job. (To refresh your memory we recommend the book *Practical Fracture Management* by Ronald McRae. This has an excellent overview of all the common fractures and their management and includes many radiographs of the more common injuries.) If in doubt, follow the guidelines below for looking at a radiograph.

CHAPTER 6

Looking at a radiograph
- Check the label (this is the radiograph of William Rhodes who is 40, taken on 20 October 2012)
- Name the bone or joint, side and the view (eg it is an anteroposterior [AP] view of the left femur)
- Describe the obvious abnormality, if there is one

Describing a fracture on a radiograph
- If shown only one film, ask if there are any other views
- **Site:** side, bone and level (divide long bones into proximal, middle and distal thirds)
- **Pattern:** transverse, oblique, spiral, complex (in children, greenstick or buckle fractures)
- **Comminution:** simple, wedge or complex (comminuted)
- **Special features:** eg avulsion fracture, depressed, involving the articular surface
- **Displacement:** estimate percentage of fracture surface in contact and shortening
- Angulation* or **tilt**
- **Axial rotation:** you need to see the joint above and below the fracture
- **Associated features:** dislocation, soft-tissue swelling, obvious compound (not easy to determine on radiograph unless dramatic), foreign bodies and pathological fracture

Do NOT say 'angulation' unless you have read up on it and fully understand it; it means the opposite to what most people think – saying 'fracture of the mid-shaft of the tibia with 20° of medial angulation' means 'the distal end of the distal fragment has swung LATERALLY'! (Use the word 'tilt' instead – 'the distal fragment is tilted laterally by about 20°'. This means what it says – much safer during exam stress!)

SECTION 3

Principles of management of fractures

Learning point

Principles of fracture management
- Resuscitation
- Reduce (if necessary)
- Hold
- Rehabilitate the limb and the patient

When discussing any given fracture consider the following six points:
1. Initial emergency measures
2. Does the fracture require reduction?
3. If reduction of the fracture is required, how will it be achieved?
4. What support is required, and for how long?
5. Consideration of soft-tissue injury?
6. Does the patient need to be admitted?

This allows you time to organise your thoughts, gives you a framework for discussing your answer, and allows the examiners to steer you to the points that they want you to discuss, without the feeling that you have missed out any important principles. You can then address the fracture that you have been asked to assess with reference to each relevant principle in greater detail.

Initial emergency measures

- Resuscitation following ATLS guidelines for all major trauma
- Temporary splint (eg sandbags, inflatable splints)
- Reposition deformed limbs immediately if overlying skin at risk
- If open fracture take photographs and swabs, cover with sterile dressings, give antibiotics and tetanus prophylaxis
- Assess clinically and radiologically

Does the fracture require reduction?

No it does not:

- If undisplaced
- If displacement likely to be corrected by remodelling (eg in children)
- If risks of anaesthesia outweigh disadvantage of deformity

Yes it does:

- If slight displacement in functionally vital area (eg articular surface)
- If significantly displaced, angled or rotated (criteria vary for each fracture)

As a general principle, lower-limb injuries need anatomical reduction to maintain the normal weight-bearing axis of the limb. The function of the upper limb is to place the hand in space; the shoulder and elbow both have a large range of motion and small residual deformities can be accommodated.

Deformity in the same plane as the joint (eg flexion extension of a femoral fracture is in the same plane as the knee) is better tolerated than deformities perpendicular to the joint (eg varus–valgus malalignment of the femur changes the weight-bearing axis through the knee). Rotation is poorly tolerated in any fracture.

How will reduction be achieved?

- **Closed** (manipulation under anaesthesia or MUA)
- **Open reduction:**
  - If MUA has failed
  - If internal fixation is required (for unstable fracture configuration and to allow early mobilisation)
  - If fracture is open
- **Continuous traction** – rarely used except in cervical spine and femur

What support is required, and for how long?

- **Non-rigid support:**
  - Broad-arm slings for support of distal limb where support of the fracture is needed (eg clavicle fractures)
  - Collar and cuff for support of distal limb where traction is desirable (eg shaft or neck of humerus)
- **Cast immobilisation:** typically plaster back-slab initially, completed or changed to lightweight cast when the swelling subsides
- **Internal fixation:** eg compression plates and screws or intramedullary devices

Internal fixation

Indications for internal fixation

- Fractures requiring open reduction
- Unstable fractures
- Intra-articular fractures
- Multiply injured patients

Advantages of internal fixation

- Anatomical reduction, absolute stability
- Allows primary bone healing
- Earlier mobilisation of joints
- Earlier discharge from hospital

Complications of internal fixation

- Infection
- Anaesthetic risk
- Failure of fixation
- Malposition of metalwork

CHAPTER 6

External fixation

Advantages of external fixation

- Rapid application
- Useful for multiple injuries
- Stabilises comminuted fractures that are unsuitable for internal fixation
- Provides fixation outside zone of injury for open fractures and allows access to the wound

Disadvantages of external fixation

- Cumbersome
- Pin-track infection/colonisation
- May hold fracture in slight distraction resulting in non-union/delayed union

Ilizarov circular frame

Advantages of Ilizarov circular frame

- Allows fine and continuous control of position, compression and distraction
- Facilitates gradual correction of deformity

Disadvantages of Ilizarov circular frame

- Requires close supervision and frequent adjustment
- Wire-track infection
- Requires specialist skills

Continuous traction

Skeletal or skin traction

- Skeletal pins (eg Steinman or Denham pins)
- Adhesive skin traction
- Now used for temporary preoperative stabilisation of adult femoral fractures and as definitive treatment of some paediatric (and a small number of adult) femoral fractures

Disadvantages of skeletal or skin traction

- Requires constant monitoring and adjustment
- Patient immobilised for many weeks, resulting in weakness and stiffness
- Risks of pressure sores, chest infection and thromboembolism

Cast bracing

- After first few weeks of cast immobilisation (allowing formation of soft callus) conversion to hinged cast allows mobilisation of joint
- Used for fractures around the elbow and the knee

Consideration of soft-tissue injury

Consider if there are open fractures, crush injury, contusions or neurovascular injury.

Open fractures

- Initial measures as above (swab, photograph, dressing, IV antibiotics, tetanus prophylaxis)
- Debridement and lavage under GA (ideally within 6 hours for heavily contaminated wounds and 24 hours for an isolated open fracture)
- Assess skin cover and plan closure (primary, split-skin graft, local flap, free flap)
- Infection risk is inversely related to time to definitive closure

Open fracture of the tibia and fibula

Classification according to the soft-tissue defect left after debridement (Gustilo and Anderson's [1976] classification of open fractures).

Type I

- Wound <1 cm long
- Little soft-tissue damage
- Simple fracture pattern with little comminution

Type II

- Wound >1 cm long
- No extensive soft-tissue damage
- Moderate contamination and fracture comminution

Type III

- Extensive soft-tissue damage
- Contamination and fracture comminution
  - Type A: soft-tissue coverage is adequate. Comminuted and segmental high-energy fractures are included regardless of wound size
  - Type B: extensive soft-tissue injuries with massive contamination; and severe fracture comminution require a local or free flap for coverage
  - Type C: arterial injury requires repair

Crush injury and severe contusion

- Beware of compartment syndrome
- Assess and treat neurological and vascular damage
- Reconstructable injury?

Mangled extremity severity score (MESS)

1–4	Energy of injury
1–3	Limb ischaemia (double score if time >6 hours)
0–2	Shock
0–2	Age of patient

MESS score >7 is indication for amputation.

Does the patient need to be admitted?

- GA or other inpatient treatment required
- Observation (eg comorbidity, multiple trauma)
- Nursing care (bed-bound, bilateral limb fractures)
- Mobilisation with physiotherapy
- Social factors (eg elderly person)
- Child abuse suspected

CHAPTER 6

SECTION 4

Complications of fractures

Complications of fractures

Early general complications
- Hypovolaemic shock
- DIC
- SIRS
- Fat embolism syndrome

Early local complications
- Arterial injury
- Nerve injury
- Compartment syndrome
- Infection
- Soft-tissue compromise

Late general complications
- Deep venous thrombosis (DVT)
- Pulmonary embolism (PE)
- Urinary tract infection (UTI)
- Respiratory tract infection
- Disuse atrophy
- Psychosocial/economic factors

Late local complications
- Delayed union/non-union/malunion
- Infection
- Joint stiffness
- Secondary osteoarthritis
- Avascular necrosis
- Myositis ossificans
- Complex regional pain syndrome – aka reflex sympathetic dystrophy or Sudeck's atrophy

---

4.1 Early general complications of fractures

Fractures and hypovolaemic shock

For more details on shock in trauma see Chapter 6, Part 1. Approximate blood loss in closed fracture:
- Pelvis 1–5 litres
- Femur 1–2.5 litres
- Tibia 0.5–1.5 litres
- Humerus 0.5–1.5 litres

Fractures and disseminated intravascular coagulation

DIC is associated with trauma and massive transfusions. It causes consumption of clotting factors and platelets, resulting in uncontrolled bleeding from injured sites. It is treated by replacement of platelets and clotting factors, with surgical control of bleeding if required. Hypothermia will exacerbate any coagulation problem. Therefore consideration of the patient's exposure and environment in the resuscitation room and operating theatre is of great importance.

Fractures and systemic inflammatory response syndrome

This is the systemic response to major trauma, mediated by changes in the autonomic nervous system and the immune system. Some patients are more susceptible to it as a result of their genetics and immune system.

Features of SIRS (must have two or more):

- Pyrexia >38°C or <36°C
- Tachycardia >90 beats/minute
- Tachypnoea >20 beats/minute or $PaCO_2$ <4.26 kPa (32 mmHg)
- WCC >12 000 cells/mm² or 10% immature (bands) forms

Patients with signs of SIRS should not be subjected to major surgery until their condition improves. The additional (surgical) trauma may exceed their physiological capacity to autoregulate the local organ and systemic circulation. This is the 'second-hit' hypothesis of trauma, and applies in particular to the intramedullary nailing of long bones, which provokes a large immunological response in patients.

Fractures and fat embolism syndrome

This complication of long-bone (especially femur) fracture presents with a petechial rash, confusion and hypoxia. The pathophysiology is not completely understood. Fat embolism syndrome is thought to occur as a result of:

- Release of lipid globules from damaged bone marrow fat cells
- Increased peripheral mobilisation of fatty acids
- Increased synthesis of triglycerides by liver

It results in embolism of the microvasculature with lipid globules. As any part of the microvasculature can be affected, the clinical manifestations are varied:

- Pulmonary: ventilation/perfusion mismatch
- Cerebral: ischaemia, infarction, oedema
- Cardiac: arrhythmias and impaired mechanical performance
- Renal: ischaemic glomerular/tubular dysfunction
- Skin: capillary damage, petechial haemorrhage

Diagnosis is made by detection of fat globules in body fluids in association with pulmonary and failure/dysfunction of at least one other organ system. Treatment is to maintain adequate tissue oxygenation. The incidence may be reduced by early stabilisation of long-bone fractures.

CHAPTER 6

4.2   Early local complications of fractures

Fractures and arterial/nerve injury

COMMON SITES OF NERVE AND ARTERIAL INJURY

Examples of common sites of injury	Structures at risk
Proximal humeral fractures/shoulder dislocation	Axillary nerve
Humeral shaft (middle and distal third)	Radial nerve
Paediatric supracondylar fracture	Radial nerve (most common), median nerve, ulnar nerve or brachial artery
Distal radial fracture	Median nerve (acute carpal tunnel syndrome)
Pelvic fracture	Lumbar–sacral plexus, iliac vessels or superior gluteal artery
Acetabular fractures/hip dislocation	Sciatic nerve
Knee dislocation	Popliteal artery and common peroneal nerve
Open tibial fracture	Any lower leg artery or nerve

Priorities in management of bleeding pelvic injury

Pelvic stabilisation can be achieved with a temporary pelvic binder, or more permanently with an external fixator. Operative surgical control of the bleeding pelvic injury has now largely been replaced by interventional vascular radiological control of bleeding.

Priorities in management of neurovascular limb injury

- Haemorrhage control
- Arterial/venous shunt
- Wound debridement
- Skeletal stabilisation
- Arterial/venous reconstruction
- Soft-tissue coverage
- Fasciotomy (if required after reperfusion)

Nerve injuries

Nerve repair may be deferred, but it is suggested that best results are obtained if it is undertaken within 10 days of injury.

- **Neuropraxia:** conduction block, axon and nerve sheath intact. Usually full recovery by 6 weeks
- **Axonotmesis:** axon divided, nerve sheath intact. May recover (at rate of 1 mm/day), but fibrosis may prevent full recovery (exploration and neurolysis may be indicated)
- **Neurotmesis:** axon and nerve sheath divided. Little chance of recovery unless primary surgical repair or nerve grafting. Unlikely to achieve full recovery, even with surgical treatment.

For further discussion of nerve repair see Trauma, Part 1.

Fractures and infection

Cellulitis

Features of cellulitis
- There is infection of the dermis and subcutaneous tissues
- Limbs are commonly affected (usually the lower leg)
- Erythema occurs with blurred demarcation to normal tissue

Microbiology of cellulitis
- Cellulitis is commonly caused by β-haemolytic streptococci (*Streptococcus pyogenes*)

Risk factors for cellulitis
- Lymphoedema
- Tinea fungal infections of the feet

Treatment of cellulitis
- Rest and elevation
- IV antibiotics

Gas gangrene

Features of gas gangrene
- Shock and septicaemia, with tachycardia, fever, confusion and rigors
- Limb is initially cool, becoming discoloured
- Bubbles of trapped CO_2 produce crepitus and may be visible on plain radiographs
- Even with the best available treatment, mortality rates are around 25%

Microbiology of gas gangrene
- Caused by *Clostridium* spp. (*C. perfringens* in 80–95% of cases):
  - Gram-positive, spore-forming rods
  - Anaerobic but will tolerate aerobic conditions
- Exotoxins produced include toxin a (responsible for haemolysis and tissue necrosis)
- Gas produced by anaerobic metabolism causes reduced tissue blood flow and acceleration of tissue necrosis
- Enzymes produced include collagenase
- Can spread by 2–3 cm/hour

Risk factors for gas gangrene
- After amputation of ischaemic limbs
- Deep penetrating injuries with tissue necrosis (eg battlefield injuries)
- GI sepsis with tissue necrosis
- Failed illegal abortion

Treatment of gas gangrene
- Surgical debridement (amputation)
- High-dose antibiotics (penicillin)
- Hyperbaric oxygen therapy (increasing the PO_2 in tissues inhibits bacteria metabolism and reduces tissue necrosis)

CHAPTER 6

Tetanus

Features of tetanus

Symptoms begin 3 days to 3 weeks from infection (typically after 7–8 days):

- Headache
- Muscle stiffness around the jaw
- Rigid abdominal muscles
- Sweating and fever

Tetanus often results from deep penetrating wounds with soil contamination. Mortality rate is approximately 50%.

Microbiology of tetanus

Tetanus is caused by *Clostridium tetani*:

- Gram-positive rods
- Obligate anaerobes

Two toxins are produced:

- Tetanospasmin (carried to the CNS; affects motor neurones)
- Tetanolysin (haemolytic)

Risk factors for tetanus

- Wounds that occurred more than 6 hours ago
- Blunt, crush or missile injuries
- Contaminated wounds
- Presence of devitalised or infected tissue

Prophylaxis for tetanus

Wound management: this involves debridement of the wound, decontamination, lavage (the solution to pollution is dilution) and consider delayed secondary closure.

Immunological prophylaxis: if patient has had three or more previous doses of tetanus toxoid (ie previous full course):

- >10 years since last dose – repeat in all cases
- >5 years since last dose – repeat for tetanus-prone wounds

If patient has had less than three previous doses of tetanus toxoid:

- Give tetanus toxoid dose
- Give tetanus immunoglobulin for tetanus-prone wounds

Treatment of tetanus

- Muscle relaxants
- Respiratory support
- Surgical debridement
- Antitoxin
- Antibiotics (penicillin)

Necrotising fasciitis

> ### Learning point
>
> Necrotising fasciitis is an infection of the dermis and subcutaneous tissues with tissue necrosis. It causes skin blisters and crepitus, with rapid advancement. Fever, septic shock and organ failure can occur. Necrotising fasciitis commonly affects the limbs or male genitalia (Fournier's gangrene).

Microbiology of necrotising fasciitis

- Commonly a synergistic infection with anaerobic and aerobic organisms
- Can occur with *S. pyogenes* infection

CHAPTER 6

Risk factors for necrotising fasciitis

- Diabetes
- Peripheral vascular disease
- Alcoholism
- Perineal injury

Treatment of necrotising fasciitis

- Blood culture
- Monitor and support organ function
- Aggressive debridement beyond the visible zone of infection
- Broad-spectrum antibiotics

Fractures and soft-tissue problems

Open fractures with soft-tissue injury or loss require soft-tissue cover. The infection rate is inversely related to the time to definitive cover (ie any delay increases the risk of infection). Soft-tissue cover may be achieved by primary closure, split-skin graft, local flaps or free microvascular flaps. If there is an associated bony defect an acute shortening procedure may be appropriate. Best results are obtained by early involvement of the plastic surgical team.

Swelling complicates all injuries – severe swelling around the fracture site may result in fracture blisters. Moderate to severe swelling will result in an increased rate of wound problems and infection. Open reduction and internal fixation should be deferred until the soft tissues permit. Ankle and calcaneal fractures are particularly prone to swelling. An unstable ankle fracture may be temporarily held in a cast or with an external fixator until the soft tissues settle.

4.3 Late local complications of fractures

Fractures and avascular necrosis

Joints with extensive, convex articular surfaces are at risk of avascular necrosis (AVN). The blood supply to subchondral bone enters the bone at a site distant from the articular surface. Fractures across this bone, carrying the blood supply, will result in AVN. Increased displacement and associated soft-tissue stripping increase the risk of AVN. Early and anatomical reduction and fixation may reduce the incidence of AVN.

Typical sites for AVN
- Femoral head from intracapsular fracture of the proximal femur
- Proximal scaphoid from a fracture of the waist of the scaphoid
- Humeral head from proximal humeral fracture (typically three- or four-part fracture where articular and tuberosity fragments are separate)
- Body of talus from a neck of talus fracture

Features of AVN
- Pain
- Chondrolysis and chondral flaps (seen on MRI)
- Articular collapse (seen on plain films)

Management of AVN
- Avoid weight bearing across the joint – may revascularise given time (revascularisation demonstrated by MRI or bone scan, or by evidence of bone resorption on plain films)

CHAPTER 6

- Revascularisation procedures such as vascularised fibula grafts in the femoral head or core decompression
- Arthrodesis or arthroplasty

Fractures and myositis ossificans

Myositis ossificans can occur after a fracture or muscle injury. It is calcification within muscle.

Typical sites for myositis ossificans

- Quadriceps
- Gluteals
- Biceps
- Intrinsic muscles of the hand

Treatment of myositis ossificans

- Differentiate from other calcifying lesions (eg osteosarcoma)
- Symptomatic treatment in the acute phase (3–6 months)
- May be excised if still symptomatic when calcification is mature (12–18 months)
- NSAIDs and radiotherapy have been used to reduce incidence but no definite benefit has been proved

Fractures and complex regional pain syndrome (CRPS)

CRPS type I

Also known as:
- Reflex sympathetic dystrophy (RSD)
- Sudeck's atrophy
- Algodystrophy
- Shoulder–hand syndrome

This is a poorly understood condition. It may be an exaggeration of the normal sympathetic response to injury. CRPS type I occurs in the upper and lower limbs. It is seen in up to 30% of cases after distal radial fracture. It may occur after any minor or major injury.

Primary clinical features of CRPS type I
- Pain (out of proportion to the injury)
- Swelling
- Stiffness
- Colour change (usually redness, but the limb may take on pale or blue coloration)

Other signs
- Temperature change
- Sudomotor changes (initially hyperhidrosis; later dry skin)
- Trophic skin changes and osteoporosis
- Palmar fibromatosis

Three stages of CRPS type I
- Stage I: pain and tenderness, with warm, dry and swollen erythematous limb
- Stage II: cool, sweaty and swollen cyanotic limb
- Stage III: stiffness, atrophy and osteoporosis

CHAPTER 6

Aetiology of CRPS type I

Many theories have been proposed for the aetiology of CRPS I:

- **Injury alters afferent neurones:** This results in altered sympathetic activity, through interaction either locally or in the cord
- **Altered sympathetic activity** (vasomotor and sudomotor) results in swelling, stiffness and colour change
- **Reduced venous drainage** perpetuates condition (this may be due to vasomotor changes, dependent limb or subclavian vein stenosis)

Treatment of CRPS type I

Usually this is a self-limiting condition in minor cases, but it may result in permanent decreased function if swelling and stiffness are allowed to persist. The cycle of pain–swelling–stiffness–pain must be broken.

- Intensive physiotherapy (and splintage if required)
- Optimised analgesia
- Sympathetic blockade (or surgical sympathectomy)

CRPS type II

This is also known as causalgia. It has the same features as CRPS type I, with a demonstrable nerve lesion. Medications such as amitriptyline and pregabalin may be helpful.

Surgical decompression and neurolysis may be of benefit in resistant cases that do not respond to non-surgical treatment.

CHAPTER 6

SECTION 5

Common fractures

5.1   Upper limb

Fractures and dislocations of the shoulder and humerus

Anterior shoulder dislocation

Mechanics of anterior shoulder dislocation

Anterior dislocation is more common than posterior dislocation of the shoulder and usually results from a fall forcing external rotation of the shoulder or a fall onto a backward-stretching arm. The head of the humerus is driven forward and lies in front of the glenoid below the coracoid process.

Associated injuries include:
- Capsule torn from glenoid anteriorly (true Bankhart's lesion)
- Labrum torn (commonly referred to as Bankhart's lesion)
- Tearing of subscapularis
- Fracture of greater tuberosity
- Hill–Sachs lesion – impression fracture on posterolateral head (from glenoid)
- Damage to axillary artery or brachial plexus

Examination of anterior shoulder dislocation
- Pain is usually severe, with no movement permitted
- Patient supports the arm with the opposite hand
- The lateral outline of the shoulder is flattened
- A small bulge may be seen and felt just below the clavicle
- It is important to check sensation over the regimental badge area for axillary and radial nerve damage (as well as distal circulation, sensation and movement)

Radiographs of anterior shoulder dislocation
A minimum of two views is required to exclude a dislocation:
- Anteroposterior view: a standard view but may be misleading. The humeral head lies below and medial to the socket in typical cases. The shadows of the humeral head and glenoid overlap
- Axillary lateral view: especially to exclude posterior dislocation if subluxation is suspected
- Translateral view: normal parabolic curve between humerus and scapula is disrupted
- Apical oblique view: if possible

Reduction techniques for anterior shoulder dislocation

Kocher's method

Carry out under sedation or GA.

For sedation, the following are mandatory:

- Adequate analgesia – usually opiates
- Sedation – usually midazolam given in 1- to 2-mg increments at least 2 minutes apart and not exceeding 6 mg in a 70-kg man unless an anaesthetist is available
- Monitoring – one dedicated nurse, continuous pulse oximetry, regular observations, anaesthetist in the building

Manipulate the joint as follows, remembering the TEAR mnemonic:

- **T**raction: holding above the patient's flexed elbow with an assistant providing countertraction
- **E**xternal rotation: rotate upper arm slowly to at least 75° and up to 90° (patient needs to be relaxed)
- **A**dduction: move flexed elbow firmly forwards and deliberately across chest
- **R**otation (internal): rotate arm back to broad-arm sling position

Hippocratic method

- Simple manual traction with the body stabilised and arm in slight abduction
- Traditionally the surgeon's heel is placed against the side of the patient's chest but a colleague can provide countertraction!

Gravitational reduction

- May be effective in recurrent cases
- It involves laying the patient prone with a sandbag under the clavicle and hanging the arm over the edge of the bed holding a weight

Post-reduction care

- Reduction must be confirmed with a radiograph
- Patients are discharged with a broad-arm sling
- Advise young patients of up to 50% recurrence rate within 2 years
- Some surgeons advocate surgical stabilisation (arthroscopic reattachment of the anterior glenoid labrum) for young sporting patients after their first dislocation
- In elderly patients stiffness is the main problem and early mobilisation (within 2 weeks) is vital
- Associated proximal humeral fractures may require reduction and fixation
- Physiotherapy for rotator-cuff strengthening and proprioceptive exercises may be required

CHAPTER 6

Posterior shoulder dislocation

In posterior dislocation the humeral head lies posterior to the glenoid. It is less common than anterior dislocation and more frequently missed.

- Usually caused by a direct blow or forced internal rotation of the abducted arm (eg during an epileptic fit)
- Arm is held in medial rotation and is locked in that position, making clinical diagnosis fairly straightforward

- Diagnostic mistakes occur because the AP radiograph may be misleading (humeral head may seem to be in contact with the glenoid). The humeral head has globular appearance because it is medially rotated (light-bulb sign). A lateral or axillary film is essential, showing posterior subluxation and sometimes indentation of humeral head
- Reduction is by traction and lateral (external) rotation while the head of the humerus is pushed forwards. Post-reduction management is as for anterior dislocation
- Recurrent posterior dislocation is rarer and more difficult to treat surgically than recurrent anterior dislocation

Clavicle fractures

Most are secondary to a direct blow on the shoulder (eg a fall on the side), and less commonly caused by transmitted force from falling on to an outstretched hand.

Fractures are most common at the junction of the middle and outer thirds or through the middle third of the clavicle. This is because of strong ligament attachments via the costoclavicular ligament medially and the coracoclavicular ligament laterally.

- **Subluxations and dislocations:** may involve acromioclavicular and sternoclavicular joints
- **Greenstick fractures:** common in children (healing is rapid and reduction not required)
- **Undisplaced fractures:** common in adults (conservative treatment only required)
- **Displaced fractures:** occur with greater violence. There is separation of the bone ends. The proximal end under the pull of the sternomastoid muscle often becomes

elevated. With greater displacement of the distal fragment there may be overlapping and shortening. Malunion of a clavicle may result in reduced shoulder abduction due to subacrominal impingement
- **Non-union:** may occur with fractures of the distal third. This is an indication for internal fixation

Other indications for internal fixation include open fracture or neurovascular injury.

Humerus fractures

> **Important nerve relationships in humerus fractures**
> - Surgical neck: the axillary nerve and circumflex humeral vessels
> - Spiral groove: running along the posterior aspect of the shaft are the radial nerve and profunda brachii vessels
> - Posterior aspect of the medial epicondyle: the ulnar nerve

Proximal humerus fractures

These fractures may involve the anatomical neck, surgical neck, greater tuberosity or lesser tuberosity, and are described in terms of how many fragments are involved (eg two-, three- or four-part). To be a separate 'part' the fragment must be of significant size and have either 1 cm of displacement or 45° of angulation. The four-part fracture has articular, greater tuberosity, lesser tuberosity and shaft fragments.

Mechanism of injury of proximal humerus fractures
- A fall onto side or direct blow to side of arm
- A fall onto outstretched hand

The upper limb acts as a strut between the hand and torso through which force is transmitted. These fractures are common in elderly people and range in severity from minimal displacement fractures, with minor angulation, to multiple-part fractures associated with dislocation at the shoulder joint.

Neer's classification of proximal humerus fractures

Group I	All fractures with: displacement <1 cm, angulation 45°
Group II	Anatomical neck fractures displaced >1 cm (can be complicated by AVN of articular surface)
Group III	Surgical neck fracture with significant displacement or angulation (can be complicated by axillary nerve injury)
Group IV	Greater tuberosity fracture, displaced by pull of supraspinatus (can be complicated by painful arc syndrome due to impingement of the greater tuberosity on the acromion process and coracoacromial ligament)
Group V	Lesser tuberosity fractures
Group VI	Fracture dislocations

Groups II–VI may be subdivided according to the number of 'parts' (eg two-part fracture).

Management of proximal humerus fractures
- Usually conservative treatment with collar and cuff or broad-arm sling
- Formal open reduction and internal fixation or hemiarthroplasty for more complicated injuries
- Start hand and elbow mobilisation from day 1
- Mobilise shoulder at 3 weeks but maintain collar and cuff for 4–5 weeks

Humeral shaft fractures

Mechanism of injury of humeral shaft fractures
- Fall onto outstretched hand
- Indirect twisting force results in spiral fracture
- Direct force to arm results in short oblique or comminuted fracture
- Seen in adults of any age, but seldom in children

Classification of humeral shaft fractures
Described in relation to the position of fracture along the shaft:
- Upper third: proximal fragment adducted by pull of now unopposed pectoralis major
- Middle third: proximal fragment tends to be abducted by action of deltoid muscle
- Lower third: supracondylar fractures

Associated radial nerve injury may occur in middle-third fractures due to the course of the radial nerve in the spiral groove on the posterior aspect of the humeral shaft.

CHAPTER 6

Management of humeral shaft fractures

- Up to 20° of AP angulation and 30° of varus–valgus angulation is acceptable for non-surgical treatment (with hanging cast followed by functional bracing)
- Open reduction and internal fixation or intramedullary nailing indicated in polytrauma, pathological fractures or where the position is unacceptable
- Plate fixation risks injury to the radial nerve
- Anterograde humeral nailing may cause shoulder impingement and pain

Fractures around the elbow

Adult supracondylar fractures

The mechanism of injury is usually from a fall onto an outstretched hand. The distal fragment is usually displaced and tilted backwards. There may be local neurovascular injury.

Management of adult supracondylar fractures can be:

- Non-surgical: if undisplaced
- ORIF: if displaced (plate on medial and lateral columns, through triceps – splitting approach or with olecranon osteotomy)
- Total elbow replacement: considered in elderly patients with very comminuted fractures

Intercondylar fractures

The injury commonly arises from a fall onto an outstretched hand with elbow flexed. The fracture extends into the joint. The condyles are split, often with significant comminution.

Management of intercondylar fractures can be:

- Non-surgical: if undisplaced
- 'Bag of bones' technique: for very displaced fractures in patients with low functional demand. Elbow is immobilised in flexion with collar and cuff for pain relief. As things settle the patient may mobilise within the limits of comfort
- ORIF: if displaced (double-plate fixation with interfragmentary screws to reconstruct the articular surface)
- Total elbow replacement: in mobile elderly patients with very comminuted fractures

Olecranon fractures

The injury often involves a fall on to the elbow point (usually adults).

Management of olecranon fractures depends on the type of injury:

- Immobilisation: with elbow flexed to 90° without distracting fracture further (suitable for undisplaced fractures).
- Screw fixation or tension-band wiring: for displaced fractures
- Plate fixation: for comminuted fractures. A rarely used alternative to plating comminuted fractures is to excise the fragments of the olecranon and secure the triceps insertion to ulna

Coronoid fractures

The mechanism of injury is most commonly associated with posterior dislocation of elbow. Coronoid fractures are classified as:

- Simple avulsion
- Half or less of coronoid
- More than half of coronoid

Management of coronoid fractures is:

- Conservative: unless more than half of the coronoid is involved
- Internal fixation: may be used to prevent recurrent dislocation

Radial head fractures

The usual mechanism of injury involves a fall onto an outstretched hand. The force is transmitted along the radial shaft to the head – striking the head on the capitulum. These fractures are common in young adults.

Management of radial head fractures depends on severity of damage to the radial head:

- Simple immobilisation for undisplaced fracture (two weeks)
- ORIF for large, displaced fragments
- Excision of severely comminuted radial head fracture with Silastic replacement

Always check for associated subluxation of the distal ulna in cases where the interosseous membrane is torn and there is upward drift of the radial shaft.

Radial neck fractures

These fractures commonly occur in children. The mechanism of injury is a fall onto an outstretched hand. In adults a similar mechanism of injury may produce a radial head fracture.

Management of radial neck fractures depends on the angulation:

- Simple immobilisation: if angulation <30%
- MUA: if angulation >30%
- If residual angle >45° or dislocated:
  - ORIF in adults
  - Open reduction only in children

The radial head should not be excised in a child.

Complications of fractures around the elbow joint
- Loss of range of movement
- Prolonged immobility
- Posterior interosseous nerve damage (in surgery near radial head)
- Myositis ossificans
- Ulnar nerve damage

Radial and ulnar fractures

Monteggia and Galeazzi fractures

If only one forearm bone is fractured and angled with its humeral and wrist attachments intact, the other forearm bone must be dislocated. Complete rupture of the interosseous membrane may give rise to severe long-term problems.

Monteggia fracture: fracture of the proximal ulna with dislocation of the radial head is called a Monteggia fracture (remember: Monty loses his head). It is relatively uncommon. It is due to a fall with forced pronation of the forearm or a direct blow on back of upper forearm.

A Galeazzi fracture is a fracture of the shaft of the radius, usually at the junction of the middle and lower third, with dislocation of the distal ulna. It is often due to a fall on the hand.

A single forearm fracture should never be accepted as a definitive diagnosis until Monteggia or Galeazzi is ruled out.

Management of Monteggia and Galeazzi fractures

Perfect reduction is seldom attainable by closed manipulation. ORIF is often required to maintain the reduction.

Forearm bone shaft fractures

It is possible to sustain a fracture of either forearm bone in isolation (eg warding off a direct blow or falling on a sharp edge). More commonly, a fall onto the outstretched hand subjects the forearm bones to indirect force that causes both to fracture.

CHAPTER 6

The ulna may angulate or be displaced, whereas the radius may be subject to axial rotation due to insertion of the pronator teres midway along the radial shaft.

If the radius is fractured proximal to this insertion, the proximal fragment will supinate due to unopposed action of the biceps insertion and the distal fragment will be pronated. The forearm should be immobilised and supinated to match the supinated proximal end. If the fracture is distal to the insertion of pronator teres, the actions of biceps plus pronator muscles are equalised. The forearm is immobilised in the neutral position.

Management of forearm bone shaft fractures

- Varies from MUA in children to ORIF in adults
- In children, angulation of up to 20° is acceptable in those aged <10
- Age >10 years: angulation of no more than 10° is acceptable
- Any rotational malalignment will compromise pronation–supination and is unacceptable

Complications of forearm shaft fractures

- Compartment syndrome
- Non-union
- Synostosis
- Malunion
- Refracture (first 6 months)
- Neurological damage

Fractures of the lower end of the radius

Colles' fracture

Learning point

- Fracture of the radius within 2.5 cm of wrist joint
- Extra-articular fracture with dorsal and radial displacement of the distal fragment
- Classic 'dinner-fork' deformity
- Radial displacement and tilt with dorsal displacement and tilt

Colles' fracture is commonly associated with fracture through the ulnar styloid. Radial displacement of the distal fragment causes avulsion of the ulna styloid through its attachment via the triangular fibrocartilage. Management of Colles' fracture depends on the degree of displacement and age. MUA or ORIF may be necessary.

Reduction of Colles' fracture

The main aim is to disimpact the radial fragment.
- Exaggerate deformity: traction; dorsal displacement
- Restore anatomical position: volar displacement
- Plaster in ulnar deviation and slight flexion

These may be performed under local (haematoma block), regional (Bier's block) or GA. The long-term success of MUA depends on the quality of the plaster of Paris cast that is subsequently applied. The cast should be padded, but not excessively. The goal should

CHAPTER 6

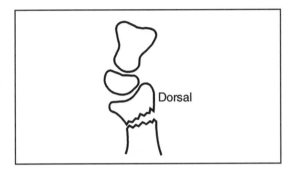

Figure 6.22 Smith's fracture

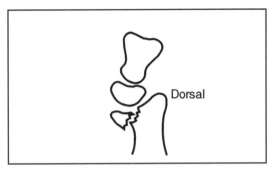

Figure 6.23 Volar fracture (Barton's fracture)

be three points of contact, with moulding spread over a large area to prevent pressure problems. The wrist should be slightly flexed and slightly ulna-deviated. Excessive angulation will contribute to median nerve problems and should be avoided.

Potential complications of Colles' fracture

* Persistent deformity or malunion
* Delayed rupture of extensor pollicis longus
* Reflex sympathetic dystrophy (also known as CRPS)
* Carpal tunnel syndrome
* Persisting stiffness
* Ulnar abutment syndrome due to radial shortening

Barton's fracture (intra-articular)

This is a fracture of the dorsal or volar lip of the distal radius with subluxation of the carpus. Management is with cast immobilisation if undisplaced. ORIF if displaced.

Smith's fracture

This is an extra-articular distal radial fracture with volar displacement. It usually occurs as a result of a fall onto the dorsum of the hand.

Fractures of the carpus (wrist)

> **Learning point**
>
> **Common injuries of the carpus (wrist)**
> * Fracture of scaphoid bone
> * Dislocation of carpal bones
> * Fractures of other carpal bones

Scaphoid fracture

The most commonly fractured wrist bone is the scaphoid, which is involved in both the radiocarpal joint and the joint between the distal and proximal carpal rows.

The blood supply to the scaphoid is variable. It commonly enters the distal part of the ligamentous ridge between the two main articular surfaces. Thus there is a risk of AVN of the proximal part of the bone if a fracture of the waist is sustained.

Due to the role of the scaphoid in two major joints, movement of fracture fragments is difficult to control. The prognosis is good in stable fractures, but poor in unstable fractures.

CHAPTER 6

Mechanism of injury
- Fall onto outstretched hand in young adults
- 'Kick back' when using jump-start handles or pulleys

Sites of scaphoid fracture
- Waist of scaphoid bone (most common)
- Proximal pole (high risk of AVN)
- Distal half (least common)

Management of scaphoid fractures
Treatment is by plaster immobilisation or internal fixation if displaced.

Scaphoid plaster
- Wrist pronated, radially deviated, moderately dorsiflexed
- Extending from metacarpophalangeal (MCP) joints (including thumb in mid-abduction), extending along forearm but not involving elbow joint
- For 6–8 weeks

If no fracture is seen on radiograph but clinical suspicion is high, immobilise in a cast for 2 weeks then repeat the radiograph.

Complications of scaphoid fractures
- Delayed union
- Non-union
- AVN (of proximal third)
- Osteoarthritis

Injuries of other carpal bones are uncommon. Treat as for uncomplicated fractures of the scaphoid (ie short period of plaster immobilisation)

Dislocation of the lunate

The lunate is a crescent-shaped bone with its base anteriorly. If it is subjected to excessive force with the hand extended it can be squeezed out of position. In the characteristic injury the lunate lies anterior to the wrist, rotated through 90° or more on a horizontal axis, so that its concave distal articular surface faces anteriorly. It may compress the median nerve.

Management of dislocation of the lunate
- MUA
- ORIF

Complications of dislocation of the lunate
- Median nerve injury
- Osteoarthritis

Perilunate dislocation of the carpus: the whole carpus is dislocated posteriorly except for the lunate, which remains congruous with the radius.

Scapholunate dissociation (rupture of the scapholunate ligament complex): the carpal bones rotate as the hand moves from radial to ulnar deviation. The rotational force is transmitted through the intrinsic carpal ligaments. Disruption of the ligaments leads to abnormal carpal biomechanics. This may lead to osteoarthritis (OA) in the long term.

5.2 Lower limb

Fractures of the proximal femur

> **Learning point**
>
> The types of proximal femur fractures differ in different age groups:
> - **Adolescents:** slipped upper femoral epiphysis
> - **Young adults:** hip dislocation (as opposed to fracture)
> - **Elderly people:** fracture of the neck of femur (seen in patients mean age n80 years; sex ratio 1 M:4 F)

It is important to appreciate the blood supply of the femur because some femoral fractures can lead to AVN of the femoral head. The blood supply of the proximal femur occurs:
- Through diaphysis
- Retinacular branches from medial and lateral femoral circumflex arteries (pass proximally within joint capsule to anastomose at junction of neck and articular surface)
- Ligamentum teres (small contribution, or no contribution in elderly people)

The retinacular vessels are disrupted in intracapsular fractures, leading to AVN of the head.

Proximal femur fractures can be divided into two groups:
- Intracapsular:
  - Subcapital
  - Transcervical
  - Basicervical
- Extracapsular:
  - Intertrochanteric
  - Subtrochanteric

There may be significant blood loss with an extracapsular fracture. These patients need careful resuscitation and observation.

Intracapsular fracture of the proximal femur

> **Garden's classification of intracapsular fractures**
>
> This is based on integrity of trabecular lines in an AP projection.
>
> **Stage I** Impacted fracture, medial cortical, trabeculae intact but angulated (undisplaced similar prognosis)
>
> **Stage II** Complete but undisplaced fracture, medial cortical trabeculae interrupted but not angulated
>
> **Stage III** Complete, partially displaced fracture with loss of trabecular alignment
>
> **Stage IV** Completely displaced fracture

Management of intracapsular fracture
- Undisplaced intracapsular fracture (Garden I and II):
  - Internal fixation with two or three parallel screws
  - Small risk of AVN or non-union
  - If this occurs, cannulated screws may be revised to a hemiarthroplasty or total hip replacement (THR)
- Displaced intracapsular fracture (Garden III and IV):
  - NICE recommends total hip replacement for fit patients and hemi-arthroplasty for patients with significant comorbidity (lack of mobility).
  - In young fit patients urgent reduction and internal fixation

CHAPTER 6

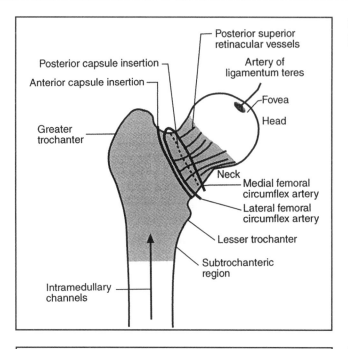

Figure 6.24
Blood supply of the femoral head

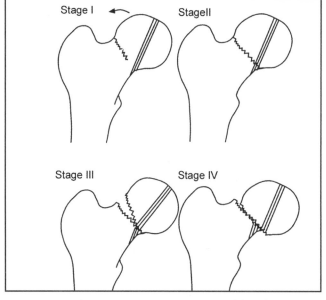

Figure 6.25
Garden's classification of intracapsular fractures

Risk of AVN is higher for Garden III and IV fractures, but accurate reduction gives excellent results in a proportion of patients.

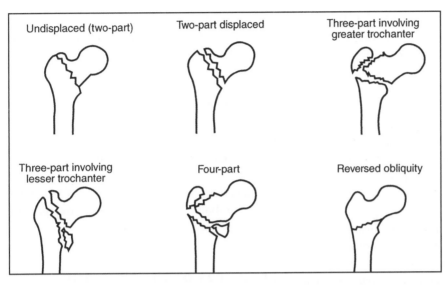

Figure 6.26
Extracapsular
fractures

Undisplaced (two-part)

Two-part displaced

Three-part involving greater trochanter

Three-part involving lesser trochanter

Four-part

Reversed obliquity

Postoperative complications of intracapsular fracture

- Infection
- Dislocation
- Femoral stem loosening and thigh pain
- Acetabular erosion

Extracapsular fracture of femur

These fractures occur from the basal part of the femoral neck to about 5 cm below the lesser trochanter. They include:

- Intertrochanteric
- Basal
- Subtrochanteric

They occur distal to the insertion of the joint capsule through an area of well-vascularised metaphyseal bone. Classification is based on the number of fragments produced by the fracture (Figure 6.26):

- Undisplaced (two-part)
- Displaced (two-part)
- Three-part involving the greater trochanter
- Three-part involving the lesser trochanter
- Four-part
- Reversed obliquity

Management of extracapsular fracture

This is with reduction and fixation with a device that transmits force from the femoral head to the femoral shaft.

- Dynamic hip screw (DHS): the screw is inserted into the neck and head and slides freely in the barrel of the plate, which is secured to femoral shaft. This allows fractures to compress
- Intramedullary fixation device: similar to DHS but force is transmitted to an intramedullary nail

Complications of proximal femur fractures

Due to comorbid factors, the mortality rate for hip fracture patients is 14–36% at 1 year. The highest mortality risk occurs within the first 4–6 months. After 1 year the mortality rate approaches that for age-matched and sex-matched controls.

CHAPTER 6

Femoral shaft fractures in adults

- Commonly the result of high-energy trauma
- Will result in blood loss of 1000–1500 ml (more if open fracture)
- Compartment syndrome is rare

First-aid treatment includes the identification of associated injuries (according to ATLS guidelines), correction of hypovolaemia and temporary splinting of the fracture (using Thomas splint with skin traction).

Femoral fractures should be stabilised as soon as possible. Fat embolism syndrome may follow fracture of the femoral shaft; the risk of this is thought to be reduced by early surgical intervention. This has to be weighed against the risks of exacerbating the systemic inflammatory response of trauma with a second operation. There is much discussion about 'early total care' (treating all injuries as soon as possible) versus 'damage control orthopaedics'. Decisions about the timing of surgery have to be made on a case-by-case basis, but monitoring physiological and biochemical parameters of inflammation may inform this decision-making process.

Femoral shaft fractures are usually treated by intramedullary nailing, but external fixation or compression plating may be used in some cases.

Distal femoral fractures in adults

Supracondylar or intercondylar distal femoral fractures in young patients are the result of high-energy trauma. They occur in the elderly population with severe osteoporosis.

The muscle attachments of the distal femur mean that these fractures are unstable. They are generally treated by open reduction and internal fixation. Locking plates (contoured to the shape of the lateral side of the distal femur) have been developed which allow the fixation to be done using a less invasive technique.

Patellar fracture

Undisplaced fractures with an intact extensor mechanism are treated non-surgically in a long-leg cast or functional brace.

Displaced fractures are treated by ORIF with a tension-band wire or screws or excision of fragments if it is un-reconstructable.

Fractures of the tibia and fibula

Tibial plateau fractures

More than 50% of patients sustaining this injury are >50 years old. Plateau fractures may be classified using the Schatzker classification. The lateral plateau is more commonly affected than the medial. These injuries may be relatively undisplaced, but can result in significant articular depression. The goal is to restore the joint surface and support this with bone graft and fixation (screw/buttress plate or Ilizarov frame). Undisplaced injuries may be treated in a hinged-knee brace.

Tibial shaft ± fibula fractures

Fractures of the tibia are more commonly open than in any other bone, and skin closure is particularly difficult because the bone is subcutaneous.

Management of tibial shaft ± fibula fractures
- Minimally displaced and slightly displaced stable fractures (eg transverse) are readily amenable to conservative treatment with an above-knee cast

- Oblique and spiral fractures are potentially unstable, but conservative management is an option if there is minimal displacement
- Displaced unstable fractures require reduction and stabilisation

Stabilisation may be achieved by one of several techniques:
- Long-leg cast: for transverse, minimally displaced fractures. May allow early weight bearing
- Tibial nail: for diaphyseal fractures. May allow early weight bearing
- Plate and screws: more useful for metaphyseal fractures. Disruption of fracture site reduces blood supply to fracture (seldom used)
- External fixator (monolateral frame): good temporary fixation. May be complicated by pin-site infection and loosening
- Circular frame (Ilizarov technique): allows great control of fragments. Does not disrupt soft tissues. Requires specialist skill to apply and care for

Complications associated with tibial fracture
- Compartment syndrome
- Soft-tissue injury: a tibial fracture is often associated with tissue damage and tissue loss. Open fractures should be treated in a centre with suitable plastic surgery facilities. It is vital to aid fracture healing and avoid infection by early skin cover
- Vascular injury: a displaced fracture of the proximal shaft may damage the trifurcation of the popliteal artery. Alternatively a distal branch may be damaged. Inform the vascular team immediately
- Delayed union and non-union: occurs in up to 20% of cases. Often occurs secondary

to the significant initial displacement, comminution and distraction, causing soft-tissue injury and devascularisation of the fracture site
- Malunion: shortening, malrotation, varus and valgus deformity of >10° may lead to secondary OA of the knee or ankle
- Ankle and subtalar joint stiffness: due to prolonged immobilisation

Ankle fractures

Classification of ankle injuries
There are numerous classifications of ankle fracture. The two most widely used systems are the Weber–AO system, which reflects on the level of the fibula fracture, and the Lange–Hansen system which refers to the position of the foot and the direction of the deforming force.

In the **Weber–AO system** fractures are classified by the level of the lateral malleolar fibular injury:
- **Type A fractures** of the fibula are below the tibial plafond and typically transverse fractures
- **Type B fractures** of the fibula begin at the level of the tibial plafond and typically extend proximally in a spiral or short oblique fashion
- **Type C fractures** of the fibula are initiated above the tibial plafond and are associated with syndesmotic injuries

The talus sits in the ankle mortise. The stability of the mortise is derived from the deltoid ligament, medial malleolus, distal tibia, syndesmosis (tibiofibular ligaments), lateral malleolus and lateral ligament complex. Disruption of the mortise with talar shift is an indication for fixation.

CHAPTER 6

Treatment of ankle injuries

Aims of treatment are to:

- Restore and maintain normal alignment of the talus with the tibia
- Ensure no future problems with instability
- Ensure realignment of the articulating surfaces to reduce the chance of developing secondary osteoarthritis

Excellent results can be obtained with conservative management in the stable fracture. Some displaced fractures may be successfully treated by MUA and cast immobilisation. However, surgical fixation is the method of choice for unstable fractures.

Indications for ankle fracture fixation

- Talar shift
- Potential talar shift
- Fibular fracture above the inferior tibiofibular joint
- Displaced medial malleolus
- Fibula shortening
- Significant displaced articular fragments

Beware of the 'isolated' deltoid (medial) ligament sprain. Check for associated high-fibula fracture and 'diastasis' at the distal tibia–fibula joint (Maisonneuve fracture).

5.3   Pelvic fractures

Mechanism of injury of pelvic fractures

Pelvic fractures occur as the result of a high-energy trauma, associated injuries are common.

The pelvic ring comprises the sacrum and two innominate bones. They are joined by ligaments that resist vertical shear, separation and rotation at the sacroiliac (SI) joints and pubic symphysis. With high-energy injuries, it is unusual to disrupt the pelvic ring in just one place. Just as in the forearm and lower leg, injuries to a bony ring come in pairs.

Pelvic injuries may be classified according to either their mechanism of injury or the stability of the pelvic ring.

Classification of pelvic fractures

Mechanism of injury – Young and Burgess classification

- **Lateral compression:** lateral force causes internal rotation of the hemipelvis, causing disruption of some SI ligaments or compression fractures of the sacrum. Internal rotation closes down the pelvic volume and bleeding is reduced. Lateral compression injuries may be associated with abdominal and chest injuries
- **AP compression:** causes external rotation of the hemipelvis (open-book injury). This increases the pelvic volume and thus the space for potential blood loss
- **Vertical shear:** vertical force causes complete disruption of the posterior arch on one side and the hemipelvis is displaced superiorly. Bleeding may be significant. There is often injury to the lumbosacral plexus
- **Combined mechanism**

Stability of posterior arch (ilium, SI joints and sacrum) – Tile–AO classification

- **Type A:** stable injuries (eg avulsion fractures, transverse fractures of the sacrum)
- **Type B:** rotationally unstable injuries, partial disruption of the posterior arch (eg open-book injury or lateral compression injury)

- **Type C:** rotationally and vertically unstable injuries, complete disruption of the posterior arch (eg vertical sheer injury)

Investigating pelvic fractures

A plain radiograph of the pelvis constitutes part of the ATLS primary survey. Plain films are poor at detecting posterior injuries. Additional information may be obtained from inlet/outlet views of the pelvis.

CT is the investigation of choice (when the patient is stable).

Management of pelvic fractures

Mechanically unstable injuries may be temporarily stabilised with a pelvic binder or external fixator. This reduces the pelvic volume and reduces bleeding by providing a stable environment for clot formation. 'Springing' a pelvis to detect a fracture displaces any clot that has formed, causes increased bleeding and should not be performed.

Many pelvic fractures can be managed conservatively, non-weight-bearing for 12 weeks.

Definitive fixation of pelvic fractures may be deferred until the patient is stable.

Acetabular fractures

Acetabular fractures are the result of high-energy trauma. They occur in association with dislocation of the hip. There is a high incidence of sciatic nerve injury.

Each innominate bone may be considered to have two columns (anterior and posterior) through which load is transferred. These columns come together in an inverted Y, with the dome of the acetabulum at the apex. The acetabulum has a posterior and anterior wall. Acetabular fractures are classified according to involvement of the columns and walls.

An AP radiograph of the pelvis gives little information on the anatomy of an acetabular fracture. A pair of oblique views (Judet views) will show the columns in more detail, but, again, CT gives the most information.

Undisplaced acetabular fractures may be treated non-surgically. Displaced fractures should be reduced and internally fixed. **Dislocated hips** should be reduced as soon as possible.

5.4 Thoracolumbar spinal injuries

Osteoporotic fractures of the thoracolumbar spine outnumber traumatic injuries by a factor of 10. All patients who present with an 'osteoporotic fracture' should be assessed to exclude other possible causes of pathological fracture such as metastatic spinal disease.

If the fracture is osteoporotic, then possible secondary causes of osteoporosis should be sought; 50% of men and 30% of women presenting with osteoporotic spinal fractures will have an underlying cause for their osteoporosis.

The majority of thoracolumbar injuries seen in the UK today are the result of RTAs and falls from a height.

Assessment of spinal injuries

- Resuscitation according to ATLS guidelines, and full examination including log-roll
- Fully document neurological function with time of examination

CHAPTER 6

- If there is an injury at one level the whole spine should be imaged to exclude an associated injury at another (10% incidence of non-contiguous injury)

Classification of spinal injuries

Spinal injuries may be classified according to the fracture and the neurological injury. The American Spinal Injury Association (ASIA) score grades normal cord function E and complete spinal cord injuries A.

Commonly used spinal fracture classification systems use the concept of columns. It is worthwhile knowing both Denis' three-column description and the AO-Magerl two-column model. It is important to note that there is a spectrum of spinal stability from normal to completely unstable and, secondly, that there is more to spinal fractures than simply either wedge fractures or burst fractures!

AO-Magerl two-column concept

The spine has an anterior column (discs and vertebral bodies), which is loaded in compression. The posterior spinal column (posterior elements and interspinous ligaments) is loaded in tension.

Fractures are graded A–C, with decreasing stability with increasing grade. A-type injuries are injuries of the anterior column only (including burst fractures). These are relatively stable. B-type injures have disruption to the posterior column. The anterior column is loaded in compression and fractures here tend to heal. The posterior column is loaded in tension and injuries here tend not to heal. B-type fractures are relatively unstable. C-type fractures have a rotational element and are very unstable.

Three-column theory of Denis

The spine has three weight-bearing columns:
- Anterior: anterior longitudinal ligament and anterior part of vertebral body and disc
- Middle: posterior part of vertebral body and disc and posterior longitudinal ligament
- Posterior: posterior elements (ligaments and bony parts)

Denis' classification is often misquoted. His original work states that, by looking at the mode of failure of the middle column, one could derive information about the stability of the spine. He did not say one column injury stable, two column unstable.

Recent classifications have tried to integrate spinal cord injury grade with a morphological fracture description and an assessment of the functional stability of the posterior spinal column (which is loaded in tension and prevents kyphosis). This aims to give a guide as to which injuries should be treated surgically.

Aims of treatment of spinal injuries
- Prevent further neurological injury
- Prevent deformity/stabilise the spine
- Restore function

A thoracolumbar injury with a cauda equina injury or cord injury with disruption of the posterior column would favour operative treatment. More complex anterior column injuries, such at those with rotation would also favour operative treatment.

Thoracolumbar injuries tend to occur at junctional areas between the cervical and thoracic spine and thoracic and lumbar spine. Fractures of T12 and L1 are most commonly seen. This is the level of the conus of the spinal cord.

Burst fractures are a common result of thoraco-lumbar trauma. Here the anterior column has failed in compression. The vertebral body has been forced out on all sides as a result of this compression and a fragment is projected backwards into the spinal canal. At the time of injury the position of this fragment would have been significantly worse than that seen when the patient is imaged. The spinal canal remodels over time and the 'retropulsed fragment' is of little significance.

5.5   Cervical spine trauma

Learning point

Assessment of the cervical spine

The cervical spine should be immobilised with collar, head blocks and tape until a fracture has been excluded clinically or radiologically.

May be cleared clinically in a fully conscious patient with no neck pain and no significant distracting injuries.

Radiographic assessment requires three views (lateral C1 to T1, AP and open-mouth view of the odontoid peg).

If plain films are inadequate or suggest a fracture then a CT scan should be obtained. A CT should be 2- to 3-mm slices from the skull base down to T4, reconstructed in all three planes.

An MR scan or flexion/extension views are helpful if ligamentous injury/instability is suspected.

Some important cervical spine injuries:
- **Jefferson's fracture:** burst fracture of C1, associated with other C-spine injuries
- **Odontoid peg fracture:** 5–10% incidence of cord injury
- **Hangman's fracture:** traumatic spondylolis-thesis of C2 on C3 (due to pars fracture C2)
- **C3–C7 injuries:** classified on mechanism of injury (ie compression/distraction and flexion/extension/lateral flexion)
- **Facet joint dislocation:** unilateral or bilateral. MRI required to assess disc injury, which may need to be cleared before the fracture is reduced, or cord compression may result. Reduced with increasing traction
- **Clay-shoveller's fracture:** avulsion fracture of spinous process of lower cervical vertebra

Treatment of cervical spine injuries

Treatment depends on the pattern and stability of the fracture and the presence or absence of neurological injury. Options include:
- **Rigid collar:** eg Philadelphia collar, which prevents flexion/extension but gives poor control over rotation
- **Cervical–thoracic orthosis:** many designs. Have better lateral flexion and rotational stability than a collar alone
- **Halo frame:** body harness with four bars linked to a ring that is fixed to the skull by four pins. More rigid than other external stabilisation devices
- **Cervical tongs:** eg Gardner–Wells tongs. Used to provide cervical traction (for reducing facet-joint dislocations)
- **Fusion/internal fixation:** with or without spinal decompression

CHAPTER 6

SECTION 6

Fractures and related injuries in children

Learning point

Bony injuries in children are different because:
- Their bone is different from adult bone
- They have an epiphysis
- They are still growing

Fractures and related childhood injuries that you should be aware of are:
- Epiphyseal injuries
- Forearm bone fractures
- Supracondylar fractures
- Condylar fractures

6.1 Paediatric bone

Differences between paediatric and adult bone:
- Higher water content
- Lower mineral content
- Greater elasticity
- Weaker than paediatric ligaments (so more fractures, fewer sprains)

Failure of paediatric bone under load conditions:
- **Compression:**
  - Buckle or torus fractures at metaphysis–diaphysis junction
- **Bending:**
  - Greenstick fractures
  - Compression on one side (cortex and periosteum intact), cortex fractured on tension side
- **Torsion:**
  - In young children causes diaphyseal spiral fractures (eg tibial fractures in toddlers)
  - In older children causes epiphyseal injuries

6.2 Epiphyseal injuries

Salter–Harris classification (most are type I or II)

Type I
- Distraction injury of growth plate
- No fracture of epiphysis or metaphysis
- Seldom results in growth disturbance

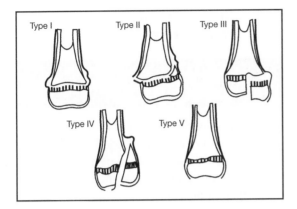

Figure 6.27 Salter–Harris classification (most are type I or II)

Type II

- Fracture through physis with a metaphyseal fragment (Thurston–Holland fragment)
- Most common type of epiphyseal injury
- Seldom results in growth disturbance

Type III

- Portion of epiphysis associated with its adjacent growth plate fractures from epiphysis
- This is intra-articular, so accurate reduction and fixation are needed

Type IV

- Separation of portion of metaphysis, physis and epiphysis
- Intra-articular injury
- This fracture pattern is commonest cause of premature growth arrest

Type V

- Rare
- Crush injury to the physis
- Disrupts growth
- Difficult to diagnose (often diagnosed in retrospect)

Epiphysial contributions to growth

GROWTH CONTRIBUTIONS OF EACH PHYSIS

Physis	Accounts for percentage of growth of that bone	Accounts for percentage of overall growth of limb
Proximal humerus	80	40
Distal humerus	20	10
Proximal radius/ulna	20	10
Distal radius/ulna	80	40
Proximal femur	30	15
Distal femur	70	40
Proximal tibia	55	27
Distal tibia	44	18

Most longitudinal growth in the arm occurs at the shoulder and wrist. In the lower limb it occurs at the knee.

Growth disturbance occurs as a result of the formation of bony bars across the physis. This occurs if the fracture is not accurately reduced, or if the injury causes disruption of the blood supply to the physis. Bars may be central (resulting in longitudinal growth arrest) or peripheral (resulting in angular deformities). Bony bars may be treated by excision and soft-tissue interposition.

6.3 Forearm bone fractures

Mechanism of injury

- Fall onto outstretched hand (eg in rollerblading accidents, climbing trees)
- Represent 45% of all paediatric fractures
- Majority of forearm fractures are of the distal radius and ulna

CHAPTER 6

The distal radial and ulnar physes provide approximately 80% of the total growth of the forearm.

There is therefore excellent remodelling potential of distal, radial and ulnar fractures in the plane of the joint only.

Complete, greenstick and torus fractures

Both complete and incomplete fractures may occur in children, but incomplete fractures are common due to the increased plasticity of children's bones.

- **A greenstick fracture** is an incomplete fracture where one cortex breaks and the other does not. It is due to forced angulation. The bone buckles on the side opposite to the causal force. There may be minimal periosteal tearing
- **A torus fracture** is due to compression. The side of the cortex buckles when it is subjected to compression

Management of forearm bone fractures in children

- Torus fracture: POP for pain relief
- Complete and greenstick fractures: require MUA or, occasionally, ORIF; above-elbow POP to prevent supination–pronation of the forearm
- Epiphyseal injuries: require MUA to reduce physis

All displaced fractures treated by manipulation (especially in children) have a risk of recurrent displacement. The patient should be seen in clinic at 1 week and repeat radiographs taken to ensure that the position remains acceptable.

6.4 Supracondylar fractures

> **Learning point**
>
> Fractures just above the elbow are common in children and risk damage to the median nerve, radial nerve and brachial artery, and development of compartment syndrome.

Mechanism of injury

These result from a fall onto an outstretched hand.

Characteristics of supracondylar fractures

- Most common in childhood – peak at age 8 years
- The distal fragment is usually displaced and tilted backwards (extension type)
- Reduction is required if the fracture is displaced
- May be associated with distal radial fracture

Management of supracondylar fractures

An uncomplicated, minimally displaced fracture should be immobilised with the elbow flexed – but in a position with no vascular compromise.

MUA percutaneous k-wires or wires through a mini-open approach to protect the ulnar nerve is indicated if there is displacement. In a displaced fracture, the lower fragment is brought into position by longitudinal traction and pressure applied behind the olecranon with the elbow flexed.

CHAPTER 6

Vigilant observation is required postoperatively for signs of brachial artery and median nerve damage due to proximal fragment impingement.

Signs of brachial artery damage in a supracondylar fracture
- Pain on passive finger extension
- Excessive bruising and swelling around the elbow
- Pain and paraesthesiae
- Loss of distal pulses
- Pallor and coldness of hand and forearm
- Progressive weakness
- Gangrene of digits due to emboli

Volkmann's ischaemic contracture may result if these signs are missed. Fortunately the extensive anastomosis around the elbow is often able to preserve perfusion even when the artery is damaged.

6.5   Condylar fractures

These are uncommon and occur mainly in children. They can cause permanent disability if not reduced adequately. They mostly involve the lateral condyle. It is easy to miss them at initial presentation because the radiographic signs may be subtle.

Growth arrest at the fracture site may occur, causing a deformity that increases with age.

6.6   Femoral fractures in children

There is a bimodal peak in the incidence of femoral fractures: 2–4 years and the early teenage years. Non-accidental injury should be suspected if a femoral fracture occurs in a child who is not yet walking. Fractures in teenagers are usually due to motor vehicle accidents.

Paediatric femoral shaft fractures may be treated initially by reduction with skin traction and a Thomas splint (or gallows traction if <3 years). Traction may be the definitive treatment in some cases. Other options include a hip spica for young children or stabilisation with multiple flexible intramedullary nails in children aged >5 years. External fixation or compression plating is also an option.

A small degree of malunion is acceptable because there is great potential for remodelling during growth. Up to 10° of varus or valgus or 30° of flexion or extension at the fracture site is acceptable. Some shortening (20 mm if <10 years, 10 mm if ≥10) may be acceptable. Overgrowth of 1 cm or so may be expected (due to disruption of the periosteum and increased local blood supply) and so the broken leg will be slightly longer than the unaffected side. Rotational malalignment should be avoided if possible, but up to 10° may be tolerated.

Distal femoral fractures in children

Distal femoral fractures can occur in teenagers as the result of high-energy trauma. This physeal injury requires accurate reduction.

CHAPTER 6

SECTION 7

Soft-tissue injuries and disorders

7.1 Soft-tissue injuries of the knee

> **Learning point**
>
> **Knee injuries**
> The inherent stability of the knee joint is dependent on the associated soft tissues. The main structures at risk in the knee are:
> **Ligaments**
> - Extra-articular:
>   - Medial collateral
>   - Lateral collateral
> - Intra-articular:
>   - Posterior cruciate
>   - Anterior cruciate
>
> **Menisci**
> **Extensor apparatus**

Ligaments

Medial collateral ligament injuries

The most common mechanism of injury is a blow to the lateral aspect of the knee – giving a valgus stress to the tibia on the femur and stressing the medial collateral ligament. The severity of injury varies from simple strain to complete rupture involving the medial meniscus due to its attachment to the medial collateral ligament. The posterior capsule can be torn and ultimately the anterior cruciate can be involved.

Lateral collateral ligament injuries

This is a less common injury than damage to the medial collateral ligament because knees are mostly injured from a lateral blow. The lateral collateral ligament is part of a complex that includes the biceps femoris tendon and fascia lata – forming attachments to the tibia, fibula and patella. All three structures may be damaged, including the cruciates in severe varus stress. The common peroneal nerve may be damaged, resulting in weakness of dorsiflexion of the foot and toes and numbness on the dorsum of the foot and lateral aspect of the lower leg.

Posterior cruciate ligament injuries (rare)

These occur when the tibia is struck and forced backwards with the knee flexed (eg the lower leg against the dashboard in front-seat passengers in RTAs, during a fall). There is loss of the profile of the knee when flexed as the tibia sags backwards. Use the posterior sag test to assess this injury.

Anterior cruciate ligament injuries (common)

The typical history is of twisting over a slightly flexed knee with the foot fixed. It is commonly seen in footballers, but the highest incidence of this injury in sports is netball. Anterior cruciate ligament (ACL) injuries may result in instability. This can be managed with physiotherapy in some cases. Surgical reconstruction can be considered.

How to differentiate a serious ligamentous knee injury from a strain

Serious ligamentous injury
- Rapid swelling within 1–2 hours of injury
- Significant haemarthrosis (complete rupture of collateral ligament may allow haemarthrosis to escape into soft tissues)
- Large effusion (allowing minimal movement)
- Sometimes surprisingly painless
- Localised tenderness (however, no localised tenderness may be elicited in cruciate injuries)
- Radiograph bony avulsion of ligamentous attachments sometimes seen

Strain
- Swelling develops over 12–24 hours
- Moderate effusion
- Painful
- Localised tenderness
- No bony injury

Interval reassessment is a useful clinical tool in the early phase, with MRI for patients with clear pathology at presentation or pathology that becomes obvious with observation.

Meniscal injuries (semilunar cartilages)

The mechanism of meniscal injuries is rotation of the tibia on the femur in the flexed weight-bearing knee (eg during skiing or football). Medial meniscal injuries are 20 times more common than lateral meniscal tears. Due to the concave shape of the medial plateau there is still a reasonable contact area between the medial femur and medial tibia, so there is a low rate of degenerative change after a medial meniscal injury. This contrasts with the lateral side, where the convex lateral tibial plateau results in a low contact area, high contact forces and a high rate of degenerative change after a lateral meniscal injury.

Most tears are vertical splits in the body of the meniscus – radial tears, which may be anterior horn or posterior horn tears. Circumferential tears may result in an unstable segment which can displace into the knee – bucket-handle tears. Horizontal cleavage tears occur in degenerate menisci.

Meniscal tears can present as a locked knee. A locked knee is an indication for a semi-urgent arthroscopy. Weight bearing on a locked knee will result in damage to the articular cartilage.

Clinical features of meniscal tears
- **Haemarthrosis:** haemarthrosis occurs with peripheral tears but not with more centrally based tears. Injuries away from the periphery at the meniscus are relatively avascular and, once torn, they do not heal
- **Joint-line tenderness**
- **Extension block to knee:** secondary to displaced tears
- **Locking of joint:** prevention of full flexion or full extension
- **Clicking, clunking**
- **Medial or lateral pain**

CHAPTER 6

Investigating meniscal tears

- Need to take radiograph to exclude other pathology
- MRI
- Arthroscopy

Extensor apparatus injuries

Mechanisms of injury

- Direct violence (eg falls against hard surface)
- Indirect violence (eg sudden muscular contraction)

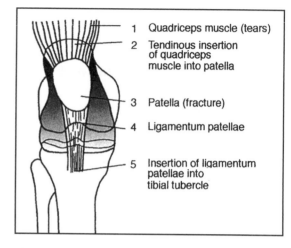

1	Quadriceps muscle (tears)
2	Tendinous insertion of quadriceps muscle into patella
3	Patella (fracture)
4	Ligamentum patellae
5	Insertion of ligamentum patellae into tibial tubercle

Figure 6.29 Sites of extensor apparatus injury

Clinical features of extensor apparatus injuries

- Mostly unable to extend knee
- Swelling
- Bruising
- Palpable gap above patella (tear of tendinous insertion of quadriceps into patella)
- Obvious displacement of patella (patella tendon rupture)
- Gap in patella

Requires radiography (AP and lateral). Tangential projections are difficult due to pain. Do not mistake a congenital bipartite or tripartite patella for a fracture.

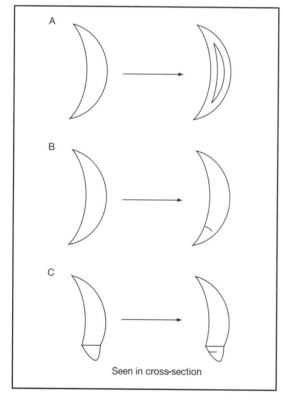

Seen in cross-section

Figure 6.28 Meniscal injuries: (A) bucket-handle tear; (B) radial tear; (C) horizontal cleavage tear

Management of extensor apparatus injuries

- **Muscle tear:** no surgical intervention; when swelling subsides, the proximal end of the muscle is prominent on thigh contraction
- **Tendon rupture** of the quadriceps tendon and patella tendon is treated by surgical repair
- **Patella fractures**
- **Vertical:** don't show on lateral view (frequently missed); treat conservatively
- **Horizontal undisplaced:** plaster immobilisation
- **Displaced:** ORIF, mostly tension-band wiring
- **Avulsion of tibial tubercle:** rare in adults; however, marked displacement must be reduced and fixed

7.2 Soft-tissue injuries of the ankle

Inversion injuries

These damage the lateral ligament. Grades of severity dependent on how much of the ligament is involved. They range from a sprain (some fibres) to complete tear or detachment from the fibula. In complete tears the talus is free to tilt, leading to chronic instability if the joint is untreated.

Eversion injuries

These stress the medial ligament which, due to its strength, tends to avulse the medial malleolus rather than tear.

Forced dorsiflexion

When the foot is dorsiflexed the distal end of the fibula moves laterally. This movement is restricted by the inferior tibiofibular ligaments and the interosseous membrane. Damage to these structures may lead to lateral displacement of the fibula and lateral drift of the talus (diastasis).

Achilles tendon rupture

- Rupture occurs when there are degenerative changes to the tendon, so more common in those aged >40 or following steroid use
- The patient feels a sudden pop and has intense pain – often think they have been kicked – even if nobody was nearby
- To assess, you palpate for a defect, then palpate while the patient plantarflexes against resistance (or stands on tiptoes)
- Compare passive plantarflexion caused by a squeeze of the calf – reduced if ruptured (may have some small movement though)
- Treatment is either conservative with a long-leg plaster with the foot plantarflexed with physiotherapy, or formal surgical tendon repair

SECTION 8

Compartment syndrome

Learning point

Compartment syndrome is inadequate tissue perfusion and oxygenation in a compartment secondary to raised pressure within that compartment. It is a surgical emergency with dire consequences if missed! Immediate diagnosis and prompt surgery are vital to save limb function.

8.1 Pathogenesis and physiology

Swelling within a compartment bounded by bone and fascia, secondary to oedema, inflammation or haematoma, will impede venous outflow, increasing the compartment pressure further. This prevents inflow of oxygenated blood. This leads to muscle ischaemia, which will increase the oedema and inflammatory response, so exacerbating the problem. It must be treated by immediate surgical decompression. Ischaemia will lead to tissue necrosis, resulting in long-term disability. Muscle necrosis and rhabdomyolysis can result in acute renal failure and death.

The most common site is the anterior compartment of the lower limb. It can occur in any fibro-osseous compartment, including hands, feet, thigh, buttock and forearm.

Causes of compartment syndrome

- Can occur after any injury
- Crush injuries
- Prolonged compression of limb (eg tight cast, prolonged surgery, collapsed patient after drug overdose)
- Occurs in both open and closed fractures
- Reperfusion injury (eg after delayed arterial repair or prolonged tourniquet time)

8.2 Diagnosis and treatment

> ### Recognising compartment syndrome
> The cardinal sign is pain that is out of proportion to the injury sustained. On examination there is muscle tenderness and the compartment feels tense. There is typically pain on passive stretch. Weakness, paraesthesia and pulses should be looked for. A pale, cool limb and loss of pulses are very late signs and suggest that the window of opportunity for successful treatment has been missed. Initially, distal circulation and pulses are normal, with warm, pink skin.

Management of compartment syndrome

If compartment syndrome is suspected clinically then plaster immobilisation and any bandaging must be removed immediately. Compartment pressures should be measured if there is doubt about the diagnosis, and if elevated (>30 mmHg [or lower if diastolic BP is low]), urgent fasciotomy must be performed. There is some disagreement between authors as to what the cut-off should be. Some published series report successful conservative treatment of patients with a compartment pressure >40 mmHg, but in these cases the difference between compartment pressure and diastolic blood pressure was >30 mmHg.

Fasciotomy for compartment syndrome in the calf requires decompression of four compartments through two incisions:

- Lateral incision: peroneal and anterior compartment – two fingers lateral to anterior border of tibia
- Medial incision: superficial and deep posterior compartments – just behind medial border of tibia

The skin and fascial incisions should extend the full length of the compartment. The incisions are left open and closed when the swelling subsides.

Regional anaesthetic techniques (such as nerve blocks, spinals or epidurals) may mask the symptoms of compartment syndrome, resulting in a missed diagnosis. Therefore these techniques should be avoided where there is a high risk of compartment syndrome (tibial shaft fractures). If these techniques must be used, or if the patient's conscious level is reduced, compartmental pressure monitoring should be considered.

CHAPTER 6

CHAPTER 7
Evidence-based Surgical Practice

Nerys Forester

SECTION 1

Surgical research and evidence-based medicine

1.1 The hierarchy of evidence

Evidence for the hypothesis can be regarded as a spectrum from the anecdotal to the rigorously tested. This generates a hierarchy of evidence:

Case reports
↓
Case series
↓
Cross-sectional surveys
(observational studies that assess prevalence across a given population, which may be performed by questionnaire or interview with participants or by review of case notes)
↓
Retrospective studies
(observational studies that test hypotheses on aetiology or treatment of disease)
↓
Prospective studies
(observational studies that test hypotheses on aetiology or treatment of disease)
↓
Randomised controlled trials (RCTs)
(studies that test hypotheses on the treatment of disease)
↓
Systematic reviews of RCTs
(may include meta-analyses)

There are advantages and disadvantages to different study designs. **The gold standard is regarded as the randomised control trial**. Studies lower down the hierarchy of evidence are usually performed to establish enough evidence to justify the cost and time-consuming nature of more rigorous testing. These studies also enable the investigator to refine the hypothesis as the evidence mounts.

Blinding

This refers to the process by which the person assessing the outcome remains unaware of the groups to which the participants have been allocated. The more people blinded to the treatment group (participants and assessors), the less likely is the introduction of observer bias. **Double-blinding** means that both the participant and the assessor are unaware of the treatment group.

Controls

A control group is a group of participants that is not exposed to the risk factor or treatment being studied. The control group must have similar characteristics to the treatment group to avoid introducing bias. This is called 'matching' and controls for differences between the two groups in terms of age, sex, socioeconomic factors and other risk factors. **Matching** aims to ensure that any differences seen are due to the factor being studied and are not influenced by other parameters. However, case–control studies are difficult to perform, and it is often more effective to control for differences between study groups using regression models.

Meta-analysis

This is a cumulative statistical test that pools the results from all the studies that have been conducted to answer a specific question. Often the difficulty with medical research is the existence of several, small studies, possibly with conflicting or inconclusive results. Meta-analyses and systematic reviews are processes used to combine relevant studies into one larger, more precise study with a single overall result.

Meta-analysis is a mathematical tool that increases the power and precision of research already performed. It is useful for detecting small but clinically important effects (eg the benefits of thrombolysis in myocardial infarction [MI]). Although meta-analysis is the method used to combine studies, it is preceded by a systematic review or search for all relevant studies.

The Cochrane Collaboration provides support for authors undertaking a systematic review. It ensures a thorough search of the available literature and helps authors to avoid missing published (and even unpublished or ongoing) work. A systematic review searches the literature in a methodical way, with strictly defined inclusion and exclusion criteria.

1.2 Evidence-based medicine (EBM)

Healthcare must be based on the best available evidence. However, there is a tremendous volume of published research out there and clinical practice tends to lag behind the research data.

CHAPTER 7

What is EBM?

> ## Learning point
>
> EBM is the application of the best research evidence to your clinical practice. It is therefore a set of strategies for keeping your clinical practice up to date.
> It involves:
> * Asking an answerable clinical question
> * Tracking down the best evidence
> * Critical appraisal of the evidence
> * Applying the evidence to clinical practice

The best research evidence involves the integration of aspects of:
* Patient values and expectations
* Clinician experience
* Audit
* Published research

Published research follows a hierarchy of evidence as outlined previously. However, research may be applicable to your own practice only if the patient groups are similar.

The practice of EBM can be broken down into the following steps:
* Ask an answerable question
* Track down the best evidence in order to answer that question
* Critically appraise that evidence
* Use that evidence in your clinical approach or management of individual patients
* Evaluate the effectiveness of applying that evidence (in individual cases and across your practice as a whole)

This structure is based on the recommendations of Professor David Sackett, formerly of the Oxford Centre for EBM.

Asking an answerable question

Clinical questions may be **background questions**, such as general questions about disease incidence or pathology, questions about disease progression or prognosis, etc.

More importantly, clinical questions may be very specific and applicable to individual patients, ie **foreground questions**. For example, in a 40-year-old woman with early breast cancer, what is the best combination of postoperative chemotherapeutics (monotherapy vs polytherapy) to prolong survival?

Clinical questions tend to fall into four categories:
* Diagnosis and screening
* Prognosis
* Causing harm (or side effects)
* Treatments

It is helpful to write down the clinical question that you want to answer and then divide it into four parts (PICO):

P The **p**atient or **p**roblem, eg early breast cancer

I The proposed **i**ntervention or treatment, eg monochemotherapy

C The **c**omparative treatment, eg polychemotherapy

O The **o**utcome, eg survival

Tracking down the best evidence

Tracking down the best available published evidence basically involves literature searching. You should be familiar with online methods of searching for literature (hospital librarians are often invaluable in performing searches or teaching search strategies).

Useful sources of evidence currently available include:
* Databases such as PubMed or Medline

(www.pubmed.org/) or the TRIP database (www.tripdatabase.com)

- Systematic reviews from the Cochrane Collaboration (www.cochrane.org)
- Appraised studies from the *Evidence-Based Medicine Journal* (www.evidence-basedmedicine.com) and the clinical evidence website (www.clinicalevidence.com)

The best evidence depends on the question that you are asking.

> Questions about **diagnosis** are best answered using cross-sectional studies. Questions about **harm** or side effects are best answered using a cohort study. Questions about **prognosis** are best answered using cohort studies. Questions about **treatment** are best answered using RCTs or systematic reviews.

1.3 Critical appraisal of the evidence

Learning point

Critical appraisal means **satisfying yourself** and **justifying to others** that evidence has sufficient validity to be applicable to your patients or questions. Critical appraisal of a paper can be performed using the mnemonic RAMBOS:

- **R**andomisation
- **A**scertainment
- **M**easurement
- **B**linding
- **O**bjective
- **S**tatistics

The hierarchy of evidence outlines important factors in the design and performance of different clinical studies. A systematic method for undertaking critical appraisal (ie quantifying validity) is outlined below.

Was the study randomised?

Randomisation is important in trials related to comparison between treatments. This is often done by computer but may be done by allocating numbered envelopes.

Look to see whether the randomised groups had similar demographics at the start of the trial (this shows that the randomisation has roughly worked).

Are there any differences between the groups (ie bias) and (if there are) which treatment will these differences favour?

How did the study ascertain the outcome?

Was the outcome measurement sensible and valid? How methodologically sound is the study?

All studies suffer from loss to follow-up. Up to 5% loss to follow-up leads to little bias. If more than 20% of patients were lost to follow-up this affects study interpretation. How were the results from patients lost to follow-up managed? Acceptable methods for managing loss to follow-up include either excluding all missing values from the subsequent analysis or carrying forward the last known measurement.

How was the outcome measured?

Both treatment groups must have the outcome measured in the same way otherwise this is a source of bias and therefore error.

Appraising the methodology

Appraisal of the evidence requires an understanding of the following:

- Study hypothesis
- Selection process
- Which patients were chosen and why
- Whether there are any sampling errors
- Whether the study has any bias (error that does not occur by chance)
- Number of participants should be determined by a power calculation at the start of the study
- Study design (eg prospective study or RCT)
- Is the study methodologically sound?

If the study relates to a **diagnostic test** it should include:

- Participants with and without the condition being tested
- Participants at all stages of the disease
- A definitive test performed separately to establish disease status, for comparison

If the study is a **cross-sectional survey** it should have:

- Validation by pilot study
- Appropriate type of survey to answer the question
- Response rate >60%

If the study is a **prospective study** it should include:

- A matched control group not exposed to the risk factor or treatment
- A degree of exposure to the risk factor (eg cigarette smoking in pack-years)
- A specific and measurable outcome
- Contribution of other prognostic risk factors to the one being studied
- Sufficient follow-up

If the study is a **retrospective survey** it should use:

- A definitive method for retrospective identification of the factor to be studied
- Control participants who had the same opportunity of exposure to the risk factor as the study group

If the study is an **RCT** it should:

- Have strict inclusion and exclusion criteria
- Be randomised according to accepted practice
- Be double-blinded (during trial, and for subsequent data analysis if possible)
- Ensure that all other treatment of the two groups is equal

If the study is a **systematic review** it should:

- Perform a thorough search for all studies eligible for inclusion
- Include assessments by more than one assessor
- Only include properly randomised studies

CHAPTER 7

Was the study blinded?

Error can be minimised by ensuring that neither the participant nor the researcher knows which treatment group the participant has been allocated to (double-blinding). Sometimes this is not possible. However, ideally the person tasked with interpretation or data analysis should remain blinded to the treatment group.

How objective was the outcome measurement?

Objectivity is important. Factual data such as survival times, blood test results or disease recurrence are more objective than patient-allocated scores or scales such as 'worse, the same, better'. Also consider the potential of the **placebo effect**.

Were the statistics used appropriate, and what do they tell you?

Statistics are discussed in detail in Section 2. Statistics essentially are a method for assessing the role of chance in reaching the result. Look for clinically meaningful measures:

- Diagnosis: likelihood ratios
- Prognosis: proportions and confidence intervals
- Treatments: absolute and relative risk reduction; numbers needed to treat

Applying evidence to clinical practice

Everyone is busy, so finding the time to search for evidence is not often high on the priority list. It may be helpful to keep a note of the answers that you find to common questions. It is also helpful to think about how you might communicate medical evidence to patients when you are explaining diagnosis, prognosis and treatment options.

1.4 Development of clinical projects

Study design

- What is the hypothesis?
- What is the aim (eg basic knowledge, improving care)?
- What is the current evidence in the literature?
- How will you test the hypothesis?
- How will you select patients to provide a representative sample and to avoid bias?
- What are the inclusion and exclusion criteria?
- How large will the study need to be to be statistically valid (power calculations)?
- What data will you collect?
- What statistical tests will be used in data interpretation?

In addition:
- Will you require ethics committee approval?
- How will the study be funded?

Study protocol

The study protocol should be written out in full, clearly stating the study design (including all the factors outlined above). The evidence from the current literature should be summarised and referenced. Patients should be given verbal and written information and all patient information sheets should be included in the protocol.

Ethics committees

> ## Learning point
>
> Ethics approval is always needed for ANY studies involving humans. Ethics will want to see evidence of:
> - Study aim and hypothesis
> - Risk–benefit analysis
> - Informed consent
> - Patient confidentiality
> - Procedures for use of human tissue (if relevant)

Ethical approval will always be required for studies involving patients, staff or animals. The study protocol should be submitted to the local ethics committee, who have a statutory requirement to oversee research.

The local ethics committee (LREC) is supervised by the main ethics committee (MREC), which is supervised by the central ethics committee (COREC).

The key ethical principles for human research are:
- Respect for autonomy (to ensure informed freedom of choice)
- Beneficence (to do good)
- Non-maleficence (to do no harm)
- Justice (to give fair and equal treatment without bias)

Ethics committees will need to be satisfied that you have taken into consideration the following factors:
- **Risk–benefit ratio:**
  - Is the risk to the research subject justified by the potential benefit of the research?

- The value of the individual outweighs the principle of 'the good of society'
- **Informed consent:**
  - Patients should be competent to consent (special cases for children; vulnerable people, eg those with learning difficulties, those who are unconscious or who are suffering from confusional states)
  - Verbal and written information should be given to all participants
  - There should be an opportunity for patients to get their questions answered
  - Patients should receive full disclosure on risks of participation
  - Ideally patients should be given time to assimilate information (often 24 hours) before giving consent
  - Written consent should be given by the patients, and signed and dated
  - Patients should be aware of their right to withdraw at any time and for any reason without compromise to their further care
- **Patient confidentiality:**
  - Assure anonymity
  - Consider adequate data storage
- **Use and storage of human tissue** (if required)
- **Aims of the study and their subsequent application**

Research funding

Options for funding include:
- University funds
- Trust funds
- Research grants (eg Royal College of Surgeons, Medical Research Council)
- Charities (eg the Wellcome Trust, disease-specific foundations)
- Drug or pharmaceutical companies

It is important that funding does not produce a conflict of interests. The researcher should be free to design, implement and run the project without undue influence from the funding body. This particularly applies to the interpretation of results if funding comes from the commercial sector.

1.5   Writing a paper

Paper content

The paper should include abstract, introduction, methods and results sections, and a discussion. All data belong in the results section.

The discussion is often the hardest part to write, but it can be structured as follows:
- A short summary of the main findings
- A comparison with other findings in the literature
- A short critical appraisal of the study, pointing out its strengths and weaknesses
- An indication of the future direction of the research

Tables and figures

Use tables and figures that are informative and economical with space; this is a much more visually pleasing way to display information than large blocks of text. However, certain journals have limits on the number that may be included (they are expensive to publish) so do combine figures if possible.

Each figure should have a legend that fully explains the figure (whereby if the figure were separated from the text you should still be able to interpret it using only the information written in the legend).

Tables can have footnotes. You can use these to indicate the important points outlined in the table or the statistically significant values.

References

Cross-reference statements in the text with the current literature and always read all papers that you use as a reference! Reference-managing computer programmes are very helpful (eg EndNote or Reference Manager) and will often contain templates for different journal styles.

Think ahead to the destination publication and look at the way that its articles are structured. If you structure and write yours in the style of that publication, it will save you time in the long run.

Learning point

Stats are important:
- To practise evidence-based medicine (investigations and treatments)
- To correctly plan and execute meaningful research

In order to get the best out of statistics:
- Think about study types and design at the beginning (type, bias, tests to use)
- **Categorise data:** this choice then determines the pathway taken for subsequent statistics to be performed:
  - Nominal
  - Ordinal
  - Metric

Measure the spread of data
- Mode, mean or median (measures of location)
  - Range and interquartile range
  - Standard deviation
  - Standard error and confidence intervals
- Test for the normal distribution of the data (normal vs skewed)
- Decide whether you need a parametric or non-parametric test
- Test for significant differences (null vs alternative hypothesis)

The increasing practice of EBM and investigation into the appropriateness of clinical therapies require a sound understanding of statistics, what they can be used for and what they actually mean. In addition, most surgeons will be involved in conducting clinical research throughout their career, and prior knowledge of statistics and research methodology is fundamental to the ability to construct well-designed trials or experimental questions that will allow appropriate data handling and interpretation.

2.1 Study types and design

There are two main types of epidemiological study design. These have been discussed in the previous section. They are categorised as:

- Observational studies
- Experimental studies

Observational studies can be descriptive or analytical. Analytical studies include case–control studies, cohort studies and cross-sectional analyses.

Experimental studies are the RCTs.

SUMMARY OF THE FEATURES AND LIMITATIONS OF DIFFERENT STUDY TYPES

Type of study	Main features	Advantages and Disadvantages
Case–control	Retrospective analysis Compares group of patients with disease with group without disease to obtain details about previous medical history/lifestyle Defines risk factors for disease First case–control study showed incidence relationship between smoking and lung cancer (Doll, 1994)	Useful for rare diseases and those with long latent periods Disadvantages are retrospective data collection and potential bias, and no information about disease
Cohort	Observational study Prospective Monitors disease development in participants without disease over time Gives disease incidence Example is Framingham Heart Study	Accurate and precise information about disease development Good for temporal associations between exposure and disease Needs large numbers over long period of time
Cross-sectional	Observational study Determines presence or absence of disease in a group of participants Gives disease prevalence	No comparative element Unable to determine cause or effect
Randomised controlled trial	Gold standard of all treatment studies! Intervention study Groups differ in treatment or intervention Equal spread of confounders (eg age, sex, social class) Single-blind: patient unaware of treatment group Double-blind: patient and investigator unaware of treatment group (difficult in surgery!)	Best way of determining treatment benefit Bias should be eliminated by randomisation (which is simple, by random number generation, stratified to ensure equal distribution of important factors across treatment groups, or blocks, to ensure patient numbers are equal within treatment groups)

Incidence is the rate of occurrence of a new disease within a population.

Prevalence is the frequency of a disease in a population at any given time.

2.2 Significance testing

In order to determine whether or not the data that you have collected between two or more groups is significantly different, a variety of statistical tests is available to test the hypothesis or study question. Usually, this is constructed in the form of the **null hypothesis**, which states that no difference exists between the two populations sampled. The subsequent tests either prove or disprove this hypothesis.

If our tests disprove the null hypothesis (or show that it is very unlikely), this means that we accept the **alternative hypothesis**, that a difference between the two groups does exist and that this relationship has not been found by chance. With all statistical tests, the null hypothesis is tested by calculating a p value (or equivalent). **The p value is the probability that the null hypothesis is true**. Hence if the p value is very small, the null hypothesis is less likely to be correct. We are usually willing to accept that we will get the answer 'wrong' 5% of the time, ie a p value of 0.05 or lower would mean that the null hypothesis was false, and that the alternative hypothesis was true.

To test our hypotheses, a number of different statistical tests are available; correct usage depends on our knowledge of the type of data collected. To determine which test we should use, we need to ask:

- Are the data metric or categorical?
- Are they normally distributed?
- Are the data from separate groups, paired groups or multiple (more than two) groups?

2.3 Types of data

Fundamental to all research is the type of data collected in a study. There are three types:

- Nominal (eg ethnic group, sex, blood group)
- Ordinal (eg scales such as Apgar, Glasgow Coma Scale [GCS])
- Metric (eg height, weight, body mass index [BMI], parity)

Nominal and ordinal data are categorical variables, and differ in the fact that nominal data cannot be put into a logical order, whereas ordinal data can. However, when considering ordinal data, when the data-sets are placed in order the differences between them are not equal – eg a GCS score of 8 is not twice as good as a GCS score of 4. A common mistake is to interpret such data as if they were metric data; ordinal numbers are not real and so they do not obey mathematical laws (eg GCS scores cannot be averaged).

In **metric** data, the numbers represent values with units and relate to each other. Metric data can be **continuous** – where the number of possible values is infinite (eg weight) – or **discrete** – where there are a finite number of values, usually whole numbers (eg number of days to discharge, number of subjects in a group, number of postop deaths).

Once the type of data collected has been identified, the data-set needs to be described in terms of:

- Location or central tendency
- Spread, scatter or dispersion

The way in which the data are described depends on the type of data that you are describing! In addition, the type of data also determines the statistical tests that you can subsequently apply.

CHAPTER 7

Measures of location

There are three measures of location:
- Mode
- Mean
- Median

The **mode** describes the most commonly occurring (most frequent) value within a data-set. It is used to describe categorical variables (eg blood group, nominal data).

The **mean** is the average value within a data-set (eg the average height or weight of a group of individuals). It can be used **only** with metric data.

The **median** is the middle value obtained within the data-set after the values have been ordered or ranked. It can be used with ordinal data (eg GCS score) but not with nominal data. It can also be used with metric data, and it may be appropriate to do so when a data-set is skewed (eg study with groups at extremes of age, data not normally distributed).

Measures of spread

Measure of spread of a data-set provides information about the number of individuals sampled and the range of values measured within a study:
- Range or interquartile range
- Standard deviation

As before, the measure of spread used to describe the data depends on the data type and measure of location used to describe it.

The **range** is the smallest to highest value obtained in the study. It can be used with both ordinal and metric data, often given when the median value is used.

The **interquartile range** describes the data spread in terms of four 'quartiles', ie the data-set is divided equally into four. The first 25% of values lie in the first quartile, with the median being the middle or 50th quartile. The interquartile range is represented by the numbers that are the 25th quartile to the 75th quartile. This way of expressing data is very sensitive to outlying values, and gives an indication of how large or small is the range within which the middle value lies.

The **standard deviation** (SD) describes the spread of the mean. It is a measure of the average distance of the individual data values from their mean, ie the variability between individuals of the factor measured.
- It can be used only to describe metric data
- The wider the spread of the values measured, the greater the distance from the mean, and so the greater the standard deviation
- Outliers have a marked effect on standard deviation
- Mathematically, standard deviation is calculated as the square root of the sum of the squares of each of the differences of each observed value from the mean value (often referred to as the square root of the variance)
- Standard deviation can be used to see if the data are normally distributed

If the values obtained are normally distributed, then 95% of these values will lie within 2 (more accurately 1.96) SDs on either side of the mean, with 99% of the values within 3 SDs on each side of the mean. So, if you cannot fit 3 SDs between the mean and the minimum or maximum value, then the data distribution is not normal, and further hypothesis testing of these values should not use parametric tests of significance.

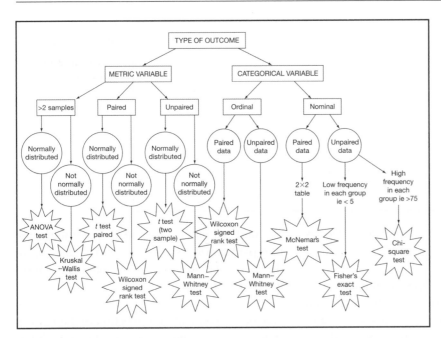

Figure 7.1 Selecting the right statistical test for your data

The **standard error** (SE) of the mean reflects the fact that your set of measurements samples only part of the population that you could have studied (eg only some of the blood pressure of people with or without hypertension), and so is unlikely to determine the population value exactly. It is the reliability with which the mean data value that you have calculated for your data-set reflects the actual mean value for the population. It therefore reflects the size of the sample studied, with large samples giving a more accurate estimation of population mean than smaller samples. Mathematically, it is derived as the standard deviation divided by the square root of the number of subjects sampled.

Hence, standard deviation describes the spread of measurements, whereas standard error of the mean tells us how good our estimate of the mean population value is.

The standard error of the mean is more useful when converted to a **confidence interval** (CI), a range of plausible values between which you can

have a degree of confidence that the true average value for the population that you have sampled will lie. This depends on the number of participants sampled and the confidence level with which you need to know the mean value. Usually this is acceptable at a 95% CI, ie the values within which the true population mean would be found 95% of the time (also described as the mean 1.96 times the standard error of the mean).

Confidence intervals are of particular value in a clinical setting. They can be used when comparing the means of two groups (eg treated vs untreated). If the confidence intervals overlap, the two groups cannot be significantly different because it is possible the true population means could be the same.

The normal distribution

If you study the frequency distribution of a data-set, most biological data can be described by a bell-shaped curve, which is symmetrical about the mean – height or weight, for example.

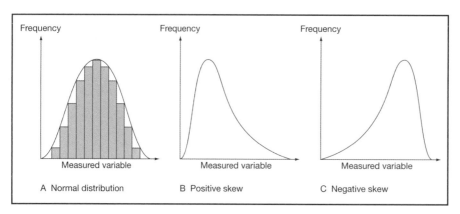

Figure 7.2 Data distribution – normal and skewed

Only metric data can be truly described as normally distributed.

Tests of normality can be applied to data-sets to calculate whether or not the values collected are normally distributed (Shapiro–Wilks and Kolmogorov–Smirnov tests). The normal distribution is fundamental to hypothesis testing, because normally distributed data can be analysed using **parametric tests**, whereas non-normally distributed data must be analysed using **non-parametric tests** (which are also used for ordinal categorical data, and work by ordering or ranking the values obtained).

Sometimes a data-set may show a **skewed distribution**, with higher frequencies of values occurring at the extremes of the values measured. These data-sets may be 'transformed to normality' using mathematical functions (eg logarithmic transformations) after which parametric tests can be used on the transformed data-set (remembering to transform the data back when the analysis is complete!).

2.4 Selecting an appropriate statistical test

Once you have described your data-set, tested for normality if appropriate, and decided whether you need parametric or non-parametric statistical tests, the flow diagram in Figure 7.1 can be used to determine the correct test to use.

However, even with the selection of the correct statistical test there is always the possibility that the result given may be incorrect – due to chance. In statistical testing two types of error are possible: type 1 and type 2.

- **Type 1 errors (α errors):** a false-positive result, ie we state that there is a difference when there is none; this error decreases with the p value and is usually accepted at 0.05 (a 95% chance that the difference observed is correct)
- **Type 2 errors (β errors):** a false-negative result, ie we state that there is no difference when there actually is one. This error usually occurs with small sample sizes, and is less important than type 1 errors; it is usually accepted as 0.2 (a 20% chance that any actual difference between the groups will be missed) or less

These errors can be used to calculate the **power** of a study, so that it can be correctly designed to minimise the risk of a study missing a true difference of clinical importance. The power of a study is $1 - β$, which is the chance of not getting a false-negative result.

CHAPTER 7

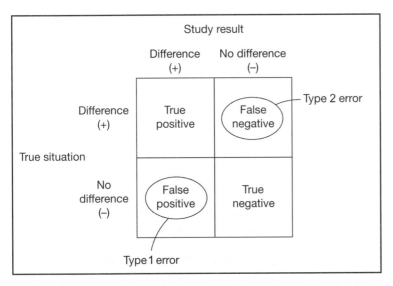

Figure 7.3 Study results and power calculations

Power calculations are used to calculate the number of samples needed within each group to show a true difference between groups, should one actually exist. They depend on the type of data collected and can be calculated mathematically, or using a normogram. They need to be done before you start the study, and require a prediction of what magnitude of difference between the groups you would consider to be clinically relevant. A statistician would be very useful, especially at an early stage, to help with calculations.

2.5 Bias and confounding

As well as effects due to chance, studies may also be subject to the effects of bias and confounding.

Bias is the distortion of the estimated effects due to a systematic difference between the two groups being compared. There are many types of bias, either due to the selection of patients (eg putting all the patients with high BP in the non-antihypertensive treatment group), or due to collection or recall of information collected in the study.

Types of bias

- **Observer bias:** may occur when measurements are made. Such bias can be intraobserver (ie the same person measures a quantity differently each time) or interobserver (ie different observers measure the same quantity differently, whereby agreement – or lack of it – is measured by a kappa coefficient)
- **Selection bias:** may occur when the study population is drawn from participants who are not wholly representative of the target population
- **Prevalence bias:** may arise when the study population is drawn from participants who are part of a special subgroup of the disorder of interest (ie not representative of all those at risk in the target population)
- **Recall bias:** this is the effect on the study of different individuals' abilities to recall events correctly
- **Information bias:** concerns mistakes made when measuring or classifying data
- **Publication bias:** even with a perfectly designed trial, research ultimately suffers from publication bias because positive studies are more likely to be published than negative ones

CHAPTER 7

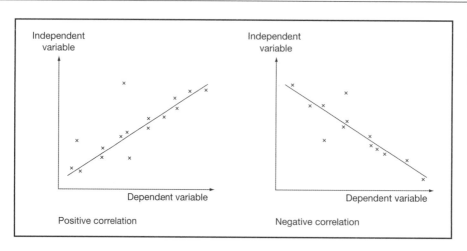

**Figure 7.4
Positive and
negative
correlations**

Confounding

Confounding occurs when the effect or outcome that you are studying is affected by another variable, such as sex, socioeconomic class or age. This is usually controlled for in a study by randomisation, mathematical modelling or stratification of data

Statistical error

This occurs when multiple statistical tests are used, for example, to compare a control group with several different patient groups. It should be remembered that if you do a test 20 times, then one time out of 20 (5%) it will be significant by chance. If using multiple tests on data-sets a correction factor must be applied to the *p* values obtained to reflect this possibility, or you should choose a test designed for *n* >2 groups, which have correction factors available as post-hoc tests (eg Bonferroni correction, Tukey test).

2.6 Correlation and regression analysis

The strength of an association between two variables can be assessed by means of a scatter plot (see figure 7.4).

Correlation is the most widely used measure of association between two variables. It does not imply causality, ie that one variable causes the change in the other variable. The strength of the association depends on how close the measured points lie to the line of best fit between the data-points. If all points fall exactly on the line there is perfect correlation, reflected by a correlation coefficient of 1. A correlation coefficient of 0 means that there is no association between the variables. The association between the variables may be positive (as one increases so does the other) or negative (one increases as the other decreases). To use Pearson's correlation coefficient each data-set compared should be normally distributed; otherwise, Spearman's coefficient should be used.

Linear regression is used to determine the nature and direction of a causal relationship between variables. It allows generation of a mathematical model that uses the value of one or more independent variables to predict another (eg using age, smoking status and waist size to predict systolic BP). The strength and significance of each independent variable within the model can be calculated and used to determine factors that significantly affect the variable of interest.

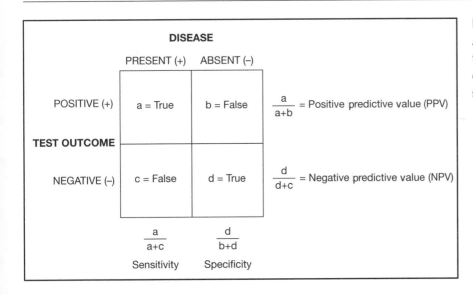

Figure 7.5
A 2 × 2 table for
the calculation
of sensitivity and
specificity

Survival analysis

Survival analysis is often used in medicine, where a recognised endpoint can be measured. This can be death, limb loss or salvage, or joint replacement failure, for example, with the time to occurrence and cumulative frequency of the number of patients reaching the endpoint in question documented. This information allows you to plot a survival curve (eg a Kaplan–Meier curve). Difficulties with this type of analysis include losses to follow-up and patients who opt out of the research programme. All patients originally included in the study should be included in analysis on an 'intention-to-treat' basis, with the worst-case scenario applied to losses to follow-up (ie assume all losses are worst outcome measures).

2.7 Sensitivity and specificity

The ability of a test to predict the presence or absence of a disease can be measured using sensitivity and specificity.

- **Sensitivity** is the ability of a test to correctly identify people with the condition (true positives). Therefore, a highly sensitive test (Sn) has a high rate of detection of the disease or condition. The false-negative rate is therefore low, so if the test is negative it effectively rules the diagnosis 'out' (remember **SnOUT**)
- **Specificity** reflects the ability of a test to correctly identify people without the condition (true negatives). Therefore, a highly specific test (Sp) has a low false-positive rate, so if the test is positive it effectively rules the diagnosis 'in' (remember **SpIN**)

The **positive predictive value** of a test is the proportion of patients that the test identifies as having the condition who actually do have the condition, whereas the **negative predictive value** is the proportion of patients that the test identifies as not having a condition who do not have the condition.

These concepts are easier to visualise after constructing a **2 × 2 table** of the possible outcomes of a test to diagnose a condition.

CHAPTER 7

565

CHAPTER 8

Ethics, Clinical Governance and the Medicolegal Aspects of Surgery

Sebastian Dawson-Bowling

This chapter covers the key areas of law, ethics and governance that together make up the way in which we maintain our standards of practice. A basic understanding of ethical and medicolegal principles is essential to the safe practice of clinical and operative surgery in the twenty-first century. As clinicians practising in increasingly litigious times, we must all take responsibility, not only for ensuring that we are aware of these principles, but also for constantly reviewing our own standards of practice, and the way that we deliver care to our patients. This will simultaneously ensure that they receive the highest possible standard of treatment, while we as clinicians minimise the risk of complaints or negligence claims.

1.1 Principles of medical ethics

Medical law does not simply deal with what is legal, but also with the more complicated issues of 'right and wrong'. It should be remembered that many legal principles are underpinned by ethical ones, eg the law of consent is clearly based around the notion of autonomy. Although a detailed discussion of ethics is beyond the scope of this book, it is therefore worth briefly looking at the key doctrines in modern medical ethics, as defined by Beauchamp and Childress.

> **Core values of modern medical ethics**
> - Respect for autonomy
> - Beneficence
> - Non-maleficence
> - Justice

Autonomy is the right of the individual to act freely, following decisions resulting from his or her own independent thought. In the clinical setting, this equates to making decisions about medical care without healthcare professionals either over-riding or trying to influence the decision. The respect for autonomy is absolutely paramount in the clinical decision-making process – a patient wishing not to undergo life-saving treatment, for example, must have his or her decision respected (provided that he or she is mentally competent to make this decision, and has not signed an Advance Directive – see Section 7).

Beneficence means, simply, doing good; for doctors, this effectively means that they must act in the best interests of their patients.

Non-maleficence is best understood by the often-quoted mantra 'First, do no harm' – a doctor must not harm his or her patient. However, in reality

CHAPTER 8

there is often a conflict, sometimes referred to as 'double effect', between beneficence and non-maleficence, in that many medical interventions cause damage to the patient , eg amputating a cancerous limb or administering a course of chemotherapy. This requires patient and doctor together to weigh up what is in the patient's best interests, always remembering that the patient's autonomy must be upheld.

Justice, often considered synonymous with fairness, is embodied by a respect for the rights and dignity of all human beings. It is often viewed as a moral obligation to ensure that one's actions are based on a fair adjudication between competing claims, which may refer to an individual's rights, or to the allocation of limited healthcare resources (see Section 6).

1.2 Confidentiality

The duty of confidentiality dates back to Hippocrates in 420 BC, subsequently reflected in

the wording of the 1948 Declaration of Geneva: 'I will respect secret which are confided in me, even after the patient dies.' More simply, the *Duties of a Doctor*, as outlined by the General Medical Council, include to 'respect patients' right to confidentiality'. Again, this can also be seen to reflect the ethical principle of respect for autonomy. This duty of confidence includes non-medical information imparted in the context of the doctor–patient relationship.

It is reasonable to assume that a patient providing information to a member of a healthcare team is consenting to this information being shared with other members of the team involved in treating the patient. Nevertheless, it is good clinical practice to inform patients of this, and to remind colleagues that the information being shared with them is confidential.

There are certain occasions when a doctor may breach the duty of confidentiality, as outlined in the box.

Exceptions to the duty of confidentiality

Consent: a patient may give permission for their health information to be shared with others not involved in providing their care, eg a group of medical students. It should be ensured that patients understand what they are agreeing to, and that consent has been given voluntarily.

Public interest: disclosure is acceptable provided that there is a 'real, immediate and serious' risk to the public. How exactly this is defined has not been fully clarified; in general, if a patient has committed, or plans to commit, a serious criminal offence then disclosure is justified. If doubts arise advice should be sought from a medical defence organisation.

Notifiable diseases, eg TB, meningitis/meningococcal septicaemia, malaria, diphtheria, salmonella. Doctors have a statutory duty to notify a 'proper officer' of the Local Authority if a notifiable disease is suspected. A notification certificate should be completed immediately a suspected notifiable disease is diagnosed, and submitted within 3 days; laboratory confirmation should not be awaited. Urgent cases should be reported verbally within 24 hours.

CHAPTER 8

Consent to treatment is dealt with in detail in Section 5, but the following points should be considered specifically with regard to the consent to disclosure of confidential information:

- **Implied consent:** when sharing information between medical teams; it is impossible to provide the best care for patients without divulging their history to the associated team. Patients can be assumed to expect that their case will be discussed within and between medical teams. The same applies to the use of their information in audit
- **Written consent** is required if a third party such as an insurance company requests information about a patient. The same applies to police and solicitors, who cannot obtain confidential information about a patient without that patient's consent. The exception to this is that a judge or court may request confidential clinical information without the patient's consent, in which instance only information that is immediately relevant to the question asked should be disclosed.

Disclosure after death: the duty to maintain the confidentiality of deceased patients is the same as for those still alive. Any previous declarations made before death pertaining to disclosure must be upheld. There may be a conflict between the law and moral issues, which may cloud decisions; in such cases advice should be sought from senior colleagues, the GMC or a medical defence organisation.

SECTION 2

Clinical governance and risk management

2.1 Overview of clinical governance

Definition: a framework through which NHS organisations are accountable for continuously improving the quality of their services and safeguarding high standards of care, by creating an environment in which excellence in clinical care will flourish (Department of Health 1998).

Two key components:
- Quality control
- Risk management

Quality control
- Audit
- Application of evidence-based medicine
- Patient feedback and satisfaction
- Personal professional development (appraisal and revalidation)

Risk management
- Error reporting
- Morbidity and mortality meetings
- Audit

National guidelines

The Bristol Inquiry brought to light failings within the NHS to set a national standard of care, and highlighted the lack of guidelines to assess the quality of care. This was the start of clinical governance. It relies on a cycle of assessment, identification of areas for improvement, implementation and reassessment; audit is at the core of the governance framework.

The overall goal of clinical governance is to produce the best possible patient care, and responsibility for this is placed with the entire clinical team. It aims to:
- Encourage the practice of evidence-based medicine
- Provide opportunities for research into improvements in practice
- Reduce variation in quality of healthcare throughout the country

2.2 Quality control

Quality control should cover every aspect of clinical care. This includes access to appropriate treatment options, the right equipment and buildings, the right education for staff, the right audit tools and access to research opportunities where appropriate.

Components of quality control
- Completing the audit cycle
- Application of evidence-based medicine
- Patient satisfaction (focus groups and surveys)
- Personal professional development (aims to maintain good surgical practice by continually updating clinical and intellectual knowledge)

Personal professional development consists of two processes:

- **Appraisal** – a process that provides feedback on doctors' performance, monitors continuing professional development and identifies shortcomings at an early stage, in order to ensure focused improvement
- **Revalidation** – all specialists must demonstrate that they continue to be fit to practise in their chosen field; this is repeated every 5 years

In both appraisal and revalidation, clinicians must show continued professional development by maintaining a **portfolio**. This should include a surgical logbook (for procedures), and evidence of attendance at meetings, involvement in academic work and appropriate training courses. These processes should enable all clinicians to uphold standards and accomplish the **guidelines** set out in the GMC's *Good Medical Practice* (2001).

2.3   Risk management

Learning point

- **Critical incident forms** – may be completed by any healthcare professional; reporting should include 'near miss' events
- **Morbidity and mortality meetings**
- **Staff concerns** – there should be a forum for staff to voice concerns about current practices and suggest improvements
- **Audit** to identify areas and extent of weak performance
- **Comparison measures** between individuals and organisations to produce guidelines to minimise risk (eg NICE, NCEPOD)

Originally developed within the corporate sector to assess complications and minimise their recurrence, risk management consists of a system or systems for identifying errors, 'near misses' and areas where practice is failing to meet accepted standards. The aim is not to apportion blame, but rather to identify areas where future problems may potentially occur, and so reduce the risk.

Incident reporting

Incident reporting systems are vital in helping NHS organisations to analyse the type, frequency and severity of incidents, and then use that information to make changes to improve care. Other industries (eg airlines) have shown that regular reporting of all incidents, including near-miss incidents, results in improvements in safety.

CHAPTER 8

A patient safety incident is any unintended or unexpected incident that could have led, or did lead, to harm for one or more patients.

Incident reporting starts at a local level with the completion of a trust incident form. These forms are assessed within the trust management structure and **serious untoward incidents** (SUIs) are identified. The forms are also fed electronically to the NHS Commissioning Board Special Health Authority (NHSCBA). The information is used to compile patient safety reports and issue safety alerts. Prior to June 2012 this role was undertaken by the Patient Safety Agency.

Serious untoward incidents

- Unexpected or avoidable death of one or more patients, staff, visitors or members of the public
- Serious harm to one or more patients, staff, visitors or members of the public or where the outcome requires life-saving intervention, major surgical/medical intervention, permanent harm or will shorten life expectancy or result in prolonged pain or psychological harm (this includes incidents graded under the NHSCBA definition of severe harm)
- A scenario that prevents or threatens to prevent a provider organisation's ability to continue to deliver healthcare services, eg actual or potential loss of personal/organisational information, damage to property, reputation or the environment, or IT failure
- Allegations of abuse
- Adverse media coverage or public concern about the organisation or the wider NHS
- One of the core set of 'never events'

'Never events' are very serious, largely preventable patient safety incidents that should not occur if the relevant preventative measures have been put in place. The list is updated yearly and all trusts are required to report these incidents. There are 25 'never events' on the 2011/2012 list:

1   Wrong site surgery
2   Wrong implant/prosthesis
3   Retained foreign object after surgery
4   Wrongly prepared high-risk injectable medication
5   Maladministration of potassium-containing solutions
6   Wrong route of administration of chemotherapy
7   Wrong route of administration of oral/enteral treatment
8   Intravenous administration of epidural medication
9   Maladministration of insulin
10 Overdose of midazolam during conscious sedation
11 Opioid overdose of an opioid-naïve patient
12 Inappropriate administration of daily oral methotrexate
13 Suicide using non-collapsible rails
14 Escape of a transferred prisoner
15 Falls from unrestricted windows
16 Entrapment in bedrails
17 Transfusion of ABO-incompatible blood components
18 Transplantation of ABO or HLA-incompatible organs
19 Misplaced naso- or orogastric tubes
20 Wrong gas administered
21 Failure to monitor and respond to oxygen saturation
22 Air embolism
23 Misidentification of patients
24 Severe scalding of patients
25 Maternal death due to postpartum haemorrhage after elective caesarean section

SUIs are investigated using a national framework provided by the NHSCBA.

2.4 Levels of clinical governance

Clinical governance is achieved at the *local* and the *national* level.

Local clinical governance

- **Trust** – audit cycle, morbidity and mortality meetings (M&Ms), risk management strategy
- **Personal** – appraisal, revalidation, continuing professional development

National clinical governance

This comprises several organisations:
- National Institute for Health and Clinical Excellence (NICE)
- Care Quality Commission
- Monitor
- National Confidential Enquiry into Patient Outcome and Death (NCEPOD)

National Institute for Health and Clinical Excellence

- Set up in 1999
- Provides guidance on 'best practice', which is centred around evidence-based research and thorough audit (see www.nice.org.uk)
- Therefore also has an indirect role in controlling NHS resource allocation

Care Quality Commission

This has replaced the Health Care Commission, formerly the CHI, the Commission for Healthcare Improvements. The CQC:

- Was established in 2009 as an independent regulator of healthcare and adult social care in England
- Has a role in assessing NHS organisations, ensuring correct implementation of clinical governance is being achieved
- Obtains feedback from both patients and NHS employees to publish reports and make recommendations about individual services/institutions

Monitor

Monitor was established in 2004 to authorise and regulate NHS foundation trusts, and is directly accountable to Parliament. The Health and Social Care Act 2012 established Monitor as the sector regulator for Health. A two-way flow of information between Monitor and the CQC assists both organisations in carrying out their respective remits. The three main functions of Monitor are to:
- Determine whether NHS trusts are ready to be granted foundation status
- Ensure that established foundation trusts comply with the stipulated conditions
- Support NHS foundation trust development.

National Confidential Enquiry into Patient Outcome and Death

- Established in 1982 as CEPOD – a joint surgical/anaesthetic venture looking at perioperative deaths
- Now comes under the umbrella of the NPSA
- Aims to review clinical practice in order to identify areas of potential improvement in the practice of surgery, endoscopy, medicine and anaesthesia
- Scottish Audit of Surgical Mortality (SASM) is the Scottish equivalent of NCEPOD

SECTION 3

Surgical outcomes, the audit cycle and clinical decision-making

3.1   Surgical outcomes

> **Prediction and measurement of surgical outcome**
>
> Tools to aid in the prediction of outcome include:
> - Research (randomised controlled trials, meta-analyses, etc)
> - Preoperative scoring systems such as:
>   - American Society of Anaesthesiologists (ASA) grade
>   - Acute Physiology and Chronic Health Evaluation (APACHE)
>   - Glasgow Coma Scale (GCS)
>
> A spectrum of measures is available for quantifying outcomes:
> - Recurrence rates after cancer surgery
> - Mortality data
> - Economics (eg length of hospital stay)
> - Databases (eg Central Cardiac Audit Database [CCAD])
> - Patient satisfaction questionnaires

Surgical outcome is defined as the end-result, of either a specific intervention or the patient's management as a whole. This may be assessed at any time point in the process of diagnosis, investigation or treatment; it should be recognised that a doctor's and patient's assessments of whether an outcome is positive or negative may differ. Outcome may be assessed subjectively (eg patient satisfaction questionnaire) or objectively (survivorship data, time to discharge, etc) and may be categorised in terms of:

- Physical health – measured against the physiological norm
- Mental health – anxiety or distress, quality of life, self-esteem
- Social health – ability to perform normal social roles

Publication of outcomes – giving national averages allows the setting of target levels for positive outcomes. Research and meta-analysis of outcome measures can give an indication of the predicted outcome for specific patient groups (eg mortality rates for colorectal liver metastasis after combined chemotherapy and liver resection, compared with chemotherapy alone).

A number of confounding factors may affect outcomes, and inferior results should never be automatically attributed to surgical error. Results may be affected by:

- Different available facilities and back-up (eg theatres, intensive therapy units [ITUs])
- Allied services (eg oncology, interventional radiology)
- Case mix of patients:
  - Cancer or disease stage

- Prediction scores (eg ASA)
- Demographics (eg age, sex, social class)

Patient satisfaction is multifactorial, often drawing on a combination of physical, mental and social health. A treatment may not achieve a cure but nevertheless be regarded as having a positive outcome for the patient if there is relief from symptoms and alleviation of anxiety.

3.2 The audit cycle

Learning point

Definition: the collective review, evaluation and improvement of practice with the common aim of improving patient care and outcomes. It is performed retrospectively.

Functions of clinical audit
- Encourages improvement in clinical procedure
- Educates all members of the team
- Raises overall quality of clinical care
- Compares your practice with current best practice
- Provides peer comparison

Audit subtypes
- **Medical audit** is doctors looking at what they do
- **Clinical audit** is interdisciplinary
- **Comparative audit** provides data from a wide group, allowing comparison of individual results with national levels or averages

The Royal College of Surgeons requires that regular audits be carried out in each surgical speciality. One consultant in each department is responsible for the audit programme, and meeting records and minutes must be kept. These must include an attendance list, the topics discussed, conclusions and recommendations, action to be taken on any unresolved topics, and a future date for reviewing the topic. Evidence of regular audit meetings is mandatory for educational approval of training posts. The process should

be consultant-led and the consultant has to be in attendance. Areas audited should include:
- Access of patients to care (eg waiting time, cancellations)
- Process (eg investigations)
- Outcome (eg deaths, complications)
- Organisation of hospital and resources
- Financial implications

Structure refers to the availability and organisation of resources required for the

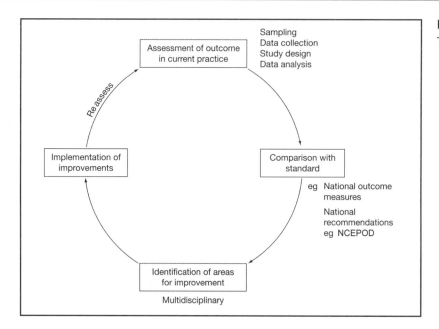

**Figure 8.1
The audit cycle**

delivery of a service (eg resources can include staff, equipment, accommodation).

Process refers to the way that the patient is received and managed by the service from time of referral to discharge.

Outcome means the results of clinical intervention.

Constructing an audit
- The **indicator** is the thing to be measured
- The **target** refers to the desired result
- **Monitoring method** encompasses the method of data collection, who is collecting it and the frequency of collection

The concept of audit as a **cycle** is an important one; once recommended changes have been implemented, the process should always be reassessed, to allow comparison not only with the national standard, but also with that previously assessed within the department. This is sometimes referred to as **closing the audit loop**.

3.3 Clinical decision-making

Learning point

The basis of decision-making
- Personal knowledge
- Senior review
- Guidelines/protocols

Four stages of decision-making
- Assessment and diagnosis (triage)
- Planning (strategy)
- Intervention (tactics)
- Evaluation (monitoring)

Personal knowledge
This may be subdivided into two types:
- Background knowledge about a disease or condition (applies to previous education and learning)

CHAPTER 8

- Foreground knowledge about a disease or condition (applies to information obtained from the individual patient's condition)

Senior review

Decision-making can be guided by someone of greater experience. This may be another doctor, or an experienced member of an allied profession such as nursing, physiotherapy, dietetics, etc. The ability to follow and understand the train of thought from someone with more experience adds to our personal knowledge of a disease, condition or treatment.

Protocols

Guidelines and protocols are developed by experts, based on pooled experience and current knowledge, and provide a framework that can accelerate the decision-making process. They are also a helpful way to teach clinical decision-making. Protocols may be expressed visually as algorithms. It should be remembered that an algorithm should be used only to treat patients falling within the specific clinical context explicitly described. Protocols must be subjected to the same audit processes as other areas of clinical care.

Assessment

Knowledge is used to recognise patterns in data collected about patients. We tend to start with a broad differential diagnosis, encompassing all diagnostic possibilities. Choosing when and where to limit data collection is important. Identifying which information was most relevant to the final diagnosis acts as a learning tool, adding to our background knowledge.

Planning and investigation

The differential diagnosis can be refined by planning and investigation. A test should generally be performed only if its results will aid in diagnosis or prognosis, or affect subsequent management. Interpretation of test results requires an understanding of probability. Tests may be interpreted differently by different clinicians, based on individual experience. All tests are subject to a degree of sensitivity and specificity, and may therefore give false positives or false negatives. Test results should therefore always be taken in the context of the clinical picture.

Intervention

There may be several treatment options; an understanding of the likely outcomes is a result of education and experience. Determining a threshold for treatment involves assessment (often performed subconsciously) of the risk–benefit ratio for that particular patient. It should be remembered that tests consume limited resources, may delay the initiation of treatment and may place the patient at risk of an adverse event from the test itself.

Evaluation

Reassessment should occur continuously – anticipating, recognising and correcting errors as circumstances change. At the end of the process, this evaluation involves feedback. On a personal or departmental level, feedback is formalised as the audit cycle (see above). Feedback allows for correction of mistakes and adds to learning by helping to reduce the risk of future error.

CHAPTER 8

3.4 Working in teams

Guidance on working in teams is available from the GMC's *Good Medical Practice* and this is summarised below.

Most doctors work in teams with colleagues from other professions. Working in teams does not change your personal accountability for your professional conduct and the care that you provide. When working in a team, you should act as a positive role model and try to motivate and inspire your colleagues. You must:

- Respect the skills and contributions of your colleagues
- Communicate effectively with colleagues within and outside the team
- Make sure that your patients and colleagues understand your role and responsibilities in the team, and who is responsible for each aspect of patient care
- Participate in regular reviews and audit of the standards and performance of the team, taking steps to remedy any deficiencies
- Support colleagues who have problems with performance, conduct or health

Sharing Information within the wider team

Sharing information with other healthcare professionals is important for safe and effective patient care.

When you refer a patient, you should provide all relevant information about the patient, including the medical history and current condition.

If you provide treatment or advice for a patient, but are not the patient's general practitioner, you should tell the GP the results of the investigations, the treatment provided and any other information necessary for the continuing care of the patient, unless the patient objects.

If a patient has not been referred to you by a GP, you should ask for the patient's consent to inform his or her GP. If you do not inform the patient's GP, you will be responsible for providing or arranging all necessary aftercare.

Delegation

Delegation involves asking a colleague to provide treatment or care on your behalf. Although you will not be accountable for the decisions and actions of those to whom you delegate, you will still be responsible for the overall management of the patient, and accountable for your decision to delegate. When you delegate care or treatment you must be satisfied that the person to whom you delegate has the qualifications, experience, knowledge and skills to provide the care or treatment involved. You must always pass on all the information about the patient and the treatment that he or she needs.

Referral

Referral involves transferring some or all of the responsibility for the patient's care, usually temporarily and for a particular purpose, such as additional investigation, care or treatment that is outside your competence. You must be satisfied that any healthcare professional to whom you refer a patient is accountable to a statutory regulatory body or employed within a managed environment. If they are not, the transfer of care will be regarded as delegation, not referral. This means that you remain responsible for the overall management of the patient, and accountable for your decision to delegate.

3.5 Dealing with conflict

Conflict is a broad term and can be experienced in a number of different ways.

Conflict with colleagues

The manner in which you handle disagreement with or between colleagues requires leadership and communication skills. In particular, objectivity and flexibility are vital. The NCEPOD has identified conflict and poor communication in the operating theatre as a major cause of surgical error, and many studies have identified a reduction in performance quality of the whole team even after just witnessing confrontation between two of its members. This is therefore not just a question of professional behaviour but has important patient safety implications.

There are many models of conflict resolution, but good principles to adhere to are:
• Listen
• Be objective and do not make the discussion personal
• Stick to patients best interests rather than fighting your corner
• Try to find more than one solution to the issue by being flexible

Aggression and violence

Violence directed against staff in the NHS is most common in frontline and mental health services. There is now an NHS syllabus for formal conflict resolution training for staff who have direct contact with the public. The training courses focus on non-physical techniques and include customer service, recognition of warning signs, de-escalation models and cultural awareness.

In addition there are now standardised pathways via NHS Protect, in conjunction with the Crown Prosecution Service, for dealing with cases of violence against staff within the NHS, and such cases should always be reported to your senior for further action.

CHAPTER 8

SECTION 4

Medical negligence

Learning point

Definition
Negligence is a tort (civil wrong) that occurs when one party breaches their duty of care owed to another, causing the latter to sustain an injury or a loss. Negligence law applies to other areas as well as medicine.

Elements of negligence
- Duty of care is owed
- This duty has been breached
- The breach has directly caused harm or loss to the person to whom the duty was owed

Defining the standard of care – the 'four Rs'
The courts have surmised that the level of care provided must accord with that of a group of peers, who would consider the standard to be:
- Reasonable
- Responsible
- Respectable
- Rational

Negligence claims in England are dealt with by the NHS Litigation Authority (NHSLA). Once liability is established, a court will award **damages**, namely monetary compensation to be paid to the claimant (plaintiff). The trust, rather than an individual doctor, tends to be liable for this payment; all hospital trusts and primary care trusts (PCTs) in England therefore make an annual financial contribution to the authority's Clinical Negligence Scheme for Trusts (CNST). The CNST is used to fund payouts incurred by any member organisations.

In 2010–11, the NHSLA received 8655 claims of clinical negligence and 4346 claims of non-clinical negligence against NHS bodies – a rise of more than 20% compared with figures for 2009–10. In the same period, £863 million was paid in connection with clinical negligence claims.

From a legal perspective, there are three **elements of negligence** that must be demonstrated. In reality, many trusts are opting increasingly for out-of-court settlements to avoid the expenditure of going to court, even where there has probably been no negligence; though in the long term there is the risk that this will encourage patients increasingly to bring claims against the NHS.

4.1 Duty of care

All doctors (along with allied professionals) have a duty to provide patients with care to an acceptable standard. In most doctor–patient encounters, it is self-evident that a duty of care exists. Equally, however, any doctor undertaking a 'Good Samaritan' act such as stopping at roadside accidents should bear in mind that, once they start to provide care, they assume a legal duty to provide it to an adequate standard.

4.2 Breach of duty

Once the duty of care has been established, a claimant must then demonstrate that the doctor failed to meet this duty – in other words, that the *standard of care* provided has fallen below the minimum acceptable level. An area that has been extensively debated in the courts is how this standard is to be quantified. The basic test remains the 'Bolam test', named after the case from 1957 (*Bolam* v. *Friern Hospital Management Committee*) in which the test was initially established.

The **Bolam test** states that a doctor is not negligent if his or her actions are supported by a 'responsible body of medical opinion'. This is felt by some to be controversial, given that it will tend to defend a doctor provided that *any* group can be found to support his or her actions, even if there is a large body of doctors who disagree. Nevertheless, to date it remains the basis for defining whether the duty of care has been breached. Subsequent cases have examined whether the judiciary is entitled to choose one body of medical opinion over another – but to date this has not been found to be the case

Defining the standard of care

How to decide what level of knowledge or clinical acumen is acceptable nevertheless remains a complex area, despite the Bolam test. For the practising clinician, it is worth bearing in mind the following points:

- **Keeping up to date** – this is a doctor's personal responsibility, eg if reports of a major new treatment are published in the mainstream medical literature, the courts would expect a doctor to keep him- or herself abreast of this. However, it is accepted that this will probably happen over a period of time; one would not be negligent for being unaware of a treatment only described the previous month, for example
- **Newly qualified doctors** still have responsibility for their clinical actions. In the *Wilsher* case (*Wilsher* v. *Essex Area Health Authority* 1986), the judge stated that it is the post, not the level of experience of the individual doctor, which defines the expected level of expertise, eg a new senior house officer (SHO) in a paediatric accident and emergency department (A&E) would be expected to practise at the level of an experienced paediatric A&E SHO
- **Lack of resources** is not a defence. If a hospital does not have facilities to offer a given service to a standard that meets the Bolam test, that particular service should not be offered at all
- **Emergencies** – although 'Good Samaritan' acts do confer a duty of care, the law recognises that there are not the same facilities at the roadside as there are in hospital. Similarly, during a major incident it is understood that the large number of patients presenting simultaneously may not allow the same level of care to be provided as would normally be expected

- **The 'thin skull rule'** states that one must take the patient as one finds them. In the *Robinson* case (*Robinson* v. *Post Office* 1974) a man with a cut leg was given a tetanus immunisation, to which he subsequently had an allergic reaction and died; the doctors were held liable for his death. This might seem unfair, and certainly other cases have not always followed the rule – nevertheless it is worth being aware of this

---

Table of cases
- *Bolam* v. *Friern Hospital Management Committee* [1957] 1 WLR 582
- *Robinson* v. *Post Office* [1974] 1 WLR 1176
- *Wilsher* v. *Essex Area Health Authority* 1986] 3 ALL ER 801

4.3   Causation

The final point required to establish liability is that the breach of duty of care led to some harm to the patient, eg if patients are administered an antibiotic that they have stated they are allergic to, and as a result suffer a severe anaphylactic reaction, the prescribing doctor has been negligent. However, if a patient believes (and states) that they are allergic, but in fact are *not*, and therefore has no reaction, then there has been no negligence. Although the doctor had a duty not to prescribe a drug to which the patient is allergic, and has breached this duty by doing so, the lack of causation of harm precludes negligence.

This is sometimes defined by the 'but for' test – but for the breach of care, would the patient not have suffered the harm? If the answer to this question is *yes* (ie they would *not* have suffered the harm), the test has been met and causation has been demonstrated. Where several factors have contributed to the harm (eg a head injury at work followed by negligent treatment in A&E), it must be shown that the negligence led to over 50% of the harm in order for the legal claim to succeed.

This has specific relevance in the area of **consent**; the doctor has a duty to provide the patient with the information needed to make an informed decision about agreeing to the treatment. If a patient can convince the court, after a complication, that he or she did not understand any given particular risk, and that if he or she had, he or she would not have agreed to the procedure, then it can be said that the doctor's failure adequately to inform *caused* the patient to suffer the complication by not allowing the patient to decide not to have the operation.

Within the modern culture of clinical governance, which is concerned very much with process and collective responsibility, most negligence claims tend to brought against trusts rather than individual doctors. Nevertheless, it is clearly important for clinicians to have a degree of understanding of the principles of medical negligence law – not so that we can practise defensive medicine, but so that we can at least avoid pitfalls that may potentially lead to liability.

Documentation

This is of crucial importance in this process. Should a case be taken to court, it is difficult for a doctor to defend his or her clinical decision-making processes if they have not been accurately recorded. This is especially so given that the clinical episode under scrutiny may relate to a previous post in a different hospital, and details may not be clearly recalled.

All entries in a patient's notes should be contemporaneous, and should include:

- Date and time
- Legible handwriting
- A clearly defined plan
- Signature
- Name in full
- Job designation
- Bleep number or contact details

These are minimum requirements, and there are numerous documented cases in which clinicians have been unable to defend their actions at a later date due to poor documentation.

Incompetence

If a breach of duty of care has not caused harm to a patient (ie there are no grounds for a negligence claim), it may still be the case that the GMC will choose to instigate incompetence proceedings against a doctor. This then becomes an issue of professional regulation, not civil law, and may result in the temporary or permanent exclusion of a doctor from the GMC's register. Conversely, it should of course be remembered that not all negligence claims lead to professional incompetence proceedings.

Gross negligence

This occurs when such a disregard of the duty of care is shown as to amount to recklessness. Should this lead to the death of a patient then this may constitute **criminal negligence** or **gross negligence manslaughter**. Such cases are then dealt with by the criminal, not civil, courts, and a custodial sentence and criminal record may ensue.

SECTION 5

'Informed' consent

The Department of Health has defined consent as 'a patient's agreement for a professional to provide care. Patients may indicate consent non-verbally … orally, or in writing'. Both morally and legally, this principle of 'informed' consent is fundamental to healthcare provision. Appropriate or 'valid' consent constitutes the sole determinant of whether any medical intervention is undertaken 'legally'.

5.1 What is consent?

Capacity

For consent to be valid, the patient must be able to:
- Understand information given to them
- Retain this information
- Process the information to form a decision
- Communicate this decision

Information required

The information provided to the patient must include:
- The nature of the disease and its likely natural history if not treated
- A basic understanding of the nature of the procedure – including postoperative course and other steps/procedures that may become necessary
- 'Serious or frequently occurring' risks
- Alternative treatment options

Battery is a common-law offence defined as any unlawful touching; this should be distinguished from **assault**, which merely implies that the victim believed that battery was about to occur – no physical contact need take place. ('Common law' refers to law established by legal precedent, as opposed to 'statute law', passed as parliamentary legislation.) However, the English court system has not upheld battery cases relating to consent on the basis that, as soon as a patient agrees to be treated to the 'general act of the treatment', there is no act of battery.

Instead, the courts have supported claims based in negligence (see Section 4). Therefore, if there is a complication after surgery, and the patient wishes to claim that he or she was not informed of the risk of this complication, the elements of negligence, in specific relation to consent, apply:
- **Duty of care** is owed to the patient to ensure that he or she receives all relevant information before agreeing to any given treatment
- **Breach** – the claimant demonstrates that this information was not provided adequately

- **Causation** – had the patient had this information he or she would not have undergone the treatment; the failure to inform of the risk can therefore be said to have *caused* the patient to have the complication.

Consent should be viewed not as an action but as an ongoing process, of which signing the consent form is only one stage. This process involves building professional trust between doctor and patient, part of which arises from the provision of sufficient information for the patient to feel that decisions that he or she makes about his or her own treatment are *informed*.

The consent form itself is not a binding contract – indeed, there is no requirement in law for the use of a form at all. Rather, it acts as a record of a discussion, or a series of discussions, that have taken place between healthcare professional(s) and patient. There is no legal 'time limit' on the validity of a patient's consent; however, many trusts suggest a counter-signature at the time of surgery if the consent form has been completed over 2 weeks earlier.

What are verbal and implied consent?

Verbal consent refers to patients stating their agreement to a medical intervention. **Implied consent** normally refers to the inference, from patients' conduct, that they agree to a procedure proposed to them. An example given in the Department of Health's *Reference Guide to Consent* is blood pressure measurement. Having explained to his or her patient that he proposes to check the blood pressure, the GP turns to find the patient proffering an arm and infers that consent to the measurement is implied. If there is ever any doubt as to whether implied consent is sufficient, it is better to err on the side

of caution and verbalise – or even write – the consent process formally.

The first area to ensure is that the patient has adequate understanding of the disease process and the likely natural history if left untreated. Subsequent to this there are three key areas, relating to the procedure itself, which must be included in the discussion.

Nature of procedure

The aims of the surgery should be fully explained, and the key steps of the operation described. It is important to confirm the patient's understanding of non-lay medical terms – even seemingly simple words such as 'suture' and 'thrombosis' may be unfamiliar. It is always the doctor's responsibility to ensure this understanding. The explanation should also provide information about the postoperative course that the patient can expect. Will there be much pain? Might a blood transfusion be needed? Will results (eg histology) have to be awaited postoperatively before the next step of the treatment?

There should be mention of any other steps or procedures, not part of the planned treatment, which may become necessary (eg conversion from laparoscopic to open abdominal surgery).

Alternative treatment options

These must be discussed. This can tie in with the discussion of the disease's natural history if wished; the patient should also understand what would happen if they had no treatment at all.

Potential complications

The doctor's duty is generally considered to be to explain the 'serious or frequently occurring risks'; how this should be defined continues to

CHAPTER 8

be debated. Very few surgeons would mention death as a potential risk of carpal tunnel decompression – yet is this correct, given that it is hard to imagine a more serious complication, however rare? Similarly, there is no clear legal guidance on what constitutes 'frequently occurring'; a rough guide might be to mention any complication with more than 1% likelihood, as well as rarer but more severe ones.

The inherent risks of anaesthesia should be discussed in detail by the anaesthetic team. However, many surgeons include 'anaesthetic complications' or a similar term among their listed complications on a surgical consent form – certainly a useful way to make sure the subject is not overlooked.

5.2   Who can obtain consent?

Numerous misconceptions exist in this area; the law sets down no stipulations about who can take a patient's consent. However, it should be stressed that it remains the operating surgeon's responsibility to ensure that the process is completed appropriately before undertaking the procedure. Clearly, the person taking consent must be sufficiently trained to have appropriate knowledge of the procedure, alternatives and inherent risks.

Although there is no legal basis for the widely held belief that to take consent 'you must be able to do the operation yourself', this is currently suggested by the GMC guidelines. Equally, it is important to be familiar with individual trust policies, which may set down additional requirements to those found in the law.

5.3   Who can give consent?

The general rule is that only patients themselves can give consent. However, for their consent to be valid, they must have the mental capacity to understand the information that they are being given, to retain it and to process it meaningfully as part of the decision-making process. They must also be capable of communicating their decision. A lack of capacity may be either temporary or permanent.

Temporary incapacity

In such cases the legal doctrine of *necessity* obviates the need for consent in the case of the unconscious patient. This principle effectively states that in certain circumstances acting unlawfully is justified if its benefits outweigh those of adhering rigidly to the law – as, for example, in the case of the unconscious patient admitted with a head injury. Two *caveats*, however, are first that the treatment undertaken must be no more extensive than absolutely necessary at the time, and second that there must be no known advance objection expressed to treatment. Non-emergency treatment should be delayed until the patient regains capacity.

Permanent incapacity

This is a complex area, covered in the Mental Capacity Act 2005 and Mental Health Act 2007. As with temporary incapacity, the guiding principles are that any treatment undertaken must be strictly in the patient's best interest, and should not be at odds with any advanced wishes expressed by the patient before loss of capacity. One change in the 2005 Act has been the introduction of the Court of Protection, a specialist court for all issues relating to lack of capacity. In non-emergency cases, surgeons wishing to treat such patients should apply to this court (see **www.hmcourts-service.gov. uk** for details). In the recent case of Ms PS, a woman with learning difficulties was treated against her will for gynaecological cancer after a ruling from the Court of Protection.

For emergencies, where time does not allow for a court application, the principles remain as they are for the unconscious patient.

Patients such as those with progressive dementia may set down an advance directive at a time while they still have capacity and, if they later lose capacity, the directive must be followed.

Children

Only parents (or those with legal parental responsibility) can legally give consent on behalf of their children. From age 16 onwards minors are deemed to have capacity to provide their own consent on their own behalf. Before this the age it must be decided whether the patient is *Gillick competent*. The Gillick case (*Gillick* v. *West Norfolk and Wisbech Area Health Authority* 1985) focused around the complaint of Mrs Gillick that a doctor acted wrongly in prescribing the oral contraceptive pill to her daughter who was under 16. The House of Lords ruled that: 'The parental right to determine … medical treatment terminates if and when the child achieves sufficient understanding and intelligence to understand fully what is proposed.' This notion of Gillick

competence has been adopted as the standard test. Interestingly, the law does not allow that minors are competent to *refuse* treatment – even if that same minor would be deemed competent to consent.

In principle, parents have the right to refuse treatment for their children. However, doctors may overrule this in certain circumstances if they believe it not to be in the child's best interests. If time allows, a court application should be made (again see **www.hmcourts-service.gov.uk** for how to do this). In the case of emergency medical treatment, the law is highly likely to support the decision of a doctor who acted against a parent's wishes in the child's best interests; however, doctors should make great efforts to obtain advice from their medical defence organisation before proceeding.

Table of cases
- *Gillick* v. *West Norfolk and Wisbech Area Health Authority* [1985] 3 ALL ER 402

Physical restrictions

Some patients, eg those with hand injuries, may be physically unable to sign a consent form. This should **not** be confused with a lack of mental capacity. Most trust consent forms have an area where a witness can sign on a patient's behalf if they are unable to sign – this should be used, *not* the mental incapacity form.

CHAPTER 8

SECTION 6

Healthcare resource allocation and the economic aspects of surgical care

Resource allocation within the NHS continues to become increasingly difficult as patient expectations increase and medical technology advances, while financial constraints tighten. It is important as surgeons to be aware of some of the key issues in this area. Assessment of economic costs and benefits aims to determine and implement the most effective strategies. The interpretation of the cost–benefit ratio depends on perspective: the patient's perspective differs from that of the doctor, the healthcare provider or the policy maker. There is also variation in the cost–benefit ratio when prophylactic surgery is considered. Benefit gained in the present tends to be considered more important than possible future benefit. The economics of surgical treatment can be divided into costs and consequences of surgery.

Costs of surgery

These include costs to patients, healthcare provider and others (eg patients' employers), and may be divided into:

- Direct medical costs (eg personnel, drugs)
- Indirect medical costs (eg overheads such as administration, buildings)
- Indirect costs of lost productivity (eg days off work)
- Intangible costs (eg pain, fear or suffering) that are difficult to quantify

Consequences of surgery

These may be:

- Positive (relief of symptoms, increased life expectancy)
- Negative (complications, period of hospital-isation, scarring)

Ethically, challenging decisions have to be made when considering who should be given preference, eg should priority be given to:

- Parents with dependent families?
- Young patients with longer life expectancy?
- Life-prolonging or life-improving treatments (eg joint replacement surgery)?
- Patients requiring cheaper interventions, thus allowing greater numbers of patients to be treated?

- Patients whose conditions may be related to lifestyle issues such as smoking or obesity?

One means of trying to answer these questions is to use the **quality-adjusted life year (QALY)**, which incorporates both the number of years that a patient can expect to live after the treatment, and his or her anticipated quality of life during this time (1 year of full health scores 1, death scores zero, 1 year of 'reduced quality' living falls in-between). There are three possible methods for assessing the economics of an intervention:

- **Cost–benefit analysis (CBA):** all costs and benefits (including intangible costs such as the value of lives lost or saved) are allocated a monetary value; CBA is calculated by the sum of the costs and benefits over a prespecified time
- **Cost–effectiveness analysis (CEA):** this is expressed in 'health units' (eg lives saved or incidence of disease); it does not put a monetary value on life. It is useful for comparison of two strategies to prevent the same condition
- **Cost–utility analysis:** this integrates the quality of life by using the QALY; it is expressed as a monetary value per QALY gained

However, some criticise QALYs as age discriminatory, also pointing out that not all interventions can be evaluated in terms of QALYs. NICE plays a role in guiding doctors' treatment choices for their patients, and part of this guidance is based on economic issues. Doctors in turn are obliged to follow this guidance:

'Once NICE guidance is published, health professionals are expected to take it fully into account when exercising their clinical judgement' (*A Guide to NICE*, 2005)

Several legal cases have challenged decisions not to provide treatment in certain conditions, either individually or nationally (an example being the challenge to the restrictions on prescribing *Aricept* [donepezil] in Alzheimer's disease). These have focused more on whether the process for reaching the decision was legal, rather than on whether the decision itself was fair.

Other cases have attempted to invoke the *right to life* as set out by the European Convention on Human Rights, saying that this right is being denied if a particular treatment (eg second-line anti-cancer therapy) is not provided. However, to date the courts have not taken this up, preferring to adopt the view that clinical decisions regarding allocation of limited treatment resources remain the remit of doctors, and ultimately the Secretary of State for Health, rather than of the courts.

For clinicians the safest course of action remains to follow guidelines where possible, and, where it is not, to discuss with colleagues (and even managers if necessary) before continuing.

CHAPTER 8

SECTION 7

Other medicolegal issues encountered in surgery

7.1   Whistle-blowing

'Act quickly to protect patients from risk if you have good reason to believe that you or a colleague may not be fit to practise.' (General Medical Council 2001)

The term 'whistle-blowing' is unfortunate in having negative connotations. The ultimate aim of bringing failings to light is to protect patients. Inappropriate or substandard practice should be reviewed with the goal of adjusting practice or providing additional training for improved professional development.

If there are concerns about a member of the team, the best course initially is to have an 'unofficial' discussion with a senior colleague, such as the lead clinician, educational supervisor or postgraduate dean. The intention is not to produce an overly defensive medical culture, but in a professional and delicate manner to help an underachiever to reach his or her full potential and provide safe care for the patients. Often, such colleagues have already realised that they are struggling, and are grateful for help, provided that it is given sensitively and discreetly.

7.2   Critical evaluation of surgical innovations

Surgery, similarly to all areas of clinical practice, is constantly evolving and this invariably leads to the introduction of both new techniques and new equipment. However, it is important to be aware of the fact that surgeons cannot simply 'try out' new treatments on patients as they wish.

It may be that such treatments are being undertaken as part of a formal research trial, and if this is the case full ethical approval must be obtained. However, even where the techniques in question are not subject to this process, certain conditions apply. *Good Surgical Practice* (2008) suggests that such innovations may include:
- A newly developed operation
- Significant modifications to an existing operation
- An operation not undertaken before in a given trust

Whichever of these applies, the principles are the same. The key considerations are:
- The patient's wellbeing must always remain the chief concern

- The surgeon(s) must liaise with colleagues of appropriate experience to discuss the intended treatment
- Any financial interest must be openly declared
- The consent process must include a frank explanation to patients of the fact that the treatment that they are to receive is new; the reasons for this, and for not applying existing treatments, should be clearly explained
- Local protocols with regard to ethics committee approval must be strictly adhered to
- Formal audit of the treatment and its outcomes is mandatory. This is essential locally for patient protection, but also to allow information to be gathered and disseminated more widely about developments in surgical practice that may ultimately benefit the wider patient population

These are important considerations, which all surgeons should understand. However, there may be times, especially in the emergency situation, where it is not possible to follow all these steps fully, in which case it is helpful to understand the legal perspective – namely that surgeons are only likely to be liable if their actions fail to meet the three criteria of the *reasonableness* test:

- It must be shown that there is a recognised existing practice
- This practice was not followed
- The treatment undertaken was one that no reasonable doctor would have undertaken

7.3 Advance directives

The term 'advance directive' means a statement explaining what medical treatment the individual would not want in the future, should that individual 'lack capacity' as defined by the Mental Capacity Act 2005. While patients retain capacity, their word over-rides anything in the advance directive. If the patient does not have capacity then the directive may be considered legally binding.

An advance directive enables an individual to think about the sort of care that he or she would like to receive if he or she no longer has the capacity to make decisions, for example about:

- Cardiopulmonary resuscitation
- The use of fluids and nutrition
- Life-saving care in the end-stages of degenerative disease, eg dementia
- Blood transfusion for Jehovah's Witnesses

An advance directive cannot be used to:

- Ask for specific medical treatment.
- Request something that is illegal (eg assisted suicide)
- Choose someone to make decisions on behalf of the patient, unless that person is given 'lasting power of attorney'
- Refuse treatment for a mental health condition (doctors are empowered to treat such conditions under Part 4 of the Mental Health Act)

A directive may be invalid:

- If it is not signed
- If there is reason to doubt its authenticity (eg if it was not witnessed)
- If it is felt that there was duress
- If there is doubt about the person's state of mind (at the time of signing)

Note that these are complex issues and should always be discussed at a senior level within the team.

7.4   Euthanasia

Learning point

Euthanasia may be subcategorised in two ways:
Active and passive
- Active – a specific act is committed to end life
- Passive – life is ended by omission

Voluntary, involuntary and non-voluntary
- Voluntary – at the patient's request
- Involuntary – life is ended against, or without, the patient's wishes
- Non-voluntary – the patient is not competent to give their opinion

'Euthanasia is the act of taking life to relieve suffering.' (*Oxford Concise Medical Dictionary* 1990)

At present, despite ongoing debate, euthanasia remains illegal in the UK, and deliberately ending a patient's life unquestionably opens a doctor to potential charges of manslaughter or even murder. However, in the 1957 case of *R* v. *Adams* the court stated that:

> '[A doctor] … is entitled to do all that is proper and necessary to relieve pain and suffering, even if the measures may incidentally shorten life.'

This suggests that there is some room for manoeuvre in this area, and certainly there have been very few criminal convictions to date. Similarly, in the case of *Airedale NHS Trust* v. *Bland* (1993) the hospital, consultant and parents applied for legal permission to withdraw enteral feeding from a patient with permanent vegetative state, which would inevitably lead to death. This withdrawal of treatment was approved by the court; however, the concomitant use of medication to accelerate death was expressly prohibited. In keeping with this, all doctors should remember that active euthanasia remains a criminal offence.

Table of cases

Airedale NHS Trust v. *Bland* [1993] 1 ALL ER 821

R v. *Adams* [1957] Crim LR 365

CHAPTER 9

Orthopaedic Surgery

Nigel W Gummerson

CHAPTER 9

Bone, muscle and joint structure and physiology

1.1 Bone physiology

Learning point

Bone is a specialised form of mesenchymally derived connective tissue. It is a dynamic structure, with more functions than the obvious one of providing an articulating framework for muscles and soft tissues. Bones respond to the biomechanical stresses encountered, with subsequent adjustments in the architecture and mass of the skeleton (Wolff's law). In addition, bones provide the major store of the body's calcium and phosphate and so plays an important role in mineral exchange.

Functions of bone
- Supports the body
- Facilitates movement
- Produces blood cells (haematopoiesis)
- Regulates calcium (haemostasis)
- Protects organs (eg thoracic cage, which also facilitates ventilation)

Hormonal control of bone activity

Hormonal control of bone activity is necessary for bone remodelling and growth, and the regulation of mineral exchange.

Calcium is the most abundant metallic element in the human body. Bone is an enormous reservoir of calcium within the body, and the main hormones acting on bone are involved with calcium homeostasis. Calcium is involved in many physiological functions (muscle contraction, intracellular messengers, control of neural excitability) and serum levels are under tight physiological regulation. Usually 50% of calcium is carried bound to albumin, and the remainder is in the free 'ionised' form. Total serum calcium is 2.2–2.6 mmol/l, depending on the bound (albumin) fraction.

Hormones acting on bone

Vitamin D
- Natural vitamin D (cholecalciferol) derived from the diet or indirect action of UV light on precursors in the skin
- Conversion to active metabolite occurs in the liver (cholecalciferol to 25-hydroxy-cholecalciferol) and kidney (to 1,25-dihydroxycholecalciferol, DHCC)
- Production of 1,25-DHCC is controlled by parathyroid hormone (PTH) and phosphate (increased PTH or decreased phosphate increases amount of 1,25-DHCC produced)
- Increased 1,25-DHCC increases calcium and phosphate absorption from the intestine, and stimulates osteoclasts, increasing bone resorption (increases serum calcium)
- Low vitamin D levels result in rickets and osteomalacia

Parathyroid hormone
- Fine regulator of calcium exchange (maintains extracellular calcium within narrow limits)
- Produced by chief cells of parathyroid glands in response to low calcium concentrations
- Target organs are bone and kidney
- Causes resorption of bone by osteoclasts in response to low serum calcium
- Decreases renal calcium excretion in response to low serum calcium (with subsequent increase in phosphate excretion) – this effect is rapid

- Primary hyperparathyroidism (eg parathyroid adenoma) causes hypercalcaemia
- Secondary hyperparathyroidism (eg renal disease resulting in increased calcium loss) causes increased secretion of PTH with resultant decalcification of bone and pathological fractures
- Hypoparathyroidism (eg surgical removal of parathyroid glands) causes hypocalcaemia with hyperphosphataemia

Calcitonin
- Opposite actions to PTH
- Produced in parafollicular (C) cells of the thyroid
- Inhibits bone resorption by osteoclasts in response to high serum calcium
- Increases renal calcium excretion in response to high serum calcium

Thyroxine (T$_4$)
- Catabolic (so breakdown of bone tissue)
- Hypercalcaemia and hypercalciuria are seen in thyrotoxicosis (low PTH level)

Growth hormone (GH)
- Normally released in response to hypoglycaemia from the pituitary gland in a negative feedback loop in the hypothalamic–pituitary axis
- Affects glucose metabolism and growth
- Stimulates production of insulin-like growth factor 1 (IGF-1) in the liver and other tissues (IGF-1 leads to increased bone growth)
- Too much GH (eg pituitary adenoma) leads to gigantism before puberty or acromegaly after the epiphyseal plates have fused. Acromegaly causes general thickening of bones and soft tissues

Glucocorticoids

High levels of glucocorticoids cause:
- Reduced bone matrix
- Increased bone resorption
- Potentiation of PTH
- Reduced calcium absorption from the gut

High levels of glucocorticoids therefore result in:
- Osteoporosis
- Fractures
- Vertebral body collapse
- Avascular necrosis of the femoral head
- Growth retardation in children

Oestrogens and androgens

Anabolic hormones which may promote epiphyseal closure.

Effects of nutrition on bone

The prime requirements for a healthy skeleton are adequate calories, calcium and vitamin D (along with phosphate, fluoride, magnesium and vitamin C). Even a very mild degree of malnutrition can lead to reduced bone density in the long term, increasing the risk of osteoporotic fractures.

Calories

Calorie deficiency and protein deficiency result in poor healing and poor recovery from fractures.

Vitamin D

Vitamin D deficiency leads to rickets (in children) and osteomalacia (in adults).

Calcium

> **Potential causes of decreased calcium absorption**
>
> **Phytates** from cereals, peas, beans and nuts reduce calcium absorption. These phytates are inactivated by the enzyme phytase. Yeast contains phytase (the human gut does not) so leavened bread is not a problem; large quantities of unleavened breads (such as chapatis) in the diet can result in inadequate calcium absorption
>
> **Steatorrhoea** (insoluble calcium soaps in the gut reduce absorption)

> **Potential causes of increased urinary calcium loss**
> - High sodium intake
> - Caffeine
> - High ratio of protein to calcium intake (only a problem when calcium intake and absorption are low)

Other important nutrients

- Magnesium: important in hydroxyapatite crystallisation
- Vitamin C: scurvy is the result of inadequate dietary vitamin C; it causes failure of collagen synthesis and clotting abnormalities, and results in subperiosteal haemorrhage
- Vitamin K
- Zinc
- Manganese
- Copper
- Boron

CHAPTER 9

Effects of ageing on the structure of bone

Continued bone resorption and formation occur throughout life. This process is known as remodelling. During growth the bone increases in size; new bone is added by endochondral ossification at the physis (increasing length) and subperiosteal appositional ossification (increasing width). Endosteal resorption expands the medullary cavity.

Between the ages of 20 and 40, cortical thickness increases, and haversian canals and intertrabecular spaces fill in, making bones heavier and stronger.

After the age of 40 there is a slow, steady loss of bone, with enlargement of the haversian spaces, thinning of the bony trabeculae and expansion of the medullary space. Bone mass decreases. This age-related osteoporosis is accelerated in women at the menopause due to oestrogen withdrawal.

With further advances in age, bone loss increases. Additional factors such as malnutrition, lack of weight-bearing exercise and chronic disease also contribute to this bone loss.

1.2 Bone structure

Learning point

Bone is a connective tissue. It is unique in that it normally mineralises. It consists of an organic matrix and an inorganic matrix.

Organic matrix (35%) is composed of bone proteins (predominantly type I collagen) and bone-forming cells – osteoprogenitor cells, osteoblasts and osteocytes (derived from osteoblasts). The generation and stimulation of these cells are regulated by cytokines and growth factors.

Inorganic matrix (65%) is composed of mainly calcium hydroxyapatite, which contains 99% of the body's calcium store and 85% of body phosphorus. The inorganic matrix also houses 65% of sodium and magnesium stores.

Bone proteins

The proteins of bone include type I collagen and non-collagenous proteins that are produced by steoblasts. Remember that bone in different situations is composed of differing amounts of bone components.

Type I collagen

This makes up 90% of the organic component. Osteoblasts deposit collagen either in a random weave (woven bone) or an orderly layered manner (lamellar bone). These differences can be seen histologically.

Non-collagenous proteins

These are bound to the matrix. They are adhesion proteins, calcium-binding proteins, mineralisation proteins, enzymes, cytokines and growth factors (eg bone morphogenetic proteins).

Bone cells

The osteoblasts and osteoclasts act in coordination and are considered the functional unit of bone. They are instrumental in the processes of bone formation and bone resorption.

Osteoprogenitor cells

- Derived from pluripotential mesenchymal stem cells
- Located in the vicinity of all bony surfaces
- The only bone cells that divide
- Daughter cells are called osteoblasts

Osteoblasts

- Derived from osteoprogenitor cells
- Their function is to build bone
- Located on the surface of bone
- Synthesise, transport and arrange the many proteins of the matrix
- Initiate mineralisation
- Express cell-surface receptors that bind to PTH, vitamin D, oestrogen, cytokines, growth factors and extracellular matrix proteins
- Role in hormonal regulation of bone resorption

Osteocytes

- Derived from osteoblasts (osteoblasts surrounded by matrix are known as osteocytes); these are mature bone cells
- Their function is to maintain bone
- Most numerous type of bone cell in mature bone
- Communicate with each other and with surface cells via a network of tunnels through the matrix (canaliculi); this network may control the fluctuations in serum calcium and phosphate by altering the concentration of these electrolytes in the local extracellular fluid

- Translate mechanical forces into biological activity (eg bone remodelling)

Osteoclasts

- Derived from haematopoietic progenitor cells of monocyte/macrophage lineage
- Their function is to resorb bone
- Cytokines are crucial for osteoclast differentiation and maturation (the interleukins IL-1, IL-3, IL-6 and IL-11, tumour necrosis factor [TNF] and granulocye–macrophage colony-stimulating factor [GM-CSF])
- Mature osteoclasts are multinucleated (15–20 nuclei)
- Found at sites of active bone resorption, close to the bone surface in pits known as Howship's lacunae

How does an osteoclast break down bone?

Osteoclast activity is initiated by binding to matrix adhesion proteins. The osteoclast cell membrane becomes modified by villous extensions on the matrix interface, which increases the surface area. The plasmalemma bordering this region forms a seal with the underlying bone, preventing leakage of digestion products and creating a self-contained extracellular space. The osteoclast acidifies this space by pumping in hydrogen ions. The solubility of the calcium hydroxyapatite increases as the pH falls. The osteoclast then releases a multitude of enzymes that break down the matrix proteins into amino acids, and liberate and activate growth factors and enzymes. Thus, as bone is broken down to its elemental units, substances are released that initiate its renewal.

Bone types

Woven bone

- Immature bone, seen in fetal skeleton, growth plates and callus
- Product of rapid bone formation
- Irregular and disorganised arrangement of collagen
- Mechanically weak
- Indicative of pathological state in adult (eg in circumstances requiring rapid repair such as fractures)
- Forms around site of infection
- Comprises the matrix of bone-forming tumours

Lamellar bone

- Regular, orderly arrangement of collagen fibres into sheets (lamellae)
- Mechanically strong
- Gradually replaces woven bone, but is deposited much more slowly
- Can be cortical (compact) or cancellous (trabecular) bone
- Cortical bone is rigid and has no marrow, with well-defined haversian canals lying parallel to the long axis of the bone providing a good vascular supply
- Cancellous bone lies inside the cortical layer, contains marrow in spaces between trabeculae and has no blood vessels (therefore osteocytes rely on diffusion from medullary blood vessels)

Periosteum

Bones are covered by periosteum, a moderately thick layer of fibrocellular tissue that is attached to the underlying bone strongly by Sharpey's fibres. There are two layers: the cambrial (inner) and the fibrous (outer).

Functions of the periosteum include:
- **Anchor:** provides a firm attachment for tendons and ligaments
- **Source of osteoprogenitor cells:** required for bone remodelling and fracture healing (loss of the periosteum significantly impairs fracture healing)
- **Nutrition:** blood vessels running within the deep layer supply the underlying bone

Development, ossification and growth of bone

Bone develops from the condensation of mesenchymal tissue during week 5 of embryonic development. Bones may ossify directly (intramembranous, as in the clavicle) or chondrocytes may produce a hyaline cartilage template that then ossifies (endochondral ossification, as in the tibia and all other long bones).

Long bone development and structure

A typical long bone develops by endochondral ossification and consists of:
- **Diaphysis** (shaft): a tube of cortical bone
- **Metaphysis:** a conical area of cancellous bone facilitating load transfer from the articular surface to the diaphysis
- **Physis:** a growth plate, the zone of growth and ossification
- **Epiphysis:** caries the articular surface and a zone of cancellous bone above dividing chondrocytes

---

The primary ossification centre of a long bone appears in the diaphysis. Secondary centres appear in the epiphysis (in some bones there can be multiple secondary centres, as in the distal humerus). At the ossification centre the chondrocytes hypertrophy and die. The cartilage becomes calcified. The majority of the diaphysis of each bone is ossified at birth.

Longitudinal growth of the bone occurs at the growth plate. Circumferential growth occurs below the periosteum. Osteogenic cells in the cambrial layer produce new bone; this layer is very thick and vascular in children.

Growth plates develop between primary and secondary centres.

The physis (or growth plate) has four zones:
- **Resting zone:** resting chondrocytes on epiphyseal side of physis
- **Proliferative zone:** dividing chondrocytes
- **Hypertrophic zone:** maturing chondrocytes
- **Zone of provisional calcification:** new bone is formed on the metaphyseal side of the physis

Physeal fractures typically occur between the hypertrophic and calcification zones.

Bone is a dynamic structure that constantly undergoes remodelling. The trabeculae are formed in response to the loads placed on the bone, and the trabecular pattern will change if the loads are changed. This is **Wolff's law**. As the bone grows, remodelling occurs throughout the whole bone.

Blood supply of bone

The vascular supply to bone is important for bone growth and healing, calcium metabolism and haematopoiesis. Five to ten per cent of the total cardiac output is distributed to the bone. Unfortunately the blood supply may also carry tumour or infection through the skeleton.

Generally, the vascular supply to a bone includes:
- **Nutrient artery:** perforates cortex of the bone and supplies bone marrow and trabecular bone
- **Vessels accompanying tendons and ligaments:** supply periosteum and adjacent bone cortex
- **Circulus vasculosus:** an arterial plexus surrounding the epiphysis derived from regional arterial branches, which supplies the epiphysis before union with the main bone; after union, vessels communicate with the vascular supply of the main bone

The arterial supply of a long bone is from four sources:
- **Nutrient artery:** supplies the diaphysis (marrow and trabeculae)
- **Metaphyseal vessels:** from the surrounding joint anastomosis; supply the epiphyseal end of the diaphysis; the metaphyseal region is the most vascularised part of bone
- **Epiphyseal vessels:** from surrounding joint vessels
- **Periosteal vessels**

Venous flow is from the cortical capillaries draining to sinusoids and then to the emissary venous system.

CHAPTER 9

1.3   Joint structure and physiology

Learning point

A joint, or articulation, is the place where two bones come together. All bones except one – the hyoid – form a joint with another bone. Joints hold bones together and allow the rigid skeleton to move.

Classification of joints

Based on function (the amount of movement they allow) there are three types of joints:

- **Immovable joints (synarthroses):** the bones are in very close contact, separated only by a thin layer of fibrous connective tissue (eg skull sutures)
- **Slightly movable joints (amphiarthroses):** characterised by bones connected by hyaline cartilage (eg manubriosternal joint)
- **Freely movable joints (diarthroses):** characterised by synovial-lined joint cavity and hyaline articular cartilage

There are six types of freely movable joints:

- **Ball and socket**, eg shoulder, hip
- **Condyloid**, eg metacarpophalangeal joints – oval-shaped condyle fits into elliptical cavity of another, allowing angular motion but not rotation
- **Saddle**, eg carpometacarpal joint of thumb
- **Pivot**, eg atlantoaxial joint
- **Hinge**, eg elbow, knee
- **Gliding**, eg vertebral column facet joints – flat or slightly flat surfaces move against each other, allowing sliding or twisting without any circular movement

Joint structure

Based on structure, there are three types of joint:

- Fibrous joints
- Cartilaginous joints
- Synovial joints

Fibrous joints

- Lack joint cavity
- Fibrous tissue unites bones

There are three types of fibrous joints:

- Sutures (eg cranial)
- Syndesmosis (eg inferior tibiofibular joint)
- Gomphosis (eg roots of teeth in alveolar socket)

Cartilaginous joints

There are two types of cartilaginous joints:

- **Primary** (synchondrosis): where bone and hyaline cartilage meet (eg between rib and costal cartilage)
- **Secondary** (symphysis): where hyaline-covered articular surfaces of two bones are united by fibrous tissue or fibrocartilage (eg pubic symphysis and intervertebral joints)

Synovial joints

Synovial joints are characterised by:

- Presence of a joint cavity
- Bones are covered with a layer of smooth hyaline cartilage to reduce friction

(occasionally fibrocartilage), eg menisci of knee
- Joint is enclosed by capsular ligament, lined with synovial membrane
- Synovial membrane produces synovial fluid, lubricating the joint
- Articulating surfaces of adjacent bones are reciprocally shaped

Hyaline cartilage is composed of chondrocytes, cartilage, gel matrix, water, collagen (mainly type II) and proteoglycans. **Articular cartilage** has no blood or nerve supply, and relies on diffusion for nutrition.

Diseases of bone

There are numerous conditions that can disturb bone development, growth or structure. They are too numerous to discuss here, and only a simplified description of a few selected examples will be given.
- **Osteogenesis imperfecta** – a disorder of type I collagen resulting in abnormal bone formation and mineralisation. The clinical presentation is variable, depending on subtype, but it may lead to fractures and progressive deformity
- **Achondroplasia** – the most common skeletal dysplasia and results in dwarfism. It is usually the result of a new mutation in the fibroblast growth factor receptor 3 gene. Patients will present with disproportionate dwarfism, the root of the limb being most affected. Radiographs will show a narrow spinal canal, short thick bones, with metaphyseal cupping and a large skull with a narrow foramen magnum

Further examples such as metabolic bone disease are discussed in Section 3.

1.4 Muscle structure and physiology

> **Learning point**
>
> All muscles share the following properties, which are interrelated and achieve movement:
> - **Contractility** (ability to shorten in response to stimuli)
> - **Excitability** (ability to react to stimulus)
> - **Extensibility** (ability to undergo stretch)
> - **Elasticity** (ability to return to original shape and size)
>
> The three types of muscle which you should be familiar with are:
> - Skeletal muscle
> - Smooth muscle
> - Cardiac muscle

Skeletal muscle

Skeletal muscle is muscle attached to the skeleton, the contraction of which brings about skeletal movements. It may also be referred to as 'striated' muscle, reflecting the presence of the alternating light and dark striations (thin and thick filaments, respectively) seen under the microscope. Skeletal muscle is under voluntary control, although it is capable of involuntary contraction. It is usually in a state of partial contraction (muscle tone). Skeletal muscle makes up 40–50% of the total body weight of a man, 30–40% in a woman.

Structure of skeletal muscle

Skeletal muscle is composed of cylindrical muscle fibres, many of which run the whole length of the muscle, and these are bound together by connective tissue. Each muscle fibre is enclosed in a cell membrane (sarcolemma) and contains:

- Myofibrils (stacked lengthways, running the entire length of the fibre, composed of thick and thin filaments called myofilaments)
- Mitochondria
- Endoplasmic reticulum
- Many nuclei
- Cellular cytoplasm (called 'sarcoplasm')

Each myofibril is made up of arrays of parallel filaments. The thick filaments have a diameter of about 15 nm and are composed of the protein myosin. The thin filaments have a diameter of about 5 nm and are composed of the protein actin, with smaller amounts of troponin and tropomyosin. A sarcomere is composed of one thick and two thin filaments, which interact to cause muscle contraction, and it is this arrangement that gives skeletal muscle its striated appearance.

Individual muscle fibres are grouped together into long bundles (fasciculi), which in turn are bunched together by connective tissue called perimysium to make up the muscle mass. The entire muscle is then surrounded by epimysium. Although each individual striated fibre can contract individually (eg the ocular muscles), muscle fibres tend to contract in groups.

Innervation of skeletal muscle

Motor neurons in peripheral nerves leading to skeletal muscles have branching axons, each of which terminates in a neuromuscular junction with a single muscle fibre. Nerve impulses passing down a single motor neurone will thus trigger contraction in all the muscle fibres at which the branches of that neurone terminate. The nerve, together with the muscle fibres that it innervates, make up a motor unit.

The size of the motor unit is small in muscles over which we have precise control, eg a single motor neurone triggers fewer than 10 fibres in the muscles controlling eye movements. In contrast, a single motor unit for a muscle such as gastrocnemius may include 1000–2000 fibres. Although the response of a motor unit is all or none, the number of motor units activated determines the strength of the response of the entire muscle.

The junction between the motor neurone and the muscle fibre is called the neuromuscular junction. Here the axon terminals of the nerve cross the endomysium of the muscle to contact the corresponding muscle fibre, at a specialised area called the motor endplate. Nerve impulses are transmitted to the muscle by release of acetylcholine, a neurotransmitter, the effect of which is to trigger an action potential in the muscle fibres.

Activation of the muscle fibre causes the myosin (in the thick filament) to bind to actin (in the thin filament), which draws the thin filament a short distance (approximately 10 nm) past the thick filament. These bonds then break (for which ATP is needed) and re-form further along the thin filament to repeat the process. As a result, the filaments are pulled past each other in a ratchet-like action, and contraction of the muscle occurs. This is called the sliding filament model of muscle contraction.

Excitation–contraction coupling

Activation of the muscle requires translation of the action potential from the motor neurone into a stimulus which causes the actin and

CHAPTER 9

myosin filaments to interact. This is achieved using calcium stores in the muscle sarcoplasmic reticulum. The arrival of the action potential triggers the release of calcium, which diffuses among the thick and thin filaments where it binds to troponin, and this initiates the contraction of the sarcomere. When the process is over, the calcium is pumped back into the sarcoplasmic reticulum and the process is ready to repeat. ATP fuels muscle contraction. The level of ATP is maintained by creatine phosphate and glycogen.

Types of muscle fibre

Two different types of muscle fibre can be found in most skeletal muscles – types I and II.

Type I fibres
- Loaded with mitochondria
- Resistant to fatigue
- Rich in myoglobin (red colour)
- Activated by slow-conducting motor neurones
- Known as 'slow-twitch' fibres
- Dominant in muscles that depend on tonus (eg posture muscles)

Type II fibres
- Few mitochondria
- Rich in glycogen
- Fatigue easily
- Low in myoglobin (whitish in colour)
- Activated by fast-conducting motor neurones
- Known as 'fast-twitch' fibres
- Dominant in muscles used for rapid movement

Most skeletal muscles contain some mixture of type I and type II fibres, but a single motor unit always contains one type or the other – never both. The ratios of type I and type II fibres can be changed by endurance training (this produces more type I fibres).

Types of muscle contraction

There are five types of skeletal muscle contraction:
- **Twitch:** a transient contraction in response to a short-lived stimulus
- **Isotonic contraction:** muscle becomes shorter and thicker with no change in tension
- **Isometric contraction:** muscle tension increases without change in muscle length
- **Treppe:** repetitive stimuli over a prolonged period causes contractions of increasing strength, followed by levelling off of tension
- **Tetanus:** rapid repeated muscle stimulation that causes a continuous contraction as the muscle cannot relax between the stimuli

Smooth muscle

Smooth muscle is found in the walls of arteries and veins, and in the respiratory, digestive and urogenital systems. It is composed of single spindle-shaped cells, which, despite the lack of visible microscopic striations, still possess thick and thin filaments; these slide against each other to achieve contraction of the cells.

Smooth muscle (like cardiac muscle) does not depend on motor neurones to be stimulated; it is innervated by the autonomic nervous system and therefore is not under voluntary control. Smooth muscle can also be made to contract by other substances released in the vicinity (paracrine stimulation, eg histamine causes contraction of the smooth muscle lining the airways), or by hormones circulating in the blood (eg oxytocin contracts the uterus to begin childbirth).

Unlike skeletal muscle, smooth muscle is not attached to bone. Compared with skeletal muscle, smooth muscle contractions and relaxation are slower, more rhythmic and

CHAPTER 9

sustained. In addition, smooth muscle lacks the calcium-binding protein troponin, instead using calmodulin to mediate contraction.

Cardiac muscle

This is a specialised form of muscle found only in the heart. Cardiac muscle is striated, and each cell contains sarcomeres with sliding filaments of actin and myosin.

Unlike skeletal muscle, the action potential that triggers cardiac muscle contraction is generated within the heart itself. Although autonomic fibres pass to the heart, they merely modulate the intrinsic rate and strength of the contractions generated.

In addition, tetany is not possible within cardiac muscle, as the muscle's refractory period is much longer than the time it takes the muscle to contract and relax.

SECTION 2

Joint pathology

Differentiating between rheumatoid arthritis and osteoarthritis

	Rheumatoid arthritis (inflammatory)	Osteoarthritis (mechanical)
Symptoms	Worst on waking Relieved by exercise Worse with rest Early morning stiffness (>30 min) Stiffness after rest (>5 min) Relieved by NSAIDs Systemic effects Possible family history Autoimmune disease	Worst at end of day Worse with exercise Relieved by rest Limited early morning stiffness (<30 min) Limited stiffness after rest (<5 min) Relieved by simple analgesics No systemic effects Previous injury, some genetic component Occupation
Signs	Soft-tissue swelling Joints warm ± erythema Systemic signs Associated pathology	Bony swelling Joints cool, no erythema No systemic signs No associated pathology
Investigations	Increased ESR, CRP Anaemia of chronic disease Positive autoantibodies Inflammatory synovial fluid	Normal ESR, CRP Normal full blood count Negative autoantibodies Non-inflammatory synovial fluid
Changes in radiograph	Periarticular osteoporosis Joint space narrowing Marginal erosions Boutonnière deformity Swan-neck deformity Subluxations and dislocations Soft-tissue swelling, symmetrical, fusiform	Heberden's nodes Bouchard's nodes Joint space narrowing Subchondral sclerosis Osteophytes Subarticular bone cysts

2.1 Osteoarthritis

> ## Learning point
>
> Osteoarthritis (OA) affects synovial joints. It presents with pain and stiffness. It may be primary or secondary.
>
> **Pathological features of OA**
> - Breakdown and loss of articular cartilage
> - Loss of joint space
> - Reparative bone response
> - Capsular fibrosis
>
> **Radiological features of OA**
> - Loss of joint space
> - Osteophyte formation
> - Juxta-articular sclerosis
> - Subarticular bone cysts

Pathogenesis of osteoarthritis

The primary lesion is damage to hyaline cartilage. Cartilage is composed of chondrocytes in an extracellular matrix, with water accounting for 70–80% of the weight. The matrix is composed of proteoglycans and non-collagenous proteins in a network of collagen fibres. Proteoglycans are hydrophilic, but swelling due to hydration is restrained by the collagen network. With normal ageing, decreased proteoglycans lead to lower water-binding capacity. This results in a thinner, stiffer cartilage with lower resilience and higher vulnerability to injury.

In early osteoarthritis (OA) increased matrix turnover is followed by a loss of proteoglycan and collagen. This cartilage is initially softer and less resistant to force, allowing further damage. Breakdown products activate the immune system leading to inflammation and tissue destruction by cytokines and degradative enzymes.

Attempts at repair lead to formation of new cartilage that may undergo ossification, forming marginal osteophytes. It also causes bony protrusions at the margins of distal interphalangeal joints – Heberden's nodes. Subchondral new bone formation leads to sclerosis.

Degeneration of cartilage can be graded:

Grade 1	Softening of articular cartilage
Grade 2	Fibrillation and fissuring
Grade 3	Partial-thickness loss, clefts and chondral flaps
Grade 4	Full-thickness loss with bone exposed

Pain in OA is due to:
- Inflamed and thickened synovium
- Muscle spasm
- Irregular exposed joint surfaces

Clinical patterns in osteoarthritis

Osteoarthritis can be either primary (with no obvious underlying cause – 20%) or secondary (following a demonstrable abnormality – 80%). The frequency of OA increases with age, and there is a genetic predisposition.

Primary osteoarthritis
- Men: middle age
- Women: old age
- 80% >70 years
- Polyarthropathy affecting mainly hands, hips, knees and spine

Secondary osteoarthritis

- Previously damaged or congenitally abnormal joint
- Any age

Causes of secondary osteoarthritis

Trauma	Intra-articular fracture
	Ligament injury (eg ACL)
	Repetitive injury
	Meniscal injury
	AVN
Inflammatory	Rheumatoid arthritis
Sepsis	Septic arthritis
Developmental	DDH
	SUFE
Unknown	Perthes' disease
Connective tissue	Hypermobility
Bone disease	Paget's disease
Neuropathic joints	Diabetes
	Syringomyelia
	Deep dorsal horn disorders
Endocrine/metabolic	Acromegaly
	Cushing's disease
	Gout and pseudogout
	Ochronosis
	Wilson's disease
	Haemochromatosis
Haematological	Haemophilia
	Sickle cell disease

ACL, anterior cruciate ligament; AVN, avascular necrosis; DDH, developmental dysplasia of the hip; SUFE, slipped upper femoral epiphysis.

Management of osteoarthritis

Management of OA depends on the stage of disease and the disability that it causes. In general it can be divided into non-surgical and surgical management.

Conservative management of OA

- Pain relief (analgesics and anti-inflammatory drugs)
- Activity modification
- Physiotherapy – maximise muscle strength and control, maintain joint range of motion
- Reduction of load (eg stick used in hand opposite to joint, weight loss)
- Non-weight-bearing exercise
- Splintage – most appropriate for OA in the hand

Surgical management of OA

Remember, consideration must be given to the age, occupation and general condition of the patient.

Surgical options are to realign, excise, fuse or replace:
- Realignment osteotomy: to alter joint biomechanics
- Joint arthrodesis: joint is fused, usually indicated for pain
- Joint arthroplasty or removal of the diseased joint: can be excision (eg Keller's procedure of the great toe, Girdlestone's procedure of the hip) or excision and replacement (eg total hip replacement or total knee replacement)

Surgical management may be indicated when non-surgical management has failed.

CHAPTER 9

2.2   Rheumatoid arthritis

Learning point

Rheumatoid arthritis (RA) is a symmetrical, inflammatory polyarthropathy with systemic manifestations. It affects vasculature, skin, heart, lungs, nerves and eyes and affects around 1% of the population, commonly women, usually in their 40s and 50s. In the acute phase, ESR and CRP levels (both measures of acute phase proteins) are raised. Eighty per cent of patients with RA have recurrent flares, 5% per cent show relentless disease progression and the remainder manifest a low-grade clinical course.

Pathology of rheumatoid arthritis

RA affects the synovial membrane, causing severe chronic synovitis. Initially it affects the small proximal joints of the hands and feet but then usually progresses symmetrically to the wrists, elbows, ankles and knees. The most common site of initial presentation is the foot.

- Infiltration of synovium by macrophages and T lymphocytes
- Inflamed synovium (**pannus**): this eventually fills the joint space and impinges on joint surfaces. Pannus formation and release of destructive enzymes and cytokines destroy underlying cartilage
- Bony erosion at the joint margin follows. Inflammation of other synovial structures, such as tendon sheaths, contributes to deformity and disability by leading to tendon rupture

- Around 20% have rheumatoid nodules. These are lesions of the subcutaneous tissue; each nodule consists of a central necrotic zone surrounded by a cellular infiltrate of macrophages and fibroblasts. They mostly occur on extensor surfaces of the arms and elbows

Aetiological theories

The aetiology of rheumatoid arthritis is uncertain but there are two main theories:
- **Microbial triggers:** Epstein–Barr virus (EBV) is the prime suspect, also *Mycobacterium tuberculosis* and *Proteus mirabilis*
- **Genetic/autoimmune disease:** linkage to HLA-DR4 points to a genetic susceptibility

Once inflammatory synovitis is initiated, an autoimmune reaction ensues. CD4 T cells are activated, with release of many cytokines. Autoantibodies are produced. Autoantibody against the Fc portion of autologous IgG is called **rheumatoid factor**. Rheumatoid factor is usually IgM but can be IgG, IgA or IgE. These factors form complexes within the synovium and synovial fluid and are partly responsible for the characteristic changes. Rheumatoid factor is positive in 20% of cases.

Clinical features of rheumatoid arthritis

- Early morning stiffness, lasting at least 1 hour before maximal improvement
- Arthritis of three or more joint areas with simultaneous soft-tissue swelling or fluid
- Arthritis of hand joints (eg wrist, metacarpophalangeal [MCP] or proximal interphalangeal [PIP] joints)
- Symmetrical arthritis (involvement of the same joint areas on both sides of the body)

- Rheumatoid nodules (subcutaneous nodules: over bony prominences or extensor surfaces or in juxta-articular regions)

Clinically, patients may present with a lack of wellbeing, warm joints, swelling, joint thickening and effusion, muscle wasting or tendon rupture causing joint deformities. For example:
- Boutonnière deformity
- Swan-neck deformity
- Z-thumb

The diagnostic criteria for RA comprise a points-based system that gives a score in each of the following four domains: joint involvement, serological parameters, duration of arthritis and acute phase proteins.

Radiological features of rheumatoid arthritis
- Loss of joint space
- Periarticular erosions
- Joint-line thickening
- Juxta-articular osteoporosis
- No osteophytes

Management of rheumatoid arthritis

The principles of management of RA are to:
- Stop synovitis
- Prevent deformity
- Reconstruct diseased joints
- Rehabilitate the patient

Medical/conservative management of RA

Prevention of synovitis relies initially on drugs:
- Initially NSAIDs and analgesics
- Disease-modifying anti-rheumatic

drugs (DMARDs) such as methotrexate, sulfasalazine, azathioprine, ciclosporin and penicillamine. Biological DMARDs such as the tumour necrosis factor α (TNF-α) blockers (eg etanercept and infliximab), IL-1 blockers, IL-6 blockers and monoclonal antibodies
- Steroids

In addition, rest and joint splintage have a role in conservative management. After acute attacks, physiotherapy and joint mobilisation are crucial.

Surgical management of RA
- Synovectomy (eg elbow, wrist)
- Arthrodesis (eg ankle, wrist, neck)
- Replacement arthroplasty (eg hip, knee, shoulder)
- Excision arthroplasty (eg radial head excision)
- Tendon reconstruction (eg hand, foot)

2.3   Gout

Gout typically affects the metatarsophalangeal joint of the great toe (in >50% of cases) but can also involve the ankle, knee or small joints of the hands.

Gout presents with recurrent attacks of acute arthritis triggered by crystallisation of monosodium urate in the joint, with asymptomatic intervals. In severe cases there is eventual development of tophaceous gout with aggregates of urates in and around joints and chronic, often crippling, gouty arthritis.

Hyperuricaemia is only present in about half of all cases.

CHAPTER 9

Aetiology of gout

- 90% primary (mostly idiopathic due to increased uric acid production or decreased excretion)
- 10% secondary to diuretics (thiazides especially), myeloproliferative/lymphoproliferative disorders and chronic renal failure

Pathological features of gout

- **Acute arthritis:** acute inflammatory synovitis stimulated by monosodium urate crystals (long, needle-shaped crystals which are negatively birefringent on microscopy). Leucocytes and macrophages release cytokines
- **Chronic arthritis:** urate precipitates in the synovial membrane after acute attacks, stimulating a pannus (inflammatory overgrowth) over the synovium and cartilage, degrading cartilage and bone. Leads to proliferation of marginal bone and bony ankylosis
- **Tophi:** urate deposition in periarticular tissues surrounded by intense inflammatory reaction involving white cells, fibroblasts and giant cells. Typical chalky exudative deposits may cause overlying skin necrosis and exude a paste of monosodium urate crystals (hence the unlikely story of the patient who kept the darts scores on the pub blackboard with his gouty hands – having no need for chalk!)
- **Kidney disease:** acute uric acid nephropathy, nephrolithiasis, chronic urate nephropathy

Associations of gout

- Obesity, type IV hyperlipidaemia, hypertension, diabetes, ischaemic heart disease

---

Radiological findings in gout

Typically seen late (>6 years after first attack). Features include:

- Soft-tissue swelling: these are 'punched-out' erosions; they start near joint margins and have a classic overhanging sclerotic margin; they are mostly set back from the articular surface
- Eccentric soft-tissue masses in a periarticular location in tophaceous gout (these calcify only rarely)
- Cartilage destruction (and hence joint-space narrowing) is not typical except in very late cases and typically there is no osteoporosis (differentiating it from RA)

Treatment of gout

- Exclude infection
- Treat acute attack: anti-inflammatory drugs (eg NSAIDs such as indometacin or, rarely, colchicine)
- Prophylaxis: reduce precipitating factors (alcohol, obesity, diuretics); decrease uric acid production (allopurinol); increase uric acid secretion (uricosurics, eg probenecid)

Beware: altering uric acid metabolism can precipitate an attack, so do not start allopurinol during an acute attack, and cover introduction of prophylactic long-term therapy with non-steroidals.

2.4   Pseudogout

Pseudogout is similar to gout (see above) but with short, rhomboid, water-soluble crystals of calcium pyrophosphate causing acute joint inflammation. These crystals are positively birefringent under polarised light microscopy. The knee is most commonly affected. It is seen more frequently with increasing age. Acute attacks may be precipitated by medical illness. It is associated with hyperparathyroidism and hypomagnesaemia. Treatment may involve rest, aspiration and steroid injections.

Chondrocalcinosis refers to the radiological appearances of calcification in the soft tissues and linear densities in the articular cartilage parallel to subchondral bone. Pseudogout and chondrocalcinosis are both forms of **pyrophosphate arthropathy**.

2.5 Osteochondritis dissecans

Learning point

Osteochondritis dissecans (note: dissecans [separating] not dessicans [drying]) occurs in young patients and is characterised by partial or complete detachment of a fragment of articular cartilage or bone. Avascular areas of subchondral bone are susceptible to microfracture; these areas do not remodel (as they are not vascularised), so subchondral bone can detach, taking articular cartilage with it.

Aetiology of osteochondritis dissecans

- Idiopathic
- Repetitive minor trauma, ligament instability, shearing forces
- Abnormal epiphyseal ossification
- Genetic
- Following high-dose steroids

Clinical presentation of osteochondritis dissecans

Presents with pain (worse with activity), swelling and joint effusions. There might be loose bodies, locking and giving way of the joint. Radiographs may show a line of demarcation in the early stages or overlying fibrocartilage (similar to that seen in non-union) or a loose body in later stages. Note that the rest of the bone is normally vascularised, thus distinguishing between osteochondritis dissecans and osteonecrosis. MRI is useful for demonstrating the size and depth of the lesion.

It commonly affects convex joint surfaces, for example:
- Knee (lateral surface of medial femoral condyle in 75%)
- Talar dome
- Elbow (capitellum) – Panner's disease
- Patella
- First metatarsal head
- Femoral head

Treatment of osteochondritis dissecans

- Rest or activity modification
- Trial of immobilisation
- Surgical intervention – pinning of the loose fragment or debridement:
  - In children, healing can occur without intervention
  - In adolescents, drilling of the defect can stimulate healing
- Autologous cartilage transplant

CHAPTER 9

SECTION 3

Bone pathology

3.1 Osteoporosis

Pathogenesis of osteoporosis

Peak bone mass, achieved in early adulthood, is determined by:

- Nutritional state
- Levels of physical activity
- Hormonal status

Approximately 3–5% of cortical bone and 15–25% of trabecular bone is remodelled yearly and the amount of bone resorbed is equal to the amount of bone formed. At the start of the fourth decade, the amount of bone resorbed exceeds that which has been formed, so there is a steady decrease in skeletal mass. Osteoblasts from elderly individuals have impaired reproductive and biosynthetic potential. Also, the non-collagenous proteins bound to the extracellular matrix, such as growth factors, lose their full impact on osteoblastic stimulation over time.

CHAPTER 9

Causes of osteoporosis

Primary osteoporosis

Postmenopausal (type 1)
- Affects women 10–20 years after the menopause – due to increased osteoclast activity
- *Senile/age-related (type 2)*
- Affects men and women aged >70 – due to reduced oteoblast activity/ availability

Secondary osteoporosis

Neoplasia
- Multiple myeloma
- Carcinomatosis
- Leukaemia

Drugs
- Anticoagulants (heparin)
- Chemotherapy
- Corticosteroids
- Anticonvulsants
- Alcohol

Endocrine disorders
- Hyperparathyroidism
- Thyroid disorders
- Hypogonadism

- Pituitary tumours
- Addison's disease
- Diabetes mellitus (type 1)

Gastrointestinal
- Malnutrition
- Malabsorption
- Vitamin C deficiency
- Vitamin D deficiency

Disease
- RA
- Ankylosing spondylitis
- TB
- Chronic renal disease

Mechanical
- Disuse
- Immobilisation

Haematological
- Thalassaemia
- Sickle cell

Fifty per cent of elderly men and 30% of elderly women presenting with an osteoporotic vertebral fracture will have an identifiable cause for their osteoporosis.

Risk factors for osteoporosis

Reduced physical activity, sedentary lifestyle

Mechanical forces are important stimuli for normal bone remodelling. There is evidence to support physical activity in prevention of bone loss (eg from observation of bone loss in paralysed, immobile limbs compared with higher bone density in athletes). Muscle contraction is the dominant source of skeletal loading.

Smoking

Smoking increases the risk of osteoporosis.

Nutritional state, low weight, alcohol

Low body mass index correlates with a higher incidence of osteoporosis. Alcohol directly reduces osteoblast function.

Hormonal influences, early menopause

Decreased oestrogen levels result in increased production of IL-1, IL-6 and TNF-α by blood monocytes and bone marrow cells. These are potent stimulators of osteoclast activity. Compensatory osteoblastic activity occurs but does not keep up with osteoclastic activity.

CHAPTER 9

617

Genetic factors

Genetic variability resulting in differences in the vitamin D receptor molecule accounts for approximately 75% of the peak bone mass achieved.

Clinical features of osteoporosis

- Presents with low-trauma fractures
- Commonly vertebral fracture in thoracic spine and lumbar spine – pain, loss of height, kyphosis
- Fracture neck of femur, pelvis and Colles' fracture of the distal radius

Investigating osteoporosis

Osteoporosis cannot be reliably detected on plain radiographs until 40–50% of the bone mass is lost. Measurement of serum calcium, phosphorus and alkaline phosphatase is not diagnostic. It is difficult to diagnose accurately because it is asymptomatic until advanced skeletal fragility manifests itself in the form of pathological fracture.

The investigation of choice is dual-energy X-ray absorptiometry (DXA scan).

Other investigations include:
- Bone biopsy (loss of normal bony trabecular pattern)
- Other quantitative radiographic imaging, eg quantitative CT

Treatment of osteoporosis

- **Prevention:** maximise peak skeletal mass by exercise, diet, calcium supplementation ± HRT (hormone replacement therapy) in the perimenopausal period
- **Exclude secondary cause**

- **Quantitative assessment of bone density:** to establish diagnosis and provide baseline to monitor response (not indicated after femoral neck fractures – here the diagnosis is already established and treatment should be instituted)
- **Treatment of fractures** (neck of femur, Colles' fractures)
- **Drug treatment of established osteoporosis**, for secondary prevention of fractures. Calcium and vitamin D supplements should be given first to correct any deficiency, and then the first-line treatment is with bisphosphonates, which reduce bone turnover. Strontium or anabolic agents such as calcitonin and teraparatide may be indicated for very low bone density, or for patients who cannot tolerate bisphosphonates or fail to respond to bisphosphonates

3.2 Rickets and osteomalacia

Learning point

Rickets in children and osteomalacia in adults arise from deranged vitamin D absorption or metabolism or, less commonly, from disorders that disturb calcium or phosphate homeostasis. The hallmark is impaired mineralisation of bone (osteoid), leading to large areas of unmineralised matrix (volume of bone is normal).

Vitamin D and calcium homeostasis

The major role of vitamin D is the maintenance of normal plasma levels of calcium and phosphorus. There are two major sources of vitamin D, endogenous synthesis and diet.

Endogenous synthesis takes place in the skin (the precursor, 7-dihydrocholesterol, in the skin is converted to vitamin D_3 by UV light).

The active form of vitamin D (produced by the kidney):

- Stimulates absorption of calcium and phosphorus in the gut
- Acts with PTH in the mobilisation of calcium from bone

- Stimulates the PTH-dependent reabsorption of calcium in the distal renal tubules

Although vitamin D collaborates with PTH in the resorption of calcium and phosphorus from bone to support blood levels, it is required for normal mineralisation of epiphyseal cartilage and osteoid matrix. It is not clear how the resorptive mechanism is mediated. The mechanism of mineralisation is also not known.

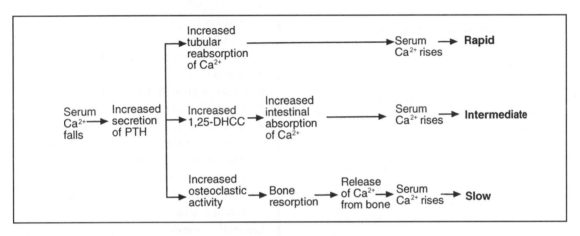

Figure 9.1 Calcium homeostasis

Predisposing conditions for rickets or osteomalacia	**Derangements in vitamin D metabolism**
Inadequate synthesis or dietary deficiency of vitamin D	- Drugs can increase degradation of vitamin D (eg phenytoin, phenobarbital, rifampicin)
- Inadequate exposure to sunlight	- Liver disease
- Dietary deficit	- Renal disease
- Poor maternal nutrition	**Phosphate depletion**
- Dark skin pigmentation	- Poor absorption, due to chronic use of antacids (phosphate binds to aluminium hydroxide)
Decreased absorption of fat-soluble vitamin D	- Excess renal tubule excretion of phosphate (eg oncogenic osteomalacia caused by mesenchymal tumours of bone and soft tissues, or prostate cancer)
- Cholestatic liver disease	
- Pancreatic insufficiency	
- Biliary tract obstruction	- X-linked inherited hypophosphataemia secondary to enzyme deficiency
- Small-bowel disease (coeliac disease and Crohn's disease)	

CHAPTER 9

Rickets (children)

Clinical features of rickets

These depend on the severity and duration of the disorder and the patient's age. Commonly symptoms include bone pain and tenderness.

In children, skeletal deformities are accentuated by the effects of gravity and muscle action on growing bones. Children are often apathetic, irritable and hypokinetic with delayed walking.

Inadequate calcification of epiphyseal cartilage leads to:
- Overgrowth of epiphyseal cartilage due to inadequate calcification and failure of cartilage cells to mature and disintegrate
- Persistence of distorted irregular masses of cartilage
- Deposition of osteoid matrix on inadequately mineralised cartilaginous remnants – enlargement and lateral expansion of osteochondral junction
- Deformation of the skeleton due to loss of rigidity of developing bones, in response to stresses to which individual bones are subjected

During the non-ambulatory stage of infancy the head and chest sustain the greatest stresses, leading to:
- Flattening of occipital bones (craniotabes), prominence of suture lines ('hot-cross bun' skull)
- Inward buckling of parietal bones
- Frontal bossing due to excess osteoid
- Squared appearance to the head
- Pigeon chest (due to pull of respiratory muscles on weak ribs) and Harrison's sulcus (indentation of lower part of the rib cage at the insertion of the diaphragm)
- Prominence of costochondral junctions (rachitic rosary)

In the ambulatory child the stresses are on the pelvis, spine and long bones. This causes:
- Increased lumbar lordosis, thoracic kyphosis (rachitic cat back)
- Bowing of legs, fractures, slipped capital epiphysis

Main radiological features in rickets
Changes due to soft bones
- Trefoil pelvis
- Scoliosis
- Biconcave vertebral bodies
- Craniotabes (soft, thinned skull)
- Bowing of diaphysis

Changes at growth plate and cortex
- Flaring/cupping of metaphysis
- Thin bony spur from metaphysis surrounding uncalcified growth plate
- Thickened, wide growth plate
- Cupping of ends of ribs
- Thin cortex due to uncalcified subperiosteal osteoid

General changes
- Looser's lines (collections of osteoid producing ribbon-like zones of incomplete radiolucency (eg medial side femoral neck, pubic rami, ribs, clavicle)
- Osteopenia
- Wide osteoid seams (indistinct fuzzy trabeculae)

Investigating rickets

Typical findings: low calcium, low phosphate, increased alkaline phosphatase (this is increased in young children normally).

Osteomalacia (adults)

Clinical features of osteomalacia

Symptoms and signs
- **Fatigue**, malaise and proximal muscle weakness
- **Bone pain** and tenderness, most often localised to the pelvis, scapula and ribs, possibly related to microfractures or pseudofractures, commonly called Looser's zones. These are radiolucent lines several millimetres thick, sharply demarcated from the adjacent bone. They are attributed to resorption of the thin bone by overlying pulsating arteries
- **Pathological fractures:** the newly formed osteoid matrix laid down by osteoblasts is inadequately mineralised, thus producing excess of osteoid. Although the contours are not affected, the bone is weak and subject to gross fracturing. It is most likely to affect vertebral bodies and femoral necks

Investigating osteomalacia
- **Treatment:** the best way to make the diagnosis of osteomalacia in most instances is a therapeutic trial of vitamin D and calcium
- **Serum calcium and vitamin D** levels are not usually helpful as they can be normal or low
- **Alkaline phosphatase (ALP) and PTH** levels are often high. The increases are due to osteoblast attempts to form new bone

Persistent failure of mineralisation leads to loss of skeletal mass, making the distinction between osteoporosis and osteomalacia difficult.

Remember, renal disease (renal osteodystrophy) is one of the most common causes of osteomalacia (and rickets), with profound effects on the skeletal system.

Management of rickets and osteomalacia
- **Prevention:** correct deficiencies, balanced diet, adequate sunlight exposure
- **Treat established disease:** eg vitamin D with calcium, calcitrol or alfacalcidol, manage renal failure, stop any implicated drugs
- **Treatment of complications:** fractures, SUFE, brace/realign deformities, osteotomy or arthroplasty if joint damage occurs

3.3 Paget's disease of the bone

Learning point

Paget's disease (osteitis deformans) was first described by James Paget in 1877 and is characterised by excessively disorganised bone turnover. There are three phases:
- **Osteolytic (initial) stage:** mediated by osteoclasts, with bone resorption causing osteolytic lesions
- **Reparative phase:** rapid bone formation is mediated by an osteoclastic or osteoblastic stage that ends with a predominance of osteoblastic activity; this results in a gain of bone mass – the newly formed bone is disordered and structurally unsound
- **Inactive phase:** a burnt-out quiescent osteosclerotic stage (dense bone mosaic but little cellular activity)

CHAPTER 9

Aetiology of Paget's disease

Usually presents in mid-adulthood (in the 40s) with a 3% prevalence in those aged >40 and 10% in those aged >90. Most commonly seen in Britain, but also in Europe, the USA, New Zealand and Australia.

The exact cause of Paget's disease is unclear. There is a genetic predisposition in up to 25% of patients, linked to certain HLA patterns. An alternative theory is that the disease is virally induced, because viral inclusions have been demonstrated within the abnormal osteoclasts.

Clinical features of Paget's disease

Many patients are asymptomatic. Any bone can be affected; usually more than one bone is involved. It is monostotic (one bone) in about 15% of cases. The axial skeleton or proximal femur is involved in up to 80% of cases. New bone formed is soft and highly vascular. It commonly occurs in the pelvis, lumbar and thoracic spine, femur, skull, sacrum, tibia and humerus. Bone-specific ALP levels will be raised when Paget's disease is active. Calcium, phosphate and PTH levels are usually normal. Calcium levels may be elevated in polyostotic (many bones) disease.

Skeletal effects of Paget's disease

- Painful affected bone
- Anterior bowing of femur and tibia
- Overgrowth of craniofacial skeleton leading to leontiasis posse (lion-like facies) and a cranium that's so heavy it becomes difficult to hold the head erect
- Invagination of base of skull secondary to increased weight with compression of posterior fossa structures
- Distortion of femoral head leading to severe osteoarthritis

- Long bones of lower limbs are affected leading to 'chalk-stick' fractures (transverse fractures)
- Compression fracture in spine may result in deformity (kyphosis) and spinal cord injury
- Secondary osteoarthritis

Neurological effects of Paget's disease

- Bone overgrowth can compress spinal and cranial nerve roots (entrapment syndromes, paraplegia, paresis)
- Headache and dizziness
- Altered mental status (platybasia)

Cardiovascular and metabolic effects of Paget's disease

- Hypervascularity of pagetic bone leads to increased blood flow that acts as an arteriovenous (AV) shunt, leading to high output cardiac failure or exacerbation of underlying cardiac disease (very rare)
- Hypercalcaemia and hypercalciuria

Tumours in Paget's disease

Benign tumours in Paget's disease
- Giant-cell reparative granuloma

Malignant tumours in Paget's disease
- Sarcoma (in 5–10% with severe polyostotic disease)
- Osteosarcoma
- Malignant fibrous histiocytoma
- Chondrosarcoma
- Giant-cell tumour

Diagnosis of Paget's disease

- **Radiological appearance:** enlarged with thick, coarse cortices and cancellous bone. Technetium isotope scanning allows visualisation of the entire skeleton, and demonstration of early lesions
- **Biochemical markers:** increased ALP and increased urinary excretion of hydroxy-proline; serum calcium and phosphate are usually normal

Treatment of Paget's disease

Medical treatment with bisphosphonates or calcitonin can reduce the rate of bone turnover. Surgical treatment may be required in cases of neurological compression, fracture or tumour.

CHAPTER 9

SECTION 4

The hip and thigh

4.1 Anatomy of the hip joint

> **Learning point**
>
> The hip is a ball-and-socket joint. It consists of the rounded head of the femur articulating with the cup-shaped acetabulum. The acetabulum (which is named after an ancient vinegar cup) is formed at the junction of the ilium, pubis and ischium.

The greater and lesser trochanters are the insertion points for a number of muscles around the hip. These prominences allow the insertion point to be offset from the shaft and alter the biomechanics of the muscle.

The greater trochanter is lateral to the femoral head and carries the attachments of:
- Piriformis
- Obturator externus
- Obturator internus

- Gluteus medius
- Gluteus minimus
- The gemelli

The lesser trochanter is on the medial aspect of the proximal femur and provides attachment for two hip flexors:
- Psoas
- Iliacus

Ligaments of the hip and joint capsule

The geometry of the hip (ball and socket) gives it a degree of intrinsic stability. This is increased still further by the acetabular labrum – a ring of fibrocartilage around the acetabulum. Three ligaments contribute to the stability of the hip joint. The most important is the Y-shaped iliofemoral ligament (of Bigelow). The other ligaments are the pubofemoral and the ischio-femoral ligaments. Ten per cent of the population have an outpouching in the anterior capsule. This results in a **psoas bursa**.

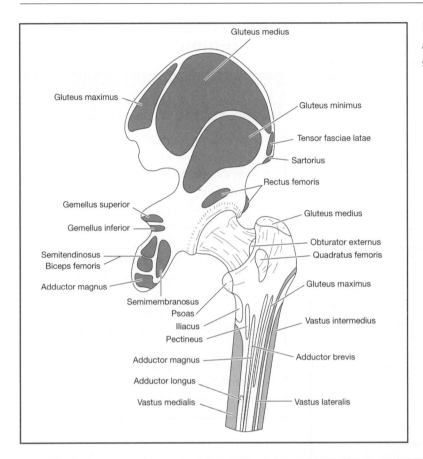

Figure 9.2 Muscles attached to the external surface of the right hip

Ligaments of the hip	Arises	Inserts	Action
Iliofemoral	Anterior inferior iliac spine	Lower and upper part of intertrochanteric line	Resists hyperextension
Pubofemoral	Superior ramus of pubis	Lower part of inter-trochanteric line	Resists extension and abduction
Ischiofemoral	Ischium	Greater trochanter	Limits extension

Blood supply of the hip joint

The hip derives its blood supply from three main vessels:

- Medial circumflex femoral artery (from profunda femoris artery)
- Lateral circumflex artery (from profunda femoris artery)
- Ligamentum teres (this contains a small vessel, which provides a negligible blood supply in the adult, but is more significant in children)

The medial and lateral circumflex femoral arteries form a vascular ring at the base of the femoral neck (outside the capsule) and give off the retinacular vessels. These enter the head around the insertion of the capsule (about 1 cm above the trochanteric crest).

There is also a contribution directly from the metaphysis. The clinical implications of the blood supply of the femur are discussed further in the companion volume.

Nerve supply and movement of the hip

The nerve supply is derived from the femoral, obturator and sciatic nerves. By understanding the principles of Hilton's law, the nerves supplying the hip joint can be remembered.

Hilton's law
The nerve trunk supplying a joint also supplies the overlying skin and the muscles that move the joint.

Movement of the hip	Main muscle groups
Flexion	Psoas and iliacus
Extension	Gluteus maximus and hamstrings
Adduction	Adductors
Abduction	Gluteus medius and minimus, tensor fasciae latae
Lateral rotation	Piriformis, obturators, quadriceps femoris and gluteus maximus
Medial rotation	Tensor fasciae latae, gluteus medius and maximus

4.2 Anatomy of the gluteal region

Learning point

The gluteal region consists of the:
- Gluteus muscles
- Tensor fasciae latae
- Piriformis
- Gemelli muscles
- Obturator internus
- Quadratus femoris

It extends from the top of the iliac crest to the gluteal buttock crease. Gluteus maximus is the largest muscle of the body, and its fibres fuse to insert in the iliotibial tract and gluteal tuberosity. It is the only gluteal muscle to be supplied by the inferior gluteal nerve. Medius and minimi are supplied by the superior gluteal nerve (L4–S1).

The greater and lesser sciatic foramina

To understand the gluteal region, it is essential to understand the two main ligaments that divide the pelvis into two, forming foramina that allow the passage of nerves and vessels from the pelvis into the lower limb. These ligaments are sacrotuberous and sacrospinous, forming the greater and lesser sciatic foramina.

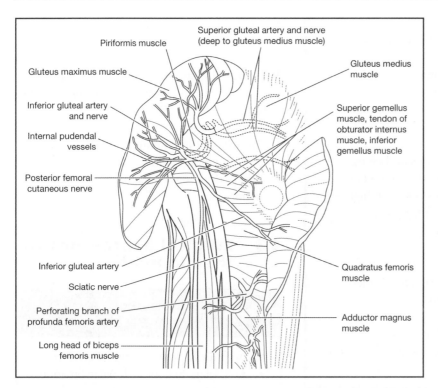

Figure 9.3 Gluteal region

Piriformis muscle

Superior gluteal artery and nerve (deep to gluteus medius muscle)

Gluteus maximus muscle

Gluteus medius muscle

Inferior gluteal artery and nerve

Superior gemellus muscle, tendon of obturator internus muscle, inferior gemellus muscle

Internal pudendal vessels

Posterior femoral cutaneous nerve

Inferior gluteal artery

Sciatic nerve

Quadratus femoris muscle

Perforating branch of profunda femoris artery

Adductor magnus muscle

Long head of biceps femoris muscle

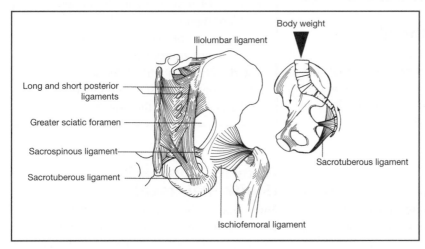

Figure 9.4 The greater and lesser sciatic foramina

Iliolumbar ligament

Body weight

Long and short posterior ligaments

Greater sciatic foramen

Sacrospinous ligament

Sacrotuberous ligament

Sacrotuberous ligament

Ischiofemoral ligament

CHAPTER 9

Structures passing through the sciatic foramina

Greater sciatic foramen:
- Superior gluteal nerves
- Superior gluteal arteries and veins
- Piriformis
- Inferior gluteal nerves
- Inferior gluteal arteries and veins
- Internal pudendal artery and vein
- Posterior cutaneous nerve of thigh, nerve to obturator internus and quadratus femoris
- Sciatic nerve
- Pudendal nerve (re-enters pelvis through the lesser sciatic foramen)

Lesser sciatic foramen:
- Pudendal nerve
- Internal pudendal artery and vein
- Nerve to obturator and internus and its tendon

Blood supply to the gluteal region

This is from two branches of the internal iliac artery which form part of two anastomoses connecting the internal iliac with the femoral arteries. The two internal iliac branches are:
- Superior gluteal artery
- Inferior gluteal artery

It is worth remembering that the superior gluteal artery lies above the piriformis muscle, whereas the inferior gluteal artery lies below piriformis as it enters the gluteal region.

The trochanteric anastomosis supplies the head of the femur and is formed by the following arteries:
- Superior gluteal
- Inferior gluteal
- Medial femoral circumflex
- Lateral femoral circumflex

The cruciate anastomosis supplies the posterior aspect of the femur and consists of branches from:
- Inferior gluteal
- Medial femoral circumflex
- Lateral femoral circumflex
- First perforating branch of the profunda femoris artery

4.3 Surgical approaches to the hip joint

Learning point

- Anterior approach (Smith–Petersen)
- Anterolateral approach (Watson–Jones)
- Direct lateral approach (modified Hardinge)
- Posterior approach (Moore or Southern approach)

The direct lateral and posterior approaches are most commonly used – and asked about in the exam.

Anterior approach (Smith–Petersen)

This approaches the joint through the internervous interval between sartorius and tensor fascia latae. Rectus femoris is detached to arrive at the anterior joint capsule. Tensor fascia latae and anterior parts of gluteus medius may be detached from the pelvis to improve access to the acetabulum.

- **Structures at risk:** lateral femoral cutaneous nerve, femoral nerve, ascending branch of lateral femoral circumflex artery
- **Common applications:** open reduction in DDH; biopsy; (less commonly) arthroplasty

Anterolateral approach (Watson–Jones)

This approaches the joint between tensor fascia latae and gluteus medius. Detaching the anterior portion of gluteus medius from its femoral insertion improves access to the femoral shaft and acetabulum.

- **Structures at risk:** femoral nerve (mostly commonly compression neuropraxia from misplaced retractors)
- **Common applications:** total hip replacement and hemiarthroplasty; open reduction of proximal femoral fractures

Direct lateral approach (modified Hardinge)

This is a lateral incision over the greater trochanter in the line of the femur (one handbreadth above, one below). The fascia latae is incised and split in the line of its fibres and the retractor inserted. The gluteal bursa is swept away. The anterior tendon of gluteus medius and vastus lateralis is divided (keeping continuity between the two), leaving a cuff on the trochanter to allow repair. Vastus lateralis may be split distally, but beware of splitting gluteus medius too far proximally (>3 cm) – the superior gluteal nerve is about 4 cm above the tip of the trochanter. Lift cut edge of gluteus medius and vastus lateralis anteriorly with the retractor showing the anterior hip capsule.

- **Common applications:** total hip replacement; hemiarthroplasty

Posterior approach (Moore or Southern approach)

The patient is placed in lateral decubitus with the hip in slight flexion. Lateral incision is made over the greater trochanter in the line of the femur (one handbreadth above the greater trochanter, one below). The fascia latae is incised and split in the line of its fibres. The middle of gluteus maximus is split in the line of its fibres. The retractor is placed under the posterior free edge of gluteus medius and the fat is swept away to expose the short external rotators (piriformis, obturator internus and the gemelli). A stay suture is placed in the short external rotators (for retraction and to allow repair at closure) which are then divided at their femoral attachments to expose the capsule. The sciatic nerve is retracted medially and protected by turning the cut ends of piriformis, obturator internus and gemelli backwards over the nerve. The capsule is opened and the hip dislocated by internally rotating the leg.

- **Structures at risk:** sciatic nerve (most commonly caught by the deep blades of the hip retractor [Charnley bow])
- **Common applications:** total hip replacement; open washout of septic arthritis; removal of loose bodies; open reduction and internal fixation of posterior acetabular fractures

CHAPTER 9

4.4 Clinical assessment of the hip joint

History

Pain, site and severity (groin? trochanter? back? buttock? thigh? knee?). Knee and spinal problems? Trouble with sitting? Trouble with stairs? Trouble with socks and shoes?

Clinical examination

Standing, trousers, shoes and socks off (don't forget to examine the spine!)

Look:

Observe walking gait:
- *From the front*
  - Pelvic tilting?
  - Quad muscle wasting
  - Rotational deformity
- *From behind*
  - Gluteal muscle wasting
  - Scoliosis?
  - Sinus or scars
- *From the side*
  - Lumbar lordosis
  - Scars

Lie patient down to assess for shortening:
- True length
- Apparent length
- Femur or tibia shortened? Flex knees to see

Feel:
- Greater trochanter
- Head of femur
- Adductor longus origin
- Lesser trochanter

Move:

Thomas' test for fixed flexion deformity/extension
- Hand behind lumbar spine
- Flex good hip fully (knee to abdomen)
- Does lumbar spine flatten and bad hip stay on bed? No fixed flexion deformity
- Does affected hip rise from the bed? Fixed flexion deformity (loss of extension)

Assess flexion

Assess abduction and adduction (in extension)

Assess internal and external rotation (at 90°)

Trendelenberg's test
- Kneel in front of standing patient
- Place your hands on anterior superior iliac spines
- Ask patient to place hands on your forearms (this allows you to watch the pelvis, to keep him or her steady, and to assess how much weight he or she needs for support on each side)
- Ask the patient to stand on the bad leg
- Does the pelvis drop on the opposite side? Test positive

Summary of findings and differential diagnosis

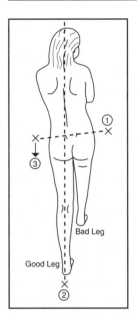

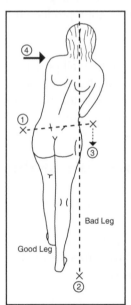

Figure 9.5a Normal or negative Trendelenberg's test. Hip is higher on the side of the lifted leg (1). Centre of gravity is over the supporting leg (2). When standing on a healthy leg, the hip abductors (gluteus medius and minimus) of the supporting leg contract to pull the pelvis down on that side (3). The pelvis is tilted so that the opposite hip is lifted (1) and the centre of gravity is brought over the supporting leg (2) so that the patient can hold steady for 30 seconds

Figure 9.5b Abnormal or positive Trendelenberg's test. Hip is not higher on the side of the lifted leg (1), or position cannot be held for 30 seconds. When standing on the affected hip, the hip abductors of the supporting leg fail to pull the pelvis down on that side (3). The opposite hip cannot be lifted (1). Do not allow the patient's upper body to tilt in compensation (4). The centre of gravity will fall outside the supporting leg if the opposite hip does not drop, so a positive Trendelenberg's test is either the opposite hip falling below the horizontal (1) or inability of the patient to hold the position

Figure 9.6 Reasons for a positive Trendelenberg's test. (1) Pain arising in the hip joint inhibiting the gluteal muscles. (2) Gluteal paralysis or weakness from polio or a muscle-wasting disease. (3) Gluteal inefficiency from coxa vara. (4) Gluteal inefficiency from congenital dislocation (developmental dysplasia) of the hip. (5) Not shown. False positive due to pain, generalised weakness, poor cooperation or bad balance (10% of patients)

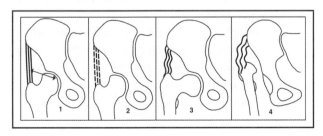

CHAPTER 9

4.5 Osteoarthritis of the hip joint

Learning point

Osteoarthritis of the hip may develop in a relatively young adult as a sequel of development dysplasia, Perthes' disease, previous sepsis or injury. In the older patient it may be secondary to rheumatoid arthritis, avascular necrosis or Paget's disease. When no underlying cause is present it is referred to as primary osteoarthritis (OA). The incidence peaks in the sixth decade, and it is usually bilateral. OA of the hip causes pain and restricted movement. Hip OA should be treated with conservative measures. If these measures fail the patient may require a hip replacement (arthroplasty).

Symptoms of osteoarthritis of the hip

The main complaint is pain – into the groin descending down the thigh. Patients may experience pain round the hip area, into the lower back; it is important to differentiate this from lumbar pathology. Stiffness can be a problem but it is not usually as marked as with knee OA. Patients are unable to cut their toenails and put on socks and shoes as the range of movement decreases.

Signs of osteoarthritis of the hip

These include:
- Antalgic gait
- Muscle wasting
- Marked restrictions of movements (internal rotation is the first to be affected)
- Shortening of the leg – either true (erosion of the acetabulum or collapse of the femoral head) or false (fixed flexion deformity)

Investigating osteoarthritis of the hip

OA of the hip may be diagnosed on the basis of the history and examination and confirmed by a plain radiograph of the pelvis (request 'AP pelvis for hips'). There is loss of joint space, osteophytes are seen around the margin of the joint, and there is sclerosis and erosion to the head of the femur and acetabulum. Consider other causes of groin pain (such as degenerate lumbar spine disease or nerve root compression) if movement of the hip does not reproduce the pain.

If the hip joint appears relatively well preserved on the plain radiographs, a diagnostic local anaesthetic (LA) injection can help to confirm or exclude the hip as the pain generator.

Managing osteoarthritis of the hip

Osteoarthritis of any joint can be treated along the following lines:
- Reduce load across the joint
- Strengthen muscles acting across the joint
- Give appropriate analgesia

In the case of the hip these things can be achieved by:
- Weight loss, modification of lifestyle and walking aids (which can reduce the load on the lower limbs by around 7 kg)
- Targeted physiotherapy
- Appropriate analgesia

Surgical treatment is indicated when non-surgical treatment has been tried but failed, and when there are significant ongoing symptoms of pain.

Surgical options for osteoarthritis of the hip

> ### Learning point
>
> The ideal examination answer to the question of surgical options includes a mention of both arthrodesis (fusion of the hip joint which is now seldom used) and osteotomy realignment of the articular surface, which may be used in selected young patients.

Total hip replacement (THR, or low-friction arthroplasty) was developed by Sir John Charnley at Wrightington in the early 1960s. It is the gold standard treatment and is highly effective.

The original (Charnley) THR consisted of a solid metal femoral prosthesis articulating with a high-density polyethylene cup. Both components were 'grouted' into place using acrylic bone cement (methylmethacrylate). This cement transmits the load from the prosthesis to the bone.

There was an explosion of competing designs, not all of which were successful. After the well-published controversy of the 3M hip replacement, there are now guidelines issued by NICE, recommending that surgeons should select a design that has 10-year follow-up with 90% survival (or if the design is less than 10 years old, that it has 3-year data which are consistent with 90% survival at 10 years).

Modern total hip replacement (THR) design

Cemented vs uncemented: the indications, surgical approach and longevity of both types are similar. Uncemented hips avoid the problems of cement loosening but will fail in different ways. There is no clear advantage of one type over the other and both are widely used.

Modular vs monoblock: modern designs of both cemented and uncemented hips are modular in design (eg a separate interchangeable head, stem and cup). This allows independent adjustment of factors such as neck length and offset, which ensures optimal soft-tissue tension and stability. Monoblock stems (combined head and stem) do not allow this flexibility.

Metal-on-polyethylene: the majority of modern total hip replacements still consist of a cobalt chrome femoral prosthesis and a polyethylene bearing acetabular cup.

Ceramic-on-polyethylene: ceramic (femoral heads) on polyethylene (acetabular cups) may give longer survival of the hip and are often used in younger patients.

Metal-on-metal: the 'resurfacing' hips and some traditional total hip replacement designs have a metal-(femoral head)-on-metal (acetabular cup) bearing. There are some concerns about wear and long-term metal ion toxicity with these designs.

Hip resurfacing: the patient's own femoral neck and head is spared and simply resurfaced with a metal cap. The acetabulum is resurfaced with a metal cup. One manufacturer has recently withdrawn its prosthesis because of high early failure rates. There is concern that this prosthesis design may give rise to high circulating levels of chromium. A florid inflammatory response has been reported in a significant number of patients.

CHAPTER 9

There is a well-documented risk of sepsis during the procedure and prophylactic antibiotics should be given in all cases. The rates of late sepsis are approximately 1%. The prosthesis may be saved in an acute infection if the infection is treated aggressively. Chronic infection is harder to 'cure' and it is likely that the prosthesis will have to be removed. Other complications include dislocation, periprosthetic fractures and aseptic loosening.

A failed THR can be revised. The rate of complications is higher for revisions than for primary arthroplasty. Modified cups, long-stemmed femoral components and bone graft can all be used to reconstruct the hip.

A failed revision can itself be revised but in some cases Girdlestone's (excision arthroplasty) procedure may be the only option. Girdlestone's procedure results in the formation of a pseudarthrosis at the hip joint. The leg is short and externally rotated. Considerable energy (and physical fitness) is required to mobilise after this procedure.

4.6   Other hip disorders

Rheumatoid arthritis of the hip

Rheumatoid arthritis usually affects the hip in the late stages of the disease. The hip joint becomes painful and stiff. A total hip arthroplasty is appropriate if non-surgical measures fail.

Avascular necrosis of the hip

See Fractures, Chapter 6, Trauma. AVN is treated by reducing the load across the joint, surgical revascularisation or arthroplasty.

'Clicking hips'

The snapping hip (coxa saltans)

- Snapping iliotibial band: the posterior iliotibial band snaps over the greater trochanter
- Snapping psoas: the iliopsoas snaps over the iliopectineal eminence

These are both treated by stretching the offending structure and rarely require surgical intervention.

Femoral acetabular impingement

Acetabular labral tears or loose bodies

- Labral tears or loose bodies can give rise to a painful clunk in the hip
- These can be evaluated using contrast MR arthography and treated by hip arthroscopy

Trochanteric bursitis

- Painful inflammation of the bursa over the greater trochanter. Patients often attribute this to the hip joint itself and may be convinced that they have osteoarthritis of the hip (they may be correct – they may have this as well)
- The pain is usually well localised, and exacerbated by lying on the side, especially at night
- Treatment is with physiotherapy, stretching, and avoidance of repetitive activity
- The diagnosis may be confirmed with ultrasonography or MRI
- There may be a role for steroid and local anaesthetic injections

Metabolic bone disorders

Covered in Section 3; they have specific implications for the hip joint.

- **Osteomalacia:** can cause insufficiency fractures of the femoral neck
- **Osteoporosis:** causes hip fractures in elderly people
- **Paget's disease:** may lead to osteoarthritis of the hip. Surgical total hip replacement may result in increased bleeding if done while the Paget's is active

3.7 Anatomy of the thigh

Learning point

The thigh is surrounded by a thick fascial sheath attaching to the inguinal ligament and bony pelvis, and descending to attach to the tibia, fibula and patella. The lateral side is condensed to form the iliotibial tract. The iliotibial tract is the insertion of the tensor fasciae latae and the insertion of part of gluteus maximus. The deep fascia penetrates the muscle and joins on to the linea aspera of the femur to divide the thigh into three compartments, each with its own muscles, nerves and arteries.

Compartments of the thigh

Compartment	Muscles	Artery	Nerve
Anterior	Iliacus Psoas Pectineus Sartorius Quadriceps femoris	Femoral artery	Femoral nerve
Medial	Adductors Gracilis Obturator externus	Profunda femoris artery and obturator artery	Obturator nerve
Posterior	Biceps femoris Semimembranosus Semitendinosus Small part of adductor magnus	Profunda femoris artery	Sciatic nerve

Femoral triangle

The femoral triangle is an important area containing:

- The femoral nerve and its branches
- The femoral sheath, the femoral artery and its branches
- The femoral vein and its tributaries
- The deep inguinal lymph nodes

The boundaries of the triangle are:

- Superiorly – inguinal ligament
- Laterally – sartorius muscle
- Medially – adductor longus muscle

The apex of the femoral triangle (which lies inferiorly) is the beginning of the adductor canal.

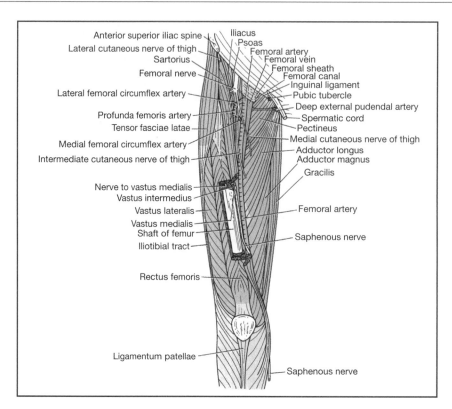

Figure 9.7 Femoral triangle and adductor canal in the right lower limb

The floor of the triangle consists of:
- Iliacus (most lateral)
- Psoas tendon
- Pectineus
- Adductor longus (most medial)

The neurovascular structures enter the femoral triangle in the order of:
- Nerve
- Artery
- Vein
- Canal

The artery, vein and canal lie within the femoral sheath. The femoral nerve is outside the femoral sheath.

For further details of the femoral sheath and femoral canal, see 'Abdominal wall and hernias' in Chapter 1, Book 2.

Adductor canal

The adductor canal is an intermuscular cleft on the medial aspect of the middle third of the thigh. It contains the:
- Terminal part of the femoral artery
- Femoral vein
- Deep lymph vessels
- Saphenous nerve
- Nerve to vastus medialis
- Terminal part of the obturator nerve

The adductor canal starts at the apex of the femoral triangle and continues down the thigh to a hiatus in adductor magnus, which allows vessels and nerve to enter the popliteal fossa. The adductor canal has three walls:
- Laterally the vastus medialis
- Posteriorly adductor longus and magnus
- Anteromedially some fibrous tissue deep to sartorius

SECTION 5

The knee

5.1 Anatomy of the knee joint

> **Learning point**
>
> The knee is a modified synovial hinge joint, allowing extension, flexion and a small amount of rotation. The articular surfaces are covered with hyaline cartilage. The joint involves three bones: the tibia, femur and patella. The fibula is not involved with articulation. The articular surface contributes only a little to the overall stability of the knee. The cruciate and collateral ligaments give considerable stability to the knee. The menisci increase the area of contact across the joint. Dynamic stability of the knee is provided by a combination of muscular and ligamentous action across the joint.

Movement of the knee

The knee joint's main movements are flexion and extension. The main muscles that contribute to the movement of the knee joint are:
- Extension: quadriceps femoris
- Flexion: hamstring, gastrocnemius, sartorius
- Rotation: popliteus

Ligaments of the knee

Cruciate ligament	Arises	Inserts into
Anterior cruciate ligament	Anterior intercondylar area of tibia	Lateral femoral condyle in the intercondylar notch
Posterior cruciate ligament	Posterior intercondylar area of tibia	Medial femoral condyle in the intercondylar notch

Each ligament has two main bundles of fibres which differentially slacken and tighten as the knee goes through its range of motion. Remember the acronym '**A BUL**l in a field' which stands for:

Anterior goes **B**ackwards, **U**pwards and **L**aterally.

Collateral ligaments
- The **medial collateral ligament** (MCL) arises from the medial femoral epicondyle and runs to the tibial surface. There are superficial and deep portions. The deep MCL has an attachment to the medial meniscus

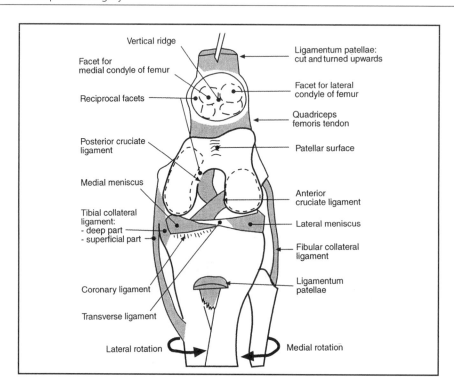

Figure 9.8 Anatomy of the left knee

Vertical ridge

Facet for medial condyle of femur

Reciprocal facets

Posterior cruciate ligament

Medial meniscus

Tibial collateral ligament:
- deep part
- superficial part

Coronary ligament

Transverse ligament

Lateral rotation

Ligamentum patellae: cut and turned upwards

Facet for lateral condyle of femur

Quadriceps femoris tendon

Patellar surface

Anterior cruciate ligament

Lateral meniscus

Fibular collateral ligament

Ligamentum patellae

Medial rotation

- The **lateral collateral ligament** runs from the lateral epicondyle and attaches to the head of the fibula. There is no lateral meniscal attachment

Menisci of the knee
- There are two crescent-shaped fibrocartilage components in the knee joint. They increase the contact area at the knee, reducing the force per unit area. (The contact area between the relatively flat tibia and convex femur would be very small were it not for the menisci)
- The **medial meniscus** is the larger and is attached to the anterior and posterior intercondylar areas of the tibia. It attaches to the capsule and the MCL
- The **lateral meniscus** is more mobile than the medial. This mobility is important because the femur internally rotates over the tibia as the knee locks in full extension.

This 'locking' (which is not the same as pathological locking) increases the stability of the knee joint in full extension and allows quadriceps to relax when standing – thus saving energy
- In full extension popliteus has a role in pulling the lateral tibial plateau forwards under the femur, thus externally rotating the femur above the tibia, unlocking the knee and allowing flexion

Bursae of the knee
There are three bursae that communicate with the knee joint. If there is injury to the knee these bursae may swell and become palpable. They are the:
- Suprapatellar bursa
- Bursa deep to the medial head of gastrocnemius
- Popliteus bursa

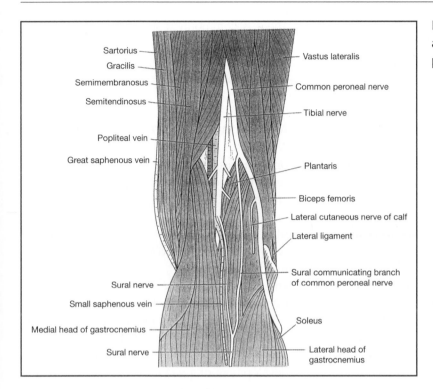

Figure 9.9 Boundaries and contents of the right popliteal fossa

An additional bursa lies deep to the lateral head of gastrocnemius. It can (but does not always) communicate with the knee joint.

The prepatellar bursa and infrapatellar bursa do not communicate with the joint and lie in front of the patella and tibial tuberosity, respectively. They may become inflamed, leading to housemaid's knee or clergyman's knee.

The bursa under the pes anserinus (sartorius, gracilis and semitendinosus insertion) may also become inflamed.

The popliteal fossa

The popliteal fossa is a diamond-shaped space at the back of the knee. Its boundaries are:
- Roof:
  - Skin
  - Superficial fascia
  - Deep fascia of the thigh
- Floor:
  - Femur
  - Posterior ligament of knee joint
  - Popliteus
- Laterally:
  - Biceps femoris
  - Lateral head of gastrocnemius
  - Plantaris
- Medially:
  - Semimembranosus
  - Semitendinosus
  - Medial head of gastrocnemius

> **Contents of the popliteal fossa**
> - Popliteal artery and its branches
> - Popliteal vein
> - Small saphenous vein
> - Common peroneal nerve
> - Tibial nerve
> - Posterior cutaneous nerve of the thigh
> - Genicular branches of the obturator nerve
> - Connective tissue
> - Lymph nodes

The deepest and the most medial structure is the artery, with the vein overlying it. The common peroneal, tibial and sural nerves are the most superficial. The popliteal artery provides branches (geniculate) to the knee and divides into anterior and posterior terminal arteries.

5.2 Surgical approaches to the knee joint

> **Learning point**
>
> - Medial parapatellar approach
> - Medial meniscectomy approach
> - Posterior approach

Medial parapatellar approach

Make a longitudinal skin incision, either in the midline or skirting the medial border of the patella. Open the joint from the medial border of the quadriceps tendon, skirting the medial side of the patella and patellar tendon (leaving a cuff of tissue for repair).

This gives unrivalled exposure of the whole joint and is used for total knee joint replacement surgery.

There is commonly a small area of numbness, regardless of where the skin incision is sited. There is an argument for siting the skin incision away from areas that are loaded when kneeling.

Medial meniscectomy approach

A much more restricted approach is used for open access to the medial meniscus, now seldom used thanks to the development of arthroscopy.

Make an incision from the medial border of the patella, heading downwards and posteriorly, roughly parallel with the medial edge of the articular surface of the medial femoral condyle. Care must be taken not to extend the incision more than 1 cm below the upper margin of the tibia, because the infrapatellar branch of the saphenous nerve is at risk. This can lead to the development of a painful neuroma. If the nerve is damaged the ends should be buried deep in the fat. The area of anaesthesia produced is not usually troublesome.

Posterior approach

This approach exposes the back of the joint capsule and is used in only a few selected cases. It involves dissecting the tibial nerve from semimembranosus, then displacing the nerve and popliteal vessels laterally and detaching the medial head of gastrocnemius from its origin. The head is also displaced laterally to protect the neurovascular bundle while exposing the joint capsule.

- **Superficial structures to avoid:** small saphenous vein, posterior femoral cutaneous nerve, medial sural cutaneous nerve
- **Deep structures to avoid:** tibial nerve, popliteal vein, popliteal artery, common peroneal nerve

Procedure box: Approaches for knee procedures

Aspiration or injection of the knee joint

- Patient is supine and relaxed, knee in full extension (contracted quadriceps makes procedure difficult for you and painful for the patient)
- Clean whole anterior aspect of the knee (eg chlorhexidine)
- Needle entry point may be medial or lateral, proximal to the superior patella pole, to enter suprapatellar pouch

Arthroscopy

- Under general anaesthesia, prepare and drape knee
- Elevate and exsanguinate and inflate tourniquet
- Check equipment before commencing
- Identify soft triangle lateral to patellar tendon, above lateral plateau and below patella
- Identify point one (small) finger-breadth above joint line
- Make horizontal or vertical incision, tip of knife aiming towards intercondylar notch (and keeping blade away from patellar tendon or lateral meniscus)
- Insert trocar and arthroscope
- Begin fluid irrigation once inside the joint
- The medial portal is sited in a similar manner – the arthroscope may be used to do this under direct vision

5.3 Clinical assessment of the knee joint

History

Pain, site and severity. Swelling? Locking? Giving way? Trouble with stairs? Kneeling and squatting difficulties?

Clinical examination

- Standing, trousers, shoes and socks off
- Then lying supine on couch

Look

- Assessment of walking gait
- Symmetry, swelling, scars, quads wasting

Feel

- Is it tender?
- Temperature
- Extensor apparatus – quads tendon, patella, patellar tendon, tibial tubercle
- Effusion – stroke test, patellar tap
- Collateral ligaments
- Joint line
- Popliteal fossa

Move

- Active and passive flexion and extension

Assessment of ligamentous stability

- Collateral (varus and valgus stress test)
- Cruciates (anterior drawer/Lachman's test, posterior sag)

continued oveleaf

- Pivot shift test: tests ability of ACL to prevent impingement of lateral tibial plateau on lateral femoral condyle. Begin with the knee in extension. Internally rotate the tibia (by dorsiflexing the foot to lock the ankle and using the foot to control rotation). Apply valgus stress by pressure over the lateral side of the leg distal to the knee. This will force the lateral tibial plateau in front of the lateral femoral condyle if ACL is deficient. As the knee is flexed, the tibia will suddenly move back to its normal position. Extending from a flexed position will reverse this process. The pivot shift test is painful and risks further damage to the menisci and so should be done once only

Assessment of menisci

- McMurray's test – pain or clicking

Patellar stability

- Apprehension test

Summary of findings and differential diagnosis

Learning point

Common pathologies affecting the knee
- Osteoarthritis
- Soft tissue injuries
- Ligaments
- Menisci
- Extensor apparatus
- Rheumatoid arthritis
- Paget's disease
- Spontaneous osteonecrosis of the knee (SONK)

Childhood disorders
- Anterior knee pain
- Patellar instability
- Osgood–Schlatter disease
- Discoid lateral meniscus
- Osteochondritis dissecans of the knee
- Genu varum/valgum
- Sinding–Larsen–Johansson syndrome
- Rickets

5.4   Osteoarthritis of the knee joint

Learning point

As with any joint, the knee can be affected by either secondary OA (where cause is known, eg trauma) or primary. Medial compartmental OA is more common than lateral OA. Asymmetrical degeneration may lead to deformity and abnormal loading through the joint, which in turn accelerates the degenerative process.

Clinical presentation of OA of the knee

The history and signs of knee OA are very similar to those of the hip or any other joint.
- Pain and stiffness that improves with exercise
- A limp and varus (occasionally valgus) deformity
- Reduced range of movement
- Swelling (effusion)
- Crepitus
- Osteophytes and synovial thickening

Investigating OA of the knee

The most useful investigation for establishing if there is OA is the plain radiograph. If there is suggestion that there may be patellofemoral OA, a skyline view may also be requested. Looking at a plain radiograph of an OA knee, there will be:

- Loss of joint space
- Osteophytes
- Periarticular sclerosis
- Bone cysts

Treatment of OA of the knee

Conservative management

This is the first-line treatment, including simple analgesia, walking aids and physiotherapy.

Joint injections

Second-line treatment may include steroid injections to relieve the symptoms, but these are often effective only for a short while. Some patients derive benefit from viscosupplementation (injections of artificial synovial fluid-type material).

Surgery

The third line of treatment is surgery:

- **Arthroscopy:** indicated for patients with true mechanical symptoms (locking and giving way) because these are likely to be due to degenerate meniscal tears or flaps and will respond to debridement. Also useful for removing loose bodies
- **Chondrocyte transplantation:** this technique is still in the experimental stage. It is suitable only for small, well-contained lesions (thus excluding the vast majority of patients with OA of the knee). Chondrocytes can be grown in culture or cartilage taken

with a bone plug from non-articular areas

- **Arthrodesis:** very rarely used because it is very disabling
- **Osteotomy:** used for young patients with unicompartmental disease. Distal femoral osteotomy or (more commonly) high tibial osteotomy can be used to realign the weight-bearing axis of the limb, shifting the line of force away from the affected compartment to the unaffected compartment
- **Replacement arthroplasty:** if all other therapies fail

Knee arthroplasty

Knee arthroplasty may replace only the affected compartment (eg unicompartmental knee replacement or patellofemoral replacement) or the whole of the tibiofemoral articulation. The total knee replacement (TKR) is misnamed because the patella is often not resurfaced during a TKR.

Arthroplasty should be considered only when non-surgical measures have failed, and the patient's quality of life is dramatically reduced due to pain (especially at night), stiffness and immobility.

As with any surgery to the lower limb, careful consideration must be given to patients with a history of steroid use, diabetes or peripheral vascular disease (PVD). Non-healing wounds can be disastrous, especially if the prosthesis becomes infected.

The large volume of the knee and its relatively superficial location mean that patients can experience some discomfort for 6–12 weeks following arthroplasty. This is in contrast to THR, where pain seems to settle very quickly.

CHAPTER 9

SECTION 6

Disorders of the foot and ankle

6.1 Anatomy of the lower leg

Peripheral nerves of the lower limb

Before the anatomy of the foot can be discussed it is important to consider the common peroneal nerve and the tibial nerve (which are the peripheral nerves of the lower limb). Many of the muscles they innervate exert their actions on the foot.

Common peroneal nerve

The smaller terminal branch of the sciatic nerve.

Motor distribution of the common peroneal nerve

Muscles of the anterior compartment of the leg are supplied by deep branches of the common peroneal nerve:

- Tibialis anterior
- Extensor hallucis longus
- Extensor digitorum longus
- Peroneus tertius
- Extensor digitorum brevis

Muscles of the peroneal (lateral) compartment of the leg are supplied by superficial branches of the peroneal nerve:

- Peroneus brevis
- Peroneus longus

The common peroneal nerve also supplies the extensor digitorum brevis in the foot.

Sensory distribution of the common peroneal nerve

- First web space (deep peroneal branch)
- Dorsum of foot, anterior and lateral side of lower limb (superficial peroneal branch)

Mechanisms of injury to the common peroneal nerve

- Fracture of fibula neck (eg direct blow to leg)
- Lateral ligament injuries of knee
- Pressure from plaster casts

Classic peroneal nerve injury

- Loss of anterior (deep) and lateral (superficial) leg muscles

- Loss of ankle and foot dorsiflexion and toe extension (foot drop)
- High-stepping gait to ensure plantarflexed foot clears the ground
- The foot is of normal appearance

Test for peroneal nerve

- Dorsiflexion against resistance, (deep branch)
- Evert foot against resistance (superficial branch)

Tibial nerve

The larger terminal branch of the sciatic nerve.

Motor distribution of the tibial nerve

- Soleus
- Tibialis posterior
- Flexor hallucis longus
- Flexor digitorum longus
- Plantaris
- Popliteus
- Gastrocnemius
- All the muscles of the sole of the foot (via the division of the tibial nerve into medial and lateral plantar nerves)

Sensory distribution of the tibial nerve

- Sole of foot
- Nail beds
- Distal phalanges
- Lateral foot and little toe skin

Note that the lateral side of the foot is supplied by the sural nerve (single cutaneous branch from tibial nerve).

Mechanism of injury to the tibial nerve

- Tibial shaft fracture
- Compartment syndrome of posterior calf
- Tight plasters
- Injuries posterior to medial malleolus
- Injuries involving tarsal tunnel

Classic tibial nerve injury

- Loss of ankle and toe flexors
- Clawing of toes
- Trophic ulceration
- Shuffling gait as the take-off phase of walking is impaired
- Muscle wasting in sole of foot
- Loss of sensation in sole of foot and distal phalanges
- Foot will be flat as the lateral longitudinal arch will have lost most of its principal supports and the medial longitudinal arch is compromised by the loss of tibialis posterior (see Section 6.5, Tibialis posterior insufficiency)

Test for tibial nerve

- Toe flexion
- Sensation on sole

6.2 Anatomy of the ankle joint

The ankle is a hinge joint (ginglymus). It is formed by the distal fibula and tibia which articulate with the body of the talus. The tibia and fibula are firmly bound together at the syndesmosis by the anterior and posterior tibofibular ligaments and the interosseous membrane. The ankle joint capsule is relatively capacious anteriorly and posteriorly, allowing movement. The capsule is reinforced laterally and medially by ligaments. The ankle may be dorsiflexed and plantarflexed. The body of the talus is wider anteriorly and in

CHAPTER 9

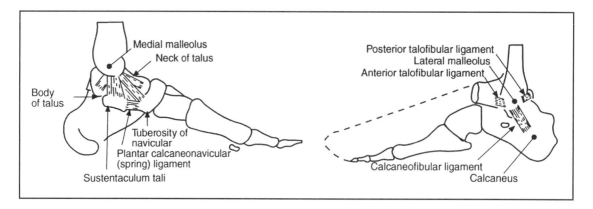

Figure 9.10 Anatomy of the ankle

full dorsiflexion it becomes firmly constrained between the malleoli, with the fibula slightly displaced laterally. In plantarflexion a greater degree of movement is possible between the talus and malleoli, so the ankle is more susceptible to injury in this position. This is because the talus is narrower posteriorly.

The principal ligaments that provide stability are:

- **Inferior tibiofibular ligaments** (anterior and posterior): these attach the fibula to the tibia, along with a weak interosseous membrane
- **Lateral ligament:** this originates from the fibula and consists of three parts – distally, the anterior and posterior slips attach to the talus and the central slip attaches to the calcaneus; this is the most common ligament to be torn
- **Medial ligament** (deltoid ligament): this is triangular in shape and extremely strong. It originates from the medial malleolus. Distally its deep fibres attach to the medial surface of the talus and the superficial fibres attach to the navicular, spring ligament and calcaneus. The medial ligament is seldom torn

6.3   Anatomy of the foot

On standing, the prominence of the heel is aligned with the tibia. The calcaneus and the first and fifth metatarsal heads form a tripod. The forefoot is connected to the hindfoot by the midtarsal joint, which is formed by the calcaneocuboid joint (medially) and the talonavicular joint (laterally). When the foot is in the plantigrade position, the axis of rotation of both the calcaneocuboid joint and the talonavicular joint align, and the foot is relatively flexible across the midtarsal joint. As the foot is plantarflexed, the heel goes into varus (inverts). These movements are coupled due to the morphology of the subtalar joint. As the heel (and calcaneus) moves into varus, the orientation of the axis of the calcaneocuboid joint moves out of line from the axis of the talonavicular joint. As the axis of these joints moves out of line, the midfoot will become relatively stiff.

The arches of the foot

Medial longitudinal arch (most important)

The bony components of the medial longitudinal arch are:

- Calcaneus

- Talus
- Navicular
- Cuneiforms
- Medial three metatarsals

> **Principal supports of the medial longitudinal arch:**
> - Spring ligament (plantar calcaneonavicular ligament): supports head of talus
> - Plantar fascia: acts as a tie by means of its attachments to the heel and metatarsal heads
> - Abductor hallucis and flexor digitorum brevis (spring ties)
> - Tibialis anterior: elevates arch and with peroneus longus forms a supporting sling
> - Tibialis posterior: adducts midtarsal joint and reinforces the action of the spring ligament
> - Flexor hallucis longus

Flattening of the medial longitudinal arch is common (pes planus).

Lateral longitudinal arch

Bony components:
- Calcaneus
- Cuboid
- Fourth and fifth metatarsals

Shallow, flattens on weight bearing.

> **Principal supports of the lateral longitudinal arch:**
> - Long and short plantar ligaments
> - Plantar fascia
> - Flexor digitorum brevis
> - Flexor digiti minimi
> - Abductor digiti minimi
> - Peroneus tertius
> - Peroneus brevis

Anterior arch

The anterior arch lies in the coronal plane and is present only in the non-weight-bearing foot.

The bony components of the arch are the metatarsal heads. Under a load the metatarsal heads flatten out and the arch disappears. The metatarsal heads are prevented from spreading out by the intermetatarsal ligaments and the intrinsic foot muscles.

Figure 9.11 Anatomy of the foot

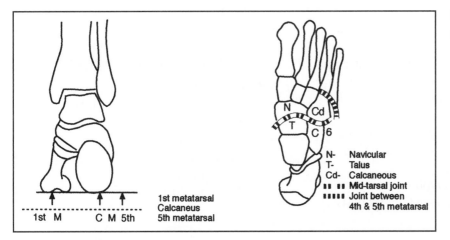

1st M   C M 5th
1st metatarsal
Calcaneus
5th metatarsal

N- Navicular
T- Talus
Cd- Calcaneous
▮▮ ▮▮ Mid-tarsal joint
▮▮▮▮▮ Joint between 4th & 5th metatarsal

CHAPTER 9

Intrinsic muscles of the foot

The intrinsic muscles of the foot play an important part in maintaining the shape of the foot. The interosseous and lumbrical muscles, through their attachment to the extensor expansions, extend the toes at the PIP and distal interphalangeal (DIP) joints. If they become weak, the unopposed flexor digitorum longus results in clawing of the toes.

6.4   Clinical assessment of the foot and ankle

History
- Pain, site and severity
- Swelling?
- Locking?
- Giving way?
- Trouble with stairs?
- Kneeling and squatting difficulties?

Clinical examination
- Standing, trousers, shoes and socks off
- Then lying supine on couch or sitting

Look

Standing
- Assessment of walking gait, note angle of foot during walking
- Legs, ankles, feet, arches, toes, obvious deformity – plantigrade foot (both heel and forefoot squarely on the floor), in-toeing, genu valgum, flat foot, eversion, inversion, splaying, proportion

Sitting
- Heel: exostosis, bursitis, talipes, old fracture
- Dorsum: exostosis from fifth metacarpal head or base, cuneiform exostosis, dorsal ganglion; check dorsalis pedis pulse
- Big toe: hallux valgus, bunion, gout, hallux rigidus, hallux flexus; callus underneath?
- Toenails: onchogryphosis, subungal exostosis, fungal infection, psoriasis
- Toes: length, clawing, hammer toe, mallet toe, quinti varus, corns
- Sole: hyperhidrosis, athlete's foot, ulcers, callus, verruca, plantar fasciitis

Feel

Tenderness
- Heel (Sever's disease, exostosis, fasciitis, bursitis, pes cavus)
- Forefoot
- Medial malleolus (tarsal tunnel syndrome)
- Big toe

Joint crepitations

Temperature

Move

Ankle joint
- Hold the shin still and grip the whole heel
- Move the foot
- There should be:
  - Plantarflexion (55° from right angle)
  - Dorsiflexion (15° from right angle)

Subtalar joint
- Hold the ankle still and grip the lower heel
- Move the heel
- There should be:
  - Inversion (10°)
  - Eversion (20°)

continued opposite

CHAPTER 9

Forefoot (midtarsal and tarsometatarsal)

- Hold the heel still and grip the forefoot
- There should be:
  - Inversion (15°)
  - Eversion (10°)
- Now check plantar and dorsal flexion of the first, fifth and third metatarsophalangeal joints
- Finally get the patient to curl the toes, then extend them

Examine the ligaments of the ankle and foot

There are three main ligaments round the ankle:

- **Lateral ligament** from fibula to talus and calcaneus
  - Feel for it below the lateral malleolus
  - Test for it by forcibly inverting the foot – if lax it will open up

- **Medial (deltoid) ligament** from the tibia to the talus, navicular, calcaneus and spring ligament
  - Very strong
  - Rarely torn without a fracture
- **Inferior tibiofibular ligament**
  - Feel for it just above the joint line on the dorsal surface of the ankle between the fibula and tibia
  - Test for it by dorsiflexing the foot (will produce pain) and trying to move the talus laterally (will displace laterally if ligament is disrupted)

Summary of findings and differential diagnosis

6.5 Other disorders of the foot and ankle

Claw toes

Clawing of toes results from a weakness of the interosseous and lumbrical muscles, which normally extend the PIP and DIP joints of the toes and flex the metatarsophalangeal (MTP) joint by their attachment to the extensor expansions. The unopposed action of flexor digitorum longus results in clawing via flexion of the DIP and PIP joints. When standing, the toe pads do not contact the ground so the weight-bearing forces are transmitted through the metatarsal heads, which are in a state of hyperextension. The results of this downward pressure are pain and callosity of the skin of the sole. Callosities form on the dorsal aspect of the toes due to their prominence in their flexed state.

Causes of claw toes

- Idiopathic
- Pes cavus
- Hallux valgus
- Poor footwear (eg high heels)
- Rheumatoid arthritis
- Underlying neurological abnormality – check the spine!

CHAPTER 9

Treatment of claw toes

- Treat cause
- Exercises for the intrinsic muscles of the foot
- Insoles to relieve weight from the metatarsal heads
- Padding to callosity
- Surgical intervention: flexor to extensor tendon transfer; excision of metatarsal heads (effective only in rheumatoid arthritis); forefoot arthroplasty

Hammer toes

This affects the second, third and fourth toes and is characterised by hyperextension of the MTP and DIP joints and flexion of the PIP joint. It is associated with hallux valgus and overcrowding of toes (eg in pointed or small shoes). Callosities form over the bony prominence on the dorsum of the PIP joint and eventually adventitious bursae develop. Secondary contractions of tendons and ligaments can occur. There is pain beneath the metatarsal head due to pressure transmitted from the PIP joint.

Treatment of hammer toes

- Remove the cause
- Corrective splinting
- Arthrodesis of PIP joint with extensor tenotomy and dorsal capsulotomy of MTP joint

Mallet toe

This is a flexion deformity of the distal interphalangeal joint. It may cause nail problems or calluses. Treatment is with chiropody, joint fusion or amputation of the distal phalanx.

Joint	Claw toe	Hammer toe	Mallet toe
MTP	Extended	Extended	Normal
PIP	Flexed	Flexed	Normal
DIP	Flexed	Extended	Flexed

Pes cavus (claw foot)

This is characterised by abnormally high longitudinal arches, produced by an imbalance in the muscles controlling the maintenance and formation of the arches. The muscle imbalance is mostly between the peroneals and the extensor compartment, and weakness of the intrinsic muscles of the toes produces clawing.

The abnormal distribution of weight in the foot leads to extensive callosities forming under the metatarsal heads and the heel. The deformity becomes worse during the growth period. A neurological cause should always be sought – check the spine!

Neurological causes of pes cavus

- Poliomyelitis
- Spinocerebellar degenerative diseases (eg Friedreich's ataxia, peroneal muscular atrophy)
- Spastic diplegia

Treatment of pes cavus

- Symptomatic (eg insoles)
- Surgery (only if sufficient disability exists)
- Lengthening of Achilles' tendon
- Calcaneal osteotomy
- Flexor-to-extensor tendon transfers

Hallux valgus

Lateral deviation of the great toe may be exacerbated by wearing footwear that is too narrow for the forefoot. An abnormally broad forefoot is predisposed to this condition. An inherited short and varus first metatarsal may also contribute. Once the valgus position of the great toe has developed, it tends to progress due to the pull of the extensor and flexor hallucis longus which increase the deformity by a bowstring mechanism.

Complications of hallux valgus

- **An exostosis** on the medial aspect of the first metatarsal head – secondary to pressure on the periosteum
- **A bunion** (inflamed adventitious bursa) produced over the prominent head of the first metatarsal by pressure and friction
- **Osteoarthritis** of the first MTP joint secondary to malalignment of the proximal phalanx
- **Further lateral drift of the great toe** results in crowding of the other toes – the great toe may pass over the second toe or, more commonly, the second toe may over-ride it
- **A displaced second toe** may develop a painful callosity, later dislocating at the MTP joint
- **Dislocation of the second toe** is an indication for surgery even in young patients

The aim of surgery is to correct the deformity and maintain the function of the great toe. Treatment varies depending on the site and degree of deformity.

Treatment options for hallux valgus

Non-surgical options

- Modify footwear – soft shoes with a broad toe box

Surgical options

- **Mild to moderate deformity:** distal soft tissue realignment procedure with distal osteotomy of the first metatarsal and bunionectomy
- **Severe deformity:** distal osteotomies are limited in the correction that they can achieve, thus for greater deformity a shaft osteotomy or proximal osteotomy is required

Note that there are more than 100 described procedures for hallux valgus.

Hallux rigidus

- Osteoarthritis of the MTP joint of the great toe
- Can be primary but is mostly secondary
- More common in men.

There are two types:
- **Adolescent:** synovitis of MTP joint following injury (eg kicking football with toe); may develop osteochondritis dissecans of first metatarsal head
- **Adult:** osteoarthritis occasionally precip-itated by injury; painful, decreased movement secondary to destruction of articular surfaces and interlocking of osteophytes

CHAPTER 9

Treatment of hallux rigidus

- Stiff-soled shoes
- Manipulation under anaesthetic ± steroid injection
- Fusion of MTP joint

Metatarsalgia

This is pain under the metatarsal heads, often associated with splay foot – a widening of the foot at that level. It is the most common cause of forefoot pain, although other causes should be excluded. It typically occurs in middle-aged women and is associated with obesity, prolonged standing, flattened medial longitudinal arches, weak intrinsic muscles, claw toes and calluses on the sole. Shoe inserts and chiropody are the first lines of treatment.

Morton's neuroma

This is a plantar or digital neuroma commonly affecting the plantar nerve running between the third and fourth metatarsal heads to the third web space. Any of the other digital nerves can be affected, usually just before the bifurcation at the toe clefts. It causes piercing pain in the foot. It typically occurs in women aged between 25 and 45. It is diagnosed by history and examination, confirmed by ultrasonography or MRI and is treated by excision.

Tibialis posterior insufficiency

The tibialis posterior is the main muscle that supports the longitudinal arch of the foot. Tibialis posterior dysfunction is thought to be the major cause of acquired adult flat feet. Obesity, prolonged standing and degenerative change are also contributory. Secondary arthritis may follow. Weight loss, physiotherapy and arch supports are the mainstays of treatment.

Rheumatoid arthritis

Deformities seen in the rheumatoid foot include pes planus, splay foot, hallux valgus, claw toes, anterior metatarsalgia and hammer toes. Surgical shoes with moulded insoles may alleviate symptoms. Fowler's arthroplasty of all the MTP joints and reconstruction of the metatarsal weight-bearing pad is a surgical option for severe cases of RA foot.

6.6 The diabetic foot

Note that the diabetic foot is covered in Chapter 9 (Vascular Surgery), in Book 2, and much of the pathology is dealt with by vascular surgeons, but there are some implications for orthopaedic surgery of the lower limb. Surgery to the diabetic foot has a higher incidence of complications. Careful assessment of the vascularity, sensation and skin of the foot is required before surgery. Occult chronic infection in the foot may result in a higher rate of infection following any lower limb surgery, especially total hip or total knee replacement.

CHAPTER 9

SECTION 7

The shoulder and humerus

7.1   Anatomy of the shoulder joint

Learning point

Three joints
- Glenohumeral
- Scapulothoracic
- Acromioclavicular

Three bones
- Scapula
- Humerus
- Clavicle

Four ligaments
- Coracohumeral ligament
- Glenohumeral ligament
- Transverse humeral ligament
- Coracoacromial ligament

Five muscles
- Deltoid
- Subscapularis
- Supraspinatus ⎫
- Infraspinatus   ⎬ Rotator cuff
- Teres minor   ⎭

Five contributors to joint stability
- Glenoid labrum
- Rotator cuff muscles
- Coracoacromial arch
  - Coracoacromial ligament
  - Tip of acromion
  - Coracoid process of the scapula
- Long head of triceps
- Capsule and ligaments

Bones of the shoulder

The 'shoulder joint' is a complex arrangement of three joints: the glenohumeral, scapulothoracic and acromioclavicular joints. The coordinated movement of the humerus, scapula and clavicle allows a considerable range of movement, governed by a multitude of soft tissue and ligamentous insertions that constrain and direct the rotations and translations of these three joints. Hence, the shoulder joint is capable of every variety of movement: flexion, extension, abduction, adduction, circumduction and rotation.

The glenohumeral joint is a ball-and-socket joint between the hemispherical head of the

CHAPTER 9

653

humerus and the shallow glenoid cavity of the scapula. The relatively large size of the humeral head in comparison with the glenoid (4:1 ratio), even when supplemented by the glenoid labrum, is an arrangement that lacks intrinsic stability. Instead, the surrounding tendons and muscles stabilise the joint. The ligaments do not contribute greatly to joint stability, because the humerus can be separated from the glenoid a considerable extent when only the ligaments remain. Their function is to limit the extremes of joint movement. Similarly, the joint capsule provides little joint stability, being relatively lax throughout the normal range of motion.

Joint stability is, therefore, derived from a combination of factors including:
- **Glenoid labrum:** a ring of fibrocartilage that deepens the glenoid fossa and is continuous above with the long head of biceps
- **Rotator cuff muscles:** tendons of these four muscles insert into and reinforce the joint capsule. The rotator cuff is the major stabilising factor for the shoulder joint
- **Coracoacromial arch:** the coracoacromial ligament, tip of acromion and coracoid process provide stability superiorly
- **Long head of triceps:** provides support inferiorly where capsule is most lax and least strong
- **Capsule and ligaments** (glenohumeral and coracohumeral): may provide a degree of additional joint stability

Ligaments of the shoulder
- **Coracohumeral ligament:** a broad band that strengthens the upper capsule. Arises from the lateral border of the coracoid process, and passes obliquely downwards and lateral to the front of the greater tuberosity of the humerus, blending with the tendon of supraspinatus

- **Glenohumeral ligament** (composed of three bands):
  - From the medial edge of the glenoid cavity to the lesser tubercle of the humerus
  - From under the glenoid cavity to the anatomical neck of the humerus
  - From the apex of the glenoid cavity to just above the lesser tubercle of the humerus
- **Transverse humeral ligament:** a broad band passing from the lesser to the greater tubercle of the humerus, converting the intertubercular groove into a canal
- **Coracoacromial ligament:** spans from the undersurface of the acromion to the lateral aspect of the coracoid and is continuous with the clavipectoral fascia. Maintains the normal relationships between the coracoid and the acromion

Muscles of the shoulder

Deltoid
This is a cape-like muscle covering the shoulder joint. Arises from the lateral third of the clavicle, lateral border of acromion and inferior lip of scapular spine. Inserts into the deltoid tuberosity of the humerus.
- Action: abducts arm, assisted initially by supraspinatus
- Innervation: axillary nerve

The rotator cuff
This is an almost complete ring of muscle and tendons formed by the tendons of the short scapular muscles, which cross the shoulder joint capsule before inserting into the greater and lesser tuberosities of the humerus. The tendons are all blended with one another, forming a cuff of muscles to reinforce the capsule.

The rotator cuff consists of the following four muscles:

Subscapularis
- Reinforces the anterior aspect of the joint capsule
- Originates on the subscapular surface, and inserts onto the anterior aspect of the lesser tuberosity of the humerus
- Action: medial rotator
- Innervation: upper and lower subscapular nerves

Supraspinatus
- Reinforces the upper aspect of the joint capsule
- Originates from the whole of the suprascapular fossa, and inserts into the upper surface of the greater tuberosity of the humerus
- Actions: shoulder abduction and lateral rotation
- Innervation: suprascapular nerve

Infraspinatus
- Reinforces the posterior aspect of the joint capsule
- Originates from the medial three-quarters of the infraspinatous fossa, and attaches to the posterior aspect of the greater tuberosity, above teres minor
- Action: lateral rotator
- Innervation: suprascapular nerve

Teres minor
- Reinforces the posterior aspect of the joint capsule
- Originates from the axillary border of the scapula, and attaches to the posterior aspect of the greater tuberosity, below infraspinatus
- Action: lateral rotation and weak adduction
- Innervation: posterior branch of axillary nerve

Movements of the shoulder
The plane of the scapula lies at about 30° to the coronal plane. Movements of the shoulder can be described relative to this scapular plane or to the coronal plane. The movements of abduction, forward flexion, external rotation and internal rotation are usually measured in clinic and given relative to the coronal plane.

When observing these movements also note any 'trick' movements such as a 'hitching' (used to help initiate abduction) and also the rhythm and ratio of movement between the scapulothoracic and glenohumeral joints.

Glenohumeral abduction
Pure abduction at the glenohumeral joint comes to an end when the greater tuberosity of the humerus impinges on the glenoid rim (approximately 85°). This can be increased if the arm is externally rotated, thus delaying impingement.

Thus external rotation is required for full abduction (about 130° at the glenohumeral joint, giving a total of 180° when combined with about 50° at the scapulothoracic joint).

Scapulothoracic movement
The scapula articulates with the clavicle and carries the glenohumeral joint. It can move independently over the underlying thoracic cage and serratus anterior. It may be elevated, depressed, rotated medially or laterally around the chest wall. It may also be tilted, changing the angle of the glenoid.

CHAPTER 9

During the first 30° of abduction, the glenohumeral joint is the primary effector. Beyond 30° there is roughly 2:1 glenohumeral to scapulothoracic movement. During the last 30° there may be a spinal contribution, ie lateral flexion of thoracic spine. An intact supraspinatus is necessary for initiation of abduction, which is then complemented by the deltoid, which raises the head of the humerus relative to the glenoid. Muscular stability of the scapula is essential for all shoulder movements.

7.2   Surgical approaches to the shoulder joint

Learning point

Two surgical approaches to the shoulder joint are commonly used:
- Anterior (deltopectoral) approach
- Lateral approach

Anterior (deltopectoral) approach

Applications
- Anterior stabilisation, joint replacement, fracture fixation

Incision
- 10–15-cm skin incision over the deltopectoral groove

Approach
- Split deltoid and pectoralis major (retracting cephalic vein)
- Retract short head of biceps medially or perform coracoid osteotomy (protecting musculocutaneous nerve)
- Divide subscapularis between stay sutures (with arm externally rotated to bring musculotendinous junction lateral to axillary nerve (which runs in quadrangular space between the humeral shaft, teres major, subscapularis and long head of triceps))
- Longitudinal capsulotomy

Lateral approach

Applications
- Used in rotator cuff repair, intramedullary nailing and fracture fixation (distal exposure limited by axillary nerve as it winds around humerus, about 5 cm below the lateral border of the acromion)

Incision
- Approximately 5-cm longitudinal incision from the tip of the acromion down the arm, posterior to the greater tuberosity

Approach
- Split deltoid in line of its fibres (a stay suture may be used to stop this split progressing more than 5 cm and putting the axillary nerve at risk)
- The subacromial bursa may be opened to expose the cuff and humeral head in the proximal portion of the wound

7.3 Clinical assessment of the shoulder joint

History

- Trauma
- Sports, hobbies and occupation
- Handedness
- Nature of pain and range of motion over which it occurs
- Dislocations – first dislocation (mechanism and subsequent treatment), number, degree of trauma required to produce dislocation and treatment needed to reduce dislocation
- Instability symptoms

Clinical examination

Shoulder fully exposed (ie shirts, vests, blouses off; bras may remain).

Look

From above, in front and behind.

Anteriorly

- Prominent sternoclavicular joint: subluxation
- Deformity of clavicle: previous fracture
- Prominent acromioclavicular (AC) joint: osteoarthritis, subluxation
- Deltoid wasting: axillary nerve palsy with loss of sensation in 'regimental badge' region, disuse atrophy
- Scars

Posteriorly

- Scapula: normal shape, small, high. Winged due to paralysis of serratus anterior (long thoracic nerve damage) or muscular incoordination

Feel

- Bony structures
  - Sternoclavicular joint
  - Clavicle
  - Acromioclavicular joint
  - Acromion
  - Coracoid
- Soft tissue
  - Subacromial space

Move

Abduction

Observe abduction from the front and behind.

Difficulty initiating abduction suggests loss of scapular control or cuff pathology and a shoulder hitch may be seen. Similarly, abnormal scapulothoracic rhythm may be seen in many shoulder conditions.

- A painful arc of motion between 60° and 120° suggests subacromial impingement
- A painful arc of motion between 170° and 180° suggests AC joint pathology

Re-test, isolating glenohumeral joint by fixing scapula with hand on top.

- Forward flexion: 0–165°
- Backward extension: 0–60°

External rotation

Test with elbow tucked into side. This is the first movement to disappear and the last to return in adhesive capsulitis (frozen shoulder).

continued oveleaf

Internal rotation

Recorded as the highest point that the fingers or hand reaches on the back (specify which, eg fingertips to T12).

Special tests of shoulder movements

- **Rotator cuff tests:**
    - Empty beer can test (supraspinatus): resisted elevation of the forearm with the humerus in plane of scapula and internal rotation (eliminates deltoid) – the position for emptying the last dregs from your beer can
    - Resisted external rotation (infraspinatus)
    - Lift-off test (subscapularis): resist lifting of the hand off the back (ie in maximal internal rotation, eliminating activity of pectoralis major)
- **Apprehension test:** used to assess anterior stability of the shoulder. The shoulder is abducted to 90° with the elbow flexed to 90°. The arm is gently externally rotated, with a positive test being when the patient becomes tense or complains of shoulder pain. Always compare sides

- **Anterior glenohumeral translation:** fixing humeral head in one hand and scapula in the other, assessing antero-posterior (AP) laxity
- **Sulcus sign:** longitudinal, downward traction on the arm may produce a visible sulcus between the acromion and the head when inferior laxity is present
- **Impingement test:** passive internal rotation of the arm with the shoulder at around 120° abduction in the scapular plane. This brings the greater tuberosity up under the acromion. The test may be repeated after a subacromial injection of local anaesthetic, confirming the diagnosis of subacromial impingement if the pain is abolished by the local anaesthetic

Summary of findings and differential diagnosis

Investigating the shoulder

Imaging of the shoulder may include:

- **Radiograph:** three views usually required (especially if dislocation is a concern). These are AP and lateral in the plane of the scapula and an axillary view. Even after trauma, a good radiographer should be able to obtain an axillary view

- **Ultrasonography:** shows cuff tears. Needs skilled and experienced operator for best results
- **CT:** good visualisation of bony anatomy. Will help define large bony Bankart lesions (avulsion fracture from anterior glenoid following anterior dislocation)
- **MRI:** shows labral tears, cuff pathology and capsular tears

7.4 Shoulder disorders

Rotator cuff pathology

Cuff pathology accounts for a third of all shoulder problems, typically in patients over 40, and increasing in incidence with increasing age. There is a spectrum of pathology from mild impingement, through small cuff tears to massive tears (>5 cm) and end-stage cuff arthropathy.

Subacromial impingement may be treated by local steroid injections and physiotherapy. Resistant cases may be treated by subacromial decompression.

Cuff tears may result from sudden traction to the arm, usually on a background of gradual attrition of the tendon. Supraspinatus is most commonly involved. This manifests as difficulty in abducting the arm. Painful abduction in impingement from a torn rotator cuff is eased when the arm is abducted in full external rotation. Revascularisation plus healing of tears and of degeneration leads to calcium deposition and subdeltoid bursitis, thus aggravating the condition.

Surgical intervention involves decompression of the rotator cuff by excising the coracoacromial ligament and part of the acromion. Tendon repairs are indicated in young patients (<65 years) with symptomatic small tears. Large tears may be repaired in elderly patients.

Arthritis of the glenohumeral joint

Degenerate change in the shoulder may result from trauma, inflammatory arthropathy (eg RA), cuff dysfunction or simply idiopathic OA.

First line of treatment is physiotherapy, analgesia and modification of activities. The vast majority of patients can be managed with these non-surgical treatments. In a small number shoulder replacement may be indicated.

The shoulder is commonly affected by RA. The disease commonly affects other joints in the upper limb. The goal of treatment is to relieve pain and allow the hand to be positioned in space to allow activities of daily living such as feeding and grooming. As a general principle, proximal joints (ie the shoulder) should be treated before distal joints.

Osteoarthritis of the acromioclavicular joint

Usually there is localised tenderness with obvious prominence of the joint from osteophyte formation.
- Physiotherapy is first-line treatment
- Excision of the distal end of the clavicle may be considered in severe cases

CHAPTER 9

Note: don't be misled by:
- Referred pain from cervical spondylosis
- Pain from irritation of nerve roots referred from neck to shoulder

Adhesive capsulitis (frozen shoulder)

Numerous aetiologies but occurs most commonly in middle-aged individuals with degenerative changes of the rotator cuff.

Clinical features of frozen shoulder

- Decreased range of movement of shoulder joint, often severe with no movement at glenohumeral joint
- External rotation is the first movement to be restricted
- Frequently there is a history of minor trauma which exacerbates existing degenerative changes and develops into a prolonged inflammatory response. Occasionally

develops after a period of immobilisation. Radiographs are mostly normal
- The classic description is of three phases – pain, freezing then thawing, with resolution over about 2 years. This description is probably a little optimistic
- Physiotherapy, steroid injection and manipulation in resistant cases have all been shown to be helpful

7.5 Anatomy of the upper arm

Learning point

- Humerus
- Muscles
- Nerves (brachial plexus and branches)
- Arteries and veins (see Chapter 12, Vascular Surgery)

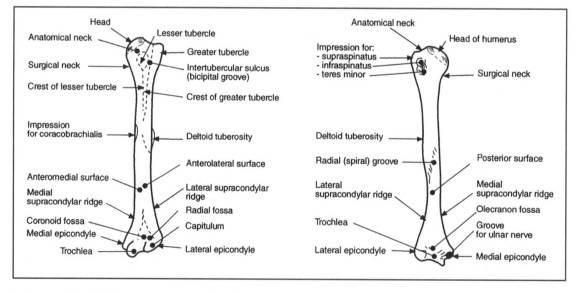

Figure 9.12 The humerus

CHAPTER 9

Anatomy of the humerus

The humerus is a long bone. The upper half is cylindrical, consisting of a head facing medially. The head is separated from the greater and lesser tubercles by the anatomical neck. The tubercles are separated by the bicipital groove and the shaft is separated from the upper half by the surgical neck.

The lower half of the humerus is flattened. Its lower end bears the capitulum laterally, which articulates with the radial head, and the trochlea medially, which articulates with the trochlear notch of the ulna. The medial and lateral epicondyles are extracapsular. The medial is larger and extends more distally.

Muscles of the upper arm

Muscle	Origin	Insertion	Action	Innervation
Coracobrachialis	Coracoid	Medial shaft of the humerus	Flexes and adducts shoulder	Musculocutaneous nerve, C5, C6, (C7)
Biceps brachii	Long head: glenohumeral labrum Short head: coracoid	Radial tuberosity and bicipital aponeurosis	Flexes elbow (when supinated) supinates forearm – from neutral and stabilises shoulder	Musculocutaneous nerve, C5, C6
Brachialis	Distal half of anterior humerus and intermuscular septa	Ulnar tuberosity and coronoid process of ulna	Major elbow flexor	Musculocutaneous nerve, C5, C6
Triceps brachii	Long head: infraglenoid tubercle of the scapula Lateral head: proximal half of the posterior surface of the shaft of the humerus Medial head: posterior shaft of humerus, distal to radial groove and both the medial and lateral intermuscular septa (deep to the long and lateral heads)	Olecranon	Extends elbow	Radial nerve, C6, C7
Anconeus	Posterior surface of the lateral epicondyle of the humerus	Lateral aspect of olecranon extending to the lateral part of ulnar body	Extends elbow and controls ulna in extension	Radial nerve, C7, C8

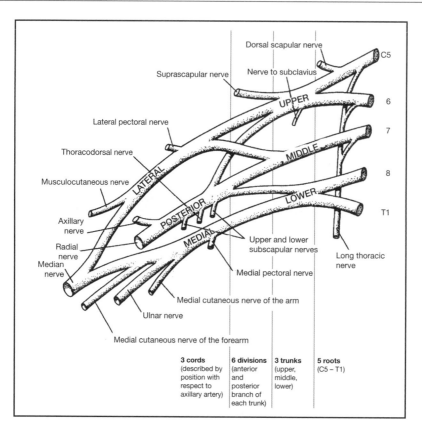

Figure 9.13 Brachial plexus

3 cords	6 divisions	3 trunks	5 roots
(described by position with respect to axillary artery)	(anterior and posterior branch of each trunk)	(upper, middle, lower)	(C5 – T1)

Important neurovascular relationships of the humerus

- **Surgical neck:** the axillary nerve and circumflex humeral vessels
- **Spiral groove** (running along the posterior aspect of the shaft): the radial nerve and profunda brachii vessels
- **Posterior aspect of the medial epicondyle:** the ulnar nerve

Nerves of the upper arm

Axillary nerve (C5, C6)

- Arises from posterior cord of the plexus
- Runs through quadrilateral space (with posterior circumflex humeral artery) to lie deep to deltoid around surgical neck of humerus
- Supplies deltoid, teres minor, shoulder joint
- Gives rise to upper lateral cutaneous nerve of arm (regimental badge sensation)

Radial nerve (C5–T1)

- Arises from posterior cord of the plexus
- Runs through lateral triangular space to lie between medial and lateral heads of triceps in the spiral groove of humerus. From here it pierces the lateral intermuscular septum to reach the anterior compartment of the forearm, lying under cover of the mobile wad (brachioradialis and extensor carpi radialis longus and brevis)
- Gives off the posterior interosseous nerve, which runs between the two heads of supinator and supplies the extensor compartment of the forearm
- Sensory braches: posterior cutaneous nerve of the arm, lower lateral cutaneous nerve of the arm, posterior cutaneous nerve of the forearm and superficial radial nerve

Musculocutaneous nerve (C5–C7)

- Arises from the lateral cord of the plexus
- Runs between the conjoined heads of coracobrachialis and lies on the deep surface of biceps, supplying coracobra-chialis, biceps and brachialis
- Gives rise to the lateral cutaneous nerve of the forearm

Median nerve (C6–T1)

- Arises from roots from the lateral and medial cords of the brachial plexus
- Median nerve initially lies lateral to the brachial artery, crossing to the medial side in the arm
- Median nerve supplies the flexor compartment of the forearm, which it enters between the two heads of pronator teres
- Deep muscles (flexor pollicis longus, ponator quadratus and half of flexor digitorum profundus) are supplied by the anterior interosseous nerve (a branch of the median nerve)
- In the hand it supplies the muscles of the thenar eminence and the lateral two lumbricals
- Median nerve passes under the transverse carpal ligament on the radial side of the tendons of flexor digitorum superficialis (in the carpal tunnel)
- Motor branch to the thenar muscles is given off on the radial side of the nerve (usually)
- Therefore, for carpal tunnel decompression the ligament is divided on the ulnar side of the nerve

Ulnar nerve (C8, T1)

- Arises from the medial cord of the plexus
- Lies in the anterior compartment of the arm down to the midpoint of the humerus, where it enters the posterior compartment by piercing the medial intermuscular septum
- Passes behind the medial epicondyle and enters the forearm between the two heads of flexor carpi ulnaris
- Runs deep to this muscle through the forearm and lateral to its tendon at the wrist
- Gives a palmar and a dorsal cutaneous branch before entering the hand to supply most of the intrinsic muscles

SECTION 8

The elbow

8.1 Anatomy of the elbow

> ### Learning point
>
> The purpose of the elbow is to enable positioning of the hand to allow function. It allows flexion and pronation–supination.
> The elbow complex consists of three joints:
> * Ulnohumeral
> * Radiohumeral
> * Proximal radioulnar
> It is generally very stable due to the congruence of the ulna and trochlea, aided by strong collateral ligaments. All three articulations are contained within a single capsule.

Movement of the elbow joint

Flexion–extension

(See Section 7.5, 'Anatomy of the upper arm' for muscles acting on the elbow.)
* Elbow flexion is performed by brachialis, biceps brachii, brachioradialis and pronator teres

* Elbow extension is performed by triceps and anconeus
* At full flexion the coronoid process lies in coronoid fossa
* At full extension, the olecranon process lies in the olecranon fossa

Due to the proximity of these components only a small disruption in their position or a small loose foreign body in one of the fossae can cause a significant restriction of movement.

Pronation–supination

The disc-shaped radial head rotates freely within the annular ligament of the elbow. The axis of pronation and supination passes through the radial head at the elbow and the attachment of the triangular fibrocartilage at the wrist.
* Pronation is performed by pronator teres and pronator quadratus
* Supination is performed by biceps (only in flexion) and supinator

Ossification centres of the elbow joint

There are six major ossification centres in the elbow, which can make interpretation of paediatric elbow radiographs challenging.

They appear in the following order (remember CRITOL):

Capitulum (3 months)
Radial head (5 years)
Internal (medial) epicondyle (7 years)
Trochlea (9 years)
Olecranon (11 years)
Lateral epicondyle (13 years)

The above ages are approximate. The ossification centres appear every 2 years and tend to appear earlier in girls than in boys.

Important neurovascular relations of the elbow joint

- The median nerve and brachial artery lie medial to the biceps tendon and superficial to brachialis
- Medially in the subcutaneous plane lie the medial cutaneous nerve of forearm, basilic and median cubital veins. The radial nerve and its posterior interosseous branch lie lateral to the biceps tendon
- Laterally in the subcutaneous plane lie the lateral cutaneous nerve of the forearm and cephalic vein
- The ulnar nerve at the elbow lies behind the medial epicondyle. The main extensor origin is from the lateral epicondyle. The main flexor origin is from the medial epicondyle

8.2 Surgical approaches to the arm and elbow joint

Learning point

Surgery on the arm and elbow joint is usually for fracture fixation, and the approach depends on the location and configuration of the fracture. Options include:
- Anterior approach to the humerus
- Anterolateral approach to the humerus
- Posterior approach to the humerus
- Lateral approach to the distal humerus
- Posterior approach to the elbow
- Posterolateral approach to the radial head and neck
- Medial approach to the elbow
- Anterolateral approach to the elbow
- Anterior approach to the cubital fossa

Anterior approach to the humerus

- Incision: extensile incision, may be as long as from coracoid, running down in the deltopectoral groove to lateral border of biceps (stopping about 5 cm above flexion crease to avoid lateral antebrachial cutaneous nerve)
- Retract biceps and pectoralis major medially and deltoid laterally to expose humeral shaft
- Split brachialis in the line of its fibres to expose distal shaft (brachialis is supplied by radial nerve laterally and musculocutaneous nerve medially)

CHAPTER 9

Anterolateral approach to the humerus

- Allows better access to the distal 25% of the humeral shaft
- Brachialis retracted medially, brachioradialis retracted laterally (both are supplied by the radial nerve, which will be seen under brachioradialis)

Posterior approach to the humerus

Common approach for open reduction and internal fixation of shaft fracture (particularly if radial nerve is injured at time of injury).

- Incision: extensile incision, may be as long as from posterior midline, 10 cm from acromion to olecranon, continuing along ulna if required
- Split triceps (lateral and long heads superficially and medial head deep)
- Radial nerve (running in spiral groove) must be identified after separating lateral head of triceps from long head of triceps

Lateral approach to the distal humerus

- Incision: 5 cm over lateral supracondylar ridge
- Incise fascia, reflecting triceps posteriorly and brachioradialis anteriorly. This will expose the anterior and posterior surfaces of the distal humerus
- The radial nerve is at risk if the incision is carried proximally

Posterior approach to the elbow

Common approach for open reduction and internal fixation of articular fracture.

- Incision: curved longitudinal posterior incision, avoiding tip of olecranon
- Ulnar nerve is identified

- The articular surface may be exposed using an olecranon osteotomy

Posterolateral approach to the radial head and neck

- Incision: from lateral epicondyle, over radial head to radial border of proximal ulna
- Divide fascia between anconeus and extensor carpi ulnaris
- Pronation of the forearm carries the posterior interosseous nerve away from the surgical field. This nerve is in danger from misplaced retractors around the radial neck
- The radial nerve lies anterior to the elbow joint capsule

Other approaches

- Medial approach to the elbow (for capitulum)
- Anterolateral approach to the elbow (for proximal radius)
- Anterior approach to the cubital fossa (for median nerve and brachial artery)

8.3 Clinical assessment of the elbow joint

History

Ask about:
- Trauma
- Sports (especially pitching and throwing and of course tennis and golf!)
- Occupation
- Handedness
- Functional deficit
- Nature and location of pain and range of motion over which it occurs
- Neurological symptoms

Clinical examination

Expose whole of upper limb including shoulder (check with examiner if shoulder not already exposed).

Look

Inspection of the elbow
- **Effusion:** earliest sign of effusion is filling out of the hollow as seen in the flexed elbow above the olecranon
- Rheumatoid nodules
- Muscle wasting
- **Carrying angle:** males approximately 11° and females approximately 13°
  - Cubitus valgus: increase in carrying angle
  - Cubitus varus: decrease in carrying angle

Feel
- Is it tender?
- Temperature
- Effusion
- Collateral ligaments
- **Epicondyles:** lateral tenderness, tennis elbow; medial tenderness, golfer's elbow
- **Olecranon**
- **Radial head:** palpate while pronating and supinating forearm

Move
- Active flexion and extension
- Pronation and supination
- Extension: (full 0°) loss of full extension is common in osteoarthritis, old fractures
- Hyperextension: up to 15° is normal, especially in women but consider Ehlers–Danlos syndrome and other connective tissue disorders
- Flexion: (145°) restriction is common in OA, RA and old fractures
- Pronation: range from neutral position (90°)

- Supination: range from neutral position (90°)
- Pronation/supination: reduced in old forearm or wrist fracture, RA, OA

Complete examination with neurological examination of upper limb (especially ulnar nerve) and vascular assessment.

Summary of findings and differential diagnosis

Investigating the elbow

For most cases AP and lateral radiographs are all that are required. These views may show:
- Fat pad signs (commonly anterior, occasionally posterior) – an effusion in the elbow is easily seen radiographically because it lifts the anterior fat pad from the distal humerus, producing a second shadow
- Fractures
- Loss of joint space
- Osteophytes
- Loose bodies

MRI and CT may have a role in selected cases.

8.4 Elbow disorders

Tennis elbow

Tennis elbow is a strain or small tears in the common extensor origin, followed by inflammatory reaction.

Usually presents in the 35–50 age group:
- Main complaint is pain on the lateral side of the elbow exacerbated by movement and holding heavy objects at arm's length with the forearm pronated
- There may be a history of excessive activity (eg dusting, sweeping, playing tennis!)

Treatment of tennis elbow

- Local steroid injections and local anaesthetics
- Topical NSAIDs
- Avoidance of pain-provoking movement – do not allow full extension of the elbow while lifting
- If conservative measures are unsuccessful, surgical exploration of extensor carpi radialis brevis may be advocated. There is (as yet) no good evidence that surgery is effective

Golfer's elbow

Similar complaint to tennis elbow but much less common. Pain is localised to the medial epicondyle at the common flexor origin. Ulnar nerve entrapment is a differential diagnosis.

Cubitus varus and cubitus valgus

Decrease (varus) or increase (valgus) in the carrying angle of the elbow follows a supracondylar or other elbow fracture in childhood.

If, after some years of observation, there is interference with function, corrective osteotomy may be performed.

In later life, a cubitus valgus deformity may be associated with a tardy ulnar nerve palsy.

Tardy ulnar nerve palsy

This is an ulnar nerve palsy characterised by slow onset. Typically presents at 30–50 years, after injury to the elbow, often sustained in childhood. Mostly seen with a cubitus valgus deformity. Ischaemic and fibrotic changes are seen in the nerve.

Treatment is transposition of nerve from behind the medial epicondyle to in front of the joint.

Ulnar neuritis and ulnar tunnel syndrome

The ulnar nerve is susceptible to compression or trauma at the elbow. There are three sites where compression or trauma can occur:

- **Medial epicondyle:** where the nerve is abnormally mobile it can be exposed to frictional damage as it slips repeatedly in front of and behind the medial epicondyle
- **The two heads of flexor carpi ulnaris:** these exert pressure as the nerve passes between them
- In the ulnar tunnel in the hand

Nerve conduction studies are very helpful in determining the level of insult but are not sensitive enough to identify early cases.

Pulled elbow (nursemaid's elbow)

This is a dislocation of the radial head, typically in children aged 2–5. It is caused by sudden traction on one arm (eg by pulling a child back suddenly if there is a car coming, or by lifting a child up by one arm).

The child presents with limited supination and tenderness over the radial head.

Reduction is achieved:
- Spontaneously (broad-arm sling)
- By firmly supinating the flexed arm while the wrist is in full radial deviation and the radius is being pushed proximally

SECTION 9

The forearm and wrist

9.1 Anatomy of the forearm

Arteries and veins of the upper limb are described in Chapter 12, Vascular surgery.

Muscles of the forearm

The flexor and extensor muscles of the forearm, together with their origins, insertions, actions and innervation, are shown in the tables on page 708.

Flexors

Muscle	Origin	Insertion	Action	Innervation
Pronator teres	Two heads, common flexor origin (medial epicondyle) and coronoid	Lateral radial shaft (pronator tuberosity)	Pronates forearm	Median nerve, C6, C7
Flexor carpi radialis	Common flexor origin and fascia of forearm	Base of second and third metacarpals	Wrist flexion and radial deviation	Median nerve, C6, C7
Palmaris longus	Common flexor origin and fascia of forearm	Flexor retinaculum and palmar aponeurosis	Vestigial muscle – weak wrist flexor	Median nerve, C6, C7
Flexor carpi ulnaris	Two heads, common flexor origin and proximal ulna shaft	Pisiform and hamate	Wrist flexion and ulnar deviation	Ulnar nerve, C8, T1
Flexor digitorum superficialis	Common flexor origin and proximal ulna and radius	Base of middle phalanx of fingers	Flexor of fingers (and wrist)	Median nerve, C7, C8, T1

continued oveleaf

CHAPTER 9

Muscle	Origin	Insertion	Action	Innervation
Flexor digitorum profundus	Proximal ulna and interosseus membrane	Base of distal phalanx of fingers	Flexes DIP joints of fingers (and wrist)	Ulnar nerve, C8, T1 and anterior interosseous branch of median nerve, C8, T1
Flexor policis longus	Anterior surface of the distal radius and interosseus membrane	Distal phalanx of thumb	Flexes IP joint of thumb	Anterior interosseous branch of median nerve, C8, T1
Pronator quadratus	Distal ulna	Distal radius	Pronates forearm	Anterior interosseous branch of median nerve, C8, T1

Extensors

Muscle	Origin	Insertion	Action	Innervation
Brachioradialis	Upper lateral supracondylar ridge of humerus	Radial styloid	Flexes elbow and returns forearm to neutral position from extremes of pronation and supination	Radial nerve, C5, C6
Extensor carpi radialis longus	Lower lateral supracondylar ridge	Base of second metacarpal	Extends and radially deviates wrist	Radial nerve, C5, C6
Extensor carpi radialis brevis	Common extensor origin	Base of third metacarpal	Extends and radially deviates wrist	Radial nerve, C6, C7
Extensor digitorum	Common extensor origin	Extensor hood – base of middle and distal phalanges of fingers	Extends fingers (and wrist)	Posterior interosseous nerve of the radial nerve, C6–8
Extensor digiti minimi	Common extensor origin	Base of middle and distal phalanx little finger	Extends and abducts little finger	Posterior interosseous nerve of the radial nerve, C6–8
Extensor carpi ulnaris	Two heads, common extensor origin and proximal ulna	Base of the fifth metacarpal	Extends and ulna deviates wrist	Posterior interosseous nerve of the radial nerve, C6–8

continued opposite

Muscle	Origin	Insertion	Action	Innervation
Supinator	Lateral epicondyle and ulna	Radial tuberosity	Supinates forearm	Radial nerve, C6
Abductor pollicis longus	Posterior surface of radius and ulna	Lateral aspect of base of first metacarpal	Adducts thumb and assists extension	Posterior interosseous nerve of the radial nerve, C6–8
Extensor pollicis brevis	Posterior surface of radius and ulna	Base of proximal phalanx of thumb	Extends thumb	Posterior interosseous nerve of the radial nerve, C6–8
Extensor pollicis longus	Posterior surface of ulna and interosseous membrane	Distal phalanx of thumb	Extends thumb	Posterior interosseous nerve of the radial nerve, C6–8
Extensor indicis	Posterior surface of ulna and interosseous membrane	Base of middle and distal phalanx of the index finger	Extends index finger	Posterior interosseous nerve of the radial nerve, C6–8

9.2 Bones of the forearm

Anatomy of the radius and ulna

> **Hints for orientating the radius and ulna in the viva**
> **Radius**
> - Distal end large and proximal end small (in contrast to ulna, which is large proximally and smaller distally)
> - Anteroposteriorly: distal end (prominent dorsal tubercle posteriorly)
> - Mediolaterally: ulnar notch faces medially to articulate with ulna distally
>
> **Ulna**
> - Proximal end large, distal end small
> - Anteroposteriorly: proximal end (trochlear notch projecting anteriorly)
> - Mediolaterally: radial notch faces laterally to articulate with radius proximally

The two bone shafts are joined by an interosseous membrane. In pronation and supination, the head of the radius rotates against the radial notch of the ulna. The radial shaft swings around the relatively fixed ulnar shaft. The distal end of the radius rotates against the head of the ulna.

CHAPTER 9

671

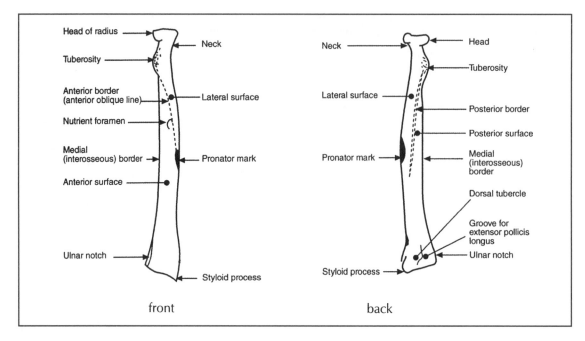

Figure 9.14 Radius (front and back)

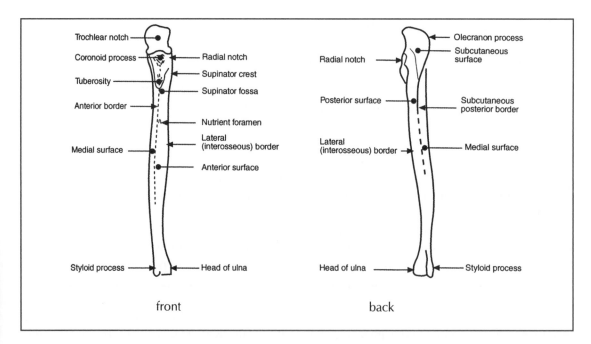

Figure 9.15 Ulna (front and back)

9.3 Bones of the wrist (the carpus)

Learning point

- Eight bones
- Two rows (proximal and distal with midcarpal joint between)
- Multiple complex articulations
Stability is derived from intrinsic and extrinsic ligaments.

The scaphoid spans the proximal and distal row, forming a link across the midcarpal joint. Most of its surface is covered in articular surface, so only a small area is available for vessels to enter this bone. This results in the problem of AVN and non-union following some scaphoid fractures.

A handy mnemonic for bones of the carpus:
So Long To Pinky, Here Comes The Thumb
(**S**caphoid, **L**unate, **T**riquetral, **P**isiform, **H**amate, **C**apitate, **T**rapezoid and **T**rapezium)

Extensor tendons

The index and little fingers have a double extensor mechanism. In addition to extensor digitorum tendon the index has an extensor indicis and the little finger has extensor digiti minimi.

The extensor tendons pass over the distal radius, contained within one of six dorsal wrist compartments. These contain (from radial to ulnar):

9.4 Bones and joints of the hand

The metacarpals, proximal phalanges and middle phalanges are a similar shape. They all have a roughly cylindrical shaft, with a flared base and bicondylar head. The distal phalanges are flattened, with a broad terminal tuft.

The base of the first metacarpal articulates with the trapezium in a saddle-shaped joint, allowing circumduction at this joint. The fifth metacarpal has a very mobile articulation with the hamate allowing opposition of the little finger. As a result this joint is prone to fracture dislocation.

The ligaments at the MCP joints are tight in flexion. The ligaments at the IP joints are tight in extension. Thus the hand should be immobilised with extended IP joints and flexed MCP joints to prevent contracture of these collateral ligaments.

The muscles and tendons of the hand are shown in the table on page 674, with descriptions of their insertions and origins, innervation and actions.

Compartment 1 (radial)	Abductor pollicis longus (APL) Extensor pollicis brevis (EPB)
Compartment 2	Extensor carpi radialis longus (ECRL) Extensor carpi radialis brevis (ECRB)
Compartment 3	Extensor pollicis longus (EPL)
Compartment 4	Extensor indicis (EI) Extensor digitorum communis (EDC)
Compartment 5	Extensor digiti minimi (EDM)
Compartment 6 (ulnar)	Extensor carpi ulnaris (ECU)

CHAPTER 9

Muscle	Origin	Insertion	Action	Innervation
Abductor pollicis brevis	Trapezium and flexor retinaculum	Base of proximal phalanx of the thumb	Abducts and flexes thumb	Recurrent branch of median nerve, C8, T1
Flexor pollicis brevis	Two heads, flexor retinaculum and floor of carpal tunnel	Base of proximal phalanx of thumb	Flexion of thumb (especially MCP joint)	Superficial head: recurrent branch of median nerve, C8, T1; deep head: deep branch of ulnar nerve, C8, T1
Opponens pollicis	Trapezium and flexor retinaculum	Lateral aspect of the first metacarpal	Opposes thumb	Recurrent branch of median nerve, C8, T1
Adductor pollicis	Floor of carpal tunnel and first, second and third metacarpals	Medial side of proximal phalanx	Adducts thumb	Deep branch of ulnar nerve, C8, T1
Palmaris brevis	Medial margin of palmar aponeurosis	Skin on ulnar border of palm	Contracts, tensing the skin – has a role in grip	Superficial branch of ulnar nerve, C8, T1
Abductor digiti quinti	Pisiform and the tendon of flexor carpi ulnaris	Base of proximal phalanx of little finger	Abducts little finger	Deep branch of ulnar nerve, C8, T1
Flexor digiti quinti brevis	Hook of hamate and flexor retinaculum	Medial aspect of the proximal phalanx of little finger	Flexes little finger	Deep branch of ulnar nerve, C8, T1
Opponens digiti quinti	Hook of hamate and flexor retinaculum	Medial aspect of the fifth metacarpal	Opposes little finger	Deep branch of ulnar nerve, C8, T1
Palmar interossei	Metacarpal shafts	Proximal phalanx and extensor hood	**Palmer add**uct (PAD)	Deep branch of ulnar nerve, C8, T1
Dorsal interossei	Metacarpal shafts	Proximal phalanx and extensor hood	**Dorsal ab**duct (DAB)	Deep branch of ulnar nerve, C8, T1
Lumbricals	Tendon of flexor digitorum profundus	Flexor hoods of fingers	Flexion and MCP joints, extension at IP joints	Medial pair: median nerve, C8, T1; and ulna pair: deep branch of ulnar nerve, C8, T1

Flexor tendons

There are five flexor tendon zones in the hand and wrist, based on anatomical factors influencing prognosis of repair (Verden zones). Injuries in zone 2 cause most problems.

Zone 1	Between the DIP and PIP joint creases distal to the insertion of flexor digitorum superficialis (FDS) Contains the flexor digitorum profundus (FDP) tendon within the distal flexor sheath
Zone 2	Between distal palmar crease and midpoint of middle phalanx Corresponds to the proximal part of the flexor tendon sheath, A1 pulley, and extends to the FDS insertion containing FDS and FDP tendons
Zone 3	Between distal margin of carpal tunnel and distal palmar crease Contains both FDS and FDP tendons but are unsheathed
Zone 4	Area of carpal tunnel Contains both FDS and FDP tendons
Zone 5	Area of wrist and forearm up to carpal tunnel

In the thumb, zone 1 is distal to the IP joint, zone 2 is over the proximal phalanx from the A1 pulley to the IP joint, zone 3 is the thenar eminence, and zones 4 and 5 are the same as for the fingers.

9.5 Surgical approaches to the forearm and wrist

Learning point

- Anterior approach to the radius (Henry's approach)
- Posterior approach to the radius
- Approach to the ulna shaft

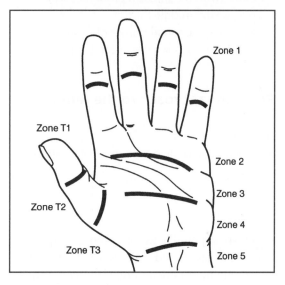

Figure 9.16 Zones of the palmar surface of the hand and wrist

Anterior approach to the radius (Henry's approach)

Incision

- Extensile approach; may be as long as from just lateral to the biceps tendon (in line of lateral epicondyle) to styloid process of the radius

Approach

- Develop plane between brachioradialis (overlying superficial branch of radial nerve) and flexor carpi radialis

CHAPTER 9

- Radial artery and venae comitantes run in this interval. There may be a significant leash of vessels proximally (leash of Henry), crossing into the brachioradialis, which may be divided
- Elevation of the insertion of supinator (with the forearm in supination to protect the posterior interosseous nerve) will expose the proximal third
- Elevation of the insertion of pronator teres and the origin of flexor digitorum superficialis (with the forearm pronated) will expose the middle third
- Elevating the radial border of pronator quadratus exposes the distal third

Posterior approach to the radius

Incision
- Lateral epicondyle of humerus to Lister's tubercle

Approach
- Develop plane between extensor carpi radialis brevis and extensor digitorum communis (abductor pollicis longus and extensor pollicis brevis emerge between these two muscles distally)
- Exposure of the proximal third through this approach requires identification of the posterior interosseous nerve and dissection of the nerve as it runs through supinator
- The middle and distal thirds may be exposed by mobilising and retracting abductor pollicis longus and extensor pollicis longus and brevis

Approach to the ulnar shaft
- The subcutaneous border of the ulna is palpable along its entire length
- It is easily exposed, reflecting extensor carpi ulnaris and flexor carpi ulnaris

Only part of each approach may be used to access the desired part of the bone. Some approaches (eg anterior approach to the radius, anterior approach to the humerus and the deltopectoral approach) are easily extended and may be combined to access the entire limb if required.

9.6 Clinical assessment of the wrist

History

Ask about:

- Trauma (mechanism, time and subsequent treatment if any)
- Occupation, hobbies and sports
- Handedness
- Functional deficit
- Nature and location of pain and range of motion over which it occurs
- Neurological symptoms

Clinical examination

Expose hands, wrists and forearms, including the elbow.

Look

- Deformity
- Swellings (ganglia, synovitis etc)

Feel

- Tenderness (bony or over tendon sheaths)
- Temperature and sweating

Move

- Range of motion (flexion, extension, radial and ulnar deviation and pronation–supination)
- Grip strength
- Special tests, eg:
    - Finklestein's test for de Quervain's tenosynovitis (pain on ulnar deviation of the wrist with the thumb adducted)
    - Ulnar impingement test (ulnar deviation in full pronation)
- Neurological assessment (carpal tunnel, ulnar tunnel, cubital tunnel syndromes)

Summary of findings and differential diagnosis

Investigating wrist problems

- **Plain films** (including four-view scaphoid series if indicated) for:
    - Fractures (and non-union/malunion)
    - Dislocations
    - Carpal instability patterns
- **MRI:** to look for scapholunate ligament injuries or triangular fibrocartilage injuries
- **Wrist arthroscopy**

SECTION 10

Disorders of the hand

10.1 Clinical assessment of the hand

History

Ask about:

- Trauma (mechanism, time and subsequent treatment if any)
- Tetanus status (for trauma cases)
- Occupation, hobbies and sports
- Handedness
- Functional deficit
- Nature and location of pain and range of motion over which it occurs
- Neurological symptoms

Clinical examination

Expose hands, wrists and forearms including the elbow.

Look

General inspection

- Deformity
- Any finger hypertrophy (eg Paget's, neurofibromatosis, arteriovenous [AV] fistula)?
- Fusiform swelling of IP joints (eg collateral ligament tears, RA)
- Mallet finger/thumb deformity

- Swan-neck deformity
- Boutonnière deformity
- Z-thumb
- Dupuytren's contracture
- Ulnar deviation of fingers at MCP joints due to joint subluxation and later dislocation in RA

Wasting of muscles

- Unilateral wasting (root, plexus or peripheral nerve lesion)
- Widespread wasting (generalised peripheral neuropathy, multiple sclerosis [MS], muscular dystrophies)

Lumps and bumps

- Heberden's nodes: bony spurs on the dorsal aspect DIP joints, most common clinical manifestation of OA
- Bouchard's nodes: osteophytes that develop at PIP joints, seen in OA

continued opposite

CHAPTER 9

- Rheumatoid nodules/synovial swellings: subcutaneous masses consisting of a collagenous capsule surrounding a fibrous core, which occur over bony prominences, most commonly over the olecranon and extensor surface of the forearm. In the hand they may appear on the dorsal and volar aspects of the fingers, impinging on digital nerves and affecting function. As they expand the centre may undergo avascular necrosis. They can erode through the skin and form draining sinuses. Treatment is by surgical excision

Dupuytren's contracture?

Appearance of nails and skin (including hair and sweating)

Feel
- Palpate individual finger and thumb joints
- Increased temperature
- Thickening, tenderness, oedema

Move
- Active and passive range of motion (best measured with a goniometer)
  - MCP joint 0–90°
  - PIP joint 0–110°
  - DIP joint 0–80°
  - Thumb IP joint flexion 80°, extension 20°
  - Thumb MCP joint 0–55°
- Test function of all joints and all tendons

Movement of the fingers
- **Flexion:** DIP – flexor digitorum profundus; PIP joint – flexor digitorum superficialis
- **Extension:** extensor digitorum communis – all MCP joints; extensor digiti indicis – index finger; extensor digiti minimi – little finger. Intrinsic muscles extend PIP and DIP joints
- **Abduction:** dorsal interossei – abduct from axis of middle finger and flex MCP joints while extending IP joints
- **Adduction:** palmar interossei – adduct to axis of middle finger and flex MCP joints while extending IP joints

Movement of the thumb
- **Flexion:** flexor pollicis longus plus thenar eminence muscle; flexor pollicis brevis
- **Extension:** extensor pollicis longus; extensor pollicis brevis
- **Abduction:** abductor pollicis longus; abductor pollicis brevis
- **Adduction:** adductor pollicis
- **Opposition:** opponens pollicis

Assess pinch grip, grip strength. Objective measurements may be obtained with dynamometer.

Summary of findings and differential diagnosis

Further assessment of the hand

Assessing hand injuries requires a thorough knowledge of hand anatomy to determine any structural damage accurately.

Hand trauma examination can be facilitated by the use of local anaesthetic blocks (eg ring block at base of digit; wrist block involving ulnar, median and radial nerves; brachial plexus block).

Remember to assess any sensory deficit before giving local anaesthetic.

Some structural damage may be only partial and therefore can be misleading in the clinical setting (eg patient may be able to flex a DIP joint but have a partial severance of the corresponding flexor digitorum profundus tendon).

In partial tears the movement, although present, will be painful and often cannot be performed against resistance.

Hand trauma assessment requires radiological assessment.

10.2 Injuries to the hand

Learning point

Extensor tendon injuries
- Mallet finger (extensor tendon of the terminal phalanx disrupted)
- Mallet thumb (rupture of EPL)
- Boutonnière deformity (lateral bands of the extensor expansion sublux volarly)
- Swan-neck deformity (shortening of extensor digitorum communis, tight interossei and rupture of FDS)

Flexor tendon injuries

Extensor tendon injuries

Extensor tendon divisions from wounds on the back of the hand are treated by primary suture and splintage in extension for around 6 weeks in association with hand physiotherapy.

Mallet finger

In mallet finger the DIP joint is flexed and cannot be extended. The cause is injury to the extensor tendon of the terminal phalanx due to forcible flexion of an extended finger (eg by a cricket ball).
- The distal extensor tendon slip is torn at its attachment to bone or it avulses a bony fragment
- The patient cannot actively straighten the terminal IP joint so when all fingers are extended the affected finger is bent at the DIP joint, although it can be passively straightened with ease
- Mallet finger can be treated with 6 weeks of splintage of DIP hyperextended and the PIP joint flexed. Some surgeons recommend 2 weeks of further night splintage
- Occasionally there is involvement of more than 50% of the articular surface of the distal phalanx, sometimes with anterior subluxation. This requires formal repair

Mallet thumb

Delayed rupture of EPL can follow Colles' fracture or in RA. This can be repaired via tendon transfer of extensor indicis.

Boutonnière deformity

Characterised by flexion of the PIP joint and hyperextension of the DIP joint, this deformity is seen in RA.
- Central slip of the extensor tendon stretches or ruptures, either from trauma or in degenerative joint disease allowing PIP joint flexion
- The lateral bands of the extensor expansion sublux volarly; the oblique retinacular ligaments shorten, resulting in hyperextension of the DIP joint
- Finally the MCP joint may hyperextend to place the finger in a more functional position

Swan-neck deformity

Characterised by flexion of the DIP joint and hyperextension of the PIP joint, this deformity is seen in RA. There are several causative factors:
- Shortening of extensor digitorum communis
- Tight interossei
- Rupture of FDS

The swan-neck deformity may initiate at either the PIP or DIP joints.
- For example, at the DIP joint it may start as a result of a mallet deformity with rupture of the distal extensor insertion
- This creates extensor imbalance and volar plate laxity leading to hyperextension of the PIP joint
- Conversely, if PIP joint hyperextension is due to synovial pannus stretching of the volar plate, then DIP joint flexion is secondary

Flexor tendon injuries

Prognosis depends on level of injury, whether one or both flexor tendons are involved, and whether injury occurs at a point at which the tendons are within the flexor sheath.

The level of injury can be described with respect to the flexor tendon zones.

Usually a primary repair can be carried out. If the repair is delayed significantly it is very difficult to reoppose severed ends because the proximal end tends to retract proximally and loses elasticity. In these situations tendon reconstruction is indicated in the compliant patient.

These injuries often involve divisions of digital nerves. These are repaired primarily. Suturing is of the epineurium only. One digital artery is sufficient blood supply to a finger/thumb; however, repair of digital arteries should be attempted using magnification.

Z-thumb deformity

Flexed MCP joint and hyperextended IP joint due to displacement of extensor tendons or ruptured FPL. Seen in RA.

10.3 Hand infections

Learning point

- Paronychia
- Apical infections
- Pulp infections
- Tendon sheath infections (suppurative flexor tenosynovitis)
- Web space infections
- Midpalmar and thenar space infections

Paronychia

Infection between the side of the nail and the lateral pulp of the finger, the eponychial fold.

- *Staphylococcus aureus* is the most common bacterial source
- Usually resolved once it is lanced

Apical infections

- Occur between the top of the nail and underlying nail bed

CHAPTER 9

Pulp infections

- Occur in the fibrofatty tissue of the fingertips
- Exquisitely tender and can lead to destruction of the distal phalanx

Tendon sheath infections (suppurative flexor tenosynovitis)

- *Staphylococcus aureus* is the most common causative organism
- Produce rapid swelling leading to a painful swollen flexed finger
- Extension exacerbates pain, which is localised to the sheath – often the base
- There is always a risk of tendon sloughing and adhesion formation
- Tendon sheath infections require urgent incision, drainage and washout, elevation, splintage and intravenous antibiotics

---

Kanavel's signs of tendon sheath infections

- Tenderness over flexor sheath
- Pain on passive extension
- Flexed posture of the digit
- Fusiform swelling of the digit

Web space infections

- Marked swelling extending to the back of the hand
- Painful, associated with systemic upset
- Can spread to adjacent web spaces or anterior aspect of palm
- Require elevation, intravenous antibiotics, and early incision and drainage

Midpalmar and thenar space infections

- These two compartments lie between the flexor tendons and the metacarpals
- Infection leads to gross swelling involving both dorsal and palmar aspects of the hand
- Unless a rapid response to antibiotics, elevation and splintage is seen, early incision and drainage are essential to preserve function

---

'Safe' or 'intrinsic plus' position of the hand

- Wrist slightly extended (20°)
- MCP joints flexed to 70°
- Interphalangeal joints fully extended

The described joint positions are those in which the collateral ligaments and volar plates are fully extended. Thus, once movement is recommenced, there should be no shortening of these ligaments or plates and, therefore, no functional problems that cannot be overcome with physiotherapy. The 'safe' position is the preferred position for splintage of the hand.

10.4 Other disorders of the hand and wrist

Learning point

- The rheumatoid hand
- De Quervain's tenosynovitis
- Trigger finger
- Dupuytren's contracture
- Ganglion cysts
- Dermoid cysts

The rheumatoid hand

Rheumatoid disease frequently affects the hands and will involve joints, tendons, muscles, nerves and arteries. In RA, MCP and PIP joints are commonly involved whereas OA has a predilection for DIP joints and the basilar joint of the thumb.

- Early changes: hand warm and moist
- Later changes: joint swelling and tenderness; synovial tendon sheath and joint thickening with effusion, muscle wasting and ultimately deformity

Tendon involvement in the rheumatoid hand

Tendon rupture, joint damage and subluxation are the main factors leading to severe deformity (swan-neck and Boutonnière deformities are covered in Section 10.2).

- Flexor pollicis longus (FPL) is the most common flexor tendon to rupture due to carpal irregularities
- Extensor tendon ruptures are often sequential, beginning in the ulnar extensors of the little and ring fingers and progressing in a radial direction

The pathogenesis of tendon damage in RA includes:

- Local infiltration from synovitis of surrounding synovial tendon sheath
- Repeated trauma from rubbing over rough bony prominences

Conservative management of the rheumatoid hand

To alleviate pain, preserve movement and minimise deformity:

- Analgesia
- Rest
- Splintage
- Physiotherapy

Surgical management of the rheumatoid hand

- **Synovectomy:** synovial thickening before joint destruction is amenable to synovectomy. This relieves pain and slows the progression of the destruction
- **Joint replacement:** in joint destruction with functional impairment, joint replacement is very helpful
- **Tendon repair:** for spontaneous rupture of tendons in RA, surgical exploration is warranted. It is often difficult to perform direct end-to-end repair due to poor quality of tendon from long-term trauma. Surgeons often need to use tendon transfer in the guise of a free tendon interposition graft or to employ end-to-side technique, hitching the ruptured tendon onto an intact extensor mechanism. This results in a mass action effect
- **Arthrodesis:** where stability is more important than flexibility (eg wrist, cervical spine)
- **Physiotherapy:** an essential part of postoperative management – as in all hand surgery

De Quervain's tenosynovitis

This is a stenosis of the tendon sheath of the first dorsal wrist compartment containing the APL (abductor pollicis longus) and EPB (extensor pollicis brevis) tendons. It occurs in inflammatory arthritides but can result from overuse, eg holding, patting and rocking a newborn. In China this is called 'mother's hand'.

- Occurs in inflammatory arthritides but may result from overuse
- Most common in women aged 30–50
- Symptoms include pain and tenderness localised to the dorsoradial aspect of the wrist, which is exacerbated by thumb movement

CHAPTER 9

Use **Finkelstein's test** to diagnose:

- The patient makes a fist over the thumb while the wrist is passively deviated in an ulnar direction
- This should elicit pain from the tension placed on the APL and EPB tendons

Differential diagnoses of de Quervain's tenosynovitis

- OA of the first CMC (carpometacarpal) joint
- OA of wrist
- Scaphoid fracture
- Wartenburg syndrome (neuritis of the superficial branch of the radial nerve)
- Intersection syndrome (tenosynovitis of the second dorsal wrist compartment where the APL and EPB tendons cross over the ECRL and ECRB tendons)

Management of de Quervain's tenosynovitis

Manage non-surgically initially with rest and avoidance of provoking movements. Steroid injections can be used. If these measures fail, then resort to surgical release of the first dorsal wrist compartment.

Trigger finger (stenosing tenosynovitis)

Thickening of the fibrous tendon sheath (usually after trauma or unaccustomed activity) leads to narrowing of the sheath (stenosing tenovaginitis or tenosynovitis). A flexor tendon of the thumb or finger may become trapped at the entrance to the sheath until in forced extension, when it passes the constriction with a snap (triggering). This results in locking of the digit in flexion that is only passively correctable. The pathology is usually related to the A1 pulley.

The most common patient is the healthy middle-aged woman; however, triggering is associated with RA, gout and diabetes. The patient's finger remains flexed when she tries to open her hands from a fist. On further effort, or with help from the other hand, it suddenly straightens with a snap. The finger clicks when she bends it and a tender nodule may be felt in front of the affected sheath.

This stenosing tenosynovitis can be injected with steroids or managed by surgical release in more intractable cases.

In RA, however, the A1 pulley should be preserved to prevent flexor tendon bowstringing and ulnar deviation of the digits. A flexor tenosynovectomy should therefore be performed.

Dupuytren's contracture

This is a proliferative fibroplasia of the palmar and digital fascia that results in the formation of nodules and cords, leading to flexion contractures of the fingers. The pathophysiology is unclear. It affects men more than women (10:1 M:F).

The exact cause is unknown.

Fingers affected by Dupuytren's contracture

- | Ring (most commonly)
- | Little
- | Middle
- | Index
- ↓ Thumb (least commonly)

Conditions associated with Dupuytren's contracture

- Familial trait (mainly)
- Diabetes mellitus
- Idiopathic
- Alcoholic cirrhosis
- Phenytoin usage (and hence epilepsy)
- Trauma

Fibromatosis of the plantar fascia (Ledderhose's disease) and penile fibromatosis (Peyronie's disease) are associated with an aggressive and often severe form of Dupuytren's disease called Dupuytren's diathesis.

Treatment of Dupuytren's contracture

Indications for surgical treatment of Dupuytren's contracture

- If the contracture causes a functional problem (such as with putting hand in trouser pocket)
- MCP joint contracture of more than 30°
- Any degree of PIP joint contracture warrants early intervention because this can be difficult to correct
- Maceration or infection of the palmar skinfolds

Surgical management of Dupuytren's contracture is now aimed at early intervention with limited or segmental fasciectomy procedures to combat the development of established joint contractures.

- **Fasciotomy:** division of diseased cords
- **Fasciectomy:** excision of diseased cords
- **Dermofasciectomy:** excision of involved overlying palmar skin requiring full-thickness skin grafting

The dissection is often difficult because the neurovascular bundles are displaced by the disease process. Involvement of skin may necessitate Z-plasty or skin excision and full-thickness skin grafting.

Postoperative management includes splintage and physiotherapy.

Complications of surgery for Dupuytren's contracture

- Nerve injury
- Vascular compromise
- Haematoma
- Infection
- Stiffness
- Recurrence

Ganglion cysts

Ganglion cysts arise from tendons or joints and are essentially a herniation of fluid from the joint or tendon sheath contained within a capsule. They communicate directly with the joint or tendon sheath.

Ganglion cysts transilluminate; however, tumours with a high water content such as soft-tissue myxoma and myxoid chondro-sarcoma may also transilluminate.

CHAPTER 9

Mucous cysts are small ganglion cysts that arise from either the radial or the ulnar aspect of the DIP joints of the fingers or thumb. They are associated with OA and often have an associated osteophyte.

Aspiration of a ganglion is the first line of treatment and this can be repeated more than once. Steroid injections have been used successfully. If resistant to these methods then surgical excision may be indicated. It is important to excise the origin of the ganglion to prevent recurrence.

Dermoid cysts

Learning point

A dermoid cyst is a cyst, deep to the skin, which is lined by skin.
Skin can become trapped in the subcutaneous tissues, either during fetal development (**congenital dermoid cyst**) or after an injury that forces skin into the deeper tissues (**acquired/implantation dermoid cyst**).

Congenital dermoid cyst

- **Definition:** congenital subcutaneous cyst caused by developmental inclusion of epidermis along lines of fusion
- **Histology:** cyst is lined by stratified squamous epithelium but, unlike epidermal (sebaceous) cysts, the wall also contains functioning epidermal appendages (such as hair follicles, and sweat and sebaceous glands)
- **Sites:** occurs at sites of fusion of skin

dermatomes, typically the lateral and medial ends of the eyebrow (external and internal angular dermoid), the midline of the nose (nasal dermoid), sublingually, the midline of the neck, and at any point in the midline of the trunk, typically the perineum and sacrum
- **Complications:** may create a bony depression. May penetrate down to the dura. A nasal dermoid may look similar to a small superficial pit but may be an extensive cyst that passes between the nasal bones towards the sphenoid sinus
- **Treatment:** rarely troublesome and rarely get infected so can be left alone. Not to be excised by an SHO on the locals list! Need an experienced surgeon in case of deep extension. May need CT scans and skull radiographs preoperatively

Acquired/implantation dermoid cyst
- **Definition:** cyst is formed after the survival of a piece of skin forcibly implanted into the subcutaneous tissues by an injury such as a small, deep cut or stab injury. The patient may not remember the injury. The histology is similar to that of the congenital dermoid
- **Sites:** occurs in areas subject to repeated trauma (such as volar aspect of fingers and palms), so tend to be troublesome, interfere with function, and can become painful and tender. Cysts arise from the subcutaneous tissue and are usually attached to neither the skin (unlike sebaceous cysts) nor the deeper structures (unlike some congenital dermoids)
- **Management:** excision. This is commonly confused with a sebaceous cyst, but the presence of a scar and history of an old injury are helpful in differentiating them. Dermoid cysts, unlike sebaceous cysts, rarely become infected

10.5 Upper limb peripheral nerve compression neuropathies

Brachial plexus injuries

Erb's palsy

This birth traction lesion usually affects C5–C7 (shoulder to elbow). Initial treatment is physiotherapy, but if there is no biceps or shoulder recovery by 4 months of age then surgery by nerve grafting should be considered.

Adult traction injury

This is usually the result of a motor vehicle accident and can affect the whole plexus. Avulsion of the roots is more common in adults than in infants. If there is total paralysis of the limb an MR scan will determine if there is root avulsion. Treatment is usually early exploration and nerve graft. If there is partial paralysis the management is usually observation for 3–5 months then, if not recovered, consider neurolysis ± grafting.

Median nerve injury

Median nerve roots

Lateral and ulnar cords of brachial plexus: C5, C6, C7, C8, T1.

Course of the median nerve

The medial root crosses in front of the third part of the axillary artery to join the lateral root. It runs downwards on the lateral side of the brachial artery, crossing to the medial side halfway down the upper arm. It is superficial here but is crossed at the elbow by the bicipital aponeurosis. It passes between the two heads of the pronator teres, separated from the ulnar artery by the ulnar head of pronator teres. It runs down behind flexor digitorum superficialis and is attached to its deep surface by connective tissue. It rests posteriorly on flexor digitorum profundus. At the wrist the median nerve emerges from the lateral border of flexor digitorum superficialis and lies behind the tendon of palmaris longus. It enters the palm, passing under flexor retinaculum, through the carpal tunnel and immediately divides into lateral and medial branches, each of which gives muscular and cutaneous terminal branches.

Median nerve branches and what they supply

Near the elbow
- Flexor digitorum superficialis
- Flexor carpi radialis
- Palmaris longus
- Pronator teres

In the forearm (via anterior interosseous branch)
- Flexor pollicis longus
- Half of flexor digitorum profundus
- Pronator quadratus

In the hand
- Motor (the LOAF muscles of the thenar eminence)
  - **L**ateral two lumbricals
  - **O**pponens pollicis
  - **A**bductor pollicis
  - **F**lexor pollicis brevis
- Sensation (of the lateral palm and lateral two and a half fingers)

Causes of damage to the median nerve

Carpal tunnel syndrome: may occur after wrist fractures

At the wrist: especially from lacerations here

In the forearm: (anterior interosseous nerve) from forearm bone fractures

Distal to the elbow: pronator teres nerve entrapment syndrome

At the elbow: eg after dislocations in children, supracondylar fractures

---

Examination of the median nerve

Inspection
Patient has rolled-up sleeves.

Look for:
- Thenar wasting
- Simian thumb (thumb appears ape-like due to thenar wasting)
- Decreased pulp of the index finger
- Cigarette burns
- Local trauma between the index and middle fingers
- Wasting of the lateral aspect of the forearm
- Benediction sign (index and middle fingers remain extended at MCP joint when patient is asked to make a fist – deinnervation of lateral two lumbricals)
- Cubitus valgus or varus (previous supracondylar fracture?)
- Scars around the elbow, forearm and wrist

Palpation
- Palpate the nerve where it is superficial at the wrist

Sensation
- Palmar side: radial side of the palm and thumb and the radial two and a half fingers
- Dorsal side: the radial two and a half fingers and the tip of the thumb

Power
- Abductor pollicis brevis: this muscle is invariably and exclusively supplied by the median nerve. Can the patient, with the hand flat on the table, palm up, lift the thumb off the table against resistance?
- Flexor pollicis longus (flex tip of thumb)
- Pronator teres (pronate arm against resistance)

Tests for carpal tunnel syndrome if relevant

- Tinel's test
- Phalen's test
- Tourniquet test

(See Carpal tunnel syndrome below.)

Carpal tunnel syndrome

Learning point

This is compression and ischaemia of the median nerve in the carpal tunnel deep to the wrist flexor retinaculum. It commonly affects women (M:F 1:8) aged 30–60.

Causes of carpal tunnel syndrome
Can occur in healthy people
- Idiopathic
- Pregnancy
- Obesity
- Occupation
- Trauma

Can occur as a sign of underlying disease
- Myxoedema
- Rheumatoid arthritis
- Acromegaly
- Diabetes
- Congestive heart failure

Clinical features of carpal tunnel syndrome

- Pain and paraesthesiae in the distribution of the median nerve in the hand (thumb and lateral two and a half fingers)
- Wasting of the thenar muscles

- Pain worse at night, especially in the early hours
- Relieved by hanging arm out of bed and shaking it
- During the day little pain is felt unless wrists are held still (eg knitting, holding a paper)
- Daytime symptoms are worse if pronator syndrome is present

Diagnostic tests for carpal tunnel syndrome
Phalen's test: ask patients to hold both wrists flexed for 1–2 minutes to see if this worsens or reproduces symptoms
Tourniquet test: apply sphygmomanometer cuff just above systolic BP for 1–2 minutes to see if this reproduces symptoms
Nerve conduction test: differentiate from cervical spondylosis involving C6 and C7

Treatment of carpal tunnel syndrome

- Conservative: wrist splints at night to prevent flexion
- Surgical: division of flexor retinaculum and decompression of nerve

Pronator syndrome

Pronator syndrome manifests itself as pain in the volar surface of the distal upper arm and forearm with loss of sensation in the radial three and a half digits.

Phalen's and Tinel's tests are negative at the wrist. Symptoms may be exacerbated by resisted pronation of the forearm.

CHAPTER 9

Anterior interosseous nerve syndrome

This is a loss of motor function in FPL, FDP index and pronator quadratus without sensory loss.

Ulnar nerve lesions

Ulnar nerve roots

Medial cord of brachial plexus: C8, T1.

Course of the ulnar nerve

It descends between the axillary artery and vein, and then runs down on the medial side of the brachial artery, as far as the middle of the arm. Here, at the insertion of coracobrachialis, the nerve pierces the medial fascial septum, accompanied by the superior ulnar collateral artery, and enters the posterior compartment of the arm. It descends behind the septum, covered posteriorly by the medial head of triceps. At the elbow it lies superficially behind the medial epicondyle of the humerus on the medial ligament of the elbow joint. It enters the forearm between the two heads of origin of the flexor carpi ulnaris (FCU). It runs down the forearm between FCU and FDP, medial to the ulnar artery. At the wrist the ulnar nerve becomes superficial again and lies between the FCU and FDS tendons, entering the palm in front of the flexor retinaculum, lateral to the pisiform base, and divides into a superficial branch that ends in muscular and cutaneous branches, and a deep branch that runs backwards between abductor digiti minimi and flexor digiti minimi, piercing opponens digiti minimi and winding around the hook of the hamate. It passes laterally in the deep palmar arch, giving off muscular branches.

Ulnar nerve branches and what they supply

In the forearm:
Muscles
- FCU
- 50% of FDP
- Skin

Dorsal cutaneous branch
- Medial skin of dorsum of hand
- Medial one and a half digits

Joints
- Elbow

In the hand:
Muscles
- Hypothenar muscles
- Interossei
- Two medial lumbricals
- Adductor pollicis

Skin
- Superficial palmar branch
- Ulnar one and a half digits
- Palmar cutaneous branch
- Medial skin of palm

Common causes of ulnar nerve palsy (distal to proximal)

Ulnar tunnel syndrome: where the nerve enters the palm via Guyon's canal, a fibro-osseous tunnel is formed between the pisiform and the hook of the hamate. Compression may also be due to a ganglion or fractured hook of the hammate. The most distal lesions affect the deep palmar branch and are entirely motor.

At the wrist: from lacerations, occupational trauma and ganglion cysts.

Distal to the elbow (compression occurs in several sites):
- As the nerve passes between the two heads of the FCU, 3–5 cm distal to the medial epicondyle. Compression here may give rise to cubital tunnel syndrome, which is characterised by intermittent numbness in the ulnar nerve distribution associated with elbow flexion and relieved by elbow extension
- As it runs along the medial head of triceps, where it is at risk in the presence of a subluxing medial head of triceps
- As it runs in the thick medial intermuscular septum

At the level of the medial epicondyle: where it is very superficial due to trauma, local friction, pressure or stretching (eg in cubitus valgus or osteoarthritis).

The arcade of Struthers: a fascial arcade of the intermuscular septum which is located 8 cm proximal to the medial epicondyle.

After supracondylar fractures: or other fractures around the elbow.

In the brachial plexus: due to trauma, traction, cervical rib, Pancoast's tumour, etc.

Examination of the ulnar nerve

Inspection
Ask patient to roll up their sleeves.

Look for
- **Claw hand:** a claw deformity most marked in the little and ring fingers due to loss of action of interossei and lumbricals. The MCP joints are thus extended and the IP joints flexed. If the ulnar nerve lesion is distal to the FDP muscle belly, then the function of FDP to the ring and little fingers will be intact, paradoxically giving a more marked flexor deformity
- **Ulceration** of the skin
- **Brittle nails**
- **Trophic changes**

- **Wasting** of the:
  - Hypothenar eminence
  - Dorsal first web space
  - Medial forearm
- **Cubitus valgus** or **varus**
- **Scars** around the elbow, forearm and wrist

Palpation
- At the elbow
- At the wrist

Sensation
- Ulnar side of the palm over the hypothenar eminence
- Ulnar one and a half fingers
- Ulnar side of the dorsum of the hand (proximal lesion)

CHAPTER 9

Power

- Interossei
- First dorsal interosseus
- Abductor digiti minimi
- Froment's test for adductor pollicis weakness:
  - Put a sheet of paper between the thumb and index finger
  - If there is no adductor pollicis power then the patient will flex thumb at the IP joint to maintain hold on paper

---

Signs of a distal ulnar nerve lesion (eg lesion at wrist)

- Flexor carpi ulnaris intact
- Ulnar half of flexor digitorum profundus is intact (paradoxically worse claw hand)
- No muscle wasting of forearm
- Sensation of ulnar side of dorsum of hand intact

Signs of a proximal ulnar nerve lesion (eg lesion at elbow)

- FCU affected (decreased abduction of little finger)
- Ulnar half of FDP affected (decreased flexion of DIP joint of little finger)
- Muscle wasting of medial forearm
- Sensation of ulnar side of dorsum of hand affected

Radial nerve injuries

Radial nerve roots

Posterior cord of brachial plexus: C5, C6, C7.

Course of the radial nerve

This arises posterior to the axillary artery. It runs with the profunda brachii artery, between the long and medial heads of triceps. It runs in the spiral groove of the humerus between the medial and lateral heads of triceps (where it is susceptible to injury in humerus fractures). It lies deep to brachioradialis. It then passes anterior to the lateral epicondyle and runs between brachialis and brachioradialis, before dividing into superficial sensory and deep posterior interosseous motor branches. The 'supinator tunnel' refers to where the fibres of the supinator muscle are arranged in two planes, between which the deep posterior interosseous branch of the radial nerve lies.

Branches of the radial nerve and what they supply

Above the elbow:
Muscles
- Triceps
- Brachialis (lateral part)
- Brachioradialis
- Extensor carpi radialis longus

Joint
- Elbow

Skin
- Posterior cutaneous branch to back of the arm and forearm

Below the elbow:
- The nerve enters the lateral cubital fossa and divides into two branches.

Posterior interosseous (deep) branch
- Runs between two heads of supinator passing into posterior compartment
- Supplies supinator and all extensors

Superficial radial branch
- Runs under brachioradialis lateral to radial artery
- Supplies skin of dorsum of hand and lateral three and a half digits

---

Examination of the radial nerve

Inspection
Ask the patient to roll up his or her sleeves.

Look for:
- Wrist drop
- Forearm wasting
- Triceps wasting

Power
- Extensors (extend fingers, extend wrist)
- Supinator (elbow extended, supinate against resistance)
- Brachioradialis (feel for it as elbow flexes against resistance)
- Triceps (extend elbow)

Sensation
- Lesions distal to the elbow (anatomical snuffbox)
- Higher lesion (back of the forearm also)

Radial nerve palsy

Motor effects
- Wrist drop (inability to extend wrist or MCP joints of all the digits)
- Forearm extensor wasting
- Brachioradialis (loss of supination) and triceps weakness suggest very high nerve lesions

Sensory effects
- Loss confined to anatomical snuffbox in distal lesions
- Loss of sensation along back of forearm suggests higher lesions

Posterior interosseous nerve palsy results in motor loss to all finger extensors but wrist drop is less marked as ECRL is spared. Also there is no sensory loss.

A dynamic wrist extension splint can be used to restore active hand function.

Causes of damage of the radial nerve

In the axilla
- 'Saturday night palsy', ie neuropraxia from sleeping with arm over the back of a chair
- Ill-fitting crutches (axillary crutches have now all but disappeared for just this reason. Most patients are now given elbow crutches)

Midhumerus
- Fractures of humerus
- Tourniquet palsies

At and below the elbow
- Elbow dislocations
- Monteggia fractures
- Ganglion cysts
- Surgical trauma

In the supinator tunnel
The course of the radial nerve from the radial head to the supinator muscle has four sites of potential compression:
- A tight fibrous band anterior to the radial head at the entrance of the supinator tunnel
- The radial recurrent vessels then fan out over the nerve (which is called the 'leash of Henry') and if tortuous may compress the nerve
- The tendinous margin of extensor carpi radialis brevis
- The proximal supinator

CHAPTER 9

SECTION 11

Orthopaedic infections

11.1 Pathology of orthopaedic infection

Learning point

Acute and chronic bone infections used to be common and were often fatal, especially in children. Antibiotics have made these infections eminently treatable.

Bacteria are usually blood-borne and there is often no obvious primary focus of infection.

In 80% of cases the organism is *Staphylococcus aureus*.

Other organisms causing infection are streptococci, pneumococci, *Haemophilus influenzae* (common in children under 2 years of age), *Staphylococcus albus* and *Salmonella* spp.

Learning point

The natural history of bone infections:
- Start at metaphysis
- Travel through cortex
- Exudate deep to periosteum lifts it
- Subperiosteal pus
- Cortex infarction
- Sequestrum – dead bone within infection
- Involucrum – new bone forming in response to infection

The pattern of infection in a bone varies depending on the age of the patient.

These variations are explained by changes in blood supply that occur with growth. Osteomyelitis can lead to septic arthritis and vice versa.

Natural history of bone infections

Bone infections almost always begin at the metaphysis. They progress through the cortex via the haversian canals, causing thrombosis of blood vessels, eventually reaching the subperiosteal region. In the first 24–48 hours an inflammatory exudate forms deep to the periosteum, elevating the membrane. The periosteum is innervated and inelastic, so this stretching causes pain.

After 24 hours frank pus develops subperiosteally. This rarely affects the growth plate because it contains no blood vessels and the periosteum is firmly attached to plate at this level. The inflammatory process progresses along the medulla, causing venous and arterial thrombosis.

The pus tracks subperiosteally, stripping the periosteum and interrupting its blood supply. In this way, progressively larger areas of cortex become involved and infarcted. The bony infarct is known as a sequestrum.

Surrounding the sequestrum, the elevated periosteum lays down new bone that encloses the dead bone within. The ensheathing mass of new bone is known as the involucrum.

In the absence of treatment the pus bursts through periosteum, tracking through muscle to reach the skin, eventually forming a sinus connecting bone to skin surface. Where pus has broken through the periosteum sinuses develop within the involucrum, and are known as cloacae (Latin for 'a drain'). Advanced pathology such as this is rare with modern treatment.

The intraosseous abscess cavity is prevented from resolving by its bony walls, which are impenetrable to both the body's normal defence mechanisms and to antibiotic treatment.

Infection and osseous blood supply

The sites at which a haematogenous infection is likely to settle are determined by the anatomy of the blood supply. The blood supply to the metaphysis, physis and epiphysis changes with growth.

In infants a few of the nutrient arteries may cross the physis. Infection of the epiphysis (and spread to the joint) is more likely.

In the growing child the nutrient artery terminates in a network of capillary loops in the metaphysis. Abnormal cells (eg sickled red blood cells) and bacteria are likely to stop here, establishing infection in the metaphysis.

In the adult, vessels will again cross the physis.

The vertebrae have nutrient vessels that cross into the discs until the age of 12 years. These vessels close with growth, and the disc becomes relatively avascular. Children under the age of 12 are therefore more likely to develop primary septic discitis than adults. In adults, the disc can become infected via spread of infection from the vertebral endplate.

The vertebrae have a valveless venous plexus (of Baston) which allows retrograde flow or local stasis around the vertebrae. This makes the vertebrae potential seeding sites for haematogenous infection or metastasis.

Spread of infection

Osteomyelitis may lead to a septic arthritis via one of several possible routes:
- Direct joint entry from the intra-articular physis (eg shoulder, elbow, wrist, hip, knee)
- Subperiosteal spread
- Spread to the epiphysis or direct epiphyseal infection and spread to the joint

CHAPTER 9

11.2 Septic arthritis

> ### Learning point
>
> Septic arthritis is the invasion of any joint by a microorganism. (This is in contrast to reactive arthritis, which is an inflammatory response to infection elsewhere in the body.) Any hot, swollen, painful joint is septic arthritis until proved otherwise. It is a potentially life-threatening condition. It can progress to systemic sepsis and destroy the affected joints.

> **Septic arthritis must be treated as a surgical emergency.**

Aetiology of septic arthritis

The aetiology of septic arthritis is still not well understood. It is clear that bacteria are in the joint, but how do they get there? There is a very low infection rate after a puncture or penetrating injury to a normal joint. It is thought that there may be a dysfunction in the synovium that allows a sufficiently large number of bacteria to enter the joint and establish an infection.

Sources of infection

- Direct inoculation (eg penetrating trauma)
- Local extension from nearby osteomyelitis
- Blood-borne from distal site or systemic infection, spread from synovium or epiphysis

Causative organisms

Common organisms

- *S. aureus* is most common in all ages
- *Neisseria gonorrhoeae* in young adults
- *H. influenzae* in neonates and infants (becoming less common because of immunisation with the 5-in-1 vaccine)
- Group B streptococci
- Pneumococci

Less common organisms

- Gram-negative rods
- *Escherichia coli*
- *Proteus* spp.
- *Pseudomonas* spp.
- Fungi

> **Risk factors for septic arthritis**
> - Very young age
> - Very old age
> - Intravenous drug abuse
> - Diabetes
> - Pre-existing joint problems

Clinical features of septic arthritis

- Restricted and painful range of motion
- General malaise
- Spiking pyrexia, rapid onset
- Joint is hot, red and swollen
- In infants it commonly affects the hip
- In children it commonly affects the knee
- In adults it most commonly affects the knee, followed by the hip, ankle, elbow, shoulder, wrist and hand

Investigating septic arthritis

Imaging

- **Radiography:** of joint may show effusion and soft-tissue swelling. Bony changes such as periarticular osteoporosis and resorption occur late and are not seen in the acute phase. Chondrocalcinosis does not exclude sepsis, but does make pseudogout or gout a more likely diagnosis. Early degenerative change may be seen in around 70% of elderly patients presenting with septic arthritis
- **Ultrasonography:** to confirm effusion and allow diagnostic aspiration of joint
- **Chest radiograph:** if tuberculosis (TB) is suspected
- **MR or isotope bone scans:** these are less useful than ultrasonography and will delay definitive treatment (they are not used often)

Microbiology

- **Blood culture**
- **Joint aspiration:** should be done in a clean environment and under sterile conditions. Large effusions of the knee are easily aspirated. The needle is inserted into the joint above the patella, either medially or laterally. The needle should not be passed through obviously infected skin. Joint aspirates should be sent for:
  - Urgent microscopy
  - Gram stain and culture
  - Uric acid (sodium urate) or calcium pyrophosphate crystals
  - Organisms
- **Gonorrhoea-specific swabs** of the urethra, cervix, throat and rectum

Other lab tests

- FBC (full blood count)
- CRP and ESR/plasma viscosity (PV) (useful for monitoring response to treatment)

- U&Es (urea and electrolytes)
- Uric acid (raised serum uric acid suggests gout, but only the presence or absence of uric acid crystals in the joint can confirm or exclude this diagnosis)

The combination of inability to weight-bear, fever, raised WCC (white cell count) and raised ESR predicts a 99% chance that sepsis is responsible. If three of these features are present the chance of sepsis is 93%.

Differential diagnosis of septic arthritis

Differential diagnosis in children

- Transient synovitis
- Acute osteomyelitis
- Haemarthrosis (usually haemophilia)
- Henoch–Schönlein purpura (small-vessel vasculitis with purpuric rash on the extensor surface of the lower limbs, buttocks and back of thighs)
- Perthes' disease

Differential diagnosis in adults

- Inflammatory or septic bursitis (especially around the knee and elbow)
- Crystal arthropathy of gout (negatively birefringent sodium urate crystals) or pseudogout (positively birefringent calcium pyrophosphate crystals)
- Osteomyelitis
- Reactive arthritis
- Haemarthrosis (anticoagulation, trauma)
- Synovitis (in rheumatoid and other inflammatory arthropathies)
- Lyme disease (caused by transmission of the spirochaete *Borrelia burgdorferi* from infected tick bites; there is an initial rash followed after several weeks by a painful effusion of the knee)

CHAPTER 9

Management of septic arthritis

> ### Learning point
>
> This must be done **without delay** because septic arthritis is a surgical emergency. Resuscitation of the patient and preservation of the articular cartilage are the priorities. The combined action of bacteria and the inflammatory response can destroy articular cartilage in a matter of hours.

Joint aspiration

See 'Investigating septic arthritis' above. This is both diagnostic and therapeutic. Aspiration will remove some of the bacteria and white blood cells (WBCs) and their products, which degrade the cartilage. It is not a substitute for surgical washout.

Surgical washout

Formal surgical washout is indicated if Gram stain or microbiology is positive, or if the index of suspicion is high. Joints such as the hip, elbow or ankle may require an arthrotomy for washout. The knee or shoulder may be washed out arthroscopically using separate portals for inflow and outflow. However, if the infection is established and loculated an arthrotomy will be required.

- Washout should be continued until the outflow is clear (3–6 litres). Remember that 'the solution to pollution is dilution'
- Washout may have to be repeated after 48 hours
- Joint immobilisation

The joint should be immobilised after washout, in a position of optimum function:

- **Shoulder** 40–50° abduction, elbow joint anterior to the coronal plane and hand in front of the mouth
- **Elbow** flexed 90° and semipronated
- **Wrist** dorsiflexed (to maintain strong grip)
- **Hip** neutral abduction and rotation
- **Knee** 5–10° flexion (to allow the foot to clear ground when walking)
- **Ankle** 90°

Antibiotics

Intravenous antibiotics may be given once joint fluid and blood have been obtained for culture.

- Initial antibiotics (eg flucloxacillin and benzylpenicillin) cover the likely organisms (eg *S. aureus* and streptococci) and are changed once the culture and sensitivity results are available
- Intravenous antibiotics are continued until there is significant clinical improvement in the condition of the patient and the affected joint, and inflammatory markers have normalised
- Oral antibiotics are given for 2–6 weeks (discuss this with your microbiologist)

Complications of septic arthritis

Early complications

- Effusion
- Soft-tissue swelling
- Muscle wasting
- Periarticular osteoporosis

Late complications

In adults
- Secondary OA
- Joint stiffness
- Fibrous/bony ankylosis

In children
- Destruction of physis
- Growth arrest or abnormality (in the case of the hip this can lead to dislocation of the hip joint)

11.3 Acute osteomyelitis

> **Learning point**
>
> Osteomyelitis is the term applied to any bacterial infection of bone. It may be classified by the route of spread:
> - Haematogenous (by blood)
> - Post-traumatic (via open wound)
> - Contiguous (from local soft-tissue infection)
>
> Osteomyelitis may present acutely with pain and features of sepsis, or chronically with established infection and radiographic changes.
>
> Infections of bone after open fractures or infections of bone or implants after joint replacement surgery represent part of the spectrum of osteomyelitis.
>
> Treatment involves resuscitation, antibiotics, splintage, aspiration or surgical debridement, and rehabilitation.

Aetiology of acute osteomyelitis

Causative organisms

Common causes
- *S. aureus* is most common in all ages
- *H. influenzae* and haemolytic streptococci in neonates and infants

Other causes
- *Salmonella* spp. in patients with sickle cell disease
- Entry from urinary tract infections (UTIs), infected intravenous access sites or ENT (ear, nose, throat) sepsis

> **Risk factors for acute osteomyelitis**
> - Very young age
> - Very old age
> - Intravenous drug abuse
> - Immunocompromise
> - Diabetes
> - Sickle cell disease

Clinical features of acute osteomyelitis
- Pain that increases in severity
- Localised bony tenderness
- Systemic toxicity and pyrexia
- Joint effusion (adjacent joints may contain an effusion but the joint itself will not be tender and some movement is possible; this contrasts with infective arthritis in which even small movements are very painful)
- Commonly metaphyseal in infants and vertebral in adults

CHAPTER 9

Differential diagnosis of osteomyelitis

- Acute suppurative arthritis (distinguish joint pain from bone pain)
- Acute RA (polyarticular)
- Subperiosteal haematoma (eg haemophilia and scurvy)
- Bone infarct secondary to sickle crisis
- Ewing's tumour

Investigating acute osteomyelitis

- **Radiograph:** there are no abnormal radiological signs in the first 10–14 days (radiological changes can appear sooner in infants). Periosteal elevation plus new bone deposition (involucrum) may be seen after 10 days. The initial radiographs provide a useful baseline and help exclude other pathologies such as Ewing's tumour
- **Isotope bone scan:** this is useful in areas of difficult localisation, such as vertebral infection. Bone scans do not show abscess formation and give no information on collections which may need drainage, so ultrasonography, CT and MRI are more useful
- **Ultrasonography:** may show a soft-tissue or subperiosteal collection, which can be aspirated under ultrasound control or drained in an open procedure
- **MRI:** gives useful information regarding size and position of bone infection and associated periosteal or soft-tissue collections
- **CT:** unlike MRI, this may be used to guide needle aspiration of collections
- **Blood cultures:** must be taken before antibiotics are commenced
- **Other investigations**
    - Bone and tissue cultures
    - FBC
    - U&Es
    - CRP
    - PV/ESR

Management of acute osteomyelitis

The priority in acute osteomyelitis is to obtain samples for culture and prescribe the correct antibiotics. Management involves the following:

- **Resuscitation**
- **Intravenous antibiotics** (after appropriate cultures have been obtained)
- **Splintage** of the affected limb (to prevent soft-tissue contracture)
- **Radiographically guided aspiration or surgical evacuation** of significant soft-tissue or subperiosteal collections (surgical evacuation is preferable for large collections; all devitalised tissue may be excised and the procedure can be repeated if required)
- **Rehabilitation** of the patient and affected limb
- The duration of the antibiotic course is controversial: 10–14 days of intravenous antibiotics followed by oral antibiotics for a total of 4–6 weeks is a reasonable plan

Sequelae, complications and prognosis of acute osteomyelitis

Before antibiotics were available, the mortality rate was about 20%; now it is approaching 0%. In 5% there are long-term sequelae:

- Recurrence
- Chronic osteomyelitis
- Septic arthritis
- Pathological fractures through devascularised bone (sequestrum), which will heal if the infection is successfully treated and the fracture is reduced and stabilised for a sufficiently long period

- Damage to the growth plate, causing either complete growth arrest or an angular deformity as part of the physis continues to grow

Brodie's abscess

This is a subacute abscess in the metaphysis of any long bone that presents with pain. It is typically seen in the distal tibia of patients under 25 years of age. Cultures may be negative. Curettage and appropriate antibiotics are generally successful.

11.4 Chronic osteomyelitis

Learning point

Chronic osteomyelitis arises from acute osteomyelitis, open fractures, or local soft-tissue infection (contiguous osteomyelitis).

Classification of chronic osteomyelitis

The Cierny–Mader classification system considers the anatomy of infection, local factors and systemic patient factors (such as smoking and vascular disease).

Classification based on anatomical stage:
- Medullary (confined to the medullary cavity)
- Superficial (periosteum and cortex)
- Localised (medulla and periosteum, with formation of draining sinus and cloacae)
- Diffuse (through-and-through infection)

Aetiology and pathogenesis of chronic osteomyelitis

The formation of sequestrum and involucrum is followed by the formation of an encasing layer of scar tissue. This results in a hypovascular area, which is poorly penetrated by the patient's immune system or antibiotics (poor blood supply). The encapsulated necrotic and infected material cannot be resorbed, and provides a continuing focus of infection. The infection will not resolve until this material is excised. Some of this material will occasionally be ejected from the sinus.

Microbiology
- *S. aureus* (most common)
- Anaerobes
- Gram-negative bacilli

Risk factors for chronic osteomyelitis
- Smoking
- Malnutrition
- Immunocompromise
- Diabetes
- Steroids
- Vascular disease (arterial and venous)
- Multiple medical comorbidities

Clinical features of chronic osteomyelitis

Chronic osteomyelitis usually involves:
- Long bones
- Vertebral bodies
- Small bones of the feet (especially in diabetes)

It usually presents with:
- Pain
- Chronic inflammation
- Sinus formation or ulceration

CHAPTER 9

701

Investigating chronic osteomyelitis

- **Plain radiograph:** diagnostic changes are usually well established in haematogenous chronic osteomyelitis. The appearance will change with treatment, but may lag behind by 10–14 days. In contiguous osteomyelitis the radiographic changes may be more subtle and difficult to distinguish from the disuse changes associated with longstanding soft-tissue infection
- **MRI:** is useful for differentiating soft-tissue infection from osteomyelitis. Both MRI and CT are adversely affected by the presence of metallic implants
- **CT:** can identify necrotic bone
- **Isotope bone scan:** is useful to localise infection in difficult areas such as the vertebral column. CT and MRI are probably more useful if available
- **CRP, PV, ESR:** inflammatory markers are useful for monitoring the response to treatment
- **Blood culture:** positive blood cultures with radiographic changes of osteomyelitis are sufficient to base the treatment on
- **Bone biopsy:** is indicated if blood cultures are negative, or if the infection does not respond to the initial treatment
- **Swabs from the sinus tract:** are seldom indicated as the tract will be colonised with many organisms, so the culture and sensitivity results will not reflect the situation in the bone

Note: check previous microbiology results. Recurrent episodes are likely to be due to the same organism, but repeated cultures are mandatory.

Management of chronic osteomyelitis

The aim is to arrest the infection and restore function.

- **Identify the organism**
- **Give intravenous antibiotics** for 2 weeks followed by 4 weeks of oral antibiotics. This total of 6 weeks from start of treatment or last surgery treats the infection and prevents infection of viable bone as it revascularises after surgical debridement
- **Improve general patient factors** such as:
  - Stop the patient from smoking
  - Correct malnutrition
  - Give hyperbaric oxygen
  - Revascularisation of an ischaemic limb by the vascular team if necessary
- **Bone and soft-tissue management** aims to:
  - Eradicate dead material (eg surgical debridement of bone, scar tissue, implants)
  - Reduce soft-tissue space (eg local flaps, free flaps, antibiotic-impregnated beads or cement)
  - Stabilise the skeleton
  - Promote fracture union and bone regeneration (the Ilizarov circular frame for distraction histiogenesis is a circular frame with multiple wires that transfix the bone. It can provide stability and fine control of movement. It can also be used to achieve compression, angular correction or distraction, resulting in the formation of new bone)

If there is ongoing infection after the end of the cycle, or if there is no response to treatment, repeat cultures and debridement, and administer antibiotics for another 6 weeks. Consider other options, such as amputation.

Sequelae and prognosis of chronic osteomyelitis

- Pain
- Recurrence
- Pathological fractures
- Sinus formation/ulceration
- Malignancies such as squamous cell carcinoma may develop in the margin of any chronic wound or sinus
- Amyloid deposited around the sinus as a result of chronic inflammation

11.5 Tuberculosis of the skeleton

Learning point

There has been a resurgence of TB in the UK. This is attributed to increased globalisation, increased incidence of immunocompromise (due to HIV) and the emergence of multidrug-resistant TB.

TB affects the joints, appendicular skeleton or (in 50% of cases) the vertebral column. Spread is haematogenous. *Mycobacterium tuberculosis* is the most common cause.

TB may mimic almost any bone pathology. It causes pain, stiffness and deformity, as well as systemic symptoms. Treatment is prolonged anti-TB chemotherapy, debridement and drainage where necessary, and reconstruction where bone destruction has caused problems.

Aetiology and pathogenesis of skeletal TB

TB may affect bones or joints (osseous TB or articular TB). Osteoarticular infection results from haematogenous spread from infection in regional lymph nodes from an initial pulmonary, gut or renal infection.

The vertebral column is affected in half of all cases. TB can affect any part of the spine, but commonly affects the thoracic region.

In the joints TB spreads to the synovium (high PO_2) or to intra-articular bone. This means that any synovial joint can be affected and any structures ensheathed in synovium (eg bursae or finger flexor tendons).

Tubercles develop in the synovial membrane, which becomes bulky and inflamed. There is an effusion within the synovial cavity. As this synovitis progresses it causes destruction of articular cartilage and adjacent bone, resulting in loss of function and fibrous ankylosis. In children, damage to the physis may cause growth arrest or angular deformity.

Is osseous TB the exudate from the infection may result in a **cold abscess**. This exudate collects in the soft tissue; the overlying skin is not red and is only slightly warm, with few signs of acute inflammation.

Microbiology of skeletal TB

Causative organisms

- *Mycobacterium tuberculosis* (most common)
- *M. bovis* (transmitted through unpasteurised cow's milk)
- *M. africanum* (confined to Africa)
- *M. avium*
- Non-tuberculous mycobacteria (NTM) (tendon sheath infection)

Characteristics

- Thin rods, alcohol-fast and acid-fast with ZN (Ziehl–Neelsen) staining
- Slow multiplication rate, best in high PO_2

Clinical features of skeletal TB

- Localised aches and pains (worse on exertion or at night)
- Increased stiffness
- Increased pain on joint movement (due to adhesion formation, muscle spasm and bone destruction; usually a single bone or joint)
- Synovial thickening and effusion in superficial joints
- Symptoms of spinal instability
- Kyphosis and abscess collection (late signs)
- Night sweats
- Anorexia and weight loss

Radiological changes of skeletal TB

These are not obvious in early disease.
- Soft-tissue swelling
- Narrowing of joint or disc space
- Osteolytic lesions in adjacent bone

TB may mimic almost any bone pathology.

Spinal TB

Spinal TB typically involves the vertebral body, but the pedicles, laminae or transverse process may be involved, and may be seen to have disappeared on the plain films.

Spinal TB may escape diagnosis until two adjacent vertebral bodies are involved, resulting in deformity.

Should treatment be delayed, progressive destruction occurs, leading to vertebral body collapse and kyphosis.

The exudate often tracks along tissue planes to present superficially:
- T12 involvement (and lumbar involvement) can lead to pus tracking along the psoas muscle to present as a 'cold' abscess in the groin
- Cervical lesions may point in the neck
- Retropharyngeal cold abscesses may cause dysphagia

The combination of granulation tissue, necrotic bone and disc material, cold abscess and spinal angulation may cause spinal cord compression. The blood supply via the anterior spinal arteries may also be compromised. Both may result in a neurological deficit, possibly paraplegia. It is not uncommon for patients to present multiple times to local medical services before spinal infection is diagnosed.

Investigation of skeletal TB

Early diagnosis and treatment are essential to preserve function. Early biopsy of involved tissue for histological and bacteriological examination should be performed. This shows acid-fast bacilli and typical tubercles.

- **Chest radiograph:** useful for excluding a primary pulmonary lesion (CT and MRI can also be used to 'hunt the primary')
- **Plain films:** may show generalised osteoporosis and 'cat bite' lesions (periarticular destruction). In osseous TB sequestrum and involucrum may be seen, but are less severe than in pyogenic osteomyelitis

- **CT:** to localise infection or for CT-guided biopsy
- **MRI:** this is useful, especially in spinal TB, to assess cord/root compression and abscess formation
- **Culture:** difficult to grow. Extended culture in specific medium (Lowenstein–Jensen) is necessary:
  - Synovial or joint fluid culture
  - Early-morning urine culture
  - Sputum culture
- **Biopsy:** for histology, ZN stain and culture
- **Tuberculin skin test:** establishes prior exposure, but does not confirm infection
- **Inflammatory markers:** FBC, CPR and PV/ESR are useful for monitoring response to treatment

Management of skeletal TB

Anti-TB chemotherapy

A combination of drugs is given in a two-phase regimen. One of the drugs should be bactericidal. The initial phase lasts for 2 months and involves three or four drugs; followed by 9–12 months with two drugs. Unfortunately all have side effects and compliance may be a problem. Poor compliance promotes the development of multidrug-resistant TB.

Treatment of TB in the appendicular skeleton

Medical treatment is the main treatment, and many infections will be arrested by this alone. Patients may need hospitalisation for immobilisation and joint splintage in the acute phase. Surgical intervention is not indicated at the synovial stage; antibiotics will arrest progression of the disease. Abscesses may need drainage and debridement if large and symptomatic. Debridement may also be required if the infection does not respond to medical treatment.

The long-term aim is to relieve pain and restore function. This is achieved by splinting the joint in the position of function. Arthrodesis or arthroplasty may be required in the long term.

Treatment of spinal TB

Medical treatment alone is highly effective in many cases.

Surgery is indicated when there is marked bone destruction and threatened severe kyphosis or a progressive neurological deficit.

The aims are to prevent and correct deformity, to prevent neurological involvement and achieve spinal stability.

Anti-TB drugs and side effects
- Ethambutol: optic neuritis, peripheral neuropathy
- Rifampicin: hepatitis, discoloured body fluids
- Isoniazid: hepatitis, neuritis (given with pyridoxine [vitamin B6] to reduce CNS side effects)
- Pyrazinamide: arthralgia
- Streptomycin: nephrotoxicity, ototoxicity

CHAPTER 9

Complications of skeletal TB

Complications of TB in the appendicular skeleton
- Recurrence
- Growth arrest/growth disturbance in children
- Joint destruction

Complications of spinal TB
- Recurrence
- Meningeal TB
- Vertebral collapse (anterior column is commonly affected, resulting in kyphosis)
- Spinal cord compression
- Mortality rate approximately 5%

11.6 Non-tuberculous spinal infections

Learning point

Infection may arise via direct inoculation (eg radiological/pain-relieving procedures) or via haematogenous spread.

Infections may affect the vertebral body, disc, posterior elements or epidural space. Pus may track through soft tissues and an abscess may point at a site distant from the infective focus.

The most common site for pyogenic infections is the lumbar spine, and the most common organism is *S. aureus*.

Microbiology of spinal infections

Common cause
- *S. aureus*

Other causes
- *E. coli*
- *Proteus* spp.
- Streptococci
- Granulomatous infections
- TB (see above)
- *Brucella* spp. (found in agricultural areas; in the UK it is found in cattle)
- *Bartonella* spp.
- Fungal infections (rare in the UK, except in immunocompromised patients)
- Parasitic infections (eg *Echinococcus* sp. which forms hydatid cysts)

Risk factors for spinal infections
- Elderly
- Intravenous drug abuse
- Rheumatoid disease
- Infective endocarditis
- Renal failure
- Alcoholism
- Immunodeficiency

Clinical features of spinal infections
- Pain and local tenderness
- Muscle spasm
- Fluctuant mass
- Sinus formation
- Angular deformity
- Neurological deficit

Investigating spinal infections

- **Inflammatory markers:** FBC, CRP, PV/ESR
- **Blood culture** (and urine culture if this is thought to be the source of infection)
- **Radiograph:** plain films are required as a baseline, but will not show changes until 14–21 days after onset of symptoms
- **Isotope bone scan:** technetium bone scans are useful for localisation of infection and become positive after 48 hours of symptoms (MRI may be negative in the early stages)
- **MRI:** extremely sensitive. Gives useful information on all elements (bone, disc, spinal cord and canal, and other soft tissue)
- **CT:** shows destruction of bone and can be used to guide needle aspiration
- **Myelography/discography:** no longer indicated

Management of spinal infections

Treatment is **non-surgical** if no progressive neurological deficit and the organism is known.

- Bedrest
- Intravenous antibiotics
- Monitoring of response (repeated examination, inflammatory markers or MRI is helpful if there is clinical deterioration, but, as the MRI changes of improvement lag behind the clinical course, it has no role in monitoring improvement)

Surgery is indicated in failed non-surgical management, if there is an unknown organism or progressive neurological deficit.

- Identify organism
- Drain collections and decompress spinal cord/nerve roots
- Achieve spinal stability

Complications of spinal infections

- Meningitis
- Epidural abscess
- Paraspinal abscess
- Spinal cord compression
- Mortality rate approximately 10%

11.7 Prosthetic joint infections

Learning point

Infection may complicate any surgical procedure, but the presence of implant materials and dead bone or soft tissue renders infection resistant to treatment. Therefore prevention of infection is a particular priority in all orthopaedic surgery. The quoted rates of infection are:
- 1–2% for total hip replacement
- 2–3% for total knee replacement

Pathogenesis of prosthetic joint infections

Exogenous (involves direct entry at time of surgery or via puncture) or haematogenous (seeding the joint from a bacteraemia of any cause).

Bacteria may form a 'biofilm' of bacteria embedded in polysaccharide on the exposed surface of the implant. Penetration of the host immune system and antibiotic to the biofilm is poor. The effectiveness of some antibiotics is reduced by the low metabolic rate of the bacteria in this biofilm.

CHAPTER 9

Chronic infection and inflammation result in bone resorption around the implant, allowing movement, and causing pain and subsequent mechanical failure of the implant if left untreated.

Microbiology of prosthetic joint infections

Most common
- *S. aureus*
- Coagulase-negative staphylococci

Other
- Gram-negative bacilli (coliforms, *Pseudomonas* spp.)
- Streptococci
- Anaerobes

Rare
- Fungi
- *Mycobacterium tuberculosis*

Often the picture is mixed (*S. aureus*, *Proteus* spp., *Pseudomonas* spp.). Skin commensals that are not normally pathogenic, such as *S. epidermidis*, may also be involved.

Risk factors for prosthetic joint infections
- Previous surgery to joint
- Prolonged operative time
- Postoperative 'superficial' infection
- Medical comorbidity

Clinical features of prosthetic joint infections
- Pain/stiffness
- Warmth around joint
- Erythema/cellulitis around wound
- Sinus formation
- Prosthetic loosening
- Systemic features of sepsis (fever, rigors)

Investigating prosthetic joint infections
- **Inflammatory markers:** such as FBC, CRP, and PV/ESR
- **Joint aspiration** (in sterile conditions): probably the most useful investigation as positive culture or Gram stain confirms the diagnosis
- **Open biopsy for histology and culture:** may be done at the first stage of joint revision; five separate microbiology samples help to reduce false-positive and false-negative results
- **Plain films:** may show bone resorption, periosteal reaction and loosening
- **Isotope bone scans or radiolabelled WBC scans:** useful in difficult cases. Isotope bone scans show increased bone turnover, which supports (but does not prove) a diagnosis of infection

---

Prevention of prosthetic joint infections

Meticulous technique

- Minimising soft-tissue trauma avoids devitalised tissue being left in wound: devitalised bone and soft tissue are excellent growth media for bacteria, and the patient's own immune system has little or no access to it. By definition it has lost its blood supply
- Minimise haematoma formation
- Avoid wound tension

Aseptic precautions

- Clean-air theatre
- Theatre discipline: head covers; masks; closure of doors
- Avoid surgery if there is ongoing chest infection or UTI
- Screening for meticillin-resistant *S. aureus* (MRSA) and decolonisation with mupirocin and chlorhexidine, along with good intravenous access management, reduces MRSA infection

Preoperative prophylactic antibiotics

- Single preoperative dose. Cephalosporins now avoided due to problems with *Clostridium difficile*

Management of prosthetic joint infections

Several management routes may be followed in these cases. The choice will depend on the patient's wishes, the nature of the infection, and the quality of bone and soft tissues.

The principles are similar to those employed in chronic osteomyelitis:

- Identify the organism
- Select antibiotics

- Improve the general condition of the patient
- Remove all non-viable material (including prostheses)
- Stabilise the skeleton
- Minimise soft-tissue dead space

- **Antibiotic suppression:** in patients who are not medically fit, or who do not wish to undergo revision surgery, long-term antibiotic suppression of the infection may be possible
- **Debridement:** if the implant is well fixed, debridement of necrotic tissue and an attempt to remove the biofilm with pulsatile lavage may allow the arrest of the infection with appropriate antibiotics
- **One-stage revision:** prosthesis and necrotic material are removed, followed by implantation of a new prosthesis. When combined with appropriate antibiotics (for 6–12 weeks) this will arrest the infection in up to 85%. Although there is less morbidity than in the two-stage revision, this not good for resistant organisms
- **Two-stage revision:** the prosthesis is debrided and removed, then a prosthetic or cement 'spacer' is used (to minimise dead space). This is followed by 6–12 weeks of antibiotics. A new prosthesis is fitted at the second stage. This has a higher 'cure' rate than the one-stage revision (95%), but also a higher morbidity
- **Excision arthroplasty:** this is for the unreconstructable failed total hip replacement (THR). Girdlestone's excision arthroplasty of the hip results in formation of a pseudarthrosis. The leg is short and the energy required to walk is increased
- **Joint fusion:** considered for infected total knee replacement (TKR)
- **Amputation:** considered for infected TKR, and occasionally for THR where there is massive femoral bone loss

CHAPTER 9

SECTION 12

Neoplasia and pathological fracture

12.1 Principles of primary bone tumours

> ### Learning point
>
> Primary bone malignancies are:
> - Rare
> - Represent <1% of all diagnosed malignancies
>
> The aim of investigation is to:
> - Identify the tumour – benign or malignant?
>   - History
>   - Radiology
>   - Biopsy (after clinical staging and by specialist centre)
> - Stage the tumour
>   - Clinically
>   - Pathologically

Some benign bone tumours can be managed expectantly. Other tumours are treated with radiotherapy, chemotherapy or surgery.

Principles of identifying a bone tumour

Bone tumours are mainly identified by history, radiology and biopsy. The main question to ask is: Is it benign or malignant? Identifying a bone tumour

History

Pain
- Ranges from dull ache to severe pain
- Not relieved by rest (unlike fracture pain)
- May be referred (eg hip or thigh pathology causing knee pain)

Swelling
- Bleeding into tumours may produce large swelling
- Tumours near a joint may result in an effusion
- Expanding tumours often noticed earlier if more distal in the limb (muscle bulk around hip and shoulder can obscure small tumours)

Classification of bone tumours

	Benign	Malignant
Bone-forming	Osteoblastoma Osteoid Osteoma	Osteosarcoma
Cartilage-forming	Chondroblastoma Osteochondroma Chondroma	Chondrosarcoma
Fibrous/fibro-osseous	Fibrous dysplasia Non-ossifying fibroma	Fibrosarcoma Malignant fibrous histiocytoma
Vessel-forming	Angioma	Angiosarcoma
Marrow		Plasma cell myeloma Lymphoma
Miscellaneous	Giant-cell tumour Brown tumour of hyperparathyroidism	Ewing's tumour Adamantinoma

Loss of function

- Neural compression (cord, root or nerve) may result in the insidious loss of function
- Pathological fractures result in acute loss of function

Incidental finding

- Investigating other problems (eg with examination, radiograph, CT, MRI) sometimes reveals unsuspected tumours

Bone tumours and lesions that resemble tumours tend to occur in particular age groups:
- Myeloma is rare in people aged <40
- Osteosarcoma occurs in 20s and 30s with a small peak in the 50s (due to malignant transformation in Paget's disease)
- Chondrosarcoma occurs at age 20–40
- Ewing's occurs at age 5–20

These four tumours represent 80% of all primary bone tumours.

CHAPTER 9

Radiology

Plain film interpretation

Ask the following four questions when interpreting plain radiographs:

1. Where is it?

- Different tumours appear in characteristic locations with the bone:
  - Diaphysis (eg Ewing's sarcoma, osteoid osteoma, lymphoma)
  - Epiphysis (eg chondroblastoma, giant cell tumour)
  - Metaphysis (eg osteoblastoma, osteosarcoma, aneurysmal bone cyst, fibrous dysplasia, non-ossifying fibroma)

2. What is the tumour doing to bone?

3. What is the bone doing in response?

- Bone destruction
- Sharp or blurred zone of transition between tumour and normal bone
- Periosteal reaction
- Slow-growing lesions produce a sharp, well-defined zone of transition, with a shell of reactive bone. Aggressive lesions produce a wide and poorly defined zone of transition with rapid bone destruction. Aggressive lesions tend to produce more periosteal reaction. Periosteal reaction is more marked in children

4. Are there any distinguishing features?

- Unique characteristics of some tumours may aid diagnosis.
- **Ultrasonography:** useful for imaging superficial soft-tissue tumours
- **MRI:** shows the soft-tissue extent of tumour and complements the information gained from CT
- **CT:** shows new bone formation and cortical destruction. Also gives better resolution than plain radiograph when imaging the lung to exclude pulmonary metastasis
- **Isotope scans:** shows extent of skeletal involvement. Does not differentiate tumour from fracture or infection

Biopsy

All imaging for clinical staging should be done before biopsy. Haematoma and oedema after biopsy will distort images and can result in radiographic misinterpretation.

The team in the specialist centre who will be providing definitive treatment should perform the biopsy. Non-specialists may inadvertently place the biopsy tract in a location that precludes limb-salvaging treatment in the future.

The biopsy technique, placement of the track and the area of the lesion from which the sample is taken should be planned with the likely diagnosis and future treatment in mind.

Ultrasonography, CT or MRI may be used to guide the biopsy. Biopsy techniques include:
- Fine-needle aspiration
- Core-needle biopsy
- Open incisional biopsy
- Open excisional biopsy

Principles of staging a bone tumour

Staging of any tumour is an attempt to define:

- The anatomical extent of the tumour
- Its capacity for local tissue destruction
- Its potential to metastasise

This information can be used to categorise patients, guide treatment and give a likely prognosis.

Clinical stage of bone tumours

- Refers to local and systemic spread of the tumour
- Established by examination and imaging (plain films, ultrasonography, MRI, CT, radioisotope scans)
- Clinical staging is repeated before surgery when preoperative adjuvant therapy has been used

Pathological stage of bone tumours

This is based on histology (sometimes immuno-histochemistry or genetics) of the lesion, giving a guide to potential for local and systemic spread. Grade of tumour is based on features (eg cellularity, pleomorphism, local infiltration, mitotic activity). There are many pathological staging systems. The Musculoskeletal Tumor Society (MSTS) system is the accepted system for bone tumours.

The Enneking (MSTS) surgical staging system uses three parameters to give a grade from 1 to 3.

Tumour grade
- G0 Benign
- G1 Low grade
- G2 High grade

Site (confined to single anatomical compartment)

Presence of metastasis

More complex systems may be used for specific tumour types.

Principles of non-surgical treatment of bone tumours

Benign tumours

- Many benign bone tumours, discovered as incidental findings, can be managed expectantly, and investigated should they become symptomatic
- Some benign tumours can undergo malignant transformation

Malignant tumours

- Some malignant tumours are chemosensitive or radiosensitive
- Neoadjuvant (preoperative) chemotherapy may be used with tumours (eg osteosarcoma and Ewing's sarcoma) to reduce the size of the tumour and enable easier excision
- Adjuvant chemotherapy has been shown to increase survival times after resection of these tumours
- Radiotherapy is useful for control of pain and for reducing local recurrence in some tumours (eg myeloma, lymphoma and Ewing's tumour)

Principles of surgical treatment of bone tumours

The aim of surgical treatment is to remove the tumour and prevent recurrence. How this is achieved will vary depending on the tumour site, type and stage. This information can be used to plan the margin of surgical resection.

- **Intralesional resection (curettage):** will leave macroscopic remnants of tumour and is appropriate only for benign lesions
- **Marginal resection:** 'shells out' the lesion in

CHAPTER 9

the plane of its pseudocapsule, which may leave microscopic remnants of tumour

- **Wide resection:** aims to remove the tumour and the pseudocapsule along with the reactive zone around the tumour, and thus remove all tumour remnants. Advances in chemotherapy and radiotherapy are allowing wide resection when previously only radical resection or amputation would have been considered

- **Radical resection:** removal of the entire bone or soft-tissue compartment to further reduce the chance of local recurrence

- **Amputation:** if radical resection or reconstruction following radical resection is not possible amputation should be considered

12.2 Primary malignant bone tumours

> **Learning point**
>
> **Osteosarcoma:** second most common primary malignant bone tumour, aggressive and metastasising, affects young people
> **Chondrosarcoma:** third most common primary malignant bone tumour
> **Ewing's sarcoma/primitive neuroectodermal tumour (PNET):** the second most common primary bone tumour in children
> **Adamantinoma:** very rare
> **Malignant fibrous histiocytoma:** lytic lesion needing wide resection
> **Lymphoma:** primary skeletal lymphoma is usually non-Hodgkin's lymphoma. Treated by radiotherapy and chemotherapy
> **Myeloma:** the most common primary malignant bone tumour

Osteosarcoma

- **Epidemiology:** second most common primary malignant bone tumour (2.5 per million in the UK). Bimodal distribution:
  - 75% of cases in people aged 10–25
  - Second smaller peak in incidence in elderly people (most of whom have Paget's disease)
- **Aetiology:** 90% idiopathic. Found in the young before epiphyseal closure; 10% secondary to underlying bone disorder (eg Paget's disease). Genetic basis: surviving retinoblastoma patients have a 500-fold risk of developing osteosarcoma

- **Site:** most arise in medullary cavity in metaphyseal ends of long bones. Distal femur > proximal tibia > proximal humerus > proximal femur > pelvis
- **Pathology:** histology reveals malignant osteoblasts producing osteoid. Metastasis and 'skip lesions' are common
- **Presentation:** painful, enlarging mass. Aggressive tumours, mostly with extensive blood-borne metastases on diagnosis; 20% have pulmonary metastases on presentation
- **Imaging:** lytic or sclerotic. Extends through cortex and periosteum, forming bulky mass. A triangular shadow is seen between the

cortex and raised periosteum (Codman's triangle). Seldom penetrates epiphyseal plate or invades into the joint. Spiral CT shows pulmonary metastasis in 20% of patients at presentation

- **Treatment:** advances in combination chemotherapy and limb-sparing surgery have significantly improved survival. Resection of pulmonary metastasis is now common practice. The 5-year survival rate is 75%. Prognosis is better in young adults, and in those with more distally located tumours. Multifocal osteosarcomas and those with a background of Paget's disease have a poor prognosis

Chondrosarcoma

- **Epidemiology:** third most common primary malignant bone tumour (1.5 per million in UK). Affects middle-aged and elderly people
- **Aetiology:** occurs anew or as a result of malignant transformation of a previously benign cartilage tumour (eg enchondromas in Ollier's disease or Maffucci syndrome)
- **Site:** within the medulla of bone (central) or on bone surface (juxtacortical). Commonly pelvis, ribs, proximal humerus and proximal femur
- **Pathology:** grading determined by examining cellularity, degree of cytological atypia and mitotic activity. Most are slow-growing and are of low to intermediate grade (85%). Seldom metastasise (but pulmonary metastases are most common)
- **Presentation:** pain or pathological fracture
- **Imaging:** prominent endosteal scalloping and cortical thickening. Destruction with bone expansion
- **Treatment:** wide surgical resection and limb salvage or amputation. Resection of pulmonary metastasis appropriate in some

patients. Radiotherapy and chemotherapy not shown to be effective

- **Outcome:** determined by the grade of the tumour. Five-year survival rates:
  - Grade 1: 90%
  - Grade 2: 81%
  - Grade 3: 43%

Ewing's sarcoma

- **Epidemiology:** second most common primary bone tumour in children; fourth most common overall. Peak incidence in 20s
- **Site:** diaphysis of long tubular bones (especially femur and flat bones of the pelvis)
- **Pathology:** small round cells of unknown origin; 85% have characteristic chromosomal translocation between chromosomes 11 and 22
- **Presentation:** pain. Enlarging mass. Sometimes associated systemic upset
- **Imaging:** lytic lesions with permeative margins give 'moth-eaten' appearance (ie wide zone of transition). Characteristic periosteal reaction produces layers of reactive bone deposited with 'onion-skin' pattern
- **Treatment:** en bloc resection and chemotherapy significantly improve 5-year survival rate (to 75%)

Primitive neuroectodermal tumour

- Essentially identical to Ewing's sarcoma in all respects except that it shows more neural differentiation. Ewing's and PNET might represent different stages of differentiation of a single tumour

CHAPTER 9

Adamantinoma

- **Epidemiology:** very rare. Typically occurs in 20s and 30s (but may occur at any age)
- **Site**: 90% in tibia
- **Pathology:** lobulated lesion. Mixture of fibrous and epithelial stroma
- **Presentation:** pain and swelling. Lesions are slow-growing and the history may be long. History of preceding trauma in 60% of cases
- **Imaging:** lobulated lytic area with surrounding sclerotic bone
- **Treatment:** wide resection and reconstruction or amputation

Malignant fibrous histiocytoma

- **Epidemiology:** affects any age
- **Site**: metadiaphysis of long bones
- **Pathology:** consists of spindle cells, histiocyte-type cells (probably derived from fibroblasts) and giant cells. Pulmonary metastases in 30% of cases
- **Presentation:** pain and swelling
- **Imaging:** lytic lesion with permeative bone destruction (wide zone of transition). Cortical destruction and minimal periosteal reaction
- **Treatment:** wide resection. The 5-year survival rate is 30–60%

Lymphoma

- **Epidemiology:** affects any age
- **Site:** femur, pelvis, humerus or vertebrae
- **Pathology:** multiple small round cells, differentiated from other small-cell tumours by their surface antigens. Primary skeletal lymphoma is usually non-Hodgkin's lymphoma
- **Presentation:** pain or soft-tissue swelling
- **Imaging:** moth-eaten lytic or sclerotic lesion
- **Treatment:** radiotherapy and chemotherapy

Myeloma

- **Epidemiology:** most common primary malignant bone tumour. Occurs at ages >50
- **Site:** any bone
- **Pathology:** monoclonal proliferation of plasma cells (B cells) producing monoclonal antibody. Plasma electrophoresis and urinalysis for Bence Jones protein are useful diagnostic tests. Bone marrow biopsy is definitive investigation
- **Presentation:** fatigue, pain and weakness
- **Imaging:** lytic lesion with little or no reactive sclerosis. Typical punched-out lesions
- **Treatment:** surgery is indicated to treat or prevent pathological fractures. Radiotherapy can alleviate bone pain. Chemotherapy may achieve disease suppression. Bone marrow transplant has potential to provide a cure

12.3 Benign bone tumours

Learning point

Osteochondroma/exostosis: most common benign tumour of bone. Bony stalk with cartilaginous cap

Echondroma: hyaline cartilage within long bone

Juxtacortical chondroma/periosteal chondroma (very rare)

Chondroblastoma: benign tumour of hyaline cartilage within physis

Chondromyxoid fibroma (very rare)

Osteoid osteoma: benign bone-forming tumour that may heal spontaneously. Characterised by pain at night that is relieved by aspirin

Osteoblastoma: a large osteoid osteoma in the spine

Bone island (incidental finding): area of lamellar bone within a background of cancellous bone

Bone infarct: infarction due to occlusion of small vessels. Radiologically appears as dense calcification

Aneurysmal bone cyst (ABC): expansive blood-filled cyst occurring in the under-20s which may heal spontaneously

Unicameral bone cyst (simple bone cyst): area of focal bone necrosis in the proximal humerus or femur which may cause pathological fracture

Giant-cell tumour (GCT): benign locally aggressive tumour in young people that is found below the subchondral plate

Fibrous dysplasia: fibro-osseous abnormality of unknown aetiology

Metaphyseal fibrous defects: fibrous cortical defect and non-ossifying fibroma (incidental finding, occasionally resulting in pathological fracture)

Haemangioma: skeletal haemangioma which can cause pain or wedge fracture

Osteochondroma (exostosis)

- **Epidemiology:** most common benign tumour of bone. Peak incidence in 20s
- **Site:** long bones, pelvis, scapula and ribs from a developmental anomaly of the epiphyseal growth plate
- **Pathology:** bony outgrowths from the surface of bone, capped with a layer of cartilage. May be single or multiple (10:1). Slow-growing and growth of lesions usually ceases with skeletal maturity. Malignant change is rare in solitary lesions, but transformation to chondrosarcoma occurs in 10% of patients with multiple lesions

- **Presentation:** mostly an incidental finding. Pain suggests possibility of malignant transformation
- **Imaging:** osteochondromas range in size from 2 cm to 15 cm and typically grow away from joint. On plain films they look like a mushroom with calcified stalk and radiolucent cap
- **Treatment:** symptomatic lesions should be resected. Asymptomatic lesions should

CHAPTER 9

717

be watched and investigated to exclude malignant transformation if they become painful

Enchondroma

- **Epidemiology:** occurs in third to fifth decades
- **Site:** found within metaphysis of long bones (commonly hands and feet, humerus, femur and tibia)
- **Pathology:** well-defined lesion of lobulated hyaline cartilage with some areas of ossification. Thought to represent areas of incomplete endochondral ossification (leaving embryonic cartilage that continues to grow within the bone). Malignant transformation occurs in approximately 1% of lesions. Difficult to differentiate histology from chondrosarcoma
- **Presentation:** mostly incidental finding. Pain suggests possibility of malignant transformation. May present with pathological fractures
- **Imaging:** elongated, oval, lytic areas. Well defined, with narrow zone of transition. Cortex preserved. Areas of calcification appear with age
- **Treatment:** symptomatic lesions to undergo curettage. Asymptomatic lesions to be watched and investigated to exclude malignant transformation if they become painful. If suspected malignancy, lesion to be resected en bloc
- **Ollier's disease:** multiple enchrondromatosis due to non-hereditary, developmental abnormality. May result in growth disturbance or deformity of affected bones; 25% risk of malignant transformation to low-grade chondrosarcoma. At-risk patients to be monitored and investigated if any lesions become symptomatic
- **Maffucci syndrome:** multiple

enchrondromatosis in association with multiple haemangiomas. Similar to Ollier's disease, a non-hereditary, developmental abnormality with high (25–100%) risk of malignant transformation

Juxtacortical chondroma (periosteal chondroma)

- **Epidemiology:** very rare. Occurs in 20s and 30s
- **Site:** beneath periosteum covering long bones (typically proximal humerus or femur)
- **Pathology:** hyaline cartilage formed below periosteum erodes into (but does not breach) cortex
- **Presentation:** mild ache or swelling
- **Imaging:** erosion and saucerisation of the cortex with buttresses of periosteal new bone formation (may overhang the lesion around its margins)
- **Treatment:** symptomatic lesions to be excised. Asymptomatic lesions to be watched and investigated to exclude malignant transformation if they become painful. If suspected malignancy, lesion should be resected en bloc

Chondroblastoma

- **Epidemiology:** occurs in 20s and 30s
- **Site:** epiphysis of long bones, with involvement of the metaphysis when the physis is closing
- **Pathology:** benign tumours of hyaline cartilage arise within physis. Composed of lobules of well-circumscribed cartilage with benign chondrocytes lying in lacunae. 'Chicken-wire' pattern of calcification
- **Presentation:** typically long history of low-grade joint-line pain (as diagnosis is often delayed)
- **Imaging:** lytic lesion in epiphysis. Lesions

seen to cross the physis if the physis is closing. Eccentric lesions affect the medulla but not the cortex
- **Treatment:** curettage (can cause premature closure of the physis resulting in growth disturbance)

Chondromyxoid fibroma
- **Epidemiology:** very rare. Peak incidence in 40s. Typically in males
- **Site:** epiphysis and metaphysis of long bones, commonly proximal tibia
- **Pathology:** chondroid areas resemble hyaline cartilage. Tumour often lobulated, sometimes with small satellite tumours that are missed on plain films (but seen with MRI). Chondroid components and variable histological features mean that this tumour may be mistaken for chondrosarcoma or chondroblastoma
- **Presentation:** vague aches and pains
- **Imaging:** round or oval, with rim of sclerotic reactive bone. May cause cortical expansion
- **Treatment:** en bloc resection with bone grafting or bone cement to fill the residual defect

Osteoid osteoma
- **Epidemiology:** affects ages 5–30
- **Site:** commonly in shaft of long bones (especially femoral neck). Also tibia, humerus and spine
- **Pathology:** benign bone-forming tumour
- **Presentation:** pain that is worse at night. Pain relieved by aspirin (caused by excess prostaglandin E_2 production)
- **Imaging:** small (<2 cm) radiolucent nidus, composed of osteoblastic tissue laying down woven bone, surrounded by reactive bone formation. Bone scan positive. CT scan can be diagnostic (shows nidus)

- **Treatment:** may heal over 2–3 years. Resection or radiofrequency ablation (if non-surgical treatment fails or is not acceptable)

Osteoblastoma
- Essentially the same as osteoid osteoma but lesions involve vertebrae and are larger
- Less surrounding reactive bone formation. Treated by curettage or excision (depending on site and stage of lesion)

Bone island
- **Epidemiology:** affects from the age of skeletal maturity onwards
- **Site:** any cancellous area except cranial vault
- **Pathology:** nodule of lamellar bone within area of cancellous bone
- **Presentation:** incidental finding
- **Imaging:** 2–20 mm area of dense bone with sharply defined zone of transition
- **Treatment:** if <2 cm and stable no treatment required. If large or expanding consider biopsy

Bone infarct
- **Epidemiology:** increasing incidence with age
- **Site:** any
- **Pathology:** infarction due to occlusion of small vessels. Rarely undergoes malignant transformation to malignant fibrous histiocytoma
- **Presentation:** incidental finding
- **Imaging:** localised area of dense calcification
- **Treatment:** none required

Aneurysmal bone cyst

- **Epidemiology:** 75% occur in people aged <20
- **Site:** metaphysis of long bones and vertebrae. Typically proximal humerus, distal femur and proximal tibia
- **Pathology:** cavity with multiple blood-filled spaces. Surrounded by thin layer of bone and periosteum. Association with other bone tumours. Some ossify spontaneously (but most are progressive and destructive)
- **Presentation:** pain and swelling
- **Imaging:** expanding radiolucent cyst
- **Treatment:** curettage and bone grafting, with local adjuvant therapy or resection for higher grades. There is a high local recurrence rate

Unicameral bone cyst (simple bone cyst)

- **Epidemiology:** occurs in first and second decades
- **Aetiology:** unknown cause. Possibly due to high intraosseous pressure and focal bone necrosis
- **Site:** metaphysis; 90% in proximal humerus and proximal femur
- **Pathology:** thin-walled cavity with cuboidal cell lining. Filled with straw-coloured or bloodstained fluid
- **Presentation:** often asymptomatic. May present after pathological fracture
- **Imaging:** multiloculated appearance (only one cavity, but ridges give loculated appearance). Thinning, but no expansion of cortex. May see fragment of cortex if fractures (fallen-crescent sign)
- **Treatment:** may resolve spontaneously. Tend to heal after fracture. If symptomatic or impending fracture consider aspiration and steroid injection

Giant-cell tumour

- **Epidemiology:** affects ages 20–40
- **Site:** epiphysis, below subchondral plate; eccentric location; 50% around the knee
- **Pathology:** benign but locally aggressive tumour. Difficult to manage. Occasionally metastasises to the lungs (transforms to osteosarcoma in rare cases). Consists of three main cell types:
  - Mononuclear fibroblastic cells
  - Mononuclear fibrohistiocytic cells
  - Multinucleated giant cells
- **Presentation:** pain
- **Imaging:** lytic, eccentric lesions with permeative interface (widened zone of transition). MRI shows high-grade GCTs extending out of cortex and beyond periosteum
- **Treatment:** curettage with local adjuvant therapy (phenol and bone cement) reduces recurrence rate to approximately 3%. Consider wide resection and allograft reconstruction for high-grade lesions

Fibrous dysplasia

- **Epidemiology:** majority present at age <30
- **Site:** any bone (but commonly ribs, facial bones, proximal tibia, humerus and femur). Affects one bone (monostotic) or many (polyostotic)
- **Pathology:** fibro-osseous abnormality of unknown aetiology. Fibrous tissue and disordered bone replace bone marrow. Malignant change rare (<0.5%). Fibrous dysplasia is a feature of Albright syndrome
- **Presentation:** pathological fracture, deformity or growth disturbance
- **Imaging:** diaphyseal lytic lesion with well-defined margins and 'ground-glass' appearance
- **Treatment:** internal fixation and bone grafting for symptomatic lesions

Metaphyseal fibrous defect (fibrous cortical defect and non-ossifying fibroma)

- **Epidemiology:** common developmental abnormality seen in first and second decades
- **Site:** metaphyseal cortex of long bones (typically distal femur, proximal tibia or distal tibia)
- **Pathology:** size 2 mm to several centimetres. Composed of collagen and fibroblasts with histiocytes and giant cells
- **Presentation:** incidental finding Occasionally results in pathological fracture
- **Imaging:** eccentric, well-defined lucencies in cortex. Sclerotic rim, but no periosteal reaction
- **Treatment:** self-heals or disappears spontaneously. Curettage and bone grafting if fracture risk is high

Haemangioma

- **Epidemiology:** young adults
- **Site:** common sites of skeletal involvement include the vertebral column, ribs and long bones
- **Pathology:** typically cavernous haemangioma in the skeleton. Dilated blood-filled vessels lined by endothelium
- **Presentation:** usually incidental finding. May present with pain. Occasionally pathological vertebral wedge fractures
- **Imaging:** thickening of the vertebral trabeculae with 'honeycomb' appearance
- **Treatment:** embolisation of symptomatic lesions

12.4 Skeletal metastases

Learning point

Metastatic tumours are the most common form of skeletal malignancy and second only to osteoporosis as the cause of pathological fractures.

Source and sites of skeletal metastases

Tumour reaches the bone via:
- Direct spread
- Lymphatic/vascular dissemination
- Intraspinal seeding

Any cancer can spread to bone, but in adults more than 80% originate from:
- Prostate
- Breast
- Lung

Other important cancers that metastasise to bone include:
- Kidney
- Thyroid

Usually skeletal metastases are multifocal, but kidney and thyroid carcinomas tend to produce solitary lesions.

In children the two main metastatic tumours are neuroblastoma and Wilms' tumour (nephroblastoma). Common sites of skeletal metastasis:
- Vertebral column
- Pelvis
- Ribs
- Skull
- Sternum

CHAPTER 9

- Proximal femur
- Humerus

Metastasis distal to the knee or elbow is rare.

Red marrow in these areas facilitates implantation and growth of tumour cells, because of its:
- Rich capillary network
- Slow blood flow
- Nutrient environment

Clinical presentation of skeletal metastases
- Pain
- Hypercalcaemia
- Pathological fractures
- Neurological complications
- Marrow suppression (presenting with anaemia)

Principles of investigation of skeletal metastases

Aims of investigation
- Confirm diagnosis
- Identify primary malignancy
- Exclude or treat complications (eg anaemia or hypercalcaemia)
- Identify other deposits

Imaging of skeletal metastases

Plain radiographs
- Show lytic or blastic lesions (but normal plain films do not exclude metastasis)
- In lytic lesions (typically breast, lung and thyroid), tumour cells secrete factors that stimulate osteoclastic bone resorption. Lytic lesions must be >1 cm and cause loss of >50% of bone matrix before they are visible on plain films

- Malignancies that elicit a sclerotic response (eg adenocarcinoma of prostate) do so by stimulating osteoblastic formation
- Most metastases produce a mixed lytic/sclerotic reaction

Bone scans
- Sensitive, cheap and rapid method for screening for skeletal metastases
- Rely on uptake of radioisotope by reactive bone (not tumour) and so do not show purely lytic lesions (eg myeloma) or rapidly growing lesions where there is no sclerotic response

CT
- Shows lytic lesions and reactive new bone formation
- Chest/abdominal/pelvic CT is helpful when looking for an unknown primary

MRI
- Shows marrow infiltration (showing the tumour tissue directly)

Identify the primary
Thorough examination:
- Thyroid examination
- Breasts in women (and men)
- Digital rectal examination of prostate in men
- FBC, electrolytes, CRP, PV/ESR, calcium, thyroid function test, liver function tests, prostate-specific antigen (PSA) in men (taken before rectal exam – otherwise PSA will be elevated)
- Serum and urine electrophoresis (for myeloma)
- Chest radiograph

If the primary is still unknown then consider:
- Chest/abdominal/pelvic CT
- Mammogram in women

If the primary remains unknown after these further investigations, biopsy of the lesion may give the required information. All cancer networks should have a team who specialise in identifying the primary in patients with a carcinoma of unknown primary site (CUPS) team.

Management of skeletal metastases

Aims of treatment of skeletal metastases
- **Control disease:** surgery, chemotherapy, radiotherapy and hormonal manipulation have roles in local and systemic control
- **Relieve bone pain:** radiotherapy and bisphosphonates are both effective
- **Maintain mobility and function**
- **Facilitate nursing care**
- **Prevent fracture**
- **Treat complications:** hypercalcaemia can cause anorexia, lethargy, confusion and coma. It is treated by intravenous rehydration and bisphosphonate (eg intravenous pamidronate) in resistant cases

Role of the orthopaedic surgeon team in management of skeletal metastases
Patients with skeletal metastasis are generally cared for by the multidisciplinary team (MDT), but the orthopaedic team has an important role in the following areas:
- **Treatment of pathological fractures:** unless the patient is moribund, stabilisation of fractures gives good pain relief and allows

nursing care. It is assumed the fracture will not unite and the fixation technique must allow load transfer for the remainder of the patient's life
- **Prophylactic intramedullary stabilisation of impending fractures:** it is generally accepted that a fracture is inevitable when 50% of a single cortex of a long bone has been destroyed by metastatic disease. Prophylactic fixation has fewer complications and is technically easier than fixation after fracture. Mirel's scoring system (based on site, pain, percentage of involvement and type of bone reaction) can be used to assess the likelihood of fracture
- **Spinal decompression and stabilisation:** 'curative' spinal resections and reconstruction for solitary spinal metastasis. Palliative stabilisation and decompression for pathological fracture or impending fracture or cord compression. The Tokuhashi score (based on tumour primary site, patient's general condition, number of spinal deposits, number of extraspinal skeletal deposits and any spinal cord injury) aims to estimate the likely survival, and can help when planning a simple palliative stabilisation or a more aggressive spinal reconstruction
- **Reconstruction for lesions around a joint** (eg total hip replacement for lesions in the femoral neck or acetabulum): this is appropriate only if the patient's life expectancy is 6 months or more, because it must be remembered that the patient would not wish to spend their last few weeks recovering from major surgery

Planning the timing of orthopaedic surgical intervention requires liaison between members of the MDT, eg radiotherapy should be deferred until after surgery, because preoperative treatment may result in increased incidence of wound infection or breakdown.

SECTION 13

Spine

13.1 Development of the spine

Learning point

The embryology of the spinal cord depends on the neural plate (the ectoderm overlying the notochord). The neural plate folds to form a neural tube in the fourth week of gestation.

The vertebrae develop from mesodermal somites and ossify in week 8 of gestation from three primary ossification centres.

Five secondary ossification centres usually unite by age 25.

The normal AP curvatures of the spine develop throughout childhood.

Embryology of the spine

By week 3 of gestation the embryo is trilaminar (ectoderm, mesoderm and endoderm), and contains the following structures:

- Notochord
- Neural plate (the ectoderm overlying the notochord)

Two ridges appear along the length of the neural plate. The edges of the neural plate fold over on either side and these folds approximate with each other to form the neural tube (Figure 9.17).

Closure of the tube begins centrally (Figure 9.18). The posterior (caudal) neuropore closes on day 24 and the anterior (cranial) neuropore on day 26. Failure to close cranially results in **anencephaly**, whereas dorsal failure results in **spina bifida**.

Not all neural ectoderm is incorporated into the neural tube. Cells at the neural plate border are known as **neural crest cells**. Neural crest cells form the following tissues:

- Dorsal root ganglia
- Chromaffin tissue in the adrenal medulla
- Melanocytes
- Sheath cells of the peripheral nervous system
- Ganglia of the autonomic nervous system

Vertebral development

The vertebrae develop from the mesodermal somites. Cartilaginous rings form in the mesoderm surrounding the neural tube. The vertebrae ossify in hyaline cartilage. This process occurs by gestational week 8.

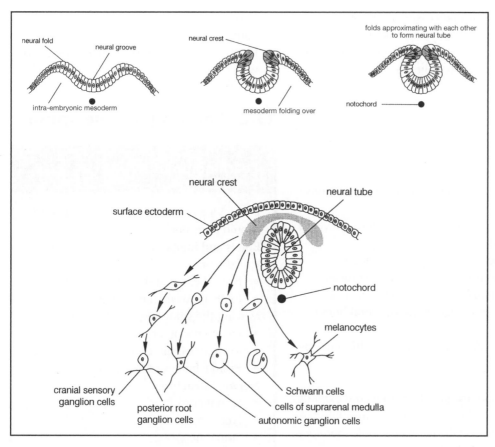

Figure 9.17 Formation of the neural tube (transverse section) in week 3 of gestation

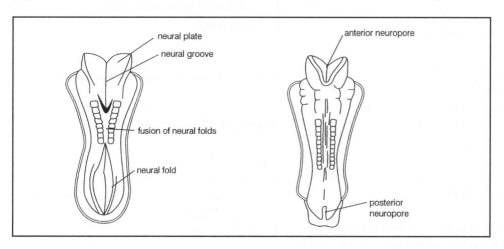

Figure 9.18 Formation of the neural tube (dorsal view) at days 22 (left) and 23 (right)

CHAPTER 9

725

There are **three primary ossification centres**, one in the centre of the body and one at each side of the vertebral arch. At birth, therefore, vertebrae have three bony parts united by cartilage.

Vertebral arches fuse in:
- C-spine by age 1
- Lumbar spine by age 6 (failure results in spina bifida occulta)

The arch fuses with the body at age 5–8 years.

Five secondary ossification centres develop during puberty:
- One at the tip of the spinous process
- One at the tip of each transverse process
- Two ring epiphyses (one at the superior and one at inferior edge of the vertebral body)

Secondary ossification centres usually unite by age 25.

Note that in the neonate the spinal cord extends to the level of the L3 (not L1 as in adults). A lumbar puncture in the neonate should therefore never be done above L3–4.

Sagittal curvatures of the spine

The normal spine is a straight line when viewed anteroposteriorly, but when viewed laterally there are four sagittal plane spinal curves:
- Cervical and lumbar (lordotic)
- Thoracic and sacrococcygeal (kyphotic)

Thoracic and sacral (primary) curves develop in the embryonic period.

Cervical and lumbar (secondary) curves develop in the fetal period but are not very obvious until infancy.

- Cervical curve develops as infants gain head control
- Lumbar curve develops as infants begin to walk

13.2 Anatomy of the spine

Learning point

In studying the anatomy of the spine one should consider:
Bones and joints
- Vertebrae
- Neural canal and neural foramina
- Joints between the vertebrae

Moving the spine
- Ligaments of the spine
- Muscles of the spine
- Biomechanics of the spine

Nervous structures
- Spinal cord
- Nerve roots
- Spinal nerves
- Peripheral nerves
- Autonomic nervous system

Blood supply
- Arteries
- Veins

Role of the spine

Structural
- Maintenance of posture
- Transmission of body weight through pelvis to lower limbs
- Locomotion

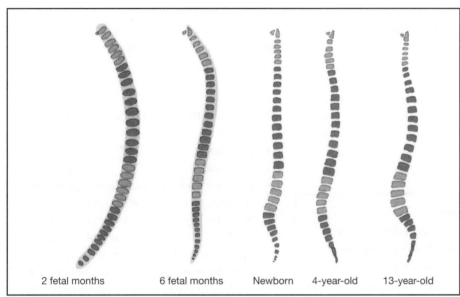

**Figure 9.19
Development
of the spine**

2 fetal months   6 fetal months   Newborn   4-year-old   13-year-old

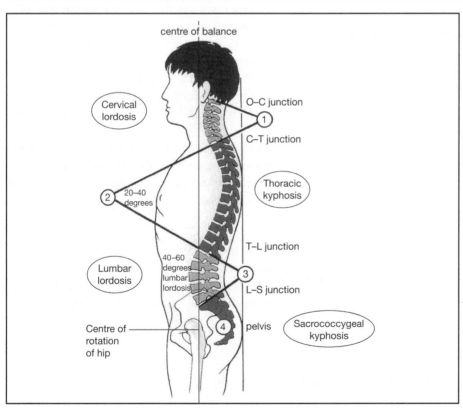

**Figure 9.20
Curvature of
the normal
spine**

centre of balance

Cervical
lordosis

O–C junction

1

C–T junction

Thoracic
kyphosis

2 20–40
degrees

T–L junction

Lumbar
lordosis

40–60
degrees
lumbar
lordosis

3

L–S junction

Centre of
rotation
of hip

4 pelvis

Sacrococcygeal
kyphosis

CHAPTER 9

Protective

- Protection of spinal cord and nerve roots

Haematopoiesis

- Haematopoietic red marrow is found in the axial skeleton (spine, pelvis and ribs), with a little within the proximal humerus and femur

---

Surface markings
- Skin dimple at posterior iliac spine level = S2 – the dimples of Venus
- Top of gluteal cleft = top of coccyx

Bones and joints of the spine

Anatomy of the vertebrae

There are 33 vertebrae:
- 24 are mobile
  - 7 cervical
  - 12 thoracic
  - 5 lumbar
- 9 are immobile
  - 5 sacral
  - 4 coccygeal

Vertebrae become larger as the sacrum is approached, then smaller towards the coccyx. Vertebral bodies contribute to about three-quarters of the length of the presacral vertebral column, and discs about a quarter.

How to describe a vertebra: vertebral elements

A typical vertebra consists of a body and an arch.

Body (anteriorly)

The body of the vertebra supports the weight of the spine and increases in size from C3 to S1.

Arch (posteriorly)

The arch protects the neural structures by forming the neural canal. It consists of:
- **Pedicles**
- **Laminae**
- **Superior and inferior articular processes (facets):** project superiorly and inferiorly from the lamina–pedicle junction. In the lumbar spine the superior and inferior facets are connected by the pars interarticularis (literally translates as the 'bit' between the joints!). In the cervical spine these articular processes together form the **lateral masses**
- **Transverse processes:** project laterally from the junction of the pedicle and laminae
- Spinous process
- **The vertebral foramen:** this is the 'hole' formed by arch and the body. All of these foramina collectively form the **spinal canal**

Muscles and ligaments attach to the spinous and transverse processes. These bony levers offset the attachment points for the muscles and improve their mechanical advantage.

How to identify a vertebra: distinguishing features

Vertebrae from different regions have distinctive features by which they can be identified.

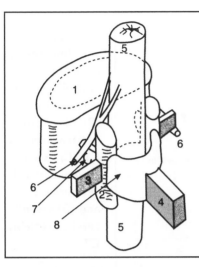

1. Vertebral body
2. Articular mass
3. Transverse process
4. Spinous process
5. Spinal cord passing through vertebral foramen
6. Nerve roots
7. Pedicle
8. Lamina

Figure 9.21 Schematic diagram of the vertebra and spinal cord

---

Distinguishing features of vertebrae

When handed a vertebra in your viva ask yourself these six questions, in this order:

1. Is it the coccyx (tiny vestigial tail)?
- Yes/No

2. Is it the sacrum (five fused vertebrae)?
- Yes/No

3. Does it have a body?
- Yes → not C1
- No, just a ring (and no spinous process) → C1

4. Is the spinous process bifid?
- Yes → cervical vertebra (hole in the transverse process [for vertebral artery] in all but C7)
- With long spinous process → C7
- With odontoid peg → C2
- With neither long spinous process nor odontoid peg → C3–C6
- No → not cervical

5. Does it have rib articulation facets on the transverse process and body?
- Yes → thoracic (slender spinous process, heart-shaped body)
- No → not thoracic

6. Has it got a big quadrilateral body?
- Yes → lumbar
- No → not a vertebra!

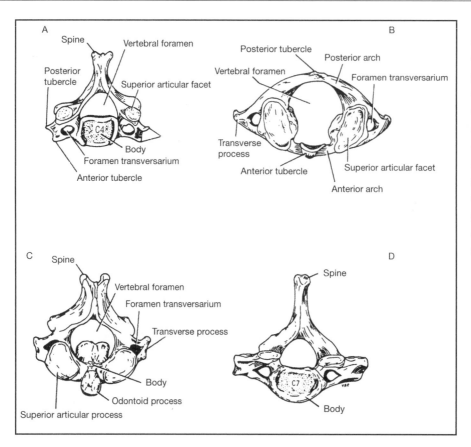

Figure 9.22 Cervical vertebrae shown from above: (A) typical cervical vertebra C4; (B) atlas or first cervical vertebra C1; (C) axis or second cervical vertebra C2; and (D) seventh cervical vertebra C7

Cervical vertebrae

- All have a hole in the medial aspect of the transverse process (TP) called the foramen transversarium (transmits the vertebral artery and vertebral vein)
- C7 foramina transversaria are smaller or may be absent (transmits only vertebral vein)
- C3–6 spinous processes are short and bifid

First, second and seventh cervical vertebrae are atypical:

- C1 is a ring with no spinous process or body
- C2 has an odontoid peg (unique feature)
- C7 has a vertebra prominens (long spinous process) and large transverse processes

Thoracic vertebrae

- Long, slender spinous processes
- Heart-shaped bodies
- All articulate with ribs, therefore have articular facets for ribs:
  - The articular process on the side of the body articulates with the head of the rib
  - The articular process on the side of the TP articulates with the tubercle of the rib
- T1–4 have some features of cervical vertebrae
- T9–12 have some features of lumbar vertebrae

Lumbar vertebrae
- Large 'typical' vertebrae

Sacrum
- Transmits the weight of the body to the pelvic girdle through sacroiliac joints
- Wedge-shaped, consisting of five fused vertebra

There are four pairs of sacral foramina:
- **Sacral promontory:** anterior projection of S1 (lateral to which are the sacral ala)
- **Median sacral crest:** five prominent ridges on dorsal surface of sacrum (fused spinous process)
- **Intermediate sacral crest:** fused articular process
- **Lateral sacral crest:** fused transverse processes

Coccyx
- Four rudimentary vertebrae (essentially bodies only)

Neural canal and neural foramen
The neural canal contains the dura and its contents, ie the spinal cord and nerve roots. It is bordered by the vertebral body anteriorly, the facet joints laterally and the laminae posteriorly. The neural foramina contain a sleeve of dura containing the nerve root as it exits laterally from the neural canal.

Joints of the spine

> ### Learning point
>
> Each vertebra from C1 to S1 articulates with the one above and the one below at three joints:
> - One intervertebral disc (transmits main axial compressive load)
> - Two zygapophyseal (facet) joints
>
> Some vertebrae have additional special joints:
> - Atlanto-occipital joint (nods the head)
> - Atlantoaxial joint (shakes the head)
> - Costotransverse joints between thoracic vertebrae and ribs (rib movements)
>
> At all levels of the spine, flexion, extension, and lateral flexion to both sides are possible.

Intervertebral discs
These are the joints between the vertebrae. They are symphyses that have fibrocartilaginous articulations designed for strength. The intervertebral discs consist of a strong annulus fibrosis containing a gelatinous nucleus pulposus.
- **The annulus fibrosus** consists of spiralling fibres of collagen orientated at 120° to each other and 30° to the cartilaginous endplates. The annulus fibres run obliquely to form concentric lamellae and insert on the rim of articular surfaces of the vertebral bodies. The layers are thinner and less numerous posteriorly
- **The nucleus pulposus** is a semi-fluid substance in contact with the hyaline endplates of articular cartilage. It acts as a shock absorber for axial forces. It consists of

CHAPTER 9

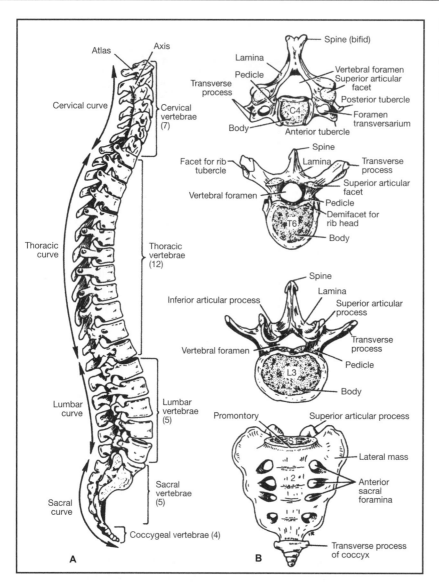

Figure 9.23 (A) Lateral view of the vertebral column; (B) general features of different kinds of vertebrae

2% cells and the rest is extracellular matrix (mostly a hydrophilic proteoglycan gel and water). In a young person this matrix is 88% water. With age there is a decrease in proteoglycan production, leading to a reduction of water in the nucleus pulposus. The nucleus pulposus is derived from the notochord and is avascular. It is nourished by diffusion from the annulus and the vertebral body vessels

The annulus fibrosis forms a ring around the nucleus pulposus, attaching to the edges of the bodies of adjacent vertebra. As a result of the elasticity of the annulus, the nucleus pulposus is under constant pressure and may herniate anteriorly or centrally. This is less likely in a young disc with a high water and proteoglycan content, which maintains a constant, even pressure around the entire circumference of the annulus fibrosus.

CHAPTER 9

If annulus fibres tear (secondary to trauma or degenerative changes) the nucleus tends to bulge posterolaterally where annulus fibres are weaker and poorly supported by the posterior longitudinal ligament.

There are no intervertebral discs
- Between first two vertebrae
- In the sacrum
- In the coccyx

Zygapophyseal (facet) joints
- Allow rotation in the thorax but not in the lumbar region

The facet joints are synovial joints between the superior articular process of one vertebra and the inferior articular process of the one above.

In the thoracic spine the plane of the facet joint lies in the arc of a circle which has its centre in the nucleus pulposus – hence axial rotation is possible in this part of the spine and C1–2 only. In contrast, the orientation of the facet joints in the lumbar region is such that rotation is blocked.

The facet joints bear some weight and help to control flexion/extension/rotation of adjacent vertebrae. Each facet is surrounded by a thin, loose articular capsule – longer and looser in the cervical spine to allow more flexion.

Facet joints are innervated by medial branches of the dorsal primary rami, which descend on the posteromedial surface of the transverse process to reach it (these are the target of the facet rhizotomy procedure).

Atlanto-occipital joints: nod the head
This is a pair of joints between the superior articular facets of the lateral masses of C1 and the occipital condyles of the skull. Their loose articular capsules permit flexion (nodding).

The skull and C1 are also connected by the anterior atlanto-occipital membrane (a continuation of the anterior longitudinal ligament) and the posterior atlanto-occipital membrane (similar to the ligamentum flavum).

Atlantoaxial joints: shake the head
These are two lateral joints and one medial joint between the dens (the odontoid peg) and the anterior arch of C1. These joints permit head rotation. The skull and C1 move as a unit with respect to C2.

Ligaments of the atlantoaxial joint include:
- **Apical ligament:** between the odontoid process and the foramen magnum
- **Alar ligaments:** either side of the apical ligament, attaching the odontoid process to the occipital condyles (limit lateral rotation and side-to-side head movements)
- **Transverse band of the cruciate ligament:** strong membrane across the inside of the anterior arch of C1 holding the odontoid peg in place to prevent it slipping backwards
- **Vertical band of the cruciate ligament:** weak membrane from C2 to the foramen magnum
- **Tectorial membrane:** continuation of the posterior longitudinal ligament attached to the foramen magnum; passes behind odontoid process covering and reinforces apical, alar and cruciate ligaments

CHAPTER 9

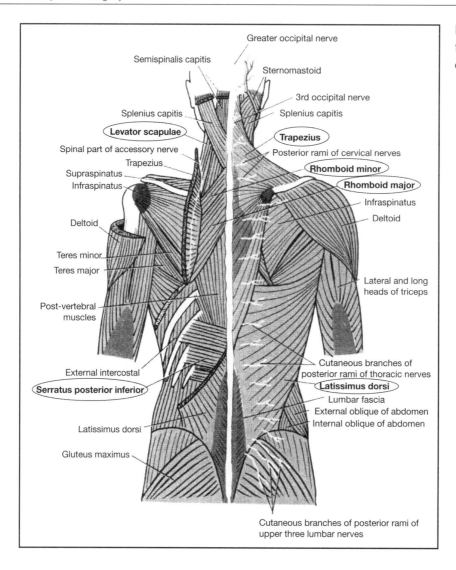

Figure 9.24 Some of the extrinsic muscles of the back (circled)

Greater occipital nerve

Semispinalis capitis

Sternomastoid

3rd occipital nerve

Splenius capitis

Splenius capitis

Levator scapulae

Trapezius

Spinal part of accessory nerve

Posterior rami of cervical nerves

Trapezius

Rhomboid minor

Supraspinatus

Rhomboid major

Infraspinatus

Infraspinatus

Deltoid

Deltoid

Teres minor

Teres major

Lateral and long heads of triceps

Post-vertebral muscles

External intercostal

Cutaneous branches of posterior rami of thoracic nerves

Serratus posterior inferior

Latissimus dorsi

Lumbar fascia

External oblique of abdomen

Internal oblique of abdomen

Latissimus dorsi

Gluteus maximus

Cutaneous branches of posterior rami of upper three lumbar nerves

Costovertebral joints: allow movement of the ribs with respiration

Costal facets are present on the sides of the bodies of the thoracic vertebrae T1–12 where the heads of the ribs articulate. In addition, T1–10 have facets on the transverse processes for articulation with the tubercles of the ribs.

Moving the spine

Ligaments of the back

The vertebral bodies are united by the anterior longitudinal ligament (ALL) and posterior longitudinal ligament (PLL).
Other ligaments include:
- Ligamentum flavum (joining the laminae – translates as yellow ligament – derives its colour from elastin content)
- Supraspinatus (strong ligaments joining the spinous processes)
- Interspinous (weak ligaments joining the spinous processes)
- Ligamentum nuchae (ligament running from C7 spinous process to posterior border of foramen magnum and external occipital crest)
- Intertransverse ligaments (joining transverse processes; strongest in the lumbar region)

Anterior longitudinal ligament
- Broad fibrous band
- Runs from sacrum to anterior tubercle of C1 (extends up from there to foramen magnum as the **anterior atlanto-occipital membrane**)
- Firmly fixed to discs (and to a greater extent to the periosteum of vertebral bodies)
- Prevents hyperextension

Posterior longitudinal ligament
- Similar to the ALL but narrower and weaker
- Runs from sacrum to atlas (extends up from there to foramen magnum as the **tectorial membrane**)
- Attaches to discs (mainly) and vertebral bodies (reinforces discs and reduces posterior herniation)
- Prevents hyperflexion

Muscles of the back

There are three groups of back muscles:
Superficial extrinsic
These are associated with the upper limb and include:
- Trapezius
- Latissimus dorsi
- Levator scapulae
- Rhomboid major and minor

Intermediate extrinsic
These are concerned with respiration and include:
- Serratus posterior superior
- Serratus posterior inferior
- Levatores costorum

Intrinsic
These are concerned with movement of the vertebral column and maintenance of posture and are the 'true' back muscles.
They are in three groups:
- Superficial intrinsic
- Intermediate intrinsic
- Deep intrinsic

CHAPTER 9

Important extrinsic muscles of the back

	Origin	Insertion	Nerve Supply	Action
Superficial extrinsic muscles				
Trapezius	Occiput, ligamentum nuchae, spinous and supraspinous ligaments from C1 to T12	Lateral clavicle, acromium and spine of scapula	Spinal part of accessory nerve and cervical nerves C3 and C4	Elevates and rotates scapula, assists with abduction of the arm
Latissimus dorsi	Posterior iliac crest, lumbar fascia, T6–12 spines and ribs 8–12	Floor of bicipital groove of the humerus	Thoracodorsal nerve	Extends, adducts and medially rotates the arm
Levator scapulae	Transverse processes of C1–4	Medial border of the scapula	Cervical nerves C3 and C4 and dorsal scapular nerve (C5)	Raises medial border of scapula
Rhomboids	Ligamentum nuchae, spines of C7 and T1 (rhomboid minor). Spines and supraspinous ligaments of T2–5 (rhomboid major)	Medial border of the scapula	Dorsal scapular nerve (C5)	Raises medial border of scapula
Intermediate extrinsic muscles				
Serratus posterior superior	Lower cervical and upper thoracic vertebrae	Upper ribs	Intercostal nerves	Raise the ribs (inspiratory muscle)
Serratus posterior inferior	Lower thoracic and upper lumbar vertebrae	Lower ribs	Intercostal nerves	Depress the ribs (expiratory muscle)
Levatores costarum	Tip of transverse process	Into the rib below the transverse process from which it arises	Posterior rami of thoracic spinal nerves	Raise the ribs (inspiratory muscle)

Intrinsic muscles

These muscles are paired muscle columns lying in longitudinal bands on each side of the spinous processes. They are supplied by branches of the dorsal primary rami and are covered dorsally by thoracolumbar fascia. The intrinsic muscles are concerned with the movement of the vertebral column and maintenance of posture. They are the 'true' back muscles.

The three layers of intrinsic muscles can be identified by the direction of their fibres:
- Superficial: pass superolaterally
- Intermediate: run longitudinally
- Deep: pass superomedially

CHAPTER 9

Intrinsic muscles

Superficial intrinsic

- Splenius capitus
- Splenius cervicis

Intermediate intrinsic

Erector spinae (sacrospinalis) are the largest muscles of the back. They divide into three columns in the superior lumbar spine from lateral to medial:

- **Iliocostalis:** from iliac crest to ribs. Named according to the region of the spine, ie ileocostalis lumborum, ileocostalis thoracis, iliocostalis cervicis
- **Longissimus:** mainly between transverse processes of vertebrae; named according to insertion site of fibres
- **Spinalis:** less significant, from spinous processes of superior lumbar and inferior thoracic region to spinous processes of superior thoracic region

Deep intrinsic

These are collectively known as the transverse spinalis muscles. They tend to extend and rotate the spine. They consist of several short muscles in the groove between the spinous processes and the transverse processes:

- **Semispinalis:** originates from about half of the vertebral column, T10 and up
- **Multifidus**
- **Rotatores**

In the cervical region there are two additional deep intrinsic muscles:

- **Interspinales:** connect adjacent spinous processes; result in extension
- **Intertransversarii:** connect adjacent transverse processes; result in rotation

Suboccipital triangle

This is a triangular area between the occipital portion of skull and the posterior aspect of atlas and axis, deep to trapezius and semispinalis capitis. There are four small muscles, deep to semispinalis capitis, that extend and rotate the head:

- Rectus capitis posterior major
- Rectus capitis posterior minor
- Inferior oblique
- Superior oblique

Other contents of the triangle include:

- Vertebral arteries
- Suboccipital nerve (dorsal ramus of C1)
- These both run in the groove on the superior surface of C1

Biomechanics of the back

Control of posture

Stability

- Intervertebral discs
- Ligaments
- Muscles
- Shape of individual vertebrae

Static control

- Vertebrae
- Joints
- Ligaments

Dynamic control

- Extrinsic muscles (polysegmental vertebral movements)
- Intrinsic muscles (monosegmental and polysegmental vertebral movements)

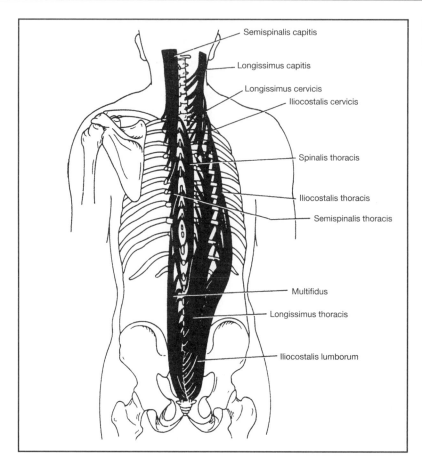

Semispinalis capitis

Longissimus capitis

Longissimus cervicis

Iliocostalis cervicis

Spinalis thoracis

Iliocostalis thoracis

Semispinalis thoracis

Multifidus

Longissimus thoracis

Iliocostalis lumborum

Figure 9.25 Some of the intrinsic muscles of the back

Forces on the spine

When comparing relative loads on the lumbar spine, take 100% to be standing.

- Lying supine is about 30% load
- Sitting is about 150% load (posterior spinal muscles contract to stabilise the spine)
- Lifting weight close to the body is just over 150% load
- Lifting and leaning is about 200% load (higher compressive forces)

Vertebral column movements

- Movement is allowed at discs and zygapophyseal (facet) joints
- C-spine and lumbar spine most mobile
- C1–2 is single most mobile segment in the spine

Thoracic stability is attributable to:

- Overlap of spinous processes (T4–T12 spinous processes overlie body of vertebra beneath)
- Thinner discs
- Attachment to ribs and sternum

Principal muscles producing movement of spine regions

	Flexion	Extension	Lateral bending and rotation
How do we move our head? **Muscles acting on C1–2**	Sternomastoid	Longissimus capitis	Rectus capitis lateralis
	Longus capitis	Rectus capitis post-major and -minor	Obliquus capitis lateralis
	Rectus capitis anterior	Obliquus capitis posterior	Sternomastoid
		Semispinalis capitis	Splenius capitis
		Splenius capitis	
How do we move our neck? **Muscles acting on C3–7**	Sternomastoid	Splenius capitis and cervicis	Sternomastoid
	Longus colli	Semispinalis capitis	Scalene muscles and cervicis
	Longus capitis	Longissimus capitis and cervicis	Splenius capitis and cervicis
		Iliocostalis	Longissimus capitis and cervicis
			Iliocostalis cervicis
			Multifidus
How do we move our back? **Muscles acting on T1–S1**	Rectus abdominis	Erector spinae mass	Psoas major and minor
	Psoas major and minor	Quadratus lumborum	Quadratus lumborum
			External and internal obliques
			Multifidus
			Iliocostalis thoracis and lumborum
			Rotatores

Nervous structures

Spinal cord anatomy

The spinal cord is part of the CNS and continuous with the brain. It runs from the medulla oblongata (foramen magnum level of skull) to the lower border of the first lumbar vertebra (in adults). Thus it occupies the upper two-thirds of the spinal canal of the vertebral column.

Spinal cord coverings

The spinal cord is surrounded by (from the outside in):

- Dura mater (loose tough covering continuous with nerve epineurium)
- Subdural space
- Arachnoid mater (loose internal covering continuous with nerve epineurium)
- Subarachnoid space (CSF filled; traversed by fibrous strands of ligamentum denticulum [thickening of pia mater] to suspend spinal cord)
- Pia mater (closely adheres to cord surface)

Features of the spinal cord

The cord is roughly cylindrical but it has two fusiform enlargements:

- Cervical enlargement (C4–T1) gives rise to the brachial plexus
- Lumbar enlargement (L2–S3) gives rise to the lumbar plexus

In the midline, anteriorly, running the length of the cord, is the deep, longitudinal cleft called the anterior median fissure. In the midline, posteriorly, is a shallower cleft called the posterior median sulcus.

Inferiorly the cord tapers off into the conus medullaris, where the filum terminale (prolongation of pia mater) descends from its apex to attach to the posterior surface of the coccyx.

Along the length of the spinal cord are attached the 31 pairs of spinal nerves which are formed from the dorsal and ventral roots. These are, in turn, attached to the spinal cord by a series of rootlets or filaments.

Composition of the spinal cord

The spinal cord is composed of an inner core of grey matter and an outer covering of white matter. There is more grey matter the more muscle is innervated at that level (hence the cervical and lumbar enlargements).

Spinal cord anatomy relative to vertebral column

In embryos, the spinal cord originally extends the entire length of the vertebral canal. The vertebral column grows faster than the spinal cord and therefore the inferior end of the spinal cord lies at higher levels (L2–3 in the neonate). This results in obliquity of the roots in the subarachnoid space. The length and obliquity of nerve roots increase as one moves caudally.

As a result, in adults the spinal cord segments do not correspond with vertebral levels, especially below T11.

- The spinal cord ends at level L1 (dural sac below this contains the cauda equina)
- The cauda equina contains L2–S5 nerve roots (until they exit below their corresponding vertebrae more distally)
- The subarachnoid space ends at S2 (inferior end of dural sac)
- The filum (consisting of connective tissue, pia and neuroglial elements) continues extradurally to insert into the dorsum of the coccyx
- The lumbar cistern is the subarachnoid space from L2 to S2

The normal level at which a lumbar puncture, spinal tap or epidural is attempted is above or below the L4 vertebra.

Procedure box: Lumbar puncture

Indications
- Aspirate CSF for culture, biochemistry, microscopy
- Epidural/spinal analgesia
- Measure intracranial pressure (ICP)
- Reduce ICP in benign intracranial hypertension (BIH)
- Inject drugs (antibiotics, chemotherapy)
- Blood patch to stop CSF leak post-procedure

Preparation
- Consent and inform
- Ensure no space-occupying lesions in brain (either no clinical signs of raised ICP or, if benign ICP or BIH suspected, normal CT scan)

Patient position: either on side or sitting with vertebral column flexed.

Procedure
- An imaginary line joining the highest points on the iliac crests passes over L4. Prep and drape back (aseptic technique)
- Infiltrate LA
- Pass lumbar puncture needle into vertebral canal above or below L4 and into CSF-filled subarachnoid space

- The depth of traversed structures from the surface varies from 2 cm in a child to 10 cm in an obese adult. These structures are:
  - Skin
  - Superficial fascia
  - Supraspinous ligament
  - Interspinous ligament
  - Ligamentum flavum
  - Areolar tissue containing the internal vertebral venous plexus
  - Dura mater
  - Arachnoid mater

Measure CSF pressure with a manometer and three-way tap (normal: 7–20 cmH$_2$O CSF with patient lying laterally).

Send specimens for microscopy, culture, protein and glucose, and other tests (virology, serology, cytology, acid-fast bacillus [AFB] for TB, oligoclonal bands for cryptococcal antigen testing, India ink stains, fungal culture, multiple sclerosis). Remove needle and place plaster over puncture site.

The patient is to lie flat for 6 hours, with neuro-observation and BP monitoring. Encourage fluid intake.

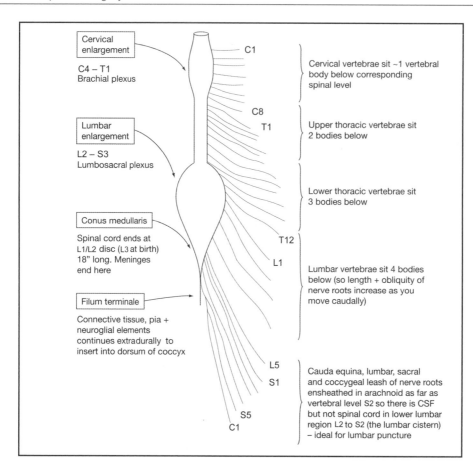

**Figure 9.26
Gross anatomy
of the spinal
cord**

Cervical
enlargement

C4 – T1
Brachial plexus

Lumbar
enlargement

L2 – S3
Lumbosacral plexus

Conus medullaris

Spinal cord ends at
L1/L2 disc (L3 at birth)
18" long. Meninges
end here

Filum terminale

Connective tissue, pia +
neuroglial elements
continues extradurally to
insert into dorsum of coccyx

C1

Cervical vertebrae sit ~1 vertebral
body below corresponding
spinal level

C8
T1

Upper thoracic vertebrae sit
2 bodies below

Lower thoracic vertebrae sit
3 bodies below

T12

L1

Lumbar vertebrae sit 4 bodies
below (so length + obliquity of
nerve roots increase as you
move caudally)

L5
S1

S5
C1

Cauda equina, lumbar, sacral
and coccygeal leash of nerve roots
ensheathed in arachnoid as far as
vertebral level S2 so there is CSF
but not spinal cord in lower lumbar
region L2 to S2 (the lumbar cistern)
– ideal for lumbar puncture

Complications of lumbar puncture

Headache: (in 25%) worse when upright. May last for days. Treat with analgesia and reassurance.

Trauma to nerve roots: nerve roots usually move out of the way of the needle. If stimulated, patients may feel a shooting pain or twitch (less common if needle is kept in the midline, but abandon procedure if symptoms persist).

Minor bleeding (traumatic tap): usually due to nicking a spinal vein. CSF appears bloody. Often stops spontaneously (increased risk in coagulopathy, severe liver disease, thrombocytopenia).

Coning: herniation of cerebellar tonsils with compression of medulla. Rare, unless patient has raised ICP. If there are clinical signs of ICP, patient must have a pre-puncture CT scan to exclude space-occupying lesions (mortality is high).

Infection: rare, if proper sterile technique used.

Spinal nerve roots and spinal nerves

There are 31 pairs of spinal nerves emerging from each spinal cord segment from the first cervical to the first coccygeal segment inclusive.

Spinal nerves arise from the spinal cord in dorsal (sensory) and ventral (motor) roots
↓
Ventral and dorsal roots unite (at lateral aspect of intervertebral foramen)
↓
Form a spinal nerve
↓
Spinal nerve leaves the foramen
↓
Divides into dorsal and ventral primary rami

- Cell bodies of axons in the ventral roots are located in the ventral grey horn
- Cell bodies of axons in the dorsal roots are located in the dorsal root ganglion, in the proximal intervertebral foramen, resting on the pedicle
- Dorsal root sleeves blend with epineurium at lateral end of intervertebral foramen

---

Note the difference between roots and ram.

Roots

Come directly off the spinal cord – not yet forming a spinal nerve.

- Ventral roots
- Postganglionic (on emerging from spinal cord)
- Carry motor fibres
- Dorsal roots
- Preganglionic (on emerging from spinal cord)
- Carry sensory fibres
- Have a dorsal root ganglion outside spinal cord

Dorsal and ventral roots unite – to form the spinal nerve.

Rami

Rami are the two main branches of the spinal nerve.

- They contain mixed motor and sensory fibres
- They supply:
  - Dorsal rami of spinal nerves supply the back
  - Ventral rami supply lateral/anterior regions of trunk/limbs

---

Relationship between nerve roots and discs

Each root passes below pedicle of the vertebra with the same name, eg the right L4 nerve root under the right pedicle of L4 exits through the intervertebral foramen between L4 and L5.

In lower spinal segments, especially where the cauda equina runs, the discrepancy between spine segment and vertebral level means several nerve roots may run past a herniating disc, eg when a L4/5 disc is herniated it may compress the exiting L4 nerve root and often the L5 nerve root that travels down to exit below L5 (see Figure 9.26). Likewise, an L5/S1 herniated disc may compress the exiting L5 nerve root and passing S1 nerve root. This may lead to some confusion when eliciting clinical signs.

Peripheral nerves, dermatomes and myotomes

Peripheral nerves

For details of the peripheral nerves of the upper and lower limbs see earlier sections of this chapter.

CHAPTER 9

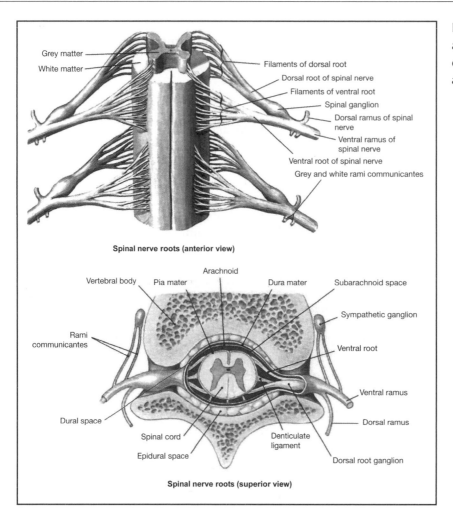

Figure 9.27 Anterior and superior views of spinal nerve roots and spinal nerves

Grey matter
White matter
Filaments of dorsal root
Dorsal root of spinal nerve
Filaments of ventral root
Spinal ganglion
Dorsal ramus of spinal nerve
Ventral ramus of spinal nerve
Ventral root of spinal nerve
Grey and white rami communicantes

Spinal nerve roots (anterior view)

Vertebral body
Pia mater
Arachnoid
Dura mater
Subarachnoid space
Sympathetic ganglion
Rami communicantes
Ventral root
Ventral ramus
Dural space
Dorsal ramus
Spinal cord
Denticulate ligament
Epidural space
Dorsal root ganglion

Spinal nerve roots (superior view)

- L1–4 make up the lumbar plexus
- L4–S4 make up the sacral plexus
- S5 plus part of S4 make up the coccygeal plexus

Dermatomes

A dermatome is an area of skin supplied by a single spinal nerve. It is thus possible to test the sensory function of individual spinal nerves by assessing sensation (usually by pinprick or light touch) in the corresponding area. For this reason you should know the dermatomes.

Myotomes

Skeletal muscle also receives segmental innervation, but most muscles are innervated by several spinal nerves. Although it is impossible to learn the segmental innervation of all the muscles, the muscle reflexes shown should be known, as they are a useful way of demonstrating motor function of the individual spinal nerves.

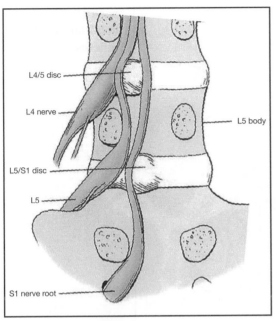

Figure 9.28 The interrelationships of L4/5 disc, L5/S1 disc and the nerve roots L4, L5 and S1

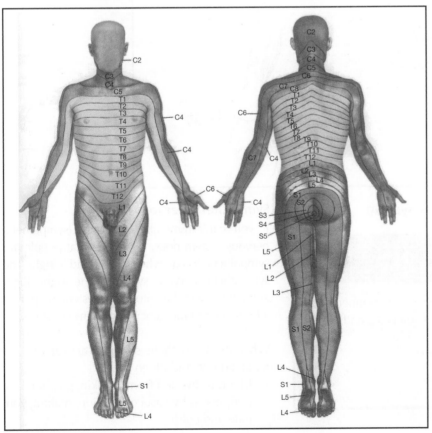

Figure 9.29
Dermatomes

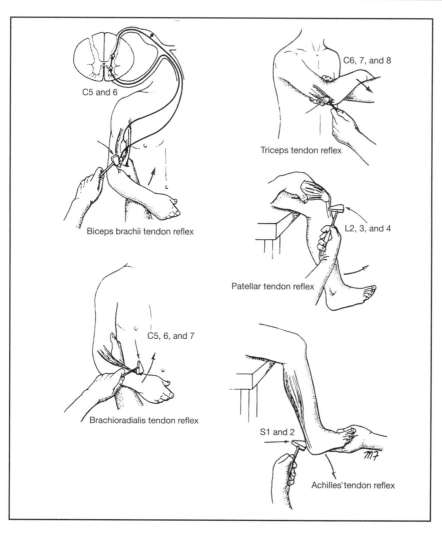

Figure 9.30 Some important tendon reflexes

C5 and 6

Biceps brachii tendon reflex

C6, 7, and 8

Triceps tendon reflex

L2, 3, and 4

Patellar tendon reflex

C5, 6, and 7

Brachioradialis tendon reflex

S1 and 2

Achilles' tendon reflex

Autonomic nervous system

> ### Learning point
>
> The autonomic nervous system innervates involuntary structures such as glands, organs and smooth muscle.
> It consists of two parts:
> - Sympathetic
> - Parasympathetic

Sympathetic nervous system

If you can't remember what the sympathetic nervous system does, remember that people are sympathetic to you when you've had a fright. The sympathetic nervous system is the fright, flight and fight part of the autonomic system, preparing a body for an emergency in response to stress.

When the sympathetic system is activated:
- Heart rate and BP go up
- Blood is diverted **from** the skin, gut, and peripheries by vasoconstriction (making you pale and cold)

CHAPTER 9

- Blood is diverted **to** the brain, heart and skeletal muscle by vasodilatation (making you alert and ready for action)
- Peristalsis and glandular activity of the gastrointestinal tract is inhibited and most sphincters are closed
- Pupils dilate, hair stands on end and sweating increases

In the sympathetic nervous system cell bodies are located in the lateral horn of the grey matter of the spinal cord. The axons synapse in the paravertebral ganglia (sympathetic trunk) and adrenal gland, which is the only organ to receive preganglionic sympathetic innervation. The sympathetic system has connections to the spinal cord at all the levels from T1 to L2 (but the rami of all spinal levels contain sympathetic fibres).

The sympathetic nervous system preganglionic fibres follow this route:

Emerge from ventral root
↓
Spinal nerve
↓
Ventral primary ramus
↓
White ramus communicans to sympathetic ganglion
↓
Ascend/descend in sympathetic trunk or synapse directly
↓
Postganglionic fibres
↓
Grey ramus communicans back to ventral rami
↓
Ventral rami back to dorsal rami
↓
Fibres distribute to blood vessels, sweat glands, sebaceous glands, erector pili muscles, peripheral nerves

Thus sympathetic trunks consist of preganglionic efferents, postganglionic efferents and afferent fibres.

Dorsal and ventral rami consist of motor fibres from the spinal canal, sensory fibres of the dorsal root ganglion and autonomic fibres.

Parasympathetic nervous system
The parasympathetic nervous system aims to conserve and restore energy and has the opposite effect to the sympathetic system.

The parasympathetic nervous system cell bodies are located in the brain and the sacral segments of the spinal cord. The ganglia are located in viscera. The system has connections to cranial and sacral parts of the spinal cord via cranial nerves III, VII, IX and X and the pelvic splanchnic nerve (S2–4).

Blood supply of the spinal cord

Arterial supply
The spinal cord is supplied by:
- A pair of descending posterior spinal arteries from the vertebral arteries (running either side of dorsal spinal nerve root)
- A single descending anterior spinal artery from the vertebral arteries (running within anterior median fissure)
- Radicular arteries

Radicular arteries
The radicular arteries arise from spinal branches of the following segmental vessels:
- Vertebral arteries
- Deep cervical arteries
- Ascending cervical arteries
- Posterior intercostal arteries

CHAPTER 9

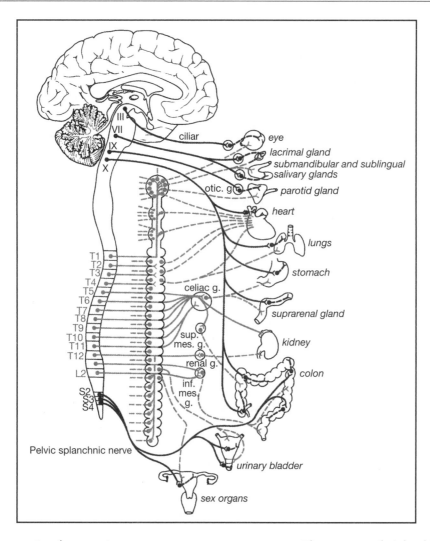

Figure 9.31 Efferent part of the autonomic nervous system

- Lumbar arteries
- Lateral sacral arteries

Radicular arteries enter the vertebral canal through the intervertebral foramina, divide into the anterior and posterior radicular arteries, then pass along the dorsal or ventral nerve root to reach the spinal cord; they pass into it as sulcal arteries.

The midthoracic (T4–8) area is the main watershed between the radicular arteries and is the most vulnerable to ischaemia.

The artery of Adamkiewicz is a particularly large anterior radicular artery. It arises on the left between T8 and T10 from an intersegmental branch of the descending aorta, and is often the major source of blood to the lower two-thirds of the spinal cord. It is at risk during scoliosis surgery.

Veins of the spinal cord

The veins of the spinal cord drain into six tortuous longitudinal channels that communicate superiorly with the veins of the brain and the venous sinuses. They drain mainly into the internal vertebral venous plexus.

The spinal veins form two loose-knit plexuses, one anteriorly and one posteriorly. Both drain along the nerve roots, communicating with:
- The vertebral venous plexus
- The segmental veins (through the intervertebral foramina) which are:
  - Vertebral in the neck
  - Azygos in the thorax
  - Lumbar in the lumbar region
  - Lateral sacral in the sacral region

The clinical implications of these links are:
- By linking the superior vena cava with segmental vessels, the venous plexus enables blood to be returned from the abdomen and pelvis to the heart
- Malignant cells can spread from the prostate to the vertebrae
- Pelvic or abdominal sepsis can result in vertebral osteomyelitis and discitis

Learning point

At MRCS level you should know:
- How to assess the spine
- Common/serious things that can go wrong with the spine
- Three common clinical presentations that these pathologies result in

13.3 Clinical assessment of the spine

Learning point

How to clinically assess the spine:
- **History**
- **Examination**
- **Use the 'red flags':** differentiate dangerous causes (need urgent intervention) from common benign pathologies (need conservative treatment and reassurance)
- **Investigation:** identify which pathology caused the clinical symptoms
- **History** of the spine and peripheral neurology

History

When taking a history for someone with a spine complaint the following facts should be elicited:
- Age
- Occupation
- Onset of pain:
  - When it started
  - Gradual or sudden
  - History of injury (including a trivial trip or sneeze)
- Past relevant history:
  - Previous similar attack
  - Previous back trouble or surgery
- Site and nature of the pain:
  - Localised or diffuse
  - Constant or related to position/ movement
  - Aggravating or alleviating factors

- Radiation of the pain:
  - Into the legs? How far? Where?
  - Character (dull, aching, sharp, knife-like)
  - Paraesthesia
- Motor involvement:
  - Weakness, wasting, or fibrillation
  - Gait, balance, drop-foot or ankles giving way
- Systemic enquiry:
  - Malaise, fever or other joints affected
  - Weight loss
  - Large-bowel or gastrointestinal symptoms
  - Genitourinary symptoms
  - Respiratory problems
  - Major neurological disturbance

Examination of the spine and peripheral neurology

Summary of examination of the neck
- Patient sits on chair; neck exposed
- Inspection:
  - Asymmetry, deformity, torticollis, muscle wasting, position of head
  - Scars, sinuses, localised tenderness
- Palpation:
  - Step deformity
  - Lateral masses and tenderness
  - Cervical rib
  - Tumour, nodes, masses, temperature
- Movements:
  - Forward flexion, extension, lateral flexion, rotation
  - Feel for crepitations

Summary of examination of the back
- Patient stands; trousers off; back to examiner
- Inspection from the back:
  - Scoliosis, swellings, scars
  - Abnormal pigmentation, hair, café-au-lait spots

- Inspection from the side: kyphosis, gibbus, lumbar curvature
- Palpation: vertebrae, lumbar muscles, sacroiliac joints, step
- Percussion: with patient bent forward
- Movements: forward flexion, extension, lateral flexion, rotation
- Lying down: rotation at hip, straight leg raise, passive dorsiflexion
- Offer (if appropriate):
  - Reverse Lasègue test
  - Tests for functional overlay
  - Tests of sacroiliac joint
  - Neurological examination of leg
  - Femoral pulses
  - Abdominal examination
  - Per rectal assessment of anal tone in acute back pain with focal neurology

Summary of neurological examination of the upper limb
- Patient sits on chair or stands; shirt off
- Look:
  - General inspection of face and neck
  - Arms (front and back; arms out)
  - Deformities, scars, tremor, muscle wasting, swollen joints
- Feel: tone
- Move (power):
  - Deltoids C5: push patient's elbows down
  - Biceps C5, C6: try to straighten patient's elbows
  - Triceps C7: try to bend patient's elbows
  - C8, T1: squeeze examiner's fingers
  - C6: pronation–supination
  - C6, C7 (radial nerve): wrist extension
  - T1 (ulnar nerve): spread fingers
  - T1 (ulnar nerve): paper between fingers
  - Median nerve: thumb to ceiling
- Coordination:
  - Alternate movement clapping test
  - Finger to nose
- Reflexes: biceps, triceps, supinator

- Sensation: pinprick, light touch
- Offer (if appropriate):
  - Joint position test, vibration sense
  - Range of movement: neck, shoulder, elbow, wrist
  - Vascular examination, pulses

Summary of neurological examination of the lower limb

- Patient sits on bed; legs out in front; trousers off
- Look: asymmetry, nystagmus, muscle wasting, fasciculation, pes cavus
- Tone: roll leg, lift and drop knee
- Power (all against resistance):
  - Hip flexors L2, L3: straight leg up
  - Hip extensors L4, L5: straight leg into bed
  - Knee flexors L5, S1: bend knee
  - Knee extensors L3, L4: straighten knee
  - Foot dorsiflexors L4, L5: flex foot
  - Foot plantarflexors S1, S2: point toes
- Coordination: heel–shin test
- Reflexes:
  - Knee jerk, ankle jerk
  - Clonus
  - Extensor reflex (Babinski's test)
- Sensation: pinprick, light touch
- Offer (if appropriate):
  - Vibration, position sense
  - Gait, Romberg's test

Assessing the spine using 'red flags'

The first question to ask when assessing the spine is:

> **Are there symptoms or signs of focal neurology (ie neural compression)?**

If there are, then you should seek a specialist opinion.

Signs of nerve root lesions in the lower limb

Root	Sensory loss	Motor weakness	Reflex
L4	Medial knee and shin	Quadriceps	Knee jerk
L5	Lateral calf and dorsum of foot	Extensor hallucis longus and ankle dorsiflexion	Tibialis posterior (but only 50% have it)
S1	Lateral border of foot	Flexor hallucis longus Ankle plantarflexion	Ankle jerk

If not then you must exclude the following underlying systemic or local disease by looking for 'red flags' such as:

- Malignant disease
- Spinal infections including TB
- Osteoporosis and spinal fractures

If the patient does have evidence of neural compression you must try to identify one of these four conditions:

- Radiculopathy (nerve root pain)
- Cauda equina syndrome
- Spinal cord compression
- Neurogenic claudication

Red flags

There are no identifiable pathological lesions to explain the pain in more than 90% patients with acute low back pain, so the diagnosis is a clinical one.

It is important to pick out any 'red flags' when taking a history or examination. These are

CHAPTER 9

features in the history or examination that are not typical of mechanical back pain, and that indicate that further investigations may discover a treatable or serious pathology.

	Red flag	Raises suspicion of
History	Major trauma; minor trauma	Spinal fracture
	Elderly; on steroids	Osteoporotic spinal fracture
	T-spine pain	Fracture, tumour, infection
	Age <20 or >55	Tumour, infection
	Night/rest pain	Tumour, infection
	Night sweats	Tumour, infection
	Weight loss	Tumour, infection
	Previous cancer history	Metastatic tumour
	Fever	Tumour, infection
	Recent bacterial infection	Infection
	Immunocompromise (intravenous drug abuse, diabetes)	Infection
	Saddle anaesthesia	Cauda equina syndrome, cord compression
	Bladder dysfunction	Cauda equina syndrome, cord compression
	Generalised ill health	Tumour, infection
	Family history of breast cancer	Tumour
	Cough, haemoptysis, per rectum bleed, haematuria	Tumour
Examination	Bruising/haematoma	Fracture
	Step deformity/local deformity	Fracture, tumour, infection
	Neurological loss with level	Cord compression by degenerative bone or disc disease, fracture, tumour, infection
	Upper motor neurone signs	Cord compression
	Severe pain on palpation	Tumour, infection, fracture
	Evidence of local infection	Infection
	Lax anal sphincter	Cauda equina syndrome, cord compression
	Perianal/perineal sensory loss	Cauda equina syndrome, cord compression
	Major motor weakness (eg bilateral foot drop)	Cauda equina syndrome, cord compression
	Cachexia, jaundice, anaemia	Tumour
	Lymphadenopathy	Tumour
	Breast or thyroid lump	Tumour
	Abnormal chest examination	Tumour

Investigating the spine

Imaging of the spine

- Plain radiographs
  - AP, lateral, oblique
  - Standing, of thoracolumbar and lumbar spine
  - Lateral bending and flexion/extension views
- CT: with/without contrast
- MRI: with/without contrast
- Radioisotope: local/whole body
- Scans: SPECT (single-photon emission CT), white cell-labelled
- Provocative tests: facet joints, discography

Non-radiological investigations of the spine

- Haematology: FBC, PV, clotting profile
- Biochemistry: U&Es, LFTs, bone biochemistry, CRP, protein electrophoresis, urinary proteins
- Microbiology: MSU, blood cultures, MC&S, aspirates, biopsies
- Histopathology: histology of biopsies
- Electrophysiology: EMGs
- Urodynamics: cystometrogram

MRI is the investigation of choice if infection or tumour are suspected.

13.4 Pathology of the spine

Learning point

Important spinal pathologies
- Spondylosis
- Disc prolapse
- Rheumatoid arthritis
- Ankylosing spondylitis
- Spinal infections
- Tumours
- Osteoporotic
- Fractures

Spondylosis

Spondylosis is the progressive, age-related degenerative changes of the spine. The worst affected areas are the midcervical and lower lumbar regions of the spine. Low back pain (Section 13.5) and cervical spine pain (Section 13.6) are considered separately.

Predisposing factors for spondylosis

- Human spines are erect not horizontal, as 'designed' evolutionally
- Extra loading on cervical and lumbar areas
- Anatomical abnormality of the spine (congenital or acquired)
- Abnormal loading of the spine (due to obesity, pregnancy, heavy work, athletic activities, injury to other joints, eg hip or knee)
- Age-related disc changes and osteoporosis (accelerate spondylosis)

CHAPTER 9

Pathological features of spondylosis

With age, the nucleus pulposus loses water content, flexibility and height. This causes the annulus fibrosus to bulge, split and herniate. The motion segment becomes unstable, causing:

- Bony osteophytes
- Facet joint hypertrophy
- Ligamentum flavum hypertrophy
- Loss of lumbar lordosis in cervical and lumbar regions
- Increased kyphosis in the thoracic regions

These changes in the curvatures cause further misalignment and more mechanical stress (a vicious circle).

Pain and symptoms of spondylosis

Pain and symptoms are due to:

- Pain from increased load on facet joints (which have sensation)
- Pain from peripheral annular fibres of the disc (discogenic pain)
- Pain, paraesthesia and motor loss from spinal nerves as exit foramina are narrowed by facet joint enlargement
- Pain, paraesthesia and motor loss from nerve roots as degenerate disc, bone or ligaments impinge on them (especially posterior osteophytes or posterolateral disc herniation)
- Pain, paraesthesia and motor loss from cord or cauda equina because the spinal canal is narrowed by disc protrusion, osteophytes and enlarged ligaments

The treatment of spondylosis in the lower back and in the neck is described in Management of lower back pain (see Section 13.5).

Disc prolapse

Prolapse of the intervertebral disc is caused by degeneration which allows nucleus pulposus to herniate through. Protective lumbar muscle spasm at the affected level is common and is probably an important factor in generating some of the back pain element of the problem (as opposed to the radicular leg pain). The muscle spasm results in loss of lumbar lordosis, decreased range of movement and a protective scoliosis.

Lateral disc protrusion

The disc often herniates posterolaterally. It commonly impinges on one or two nerve roots. Signs are mostly unilateral and localised to the particular nerve root that is involved. It is rare in the thoracic region and common in the lumbar region. It can be diagnosed clinically but confirmed by MRI/CT. The disc between L5 and S1 is most commonly implicated, followed by that between L4/5 and L3/4.

Patients usually recover with rest and physiotherapy. Surgical treatment may be required.

Central disc protrusion

If the disc prolapses posteriorly, it may directly compress the spinal cord (above L2) or the cauda equina (below L2). This is a much more serious emergency than a lateral disc protrusion. If there are signs of cord compression or cauda equina syndrome (such as bladder disturbance and bilateral lower limb signs) this warrants immediate emergency surgical exploration. If this is delayed, permanent neurological deficit may result.

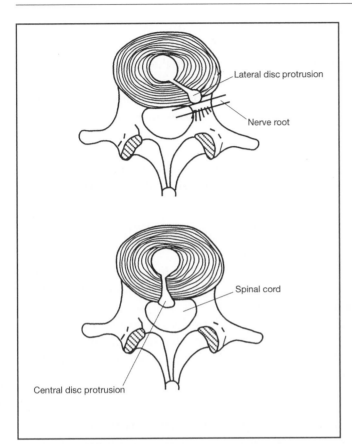

Figure 9.32a Lateral disc protrusion

Figure 9.32b Central disc protrusion

Management of acute disc prolapse

Patients with acute disc prolapse fall into three groups:

Group 1
- No neurology
- Surgery rarely indicated
- Rest, analgesia and physiotherapy

Group 2
- Radicular symptoms only
- 85% settle without surgery, but may need discectomy or laminectomy if they don't settle (eg for sciatica)

Group 3
- Significant neurology
- Urgent surgical decompression mandatory (eg for cord compression, cauda equina syndrome)

Rheumatoid arthritis in the spine

Rheumatoid arthritis is an erosive polyarthropathy that can affect any synovial joint. It commonly affects the joints of the cervical spine, especially those between C1 and C2.

Pathology of spinal RA

For the general pathology of RA see Section 2.2.

C1–2

- Inflammatory hypertrophic synovium (pannus) forms behind the odontoid peg
- Together with instability from laxity of the transverse ligament, this causes an increased interval between odontoid peg and atlas – the atlanto–dens interval (ADI)
- Erosions of lateral masses of C1 and C2 may cause vertical subluxation and impaction of the odontoid peg into the foramen magnum (basilar invagination or cranial settling)
- Fixed deformity may predispose to fracture
- Spinal cord and brainstem (neuroaxial) compression follow these changes

Below C1–2 (subaxial)

- RA affects the subaxial spine to cause two things:
  - Increase in age-related changes
  - Reducible then irreducible subluxation of cervical vertebrae
- Whole subaxial spine can show successive subluxation (subaxial staircase) in advanced disease
- Spinal cord compression follows these changes

Clinical signs and symptoms of spinal rheumatoid arthritis

- Pain radiating to the vertex of the skull (from stretching occipital nerve)
- CO_2 retention and nocturnal hypoxia can cause nightmares (due to mild medullary failure)
- Numb hands, spastic paraparesis, and hyper-reflexia from spinal cord compression
- Neurological signs may be absent

Investigating spinal rheumatoid arthritis

- Plain radiograph (flexion and extension) to show subluxations and whether they are reducible
- MRI to show signs of neuroaxial compression, presence of pannus and signal change within spinal cord indicating damage

Ankylosing spondylitis

- Idiopathic inflammatory disease
- Mainly localised to spine
- Affects young men (M:F ratio 5:1)
- Age of onset 15–25 years
- More common in western Europe
- Unknown cause
- 90–95% have HLA-B27 (although most people with HLA-B27 do not have ankylosing spondylitis, so HLA-B27 is not a useful diagnostic test)
- 25% of relatives affected

Distribution and clinical picture of ankylosing spondylitis

- Sacroiliac joints typically affected (forms part of diagnostic criteria)
- Vertebral joints often affected
- Hips and shoulders sometimes affected

- Small joints of hands and feet very rarely affected
- May present as asymmetrical peripheral arthritis, usually of large, weight-bearing joints
- May complain of painful heels at site of insertion of Achilles' tendon

Pathology of ankylosing spondylitis

Inflammation of ligamentous insertions
↓
Formation of granulation tissue
↓
Erosion of articular cartilage and bone
↓
Replacement by fibrous tissue
↓
Ossification of fibrous tissue
↓
Ankylosis (fusion)

- Marginal syndesmophytes are spurs, vertically oriented in the line of fibres of the ALL and PLL
- Vertebral bodies are 'squared off'
- Facet joints show smooth ascending circumferential ankylosis (starting in lumbar, to cervical)

Clinical features of ankylosing spondylitis

- **Low back pain:** differentiated from mechanical low back pain because it is typically worse in the morning and eases with exercise, whereas mechanical back pain is brought on by exercise
- **Stiff spine:** decreased movement in all directions (especially extension)
- **Deformity:** loss of lumbar lordosis and a fixed kyphosis, compensated for by

extension of the cervical spine in an attempt to keep the visual axis horizontal (otherwise they are looking at their feet) – producing a stooped 'question mark' posture. But beware, this condition may be completely undetected if the patient is propped up in a hospital bed. Get him to try to look at the ceiling. When asked to turn his head the patient turns his whole body
- **Chest expansion:** this is reduced and there is a prominent abdomen because the patient breathes by increased diaphragmatic excursion

Wall test
If a healthy person stands with his back against the wall, the heels, bum, scapula and occiput should all be able to touch the wall simultaneously. If spine extension is diminished this is impossible.

Associated diseases
Ankylosing spondylitis is also associated with inflammatory bowel disease, Reiter syndrome, *Yersinia* arthritis, acute anterior uveitis and psoriatic arthritis.

Extraskeletal manifestations
- Iritis (30%)
- Aortitis (4%)
- Apical pulmonary fibrosis
- Cardiac conduction defects (10%)
- Neurological complications: tetraplegia or paraplegia due to atlantoaxial dislocation or traumatic fracture of the rigid spine. Sciatica is also common
- Secondary amyloidosis

CHAPTER 9

Investigating ankylosing spondylitis

- ESR elevated

Radiological features

- Typical loss of lumbar lordosis, increased thoracic kyphosis and compensatory C-spine extension seen on lateral views
- Fuzziness or erosion of sacroiliac joints is typical
- Ossification of the intervertebral discs (syndesmophytes) bridges the intervertebral space, giving a typical bamboo spine appearance on AP views

Treatment of ankylosing spondylitis

- Analgesia (non-steroidals)
- Exercise and intensive physiotherapy (mainstay of preventing deterioration)
- Postural training
- Joint replacement (eg hips) may be needed but outcome very poor
- Vertebral osteotomy (severe flexion deformity can be partially corrected). Ankylosing spondylitis predisposes to poor fusion and non-union is common; the fused spine acts as a single, long lever (similar to a long bone) so multiple fixation points above an osteotomy (or fracture) are required

Spinal infections

See also Section 11.

> The axiom is:
>
> Good disc, bad disease (tumour)
>
> Bad disc, good disease (infection)

Metastasis and tumours of the spine

See also Section 12.

Metastasis to the spine

- Secondary spread of tumour occurs often in patients aged >50
- Metastatic deposits to the spine can cause vertebral body erosion, vertebral collapse or fracture and nerve root, cord or cauda equina compression
- Most common route is haematogenous
- Renal cancers may directly invade the spine
- Lytic lesions are due to osteoclastic activity
- Sclerotic lesions are due to osteoblastic activity (eg prostate)
- Neural compromise occurs when direct pressure of the expanding lesion or vertebral collapse leads to kyphosis or scoliosis

> **Primary tumours that commonly metastasise to bone**
> Use this medical student trick to remember:
> **B**reast, **B**rostate (prostate), **B**ridley (kidney), **B**ronchus, **B**yroid (thyroid), **B**ladder
> Cancers of the gastrointestinal tract can metastasise to bone, but not as often as you might expect, considering how common these cancers are.

Primary tumours of the spine

Primary tumours can affect the spine and can also cause pathological fractures, deformity and cord, root and nerve compression. They can be classified as:

- Tumours of bone (eg myeloma, osteoma, osteoblastoma, metastasis)
- Tumours of covering layers (eg neurofibroma, schwannoma, meningioma)
- Tumours of spinal cord (eg glioma, ependymoma, astrocytoma)

Cysts within the spinal canal can present like a tumour with nerve root pain and neurological loss (eg degenerative facet joint cysts and arachnoid Tarlov cysts).

Osteoporosis and fractures of the spine

- Senile osteoporotic kyphosis is seen in postmenopausal women
- There is anterior vertebral wedging, pathological fracture, radiographic evidence of decalcification and disturbed serum chemistry. Deformity is typical, with increased lumbar lordosis, thoracic kyphosis and cervical lordosis (think of the classic 'little old lady' posture). Pain may be a feature if fractures are present
- Treatment is directed towards controlling underlying osteoporosis

Learning point

Three common clinical presentations of spinal pathology (each of these can be caused by almost all of the important spinal pathologies discussed above):
- Lower back pain
- Neck pain
- Spinal deformity

13.5 Lower back pain

Learning point

There are six causes of back pain, which we will discuss in this section:
- Mechanical back pain
- Nerve root pain (radiculopathy)
- Spinal cord compression
- Cauda equina syndrome
- Neurogenic claudication
- Coccodynia
Almost all of the other spinal pathologies discussed in this chapter may also present with back pain.

Lower back pain is one of the most common symptoms reported to the GP. It is experienced to some extent by >90% of the UK population at some time in their lives. It is a major cause of time off work and of registered disability, and is a significant cost to society.

Most patients have chronic mechanical back pain or temporary, self-resolving, acute nerve root pain due to prolapsed discs. The mainstays of treatment are analgesia, rehabilitation and reassurance. However, a few patients have serious general underlying pathology (eg tumour, infection or osteoporotic fracture) which must be investigated and diagnosed.

Another group of patients are at risk of serious permanent neurological disability caused by cord compression, cauda equina or prolonged nerve root compression, and they must be diagnosed and treated as a matter of urgency.

CHAPTER 9

You must be able to spot the features of the history and examination that raise suspicions of serious pathology. Then you can decide which of the vast numbers of people with backache warrant further investigation.

Causes of back pain

Age 0–10
- Scoliosis (idiopathic scoliosis should not be painful and pain in this population should be investigated)
- Spondylolisthesis
- Spinal infections

Age 11–20
- Scoliosis (idiopathic scoliosis should not be painful and pain in this population should be investigated)
- Scheuermann's kyphosis
- Non-specific back pain

Age 21–40
- Non-specific back pain
- Prolapsed intervertebral disc
- Spondylolisthesis
- Spinal fracture
- Ankylosing spondylitis
- Coccydynia
- Spinal infection

Age 40–60
- Non-specific back pain
- Prolapsed intervertebral disc
- Spondylolisthesis
- Spondylosis
- Secondary OA
- Spinal metastasis
- Coccydynia
- Spinal infections
- Paget's disease
- RA

Age >60
- OA
- Senile kyphosis
- Osteoporosis
- Osteomalacia
- Spinal metastases
- Spinal infections
- Pathological fracture due to any of the above

Non-specific back pain

Also known as mechanical back pain, non-specific back pain is caused by irritation of facet joints, ligaments and muscles, usually due to degenerative changes or spondylosis.

- It is the most common cause of low back pain
- It produces dull, aching pain in the low back, upper buttocks, outside the pelvis and lateral aspects of the thighs. It may radiate to the knees, but no further
- It is aggravated by activity
- There may be a history of minor injury
- There is a good range of movement of the spine and no positive neurological signs

This almost ubiquitous disorder is generally self-limiting, but recovery may be prolonged. It is important that this is a diagnosis of exclusion, and that all serious underlying pathology has been excluded by carefully asking about and examining for any 'red flags'.

Management of non-specific back pain

Physiotherapy, local heat, education about lifting techniques, and avoiding heavy manual work or hobbies are useful. Losing weight and strengthening abdominal muscles by supervised exercise is also advised. In some cases orthotics (a supportive corset) or a local injection of steroids may be indicated. Surgery is not generally indicated. Some surgeons advocate fusion of the motor segments causing pain, but this is controversial, and conservative treatment should be followed in the first instance.

Social or psychological factors may prolong or embellish symptoms and signs. Non-physical factors must be taken into consideration, especially when dealing with someone with chronic back pain. The biopsychological model of low back pain recognises the fact that these patients may need psychological support and encouragement.

Nerve root pain (radiculopathy/sciatica)

This is caused most commonly by posterolateral disc protrusion, but can also be caused by other space-occupying lesions such as tumour, infection, rheumatoid disease or osteophytes secondary to spondylosis.

Radiculitis is defined as pain in the distribution of the nerve root. Radiculopathy is dermatomal sensory loss, and possible muscle weakness and reflex loss relating to the particular nerve root involved. The neurological disturbance is segmental and dependent on the level of prolapse.

In 1.5% of cases of low back pain there is an associated radiculopathy due to a herniated disc. Sciatica is the typical clinical presentation and it usually presents in people aged 30–55.

Sciatic pain extends past the knee and on to the foot/ankle.

Management of nerve root pain

Once significant neurological signs and underlying pathology are excluded, all cases of acute disc prolapse are first treated by conservative methods:

- Rest
- Analgesia ± muscle relaxants
- Physiotherapy

If, however, there is an unsatisfactory response or where residual symptoms are severe, further investigation by MRI (preferably) or CT is undertaken with a view to exploratory surgery.

If the patient has radicular symptoms (eg sciatica) 85% will settle after 6 weeks of conservative treatment as above. These patients are usually previously healthy, working people who suddenly find themselves in excruciating pain that renders them immobile, and it is often difficult to explain to them that no urgent procedure is indicated. The person who invents a cure for acute sciatica and spares these poor people the 6 weeks of gradually abating agony would soon become very rich. Studies have shown no benefit in early surgery, bedrest for more than 48 hours, local joint injections, epidurals, transcutaneous nerve stimulation, radiofrequency facet denervation, lumbar supports, traction or acupuncture when compared with simple rest, analgesia and physiotherapy.

If the patient does not settle after 6 weeks, surgery may be considered; 5–10% of patients with sciatica will eventually require surgery (see 'Surgical management of lower back pain' below).

Spinal cord compression

Also known as myelopathy, this is commonly caused by central disc protrusion but can also be caused by tumours, infection, trauma, ankylosing spondylitis and Paget's disease, which narrows the spinal canal.

Symptoms include numbness, clumsiness and weakness of the legs (or the hands in cervical spinal cord compression), difficulty in walking, sensory impairment and difficulty in bladder control. Symptoms may present suddenly, gradually or with stepwise deterioration. This is an orthopaedic/neurosurgical emergency, and urgent MRI and discussion with the relevant specialist are mandatory.

Decompression methods are described below (see 'Surgical management of lower back pain').

Cauda equina syndrome

If the narrowing of the spinal canal described above occurs below the level of L2, it is not the spinal cord that is compressed but the cauda equina. Cauda equina syndrome is usually the result of a large, central rupture of the disc at L4–5 and constitutes 1–2% of all operated discs. It can also occur at other levels between L2 and S2, and can be caused by any of the pathologies that cause spinal cord compression listed above.

The typical patient presents with sphincter disturbance (urinary retention, urinary incontinence, saddle anaesthesia, lax anal sphincter), bilateral sciatica, significant motor weakness often involving more than one motor root, low back pain and sexual dysfunction. Similar to spinal cord compression, this is an emergency that necessitates urgent imaging and referral for surgery.

Neurogenic claudication

Neurogenic claudication is caused by spinal stenosis (a narrowing of the sagittal diameter of the spinal canal) and presents as vague backache, morning stiffness, and aching in the legs when walking or standing. There may

be temporary motor paralysis, leg cramps or paraesthesiae related to exercise, and the legs may 'give way' after walking a certain distance. Flexion relieves symptoms by increasing canal diameter so the pain is relieved by sitting down.

They may be referred to the vascular clinic on suspicion of peripheral vascular disease, but have variable claudication distance, good peripheral pulses and segmental rather than stocking-distribution sensory loss. Compression of the nerve root in the thecal sac or root canal causes pain and impaired blood flow. Spinal stenosis is common in achondroplasia. MRI, CT or myelography may help to confirm the diagnosis.

Surgery is the only treatment that will alter the anatomical cause of the symptoms. A lumbar laminectomy with undercutting of the facets, or multiple laminotomies to decompress the roots in the lateral recesses, results in a good outcome for 55–87% of patients. (See 'Surgical management of lower back pain' below.)

Coccydynia

This is pain in the coccygeal area. It has been previously poorly understood and the patients complaining of it have been labelled as hypochondriac. However, it is a very real, chronic, painful syndrome; 60% of cases trace back to an episode of trauma or childbirth.

Per rectum examination excludes more serious pathology. MRI can help exclude rare sacral tumours.

Treatment is physiotherapy. If this does not work, long-acting steroids injected into the pericoccygeal plexus of nerves combined with a sacrococcygeal manipulation will cure >90%.

Excision of the coccyx (coccygectomy) should be reserved for a very small number of patients who do not respond to prolonged intensive conservative treatment. Early excision carries a poor prognosis.

Surgical management of lumbar spinal pathology

Surgical decompression of the lumbar spine

The aim of surgical spinal decompression is to relieve pressure on nerve roots, spinal cord or cauda equina, usually from a herniated disc but occasionally by bony or ligamentous enlargement.

Microdiscectomy

- **Aim:** to remove herniated disc fragment and decompress nerve root, spinal cord or cauda equina
- **Indications:** disc herniation causing compression of nerve root, spinal cord or cauda equina. It is the gold standard approach
- **Approach:** posterior (transcanalicular)
- **Principles:** using an operating microscope, a small posterior lumbar incision is made, the ligamentum flavum is removed (with or without an additional foramenotomy), and the herniated disc fragment removed after identifying the nerve root and theca. Usually the disc space is entered and any additional disc fragments are removed
- **Results:** success rates of 75% at 10 years
- **Complications:** infection, haematoma, nerve root damage and dural tear with CSF leak

Laminectomy

- **Aim:** to remove spinous process and medial half of each facet

- **Indications:** if the disc is large (common in cauda equina syndrome). Also used with undercutting of the facet joints in treating neurogenic claudication (see below). Lumbar spinal stenosis is cured by laminectomy in 75–80% of cases
- **Approach:** posterior (transcanalicular)
- **Principles:** performed with a discectomy, which allows thorough decompression of the nerve root and clearing of debris from the intervertebral disc space. This makes the operated segment unstable so fusion may be required (see later). Risk of instability is high in stenosis with scoliosis or spondylolisthesis, or extensive resection of facet joint

Intradiscal extracanalicular approaches

- **Aim:** to achieve decompression with minimal intervention and avoid scarring around the nerve root
- **Indications:** contained discs – small disc herniations that have not breached the outer annulus. These techniques are not as commonly used as traditional discectomy and laminectomy
- **Approach:** lateral to canal and direct into disc space
- **Principles:** the aim is to decompress the nucleus and thereby improve disc compliance, but it is often difficult to treat the posterolateral disc herniation itself through this approach

Foraminotomy

- Undercutting the superior facet joint is used for decompression when there is a localised hypertrophied facet joint
- It is also used to treat neurogenic claudication in conjunction with a laminectomy

CHAPTER 9

Fusion procedures of the lumbar spine

This is indicated in the presence of a deformity that changes the balance of the spine, such as scoliosis, post-traumatic kyphosis and spondylolisthesis. Extensive surgical decompression produces motion segment instability so there are indications, especially in a degenerate spine, to perform a fusion at the same time as the decompression. Patients should be aware that although the deformity may be improved and the instability corrected, pain may persist.

There is no evidence to support spinal fusion in the absence of a deformity or a loss of balance. Furthermore, back pain resulting from multilevel degenerative disc disease, especially in a young patient, is not an indication for fusion.

Posterolateral or intertransverse fusion

- **Aim:** to produce circumferential arthrodesis (firm fusion of posterior and anterior aspects of the vertebrae) between two adjacent vertebrae
- **Approach:** posterolateral gutter exposed on both sides
- **Principles:** the transverse processes, pars interarticularis and facet joints of adjacent levels are fused by decortication and bone grafting. Screws may also be used

Posterior lumbar interbody fusion

- **Aim:** to produce circumferential arthrodesis between two adjacent vertebrae
- **Approach:** posterior midline
- **Principles:** disc contents are removed with a wide decompression. Endplates are denuded of cartilage. Intervertebral space is filled with bone graft to allow interbody fusion. Cages, ramps and screws may be used

Transforaminal lumbar interbody fusion

- **Aim:** to produce circumferential arthrodesis between two adjacent vertebrae
- **Approach:** intradiscal, extracanicular (avoids potential neurological complications of posterior lumbar interbody fusion [PLIF])
- **Principles:** disc contents are removed with a wide decompression. Endplates are denuded of cartilage. Intervertebral space is filled with bone graft to allow interbody fusion. Cages, ramps and screws may be used

Anterior lumbar interbody fusion

- **Aim:** to produce fusion between adjacent vertebrae (not a circumferential fusion unless posterior fusion also performed)
- **Approach:** transperitoneal or retroperitoneal (can be performed by minimally invasive techniques)
- **Principles:** the whole nucleus of the disc is excised as in PLIF, and bone graft in a cage or femoral bone ring is inserted into the intervertebral space

Results and complications of fusion procedures

- Pain may persist
- Reduced mobility of spine
- Compensatory hypermobility in adjacent levels
- Floating fusion (if a fusion is carried out in the lumbar spine above an unfused level it is called 'floating' because there is potential for degenerative change above and below the fused level)

Disc replacement

- **Aim:** an alternative to fusion, to maintain segmental motion after partial or total discectomy (avoiding compensatory hypermobility in adjacent levels)

- **Principles:** after discectomy, replaces nucleus or whole disc with prosthesis (rather than leaving joint unstable or going for fusion)
- **Results and complications:** studies suggest may be as effective as fusion procedures, but concerns about revision limit its use

13.6 Neck pain

Learning point

Most common cervical ailments that are amenable to surgery are due to:
- Acute cervical disc prolapse
- Cervical spondylosis (degeneration)
- Rheumatoid arthritis

All of these pathologies may result in:
- Spinal cord compression (myelopathy) and/or
- Nerve root compression (radiculopathy/brachalgia)

The usual treatment for muscular neck pain (without myelopathy or radicu-lopathy) is:
- Manipulative therapy
- Early mobilisation
- Avoidance of a collar

Most settle in 5–6 weeks.

Pathology of neck pain

Acute cervical disc

Cervical disc prolapse can be sudden or gradual and occurs in a younger age group (<40). There is usually associated radiculopathy. Brachalgia is the upper limb version of sciatica, caused by pressure on the nerve roots, in the same way that sciatica compresses the nerve roots. Brachalgia is typically unilateral and affects a dermatomal distribution, depending on the nerve root affected. It presents as pain, paraesthesia or weakness.

Signs include muscle spasm, local tenderness, loss of range of motion and loss of lordosis in the neck. C5–8 nerve root signs are the most common. C5–6 and C6–7 are the most common levels affected (these are the most mobile segments in the young).

Radiographs sometimes show loss of lordosis but usually no loss of disc height.

Management of cervical disc prolapse

Although, similar to lumbar disc prolapse, this condition is excruciatingly painful, it usually settles with time, analgesics, muscle relaxants, anti-inflammatories and physiotherapy. This is one of the rare occasions where short-term use of a soft collar may be helpful.

If there is a significant neurological loss or any sign of cord compression then an MRI is indicated. If the pain shows no sign of settling at 6 weeks an MRI and consideration of surgical decompression is indicated. (See 'Surgical management of neck pain' overleaf.)

Cervical spondylosis

This is an age-related disc and joint degenerative change (see Section 13.4). It usually presents in middle age (>40) and has gradual onset. Similar to disc prolapse, the mobile segments of C5–6 and C6–7 are most frequently affected. Patients may present with pain, stiffness, occasional radiculopathy (sensory more than motor) and, rarely, signs of cord compression.

CHAPTER 9

Radiographs show loss of disc height, posterior osteophytes and facet joint degeneration. In most people it is an incidental finding and does not cause significant symptoms.

Management of cervical spondylosis

Once the symptoms of cervical spondylotic myelopathy have developed, complete remission is rare and results of surgery disappointing. The main aim of surgery is to prevent further neurological deterioration. Methods include posterior laminectomy, anterior cervical discectomy or anterior foramenotomy with bone graft; spacers or cages often used to restore disc space (see 'Surgical management of neck pain').

Rheumatoid arthritis of the cervical spine

This pathology is seen in elderly people, often with advanced rheumatoid disease. Women are affected more commonly than men.

RA of the cervical spine presents with restriction of neck movements and neck pain in a rheumatoid patient. It can present with sudden death because there is potential for pressure on the brainstem with atlantoaxial subluxation. Also tetraparesis (weakness in all limbs) and occipital neuralgia (pain radiating to back of the head) are seen. Radicular symptoms and cord compression are common.

It occurs typically in C1–2, with the subaxial spine affected less often. Radiographs show atlantoaxial slip.

Management of RA of the cervical spine

Treatment involves traction and fusion. See 'Surgical management of neck pain'.

Surgical management of neck pain

Surgery of disc prolapse and spondylosis

- **Aim:** to prevent further neurological deterioration rather than restore neurology that has been lost, or to cure pain
- **Approach:** anterior is indicated for anterior disease such as osteophyte or herniated disc
- **Procedures:**
  - Anterior cervical discectomy and fusion (ACDF) involves removing the disc and inserting iliac crest bone graft
  - Vertebrectomy with cage plate fusion is a more radical decompression with a synthetic spacer
  - Multilevel degeneration necessitates a posterior cervical laminectomy, laminoplasty or split laminectomy. The main disadvantage of a laminectomy is that it is potentially destabilising

Surgical management of C1–2 rheumatoid arthritis

- **Aims:** to fuse C1 to C2 preventing rotation, flexion, extension and anteroposterior translation of C1 on C2
- **Indications** for surgery of C1–2:
  - Intractable, intolerable, greater occipital neuralgia
  - Cervical myelopathy
  - Increasingly severe subluxation of C1–2
- **Procedures:**
  - If subluxation is reducible then treatment is by C1–2 fusion, for which there are many methods, using screws, wires and bone grafts
  - Postoperatively the neck is placed in a collar for 3 months
  - If subluxation is reducible only after traction, a posterior occipitocervical fusion is indicated using internal

implants and bone grafts

- If subluxation is irreducible even after traction a transoral excision of the odontoid peg is combined with occipito-cervical fusion

Surgical management of subaxial RA

- In single-level reducible subluxation, anterior cervical discectomy with bone grafting may be adequate
- In irreducible subluxation, corpectomy is performed. The central vertebral body is removed and replaced with bone graft from iliac crest

Preoperative precautions in cervical RA

- Care when positioning patients
- Screen for anaemia
- Cover with oral steroids (intravenous perioperatively)
- Give prophylactic antibiotics if immuno-compromised by steroids
- Preoperative neurological assessment with scoring system (eg Ranwat's system) used to decide if patient will benefit from cervical spine surgery. If the patient is crippled or bed-bound, significant neurological recovery is unlikely

Complications of cervical spine surgery

- Fusion rates vary (high for transarticular screw fixations; low for occipitocervical fusion)
- Tetraplegia (rare but serious)
- Mortality (5% for transoral odontoidectomy)

13.7 Spinal deformity

Unlike spine pain, which occurs mainly in the cervical and lumbar regions, spinal deformity occurs more commonly in the thoracic spine.

Learning point

Types of spinal deformity:
Kyphosis
- Postural
- Osteoporotic
- Scheuermann's kyphosis
- Neuromuscular
- Congenital
- Degenerative (senile)
- Pathological
- Ankylosing spondylitis
- Paget's disease
- Infection
- Fracture

Scoliosis
- Idiopathic
- Degenerative
- Congenital
- Neuromuscular
- Postural

Spondylolisthesis
- Congenital or dysplastic (type I)
- Isthmic (type II)
- Degenerative (type III)
- Traumatic (type IV)
- Pathological (type V)

May occasionally be Iatrogenic

Spinal dysraphism
- Meningocele
- Myelomeningocele
- Spina bifida occulta
- Diastematomyelia
- Spina bifida cystica

Kyphosis

Kyphosis is an increased forward curvature of the thoracic spine, obvious when viewed from the side.

Kyphosis can be classified according to the shape of the deformity:
- **Regular kyphosis:** a gradually increasing curvature
- **Angular kyphosis:** (gibbus) where there is an abrupt alteration in the thoracic curvature accompanied by a prominent spinous process. Angular kyphosis suggests an underlying pathology such as spinal infection or fracture

Or it can be classified according to fixity:
- **Mobile:** as in postural kyphosis and some neuromuscular kyphosis
- **Fixed:** as in ankylosing spondylitis and senile kyphosis

Postural kyphosis
- Common in adolescent girls, causing a rounded back and drooping shoulders
- Regular mobile kyphosis which just needs postural correction
- May be related to an increased lumbar lordosis due to abnormal forward tilting of the pelvis, flexion contracture of the hips or developmental dysplasia of the hip
- No need for surgery

Osteoporotic kyphosis
See Osteoporosis (Section 13.4).
- Seen in postmenopausal women or those on long-term steroids
- Caused by anterior vertebral wedging and often pathological fractures (which are painful)

- It is a fixed kyphosis (usually regular) but fractures may cause a gibbus
- Osteomalacia presents similarly
- Treatment is directed at biochemical abnormality (see Section 13.4)
- Treatment by percutaneous injection of cement under image intensification (vertebroplasty) has a role in the management of a painful segment

Scheuermann's kyphosis
- Thought to be a growth disturbance of the thoracic vertebral bodies (ie anterior wedging)
- Clinical definition is 5° of wedging in an individual vertebra and >40° kyphosis overall
- Cause unknown
- Patients complain of mild backache and deformity. Mobility is impaired. There is marked fixed regular kyphosis and a compensatory increase in lumbar lordosis
- Secondary OA and disc herniation are common
- Surgical treatment reserved for large deformities

Neuromuscular kyphosis
- May result from muscle weakness secondary to anterior poliomyelitis or muscular dystrophy
- Usually a regular kyphosis that starts as mobile but becomes fixed over time

Degenerative (senile) kyphosis
- Secondary to age-related degenerative changes of the spine (see Section 13.4)
- Intervertebral discs lose height (patient becomes progressively stooped and shorter)
- Kyphosis is fixed and regular

- Pain may occur if associated OA
- Condition is accelerated by osteoporosis or osteomalacia (also common in elderly people)

Pathological kyphosis

Kyphosis may be an indication of underlying disease. Always exclude:
- Ankylosing spondylitis: fixed, regular, diagnostic radiographs
- Paget's disease: fixed, regular, other bony deformities
- Infection: fixed, angular, painful, associated symptoms
- Fracture: old fractures are fixed, angular and seen on radiograph
- Calve's disease: a childhood disorder where a single vertebral body is deformed, usually grossly flattened. Thought to be due to eosinophilic granuloma. Symptoms resolve spontaneously but it can result in an angular fixed kyphosis that needs surgery

Scoliosis

This is defined as a lateral curvature of the spine >10° as measured using Cobb's method on a standing radiograph.

Scoliosis may be:
- Structural (due to deformity of vertebrae)
- Non-structural (compensatory, postural or secondary to pain and spasm)
- In most patients the cause of scoliosis is unknown (idiopathic). The lateral bend is associated with spinal rotation, which in turn leads to rotation of the thoracic cage and rib deformities

Cobb's angle

The magnitude of the curve in scoliosis is commonly determined by measurement of Cobb's angle, which is derived from a standard posteroanterior standing radiograph of the spine.

Cobb's angle is the angle formed between two lines: a line drawn perpendicular to the top of the superior vertebrae of the scoliotic curve, and another line perpendicular to the bottom of the inferior vertebrae.

Classification of scoliosis

- **Postural scoliosis:** this is a non-structural compensatory scoliosis (eg pelvic obliquity secondary to hip or leg inequality). When the legs are squared the scoliosis disappears
- **Congenital scoliosis:** these are structural abnormalities of the vertebrae. Vertebral abnormalities (eg hemivertebrae, fused vertebrae, absent or fused ribs) occur as the result of failures of vertebral formation or vertebral segmentation during embryonic development. Congenital scoliosis (and other early-onset forms of scoliosis) pose a risk to the life of the child. The spinal deformity restricts lung development, leading to increased mortality in early adulthood
- **Neuromuscular scoliosis:** this may be caused by cerebral palsy, poliomyelitis, syringomyelia, Friedreich's ataxia, Duchenne muscular dystrophy, neurofibromatosis or post-traumatic paralysis. Often the main problem is balance (eg sitting upright in a wheelchair)
- **Degenerative scoliosis:** occurs in elderly patients due to facet joint failure. It is often associated with spondylolisthesis

CHAPTER 9

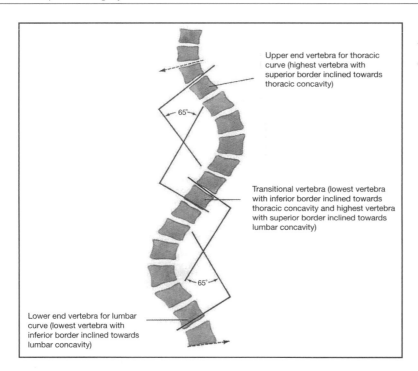

Figure 9.33 Cobb's method for measurement of curvature of the spine

Upper end vertebra for thoracic curve (highest vertebra with superior border inclined towards thoracic concavity)

65°

Transitional vertebra (lowest vertebra with inferior border inclined towards thoracic concavity and highest vertebra with superior border inclined towards lumbar concavity)

65°

Lower end vertebra for lumbar curve (lowest vertebra with inferior border inclined towards lumbar concavity)

- **Idiopathic scoliosis:** this is the most common of the structural scolioses. It has an unknown cause. There is usually one (occasionally two) distinct levels at which several vertebrae are affected, forming the fixed primary curve. Above and below this curve are compensatory mobile secondary curves. The primary curve has rotational deformity: the spinous processes rotate into the concavity and the bodies (which carry the ribs) rotate into the convexity, causing a hump or hunchback. The spinal deformity is associated with shortening of the trunk, and there may be impairment of cardiac and respiratory function if it develops before the age of 5–6 years. The age of onset is used to divide idiopathic scoliosis:
  - **Early-onset idiopathic:** the sex ratio is 3M:2F; 90% curve to the left. Associated with ipsilateral craniofacial deformity (may resolve but severe if progressive).

Respiratory compromise secondary to scoliosis may occur in infants due to failed development of alveoli
  - **Late-onset idiopathic:** the sex ratio is 1M:10F (for large curves); 90% curve to the right. Rib hump exaggerates deformity

History of scoliosis

This is a cosmetic deformity with aching pain. Severe pain is unusual, and must exclude bone tumour. Family history is important, so also enquire about pregnancy, and birth (cerebral palsy, birth anoxia).

Examination of scoliosis

Note any skin pigmentation, dimples or hairy patches. Stand behind the patient, ask them to lean forwards and note any rib hump, and the direction of convex curve (direction of scoliosis).

Assess balance by placing a plumb line on the occiput and seeing the curve in relation to the sacrum. In an unbalanced spine, a plumb line will pass lateral to the lumbosacral junction instead of bisecting the junction as it does in the balanced spine. Measure leg lengths to ensure that the curve is not just postural.

Prognosis in scoliosis

Determinants of progression are patient gender, future growth potential and the curve magnitude at the time of diagnosis.

- Females have a risk of curve progression ten times higher than males
- The greater the growth potential and the larger the curve, the greater the likelihood of curve progression

Evaluation of growth potential is done by assessing the Tanner stage and the Risser grade:

- **Tanner stages** 2–3 occur just after onset of pubertal growth spurt and are the time of maximum progression of scoliosis
- **Risser grades** 0–5 give a useful estimate of how much skeletal growth remains by grading the progress of bony fusion of the iliac apophysis. The iliac apophysis ossifies in a predictable fashion from anterolateral to posteromedial, along the iliac crest

Treatment of scoliosis

Surgery is for:

- Curves of >30° that are cosmetically unacceptable
- Prepubertal children with progressive curves
- Surgery does not alter back pain in scoliosis

The incidence of back pain in late-onset idiopathic scoliosis is the same as in the general population. Surgery is usually a single-stage posterior instrumented correction with multiple pedicle screw. Larger, stiffer curves may require an anterior and posterior approach.

Non-surgical treatments are controversial but include exercises and bracing. There is no evidence that either of these treatments can alter the natural history of the underlying curve, but physiotherapy is helpful where there is an element of muscular back pain.

Spondylolisthesis

Spondylolisthesis means 'vertebra slips' in Greek, and it refers to the forward translation of one vertebra relative to another. This is the most common spinal deformity seen in general orthopaedic practice.

Pathogenesis of spondylolisthesis

- When standing, the L5 vertebra carries the weight of the trunk
- The L5 vertebra rests on S1, which slopes downwards anteriorly. The main thing stopping L5 from slipping forwards on S1 is the inferior articular process of L5 in contact with the superior articular processes of the sacrum
- The part of L5 immediately anterior to the inferior articular process (the pars interarticularis) may fracture or have a defect either unilaterally or bilaterally (spondylolysis), allowing forward slippage of L5 on S1 (spondylolisthesis)
- Although typically seen at the L5/S1 level it can occur at other levels (eg L4 on L5)

Classification of spondylolisthesis

The Wiltse, Macnab and Newman classification system outlines the most common causes of vertebral translation in an anterior direction. There are six categories in the system.

CHAPTER 9

Type I: congenital spondylolisthesis

This is characterised by the presence of dysplastic sacral facet joints allowing forward translation of one vertebra relative to another. Orientation of facets in an axial or sagittal plane may allow for forward translation, producing undue stress on the pars, resulting in a fracture. There are three subtypes:

- IA: associated with spina bifida
- IB: adult variety
- IC: other congenital variety

Type II: isthmic spondylolisthesis

This is caused by development of stress fracture of the pars interarticularis. There are three subtypes:

- IIA: repeated stress fractures, and defect fills with fibrous tissue (most common)
- IIB: pars elongates due to repeated microfractures (but is intact)
- IIC: acute pars fracture (unstable)

Type III: degenerative spondylolisthesis

This is commonly caused by intersegmental instability produced by facet arthropathy. This variation usually occurs in the adult population and, in most cases, does not progress beyond a grade 1 spondylolisthesis (see grading system below). Most commonly at L4–5 level.

Type IV: traumatic spondylolisthesis

This can, in rare instances, result from acute stresses (trauma) to the facet or pars. Similar to type IIC but affects posterior elements except pars.

Type V: pathological spondylolisthesis

Any bone disorder can destabilise the facet mechanism, producing pathological spondylolisthesis.

Type VI: iatrogenic spondylolisthesis

This may occur if an over-zealous surgeon performs too great a facetectomy.

Grading of spondylolisthesis

The **Meyerding grading system** for spondylolisthesis is the most commonly used. The degree of slippage is measured as the percentage of distance that the anteriorly translated vertebral body has moved forwards relative to the superior endplate of the vertebra below:

Grade 1   0–25% slippage

Grade 2   26–50% slippage

Grade 3   51–75% slippage

Grade 4   76–100% slippage

Grade 5   >100% slippage (spondyloptosis)

Clinical presentation and management of spondylolisthesis

Both spondylosis and spondylolisthesis give rise to low back pain that radiates into the buttocks.

Neurological symptoms occur if there is disc prolapse or stretching of the cauda equina or nerve roots.

Treatment is by local fusion, with or without disc excision and further decompression as needed.

Spinal dysraphism (neural tube defects)

Spinal dysraphism, or neural tube defects, is the general term for embryonic failure of neural tube development and failure of posterior midline fusion of the vertebral arch. It usually occurs in the lumbosacral spine.

The incidence of neural tube defects is falling.

There are a number of reasons for this, such as improved maternal nutrition, periconceptual folic acid supplements and antenatal screening.

Spina bifida cystica

Posterior spine elements (laminae, facets and spinous processes) fail to develop, allowing the contents of the spinal canal to prolapse through the defect.

Myelomeningocele

This is a severe form of spina bifida cystica where the spinal cord and nerve roots prolapse through the posterior defect. It is the most common neural tube defect.

- Open myelomeningocele means the spinal cord is open and CSF can escape through the defect
- In a closed myelomeningocele the neural tube is fully developed and covered by a membrane

The most common site is the lumbar spine, although extensive lesions may extend up to involve the thoracic cord. Sensory and motor function below the segmental level of the neural tube defect is absent. Involvement of the lower limbs depends on the level.

Treatment of myelomeningocele

Priorities of treatment include skin closure within 48 hours. This then causes hydrocephalus, necessitating a ventriculoperitoneal shunt.

Limb deformities are treated by stretch exercises and strapping or splinting for 6–12 months.

When the child is slightly older, open correction is indicated. Proximal deformities are corrected before distal ones. This entails dividing and transferring the tendons, and then correcting the bony deformity. It is rare for children with anything above a sacral defect to walk unaided.

Urinary problems develop in 90% due to neural involvement of sacral nerves to the bladder (intravenous urogram investigation or urinary diversion needed).

Meningocele

This is rare. There is a dorsal bony defect in the spinal column and the meninges are skin-covered. The neural tube is closed and there should be no neurological damage.

Spina bifida occulta

This mild form of spinal dysraphism is said to affect up to 20% of the population but most are asymptomatic. It may be associated with a hairy patch, dimple or birthmark, but not with overlying muscle or skin abnormalities. Occasionally it can cause a spastic gait or bladder dysfunction.

Diastematomyelia

A fibrous, cartilaginous or bony spur splits the spinal cord. As the child develops, the spinal cord is 'tethered' by this spur and this can cause neurological deficits. Sometimes this is manifest only during puberty. It can present with weak legs and cauda equina syndrome.

CHAPTER 9

13.8 Surgery to the thoracic spine

The posterior approach is not suitable for the thoracic spine because the spinal cord cannot be retracted towards the midline without causing significant neurological problems. In the lumbar spine, the cauda equina can be moved aside, so the posterior approach is possible.

Surgical approaches for a persistently symptomatic thoracic disc are anterior via thoracotomy, posterior or costotransverse incisions.

Anterior, posterior, and costotransverse approaches

The costotransverse approach was common in the era of TB of the spine. However, due to the destruction of the muscles and painful dissection, it has largely been replaced by either the anterior or the posterior approach. Generally, if the pathology is anterior (ie in the vertebral body) a thoracotomy is performed and excision or reconstruction of the spinal column is achieved. If the posterior elements are involved (ie lamina or pedicles) a posterior muscle strip and fusion are performed.

Spinal column reconstruction

The aim of spinal column reconstruction is to correct the alignment of the spine. This may be achieved by an anterior approach, a posterior approach or both approaches. General principles are that discs and facet joints are removed, correction is achieved and bone graft is placed around the area to be fused. This is augmented with instrumented titanium metalwork in the way of cages and plates (anteriorly), and screws, hooks and rods (posteriorly). Metalwork will fail unless fusion occurs, and recently bone morphometric proteins (BMPs) have begun to play a role in accelerating fusion of the spine.

Excision of thoracic disc

Thoracic disc herniation is rare but can be very symptomatic because the spinal canal is narrow at this level. Approaches are transthoracic (ie thoracotomy), which has the advantage of not touching the spinal cord at all, but the disadvantages associated with a thoracotomy. Alternatively, a transpedicular approach entails a lateral approach through a midline incision, drilling down one pedicle. The herniated disc is removed piecemeal lateral to the spinal cord and may be difficult if the disc is calcified because it may impinge on the spinal cord on removal, but this has the advantage of avoiding a thoracotomy. Recently, thoracoscopic approaches have been used.

Decompression

Decompression is a general term for removing the pressure from the spinal cord. This may be done via an anterior approach, such as a discectomy or vertebrectomy, or a posterior approach, such as a laminectomy. Decompression is often combined with a fusion procedure to avoid progressive kyphosis of the spine.

Section 14

Complications of orthopaedic surgery

General complications
General complications of anaesthesia
General complications of orthopaedic surgery
- Mortality
- Myocardial infarction (MI)
- Bleeding
- Deep vein thrombosis (DVT)
- Pulmonary embolism (PE)
- Reaction to methylmethacrylate bone cement
- Fat embolism syndrome

Local complications
- Soft-tissue swelling
- Haematoma
- Infection
- Neurovascular damage
- Non-union
- Malunion
- Periprosthetic fracture
- Implant failure
- Chronic pain
- Loss of function

Venous thromboembolism and pulmonary embolism

Orthopaedic surgery carries a high risk of development of DVT (40–80% after total knee replacement) and proximal vein thrombosis (10–30%). The main risk factors are:
- Prolonged immobility (>4 days)
- Surgery of pelvis, hip, lower limb
- Prolonged operating time in both elective and emergency surgery
- Elderly population
- Fractured neck of femur
- Often associated with blood transfusion, increased risk of DVT
- Joint replacement

Details of DVT and PE are found in Chapter 9, Vascular surgery, Book 2.

An individual patient's risk of DVT/PE should be assessed and prophylactic treatment given if indicated. For some procedures the risks of bleeding may outweigh any potential benefit of anticoagulation (eg spinal surgery). Upper limb procedures carry a very low risk of DVT/PE.

CHAPTER 9

775

NICE (National Institute for Health and Clinical Excellence) has published guidance on DVT and PE prophylaxis. There is still no clear consensus on the treatment of patients whose lower limbs are immobilised in a cast with no surgical treatment (eg conservatively treated ankle fractures).

Anti-embolism compression stockings are very difficult to fit accurately in orthopaedic patients. Postoperative swelling in one or both legs means that the anti-embolism compression may cause problems due to locally constrictive bands. Intermittent pneumatic compression calf or foot pumps are a viable alternative.

Soft-tissue swelling

This can be avoided by:
- Elevating the limb during surgery and postoperatively
- Ensuring that dressings are not too tight
- Early mobilisation

Haematoma

May be avoided by:
- Meticulous haemostasis
- Use of suction drains? There is currently no evidence for or against the use of suction drains

Infection

Implanting prosthetic material into the body increases the risk of infection and makes infection more difficult to deal with when it does occur. A lower number of colony-forming units (of bacteria) are required to initiate an infection when an implant is present. Once established, infection around an implant is difficult to eradicate. Antibiotic penetration to the material immediately adjacent to the prosthesis is poor. The patient's immune cells may not reach the outer surface of the prosthesis. Some bacteria may establish a relatively low-grade infection, with a 'biofilm' around the prosthetic material. Antibiotics are less effective in low-grade infection because the mechanism of action for many antibiotics is to disrupt the process of bacterial division and multiplication.

Orthopaedic surgical procedures are usually performed in a laminar flow theatre. The laminar flow canopy is designed to give a large number of air changes and reduce the level of particulate material (which may be carrying bacteria) within the surgical field. Good theatre discipline (hats, masks, etc) will also reduce the rate of infection. Prophylactic antibiotics are given whenever prosthetic material is implanted. The choice of antibiotic is usually dictated by local policy, but must cover the common infection organisms (eg *S. aureus*). Cephalosporins have fallen out of favour as prophylactic antibiotics because they increase the rate of infection with *C. difficile*.

MRSA (meticillin-resistant *S. aureus*) is a problem that is now endemic within the healthcare system. Elective orthopaedic patients are screened for MRSA, and treated when it is found. Acute orthopaedic admissions (trauma patients) are all routinely treated for MRSA (with nasal mupuricin and chlorhexidine washes) in the author's institution.

Common orthopaedic problems in children

Learning point

Orthopaedic problems in children include:

The limping child
- Transient synovitis
- Developmental dysplasia of the hip (DDH)
- Perthes' disease
- Slipped upper femoral epiphysis (SUFE)
- Trauma
- Paediatric arthropathy
- Bone disease, eg rickets or skeletal dysplasia
- Systemic disease causing limp

Problems with the foot
- Congenital talipes equinovarus
- Flat foot

Angular and rotational deformities of the leg
- Genu varum
- Genu valgum

In-toeing
- Metatarsus adductus
- Excessive femoral anteversion
- Internal tibial torsion

Knee problems
- Patellar instability
- Anterior knee pain
- Discoid lateral meniscus
- Osteochondritis dissecans of the knee
- Osgood–Schlatter disease
- Sinding–Larsen–Johansson syndrome

Metabolic bone disease
- Rickets
- Skeletal dysplasia
- Osteogenesis imperfecta

Other paediatric orthopaedic problems
- Obstetric brachial plexus palsy
- Spinal abnormalities
- Cerebral palsy

CHAPTER 9

Children can present with a number of complaints to the orthopaedic surgeon. The ones that we think you need to know about are listed above. Most are dealt with in this chapter, but some are to be found elsewhere in this book.

15.1 The limping child

Learning point

There are a number of conditions affecting the lower limb in childhood. They cannot be reliably distinguished from each other at the initial presentation, although age at presentation helps. The clinical features uniting these conditions are:
- Limp
- Decreased range of movement
- Pain

Causes of a limping child
- Transient synovitis
- Developmental dysplasia of the hip
- Perthes' disease
- Slipped upper femoral epiphysis
- Trauma (soft tissue)
- Fracture (traumatic) of the lower limb
- Fracture (pathological) of the lower limb
  - Bone cysts
  - Bone tumours
  - Osteogenesis imperfecta
  - Non-accidental injury
- Paediatric arthropathy
  - Septic arthritis
  - Juvenile chronic arthritis
  - Haemophilia causing haemarthrosis
  - Rheumatic fever

- Bone disease
  - Osteomyelitis
  - Bone tumours
- Systemic disease causing limp
  - Henoch–Schönlein purpura
  - Sickle cell disease
  - Neuromuscular disease

History and examination of a limping child

History in a limping child
- Was the onset acute or gradual? Alternatively, was there gradual onset with an acute increase in pain (eg acute on chronic slip in SUFE)?
- Are there associated symptoms, such as headache, fever, rash or previous joint problems?
- Was there recent trauma?
- Is the history consistent with the injuries? Consider non-accidental injury if vague or inconsistent history
- Has there been an illness, such as upper respiratory tract or gastrointestinal symptoms, in the last 2–3 weeks?
- What about the site and severity of the pain? Pain from the hip joint may be felt in the thigh or knee. Weight-bearing status should be documented

Examination of a limping child
- General (temperature, rash, ENT examination)
- Observation of gait (protecting one joint; heel or toe walking; favouring medial or lateral side of the foot)
- Spine (spinal deformity/tenderness)
- Position of hip and knee at rest (joint effusions result in slight flexion, abduction and external rotation of the hip, or slight

flexion of the knee at rest as the child tries to reduce intra-articular pressure)
- Active/passive range of motion of hips and ankles
- Leg length
- Joint swelling, joint temperature, erythema
- Long-bone tenderness, especially along the anterior border of the tibia (toddler's fracture of tibia?)
- Ankle swelling/tenderness
- Wounds or foreign bodies between the toes or on the sole of the foot
- Neurological examination

Investigating a limping child

Limping due to acute sepsis must not be missed because delayed diagnosis and treatment result in irreparable joint damage.

- **FBC:** elevated WCC suggests infection somewhere but does not prove that the joint is the focus
- **ESR or PV/CRP:** these inflammatory markers do not prove or exclude the diagnosis of sepsis, but they provide a useful marker of the response to treatment of infections. They may be raised in many inflammatory conditions, including all the paediatric arthropathies
- **Ultrasonography:** this will show or exclude a hip effusion. The hip may be aspirated under ultrasound guidance if required. In neonates, infants and young children, ultrasonography is more useful than plain films. Transient synovitis is the most common cause of a hip effusion
- **Plain radiograph:** plain films of the painful joint or bone should be obtained to exclude fractures, Perthes' disease and SUFE. (Note: full radiographic evaluation of any bone or joint requires a minimum of two orthogonal views)

- **Joint aspirate:** this investigation is mandatory to confirm or exclude septic arthritis in cases where suspicion is high. A Gram stain will often help determine the initial antibiotic regimen until the culture and sensitivity results are available
- **Blood culture:** cultures must be obtained before any antibiotics are given. If the suspicion of sepsis is high antibiotics should be given after cultures are obtained. There is no need to wait for the culture results

In less common cases, titres of rheumatoid factor (RF) and anti-streptolysin O may be useful (eg in paediatric arthropathy, Henoch–Schönlein purpura).

Kocher criteria

The Kocher criteria are very helpful in diagnosing joint sepsis in children. The criteria are:
- Unable to weight-bear on the affected limb
- ESR >40 mm/h
- A history of fever (>38.5°C) (not necessarily fever at the precise time of examination)
- WCC >12.0 × 10^9/l

When all four are present there is a 99% chance of septic arthritis; it is only 3% if just one criterion is present (3/4 = 93% and 2/4 = 40%).

Transient synovitis (irritable hip)

Transient synovitis is the most common cause of hip pain in children. The aetiology is unknown.

Transient synovitis is not a true arthropathy because there is no joint damage. It is a synovitis and effusion in response to an upper respiratory tract infection (URTI) or similar. The effusion causes pain and a limp, and in most cases resolves completely.

CHAPTER 9

It affects 3% of children aged 3–8 years with a M:F ratio of 2:1.

Children may present with a low-grade fever and pain in the groin, thigh or knee. (Pain from the hip joint may be referred to any area that is supplied by a nerve innervating the muscle which crosses the joint; this is Hilton's law.)

There may be a history of recent URTI or other viral infection. All children presenting with these signs should be investigated to exclude infection, SUFE, Perthes' disease and other inflammatory arthropathies.

Blood tests and radiographs will be normal in cases of transient synovitis. Ultrasonography can show an effusion, but hip aspirate will show no bacterial growth.

Treatment is bed rest and analgesia.

A proportion of these cases represent the early presentation of Perthes' disease (<4%) so some form of follow-up is recommended.

Developmental dysplasia of the hip

DDH was formerly known as CDH (congenital dislocation of the hip). It is not called CDH anymore because:
- It is a spectrum of disease
- CDH suggests that a dislocation was present at birth and thus missed by the paediatrician, which is not usually the case

DDH encompasses a range of pathology from mild dysplasia of the acetabulum to irreducible dislocation. Many children will have hips that are normal to examination at birth. Therefore diagnosis is difficult, but the success of treatment is related to age at diagnosis.

Incidence is 1 per 1000 live births.

The left hip is affected more than the right in a ratio of 3:1 (20% are bilateral).

Risk factors for DDH
- Breech presentation (and other obstetric problems such as oligohydramnios, prematurity, caesarean section)
- First-born
- Female sex (M:F ratio of 1:4–1:8)
- Family history of DDH (tenfold increase in risk if a first-degree relative has the condition)
- Ethnic factors:
  - More common in white children than in African children
  - High rates in Navajo Indians and Lapps, who swaddle their children (ie with legs extended and adducted)
  - Low rates in Chinese and African populations where children are carried across the back or chest with legs abducted

Conditions associated with DDH
- Congenital talipes equinovarus (25% have DDH)
- Torticollis (20% have DDH)
- Metatarsus adductus (10% have DDH)
- Other congenital abnormalities or syndromes (especially neuromuscular problems)

Diagnosis of DDH
- By clinical examination
- Some debate as to whether all children should be screened by ultrasound examination
- UK Department of Health recommends that all children are screened at intervals up to age 21 months

- UK law states that all children must be examined at birth

Diagnosis in neonates

Two tests, when used in combination, can elicit a dislocated hip, assess its reducibility and diagnose an unstable hip that is dislocatable. These are:

- Ortolani's test
- Barlow's provocative test

Ortolani's test: Is there a reducible dislocation or subluxation?

Flex the knees.
Place hands so that thumbs lie over the medial aspect of the thigh and the fingers lie over the trochanters.
Flex the hips to a right angle. Slowly and gently abduct the hips.
If a hip is dislocated the femoral head will be felt slipping into the acetabulum as full abduction is approached.
If abduction is restricted, this may represent an irreducible dislocation.

Diagnosis in children of 3 months of age to walking age

- Decreased abduction
- Asymmetrical skinfolds indicate DDH (unreliable discriminator; 20% of normal children may have asymmetrical skinfolds)

Diagnosis in walking children

- Look for Trendelenburg's gait

Barlow's provocative test: Is the hip dislocatable?

If Ortolani's test is negative, the hip may still be unstable.
Fix the pelvis between the symphysis and the sacrum with one hand.
With the thumb of the other hand attempt to dislocate the hip by gentle but firm backward pressure.
If the head is subluxed backwards, its reduction should be achieved by forward finger pressure or wider abduction. If a hip is dislocated the femoral head will be felt slipping into the acetabulum as full abduction is approached.
If abduction is restricted, this may represent an irreducible dislocation.

The order of examination should be Ortolani–Barlow–Ortalani (O-B-O). The questions in the mind of the examiner when performing this test are:
- Is the hip out? Can I reduce it?
- If the hip is in, can I dislocate it?
- If it dislocates can it be re-reduced?

Imaging of DDH

Ultrasonography

- Hips with abnormal physical examination findings should be evaluated by ultrasonography
- Best performed at 2-week stage (when most lax capsules will have tightened up)
- Lessens the likelihood of unnecessary splintage (a complication of this is avascular necrosis of the femoral head)

CHAPTER 9

Plain radiograph

Radiographs (AP with hips extended and neutral abduction) are helpful after 4–5 months when the femoral capital epiphysis begins to ossify. The ossific nucleus should lie below Hilgenreiner's line and medial to Perkin's line. Shenton's line should follow a smooth curve.

- **Shenton's line** is an arc from the lesser trochanter, up the neck and inferior to the superior pubic ramus
- **Hilgenreiner's horizontal line** is a transverse line through the triradiate cartilage
- **Perkin's vertical line** is drawn at the lateral margin of the acetabulum (perpendicular to Hilgenreiner's line)

The line of the acetabular roof is used to calculate the acetabular index, which should be less than 30°.

Management of DDH

The aim of treatment is to achieve a stable, congruent hip joint with good cover.

Neonate to age 6 months at diagnosis

- Up to 90% of dislocatable hips will stabilise after 2–3 weeks
- Dislocated but reducible and persistently dislocatable hips should all be treated with splintage (eg with a Pavlik harness)
- Hips should be monitored to ensure they remain reduced (ultrasonography)
- Maintain splintage for 4–6 weeks and longer for children who present later
- A Pavlik harness allows motion with a controlled range of abduction and flexion and is preferable to rigid splintage
- Dislocated and irreducible hips should be treated surgically (see below) when the ossific nucleus has appeared

6 months to 18 months at diagnosis

- Gentle closed reduction (with or without an adductor tenotomy) is the first line of treatment. If this cannot be achieved then an arthrogram is indicated to assess any soft-tissue block to reduction (such as enlargement and inversion of the labrum or enlarged ligamentum teres)
- Open reduction may then be performed
- Reduction is held with a hip spica cast at 60° abduction and 90° of flexion

18 months to 3 years old at diagnosis

- Open reduction with or without femoral varus derotation osteotomy

3 years to 8 years old at diagnosis

- Open reduction with femoral varus derotation osteotomy and pelvic osteotomy

Over 8 years old at diagnosis

- Late-presenting cases should be treated non-surgically, with a plan for total hip replacement as a young adult when symptoms justify surgical intervention

Follow-up of DDH

Children with 'successfully' treated DDH should be followed up, at least until they are walking normally. The WHO (World Health Organisation) recommends follow-up to age 5.

Perthes' disease

Perthes' disease is characterised by idiopathic osteonecrosis of the proximal femoral epiphysis resulting in flattening and fragmentation of the epiphysis.

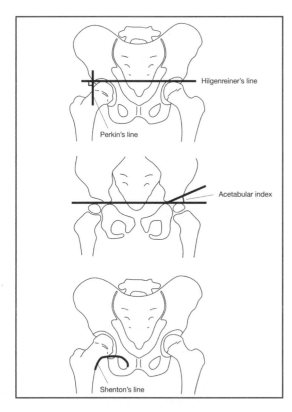

Figure 9.34 Diagnosis of developmental dysplasia of the hip on plain radiographs

There is a cycle of avascular necrosis followed by deformation and subsequent revascularisation; the cycle is approximately 2–4 years.
- Cause unknown
- Incidence 1 in 10 000

Risk factors for Perthes' disease
- Age 3–12 years (commonly 5–7)
- Male sex (M:F ratio is 4:1)
- Small-for-age children
- Delayed bone maturation

Stages of Perthes' disease
- **Initial phase** ('the head is dead'): trabecular fractures result in the crescent sign

- **Resorption stage:** resorption of bone results in rarefaction on plain radiographs
- **Reparative phase:** creeping substitution of new bone formation replaces the dead head

Diagnosis of Perthes' disease
Children present with limp and pain. Haematological investigations are normal.

Radiological changes are usually well established by the time the child presents. Radiographic features (with increasing severity) are:
- Subchondral crescent-shaped radiolucent line
- Calcification lateral to epiphysis
- Metaphyseal rarefaction
- Lateral extrusion of head
- Abnormal physeal growth
- Gage's sign (lateral epiphyseal rarefaction)

Management of Perthes' disease
The condition can be classified on the radiological appearance into groups of varying severity. In general, prognosis is dependent on the extent of the area of the femoral head that is involved and the age at onset.

The aim of treatment is to prevent deformity and restore motion. Containment of the femoral head prevents deformity.

A more spherical head and therefore a more congruous joint will decrease the risk of degenerative arthritis in the future.

Influence of age in the management of Perthes' disease
- **<6 years at onset:** symptomatic treatment only and good outcome expected

CHAPTER 9

- **6–8 years old at onset:** containment by brace or surgical intervention
- **>8 years at onset:** containment by surgical intervention (by femoral and/or pelvic osteotomy)

Slipped upper femoral epiphysis

This is a displacement of the upper femoral epiphysis (femoral head) from the femoral neck as a result of mechanical failure of the cartilaginous physis. SUFE is rare, affecting 3 per 100 000 children (bilateral in 25%).

Risk factors for SUFE

- Obesity
- Male gender (M:F ratio 5:1)
- Hormonal abnormalities (increased growth hormone, decreased sex hormones, hypothyroidism)

Aetiology of SUFE

- Usually related to puberty (boys 14–16; girls 11–13). The growth spurt of puberty is thought to result in a weaker perichondrial ring which weakens the physis
- Normal forces on the hip may then result in a slip

Diagnosis of SUFE

- SUFE is difficult to diagnose. It is often thought to be a strain
- Pain is localised to the thigh or knee. Acute-on-chronic presentation is common
- The leg is externally rotated with mild shortening, decreased abduction and increased adduction
- The epiphysis almost always slips backwards
- If severe it can be seen easily on an AP

radiograph; otherwise it is essential to obtain a lateral view
- Slips are graded radiologically according to the extent of displacement of the epiphysis on the neck

Management of SUFE

- Minor to moderate slips should be pinned in situ with one cannulated hip screw
- Reduction of a SUFE has a high risk of avascular necrosis (AVN)
- Some surgeons recommend preoperative traction to slowly reduce a severe slip, but many advocate pinning in situ
- Delayed femoral neck osteotomy may be indicated

Follow-up of SUFE

The incidence of bilateral slip is variable but is at least 20%. Therefore one should monitor the other hip during treatment and follow-up.

Many surgeons advocate prophylactic pinning of the other hip if there are any concerns regarding compliance with follow-up.

Fractures and the limping child

Trauma is the most common explanation for the acutely limping child. Traumatic fractures are dealt with in Chapter 6.

Pathological fractures are fractures through abnormal bone which occur after an impact or minor injury that would not be expected to cause a fracture in normal bone.

Common causes of pathological fracture in a child are:
- Bone cyst
- Tumour

- Osteogenesis imperfecta
- Non-accidental injury

Non-accidental injury

Careful evaluation (and documentation) of the mechanism of injury is required in all paediatric injuries.

- Is the history consistent with the injuries seen?
- Is the child crawling, toddling or walking, and is this consistent with the reported mechanism of injury and injuries sustained?
- Are there multiple injuries of differing ages?
- Bruises and specific fractures, such as corner fractures (avulsion fractures from the metaphysis from twisting injuries) are suggestive of abuse

In cases of concern:

- Help is available from paediatricians
- Our primary duty of care is to ensure a safe environment for the child; in case of doubt refer to paediatrics for an opinion
- Other explanations (eg osteogenesis imperfecta, rickets and leukaemia) should be considered and investigated as appropriate

Other arthropathies causing a limp in a child

Septic arthritis

Septic arthritis is a surgical emergency because the pus can destroy the articular cartilage within hours. Diagnosis in children (and indeed adults) may be difficult and the possibility of sepsis should always be considered. If treated early and appropriately the joint may return to normality. Ongoing infection may result in destruction of cartilage, bone and ligaments. Damage to the blood supply may result in AVN.

Juvenile idiopathic arthritis

Juvenile idiopathic arthritis (JIA) is a diagnosis of exclusion. Other causes of inflammatory arthropathy must be ruled out. It can be seronegative or seropositive. Knees, wrists and ankles are commonly affected.

There are three types of JIA:

- **Pauciarticular:** most common, involves fewer than five joints, good prognosis
- **Polyarticular:** involves five joints or more, responds well to treatment but may persist to adulthood
- **Systemic (Still's disease):** high fever, rash, pericarditis, hepatosplenomegaly, poor prognosis

Diagnostic criteria are:

- Onset before age 16
- More than one joint affected with swelling or tenderness or loss of motion
- >6 weeks' duration

The aim of management is to relieve pain, prevent deformity and preserve function.

Haemophilia-related haemarthrosis

This involves a deficiency of clotting factor (factor VIII in haemophilia A and factor IX in haemophilia B). It is a sex-linked recessive disease that affects 10 per 100 000 male births.

- Multiple bleeds into joints result in pain, stiffness and early OA
- Treatment aims to reduce bleeds and restore motion
- Synovectomy has a role for some joints (joint damage is the result of synovitis

and pannus formation that is triggered by recurrent haemarthrosis)

Haemarthrosis may result in a clinical picture that is similar to sepsis in young children. The knee, elbow, ankle, shoulder and hip are most commonly affected.

Rheumatic fever

Acute rheumatic fever is a result of *Streptococcus pyogenes* infection. It typically affects children aged 5–12 years. Anti-streptococcal antibodies can result in carditis, polyarthritis, chorea, subcutaneous nodules or a rash (erythema marginatum, which is a classic macular rash with 'snake-like' borders).

15.2 Problems with the foot in children

> ### Learning point
>
> - Congenital talipes equinovarus (CTEV)
> - Talipes calcaneus
> - Flat feet

Congenital talipes equinovarus

This is commonly called club-foot. It is the most common of the congenital foot abnormalities, with an incidence of 3 per 1000 live births.
- Right foot more commonly affected than the left
- 50% of cases are bilateral

Causes of CTEV

The aetiology is unknown. Thought to be polygenic inheritance of nerve or muscle abnormalities which results in an imbalance across the hindfoot, leading to characteristic equinus and varus of the heel, and supination and adduction of the forefoot (the foot points downwards and inwards); this may be exacerbated by mechanical factors in utero.

CTEV has a familial link (10% incidence if one first-degree relative has the condition).

Most cases are thought to be idiopathic, but certain abnormalities are associated with CTEV:
- Myelomeningocele
- Neuromuscular disorders (all children with CTEV require full neurological examination)
- Reduction deformities or amniotic bands
- Generalised bone problems (eg arthrogryposis)

Diagnosis of CTEV

The diagnosis is usually obvious from birth, but fixed (pathological) club-foot must be distinguished from a postural deformity. The newborn child often holds the foot in plantar flexion and inversion, so observe as the child kicks. If the foot is maintained in that position, lightly scratch the lateral side of the foot. If normal, the child will respond by dorsiflexing the foot and fanning the toes. In a normal foot it should be easy to dorsiflex the foot into contact with the tibia. In club-foot, both the hindfoot and forefoot are abnormal, so:
- **Hindfoot:** fixed in equinus and varus; the heel is not in line with the lower leg
- **Forefoot:** fixed in varus, with subluxation of the talonavicular joint; posteromedial soft tissues are tight and underdeveloped

Severe cases are characterised by rigidity of the foot, constriction rings and deep sole clefts. Calf muscle wasting is a common and permanent feature.

Management of CTEV

Corrective non-surgical treatment should be attempted in all cases. It is achieved with serial casting – the Ponseti technique. This should be commenced early. The Ponseti technique has eliminated the need for surgical correction in the vast majority of cases.

The response to conservative treatment dictates the need for surgery. Unsuccessful cases require lengthening of tight structures, open reduction and fixation of the subluxed joint.

A single-stage surgical procedure is preferred. Aftercare involves a period of immobilisation and then physiotherapy to rehabilitate.

Follow-up of CTEV

Children with successfully treated CTEV should be followed up until the foot is normal and there is no residual deformity.

Talipes calcaneus

This is a much rarer condition in which the dorsum of the foot lies against the shin.

Flat feet

Flat feet (involving loss of the medial longitudinal arch) may be flexible or relatively fixed. The flexible, painless, flat foot (pes planus) requires no treatment. Painful fixed flat feet require further assessment to determine the underlying cause (eg tarsal coalition or neurological disorders).

15.3 Angular and rotational deformities of the lower limb in children

> **Learning point**
>
> **Genu varum**
> **Genu valgum**
> **In-toeing**
> - Excessive femoral anteversion
> - Metatarsus adductus
> - Internal tibial torsion

Genu varum

Neonates have maximal varus of the knee.

This progresses to maximal physiological valgus at around 4 years of age (10°). This should improve to the normal physiological valgus of 3–7° at the age of 8 years.

Persistent varus, short stature or varus thrust with ambulation suggests a pathological rather than a physiological process. Any process that disrupts the growth at the proximal tibial or distal femoral epiphysis (such as trauma, infection, skeletal dysplasia, vascular insults or tumour) can result in varus/valgus malalignment.

Pathological varus is caused by vitamin D deficiency, tumour, trauma, infection, Blount's disease, dysplasia or congenital deformity.

Blount's disease

This results in progressive varus of the knee due to asymmetrical growth of the proximal tibial physis. It is more common in African–Caribbean and Scandinavian children. The aetiology is unknown.

CHAPTER 9

The disease is treated by prevention of progressive deformity using orthotics, and corrective osteotomy if this fails.

Genu valgum

This may be normal in children aged 2–6 years. Pathological valgus is caused by dysplasia, infection, trauma, neoplasia or renal disease.

Many cases will correct with growth. If the intermalleolar distance exceeds 8 cm at age 10, consider surgery.

Hemiepiphysiodesis occurs before skeletal maturity (fusion of half of the physis to arrest growth on one side and correct deformity). Osteotomy should be performed after skeletal maturity.

> Remember: in vaLgus the distal bone deviates Laterally.

In-toeing

Causes in normal children:
- Genu valgum and pronated foot
- Excessive femoral anteversion
- Internal tibial torsion
- Metatarsus adductus

Rotational alignment may be assessed by measuring the angles between the axis of the foot, the axis of the ankle (across the malleoli) and the femur (with the patient prone and the knee at 90°).

Excessive femoral anteversion

Some 40° of femoral anteversion is found in the neonate, reducing to 10–15° in children up to the age of 10. Excessive anteversion after the age of 8 should be assessed with a CT scan and may be treated with a femoral derotation osteotomy.

Internal tibial torsion

The normal thigh–foot angle is 0–20°. Internal tibial torsion is a normal finding up to the age of 3 and will almost always correct without intervention.

Metatarsus adductus

The presence of forefoot varus with a neutral hindfoot is a benign condition that has been related to the fetal position in utero and is associated with sleeping prone. It is treated by stretching or serial splintage; 10% of these children have DDH.

15.4 Knee problems in children

Learning point

- Patellar instability
- Anterior knee pain
- Discoid lateral meniscus
- Osteochondritis dissecans of the knee
- Osgood–Schlatter disease
- Sinding–Larsen–Johansson syndrome

Patellar instability

Patellar stability is achieved by:
- **Bony stability** (patella and trochlea, along with tibiofemoral alignment)
- **Static structures** (patellar tendon and medial patellofemoral ligament)
- **Dynamic stability** with proprioceptive

feedback (quadriceps muscle, especially vastus medialis oblique [VMO] fibres)

Acute dislocation of the patella results in tearing of the medial patellofemoral ligament. Dislocation is easily reduced by extending the knee. Bony abnormalities increase the risk of patellar instability or dislocation.

The aim of treatment after an acute dislocation is to restore knee function and prevent recurrence. Osteochondral patellar fractures may be seen on a 'skyline view' of the patellofemoral joint. These should be fixed if present.

Surgical treatment of recurrent dislocation may include soft-tissue release/reconstruction or bony realignment procedures.

Anterior knee pain

Anterior knee pain results from patella maltracking. It is commonly found in young girls and women. There may be a family history of patellofemoral problems. Mild, non-specific soft-tissue laxity may be present.

The aim of treatment is to improve the function of the dynamic stabilisers of the patellofemoral joint by improving proprioception and quads function (especially the VMO).

Discoid lateral meniscus

Incidence is 1.5–5% in the West, but 15% in Japan. Children may present between the ages of 6 and 12 with clicking or instability symptoms in severe cases.

The aim of treatment is to preserve and, if necessary, refashion the meniscus.

Osteochondritis dissecans of the knee

This most commonly affects the lateral portion of the medial femoral condyle. MRI is used to assess the integrity of overlying cartilage and bone healing.

Stable lesions may be treated with modification of activities and analgesia. Loose or free fragments should be reduced and stabilised with bioabsorbable pins.

Osgood–Schlatter disease

This is a traction apophysitis of the tibial tubercle.
- Affects children aged 10–15 years
- More common in males (M:F 3:1)
- Caused by repeated microtrauma to the tibial apophysis
- Patients have very specific point tenderness over the tibial tubercle
- Treated by modification of activities, stretching and quads strengthening

Sinding–Larsen–Johansson syndrome

This involves traction apophysitis of the distal patellar pole or tears in the proximal patellar tendon.
- Affects children aged 10–15 years
- Caused by repeated microtrauma to the patella–tendon junction
- Patients have specific point tenderness over distal patellar pole
- Treatment is by modification of activities, stretching and quads strengthening
- May coexist with Osgood–Schlatter disease, but is much less common

CHAPTER 9

15.5 Metabolic bone diseases

Rickets

See Section 3, Bone pathology.

Rickets is childhood vitamin D deficiency. It is characterised by a normal rate of osteoid formation but an inadequate rate of mineralisation.

Radiographic changes include:
- Diaphyseal bowing
- Metaphyseal flaring
- Physeal widening

Biochemical abnormalities include:
- Low serum calcium
- Low serum phosphate
- Increased alkaline phosphatase

Skeletal dysplasia

Most cases of skeletal dysplasia result in short stature. Dwarfism is defined as a standing height below the third centile, and it is either proportionate or disproportionate.

Skeletal dysplasias tend to produce disproportionate dwarfism, with the limbs or trunk affected.

Achondroplasia

This is the most common and best-known skeletal dysplasia.
- Incidence 1 per 40 000
- Normal intelligence and normal development of cognitive skills
- Delayed development of motor skills
- 80–90% of cases are the result of a new mutation in an autosomal dominant gene

Genu varum (with or without recurvatum) is common.

Osteogenesis imperfecta

A mutation in the gene coding for type I collagen results in imperfect bones, teeth, ligaments and sclera. These children may suffer numerous pathological fractures and may be mistakenly diagnosed as the victims of NAI (non-accidental injury).

Incidence is 1 in 20 000 births.

The table summarises the types, features and mode of inheritance of osteogenesis imperfecta.

Type	Inheritance	Features
I	Autosomal dominant	Blue sclera, no deformity, early hearing loss, mild bony fragility
II	Autosomal dominant or recessive	Usually fatal in perinatal period
III	Autosomal recessive	White sclera, intrauterine fractures, very short stature
IV	Autosomal dominant	Light sclera, bowing of long bones, usually more severe than type I. This mild form is often associated with the misdiagnosis of non-accidental injury

15.6 Other paediatric problems

Obstetric brachial plexus palsy

Risk factors

- Birth weight >4000 g
- Breech presentation
- Shoulder dystocia
- Long labour
- Forceps delivery

Types of obstetric brachial plexus palsy

- **Erb–Duchenne palsy** results from damage at the C5–6 roots. The deltoid, rotator cuff, elbow flexors and wrist extensors are affected, resulting in the so-called 'waiter's tip' deformity
- **Klumpke's palsy:** results from damage at the C8–T1 roots. Wrist flexors and the intrinsic muscles of the hand are affected
- **Total plexus:** results from damage at all roots (with or without Horner syndrome)

Treatment of obstetric brachial plexus palsy

- Referral to a specialist centre
- Physiotherapy (to prevent deformity)
- Monitor recovery
- Surgery (eg neurolysis, nerve grafting, nerve transfer)

Cerebral palsy

Cerebral palsy is a fixed, non-progressive brain lesion that occurs during development and maturation of the brain (prenatal period to around 2 years).

Incidence is 2 per 1000 live births.

The spectrum of presentation of cerebral palsy is very wide. Mild cases may present with minor gait problems. Children with whole-body involvement are severely disabled and rely on carers for all their needs.

Causes of cerebral palsy

- Prenatal factors (alcohol, drugs, maternal diabetes, hypothyroidism)
- Prematurity or birth trauma
- Encephalitis, meningitis
- Trauma
- Asphyxia

Management of cerebral palsy

The aims of treatment are education, communication, independence in activities of daily living and mobility.

Surgery for cerebral palsy

Surgery is indicated where non-surgical treatment has failed. Surgical intervention may control spastic deformity, correct fixed deformity or correct secondary bony deformity.

Ten per cent of children may benefit from surgery.

CHAPTER 9

CHAPTER 10

Paediatric surgery

Stuart J O'Toole, Juliette Murray, Susan Picton and David Crabbe

SECTION 1

Children as surgical patients

Children are not mini-adults. They differ anatomically, physiologically and psychologically from adults.

Anatomical differences

- Size
- Respiratory system (eg differences in tracheal length and position)
- Abdominal and pelvic dimensions and the relative size and positions of certain organs
- Skeletal structure and structure of the spine

Physiological differences

- The body's surface area relative to body mass is greater in children than in adults
- Fluids and electrolytes: children have a higher total body water
- Hepatic functions (eg clotting)
- Metabolic rate, thermoregulation and nutritional requirements
- In water loss through the gastrointestinal tract
- In the urine-concentrating capacity of the kidney
- In respiratory rate and respiratory pattern (eg nose breathing)
- In heart rate and response to stress
- In neurological functions

Psychological and emotional differences

- Developmental milestones
- Regression with illness

1.1 Anatomy in children

Learning point

The important anatomical distinctions between children and adults are:
- Size
- Airway
- Abdomen and pelvis
- Abdominal organs
- Male genitalia
- Spinal cord

Size in children

An obvious difference between children and adults is size:
- A child's size varies with age and the most rapid changes occur within the first year
- Fluid and drug dosages are calculated by weight

To estimate a child's weight use:
$$\text{weight (kg)} = (\text{age} + 4) \times 2$$

The ratio of body surface area to weight decreases with age due to increasing size; neonates and infants are small and therefore lose heat rapidly (see 'Thermoregulation' in Section 1.2).

The airway in children

Several factors can make endotracheal intubation of an infant difficult:
- The head of an infant is large compared with the rest of the body and the neck is short, so the resting position of the head is in flexion

- The glottic aperture is more anteriorly inclined and higher than in adults
- The epiglottis is inclined more posteriorly than in adults
- The trachea is significantly shorter (4 cm not 12 cm) and narrower (5 mm not 2 cm) than in adults
- The trachea lies further to the right of the midline than in adults
- The tracheal bifurcation lies at T3, not T6 as in adults
- A large tongue and adenoids will obscure the view
- The narrowest part of a child's airway is the cricoid, so uncuffed endotracheal tubes should be used because a cuff can cause pressure necrosis

Until 2 months of age, infants are obligate nasal breathers due to their large tongues. Do not block the nostril of a baby who has a nasogastric (NG) tube in the other nostril!

The left brachiocephalic vein runs across the trachea higher in the child than in adults – above the suprasternal notch – so it can get in the way if performing a tracheostomy.

Children breathe rapidly because of a high metabolic rate and they have limited oxygen reserves. They become hypoxic rapidly so you have less time to intubate. The normal respiratory rate of a neonate is 30–60 breaths/min, falling to around 15–20 breaths/minute in a 10-year-old.

Intercostal, subcostal and sternal recession are signs of respiratory distress. Grunting on expiration is a sign of severe respiratory distress in infants.

Abdomen and pelvis in children

The abdomen extends from the costal margin to the pelvic brim. In **adults** the abdomen is longer than it is wide. Therefore in adults the midline vertical laparotomy incision gives best access to most intra-abdominal organs. In **neonates** the abdomen is wider than it is long. Therefore in neonates the transverse laparotomy incision gives the best access to most intra-abdominal organs.

Scars will grow with children and get progressively larger, so paediatric surgeons must plan their incisions carefully. Scars will migrate – a supraumbilical scar may end up near the costal margin when the child has grown up.

Abdominal organs in children

There are several differences in the proportions and positions of abdominal organs of children compared with adults:

- The liver and spleen are proportionally larger in children
- The pelvis is shallower in children
- Organs that are housed in the pelvis in adults are above the pelvic brim in children
- This difference in position of organs means that:
  - Lower abdominal incisions should be made with care
  - Suprapubic catheterisation is quite straightforward in children, but access to the bladder is much higher in children
- The caecum (and appendix) sit higher in infants, migrating down to the right iliac fossa (RIF) by age 3 or 4

Important definitions

- **Premature** infants are those born before 38 weeks' gestation
- **Neonates** are children between birth and 44 weeks' post-conceptional age (neonates are also infants)
- **Infants** are children between birth and 52 weeks
- **Preschool** children are aged between 1 and 4 years
- **Abortion** is when a child is born dead before 28 weeks' gestation (includes deaths due to natural causes, as well as deliberate termination)
- **Stillbirth** occurs when a child is born dead after 28 weeks' gestation
- **Perinatal mortality** is the number of stillbirths and deaths in the first week of life. This accounts for around 1% of deliveries in the UK
- **Neonatal mortality** is the number of deaths in the first 28 days of life regardless of gestational age (about 6 per 1000 live births in the UK)
- **Infant mortality** is the number of deaths in the first year of life (about 10 per 1000 live births in the UK). It includes neonatal mortality

1.2 Physiology in children

Learning point

The important physiological differences between children and adults include:
- Thermoregulation
- Fluids and electrolytes
- Hepatic immaturity
- Nutrition and energy metabolism
- The gastrointestinal (GI) tract
- Renal function
- Respiratory system
- Cardiovascular system
- Nervous system

Thermoregulation

Neonates are more susceptible to hypothermia than adults. They have a larger surface area to weight ratio, less subcutaneous fat and less vasomotor control over skin vessels. Neonates cannot shiver and have no voluntary control over temperature regulation. In addition, premature infants have smaller stores of brown fat.

Precautions should be taken to ensure that they do not become hypothermic during surgery:
- Keep the operating theatre temperature high (naked infants need an ambient temperature of 31.5°C)
- Infants should be well wrapped up
- Respiratory gases should be warmed and humidified
- Use warming blankets
- Infuse warm intravenous (IV) fluids
- During surgery wrap wool around the head and exposed extremities
- Warm the aqueous topical sterilising 'prep'

- Use adhesive waterproof drapes to prevent the infant getting wet
- Limit exposure of the extra-abdominal viscera

Fluids and electrolytes
- Total body water in a neonate is about 800 ml/kg (80%), falling to about 600 ml/kg (60%) at 1 year
- A third is extracellular fluid, and the remainder is intracellular
- Circulating blood volume is almost 100 ml/kg at birth, falling to 80 ml/kg at 1 year
- Term neonates require transfusion if >30 ml blood is lost during a surgical procedure (one to two small swabs)

Signs of dehydration in children
Dehydration in children is traditionally estimated as < 5% (mild), 5–10% (moderate) and >10% (severe). This is an arbitrary definition and is used as a guide to aid fluid resuscitation.

Signs of dehydration in children

	Mild	Moderate	Severe
Thirst	+	+	+
Decreased urine output	+	+	+
Sunken fontanelle	–	+	+
Tachycardia	–	±	+
Drowsiness	–	±	+
Hypotension	–	–	±

Fluid requirements are estimated on the following basis:

- Normal insensible losses: respiration, GI losses, sweating
- Maintenance of urine output: excretion of urea, etc

- Replacement of abnormal losses: blood loss, vomitus, pre-existing dehydration, etc

Normal maintenance fluid and electrolyte requirements, based on weight, are shown in the table.

Normal maintenance fluid and electrolyte requirements

Body weight (kg)	Fluid requirements (ml/kg per day)	Sodium (mmol/kg per day)	Potassium (mmol/kg per day)
0–10	100 (4 ml/kg per h)	3	2
10–20	50 (2 ml/kg per h)	2	1
20+	20 (1 ml/kg per h)	1	1

Maintenance fluid and electrolyte requirements decrease incrementally as weight increases. So 25-kg child would require (100 ml × 10 kg) + (50 ml × 10 kg) + (20 ml × 5 kg) = 1600 ml over 24 h or 67 ml/h.

- For a newborn infant give 60 ml/kg per day for days 1–2, then 90 ml/kg per day on day 3
- A good choice for maintenance IV fluids for children undergoing surgery is 0.45% saline + 5% dextrose + 10 mmol potassium chloride (per 500 ml IV fluid)
- Replace NG aspirates with equal volumes of 0.9% saline + 10 mmol potassium chloride per 500 ml

Traditionally, paediatricians have limited the amount of sodium that a child receives in IV fluids. This is why fluids such as 0.15% saline and 10% dextrose are prevalent on paediatric wards. Certainly, in babies the concern over the risk of hypoglycaemia has governed this practice. However, over recent years it has become increasingly obvious that children and infants who are sick, and particularly those with a surgical pathology, are at risk of developing life-threatening hyponatraemia. Recent patient safety alerts have highlighted the importance of avoiding hypotonic fluids during resuscitation and the perioperative period. If there is concern about hypoglycaemia then fluids such as 0.9% saline and 5% dextrose can be used.

Neonatal hepatic immaturity

Vitamin K can be given to premature infants if the immature liver is not producing clotting factors; otherwise haemorrhagic disease of the newborn may result. Drug doses in premature infants must be decreased. Glycogen stores are small, resulting in hypoglycaemia after short periods of starvation. Poor glucuronyl transferase activity and high haemoglobin load can lead to physiological jaundice.

Nutrition and energy metabolism

Neonates have a high metabolic requirement compared with adults, mainly because they are so poorly insulated and need to work harder to maintain their core body temperature, and also because they are growing so fast. They therefore need more oxygen (oxygen consumption is 6–8 ml/kg per min compared with 2–4 ml/kg per min in adults). They also need more fuel in the form of calories. They require 100 kcal/kg per day – more than twice as many as adults.

Enteral fluid requirements are 150 ml/kg per day (more than IV requirements because enterally fed babies use energy to digest the food and lose more fluid in bulky stools). Before birth the principal energy substrate is glucose; after birth it comes from free fatty acids and glycerol.

Gastrointestinal tract

Infants lose more water through their alimentary tract than adults, and this loss can become very important in ill, dehydrated children. The reasons for the increased losses are:
- Small total surface area (villi undeveloped)
- Children lose their absorptive capacity when ill
- Disaccharide intolerance (common)
- Gastroenteritis (common)

Renal function

An adult responds to dehydration by passing a small volume of more concentrated urine, reabsorbing sodium and so retaining water. Neonates are less able to concentrate urine and so dehydrate more easily. They have a lower glomerular filtration rate (GFR) and lose more sodium in their urine.

Respiratory system

The respiratory rate in neonates is fast due to an increased oxygen demand (see above), usually between 30 and 60 breaths/minute, but it can vary from minute to minute. When increased respiratory effort is required the respiratory rate increases but the tidal volume does not. At birth,

50% of alveoli are not developed and the tidal volume is about 20 ml (7 ml/kg). Respiratory distress in infants may lead to hypocalcaemia, which may in turn lead to twitching and seizures.

Surfactant is required for lungs to work properly, and premature neonates do not secrete enough of this.

From a surgical point of view young children and infants breathe using their diaphragm and not their intercostal muscles. This means, first, that a child's abdomen usually moves in and out with respiration; if they have peritoneal signs then it will remain still. Second, a child can develop significant respiratory embarrassment secondary to abdominal distension. In a neonate this can result in a child requiring intubation and mechanical ventilation purely due to abdominal distension.

Cardiovascular system

In utero pulmonary vascular resistance is high. Blood bypasses the lungs (right-to-left shunting) through the foramen ovale at the atrial level and the ductus arteriosus (left pulmonary artery to aorta) – this is the fetal circulation. Before birth the pressure in the right atrium is higher than in the left so the blood moves (shunts) from the right to the left atrium.

At birth, with the first breath, pulmonary vascular resistance falls abruptly. Blood no longer returns to the right atrium from the placenta. These two things reduce the pressure in the right atrium. Simultaneously, blood begins to flow into the left atrium from the lungs. This increases the pressure in the left atrium. Shunting at the atrial level ceases and the ductus starts to close. Any condition that impairs gas exchange in the lungs (eg diaphragmatic hernia) may result in persistence of the fetal circulation (PFC).

From a physiological point of view children have a high heart rate and a very labile circulation. The heart rate is high in infants and declines with age (see table).

- Newborn: 100–150 beats/min
- 1 year: 70–110 beats/min
- 5 years: 65–110 beats/min

Stroke volume varies little in infants, so the cardiac output is dependent on heart rate alone. Cardiac output increases with increasing heart rate.

Age	Pulse (resting) (beats/min)	Respiratory rate (breaths/min)	BP systolic (mmHg)	BP diastolic (mmHg)
Premature	120–170	40–70	55–75	35–45
0–3 months	100–150	35–55	65–85	45–55
3–6 months	90–120	30–45	70–90	50–65
6–12 months	80–120	25–40	80–100	55–65
1–3 years	70–110	20–30	90–105	55–70
3–6 years	65–110	20–25	95–110	60–75
6–12 years	60–95	14–22	100–120	60–75
>12 years	55–85	12–18	110–135	65–85

Recognising shock in children is more subtle than in adults. The most important signs are tachycardia, tachypnoea and decreased capillary return. A capillary return >2 s is often quoted, but it should be remembered that in a warm infant the capillary return is almost instantaneous. The variation in physiological parameters that make up the assessment of vital signs in a child can be difficult to remember for an adult surgeon with only occasional exposure to children. Recently most hospitals have adopted age-specific TPR (temperature, pressure, respiration) charts (Children's Early Warning Score or CEWS) to alert nursing staff to values that are abnormal.

It goes without saying that hypotension is a late sign in a child and bradycardia is a sign of impending cardiac arrest.

Nervous system

The blood–brain barrier is underdeveloped and myelination is not complete at birth. This means that opiates and fat-soluble drugs have greater efficacy on the brain and can lead to respiratory depression.

Recently concern has been raised in the literature that the developing central nervous system (CNS) is at risk from certain forms of anaesthetics. This is based on the use of high doses of anaesthetic agents in animal models. The Association of Paediatric Anaesthetists of the UK has suggested that the current evidence is not strong, but it would be reasonable to consider delaying non-essential procedures until after 6 months of age and to use local anaesthetic techniques to reduce the doses of certain anaesthetic drugs would be wise.

1.3 Caring for a child in hospital

Learning point

When caring for a child in hospital it is important to:
- Have good communication skills
- Be aware of developmental milestones
- Understand consent issues
- Be able to:
  - Relieve pain
  - Gain vascular access
  - Resuscitate a critically ill child

Communication with children and parents

Communication is vital with both accompanying adults and the child. You won't gain their trust if you ignore them and speak only to the adults.
- Introduce yourself, say who you are and why you are there
- Find out who they are – don't assume that the accompanying adult is a parent
- Sit down – don't tower over the child
- Smile, be friendly, have good eye contact and avoid jargon
- Do not expect to take a systematic history – be flexible and build a rapport

The priority is to obtain and maintain the trust of the child and parent. You can fill in the gaps of the history at the end of the discussion by quizzing the parents, nurses, social workers, etc. Let the child sit on mum's lap while you talk, examine or take blood. Be honest – don't say 'This won't hurt a bit,' but something like 'There will be a little sting now and then we'll give you a sticker for being brave.'

Don't push the child for information; children often can't recall timescales ('When did the pain start?' is not as good a question as 'Did you feel alright when you were at school today?') and they are poor at localising pain. They may make up an answer if they feel under pressure.

Be reassuring but not unrealistic: wait until you have all the information before you reassure the parents. It's no good saying 'Don't worry, he'll be fine,' before you have fully assessed the child. For most parents, watching their child be rushed into surgery in the middle of the night is not fine. Find out the facts, then be specific.

Make sure that the right people get the right information – do mum and dad know she's in hospital and may be going for surgery, or are aunty and granddad keeping it from them for some reason? You usually need parental or official guardian consent.

Developmental milestones

If you ask a 1-year-old a question and expect a sensible answer, or ask the parents of a 5-year-old girl to put her pants back on after examining her in clinic, the child's parents will lose confidence in you immediately and assume that all your medical diagnostic skills and advice are worthless. If you have small children in your family these things will be obvious to you; if not, keep them in mind. Don't forget that many children regress by about a year when they are ill – a lucid 4-year-old schoolgirl may cry for mum and go back into nappies; a football-playing 10-year-old may need his favourite blanket, wet the bed and refuse to speak to anyone he doesn't trust.

Developmental milestones

6 weeks	Social smiles, turns head to sound, can hold head up, follows with eyes
4 months	Smiles spontaneously, starts to babble, rolls from tummy to back
6 months	Starts to sit unsupported, puts things in mouth, babbles sounds, eg 'oh', 'ah'
9 months	Crawls, babbles, eg 'mamamama', understands 'no', clingy with familiar adults
10–15 months	Obeys commands, eg 'clap', nervous with strangers, copies gestures
12 months	First words, eg 'milk', has favourite things and people, recognises objects
12–18 months	Takes first steps, may get frustrated/have temper tantrums, points to things
18 months	Drinks from a beaker, eats with a spoon, may walk up steps and run
2 years	Two words together, eg 'more please', walks up and down stairs, copies others
2–3 years	Potty trains, names items in picture book, starts to play with other children
3 years	Knows own name and gender, starts state nursery school (2–3 h/day)
5 years	Starts primary school, may like to sing, dance and act, can draw a person
11 years	Starts secondary school

Consent and ethics for children

Children and consent

At age 16 a young person can be treated as an adult and presumed to have capacity to decide. Below the age of 16 children may have the capacity to decide, depending on their ability to understand what is involved.

Where a competent child refuses treatment, a person with parental responsibility or the court may authorise investigation or treatment that is in the child's best interests. When a child is under 16 and is not competent, a person with parental responsibility may authorise treatments that are in the child's best interest.

Those with parental responsibility may refuse intervention on behalf of an incompetent child aged <16, but you are not bound by that refusal and may seek a ruling from the court. In an emergency, you may treat an incompetent child against the wishes of those with parental responsibility if you consider it is in the child's best interests, provided that it is limited to that treatment which is reasonably required in that emergency, eg you can give a life-saving blood transfusion to the incompetent child of Jehovah's Witness parents who refuse to consent, but not to a competent Jehovah's Witness who refuses consent himself, whatever his age. For further discussion see Chapter 8.

Pregnant women and consent

The right to decide applies equally to pregnant women as to other patients, and includes the right to refuse treatment where the treatment is intended to benefit the unborn child.

Analgesia in children

Pain assessment

This can be difficult in small children and their analgesia is often less than they need. Giving regular analgesia is better than waiting until a child becomes very sore because they may not be able to articulate their pain effectively. Patient-controlled analgesia (PCA) can be useful in older children.

Look for:
- Advice from the parents: they know the child best and rarely overestimate the pain
- Signs in the child:
  - Inconsolable crying or being unusually quiet
  - Not moving freely around the bed; reluctant to get up
  - Protecting the painful area
  - Pallor, tachypnoea, tachycardia

Pain charts can be used for older children. You can also try distracting the child with a toy or a story.

Vascular access in children
The following methods can be used for vascular access:
- **Peripheral line:** cubital fossa, dorsum of hand, scalp, femoral vein, long saphenous vein, foot (remember EMLA)
- **Peripheral long line:** cubital fossa, long saphenous vein
- **Central venous catheterisation** (under expert supervision only): internal/external jugular, femoral vein
- **Intraosseous trephine needle into tibia** (1–3 cm below tubercle): complications include through-and-through bone penetration, sepsis, osteomyelitis, compartment syndrome, haematoma, abscess, growth plate injury. Arterial access is via radial artery or femoral artery

Resuscitation of the critically ill child
Read in more detail about techniques for resuscitation of children in the *Paediatric Advanced Life Support* guidelines 2010 (www.resus.org.uk/pages/pals.pdf).

The basic principles to remember are:
- Summon help
- ABC (Airway, Breathing, Circulation)
- Clear airway. Give 100% oxygen. Ventilate artificially if necessary
- Establish IV access (always difficult in children)
- If the child has collapsed insert an intraosseous needle 2 cm below the tibial tuberosity
- Give initial bolus of 20 ml/kg fluid (0.9% saline, plasma substitutes, 4.5% albumin are all acceptable)
- Repeat boluses according to response. Start maintenance infusions

ADVANTAGES AND DISADVANTAGES OF ANALGESICS IN CHILDREN

Painkiller	What is it?	Pros	Cons
Paracetamol	Central cyclo-oxygenase (COX) inhibitor	Widely used Few side effects Oral or PR	Not anti-inflammatory Beware in children with jaundice
Ibuprofen	NSAID	Anti-inflammatory Oral or PR	Beware in asthma, blood disorders and gastric ulceration
Diclofenac	NSAID	Oral or PR (tastes horrible so give rectally if possible)	
EMLA	Eutectic mixture of local anaesthetic (2.5% lidocaine and 2.5% prilocaine) Topical local anaesthetic	'Magic cream' for taking blood or cannulation Works after 45 mins; lasts for an hour	Not to be used on broken skin
Ametop™	4% amethocaine (tetracaine) Topical local anaesthetic	'Magic cream' as above Works after 35 mins; lasts for 4–6 hours	
Morphine	Opiate	IV or oral in small frequent doses Effective analgesia Nausea not as bad as in adults Sedative	Beware respiratory depression Infants have under-developed blood–brain barrier and so are more susceptible to fat-soluble opiates Excretion by liver and kidney is slower than in adults
Pethidine	Opiate	IV only	

SECTION 2

Neonatal surgery

Embryology of the GI tract

By the third gestational week the embryo is trilaminar and consists of the notochord, intraembryonic mesoderm, intraembryonic coelom and neural plate. The intraembryonic coelom is formed by the reabsorption of the intraembryonic mesoderm.

In the fourth gestational week the previously flat embryonic disc folds in the cephalocaudal direction and transversely. This leads to formation of the endoderm-lined cavity, which forms the

2.1 Gastrointestinal tract

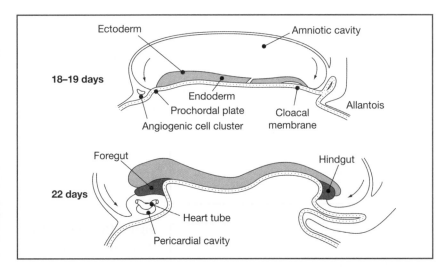

Figure 10.1 Sagittal section through the embryo showing formation of the primitive endoderm-lined gut

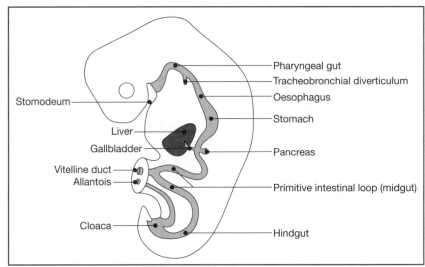

Figure 10.2 Formation of the gastrointestinal tract at week 4 of gestation showing foregut, midgut and hindgut

primitive gut. It extends from the buccopharyngeal membrane to the cloacal membrane. It is divided into the pharyngeal gut, foregut, midgut and hindgut. The endodermal lining of the primitive gut gives rise to the epithelial lining of the gut, whereas mesoderm provides the muscular parts.

The pharyngeal gut

This extends from the buccopharyngeal membrane to the tracheobronchial diverticulum.

The foregut

This gives rise to the trachea and oesophagus, stomach, duodenum, liver, pancreas and spleen. The **trachea** develops from the tracheobronchial diverticulum, which becomes separated from the foregut by the **oesophagotracheal septum**. The lung buds develop from the blind end of the trachea. These lung buds give rise to the segmental bronchi and expand into the pericardioperitoneal cavity. Abnormal closure of the oesophagotracheal septum can lead to tracheooesophageal fistula.

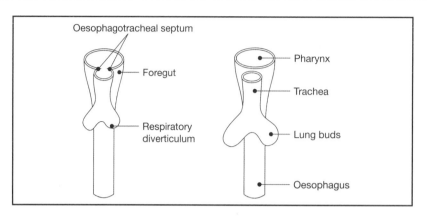

Figure 10.3 The foregut during week 4 of gestation

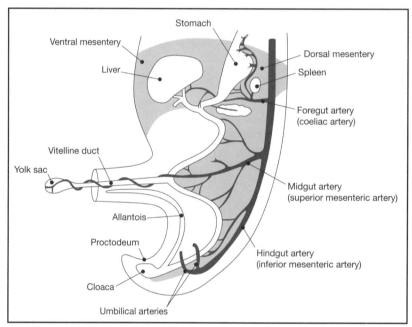

Figure 10.4 The midgut of a 5-week embryo

Formation of the **stomach** occurs when the dorsal mesentery lengthens, the gut tube rotates clockwise and the liver bud migrates to the right side of the dorsal body wall. This also gives the **duodenum** its 'C' shape.

The **liver** develops from the hepatic diverticulum, which is an endodermal outgrowth from the distal end of the foregut. The bile duct is formed from the connection between the liver and the foregut.

The uncinate process of the **pancreas** is formed from the ventral pancreatic bud, which is closely associated with the hepatic diverticulum. The body of the pancreas is formed from the dorsal pancreatic bud. The ventral pancreatic duct rotates clockwise to join the dorsal pancreatic duct.

The **spleen** is a foregut derivative of the left face of the dorsal mesentery.

The midgut

This extends from the entrance of the bile duct to the junction of the proximal two-thirds and distal third of the transverse colon. The midgut of a 5-week embryo is shown in Figure 10.4. The dorsal mesentery of the midgut extends rapidly, producing physiological herniation in the sixth week.

The cephalic limb of the midgut grows rapidly to hang down on the right side of the dorsal mesentery. The gut rotates around the axis formed by the superior mesenteric artery (SMA) 270° in an anticlockwise direction. The gut returns to the abdominal cavity in week 10.

The hindgut

This gives rise to the distal third of the transverse colon, descending colon, sigmoid colon, rectum and upper half of the anal canal.

In addition, the endoderm of the hindgut gives rise to the lining of the bladder and urethra. The **urorectal septum**, a transverse ridge arising between the allantois and the hindgut, grows to reach the cloacal membrane, to divide it into the urogenital membrane anteriorly and the anal membrane posteriorly. The **anal pit** forms in the ectoderm over the anal membrane and this ruptures in week 9 to form a connection between the rectum and outside. Figure 10.5 shows successive stages of development of the cloacal region.

Developmental abnormalities of the GI tract

Gastroschisis

- Incidence 1 in 3000 but increasing
- Most identified on prenatal ultrasonography
- Defect in abdominal wall to the right of an otherwise normal umbilicus
- No sac
- The bowel is eviscerated and, as a result of contact with amniotic fluid, thickened and matted
- Associated malformations are uncommon except intestinal atresias (10%)
- Immediate management consists of covering the exposed bowel with clingfilm and closure of the defect as rapidly as possible
- Preformed spring-loaded silos are now available that can be applied on the neonatal unit; many units use this as their first treatment and allow the bowel to reduce into the abdomen by gravity. Once

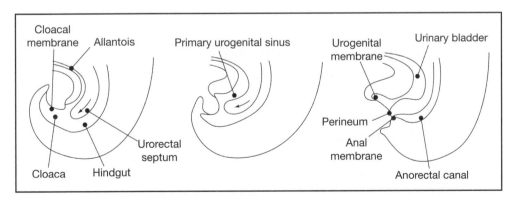

Figure 10.5 The cloacal region at successive stages in development

the bowel has been reduced the defect can be closed in the operating room or even on the ward

- Total parenteral nutrition (TPN) may be required for many weeks until intestinal function resumes
- Long-term outcome is excellent

Exomphalos (omphalocele)

- Incidence 1 in 3000 but reducing due to antenatal diagnosis and selective termination
- Characterised by a hernia into the base of the umbilical cord, ie covered by a sac (amnion)
- Identifiable on antenatal ultrasonography
- Classified as exomphalos major if defect >5 cm in diameter and exomphalos minor if <5 cm
- Associated malformations in 50% – chromosomal defects (trisomies) and cardiac defects
- Treatment consists of closure of the defect in one or more stages
- In children with a very large exomphalos the abdominal cavity may not be large enough to accept all the bowel. These cases can be treated conservatively and left to epithelialise. The hernia contents are then gradually reduced into the abdomen, with a formal closure before 1 year of age
- Prognosis depends on associated malformations

Oesophageal atresia and tracheo-oesophageal fistula

- Incidence 1 in 3500
- Maternal polyhydramnios common, although diagnosis rarely made before birth
- Present at birth as a 'mucousy' baby, choking or turning blue on feeding

Associated malformations present in 50% – the **VACTERL** association:

V	**V**ertebral anomalies
A	**A**norectal anomalies
C	**C**ardiac
TE	**T**racheo-**o**esophageal
R	**R**enal
L	**L**imb

Diagnosis is confirmed by attempting to pass an NG tube and taking a chest radiograph. There are tube coils in the upper thorax. Gas in the stomach indicates a fistula between the trachea and the distal oesophagus (tracheo-oesophageal fistula or TOF); 75% of babies with oesophageal atresia (OA) will have a TOF; 10% will have isolated OA, usually associated with a long gap; the remainder will have an isolated TOF or upper and lower pouch TOFs.

- Treatment involves disconnection of the TOF and then anastomosis of the upper and lower oesophagus through a right thoracotomy
- Complications include anastomotic leak (particularly if the gap is long), anastomotic stricture, gastro-oesophageal reflux and recurrent fistula
- Long gaps may require oesophageal replacement

Duodenal atresia

- Incidence 1 in 5000
- A third have Down syndrome
- Present at birth with bile-stained vomiting
- Diagnosis confirmed by 'double-bubble' sign of gas in stomach and proximal duodenum on abdominal radiograph
- Treatment consists of side-to-side duodenoduodenostomy
- May be associated with annular pancreas

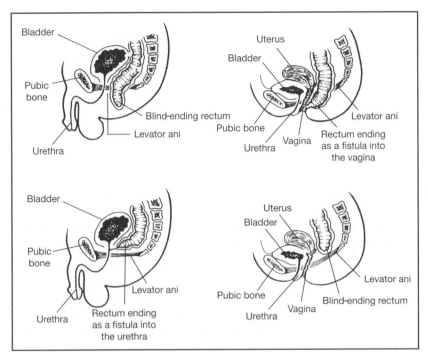

Figure 10.6 Congenital anorectal anomalies

Labels in figure (top left): Bladder, Pubic bone, Urethra, Blind-ending rectum, Levator ani

Labels in figure (top right): Uterus, Bladder, Pubic bone, Urethra, Vagina, Levator ani, Rectum ending as a fistula into the vagina

Labels in figure (bottom left): Bladder, Pubic bone, Urethra, Levator ani, Rectum ending as a fistula into the urethra

Labels in figure (bottom right): Uterus, Bladder, Pubic bone, Urethra, Vagina, Levator ani, Blind-ending rectum

Small-bowel atresia

- Incidence 1 in 3000
- Aetiology is vascular: Barnard (of heart transplant fame) and Louw produced experimental atresias in puppies by ligating mesenteric blood vessels in utero
- Pathology varies, depending on how deep in the mesentery the vascular accident occurs, from an atresia in continuity with a mucosal membrane to a widely separated atresia with a V-shaped mesenteric defect and loss of gut
- 10% of atresias are multiple
- Babies present shortly after birth with bile-stained vomiting (a cardinal symptom of intestinal obstruction in children) and abdominal distension
- Diagnosis is confirmed by abdominal radiography: multiple fluid levels
- Treatment is laparotomy and end-to-end anastomosis

Anorectal malformation

- Incidence 1 in 5000 but much higher than this in the Asian subcontinent
- Associated malformations: VACTERL association (as above)
- Should be identified at birth
- Present with failure to pass meconium, abdominal distension and bile-stained vomiting
- Precise anatomy varies but they can be subdivided into high and low/intermediate anomalies in boys and girls

Low and intermediate anorectal anomalies

- Rectum present and passes through a normal sphincter complex
- In boys there is a tiny fistulous track to the surface of the perineum, often anteriorly onto the scrotum

- If meconium is visible a local 'cut-back' procedure can be performed to open the fistula back to the rectum in anticipation of normal continence

In girls the rectum usually opens into the back of the introitus – a rectovestibular fistula. This abnormality is classified as intermediate and, although normal continence is ultimately to be expected, reconstruction involves division of a common wall between rectum and vagina. For this reason treatment involves a three-stage procedure with defunctioning colostomy, anorectal reconstruction and then closure of the stoma.

High anorectal anomalies
- Rare in girls, common in boys
- Sphincter complex poorly developed and prospects for continence are not good

In boys the rectum makes a fistulous connection with the urethra and a three-stage procedure is essential. After the first stage a cystogram and descending contrast study through the colostomy are necessary to define the anatomy of the defect. Reconstruction most commonly involves a posterior sagittal anorectoplasty (PSARP) performed through a midline perineal incision.

Midgut malrotation and volvulus

As the physiological intrauterine midgut hernia reduces, the mesentery normally rotates to bring the caecum to lie in the RIF and duodenojejunal (DJ) flexure to lie to the left of the midline. The midgut mesentery thus extends diagonally across the back of the abdominal cavity and provides a broad stable pedicle for the SMA to supply the bowel. Malrotation, failure of this normal rotation, leaves the caecum high in the right upper quadrant (RUQ) and the DJ flexure mobile in the midline. The result is a narrow base for the midgut mesentery and a narrow mobile pedicle through which the SMA runs. Malrotation is usually asymptomatic and detected only by contrast meal and follow-through.
- Midgut malrotation predisposes to midgut volvulus – the narrow base to the mesentery twists
- Immediate effect is a high intestinal obstruction at duodenal level, rapidly followed by infarction of the entire midgut from the DJ flexure to the splenic flexure
- Symptoms are bile-stained vomiting and later collapse
- Abdominal radiograph is similar to duodenal atresia with a double bubble and a paucity of gas elsewhere in the abdomen
- Diagnosis confirmed by urgent (middle of the night) upper GI contrast study

Treatment is urgent laparotomy to untwist the bowel. If bowel viability is doubtful perform second-look laparotomy after 24 hours. If the bowel is healthy perform a **Ladd procedure:** mobilise the caecum, straighten the duodenal loop; run the duodenum down to the RIF, return small bowel to the right side of the abdomen and return large bowel to the left side. The caecum then lies in the left upper quadrant (LUF) so an appendicectomy is performed. The Ladd procedure stabilises the base of the mesentery by reversing normal rotation, preventing further volvulus.

Prognosis depends on how much gut is viable.

Meconium ileus
- Incidence about 1 in 2500
- Associated with cystic fibrosis (CF) – 15% of children with CF present with meconium ileus

- Meconium is thick and viscous because of a lack of pancreatic enzymes; this causes an intraluminal intestinal obstruction in the ileum
- Distended obstructed bowel may perforate or undergo volvulus in utero. Although sterile this causes a vigorous inflammatory reaction associated with calcification in the peritoneal cavity, subsequently visible on abdominal radiography

Treatment involves relieving the intestinal obstruction. Provided that there is no evidence of intrauterine perforation, obstruction may be relieved by Gastrografin enema. Hypertonic contrast draws fluid into the bowel lumen and its detergent effect loosens inspissated meconium. This is frequently not successful, or meconium ileus is complicated by previous perforation, in which case laparotomy is required. The most common surgical management in complicated forms of meconium ileus is the temporary formation of ileostomies to allow the bowel to function and the meconium to be cleared.

After correction of the intestinal obstruction, careful management of the CF is required; this involves long-term flucloxacillin (to prevent staphylococcal chest infections) and pancreatic enzyme supplements.

Meconium ileus equivalent (MIE) is a complication in later childhood that results from inadequate levels of enzymes.

Hirschsprung's disease

- Incidence is 1 in 5000. Sometimes familial and a known association with Down syndrome
- Hirschsprung's disease is caused by a failure of ganglion cells (neural crest origin) to migrate down the hindgut. Coordinated

peristalsis is impossible without ganglion cells and so there is a functional intestinal obstruction at the junction (transition zone) between normal bowel and the distal aganglionic bowel. In 80% of cases the transition zone is in the rectum or sigmoid – short-segment disease; in 20% of cases the entire colon is involved – long-segment disease

- Presentation: 99% of normal neonates pass meconium within 24 hours of delivery.
- Hirschsprung's disease usually presents within the first few days of life with a low intestinal obstruction, failure to pass meconium, abdominal distension and bile-stained vomiting. Occasionally children with short-segment disease escape detection in the neonatal period, presenting later with chronic constipation
- Diagnosis: abdominal radiograph shows a distal intestinal obstruction and the diagnosis is confirmed by rectal biopsy – no ganglion cells in the submucosa. In neonates rectal suction biopsy is performed, in older children an open rectal strip biopsy

Treatment is surgical, traditionally involving a three-stage procedure: defunctioning colostomy with multiple biopsies to confirm the site of the transition zone, a pull-through procedure to bring ganglionic bowel down to the anus and, finally, closure of the colostomy. Many surgeons now perform a single-stage pull-through in the neonatal period, managing initial intestinal obstruction with rectal washouts. Long-term results of surgical treatment are satisfactory; about 75% of children have normal bowel control, 15–20% partial control and 5% never gain control.

The main complication of Hirschsprung's disease is enterocolitis, a dramatic condition characterised by abdominal distension, bloody watery

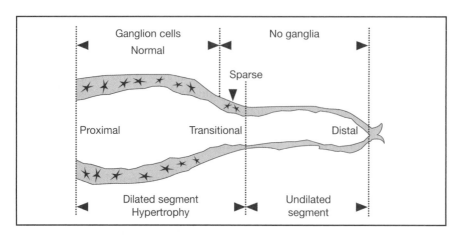

Figure 10.7 Histopathology of Hirshsprung's disease

diarrhoea, circulatory collapse and septicaemia, often associated with *Clostridium difficile* toxin in the stools. The mortality rate from enterocolitis can be as high as 10%. Although enterocolitis is more common in early childhood it can occur at any time. Any child/adult who has a history of Hirschsprung's disease and presents with fever, diarrhoea and abdominal distension should be treated carefully. If colonic distension is apparent on a radiograph then IV access needs to be established, antibiotics started and the rectum decompressed with rectal washouts.

Necrotising enterocolitis

Necrotising enterocolitis (NEC) is an acute inflammatory condition of the neonatal bowel that may be associated with areas of bowel necrosis and a systemic inflammatory syndrome. It is more common in premature infants but can also be observed in term babies (incidence 1 in 250 at birthweight >1500 g and much higher for babies <1500 g).

Aetiology is probably multifactorial. Some cases cluster in epidemics, suggesting an infectious aetiology, but a single causative organism has not been identified. Organisms isolated from stool cultures from affected babies are also isolated from healthy babies. The translocation of intestinal flora across an incompetent mucosa may play a role in systemic involvement. Bacteria overwhelm the immature intestine, causing local inflammation and a systemic inflammatory response syndrome. Ischaemia and/or reperfusion injury may play a role.

- Symptoms: include feeding intolerance, delayed gastric emptying, abdominal distension and tenderness, ileus, passage of blood per rectum (haematochezia). Perforation may occur and cause generalised peritonitis
- Signs: include lethargy, abdominal wall erythema (advanced), gas in the bowel wall and the portal vein, signs of shock (decreased peripheral perfusion, apnoea, cardiovascular collapse)
- Management: supportive: nil by mouth with nutrition delivered parenterally (though this can cause cholestasis and jaundice); surgical resection is indicated for bowel necrosis and perforation
- Early complications: perforation, sepsis, shock, collapse
- Late complications: strictures, malabsorption syndromes, failure to thrive

Mortality rates range from 10% to 44% in infants weighing <1500 g, compared with a 0–20% mortality rate for babies weighing over 2500 g. Extremely premature infants (1000 g) are particularly vulnerable, with reported mortality rates of 40–100%.

2.2 Diaphragm

Embryology of the diaphragm

Figure 10.8 shows the diaphragm in the fourth month of gestation. It develops from the following embryonic structures:

- Transverse septum (the origin of the central tendon)
- Oesophageal (dorsal) mesentery
- Pleuroperitoneal membranes
- 3rd, 4th and 5th cervical somites

Congenital diaphragmatic herniation

- Incidence is 1 in 2500
- Main problem is pulmonary hypoplasia and not the diaphragmatic hernia
- Posterolateral (Bochdalek) defects are most common
- 90% are left-sided
- Anterior (Morgagni) defects are rare
- Most CDHs are now identified on antenatal ultrasonography
- Initial management consists of endotracheal intubation, paralysis, sedation and mechanical ventilation
- If oxygenation is good (ie pulmonary hypoplasia is not severe), repair of the diaphragmatic defect is undertaken after a few days, by either primary suture or insertion of a prosthetic patch (Gore-Tex)
- About two-thirds survive and long-term problems are rare

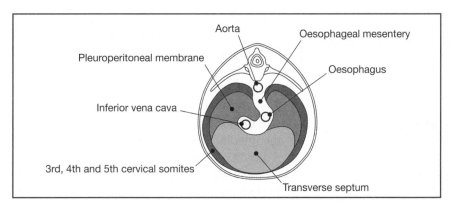

Figure 10.8 Transverse section of diaphragm at the fourth month of gestation

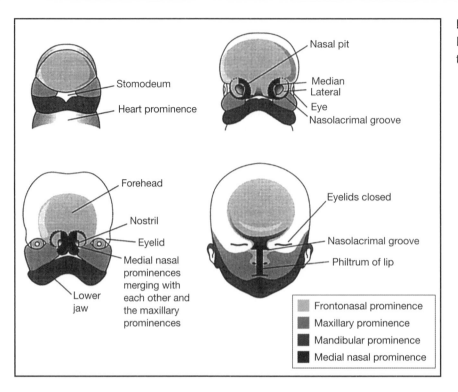

**Figure 10.9
Development of
the human face**

Labels in figure:
Stomodeum
Heart prominence
Nasal pit
Median
Lateral
Eye
Nasolacrimal groove
Forehead
Nostril
Eyelid
Medial nasal prominences merging with each other and the maxillary prominences
Lower jaw
Eyelids closed
Nasolacrimal groove
Philtrum of lip

Frontonasal prominence
Maxillary prominence
Mandibular prominence
Medial nasal prominence

2.3   Lip and palate

Learning point

Embryological disorders of the lip and palate are common and often need surgical correction. An appreciation of the embryology of the face and palate, and an understanding of the main cleft lip and palate abnormalities, are probably all that you need to know at this stage.

Embryology of the face and palate

Development of the face

The stages of development of the human face are illustrated in Figure 10.9 above. The facial primordia appear in the fourth week around the stomodeum. The five facial primordia are:

* The frontonasal prominence
* The maxillary prominences (paired)
* The mandibular prominences (paired)

They are active centres of growth and the face develops mainly between weeks 4 and 8.

Nasal placodes (the primitive nose and nasal cavities) develop in the frontonasal prominence by the end of week 4. The mesenchyme around the placodes proliferates to form elevations – the medial and lateral nasal prominences. The **maxillary prominences** proliferate and grow medially towards each other. This pushes the medial nasal placodes into the midline. A groove is formed between the lateral nasal prominence and the maxillary prominence and the two sides of these prominences merge by the end of week 6.

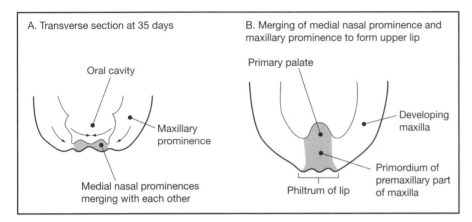

**Figure 10.10
Development of
the palate**

As the medial nasal prominences merge they give rise to the **intermaxillary segment**. This develops into the philtrum of the upper lip, septum of the premaxilla, and the primary palate and nasal septum. The maxillary prominences form the upper cheek and most of the upper lip, whereas the mandibular prominences give rise to the chin, lower lip and lower cheek region.

Development of the palate

The palate develops from week 5 to week 12, from the primary palate and secondary palate. Figure 10.10 shows the development of the palate. The primary palate develops from the deep part of the intermaxillary segment of the maxilla, during the merging of the medial nasal prominences. It forms only a small part of an adult's palate. The secondary palate forms the hard and soft palates, from the lateral palatine processes that extend from the internal aspects of the maxillary prominences. They approach each other and fuse in the midline, along with the nasal septum and posterior part of the primary palate.

Cleft lip and palate

There are two major groups of cleft lip and palate:

- Clefts involving the upper lip and anterior part of the maxilla, with or without involvement of parts of the remaining hard and soft regions of the palate
- Clefts involving hard and soft regions of the palate

Cleft lip and palate is thought to have some genetic basis. Teratogenic factors are largely unknown, but vitamin B complex deficiency in pregnancy may have an aetiological role. The risk of having a second affected child is 4% compared with 0.1% in the general population.

SECTION 3

Paediatric urology

3.1 Embryology of the genitourinary tract

Urinary tract embryology

See Figure 10.11

Intermediate mesoderm

The intermediate mesoderm gives rise to three distinct areas: the pronephros, mesonephros and the metanephros. The pronephros and mesonephros represent primitive renal units that disappear ultimately, and the metanephros gives rise to the functioning kidney. The mesonephros gives rise to the **mesonephric duct** (also called the wolffian duct); this drains into the **cloaca**. By 9 weeks the mesonephric organ has disappeared

The mesonephric duct plays a role in development of the male genital system but disappears in the female; a bud from it is involved in the formation of the ureter/renal pelvis. The metanephros appears in week 5 and will give rise to the excretory system of the definitive kidney (see below).

Formation of the definitive kidney

This has two main components:

1. The **metanephric organ** gives rise to the excretory system, ie glomeruli and renal tubules, all the way to the distal convoluted tubule
2. The **ureteric bud** grows out of the mesonephric duct close to its entrance to the cloaca and penetrates the metanephric tissue, giving rise to the ureter, renal pelvis, calyces and collecting tubules

Nephrons continue to be formed until birth, at which time there are about 1 million in each kidney.

The metanephric organ arises in the pelvic region. The kidney comes to lie in the abdomen mainly because of growth of the body in the lumbar and sacral regions. Its blood supply is received sequentially as it ascends directly from

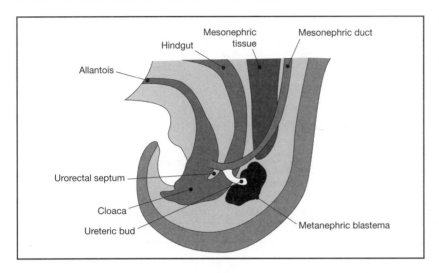

Figure 10.11 The development of the urinary tract at week 5

the aorta, with lower vessels degenerating as new arteries develop above. Abnormalities in ascent are responsible for both **pelvic** kidneys and **horseshoe** kidneys.

Development of the bladder and urethra

The bladder and urethra are derived from the **urogenital sinus**. This is the anterior part of the cloaca, which is separated from the posterior anal canal by the **urorectal septum**.

Three portions of the urogenital sinus can be distinguished:
1. The upper part becomes the urinary bladder; this is initially continuous with the **allantois**. When the allantois is obliterated a thick fibrous cord, the **urachus**, remains and connects the apex of the bladder with the umbilicus. In adults it is known as the **median umbilical ligament**
2. The middle narrow part gives rise to the prostatic and membranous parts of the urethra in the male
3. The phallic part develops differently in the two sexes (see below)

Although most of the bladder is derived from the endoderm of the urogenital sinus, the **trigone of the bladder is derived from mesoderm**. This is because of absorption of the ureters, which were outgrowths from the mesonephric ducts.

The prostate begins to develop at the end of the third month from outgrowths of endoderm in the prostatic urethra. In the female these outgrowths form the urethral and paraurethral glands.

Genital system embryology

The default situation is female. In the presence of a Y chromosome a testis-determining factor is produced and this leads to male development. The gonads do not acquire male or female morphology until week 7.

The development of the urogenital sinus is shown in Figure 10.12.

Development of the gonads

These appear initially as a pair of longitudinal ridges medial to the mesonephros. Germ cells migrate here from the yolk sac by amoeboid

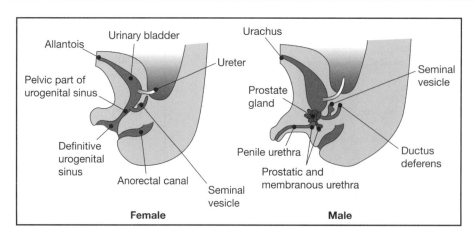

Figure 10.12 Development of the urogenital sinus

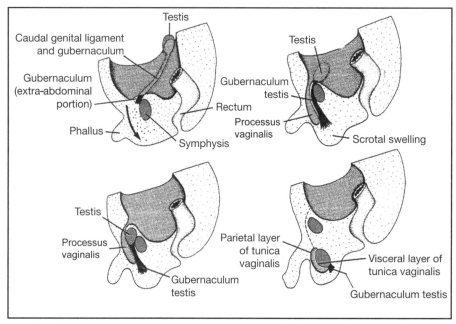

Figure 10.13 Descent of the testis

movement and arrive by week 5, invading by week 6. At the same time as the germ cells arrive primitive sex cords develop within the gonads.

Testes

- If the germ cells carry an XY sex chromosome complex, **testis-determining factor** is produced and the primitive sex cords proliferate to form the medullary

cords. The tunica albuginea forms to separate these from the surface epithelium
- By week 8, **Leydig cells** in the testis produce testosterone and this influences sexual differentiation of the genital ducts and external genitalia (see below)
- The medullary cords remain solid until puberty, when they acquire a lumen and form the seminiferous tubules. These join with the excretory tubules of the

mesonephric system, which becomes the epididymis, vas deferens, seminal vesicles and ejaculatory ducts

Ovaries

- In the ovary the medullary cords degenerate
- The germ cells become oogonia and these are surrounded by follicular cells

Descent of the gonads

Descent of the testes

The testis is initially an intra-abdominal organ that migrates to the scrotum. The factors that control this are not entirely clear. Abnormalities of descent are important clinically in terms of undescended or ectopic testes. Figure 10.13 shows the normal descent of the testis.

- The **gubernaculum** extends from the caudal pole of the testes and extends down to the inguinal region. The testis migrates along this and reaches the inguinal canal by 7 months and the external inguinal ring by 8 months
- During descent the origin of the blood supply to the testis from the lumbar aorta is retained and the testicular vessels lengthen
- An evagination of the abdominal peritoneum, the **processus vaginalis** accompanies the testis as it descends into the scrotum. This evagination forms the **tunica vaginalis**. The processes vaginalis normally closes in the 1st year after birth. If it remains open it can be associated with a congenital inguinal hernia or hydrocele of the testis/cord

(For discussion of testicular torsion see 'Disorders of the scrotum and penis' in Chapter 8, Book 2).

Descent of the ovaries

- The ovary becomes attached to the tissues of the genital fold by the gubernaculum and uterovaginal canal, giving rise to the ovarian and round ligaments, respectively
- The mesentery, which descends with the ovary, becomes the broad ligament

The genital duct system

In the indifferent stage of development embryos possess two pairs of genital ducts, **mesonephric ducts** and **paramesonephric ducts** (also called müllerian ducts). Essentially the paramesonephric ducts degenerate in the male and the mesonephric ducts degenerate in the female.

Genital ducts in the male

- In the presence of testis-determining factor, **müllerian inhibiting substance** (MIS) is produced by Sertoli cells in the testis. This causes regression of the paramesonephric ducts. The only bit that remains is a small portion at their cranial and caudal ends, the **appendix testis** and **utriculus** respectively
- The mesonephric duct forms the epididymis, the vas deferens, seminal vesicles and ejaculatory ducts

Genital ducts in the female

- In the absence of MIS, the paramesonephric ducts remain and develop into the main genital ducts of the female. The upper parts form the uterine tubes (fallopian tubes) and the caudal parts fuse to form the uterine canal
- The upper third of the vagina is also derived from the uterine canal. The lower two-thirds are derived from invagination of the urogenital sinus

- The mesonephric duct system disappears, although occasionally a small caudal portion may remain and later in life this may form a **Gartner cyst**

Development of the external genitalia

The cloacal folds form around the cloaca and anteriorly these are the **urethral folds** (posteriorly the anal folds). The urethral folds fuse anteriorly to form the **genital tubercle**.

Genital swellings appear at either side of the urethral folds.

External genitalia in the male
- The genital tubercle becomes the **phallus**
- The urethral folds form the **penile urethra**
- The genital swellings fuse and form the **scrotum**
- Failure of fusion of the urethral folds leads to **hypospadias** – this occurs in 3 in 1000 births

External genitalia in the female
- The genital tubercle elongates only slightly and forms the **clitoris**
- The urethral folds do not fuse as in the male, but develop into the **labia minora**
- The genital swellings enlarge and form the **labia majora**

3.2 Congenital renal abnormalities

> ### Learning point
>
> **Abnormalities of number or size**
> - Renal agenesis and hypoplasia
> - Supernumerary kidneys
>
> **Abnormalities of structure**
> - Aberrant vasculature
> - Parenchymal anomalies
>
> **Abnormalities of ascent**
> - Pelvic kidney
> - Horseshoe kidney

Bilateral renal agenesis (Potter syndrome)
- Rare – 3.5 in 10 000 births
- Characteristic features are oligohydramnios and secondary characteristic facial appearance
- Pulmonary hypoplasia leads to stillbirth (40%) or death within the first few days

Unilateral renal agenesis
- Incidence 1 in 1100 births
- Often an incidental clinical finding
- Common additional abnormalities include ipsilateral agenesis of vas deferens or ovaries

Aberrant renal vasculature
Aberrant vasculature with multiple arteries or veins is common. This is clearly important to bear in mind during operations on the kidney. Lower pole vessels are a common cause of pelviureteric obstruction in children.

Renal cysts and polycystic kidneys

Cystic disease is the most common space-occupying lesion in the kidney. Cysts may be simple and solitary or part of a polycystic condition. Cystic tumours may also occur (see below).

Simple renal cyst

- May be solitary, multiple or bilateral, and are usually benign
- Degenerative cysts can occur in elderly people, lined with cuboidal epithelium
- Asymptomatic unless there is infection or haemorrhage into the cyst
- Complex cysts (calcification, septa) may be associated with malignancy
- Usually untreated unless there is proven tumour or continued symptoms

Infantile polycystic kidneys

This recessive genetic condition causes cystic changes of the renal tubules. Cysts are small and numerous (<5 mm). Infantile polycystic kidneys cause rapid-onset renal failure and are associated with cystic liver disease with periportal fibrosis and portal hypertension.

Adult polycystic kidneys

An autosomal dominant condition causing cystic change in the kidney. Cysts are present at birth and progressively enlarge to compress the renal parenchyma. This occurs at a variable rate and is a common cause of end-stage chronic renal failure (CRF) which often presents in the fourth or fifth decade.

Symptoms

- Abdominal discomfort due to enlarging organs
- Colic and haematuria (spontaneous bleed into cyst)
- Hypertension and CRF

Associations

- Cystic change in other organs (especially liver, spleen and pancreas)
- Berry aneurysms of the circle of Willis
- Mitral valve prolapse

Other cystic conditions

Von Hippel–Lindau syndrome

- Risk of malignant cyst transformation to renal cell carcinoma
- Neurofibromatosis and cerebral haemangioma

Tuberous sclerosis

- Renal cysts and angiomyolipoma
- Adenoma sebum
- Cerebral hamartoma, learning difficulties and epilepsy

Medullary sponge kidney

- Cystic dilatation of the terminal collecting ducts
- Urinary stasis (causes calculi in dilated ducts and infection)
- Often asymptomatic but may have hypercalciuria or renal tubular acidosis

Parenchymal anomalies include lobulation and congenital cysts.

Pelvic kidney

- Arrest of ascent of the kidneys during development causes pelvic kidney
- Incidence is 1 in 2500
- More prone to stone disease and infection
- Associated genital abnormalities in 20%

Horseshoe kidney

- Occurs in 1 in 400 individuals
- Fusion occurs before the kidneys have rotated on the long axis and the inferior mesenteric artery (IMA) prevents full ascent
- Blood supply is variable and the horseshoe lies at L3–5
- Ureter enters bladder ectopically and urinary stasis is common
- May be detected incidentally (33%) or palpated as a midline mass
- Complications include urinary tract infection (UTI), stones and pelviureteric junction (PUJ) obstruction

Crossed renal ectopia

- This is location of a kidney on the opposite side to where its ureter inserts into the bladder
- It is associated with fusion in 90%
- Most are asymptomatic

3.3 Congenital ureteric and urethral abnormalities

> **Learning point**
>
> **Ureteric congenital abnormalities**
> - Abnormalities of **number** or **size**:
>   - Ureteric duplication (unilateral or bilateral)
> - Abnormalities of **structure**:
>   - Ureteric diverticula
>   - Ureterocele
>   - Ectopic and retrocaval ureter
> - Abnormalities of **function**:
>   - PUJ obstruction
>   - Vesicoureteric reflux (VUR)
>   - Urethral congenital abnormalities
> - Abnormalities of **structure**:
>   - Posterior urethral valves
>   - Failure of fusion (eg epispadias, hypospadias)

Ureteric duplication

Duplication is common and can predispose to urinary stasis and UTI. It occurs in 1% of the population and is usually unilateral. Most (90%) are incomplete, with fusion of the ureters before the ureteric orifice. In complete duplication, the ureter serving the upper renal moiety will lie distally (Meyer–Weigert law) and is prone to distal obstruction from it either terminating in a ureterocele or inserting in an ectopic position. An ectopically inserted ureter into the vagina of a young girl is an unusual cause of incontinence. The lower moiety ureter is inserted higher in the bladder. Very occasionally it can be obstructed at the level of the pelvis, but more commonly it is predisposed to reflux. Renal dysplasia is common in both lower- and upper-pole moieties with marked reduction in function.

Ureterocele

This is cystic dilatation of the intramural part of the ureter. It most commonly occurs in association with the upper-pole ureter of a duplex system, but can occur in a single ureter.

Retrocaval ureter

An abnormality of development of the posterior cardinal veins may lead to the ureter lying behind the inferior vena cava (IVC); this is more common on the right. Compression of the ureter can occur between the IVC and the vertebrae.

Pelviureteric junction obstruction

This is a functional obstruction of the ureter at the level of the PUJ which is thought to be congenital in origin. Although it is congenital, the problem may not become clinically apparent until later life; 25% of cases are bilateral and boys are more prone to this than girls. It may be due to congenital narrowing, an aperistaltic segment or kinking of the ureter as it leaves the pelvis. Back pressure causes renal parenchymal damage.

Presentation of PUJ obstruction

- With increasing use of prenatal ultrasonography, fetal hydronephrosis may be detected. In most of these children the significance of this hydronephrosis is uncertain. Spontaneous resolution is the norm and surgery is performed only if there is progressive dilatation, symptoms or a drop in ipsilateral renal function
- In children or adults the classic finding is of intermittent abdominal or flank pain. In adults it may occur after ingestion of alcohol for the first time (causes a diuresis and acute renal pelvic distension)

- Other possible presentations are with failure to thrive, recurrent UTIs or a palpable kidney

Investigation of PUJ obstruction

- **Ultrasonography** will confirm hydronephrosis but cannot confirm obstruction
- Diuretic renography using MAG-3 will delineate the function of the kidney and will show delay in drainage if there is obstruction. Unfortunately this test is unreliable in infants and an obstructed curve on a MAG-3 scan does not necessarily mean obstruction
- An intravenous urogram (VU) is not routinely performed for the diagnosis or assessment of PUJ obstruction. If anatomical detail is required a MR urogram would be performed

Management of PUJ obstruction

The indications for surgical management of PUJ obstruction are the development of symptoms, increasing hydronephrosis on serial ultrasound scans or a drop in renal function. If the kidney is functioning poorly (differential function <15%) then a nephrectomy may be considered. If the function is good surgery to relieve the obstruction would be indicated. The surgical options are a dismembered retroperitoneal pyeloplasty by an open or a laparoscopic approach if the child is old enough and the parents are suitably counselled about the slightly higher risk of reoperation. Endoscopic approaches to dilate or burst the PUJ are an alternative to definitive surgery, but the long-term results are not as good.

Op box: Anderson–Hynes pyeloplasty

Indications
- PUJ obstruction

Preop preparation
- Prophylactic antibiotic therapy is used for moderate to severe renal pelvic dilatations to reduce the incidence of UTI and damage to the renal parenchyma. Important preoperative investigations include ultrasonography and renal excretion studies (see above). Consent with intraoperative hazards and postoperative complications in mind

Patient positioning
- The procedure is performed under GA. It may be performed open or laparoscopically

Incision
- Flank, dorsal lumbotomy or anterior extraperitoneal approach. Four ports are required for the laparoscopic approach

Principles of the procedure
- Essentially the repair consists of transection of the ureter, excision of the narrowed segment, spatulation, and anastomosis to the most dependent portion of the renal pelvis to improve drainage. Anastomosis is performed using fine absorbable sutures and should be watertight and tension-free. Placement of a ureteric stent is down to the surgeon's preference (many try to avoid this in children as a further anaesthetic is required to remove the stent)

Intraoperative hazards
- Laceration of the vessels to the lower pole (close proximity to the ureter in 40% of cases and must be avoided)

Closure
- Close in layers with absorbable sutures

Postop
- Postoperative evaluation is performed by renal scan or excretory urography at 2–3 months. A further evaluation with ultrasonography is recommended at 12–24 months, but, beyond that, late problems are uncommon in the absence of symptoms
- A successful outcome does not always mean an improvement in the differential renal function as measured by renography. In most cases, the pyeloplasty improves the degree of hydronephrosis and washout on the renogram
- The symptoms of pain, infection and haematuria, if present before surgery, resolve along with the improvement of hydronephrosis

Complications
High success rate (90–95%) with few complications.
- Early: anastomotic leak and extravasation of urine
- Late: anastomotic stricturing and secondary PUJ obstruction

Vesicoureteric reflux

This occurs due to malfunction of a physiological valve at the vesicoureteric junction (VUJ). It may be congenital or acquired secondary to high bladder pressure in neurological disease or obstruction. It is five times more common in girls, although in the first year of life boys predominate. Vesicoureteric reflux (VUR) is intimately associated with dysfunctional voiding and it is likely that a lot of cases of VUR are caused by this. One must always remember that VUR can be a symptom of another pathology and not a disease entity in itself.

Renal damage and ureteric dilatation occur due to reflux of urine back up the ureter. This is exacerbated if the urine is infected. The condition can disappear spontaneously in many children but a small number may develop renal damage. Although in some cases VUR is diagnosed prenatally, most cases are diagnosed during the investigation of a UTI. Management is usually with prophylactic antibiotics; surgery is reserved for patients with break-through UTIs or progressive renal damage.

Posterior urethral valves

This is the most common cause of bladder outflow obstruction in boys. Severe forms cause problems in utero with hydronephrosis and oligohydramnios. Less severe obstruction presents later with poor stream, a palpable bladder or non-specific symptoms such as failure to thrive. It is treated with valve ablation per urethra or occasionally by urinary diversion such as a vesicostomy. Although resection of the valves is straightforward the long-term prognosis of the condition is influenced by residual dysfunction of the bladder and dysplasia of the kidneys. Boys with posterior urethral valves require long-term follow-up of their renal and bladder function.

Epispadias and bladder exstrophy

This results from failed midline fusion of midline structures below the umbilicus. The bladder mucosa is present as a small plaque on the anterior abdominal wall and the penis is upturned, with the meatus opening onto the dorsum. Other features can include split symphysis, low umbilicus, bifid clitoris, apparently externally rotated lower limbs, undescended testes and poorly developed scrotum. It is more common in boys. Treatment is by surgical reconstruction of the bladder. However, complications include damage to the upper tracts due to obstruction and reflux and adenocarcinoma of the original bladder mucosa. In adult life, incontinence, renal damage and vaginal stenosis can occur.

Hypospadias

In this condition the external urethral meatus lies on the ventral surface of the penis. Severity varies from a slightly displaced meatus to a perineal meatus (Fig. 8.14). The incidence is 1 in 125 boys. Associated features include undescended testis, inguinal hernia, bifid scrotum, chordee, and renal and ureteric abnormalities.

Management of hypospadias

Surgery is performed between the ages of 9 and 18 months and varies according to the classification of the deformity.

Many operations have been described for hypospadias; none is universally used. The principles of surgery are to correct the chordee and provide a straight penis, to reconstruct the urethra so that it reaches the distal glandular portion of the penis and to ensure that any surgery performed does not result in any urethral obstruction. Distal forms of hypospadias can be performed in a single stage; more proximal forms may require the use of free preputial grafts and are performed in two stages.

3.4 Developmental abnormalities of the genital tract

Learning point

- Disorders of testicular descent
- Intersex

Undescended testis

Children with a testicle absent from the hemiscrotum can have:

- A **retractile testicle** – sits high in the scrotum or in the inguinal canal but can be milked into the scrotum and stays in the scrotum with minimal tension
- An **undescended testicle** – during development the testicle has been arrested somewhere along the course of normal descent
- A **maldescended/ectopic** testicle – situated somewhere other than the course of normal descent
- A truly **absent testicle** (very rare)

Consider the following:
- Is it retractile?
- Is it truly undescended?
- Can it be felt on physical examination?

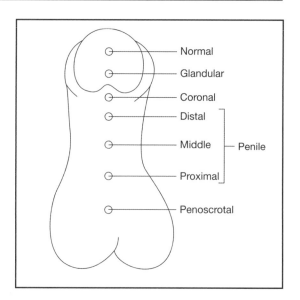

Figure 10.14 Classification of hypospadias by meatal position

Is it retractile?

Parents report seeing it at bath-time. The scrotum is normally developed. The testicle can be felt in the inguinal canal and coaxed into the scrotum on examination. No further intervention is needed – the testicle is likely to be present all of the time in the scrotum by puberty. Follow up to check.

Is it truly undescended?

The testis requires a temperature of 32°C to develop and function normally. If the testis does not reach the scrotum at the appropriate time it will have decreased fertility potential and an increased (10-fold) risk of malignancy. In addition the testis has a higher risk of torsion and trauma. Therefore undescended testes should be placed in the scrotum (orchidopexy) in early childhood. The current recommendation is that this should be before age 1 year.

Can it felt on physical examination or is it not palpable?

Old textbooks have placed great store on whether a testis is undescended or ectopic. In practical terms this is not relevant for management. The important distinction is whether or not an undescended testis can be felt in the groin on physical examination. If the testis is palpable, a day-case orchidopexy can be performed and the testis located in the groin. This procedure is performed under a general anaesthetic augmented with a local anaesthetic block. A transverse groin incision is performed and the testis located and mobilised. Most undescended testes have an associated patent processus vaginalis (PPV), so an inguinal herniotomy is usually an integral part of a routine orchidopexy. Further mobilisation of the testis is achieved by a retroperitoneal dissection to free lateral tethering or 'Ladd bands'. The testis is then removed from the coverings of the tunica vaginalis and placed in a subdartos pouch within the scrotum. Care is taken not to twist the cord as the testis is pulled into the scrotum.

If the testis is not palpable there is a chance that it is not present, is present within the abdomen or is too small to be felt. Radiological investigations are not indicated in this situation; the child is admitted for a laparoscopy to locate the testis, remove it if it looks small and atrophic, or confirm beyond reasonable doubt that it is not present. Around 6% of testes may be truly absent; at the time of laparoscopy both a blind-ending vas and vessels must be identified. If a good testis is found within the abdomen or just entering the groin at surgery it can be brought down into the scrotum by either a single-stage laparoscopic orchidopexy or a two-stage 'Fowler–Stevens' laparoscopic procedure. In the two-stage approach the short testicular vessels are divided, and at a subsequent operation the testis is brought into the scrotum, using the blood supply that runs with the vas.

Bilateral undescended testes

Bilateral undescended testes may represent a true disorder of sexual development, especially if this is associated with hypospadias. Infants

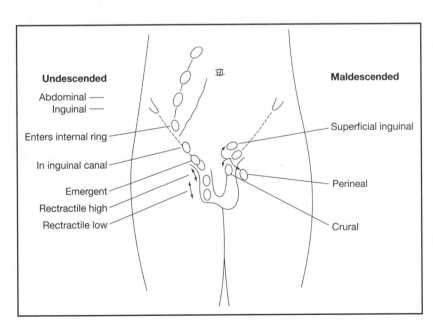

Figure 10.15 Ectopic positions for an incompletely descended or maldescended testicle

Undescended
Abdominal —
Inguinal —
Enters internal ring —
In inguinal canal —
Emergent —
Rectractile high —
Rectractile low —

Maldescended
— Superficial inguinal
— Perineal
— Crural

with bilateral undescended testes need to be assessed by an experienced paediatrician before discharge and consideration given to performing a karyotype analysis. Assuming that there is no underlying abnormality bilateral undescended testes are managed in the same was as unilateral undescended testis; however, the risk of future fertility problems is much higher.

Intersex

Congenital adrenal hyperplasia

This is an autosomal recessive disorder characterised by the absence of certain enzymes in the pathway of cortisol and aldosterone synthesis from cholesterol. It results in excess androgen levels and therefore virilisation in affected females. Affected males may present with adrenal crisis in early life. The most common form is 21-hydroxylase deficiency. Management consists of IV fluids, glucose and hydrocortisone. Long-term management includes hydrocortisone and surgical correction of virilised external genitalia in girls in the first year.

Klinefelter syndrome

This is a condition in which males have an extra X chromosome – 47,XXY. The incidence is 1 in 1000 boys. Clinical features include increased height, mild learning disabilities, gynaecomastia and infertility. The testes may be small and incompletely descended.

Testicular feminisation

Affected individuals are chromosomally XY but present as females due to complete androgen insensitivity of the genitalia. Patients may present with an inguinal hernia containing a testis or later in life with amenorrhoea.

3.5 Genetic abnormalities of the urogenital tract

Learning point

The *WT1* gene is a suppressor gene coding for Wilms tumour (see Section 4 'Paediatric oncology'). It is a transcription protein that is expressed primarily in the developing gonads and embryonic kidneys to regulate expression of its target genes. These genes are responsible for differentiation of the renal epithelial cells during development.

Denys–Drash syndrome

Denys–Drash syndrome is a very rare syndrome caused by point mutations of the *WT1* gene. It is a triad of:

- Congenital nephropathy (mesangial sclerosis)
- Wilms tumour
- Intersex disorders (gonadal dysgenesis with male pseudohermaphroditism)

WAGR syndrome

This is due to the complete deletion of the *WT1* gene and the contiguous loss of neighbouring genes in this region of chromosome 11. WAGR syndrome affects the development of seemingly disparate areas of the body, including the kidney, genitourinary system, iris of the eye and the CNS. It consists of:

- Wilms tumour
- Aniridia
- Genitourinary malformations (structural urinary tract abnormalities without nephropathy)
- Learning disabilities

3.6 Foreskin abnormalities in children

Learning point

- Phimosis
- Balanoposthitis
- Balanitis xerotica obliterans (BXO)

Anatomy of the foreskin

The foreskin consists of a single layer of skin which is adherent to the shaft of the penis and folded over at the end to create the meatus or preputial orifice. The inner layer of the foreskin is called the mucosal layer. In neonates the prepuce is adherent to the glans and does not begin to separate until the age of 1 year. The spontaneous separation of the glans and prepuce may not be complete until age 5 or older; in fact residual preputial adhesions can sometimes be seen in adolescent boys.

Procedure box: circumcision

Indications
- True phimosis, recurrent balanoposthitis, BXO, recurrent UTIs, religious reasons

Preop preparation and consent
- The procedure is usually performed under GA but in very rare cases it may be performed using regional anaesthesia in a penile block. It is commonly performed as a day case

Patient position
- Supine

Procedure
- The penis and foreskin are thoroughly cleaned to remove smegma (cleaning may have to be resumed after the initial incision if the foreskin is very tight)
- The two layers of the foreskin are cut vertically from the preputial orifice towards the coronal sulcus
- The distal skin is then removed circumferentially in layers using scissors, being careful to leave sufficient skin in place for suturing (and in adults, for erection). Bleeding is controlled with bipolar diathermy
- The frenular artery may require a suture

Closure
- The edges of the skin are then sutured together using a fine absorbable suture
- Dressings are not required routinely

Intraoperative hazards
- Damage to the penile head

Complications
- Haemorrhage (usually from the frenular artery; often stops with prolonged compression but may require return to theatre)
- Wound infection (uncommon, but can occur)
- Acute retention of urine from pain

Phimosis

The normal infantile adhesion of the prepuce to the glans is referred to as a 'physiological' phimosis. On examination of the normal infant foreskin it has a narrow, blanching, bottle-neck appearance, and is soft and unscarred. A pathological or 'true' phimosis is due to infection or disease and is characterised by pale hard tissue at the preputial orifice. A 'paraphimosis' occurs when a retracted foreskin has not been correctly replaced, leaving a tight and irreducible band around the penis, at the level of the coronal sulcus, complicated by preputial and glandular oedema.

Ballooning of the foreskin occurs when urine becomes trapped during micturition. It may then discharge later and can present as wetting. It is otherwise asymptomatic and resolves spontaneously and so is not an indication for circumcision.

Balanoposthitis

This is an acute pyogenic infection of the prepuce. It is most common in under-5s with non-retractile foreskins. It is treated with antibiotics. Circumcision is offered if there are recurrent episodes of true infection requiring systemic antibiotics. Irritation and redness at the tip of the foreskin are common and is not necessarily balanoposthitis.

Balanitis xerotica obliterans

This affects 0.6% of boys aged up to 15 years. Scarring and collagen deposition occur on the glans and foreskin. The aetiology is unknown. BXO is the usual cause of 'true phimosis'. It can affect the urethra and be associated with strictures. Treatment is circumcision.

Circumcision

Every year many children are circumcised unnecessarily. The normal infant prepuce is not designed to retract from an early age; it is designed to protect the glans from contact with urine in the nappy. A non-retractile prepuce is not an indication for circumcision in young children.

Alternatives to circumcision:
- Low-dose steroids may speed up separation of preputial adhesions
- Prepucioplasty allows preservation of the foreskin

3.7 Urinary tract infections in children

Learning point

UTIs are common in children but may indicate an underlying renal tract abnormality, so need further investigation in the form of urinalysis and ultrasonography. Certain groups of children need further investigation. The pathogen is usually *Escherichia coli* and the management is antibiotics and appropriate investigation.

Epidemiology of UTIs in children

Incidence throughout childhood is 5% in girls and 1.5% in boys. UTIs, however, are more common in boys in the first 12 months of life.

Pathogenesis of UTIs in children

E. coli is the causative organism in 85% of cases; 30–50% of children investigated for UTI are found to have some underlying urinary tract abnormality but it is doubtful whether all of these are actually responsible for the UTIs. The most common abnormality found is VUR, found in 30% of patients presenting with a UTI.

Presentation of UTIs in children

The clinical features often are non-specific, particularly in children under the age of 2. Older children have symptoms similar to those seen in adults.

Presentation of UTIs in children

- Sepsis
- Haematuria
- Lethargy
- Failure to thrive
- Vomiting
- Pain
- Mass
- Abdominal distension

Investigating UTIs in children

It is important to be careful during specimen collection because over-diagnosis of UTI is common due to contamination and leads to unnecessary investigation in many children. Options in very young children include:

- Clean-catch urine in boys
- Collection bags (the routine method)
- Suprapubic aspiration (sometimes required)

Many clinicians would recommend that all children with a febrile UTI should be investigated to exclude underlying urological abnormalities and reflux that may predispose to renal scarring. However, these National Institute for Health and Clinical Excellence (NICE) guidelines have been introduced to reduce the burden of investigation to the child and the wider health service:

- Children aged <6 months are investigated using ultrasonography 6 weeks after the infection. If the UTI has atypical features (see box below) then more urgent ultrasound can be performed. Further investigations are also performed: a micturating cystourethrogram is undertaken to look for VUR and urethral abnormalities in boys and a DMSA (dimercaptosuccinic acid) scan to look for differential renal function and scarring
- Children between 6 months and 3 years are investigated only if there are recurrent UTIs or the UTI has atypical features. In these cases an ultrasound scan and DMSA scan are performed.
- Children older than 3 years are investigated with an ultrasound if they have an atypical UTI, or with an ultrasound and DMSA scan if they have recurrent UTIs

---

Atypical UTI includes:

- Seriously ill child
- Poor urine flow
- Abdominal or bladder mass
- Raised creatinine
- Septicaemia
- Failure to respond to treatment with suitable antibiotics within 48 hours
- Infection with non-*E. coli* organisms

Management of UTIs in children

In the acute setting, antibiotic treatment is clearly required and this may be oral or intravenous, depending on the severity of the infection. Prophylactic antibiotics are often then prescribed until investigations have been completed because there is a risk of continued renal scarring. Further management depends on any other abnormalities found on investigation.

3.8 The acute scrotum in childhood

Learning point

Acute scrotal pain may also present as lower abdominal pain so always examine the genitalia. Causes of acute scrotal pain in children are:

- Torsion of the testis
- Torsion of the appendix testis
- Acute nephritic syndrome
- Epididymitis
- Orchitis
- Incarcerated hernia
- Patent processus vaginalis (congenital hydrocele)
- Testicular tumour
- Idiopathic scrotal oedema
- Henoch–Schönlein purpura

As a result of the consequences of untreated torsion an acute testicle in a child should always merit referral to a paediatric surgeon or urologist immediately, and may need emergency surgery within the hour. Genitalia should be examined in any child presenting with lower abdominal pain so that torsion is not missed.

For in-depth discussion of the pathology, diagnosis and management of these conditions in the adult see Chapter 8, Book 2.

Specific differences in children

The three most common causes of an acute scrotum are torsion of the testis, epididymo-orchitis and torsion of the appendix testis. The main difference in children is the likelihood of this occurring. Figure 10.16 shows the relative frequency of the various conditions at different ages.

In most boys the most common cause of an acute scrotum is **torsion of the appendix testis** 'the hydatid of Morgagni'. The hydatid of Morgagni is present in 90% of boys. Just before puberty the hormonal changes cause an increase in size of the hydatid and it is more prone to torsion. When infarcted it may be seen through the skin as a blue dot on top of a normally-lying and non-tender testis. At surgical exploration the hydatid is excised but, unlike torsion of the testis itself, there is no requirement for contralateral scrotal exploration.

Infection

Epididymitis occurs in infancy and the teenage years (due to reflux of infected urine retrogradely through the vas deferens). Torsion of the testis must be excluded by ultrasonography and a UTI demonstrated if possible. Orchitis is very rare before puberty.

Other differences

The majority of boys are born with a processus vaginalis still patent and this allows fluid to track into the scrotum (labia majora in girls). This produces a swelling that can be tense and look quite alarming. Intraperitoneal blood and pus can also track down through this PPV and present as a painful scrotal swelling. If the PPV is large enough, omentum and bowel can be incarcerated within it. Assessment of the acute scrotum in a child must take account of these possibilities.

Some systemic medical conditions can also present as an acute scrotum. Henoch–Schönlein purpura is a vasculitis that presents with a purpuric rash on the legs and buttocks, but can also masquerade as an acute scrotum. Likewise, acute nephritic syndrome can present with an acute scrotum. A thorough general physical examination and a urinalysis is always recommended.

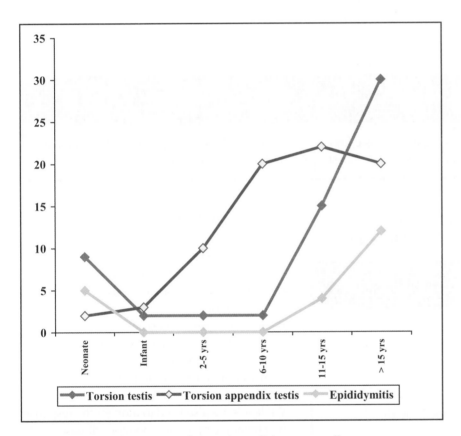

Figure 10.16 The frequency of scrotal conditions according to age

SECTION 4

Paediatric oncology

Learning point

The surgical syllabus requires a basic knowledge of the childhood malignancies that you may come across, their clinical features, investigation and principles of management.

4.1 Investigations in paediatric oncology

Learning point

Biochemistry
- AFP (α-fetoprotein)
- β-hCG (human chorionic gonadotropin)
- Urine tests
- VMA (vanillylmandelic acid)
- Catecholamines

Imaging
- Ultrasonography
- Radiography
- Angiography
- Computed tomography
- Magnetic resonance imaging
- MIBG (meta-iodobenzylguanidine) scintigraphy

Biochemistry

α-Fetoprotein

AFP level is used for the diagnosis of:
- Tumours of the ovary or testis
- Liver tumours
- Sacrococcygeal teratomas
- And for any other masses that could be teratomas or germ cell tumours (eg mediastinal, retroperitoneal)

AFP levels are also used to monitor the response to chemotherapy or monitor disease after surgical resection of mature teratomas. It is difficult to interpret in newborn babies and does not fall to normal adult levels until around the age of 6 months.
- Normal ranges for infants have been developed
- Normal adult levels are <10 kU/l

β-Human chorionic gonadotropin

- Normally <5 mIU/ml
- May be raised in patients with germ cell tumours
- Raised in pregnancy

Vanillylmandelic acid

- Raised in patients with neuroblastoma

Catecholamines

Phaeochromocytomas can secrete adrenaline, noradrenaline, dopamine, metanephrine and normetanephrine.

Most labs will give the dopamine, noradrenaline and adrenaline levels routinely. For phaeochromocytoma it is better to take a timed 24-hour urine specimen because secretion can be intermittent and a spot urine may therefore be misleadingly normal.

- Increased urinary catecholamine metabolites can be detected in about 90% of patients with neuroblastoma
- Dopamine, HVA (homovanillic acid) or HMMA (4-hydroxy-3-methoxymandelic acid) may also be raised in neuroblastoma. Spot urine tests are adequate for detecting raised levels

Imaging

Ultrasonography in paediatric oncology

Used initially for flank masses to try to distinguish Wilms tumour, neuroblastoma and hepatoblastoma. Distinction between Wilms tumour and neuroblastoma is important because the technique of biopsy is different: Wilms tumour should be needle-biopsied (an open

biopsy would upstage the tumour) whereas a 1 cm³ sample is needed for the diagnosis of neuroblastoma because cytogenetics are essential in determining treatment.

- **RUQ masses:** ultrasonography of RUQ masses should be able to tell whether or not the mass is within the liver. If a kidney is pushed down by the mass but is intact, then neuroblastoma is more likely. Wilms tumour usually replaces the whole of the kidney which is therefore not indentifiable. CT will give further information
- **Wilms tumour:** ultrasonography should be used in Wilms tumour to determine whether the renal vessels are patent and if blood flow is normal. Tumour in the renal vein or vena cava is important in the staging of Wilms tumour
- **Abdominal tumours:** also in liver tumours, tumour in the extrahepatic vasculature is very important in staging. Therefore, Doppler ultrasonography should be performed for abdominal tumours
- **Masses in the limbs:** ultrasonography is the initial investigation for masses in the limbs in order to determine whether the mass is solid or cystic and whether there is blood flow within the mass
- **Pelvic tumours:** ultrasonography is useful alongside CT in imaging pelvic tumours such as rhabdomyosarcomas or gonadal tumours

Radiographs in paediatric oncology

Plain radiographs are the initial investigation for chest masses, particularly to exclude any airway compression. Plain films of the abdomen may identify calcification in an abdominal neuroblastoma – but CT is much more useful now. Radiographs of limbs with soft-tissue tumours may identify any bony destruction but MRI is much more sensitive.

Angiography in paediatric oncology

Used to aid the surgeon before complex resections such as partial hepatectomy.

CT in paediatric oncology

Used for abdominal tumours to distinguish between Wilms tumour and neuroblastoma. Essential for staging as CT will identify whether there is significant local lymphadenopathy. CT is also used for pelvic tumours such as ovarian germ cell tumours and for staging of testicular tumours (looking for lymphadenopathy). Chest CT is used for staging of any tumours likely to metastasise to the chest (eg Wilms tumour, sarcoma, hepatoblastoma, neuroblastoma).

MRI in paediatric oncology

This has replaced CT for limb tumours such as soft-tissue sarcomas. It is also superior to CT for imaging nasopharyngeal tumours such as nasopharyngeal rhabdomyosarcoma and carcinoma (particularly important for identifying the extent, eg invasion of the base of skull). MRI is the investigation of choice for paraspinal tumours (such as neuroblastoma, ganglio-neuroma, paraspinal rhabdomyosarcoma) and to identify whether there is intraspinal extension.

MIBG scintigraphy in paediatric oncology

This is used for staging of neuroblastoma and phaeochromocytoma. It is indicated to evaluate bone and soft-tissue sites of disease; it is taken up by catecholaminergic cells (which includes most neuroblastomas) and can therefore be used to assess both the primary site and metastatic sites. ^{99m}Tc-labelled diphosphonate scintigraphy is used to assess bony metastases and is indicated for all tumours that can metastasise to bone (neuroblastoma, sarcoma).

4.2 Chemotherapy and radiotherapy in paediatric oncology

Learning point

Chemotherapy has a tremendously important role in virtually all malignant tumours in children.
- Most childhood tumours are chemosensitive
- Chemotherapy may be used preoperatively or postoperatively
- Similar to adults, children are susceptible to **general** and **organ-specific complications**

Radiotherapy may be indicated for incompletely resected childhood tumours and some metastases.

Principles of chemotherapy in paediatric oncology

Most paediatric tumours are chemosensitive (including Wilms tumour, neuroblastoma, hepatoblastoma, rhabdomyosarcoma and germ cell tumour) – even for stage I, completely resected tumours, the addition of some chemotherapy will improve survival.

Many tumours are treated with **neoadjuvant chemotherapy** (ie tumours are biopsied and then treated with chemotherapy to shrink the tumour before surgery).

After resection the child will have further chemotherapy (**adjuvant chemotherapy**) to ensure that there is no microscopic residual disease.

Main general complications of chemotherapy in paediatric tumours

- Bone marrow suppression
- Sepsis
- Bleeding
- Nausea and vomiting

Organ-specific complications of chemotherapy in paediatric tumours

- Nephrotoxicity
- Ototoxicity
- Hepatotoxicity
- Cardiac toxicity

Radiotherapy in paediatric oncology

Indications for radiotherapy in paediatric oncology

- Radiotherapy is indicated for incompletely resected tumours (Wilms tumour, neuroblastoma, rhabdomyosarcoma)
- Chest radiotherapy is also used for some chest metastases (sarcoma, Wilms tumour)

Principles of radiotherapy in paediatric oncology

- Usually used to treat the initially involved area, even when initial chemotherapy has resulted in reduction of tumour volume
- Given in fractions on a daily basis
- Young children need a daily GA
- Dose is calculated on the basis of the radiosensitivity and the normal tissue tolerance

Complications of radiotherapy in paediatric oncology

- In the short term skin erythema is common and uncomfortable

- Irradiation of the abdomen involving bowel can cause diarrhoea and mucositis
- Late complications include bowel strictures
- Outside the CNS the main long-term consequences are poor tissue growth resulting in cosmetic problems

Paediatric cancers in surgical practice

Learning point

Liver tumours
Rhabdomyosarcoma
Neuroblastoma
Nephroblastoma (Wilms tumour)
Germ cell tumours

Liver tumours (hepatoblastoma and hepatocellular carcinoma)

The median age for hepatoblastoma is 1 year and the median age for hepatocellular carcinoma (HCC) is 12 years. They present with an abdominal mass. Hepatoblastoma is a chemosensitive tumour that can occur in association with Beckwith–Wiedemann syndrome.

Staging of liver tumours

- Serum AFP both to aid diagnosis and for monitoring response to treatment, and for follow-up to identify relapse, plus CT or MR scan of the liver and CT of the chest to identify metastases
- Staging of hepatoblastoma uses the PRETEXT system, which considers the number of liver segments involved and whether there is hepatic vein or portal vein involvement

Diagnosis of liver tumours

- By liver needle biopsy, after which patients are treated with chemotherapy
- Follow-up imaging before tumour resection should be with MRI to identify exactly the surgery required to ensure a complete resection

Treatment of liver tumours

- Further chemotherapy is given after resection to treat any microscopic residual tumour
- Successful treatment requires complete surgical excision
- If complete resection is not possible liver transplantation is indicated if disease is localised to the liver
- Overall outlook is very good at over 80%, and even for the most advanced stage the survival rate is about 70%

Rhabdomyosarcoma

Arising from striated muscle, this tumour is the most common soft-tissue sarcoma of childhood. It can develop even in sites where striated muscle is not normally found, such as the bladder. It can therefore arise from virtually any site in the body.

Presentation of rhabdomyosarcoma

- Depends on the site, but can vary from a mass in the limbs, a nasopharyngeal tumour presenting with unilateral nasal obstruction and bleeding, to haematuria or urinary obstruction if the tumour is located in the bladder or prostate
- Paratesticular tumours present with a testicular mass

Prognosis of rhabdomyosarcoma

- Depends on the site (eg orbital rhabdomyosarcoma has an excellent outcome), surgical resectability, and histological subtype
- The embryonal subtype has a better prognosis than the alveolar, which has a greater propensity for dissemination
- Head and neck tumours and tumours of the genitourinary tract are rarely alveolar
- Varies from >90% for orbital rhabdomyosarcoma to <10% for widely metastatic alveolar rhabdomyosarcoma

Investigating rhabdomyosarcoma

- Initial investigations include CT or MRI of the primary tumour and identification of local lymphadenopathy
- Bone scan and bone marrow biopsy and CT of the chest for staging
- Various staging systems have been devised and many are based on the degree of surgical removal; the TNM staging system is based on pretreatment assessment and has also been applied to paediatric sarcomas

Treatment of rhabdomyosarcoma

- Consists of a diagnostic biopsy followed by chemotherapy
- The tumour is resected after shrinkage with chemotherapy
- Complete resection is extremely important for survival and if this is not possible postoperative radiotherapy will be needed to ensure adequate local control
- Chemotherapy is also essential to treat metastatic disease. Individual sites of metastatic disease should also be treated with radiotherapy (eg lung metastases and bone metastases)

- Disease which has disseminated to the bone marrow has a poor outlook. Treatment is intensified in this situation using myeloablative chemotherapy

Neuroblastoma

Neuroblastoma is the most common extracranial solid tumour in childhood. It arises from primordial neural crest cells (adrenal medulla and sympathetic ganglia anywhere from the ethmoid to the pelvis). Neuroblastoma displays a diverse clinical behaviour from spontaneous regression and maturation to ganglioglioma in some infants, to widely metastatic malignant behaviour in older children. Patients may present with an abdominal mass, a paraspinal mass or often symptoms of disseminated disease such as bone marrow failure due to marrow infiltration.

Investigating neuroblastoma

- At presentation this should include: CT scan of the primary tumour to determine whether there is local lymphadenopathy; MRI if the tumour is paraspinal to exclude spinal cord compression; MRI of the head if there are obvious deposits such as proptosis; MIBG scan, bone scan, bone marrow aspirate and biopsy and urine catecholamines
- The primary tumour should be biopsied using an open biopsy approach to ensure sufficient tissue is obtained for a fresh sample to be sent to cytogenetics as well as to the histopathologist for diagnosis

Staging of neuroblastoma

- A specific staging system has been devised – the International Neuroblastoma Staging System (INSS)
- In infants, stage IVs is a distinct entity, with disseminated disease, lack of adverse cytogenetics (ie lack of *mycN* amplification and other typical poor prognostic cytogenetic abnormalities) and the potential for spontaneous resolution without chemotherapy
- Stage IVs is defined by stage I or II local disease with distant disease in the skin, bone marrow and liver but without bone metastases

Treatment of neuroblastoma

- Localised neuroblastoma stage I or II can be treated with surgical resection alone if the cytogenetics are favourable
- Stage III and IV disease requires intensive chemotherapy followed by surgery after tumour response
- Children with stage IV disease have a poor outlook and are therefore treated aggressively with myeloablative chemotherapy after the delayed surgical resection to try to eliminate microscopic residual disease. This has improved the outcome somewhat

Wilms tumour (nephroblastoma)

This is the most common primary malignant renal tumour of childhood, representing 8% of solid tumours in children. Wilms tumours tend to present at age 3–4 years with fever, abdominal swelling and/or haematuria; 5–10% of these tumours are bilateral. They are of embryonic origin and thought to be due to a loss of a tumour suppressor gene on chromosome 11 (the *WT1* gene).

- May occur as part of syndrome WAGRI (**W**ilms, **a**niridia, **g**enitourinary **a**bnormalities and mental **r**etardation)
- May also be a part of Denys– Drash syndrome or associated with hemihypertrophy

Investigating Wilms tumour

- CT of primary and the chest to identify lung metastases
- Also Doppler ultrasonography to exclude tumour in the renal vein or vena cava
- Diagnosis is by needle biopsy to exclude other rarer renal tumours
- Open biopsy would upstage the tumour and should be avoided

Treatment of Wilms tumour

- Chemotherapy before a delayed surgical resection
- The tumour is often separated from the rest of the kidney by a pseudocapsule although this may be breached by very aggressive tumours
- Radiotherapy to the tumour bed is indicated if the tumour is not completely microscopically excised. Radiotherapy to the lungs is also indicated if there has been lung metastasis
- Further chemotherapy after tumour excision, depending on the post-surgical stage
- Partial nephrectomy is considered only if there is bilateral disease, in order to retain some renal tissue

Prognosis of Wilms tumour

- Outlook is very good, with survival rates >90% for stages I and II, >80% for stage III and about 65% for stage IV (distant metastatic tumour)
- Anaplastic variants of Wilms tumour have a poorer prognosis than classic Wilms tumour

Germ cell tumours

Germ cell tumours can be benign or malignant, within the gonads or extragonadal. They arise from pluripotential or primordial germ cells.

Sacrococcygeal teratomas are the most common of the germ cell tumours; 80% of sacrococcygeal teratomas are benign. Presentation is with an obvious mass but some can be entirely presacral without an external mass. These may present with constipation, urinary frequency or lower extremity weakness. Treatment is surgical resection including the coccyx in the neonatal period. Follow-up should include AFP measurement. Any rise above the normal value for gestational age would indicate relapse of the malignant yolk sac tumour.

Other germ cell tumours include **germinomas**, which most commonly arise in the ovary, anterior mediastinum or pineal gland, and can also arise in undescended testes. AFP may be negative in pure germinomas but these are often mixed tumours and therefore other elements of the tumour may produce AFP. **Embryonal carcinomas** are negative for AFP. **Endodermal sinus tumours** (yolk sac tumours) are the most common malignant germ cell tumours in children. They can arise in the sacrococcygeal area or the ovary in older children and are AFP-positive. **Teratomas** arise from the three germinal layers and can therefore be composed of a wide variety of tissues. They can be mature, immature or with malignant components.

All of these germ cell tumours can present with a mass in the ovary, testis, retroperitoneum or sacrococcygeal region. Those in the chest may be an incidental finding on radiography or present with symptoms of tracheal compression.

Staging of germ cell tumours

- Various staging systems exist but generally they are staged on surgical resectability and the presence or absence of distant metastases
- Spread is to local lymph nodes, lung or liver

Treatment of germ cell tumours

- Benign tumours are treated by surgical resection alone
- Malignant germ cell tumours should be resected totally if possible, followed by chemotherapy, followed by definitive surgery if residual tumour is still present

Prognosis of germ cell tumours

- These are chemosensitive and the outlook is generally good (>80% survival overall)

SECTION 5

Paediatric general surgery

> ### Learning point
>
> The field of paediatric general surgery is worthy of an entire textbook in its own right, but
> for the MRCS exam you should have an appreciation of a few important topics that we have
> highlighted here. Many of these conditions are covered in more detail in other sections of this
> book and its companion volume.
>
> **General surgical conditions in children**
> * Pyloric stenosis
> * Groin hernia (see also Chapter 1, Abdominal Surgery, Book 2)
> * Umbilical conditions
>   * Umbilical site problems
>   * Umbilical hernia (see also Chapter 1, Abdominal Surgery, Book 2)
>
> **Jaundice in neonates**
> * Biliary atresia
> * Choledochal cysts
>
> **Conditions causing acute abdominal pain in children**
> **(see also Chapter 1, Abdominal Surgery, Book 2)**
> * Appendicitis
> * Gastroenteritis
> * Bacterial enterocolitis
> * Intussusception
> * Malrotation and volvulus
> * Bleeding or infected Meckel's diverticulum
> * Constipation
> * Mesenteric adenitis
> * UTI (see 'Paediatric urology' in this chapter)
> * Testicular torsion (see Chapter 8, Urological Surgery, Book 2)
> * Obstructed/strangulated hernia
>
> For other paediatric conditions see the appropriate chapter (eg for thyroglossal cyst see
> Chapter 5, Head and Neck Surgery, Book 2).

5.1 Pyloric stenosis

Learning point

This is a hypertrophy of the circular pyloric muscles that causes gastric outlet obstruction. Its aetiology is unknown. It affects 1 in 300 newborn babies, is four times more common in boys and presents with projectile non-bilious vomiting in the first 2 months of life. Treatment is surgical pyloromyotomy.

Clinical features of pyloric stenosis

- Gradual onset of non-bilious vomiting between 3 and 6 weeks of age – becomes projectile
- Symptoms may start earlier but are very rare after 3 months. In between vomiting the baby feeds hungrily
- May have severe dehydration
- Hypochloraemic/hypokalaemic metabolic alkalosis: baby vomits repeatedly, losing hydrogen ions; kidney compensates by exchanging potassium and sodium for hydrogen ions; often associated with jaundice (see Chapter 1, Abdominal Surgery, Book 2)

Investigating pyloric stenosis

- Clinical diagnosis: palpate olive-shaped pyloric enlargement (also referred to as a pyloric 'tumour') just above the umbilicus during a 'test feed'. May see visible peristalsis
- Confirm diagnosis by ultrasonography (thickened elongated pylorus) or barium meal

Treatment of pyloric stenosis

- Stop oral feeding
- Give IV infusion of 5% dextrose, 0.45% saline plus 10 mmol potassium chloride per 500 ml until alkalosis corrects (usually 24–48 hours)
- Anaesthesia is not safe until the alkalosis is corrected because of the risk of postoperative apnoea

Long-term surgical outcome

Surgery is generally very successful; the pylorus returns to normal. Gastric investigation of these patients when they reach adulthood shows normal capacity and function.

CHAPTER 10

Op box: Ramstedt pyloromyotomy

Indications
- Pyloric stenosis

Preop preparation
- Nil by mouth (NBM) and NG tube, correction of alkalosis. The procedure is performed under GA. It may be done as an open procedure or, increasingly, as a laparoscopic technique

Incision
- Right upper transverse incision or a circumumbilical incision

Principles of procedure
- The pylorus is delivered through the incision with care not to put the stomach under too much tension
- It can be identified by the prepyloric vessel
- The pyloromyotomy involves a longitudinal incision from the antrum to the duodenum through the hypertrophied circular muscle layers (note that the muscle fibres change direction at the duodenum)
- The muscle is further opened by spreading with a pyloric spreader
- It is important not to breach the mucosa. Breach of the mucosa can be identified by inflating the stomach with air

Intraoperative hazards
- Perforation of the gastric mucosa

Closure
- Close in layers with absorbable sutures

Postop
- The NG tube can be removed early if there is no damage to the mucosa but it is left in place if there has been any perforation
- Postoperative feeding can resume after 6 hours (some vomiting will still occur initially due to gastric atony, but it will settle)

Complications
- Main complication is inadvertent perforation of the duodenal mucosa (repair with absorbable suture and cover with omental patch)
- Incomplete myotomy
- Wound infection

5.2   Groin hernias

Learning point

Groin hernias in children are usually indirect inguinal hernias. Emergency management differs from that of adult hernias (reduction by taxis is recommended in children) and surgical treatment is herniotomy, not herniorrhaphy as in adults.

Inguinal hernias

- Almost invariably indirect in children
- More common in boys than girls; more common on the right side due to later descent of the right testis
- 15% are bilateral
- Bilateral inguinal hernia in a girl is a rare presentation of testicular feminisation syndrome; chromosome studies may be necessary
- Treatment is surgical and consists of a herniotomy – the sac is dissected free from vas and vessels then transfixion-ligated at the deep ring (see Chapter 1, Abdominal Surgery)
- Herniorrhaphy, repair of the posterior wall of the canal, is unnecessary

Incarcerated inguinal hernia

Inguinal hernias in infants should be repaired within 2 weeks of diagnosis because the risk of incarceration is high. Risk of incarceration lessens after the age of 1. Incarceration results in an intestinal obstruction and there is a 30% risk of testicular infarction due to pressure on the gonadal vessels. Treatment involves resuscitation then reduction by taxis. Most hernias can be reduced safely. If not reduced, proceed to laparotomy. If the hernia has been reduced then herniotomy is performed after 24–48 hours to allow oedema to settle.

Femoral hernias

Very rare in children. Treatment follows the same principles as for adults (see Chapter 1, Abdominal Surgery, Book 2).

5.3   Umbilical disorders

Learning point

- Infection
- Herniation

Omphalitis

This is infection of the umbilical site. It is characterised by erythema and discharge of pus. It is common in the developing world and is also associated with immunodeficiency (neutrophil defects cause delay in separation of the cord), perinatal sepsis and low birthweight. It can lead to fasciitis and in severe cases may need debridement.

Umbilical hernia

> **Remember the rule of 3s**
> - 3% of live neonates have umbilical hernias
> - Only 3 per 1000 need an operation
> - Operate on after the age of 3 (many surgeons wait until age 5)
> - They recur in the 3rd trimester of pregnancy

Epidemiology of umbilical hernia

- 3% of neonates have umbilical hernias; most resolve spontaneously
- 3 in 1000 live births need surgery
- More common in black children

Anatomy of umbilical hernia

- Peritoneal sac penetrates through linea alba at the umbilical cicatrix to lie in subcutaneous tissues beneath the skin cicatrix
- There is a narrow, rigid neck at the aponeurosis

Prognosis of umbilical hernia

- All decrease in size as the child grows
- Few persist after puberty
- Some cause disfigurement or incarcerate (but strangulation is virtually unknown)
- Only a minority need an operation
- Must preserve the umbilicus to avoid stigmatising the child
- Simple repair, Mayo 'vest-over-pants' repair, on adult (see Chapter 1, Book 2)
- Absorbable sutures used

5.4 Jaundice in neonates

> **Learning point**
>
> **Physiological causes of neonatal jaundice**
> - Bilirubin <200 μmol/l
> - This can be due to hepatic immaturity or breastfeeding
>
> **Medical causes of neonatal jaundice**
> - Rhesus haemolytic disease
> - ABO incompatibility
> - Congenital spherocytosis
> - G6PD (glucose-6-phosphate dehydrogenase) deficiency
> - Hypothyroidism
> - Congenital and acquired infections
>
> **Surgical causes of neonatal jaundice**
> - Biliary atresia
> - Choledochal cysts
> - Spontaneous perforation of the bile duct
> - Inspissated bowel syndrome (within the common bile duct)
> - Tumours of the extrahepatic bile ducts

Gallstones and acute gallbladder distension must not be forgotten when managing children with an unknown cause of jaundice.

Biliary atresia

Of unknown aetiology. The extrahepatic bile ducts are destroyed by inflammation. It occurs in 1 in 14 000 live births and is equally common in boys and girls. Clinical features include jaundice, hepatosplenomegaly, pale stools and dark urine. The inflammation can be confined to the common bile duct or extend to the right and left hepatic ducts.

Treatment includes biliary–enteric anastomosis, portoenterostomy, or liver transplantation if these fail. Long-term sequelae include portal hypertension and cirrhosis.

Choledochal cysts

These occur due to a congenital weakness in the wall of the biliary tree and a functional obstruction at the distal end. They are investigated by ultrasonography and endoscopic retrograde cholangiopancreatography (ERCP). Treatment consists of excision of the cyst.

5.5 Conditions causing acute abdominal pain in children

> **Learning point**
>
> **Conditions causing acute abdominal pain in children**
> - Appendicitis
> - Gastroenteritis
> - Intussusception
> - Malrotation and volvulus
> - Meckel's diverticulum
> - Mesenteric adenitis
> - Constipation
> - Inflammatory bowel disease

Appendicitis

Three children in 1000 per year have their appendix removed. Appendicitis can occur at any age but is more common at age >5 years. Children may present with abdominal pain, vomiting and peritonism (the McBurney triad). Infants may show more non-specific features such as anorexia, vomiting, irritability and fever.

The mortality of appendicitis is higher in infants than in adults and the diagnosis is often missed and surgery delayed.

Treatment consists of appendicectomy after appropriate IV fluid replacement and antibiotics (see Chapter 1, Abdominal Surgery, Book 2).

Gastroenteritis

This is common in children and toddlers. It presents with diarrhoea and vomiting ± pyrexia and dehydration (especially in very young children). It is commonly viral but may be bacterial in nature. Common pathogens are:
- Rotavirus
- *Campylobacter* spp.
- *E. coli*
- *Salmonella* spp.

There may be a history of exposure to other infected children (common passage of rotavirus) or potentially infected foodstuffs. Remember parasites as a cause of diarrhoea and vomiting in children who live or have travelled abroad (eg *Giardia*, *Cryptosporidium* spp. and amoebiasis).

Intussusception

Incidence is 1 in 500, with a peak incidence at age 5–9 months. The majority occur in association with viral infections. An enlarged Peyer's patch in the ileum acts as the **lead point**. Intussusception in older children and adults is more likely to have a **pathological lead point,** eg a polyp or Meckel's diverticulum.

The intussusception then causes a small-bowel obstruction. The intussuscepted segment becomes engorged (with rectal bleeding) and eventually gangrenous – perforation and peritonitis follow this.

The most common site for an intussusception is ileocolic; ileoileal is less common. Small-bowel intussusception can occur as a postoperative complication, typically after nephrectomy in infants.

Clinical features of intussusception

- **Typical presentation:** spasms of colic with pallor, screaming and drawing up of legs
- The child falls asleep between episodes and later develops bile-stained vomiting and rectal bleeding (redcurrant-jelly stools)
- **Clinical signs:** ill, listless, dehydrated child. The child may become desperately ill from shock. Intussusception is palpable as a sausage-shaped mass in about a third. There is blood on rectal examination. Occasionally the tip of the intussusception is palpable per rectum. Signs of peritonitis indicate perforation

Investigating intussusception

- Abdominal radiograph shows small-bowel obstruction. May see a soft-tissue mass
- Ultrasonography is characteristic (target sign)
- On barium enema (old-fashioned) intussuscipiens shows up as a 'coiled spring'

Treatment of intussusception

- Resuscitation
- ABC
- Often require large volumes of plasma to restore perfusion
- IV antibiotics
- Analgesia
- NG tube

If the child can be resuscitated and there is no evidence of peritonitis and an expert paediatric radiologist is available, then attempt to reduce the intussusception pneumatically by rectal insufflation of air or carbon dioxide. Risks are incomplete reduction and perforation. The latter can be particularly dangerous because a tension pneumoperitoneum develops very rapidly. Facilities for immediate laparotomy must be available. Perform laparotomy if pneumatic reduction has failed or is contraindicated. Use a right upper transverse incision. The distal bowel is gently compressed to reduce the intussusception. If the serosa starts to split the reduction should be abandoned and a limited resection performed.

Outcome of treatment

Recurrence rate is about 10% whether treated radiologically or by surgery. Further recurrence raises the question of a pathological lead point.

Malrotation and volvulus

Malrotation of the midgut results in a narrow free pedicle with a predisposition to twist around the SMA as a volvulus. Acute volvulus presents during the neonatal period but may occur at any age. It may also be recurrent. Symptoms are bilious vomiting, abdominal distension and tenderness, and there can be rectal bleeding. The midgut becomes ischaemic and may infarct. Abdominal radiography shows duodenal obstruction with absent distal bowel gas. Prompt resuscitation and laparotomy for the Ladd procedure and resection of any necrotic areas is indicated.

Meckel's diverticulum

May mimic the presentation of appendicitis or present with bleeding, perforation, intussusception, volvulus or intestinal obstruction. Haemorrhage or perforation may be due to the presence of gastric mucosa within the diverticulum. See Chapter 1, Abdominal Surgery, Book 2.

Mesenteric adenitis

Vague central abdominal pain can accompany an upper respiratory tract infection, due to inflammation of the mesenteric lymph nodes and subsequent mild peritoneal reaction. Features that distinguish it from appendicitis include cervical lymphadenopathy, headache, mild abdominal pain, shifting tenderness and pyrexia >38°C. It occurs most commonly between the ages of 5 and 10 years. For more details see Chapter 1, Book 2, Abdominal Surgery.

Constipation

Causes of constipation in childhood

- Hypothyroidism
- Hypercalcaemia
- Neuromuscular disorders
- Hirschsprung's disease
- Febrile illness in older children

Chronic constipation may lead to abdominal pain, anorexia, vomiting, failure to thrive, UTIs and faecal soiling.

Soiling occurs due to the accumulation of faeces within the rectum and the resulting acquired megacolon. This leads to distension of the external sphincter and eventual failure of the external sphincter.

Anal irritation and tears can occur due to pain on defecation, leading to a cycle of faecal retention.

Management of constipation

- Treat the precipitating cause if applicable
- A short course of oral laxatives is most often successful
- A course of enemas can be considered in more refractory cases
- This should be supplemented with high fluid and roughage intake

Inflammatory bowel disease

There are about 1000 children with inflammatory disease (IBD) in the UK. The number of children with Crohn's disease is increasing. The presentation, diagnosis and treatment are similar to those in adults – see Chapter 1, Abdominal Surgery, Book 2.

Children tend to present with extra-gastrointestinal symptoms. Surgery for children who are malnourished because of the severity of their IBD should be performed early to avoid stunting of growth.

CHAPTER 11

Plastic Surgery

Stuart W Waterston

Hand surgery and the management of burns are also essential parts of plastic surgery. Hand surgery is covered in Orthopaedic Surgery (Chapter 9) and burns are discussed in Trauma, (Chapter 6) Book 1 of this series.

CHAPTER 11

SECTION 1

Anatomy and physiology of the skin

1.1 Anatomy of the skin

Skin consists of two main layers – epidermis and dermis – separated by a basal lamina that anchors the two layers. Epidermis is a stratified squamous epithelium that consists of five layers. Four main cell types are found in the epidermis: keratinocytes (the majority), melanocytes, Langerhans cells and Merkel cells. The skin also has a number of epidermal appendages – sweat glands, hair follicles, sebaceous glands and nails. These are important structures in the process of wound healing.

The five layers of the **epidermis** are:
1. **Stratum germinativum** (or basale): basal layer, only layer that is actively proliferating. Cells move towards surface from here

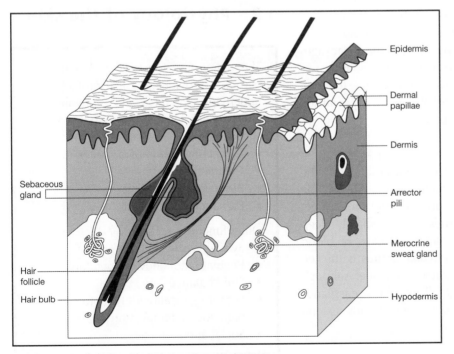

Figure 11.1 The structure of the skin

Epidermis

Dermal papillae

Dermis

Arrector pili

Merocrine sweat gland

Hypodermis

Sebaceous gland

Hair follicle

Hair bulb

2. **Stratum spinosum:** layer several cells deep, keratinocytes with spinous processes that meet neighbouring cells

3. **Stratum granulosum:** mature keratinocytes containing cytoplasmic granules of keratohyalin, giving 'granular' appearance

4. **Stratum lucidum:** found only in the thick skin of the palm of the hand and sole of the foot. Highly keratinised cells, with progressive loss of cellular structures as cells become filled with keratin

5. **Stratum corneum:** most superficial layer. Cells no longer possess nuclei or intracellular structures and are filled with keratin. Very variable in thickness depending on site

Keratinocytes are the most common epidermal cell. These are synthesised in the basal layer and progress through the layers of the epidermis until they are lost by sloughing off. They provide the barrier function of skin. **Melanocytes** (10% of epidermal cells) are neural crest-derived cells found in the basal layer of the epidermis. They produce melanin, which is responsible for the colour of the skin. Melanocytes pass packages of melanin (melanosomes) to keratinocytes. **Langerhans cells** have an immune function within the skin and **Merkel cells** are a specialised form of mechanoreceptor.

The **dermis** (95% of skin thickness) is a connective tissue layer responsible for the strength, elasticity and vascularity of the skin. Dermis can be divided into two distinct layers: **papillary dermis** is immediately deep to epidermis and contains a plexus of blood vessels and nerves; **reticular dermis** is thicker, and contains denser connective tissue. Although structures such as hair follicles and sweat glands are epidermal structures, they usually extend through the dermis and into the subcutaneous layer. **Collagen** is the main component of connective tissue and is responsible for the strength of the dermis. Collagen type I is most common in the skin, and present in a ratio to type III collagen of approximately 4:1. Dermis also contains elastin fibres, responsible for the elastic properties of skin, and ground substance, consisting of glycosaminoglycan molecules.

Knowledge of the **blood supply of the skin** is important in the planning of surgical incisions and for reconstructive surgery. It is essentially a continuous network of blood vessels, originating from deep vessels, which then supply a system of interconnecting vessels (known as perforators), and go on to supply a series of vascular plexuses, particularly within the dermis. Perforators may pass directly to the skin through connective tissue septa, or pass indirectly, through other structures such as muscle.

1.2 Physiology of the skin

The major function of the skin is as a barrier. It provides physical protection to underlying structures and is involved in the immunological response to damage by agents such as:

- Direct physical trauma
- Chemicals
- Biological agents
- Radiation, eg sunlight

Other functions include:

- Synthesis of vitamin D
- Regulation of body temperature
- Fluid balance
- Sensory – location of receptors for pain, touch, temperature
- Social and aesthetic

SECTION 2
Pathology of the skin

2.1   Benign skin lesions

Seborrhoeic keratosis

Common benign epidermal lesions of highly variable appearance, often multiple. They usually occur in older age groups and may be an inherited trait. They may occur in any site except palms/soles and lips and have a tendency to occur along skin cleavage lines. They are often raised and waxy in appearance and may become pigmented. The main indication for treatment is irritation, or if the patient finds the lesions cosmetically unacceptable. Seborrhoeic keratosis may be effectively managed by cryotherapy, curettage or shave excision.

Dermatofibroma

Pink, firm, papular lesions, dermal in origin, commonly arising on the legs. The aetiology is unknown but patients commonly report a history of trauma at the site. Once developed, the lesions usually remain unchanged. They must be differentiated from amelanotic melanoma or dermatofibrosarcoma protruberans. These malignant conditions may have a similar appearance. If required, dermatofibromas can be managed by excision.

Sebaceous hyperplasia

This is a common condition, usually affecting the face of older patients, and is a result of enlargement of sebaceous glands. The aetiology is unknown. It presents as small papule, sometimes with associated telangiectasia. It is often misdiagnosed as basal cell carcinoma.

Epidermoid cysts

These are intradermal/subcutaneous lesions that arise from epidermal structures – commonly hair follicles. They develop commonly on the trunk, neck and face and are seen clinically as yellowish nodular lesions associated with a punctum. They are fixed to skin but mobile on subcutaneous tissues. Patients may give a history of discharge of foul-smelling, stringy, 'cheesy' material. Cysts can rupture, resulting in irritation of the surrounding tissues, or become infected and present as abscesses. Management is by complete surgical excision of the cyst and overlying punctum. It is reasonable to excise these lesions because the scarring that results from infection of the cyst is usually worse than that of elective excision. Infected lesions should be drained and allowed to settle; if they recur, then the residual cyst can be excised.

Gardner syndrome is an autosomal dominant condition that presents with multiple epidermal cysts, osteomas of the jaw and gastrointestinal polyps. It is a variant of familial adenomatous polyposis (FAP). Polyps have a 100% risk of undergoing malignant transformation.

Beware of patients presenting with an 'infected discharging cyst' along the border of the mandible. This may in fact represent a discharging dental abscess, and the state of the patient's dentition should be carefully evaluated.

Trichilemmal (pilar) cyst

This is indistinguishable from an epidermal cyst except through the absence of an overlying punctum. It is derived from the outer root sheath of hair follicles. Most (90%) occur on the scalp. They are usually removed by direct incision over the lesion, which is easily dissected from surrounding tissues.

Dermoid cyst

This may be congenital or acquired. **Congenital dermoid cysts** are usually the result of entrapment of epidermal tissue along lines of embryological fusion. A common variant is the external angular dermoid, which presents as a subcutaneous (submuscular) swelling at the superolateral aspect of the orbit. These are managed by excision. Dermoid cysts presenting in the facial midline, particularly between the nasal tip and the forehead, may be associated with intracranial extension and should be evaluated by imaging before any attempt at excision is made. Excision may require a transcranial approach.

Acquired dermoid cysts ('implantation dermoids') are the result of trapping of epidermal material deeper in the skin or subcutaneous

tissues, usually as the result of trauma. They are often associated with an overlying or adjacent scar. Management is by excision.

Pilomatrixoma

This is a benign skin appendage tumour that shows some features of hair follicle cells. It is usually seen on the face in children. It presents as a characteristic, 'stony hard' nodule, which is slowly growing. Management is by excision.

Neurofibroma and neurofibromatosis

A neurofibroma is a benign nerve sheath tumour found along the course of a peripheral nerve. It may be asymptomatic or can be associated with compressive symptoms.

Neurofibromatosis (NF) is an inherited neurocutaneous syndrome, of which there are a number of variants. NF type 1 (von Recklinghausen's disease) is the most common, and is characterised by multiple dermal and subcutaneous neurofibromas, café-au-lait marks (light-brown macular patches) and axillary freckling. It is inherited as an autosomal dominant, with a defect on chromosome 17. Extracutaneous involvement includes scoliosis, epilepsy, learning difficulties, cardiopulmonary problems, ocular involvement, association with certain malignancies and a risk of sarcomatous degeneration of the neurofibromas.

Benign pigmented lesions

A naevus (mole) is a benign skin tumour composed of melanocyte-derived naevus cells that are grouped in various levels throughout the skin. They may present at birth (congenital naevi) or, more commonly, develop throughout childhood to a peak in adolescence (acquired naevi). Naevi may change appearance over time, usually starting as a flat pigmented lesion and becoming progressively elevated. They may regress completely with time.

Types of naevus

Junctional naevi are flat lesions formed by nests of naevus cells at the dermo-epidermal junction. **Compound naevi** are the result of naevus cells at the dermo-epidermal junction and various levels through the dermis. They are usually slightly raised and may be hairy. An **intradermal naevus** is an elevated fleshy lesion, with an irregular surface, which may be pigmented but is often flesh coloured. Some naevi may develop a symmetrical area of hypopigmentation surrounding them – these are known as **halo naevi**. The halo is the result of an inflammatory response, and the naevus usually disappears subsequent to the development of a halo. A **blue naevus** is a bluish-coloured lesion that is the result of heavily pigmented melanocytes in the deeper parts of the dermis. Although usually benign, the intensity of pigmentation may raise concerns.

Spitz naevus is a benign lesion, often occurring on the face of a child. It is variable in colour and appearance, but has characteristic features on dermatoscopy. Histologically, it may resemble a melanoma, and as a result may cause diagnostic difficulty (they were previously termed 'juvenile melanoma'). Management should be by excision and reassurance.

2.2 Premalignant lesions

Giant congenital melanocytic naevi are, by definition, lesions present at birth. Exactly what constitutes a 'giant' congenital naevus is variable, but a reasonable definition is a lesion >20 cm in diameter (or predicted to achieve that size by adulthood) or covering >2% body surface area or >1% in the head and neck. These lesions change over time, often becoming thicker and hairy. There is a definite risk of malignant transformation to melanoma (overall risk 7.5%, although widely variable rates are reported). Management is controversial.

Sebaceous naevus is a hamartoma of sebaceous glands and hair follicles. It forms pale, raised, waxy plaques, with an irregular surface, and is often seen on the scalp. There is a risk of development of basal cell carcinoma; the overall risk is debatable, but may be up to 20%. Management is by excision.

Actinic keratosis (also known as solar keratosis) is a crusty lesion that usually occurs in sun-exposed areas; it has a risk of transformation into squamous cell carcinoma. It may be effectively managed by non-surgical methods.

Bowen's disease represents squamous cell carcinoma in situ. It usually presents as a reddish plaque lesion, particularly on the limbs of elderly women. A more aggressive version affecting the glans penis is known as erythroplasia of Queyrat.

Keratoacanthoma is a rapidly growing mass of squamous cells with a central keratin plug, which is said to resemble a small volcano. These are histologically indistinguishable from an early squamous cell carcinoma. Conservative management usually results in complete resolution with a small residual scar, but management as per squamous cell carcinoma is often recommended.

Paget's disease is intraepithelial adenocarcinoma. The classic mammary form is an eczema-like skin change around a nipple, and usually suggests an underlying breast malignancy. Extramammary

Paget's disease usually involves the genital or perianal regions, and may also be associated with underlying malignancy, although this is less common than the mammary form. Management is usually surgical.

2.3 Non-melanoma skin malignancy

Basal cell carcinoma (rodent ulcer)

> **Learning point**
>
> - Most common skin malignancy, slow growing and locally invasive, but little potential to metastasise
> - UV exposure is major aetiological factor
> - Various subtypes; classic nodular lesions have rolled 'pearly' edge with telangiectasias
> - Manage according to UK guidelines

A malignant tumour of the epidermis that represents both the most common malignancy diagnosed overall and the most common type of skin malignancy. It originates from cells in the stratum germinativum of hair-bearing skin. Sun damage is the primary aetiological factor, although basal cell carcinoma (BCC) may be associated with immunosuppression. A predisposition to the development of BCC may occur in patients with a sebaceous naevus, or in patients with basal cell naevus (Gorlin) syndrome, which is an autosomal dominant condition secondary to a defect in a tumour suppressor gene. Most BCCs occur in older, white patients, and most often affect the head and neck area.

There are a number of subtypes of BCC. The classic nodular lesion is the most common, and tends to have a rolled edge with a 'pearly' appearance, telangiectasias and an area of central ulceration. BCCs often contain melanocytes and may be pigmented. 'Morphoeic' lesions may be large with ill-defined borders. These are aggressive lesions that can be difficult to treat.

BCC is slow growing but can be locally invasive and destroy underlying structures. Metastasis is extremely rare.

> **High-risk BCC lesions**
> The British Association of Dermatologists has produced guidelines on the management of BCC, updated in 2008. Lesions are considered 'high risk' and thus more difficult to treat if they have the following characteristics:
> - Tumour site – eyes, ears, lips, nose, nasolabial folds (sites of embryonic fusion)
> - Tumour size >2 cm, especially in high-risk sites
> - Histological subtype – morphoeic, infiltrative, micronodular
> - Poorly defined macroscopic margins
> - Recurrent lesions
> - Perineural or perivascular involvement
> - Immunosuppressed patient

BCCs may be managed both surgically and non-surgically. Surgical excision using the Mohi technique should result in a cure rate of up to 99%. Standard surgical excision with a 3-mm margin of normal skin will remove 85% of low-risk lesions. Destructive therapies such as curettage or cryosurgery are less effective and may not provide tissue for histology. Radiotherapy is as effective as standard surgery but should not be used in sensitive sites such as the periocular area. It is usually reserved for those unable or unwilling to undergo surgical excision. Photodynamic therapy is also an effective treatment for BCCs.

Patients with a completely excised BCC do not require long-term follow-up, but they should be counselled that more than half of patients will develop a new BCC within 5 years. They are also at increased risk from other types of skin malignancy.

Management of an incompletely excised BCC is controversial. Up to half may recur. Low-risk lesions incompletely excised on a lateral margin may be managed by observation.

Squamous cell carcinoma

Learning point

- A common epidermal tumour, locally destructive with potential for metastatic spread
- UV exposure, immunosuppression and chronic wounds are important aetiological factors
- Management is ideally surgical, according to UK guidelines

Squamous cell carcinoma (SCC) is a common invasive malignant epidermal tumour that is locally destructive and has a low but significant potential for metastasis to lymph nodes. It arises from cells of the stratum spinosum and epidermal appendages.

Aetiology of SCC

Sun exposure is the major aetiological factor for the development of SCC. Other predisposing factors include:
- Carcinogen exposure – pesticides, arsenic, hydrocarbons, viruses (human papillomavirus, herpesviruses), radiation
- Immunosuppression – significantly increased risk in transplant recipients
- Premalignant lesions – Bowen's disease, actinic keratosis
- Genetic disease – xeroderma pigmentosum
- Chronic wounds – scars, burns, venous ulcers, pressure sores, sinuses etc. These are commonly referred to as a 'Marjolin ulcer'

SCC commonly presents in older, fair-skinned individuals, usually with a history of sun exposure or other predisposing factors. The clinical features may be variable, but it is usually a keratinising or crusted tumour, although it may present as an ulcer with no evidence of keratinisation.

Histologically, SCC may be classified according to the degree of differentiation of the cells (well, moderate, poorly and undifferentiated – the Broder classification). It may also be classified according to histological subtype. Both of these have prognostic significance.

The British Association of Dermatologists has produced guidelines on the management of SCC, updated in 2009. These provide both prognostic and management information.

Risk of metastasis in SCC

The metastatic potential of SCC is influenced by the following factors (and such lesions are classified as high risk):

- Site (increasing order):
  - Sun-exposed sites (not lip/ear)
  - Lip
  - Ear
  - Non-sun-exposed sites, eg perineum
  - Chronically inflamed/irritated/irradiated areas/burn scars, Bowen's disease
- Size >2 cm (metastases in up to 30%)
- Depth >4 mm (metastases in up to 45%)
- Histological features:
  - Subtype – certain histological subtypes have better prognosis, eg verrucous subtype
  - Differentiation – three times increased metastatic rate for poorly differentiated lesions compared with well-differentiated ones
  - Perineural and lymphovascular space involvement
- Immunosuppression – poorer prognosis in immunosuppressed patients
- Recurrence – recurrent lesions carry a worse prognosis

Management of SCC

Patients presenting with a primary cutaneous SCC should have the relevant lymph node basins assessed and staged if any abnormality is found.

Management of the primary lesion is ideally surgical because this provides tissue for histological assessment and allows the adequacy of excision to be assessed. Standard surgical excision for low-risk lesions involves a 4-mm margin of normal skin, and would be expected to clear 95% of lesions. High-risk lesions should have a margin of at least 6 mm of normal skin.

Follow-up of patients with cutaneous SCC varies, but, in general, 75% of recurrences will be seen within 2 years and 95% within 5 years. Lymph node basins should be assessed at follow-up. Patients are at risk of further lesions or other skin malignancies.

A **Marjolin ulcer** is an SCC arising in an area of chronic irritation or inflammation. It is classically associated with burn scars, and may be seen in up to 2% of long-standing burn scars. It is thought that prolonged wound healing results in an abnormal keratinocyte population that is prone to malignant transformation. Marjolin's ulcer usually develops in long-standing wounds/scars, but in rare instances an acute form is seen. Ulceration or abnormality developing within a wound should raise the possibility of this diagnosis. Marjolin's ulcer tends to be an aggressive form of SCC, with a high metastatic rate. Management is surgical. Management of lymph node basins is needed, and adjuvant therapy may be required.

Merkel cell carcinoma

This is a rare, but aggressive, malignancy of neuroendocrine origin, seen almost exclusively in elderly white patients. UV exposure and immunosuppression are aetiological factors, but recently a possible viral aetiology has been suggested, with Merkel cell polyomavirus found in up to 80% of cases.

It commonly affects the head and neck, and presents as red dermal nodules 2–4 mm in diameter. Metastasis to lymph nodes is very common. Distant metastasis is also common and associated with a very poor prognosis. Management is surgical, but radiotherapy and chemotherapy should be considered as adjuvant therapy.

Sebaceous carcinoma

This arises from the epithelial lining of sebaceous glands, and three-quarters occur in the eyelid, representing the fourth most common eyelid tumour, after BCC, SCC and melanoma. Small nodular lesions are often misdiagnosed. Local recurrence and metastasis are relatively common. Management is excision plus consideration of adjuvant therapy.

Dermatofibrosarcoma protruberans

This is a locally aggressive dermal tumour, with high local recurrence rates but a low metastatic rate. It usually occurs in younger patients and presents as a solitary red nodular lesion. It is thought to be the result of a genetic defect in the production of platelet-derived growth factor β. Surgical treatment with wide margins is required. In the rare cases of metastasis, spread to the lungs is common and carries a poor prognosis.

2.4 Melanoma

Learning point

- Melanoma is an invasive tumour of melanocytes, with significant metastatic potential
- Multifactorial aetiology but UV exposure very important
- Increasing in incidence, more common in more affluent portions of the population
- Important prognostic factors include Breslow thickness, ulceration, mitotic rate and regional lymph node status
- Mainstay of management is surgery – role of adjuvant therapies currently within clinical trials

Aetiology of melanoma

Malignant melanoma is an invasive malignant tumour of melanocytes, with significant metastatic potential. It has been steadily increasing in incidence, with almost 12 000 new cases in the UK in 2008. It is strongly associated with exposure to solar radiation, with both UVA and UVB radiation being implicated, although the aetiology is multifactorial. It is more common in females, and, although most cases affect older people, just over a quarter occur in patients aged <50 years. Unusually, it has a positive correlation with affluence, which is related to greater sun exposure in more affluent groups.

Most melanomas arise anew, rather than from pre-existing lesions. Assessment of pigmented lesions can be difficult, but various features should raise the potential diagnosis of melanoma.

Lesion characteristics suggestive of melanoma

The ABCDE system is useful and easy to remember:
- **A**symmetry in two axes
- **B**order irregularity
- **C**olour (usually more than two)
- **D**iameter (>6 mm)
- **E**volution of lesion with time/ **E**levation/**E**nlargement

Dermatoscopy performed by those appropriately trained in the technique may be useful for assessment of suspicious lesions, but, excision biopsy and histological assessment remain the gold standard.

Suspicious lesions should ideally be excised

with a 2-mm margin and a cuff of subcutaneous tissue. Incisional biopsy of a melanoma may give misleading information and result in inadequate initial treatment. Incisional biopsy of the most suspicious area of a lesion should be performed only if simple complete excision is not possible.

Patients presenting with a suspected primary cutaneous melanoma should have relevant lymph node basins assessed and staged if any abnormality is found.

Management of melanoma

The British Association of Dermatologists has produced British guidelines on the management of melanoma, revised in 2010. The following information is based on this guideline.

Management of the patient with cutaneous melanoma should ideally be under the auspices of a multidisciplinary team that has access to dermatology, oncology and plastic surgery services.

Once the initial lesion had been excised, histopathological assessment should be reported in a standard fashion with comments on a number of factors. The single most important factor in prognosis and planning of treatment is the **Breslow thickness**. This is measured from the granular layer of epidermis to the deepest involved cells in the dermis, to the nearest 0.1 mm. Ulceration of the lesion is important, as is an assessment of the mitotic rate of malignant cells per mm^2. This information will give a pathological staging.

Pathological staging

Pathological stage (T)	Thickness (mm)	Ulceration/Mitotic rate (MR)
T1a	<1	No ulceration/ MR <1/mm^2
T1b	<1	Ulceration/ MR >1/mm^2
T2a	1.01–2.0	No ulceration
T2b	1.01–2.0	Ulceration
T3a	2.01–4.0	No ulceration
T3b	2.01–4.0	Ulceration
T4a	>4	No ulceration
T4b	>4	Ulceration

Other information that may be included in the histology report includes melanoma subtype, eg superficial spreading, nodular; growth phase; lymphatic/vascular or perineural invasion; evidence of regression or lymphocytic infiltration; and the presence of any microsatellites (predictive of nodal recurrence). Once the Breslow thickness of the lesion is known, wide excision of the affected area can by planned to remove micrometastases and reduce the risk of local recurrence. A number of trials regarding excision margins for melanoma have been performed, and current accepted practice is as follows.

Breslow thickness (mm)	Excision margin (cm)
≤1	1
1.01–2.0	1–2
2.01–4.0	2–3
>4	3

Managing the regional lymph nodes in melanoma

Assessment and management of regional lymph node basins in patients with melanoma is a controversial subject. In the patient who is clinically node-positive at presentation, fine-needle cytology should be performed to confirm the diagnosis, and a lymph node dissection undertaken. In the patient who is clinically node-negative on presentation, it is recognised that there is no value in elective lymph node dissection. Options therefore include simple clinical follow-up, clinical follow-up plus assessment of node basins by imaging, or formal assessment of node basins using the sentinel node biopsy (SNB) technique.

The SNB technique aims to identify the first draining lymph node of a given area using a combination of lymphoscintigraphy with a radioisotope, and injection of a blue dye around the primary lesion, which is rapidly taken up by the lymphatics and stains the sentinel node blue. This node can then be located using a gamma probe and visual assessment for the blue colour. This node is then assessed by histology and immunohistochemistry and, if positive for melanoma, a completion lymph node dissection is undertaken. Although it is accepted that patients with a negative sentinel node have a better overall prognosis, it is not clear that assessment of the sentinel node and subsequent node dissection confers any long-term survival benefit when compared with those patients who have undergone clinical follow-up. The SNB technique has a false-negative rate, and morbidity of the procedure is around 5%, including some patients who get troublesome lymphoedema. A number of trials about the SNB technique for melanoma are ongoing; however, information from the technique is incorporated into the latest staging guidelines, and the recommendation of the UK group is that all patients with melanoma stage T1b or greater should be considered for SNB.

Staging for melanoma

Staging of melanoma is according to the AJCC (2009) guidelines.

For patients who present as stage I/II, no further investigation of asymptomatic patients is required before management of the primary lesion. Stage III patients should have a CT scan of the head (controversial), chest, abdomen and pelvis, before node dissection. Stage IV patients should have whole-body CT and measurement of serum lactate dehydrogenase (LDH), plus consideration of the use of positron-emission tomography (PET).

The use of adjuvant chemo-/radiotherapy in melanoma has not currently been shown to confer any survival benefit, but may be undertaken as part of a clinical trial.

Follow-up for melanoma

Melanoma patients generally require long-term follow-up to detect recurrence/spread and monitor for the development of further skin malignancies. Individual units may have their own follow-up protocols.

Based on the 2010 British guidelines, patients with in-situ melanoma can be discharged immediately with advice. Patients with very early invasive melanoma (stage Ia) may be safely discharged at 1 year. Patients with stage Ib/II melanoma should be followed up for at least 5 years, usually 3-monthly for 3 years then 6-monthly to 5 years. Patients with stage III or greater should have a minimum of 10 years of follow-up, with yearly follow-up beyond 5 years.

AJCC guidelines

T			N			M		
T	Thickness (mm)	Ulceration/ mitotic rate (MR)	N	Number of nodes	Tumour Burden	M	Site	Serum LDH
T1a	<1	No ulceration; MR <1/mm²	N0	0	0	M0	None	Normal
T1b	<1	Ulceration; MR > 1/mm²	N1a	1	Microscopic	M1a	Distant skin or subcutaneous or nodal	Normal
T2a	1.01–2.0	No ulceration	N1b	1	Macroscopic	M1b	Lung	Normal
T2b	1.01–2.0	Ulceration	N2a	2–3	Microscopic	M1c	Other viscera Distant	Normal Elevated
T3a	2.01–4.0	No ulceration	N2b	2–3	Macroscopic			
T3b	2.01–4.0	Ulceration	N2c	2–3	In transit, or satellites but no metastatic nodes			
T4a	>4	No ulceration	N3	4+, matted, or in transit, or satellites with metastatic nodes				
T4b	>4	Ulceration						

Based on this staging, a clinical stage and estimate of prognosis may be given.

Clinical stage	TNM classification	5-year survival rate (%)
Ia	T1aN0M0	95
Ib	T1bN0M0 T2aN0M0	89–91
IIa	T2bN0M0 T3aN0M0	77–79
IIb	T3bN0M0 T4aN0M0	63–67
IIc	T4bN0M0	45
IIIa	T1–4aN1a/2a	63–69
IIIb	T1–4bN1a/2a T1–4aN1b/2b/2c	46–53
IIIc	T1–4bN1b/2b/2c Any T N3	24–29
IV	Any T/N, M1	7–19

The principles of wound assessment and management are core knowledge and skills for any surgeon. A wound is the end-result of damage to the skin or other structures secondary to some form of trauma, whether accidental, eg after an assault, or intentional, eg a surgical incision.

3.1 Types of wound

Traumatic wounds are commonly a combination of a number of different types of wounds. The type of wound and mechanism of injury will give an indicator of the likely management requirements.

Abrasions are the result of rubbing or scraping of skin and may range from minor superficial injuries that will heal with good results, to significant wounds with large areas of tissue loss and contamination with foreign material, which commonly result in large areas of poor scarring. A common example is the so-called 'road rash' seen in road traffic accident (RTA) victims.

Lacerations involve tearing of a tissue or organ. The tissue is forcibly stretched and fails, resulting in a wound with irregular edges and potentially compromised vascularity. An **incised wound** is produced by a sharp object such as a knife or scalpel, and usually has clean, well-defined, viable wound edges.

De-gloving is a type of laceration, in which skin is sheared from underlying tissues by rotational and/or crushing forces. This may occur in more than one tissue plane. Skin vascularity is compromised because feeding vessels are torn. The external appearance of the wound may be relatively minor, despite the major underlying damage. This type of injury is often caused when a limb is caught beneath a vehicle wheel or in rotating machinery.

Avulsion involves tearing or forcible separation of a structure from its origin, eg the traumatic avulsion of a limb in machinery. Avulsion implies a major transfer of energy. Avulsion injury is often a contraindication to replantation because the internal structure of the avulsed part is severely disrupted.

A **crush** injury results in tissue damage from a compressive force, and may result in significant tissue and microvascular damage.

Wound assessment

Viability of tissue in traumatic wounds can be difficult to assess and judgement comes with experience. Assessment of viability is based on evidence of tissue vascularity, with the presence of a normal capillary refill time and bleeding from cut wound edges as indicators of viability. Discoloration of subcutaneous tissues and thrombosis of vessels are usually indicators of dubious viability.

3.2 Wound management

Wound debridement

Debridement is the process of removing dead, non-viable or infected tissue and foreign material from a wound, and represents an essential step in wound management to allow optimal wound healing, or as preparation for wound closure.

Debridement may be considered as surgical ('sharp'), mechanical, autolytic, chemical or biological.

Surgical debridement involves selective excision of dubious tissue to achieve a healthy wound. It may be staged to potentially preserve questionable tissue in special areas, eg the face.

Mechanical debridement, eg scrubbing, or the use of certain dressings, may be used as a non-selective method of wound debridement. Hydrotherapy and hydrosurgical systems (eg VersaJet) are forms of mechanical debridement.

Chemical debridement involves the use of enzymes and other compounds to remove necrotic tissue. **Autolytic debridement** involves allowing non-viable tissue to separate from the wound bed as a result of the body's own wound healing processes. It is promoted by dressings that retain moisture within the wound. It is very selective, but can take a significant amount of time. **Biological debridement** involves the use of maggots to clear a wound of necrotic tissue. It can be very effective and is highly selective, but requires time and experience, and may be unacceptable to some patients.

Wound closure

Wound closure/reconstruction may be achieved by a number of methods ranging from simple to complex. The concept of the 'reconstructive ladder' was devised as a stepwise progression in wound closure techniques from simple to complex. However, with modern reconstructive surgery techniques and free tissue transfer, it may be that a more complex form of reconstruction will achieve the best result, both functionally and cosmetically, and should be considered before simpler techniques. This is sometimes referred to as the 'reconstructive elevator'.

Healing by secondary intention is when the wound is left to heal from the base and edges, and by the process of wound contraction. It is effective and appropriate in certain circumstances, eg after drainage of an abscess. Prolonged healing may result in poor scarring.

Primary closure is direct apposition of wound edges, and is appropriate for clean wounds with minimal tissue loss, which can be closed without excessive tension or distortion of surrounding structures. Delayed primary closure is direct closure of a wound that has been left open for a period of time.

3.3 Soft-tissue reconstruction

Tissue expansion

Tissue expansion is a process that allows an area of skin to be expanded as a result of its inherent viscoelastic properties. When a force is applied to skin over time, collagen fibres straighten and realign, elastin fibres fragment, and the composition of tissue ground substance is altered (this process is known as 'creep'). With time, the force required to maintain the expanded tissue decreases (stress relaxation). Tissue expansion is usually achieved with the use of a subcutaneous silicone balloon (expander) with a filling port.

The advantages of tissue expansion are that it allows use of adjacent donor sites and tissue with the correct properties, and potentially limits donor site morbidity. Disadvantages include multiple procedures/outpatient visits, temporary aesthetic deformity during expansion, and the complications of the expansion process (infection, extrusion of expander, etc).

Skin grafts

Skin grafting is the process of transferring a piece of skin without a blood supply from one site in the body to another, where the graft will obtain a blood supply and heal. Skin grafting requires a healthy, vascularised recipient site, free of infection or malignancy. Skin grafts may be considered as **split** or **full thickness**.

Split-skin grafts consist of epidermis and variable amounts of dermis that are harvested by means of a specialised knife or powered instrument known as a dermatome. As epidermal elements are left behind at the donor site (eg in hair follicles), the donor site can re-epithelialise.

Advantages of split-thickness grafts include:

- Donor site will heal by re-epithelialisation and may be reharvested
- Large available donor area (essentially entire body surface)
- Can cover large areas by use of 'meshing' technique
- Contour well to complex wounds

Disadvantages include:

- Poor matching of colour and texture
- Meshed pattern may be visible
- Significant contraction with healing

Meshing of split-skin grafts allows a lattice pattern to be cut in the graft, which in turn allows the graft to be expanded to cover a larger area for a given size of graft. It also allows the graft to contour to awkward wounds, and allows fluid to escape that may otherwise compromise healing.

Full-thickness skin grafts consist of the entire dermis and epidermis and, as a consequence, donor sites require closure and are more limited. Common donor sites include postauricular skin, supraclavicular fossa, medial arm and groin. Donor sites above the clavicles have better colour match for facial defects. Advantages of full-thickness grafts include better cosmesis and less contraction with time. Full-thickness grafts may grow in children.

Disadvantages include limited donor sites and the need to close the donor site.

The process of skin graft healing ('take') involves four phases:

1. Adherence – fibrin bond between graft and recipient site. This may be disrupted by shearing forces or bacterial proteases
2. Plasmatic imbibition – process of nutrition of graft before establishment of a blood supply by absorption of interstitial fluid
3. Revascularisation – exact method unknown, but occurs by a number of processes
4. Maturation – contraction of wound and graft

Graft failure may result from any process disrupting the above sequence, eg:
- Avascular bed/inadequately prepared wound
- Infection
- Haematoma/seroma
- Shearing forces
- Systemic problems – infection/malnutrition/malignancy/steroids
- Technical error

Flaps

> A flap is a vascularised unit of tissue that is moved from a donor to a recipient site, and is a key concept in reconstructive plastic surgery.

Flaps may be classified in a variety of ways:
- According to the type of tissue within the flap (eg skin/muscle/bone)
- The blood supply of the flap
- The relationship of the flap to the defect (eg local, regional, distant/free)
- The movement of the flap to the defect (eg rotation, advancement, transposition, interpolation)

A flap may consist of one or more types of tissue, and is named accordingly. A flap consisting of muscle and skin is a musculocutaneous flap, and of fascia and skin is a fasciocutaneous flap.

A **'random pattern'** flap has no named directional blood vessel providing its blood supply. Common examples are cutaneous flaps used for reconstruction of small facial defects after excision of skin lesions. An 'axial' flap has an identifiable source vessel running within the flap. A perforator flap is based on a blood vessel (perforator) travelling from a source vessel, either through muscle or directly to skin.

A **'local' flap** is usually adjacent to the defect to be reconstructed. Again, facial cutaneous flaps are common examples. A 'Z-plasty' is also a useful local flap technique for management of scar contractures and reorientation of scars.

A **'regional' flap** is moved from a donor site nearby but not necessarily adjacent to the defect. The use of latissimus dorsi, moved from the back in breast reconstruction is a good example of this type.

A **'free' flap** is detached from its blood supply at the donor site, and the flap vessels are connected to vessels at the recipient site.

The reconstructive surgeon can use flaps to bring well-vascularised tissue to a defect, or replace missing tissue with a similar tissue type. Flaps may be used to restore sensation and/or functionality by bringing a nerve supply or a functioning muscle, or for limb salvage by restoring blood supply in an ischaemic limb. Improving knowledge of flap techniques means that flaps may be taken from areas with the minimum of morbidity at the donor site.

Common flaps

Common flaps used in reconstruction include:

- Latissimus dorsi
- Scapular and parascapular flaps
- Radial forearm flap
- Rectus abdominis/DIEP (deep inferior epigastric artery perforator) flaps
- Gracilis flap
- Anterolateral thigh flap
- Fibular flap

Latissimus dorsi

Flaps based on latissimus dorsi and the thoracodorsal vessels are commonly used for breast and chest wall reconstruction, and for free tissue transfer where a large area of coverage is required. The skin overlying latissimus dorsi may also be harvested as a perforator-based flap.

Scapular and parascapular flaps

Flaps based on the circumflex scapular arterial system provide a versatile source of fasciocutaneous flaps. Bone from the lateral edge of the scapula can also be harvested. As regional flaps, they can be used to resurface the axilla and release axillary contractures. Used as a free tissue transfer, they provide a useful source of pliable skin, with an excellent donor site.

Radial forearm flap

Flaps based on the radial artery provide a useful source of thin fasciocutaneous flaps as virtually the entire volar forearm skin can be harvested if required. They may be used as pedicled flaps for hand and upper limb coverage or as a free flap for head and neck/intraoral reconstruction. The major downside of this flap is the donor site. This may be closed directly for small flaps, but for larger flaps a skin graft is required, which may result in a poor aesthetic outcome.

Rectus abdominis/DIEP flaps

Flaps based on rectus abdominis and the inferior epigastric arterial system are commonly used in breast, chest and pelvic reconstruction. Rectus abdominis and the overlying skin, based on the deep inferior epigastric artery, may be pedicled into the pelvis to fill defects after oncological resection. Based on the deep superior epigastric artery, this flap may be used as a pedicled flap for chest wall and sternal reconstruction. Harvesting of rectus abdominis may lead to a significant risk of abdominal wall weakness and hernia. This donor site is now more frequently used for the DIEP flap. This harvests similar skin territory, but is based on the source artery and its perforating vessels through the rectus muscle, which are dissected free, leaving the muscle intact.

Gracilis flap

Gracilis is a long thin muscle with consistent vascular anatomy (via profunda femoris or medial circumflex femoral systems) that is useful as both a regional flap for perineal reconstruction and a free tissue transfer. Innervation of the muscle is via the anterior branch of the obturator nerve. The muscle may be harvested and transferred as a functional reconstruction, eg to restore biceps function. Donor site morbidity is minimal. The skin overlying the muscle can also be taken in various patterns, but it is less reliable as a musculocutaneous flap.

CHAPTER 11

Anterolateral thigh flap

Flaps based on perforating vessels from the descending branch of the lateral circumflex femoral artery, via the septum between rectus femoris and vastus lateralis, or more commonly through vastus lateralis, are a versatile source of large fasciocutaneous flaps with an excellent donor site. Portions of vastus lateralis may also be harvested. Long pedicle lengths can be achieved, making this source a useful donor site for a variety of uses. It is most commonly used as a free tissue transfer, but may also be pedicled into the groin, or for perineal reconstruction. The downside to this donor site is the somewhat variable vascular anatomy.

Fibular flap

Vessels from the peroneal artery supply the fibula and an area of overlying skin of the lateral leg. The vascular anatomy is relatively consistent but the dissection can be tricky. It is a very useful source of a long segment of vascularised bone, and is commonly used for mandibular reconstruction. The reliability of the overlying skin paddle is variable.

List of Abbreviations

5-HIAA	5-hydroxyindole acetic acid
A&E	accident and emergency (department)
AAA	abdominal artery aneurysm
ABC	aneurysmal bone cyst
ABGs	arterial blood gases
ACh	acetylcholine
ACL	anterior cruciate ligament
ACPGBI	Association of Coloproctology of Great Britain and Ireland
ACTH	adrenocorticotropic hormone
ADH	antidiuretic hormone (vasopressin)
AF	atrial fibrillation
AFB/s	acid-fast bacillus/bacilli
AFP	alphafetoprotein
AIDS	acquired immunodeficiency syndrome
ALI	acue lung injury
ALL	anterior longitudinal ligament
ALP	alkaline phosphatase
ANP	atrial natriuretic peptide
AP	anteroposterior
APBI	ankle–brachial pressure index
APC	antigen-presenting cell
APKD	adult polycystic kidney disease
APL	abductor pollicis longus
APTT	activated partial thromboplastin time
ARDS	adult respiratory distress syndrome
ARF	acute renal failure
ASIS	anterior superior iliac spine
ATLS	advanced trauma life support
ATP	adenosine triphosphate
AV	arteriovenous
AVM	arteriovenous malformation
AVN	avascular necrosis
AVPU	alert, verbal stimuli (responds to), pain (responds to), unresponsive
BAL	bronchoalveolar lavage
BCG	bacille Calmette–Guérin
BIH	benign intercranial hypertension
BiPAP	bi-level positive airway pressure
BM	blood glucose monitoring
BMI	body mass index
BP	blood pressure
BPH	benign prostatic hyperplasia
BXO	balanitis xerotica obliterans
CAH	congenital adrenal hyperplasia
CAPD	continuous ambulant peritoneal dialysis
CDH	congenital diaphragmatic hernia(tion)
CDT	*Clostridium difficile* toxin
CEA	carcinoembryonic antigen
CF	cystic fibrosis
CIS	carcinoma in situ
CJD	Creutzfeldt–Jacob disease
CK	creatine kinase
CMC	carpometacarpal (joint)
CMV	cytomegalovirus, controlled mechanical ventilation
CNS	central nervous system
CO	carbon monoxide; cardiac output
COPD	chronic obstructive pulmonary disease
COREC	Central Office for Research Ethics Committees
COX	cyclo-oxygenase
CPAP	continuous positive-pressure airway pressure (ventilation)
CPB	cardiopulmonary bypass
CPPS	chronic pelvic pain syndrome
CRC	colorectal cancer
CREST	calcinosis, Raynauld's, oesophageal dysfunction, sclerodactyly, telangectasia
CRF	chronic renal failure
CRH	corticotropin-releasing factor
CRP	C-reactive protein
CSF	cerebrospinal fluid
CT	computed tomography
CTEV	congenital talipes equinovarus
CVA	cerebrovascular accident
CVP	central venous pressure
CXR	chest X-ray

DDH	developmental dysplasia of the hip		GCS	Glasgow Coma Scale
DEXA/			GFR	glomerular filtration rate
	DXA	dual-energy X-ray absorptiometry	GH	growth hormone
DHCC	dihydroxycholecalciferol		GI	gastrointestinal
DHS	dynamic hip screw		GM-CSF	granulocyte-macrophage colony-stimulating factor
DIC	disseminated intravascular coagulation		GnRH	gonadotropin-releasing hormone
DIP	distal interpharyngeal (joint)		HAART	highly active antiretroviral therapy
DMARD	disease-modifying anti-rheumatic drug		HCC	hepatocellular carcinoma
			hCG	human chorionic gonadotropin
DMSA	dimercaptosuccinic acid		HDU	high-dependency unit
DPG	2,3 diphosphoglycerate		HER-2	human epidermal growth factor receptor-2
DPL	diagnostic peritoneal lavage			
DVT	deep vein thrombosis		HiB	Haemophilus influenzae type B
EBV	Epstein–Barr virus		HIV	human immunodeficiency virus
ECG	electrocardiogram		HLA	human leucocyte antigen
ECM	extracellular matrix		HNPCC	hereditary non-polyposis colon cancer
ECRL	extensor carpi radialis longus			
ECU	extensor carpi ulnaris		HPV	human papillomavirus
EDL	extensor digitorum longus		HR	heart rate
EHL	extensor hallucis longus		HSP	heat-shock protein
ELISA	enzyme-linked immunosorbent assay		HSV	herpes simplex virus
ELN	external laryngeal nerve		HTLV-1	human T-cell lymphotropic virus 1
EMD	electromechanical dissociation		IARC	International Agency for Research on Cancer
EMG	electromyogram			
EMLA	eutectic mixture of local anaesthetic		ICAM	intercellular adhesion molecule
ENT	ear, nose and throat (department)		ICP	intracranial pressure
EPB	extensor pollicis brevis		IDDM	insulin-dependant diabetes mellitus
ER	(o)estrogen receptor		IFN	interferon
ESR	erythrocyte sedimentation rate		IGF	insulin-like growth factor
ET	endotracheal tube		IHD	ischaemic heart disease
EUA	examination under anaesthetic		IL	interleukin
FAP	familial adenomatous polyposis		INR	international normalised ratio
FBC	full blood count		INSS	international neuroblastoma staging system
FCU	flexor carpi ulnaris			
FDL	flexor digitorum longus		ITP	idiopathic thrombocytopenic purpura
FDP	flexor digitorum profundus		ITU	intensive therapy unit
FDS	flexor digitorum superficialis		IV	intravenous
FEV_1	forced expiratory volume in 1 second		IVU	intravenous urethrogram
FHL	flexor hallucis longus		JGA	juxtaglorerular apparatus
FMD	fibromuscular dysplasia		JIA	juvenile idiopathic arthritis
FNA/C	fine-needle aspiration / cytology		JVP	jugular venous pressure (or pulse)
FVC	forced vital capacity		KUB	kidneys, ureters, bladder
GA	general anaesthesia		LA	local anaesthetic
GCA	giant-cell tumour		LDH	lactate dehydrogenase
			LFTs	liver function tests

LIF	left iliac fossa		PaO_2	partial pressure of oxygen (arterial)
LMWH	low-molecular-weight heparin		PAP	pulmonary artery pressure
LP	lumbar puncture		PAS	para-aminosalicylic acid
LREC	local research ethics committee		PAWP	pulmonary artery wedge pressure
LUQ	Left upper quadrant		PCA	patient-controlled analgesia
LVH	left ventricular hypertrophy		PCL	posterior cruciate ligament
MAC	*Mycobacterium avium* complex, membrane attack complex		PCP	*Pneumocystis carinii* pneumonia
MALT	mucosa-associated lymphoid tissue		PDA	patent ductus arteriosus
MAP	mean arterial pressure		PE	pulmonary embolism
MC&S	microscopy, culture and sensitivity		PEEP	peak end-expiratory pressure
MCP	metacarpophalangeal (joint)		PET	positron-emission tomography
MDT	multidisciplinary team		PFTs	pulmonary function tests
MEN	multiple endocrine neoplasia		PG	prostaglandin
MHC	major histocompatibility complex		PIP	proximal interpharyngeal (joint)
MI	myocardial infarction		PLL	posterior longitudinal ligament
MIBG	meta-iodobenzylguanidine		PNET	primitive neuroectodermal tumour
MODS	multiorgan dysfunction syndrome		POP	plaster of Paris
MREC	multicentre research ethics committee		PP	pulse pressure
			PPI	proton pump inhibitor
MRI	magnetic resonance imaging		PPV	patent processus vaginalis
MRSA	meticillin-resistant *Staphylococcus aureus*		PSA	prostate-specific antigen
			PSIS	posterior superior iliac spine
MRTB	multidrug-resistant TB		PT	prothrombin time
MS	multiple sclerosis		PTFE	polytetrafluoroethylene
MST	morphine suphate tablet		PTH	parathyroid hormone
MTP	metatarsophalangeal (joint)		PV	plasma viscosity
MUA	manipulation under anaesthetic		PVD	peripheral vascular disease
NAD	nicotine adenine dinucleotide		PVDF	polyvinylidene fluoride (suture)
NCEPOD	National Confidential Enquiry into Patient Outcome and Death		PVR	peripheral vascular resistance
			RA	rheumatoid arthritis
NF	neurofibromatosis		RBC	red blood cell
NG	nasogastric		RIF	right iliac fossa
NHL	non-Hodgkin lymphoma		RTA	road traffic accident
NICE	National institute for Health and Clinical Excellence		RUQ	right upper quadrant
			SBP	systolic blood pressure
NPSA	National Patient Safety Agency		SIMV	synchronised intermittent mandatory ventilation
NSAID	non-steroidal anti-inflammatory drug			
NSCLC	non-small-cell lung carcinoma		SIRS	systemic inflammatory response syndrome
OA	osteoarthritis			
OCP	oral contraceptive pill		SLE	systemic lupus erythematosus
ORIF	open reduction plus internal fixation		SMA	superior mesenteric artery
PA	pulmonary artery		SPECT	single-photon emission computed tomography
$PaCO_2$	partial pressure of carbon dioxide (arterial)			
			SSRI	selective serotonin reuptake inhibitors
PAN	polyarteritis nodosa		SUFE	slipped upper femoral epiphysis
			SVC	superior vena cava

TB	tuberculosis		US(S)	ultrasound (scan)
Tc	technetium		UTI	urinary tract infection
TCA	tricyclic antidepressant		VC	vital capacity
TCC	transitional cell carcinoma		VDRL	Venereal Disease Research
THR	total hip replacement			Laboratory (test for syphilis)
TKR	total knee replacement		VEGF	vascular endothelial growth factor
TNM	tumour, node, metastasis		VF	ventricular fibrillation
TPN	total parenteral nutrition		VIP	vasoactive intestinal peptide
TRAM	transverse rectus abdominis		VSD	ventricular septal defect
	myocutaneous (flap)		VT	ventricular tachycardia
TRH	thyrotropin-releasing hormone		VUJ	vesicoureteric junction
TSH	thyroid-stimulating hormone		VUR	vesicoureteric reflux
TT	thrombin time		WAGR	Wilms tumour, aniridia, genitourinary
TTP	thrombotic thrombocytopenic			abnormalities, learning difficulties
	purpura		WBC	white blood cells
U&Es	urea and electrolytes		WCC	white cell count
UICC	Union Internationale Contre le		ZN	Ziehl–Neelsen (stain)
	Cancre			

Bibliography

Books:

Anderson ID (1999) *Care of the Critically Ill Surgical Patient*. London: Arnold.

Armstrong RF, Salmon JB (1997) *Critical Care Cases*. New York, Oxford University Press.

Berne RM, Levy MN (eds) (1996) *Principles of Physiology* (2nd edition). London: Mosby.

Bersten A, Soni N, Oh TE (2003) *Oh's Intensive Care Manual* (5th edition). London: Butterworth Heinemann.

Blandy J (1998) *Lecture Notes on Urology* (5th edition). Oxford: Blackwells.

Brown N (1997) *Symptoms and Signs of Surgical Disease* (3rd edition). London: Arnold.

Calne R, Pollard SG (1991) *Operative Surgery*. London: Gower Medical.

Cooke RS, Madehavan N, Woolf N (2001) Surgeons in Training Education Programme (*STEP™*). London: Royal College of Surgeons of England.

Corson JD, Williamson RCN (2001) *Surgery*. London: Mosby.

Craft TM, Nolan J, Parr M (1999) *Key Topics in Critical Care*. Oxford: Bios Scientific Publishers.

Ellis H (1997) *Clinical Anatomy: A Revision and Applied Anatomy for Clinical Students* (9th edition). Oxford: Blackwell Science.

Farr RF, Allisy-Roberts PJ (1988) *Physics for Medical Imaging*. London: WB Saunders.

Goldhill DR, Withington PS (1997) *Textbook of Intensive Care*. London: Chapman & Hall.

Green DP (ed) (1993) *Fracture of the Metacarpals and Phalanges in Operative Hand Surgery*. London: Churchill Livingstone.

Hillman K, Bishop G (1996) *Clinical Intensive Care*. Philadelphia: Lippincott-Raven.

Hinds CJ, Watson JD (1996) *Intensive Care: A Concise Textbook*. London: WB Saunders.

Hobbs G, Mahajan R (2000) *Imaging in Anaesthesia and Critical Care*. Edinburgh: Churchill Livingstone.

Kirk RM, Mansfield AO, Cochrane JPS (1999) *Clinical Surgery in General* (3rd edition). Edinburgh: Churchill Livingstone.

Kleihues P, Cavanee WK (eds) (2000) *WHO Classification of Tumours of the Nervous System*. Lyon: IARC Press.

Mann CV, Russell RCG, Williams NS (1995) *Bailey and Love's Short Practice of Surgery* (22nd edition). London: Chapman and Hall.

Marino P (1998) *The ICU Book*. Philadelphia: Lippincott Williams & Wilkins.

Martin E (1990) *Concise Medical Dictionary*. New York: Oxford Press.

McConachie I (1999) *Handbook of ICU Therapy*. Cambridge: Greenwich Medical Media.

Mokbel K (1999) *Concise Notes on Oncology*. Newbury: Petroc Press.

Pallis C, Harley DH (1996) *ABC of Brainstem Death* (2nd edition). London: BMJ Publishing Group.

Paw GW, Park GR (2000) *Handbook of Drugs in Intensive Care*. Cambridge: Greenwich Medical Media.

Sadler TW (1990) *Langman's Medical Embryology* (6th edition). Philadelphia: Williams & Wilkins.

Sinnatamby CS (1999) *Last's Anatomy, Regional and Applied* (10th edition). London: Churchill Livingstone.

Smith AB (2004) *Infectious Diseases: An Exploration* (2nd edition). London: Churchill Livingstone.

Webb AJ, Shapiro MJ, Singer M, Suter PM (1999) *Oxford Textbook of Critical Care*. Oxford: Oxford University Press.

Whittaker RH, Borley NR (2000) *Instant Anatomy* (2nd edition). Oxford: Blackwell Science.

Woolf N (1998) *Pathology: Basic and Systemic*. London: WB Saunders.

Yentis SM, Hirsch NP, Smith GB (2000) *Anaesthesia and Intensive Care A to Z: An Encyclopaedia of Principles and Practice*. London: Butterworth Heinemann.

Peer-reviewed publications:

Bartlesman JF, Hameeteman W, Tytgat GN, *et al.* (1966) 'Principles and practice of screening for disease' *American Journal of Gastroenterology*, 91: 1507–1516.

Cole LJ, Nowell PC (1965) 'Radiation carcinogenesis: the sequence of events' *Science*, 150: 1782–1786.

Copeland GP, Jones D and Walters M. (1991) POSSUM: A scoring System for Surgical Audit *BJS*: 78;356-360

Doll R (1994) 'Mortality in relation to smoking: 40 years' observation on male British doctors' *British Medical Journal*, 309: 901–911.

General Medical Council (1998) *Seeking Patient's Consent: The Ethical Considerations*. London: GMC.

Helfet DL, Howey T, Sanders R, Johansen K (1990) 'Limb salvage versus amputation: Preliminary results of the mangled extremity severity score' *Clinical Orthopaedics*, 256: 80–86.

Irving M, Carlson GL (1998) 'Interocutaneous fistulae' *Surgery*, 16(10): 217–222.

Jenkins TPN (1976) 'The burst abdominal wound: A mechanical approach' *British Journal of Surgery*, 63: 873–876.

Kessler RC, Sonnega A, Bromet E, Hughes M, Nelson CB (1995) 'Posttraumatic stress disorder in the National Comorbidity Survey' *Archives of General Psychiatry*, 52(12): 1048–1060.

Knudson AG Jr (1974) 'Heredity and human cancer' *American Journal of Pathology*, 77(1): 77–84.

Medical Research Council (1976) *Memorandum no. 45. Aids to the examination of the peripheral nervous system*. London: HMSO.

Mitchell CL, Fleming JL, Allen R, Glenney C, Sanford GA (1958) Osteotomy-bunionectomy for halux valgus. *Journal of Bone and Joint Surgery*, 40(A): 41–60.

Marsden JR, Newton-Bishop JA, Burrows L, Cook M, Corrie PG, Cox NH, Gore ME, Lorigan P, Mackie R, Nathan P, Peach H, Powell B, Walker C; British Association of Dermatologists (BAD) Clinical Standards Unit. (2010) Revised UK guidelines for the management of cutaneous melanoma 2010. *J Plast Reconstr Aesthet Surg*. 63(9):1401-19.

RJ Motley, PW Preston, CM Lawrence. Multi-professional guidelines for the management of the patient with primary cutaneous squamous cell carcinoma 2009 - *update of the original guideline which appeared in BJD, Vol. 146, No. 1, January 2002 (p18-25)*

Nowell PC (1976) 'The clonal evolution of tumor cell populations' *Science*, 194: 23–28.

Oken MM, Creech RH, Yormey DC, *et al.* (1982) 'Toxicity and response criteria of the Eastern Co-operative Oncology Group' *American Journal of Clinical Oncology*, 5: 649–655.

Poldermans D et al. (2009) Guidelines for pre-operative cardiac risk assessment and perioperative cardiac management in non-cardiac surgery: The Task Force for Preoperative Cardiac Risk Assessment and Perioperative Cardiac Management in Non-cardiac Surgery of the European Society of Cardiology (ESC) and endorsed by the European Society of Anaesthesiology (ESA) *European Heart Journal* 30, 2769–2812

Salter RB, Harris WR (1963) 'Injuries involving epiphyseal plate' *Journal of Bone and Joint Surgery*, 45(A): 587–621.

McGaughey J, Alderdice F, Fowler R, Kapila A, Mayhew A, Moutray M.(2007) Outreach and Early Warning Systems (EWS) for the prevention of intensive care admission and death of critically ill adult patients on general hospital wards. *Cochrane Database Syst Rev.* 3:CD005529.

Associated Publications:

American College of Surgeons, ATLS manual, 9th edition (revised Sept 2012) GMC (2001) *Good Medical Practice*

GMC (2008) *Consent: patients and doctors making decisions together* [www.gmc-uk.org/guidance/ethical_guidance/consent_guidance_index.asp (last accessed Sept 2012)]

NCEPOD (2011) *Knowing the Risk: A review of the Perioperative Care of Surgical Patients* [www.ncepod.org.uk/2011report2/downloads/POC_fullreport.pdf (last accessed Sept 2012)]

Royal College of Surgeons of England (1993) *Clinical Guidelines on the management of groin hernia in adults*. Report from a working party convened by the Royal College of Surgeons. London: RCS.

Wilson JMG, Junger G (1968) *Principles and practice of screening for disease*. Public Health Papers, no. 34. Geneva: World Health Organization.

Websites:

Adjuvant Online: www.adjuvantonline.com (last accessed Sept 2012)

BMJ clinical evidence database: www.clinicalevidence.com (last accessed Sept 2012)

Cochrane Collaboration: www.cochrane.org (last accessed Sept 2012)

EBM: www.evidence-basedmedicine.com (last accessed Sept 2012)

European System for Cardiac Operative Risk Evaluation: www.euroscore.org (last accessed Sept 2012)

General Medical Council (GMC): www.gmc-uk.org (last accessed Sept 2012)

National Institute for Clinical Excellence: www.nice.org.uk (last accessed Sept 2012)

NHS cancer screening programmes: www.cancerscreening.nhs.uk (last accessed Sept 2012)

Risk prediction models for surgery: www.riskprediction.org.uk (last accessed Sept 2012)

Royal College of Surgeons of England: www.rcseng.ac.uk (last accessed Sept 2012)

Scottish Intercollegiate Guidelines Network (SIGN): www.sign.ac.uk (last accessed Sept 2012)

The Ileostomy and Internal Pouch Support Group: www.the-ia.org.uk (last accessed Sept 2012)

Turning Research Into Practice: www.tripdatabase.com (last accessed Sept 2012)

UK Resuscitation Council: www.resus.org.uk (last accessed Sept 2012)

US National Library of Medicine citations database: www.pubmed.org (last accessed Sept 2012)

World Health Organization: www.who.int (last accessed Sept 2012)

Index